Why You Need This New Edition

If you are wondering why you should add this new ninth edition of *Literature for Composition* to your personal library, here are five good reasons:

1. **A new Chapter 1, "How to Write an Effective Essay: A Crash Course,"** gives you an easy-to-use reference that allows you to quickly preview the writing process at a glance.
2. **Six new student essays** provide helpful models of how students have completed essays on a wide array of topics. You will find a total of nineteen student essays in this new edition.
3. **Two new thematic units**—"The World Around Us" and "The Sporting Life"—offer you additional ideas for writing papers.
4. **Greater fiction coverage offers forty-five stories,** ranging from Aesop to renowned science fiction writers Ray Bradbury and Arthur Clark to today's leading writers Lydia Davis, Alice Munro, and Tobias Wolff.
5. **An Appendix with the new 2009 MLA guidelines** is a terrific reference for writing papers that conform to these changes.

PEARSON

NINTH EDITION

Literature for Composition

Essays, Stories, Poems, and Plays

Sylvan Barnet
Tufts University

William E. Cain
Wellesley College

William Burto
University of Massachusetts at Lowell

Longman

Boston Columbus Indianapolis New York San Francisco Upper Saddle River
Amsterdam Cape Town Dubai London Madrid Milan Munich Paris Montreal Toronto
Delhi Mexico City São Paulo Sydney Hong Kong Seoul Singapore Taipei Tokyo

Acquisitions Editor: Vivian Garcia
Development Editor: Katharine Glynn
Senior Supplements Editor: Donna Campion
Executive Marketing Manager: Joyce Nilsen
Production Manager: Eric Jorgensen
Project Coordination, Text Design, and Electronic Page Makeup:
Nesbitt Graphics, Inc.
Cover Design Manager: John Callahan
Cover Designer: Laura Shaw
Cover Image: *Two Women Reading* by Sylvia Plath, Courtesy Lilly Library, Indiana University, Bloomington, IN, and the Plath estate
Image Permission Coordinator: Debbie Latronica/Image Resource Center
Senior Manufacturing Buyer: Alfred C. Dorsey
Printer and Binder: Quebecor World Book Services/Taunton
Cover Printer: Lehigh/Phoenix Color, Hagerstown

For permission to use copyrighted material, grateful acknowledgment is made to the copyright holders on pages 1386–95, which are hereby made part of this copyright page.

Library of Congress Cataloging-in-Publication Data
Literature for composition : Reading and writing arguments about essays, stories, poems, and plays / [edited by] Sylvan Barnet, William Burto, William E. Cain.—9th ed.
p. cm.
Includes bibliographical references and index.
ISBN 978-0-205-74359-9
1. College readers. 2. English language—Rhetoric—Problems, exercises, etc. 3. Criticism—Authorship—Problems, exercises, etc. 4. Academic writing—Problems, exercises, etc. I. Barnet, Sylvan. II. Burto, William. III. Cain, William E., 1952-
PE1417.L633 2010
808—dc22 2009040979

1 2 3 4 5 6 7 8 9 10—QWT—12 11 10 09 08 07

Longman
is an imprint of

www.ablongman.com

ISBN 10: 0-205-74359-5
ISBN 13: 978-0-205-74359-9

Contents

CHAPTER 3 The Reader as Writer 45

CHAPTER 4 Reading Literature Closely: Argument 88

CHAPTER 9 Research Writing with Sources 309

PART II

Up Close: Thinking Critically about Literary Works and Literary Forms 321

CHAPTER 10 Critical Thinking: Arguing with Oneself, Asking Questions, and Making Comparisons 323

CHAPTER 11 A Brief Guide: Writing about Literature 334

CHAPTER 12 Reading and Writing about Essays 339

CHAPTER 13 Reading and Writing about Stories 355

CHAPTER 14 Thinking Critically: A Case Study about Flannery O'Connor 403

CHAPTER 20 Love and Hate 678

CHAPTER 21 Making Men and Women 740

Stories

Poems

Play

CHAPTER 22 Innocence and Experience 843

Short Views

Essay

Stories

Poems

Play

CHAPTER 23 The Sporting Life 1027

Short Views

Essay

Stories

Poems

Play

CHAPTER 24 Identity in America 1073

Short Views

Essays

Stories

Poems

Plays

CHAPTER 25 American Dreams and Nightmares 1184

Short Views

Essays

Stories

Poems

APPENDIX B Remarks about Manuscript Form 1362

APPENDIX C How Much Do You Know about Citing Sources? A Quiz with Answers 1379

Contents by Genre

Essays

Stories

Poems

Plays

MyLitLab Contents

Fiction

James Baldwin Biography, Bibliography, Critical Archive
Sonny's Blues: Longman Lecture

Toni Cade Bambara Biography
The Lesson: Longman Lecture

Ambrose Bierce Biography
An Occurrence at Owl Creek Bridge: Video Essay, Critical Essay

T. Coraghessan Boyle Biography
Greasy Lake: Critical Essay

Raymond Carver Biography, Bibliography, Critical Essay
Cathedral: Longman Lecture

Willa Cather Biography/Photos, Bibliography, Critical Archive
Paul's Case: Video, Audio, Critical Essay

Anton Chekhov Biography, Bibliography, Critical Archive

Kate Chopin Biography, Bibliography, Critical Archive
Désirée's Baby: Longman Lecture
The Storm: Longman Lecture, Interactive Reading, Student Paper, Critical Essay
The Story of an Hour: Longman Lecture

Joseph Conrad Biography
Heart of Darkness: Longman Lecture

William Faulkner Biography/Photos, Bibliography, Critical Archive
Barn Burning: Video (2), Audio (2), Critical Essay (2)
A Rose for Emily: Critical Essay

F. Scott Fitzgerald Biography

Charlotte Perkins Gilman Biography, Bibliography, Critical Archive
The Yellow Wallpaper: Critical Essay

Nathaniel Hawthorne Biography, Bibliography, Critical Archive
Young Goodman Brown: Longman Lecture

Ernest Hemingway Biography, Bibliography, Critical Archive
A Clean Well-Lighted Place: Critical Essay

Shirley Jackson Biography
The Lottery: Interactive Reading, Critical Essay

Gish Jen Biography
In the American Society: Longman Lecture

James Joyce Biography, Bibliography, Critical Archive
Araby: Longman Lecture, Interactive Reading

Ursula K. Le Guin Biography
The Ones Who Walk Away from Omelas: Student Paper

Katherine Mansfield Biography
Miss Brill: Interactive Reading, Critical Essay

Bobbie Ann Mason Biography
Shiloh: Longman Lecture

Guy de Maupassant Biography
The Necklace: Interactive Reading

Joyce Carol Oates Biography, Bibliography, Critical Archive
Where Are You Going, Where Have You Been?: Longman Lecture

Tim O'Brien Biography
The Things They Carried: Longman Lecture

Flannery O'Connor Biography, Bibliography, Critical Archive
A Good Man Is Hard to Find: Critical Essay, Interactive Reading, Longman Lecture

Edgar Allan Poe Biography/Photos, Bibliography, Critical Archive
Ligeia: Longman Lecture
The Tell-Tale Heart: *Longman Lecture, Video, Critical Essay*

Katherine Anne Porter Biography/Photos
The Jilting of Granny Weatherall: Video, Audio, Critical Essay

Isaac Bashevis Singer Biography

Amy Tan Biography, Bibliography, Critical Archive
A Pair of Tickets: Critical Essay

Poetry

Drama

Preface to Instructors

Literature for Composition is based on the assumption that students in composition or literature courses should encounter first-rate writing—not simply competent prose but the powerful reports of experience that have been recorded by highly skilled writers of the past and present, reports of experiences that must be shared.

Our view is not original. A thousand years ago in Japan, Lady Murasaki (978?–1026) wrote a scene in *The Tale of Genji* in which some of her characters talk about reading fiction, and one of them offers his opinion as to why an author writes:

> Again and again writers find something in their experience, or see something in the life around them, that seems so important they cannot bear to let it pass into oblivion. There must never come a time, the writer feels, when people do not know about this.

We assume that you share our belief that the study of such writing offers pleasure and insight into life and also leads to increased skill in communicating.

What is New in the Ninth Edition?

Instructors familiar with earlier editions will notice that we retain our emphasis on critical thinking and argument, but we have made many substitutions in the literary works, most notably by substantially increasing the number of short stories. For the convenience of instructors who have used an earlier edition, we briefly summarize here the major changes:

Increased Emphasis on Writing

The most obvious additions here are:

- **A new opening chapter**, "How to Write an Effective Essay: A Crash Course."
- **Six new essays by students**, some with the preliminary jottings, provide a total of nineteen student essays. These selections are not offered simply as models of excellence. Rather, they vary in strength, thereby allowing—unlike essays written in a course that an instructor is currently teaching—for uninhibited class discussions.
- Each new thematic unit, like the others, begins with Short Views, brief statements ranging from epigrammatic sentences to a paragraph. These memorable and provocative comments, followed by topics for writing, can also be juxtaposed with the readings in the chapter.
- Moreover, every literary selection is followed by questions that serve as writing prompts.
- **The new MLA guidelines** from the seventh edition of the *MLA Handbook* are clearly summarized for students. The updated source citation requirements are incorporated in all sample student papers.
- A new appendix, Appendix C, consists of a class-tested quiz on the topic of plagiarism and citation of sources.

Two New Thematic Units

- "The World Around Us." Among the authors represented in the twenty-three readings in the first new chapter are Thoreau, Bill McKibben, Aesop, Sarah Orne Jewettt, Sylvia Plath, and—in a casebook—Robert Frost.
- "The Sporting Life." Among the authors in the second new chapter are James Michener, Sherwood Anderson, Mary Robison, and Tobias Wolff.

Key Features

Here are the key features in the ninth edition of *Literature for Composition.*

- **Extensive instruction in composition:** Students are guided through the entire process of writing (especially writing arguments), beginning with generating ideas (for instance, by listing or by annotating a text), developing a thesis, supporting the thesis with evidence, and on through the final stages of documenting and editing. Nineteen examples of student writing are included; most are prefaced with the students' preliminary notes, and some are annotated or otherwise analyzed.
- **Strategies for writing effective arguments:** The ninth edition focuses on argument and evaluation, not only in the case studies but also in the topics (headed "Joining the Conversation: Critical Thinking and Writing") that follow every reading. We emphasize the importance of questioning your own assumptions—a key principle in critical thinking—and we also emphasize the importance of providing evidence in the course of setting forth coherent, readable arguments.
- **Wide range of literary selections:** The book includes some three hundred selections, ranging from ancient classics such as Sophocles' *Antigonê* to Billy Collins's poem about the attack on the World Trade Center.
- **Abundant visual material, with suggestions about visual analysis:** The book is rich in photographs, paintings, and facsimiles of manuscripts. The images are chosen to enhance the student's understanding of particular works of literature. For example, we include photos of Buffalo Bill and a facsimile of a draft of E. E. Cummings's poem about Buffalo Bill (to our knowledge, never before published in a textbook). Similarly, we include previously unpublished typescript pages of Faulkner's "A Rose for Emily," thereby helping students to think about the kinds of choices and changes that a serious writer makes.
- **Introductory genre anthology:** After preliminary chapters on getting ideas and thinking critically, students encounter chapters devoted to essays, fiction, drama, and poetry.
- **Thematic anthology:** The chapters in Part 3 are arranged under nine themes: The World Around Us, Journeys, Love and Hate, Making Men and Women, Innocence and Experience, The Sporting Life, Identity in America, American Dreams and Nightmares, and Law and Disorder.
- **Case studies:** The five case studies presented in this book give a variety of perspectives for writing arguments and organizing research: William Faulkner's "A Rose for Emily" (page 236), Flannery O'Connor (page 403), Emily Dickinson (page 532), Comparing Poems and Pictures (page 567), Robert Frost (page 609), and *Hamlet* (page 897).

- **Extensive material on research and the Internet:** Because instructors are increasingly assigning research papers, the ninth edition includes material on short, medium, and long research papers, and it provides up-to-date instruction on evaluating, using, and citing electronic sources.
- **Words and Images:** The visual material includes a color insert section entitled "Word and Image" that presents twelve works of art that are the subjects of poems. Students analyze the poems and paintings and offer evidence to support their arguments.
- **Checklists:** Eighteen checklists focus on topics such as writing with a computer, revising paragraphs, editing a draft, and using the World Wide Web. Students can use these checklists to become peer readers of their writing.

Organization

Although *Literature for Composition* is in large part an anthology of literature, it is much more, offering extensive instruction in writing, especially writing arguments.

Part I, "Getting Started: From Response to Argument," consists of ten chapters with some sixty short works of literature. The aim of all the chapters in this part is to help students read and respond—in writing. Chapter 1 is a crash course, a quick review for students who have already taken a course in composition. The next three chapters discuss annotating, free writing, and listing; Chapters 5 and 6 discuss writing explications and analyses; Chapters 7 through 9 cover arguing and research. These chapters include thirteen examples of student writing, most of which are accompanied by the preliminary journal entries or drafts that helped produce them.

Part II, "Up Close: Thinking Critically about Literary Works and Literary Forms," begins with a discussion of critical thinking (Chapter 10). This chapter invites students to use comparison to analyze E. E. Cummings's poem "Buffalo Bill 's". A photograph of Buffalo Bill and Sitting Bull is shown as is the manuscript draft of the poem. Chapter 11, "A Brief Guide: Writing about Literature," is a brief survey that functions as a preface to the next eight chapters, which introduce students to four genres: the essay (Chapter 12), fiction (Chapters 13 and 14), drama (Chapter 15), and poetry (Chapters 16–17). The chapter on the essay includes two essays, and additional essays appear in the later thematic chapters. The three chapters on fiction present two stories, with a case study on Flannery O'Connor. The chapter on drama includes two plays; the two chapters on poetry include twenty-nine poems followed by case studies on Emily Dickinson (ten poems) and on poems about pictures (twelve poems). Suggested topics for discussion and examples of student writing; (annotations, journal entries, drafts, and final essays) help students think critically and develop arguments about the material. Part II, then, offers a small anthology of literature organized by genre, as well as abundant guidance in thinking and writing about literature.

About 150 literary texts appear in Parts I and II; another 160 appear in Part III, "Standing Back: A Thematic Anthology," where the chapters are grouped into nine themes: The World Around Us, Journeys, Love and Hate, Making Men and Women, Innocence and Experience, The Sporting Life, Identity in America, American Dreams and Nightmares, and Law and Disorder. Here, as earlier, almost all of the essays, stories, plays, and poems are followed by questions to stimulate critical thinking and writing arguments.

The book concludes with three appendixes: "Writing about Literature: An Overview of Critical Strategies," "Remarks about Manuscript Form," and "How Much Do You Know about Citing Sources? A Quiz with Answers." The material on manuscript form may seem to be yet another discussion of writing, and some readers may wonder why it is put near the back of the book. The explanation is that we see manuscript form as the final packaging of a product that develops during a complicated process, a process that begins with reading, responding, and finding a topic, a thesis (supported by evidence), and a voice, not with worrying about the width of margins or the form of citations. The last thing done in writing an essay, and therefore one of the last things we present in our book, is to set it forth in a pleasing and logical physical form fit for each reader's consumption. The quiz on plagiarism is a fresh and engaging look at a topic of enormous concern to students and instructors.

Resources for Students and Instructors

For Students

- The *new* ***MyLiteratureLab.com*** is a dynamic interactive online resource designed to accompany *Literature for Composition* and help students in their literature course. New assets include an eAnthology with 200 additional selections, Multimedia Instructional Resources, a Composing space for drafting and revising, and Gradebook built specifically for courses with a heavy writing component. The Longman Lectures—evocative, richly illustrated audio readings—engage students and give advice on how to read, interpret, and write about literary works and are read by Longman authors, including X. J. Kennedy. This powerful program also features Diagnostic Tests, Interactive Readings with clickable prompts, film clips of selections in *Literature for Composition,* Writers on Writing (video interviews with distinguished authors and poets that inspire students to explore their creativity), sample student papers, Literature Timelines, and Avoiding Plagiarism. *MyLiteratureLab.com* can be packaged at no additional cost with most Longman literature titles. It's the perfect resource for online literature-based composition and introduction to literature courses and can be delivered within Course Compass, Web CT, or Blackboard course management systems.
- ***Sourcebooks Shakespeare*** is a revolutionary book and CD format that offers the complete text of a Shakespeare play with rich illustrations, extensive explanatory and production notes, and a glossary. An accompanying audio CD—narrated by actor Sir Derek Jacobi—features recordings from memorable productions to contrast different interpretations of the play and its characters.

For Instructors

- ***Instructor's Manual*** with detailed comments and suggestions for teaching each selection is available. This important resource, entirely written by the authors of the text, also contains references to critical articles and books that we have found to be the most useful.
- ***Penguin Discount Novel Program*** offers, in cooperation with Penguin Group USA, a variety of Penguin paperbacks at a significant discount—almost sixty percent off the retail price—when packaged with any Pearson title. To review the list of titles available, visit the Pearson Penguin Group USA Web site at *www.pearsonhighered.com/penguin.*

- ***Video Program*** is an impressive selection of videotapes that is available to qualified adopters to enrich students' experience of literature. The videos include selections from William Shakespeare, Sylvia Plath, Ezra Pound, and Alice Walker. Contact your Pearson Longman sales representative to see if you qualify.
- ***The Longman Electronic Testbank for Literature*** features various objective questions on major works of fiction, short fiction, poetry, and drama. With this user-friendly CD-ROM, instructors simply choose questions from the electronic testbank, then print out the completed test for distribution.

Contact Us

For examination copies of any of these books, CDs, videos, and programs, contact your Pearson Longman sales representative, or write to Literature Marketing Manager, Pearson Education, 51 Madison Avenue, New York, NY 10010. For examination copies only, call (800) 922-0579. To order an examination copy online, go to *http:/www.pearsonhighered.com* or send an e-mail to exam.copies@pearson.

Acknowledgments

In preparing the first eight editions of *Literature for Composition,* we were indebted to Elizabeth Addison, Jonathan Alexander, James Allen, Kathleen Anderson-Wyman, Patricia Baldwin, Mary J. Balkun, Daniel Barwick, David Beach, Phyllis Betz, Margaret Blayney, Bertha Norman Booker, John P. Boots, Pam Bourgeois, Noelle Brada-Williams, Carol Ann Britt, Jennifer Bruer, Robin W. Bryant, Sharon Buzzard, Kathleen Shine Cain, Diana Cardenas, William Carpenter, Mike Chu, Alan P. Church, Dennis Ciesielski, Arlene Clift-Pellow, Walter B. Connolly, Stanley Corkin, Linda Cravens, Bruce Danner, Donald A. Daiker, Phebe Davidson, Beth DeMeo, John Desjarlais, Emily Dial-Driver, John Dobelbower, Ren Draya, James Dubinsky, Gail Duffy, Bill Elliott, Leonard W. Engel, William Epperson, Martin J. Fertig, Elinor C. Flewellen, Kay Fortson, Marie Foster, Donna Friedman, Larry Frost, Loris Galford, Chris Grieco, Jessica Beth Gordon, Susan Grimland, Debbie Hanson, Dorothy Hardman, Sandra H. Harris, Syndey Harrison, Sally Harrold, Tom Hayes, Keith Haynes, Michael Hennessey, Mary Herbert, Ana B. Hernandez, Maureen Hoag, Allen Hoey, Diane Houston, Clayton Hudnall, Joyce A. Ingram, Craig Johnson, Michael Johnson, Angela Jones, Kristianne Kalata, Rodney Keller, Beth Kemper, Alison Kuehner, Donya Lancaster, Regina Lebowitz, Margaret Lindgren, John Loftis, Robert Lynch, Maria Makowiecka, Phil Martin, Dennis McDonald, Sara McKnight Boone, Delma McLeod-Porter, Linda McPherson, Bill McWilliams, Martin Meszaros, Zack Miller, JoAnna S. Mink, Dorothy Minor, Wayne Moore, Charles Moran, Patricia G. Morgan, Nancy Morris, Jonathan Morrow, Christina Murphy, Richard Nielson, Torria Norman, David Norlin, Marsha Nourse, John O'Connor, Chris Orchard, Phyllis Orlicek, Eric Otto, Suzanne Owens, Janet Palmer, James R. Payne, Stephanie Pelkowski, Don K. Pierstorff, Gerald Pike, Louis H. Pratt, John Prince, Michael Punches, Bruce A. Reid, Thomas Reynolds, Linda Robertson, Lois Sampson, Terry Santos, Sigmar J. Schwarz, Jim Schwartz, Robert Schwegler, Linda Scott, Herbert Shapiro, William Shelley, Janice Slaughter, David Slater, Martha Ann Smith, Tiga Spitsberg, Judith Stanford, Pam Stinson, Darlene Strawser, Geri Strecker, Jim Streeter, Anthony Stubbs, David Sudol, Beverly Swan, Leesther Thomas, Raymond L. Thomas, Susan D. Tilka, Mary Trachsel, Dorothy Trusock, Billie Varnum, John H. Venne, Mickey Wadia, Nancy Walker, Betty Weldon, Patrick White, Bertha Wise, Arthur Wohlgemuth, Cary Wolfe, Sallie Woolf, Linda Woodson, Kathy J. Wright, Carlson Yost, Dennis Young, and Gary Zacharias.

For the eighth and ninth editions, we want to thank Larry Armstrong, Itawamba Community College; William D. Atwill, University of North Carolina Wilmington; Daniel Bender, Pace University; Billie Bennet, University of Georgia; Mary Anne Bernal, Alamo Community College District; Kenneth R. Bishop, Itawamba Community College; Evelyn Cartright, Barry University; Allan Chavkin, Texas State University; Alan P. Church, University of Texas at Brownsville; Thomas Deans, University of Connecticut, Storrs; Gareth Euridge, Tallahassee Community College; Charlene Gill, Texas State University, San Marcos; Esther Godfrey, University of Tennessee; Dwonna Goldstone, Austin Peay State University; Kim Greenfield, Lorain County Community College; Elizabeth Howells, Armstrong Atlantic State University; Glenn Klopfenstein, Passaic County Community College; Theresa René LeBlanc, Texas State University, San Marcos; Kate Massengale, University of New Mexico; Sean Nighbert, St. Philip's College; Sharon Prince, Wharton County Junior College; David Raymond, Northern Maine Community College; Daniel Schierenbeck, Central Missouri State University; Jonathon Wild, Cloud Community College; and Rebecca Wright, State University of New York at Buffalo.

For many e-mails and conversations about the ninth edition, and for help with its preparation, we are grateful to Vivian Garcia and Katharine Glynn at Longman. We wish also to thank Virginia Creeden, who secured copyright permission for the texts, and Rona Tucillo, who secured permission for the images. Aaron Downey at Nesbitt Graphics and Eric Jorgensen at Longman expertly coordinated the efforts of publisher, authors, copyeditor, proofreader, and compositor. We also thank the copyeditor, Stephanie Magean. In short, we have been fortunate in our associates.

Bill Cain would like to thank his wife Barbara and his daughters Julia and Isabel for their love and support.

SYLVAN BARNET
WILLIAM E. CAIN
WILLIAM BURTO

PART I

Getting Started

From Response to Argument

CHAPTER 1

How to Write an Effective Essay: A Crash Course

What is written without effort, in general is read without pleasure.

SAMUEL JOHNSON

Later pages will speak in detail about the writing process, but here we can offer a brief overview.

The Basic Strategy

Students have assured us that these suggestions are helpful.

- **Choose a topic and a tentative thesis,** an *argument*.
- **Generate ideas,** for instance, by asking yourself questions such as "Why did the author—a woman—tell the story from the point of view of this male character rather than that female character?" and "Does this story give me some insight into life?"
- **Make a tentative outline** of points you plan to make.
- **Rough out a first draft,** working from your outline (don't worry about spelling, punctuation, etc.) but don't hesitate to depart from the outline when new ideas come to you in the process of writing.
- **Make large-scale revisions** in your draft by reorganizing, or by adding details to clarify and support assertions, or by deleting or combining paragraphs.
- **Make small-scale revisions** by revising and editing sentences, checking spelling and grammar.
- **Revise your opening and concluding paragraphs.** Be certain that they are *interesting*, not mere throat-clearing and not mere summary.
- **Have someone read your revised draft** and comment on it.
- **Revise again,** taking into account the reader's suggestions.
- Read this latest version and **make further revisions as needed,** so that your thesis—your argument—is evident.
- **Proofread** your final version.

All writers must work out their own procedures and rituals, but the following basic suggestions will help you write effective essays. They assume that you have annotated the margins of the text and have jotted notes on index cards, but you can easily adapt the principles if you use a laptop. If your paper involves using sources, consult also Chapter 9, "Research: Writing with Sources."

Looking Closely: Approaching a First Draft

- **Look at the work or works carefully.**
- **Choose a worthwhile and compassable subject,** something that interests you and is not so big that your handling of it must be superficial. As you work, shape your topic, narrowing it, for example, from "Characterization in Updike's 'A & P'" to "Updike's Use of Contrasting Characters in 'A & P.'"
- **Keep your purpose in mind.** Although your instructor may ask you, perhaps as a preliminary writing assignment, to jot down your early responses—your initial experience of the work—it is more likely that he or she will ask you to write an analysis in which you will connect details, draw inferences, and argue that such-and-such is the case. That is, almost surely you will be asked to do more than write a summary or to report your responses; you probably will be expected to support a *thesis*, to make a claim, to offer an *argument*: "The metaphors are chiefly drawn from nature and, broadly speaking, they move from sky and sea to the earth, to human beings, which is to say that they become closer at hand, more immediate, more personal."

Don't expect to have a sound thesis at the very beginning of your work on the essay. The thesis will probably come to you only after you have done some close looking and have stimulated ideas by asking yourself questions. Almost surely you will see that the initial thesis needs to be modified in the light of evidence that you encounter. In short, your thesis will evolve in the course of thinking about what you are looking at.

An essay that evaluates a work will not only offer a value judgment but will also support the judgment with evidence. Yet even an explication—a sort of line-by-line paraphrase (see Chapter 5)—presents an argument, holding that the work means such-and-such. In thinking about your purpose, remember, too, that your *audience* will in effect determine the amount of detail that you must give. Although your instructor may in reality be your only reader, probably you should imagine that your audience consists of people pretty much like your classmates—intelligent but not especially familiar with the topic on which you have recently become a specialist. In putting yourself into the shoes of your imagined readers, think of reasonable objections the readers might raise, and respond appropriately to these objections.

1. **Keep looking at the literary work you are writing about.** Jot down notes on all relevant matters.
   - You can generate ideas for writing about the issues raised by essays, stories, poems, and plays by asking yourself questions such as those given on pages 349–50, 365–67, 443–44, and 519–20.
   - As you look and think, reflect on your observations and record them.
   - When you have an idea, jot it down, perhaps on a Post-it note attached to the margin of the book page; don't assume that you will remember it when you begin writing. Many people—if they are not taking notes on a computer—find that 4 × 6 index cards are handy for those notes that will not fit in the margins.
   - If you do use cards, put only one point on each card, and write a brief caption on the card (e.g., "Significance of title," or "Night = death???" Later you can arrange the cards so that the relevant notes are grouped together.

2. **When taking notes from secondary sources, do not simply highlight or photocopy.**
   - Take brief notes, *summarizing* important points and jotting down your own critiques of the material.
   - Read the material analytically, thoughtfully, with an open mind and a questioning spirit.
   - When you read in this attentive and tentatively skeptical way, you will find that the material is valuable not only for what it tells you but also for the ideas that you yourself produce in responding to it.

Writing your paper does not begin when you sit down to write a draft; rather, it begins when you write your first thoughtful notes.

3. **Sort out your notes, putting together what belongs together.** Three separate cards with notes about the texture of the materials of a building, for instance, probably belong together. Reject cards irrelevant to your topic.
4. **Organize your notes into a reasonable sequence.** Your notes contain ideas (or at least facts that you can think about); now the packets of cards have to be put into a coherent sequence. When you have made a tentative arrangement, review it; you may discover a better way to group your notes, and you may even want to add to them. If so, start reorganizing.

A tripartite organization usually works. For this structure, tentatively plan to devote your opening paragraph(s) to a statement of the topic or problem and a proposal of your hypothesis or thesis. The essay can then be shaped into three parts:

- a beginning, in which you identify the work(s) that you will discuss, giving the necessary background and, in a sentence or two, setting forth your underlying argument, your thesis;
- a middle, in which you develop your argument, chiefly by offering evidence and by taking account of reasonable possible objections to your argument; and
- a conclusion, in which you wrap things up, perhaps by giving a more general interpretation or by setting your findings in a larger context. (To read more about concluding paragraphs, see pages 3, 19, 62, 148–49, 193.)

In general, organize the material from the simple to the complex in order to ensure intelligibility. For instance, if you are discussing the structure of a poem, it probably will be best to begin with the most obvious points and then to turn to the subtler but perhaps equally important ones. Similarly, if you are comparing two characters, it may be best to move from the most obvious contrasts to the least obvious. When you have arranged your notes into a meaningful sequence, you have begun a key step: dividing your material into paragraphs.

5. **Get it down on paper.** Most essayists find it useful to jot down some sort of **outline,** a map indicating the main idea of each paragraph and, under each main idea, supporting details that give it substance. An outline—not necessarily anything highly formal, with capital and lowercase letters and Roman and Arabic numerals, but merely key phrases in some sort of order—will help you to overcome the paralysis called "writer's block" that commonly afflicts professional as well as student writers. For an example of a student's rough outline, see the jottings on page 21 that were turned into an essay on page 17.

A page of paper with ideas in some sort of sequence, however rough, ought to encourage you. You will discover that you do have something to say. And so, despite the temptation to sharpen another pencil or to have another cup of coffee or to get some new software, the best thing to do at this point is to follow the advice of Isaac Asimov, author of 225 books: "Sit down and start writing."

If you do not feel that you can work from note cards and a rough outline, try another method: Get something down on paper, writing (preferably on a word processor) freely, sloppily, automatically, or whatever, but allow your ideas about what the work means to you and how it conveys its meaning—rough as your ideas may be—to begin to take visible form. If you are like most people, you cannot do much precise thinking until you have committed to paper at least a rough sketch of your initial ideas. At this stage you are trying to find out what your ideas are, and in the course of getting them down on paper you will find yourself generating new ideas. We *think* with words. Later you can push and polish your ideas into shape, perhaps even deleting all of them and starting over, but it is a lot easier to improve your ideas once you see them in front of you than it is to do the job in your head. On paper, one word leads to another; in your head, one word often blocks another.

Just keep going; you may realize, as you near the end of a sentence, that you no longer believe it. Okay; be glad that your first idea led you to a better one, and pick up your better one and keep going with it. What you are doing is, in a sense, by trial and error pushing your way not only toward clear expression but also toward sharper ideas and richer responses.

Revising: Achieving a Readable Draft

Good writing is *re*writing. The evidence? Heavily annotated drafts by Chekhov, Keats, Hemingway, Tolstoy, Woolf—almost any writer you can name. Of course, it is easy enough to spill out words, but, as the dramatist Richard Sheridan said 200 years ago, "Easy writing's curst hard reading." Good writers find writing is difficult because they care; they care about making sense, so they will take time to answer reasonable objections to their arguments, and to find the exact words, the words that enable them to say precisely what they mean, so their readers will get it right. And they care about holding a reader's attention; they recognize that part of the job is to be interesting.

1. **Keep looking and thinking,** asking yourself questions and providing tentative answers, searching for additional material that strengthens or weakens your main point, and take account of it in your outline or draft.

Now is probably the time to think about a title for your essay. It is usually a good idea to let your reader know what your topic is—which works of literature you will discuss—and what your approach is. For instance, your topic might be Kate Chopin's "Désirée's Baby"—a story about the response to a white woman who gives birth to a black infant—and your approach might be that it is still relevant today. At this stage your title is still tentative, but thinking about a title will help you to organize your thoughts and to determine which of your notes are relevant and which are not. Remember, the title that you settle on is the first part of the paper that your reader encounters. You will gain the reader's goodwill by providing a helpful, interesting title.

2. **With your outline or draft in front of you, write a more lucid version,** checking your notes for fuller details. You probably wrote your draft on a computer, but do not try to revise it now merely by reading the monitor. Print a hard copy and revise it with pen or pencil. You need to read the essay more or less as your instructor will read it. True, the process of revising by hand takes more time than revising on a computer, but time is exactly what you need to devote to the process of revision. When you wrote your first draft, you perhaps were eager to pour out words, to find out what you thought, what you knew, what you did not know, but now, in the revising stage, you need to write slowly, thoughtfully. Later you will keyboard the handwritten revisions into the computer.

In revising an early draft it is probably best to start by concentrating on *large-scale revisions*—reorganization, additions (for instance, you may now see that you need to define a term, or to give an example, or to quote, as evidence, from the work you are discussing). You probably will also make substantial deletions, because you now see that some sentences or paragraphs, although interesting in themselves, are redundant or irrelevant.

Although it is best to start with large-scale revisions (i.e., with what teachers of composition somewhat grandly call "global revision"), the truth is that when most writers revise, whether they are experienced or inexperienced, they do not proceed methodically. Rather, they jump around, paying attention to whatever attracts their attention at the moment, like a dog hunting for fleas, and that is not a bad way to proceed. Still, here we can say that you might at least plan to work in the following sequence:

- **Introductory matters:** Make sure that your title and opening paragraph(s) give your readers an idea of where you will be taking them. Is your thesis evident?
- **Matters of organization:** If some of your material now seems to be in the wrong place, cut and paste. The Golden Rule: "Put together what belongs together." Is your concluding paragraph conclusive without being merely repetitive?
- **Evidence:** Make sure that your assertions are supported by evidence, evidence is of varying sorts, ranging from details in the works that you are talking about to quotations from appropriate sources.
- **Counter-evidence:** Consider the objections that a reasonable reader might raise to some or all of your points, and explain why these objections are not substantial.
- **Coherence in sentences, in paragraphs, and between paragraphs:** Usually this is a matter of adding transitional words and phrases (*furthermore, therefore, for instance, on the other hand*).
- **Tone:** Remember, your sentences inevitably convey information not only about your topic but about you yourself. Do the sentences suggest stuffiness? Or are they too informal, inappropriately casual?
- **Editorial matters:** Check the spelling of any words that you are in doubt about, check the punctuation, and check the form of footnotes and bibliography (list of works cited).

If you find that some of the points in your earlier jottings are no longer relevant, eliminate them; but make sure that the argument flows from one point to the next. It is not enough to keep your thesis in mind; you must keep it in the reader's mind. As you write, your ideas will doubtless become clearer, and some may prove to be poor ideas. (We rarely know exactly what our ideas are until we set them down on paper. As the little girl said, replying to the suggestion that she should think before she speaks, "How do I know what I think until I see what I say?") Not until you have written a draft do you really have a strong sense of what you feel and know, and of how good your essay may be.

If you have not already made an outline at this stage, it is probably advisable to make one, to ensure that your draft is reasonably organized. Jot down, in sequence, each major point and each subpoint. You may find that some points need amplification, or that a point made on page 3 really ought to go on page 1.

Later you will concern yourself with *small-scale revisions* (polishing sentences, clarifying transitions, varying sentence structure if necessary, checking spelling and documentation).

3. **After a suitable interval, preferably a few days, again revise and edit the draft.** To write a good essay, you must be a good reader of the essay you are writing. We are not talking at this stage about proofreading or correcting spelling errors, though you will need to do that later. Van Gogh said, "One becomes a painter by painting." Similarly, one becomes a writer by writing—and by rewriting, by revising. In revising their work, writers ask themselves many questions:
   - Do I mean what I say?
   - Do I say what I mean? (Answering this question will generate other questions: Do I need to define my terms? Add examples to clarify? Reorganize the material so that a reader can grasp it?)

> ***A Rule for Writers:*** Put yourself in the reader's shoes to make sure that the paper not only has an organization but also that the organization will be clear to your reader. If you imagine a classmate as the reader of the draft, you may find that you need to add transition words (*for instance, on the other hand*), clarify definitions, and provide additional supporting evidence.

During this part of the process of writing, read the draft in a skeptical frame of mind. You engaged in critical thinking if you made use of sources. Apply the same questioning spirit to your own writing. In taking account of your doubts, you will probably unify, organize, clarify, and polish the draft.

Reminder: If you have written your draft on a word processor, do not try to revise it on the monitor. Print the entire draft, and then read it—as your reader will be reading it—page by page, not screen by screen. Almost surely you will detect errors in a hard copy that you miss on the screen. Only by reading the printed copy will you be able to see if, for instance, paragraphs are too long.

After producing a draft that seems good enough to show to someone, writers engage in yet another activity. They edit. **Editing** includes such work as checking the accuracy of quotations by comparing them with the original, checking a dictionary for the spelling of doubtful words, and checking a handbook for doubtful punctuation—for instance, whether a comma or a semicolon is needed in a particular sentence.

CHECKLIST: *Revising a Draft*

Have I asked myself the following questions?

- Does the draft fulfill the specifications (e.g., length, scope) of the assignment?
- Does the draft have a point, a focus?
- Is the title interesting and informative? Does it create a favorable first impression?
- Are the early paragraphs engaging, and do they give the reader a fairly good idea of what will follow, perhaps by naming the works of art and the approach?
- Are arguable assertions supported with evidence?
- Are the readers kept in mind, for instance, by defining terms that they may be unfamiliar with? Are possible reasonable objections faced and adequately answered?
- If any quotations are included, are they adequately introduced rather than just dumped into the essay? Are quotations as brief as possible? Might summaries (properly credited to the sources) be more effective than long quotations?
- Are *all* sources cited, including Internet material?
- Is the organization clear, reasonable, and effective? (Check by making a quick outline.)
- Does the final paragraph nicely round off the paper, or does it merely restate—unnecessarily—what is by now obvious?
- Does the paper include whatever visual materials the reader needs to see?

Peer Review

Almost all professional writers get help—from friends, from colleagues, and especially from editors who are paid to go over their manuscripts and call attention to matters that need clarification. If possible, get a fellow-student to read your manuscript and to give you his or her responses. Do not confuse this sort of help—recommended by all instructors—with plagiarism, which is the unacknowledged borrowing of words or ideas or both. Your reader is not rewriting the paper for you, but merely is suggesting that (for instance) your title is misleading, and that here you need a clear example, there you are excessively repetitive, and so forth. If you are unfamiliar with the process of peer review and have any doubts about the nature of plagiarism, we urge you to read the discussions on pages 9–10, 318–19, and Appendix C.

If peer review is a part of the writing process in your course, the instructor may distribute a sheet with suggestions and questions. The preceding checklist is an example of such a sheet.

Preparing the Final Version

1. **If you have received comments from a reader, consider them carefully.** Even if you disagree with them, they may alert you to places in your essay that need revision, such as clarification.

In addition, if a friend, a classmate, or another peer reviewer has given you some help, acknowledge that person in a footnote or endnote. (If you look at almost any book, you will notice that the author acknowledges the help of friends and colleagues. In your own writing follow this practice.) Here are sample acknowledgments from papers by students:

> I wish to thank Anna Aaron for numerous valuable suggestions.
>
> I wish to thank Paul Gottsegen for calling my attention to passages that needed clarification, and Jane Leslie for suggesting the comparison between Sammy in Updike's "A & P" and the unnamed narrator in Joyce's "Araby."

2. **Write, type, or print a clean copy,** following the principles concerning margins, pagination, footnotes, and so on, set forth in Appendix B.
3. **If you have borrowed any ideas, be sure to give credit,** usually in footnotes, to your sources. Remember that plagiarism is not limited to the unacknowledged borrowing of words; a borrowed idea, even when put into your own words, requires acknowledgment. (On giving credit to sources, see pages 318–19.)
4. **Proofread a hard copy, make corrections as necessary, and reprint.**

All of this adds up to a recipe in a famous Victorian cookbook: "First catch your hare, then cook it."

CHAPTER 2

The Writer as Reader

Interviewer: Did you know as a child you wanted to be a writer?
Toni Morrison: No. I wanted to be a reader.

Reading and Responding

Learning to write is in large measure learning to read. The text you should read most carefully is the one you yourself write, an essay—probably an argument defending an interpretation. It may start as a jotting in the margin of a book you are reading or as a brief note in a journal, and it will go through several drafts before it becomes an essay. To produce something that another person will find worth reading, you must read each draft with care, trying to imagine the effect your words are likely to have on your reader. In writing about literature, you will apply some of the same critical skills to your reading; that is, you will examine your responses to what you are reading and will try to account for them.

Let's begin by looking at a very short story by Kate Chopin (1851–1904). (The name is pronounced in the French way, something like "show pan.") Kate O'Flaherty, born into a prosperous family in St. Louis, in 1870 married Oscar Chopin, a French-Creole businessman from Louisiana. They lived in New Orleans, where they had six children. Oscar died of malaria in 1882, and in 1884 Kate returned to St. Louis, where, living with her mother and children, she began to write fiction.

KATE CHOPIN

Ripe Figs

Maman-Nainaine said that when the figs were ripe Babette might go to visit her cousins down on the Bayou-Lafourche where the sugar cane grows. Not that the ripening of figs had the least thing to do with it, but that is the way Maman-Nainaine was.

It seemed to Babette a very long time to wait; for the leaves upon the trees were tender yet, and the figs were like little hard, green marbles.

But warm rains came along and plenty of strong sunshine, and though Maman-Nainaine was as patient as the statue of la Madone, and Babette as restless as a humming-bird, the first thing they both knew it was hot summertime. Every day Babette danced out to where the fig-trees were in a long line against the fence. She walked slowly beneath them, carefully peering between the gnarled, spreading branches. But each time she came disconsolate away again. What she saw there finally was something that made her sing and dance the whole long day.

When Maman-Nainaine sat down in her stately way to breakfast, the following morning, her muslin cap standing like an aureole about her white, placid face, Babette approached. She bore a dainty porcelain platter, which she set down before her godmother. It contained a dozen purple figs, fringed around with their rich, green leaves.

"Ah," said Maman-Nainaine arching her eyebrows, "how early the figs have ripened this year!"

"Oh," said Babette. "I think they have ripened very late."

"Babette," continued Maman-Nainaine, as she peeled the very plumpest figs with her pointed silver fruit-knife, "you will carry my love to them all down on Bayou-Lafourche. And tell your Tante Frosine I shall look for her at Toussaint—when the chrysanthemums are in bloom."

[1893]

Reading as Re-creation

If we had been Chopin's contemporaries, we might have read this sketch in *Vogue* in 1893 or in an early collection of her works, *A Night in Acadie* (1897). But we are not Chopin's original readers, and, since we live more than a century later, we inevitably read "Ripe Figs" in a somewhat different way. And this gets us to an important truth about writing and reading. A writer writes, sets forth his or her meaning, and attempts to guide the reader's responses, as we all do when we write a letter home saying that we're thinking of dropping a course or asking for news or money. To this extent, the writer creates the written work and puts a meaning in it.

But the reader, whether reading that written work as a requirement or for recreation, *re-creates* it according to his or her experience and understanding. For instance, if the letter-writer's appeal for money is too indirect, the reader may miss it entirely or may sense it but feel that the need is not urgent. If, on the other hand, the appeal is direct or demanding, the reader may feel imposed upon, even assaulted. "Oh, but I didn't mean it that way," the writer later protests. Nevertheless, that's the way the reader took it. The letter is "out there," a physical reality standing between the writer and the reader, but its *meaning* is something the reader as well as the writer makes.

Since all readers bring themselves to a written work, they each bring something individual. Although many of Chopin's original readers knew that she wrote chiefly about the people of Louisiana, especially Creoles (descendants of the early French and Spanish settlers), Cajuns (descendants of the French whom the British had expelled from Canada in the eighteenth century), African Americans, and mulattoes, those readers must have varied in their attitudes about such people. And many of today's readers do *not* (before they read a work by Chopin) know anything about her subject. Some readers may know where Bayou-Lafourche is, and they may have notions about what it looks like, but most readers will not; indeed, many readers will not know that a bayou is a sluggish, marshy inlet or outlet of a river or lake.

Moreover, even if a present-day reader in Chicago, Seattle, or Juneau knows what a bayou is, he or she may assume that "Ripe Figs" depicts a way of life still current, whereas a reader from Louisiana may see in the work a depiction of a lost way of life, a depiction of the good old days (or perhaps of the bad old days, depending on the reader's point of view). Much depends, we can say, on the reader's storehouse of experience.

To repeat: Reading is a *re*-creation; the author has tried to guide our responses, but inevitably our own experiences, as well as our ethnic background and education, contribute to our responses. You may find useful a distinction that E. D. Hirsch makes in *Validity in Interpretation* (1967). For Hirsch,

- the *meaning* in a text is the author's intended meaning;
- the *significance* is the particular relevance for each reader.

In this view, when you think about meaning you are thinking about what the author was trying to say and to do—for instance, to take an old theme and treat it in a new way. When you think about significance, you are thinking about what the work does for you—it enlarges your mind, deepens your understanding of love or grief, offends you by its depiction of women, or produces some other effect.

Collecting Evidence, Making Reasonable Inferences

Does this mean, then, that there is no use talking (or writing) about literature, since all of us perceive it in our relatively private ways, rather like the seven blind men in the fable? One man, you will recall, touched the elephant's tail (or was it his trunk?) and said that the elephant is like a snake; another touched the elephant's side and said the elephant is like a wall; a third touched the elephant's leg and said the elephant is like a tree, and so on. This familiar story is usually told in order to illustrate human limitations, but notice, too, that each of the blind men *did* perceive an aspect of the elephant—an elephant is massive, like a wall or a tree, and an elephant is (in its way) remarkably supple, as you know if you have given peanuts to one.

As readers we can and should make an effort to understand what an author seems to be getting at. For instance, we should make an effort to understand unfamiliar words. Perhaps we shouldn't look up every word that we don't know, at least on the first reading, but if certain unfamiliar words are repeated and thus seem especially important, we will want to look them up.

It happens that in "Ripe Figs" a French word appears: "*Tante* Frosine" means "*Aunt* Frosine." Fortunately, the meaning of the word is not crucial, and the context probably makes it clear that Frosine is an adult, which is all that we really need to know about her. But a reader who does not know that chrysanthemums bloom in late summer or early autumn will miss part of Chopin's meaning. The point is this: The writer is pitching, and she expects the reader to catch.

On the other hand, although writers tell us a good deal, they cannot tell us everything. We know that Maman-Nainaine is Babette's godmother, but we don't know exactly how old Maman-Nainaine and Babette are. Further, Chopin tells us nothing of Babette's parents. It *sounds* as though Babette and her godmother live alone, but readers' opinions may differ. One reader may argue that Babette's parents must be dead or ill, whereas another may argue that the status of her parents is irrelevant and that what counts is that Babette is supervised by only one person, a mature woman.

In short, a text includes **indeterminacies** (passages that careful readers agree are open to various interpretations) and **gaps** (things left unsaid in the story, such as why a godmother rather than a mother takes care of Babette). As we work our way through a text, we keep reevaluating what we have read, pulling the details together to make sense of them, in a process called **consistency building.**

Whatever the gaps, careful readers are able to collect evidence and to draw many reasonable inferences about Maman-Nainaine. What are some of these? We can list them:

She is older than Babette.
She has a "stately way," and she is "patient as the statue of la Madone."
She has an odd way (is it exasperating, or engaging, or a little of each?) of connecting actions with the seasons.
Given this last point, she seems to act slowly, to be very patient.
She apparently is used to being obeyed.

You may at this point want to go back and reread "Ripe Figs," to see what else you can say about Maman-Nainaine.

And now what of Babette?

She is young.
She is active and impatient ("restless as a humming-bird").
She is obedient.

And at this point, too, you may want to add to the list.

If you do add to the list, you might compare your additions with those of a classmate. The two of you may find that you disagree about what may reasonably be inferred from Chopin's words. Suppose, for instance, that your classmate said that although Babette is outwardly obedient, inwardly she probably hates Maman-Nainaine. Would you agree that this assertion is an acceptable inference? If you don't agree, how might you go about trying to convince your classmate that such a response is not justified? What arguments (supported by what evidence) would you offer?

We are speaking here of an activity of mind called **critical thinking,** a topic discussed in the next chapter.

Reading with Pen in Hand

It's probably best to read a work of literature straight through, enjoying it and letting yourself be carried along to the end. But then, when you have an overall view, you'll want to read it again, noticing (for example) how certain innocent-seeming details given early in the work prove to be important later.

Perhaps the best way to read attentively is, after a first reading, to mark the text, underlining or highlighting passages that seem especially interesting, and to jot notes or queries in the margins. (*Caution*: Annotate and highlight, but don't get so carried away that you highlight whole pages.)

Recording Your First Responses

Another useful way of getting at the meaning of a work of literature is to jot down your initial responses to it, recording your impressions as they come to you in any order—almost as though you're talking to yourself. Since no one else is going to read your notes, you can be entirely free and at ease. You can write in sentences or not; it's up to you.

You can jot down these responses either before or after you annotate the text. Some readers find that annotating the text helps to produce ideas for further jottings,

KATE CHOPIN
Ripe Figs

Maman-Nainaine said that when the figs were ripe Babette might go to visit her cousins down on the Bayou-Lafourche where the sugar cane grows. Not that the ripening of figs had the least thing to do with it, but that is the way Maman-Nainaine was.

It seemed to Babette a very long time to wait; for the leaves upon the trees were tender yet, and the figs were like little hard, green marbles.

But warm rains came along and plenty of strong sunshine, and though Maman-Nainaine was as patient as the statue of la Madone, and Babette as restless as a humming-bird, the first thing they both knew it was hot summertime. Every day Babette danced ~~out to~~ where the fig-trees were in a long line against the fence. She walked slowly beneath them, carefully peering between the gnarled, spreading branches. But each time she came disconsolate away again. What she saw there finally was something that made her sing and dance the whole long day.

When Maman-Nainaine sat down in her stately way to breakfast, the following morning, her muslin cap standing like an aureole about her white, placid face, Babette approached. She bore a dainty porcelain platter, which she set down before her godmother. It contained a dozen purple figs fringed around with their rich, green leaves.

"Ah," said Maman-Nainaine arching her eyebrows, "how early the figs have ripened this year!"

"Oh," said Babette. "I think they have ripened very late."

"Babette," continued Maman-Nainaine, as she peeled the very plumpest figs with her pointed silver fruit-knife, "you will carry my love to them all down on Bayou-Lafourche. And tell your Tante Frosine I shall look for her at Toussaint—when the chrysanthemums are in bloom."

Handwritten annotations: ? (Bayou) · strange · contrast between M-N and B · another contrast · Check? this · ceremonious · nice echo contrast like a song · time passes fast for M-N slowly for B · is M-N herself like a plump fig? · B entrusted with a message of love · opens with figs; ends with chrys. (autumn) · fulfillment? Equivalent to figs ripening?

but others prefer to jot down a few thoughts immediately after a first reading, and then, stimulated by these thoughts, they reread and annotate the text.

Write whatever comes into your mind, whatever the literary work triggers in your own imagination, whatever you think are the important ideas or values of your own experience.

Here is a student's first response to "Ripe Figs":

> This is a very short story. I didn't know stories were this short, but I like it because you can get it all quickly and it's no trouble to reread it carefully. The shortness, though, leaves a lot of gaps for the reader to fill in. So much is not said. Your imagination is put to work.
>
> But I can see Maman-N sitting at her table—pleasantly powerful—no one you would want to argue with. She's formal and distant—and definitely has quirks. She wants to postpone Babette's trip, but we don't know why.

And you can sense B's frustration. But maybe she's teaching her that something really good is worth waiting for and that anticipation is as much fun as the trip. Maybe I can develop this idea.

Another thing. I can tell they are not poor–from two things. The pointed silver fruit knife and the porcelain platter, and the fact that Maman sits down to breakfast in a "stately" way. They are the leisure class. But I don't know enough about life on the bayous to go into this. Their life is different from mine; no one I know has that kind of peaceful rural life.

Identifying Your Audience and Purpose

Now, suppose that you are beginning the process of writing about "Ripe Figs" for someone else, not for yourself. The first question to ask yourself is: "For whom am I writing?" That is, who is your *audience*? (Of course, you probably are writing because an instructor has asked you to do so, but you must still imagine an audience. Your instructor may tell you, for instance, to write for your classmates, or to write for the best teacher you had in high school.)

- If you are writing for people who already are familiar with some of Chopin's work, you won't have to say much about the author, but
- if you are writing for an audience that perhaps has never heard of Chopin, you may want to include a brief biographical note of the sort we gave.
- If you are writing for an audience that, you have reason to believe, has read several works by Chopin, you may want to make some comparisons, explaining—really arguing—that "Ripe Figs" resembles or differs from Chopin's other work.

In a sense, the audience is your collaborator; it helps you to decide what you will say. You are also helped by your sense of *purpose*. If your aim is to introduce readers to Chopin, you will make certain points that reflect this purpose. If your aim is to tell people what you think "Ripe Figs" means to say about human relationships, or about time, you will say some different things. If your aim is to have a little fun and to entertain an audience that is already familiar with "Ripe Figs," you may decide to write a parody (a humorous imitation) of the story.

Your Turn: Arguing a Thesis in an Essay

Let's assume that you want to describe "Ripe Figs" to someone who has not read it. You will briefly summarize the action, such as it is, and will mention where it takes place; who the characters are, including what their relationship is; and what, if anything, happens to them. Beyond that, you'll try to explain as honestly as you can what makes "Ripe Figs" appealing or interesting—or trifling, or boring, or whatever. That is, you will *argue* a thesis, even though you almost surely will not say anything as formal as "In this essay I will argue that . . ." or "This essay will attempt to prove that . . ." Your essay nevertheless will essentially be an argument because (perhaps after a brief summary of the work) you will be pointing to the evidence that has caused you to respond as you did.

A Sample Essay by a Student

Here is an essay that a student, Antonia Tenori, wrote for this assignment.

Tenori 1

Antonia Tenori

Professor Lee

English 102

11 February 2009

Images of Ripening in Kate Chopin's "Ripe Figs"

Very little happens in Kate Chopin's one-page story, "Ripe Figs." Maman-Nainaine tells her goddaughter Babette that she may "visit her cousins down on the Bayou-Lafourche" "when the figs were ripe"; the figs ripen, and Babette is given permission to go. So little happens in "Ripe Figs" that the story at first appears merely to be a character sketch that illustrates, through Babette and her godmother, the contrast between youth and age. But by means of the natural imagery of the tale, Chopin suggests more than this: She asks her readers to see the relationship of human time to nature's seasons, and she suggests that, try as we may to push the process of maturity, growth or "ripening" happens in its own time.

The story clearly contrasts the impatience of youth with the patience and dignity that come with age. Babette, whose name suggests she is still a "little baby," is "restless as a humming-bird." Each day when she eagerly goes to see if the figs have ripened, she doesn't simply walk but she dances. By contrast, Maman-Nainaine has a "stately way," she is "patient as the statue of la Madone," and there is an "aureole"—a radiance—"about her white,

Tenori 2

placid face." The brief dialog near the end of the story also emphasizes the difference between the two characters. When the figs finally ripen, Maman-Nainaine is surprised (she arches her eyebrows), and she exclaims, "how early the figs have ripened this year!" Babette replies, "I think they have ripened very late."

Chopin is not simply remarking here that time passes slowly for young people, and quickly for old people. She suggests that nature moves at its own pace regardless of human wishes. Babette, young and "tender" as the fig leaves, can't wait to "ripen." Her visit to Bayou-Lafourche is not a mere pleasure trip, but represents her coming into her own season of maturity. Babette's desire to rush this process is tempered by a condition that her godmother sets: Babette must wait until the figs ripen, since everything comes in its own season. Maman-Nainaine recognizes the patterns of the natural world, the rhythms of life. By asking Babette to await the ripening, the young girl is asked to pay attention to the patterns as well.

Chopin further suggests that if we pay attention and wait with patience, the fruits of our own growth will be sweet, plump, and beautiful, like the "dozen purple figs, fringed around with their rich, green leaves," that Babette finally offers her godmother. Chopin uses natural imagery effectively, interweaving the young girl's growth with the rhythms of the seasons. In this way, the reader is connected with both processes in an intimate and inviting way.

[New page]

Tenori 3

Work Cited

Chopin, Kate. "Ripe Figs." *Literature for Composition*. Ed. Sylvan Barnet, William Burto, and William E. Cain. 9th ed. New York: Longman, 2010. 11–12. Print.

The Argument Analyzed

- The title of the essay is informative; it clearly indicates the focus of the analysis. Notice, too, that it is much more interesting than "An Analysis of a Story" or "An Analysis of Kate Chopin's 'Ripe Figs'" or "'Ripe Figs': A Study" or "An Analysis of Imagery." In your own essays, construct titles that inform and interest your reader.
- The first sentence names the author and title. Strictly speaking, this information is redundant, since it appears in the title, but it is customary to give the author's full name and the title of the work early in the essay, and it is essential to give such information if it is not in the title.
- The second sentence offers enough plot summary to enable the reader to follow the discussion. But notice that the essay as a whole is much more than a summary of the plot. Summary here is offered early, merely to make the analysis intelligible. Chiefly, the opening paragraph presents one view (the view that Antonia believes is inadequate); then, after a transitional "but," offers a second view and presents a thesis—the point that Antonia will argue.

  Perhaps the most common error students make in writing about literature is to confuse a summary of the plot with a thoughtful analysis of the work. A little plot-telling is acceptable, to remind your reader of what happens, but normally your essay will be devoted to setting forth a thesis about a work, and supporting the thesis with evidence. Your readers do not want to know what happens in the work; they want to know what you make out of the work—how you interpret it, or why you like or dislike it.
- In the second paragraph, Antonia supports her thesis by providing brief quotations. These quotations are not padding; rather, they are evidence supporting her assertion that Chopin "contrasts the impatience of youth with the patience and dignity that come with age."
- In the third paragraph Antonia develops her thesis ("Chopin is not simply . . . She suggests . . .")
- The final paragraph begins with a helpful transition ("Chopin *further* suggests"), offers additional evidence, and ends with a new idea (about the reader's response to the story) that takes the discussion a step further. The essay avoids the deadliest kind of conclusion, a mere summary of the essay

("Thus we have seen," or some such words). Antonia's effective final sentence nicely draws the reader into the essay. (Effective final sentences are hard to write, but we give advice about them on pages 3, 19, 62, 148–49, and 193.)

Antonia Tenori wrote this paper for an assignment early in the semester, and it's worth noting that students were told to write "about 500 words (two double-spaced typed pages)." If

- the first question to ask is "To whom am I writing?"
- the second question to ask is, "What is the length of the assignment?"

The answer to this second question will provide two sorts of guidance: It will give you some sense of how much time you should devote to preparing the paper—obviously an instructor expects you to spend more time on a ten-page paper than on a one-page paper—and, second, it will give you a sense of how much detail you can include. For a short paper—say, 1–2 pages—you will need to make your main point with a special kind of directness; you will not have space for lots of details, just those that support the main point. This is what Antonia aims to achieve in her second and third paragraphs, where she highlights the term "ripens" and briefly, but effectively, develops its implications. For a longer paper, 3–5 pages, or one that is longer still, you can examine the characters, setting, and central themes in greater depth, and can focus on more details in the text to strengthen your analysis.

Behind the Scenes: Tenori's Essay, from Early Responses to Final Version

This essay is good because it is clear and interesting, and especially because it helps to develop a reader's understanding and enjoyment of Chopin's story. Now let's go backstage, so to speak, to see how Antonia Tenori turned her notes into an effective final draft.

Tenori's Earliest Responses. After reading the story, Antonia annotated it, marking whatever she thought especially noteworthy. She then jotted down ideas in the Notebook application from Circus Ponies Software, although she could just as easily have used several other applications. Is "Ripe Figs" a story, or is it just a character sketch? (She put her responses on a page for that topic.) What contrasts are notable? (She recorded the material on another notebook page.) What words or phrases or images are unusual? (She recorded the material on another notebook page.) A day later, when she returned to work on her paper, stimulated by another reading of "Ripe Figs" and by a review of her notes, Antonia made additional jottings.

Organizing Notes. When the time came to turn the notes into a draft and the revised draft into an essay, she reviewed the notes and added further thoughts. Next, she organized the note pages, putting together into one section whatever pages she had about (for instance) characterization, and putting together, into another section, whatever note pages she had about (again, for instance) the seasons. Reviewing the notes in each section, and on the basis of the review (after making a backup copy) deleting a few pages that no longer seemed useful and moving an occasional page into a different section (via the Contents view), Antonia started to think about how she might organize her essay.

As a first step in settling on an organization, she arranged the notebook sections into a sequence that seemed reasonable to her. It made sense, she thought, to begin with a brief biographical sketch of Chopin, but she soon decided not to include this material because the reader would probably already know it, and in any case it was not relevant to the argument she planned to set forth. She then decided to go on to some large points about the story, then to refine some of these points, and finally to offer some sort of conclusion. This organization, she felt, was reasonable and would enable her reader to follow her argument easily.

Preparing a Preliminary Outline. In order to get a clearer idea of where she might be going, Antonia then typed an outline following the sequence of her note packets—the gist of what at this stage seemed to be the organization of her chief points in the OmniOutliner (Omni Group), although she could just as easily have used the Outline view in Microsoft Word, or, again, she could have used pen and paper. In short, she prepared a map or rough outline so that she could easily see, almost at a glance, if each part of her paper would lead coherently to the next part.

Antonia realized that in surveying her outline she might become aware of points that she should have included but that she had instead overlooked. Below we print her outline, and the revised version.

First Outline

- Bio of Chopin
- Plot summary
- Characterization
  - Babette
  - Maman-N
- Contrasts
  - Youth: activity, impatient
  - Age: stately, "statue"
- Differences in perception of nature
- Point? Meaning?

Revised Outline

- Little plot, emph. on contrasting characters
- Characters related to seasons
- Contrasts
  - spring vs autumn
  - youth vs maturity
  - impatience vs patience (?)
- Significance, meaning
  - Maman-N as teacher
  - some things can't be hurried
  - implication that B is maturing, can carry message, will become aware of the changing seasons, and that there is a right time for each action

Remember, a tentative outline is not a straitjacket that determines the shape of the final essay. To the contrary, it is a preliminary map that, when examined, helps the writer to see not only pointless detours—these will be eliminated in the draft—but also undeveloped areas that need to be worked up. As the two versions of Antonia's outline indicate, after drafting her map she made some important changes before writing a first draft.

Writing a Draft. Working from her thoughtfully revised outline, Antonia wrote a first draft, which she then revised into a second draft. The second draft, when further revised, became the final essay. Modern word processors such as Microsoft Word allow you to track the revisions made to a document, and look at different versions of a document. However, many writers find comfort in having a printed copy of each draft to go over with a pen; the desired changes can then be made (and kept track of) on the computer.

For more about writing with a computer, see pages 62–63 and 315.

Other Possibilities for Writing

You might write a paper of a very different sort. Consider the following possibilities:

1. Write a sequel, moving from fall to spring.
2. Write a letter from Babette, at Bayou-Lafourche, to Maman-Nainaine.
3. Imagine that Babette is now an old woman, writing her memoirs. What does she say about Maman-Nainaine?
4. Write a narrative based on your own experience of learning a lesson in patience.

Looking Closely at Two Contemporary Mini-Stories: Lydia Davis's "Childcare" and "City People"

Lydia Davis

Lydia Davis, born in 1947 in Northampton, Massachusetts, grew up in New York City and then lived for several years in France and Ireland. She has translated French literature into English, and written several books of stories. Among her awards is a MacArthur Fellowship.

Childcare

It's his turn to take care of the baby. He is cross.
He says, "I never get enough done."
The baby is in a bad mood, too.
He gives the baby a bottle of juice and sits him well back in a big armchair.
He sits himself down in another chair and turns on the television.
Together they watch *The Odd Couple.*

[2007]

In Davis's *Varieties of Disturbance,* the book from which we reprint "Childcare," the story appears in the middle of a page that is otherwise blank. The very appearance on the page is part of the performance, and it is also part of—dare we say?—the meaning. We see a largely blank page, a bare world, not much to look at, not much to make life rich. What do we know about the inhabitants of this world?

- The unnamed man (he is merely "he") is "cross," and the unnamed baby "is in a bad mood, too."
- The next thing we learn about the man is what we deduce from his statement, "I never get enough done." Ah, he is someone who wants to accomplish something. That sounds admirable.
- But he thinks the temporary job ("it's his turn") of caring for the baby interferes with his unspecified aspirations. That sounds not so nice, and we may wonder, "What sort of a guy is this who resents caring for his infant?"

"Once upon a time, they lived happily ever after."

The next things we learn dispose us favorably toward the man:

- "He gives the baby a bottle of juice and sits him well back in a big armchair." This business of sitting the child "well back in a big armchair" suggests that the man takes some care to make sure that the child is secure, is safely placed. We like that, we are reassured.
- The man then sits down in another chair and "turns on the television." Television? We might have thought that this man who can "never get enough done" would balance his checkbook, or read the newspaper, or answer a letter, but no, he watches television. That's not a crime, but for a guy who complains that he "can never get enough done," it does seem a bit much.
- The final sentence is, "Together they watch *The Odd Couple*." Surely the thought crosses a reader's mind that these two are themselves an odd couple, and the reader may reasonably conclude that in some ways the man—cross, claiming that he can't get anything done—is as infantile as the baby.

It's a story told very simply, chiefly in simple sentences, "He says," "The baby is," "He gives," etc. Only twice does the author use compound sentences (simple sentences joined by a conjunction, in this case the most child-like of all conjunctions, "and," the language found in Dick and Jane children's books). Not much happens in this very simply told story, but it tells us all that we need to know about the unnamed man. And perhaps it tells us something about life, even about our own lives, for instance about the disparity between our own grand view of ourselves and the simple reality.

Now for a second very short story by Lydia Davis.

City People

They have moved to the country. The country is nice enough: there are quail sitting in the bushes and frogs peeping in the swamps. But they are uneasy. They quarrel more often. They cry, or she cries and he bows his head. He is pale all the time now. She wakes in a panic at night, hearing him sniffle. She wakes in a panic again, hearing a car go up the driveway. In the morning there is sunlight on their faces but mice are chattering in the walls. He hates the mice. The pump breaks. They replace the pump. They poison the mice. Their neighbor's dog barks. It barks and barks. She could poison the dog.

"We're city people," he says, "and there aren't any nice cities to live in."

[2001]

Joining the Conversation: Critical Thinking and Writing

1. What elements of performance—perhaps we can say Davis's craftsmanship—do you see in this tiny narrative?
2. Does the story give at least a tiny glimpse of some aspect of life? Please explain.
3. We are not told *why* these people have moved from the city to the country. Is it reasonable to offer a guess? If you think a reader can plausibly guess why they moved, what, in your view, is the reason for the move?

A Story, with a Student's Notes and Final Essay

RAY BRADBURY

Ray Bradbury (b. 1920) was born in Waukegan, Illinois, and educated there and in Los Angeles. While a high school student he published his first science fiction in the school's magazine, and by 1941 he was publishing professionally. The story printed here is from The Martian Chronicles *(1950), a collection of linked short stories. Among his other works are* Fahrenheit 451 *(1953),* Something Wicked This Way Comes *(1962), and* Death Is a Lonely Business *(1985).*

August 2026: There Will Come Soft Rains

In the living room the voice-clock sang, *Tick-Tock, seven o'clock, time to get up, time to get up, seven o'clock!* as if it were afraid that nobody would. The morning house lay empty. The clock ticked on, repeating and repeating its sounds into the emptiness. *Seven-nine, breakfast time, seven-nine!*

In the kitchen the breakfast stove gave a hissing sigh and ejected from its warm interior eight pieces of perfectly browned toast, eight eggs sunny-side up, sixteen slices of bacon, two coffees, and two cool glasses of milk.

"Today is August 4, 2026," said a second voice from the kitchen ceiling, "in the city of Allendale, California." It repeated the date three times for memory's sake. "Today is Mr. Featherstone's birthday. Today is the anniversary of Tilita's marriage. Insurance is payable, as are the water, gas, and light bills."

Somewhere in the walls, relays clicked, memory tapes glided under electric eyes.

5 *Eight-one, tick-tock, eight-one o'clock, off to school, off to work, run, run, eight-one!* But no doors slammed, no carpets took the soft tread of rubber heels. It was raining outside. The weather box on the front door sang quietly: "Rain, rain, go away; rubbers, raincoats for today. . . ." And the rain tapped on the empty house, echoing.

Outside, the garage chimed and lifted its door to reveal the waiting car. After a long wait the door swung down again.

At eight-thirty the eggs were shriveled and toast was like stone. An aluminum wedge scraped them into the sink, where hot water whirled them down a metal throat which digested and flushed them away to the distant sea. The dirty dishes were dropped into a hot washer and emerged twinkling dry.

Nine-fifteen, sang the clock, *time to clean.*

Out of warrens in the wall, tiny robot mice darted. The rooms were acrawl with the small cleaning animals, all rubber and metal. They thudded against chairs, whirling their mustached runners, kneading the rug nap, sucking gently at hidden dust. Then, like mysterious invaders, they popped into their burrows. Their pink electric eyes faded. The house was clean.

10 *Ten o'clock.* The sun came out from behind the rain. The house stood alone in a city of rubble and ashes. This was the one house left standing. At night the ruined city gave off a radioactive glow which could be seen for miles.

Ten-fifteen. The garden sprinklers whirled up in golden founts, filling the soft morning air with scatterings of brightness. The water pelted windowpanes, running down the charred west side where the house had been burned evenly free of its white paint. The entire west face of the house was black, save for five places. Here the silhouette in paint of a man mowing a lawn. Here, as in a photograph, a woman bent to pick flowers. Still farther over, their images burned on wood in one titanic instant, a small boy, hands flung into the air; higher up, the image of a thrown ball, and opposite him a girl, hands raised to catch a ball which never came down.

The five spots of paint—the man, the woman, the children, the ball—remained. The rest was a thin charcoaled layer.

The gentle sprinkler rain filled the garden with falling light.

Until this day, how well the house had kept its peace. How carefully it had inquired, "Who goes there? What's the password?" and, getting no answer from lonely foxes and whining cats, it had shut up its windows and drawn shades in an old-maidenly preoccupation with self-protection which bordered on a mechanical paranoia.

15 It quivered at each sound, the house did. If a sparrow brushed a window, the shade snapped up. The bird, startled, flew off! No, not even a bird must touch the house!

The house was an altar with ten thousand attendants, big, small, servicing, attending, in choirs. But the gods had gone away, and the ritual of the religion continued senselessly, uselessly.

Twelve noon.

A dog whined, shivering, on the front porch.

The front door recognized the dog voice and opened. The dog, once huge and fleshy, but now gone to bone and covered with sores, moved in and through the house, tracking mud. Behind it whirred angry mice, angry at having to pick up mud, angry at inconvenience.

For not a leaf fragment blew under the door but what the wall panels flipped open and the copper scrap rats flashed swiftly out. The offending dust, hair, or paper, seized in miniature steel jaws, was raced back to the burrows. There, down tubes which fed into the cellar, it was dropped into the sighing vent of an incinerator which sat like evil Baal in a dark corner.

The dog ran upstairs, hysterically yelping to each door, at last realizing, as the house realized, that only silence was here.

It sniffed the air and scratched the kitchen door. Behind the door, the stove was making pancakes which filled the house with a rich baked odor and the scent of maple syrup.

The dog frothed at the mouth, lying at the door, sniffing, its eyes turned to fire. It ran wildly in circles, biting at its tail, spun in a frenzy, and died. It lay in the parlor for an hour.

Two o'clock, sang a voice.

Delicately sensing decay at last, the regiments of mice hummed out as softly as blown gray leaves in an electrical wind.

Two-fifteen.

The dog was gone.

In the cellar, the incinerator glowed suddenly and a whirl of sparks leaped up the chimney.

Two thirty-five.

Bridge tables sprouted from patio walls. Playing cards fluttered onto pads in a shower of pips. Martinis manifested on an oaken bench with egg-salad sandwiches. Music played.

But the tables were silent and the cards untouched.

At four o'clock the tables folded like great butterflies back through the paneled walls.

Four-thirty.

The nursery walls glowed.

Animals took shape: yellow giraffes, blue lions, pink antelopes, lilac panthers cavorting in crystal substance. The walls were glass. They looked out upon color and fantasy. Hidden films clocked through well-oiled sprockets, and the walls lived. The nursery floor was woven to resemble a crisp, cereal meadow. Over this ran aluminum roaches and iron crickets, and in the hot still air butterflies of delicate red tissue wavered among the sharp aroma of animal spoors! There was the sound like a great matted yellow hive of bees within a dark bellows, the lazy bumble of a purring lion. And there was the patter of okapi feet and the murmur of a fresh jungle rain, like other hoofs, falling upon the summer-starched grass. Now the walls dissolved into distances of parched weed, mile on mile, and warm endless sky. The animals drew away into thorn brakes and water holes.

It was the children's hour.

Five o'clock. The bath filled with clear hot water.

Six, seven, eight o'clock. The dinner dishes manipulated like magic tricks, and in the study a *click*. In the metal stand opposite the hearth where a fire now blazed up warmly, a cigar popped out, half an inch of soft gray ash on it, smoking, waiting.

Nine o'clock. The beds warmed their hidden circuits, for nights were cool here.

40 *Nine-five.* A voice spoke from the study ceiling:

"Mrs. McClellan, which poem would you like this evening?"

The house was silent.

The voice said at last, "Since you express no preference, I shall select a poem at random." Quiet music rose to back the voice. "Sara Teasdale. As I recall, your favorite. . . .

There will come soft rains and the smell of the ground,
And swallows circling with their shimmering sound;

And frogs in the pools singing at night,
And wild plum trees in tremulous white;

Robins will wear their feathery fire,
Whistling their whims on a low fence-wire;

And not one will know of the war, not one
Will care at last when it is done.

Not one would mind, neither bird nor tree,
If mankind perished utterly;

And Spring herself, when she woke at dawn
Would scarcely know that we were gone."

45 The fire burned on the stone hearth and the cigar fell away into a mound of quiet ash on its tray. The empty chairs faced each other between the silent walls, and the music played.

At ten o'clock the house began to die.

The wind blew. A falling tree bough crashed through the kitchen window. Cleaning solvent, bottled, shattered over the stove. The room was ablaze in an instant!

"Fire!" screamed a voice. The house lights flashed, water pumps shot water from the ceilings. But the solvent spread on the linoleum, licking, eating, under the kitchen door, while the voices took it up in chorus: "Fire, fire, fire!"

The house tried to save itself. Doors sprang tightly shut, but the windows were broken by the heat and the wind blew and sucked upon the fire.

50 The house gave ground as the fire in ten billion angry sparks moved with flaming ease from room to room and then up the stairs. While scurrying water rats squeaked from the walls, pistoled their water, and ran for more. And the wall sprays let down showers of mechanical rain.

But too late. Somewhere, sighing, a pump shrugged to a stop. The quenching rain ceased. The reserve water supply which had filled baths and washed dishes for many quiet days was gone.

The fire crackled up the stairs. It fed upon Picassos and Matisses in the upper halls, like delicacies, baking off the oily flesh, tenderly crisping the canvases into black shavings.

Now the fire lay in beds, stood in windows, changed the colors of drapes!

And then, reinforcements.

55 From attic trapdoors, blind robot faces peered down with faucet mouths gushing green chemical.

The fire backed off, as even an elephant must at the sight of a dead snake. Now there were twenty snakes whipping over the floor, killing the fire with a clear cold venom of green froth.

But the fire was clever. It had sent flames outside the house, up through the attic to the pumps there. An explosion! The attic brain which directed the pumps was shattered into bronze shrapnel on the beams.

The fire rushed back into every closet and felt of the clothes hung there.

The house shuddered, oak bone on bone, its bared skeleton cringing from the heat, its wire, its nerves revealed as if a surgeon had torn the skin off to let the red veins and capillaries quiver in the scalded air. Help, help! Fire! Run, run! Heat snapped mirrors like the brittle winter ice. And the voices wailed, Fire, fire, run, run, like a tragic nursery rhyme, a dozen voices, high, low, like children dying in a forest, alone, alone. And the voices fading as the wires popped their sheathings like hot chestnuts. One, two, three, four, five voices died.

In the nursery the jungle burned. Blue lions roared, purple giraffes bounded off. The panthers ran in circles changing color, and ten million animals, running before the fire, vanished off toward a distant steaming river. . . .

Ten more voices died. In the last instant under the fire avalanche, other choruses, oblivious, could be heard announcing the time, playing music, cutting the lawn by remote-control mower, or setting an umbrella frantically out and in the slamming and opening front door, a thousand things happening, like a clock shop when each clock strikes the hour insanely before or after the other, a scene of maniac confusion, yet unity; singing, screaming, a few last cleaning mice darting bravely out to carry the horrid ashes away! And one voice, with sublime disregard for the situation, read poetry aloud in the fiery study, until all the film spools burned, until all the wires withered and the circuits cracked.

The fire burst the house and let it slam flat down, puffing out skirts of spark and smoke.

In the kitchen, an instant before the rain of fire and timber, the stove could be seen making breakfasts at a psychopathic rate, ten dozen eggs, six loaves of toast, twenty dozen bacon strips, which, eaten by fire, started the stove working again, hysterically hissing!

The crash. The attic smashing into kitchen and parlor. The parlor into cellar, cellar into sub-cellar. Deep freeze, armchair, film tapes, circuits, beds, and all like skeletons thrown in a cluttered mound deep under.

Smoke and silence. A great quantity of smoke.

Dawn showed faintly in the east. Among the ruins, one wall stood alone. Within the wall, a last voice said, over and over again and again, even as the sun rose to shine upon the heaped rubble and steam:

"Today is August 5, 2026, today is August 5, 2026, today is . . ."

[1951]

Joining the Conversation: Critical Thinking and Writing

1. What do you know about the family in the story? Does it seem to be a typical family?
2. What does the poem seem to say about the relationship between nature and human beings? In what way, if any, is the poem relevant to the rest of the story?
3. Do you take the story to be mere fantasy, or, on the other hand, do you take it to be a comment on our life? Or neither? Explain.

4. If possible, characterize your final response to the story. Did the story create uneasiness, a sense of your own involvement in a sadly deficient society? Or perhaps, on the other hand, the story created in you a sense of satisfaction, a sense that your own life is superior to the life depicted here.

Student Essay, with Preliminary Notes

Here is one student's response to Bradbury's story, preceded by the notes that the student used in preparing a draft. Notice that the final essay does not slavishly follow the notes. For instance, although the student jotted down four possible titles for her essay, none of these is the title that she finally settled on.

Possible title:
Bradbury's Meaning for us
Bradbury and Today
Learning from Literature/Bradbury's Lesson
Bradbury's Lesson for us
~~Begin by quoting first sentence~~
begin with joke about airline?? ✓
~~Define science fiction?~~
technology today-can do almost everything-but is this really LIVING?
Maybe such a life is a living death. Evidence??
End essay:
Does Bradbury show us our future?
A wake-up call. 2026 is not really very far away
~~end with example of unnecessary technology~~

Daniels 1

Esther Daniels

Professor Izzard

English 101a

12 October 2009

The Lesson of "August 2026"

Before discussing some of the implications of Ray Bradbury's short story, "August 2026: There Will Come Soft Rains," I want to tell a little joke. The joke goes like this. Passengers are seated on the latest kind of airplane, a plane that

Daniels 2

files without a pilot because all of the controls are operated mechanically, and the entire flight has been preprogramed. After all the passengers have boarded the plane, and the door has closed, and the passengers, in accordance with the pre-recorded announcement, have fastened their seat-belts, the plane begins to taxi for a take-off. As the plane moves down the runway, the sound system says, in its flat mechanical voice, "You are now beginning your flight on the most technologically advanced airplane ever designed. There is no pilot or copilot, and there are no flight attendants. Everything has been preprogrammed. The plane will taxi for 60 seconds and then will take off. Nothing can go wrong . . . nothing can go wrong . . . nothing can . . . nothing can . . . nothing can. . . ."

None of us has been on such a plane, but we probably all have had, in a mild way, the sort of experience that the joke implies. We have bought some wonderful gadget—let's say an alarm clock, and we have programmed it according to the complicated instructions, and it has failed to go off the next morning. Apparently we had set it for p.m, instead of a.m., but we still don't see what we did wrong. Or, try as we may we cannot change the margins on the computer. Or the airline has put our luggage on the wrong airplane. Or . . .

None of us wants to give up the wonderful devices we rely on—let's say the automobile, the computer, the ipod. We can even attend an English composition class, and, if we think it is boring, we can silently be exchanging messages with a friend a thousand

Daniels 3

miles away. Despite these pleasures and these great conveniences, there are times, I think, when most of us must wonder, "Are we really living, or are our machines doing the living for us?" In "August 2026: There Will Come Soft Rains," Ray Bradbury gives us a glimpse—with great exaggeration, of course—of what our lives may seem like in the future. Preprogrammed sounds wake people up, mechanisms prepare food and clean the house, and other mechanisms provide entertainment. If they don't make a choice, a machine chooses something on their behalf. Are the people who are served by these devices happy? We don't know, because there are no people in Bradbury's story. They have all been incinerated, and only their silhouettes survive on the wall of the house. But we, as readers of the story, probably feel that although everything was provided for these people, they could not really have been happy. Things are *too* programmed; the people who lived in this society must have become almost like machines themselves. Probably none of us wants to say that in our own lives we actually want difficulties, but, still, when we read Bradbury's story we probably say that we would not want to live in a society that was as highly programed with labor-saving devices as Bradbury shows.

And yet, that is the way we seem to be going, with faster computers, smarter houses. You can now, from your place of work, phone your home and turn the oven on and set the temperature and the duration, so that when you get home the beef has been roasted to medium-rare.

Daniels 4

Bradbury first published the story in 1951, so the story was set seventy-five years in the future. It was set, we can say, at a time when most of his readers would probably not still be alive. But today, 2026 is not all that far from us. Most of us who today are reading this story will still be alive in 2026, unless, as the story warns us, we allow our technology—gadgets that can do just about anything—to blow ourselves up. Bradbury's "August 2026: There Will Come Soft Rains" is a wake-up call, a call that we ought to heed. We have somehow let our technical knowledge outrun not only our wisdom but our sense of how to live decent meaningful lives, lives of fun, truly *human* lives, not just lives in which everything is easy, everything is done for us. We are allowing our gadgets to do our living for us—and they may kill us. We are barely living, we are sleep-walking. This cannot go on without some sort of catastrophic ending. To quote the first line of Ray Bradbury's story, it is *"time to get up, time to get up."*

[New page]

Daniels 5

Work Cited

Bradbury, Ray. "August 2026: There Will Come Soft Rains," *Literature for Composition*. Ed. Sylvan Barnet, William Burto, and William E. Cain. 9th ed. New York: Longman, 2010. 24–28. Print.

Joining the Conversation: Critical Thinking and Writing

1. Do you think that Esther Daniels has done a good job in her title and opening paragraph? Please explain.
2. What is Esther's thesis? Where does she state it?
3. Do you think Esther has provided sufficient evidence for her thesis?
4. Evaluate the final paragraph. Is it effective?

Stories for Analysis

MICHELE SERROS

Michele Serros, born in Oxnard, California, in 1966, published her first book of poems and stories, Chicana Falsa and Other Stories of Death, Identity and Oxnard, *while she was still a student at Santa Monica City College. We reprint a story from her second book,* How to Be a Chicana Role Model *(2000), which achieved national attention.*

Senior Picture Day

Sometimes I put two different earrings in the same ear. And that's on a day I'm feeling preppy, not really new wave or anything. One time, during a track meet over at Camarillo High, I discovered way too late that I'd forgot to put on deodorant and that was the worst 'cause everyone knows how snooty those girls at Camarillo can be. Hmmm. Actually the worst thing I've ever forgotten to do was take my pill. That happened three mornings in a row and you can bet I was praying for weeks after that.

So many things to remember when you're seventeen years old and your days start at six A.M. and sometimes don't end until five in the afternoon. But today of all days there's one thing I have to remember to do and that's to squeeze my nose. I've been doing it since the seventh grade. Every morning with my thumb and forefinger I squeeze the sides of it, firmly pressing my nostrils as close as they possibly can get near the base. Sometimes while I'm waiting for the tortilla to heat up, or just when I'm brushing my teeth, I squeeze. Nobody ever notices. Nobody ever asks. With all the other shit seniors in high school go through, squeezing my nose is nothing. It's just like some regular early-morning routine, like yawning or wiping the egg from my eyes. Okay, so you might think it's just a total waste of time, but to tell you the truth, I do see the difference. Just last week I lined up all my class pictures and could definitely see the progress. My nose has actually become smaller, narrower. It looks less Indian. *I* look less Indian and you can bet that's the main goal here. Today, when I take my graduation pictures, my nose will look just like Terri's and then I'll have the best picture in the year-book. I think about this as Mrs. Milne's Duster comes honking in the driveway to take me to school.

Terri was my best friend in seventh grade. She came from Washington to Rio Del Valle Junior high halfway through October. She was the first girl I knew who had contact lenses and *four* pairs of Chemin de Fers. Can you believe that? She told everyone that her daddy was gonna build 'em a swimming pool for the summer. She told me that I could go over to swim anytime I wanted. But until then, she told me, I could go over and we could play on her dad's CB.[1]

"You dad's really got a CB?" I asked her.

5 "Oh, yeah," she answered, jiggling her locker door. "You can come over and we can make up handles for ourselves and meet lots of guys. Cute ones."

"Whaddaya mean, handles?" I asked.

"Like names, little nicknames. I never use my real name. I'm 'G.G.' when I get on. That stands for Golden Girl. Oh, and you gotta make sure you end every sentence with 'over.' You're like a total nerd if you don't finish with 'over.' I never talk to anyone who doesn't say 'over.' They're the worst."

Nobody's really into citizen band radios anymore. I now see 'em all lined up in pawnshops over on Oxnard Boulevard. But back in the seventh grade, everyone was getting them. They were way better than using a phone 'cause, first of all, there was no phone bill to bust you for talking to boys who lived past the Grade and second, you didn't have your stupid sister yelling at you for tying up the phone line. Most people had CBs in their cars, but Terri's dad had his in the den.

When I showed up at Terri's to check out the CB, her mama was in the front yard planting some purple flowers.

10 "Go on in already." She waved me in. "She's in her father's den."

I found Terri just like her mama said. She was already on the CB, looking flustered and sorta excited.

"Hey," I called out to her, and plopped my tote bag on her dad's desk.

She didn't answer but rather motioned to me with her hands to hurry up. Her mouth formed an exaggerated, "Oh, *my* God!" She held out a glass bowl of Pringles and pointed to a glass of Dr Pepper on the desk.

It turned out Terri had found a boy on the CB. An older *interested* one. He was fifteen, a skateboarder, and his handle was Lightning Bolt.

15 "Lightning Bolt," he bragged to Terri. "Like, you know, powerful and fast. That's the way I skate. So," he continued, "where you guys live? Over."

"We live near Malibu." Terri answered. "Between Malibu and Santa Barbara. Over."

"Oh, excuse me, fan-ceee. Over."

"That's right." Terri giggled. "Over."

We actually lived in Oxnard. Really, in El Rio, a flat patch of houses, churches, and schools surrounded by lots of strawberry fields and some new snooty stucco homes surrounded by chainlink. But man, did Terri have this way of making things sound better. I mean, it *was* the truth, geographically, and besides it sounded way more glamorous.

20 I took some Pringles from the bowl and thought we were gonna have this wonderful afternoon of talking and flirting with Lightning Bolt until Terri's dad happened to come home early and found us gabbing in his den.

"What the . . . !" he yelled as soon as he walked in and saw us hunched over his CB. "What do you think this is? Party Central? Get off that thing!" He grabbed the receiver from Terri's hand. "This isn't a toy! It's a tool. A tool for communication, you don't use it just to meet boys!"

[1]**CB** Citizens Band (a radio frequency used by the general public to talk to one another over a short distance).

"Damn, Dad," Terri complained as she slid off her father's desk. "Don't have a cow." She took my hand and led me to her room. "Come on, let's pick you out a handle."

When we were in her room, I told her I had decided on Cali Girl as my handle.

"You mean, like California?" she asked.

"Yeah, sorta."

"But you're Mexican."

"So?"

"So, you look like you're more from Mexico than California."

"What do you mean?"

"I mean, California is like, blond girls, you know."

"Yeah, but I *am* Californian. I mean, real Californian. Even my great-grandma was born here."

"It's just that you don't look like you're from California."

"And you're not exactly golden," I snapped.

We decided to talk to Lightning Bolt the next day, Friday, right after school. Terri's dad always came home real late on Fridays, sometimes even early the next Saturday morning. It would be perfect. When I got to her house the garage door was wide open and I went in through the side door. I almost bumped into Terri's mama. She was spraying the house with Pine Scent and offered me some Hi-C.

"Help yourself to a Pudding Pop, too," she said before heading into the living room through a mist of aerosol. "They're in the freezer."

Man, Terri's mama made their whole life like an afternoon commercial. Hi-C, Pringles in a bowl, the whole house smelling like a pine forest. Was Terri lucky or what? I grabbed a Pudding Pop out of the freezer and was about to join her when I picked up on her laugh. She was already talking to Lightning Bolt. Dang, she didn't waste time!

"Well, maybe we don't ever want to meet you," I heard Terri flirt with Lightning Bolt. "How do you know we don't already have boyfriends? Over."

"Well, you both sound like foxes. So, uh, what *do* you look like? Over."

"I'm about five-four and have green eyes and ginger-colored hair. Over."

Green? Ginger? I always took Terri for having brown eyes and brown hair.

"What about your friend? Over."

"What about her? Over."

Oh, this was about me! I *had* to hear this. Terri knew how to pump up things good.

"I mean, what does she look like?" Lightning Bolt asked. "She sounds cute. Over."

"Well . . ." I overheard Terri hesitate. "Well, she's real skinny and, uh . . ."

"I like skinny girls!"

"You didn't let me finish!" Terri interrupted. "And you didn't say 'over.' Over."

"Sorry," Lightning Bolt said. "Go ahead and finish. Over."

I tore the wrapper off the Pudding Pop and continued to listen.

"Well," Terri continued. "She's also sorta flat-chested, I guess. Over."

What? How could Terri say that?

"Flat-chested? Oh yeah? Over." Lightning Bolt answered.

"Yeah. Over."

Terri paused uncomfortably. It was as if she knew what she was saying was wrong and bad and she should've stopped but couldn't. She was saying things about a friend, things a real friend shouldn't be saying about another friend, but now there was a boy involved and he was interested in that other friend, in me, and her side was losing momentum. She would have to continue to stay ahead.

55 "Yeah, and she also has this, this nose, a nose like . . . like an *Indian*. Over."

"An, Indian?" Lightning Bolt asked. "What do ya mean an Indian? Over."

"You know, *Indian*. Like powwow Indian."

"Really?" Lightning Bolt laughed on the other end. "Like Woo-Woo-Woo Indian?" He clapped his palm over his mouth and wailed. A sound I knew all too well.

"Yeah, just like that!" Terri laughed. "In fact, I think she's gonna pick 'Li'l Squaw' as her handle!"

60 I shut the refrigerator door quietly. I touched the ridge of my nose. I felt the bump my mother had promised me would be less noticeable once my face "filled out." The base of my nose was far from feminine and was broad, like, well, like Uncle Rudy's nose, Grandpa Rudy's nose, and yeah, a little bit of Uncle Vincente's nose, too. Men in my family who looked like Indians and here their Indian noses were lumped together on me, on my face. My nose made me look like I didn't belong, made me look less Californian than my blond counterparts. After hearing Terri and Lightning Bolt laugh, more than anything I hated the men in my family who had given me such a hideous nose.

I grabbed my tote bag and started to leave out through the garage door when Terri's mama called out from the living room. "You're leaving already?" she asked. "I know Terri would love to have you for dinner. Her daddy's working late again."

I didn't answer and I didn't turn around. I just walked out and went home.

And so that's how the squeezing began. I eventually stopped hanging out with Terri and never got a chance to use my handle on her dad's CB. I know it's been almost four years since she said all that stuff about me, about my nose, but man, it still stings.

65 During freshman year I heard that Terri's dad met some lady on the CB and left her mama for this other woman. Can you believe that? Who'd wanna leave a house that smelled like a pine forest and always had Pudding Pops in the freezer?

As Mrs. Milne honks from the driveway impatiently, I grab my books and run down the driveway, squeezing my nose just a little bit more. I do it because today is Senior Picture Day and because I do notice the difference. I might be too skinny. My chest might be too flat. But God forbid I look too Indian.

[2000]

Joining the Conversation: Critical Thinking and Writing

1. If someone asked you to write an essay about your body, would you find the assignment easy or difficult? Please explain.
2. a. Please describe the impression that this portrait sculpture (shown on the following page) of the most famous Maya king, Pakal the Great, makes on you.
   b. When we say that a person is handsome or beautiful or striking-looking, what do we mean? Is this just a strong feeling that we have, or is it a strong feeling that we could explain and support through an argument? Support you answer in an argument of 250–500 words (probably two or three paragraphs).

3. Which statement has the greater effect on you: "That person is very attractive" or "That person is highly intelligent"? Do you think that most people would agree with you? Could you present an argument that would convince others to agree with you? What would your argument consist of? What would be your evidence? Set forth your argument in 250–500 words.

One of the most important Maya portrait sculptures shows Pakal the Great, with an ample nose. Maya portrait sculpture (mid-seventh century).

4. How would you characterize the narrator? Do you regard her with amusement, pity, contempt, sympathy—or all of the above, or none? Please explain.
5. Briefly recounted within this story about the narrator is another story about Terri's parents. Why do you suppose Serros included this story?

GUY DE MAUPASSANT

Born and raised in Normandy, the French novelist and short-story writer Guy de Maupassant (1850–1893) studied law in Paris, then served in the Franco-Prussian War. Afterward he worked for a time as a clerk for the government until, with the support of the novelist Gustave Flaubert (a friend of Maupassant's mother) and later Emile Zola, he decided to pursue a career as a writer. Ironic and pointed, detached yet compassionate, Maupassant explores human folly and its both grim and comic consequences. His first great success came in April 1880, with the publication of the story "Boule de Suif" ("Ball of Fat"), about a prostitute traveling by coach, with a number of bourgeois companions, through Prussian-occupied France during wartime. Maupassant published six novels, including Bel-Ami *(1885) and* Pierre et Jean *(1888), and a number of collections of stories, before his untimely death from the effects of syphilis, a month short of his forty-third birthday. Like many of his stories, "The Necklace" uses realistic observation and keenly chosen detail to tell its story of a misunderstanding and the years of hard labor that follow from it.*

The Necklace

Translated by Marjorie Laurie

She was one of those pretty and charming girls who are sometimes, as if by a mistake of destiny, born in a family of clerks. She had no dowry, no expectations, no means of being known, understood, loved, wedded by any rich and distinguished man; and she let herself be married to a little clerk at the Ministry of Public Instruction.

She dressed plainly because she could not dress well, but she was as unhappy as though she had really fallen from her proper station, since with women there is neither caste nor rank: and beauty, grace and charm act instead of family and birth. Natural fineness, instinct for what is elegant, suppleness of wit, are the sole hierarchy, and make from women of the people the equals of the very greatest ladies.

She suffered ceaselessly, feeling herself born for all the delicacies and all the luxuries. She suffered from the poverty of her dwelling, from the wretched look of the walls, from the worn-out chairs, from the ugliness of the curtains. All those things, of which another woman of her rank would never even have been conscious, tortured her and made her angry. The sight of the little Breton peasant who did her humble housework aroused in her regrets which were despairing, and distracted dreams. She thought of the silent antechambers hung with Oriental tapestry, lit by tall bronze candelabra, and of the two great footmen in knee breeches who sleep in the big armchairs, made drowsy by the heavy warmth of the hot-air stove. She thought of the long *salons*[1] fitted up with ancient silk, of the delicate furniture carrying priceless curiosities, and of the coquettish perfumed boudoirs made for talks at five o'clock with intimate friends, with men famous and sought after, whom all women envy and whose attention they all desire.

When she sat down to dinner, before the round table covered with a tablecloth three days old, opposite her husband, who uncovered the soup tureen and declared with an enchanted air, "Ah, the good *pot-au-feu*![2] I don't know anything better than that," she thought of dainty dinners, of shining silverware, of tapestry which peopled the walls with ancient personages and with strange birds flying in the midst of a fairy forest; and she thought of delicious dishes served on marvelous plates, and of the whispered gallantries which you listen to with a sphinxlike smile, while you are eating the pink flesh of a trout or the wings of a quail.

[1]***salons*** drawing-rooms. [2]***pot-au-feu*** stew.

She had no dresses, no jewels, nothing. And she loved nothing but that; she felt made for that. She would so have liked to please, to be envied, to be charming, to be sought after.

She had a friend, a former schoolmate at the convent, who was rich, and whom she did not like to go and see any more, because she suffered so much when she came back.

But one evening, her husband returned home with a triumphant air, and holding a large envelope in his hand.

"There," said he. "Here is something for you."

She tore the paper sharply, and drew out a printed card which bore these words:

"The Minister of Public Instruction and Mme. Georges Ramponneau request the honor of M. and Mme. Loisel's company at the palace of the Ministry on Monday evening, January eighteenth."

Instead of being delighted, as her husband hoped, she threw the invitation on the table with disdain, murmuring:

"What do you want me to do with that?"

"But, my dear, I thought you would be glad. You never go out, and this is such a fine opportunity. I had awful trouble to get it. Everyone wants to go; it is very select, and they are not giving many invitations to clerks. The whole official world will be there."

She looked at him with an irritated glance, and said, impatiently:

"And what do you want me to put on my back?"

He had not thought of that; he stammered:

"Why, the dress you go to the theater in. It looks very well, to me."

He stopped, distracted, seeing his wife was crying. Two great tears descended slowly from the corners of her eyes toward the corners of her mouth. He stuttered:

"What's the matter? What's the matter?"

But, by violent effort, she had conquered her grief, and she replied, with a calm voice, while she wiped her wet cheeks:

"Nothing. Only I have no dress and therefore I can't go to this ball. Give your card to some colleague whose wife is better equipped than I."

He was in despair. He resumed:

"Come, let us see, Mathilde. How much would it cost, a suitable dress, which you could use on other occasions, something very simple?"

She reflected several seconds, making her calculations and wondering also what sum she could ask without drawing on herself an immediate refusal and a frightened exclamation from the economical clerk.

Finally, she replied, hesitatingly:

"I don't know exactly, but I think I could manage it with four hundred francs."

He had grown a little pale, because he was laying aside just that amount to buy a gun and treat himself to a little shooting next summer on the plain of Nanterre, with several friends who went to shoot larks down there, of a Sunday.

But he said:

"All right. I will give you four hundred francs. And try to have a pretty dress."

The day of the ball drew near, and Mme. Loisel seemed sad, uneasy, anxious. Her dress was ready, however. Her husband said to her one evening:

"What is the matter? Come, you've been so queer these last three days."

And she answered:

"It annoys me not to have a single jewel, not a single stone, nothing to put on. I shall look like distress. I should almost rather not go at all."

He resumed:

35 "You might wear natural flowers. It's very stylish at this time of the year. For ten francs you can get two or three magnificent roses."

She was not convinced.

"No; there's nothing more humiliating than to look poor among other women who are rich."

But her husband cried:

"How stupid you are! Go look up your friend Mme. Forestier, and ask her to lend you some jewels. You're quite thick enough with her to do that."

40 She uttered a cry of joy:

"It's true. I never thought of it."

The next day she went to her friend and told of her distress.

Mme. Forestier went to a wardrobe with a glass door, took out a large jewel-box, brought it back, opened it, and said to Mme. Loisel:

"Choose, my dear."

45 She saw first of all some bracelets, then a pearl necklace, then a Venetian cross, gold and precious stones of admirable workmanship. She tried on the ornaments before the glass, hesitated, could not make up her mind to part with them, to give them back. She kept asking:

"Haven't you any more?"

"Why, yes. Look. I don't know what you like."

All of a sudden she discovered, in a black satin box, a superb necklace of diamonds, and her heart began to beat with an immoderate desire. Her hands trembled as she took it. She fastened it around her throat, outside her high-necked dress, and remained lost in ecstasy at the sight of herself.

Then she asked, hesitating, filled with anguish:

50 "Can you lend me that, only that?"

"Why, yes, certainly."

She sprang upon the neck of her friend, kissed her passionately, then fled with her treasure.

The day of the ball arrived. Mme. Loisel made a great success. She was prettier than them all, elegant, gracious, smiling, and crazy with joy. All the men looked at her, asked her name, endeavored to be introduced. All the attachés of the Cabinet wanted to waltz with her. She was remarked by the minister himself.

She danced with intoxication, with passion, made drunk by pleasure, forgetting all, in the triumph of her beauty, in the glory of her success, in a sort of cloud of happiness composed of all this homage, of all this admiration, of all these awakened desires, and of that sense of complete victory which is so sweet to a woman's heart.

55 She went away about four o'clock in the morning. Her husband had been sleeping since midnight, in a little deserted anteroom, with three other gentlemen whose wives were having a very good time. He threw over her shoulders the wraps which he had brought, modest wraps of common life, whose poverty contrasted with the elegance of the ball dress. She felt this, and wanted to escape so as not to be remarked by the other women, who were enveloping themselves in costly furs.

Loisel held her back.

"Wait a bit. You will catch cold outside. I will go and call a cab."

But she did not listen to him, and rapidly descended the stairs. When they were in the street they did not find a carriage; and they began to look for one, shouting after the cabmen whom they saw passing by at a distance.

They went down toward the Seine, in despair, shivering with cold. At last they found on the quay one of those ancient noctambulant coupés which, exactly as if they were ashamed to show their misery during the day, are never seen round Paris until after nightfall.

It took them to their door in the Rue des Martyrs, and once more, sadly, they climbed up homeward. All was ended, for her. And as to him, he reflected that he must be at the Ministry at ten o'clock.

She removed the wraps which covered her shoulders, before the glass, so as once more to see herself in all her glory. But suddenly she uttered a cry. She no longer had the necklace around her neck!

Her husband, already half undressed, demanded:

"What is the matter with you?"

She turned madly toward him:

"I have—I have—I've lost Mme. Forestier's necklace."

He stood up, distracted.

"What!—how?—impossible!"

And they looked in the folds of her dress, in the folds of her cloak, in her pockets, everywhere. They did not find it.

He asked:

"You're sure you had it on when you left the ball?"

"Yes, I felt it in the vestibule of the palace."

"But if you had lost it in the street we should have heard it fall. It must be in the cab."

"Yes. Probably. Did you take his number?"

"No. And you, didn't you notice it?"

"No."

They looked, thunderstruck, at one another. At last Loisel put on his clothes.

"I shall go back on foot," said he, "over the whole route which we have taken to see if I can find it."

And he went out. She sat waiting on a chair in her ball dress, without strength to go to bed, overwhelmed, without fire, without a thought.

Her husband came back about seven o'clock. He had found nothing.

He went to Police Headquarters, to the newspaper offices, to offer a reward: he went to the cab companies—everywhere, in fact, whither he was urged by the least suspicion of hope.

She waited all day, in the same condition of mad fear before this terrible calamity.

Loisel returned at night with a hollow, pale face; he had discovered nothing.

"You must write to your friend," said he, "that you have broken the clasp of her necklace and that you are having it mended. That will give us time to turn round."

She wrote at his dictation.

At the end of a week they had lost all hope.

And Loisel, who had aged five years, declared:

"We must consider how to replace that ornament."

The next day they took the box which had contained it, and they went to the jeweler whose name was found within. He consulted his books.

"It was not I, madame, who sold that necklace; I must simply have furnished the case."

90 Then they went from jeweler to jeweler, searching for a necklace like the other, consulting their memories, sick both of them with chagrin and anguish.

They found, in a shop at the Palais Royal, a string of diamonds which seemed to them exactly like the one they looked for. It was worth forty thousand francs. They could have it for thirty-six.

So they begged the jeweler not to sell it for three days yet. And they made a bargain that he should buy it back for thirty-four thousand francs, in case they found the other one before the end of February.

Loisel possessed eighteen thousand francs which his father had left him. He would borrow the rest.

He did borrow, asking a thousand francs of one, five hundred of another, five louis here, three louis[3] there. He gave notes, took up ruinous obligations, dealt with usurers and all the race of lenders. He compromised all the rest of his life, risked his signature without even knowing if he could meet it; and, frightened by the pains yet to come, by the black misery which was about to fall upon him, by the prospect of all the physical privation and of all the moral tortures which he was to suffer, he went to get the new necklace, putting down upon the merchant's counter thirty-six thousand francs.

95 When Mme. Loisel took back the necklace, Mme. Forestier said to her, with a chilly manner:

"You should have returned it sooner; I might have needed it."

She did not open the case, as her friend had so much feared. If she had detected the substitution, what would she have thought, what would she have said? Would she not have taken Mme. Loisel for a thief?

Mme. Loisel now knew the horrible existence of the needy. She took her part, moreover, all of a sudden, with heroism. That dreadful debt must be paid. She would pay it. They dismissed their servant; they changed their lodgings; they rented a garret under the roof.

She came to know what heavy housework meant and the odious cares of the kitchen. She washed the dishes, using her rosy nails on the greasy pots and pans. She washed the dirty linen, the shirts, and the dishcloths, which she dried upon a line; she carried the slops down to the street every morning, and carried up the water, stopping for breath at every landing. And, dressed like a woman of the people, she went to the fruiterer, the grocer, the butcher, her basket on her arm, bargaining, insulted, defending her miserable money sou by sou.

100 Each month they had to meet some notes, renew others, obtain more time.

Her husband worked in the evening making a fair copy of some tradesman's accounts, and late at night he often copied manuscript for five sous a page.

And this life lasted for ten years.

At the end of ten years, they had paid everything, everything, with the rates of usury, and the accumulations of the compound interest.

Mme. Loisel looked old now. She had become the woman of impoverished households—strong and hard and rough. With frowsy hair, skirts askew, and red hands, she talked loud while washing the floor with great swishes of water. But sometimes, when her husband was at the office, she sat down near the window, and she thought of that gay evening of long ago, of the ball where she had been so beautiful and so fêted.

[3]**louis** a gold coin worth 20 francs.

105 What would have happened if she had not lost that necklace? Who knows? Who knows? How life is strange and changeful! How little a thing is needed for us to be lost or to be saved!

But, one Sunday, having gone to take a walk in the Champs Elysées to refresh herself from the labor of the week, she suddenly perceived a woman who was leading a child. It was Mme. Forestier, still young, still beautiful, still charming.

Mme. Loisel felt moved. Was she going to speak to her? Yes, certainly. And now that she had paid, she was going to tell her all about it. Why not?

She went up.

"Good day, Jeanne."

110 The other, astonished to be familiarly addressed by this plain goodwife, did not recognize her at all, and stammered:

"But—madam!—I do not know—You must be mistaken."

"No. I am Mathilde Loisel."

Her friend uttered a cry.

"Oh, my poor Mathilde! How you are changed!"

115 "Yes, I have had days hard enough, since I have seen you, days wretched enough—and that because of you!"

"Of me! How so?"

"Do you remember that diamond necklace which you lent me to wear at the ministerial ball?"

"Yes. Well?"

"Well, I lost it."

120 "What do you mean? You brought it back."

"I brought you back another just like it. And for this we have been ten years paying. You can understand that it was not easy for us, us who had nothing. At last it is ended, and I am very glad."

Mme. Forestier had stopped.

"You say that you bought a necklace of diamonds to replace mine?"

"Yes. You never noticed it, then! They were very like."

125 And she smiled with a joy which was proud and naïve at once.

Mme. Forestier, strongly moved, took her two hands.

"Oh, my poor Mathilde! Why, my necklace was paste. It was worth at most five hundred francs!"

[1885]

Joining the Conversation: Critical Thinking and Writing

1. What do we learn about Mme. Loisel from the first six paragraphs of the story? What is your response to the narrator's generalizations about women in paragraph 2?
2. Is Maupassant's point that Mme. Loisel is justly punished for her vanity and pride? What about her husband, and the impact of the apparent loss of the necklace on his life?
3. In paragraph 98, as Mme. Loisel decides she must pay the debt, Maupassant writes: "She took her part, moreover, all of a sudden, with heroism." Why the word "heroism"? Isn't this a strange way to characterize Mme. Loisel's behavior?

4. Maupassant, in a discussion of fiction, said that a serious writer's goal

> is not to tell a story to entertain us, or to appeal to our feelings, but to make us to think, and to make us understand the hidden meaning of events. By dint of having observed and having meditated, the writer sees the world, facts, people, and things in a distinctive way, a way that is the result of all of his thoughtful observation. It is this personal view of the world that a writer strives to communicate to us. . . . To make the spectacle of life as moving to us as it has been to him, he must bring life before our eyes with scrupulous accuracy. He must construct his work with great skill—his art must seem artless—so that we cannot detect his contrivance or see his intentions.

Among the big ideas in these few sentences are these: (a) The purpose of fiction is "to make us understand the hidden meaning of events"; (b) writers give us a "personal view"; (c) readers should be moved by the story but should not be aware that the artist has imposed a personal view on them. Do you think that "The Necklace" effectively illustrates Maupassant's points? What might be "the hidden meaning of events"? What would you guess is Maupassant's "personal view"? Would you agree that the story is so skillfully constructed that we are unaware of the author's methods and of his intentions?

5. Have you ever done something, tried to make up for it, and then discovered later that you had not done what you thought you did after all? How did this make you feel?

Chapter 3

The Reader as Writer

All there is to writing is having ideas. To learn to write is to learn to have ideas.

Robert Frost

Developing a Thesis, Drafting, and Writing an Argument

Prewriting: Getting Ideas

How do writers "learn to have ideas"? Among the methods are these: reading with a pen or pencil in hand, so that (as we have already seen) you can annotate the text; keeping a journal, in which you jot down reflections about your reading; talking with others (including your instructor) about the reading.

Let's take another look at the first of these, annotating.

Annotating a Text

In reading, if you own the book don't hesitate to mark it up, indicating (by highlighting or underlining or by making marginal notes) what puzzles you, what pleases or interests you, and what displeases or bores you. Later you'll want to think further about these responses, asking yourself, on rereading, if you still feel that way, and if not, why not; but these first responses will get you started.

Annotations of the sort given on page 15, which chiefly call attention to contrasts, indicate that the student is thinking about writing an analysis of the story. That is, she is thinking of writing an essay in which she will examine the parts of a literary work either in an effort to see how they relate to each other or in an effort to see how one part relates to the whole.

More about Getting Ideas: A Second Story by Kate Chopin

Let's look at a story that is a little longer than "Ripe Figs," and then we'll discuss how in addition to annotating you might get ideas for writing about it.

The Story of an Hour

Knowing that Mrs. Mallard was afflicted with a heart trouble, great care was taken to break to her as gently as possible the news of her husband's death.

It was her sister Josephine who told her, in broken sentences, veiled hints that revealed in half concealing. Her husband's friend Richards was there, too, near her. It was he who had been in the newspaper office when intelligence of the railroad disaster was received, with Brently Mallard's name leading the list of "killed." He had only taken the time to assure himself of its truth by a second telegram, and had hastened to forestall any less careful, less tender friend in bearing the sad message.

She did not hear the story as many women have heard the same, with a paralyzed inability to accept its significance. She wept at once, with sudden, wild abandonment, in her sister's arms. When the storm of grief had spent itself she went away to her room alone. She would have no one follow her.

There stood, facing the open window, a comfortable, roomy armchair. Into this she sank, pressed down by a physical exhaustion that haunted her body and seemed to reach into her soul.

5 She could see in the open square before her house the tops of trees that were all aquiver with the new spring life. The delicious breath of rain was in the air. In the street below a peddler was crying his wares. The notes of a distant song which some one was singing reached her faintly, and countless sparrows were twittering in the eaves.

There were patches of blue sky showing here and there through the clouds that had met and piled above the other in the west facing her window. She sat with her head thrown back upon the cushion of the chair quite motionless, except when a sob came up into her throat and shook her, as a child who has cried itself to sleep continues to sob in its dreams.

She was young, with a fair, calm face, whose lines bespoke repression and even a certain strength. But now there was a dull stare in her eyes, whose gaze was fixed away off yonder on one of those patches of blue sky. It was not a glance of reflection, but rather indicated a suspension of intelligent thought.

There was something coming to her and she was waiting for it, fearfully. What was it? She did not know; it was too subtle and elusive to name. But she felt it, creeping out of the sky, reaching toward her through the sounds, the scents, the color that filled the air.

Now her bosom rose and fell tumultuously. She was beginning to recognize this thing that was approaching to possess her, and she was striving to beat it back with her will—as powerless as her two white slender hands would have been.

10 When she abandoned herself a little whispered word escaped her slightly parted lips. She said it over and over under her breath: "Free, free, free!" The vacant stare and the look of terror that had followed it went from her eyes. They stayed keen and bright. Her pulses beat fast, and the coursing blood warmed and relaxed every inch of her body.

She did not stop to ask if it were not a monstrous joy that held her. A clear and exalted perception enabled her to dismiss the suggestion as trivial.

She knew that she would weep again when she saw the kind, tender hands folded in death; the face that had never looked save with love upon her, fixed and gray and dead. But she saw beyond that bitter moment a long procession of years to come that would belong to her absolutely. And she opened and spread her arms out to them in welcome.

There would be no one to live for her during those coming years; she would live for herself. There would be no powerful will bending her in that blind persistence with which men and women believe they have a right to impose a private will upon a fellow creature. A kind intention or a cruel intention made the act seem no less a crime as she looked upon it in that brief moment of illumination.

And yet she had loved him—sometimes. Often she had not. What did it matter! What could love, the unsolved mystery, count for in face of this possession of self-assertion which she suddenly recognized as the strongest impulse of her being.

"Free! Body and soul free!" she kept whispering.

Josephine was kneeling before the closed door with her lips to the keyhole, imploring for admission. "Louise, open the door! I beg; open the door—you will make yourself ill. What are you doing, Louise? For heaven's sake open the door."

"Go away. I am not making myself ill." No; she was drinking in a very elixir of life through that open window.

Her fancy was running riot along those days ahead of her. Spring days, and summer days, and all sorts of days that would be her own. She breathed a quick prayer that life might be long. It was only yesterday she had thought with a shudder that life might be long.

She arose at length and opened the door to her sister's importunities. There was a feverish triumph in her eyes, and she carried herself unwittingly like a goddess of Victory. She clasped her sister's waist, and together they descended the stairs. Richards stood waiting for them at the bottom.

Some one was opening the front door with a latchkey. It was Brently Mallard who entered, a little travel-stained, composedly carrying his gripsack and umbrella. He had been far from the scene of accident, and did not even know there had been one. He stood amazed at Josephine's piercing cry; at Richards' quick motion to screen him from the view of his wife.

But Richards was too late.

When the doctors came they said she had died of heart disease—of joy that kills.

[1894]

Brainstorming for Ideas for Writing

Unlike annotating, which consists of making brief notes and small marks on the printed page, "brainstorming"—the free jotting down of ideas—asks that you jot down whatever comes to mind, without inhibition. Don't worry about spelling, about writing complete sentences, or about unifying your thoughts; just let one thought lead to another. Later you can review your jottings, deleting some, connecting with arrows others that are related, expanding still others, but for now you want to get going, and so there is no reason to look back.

Thus you might jot down something about the title:

> Title speaks of an hour, and story covers an hour, but maybe takes five minutes to read.

And then, perhaps prompted by "an hour," you might happen to add something to this effect:

> Doubt that a woman who got news of the death of her husband could move from grief to joy within an hour.

Your next jotting might have little or nothing to do with this issue; it might simply say

> Enjoyed "Hour" more than "Ripe Figs" partly because "Hour" is so shocking.

And then you might ask yourself

> By shocking, do I mean "improbable," or what? Come to think of it, maybe it's not so improbable. A lot depends on what the marriage was like.

Focused Free Writing

Focused, or directed, free writing is a method related to brainstorming that some writers use to uncover ideas they may want to write about. Concentrating on one issue—for instance, a question that strikes them as worth puzzling over (What kind of person is Mrs. Mallard?)—they write at length, nonstop, for perhaps five or ten minutes.

Writers who find free writing helpful put down everything they can think of that bears on the one issue or question they are examining. They do not stop at this stage to evaluate the results, and they do not worry about niceties of sentence structure or of spelling. They just pour out their ideas in a steady stream of writing, drawing on whatever associations come to mind. If they pause in their writing, it is only to refer to the text, to search for more detail—perhaps a quotation—that will help them answer their question.

After the free-writing session, these writers usually go back and reread what they have written, highlighting or underlining what seems to be of value. Of course they find much that is of little or no use, but they also usually find that some strong ideas have surfaced and have received some development. At this point the writers are often able to make a rough outline and then begin a draft.

Here is an example of one student's focused free writing:

> What do I know about Mrs. Mallard? Let me put everything down here I know about her or can figure out from what Kate Chopin tells me. When she finds herself alone after the death of her husband, she says, "Free. Body and soul free" and before that she said, "Free, free, free" three times. So she has suddenly perceived that she has not been free; she has been under the influence of a "powerful will." In this case it has been her husband, but she says no one, man nor woman, should impose their will on anyone else. So it's not a feminist issue—it's a power issue. No one should push anyone else around is what I guess Chopin means, force someone to do what the other person wants. I used to have a friend that did that to me all the time; he had to run everything. They say that fathers–before the women's movement—used to run things, with the father in charge of all the decisions, so maybe this is an honest reaction to having been pushed around by a husband. I think Mrs. Mallard is a believable character, even if the plot is not all that believable—all those things happening in such quick succession.

Listing

In your preliminary thinking you may find it useful to make lists. In the previous chapter we saw that listing the traits of the two characters was helpful in thinking about Chopin's "Ripe Figs":

Maman-Nainaine
- older than Babette
- "stately way"
- "patient as the statue of la Madone"
- connects actions with seasons
- expects to be obeyed

Babette
young
active and impatient
obedient

For "The Story of an Hour" you might list Mrs. Mallard's traits; or you might list the stages in her development. Such a list is not the same as a summary of the plot. The list helps the writer to see the sequence of psychological changes.

weeps (when she gets the news)
goes to room, alone
"pressed down by a physical exhaustion"
"dull stare"
"something coming to her"
strives to beat back "this thing"
"Free, free, free!" The "vacant stare went . . . from her eyes"
"A clear and exalted perception"
rejects Josephine
"she was drinking in a very elixir of life"
gets up, opens door, "a feverish triumph in her eyes"
sees B., and dies

Unlike brainstorming and annotating, which let you go in all directions, listing requires that you first make a decision about what you will be listing—traits of character, images, puns, or whatever. Once you make the decision, you can then construct the list, and with a list in front of you, you will see patterns that you were not fully conscious of earlier.

Asking Questions

If you feel stuck, ask yourself questions. You'll recall that the assignment on "Ripe Figs" in effect asked the students to ask themselves questions about the work—for instance, questions about the relationship between the characters—and about their responses to it: "You'll try to explain as honestly as you can what makes 'Ripe Figs' appealing or interesting—or trifling, or boring."

If you are thinking about a work of fiction, ask yourself questions about the plot and the characters—are they believable, are they interesting, and what does it all add up to? What does the story mean to *you*?

One student found it helpful to jot down the following questions:

Plot
Ending false? Unconvincing? Or prepared for?

Character?
Mrs. M. unfeeling? Immoral?
Mrs. M. unbelievable character?
What might her marriage have been like? Many gaps.
(Can we tell what her husband was like?)
"And yet she loved him–sometimes" Fickle? Realistic?
What is "this thing that was approaching to possess her"?

Symbolism
Set on spring day = symbolic of new life?

You don't have to be as tidy as this student. You may begin by jotting down notes and queries about what you like or dislike and about what puzzles or amuses you. What follows are the jottings of another student, Janet Vong. They are, obviously, in no particular order—the student is "brainstorming," putting down whatever occurs to her—though it is equally obvious that one note sometimes led to the next:

> Title nothing special. What might be a better title?
> Could a woman who loved her husband be so heartless?
> Is she heartless? Did she love him?
> What are (were) Louise's feelings about her husband?
> Did she want too much? What did she want?
> Could this story happen today? Feminist interpretation?
> Sister (Josephine)—a busybody?
> Tricky ending—but maybe it could be true.
> "And yet she had loved him—sometimes. Often she had not."
>   Why does one love someone "sometimes"?
> Irony: plot has reversal. Are characters ironic too?

These jottings helped this reader-writer think about the story, find a special point of interest, and develop a thoughtful argument about it.

Keeping a Journal

A journal is not a diary, a record of what the writer did during the day ("today I read Chopin's 'Hour'"). Rather, a journal is a place to store some of the thoughts you may have inscribed on a scrap of paper or in the margin of the text, such as your initial response to the title of a work or to the ending. It is also a place to jot down further reflections, such as thoughts about what the work means to you, and what was said in the classroom about writing in general or specific works.

You will get value from your journal if you write an entry at least once a week, but you will get much more if you write entries after reading each assignment and after each class meeting. You may, for instance, want to reflect on why your opinion is so different from that of another student, or you may want to apply a concept such as *character* or *irony* or *plausibility* to a story that later you may write about in an essay. Comparisons are especially helpful: How does this work (or this character, or this rhyme scheme) differ from last week's reading?

You might even make an entry in the form of a letter to the author or from one character to another. You might write a dialogue between characters in two works or between two authors, or you might record an experience of your own that is comparable to something in the work.

A student who wrote about "The Story of an Hour" began with the following entry in his journal. In reading this entry, notice that one idea stimulates another. The student was, quite rightly, concerned with getting and exploring ideas, not with writing a unified paragraph.

> Apparently a "well-made" story, but seems clever rather than moving or real. Doesn't seem plausible. Mrs. M's change comes out of the blue–maybe some women might respond like this, but probably not most.
>
> Does literature deal with unusual people, or with usual (typical?) people? Shouldn't it deal with typical? Maybe not. (Anyway, how can I know?) Is "typical" same as "plausible"? Come to think of it, prob. not.
>
> Anyway, whether Mrs. M is typical or not, is her change plausible, believable? Think more about this.

Why did she change? Her husband dominated her life and controlled her actions; he did "impose a private will upon a fellow creature." She calls this a crime, even if well-intentioned. Is it a crime?

Arguing with Yourself: Critical Thinking

In our discussion of annotating, brainstorming, free writing, listing, asking questions, and keeping a journal, the emphasis has been on responding freely rather than in any highly systematic or disciplined way. Something strikes us (perhaps an idea, perhaps an uncertainty), and we jot it down. Even before we finish jotting it down we may go on to question it, but probably not; at this early stage it is enough to put onto paper some thoughts, rooted in our first responses, and to keep going.

The almost random play of mind that is evident in brainstorming and in the other activities already discussed is of course a kind of thinking, but the term **critical thinking** (which we addressed briefly in our first chapter) is reserved for something different. When we think critically, we skeptically scrutinize our own ideas—for example, by searching out our underlying assumptions, or by evaluating what we have quickly jotted down as evidence. We have already seen some examples of this sort of analysis of one's own thinking in the journal entries, where a student wrote that literature should probably deal with "typical" people, then wondered if "typical" and "plausible" were the same, and then added "probably not."

Speaking broadly, critical thinking is rational, logical thinking. In thinking critically, writers

- scrutinize their **assumptions;**
- **define** their terms;
- test the **evidence** they have collected, even to the extent of looking for **counterevidence;** and
- revise their **thesis** when necessary, in order to make the argument as complete and convincing as possible.

Let's start with **assumptions.** If I say that a story is weak because it is improbable, I ought to think about my assumption that improbability is a fault. I can begin by asking myself if all good stories—or all the stories that I value highly—are probable. I may recall that among my favorites is *Alice in Wonderland* (or *Gulliver's Travels* or *Animal Farm*)—so I probably have to withdraw my assumption that improbability in itself makes a story less than good. I may go on to refine the idea and decide that improbability is not a fault in satiric stories but is a fault in other kinds, but that is not the same as saying bluntly that improbability is a fault.

The second aspect of critical thinking, **definition,** here does not refer chiefly to defining technical terms such as "meter" for the benefit of readers who may be unfamiliar with the special language of literary criticism; rather, we are now speaking about the need to define controversial terms. For instance, if you are arguing that a particular story is sentimental, you almost surely will have to define what you mean by "sentimental" because the word has several meanings.

The third aspect of critical thinking that we have isolated—testing the **evidence** largely by searching for **counterevidence** within the literary work—involves rereading the work to see if we have overlooked material or have taken a particular detail out of context. If, for instance, we say that in "The Story of an Hour" Josephine is a busybody, we should reexamine the work to make sure that she indeed is meddling needlessly and is not offering welcome or necessary assistance. Perhaps the original observation will stand up, but perhaps on rereading the story we may feel, as we examine each of Josephine's actions, that she cannot reasonably be characterized as a busybody.

Different readers may come to different conclusions; the important thing is that all readers should subject their initial responses to critical thinking, testing their responses against all of the evidence. Remember, your instructor probably expects you to hand in an essay that is essentially an **argument,** a paper that advances a thesis of your own, and therefore you will revise your drafts if you find counterevidence. The **thesis** (the point) might be that

- the story is improbable, or
- the story is typical of Chopin, or
- the story is anti-woman, or
- the story is a remarkable anticipation of contemporary feminist thinking.

Whatever your thesis, it should be able to withstand scrutiny: That is what a good argument does. You may not convince every reader that you are unquestionably right, but you should make every reader feel that your argument is thoughtful. If you read your notes and then your drafts critically, you probably will write a paper that meets this standard.

One last point, or maybe it's two. Just as your first jottings probably won't be the products of critical thinking, your first reading of the literary work probably *won't* be a critical reading. It is entirely appropriate to begin by reading simply for enjoyment. After all, the reason we read literature (or listen to music, or go to an art museum, or watch dancers) is to derive pleasure. It happens, however, that in this course you are trying to deepen your understanding of literature, so you are *studying* literature. On subsequent readings, therefore, you will read the work critically, carefully noting the writer's view of human nature and the writer's ways of achieving certain effects.

This business of critical thinking is important. We will discuss it yet again, on pages 186–87, in talking about interpretations of literature.

Arguing a Thesis

If you think critically about your early jottings and about the literary work itself, you probably will find that some of your jottings lead to dead ends, but some will lead to further ideas that hold up under scrutiny. What the thesis of the essay will be—the idea that will be asserted and *argued* (supported with evidence)—is still in doubt, but there is no doubt about one thing: A good essay will have a thesis, a point, an argument. You ought to be able to state your point in a **thesis sentence.**

Consider these candidates as possible thesis sentences:

1. Mrs. Mallard dies soon after hearing that her husband has died.

True, but scarcely a point that can be argued or even developed. About the most the essayist can do with this sentence is amplify it by summarizing the plot of the story, a task not worth doing unless the plot is unusually obscure. An essay may include a sentence or two of summary to give readers their bearings, but a summary is not an essay.

2. The story is a libel on women.

In contrast to the first statement, this one can be developed into an argument. Probably the writer will try to demonstrate that Mrs. Mallard's behavior is despicable. Whether this point can be convincingly argued is another matter; the thesis may be untenable, but it is a thesis. A second problem, however, is this: Even if the writer demonstrates that Mrs. Mallard's behavior is despicable, he or she will have to go on to demonstrate that the presentation of one despicable woman constitutes a libel on women in general. That's a pretty big order.

3. The story is clever but superficial because it is based on an unreal character.

Here, too, is a thesis—a point of view that can be argued. Whether this thesis is true is another matter. The writer's job will be to support it by presenting evidence. Probably the writer will have no difficulty in finding evidence that the story is "clever"; the difficulty will be in establishing a case that the characterization of Mrs. Mallard is "unreal." The writer will have to set forth some ideas about what makes a character real and then will have to show that Mrs. Mallard is an unreal (unbelievable) figure.

4. The irony of the ending is believable partly because it is consistent with earlier ironies in the story.

The student who wrote the essay printed on page 59 began by drafting an essay based on the third of these thesis topics, but as she worked on a draft she found that she could not support her assertion that the character was unconvincing. In fact, she came to believe that although Mrs. Mallard's joy was the reverse of what a reader might expect, several early reversals in the story helped to make Mrs. Mallard's shift from grief to joy acceptable.

CHECKLIST: *Thesis Sentence*

- Does the sentence make a claim rather than merely offer a description?
- Is the claim arguable rather than self-evident, universally accepted, and of little interest?
- Can evidence be produced to support the claim?
- Is the claim narrow enough to be convincingly supported in a paper written within the allotted time, and of the assigned length?

Drafting Your Argument

After jotting down notes and then adding more notes stimulated by rereading and further thinking, you should be able to formulate a tentative thesis. At this point most writers find it useful to clear the air by glancing over their preliminary notes and by jotting down the thesis and a few especially promising notes—brief statements of what they think their key points may be. These notes may include some brief key quotations that the writer thinks will help to support the thesis.

Here are the selected notes (not the original brainstorming notes, but a later selection from them, with additions) and a draft (below) that makes use of them.

> title? Ironies in an Hour (?) An Hour of Irony (?) Kate Chopin's Irony (?)
> thesis: irony at end is prepared for by earlier ironies
> chief irony: Mrs. M. dies just as she is beginning to enjoy life
> smaller ironies: 1. "sad message" brings her joy
> 2. Richards is "too late" at end
> 3. Richards is too early at start

These notes are in effect a very brief **outline.** Some writers at this point like to develop a fuller outline, but most writers begin with only a brief outline, knowing that in the process of developing a draft from these few notes additional ideas will arise. For these writers, the time to jot down a detailed outline is *after* they have written a first or second draft. The outline of the written draft will, as we shall see, help them to make sure that their draft has an adequate organization, and that main points are developed.

A Sample Draft: "Ironies in an Hour"

Now for the student's draft—not the first version, but a revised draft with some of the irrelevancies of the first draft omitted and some evidence added.

The numbers in parentheses refer to the page numbers from which the quotations are drawn, though with so short a work as "The Story of an Hour," page references are hardly necessary. Check with your instructor to find out if you must always give citations. (Detailed information about how to document a paper is given on pages 1366–78.)

Bridas 1

Jennifer Bridas

Professor Lester

English 1102

3 March 2009

Ironies in an Hour

After we know how the story turns out, if we reread it we find irony at the very start, as is true of many other stories. Mrs. Mallard's friends assume, mistakenly, that Mrs. Mallard was deeply in love with her husband, Brently Mallard. They take great care to tell her

Bridas 2

gently of his death. The friends mean well, and in fact they do well. They bring her an hour of life, an hour of freedom. They think their news is sad. Mrs. Mallard at first expresses grief when she hears the news, but soon she finds joy in it. So Richards's "sad message" (46), though sad in Richards's eyes, is in fact a happy message.

Among the ironic details is the statement that when Mallard entered the house, Richards tried to conceal him from Mrs. Mallard, but "Richards was too late" (47). This is ironic because earlier Richards "hastened" (46) to bring his sad message; if he had at the start been "too late" (47), Brently Mallard would have arrived at home first, and Mrs. Mallard's life would not have ended an hour later but would simply have gone on as it had before. Yet another irony at the end of the story is the diagnosis of the doctors. The doctors say she died of "heart disease—of joy that kills" (47). In one sense the doctors are right: Mrs. Mallard has experienced a great joy. But of course the doctors totally misunderstand the joy that kills her.

The central irony resides not in the well-intentioned but ironic actions of Richards, or in the unconsciously ironic words of the doctors, but in her own life. In a way she has been dead. She "sometimes" (46) loved her husband, but in a way she has been dead. Now, his apparent death brings her new life. This new life comes to her at the season of the year when "the tops of trees . . . were all aquiver with the new spring life" (46). But, ironically, her new life will last only an hour. She looks forward to "summer days" (47) but she will not see even the end of this spring day. Her

Bridas 3

years of marriage were ironic. They brought her a sort of living death instead of joy. Her new life is ironic too. It grows out of her moment of grief for her supposedly dead husband, and her vision of a new life is cut short.

[New page]

Bridas 4

Work Cited

Chopin, Kate. "The Story of an Hour." *Literature for Composition.* Ed. Sylvan Barnet, William Burto, and William E. Cain. 9th ed. New York: Longman, 2010. 45–47. Print.

Revising an Argument

The draft, although thoughtful and clear, is not yet a finished essay. The student went on to improve it in many small but important ways.

First, the draft needs a good introductory paragraph, a paragraph that will let the **audience**—the readers—know where the writer will be taking them. (In Chapter 6 we discuss introductory paragraphs.) Doubtless you know from your own experience as a reader that readers can follow an argument more easily—and with more pleasure—if early in the discussion the writer tells them what the argument is. (The title, too, can strongly suggest the thesis.) Second, some of the paragraphs could be clearer.

In revising paragraphs—or, for that matter, in revising an entire draft—writers unify, organize, clarify, and polish.

1. **Unity** is achieved partly by eliminating irrelevancies. Notice that in the final version, printed on pages 59–61, the writer has deleted "as is true of many other stories."
2. **Organization** is largely a matter of arranging material into a sequence that will assist the reader to grasp the point.
3. **Clarity** is achieved largely by providing concrete details and quotations—these provide evidence—to support generalizations and by providing helpful transitions ("for instance," "furthermore," "on the other hand," "however").

4. **Polish** is small-scale revision. For instance, the writer deletes unnecessary repetitions. In the second paragraph of the draft, the phrase "the doctors" appears four times, but it appears only three times in the final version of the paragraph. Similarly, in polishing, a writer combines choppy sentences into longer ones and breaks overly long sentences into shorter ones.

Later, after producing a draft that seems close to a finished essay, writers engage in yet another activity. They edit.

5. **Editing** includes checking the accuracy of quotations by comparing them with the original, checking a dictionary for the spelling of doubtful words, and checking a handbook for doubtful punctuation—for instance, whether a comma or a semicolon is needed in a particular sentence.

Outlining an Argument

Whether or not you draw up an outline as a preliminary guide to writing a draft, you will be able to improve your draft if you prepare an outline of what you have written. (If you write on a word processor, it is probably especially important that you make an outline of your written draft. Writing on a word processor is—or seems—so easy, so effortless, that often we just tap away, filling screen after screen with loosely structured material.) For each paragraph in your draft, jot down the main point of the topic sentence or topic idea. Under each of these sentences, indented, jot down key words for the idea(s) developed in the paragraph. Thus, in an outline of the draft we have just looked at, for the first two paragraphs you might make these jottings:

story ironic from start
- friends think news is sad
- Ms. M. finds joy

some ironic details
- Richards hastened, but "too late"
- doctors right and also wrong

An outline of what you have written will help you to see if your draft is adequate in three important ways. The outline will show you:

1. the sequence of major topics,
2. the degree of development of these topics, and
3. the argument, the thesis.

By studying your outline you may see that your first major point (probably after an introductory paragraph) would be more effective as your third point, and that your second point needs to be further developed.

An outline of this sort is a brief version of your draft, perhaps even using some phrases from the draft. But consider making yet another sort of outline, an outline indicating not what each paragraph says but what each paragraph *does*. An attempt at such an outline of the three-paragraph draft of the essay on "The Story of an Hour" might look something like this:

1. The action of the friends is ironic.
2. Gives some specific (minor) details about ironies.
3. Explains "central irony."

We ought to see a red flag here. The aim of this sort of outline is to indicate what each paragraph *does*, but the jotting for the first paragraph does not tell us what the paragraph does; rather, it more or less summarizes the content of the paragraph. Why? Because the paragraph doesn't *do* much of anything. It does not clearly introduce the thesis, or define a crucial term, or set the story in the context of Chopin's other work.

An outline indicating the function of each paragraph will force you to see if your essay has an effective structure. We will see that the student later wrote a new opening paragraph for the essay on "The Story of an Hour."

Soliciting Peer Review, Thinking about Counterarguments

Your instructor may encourage or even require you to discuss your draft with another student or with a small group of students. That is, you may be asked to get a review from your peers. Such a procedure is helpful in several ways. First, it gives the writer a real audience, readers who can point to what pleases or puzzles them, who make suggestions, who may often disagree with the writer or with each other, and who frequently, though not intentionally, *misread*. Though writers don't necessarily like everything they hear (they seldom hear "This is perfect. Don't change a word!"), reading and discussing their work with others almost always gives them a fresh perspective on their work, and a fresh perspective may stimulate thoughtful revision. (Having your intentions misread because your writing isn't clear enough can be particularly stimulating.)

Your reviewers may suggest that you have overlooked evidence that works against your interpretation. Obviously you will either have to revise your interpretation or you will have to show that in fact the supposed counterevidence really does not weaken your interpretation.

The writer whose work is being reviewed is not the sole beneficiary. When students serve as readers for each other, they become better readers of their own work and consequently better revisers. As we said in Chapter 2, learning to write is in large measure learning to read.

If peer review is a part of the writing process in your course, the instructor may distribute a sheet with some suggestions and questions. Here is an example of such a sheet.

QUESTIONS FOR PEER REVIEW — ENGLISH 125A

Read each draft once, quickly. Then read it again, with the following questions in mind.

1. What is the essay's topic? Is it one of the assigned topics, or a variation from it? Does the draft show promise of fulfilling the assignment?
2. Looking at the essay as a whole, what thesis (main idea) is stated or implied? If implied, state it in your own words.
3. Is the thesis plausible? How might the argument be strengthened?
4. Looking at each paragraph separately:
   a. What is the basic point? (If it isn't clear to you, ask for clarification.)

b. How does the paragraph relate to the essay's main idea or to the previous paragraph?
c. Should some paragraphs be deleted? Be divided into two or more paragraphs? Be combined? Be put elsewhere? (If you outline the essay by jotting down the main point of each paragraph, it will help you to answer these questions.)
d. Is each sentence clearly related to the sentence that precedes and to the sentence that follows?
e. Is each paragraph adequately developed?
f. Are there sufficient details—perhaps brief, supporting quotations from the text?

5. What are the paper's chief strengths?
6. Make at least two specific suggestions that you think will assist the author to improve the paper.

Final Version of the Sample Essay: "Ironies of Life in Kate Chopin's 'The Story of an Hour'"

Here is the final version of the student's essay. The essay submitted to the instructor had been retyped; but here, so that you can easily see how the draft has been revised, we print the draft with the final changes written in by hand.

Bridas 1

Jennifer Bridas

Professor Lester

English 1102

9 March 2009

Ironies of Life in Kate Chopin's "The Story of an Hour"

~~Ironies in an Hour~~

Despite its title, Kate Chopin's "The Story of an Hour" ironically takes only a few minutes to read. In addition, the story turns out to have an ironic ending, but on rereading it one sees that the irony is not concentrated only in the outcome of the plot—Mrs. Mallard dies just when she is beginning to live—but is also present in many details.

After we know how the story turns out, if we reread it we find irony at the very start. ~~as is true of many other stories.~~ Because Mrs. Mallard's friends and her sister assume, mistakenly, that ~~Mrs. Mallard~~ she was deeply in love with her husband, Brently Mallard, ~~They~~ they take great

Bridas 2

care to tell her gently of his death. ~~The friends~~ *They* mean well, and in fact they *do* well*;* ~~They~~ bring*ing* her an hour of life, an hour of *joyous* freedom*,* *but it is ironic that* They think their news is sad. *True,* Mrs. Mallard at first expresses grief when she hears the news, but soon *(unknown to her friends)* she finds joy in it. So Richards's "sad message" (46), though sad in Richards's eyes, is in fact a happy message.

Among the *small but significant* ironic details is the statement *near the end of the story* that when Mallard entered the house, Richards tried to conceal him from Mrs. Mallard, but "Richards was too late" (47). This is ironic because *almost at the start of the story, in the second paragraph,* ~~earlier~~ Richards "hastened" (46) to bring his sad message; if he had at the start been "too late" (47), Brently Mallard would have arrived at home first, and Mrs. Mallard's life would not have ended an hour later but would simply have gone on as it had before. Yet another irony at the end of the story is the diagnosis of the doctors. The doctors say she died of "heart disease—of joy that kills" (47). In one sense ~~the doctors~~ *they* are right: Mrs. Mallard *for the last hour* experienced a great joy. But of course the doctors totally misunderstand the joy that kills her. *It is not joy at seeing her husband alive, but her realization that the great joy she experienced during the last hour is over.*

All of these ironic details add richness to the story, but The central irony resides not in the well-intentioned but ironic actions of Richards, or in the unconsciously ironic words of the doctors, but in ~~her~~ *Mrs. Mallard's* own life. ~~In a way she has been dead.~~ She "sometimes" (46) loved her husband, but in a way she has been dead*, a body subjected to her husband's will*. Now, his apparent death brings her new life. *Appropriately* This new life comes to her at the season of the year when "the tops of trees . . . were all aquiver with the new spring life" (46). But, ironically, her new life will last only an hour. *She is "free, free, free"—but only until her husband walks through the doorway.* She looks forward to "summer days" (47) but she will not see even the

Bridas 3

end of this spring day. ~~H~~er years of marriage were ironic. *If*, ~~They brought~~ *bringing* her a sort of living death instead of joy. ~~H~~er new life is ironic too, ~~I~~t grows out of her moment of grief for *not only because* her supposedly dead husband, ~~and her vision of a new life~~ *but also because her vision of "a long progression of years"* is cut short *within an hour on a spring day*.

[New page]

Bridas 4

Work Cited

Chopin, Kate. "The Story of an Hour." *Literature for Composition*. Ed. Sylvan Barnet, William Burto, and William E. Cain. 9th ed. New York: Longman, 2010. 45–47. Print.

A Brief Overview of the Final Version

Finally, as a quick review, let's look at several principles illustrated by this essay.

- The **title of the essay** is not merely the title of the work discussed; it should give the reader a clue, a small idea of the essayist's topic. Because your title will create a crucial first impression, make sure that it is interesting.
- The **opening or introductory paragraph** does not begin by saying "In this story . . ." Rather, by naming the author and the title, it lets the reader know exactly what story is being discussed. It also develops the writer's *thesis* so readers know where they will be going.
- The **organization** is effective. The smaller ironies are discussed in the second and third paragraphs, the central (chief) irony in the last paragraph. That is, the essay does not dwindle or become anticlimactic; the argument builds up from the least important to the most important point. Again, if you outline your draft you will see if it has an effective organization.
- Some **brief quotations** are used, both to provide evidence and to let the reader hear—even if only fleetingly—Kate Chopin's writing.
- The essay is chiefly devoted to **analysis** (*how* the parts relate to each other), not to summary (a brief restatement of the happenings). The writer, properly assuming that the reader has read the work, does not tell the plot in

great detail. But, aware that the reader has not memorized the story, the writer gives helpful reminders.
- The **present tense** is used in narrating the action: "Mrs. Mallard dies"; "Mrs. Mallard's friends and relatives all assume."
- Although a **concluding paragraph** is often useful—if it does more than merely summarize what has already been clearly said—it is not essential in a short analysis. In this essay, the last sentence explains the chief irony and therefore makes an acceptable ending.
- Documentation is given according to the form set forth in Appendix B.
- There are no typographical errors. The author has proofread the paper carefully.

Writing on Your Computer

In the preceding chapter we talked about "reading with pen in hand," and we really meant a pen—or a pencil—with which, in your early stage of interacting with the text, you will underline or circle or connect with arrows words and phrases. But when it comes to jotting down ideas, or sketching an outline, or drafting an essay, many students use a computer or a word processor. Further, you can receive valuable help from reference books and handbooks on style and usage, from computer programs (which check the spelling and grammar of documents), and from Internet resources. Although no computer program or Internet site can write and revise a paper for you, it can help you to detect mistakes and weak spots in your work that you can then proceed to remedy.

✓ CHECKLIST: *Writing with a Computer*

Prewriting

- ☐ Take notes. Try listing, then linking and clustering your ideas. Use an outline if you find it helpful.
- ☐ Check that your transcriptions are accurate if you quote.
- ☐ Keep your notes together in one file.
- ☐ Organize your sources in a bibliography.
- ☐ *Always back up your material.*
- ☐ Print out your notes.

Preparing a First Draft

- ☐ Use your notes—move them around in blocks. Expand on your ideas.
- ☐ Incorporate notes to yourself in your first draft.
- ☐ Read your draft on the screen to check for errors.
- ☐ Print out a copy of your first draft.

Working with Your Draft

- ☐ Revise your printed draft with pen or pencil. Incorporate these changes into your computer file.

- Read your corrected draft on the screen; then print out a fresh copy.
- Repeat these steps as many times as necessary.

Responding to Peer Review

- Give a copy to a peer for comments and suggestions.
- Respond appropriately to your reviewer, making changes in your computer file.
- Print out your revised version and reread it.

Preparing a Final Copy

- If there are only a few changes, make them on your printed copy. Otherwise, incorporate your changes in your computer file and print out your final copy.

Your Turn: Additional Stories for Analysis

Kate Chopin

For a biographical note, see page 11.

Désirée's Baby

As the day was pleasant, Madame Valmondé drove over to L'Abri to see Désirée and the baby.

It made her laugh to think of Désirée with a baby. Why, it seemed but yesterday that Désirée was little more than a baby herself; when Monsieur in riding through the gateway of Valmondé had found her lying asleep in the shadow of the big stone pillar.

The little one awoke in his arms and began to cry for "Dada." That was as much as she could do or say. Some people thought she might have strayed there of her own accord, for she was of the toddling age. The prevailing belief was that she had been purposely left by a party of Texans, whose canvas-covered wagon, late in the day, had crossed the ferry that Coton Maïs kept, just below the plantation. In time Madame Valmondé abandoned every speculation but the one that Désirée had been sent to her by a beneficent Providence to be the child of her affection, seeing that she was without child of the flesh. For the girl grew to be beautiful and gentle, affectionate and sincere,—the idol of Valmondé.

It was no wonder, when she stood one day against the stone pillar in whose shadow she had lain asleep, eighteen years before, that Armand Aubigny riding by and seeing her there, had fallen in love with her. That was the way all the Aubignys fell in love, as if struck by a pistol shot. The wonder was that he had not loved her before; for he had known her since his father brought him home from Paris, a boy of eight, after his mother died there. The passion that awoke in him that day, when he saw her at the gate, swept along like an avalanche, or like a prairie fire, or like anything that drives headlong over all obstacles.

5 Monsieur Valmondé grew practical and wanted things well considered: that is, the girl's obscure origin. Armand looked into her eyes and did not care. He was reminded that she was nameless. What did it matter about a name when he could give her one of the oldest and proudest in Louisiana? He ordered the *corbeille*[1] from Paris, and contained himself with what patience he could until it arrived, then they were married.

Madame Valmondé had not seen Désirée and the baby for four weeks. When she reached L'Abri she shuddered at the first sight of it, as she always did. It was a sad looking place, which for many years had not known the gentle presence of a mistress, old Monsieur Aubigny having married and buried his wife in France, and she having loved her own land too well ever to leave it. The roof came down steep and black like a cowl, reaching out beyond the wide galleries that encircled the yellow stuccoed house. Big, solemn oaks grew close to it, and their thick-leaved, far-reaching branches shadowed it like a pall. Young Aubigny's rule was a strict one, too, and under it his negroes had forgotten how to be gay, as they had been during the old master's easy-going and indulgent lifetime.

The young mother was recovering slowly, and lay full length, in her soft white muslins and laces, upon a couch. The baby was beside her, upon her arm, where he had fallen asleep, at her breast. The yellow nurse woman sat beside a window fanning herself.

Madame Valmondé bent her portly figure over Désirée and kissed her, holding her an instant tenderly in her arms. Then she turned to the child.

"This is not the baby!" she exclaimed, in startled tones. French was the language spoken at Valmondé in those days.

10 "I knew you would be astonished," laughed Désirée, "at the way he has grown. The little *cochon de lait!*[2] Look at his legs, mamma, and his hands and fingernails,—real fingernails. Zandrine had to cut them this morning. Isn't it true, Zandrine?"

The woman bowed her turbaned head majestically, "Mais si,[3] Madame."

"And the way he cries," went on Désirée, "is deafening. Armand heard him the other day as far away as La Blanche's cabin."

Madame Valmondé had never removed her eyes from the child. She lifted it and walked with it over to the window that was lightest. She scanned the baby narrowly, then looked as searchingly at Zandrine, whose face was turned to gaze across the fields.

"Yes, the child has grown, has changed," said Madame Valmondé, slowly, as she replaced it beside its mother. "What does Armand say?"

15 Désirée's face became suffused with a glow that was happiness itself.

"Oh, Armand is the proudest father in the parish, I believe, chiefly because it is a boy, to bear his name; though he says not—that he would have loved a girl as well. But I know it isn't true. I know he says that to please me. And mamma," she added, drawing Madame Valmondé's head down to her, and speaking in a whisper, "he hasn't punished one of them—not one of them—since baby is born. Even Négrillon, who pretended to have burnt his leg that he might rest from work—he only laughed, and said Négrillon was a great scamp. Oh, mamma, I'm so happy; it frightens me."

What Désirée said was true. Marriage, and later the birth of his son had softened Armand Aubigny's imperious and exacting nature greatly. This was what

[1]***corbeille*** wedding gifts from the groom to the bride. [2]***cochon de lait*** suckling pig (French).
[3]***Mais si*** certainly (French).

made the gentle Désirée so happy, for she loved him desperately. When he frowned she trembled, but loved him. When he smiled, she asked no greater blessing of God. But Armand's dark, handsome face had not often been disfigured by frowns since the day he fell in love with her.

When the baby was about three months old, Désirée awoke one day to the conviction that there was something in the air menacing her peace. It was at first too subtle to grasp. It had only been a disquieting suggestion; an air of mystery among the blacks; unexpected visits from far-off neighbors who could hardly account for their coming. Then a strange, an awful change in her husband's manner, which she dared not ask him to explain. When he spoke to her, it was with averted eyes, from which the old love-light seemed to have gone out. He absented himself from home; and when there, avoided her presence and that of her child, without excuse. And the very spirit of Satan seemed suddenly to take hold of him in his dealings with the slaves. Désirée was miserable enough to die.

She sat in her room, one hot afternoon, in her *peignoir*, listlessly drawing through her fingers the strands of her long, silky brown hair that hung about her shoulders. The baby, half naked, lay asleep upon her own great mahogany bed, that was like a sumptuous throne, with its satin-lined half-canopy. One of La Blanche's little quadroon boys—half naked too—stood fanning the child slowly with a fan of peacock feathers. Désirée's eyes had been fixed absently and sadly upon the baby, while she was striving to penetrate the threatening mist that she felt closing about her. She looked from her child to the boy who stood beside him, and back again; over and over. "Ah!" It was a cry that she could not help; which she was not conscious of having uttered. The blood turned like ice in her veins, and a clammy moisture gathered upon her face.

She tried to speak to the little quadroon boy; but no sound would come, at first. When he heard his name uttered, he looked up, and his mistress was pointing to the door. He laid aside the great, soft fan, and obediently stole away, over the polished floor, on his bare tiptoes.

She stayed motionless, with gaze riveted upon her child, and her face the picture of fright.

Presently her husband entered the room, and without noticing her, went to a table and began to search among some papers which covered it.

"Armand," she called to him, in a voice which must have stabbed him, if he was human. But he did not notice. "Armand," she said again. Then she rose and tottered towards him. "Armand," she panted once more, clutching his arm, "look at our child. What does it mean? tell me."

He coldly but gently loosened her fingers from about his arm and thrust the hand away from him. "Tell me what it means!" she cried despairingly.

"It means," he answered lightly, "that the child is not white; it means that you are not white."

A quick conception of all that this accusation meant for her nerved her with unwonted courage to deny it. "It is a lie; it is not true, I am white! Look at my hair, it is brown; and my eyes are gray, Armand, you know they are gray. And my skin is fair," seizing his wrist. "Look at my hand; whiter than yours, Armand," she laughed hysterically.

"As white as La Blanche's," he returned cruelly; and went away leaving her alone with their child.

When she could hold a pen in her hand, she sent a despairing letter to Madame Valmondé.

"My mother, they tell me I am not white. Armand has told me I am not white. For God's sake tell them it is not true. You must know it is not true. I shall die. I must die. I cannot be so unhappy, and live."

The answer that came was as brief:

"My own Désirée: Come home to Valmondé; back to your mother who loves you. Come with your child."

When the letter reached Désirée she went with it to her husband's study, and laid it open upon the desk before which he sat. She was like a stone image: silent, white, motionless after she placed it there.

In silence he ran his cold eyes over the written words. He said nothing. "Shall I go, Armand?" she asked in tones sharp with agonized suspense.

"Yes, go."

"Do you want me to go?"

"Yes, I want you to go."

He thought Almighty God had dealt cruelly and unjustly with him; and felt, somehow, that he was paying Him back in kind when he stabbed thus into his wife's soul. Moreover he no longer loved her, because of the unconscious injury she had brought upon his home and his name.

She turned away like one stunned by a blow, and walked slowly towards the door, hoping he would call her back.

"Good-by, Armand," she moaned.

He did not answer her. That was his last blow at fate.

Désirée went in search of her child. Zandrine was pacing the sombre gallery with it. She took the little one from the nurse's arms with no word of explanation, and descending the steps, walked away, under the live-oak branches.

It was an October afternoon; the sun was just sinking. Out in the still fields the negroes were picking cotton.

Désirée had not changed the thin white garment nor the slippers which she wore. Her hair was uncovered and the sun's rays brought a golden gleam from its brown meshes. She did not take the broad, beaten road which led to the far-off plantation of Valmondé. She walked across a deserted field, where the stubble bruised her tender feet, so delicately shod, and tore her thin gown to shreds.

She disappeared among the reeds and willows that grew thick along the banks of the deep, sluggish bayou; and she did not come back again.

Some weeks later there was a curious scene enacted at L'Abri. In the centre of the smoothly swept back yard was a great bonfire. Armand Aubigny sat in the wide hallway that commanded a view of the spectacle; and it was he who dealt out to a half dozen negroes the material which kept this fire ablaze.

A graceful cradle of willow, with all its dainty furbishings, was laid upon the pyre, which had already been fed with the richness of a priceless *layette*. Then there were silk gowns, and velvet and satin ones added to these; laces, too, and embroideries; bonnets and gloves; for the *corbeille* had been of rare quality.

The last thing to go was a tiny bundle of letters; innocent little scribblings that Désirée had sent to him during the days of their espousal. There was the remnant of one back in the drawer from which he took them. But it was not Désirée's; it was part of an old letter from his mother to his father. He read it. She was thanking God for the blessing of her husband's love:—

"But, above all," she wrote, "night and day, I thank the good God for having so arranged our lives that our dear Armand will never know that his mother, who adores him, belongs to the race that is cursed with the brand of slavery."

[1892]

Joining the Conversation: Critical Thinking and Writing

1. Let's start with the ending. Readers find the ending powerful, but they differ in their interpretations of it. Do you think that when Armand reads the letter he learns something he had never suspected or, instead, something that he had sensed about himself all along? Find evidence in the text to support your view.
2. Describe Désirée's feelings toward Armand. Do you agree with the student who told us, "She makes him into a God"?
3. Chopin writes economically: each word counts, each phrase and sentence is significant. What is she revealing about Armand (and perhaps about the discovery he has made) when she writes, "And the very spirit of Satan seemed suddenly to take hold of him in his dealings with the slaves"?
4. Is this story primarily a character study, or is Chopin seeking to make larger points in it about race, slavery, and gender?

A Student's Analysis

Hodges 1

Gus Hodges

Professor Durocher

English 125, section B

15 October 2010

Race and Identity in "Désirée's Baby"

"Désirée's Baby," says the literary scholar Emily Toth, is "a shocking story" that deals with the death of "a beautiful young woman"—the subject that, she notes, Edgar Allan Poe identified as "the perfect subject for poetry" (145). But in my view this story is shocking because it connects sexuality and race. It is not just that Désirée suffers a cruel fate, but that she does so because of her race, or, rather, the race that her husband Armand believes she belongs to. The tragic revelation is that Armand, not Désirée, is the person of mixed blood and thus is the cause or source of the mixed blood of their child.

Hodges 2

In a key passage midway through the story, Chopin brings the Désirée/Armand relationship into focus:

> When the baby was about three months old, Désirée awoke one day to the conviction that there was something in the air menacing her peace. It was at first too subtle to grasp. It had only been a disquieting suggestion; an air of mystery among the blacks; unexpected visits from far-off neighbors who could hardly account for their coming.
>
> Then a strange, an awful change in her husband's manner, which she dared not ask him to explain. When he spoke to her, it was with averted eyes, from which the old love-light seemed to have gone out. He absented himself from home; and when there, avoided her presence and that of her child, without excuse. And the very spirit of Satan seemed suddenly to take hold of him in his dealings with the slaves. Désirée was miserable enough to die. (65)

Chopin relates the action from Désirée's point of view—what she is seeing, thinking, feeling, fearing, as she and her husband grow estranged. But, at the same time, Chopin makes the reader aware of Armand. She prompts us to imagine, for ourselves, what might be leading him to shun his wife and child and, furthermore, what might account for his Satan-like treatment of his slaves.

This is a powerful insight on Chopin's part. As the story unfolds, it becomes clear that Armand has turned against Désirée because, to his horror and disgust, he has discovered that she

Hodges 3

possesses black—that is, "not white"—blood. To him, his family has been made impure, contaminated. He feels betrayed, and he takes out his wrath on his wife and child: he cannot bear to be in their presence. In addition, he unleashes his wrath on his slaves; they become the objects of his fury about his family, which is not what he thought it was.

Chopin is showing the tyranny of male authority and power, but, again, she is relating it to race. Armand becomes abusive—psychologically, emotionally, and physically violent—as a result of his reaction to the presence of blackness in his domestic life. This is intolerable to him, and he drives Désirée and the baby away, as if their disappearance could cancel out all memories of them.

The conclusion of the story is shocking: Armand learns that his child is "not white" not because of Désirée but because of himself. It was his mother who was "cursed with the brand of slavery," and she and her husband (Armand's father) sought to conceal this fact from him. Armand comes to despise his wife and child when he learns—or so it seems—that Désirée is black: this is the explanation that he gives to himself and to Désirée. He loathes himself for making such a marriage in the first place.

I am not sure I can prove this, but I have the feeling that Chopin wants us to perceive an ambiguity in the ending of her story. The meaning on the surface is that when Armand reads his mother's letter, he suddenly realizes what he had never known. But there may be a deeper meaning. Possibly it is the case that now Armand is finding confirmation from his mother of an

Hodges 4

identity—who he is—that he has known was, or could be, true. Driving away Désirée is, in truth, a desperate effort to cast out the self that is "not white."

The more we delve into "Désirée's Baby," the more it becomes Armand's story: to me, he is its central character. In this respect, it is noteworthy that when the story was first published in a magazine, it was titled "The Father of Désirée's Baby" (Knights xxv). I think that this title is better than the one that Chopin settled on, because it puts the focus on Armand. It could be that in the end he learns the truth about who he is. It also could be that in the end he is forced to see something he might have suspected all along—something he could not believe ever could be possible.

We thus find ourselves asking a two-part question about Armand: What does he know, and what might he not want to know? Could he really have been so blind as never to have imagined the possibility that he at last discovers at the end—that the "not white" blood is his own? Perhaps. To me, however, it seems just as likely that he suspected this possibility but could not face it. We do not want to accept the truth about who we might be, about who we are.

[New page]

Hodges 5

Works Cited

Chopin, Kate. "Désirée's Baby." *Literature for Composition*. Ed. Sylvan Barnet, William Burto, and William E. Cain. 9th ed. New York: Longman, 2010. 63–66. Print.

Hodges 6

Knights, Pamela. "Introduction." *The Awakening, and Other Stories*. New York: Oxford U, 2000. ix–xliii. Print.

Toth, Emily. *Unveiling Kate Chopin*. Jackson: U of Mississippi, 1999. Print.

Joining the Conversation: Critical Thinking and Writing

1. Has the writer chosen a good title for his paper?
2. Do you think it is good strategy to begin a paper with a quotation from a secondary source?
3. Notice that this student begins his closing paragraph with a question. Is this effective or not?
4. Do you agree with this student's decision to center his paper on a single lengthy quote?
5. Let's now consider the paper as a whole. What is the writer's thesis? Does the writer provide evidence? Does he prove his thesis?
6. If you could give the writer of this paper one piece of advice for improving his paper, what would it be?
7. This student makes an intriguing claim about Armand. Do you agree with him or not? Can you locate evidence in the text to support the student's feeling about what Armand has known, or might have known, all along?
8. Do you think that the final paragraph is effective?

KATE CHOPIN

For a biographical note, see page 11.

The Storm

I

The leaves were so still that even Bibi thought it was going to rain. Bobinôt, who was accustomed to converse on terms of perfect equality with his little son, called the child's attention to certain sombre clouds that were rolling with sinister intention from the west, accompanied by a sullen, threatening roar. They were at Friedheimer's store and decided to remain there till the storm had passed. They sat within the door on two empty kegs. Bibi was four years old and looked very wise.

"Mama'll be 'fraid, yes," he suggested with blinking eyes.

"She'll shut the house. Maybe she got Sylvie helpin' her this evenin'," Bobinôt responded reassuringly.

"No; she ent got Sylvie. Sylvie was helpin' her yistiday," piped Bibi.

Bobinôt arose and going across to the counter purchased a can of shrimps, of which Calixta was very fond. Then he returned to his perch on the keg and sat stolidly holding the can of shrimps while the storm burst. It shook the wooden store and seemed to be ripping great furrows in the distant field. Bibi laid his little hand on his father's knee and was not afraid.

II

Calixta, at home, felt no uneasiness for their safety. She sat at a side window sewing furiously on a sewing machine. She was greatly occupied and did not notice the approaching storm. But she felt very warm and often stopped to mop her face on which the perspiration gathered in beads. She unfastened her white sacque at the throat. It began to grow dark, and suddenly realizing the situation she got up hurriedly and went about closing windows and doors.

Out on the small front gallery[1] she had hung Bobinôt's Sunday clothes to air and she hastened out to gather them before the rain fell. As she stepped outside, Alcée Laballière rode in at the gate. She had not seen him very often since her marriage, and never alone. She stood there with Bobinôt's coat in her hands, and the big rain drops began to fall. Alcée rode his horse under the shelter of a side projection where the chickens had huddled and there were plows and a harrow piled up in the corner.

"May I come and wait on your gallery till the storm is over, Calixta?" he asked.

"Come 'long in, M'sieur Alcée."

His voice and her own startled her as if from a trance, and she seized Bobinôt's vest. Alcée, mounting to the porch, grabbed the trousers and snatched Bibi's braided jacket that was about to be carried away by a sudden gust of wind. He expressed an intention to remain outside, but it was soon apparent that he might as well have been out in the open: the water beat in upon the boards in driving sheets, and he went inside, closing the door after him. It was even necessary to put something beneath the door to keep the water out.

"My! what a rain! It's good two years sence it rain' like that," exclaimed Calixta as she rolled up a piece of bagging and Alcée helped her to thrust it beneath the crack.

She was a little fuller of figure than five years before when she married; but she had lost nothing of her vivacity. Her blue eyes still retained their melting quality; and her yellow hair, dishevelled by the wind and rain, kinked more stubbornly than ever about her ears and temples.

The rain beat upon the low, shingled roof with a force and clatter that threatened to break an entrance and deluge them there. They were in the dining room—the sitting room—the general utility room. Adjoining was her bed room, with Bibi's couch along side her own. The door stood open, and the room with its white, monumental bed, its closed shutters, looked dim and mysterious.

Alcée flung himself into a rocker and Calixta nervously began to gather up from the floor the lengths of a cotton sheet which she had been sewing.

[1]**gallery** porch, or passageway along a wall, open to the air but protected by a roof supported by columns.

15 "If this keeps up, *Dieu sait*[2] if the levees goin' to stan' it!" she exclaimed.

"What have you got to do with the levees?"

"I got enough to do! An' there's Bobinôt with Bibi out in that storm—if he only didn' left Friedheimer's!"

"Let us hope, Calixta, that Bobinôt's got sense enough to come in out of a cyclone."

She went and stood at the window with a greatly disturbed look on her face. She wiped the frame that was clouded with moisture. It was stiflingly hot. Alcée got up and joined her at the window, looking over her shoulder. The rain was coming down in sheets obscuring the view of far-off cabins and enveloping the distant wood in a gray mist. The playing of the lightning was incessant. A bolt struck a tall chinaberry tree at the edge of the field. It filled all visible space with a blinding glare and the crash seemed to invade the very boards they stood upon.

20 Calixta put her hands to her eyes, and with a cry, staggered backward. Alcée's arm encircled her, and for an instant he drew her close and spasmodically to him.

"*Bonté!*"[3] she cried, releasing herself from his encircling arm and retreating from the window, "the house'll go next! If I only knew w'ere Bibi was!" She would not compose herself; she would not be seated. Alcée clasped her shoulders and looked into her face. The contact of her warm, palpitating body when he had unthinkingly drawn her into his arms, had aroused all the old-time infatuation and desire for her flesh.

"Calixta," he said, "don't be frightened. Nothing can happen. The house is too low to be struck, with so many tall trees standing about. There! aren't you going to be quiet? say, aren't you?" He pushed her hair back from her face that was warm and steaming. Her lips were as red and moist as pomegranate seed. Her white neck and a glimpse of her full, firm bosom disturbed him powerfully. As she glanced up at him the fear in her liquid blue eyes had given place to a drowsy gleam that unconsciously betrayed a sensuous desire. He looked down into her eyes and there was nothing for him to do but to gather her lips in a kiss. It reminded him of Assumption.[4]

"Do you remember—in Assumption, Calixta?" he asked in a low voice broken by passion. Oh! she remembered; for in Assumption he had kissed her and kissed and kissed her; until his senses would well nigh fail, and to save her he would resort to a desperate flight. If she was not an immaculate dove in those days, she was still inviolate; a passionate creature whose very defenselessness had made her defense, against which his honor forbade him to prevail. Now—well, now—her lips seemed in a manner free to be tasted, as well as her round, white throat and her whiter breasts.

They did not heed the crashing torrents, and the roar of the elements made her laugh as she lay in his arms. She was a revelation in that dim, mysterious chamber; as white as the couch she lay upon. Her firm, elastic flesh that was knowing for the first time its birthright, was like a creamy lily that the sun invites to contribute its breath and perfume to the undying life of the world.

25 The generous abundance of her passion, without guile or trickery, was like a white flame which penetrated and found response in depths of his own sensuous nature that had never yet been reached.

[2]***Dieu sait*** God only knows. [3]***Bonté !*** Heavens!

[4]**Assumption** a parish (i.e., a county) in southeast Louisiana.

When he touched her breasts they gave themselves up in quivering ecstasy, inviting his lips. Her mouth was a fountain of delight. And when he possessed her, they seemed to swoon together at the very borderland of life's mystery.

He stayed cushioned upon her, breathless, dazed, enervated, with his heart beating like a hammer upon her. With one hand she clasped his head, her lips lightly touching his forehead. The other hand stroked with a soothing rhythm his muscular shoulders.

The growl of the thunder was distant and passing away. The rain beat softly upon the shingles, inviting them to drowsiness and sleep. But they dared not yield.

The rain was over; and the sun was turning the glistening green world into a place of gems. Calixta, on the gallery, watched Alcée ride away. He turned and smiled at her with a beaming face; and she lifted her pretty chin in the air and laughed aloud.

III

Bobinôt and Bibi, trudging home, stopped without at the cistern to make themselves presentable.

"My! Bibi, w'at will yo' mama say! You ought to be ashame'. You oughtn' put on those good pants. Look at 'em! An' that mud on yo' collar! How you got that mud on yo' collar, Bibi? I never saw such a boy!" Bibi was the picture of pathetic resignation. Bobinôt was the embodiment of serious solicitude as he strove to remove from his own person and his son's the signs of their tramp over heavy roads and through wet fields. He scraped the mud off Bibi's bare legs and feet with a stick and carefully removed all traces from his heavy brogans. Then, prepared for the worst—the meeting with an over-scrupulous housewife, they entered cautiously at the back door.

Calixta was preparing supper. She had set the table and was dripping coffee at the hearth. She sprang up as they came in.

"Oh, Bobinôt! You back! My! but I was uneasy. W'ere you been during the rain? An' Bibi? he ain't wet? he ain't hurt?" She had clasped Bibi and was kissing him effusively. Bobinôt's explanations and apologies which he had been composing all along the way, died on his lips as Calixta felt him to see if he were dry, and seemed to express nothing but satisfaction at their safe return.

"I brought you some shrimps, Calixta," offered Bobinôt, hauling the can from his ample side pocket and laying it on the table.

"Shrimps! Oh, Bobinôt! you too good fo' anything!" and she gave him a smacking kiss on the cheek that resounded. "*J'vous reponds,*[5] we'll have a feas' to night! umph-umph!"

Bobinôt and Bibi began to relax and enjoy themselves, and when the three seated themselves at table they laughed much and so loud that anyone might have heard them as far away as Laballière's.

IV

Alcée Laballière wrote to his wife, Clarisse, that night. It was a loving letter, full of tender solicitude. He told her not to hurry back, but if she and the babies liked it at Biloxi, to stay a month longer. He was getting on nicely; and though he missed

[5]***J'vous reponds*** Take my word; let me tell you.

them, he was willing to bear the separation a while longer—realizing that their health and pleasure were the first things to be considered.

V

As for Clarisse, she was charmed upon receiving her husband's letter. She and the babies were doing well. The society was agreeable; many of her old friends and acquaintances were at the bay. And the first free breath since her marriage seemed to restore the pleasant liberty of her maiden days. Devoted as she was to her husband, their intimate conjugal life was something which she was more than willing to forego for a while.

So the storm passed and everyone was happy.

[1898]

Writing about "The Storm"

As we said earlier, what you write will depend partly on your audience and on your purpose, as well as on your responses (for instance, pleasure or irritation). Consider the *differences* among these assignments:

1. Assume that you are trying to describe "The Storm" to someone who has not read it. Briefly summarize the action, and then explain why you think "The Storm" is (or is not) worth reading.
2. Assume that your readers are familiar with "The Story of an Hour." Compare the implied attitudes, as you see them, toward marriage in that story and "The Storm."
3. Write an essay arguing that "The Storm" is (or is not) immoral, or (a different thing) amoral. (By the way, because one of her slightly earlier works, a short novel called *The Awakening*, was widely condemned as sordid, Chopin was unable to find a publisher for "The Storm.")
4. In Part IV we are told that Alcée wrote a letter to Clarisse. Write his letter (500 words). Or write Clarisse's response (500 words).
5. You are writing to a high school teacher, urging that one of the four stories by Chopin be taught in high school. Which one do you recommend, and why?
6. Do you think "The Storm" would make a good film? Why? (And while you are thinking about Chopin and film, think about what devices you might use to turn "Ripe Figs," "The Story of an Hour," or "Désirée's Baby" into an interesting film.)

JOHN STEINBECK

John Steinbeck (1902–1968) was born in Salinas, California, and much of his fiction concerns this landscape and its people. As a young man he worked on ranches, farms, and road gangs, and sometimes attended Stanford University—he never graduated—but he wrote whenever he could find the time. His early efforts at writing, however, were uniformly rejected by publishers. Even when he did break into print, he did not achieve much notice for several years: a novel in 1929, a book of stories in 1932, and another novel in 1933 attracted little attention. But the publication of Tortilla Flat (1935), a novel about Mexican Americans, changed all that. It was followed by other successful novels—In Dubious Battle (1936) and Of Mice and Men (1937)—and by The Long Valley (1938), a collection of stories that included "The Chrysanthemums." His next book, The Grapes of Wrath (1939), about dispossessed sharecropper migrants from the Oklahoma dustbowl, was also immensely popular and won a Pulitzer Prize. During World War II Steinbeck sent reports from battlefields in Italy and Africa. In 1962 he was awarded the Nobel Prize in Literature.

The Chrysanthemums

The high grey-flannel fog of winter closed off the Salinas Valley[1] from the sky and from all the rest of the world. On every side it sat like a lid on the mountains and made of the great valley a closed pot. On the broad, level land floor the gang plows bit deep and left the black earth shining like metal where the shares had cut. On the foothill ranches across the Salinas River, the yellow stubble fields seemed to be bathed in pale cold sunshine, but there was no sunshine in the valley now in December. The thick willow scrub along the river flamed with sharp and positive yellow leaves.

It was a time of quiet and of waiting. The air was cold and tender. A light wind blew up from the southwest so that the farmers were mildly hopeful of a good rain before long; but fog and rain do not go together.

Across the river, on Henry Allen's foothill ranch there was little work to be done, for the hay was cut and stored and the orchards were plowed up to receive the rain deeply when it should come. The cattle on the higher slopes were becoming shaggy and rough-coated.

Elisa Allen, working in her flower garden, looked down across the yard and saw Henry, her husband, talking to two men in business suits. The three of them stood by the tractor shed, each man with one foot on the side of the little Fordson.[2] They smoked cigarettes and studied the machine as they talked.

5 Elisa watched them for a moment and then went back to her work. She was thirty-five. Her face was lean and strong and her eyes were as clear as water. Her figure looked blocked and heavy in her gardening costume, a man's black hat pulled low down over her eyes, clod-hopper shoes, a figured print dress almost completely covered by a big corduroy apron with four big pockets to hold the snips, the trowel and scratcher, the seeds and the knife she worked with. She wore heavy leather gloves to protect her hands while she worked.

She was cutting down the old year's chrysanthemum stalks with a pair of short and powerful scissors. She looked down toward the men by the tractor shed now and then. Her face was eager and mature and handsome; even her work with the scissors was over-eager, over-powerful. The chrysanthemum stems seemed too small and easy for her energy.

She brushed a cloud of hair out of her eyes with the back of her glove, and left a smudge of earth on her cheek in doing it. Behind her stood the neat white farm house with red geraniums close-banked around it as high as the windows. It was a hard-swept looking little house with hard-polished windows, and a clean mud-mat on the front steps.

[1]**the Salinas Valley** a fertile area in central California.
[2]**Fordson** a two-door Ford car.

Elisa cast another glance toward the tractor shed. The strangers were getting into their Ford coupe. She took off a glove and put her strong fingers down into the forest of new green chrysanthemum sprouts that were growing around the old roots. She spread the leaves and looked down among the close-growing stems. No aphids were there, no sowbugs or snails or cutworms. Her terrier fingers destroyed such pests before they could get started.

Elisa started at the sound of her husband's voice. He had come near quietly, and he leaned over the wire fence that protected her flower garden from cattle and dogs and chickens.

10 "At it again," he said. "You've got a strong new crop coming."

Elisa straightened her back and pulled on the gardening glove again. "Yes. They'll be strong this coming year." In her tone and on her face there was a little smugness.

"You've got a gift with things," Henry observed. "Some of those yellow chrysanthemums you had this year were ten inches across. I wish you'd work out in the orchard and raise some apples that big."

Her eyes sharpened. "Maybe I could do it, too. I've a gift with things, all right. My mother had it. She could stick anything in the ground and make it grow. She said it was having planters' hands that knew how to do it."

"Well, it sure works with flowers," he said.

15 "Henry, who were those men you were talking to?"

"Why, sure, that's what I came to tell you. They were from the Western Meat Company. I sold those thirty head of three-year-old steers. Got nearly my own price, too."

"Good," she said. "Good for you."

"And I thought," he continued, "I thought how it's Saturday afternoon, and we might go into Salinas for dinner at a restaurant, and then to a picture show—to celebrate, you see."

"Good," she repeated. "Oh, yes. That will be good."

20 Henry put on his joking tone. "There's fights tonight. How'd you like to go to the fights?"

"Oh, no," she said breathlessly. "No, I wouldn't like fights."

"Just fooling, Elisa. We'll go to a movie. Let's see. It's two now. I'm going to take Scotty and bring down those steers from the hill. It'll take us maybe two hours. We'll go in town about five and have dinner at the Cominos Hotel. Like that?"

"Of course I'll like it. It's good to eat away from home."

"All right, then. I'll go get up a couple of horses."

25 She said, "I'll have plenty of time to transplant some of these sets, I guess."

She heard her husband calling Scotty down by the barn. And a little later she saw the two men ride up the pale yellow hillside in search of the steers.

There was a little square sandy bed kept for rooting the chrysanthemums. With her trowel she turned the soil over and over, and smoothed it and patted it firm. Then she dug ten parallel trenches to receive the sets. Back at the chrysanthemum bed she pulled out the little crisp shoots, trimmed off the leaves of each one with her scissors and laid it on a small orderly pile.

A squeak of wheels and plod of hoofs came from the road. Elisa looked up. The country road ran along the dense bank of willows and cottonwoods that bordered the river, and up this road came a curious vehicle, curiously drawn. It was an old springwagon, with a round canvas top on it like the cover of a prairie schooner. It was drawn by an old bay horse and a little grey-and-white burro. A big stubble-bearded man sat between the cover flaps and drove the crawling team. Underneath the wagon, between the hind wheels, a lean and rangy mongrel dog walked sedately. Words were painted on the canvas, in clumsy, crooked letters. "Pots, pans, knives, sisors, lawn mores, Fixed." Two rows of articles, and the triumphantly definitive "Fixed" below. The black paint had run down in little sharp points beneath each letter.

Elisa, squatting on the ground, watched to see the crazy, loose-jointed wagon pass by. But it didn't pass. It turned into the farm road in front of her house, crooked old wheels skirling and squeaking. The rangy dog darted from between the wheels and ran ahead. Instantly the two ranch shepherds flew out at him. Then all three stopped, and with stiff and quivering tails, with taut straight legs, with ambassadorial dignity, they slowly circled, sniffing daintily. The caravan pulled up to Elisa's wire fence and stopped. Now the newcomer dog, feeling out-numbered, lowered his tail and retired under the wagon with raised hackles and bared teeth.

30 The man on the wagon seat called out, "That's a bad dog in a fight when he gets started."

Elisa laughed. "I see he is. How soon does he generally get started?"

The man caught up her laughter and echoed it heartily. "Sometimes not for weeks and weeks," he said. He climbed stiffly down, over the wheel. The horse and the donkey drooped like unwatered flowers.

Elisa saw that he was a very big man. Although his hair and beard were greying, he did not look old. His worn black suit was wrinkled and spotted with grease. The laughter had disappeared from his face and eyes the moment his laughing voice ceased. His eyes were dark, and they were full of the brooding that gets in the eyes of teamsters and of sailors. The calloused hands he rested on the wire fence were cracked, and every crack was a black line. He took off his battered hat.

"I'm off my general road, ma'am," he said. "Does this dirt road cut over across the river to the Los Angeles highway?"

35 Elisa stood up and shoved the thick scissors in her apron pocket. "Well, yes, it does, but it winds around and then fords the river. I don't think your team could pull through the sand."

He replied with some asperity. "It might surprise you what them beasts can pull through."

"When they get started?" she asked.

He smiled for a second. "Yes. When they get started."

"Well," said Elisa, "I think you'll save time if you go back to the Salinas road and pick up the highway there."

40 He drew a big finger down the chicken wire and made it sing. "I ain't in any hurry, ma'am. I go from Seattle to San Diego and back every year. Takes all my time. About six months each way. I aim to follow nice weather."

Elisa took off her gloves and stuffed them in the apron pocket with the scissors. She touched the under edge of her man's hat, searching for fugitive hairs. "That sounds like a nice kind of way to live," she said.

He leaned confidentially over the fence. "Maybe you noticed the writing on my wagon. I mend pots and sharpen knives and scissors. You got any of them things to do?"

"Oh, no," she said quickly. "Nothing like that." Her eyes hardened with resistance.

"Scissors is the worst thing," he explained. "Most people just ruin scissors trying to sharpen 'em, but I know how. I got a special tool. It's a little bobbit kind of thing, and patented. But it sure does the trick."

45 "No. My scissors are all sharp."

"All right, then. Take a pot," he continued earnestly, "a bent pot, or a pot with a hole. I can make it like new so you don't have to buy no new ones. That's a saving for you."

"No," she said shortly. "I tell you I have nothing like that for you to do."

His face fell to an exaggerated sadness. His voice took on a whining undertone. "I ain't had a thing to do today. Maybe I won't have no supper tonight. You see I'm off my regular road. I know folks on the highway clear from Seattle to San Diego. They save their things for me to sharpen up because they know I do it so good and save them money."

"I'm sorry," Elisa said irritably. "I haven't anything for you to do."

50 His eyes left her face and fell to searching the ground. They roamed about until they came to the chrysanthemum bed where she had been working. "What's them plants, ma'am?"

The irritation and resistance melted from Elisa's face. "Oh, those are chrysanthemums, giant whites and yellows. I raise them every year, bigger than anybody around here."

"Kind of a long-stemmed flower? Looks like a quick puff of colored smoke?" he asked.

"That's it. What a nice way to describe them."

"They smell kind of nasty till you get used to them," he said.

55 "It's a good bitter smell," she retorted, "not nasty at all."

He changed his tone quickly. "I like the smell myself."

"I had ten-inch blooms this year," she said.

The man leaned farther over the fence. "Look. I know a lady down the road a piece, has got the nicest garden you ever seen. Got nearly every kind of flower but no chrysanthemums. Last time I was mending a copper-bottom wash-tub for her (that's a hard job but I do it good), she said to me, 'If you ever run acrost some nice chrysanthemums I wish you'd try to get me a few seeds.' That's what she told me."

Elisa's eyes grew alert and eager. "She couldn't have known much about chrysanthemums. You *can* raise them from seed, but it's much easier to root the little sprouts you see there."

60 "Oh," he said. "I s'pose I can't take none to her, then."

"Why yes you can," Elisa cried. "I can put some in damp sand, and you can carry them right along with you. They'll take root in the pot if you keep them damp. And then she can transplant them."

"She'd sure like to have some, ma'am. You say they're nice ones?"

"Beautiful," she said. "Oh, beautiful." Her eyes shone. She tore off the battered hat and shook out her dark pretty hair. "I'll put them in a flower pot, and you can take them right with you. Come into the yard."

While the man came through the picket gate Elisa ran excitedly along the geranium-bordered path to the back of the house. And she returned carrying a big red flower pot. The gloves were forgotten now. She kneeled on the ground by the starting bed and dug up the sandy soil with her fingers and scooped it into the bright new flower pot. Then she picked up the little pile of shoots she had prepared. With her strong fingers she pressed them into the sand and tamped around them with her knuckles. The man stood over her. "I'll tell you what to do," she said. "You remember so you can tell the lady."

65 "Yes, I'll try to remember."

"Well, look. These will take root in about a month. Then she must set them out, about a foot apart in good rich earth like this, see?" She lifted a handful of dark soil for him to look at. "They'll grow fast and tall. Now remember this: In July tell her to cut them down, about eight inches from the ground."

"Before they bloom?" he asked.

"Yes, before they bloom." Her face was tight with eagerness. "They'll grow right up again. About the last of September the buds will start."

She stopped and seemed perplexed. "It's the budding that takes the most care," she said hesitantly. "I don't know how to tell you." She looked deep into his eyes, searchingly. Her mouth opened a little, and she seemed to be listening. "I'll try to tell you," she said. "Did you ever hear of planting hands?"

70 "Can't say I have, ma'am."

"Well, I can only tell you what it feels like. It's when you're picking off the buds you don't want. Everything goes right down into your fingertips. You watch your fingers work. They do it themselves. You can feel how it is. They pick and pick the buds. They never make a mistake. They're with the plant. Do you see? Your fingers and the plant. You can feel that, right up your arm. They know. They never make a mistake. You can feel it. When you're like that you can't do anything wrong. Do you see that? Can you understand that?"

She was kneeling on the ground looking up at him. Her breast swelled passionately.

The man's eyes narrowed. He looked away self-consciously. "Maybe I know," he said. "Sometimes in the night in the wagon there—"

Elisa's voice grew husky. She broke in on him, "I've never lived as you do, but I know what you mean. When the night is dark—why, the stars are sharp-pointed, and there's quiet. Why, you rise up and up! Every pointed star gets driven into your body. It's like that. Hot and sharp and—lovely."

75 Kneeling there, her hand went out toward his legs in the greasy black trousers. Her hesitant fingers almost touched the cloth. Then her hand dropped to the ground. She crouched low like a fawning dog.

He said, "It's nice, just like you say. Only when you don't have no dinner, it ain't."

She stood up then, very straight, and her face was ashamed. She held the flower pot out to him and placed it gently in his arms. "Here. Put it in your wagon, on the seat, where you can watch it. Maybe I can find something for you to do."

At the back of the house she dug in the can pile and found two old and battered aluminum saucepans. She carried them back and gave them to him. "Here, maybe you can fix these."

His manner changed. He became professional. "Good as new I can fix them." At the back of his wagon he set a little anvil, and out of an oily tool box dug a small machine hammer. Elisa came through the gate to watch him while he pounded out the dents in the kettles. His mouth grew sure and knowing. At a difficult part of the work he sucked his under-lip.

80 "You sleep right in the wagon?" Elisa asked.

"Right in the wagon, ma'am. Rain or shine I'm dry as a cow in there."

"It must be nice," she said. "It must be very nice. I wish women could do such things."

"It ain't the right kind of a life for a woman."

Her upper lip raised a little, showing her teeth. "How do you know? How can you tell?" she said.

85 "I don't know, ma'am," he protested. "Of course I don't know. Now here's your kettles, done. You don't have to buy no new ones."

"How much?"

"Oh, fifty cents'll do. I keep my prices down and my work good. That's why I have all them satisfied customers up and down the highway."

Elisa brought him a fifty-cent piece from the house and dropped it in his hand. "You might be surprised to have a rival some time. I can sharpen scissors, too. And I can beat the dents out of little pots. I could show you what a woman might do."

He put his hammer back in the oily box and shoved the little anvil out of sight. "It would be a lonely life for a woman, ma'am, and a scarey life, too, with animals creeping under the wagon all night." He climbed over the singletree, steadying himself with a hand on the burro's white rump. He settled himself in the seat, picked up the lines. "Thank you kindly, ma'am," he said. "I'll do like you told me; I'll go back and catch the Salinas road."

90 "Mind," she called, "if you're long in getting there, keep the sand damp."

"Sand, ma'am? . . . Sand? Oh, sure. You mean around the chrysanthemums. Sure I will." He clucked his tongue. The beasts leaned luxuriously into their collars. The mongrel dog took his place between the back wheels. The wagon turned and crawled out the entrance road and back the way it had come, along the river.

Elisa stood in front of her wire fence watching the slow progress of the caravan. Her shoulders were straight, her head thrown back, her eyes half-closed, so that the scene came vaguely into them. Her lips moved silently, forming the words "Good-bye—good-bye." Then she whispered, "That's a bright direction. There's a glowing there." The sound of her whisper startled her. She shook herself free and looked about to see whether anyone had been listening. Only the dogs had heard. They lifted their heads toward her from their sleeping in the dust, and then stretched out their chins and settled asleep again. Elisa turned and ran hurriedly into the house.

In the kitchen she reached behind the stove and felt the water tank. It was full of hot water from the noonday cooking. In the bathroom she tore off her soiled clothes and flung them into the corner. And then she scrubbed herself with a little block of pumice, legs and thighs, loins and chest and arms, until her skin was scratched and red. When she had dried herself she stood in front of a mirror in her bedroom and looked at her body. She tightened her stomach and threw out her chest. She turned and looked over her shoulder at her back.

After a while she began to dress, slowly. She put on her newest underclothing and her nicest stockings and the dress which was the symbol of her prettiness. She worked carefully on her hair, penciled her eyebrows and rouged her lips.

95 Before she was finished she heard the little thunder of hoofs and the shouts of Henry and his helper as they drove the red steers into the corral. She heard the gate bang shut and set herself for Henry's arrival.

His step sounded on the porch. He entered the house calling, "Elisa, where are you?"

"In my room, dressing. I'm not ready. There's hot water for your bath. Hurry up. It's getting late."

When she heard him splashing in the tub, Elisa laid his dark suit on the bed, and shirt and socks and tie beside it. She stood his polished shoes on the floor beside the bed. Then she went to the porch and sat primly and stiffly down. She looked toward the river road where the willow-line was still yellow with frosted leaves so that under the high grey fog they seemed a thin band of sunshine. This was the only color in the grey afternoon. She sat unmoving for a long time. Her eyes blinked rarely.

Henry came banging out of the door shoving his tie inside his vest as he came. Elisa stiffened and her face grew tight. Henry stopped short and looked at her. "Why—why, Elisa. You look so nice!"

"Nice? You think I look nice? What do you mean by 'nice'?"

Henry blundered on. "I don't know. I mean you look different, strong and happy."

"I am strong? Yes, strong. What do you mean 'strong'?"

He looked bewildered. "You're playing some kind of a game," he said helplessly. "It's a kind of a play. You look strong enough to break a calf over your knee, happy enough to eat it like a watermelon."

For a second she lost her rigidity. "Henry! Don't talk like that. You didn't know what you said." She grew complete again. "I'm strong," she boasted. "I never knew before how strong."

Henry looked down toward the tractor shed, and when he brought his eyes back to her, they were his own again. "I'll get out the car. You can put on your coat while I'm starting."

Elisa went into the house. She heard him drive to the gate and idle down his motor, and then she took a long time to put on her hat. She pulled it here and pressed it there. When Henry turned the motor off she slipped into her coat and went out.

The little roadster bounced along on the dirt road by the river, raising the birds and driving the rabbits into the brush. Two cranes flapped heavily over the willow-line and dropped into the river-bed.

Far ahead on the road Elisa saw a dark speck. She knew.

She tried not to look as they passed it, but her eyes would not obey. She whispered to herself sadly, "He might have thrown them off the road. That wouldn't have been much trouble, not very much. But he kept the pot," she explained. "He had to keep the pot. That's why he couldn't get them off the road."

The roadster turned a bend and she saw the caravan ahead. She swung full around toward her husband so she could not see the little covered wagon and the mismatched team as the car passed them.

In a moment it was over. The thing was done. She did not look back.

She said loudly, to be heard above the motor, "It will be good, tonight, a good dinner."

"Now you're changed again," Henry complained. He took one hand from the wheel and patted her knee. "I ought to take you in to dinner oftener. It would be good for both of us. We get so heavy out on the ranch."

"Henry," she asked, "could we have wine at dinner?"

"Sure we could. Say! That will be fine."

She was silent for a while; then she said, "Henry, at those prize fights, do the men hurt each other very much?"

"Sometimes a little, not often. Why?"

"Well, I've read how they break noses, and blood runs down their chests. I've read how the fighting gloves get heavy and soggy with blood."

He looked around at her. "What's the matter, Elisa? I didn't know you read things like that." He brought the car to a stop, then turned to the right over the Salinas River bridge.

"Do any women ever go to the fights?" she asked.

"Oh, sure, some. What's the matter, Elisa? Do you want to go? I don't think you'd like it, but I'll take you if you really want to go."

She relaxed limply in the seat. "Oh, no. No. I don't want to go. I'm sure I don't." Her face was turned away from him. "It will be enough if we can have wine. It will be plenty." She turned up her coat collar so he could not see that she was crying weakly—like an old woman.

[1937]

Joining the Conversation: Critical Thinking and Writing

1. In the first paragraph of the story, the valley, shut off by fog, is said to be "a closed pot." Is this setting significant? Would any other setting do equally well? Why, or why not?
2. What physical descriptions in the story—literal or figurative—suggest that Elisa is frustrated?
3. Describe Elisa and Henry's marriage.
4. In an argument, evaluate the view that Elisa is responsible for her troubles.

ANTON CHEKHOV

Anton Chekhov (1860–1904) was born in Russia, the son of a shopkeeper. While a medical student at Moscow University, Chekhov wrote stories, sketches, and reviews to help support his family and to finance his education. In 1884 he received his medical degree, began to practice medicine, published his first book of stories, and suffered the first of a series of hemorrhages from tuberculosis. In his remaining twenty years, in addition to writing several hundred stories, he wrote plays, half a dozen of which have established themselves as classics. He died from tuberculosis at the age of 44.

Misery

Translated by Constance Garnett

"To Whom Shall I Tell My Grief?"

The twilight of evening. Big flakes of wet snow are whirling lazily about the street lamps, which have just been lighted, and lying in a thin soft layer on roofs, horses' backs, shoulders, caps. Iona Potapov, the sledgedriver, is all white like a ghost. He sits on the box without stirring, bent as double as the living body can be bent. If a regular snowdrift fell on him it seems as though even then he would not think it necessary to shake it off. . . . His little mare is white and motionless too. Her stillness, the angularity of her lines, and the stick-like straightness of her legs make her look like a halfpenny gingerbread horse. She is probably lost in thought. Anyone who has been torn away from the plough, from the familiar gray landscapes, and cast into this slough, full of monstrous lights, of unceasing uproar and hurrying people, is bound to think.

It is a long time since Iona and his nag have budged. They came out of the yard before dinner-time and not a single fare yet. But now the shades of evening are falling on the town. The pale light of the street lamps changes to a vivid color, and the bustle of the street grows noisier.

"Sledge to Vyborgskaya!" Iona hears. "Sledge!"

Iona starts, and through his snow-plastered eyelashes sees an officer in a military overcoat with a hood over his head.

"To Vyborgskaya," repeats the officer. "Are you asleep? To Vyborgskaya!"

In token of assent Iona gives a tug at the reins which sends cakes of snow flying from the horse's back and shoulders. The officer gets into the sledge. The sledge-driver clicks to the horse, cranes his neck like a swan, rises in his seat, and more from habit than necessity brandishes his whip. The mare cranes her neck, too, crooks her stick-like legs, and hesitatingly sets off. . . .

"Where are you shoving, you devil?" Iona immediately hears shouts from the dark mass shifting to and fro before him. "Where the devil are you going? Keep to the r-right!"

"You don't know how to drive! Keep to the right," says the officer angrily.

A coachman driving a carriage swears at him; a pedestrian crossing the road and brushing the horse's nose with his shoulder looks at him angrily and shakes the snow off his sleeve. Iona fidgets on the box as though he were sitting on thorns, jerks his elbows, and turns his eyes about like one possessed, as though he did not know where he was or why he was there.

"What rascals they all are!" says the officer jocosely. "They are simply doing their best to run up against you or fall under the horse's feet. They must be doing it on purpose."

Iona looks at his fare and moves his lips. . . . Apparently he means to say something, but nothing comes out but a sniff.

"What?" inquires the officer.

Iona gives a wry smile, and straining his throat, brings out huskily: "My son . . . , er . . . my son died this week, sir."

"H'm! What did he die of?"

Iona turns his whole body round to his fare, and says:

"Who can tell! It must have been from fever. . . . He lay three days in the hospital and then he died. . . . God's will."

"Turn round, you devil!" comes out of the darkness. "Have you gone cracked, you old dog? Look where you are going!"

"Drive on! drive on! . . ." says the officer. "We shan't get there till tomorrow going on like this. Hurry up!"

The sledge-driver cranes his neck again, rises in his seat, and with heavy grace swings his whip. Several times he looks round at the officer, but the latter keeps his eyes shut and is apparently disinclined to listen. Putting his fare down at Vyborgskaya, Iona stops by a restaurant, and again sits huddled up on the box. . . . Again the wet snow paints him and his horse white. One hour passes, and then another. . . .

Three young men, two tall and thin, one short and hunchbacked, come up, railing at each other and loudly stamping on the pavement with their galoshes.

"Cabby, to the Police Bridge!" the hunchback cries in a cracked voice. "The three of us, . . . twenty kopecks!"

Iona tugs at the reins and clicks to his horse. Twenty kopecks is not a fair price, but he has no thoughts for that. Whether it is a rouble or whether it is five kopecks does not matter to him now so long as he has a fare. . . . The three young men, shoving each other and using bad language, go up to the sledge, and all three try to sit down at once. The question remains to be settled: Which are to sit down and which one is to stand? After a long altercation, ill-temper, and abuse, they come to the conclusion that the hunchback must stand because he is the shortest.

"Well, drive on," says the hunchback in his cracked voice, settling himself and breathing down Iona's neck. "Cut along! What a cap you've got, my friend! You wouldn't find a worse one in all Petersburg. . . ."

"He-he! . . . he-he! . . ." laughs Iona. "It's nothing to boast of!"

"Well, then, nothing to boast of, drive on! Are you going to drive like this all the way? Eh? Shall I give you one in the neck?"

"My head aches," says one of the tall ones. "At the Dukmasovs' yesterday Vaska and I drank four bottles of brandy between us."

"I can't make out why you talk such stuff," says the other tall one angrily. "You lie like a brute."

"Strike me dead, it's the truth! . . ."

"It's about as true as that a louse coughs."

"He-he!" grins Iona. "Me-er-ry gentlemen!"

"Tfoo! the devil take you!" cries the hunchback indignantly. "Will you get on, you old plague, or won't you? Is that the way to drive? Give her one with the whip. Hang it all, give it her well."

Iona feels behind his back the jolting person and quivering voice of the hunchback. He hears abuse addressed to him, he sees people, and the feeling of loneliness begins little by little to be less heavy on his heart. The hunchback swears at him, till he chokes over some elaborately whimsical string of epithets and is overpowered by his cough. His tall companions begin talking of a certain Nadyezhda Petrovna. Iona looks round at them. Waiting till there is a brief pause, he looks round once more and says:

"This week . . . er . . . my . . . er . . . son died!"

"We shall all die, . . ." says the hunchback with a sigh, wiping his lips after coughing. "Come, drive on! drive on! My friends, I simply cannot stand crawling like this! When will he get us there?"

"Well, you give him a little encouragement . . . one in the neck!"

"Do you hear, you old plague? I'll make you smart. If one stands on ceremony with fellows like you one may as well walk. Do you hear, you old dragon? Or don't you care a hang what we say?"

And Iona hears rather than feels a slap on the back of his neck.

"He-he! . . ." he laughs. "Merry gentlemen . . . God give you health!"

"Cabman, are you married?" asks one of the tall ones.

"I? He-he! Me-er-ry gentlemen. The only wife for me now is the damp earth. . . . He-ho-ho! . . . The grave that is! . . . Here my son's dead and I am alive. . . . It's a strange thing, death has come in at the wrong door. . . . Instead of coming for me it went for my son. . . ."

And Iona turns round to tell them how his son died, but at that point the hunchback gives a faint sigh and announces that, thank God! they have arrived at last. After taking his twenty kopecks, Iona gazes for a long while after the revelers, who disappear into a dark entry. Again he is alone and again there is silence for him. . . . The misery which has been for a brief space eased comes back again and tears his heart more cruelly than ever. With a look of anxiety and suffering Iona's eyes stray restlessly among the crowds moving to and fro on both sides of the street: can he not find among those thousands someone who will listen to him? But the crowds flit by heedless of him and his misery. . . . His misery is immense, beyond all bounds. If Iona's heart were to burst and his misery to flow out, it would flood the whole world, it seems, but yet it is not seen. It has found a hiding-place in such an insignificant shell that one would not have found it with a candle by daylight. . . .

Iona sees a house-porter with a parcel and makes up his mind to address him. "What time will it be, friend?" he asks.

"Going on for ten. . . . Why have you stopped here? Drive on!"

Iona drives a few paces away, bends himself double, and gives himself up to his misery. He feels it is no good to appeal to people. But before five minutes have passed he draws himself up, shakes his head as though he feels a sharp pain, and tugs at the reins. . . . He can bear it no longer.

"Back to the yard!" he thinks. "To the yard!"

And his little mare, as though she knew his thoughts, falls to trotting. An hour and a half later Iona is sitting by a big dirty stove. On the stove, on the floor, and on the benches are people snoring. The air is full of smells and stuffiness. Iona looks at the sleeping figures, scratches himself, and regrets that he has come home so early. . . .

"I have not earned enough to pay for the oats, even," he thinks. "That's why I am so miserable. A man who knows how to do his work, . . . who has had enough to eat, and whose horse has had enough to eat, is always at ease. . . ."

In one of the corners a young cabman gets up, clears his throat sleepily, and makes for the waterbucket.

"Want a drink?" Iona asks him.

"Seems so."

"May it do you good. . . . But my son is dead, mate. . . . Do you hear? This week in the hospital. . . . It's queer business. . . ."

Iona looks to see the effect produced by his words, but he sees nothing. The young man has covered his head over and is already asleep. The old man sighs and scratches himself. . . . Just as the young man had been thirsty for water, he thirsts for speech. His son will soon have been dead a week, and he has not really talked to anybody yet. . . . He wants to talk of it properly, with deliberation. . . . He wants to tell how his son was taken ill, how he suffered, what he said before he died, how he died. . . . He wants to describe the funeral, and how he went to the hospital to get his son's clothes. He still has his daughter Anisya in the country. . . . And he wants to talk about her too. . . . Yes, he has plenty to talk about now. His listener ought to sigh and exclaim and lament. . . . It would be even better to talk to women. Though they are silly creatures, they blubber at the first word.

"Let's go out and have a look at the mare," Iona thinks. "There is always time for sleep. . . . You'll have sleep enough, no fear. . . ."

He puts on his coat and goes into the stables where his mare is standing. He thinks about oats, about hay, about the weather. . . . He cannot think about his son when he is alone. . . . To talk about him with someone is possible, but to think of him and picture him is insufferable anguish. . . .

"Are you munching?" Iona asks his mare, seeing her shining eyes. "There, munch away, munch away. . . . Since we have not earned enough for oats, we will eat hay. . . . Yes, . . . I have grown too old to drive. . . . My son ought to be driving, not I. . . . He was a real coachman. . . . He ought to have lived. . . ."

Iona is silent for a while, and then he goes on:

"That's how it is, old girl. . . . Kuzma Ionitch is gone. . . . He said goodby to me. . . . He went and died for no reason. . . . Now, suppose you had a little colt, and you were mother to that little colt. . . . And all at once that same little colt went and died. . . . You'd be sorry, wouldn't you? . . ."

The little mare munches, listens, and breathes on her master's hands. Iona is carried away and tells her all about it.

[1886]

Joining the Conversation: Critical Thinking and Writing

1. What do you admire or not admire about Chekhov's story? Why? Set forth your response in an argument.
2. Try to examine in detail your response to the ending and develop an argument about it. Do you think the ending is, in a way, a happy ending? Would you prefer a different ending? For instance, should the story end when the young cabman falls asleep? Or when Iona sets out for the stable? Or can you imagine a better ending? If so, what?

CHAPTER 4

Reading Literature Closely: Argument

Literature is news that STAYS news.

EZRA POUND

Poets . . . present for inspection "imaginary gardens with real toads in them."

MARIANNE MOORE

All you can be sure about in a political-minded writer is that if the work should last you will have to skip the politics when you read it.

ERNEST HEMINGWAY

We shall not cease from exploration
And the end of all our exploring
Will be to arrive where we started
And to know the place for the first time.

T. S. ELIOT

Beginning with Proverbs

Proverbs as Literature

At the end of this chapter we will ask you to look again at these four quotations, but you may want to read them a second time right now, and perhaps your mind will return to one or more even as you read our words.

Let's begin thinking about literature and argument—Do literary works offer arguments?—by examining what is probably the briefest form of literature, the proverb. We say that proverbs are literature for two reasons:

- Proverbs use words as much for their connotations (their associations or resonances) as for their denotations (the literal meanings of words).
- Proverbs are much concerned with shaping coherent worlds of their own; they can be thought of as tiny short poems.

Consider these proverbs, selected almost at random:

Red sky at night, sailors delight;
Red sky in morning, sailors take warning.
Birds of a feather flock together.
A stitch in time saves nine.
Look before you leap.
Waste not, want not.

The first of these, whether true or not, means exactly what it says, and to that extent it does not illustrate our claim that proverbs rely as much on the connotations or associations of words as on the denotations. "Red" means "red," "sky" means "sky," and so on. But notice that the proverb is "literary" in other aspects: It uses repetition (*red sky . . . red sky, sailors . . . sailors*), rhyme (*night/delight, morning/warning*), and a parallel structure. This tiny poem's assertions about weather may or may not be true, but the sentence affords pleasure,

- partly by the sounds and the structure, and
- partly by the comforting implication that we live in a unified, predictable (even if sometimes threatening) world.

Proverbs as Arguments

If the proverb offers an argument, the argument is implicit: *Because* a red sky at night (usually) precedes a calm day, sailors *ought* to be pleased, and *because* a red sky in the morning (usually) precedes a stormy day, sailors *ought* to be cautious.

What we are saying about argument is this: In an argument, certain statements are given *as reasons for* other statements. "Argument," by its use of reasons, can thus be distinguished from other forms of writing, such as exposition ("In order to do this card trick, you will need to separate the black cards from the red cards"), and description ("The mountain is X feet tall") and narration ("After climbing the mountain, they rested for an hour, and then began the descent").

In "Birds of a feather flock together" we again find rhyme, but now we also find words used not literally but metaphorically. Just as the assertion that "the early bird catches the worm" is not mainly a comment about birds but about human beings, when people talk about "birds of a feather" they are not really talking about "warm-blooded, egg-laying, feathered vertebrates with forelimbs modified to form wings" (*The American Heritage Dictionary of the English Language,* 3rd edition). If there is an argument in this assertion, it is not made explicit; rather, it is implicit, something along these lines: Just as similar birds fly together, so similar human beings *naturally* (it is implied) find each other's company congenial.

In fact, we can put the advice even more strongly: "Look around, and you will see that nature tells us to stick with our kind," or maybe even "Don't choose a mate whose ethnicity or culture is notably different from your own." The proverb thus might be *used as* an argument: Someone might caution a friend against a religious intermarriage by offering the proverb as a *reason*, and even as *evidence.* Why shouldn't A marry B? Well, you know, "Birds of a feather flock together, that's nature's way." In "Red sky at night," the speaker suggests that a constant *physical* law governs nature; in "Birds of a feather," the speaker suggests there is a constant *social* law, and the speaker might even think a *moral* law is implied.

In "A stitch in time saves nine," as with "Birds of a feather," we get language that is used not in its literal sense but in its metaphoric (suggestive) sense. The speaker is not really talking about making a small repair on clothing so that a larger repair will not later be needed; rather, the speaker is using a metaphor, saying one thing but meaning another. (Robert Frost once said that poetry provides the one permissible way of saying one thing and meaning another.) "A stitch in time" is not about sewing but is about all sorts of prudent early actions, and the metaphor is emphasized, is made especially memorable, by alliteration (the repetition of the initial *s* in *stitch* and *saves*) and by a near-rhyme (*time, nine*). Here again there is an implication of an unchanging, coherent world, a predictable world in which people can live happy lives if they grasp the basic principles. (Modern proverbs of this sort include "Garbage in, garbage out"—a nice parallel construction with a nice contrast—and "There is no such thing as a free lunch.")

We leave it to you to think for a moment about the language and the structure of "Look before you leap" and "Waste not, want not."

Are Proverbs True? Is Literature True?

At this point we want to call attention to a curious fact: Proverbs—partly because they are so concise, so authoritative, so effective in their use of alliteration and of rhyme—are widely accepted as true, and many people who quote proverbs silently congratulate themselves on their own wisdom. But if proverbs are true, how can we account for proverbs that contradict other proverbs: "Look before you leap," yes, but "He who hesitates is lost." "Out of sight, out of mind," yes, but "Absence makes the heart grow fonder." "The bigger the better," yes, but "Good things come in small packages." "Many hands make light the work," yes, but "Too many cooks spoil the broth." Or, to return to "Birds of a feather flock together," we must remember too that "Opposites attract."

We are hinting, not subtly, that if literary works offer (or seem to offer) arguments, if, when we hear them, they seem convincing and memorable, they do not offer arguments of the sort that you yourself will be writing in your courses, where you will be expected to assert a thesis and support it with reasons that convince the reader that you do indeed have a strong case. We have just made a case ourselves: we have argued that although proverbs are memorable and pleasurable because

- they exploit such linguistic resources as alliteration (*look . . . leap*), rhyme (*night . . . delight*), metaphor (*birds* for human beings), and parallel constructions (*garbage in, garbage out*);
- they imply a comfortingly unified world; and
- their conciseness implies a wise speaker for whom few words suffice,

proverbs do not in fact convey—much less prove—incontrovertible truths.

We have supported our argument, our **thesis,** by citing as **evidence** proverbs that contradict other proverbs. In our view, although proverbs offer or seem to offer arguments, we value them because—like all literature—they offer intense views of life, views that, while we are under their spell, cause us to say, "Ah, yes, I think I sort of had some thoughts along this line, and now I see and feel more clearly." But no work of literature tells the whole truth. Even though we may, after some experience or other, find our minds turning to some proverb that seems to have anticipated the experience ("Ah, yes, I should have remembered that too many cooks spoil the broth"), we don't turn to proverbs, or to any other literature, for arguments about life.

In a way, we are describing a paradox: A literary work is and is not an argument. It is an argument in the sense that through it the author expresses a view of life, an understanding of who we are and how we think and feel. But the author of a literary work—a good one—seeks to give us pleasure, stimulating our minds and affecting our hearts. If an author wanted solely to present an argument, he or she might have written an argumentative essay rather than a poem, a story, or a play. Literature, then, can be understood as an argument, but it is much more than that; it is an exploration, an invitation to feel deeply and to reflect.

Think, for instance, about a play by Shakespeare that you have read or seen, perhaps *Romeo and Juliet*. We might for a moment be inclined to say that it has the force of argument: The play shows that fate conspires against the happiness of young lovers. At the very beginning the Chorus tells us that

> From forth the *fatal* loins of these two foes,
> A pair of *star-crossed* lovers take their life.

But we could say that the whole of *Romeo and Juliet* conveys a different argument, a different lesson or message: The folly of parents can have terrible and tragic consequences for their children. In truth, *Romeo and Juliet*, with great beauty and complexity, offers a range of arguments, insights, and ideas. It cannot be reduced to one. And even if it could (which it cannot), all we would need to do is to turn to *A Midsummer Night's Dream*, a work by the same author, where we find young lovers facing much opposition and difficulty and, in a wonderful comic resolution, triumphing.

Why *do* we turn to literature, if not for arguments that tell us how to live? What does a work of literature offer us? Consider this comment by Salman Rushdie:

> The liveliness of literature lies in its exceptionality, in being the individual, idiosyncratic vision of one human being in which, to our delight and great surprise, we may find our own vision reflected.

Arguments in Lyric Poems

Sometimes a poem does make arguments of the sort that we touched on: The speaker of the poem offers *reasons*. Perhaps the commonest topic in such poems is the invitation to love. The male speaker urges the woman to yield to his pleas:

- The commonest *reason* offered is that time is short, and
- the commonest *evidence* offered is that we have only one life to live, and that, like the flowers, we will soon be gone.

In short, the speaker points to evidence available to all eyes, and draws an apparently irrefutable conclusion.

Elsewhere in this book we print a seventeenth-century poem on this motif, Robert Herrick's "To the Virgins, to Make Much of Time" (page 180). Here is the first stanza:

> Gather ye rosebuds while ye may,
>   Old Time is still a-flying
> And the same flower that smiles today,
>   Tomorrow will be dying.

And the final stanza:

> Then be not coy, but use your time;
>   And while ye may, go marry;
> For having lost but once your prime,
>   You may forever tarry.

Notice that the final stanza begins with "Then," that is, "therefore." The speaker has argued his case, offered his evidence—just look around you at the flowers—and now draws what presumably is the obvious conclusion. The motif is *carpe diem,* Latin for "seize the day," and it has been a common theme in Western poetry for two thousand years.

Here is another poem that bases an argument on the brevity of the flower, but in this case the poet is not urging a woman to make love. Conceivably he is speaking to someone who has asked him why he is wandering in the park, but surely we feel he is speaking to *himself,* meditating—and, moreover, he is voicing *our* thoughts; or, rather, he is giving voice to thoughts that we make our own.

A. E. Housman

Loveliest of trees, the cherry now

Loveliest of trees, the cherry now
Is hung with bloom along the bough,
And stands about the woodland ride
Wearing white for Eastertide.

Now, of my threescore years and ten,
Twenty will not come again,
And take from seventy springs a score,
It only leaves me fifty more.

And since to look at things in bloom
Fifty springs are little room,
About the woodland I will go
To see the cherry hung with snow.

[1986]

What is the argument here, the presentation of reasons in support of a thesis? We have

- a thesis (live for the moment);
- evidence (experience shows us that flowers die, that is, living things are transient);
- additional evidence: The Hebrew Bible tells us that our years are "three score and ten"; and
- a conclusion: Therefore (Housman's word is "since") take advantage of every moment.

The evidence, primarily drawn from nature and from an authoritative book, is reinforced with *statistics,* a mathematical proof (seventy minus twenty is fifty). One can hardly ask for a poem that is more clearly an argument.

But of course if we value the poem it is not because the poet has argued us into a belief and into a course of action. Rather, we value the poem because its wit gives us pleasure—who before Housman (1859–1936) ever thought of offering a statistical proof to go out and enjoy nature?—and we value it also because we enjoy being in the presence of this young man who, at the age of twenty, frets that he has *only* another fifty years to live. And there are other things in the poem that we value—for instance, the perception, in the final line, that the cherry blossoms of the spring look rather as though the tree is decked with wintertime snow.

This last image does indeed bring into this celebration of the brevity of spring a hint of coldness, winter, and, by extension, death. We hope that you have enjoyed the poem, but we are inclined to doubt that the speaker's argument has convinced you to adopt a position that is new to you.

Here is another poem in which the speaker offers an argument, this time in an effort to persuade a woman to go to bed with him. He begins by calling her attention to a flea ("Mark but this flea") that has bitten both of them and therefore contains the blood of each.

JOHN DONNE

The Flea

Mark but this flea, and mark in this
How little that which thou deny'st me is;
It sucked me first, and now sucks thee,
And in this flea our two bloods mingled be;
Thou know'st that this cannot be said
A sin, nor shame, nor loss of maidenhead;
    Yet this enjoys before it woo,
    And pampered swells with one blood made of two,
    And this, alas, is more than we would do.

Oh stay, three lives in one flea spare,
Where we almost, yea, more than married are.
This flea is you and I, and this
Our marriage bed and marriage temple is;
Though parents grudge, and you, we are met
And cloistered in these living walls of jet.
    Though use° make you apt to kill me,
    Let not to that, self-murder added be,
    And sacrilege, three sins in killing three.

Cruel and sudden, hast thou since
Purpled thy nail in blood of innocence?
Wherein could this flea guilty be,
Except in that drop which it sucked from thee?
Yet thou triumph'st and say'st that thou
Find'st not thyself, nor me the weaker now.
    'Tis true. Then learn how false fears be:
    Just so much honor, when thou yield'st to me,
    Will waste, as this flea's death took life from thee.

[1633]

Joining the Conversation: Critical Thinking and Writing

1. What has the woman done between the second and the third stanza? (Notice that the third stanza begins "Cruel and sudden, hast thou since / Purpled thy nail in blood of innocence").

°**16 use** custom.

2. Briefly state the speaker's arguments. Notice that in lines 25–26 he introduces a new argument.

Fables and Arguments

Let's return to specific short works of literature by taking a look at a form of literature that, like the proverb, very much urges us to adopt a certain view, or to adopt a certain kind of behavior, and that therefore can be thought of as offering an argument. For many centuries, literature has been justified on two grounds: It is *useful*, or it is *pleasing*, or both. A story with a moral presumably is useful; a catchy song (however nonsensical the words) presumably is pleasing. Often a work is both useful and pleasing. We have seen that proverbs can provide some guidance, and certainly they provide pleasure at least to those who utter them, and we have seen that Housman's "Loveliest of Trees" and Donne's "The Flea"—we hope these poems gave you pleasure—offer "proof" of how to behave in certain circumstances.

Like the works that we have already looked at in this chapter, the fables attributed to Aesop, a Greek of the sixth century B.C.E., engagingly teach lessons by narrating brief encounters that seem instructive. That is, even though the stories with their talking animals are utterly fanciful, we draw homely morals from them. Among famous examples are the stories of the hare and the tortoise, the boy who cried "Wolf," the wolf in sheep's clothing, and the ant and the grasshopper. Here is a fable concerning two mice. (On page 582 we reprint the fable of the ant and the grasshopper.)

AESOP

The City Mouse and the Country Mouse

A country mouse invited a city mouse for a visit. The country mouse lived a simple life, but he generously gave his friend whatever nuts and other bits of food he had been able to garner. He knew that the city mouse was used to better food, but he hoped that this would be adequate. The city mouse sniffed and said, "Doubtless this is all very healthy, but you are wasting your life in this bleak countryside. You only live once, and if you don't eat the fine food of the city now, you may never get another chance. Come to town, and I'll show you how to live." The country mouse was tempted, and off he went with the city mouse to live in a mansion. The city mouse showed the fine furnishings, and then they went into the dining room to partake of the remains of a banquet. The country mouse, eating cheese and cake, was in heaven, and was about to decide to stay forever when the people of the house returned to the room. The mice rushed to hide, but they could not come out even when the people left, because a cat came into the room. When the cat finally left, the country mouse said goodbye to the city mouse: "I'd rather live on barley and be free from fear, than live on cheese and be in constant terror."

The moral: Peace of mind is preferable to the uncertainties of luxury.

[Sixth century B.C.E.]

Joining the Conversation: Critical Thinking and Writing

1. Complete one or both of the following fables. You may want to attach a moral to the end, but constructing a moral is less important than writing dialogue that (a) fits the speakers and (b) advances the story, bringing it to a natural end—a point where there is no more to be said, in effect bringing an argument to a decisive conclusion. To do the first of these things, you will have to put yourself, in some degree, into the minds of the characters—that is, to engage in the sort of act of impersonation that writers of stories, poems, and plays do. To do the second—that is, to advance the story and bring this fictional argument to an end—you will have to conceive of a plot, a unified action whose end is implicit in its beginning.
   a. A hare addressed the other animals, claiming that they all should have a fair share of whatever any animal caught. The donkey said, "[Invent a sentence or two]." Then the fox said, "[Invent a sentence or two]." Finally the lion spoke: "[Invent a sentence or two]."
   b. An old hound had been a fine hunter in its youth, but now it had lost its strength. One day when the hound pursued and caught a boar but was unable to hold it, the huntsman said, "[Invent a sentence]." The hound replied, "[Invent a sentence]."
2. Construct a fable out of the following material:
   a. An orange [or a flower, or a rusty ax, or whatever you wish] was in a field, and along came a [whatever animal you wish] and a [some other animal of your choice]. The [first animal] said, "[Invent a sentence or two]." To which the [other animal] replied, "[Invent a sentence or two]." (If you wish, you can use three animals.)
   b. A stork happened to alight on a chimney where a sparrow was sitting. The stork said, "[Invent a sentence or two]," to which the sparrow replied, "[Invent a sentence or two]."
   c. At a racetrack a horse from Washington, D.C. found itself next to a horse from Texas. "Look," said the Washington horse, "[Complete the fable.]"
3. Take a proverb (for instance, "A stitch in time saves nine," or "People who live in glass houses shouldn't throw stones") and invent an illustrative fable to which the moral can be attached.

Thinking Further about "Messages" in Literature: Two Mini-Stories and Two Poems

We have been arguing—largely by quoting brief examples of highly engaging literature—that although works of literature may offer arguments, may (so to speak) send messages, a reader's pleasure in the work is not dependent on the truth of the message. Rather, literary works hold our interest and give us pleasure because they *effectively* use language. If they provide us with knowledge, it is knowledge of the sort that T. S. Eliot mentions in one of the epigraphs we use at the head of this chapter:

> We shall not cease from exploration
> And the end of all our exploring
> Will be to arrive where we started
> And to know the place for the first time.

Let's look at two additional short pieces. The first is by a contemporary Chinese-American writer who writes both in Chinese and in English.

EMILY WU

The Lesson of the Master

In fourteenth-century China a Buddhist monk named Tung-ming, who was also a painter, was fortunate in having a merchant who supported him by buying his ink-paintings. Tung-ming excelled in his art, a very difficult art because an Asian ink painting, unlike a Western oil painting, cannot be changed as the artist works on it. Once the brush touches the paper, the ink makes its mark, and it cannot be removed. The brushstroke cannot even be widened or lengthened because a knowledgeable observer will easily detect the change, the places where the first stroke was widened or extended or whatever; the painting's lack of grace and spontaneity will be evident. Part of the beauty of ink painting is that the viewer understands the difficulty, and appreciates the skill that is evident in each line.

Tung-ming excelled in paintings of plum branches, but one day the merchant, who was a wholesaler of fish, asked him if he would paint a carp. The monk assured the merchant that he would paint the picture, and he then departed. A week passed. Then two weeks. Then three weeks, and still there was no painting. It was not that the merchant and the monk did not meet. No, they met every few days because the merchant often invited the monk to dinner. And in the past the monk sometimes invited the merchant to have a cup of tea at the temple and to discuss matters of Buddhism, but he had not invited the merchant since the conversation about the carp.

After the second week the merchant began to fret: "Have I offended Tung-ming?" he wondered. "Might he think that I don't sufficiently appreciate his paintings of plum blossoms?" And: "Is it possible that he thinks it is vulgar of me to ask for a picture of a fish because I am a fish merchant?" And: "Could it be that he thinks, because I am a specialist in fish, I will notice that in fact his picture of a carp is not very good, that he can't catch the essence of its fishiness?" Day after day, week after week, month after month the merchant tormented himself with such thoughts.

Now that months had gone by, the merchant summoned up the courage to ask Tung-ming if they might not, for a change, meet at the temple and have a cup of tea. Tung-ming agreed.

On the appointed day they met in the monk's quarters, drank tea, talked about Buddhist matters and other things, and then the merchant—having noticed that brush, ink-cake, and paper were in view—nervously broached the subject of the picture of the carp. Tung-ming ground some fresh ink from an ink-cake, added some water, dipped the brush in the ink, stood over the paper, paused for five seconds (but the pause seemed like eternity to the merchant) and then, in another five seconds, with five strokes brushed a marvelous silvery-gray carp and handed the sheet to the merchant.

The merchant was beside himself with joy. When he recovered his composure, he hesitantly asked Tung-ming why he had not produced a picture months earlier. Tung-ming walked across the room, opened the door of a cabinet, and hundreds of sheets of paper—each with a picture of a carp—streamed to the floor.

[2006]

Joining the Conversation: Critical Thinking and Writing

1. In one sentence tell the *plot* of the story (*what happens* in it) and in a second sentence summarize the *theme* of the story (what the happenings *add up to,* what the story is *about*).
2. Although the title of a story may be the last thing the author writes, it is the first thing that the reader encounters, and it is therefore highly important. Emily Wu called her story "The Lesson of the Master" but she *might* have called it "A Very Short Story," or "Tung-ming's Fish" or "A Fishy Story" or "The Patron and the Painter" or "The Painter and the Patron" or "Easy When You Know How" or. . . . Consider the original title and the six alternate titles. In a short argumentative essay—maybe two paragraphs—explain why you think a certain title is the best. Can you think of a title that is better than the original and the proposed alternatives? If so, state it and in an effective argument explain why you think it is better.
3. Was this story (originally written in Chinese) worth translating, and was it worth your time as a reader? Do you think you will remember this story six months from now? Please explain your position in a short argumentative essay.
4. Is there a literary work—perhaps even a nursery rhyme or a fairy tale—that you read a long time ago and that has stayed in your mind? If so, *why* has it remained with you? The moral? The catchiness of the sounds (as in "Jack and Jill/Went up a hill")? Sharply-drawn characters? A surprising plot? Please explain, in a short argumentative essay, that is, in an essay that offers reasons.

Finally, let's look at another mini-story and two poems—and we hope you will then look again at the four quotations with which we began this chapter.

JESSE LEE KERCHEVAL

Jesse Lee Kercheval was born in France but received her bachelor's degree from Florida State University and her master's degree (in creative writing) from the University of Iowa. The author of several books of poetry and of fiction, as well as a book about how to write fiction (Building Fiction *[1997]), Kercheval has received numerous awards. She teaches at the University of Wisconsin, Madison. The story we include here was written in response to a challenge to write a short story consisting of no more than 300 words.*

As this story indicates, Çarpathia *was the ship that in 1912 picked up survivors from the* Titanic, *after the* Titanic *struck an iceberg and sank.*

Carpathia

It happened on my parents' honeymoon. The fourth morning out from New York, Mother woke to find the *Carpathia* still, engines silent. She woke Father; they rushed to the deck in their nightgowns. The first thing they saw was the white of an ocean filled with ice, then they saw white boats, in groups of two or three, pulling slowly toward the *Carpathia*. My father read the name written in red across their bows—*Titantic*. The sun was shining. Here and there a deck chair floated on the calm sea. There was nothing else.

The survivors came on board in small groups. Women and children. Two sailors for each boat. The women of the *Carpathia* went to the women of the *Titanic,* wrapping them in their long warm furs. My mother left my father's side to go to them. The women went down on their knees on the deck and prayed, holding each other's children. My father stood looking at the icy water where, if he had been on the other ship, he would be.

When the *Carpathia* dropped off the survivors in New York, my parents too got off and took the train home, not talking much, the honeymoon anything but a success. At the welcome-home party, my father got drunk. When someone asked about the *Titanic,* he said, "They should have put the men in the lifeboats. Men can marry again, have new families. What's the use of all those widows and orphans?" My mother, who was standing next to him, turned her face away. She was pregnant, eighteen. She was the one drowning. But there was no one there to rescue her.

Joining the Conversation: Critical Thinking and Writing

1. In the second paragraph, the second and third sentences have no verbs. Do you suppose verbs have been omitted simply because the author was limited to 300 words, or are these two sentences more effective than they would be if they were equipped with verbs? Explain.
2. The speaker's father offers an argument—that is, he advances a thesis. Is the story about the issue that he raises—in effect, that the traditional doctrine of "women and children first" is misguided—or is it about something else. If something else, what is it about?
3. What is the narrator's attitude toward her father? Toward her mother?
4. Please complete the following sentence: "The lesson that this story teaches is . . . ." What is your evidence for this?
5. A teacher of creative writing, commenting on this story, says, "its ending is exactly right." Do you agree? Please explain.

ROBERT FROST

Robert Frost (1874–1963) was born in California. After his father's death in 1885 Frost's mother brought the family to New England, where she taught in high schools in Massachusetts and New Hampshire. Frost studied for part of one term at Dartmouth College in New Hampshire, then did odd jobs (including teaching), and from 1897 to 1899 was enrolled as a special student at Harvard. He then farmed in New Hampshire, published a few poems in local newspapers, left the farm and taught again, and in 1912 left for England, where he hoped to achieve more popular success as a writer. By 1915 he had won a considerable reputation, and he returned to the United States, settling on a farm in New Hampshire and cultivating the image of the country-wise farmer-poet. In fact he was well read in the classics, the Bible, and English and American literature.

Design

I found a dimpled spider, fat and white,
On a white heal-all, holding up a moth
Like a white piece of rigid satin cloth—
Assorted characters of death and blight
Mixed ready to begin the morning right,
Like the ingredients of a witches' broth—
A snow-drop spider, a flower like a froth,
And dead wings carried like a paper kite.

What had that flower to do with being white,
The wayside blue and innocent heal-all?
What brought the kindred spider to that height,
Then steered the white moth thither in the night?
What but design of darkness to appall?—
If design govern in a thing so small.

[1936]

Joining the Conversation: Critical Thinking and Writing

1. Do you find the spider, as described in line 1, cute or disgusting? Why?
2. What is the effect of "If" in the last line?
3. The word *design* can mean "pattern" (as in "a pretty design"), or it can mean "intention," especially an evil intention (as in "He had designs on her"). Does Frost use the word in one sense or in both? Explain.
4. Is Frost offering an argument? If so, what is it?

LINDA PASTAN

Linda Pastan was born in New York City in 1932 and educated at Radcliffe College, Simmons College, and Brandeis University. The author of ten books of poems, she has won numerous prizes, including a Pushcart Prize and the 2003 Ruth Lilly Poetry Prize, and she has received a grant from the National Endowment for the Arts.

Ethics

In ethics class so many years ago
our teacher asked this question every fall:
if there were a fire in a museum
which would you save, a Rembrandt painting
or an old woman who hadn't many

years left anyhow? Restless on hard chairs
caring little for pictures or old age
we'd opt one year for life, the next for art
and always half-heartedly. Sometimes
the woman borrowed my grandmother's face
leaving her usual kitchen to wander
some drafty, half-imagined museum.
One year, feeling clever, I replied
why not let the woman decide herself?
Linda, the teacher would report, eschews
the burdens of responsibility.
This fall in a real museum I stand
before a real Rembrandt, old woman,
or nearly so, myself. The colors
within this frame are darker than autumn,
darker even than winter—the browns of earth,
though earth's most radiant elements burn
through the canvas. I know now that woman
and painting and season are almost one
and all beyond saving by children.

[1980]

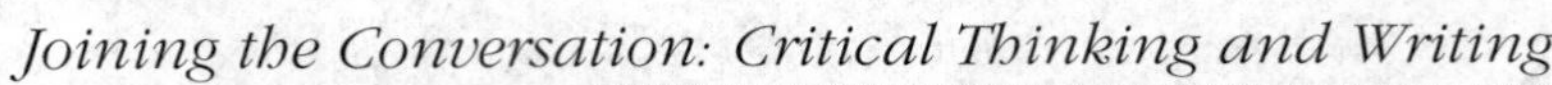

Joining the Conversation: Critical Thinking and Writing

1. What do we know about the teacher in the poem? Do you think you would like to take a course with this teacher? Why?
2. Lines 3–6 report a question that a teacher asked. Does the rest of the poem answer the question? If so, what is the answer? If not, what does the rest of the poem do?
3. Do you assume that, for this poem, the responses of younger readers (say, ages 17–22) as a group would differ from those of older readers? If so, set forth your response in a short argumentative essay.
4. Do you think high schools should offer courses in ethics? If so, do you think the question posed by the teacher in the poem is an appropriate question for such a course? And do you think that Pastan's poem suggests that high schools should or should not teach such courses?

Having read and thought about several proverbs and short fictions and a contemporary poem, you may now want to return to the four epigraphs that we printed at the beginning of this chapter (page 88). If someone were to ask you to explain what Ezra Pound and Marianne Moore might mean, what would you say? And would you agree?

If you have read a novel by a "politically-minded author," do you agree with Hemingway that if the novel lasts, future readers "will have to skip the politics"? Please explain.

And do you agree with Eliot that thus far your exploration with literature has brought you back to where you began but that now for the first time you can know—at least to some degree—the place?

Chapter 5

Reading Literature Closely: Explication

What Is Literature?

Perhaps the first thing to say is that it is impossible to define *literature* in a way that will satisfy everyone. And perhaps the second thing to say is that in the last twenty years or so, some serious thinkers have argued that it is impossible to set off certain verbal works from all others, and on some basis or other to designate them as literature. For one thing, it is argued, a work is just marks on paper or sounds in the air. The audience (reader or listener) turns these marks or sounds into something with meaning, and different audiences will construct different meanings out of what they read or hear. There are *texts* (birthday cards, sermons, political speeches, magazines, novels that sell by the millions and novels that don't sell at all, poems, popular songs, editorials, and so forth), but there is nothing that should be given the special title of literature.

Although there is something to be said for the idea that *literature* is just an honorific word and not a collection of work embodying eternal truths and eternal beauty, let's make the opposite assumption, at least for a start. Let's assume that certain verbal works are of a distinct sort—whether because the author shapes them, or because a reader perceives them a certain way—and that we can call these works literature. But what are these works like?

Literature and Form

We all know why we value a newspaper or a textbook or an atlas, but why do we value a verbal work that doesn't give us the latest news or important information about business cycles or the names of the capitals of nations? About a thousand years ago a Japanese woman, Shikibu Murasaki, or Lady Murasaki (978?–1026), offered an answer in *The Tale of Genji,* a book often called the world's first novel. During a discussion about reading fiction, one of the characters gives an opinion as to why a writer tells a story:

> Again and again writers find something in their experience, or see something in the life around them, that seems so important they cannot bear to let it pass into oblivion. There must never come a time, the writer feels, when people do not know about this.

Literature is about human experiences, but the experiences in literature are not simply the shapeless experiences—the chaotic passing scene—captured by a mindless, unselective video camera. Poets, dramatists, and storytellers find or impose a shape on scenes (for instance, the history of two lovers), giving readers things to value—written or spoken accounts that are memorable not only for their content but also for their *form*—the shape of the speeches, of the scenes, of the plots.

(In a little while we will see that form and content are inseparable, but for the moment, for our purposes, we can talk about them separately.)

Because this discussion of literature is brief, we will illustrate the point by looking at one of the briefest literary forms, the proverb. Consider this statement:

> A rolling stone gathers no moss.

Now let's compare it with a **paraphrase** (a restatement, a translation into other words):

> If a stone is always moving around, vegetation won't have a chance to grow on it.

What makes the original version more powerful, more memorable? Surely much of the answer is that the original is more concrete and its form is more shapely. At the risk of being heavy-handed, we can analyze the shapeliness thus: *Stone* and *moss* (the two nouns in the sentence) each contain one syllable; *rolling* and *gathers* (the two words of motion) each contain two syllables, with the accent on the first syllable. Notice, too, the nice contrast between stone (hard) and moss (soft).

The reader probably *feels* this shapeliness unconsciously rather than perceives it consciously. That is, these connections become apparent when one starts to analyze, but the literary work can make its effect on a reader even before the reader analyzes the work. As T. S. Eliot said in his essay on Dante (1929), "Genuine poetry can communicate before it is understood." Indeed, our *first* reading of a work, when, so to speak, we are all eyes and ears (and the mind is highly receptive rather than sifting for evidence), is sometimes the most important reading. Experience proves that we can feel the effects of a work without yet understanding *how* the effects are achieved.

Probably most readers will agree that

- the words in the proverb are paired interestingly and meaningfully;
- the sentence is not simply some information but is also (to quote one of Robert Frost's definitions of literature) "a performance in words";
- what the sentence *is*, we might say, is no less significant than what the sentence *says*;
- the sentence as a whole forms a memorable picture, a small but complete world, hard and soft, inorganic and organic, inert and moving;
- the idea set forth is simple—partly because it is highly focused and therefore it leaves out a lot—but it is also complex;
- by virtue of the contrasts, and, again, even by the pairing of monosyllabic nouns and of disyllabic words of motion, it is unified into a pleasing whole.

For all of its specificity and its compactness—the proverb contains only six words—it expands our minds.

A Brief Exercise: Take a minute to think about some other proverb, for instance "Look before you leap," "Finders keepers," "Haste makes waste," or "Absence makes the heart grow fonder." Paraphrase it, and then ask yourself why the original is more interesting, more memorable, than your paraphrase.

Form and Meaning

Let's turn now to a work not much longer than a proverb—a very short poem by Robert Frost (1874–1963).

The Span of Life

The old dog barks backward without getting up.
I can remember when he was a pup.

Read the poem aloud once or twice, physically experiencing Frost's "performance in words." Notice that the first line is harder to say than the second line, which more or less rolls off the tongue. Why? Because in the first line we must pause between *old* and *dog,* between *backward* and *without,* and between *without* and *getting*—and in fact between *back* and *ward.* Further, when we read the poem aloud, or with the mind's ear, in the first line we hear four consecutive stresses in "old dog barks back," a noticeable contrast to the rather jingling "when he was a pup" in the second line.

No two readers will read the lines in exactly the same way, but it is probably safe to say that most readers will agree that in the first line they may stress fairly heavily as many as eight syllables, whereas in the second line they may stress only three or four:

The óld dóg bárks báckward withoút gétting úp.
Í can remémber when hé was a púp.

And so we can say that the form (a relatively effortful, hard-to-speak line followed by a bouncy line) shapes and is part of the content (a description of a dog that no longer has the energy or the strength to leap up, followed by a memory of the dog as a puppy).

Thinking further about Frost's poem, we notice something else about the form. The first line is about a dog, but the second line is about a dog *and* a human being ("*I* can remember"). The speaker must be getting on, too. And although nothing is said about the dog as a *symbol* of human life, surely the reader, prompted by the title of the poem, makes a connection between the life span of a dog and that of a human being. Part of what makes the poem effective is that this point is *not* stated explicitly, not belabored. Readers have the pleasure of making the connection for themselves—under Frost's careful guidance.

Everyone knows that puppies are frisky and that old dogs are not—though perhaps not until we encountered this poem did we think twice about the fact that "the old dog barks backward without getting up." Or let's put it this way:

- Many people may have noticed this behavior, but
- perhaps only Frost thought (to use Lady Murasaki's words), "There must never come a time . . . when people do not know about this." And,
- fortunately for all of us, Frost had the ability to put his perception into memorable words.

Part of what makes this performance in words especially memorable is the *relationship* between the two lines. Neither line in itself is anything very special, but because of the counterpoint the whole is more than the sum of the parts. Skill in handling language, obviously, is indispensable if the writer is to produce literature. A person may know a great deal about dogs and may be a great lover of dogs, but knowledge and love are not enough equipment to write even a two-line poem about a dog (or the span of life, or both). Poems, like other kinds of literature, are produced by people who know how to delight us with verbal performances.

We can easily see that Robert Frost's "The Span of Life" is a work of literature—a work that uses language in a special way—if we contrast it with another short work in rhyme:

> Thirty days hath September,
> April, June, and November;
> All the rest have thirty-one
> Excepting February alone,
> Which has twenty-eight in fine,
> Till leap year gives it twenty-nine.

This information is important, but it is only information. The lines rhyme, giving the work some form, but there is nothing very interesting about it. (Perhaps you will want to take issue with this opinion.) The poem is true and therefore useful, but it is not of compelling interest, probably because it only *tells* us facts rather than *shows* or *presents* human experience. We all remember the lines, but they offer neither the pleasure of an insight nor the pleasure of an interesting tune. "Thirty days" has nothing of what the poet Thomas Gray said characterizes literature: "Thoughts that breathe, and words that burn."

Reading in Slow Motion

In this chapter, and in the next, we focus on the skills that careful study of literary language requires. "Close reading" is perhaps the most familiar name for this technique of heightened responsiveness to the words on the page. But another, employed by the literary critics Reuben A. Brower and Richard Poirier, may be even better. They refer to "reading in slow motion." Brower, for example, speaks of "slowing down the process of reading to observe what is happening, in order to attend very closely to the words, their uses, and their meanings." This sort of reading, he explains, involves looking and listening with special alertness, slowly, without rushing or feeling impatient if a work puzzles us at first encounter.[1]

As Brower and Poirier point out, sometimes we are so intrigued or moved by a writer's operations with words that we are led to "slow down" in our reading, lingering over verbal details and vivid images—"a watersmooth-silver / stallion" in Cummings's poem about Buffalo Bill (page 327), or "Babette danced out to where the fig-trees were," in Chopin's "Ripe Figs" (page 11). Or else, we find that we want to return to a poem, or to a key section of a story or scene in a play, to articulate—"slow motion" style—why it has affected us as powerfully as it did.

"Close" or slow-motion reading can help you to understand and enjoy a work that at first seems strange or obscure. When we examine a piece of literature with care and intensity, we are not taking it apart in a destructive way but, instead, are seeking to satisfy our curiosity about how the writer organized it. And almost always, our increased *understanding* of the work results in increased

[1]The quotation is taken from Brower's introduction to *In Defense of Reading: A Reader's Approach to Literary Criticism*, ed. Reuben A. Brower and Richard Poirier (1962). See also Brower, *The Fields of Light: An Experiment in Critical Reading* (1951); and Poirier, *Poetry and Pragmatism* (1992).

enjoyment. Very few poems have been made worse by close reading, and many have been made better—made, that is, more accessible and interesting, deeper, and more rewarding.

This point is clarified when we recall what it's like to watch a scene from a movie in slow motion, or a TV replay in slow motion of a touchdown run in a football game. In slow-motion film we perceive details we might otherwise miss—the subtle changes in expression on an actress's face, for example, or the interplay of gestures among several performers at a climactic moment in the action. Similarly, seeing a touchdown multiple times in slow motion, and perhaps from a half-dozen camera angles, reveals to us how the play developed, who made the crucial blocks, where the defense failed. The touchdown was exciting when it took place; and it remains exciting—and frequently it becomes more so—when we slow it down in order to study and talk about it.

This chapter deals with explication, and the next with analysis. Both are based on the principle that responding well to literature means:

- acquiring the ability to read it closely;
- practicing this skill to become better and better at it;
- explaining and demonstrating in critical essays what we have learned.

But the two terms, while related to one another, differ in emphasis. An **explication** moves from beginning to end of an entire work (if it is fairly short) or of a section of a work; it is sustained, meticulous, thorough, systematic. An analysis builds upon the habits of attention that we have gained from explicating texts and passages of texts.

When we engage in analysis of literature, we are doing so as part of presenting an argument, a thesis, about a work. What is the central theme in this short story by Welty or that one by Updike? What is the most compelling insight into the nature of love that Adrienne Rich offers in this or that group of poems about men and women? Does Hamlet delay—and if he does, why? To deal with questions like these, we have to read the text closely and study its language carefully, but we must be selective in the pieces of textual evidence that we offer. To be sure, we can explicate a single speech in Hamlet, or an exchange between characters. But it would be a daunting assignment in a short critical essay to explicate an entire scene, and impossible to explicate the entire play from start to finish.

Analysis goes hand in hand with the job of presenting and proving a thesis; it goes hand in hand with explication as well, taking the form of close reading, of reading in slow motion, as its foundation. But rather than say more about analysis here, let's turn to explication first and learn what we can discover about literature through it. As you'll see, one of the things we quickly realize is that close reading of literary works makes us not only better readers but also better writers attuned more sharply and sensitively to the organization of the language in our own prose.

Explication

A line-by-line or episode-by-episode commentary on what is going on in a text is an explication (literally, unfolding or spreading out). An explication does not deal with the writer's life and times, and it is not a paraphrase, a rewording—though it may include paraphrase. Rather, it is a commentary that reveals your sense of the meaning of the work and its structure. When we explicate a text, we ask questions about the meanings of words, the implications of metaphors and images, the speaker's tone of voice as we initially hear it and it develops and perhaps changes. How is this literary work put together? How did the writer organize it to prompt from me the response I had (and am having) to it? How does it begin, and what happens next, and next after that? And so on, through to the end.

It takes some skill to work your way along in an explication without saying, "In line one . . . In the second line . . . In the third line . . ." This sounds mechanical and formulaic. Make good use of transitional words and phrases, so that your commentary will feel to your reader more natural, with a better pace and rhythm. For example: "The speaker begins by suggesting . . . The poem then shifts in direction . . . In the next paragraph, however, the narrator implies . . ."

A Sample Explication

The following short poem is by Langston Hughes (1902–1967), an African American writer. Hughes was born in Joplin, Missouri, lived part of his youth in Mexico, spent a year at Columbia University, served as a merchant seaman, and worked in a Paris nightclub, where he showed some of his poems to Alain Locke, an influential critic, educator, and strong advocate of African American literature. When he returned to the United States, Hughes went on to publish fiction, plays, essays, and biographies; he also founded theaters, gave public readings, and was, in short, an important force.

Harlem

What happens to a dream deferred?

Does it dry up
like a raisin in the sun?
Or fester like a sore—
And then run?
Does it stink like rotten meat?
Or crust and sugar over—
like a syrupy sweet?

Maybe it just sags
like a heavy load.

Or does it explode?

[1951]

Different readers will respond at least somewhat differently to any work. On the other hand, since writers want to communicate, they try to control their readers' responses, and they count on their readers to understand the denotations of words as they understand them. Hughes assumed that his readers knew that Harlem was the site of a large African American community in New York City. A reader who confuses the title of the poem with Haarlem in the Netherlands will wonder what this poem is saying about the tulip-growing center in northern Holland. Explication is based on the assumption that the poem contains a meaning and that by studying the work thoughtfully we can unfold the meaning or meanings.

Let's assume that the reader understands Hughes is talking about Harlem, New York, and that the "dream deferred" refers to the unfulfilled hopes of African Americans who live in a society dominated by whites. But Hughes does not say "hopes," he says "dream," and he does not say "unfulfilled," he says "deferred." You might ask yourself exactly what differences there are between these words. Next, after you have read the poem several times, you might think about which expression is better in the context, "unfulfilled hopes" or "dream deferred," and why.

Working Toward an Explication

In preparing to write an explication, first write on a computer, or type or handwrite, the complete text of the work that you will explicate—usually a poem but sometimes a short passage of prose. *Don't* photocopy it; the act of typing or writing it will help you to get into the piece, word by word, comma by comma. Type or write it *double-spaced*, so that you will have plenty of room for annotations as you study the piece. It's advisable to make a few photocopies (or to print a few copies, if you are using a computer) before you start annotating, so that if one page gets too cluttered you can continue working on a clean copy. Or you may want to use one copy for a certain kind of annotations—let's say those concerning imagery—and other copies for other kinds of notes—let's say those concerning meter or wordplay. If you are writing on a computer, you can highlight words, boldface them, put them in capitals (for instance, to indicate accented syllables), and so forth.

Let's turn to an explication of the poem, a detailed examination of the whole. Here are the preliminary jottings of a student, Bill Horner.

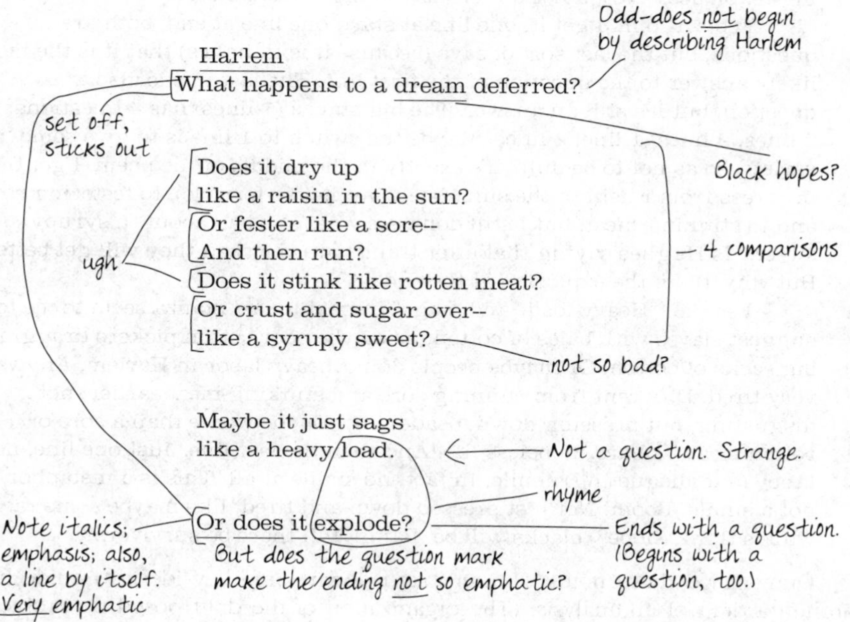

These annotations chiefly get at the structure of the poem, the relationship of the parts. Horner notices that the poem begins with a line set off by itself and ends with a line set off by itself, and he also notices that each of these lines is a question. Further, he indicates that each of these two lines is emphasized in other ways: The first begins farther to the left than any of the other lines—as though the other lines are subheadings or are in some way subordinate—and the last is italicized.

Some Journal Entries

Bill Horner later wrote entries in his journal:

> Feb. 18. Since the title is "Harlem," it's obvious that the "dream" is by African American people. Also, obvious that Hughes thinks that if the "dream" doesn't become real there may be riots ("explode"). I like "raisin in the sun" (maybe because I like the play), and I like the business about "a syrupy sweet"—much more pleasant than the festering sore and the rotten meat. But if the dream becomes "sweet," what's wrong with that? Why should something "sweet" explode?
>
> Feb. 21. Prof. McCabe said to think of structure or form of a poem as a sort of architecture, a building with a foundation, floors, etc., topped by a roof—but since we read a poem from top to bottom, it's like a building upside down. Title is foundation (even though it's at top); last line is roof, capping the whole. As you read, you add layers. Foundation of "Harlem" is a question (first line). Then, set back a bit from foundation, or built on it by white space, a tall room (7 lines high, with 4 questions); then, on top of this room, another room (lines, statement, not a question). Funny; I thought that in poems all stanzas are the same number of lines. Then—more white space, so another unit—the roof. Man, this roof is going to fall in—"explodes." Not just the roof, maybe the whole house.
>
> Feb. 21, p.m. I get it; one line at start, one line at end; both are questions, but the last sort of says (because it is in italics) that it is the most likely answer to the question of the first line. The last line is also a question, but it's still an answer. The big stanza (7 lines) has 4 questions: 2 lines, 2 lines, 1 line, 2 lines. Maybe the switch to 1 line is to give some variety, so as not to be dull? It's exactly in the middle of the poem. I get the progress from raisin in the sun (dried, but not so terrible), to festering sore and to stinking meat, but I still don't see what's so bad about "a syrupy sweet." Is Hughes saying that after things are very bad they will get better? But why, then, the explosion at the end?
>
> Feb. 23. "Heavy load" and "sags" in next-to-last stanza seem to me to suggest slaves with bales of cotton, or maybe poor cotton pickers dragging big sacks of cotton. Or maybe people doing heavy labor in Harlem. Anyway, very tired. Different from running sore and stinking meat earlier; not disgusting, but pressing down, deadening. Maybe worse than a sore or rotten meat—a hard, hopeless life. And then the last line. Just one line, no fancy (and disgusting) simile. In fact, no simile at all. This is a metaphor, not a simile. Boom! Not just pressed down and tired, like maybe some racist whites think (hope?) blacks will be. Bang! Will there be survivors?

Drawing on these notes, Horner jotted down some key ideas to guide him through a draft of an analysis. (The organization of the draft posed no problem; the writer simply followed the organization of the poem.)

11 lines; short, but powerful; explosive
Question (first line)
answers (set off by space and also indented)
"raisin in the sun": shrinking
"sore" } disgusting
"rotten meat"
"syrupy sweet": relief from disgusting comparisons
final question (last line): explosion?
explosive (powerful) because:
short, condensed, packed
in italics
stands by self-like first line
no fancy comparison; very direct

A Sample Essay by a Student (Final Version): "Langston Hughes's 'Harlem'"

Here is Bill Horner's final essay:

Horner 1

Bill Horner

Professor McCabe

English 122

10 March 2009

Langston Hughes's "Harlem"

"Harlem" is a poem that is only eleven lines long, but it is charged with power. It explodes. Hughes sets the stage, so to speak, by telling us in the title that he is talking about Harlem, and then he begins by asking, "What happens to a dream deferred?" The rest of the poem is set off by being indented, as though it is the answer to his question. This answer is in three parts (three stanzas, of different lengths).

Horner 2

In a way, it is wrong to speak of the answer, since the rest of the poem consists of questions, but I think Hughes means that each question (for instance, does a "deferred" hope "dry up / like a raisin in the sun?") really is an answer, something that really has happened and that will happen again. The first question, "Does it dry up / like a raisin in the sun?," is a famous line. To compare hope to a raisin dried in the sun is to suggest a terrible shrinking. The next two comparisons are to a "sore" and to "rotten meat." These comparisons are less clever, but they are very effective because they are disgusting. Then, maybe because of the disgusting comparisons, he gives a comparison that is not at all disgusting. In this comparison he says that maybe the "dream deferred" will "crust over— / like a syrupy sweet."

The seven lines with four comparisons are followed by a stanza of two lines with just one comparison:

> Maybe it just sags
> like a heavy load.

So if we thought that this postponed dream might finally turn into something "sweet," we were kidding ourselves. Hughes comes down to earth, in a short stanza, with an image of a heavy load, which probably also calls to mind images of people bent under heavy loads, maybe of cotton, or maybe just any sort of heavy load carried by African Americans in Harlem and elsewhere.

The opening question ("What happens to a dream deferred?") was followed by four questions in seven lines, but now, with

Horner 3

"Maybe it just sags / like a heavy load," we get a statement, as though the poet at last has found an answer. But at the end we get one more question, set off by itself and in italics: "Or does it explode?" This line itself is explosive for three reasons: It is short, it is italicized, and it is a stanza in itself. It's also interesting that this line, unlike the earlier lines, does not use a simile. It uses a metaphor. It's almost as though Hughes is saying, "O.K., we've had enough fancy ways of talking about this terrible situation; here it is, 'boom.'"

[New page]

Horner 4

Work Cited

Hughes, Langston. "Harlem." *Literature for Composition*. Ed. Sylvan Barnet, William Burto, and William E. Cain. 9th ed. New York: Longman, 2010. 106. Print.

Joining the Conversation: Critical Thinking and Writing

1. The student's explication suggests that the comparison with "a syrupy sweet" deliberately misleads the reader into thinking the ending will be happy, and it thus serves to make the real ending even more powerful. In class another student suggested that Hughes may be referring to African Americans who play Uncle Tom, people who adopt a smiling manner in order to cope with an oppressive society. Which explanation do you prefer, and why? What do you think of combining the two?

Does some method or principle help us decide which interpretation is correct? Can we, in fact, talk about a "correct" interpretation, or only about a plausible or implausible interpretation and an interesting or uninteresting interpretation?

2. In *The Collected Poems of Langston Hughes* (1994), the editors title this poem "Harlem." But in the *Selected Poems of Langston Hughes* (1959), published when the poet was still alive, the poem is titled "Dream Deferred." Which title do you think is more effective? Do you interpret the poem differently depending on how it is titled? How might a reader—who knew nothing about Hughes—respond to the poem if he or she came upon it with the title "Dream Deferred"?

Note: Another explication (of W. B. Yeats's "The Balloon of the Mind") appears in Chapter 16.

Explication as Argument

We have said that an explication unfolds or opens up or interprets a work by calling attention to such things as the speaker's tone of voice and the implications in images. It might seem, then, to be an objective report, the sort of explanatory writing that is called expository rather than argumentative.

But in fact, because literature makes considerable use of connotations and symbolic meanings—"A rolling stone gathers no moss" is not essentially a statement about stones and moss but about something else—readers may differ in what they take the words to mean. The writer of an explication not only examines the meanings of specific words and images but also, having come to a conclusion about what the details add up to, argues an interpretation, supports a thesis.

What distinguishes argument from exposition is this: In argument, some statements are offered as *reasons* for others. Because writers of arguments assume that their readers may not at the outset share their views, in their writing they offer evidence to support their assertions.

If you reread Bill Horner's explication of "Harlem," you will notice that in speaking of the line "Or does it explode?" Horner says, "This line is explosive for three reasons." He then specifies the three reasons. That is, he argues his case, presenting three pieces of supporting evidence: Hughes's line is short, it is italicized, and it is a stanza in itself.

True, much of Horner's explication does consist of expository writing when he says that the poem consists of "three parts (three stanzas, of different lengths)." There can be little disagreement between writer and reader here—although, come to think of it, a reader might respond, "No, the title is also part of the poem, so the poem consists of four parts." A reader who is looking for an argument—in the sense of a quarrel, not in the sense of a reasoned discussion—can find it with almost any piece of writing. But, again, our point is that because expository writing does not assume a difference of opinion, it chiefly sets forth information rather than seeks to make a case. Argumentative writing, on the other hand, assumes that it must set forth information in a way that persuades the reader of its truth, which means that it must give evidence.

Pure exposition—let's say, information about how to register for classes, or information about what is likely to be on the final examination—is not concerned with persuading readers to accept a thesis. But an explication, even though it might seem only to clarify the meanings of the words in a poem, argues a thesis about the work as a whole.

Notice Bill Horner's opening sentence:

> **"Harlem" is a poem that is only eleven lines long, but it is charged with power.**

What is Horner's thesis? Certainly not that the poem is "only eleven lines long"—a writer hardly needs to argue a reader into believing this assertion. Rather, Horner's thesis is that the poem "is charged with power." In the rest of the explication he offers evidence that supports this assertion. To persuade us, he points out that certain lines are indented, that certain figures of speech have certain implications, and that the last stanza is italicized and consists of only one line.

You may disagree: You may not think the poem "is charged with power," and you may think that Horner has misread certain lines. We have already mentioned, in our first topic for "Critical Thinking and Writing," that when Horner offered this interpretation in class, another student saw a different meaning in "syrupy sweet" (line 8). But if you disagree, whether with the reading as a whole or with the interpretation of a single image, it's not enough to assert that you disagree. You will have to offer an argument, which is to say you will have to set forth reasons in your effort to persuade your readers.

Your goal, in an explication, is to present your insights about the details of the poem's language. But even more, you want these insights to add up to something as a whole. When related to one another, they should enable your reader to understand the poem, overall, more clearly, and to enjoy it more fully. Ask yourself, as you study the poem and develop your draft of the paper,

> **What is my thesis (my central point, my argument)?**

This question will help you to make your essay coherent and unified. It is a reminder that an explication is more than a set of observations about this and that detail. The best explications make use of the details to teach the reader something new about the poem as a whole.

CHECKLIST: *Drafting an Explication*

Overall Considerations

- ☐ Does the poem imply a story of some sort, for instance the speaker's account of a love affair, or of a response to nature? If so, what is its beginning, middle, and end?
- ☐ If you detect a story in the speaker's mind, a change of mood—for instance a shift from bitterness that a love affair has ended to hope for its renewal—is this change communicated in part by the connotations of certain words? By syntax? By metrical shifts?
- ☐ Do the details all cohere into a meaningful whole? If so, your explication will largely be an argument on behalf of this thesis.

Detailed Considerations

- ☐ If the poem has a title other than the first line, what are the implications of the title?

(*continued*)

Detailed Considerations (continued)

- Are there clusters or patterns of imagery, for instance religious images, economic images, or images drawn from nature? If so, how do they contribute to the meaning of the poem?
- Is irony (understatement or overstatement) used? To what effect?
- How do the connotations of certain words (for instance, *dad* rather than *father*) help to establish the meaning?
- What are the implications of the syntax—for instance, of notably simple or notably complex sentences? What do such sentences tell us about the speaker?
- Do metrical variations occur, and if so, what is their significance?
- Do rhyming words have some meaningful connection, as in the clichés *moon* and *June, dove* and *love*?
- What are the implications of the poem's appearance on the page—for example, of an indented line, or of the stanzaic pattern? (For instance, if the poem consists of two stanzas of four lines each, does the second stanza offer a reversal of the first?)

Why Write? Purpose and Audience

In Chapter 2 we briefly discussed audience and purpose, but a few further words may be useful. People write explications (as well as other essays on literature) not only to communicate with others but also to clarify and to account for their responses to material that interests or excites or frustrates them. In putting words on paper you will have to take a second and a third look at what is in front of you and at what is within you. And so the process of writing is a way of learning. The last word is never said about complex thoughts and feelings, but when we write we hope to make at least a little progress in the difficult but rewarding job of talking about our responses. We learn, and then we hope to interest our reader because we are communicating our responses to material that for one reason or another is worth talking about.

When you write, you transform your responses into words that will let your reader share your perceptions, your enthusiasms, and even your doubts. This sharing is, in effect, teaching. Students often think that they are writing for the teacher, but this is a misconception. When you write, *you* are the teacher. An essay on literature is an attempt to help someone to see something as you see it.

If you are not writing for the teacher, for whom are you writing? For yourself, of course, but also for others. Occasionally, in an effort to help you develop an awareness that what you write depends partly on your audience, your instructor may specify an audience, suggesting that you write for high school students or for the readers of the *New Yorker* or *Sports Illustrated*. But if an audience is not specified, write for your classmates.

- If you keep your classmates in mind as your audience, you will *not* write, "William Shakespeare, England's most famous playwright," because such a remark seems to imply that your reader does not know Shakespeare's nationality or trade.
- On the other hand, you *will* write, "Sei Shōnagon, a lady of the court in medieval Japan," because you can reasonably assume that your classmates do not know who she is.

Your Turn: Poems for Explication

The basic assignment is to explicate the poems, but your instructor may also ask you to respond to some or all of the questions that follow each poem.

WILLIAM SHAKESPEARE

William Shakespeare (1564–1616), born in Stratford-upon-Avon in England, is chiefly known as a dramatic poet, but he also wrote nondramatic poetry. In 1609 a volume of 154 of his sonnets was published, apparently without his permission. Probably he chose to keep his sonnets unpublished not because he thought that they were of little value but because it was more prestigious to be an amateur (unpublished) poet than a professional (published) poet. Although the sonnets were published in 1609, they were probably written in the mid-1590s, when there was a vogue for sonneteering. A contemporary writer in 1598 said that Shakespeare's "sugred Sonnets [circulate] among his private friends."

Sonnet 73

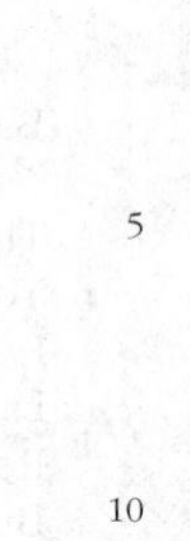

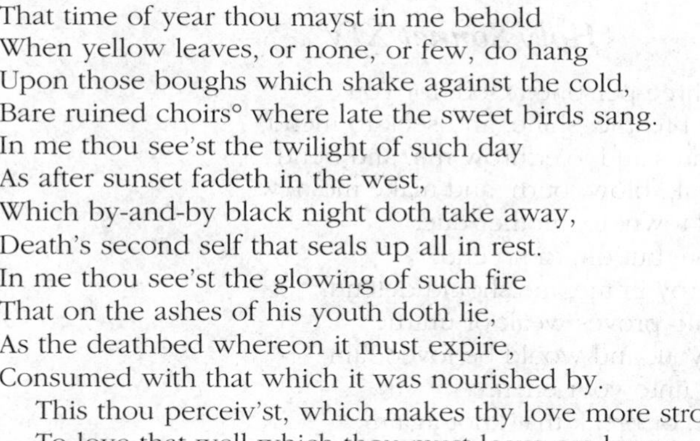

That time of year thou mayst in me behold
When yellow leaves, or none, or few, do hang
Upon those boughs which shake against the cold,
Bare ruined choirs° where late the sweet birds sang.
In me thou see'st the twilight of such day
As after sunset fadeth in the west,
Which by-and-by black night doth take away,
Death's second self that seals up all in rest.
In me thou see'st the glowing of such fire
That on the ashes of his youth doth lie,
As the deathbed whereon it must expire,
Consumed with that which it was nourished by.
    This thou perceiv'st, which makes thy love more strong,
    To love that well which thou must leave ere long.

4 choir the part of the church where services were sung.

Joining the Conversation: Critical Thinking and Writing

1. In the first quatrain (the first four lines) to what "time of year" does Shakespeare compare himself? In the second quatrain (lines 5–8) to what does he compare himself? In the third? If the sequence of the three quatrains were reversed, what would be gained or lost?
2. In line 8, what is "Death's second self"? What implications do you perceive in "seals up all in rest," as opposed, for instance, to "brings most welcome rest"?
3. In line 13, exactly what is "This"?

4. In line 14, suppose in place of "To love that well which thou must leave ere long," Shakespeare had written "To love me well whom thou must leave ere long." What if anything would have been gained or lost?
5. What insights into your own feelings and experiences does this poem give you? Please explain, being as specific as you can.

JOHN DONNE

John Donne (1572–1631) was born into a Roman Catholic family in England, but in the 1590s he abandoned that faith. In 1615 he became an Anglican priest and soon was known as a great preacher. One hundred sixty of his sermons survive, including one with the famous line "No man is an island, entire of itself; every man is a piece of the continent, a part of the main; if a clod be washed away by the sea, Europe is the less . . . ; and therefore never send to know for whom the bell tolls; it tolls for thee." From 1621 until his death he was dean of St. Paul's Cathedral in London. His love poems (often bawdy and cynical) are said to be his early work, and his "Holy Sonnets" (among the greatest religious poems written in English) his later work.

Holy Sonnet XIV

Batter my heart, three-personed God; for you
As yet but knock, breathe, shine, and seek to mend;
That I may rise and stand, o'erthrow me, and bend
Your force, to break, blow, burn, and make me new.
I, like an usurped town, to another due,
Labor to admit you, but oh, to no end.
Reason, your viceroy in me, me should defend,
But is captived, and proves weak or untrue
Yet dearly I love you, and would be loved fain,
But am betrothed unto your enemy:
Divorce me, untie, or break that knot again,
Take me to you, imprison me, for I
Except you enthrall me, never shall be free,
Nor ever chaste, except you ravish me.

[1633]

Joining the Conversation: Critical Thinking and Writing

1. Explain the paradoxes (apparent contradictions) in lines 2, 3, 13, and 14. Explain the double meanings of "enthrall" (line 13) and "ravish" (line 14).
2. In lines 1–4, what is God implicitly compared to (considering especially lines 2 and 4)? How does this comparison lead into the comparison that dominates lines 5–8? What words in lines 9–12 are especially related to the earlier lines?
3. What is gained by piling up verbs in lines 2–4?
4. Are sexual references necessarily irreverent in a religious poem? Please present a brief argument in which you say "Yes," and then another in which you say "No." Make each argument as convincing as you can.

Emily Brontë

Emily Brontë (1818–1848) spent most of her short life (she died of tuberculosis) in an English village on the Yorkshire moors. The sister of Charlotte Brontë (author of Jane Eyre*) and of Anne Brontë, Emily is best known for her novel* Wuthering Heights *(1847), but she was a considerable poet, and her first significant publication (1846) was in a volume of poems by the three sisters.*

Spellbound

The night is darkening round me,
The wild winds coldly blow;
But a tyrant spell has bound me
And I cannot, cannot go.

The giant trees are bending
Their bare boughs weighed with snow.
And the storm is fast descending,
And yet I cannot go.

Clouds beyond clouds above me,
Wastes beyond wastes below;
But nothing drear can move me;
I will not, cannot go.

[1837]

Joining the Conversation: Critical Thinking and Writing

1. What exactly is a "spell," and what does it mean to be "spellbound"?
2. What difference, if any, would it make if the first line said "has darkened" instead of "is darkening"?
3. What difference would it make, if any, if lines 4 and 12 were switched?
4. What does "drear" (line 11) mean? Is this word too unusual? Should the poet have used a more familiar word?
5. Describe the speaker's state of mind. Have you ever experienced anything like this yourself? What was the situation and how did you move beyond it?

Li-Young Lee

Li-Young Lee was born in 1957 in Jakarta, Indonesia, of Chinese parents. In 1964 his family brought him to the United States. He was educated at the University of Pittsburgh, the University of Arizona, and the State University of New York, Brockport. He now lives in Chicago, where he works as an artist.

I Ask My Mother to Sing

She begins, and my grandmother joins her.
Mother and daughter sing like young girls.
If my father were alive, he would play
his accordion and sway like a boat.

I've never been in Peking, or the Summer Palace,
nor stood on the great Stone Boat to watch
the rain begin on Kuen Ming Lake, the picnickers
running away in the grass.

But I love to hear it sung;
how the waterlilies fill with rain until
they overturn, spilling water into water,
then rock back, and fill with more.

Both women have begun to cry.
But neither stops her song.

[1986]

Joining the Conversation: Critical Thinking and Writing

1. Why might the speaker ask the women to sing?
2. Why do the women cry? Why do they continue to sing?
3. Is this poem simple, or complex? Both? Please point to specific details to support your argument.

Randall Jarrell

Randall Jarrell (1914–1965)—in the second name the accent is on the second syllable—was educated at Vanderbilt, where he majored in psychology. After serving with the air force in World War II as a control tower operator, he taught in several colleges and universities, meanwhile establishing a reputation as a poet and as a literary critic.

The Death of the Ball Turret Gunner

From my mother's sleep I fell into the State,
And I hunched in its belly till my wet fur froze.
Six miles from earth, loosed from its dream of life,
I woke to black flak and the nightmare fighters.
When I died they washed me out of the turret with a hose.

[1955]

Jarrell has furnished an explanatory note: "A ball turret was a plexiglass sphere set into the belly of a B-17 or B-24, and inhabited by two .50 caliber machine-guns and one man, a short small man. When this gunner tracked with his machine-guns a fighter attacking his bomber from below, he revolved with the turret;

hunched upside-down in his little sphere, he looked like the fetus in the womb. The fighters which attacked him were armed with cannon firing explosive shells. The hose was a steam hose."

Joining the Conversation: Critical Thinking and Writing

1. What is implied in the first line? In "I woke to . . . nightmare"? Taking account of the title, do you think "wet fur" is literal or metaphoric or both? Do you find the simplicity of the last line anticlimactic? How does it continue the metaphor of birth?
2. Why do you think Jarrell ended each line with punctuation?

Chapter 6

Reading Literature Closely: Analysis

Analysis

Explication is a method used chiefly in the study of fairly short poems or brief extracts from essays, stories, novels, and plays. In writing about works longer than a page or two, a more common approach than explicating is **analyzing** (literally, separating into parts in order to better understand the whole). An analysis of, say, *The Color Purple* may consider the functions of the setting or the uses that certain minor characters serve; an analysis of *Hamlet* may consider the comic passages or the reasons for Hamlet's delay; an analysis of *Death of a Salesman* may consider the depiction of women or the causes of Willy Loman's failure. In effect, an analytic essay usually advances a thesis, and offers arguments—reasons, evidence—in support of the thesis.

Most of the writing that you will do in college—not only in your English courses but in courses in history, sociology, economics, fine arts, and philosophy—will involve **analysis,** a method we commonly use in thinking about complex matters and in attempting to account for our responses. Watching Venus Williams play tennis, we may admire her serve, or her backhand, or the execution of several brilliant plays, and then think more generally about the concentration and flexibility that allow her to capitalize on her opponent's momentary weakness. And of course when we want to improve our own game, we try to analyze our performance. When writing is our game, we analyze our responses to a work, trying to name them and account for them. We analyze our notes, looking for ideas that connect, searching for significant patterns, and later we analyze our drafts, looking for strengths and weaknesses. Similarly, in peer review we analyze the draft of a fellow student, seeing how the parts (individual words, sentences, whole paragraphs, the tentative title, and so on) relate to one another and fit together as a whole.

To develop an analysis of a work, we tend to formulate questions and then to answer them. We ask a variety of questions:

- What is the function of the setting in this story or play?
- Why has this character been introduced?
- What is the author trying to tell us?
- How exactly can I describe the tone?
- What is the difference in assumptions between this essay and that one?

This book contains an anthology of literary works for you to respond to and then write about, and after most of the works we pose some questions. We also pose general questions on essays, fiction, drama, and poetry. These questions may stimulate your thinking and thus help you write. Our concern as teachers of writing is not so much with the answers to these questions; we believe and we ask you to believe that there are in fact no "right answers," only more or less persuasive ones, to most questions about literature—as about life. Our aim is to help you to pose questions that will stimulate your thinking.

Analyzing a Story from the Hebrew Bible: The Judgment of Solomon

A brief analysis of a very short story about King Solomon, from the Hebrew Bible (often called the Old Testament), may be useful here. Because the story is short, the analysis can consider all or almost all of the story's parts, and therefore the analysis can seem relatively complete. ("*Seem* relatively complete" because the analysis will in fact be far from complete, since the number of reasonable things that can be said about a work is almost as great as the number of readers. And a given reader might, at a later date, offer a different reading from what the reader offers today.)

The following story about King Solomon, customarily called the Judgment of Solomon, appears in the Hebrew Bible, in the latter part of the third chapter of the book called 1 Kings or First Kings, probably written in the mid-sixth century B.C.E. The translation is from the King James Version of the Bible (1611).

Two expressions in the story need clarification: (1) The woman who "overlaid" her child in her sleep rolled over on the child and suffocated it; and (2) it is said of a woman that her "bowels yearned upon her son," that is, her heart longed for her son. (In Hebrew psychology, the bowels were thought to be the seat of emotion.)

The Judgment of Solomon

Then came there two women, that were harlots, unto the king, and stood before him. And the one woman said, "O my lord, I and this woman dwell in one house, and I was delivered of a child with her in the house. And it came to pass the third day after that I was delivered, that this woman was delivered also: and we were together; there was no stranger in the house, save we two in the house. And this woman's child died in the night; because she overlaid it. And she arose at midnight, and took my son from beside me, while thine handmaid slept, and laid it in her bosom, and laid her dead child in my bosom. And when I rose in the morning to give my child suck, behold, it was dead: but when I considered it in the morning, behold, it was not my son, which I did bear."

And the other woman said, "Nay; but the living is my son, and the dead is thy son." And this said, "No; but the dead is thy son, and the living is my son." Thus they spake before the king.

Then said the king, "The one saith, 'This is my son that liveth, and thy son is dead': and the other saith, 'Nay; but thy son is the dead, and my son is the living.'" And the king said, "Bring me a sword." And they brought a sword before the king. And the king said, "Divide the living child in two, and give half to the one, and half to the other."

Then spake the woman whose the living child was unto the king, for her bowels yearned upon her son, and she said, "O my lord, give her the living child, and in no wise slay it." But the other said, "Let it be neither mine nor thine, but divide it."

5 Then the king answered and said, "Give her the living child, and in no wise slay it: she is the mother thereof."

And all Israel heard of the judgment which the king had judged; and they feared the king, for they saw that the wisdom of God was in him to do judgment.

Analyzing the Story

Let's begin by analyzing the **form** or the shape of the story. One form or shape that we notice is this:

> The story moves from a problem to a solution.

We can also say, still speaking of the overall form, that

> the story moves from quarreling and talk of death to unity and talk of life.

In short, it has a happy ending, a form that (because it provides an optimistic view of life and also a sense of completeness) gives most people pleasure.

In thinking about a work of literature, it is always useful to take notice of the basic form of the whole, the overall structural pattern. Doubtless you are already familiar with many basic patterns, for example,

> tragedy (joy yielding to sorrow) and
> romantic comedy (angry conflict yielding to joyful union).

If you think even briefly about verbal works, you'll notice the structures or patterns that govern songs, episodes in soap operas, political speeches (beginning with the candidate's expression of pleasure at being in Duluth, and ending with "God bless you all"), detective stories, westerns, and so on. And just as viewers of a western film experience one western in the context of others, so readers experience one story in the context of similar stories, and one poem in the context of others.

Second, we can say that the Judgment of Solomon is a sort of detective story: There is a death, followed by a conflict in the testimony of the witnesses, and then a solution by a shrewd outsider. Consider Solomon's predicament. Ordinarily in literature, characters are sharply defined and individualized, yet the essence of a detective story is that the culprit should *not* be easily recognized as wicked, and here nothing seems to distinguish the two petitioners. Solomon is confronted by "two women, that were harlots." Until late in the story—that is, up to the time Solomon suggests dividing the child—they are described only as "the one woman," "the other woman," "the one," "the other."

Does the story suffer from weak characterization? If we think analytically about this issue, we realize that the point surely is *not* to make each woman distinct. Rather, the point is (until late in the story) to make the women as alike as possible, so that we cannot tell which of the two is speaking the truth. Like Solomon, we have nothing to go on; neither witness is known to be more honest than the other, and there are no other witnesses to support or refute either woman.

Analysis is concerned with

- seeing the relationships between the parts of a work, but it is also concerned with
- taking notice of what is *not* in the work.

A witness would destroy the story, or turn it into an utterly different story. Another thing missing from this story is an explicit editorial comment or interpretation, except for the brief remark at the end that the people "feared the king." If we had read the story in the so-called Geneva Bible (1557–1560), which is the translation of the Bible that Shakespeare was familiar with, we would have found a marginal comment: "Her motherly affection herein appeareth that she had rather endure the rigour of the lawe, than see her child cruelly slaine." Would you agree that it is better, at least in this story, for the reader to draw conclusions than for the storyteller explicitly to point them out?

Solomon wisely contrives a situation in which these two claimants, who seem so similar, will reveal their true natures: The mother will reveal her love, and the liar will reveal her hard heart. The early symmetry (the identity of the two women) pleases the reader, and so does the device by which we can at last distinguish between the two women.

But even near the end there is a further symmetry. To save the child's life, the true mother gives up her claim, crying out, "Give her the living child, and in no wise slay it." The author (or, rather, the translator who produced this part of the King James Version) takes these very words, with no change whatsoever, and puts them into Solomon's mouth as the king's final judgment. Solomon too says, "Give her the living child, and in no wise slay it," but now the sentence takes on a new meaning. In the first sentence, "her" refers to the liar (the true mother says to give the child to "her"); in Solomon's sentence, "her" refers to the true mother: "Give her the living child. . . ." Surely we take pleasure in the fact that the very words by which the mother renounces her child are the words that (1) reveal to Solomon the truth, and that (2) Solomon uses to restore the child to his mother.

This analysis has chiefly talked about the relations of parts, and especially it has tried to explain why the two women in this story are *not* distinct until Solomon finds a way to reveal their distinctive natures: If the story is to demonstrate Solomon's wisdom, the women must seem identical until Solomon can show that they differ. But the analysis could have gone into some other topic. Let's consider several possibilities.

A student might begin by asking this question: "Although it is important for the women to be highly similar, why are they harlots?" (It is too simple to say that the women in the story are harlots because the author is faithfully reporting a historical episode in Solomon's career. The story is widely recognized as a folktale, found also in other ancient cultures.) One possible reason for making the women harlots is that the story demands that there be no witnesses; by using harlots, the author disposed of husbands, parents, and siblings who might otherwise be expected to live with the women. A second possible reason is that the author wanted to show that Solomon's justice extended to all, not only to respectable folk. Third, perhaps the author wished to reject or to complicate the stereotype of the harlot as a thoroughly disreputable person. The author rejected or complicated the harlot by introducing another (and truer?) stereotype, the mother as motivated by overwhelming maternal love.

Other Possible Topics for Analysis

1. Another possible kind of analytic essay might go beyond the structure of the individual work, to the relation of the work to some larger whole. For instance, the writer might approach the Judgment of Solomon from the point of view of gender criticism (discussed in Appendix A): In this story, it might be argued, wisdom is an attribute only of a male; women are either deceitful or emotional. From this point the writer might set out to create a research essay on gender in a larger whole, certain books of the Hebrew Bible.

2. We might also analyze the story in the context of other examples of what scholars call Wisdom Literature (the Book of Proverbs, and Ecclesiastes, for instance). Notice that Solomon's judgment leads the people to *fear* him—because his wisdom is great, formidable, and God-inspired.

It happens that we do not know who wrote the Judgment of Solomon, but the authors of most later works of literature are known, and therefore some critics seek to analyze a given work within the context of the author's life. Evidence drawn from the author's biography would be used to support an interpretation. For some other critics, the larger context would be the reading process, which includes the psychology of the reader. (Biographical criticism and reader-response criticism are discussed in Appendix A.)

3. Still another analysis—again, remember that a work can be analyzed from many points of view—might examine two or more translations of the story. You do not need to know Hebrew in order to compare this early seventeenth-century translation with a twentieth-century version such as the New Jerusalem Bible or the Revised English Bible. You might argue that one version is, on literary grounds, more effective. Such an essay might include an attempt, by means of a comparison, to analyze the effect of the archaic language of the King James Version. Does the somewhat unfamiliar language turn a reader off, or does it add mystery or dignity or authority to the tale, valuable qualities perhaps not found in the modern version? By the way, in the Revised English Bible, Solomon does *not* exactly repeat the mother's plea. The mother says, "Let her have the baby," and Solomon then says, "Give the living baby to the first woman." In the New Jerusalem Bible, after the mother says, "Let them give her the live child," Solomon says, "Give the live child to the first woman." If you prefer one version to the other two, why not try to analyze your preference?

Finally, it should be mentioned that an analysis of the structure of a work, in which the relationships of the parts to the whole are considered, allows the work to be regarded as independent of the external world. If we argue, say, that literature should in all respects reflect life, and we want to analyze the work against reality as we see it, we may find ourselves severely judging the Judgment of Solomon. We might ask if it is likely that a great king would bother to hear the case of two prostitutes quarreling over a child, or if it is likely that the false claimant would really call for the killing of the child. Similarly, to take an absurd example, an analysis of this story in terms of its ability to evoke laughter would be laughable. The point: An analysis will be interesting and useful to a reader only insofar as the aim of the analysis seems reasonable.

Analyzing a Story from the New Testament: The Parable of the Prodigal Son

Let's now look at another brief story from the Bible, this one from the Gospel according to St. Luke, in the New Testament. Luke, the author of the third of the four Gospels, was a second-generation Christian. He probably was a Roman, though some early accounts refer to him as a Syrian; in any case, he wrote in

Greek, probably composing the Gospel about 80–85 C.E. In Chapter 15, verses 11–32, Luke reports a story that Jesus told. This story, which occurs only in Luke's Gospel, is of a type called a **parable,** an extremely brief narrative from which a moral may be drawn.

The Parable of the Prodigal Son

And he said, "A certain man had two sons: and the younger of them said to his father, 'Father, give me a portion of goods that falleth to me.' And he divided unto them his living. And not many days after, the younger son gathered all together, and took his journey into a far country, and there wasted his substance with riotous living.

"And when he had spent all, there arose a mighty famine in that land, and he began to be in want. And he went and joined himself to a citizen of that country, and he sent him into his fields to feed swine. And he would fain have filled his belly with the husks that the swine did eat: and no man gave unto him. And when he came to himself, he said, 'How many hired servants of my father's have bread enough and to spare, and I perish with hunger? I will arise and go to my father, and will say unto him, "Father, I have sinned against heaven, and before thee, and am no more worthy to be called thy son: make me as one of thy hired servants."'

"And he arose, and came to his father. But when he was yet a great way off, his father saw him, and had compassion, and ran, and fell on his neck, and kissed him. And the son said unto him, 'Father, I have sinned against heaven, and in thy sight, and am no more worthy to be called thy son.' But the father said to his servants, 'Bring forth the best robe, and put it on him, and put a ring on his hand, and shoes on his feet. And bring hither the fatted calf, and kill it, and let us eat, and be merry. For this my son was dead, and is alive again; he was lost, and is found.' And they began to be merry.

"Now his elder son was in the field, and as he came and drew nigh to the house, he heard music and dancing. And he called one of the servants, and asked what these things meant. And he said unto him 'Thy brother is come, and thy father hath killed the fatted calf, because he hath received him safe and sound.' And he was angry, and would not go in: therefore came his father out, and entreated him. And he answering said to his father 'Lo, these many years do I serve thee, neither transgressed I at any time thy commandment, and yet thou never gavest me a kid, that I might make merry with friends: but as soon as this thy son was come, which hath devoured thy living with harlots, thou hast killed for him the fatted calf.' And he said unto him, 'Son, thou art ever with me, and all that I have is thine. It was meet that we should make merry, and be glad: for this thy brother was dead, and is alive again: and was lost, and is found.'"

Joining the Conversation: Critical Thinking and Writing

1. In talking about the Judgment of Solomon we commented on certain repetitions (e.g., *two* women) and contrasts (e.g., troubled beginning, happy ending), which help to give shape to the story. What parallels or contrasts (or both) do you find in the parable of the prodigal son? What *function* does the older brother serve? If he were omitted, what if anything would be lost? (Characterize him, partly by comparing him with the younger brother and with the father.)

2. Is the father foolish and sentimental? Do you approve or disapprove of his behavior at the end? In a short argumentative essay (250–500 words) support your thesis.
3. Jesus told the story, so it must have had a meaning consistent with his other teachings. Christians customarily interpret the story as meaning that God (like the father in the parable) rejoices in the return of a sinner. What meaning, if any, can it have for readers who are not Christians? Explain.
4. Does this parable present an argument? Can you offer a counterargument to the parable?

Summary

At this point we want to distinguish clearly between *analysis* and *summary*. A summary is a synopsis of the main points of a work; a summary of a work of literature usually gives the gist of the plot. It lets the reader know that X happened, then Y happened, then Z happened, but it does *not* concern itself, for instance, with evaluating whether the happenings are plausible. Normally in your analytic/argumentative essays you will not summarize because you can assume that your readers are familiar with the works you are discussing, but if, for instance, you are comparing an assigned text with another text that your readers probably don't know, you may want to offer a summary in order to help them follow the argument that you will be developing.

Consider this summary of Chopin's "The Story of an Hour" (page 45):

> A newspaper office reports that Brently Mallard has been killed in a railroad accident. When the news is gently broken to Mrs. Mallard by her sister Josephine, Mrs. Mallard weeps wildly and then shuts herself up in her room, where she sinks into an armchair. Staring dully through the window, she sees the signs of spring, and then an unnameable sensation possesses her. She tries to reject it but finally abandons herself to it. Renewed, she exults in her freedom, in the thought that at last the days will be her own. She finally comes out of the room, embraces her sister, and descends the stairs. A moment later her husband—who in fact had not been in the accident—enters. Mrs. Mallard dies—of the joy that kills, according to the doctors' diagnosis.

Here are a few principles that govern summaries:

1. A summary is **much briefer than the original.** It is not a paraphrase—a word-by-word translation of someone's words into your own. A paraphrase is usually at least as long as the original, whereas a summary is rarely longer than one-fourth of the original and is usually much shorter. A novel may be summarized in a few paragraphs, or even in one paragraph.
2. A summary **usually achieves its brevity by omitting almost all of the concrete details of the original** and by omitting minor characters and episodes. Notice that the summary of "The Story of an Hour" omits the friend of the family, omits specifying the signs of spring, and omits the business of the sister imploring Mrs. Mallard to open the door.

3. A summary is **as accurate as possible,** given the limits of space. It has no value if it misrepresents the point of the original.
4. A summary is **normally written in the present tense.** Thus "A newspaper office reports . . . , Mrs. Mallard weeps. . . ."
5. If the summary is brief (say, fewer than 250 words), it **may be given as a single paragraph.** If you are summarizing a long work, you may feel that a longer summary is needed. In this case your reader will be grateful to you if you divide the summary into paragraphs. As you draft your summary, you may find **natural divisions.** For instance, the scene of the story may change midway, giving you the opportunity to use two paragraphs. Or you may want to summarize a five-act play in five paragraphs.
6. The writer of a summary **need not make the points in the same order as that of the original.** If the writer of an essay has delayed revealing the main point until the end of the essay, the summary may rearrange the order, stating the main point first. Occasionally, if the original author has presented an argument in a disorderly or confusing sequence, a summary is written to disengage the author's argument from its confusing structure.
7. Because a summary is openly based on someone else's views, it is usually **not necessary to use quotation marks** around key words or phrases from the original. Nor is it necessary to repeat "he says" or "she goes on to prove." From the opening sentence of a summary it should be clear that what follows is what the original author says.

Summaries have their place in essays, but remember that a summary is not an analysis; it is only a summary.

Paraphrase

Like a summary, a paraphrase is *not* an analysis. A **paraphrase** is a restatement—a sort of translation in the same language—of material that may in its original form be somewhat obscure to a reader. A native speaker of English will not need a paraphrase of "Thirty days hath September," though a nonnative speaker might be puzzled by two things, the meaning of *hath* and the inverted word order. For such a reader, "September has thirty days" would be a helpful paraphrase.

Although a paraphrase seeks to make clear the basic meaning of the original, if the original is even a little more complex than "Thirty days hath September" the paraphrase will—in the process of clarifying something—lose something, since the substitution of one word for another will change the meaning. "Shut up" and "Be quiet" do not say exactly the same thing; the former (in addition to asking for quiet) says that the speaker is rude, or perhaps it says that the speaker feels little respect for the auditor, but the paraphrase loses all of this.

Still, a paraphrase can be a first step in helping a reader to understand a line that includes an obsolete word or phrase, or a word or phrase that is current only in one region. In a poem by Emily Dickinson (1830–1886), the following line appears:

> The sun engrossed the East. . . .

"Engrossed" here has (perhaps among other meanings) a special commercial meaning, "to acquire most or all of a commodity; to monopolize the market," so a paraphrase of the line might go thus:

> The sun took over all of the east.

It is worth mentioning, that you should have at your elbow a good desk dictionary, such as *The American Heritage Dictionary of the English Language*, 4th edition. Writers—especially poets—expect you to pay close attention to every word. If a word puzzles you, look it up.

Idioms, as well as words, may puzzle a reader. The Anglo-Irish poet William Butler Yeats (1865–1939) begins one poem with

> The friends that have it I do wrong. . . .

Because the idiom "to have it" (meaning "to believe that," "to think that") is unfamiliar to many American readers today, a discussion of the poem might include a **paraphrase**—a rewording, a translation into more familiar language, such as

> The friends who think that I am doing the wrong thing. . . .

Perhaps the rest of the poem is immediately clear, but in any case here is the entire poem, followed by a paraphrase:

> The friends that have it I do wrong
> When ever I remake a song,
> Should know what issue is at stake:
> It is myself that I remake.

Now for the paraphrase:

> The friends who think that I am doing the wrong thing when I revise one of my poems should be informed what the important issue is: I'm not just revising a poem—rather, I am revising myself (my thoughts, feelings).

Here, as with any paraphrase, the meaning is not translated exactly; there is some distortion. If "song" in the original is clarified by "poem" in the paraphrase, it is also altered; the paraphrase loses the sense of lyricism that is implicit in "song." Further, "Should know what issue is at stake" (in the original) is ambiguous. Does "should" mean "ought," as in "You should know better than to speak so rudely," or does it mean "deserve to be informed," as in "You ought to know that I am thinking about quitting"?

Granted that a paraphrase may miss a great deal, a paraphrase often helps you, or your reader, to understand at least the surface meaning, and the act of paraphrasing will usually help you to understand at least some of the implicit meaning. Furthermore, a paraphrase makes you see that the original writer's words (if the work is a good one) are exactly right, better than any words we might substitute. It becomes clear that the thing said in the original—not only the rough "idea" expressed but the precise tone with which it is expressed—is a sharply defined experience.

For information concerning paraphrase in connection with using secondary sources, see page 318 and also Appendix B.

Comparison: An Analytic Tool

Analysis frequently involves comparing. A moment ago we asked you to compare the older brother with the younger brother and the father in the parable of the prodigal son. When we compare, we examine things for their resemblances to and differences from other things. Strictly speaking, if you emphasize the differences rather than the similarities, you are contrasting rather than comparing, but we need not preserve this distinction: we can call both processes **comparing.**

Although your instructor may ask you to write a comparison of two works of literature, the *subject* of the essay is the works; comparison is simply an effective analytic technique to show some of the qualities in the works. You might compare Chopin's use of nature in "The Story of an Hour" (page 45) with the use of nature in another story, in order to reveal the subtle differences between the stories, but a comparison of works utterly unlike can hardly tell the reader or the writer anything.

Something should be said about organizing a comparison, say between the settings in two stories, between two characters in a novel (or even between a character at the end of a novel and the same character at the beginning), or between the symbolism of two poems. Probably, a student's first thought after making some jottings is to discuss one half of the comparison and then go on to the second half. Instructors and textbooks (though not this one) usually condemn such an organization, arguing that the essay breaks into two parts and that the second part involves a good deal of repetition of categories set up in the first part. Usually, they recommend that the students organize their thoughts differently, somewhat along these lines:

1. First similarity
   a. First work (or character, or characteristic)
   b. Second work
2. Second similarity
   a. First work
   b. Second work
3. First difference
   a. First work
   b. Second work
4. Second difference
   a. First work
   b. Second work

and so on, for as many additional differences as seem relevant. If you wish to compare *Huckleberry Finn* with *The Catcher in the Rye*, you might organize the material thus:

1. First similarity: the narrator and his quest
   a. Huck
   b. Holden
2. Second similarity: the corrupt world surrounding the narrator
   a. Society in *Huck*
   b. Society in *Catcher*
3. First difference: degree to which the narrator fulfills his quest and escapes from society
   a. Huck's plan to "light out" to the frontier
   b. Holden's breakdown

Here is another way to organize a comparison and contrast:

1. First point: the narrator and his quest
   - **a.** Similarities between Huck and Holden
   - **b.** Differences between Huck and Holden
2. Second point: the corrupt world
   - **a.** Similarities between the worlds in *Huck* and *Catcher*
   - **b.** Differences between the worlds in *Huck* and *Catcher*
3. Third point: degree of success
   - **a.** Similarities between Huck and Holden
   - **b.** Differences between Huck and Holden

A comparison need not employ either of these structures. There is even the danger that an essay employing either of them may not come into focus until the essayist stands back from the seven-layer cake and announces in the concluding paragraph that the odd layers taste better. In your preparatory thinking, you may want to make comparisons in pairs:

- good-natured humor: the clown in *Othello*, the clownish grave-digger in *Hamlet*
- social satire: the clown in *Othello*, the grave-digger in *Hamlet*
- relevance to main theme:
- length of role:

But before writing the final version, you must come to some conclusions about what these add up to.

This final version should not duplicate the thought processes; rather, it should be organized so as to make the point—the thesis—clearly and effectively. After reflection, you may believe that

- although there are superficial similarities between the clown in *Othello* and the clownish grave-digger in *Hamlet*,
- there are essential differences.

In the finished essay, a writer will not wish to obscure the main point by jumping back and forth from play to play, working through a series of similarities and differences. It may be better to discuss the clown in *Othello* and then to point out that although the grave-digger in *Hamlet* resembles him in A, B, and C, the grave-digger also has other functions (D, E, and F) and is of greater consequence to *Hamlet* than the clown is to *Othello*. Some repetition in the second half of the essay ("The grave-digger's puns come even faster than the clown's . . .") will bind the two halves into a meaningful whole, making clear the degree of similarity or difference. The point of the essay is not to list pairs of similarities or differences but to illuminate a work or works by making thoughtful comparisons.

Although in a long essay the writer cannot postpone until page 30 a discussion of the second half of the comparison, in an essay of fewer than ten pages nothing is wrong with setting forth half of the comparison and then, in light of it, the second half. The essay will break into two unrelated parts if the second half makes no use of the first or if it fails to modify the first half, but not if the second half looks back to the first half and calls attention to differences that the new material reveals. Students ought to learn how to write an essay with interwoven comparisons, but they ought also to know that a comparison may be written in another, simpler and clearer way.

Finally, a reminder: **The purpose of a comparison is to call attention to the unique features of something by holding it up against something similar but significantly**

different. You can compare Macbeth with Banquo (two men who hear a prophecy but who respond differently), or Macbeth with Lady Macbeth (a husband and wife, both eager to be monarchs but differing in their sense of the consequences), or Hamlet and Holden Caulfield (two people who see themselves as surrounded by a corrupt world), but you can hardly compare Holden with Macbeth or with Lady Macbeth—there simply aren't enough points of resemblance to make it worth your effort to call attention to subtle differences.

If the differences are great and apparent, a comparison is a waste of effort; you are arguing about something that is not really arguable. ("Blueberries are different from elephants. Blueberries do not have trunks. And elephants do not grow on bushes.") Indeed, a comparison between essentially and evidently unlike things can only obscure, for by making the comparison the writer implies that significant similarities do exist, and readers can only wonder why they do not see them. The essays that do break into two halves are essays that make uninstructive comparisons: the first half tells the reader about five qualities in Alice Walker, the second half tells the reader about five different qualities in Toni Morrison.

A Sample Essay by a Student: "Two New Women"

A student in an introductory class was asked to compare any two of the three stories by Kate Chopin ("Ripe Figs," page 11; "The Story of an Hour," page 45; "The Storm," page 71). She settled on "The Story of an Hour" and "The Storm." We print the final version of her essay, preceded by a page of notes (a synthesis of earlier notes) that she prepared shortly before she wrote her first draft.

Resemblances or differences greater?

Resemblances
Theme: release from marital bonds; liberated women
Setting: nature plays a role in both; springtime in "Hour," storm in "Storm"
Characterization: in both stories, no villains
forces of nature compel;
Clarisse presumably happier without husband
both seem to emphasize roles of women
Differences
Ending: "Hour" sad (LM unfulfilled); "Storm" happy; all characters seem content
But endings different in that "Hour" ends suddenly, surprise; "Storm" not surprising at very end.

Overall view (theme?)
"Hour" very restricted view; only one person is of much interest (LM); Josephine interesting only in terms of LM (contrast).
In "Storm," Cal. and Alc. interesting; but also interesting are simple Bobinot and even the child, and also even Clarisse, who sort of has the last word

Possible titles
Two Women
New Women
Tragic Louise, Comic Calixta
Louise, Calixta, and Clarisse

Hernandez 1

Linda Hernandez

Professor Welsh

English 102

2 November 2009

Two New Women

It is not surprising that two stories by an author somewhat resemble each other. What is especially interesting about Kate Chopin's "The Story of an Hour" and "The Storm" is that although they both deal with women who achieve a sense of new life or growth outside of the bonds of marriage, the stories differ greatly in what we call tone. "The Story of an Hour" is bittersweet, or perhaps even bitter and tragic, whereas "The Storm" is romantic and in some ways comic.

The chief similarity is that Louise Mallard in "The Story of an Hour" and Calixta in "The Storm" both experience valuable, affirming, liberating sensations that a traditional moral view would condemn. Mrs. Mallard, after some moments of deep grief, feels a great sense of liberation when she learns of the death of her husband. She dies almost immediately after this experience, but even though she is never physically unfaithful to her husband, there is a sort of mental disloyalty, at least from a traditional point of view. Calixta's disloyalty is physical, not merely mental. Unlike Louise Mallard, Calixta does go to bed with a man who is not her husband. But Calixta, as we will see, is treated just about as sympathetically as is Mrs. Mallard.

Hernandez 2

Louise Mallard is sympathetic because she does grieve for her husband, and because Chopin suggests that Mallard's sense of freedom is natural, something associated with the spring, the "delicious breath of rain," and "the tops of trees that were all aquiver with the new spring life" (46). Furthermore, Chopin explicitly says that Mallard loved her husband. But Chopin also tells us that one aspect of the marriage was a "powerful will bending her" (46). For all of these reasons, then—Mrs. Mallard's genuine grief, the association of her new feeling with the power of nature, and the assertion that Mrs. Mallard loved her husband but was at least in some degree subject to his will—the reader sympathizes with Mrs. Mallard.

In her presentation of Calixta, too, Chopin takes care to make the unfaithful woman a sympathetic figure. As in "The Story of an Hour," nature plays a role. Here, instead of nature or the outside world being a parallel to the woman's emotions, nature in the form of a storm exerts pressure on the woman. We are told that "the water beat in upon the boards in driving sheets" (72), and a bolt of lightning causes Calixta to stagger backward, into Alcée's arms. These forces of outside nature are parallel to a force of nature within Calixta. Chopin tells us that during the sexual union Calixta's "firm, elastic flesh . . . was knowing for the first time its birthright" (73). And in one additional way, too, Chopin guards against the reader condemning Calixta. We learn, at the end of the story, that

Hernandez 3

Alcée's wife, Clarisse, is quite pleased to be free from her husband for a while:

> And the first free breath since her marriage seemed to restore the pleasant liberty of her maiden days. Devoted as she was to her husband, their intimate conjugal life was something which she was more than willing to forego for a while. (75)

Since Clarisse is portrayed as somewhat pleased to be relieved of her husband for a while, we probably do not see Alcée as a villainous betrayer of his wife. The story seems to end pleasantly, like a comedy, with everybody happy.

In Louise Mallard and in Calixta we see two women who achieve new lives, although in the case of Louise Mallard the reader is surprised to learn in the last sentence that the achievement lasts only a few moments. By "new lives" I mean emancipation from their husbands, but what is especially interesting is that in both cases Chopin guides the reader to feel that although in fact both women behave in ways that would be strongly condemned by the codes of Chopin's day, and even by many people today, neither woman (as Chopin presents her) is blameworthy. Mrs. Mallard is presented almost as a tragic victim, and Calixta is presented almost as a figure in a very pleasant comedy.

[New page]

Hernandez 4

Work Cited

Chopin, Kate. "The Storm." *Literature for Composition*. Ed. Sylvan Barnet, William Burto, and William E. Cain. 9th ed. New York: Longman, 2010. 71–75. Print.

Looking at the Essay

A few comments on this student's essay may be useful.

- The title announces the *topic*.
- The first paragraph announces the *thesis*, the point that will be argued.
- The second paragraph begins by getting directly to the point: "The chief similarity is . . ."
- The third paragraph clearly advances the argument by giving *evidence*, introduced by a word that implies reasoning, "because."
- The writer provides further evidence by using short relevant quotations from the story.
- The final paragraph summarizes but does not boringly repeat; i.e., it does not merely say "Thus we see. . . ." Rather, it presents the material freshly.

Joining the Conversation: Critical Thinking and Writing

We like this essay, but perhaps you have a different view. In any case, what grade would you give this essay? Why? Be as specific as possible in calling attention to what you see as its strengths and weaknesses.

CHECKLIST: *Revising a Comparison*

- ☐ Does it makes sense to compare these things? (What question will the comparison help to answer? What do you hope your reader will learn?)
- ☐ Is the point of the comparison—the reason for making it—clear? Is the point stated in a thesis sentence?
- ☐ Does the comparison cover all significant similarities and differences?
- ☐ Is the comparison readable; that is, is it clear and yet not tediously mechanical?

(*continued*)

Revising a Comparison (continued)

- Is the organization that is used—perhaps treating one text first and then the other, or perhaps shifting back and forth between texts—the best way to make this comparison?
- If the essay offers a value judgment, is the judgment fair? Does the essay offer enough evidence to bring a reader into at least partial agreement?

Evaluation in Explication and Analysis

When we evaluate, we say how good, how successful, how worthwhile, something is. If you reread the student's essay on "Harlem," you'll notice that he implies that the poem is worth reading. He doesn't say "In this excellent poem," but a reader of the essay probably comes away with the impression that the student thinks the poem is excellent. The writer might have included a more explicit evaluation, along these lines:

> In "Harlem," every word counts, and every word is effective. The image of the "heavy load" that "sags" is not as unusual as the image of the raisin in the sun, but it nevertheless is just right, adding a simple, powerful touch just before the explosive ending.

In any case, if an essay argues that the parts fit together effectively, it almost surely is implying a favorable evaluation. But only "*almost* surely." We might argue that the parts fit, and so on, but that the work is immoral, or trivial, or unpleasant, or untrue to life. Even though it might be granted that the work is carefully constructed, the final evaluation of the work might be low. Evaluations are based on standards. If you offer an evaluation, make certain that your standards are clear to the reader.

Notice in the following three examples of evaluations of J. D. Salinger's *The Catcher in the Rye* that the writers let their readers know what their standards are. Each excerpt is from a review that was published when the book first appeared. In the first, Anne L. Goodman, writing in the *New Republic* (16 July 1951), began by praising Salinger's earlier short stories and then said this about the novel:

> But the book as a whole is disappointing, and not merely because it is a reworking of a theme that one begins to suspect must obsess the author. Holden Caulfield, the main character who tells his own story, is an extraordinary portrait, but there is too much of him. He describes himself early on and, with the sureness of a wire recording, he remains strictly in character throughout.

Goodman then quotes a longish passage from *The Catcher*, and says,

> In the course of 277 pages the reader wearies of this kind of explicitness, repetition, and adolescence, exactly as one would weary of Holden himself.

Goodman lets us know that, in her opinion, (1) a book ought not simply to repeat a writer's earlier books, and that, again in her opinion, (2) it's not enough to give a highly realistic portrait of a character; if the character is not a sufficiently interesting person, in the long run the book will be dull.

Another reviewer, Virgilia Peterson, writing in the *New York Herald Tribune Book Review* (15 July 1951), found the book realistic in some ways, but unrealistic and therefore defective because its abundant profanity becomes unconvincing:

> There is probably not one phrase in the whole book that Holden Caulfield would not have used upon occasion, but when they are piled upon each other in cumulative monotony, the ear refuses to believe.

Peterson concluded her review, however, by confessing that she did not think she was in a position to evaluate a book about an adolescent, or at least *this* adolescent.

> . . . it would be interesting and highly enlightening to know what Holden Caulfield's contemporaries, male and female, think of him. Their opinion would constitute the real test of Mr. Salinger's validity. The question of authenticity is one to which no parent can really guess the reply.

Here again the standard is clear—authenticity—but the writer confesses that she isn't sure about authenticity in this matter, and she defers to her juniors. Peterson's review is a rare example of an analysis offered by a writer who confesses an inability to evaluate.

Finally, here is a brief extract from a more favorable review, written by Paul Engle and published in the *Chicago Sunday Tribune Magazine of Books* (15 July 1951):

> The book ends with Holden in a mental institution, for which the earlier events have hardly prepared the reader. But the story is an engaging and believable one for the most part, full of right observations and sharp insight, and a wonderful sort of grasp of how a boy can create his own world of fantasy and live form.

The first sentence implies that a good book prepares the reader for the end, and that in this respect *The Catcher* is deficient. The rest of the paragraph sets forth other standards that *The Catcher* meets (it is "engaging and believable," "full of right observations and sharp insight"), though one of the standards in Engle's last sentence ("live form") strikes us as obscure.

Choosing a Topic and Developing a Thesis in an Analytic Paper

Because Hughes's "Harlem" is very short, the analysis may discuss the entire poem. But a short essay, or even a long one, cannot discuss all aspects of a play or a novel or even of a long story. If you are writing about a long work, you'll have to single out an appropriate topic.

What is an appropriate topic? First, it must be a topic that you can work up some interest in or your writing will be mechanical and dull. (We say "work up some interest" because interest is commonly the result of some effort.) Second, an appropriate topic is compassable—that is, it is something you can cover with reasonable attention to detail in the few pages (and few days) you have to devote to it. If a work is fairly long, almost surely you will write an analysis of some part.

Unless you have lots of time for reflection and revision, you cannot write a meaningful essay of 500 words or even 1,000 words on "Shakespeare's *Hamlet*" or "The Fiction of Alice Walker." You cannot even write on "Character in *Hamlet*" or "Symbolism in Walker's *The Color Purple.*" And probably you won't really want to write on such topics anyway. Probably *one* character or *one* symbol has caught your interest. Think of something in your annotations or "response" notes (described in Chapter 2) that has caught your attention. Trust your feelings; you are likely onto something interesting.

In Chapter 3 we talked about the value of asking yourself questions. To find an appropriate topic, ask yourself such questions as the following:

1. *What purpose does this serve?* For instance, why is this scene in the novel or play? Why is there a comic grave-digger in *Hamlet?* Why are these lines unrhymed? Why did the author call the work by this title?
2. *Why do I have this response?* Why do I feel that this work is more profound (or amusing, or puzzling) than that work? How did the author make this character funny or dignified or pathetic? How did the author communicate the idea that this character is a bore without boring me?

The first of these questions, "What purpose does this serve?" requires that you identify yourself with the author, wondering, for example, whether this opening scene is the best possible for this story. The second question, "Why do I have this response?" requires that you trust your feelings. If you are amused or puzzled or annoyed, assume that these responses are appropriate and follow them up, at least until a rereading of the work provides other responses. If you jot down notes reporting your responses and later think about them, you will probably find that you can select a topic.

A third valuable way to find a thesis is to test a published comment against your response to a particular work. Perhaps somewhere you have seen—for instance, in a textbook—a statement about the nature of fiction, poetry, or drama. Maybe you have heard that a tragic hero has a "flaw." Don't simply accept the remark. Test it against your reading of the work. And interpret the word *published* broadly. Students and instructors publish their opinions—offer them to a public—when they utter them in class. Think about something said in class; students who pay close attention to their peers learn a great deal.

Given an appropriate topic, you will find your essay easier to write and the finished version of it clearer and more persuasive if, at some point in your preparation, in note taking or in writing a first draft, you have converted your topic into a *thesis* (a proposition, a point, an argument) and constructed a *thesis statement* (a sentence stating your overall point).

Let's dwell a moment on the distinction between a topic and a thesis. It may be useful to think of it this way: A topic is a subject (for example, "The Role of Providence in *Hamlet*"); to arrive at a thesis, you have to make an arguable assertion (for example, "The role of Providence in *Hamlet* is not obvious, but it is crucial").

Some theses are more promising than others. Consider this thesis:

The role of Providence in Hamlet is interesting.

This sentence asserts a thesis, but it is vague and provides little direction, little help in generating ideas and in shaping your essay. Let's try again. It's almost always necessary to try again and again, for the process of writing is in large part a process of trial and error, of generating better and better ideas by evaluating—selecting or rejecting—ideas and options.

> The role of Providence is evident in the Ghost.

This is much better, and it could stimulate ideas for an interesting essay. Let's assume the writer rereads the play, looking for further evidence, and comes to believe that the Ghost is only one of several manifestations of Providence. The writer may stay with the Ghost or may (especially if the paper is long enough to allow for such a thesis to be developed) alter the thesis thus:

> The role of Providence is not confined to the Ghost but is found also in the killing of Polonius, in the surprising appearance of the pirate ship, and in the presence of the poisoned chalice.

Strictly speaking, the thesis here is given in the first part of the sentence ("The role of Providence is not confined to the Ghost"); the rest of the sentence provides an indication of how the argument will be supported.

Every literary work suggests its own topics for analysis to an active reader, and all essayists must set forth their own theses, but if you begin by seeking to examine one of your responses, you will soon be able to stake out a topic and to formulate a thesis.

A suggestion: With two or three other students, formulate a thesis about Kate Chopin's "The Storm" (in Chapter 3). By practicing with a group you will develop a skill that you will use when you have to formulate a thesis on your own.

Analyzing a Story

If a story is short enough, you may be able to examine everything in it that you think is worth commenting on, but even if it is short you may nevertheless decide to focus on one element, such as the setting, or the construction of the plot, or the connection between two characters, or the degree of plausibility. Here is a story by James Thurber (1894–1961), the American humorist. It was first published in 1939.

James Thurber

The Secret Life of Walter Mitty

"We're going through!" The Commander's voice was like thin ice breaking. He wore his full-dress uniform, with the heavily braided white cap pulled down rakishly over one cold gray eye. "We can't make it, sir. It's spoiling for a hurricane, if you ask me." "I'm not asking you, Lieutenant Berg," said the Commander. "Throw on the power lights! Rev her up to 8,500! We're going through!" The pounding of the cylinders increased: ta-pocketa-pocketa-pocketa-*pocketa-pocketa*. The Commander stared at the ice forming on the pilot window. He walked over and twisted a row of complicated dials. "Switch on No. 8 auxiliary!" he shouted. "Switch on No. 8 auxiliary!" repeated Lieutenant Berg. "Full strength in No. 3 turret!" shouted the Commander. "Full strength in No. 3 turret!" The crew, bending to their various tasks in the huge, hurtling eight-engined Navy hydroplane, looked at each other and grinned. "The Old Man'll get us through," they said to one another. "The Old Man ain't afraid of Hell!" . . .

"Not so fast! You're driving too fast!" said Mrs. Mitty. "What are you driving so fast for?"

"Hmm?" said Walter Mitty. He looked at his wife, in the seat beside him, with shocked astonishment. She seemed grossly unfamiliar, like a strange woman who had yelled at him in a crowd. "You were up to fifty-five," she said. "You know I don't like to go more than forty. You were up to fifty-five." Walter Mitty drove on toward Waterbury in silence, the roaring of the SN202 through the worst storm in twenty years of Navy flying fading in the remote, intimate airways of his mind. "You're tensed up again," said Mrs. Mitty. "It's one of your days. I wish you'd let Dr. Renshaw look you over."

Walter Mitty stopped the car in front of the building where his wife went to have her hair done. "Remember to get those overshoes while I'm having my hair done," she said. "I don't need overshoes," said Mitty. She put her mirror back into her bag. "We've been all through that," she said, getting out of the car. "You're not a young man any longer." He raced the engine a little. "Why don't you wear your gloves? Have you lost your gloves?" Walter Mitty reached in a pocket and brought out the gloves. He put them on, but after she had turned and gone into the building and he had driven on to a red light, he took them off again. "Pick it up, brother!" snapped a cop as the light changed, and Mitty hastily pulled on his gloves and lurched ahead. He drove around the streets aimlessly for a time, and then he drove past the hospital on his way to the parking lot.

5 . . . "It's the millionaire banker, Wellington McMillan," said the pretty nurse. "Yes?" said Walter Mitty, removing his gloves slowly. "Who has the case?" "Dr. Renshaw and Dr. Benbow, but there are two specialists here, Dr. Remington from New York and Dr. Pritchard-Mitford from London. He flew over." A door opened down a long, cool corridor and Dr. Renshaw came out. He looked distraught and haggard. "Hello, Mitty," he said. "We're having the devil's own time with McMillan, the millionaire banker and close personal friend of Roosevelt. Obstreosis of the ductal tract. Tertiary. Wish you'd take a look at him." "Glad to," said Mitty.

In the operating room there were whispered introductions: "Dr. Remington, Dr. Mitty, Mr. Pritchard-Mitford, Dr. Mitty." "I've read your book on streptothricosis," said Pritchard-Mitford, shaking hands. "A brilliant performance, sir." "Thank you," said Walter Mitty. "Didn't know you were in the States, Mitty," grumbled Remington. "Coals to Newcastle, bringing Mitford and me up here for a tertiary." "You are very kind," said Mitty. A huge, complicated machine, connected to the operating table, with many tubes and wires, began at this moment to go pocketa-pocketa-pocketa. "The new anesthetizer is giving way!" shouted an interne. "There is no one in the East who knows how to fix it!" "Quiet, man!" said Mitty, in a low, cool voice. He sprang to the machine, which was now going pocketa-pocketa-queep-pocketa-queep. He began fingering delicately a row of glistening dials. "Give me a fountain pen!" he snapped. Someone handed him a fountain pen. He pulled a faulty piston out of the machine and inserted the pen in its place. "That will hold for ten minutes," he said. "Get on with the operation." A nurse hurried over and whispered to Renshaw, and Mitty saw the man turn pale. "Coreopsis has set in," said Renshaw nervously. "If you would take over, Mitty?" Mitty looked at him and at the craven figure of Benbow, who drank, and at the grave, uncertain faces of the two great specialists. "If you wish," he said. They slipped a white gown on him: he adjusted a mask and drew on thin gloves; nurses handed him shining . . .

"Back it up, Mac! Look out for that Buick!" Walter Mitty jammed on the brakes. "Wrong lane, Mac," said the parking-lot attendant, looking at Mitty closely. "Gee. Yeh," muttered Mitty. He began cautiously to back out of the lane marked

"Exit Only." "Leave her sit there," said the attendant. "I'll put her away." Mitty got out of the car. "Hey, better leave the key." "Oh," said Mitty, handing the man the ignition key. The attendant vaulted into the car, backed it up with insolent skill, and put it where it belonged.

They're so damn cocky, thought Walter Mitty, walking along Main Street; they think they know everything. Once he had tried to take his chains off, outside New Milford, and he had got them wound around the axles. A man had had to come out in a wrecking car and unwind them, a young, grinning garageman. Since then Mrs. Mitty always made him drive to the garage to have the chains taken off. The next time, he thought, I'll wear my right arm in a sling; they won't grin at me then. I'll have my right arm in a sling and they'll see I couldn't possibly take the chains off myself. He kicked at the slush on the sidewalk. "Overshoes," he said to himself, and he began looking for a shoe store.

When he came out into the street again, with the overshoes in a box under his arm, Walter Mitty began to wonder what the other thing was his wife had told him to get. She had told him, twice, before they set out from their house for Waterbury. In a way he hated these weekly trips to town—he was always getting something wrong. Kleenex, he thought, Squibb's, razor blades? No. Toothpaste, toothbrush, bicarbonate, carborundum, initiative and referendum? He gave it up. But she would remember it. "Where's the what's-its-name?" she would ask. "Don't tell me you forgot the what's-its-name." A newsboy went by shouting something about the Waterbury trial.

10 . . . "Perhaps this will refresh your memory." The District Attorney suddenly thrust a heavy automatic at the quiet figure on the witness stand. "Have you ever seen this before?" Walter Mitty took the gun and examined it expertly. "This is my Webley-Vickers 50.80," he said calmly. An excited buzz ran around the courtroom. The Judge rapped for order. "You are a crack shot with any sort of firearms, I believe?" said the District Attorney, insinuatingly. "Objection!" shouted Mitty's attorney. "We have shown that the defendant could not have fired the shot. We have shown that he wore his right arm in a sling on the night of the fourteenth of July." Walter Mitty raised his hand briefly and the bickering attorneys were stilled. "With any known make of gun," he said evenly, "I could have killed Gregory Fitzhurst at three hundred feet *with my left hand*." Pandemonium broke loose in the courtroom. A woman's scream rose above the bedlam and suddenly a lovely, dark-haired girl was in Walter Mitty's arms. The District Attorney struck at her savagely. Without rising from his chair, Mitty let the man have it on the point of the chin. "You miserable cur!" . . .

"Puppy biscuit," said Walter Mitty. He stopped walking and the buildings of Waterbury rose up out of the misty courtroom and surrounded him again. A woman who was passing laughed. "He said 'Puppy biscuit,'" she said to her companion. "That man said 'Puppy biscuit' to himself." Walter Mitty hurried on. He went into an A. & P., not the first one he came to but a smaller one farther up the street. "I want some biscuit for small, young dogs," he said to the clerk. "Any special brand, sir?" The greatest pistol shot in the world thought a moment. "It says 'Puppies Bark for It' on the box," said Walter Mitty.

His wife would be through at the hairdresser's in fifteen minutes, Mitty saw in looking at his watch, unless they had trouble drying it; sometimes they had trouble drying it. She didn't like to get to the hotel first; she would want him to be there waiting for her as usual. He found a big leather chair in the lobby, facing a window, and he put the overshoes and the puppy biscuit on the floor beside it. He picked up an old copy of *Liberty* and sank down into the chair. "Can Germany

Conquer the World through the Air?" Walter Mitty looked at the pictures of bombing planes and of ruined streets.

. . . "The cannonading has got the wind up in young Raleigh, sir," said the sergeant. Captain Mitty looked up at him through tousled hair. "Get him to bed," he said wearily. "With the others. I'll fly alone." "But you can't, sir," said the sergeant anxiously. "It takes two men to handle that bomber and the Archies are pounding hell out of the air. Von Richtman's circus is between here and Saulier." "Somebody's got to get that ammunition dump," said Mitty. "I'm going over. Spot of brandy?" He poured a drink for the sergeant and one for himself. War thundered and whined around the dugout and battered at the door. There was a rending of wood and splinters flew through the room. "A bit of a near thing," said Captain Mitty carelessly. "The box barrage is closing in," said the sergeant. "We only live once, Sergeant," said Mitty, with his faint, fleeting smile. "Or do we?" He poured another brandy and tossed it off. "I never see a man could hold his brandy like you, sir," said the sergeant. "Begging your pardon, sir." Captain Mitty stood up and strapped on his huge Webley-Vickers automatic. "It's forty kilometers through hell, sir," said the sergeant. Mitty finished one last brandy. "After all," he said softly, "what isn't?" The pounding of the cannon increased; there was the rat-tat-tatting of machine guns, and from somewhere came the menacing pocket-pocketa-pocketa of the new flame-throwers. Walter Mitty walked to the door of the dugout humming "Auprès de Ma Blonde." He turned and waved to the sergeant. "Cheerio!" he said. . . .

Something struck his shoulder. "I've been looking all over this hotel for you," said Mrs. Mitty. "Why do you have to hide in this old chair? How did you expect me to find you?" "Things close in," said Walter Mitty vaguely. "What?" Mrs. Mitty said. "Did you get the what's-its-name? The puppy biscuit? What's in that box?" "Overshoes," said Mitty. "Couldn't you have put them on in the store?" "I was thinking," said Walter Mitty. "Does it ever occur to you that I am sometimes thinking?" She looked at him. "I'm going to take your temperature when I get you home," she said.

15 They went out through the revolving doors that made a faintly derisive whistling sound when you pushed them. It was two blocks to the parking lot. At the drugstore on the corner she said, "Wait here for me. I forgot something. I won't be a minute." She was more than a minute. Walter Mitty lighted a cigarette. It began to rain, rain with sleet in it. He stood up against the wall of the drugstore, smoking. . . . He put his shoulders back and his heels together. "To hell with the handkerchief," said Walter Mitty scornfully. He took one last drag on his cigarette and snapped it away. Then, with that faint, fleeting smile playing about his lips, he faced the firing squad; erect and motionless, proud and disdainful, Walter Mitty the Undefeated, inscrutable to the last.

[1939]

Working Toward a Thesis: Journal Entries

Before reading the following entries about "The Secret Life of Walter Mitty," write some of your own. You may want to think about what (if anything) you found amusing in the story, or about whether the story is dated, or about some aspect of Mitty's character or of his wife's. But the choice is yours.

A student wrote the following entry in her journal after the story was discussed in class.

> March 21. Funny, I guess, especially the business about him as a doctor performing an operation. And that "pocketa-pocketa," but I don't think that it's as hysterical as everyone else seems to think it is. And

how could anyone stand being married to a man like that? In fact, it's a good thing he has her to look after him. He ought to be locked up, driving into the "Exit Only" lane, talking to himself in the street, and having those crazy daydreams. No wonder the woman in the street laughs at him.

March 24. He's certainly a case, and she's not nearly as bad as everyone was saying. So she tells him to put his overshoes on; well, he ought to put them on, since Thurber says there is slush in the street, and he's no kid anymore. About the worst I can say of her is that she seems a little unreasonable in always wanting him to wait for her, rather than sometimes the other way around, but probably she's really telling him not to wander off, because if he ever drifts away there'll be no finding him. The joke, I guess, is that he's supposed to have these daydreams because he's henpecked, and henpecked men are supposed to be funny. Would people find the story just as funny if she had the daydreams, and he bullied her?

Developing the Thesis: Making Lists

In preparation for writing a draft, the student reread the story and jotted down some tentative notes based on her journal and on material that she had highlighted in the text. (At this point you may want to make your own list, based on your notes.)

Mitty helpless: he needs her
chains on tires
enters Exit Only
~~Waterbury~~
cop tells him to get going
fantasies

wife a nag? → causes his daydreams? Evidence?
makes him get to hotel first
overshoes
backseat driver?

"Does it ever occur to you that I am sometimes thinking?" Is he thinking, or just having dreams?

M. confuses Richthoven with someone called Richtman.

funny--or anti-woman? Would it be funny if he nagged her, and *she* had daydreams?

Next, the student wrote a draft; then she revised the draft and submitted the revision (printed here) to some classmates for peer review. (The number enclosed within parentheses cites the page number of a quotation.)

Sample Draft by a Student: "Walter Mitty Is No Joke"

Lee 1

Susan Lee

Professor Markus

English 102

5 April 2009

Walter Mitty Is No Joke

James Thurber's "The Secret Life of Walter Mitty" seems to be highly regarded as a comic story about a man who is so dominated by his wife that he has to escape through fantasies. In my high school course in English, everyone found Mitty's dreams and his wife's bullying funny, and everyone seems to find them funny in college, too. Everyone except me.

If we look closely at the story, we see that Mitty is a pitiful man who needs to be told what to do. The slightest glimpse of reality sets him off on a daydream, as when he passes a hospital and immediately begins to imagine that he is a famous surgeon, or when he hears a newsboy shouting a headline about a crime and he imagines himself in a courtroom. The point seems to be that his wife nags him, so he escapes into daydreams. But the fact is that she needs to keep after him, because he needs someone to tell him what to do. It depends on what one considers nagging. She tells him he is driving too fast, and (given the date of the story, 1939) he probably is, since he is going 55 on a slushy or snowy road. She tells him to wear overshoes, and he probably ought to, since the weather is bad. He resents all of

Lee 2

these orders, but he clearly is incompetent, since he delays when the traffic light turns from red to green, and he enters an "Exit Only" lane in a parking lot. We are also told that he cannot put chains on tires.

In fact, he cannot do anything right. All he can do is daydream, and the dreams, though they *are* funny, are proof of his inability to live in the real world. When his wife asks him why he did not put the overshoes on in the store, instead of carrying them in a box, he says, "Does it ever occur to you that I am sometimes thinking?" (142). But he does not "think," he just daydreams. Furthermore, he cannot even get things straight in his daydreams, since he gets everything mixed up, confusing Richthoven with Richtman, for example.

Is "The Secret Life of Walter Mitty" really a funny story about a man who daydreams because he is henpecked? Probably it is supposed to be so, but it is also a story about a man who is lucky to have a wife who can put up with him and keep him from getting killed on the road or lost in town.

[New page]

Lee 3

Work Cited

Thurber, James. "The Secret Life of Walter Mitty." *Literature for Composition*. Ed. Sylvan Barnet, William Burto, and William E. Cain. 9th ed. New York: Longman, 2010. 139–42. Print.

Developing an Argument

Introductory Paragraphs

As the poet Byron said, at the beginning of a long part of a long poem, "Nothing so difficult as a beginning." Woody Allen thinks so, too. In an interview he said that the toughest part of writing is "to go from nothing to the first draft."

We can give two pieces of advice:

1. *The opening paragraph is unimportant.* It's great if you can write a paragraph that will engage your readers and let them know where the essay will be taking them, but if you can't come up with such a paragraph, just put down anything in order to prime the pump.
2. *The opening paragraph is extremely important.* It must engage your readers, and probably by means of a thesis sentence it should let the readers know where the essay will be taking them.

The contradiction is, however, only apparent, not real. The first point is relevant to the opening paragraph of a *draft*; the second point is relevant to the opening paragraph of the *final version.* Almost all writers—professionals as well as amateurs—find that the first paragraphs in their drafts are false starts. Don't worry about the opening paragraphs of your draft; you'll want to revise your opening later anyway. (Surprisingly often your first paragraph may simply be deleted; your second, you may find, is where your essay truly begins.)

When writing a first draft you merely need something—almost anything may do—to break the ice. But in your finished paper the opening cannot be mere throat-clearing. The opening should be interesting.

Among the commonest ***un*interesting openings** are these:

1. A dictionary definition ("Webster says . . .").
2. A restatement of your title. The title is (let's assume) "Romeo's Maturation," and the first sentence says, "This essay will study Romeo's maturation." True, there is an attempt at a thesis statement here, but no information beyond what has already been given in the title. There is no information about you, either—that is, no sense of your response to the topic, as is present in, say, "*Romeo and Juliet* covers less than one week, but within this short period Romeo is impressively transformed from a somewhat comic infatuated boy to a thoughtful tragic hero."
3. A platitude, such as "Ever since the beginning of time men and women have fallen in love." Again, such a sentence may be fine if it helps you to start drafting, but because it sounds canned and because it is insufficiently interesting, it should not remain in your final version.

What is left? What *is* a good way for a final version to begin? Your introductory paragraph will be interesting if it gives information, and it will be pleasing if the information provides a focus—that is, if it goes beyond the title in letting the reader know exactly what your topic is and where you are headed.

Let's assume that you agree: An opening paragraph should be *interesting* and *focused.* Doubtless you will find your own ways of fulfilling these goals, but you might consider using one of the following time-tested methods.

1. *Establish a connection between life and literature.* We have already suggested that a platitude (for instance, "Ever since the beginning of time men

and women have fallen in love") usually makes a poor beginning because it is dull, but you may find some other way of relating the work to daily experience. For instance:

Doubtless the popularity of *Romeo and Juliet* (the play has been with us for more than four hundred years) is partly due to the fact that it deals with a universal experience. Still, no other play about love is so much a part of our culture that the mere mention of the names of the lovers immediately calls up an image. But when we say that So-and-so is "a regular Romeo," exactly what do we mean? And exactly what sort of lover is Romeo?

2. *Give an overview.* Here is an example:

Langston Hughes's "Harlem" is about the destruction of the hopes of African Americans. More precisely, Hughes begins by asking "What happens to a dream deferred?" and then offers several possibilities, the last of which is that it may "explode."

3. *Include a quotation.* The previous example illustrates this approach, also. Here is another example:

One line from Langston Hughes's poem "Harlem" has become famous, "A raisin in the sun," but its fame is, in a sense, accidental; Lorraine Hansberry happened to use it for the title of a play. Doubtless she used it because it is impressive, but in fact the entire poem is worthy of its most famous line.

4. *Use a definition.* We have already suggested that a definition such as "Webster says . . ." is boring and therefore unusable, but consider the following:

When we say that a character is the hero of a story, we usually mean that he is the central figure, and we probably imply that he is manly. But in Kafka's "The Metamorphosis" the hero is most *un*manly.

5. *Introduce a critical stance.* If your approach is feminist, or psychoanalytic, or Marxist, or whatever, you may want to say so at the start. Here's an example:

    Feminists have called our attention to the unfunny sexism of mother-in-law jokes, comments about women hooking men into marriage, and so forth. We can now see that the stories of James Thurber, long thought to be wholesome fun, are unpleasantly sexist.

We are not saying that these are the only ways to begin, and we certainly are not suggesting that you pack all five into the opening paragraph. We are saying only that after you have done some brainstorming and written some drafts, you may want to think about using one of these methods for your opening paragraph.

An Exercise: Write (either by yourself or in collaboration with one or two other students) an opening paragraph for an essay on one of Kate Chopin's stories and another for an essay on Hughes's "Harlem." (To write a useful opening paragraph you will first have to settle on the essay's thesis.)

Middle Paragraphs

The middle, or body, of your essay will develop your thesis by offering supporting evidence. Ideas for the body should emerge from the sketchy outline that you made after you reviewed your brainstorming notes or journal.

1. *Be sure that each paragraph makes a specific point.* This point should be sufficiently developed with evidence. (A brief quotation is often the best evidence.)
2. *Be sure that each paragraph is coherent.* Read each sentence, starting with the second sentence, to see how it relates to the preceding sentence. Does it clarify, extend, reinforce, add an example? If you can't find the relationship, the sentence probably does not belong where it is. Rewrite it, move it, or strike it out.
3. *Be sure that the connections between paragraphs are clear.* Transitional words and phrases, such as "Furthermore," "On the other hand," and "In the next stanza," will often give readers all the help they need in seeing how your points are connected.
4. *Be sure that the paragraphs are in the best possible order.* A good way to test the organization is to jot down the topic sentence or topic idea of each paragraph, and then to see if your jottings are in a reasonable sequence.

Concluding Paragraphs

Concluding paragraphs, like opening paragraphs, are especially difficult, if only because they are so conspicuous. Readers often skim first paragraphs and last paragraphs to see if an essay is worth reading. With conclusions, as with openings, say something interesting. It is not interesting to say, "Thus we see that Mrs. Mitty . . ." (and here you go on to echo your title or your first sentence).

What to do? When you are revising a draft, you might keep in mind the following widely practiced principles. They are not inflexible rules, but they often work.

1. *Hint that the end is near.* Expressions such as "Finally," "One other point must be discussed," and "In short," alert the reader that the end is near and help to prevent the reader from feeling that the essay ends abruptly.
2. *Perhaps reassert the thesis, but put it in a slightly new light.* Replace "I have shown that Romeo and Hamlet are similar in some ways" with this:

   These similarities suggest that in some respects Romeo is an early study for Hamlet. Both are young men in love, both seek by the force of their passion to shape the world according to their own desires, and both die in the attempt. But compared with Hamlet, who at the end of the play understands everything that has happened, Romeo dies in happy ignorance; Romeo is spared the pain of knowing that his own actions will destroy Juliet, whereas Hamlet dies with the painful knowledge that his kingdom has been conquered by Norwegian invaders.

3. *Perhaps offer an evaluation.* You may find it appropriate to conclude your analysis with an evaluation such as this:

   Romeo is as convincing as he needs to be in a play about young lovers, but from first to last he is a relatively uncomplicated figure, the ardent lover. Hamlet is a lover, but he is also a good deal more, a figure whose complexity reveals a more sophisticated or a more mature author. Only five or six years separate Romeo and Juliet from Hamlet, but one feels that in those few years Shakespeare made a quantum leap in his grasp of human nature.

4. *Perhaps include a brief significant quotation from the work.* Here's an example:

   Romeo has won the hearts of audiences for almost four centuries, but, for all his charm, he is in the last analysis concerned only with fulfilling his own passion. Hamlet, on the other hand, at last fulfills not only his own wish but that of the Ghost, his father. "Remember me," the Ghost says, when he first appears to Hamlet and asks for revenge. Throughout the play Hamlet does remember the Ghost, and finally, at the cost of his own life, Hamlet succeeds in avenging his dead father.

Coherence in Paragraphs: Using Transitions

In addition to having a unified point and a reasonable organization, a good paragraph is **coherent;** that is, the connections between ideas in the paragraph are clear. Coherence can often be achieved by inserting the right transitional words or by taking care to repeat key words.

Richard Wagner, commenting on his work as a composer of operas, once said "The art of composition is the art of transition," for his art moved from note to note, measure to measure, scene to scene. **Transitions** establish connections between ideas; they alert readers to the way in which you are conducting your argument. Here are some of the most common transitional words and phrases.

1. **Amplification or likeness:** similarly, likewise, and, also, again, second, third, in addition, furthermore, moreover, finally
2. **Emphasis:** chiefly, equally, indeed, even more important
3. **Contrast or concession:** but, on the contrary, on the other hand, by contrast, of course, however, still, doubtless, no doubt, nevertheless, granted that, conversely, although, admittedly
4. **Example:** for example, for instance, as an example, specifically, consider as an illustration, that is, such as, like
5. **Consequence or cause and effect:** thus, so, then, it follows, as a result, therefore, hence
6. **Restatement:** in short, that is, in effect, in other words
7. **Place:** in the foreground, further back, in the distance
8. **Time:** afterward, next, then, as soon as, later, until, when, finally, last, at last
9. **Conclusion:** finally, therefore, thus, to sum up

✓ CHECKLIST: *Revising Paragraphs*

- ☐ Does the paragraph *say* anything? Does it have substance, or is it mere padding?
- ☐ Does the paragraph have a topic sentence? If so, is it in the best place? If the paragraph doesn't have a topic sentence, might adding one improve the paragraph? Or does it have a clear topic idea?
- ☐ If the paragraph is an opening paragraph, is it interesting enough to attract and to hold a reader's attention? If it is a later paragraph, does it easily evolve out of the previous paragraph and lead into the next paragraph?
- ☐ Does the paragraph contain some principle of development—for instance, from general to particular?
- ☐ Does each sentence clearly follow from the preceding sentence? Have you provided transitional words or cues to guide your reader? Would it be useful to repeat certain key words, for clarity?
- ☐ What is the purpose of the paragraph? Do you want to summarize, or tell a story, or give an illustration, or concede a point, or what? Is your purpose clear to you, and does the paragraph fulfill your purpose?
- ☐ Is the closing paragraph effective, and not an unnecessary restatement of the obvious?

Review: Writing an Analysis

Each writing assignment will require its own kind of thinking, but here are a few principles that usually are relevant:

1. Assume that your reader has already read the work you are discussing but is not thoroughly familiar with it—and of course does not know what you think and how you feel about the work. Early in your essay name the author, the work, and your thesis.
2. Do not tell the plot (or, at most, summarize it very briefly); instead, tell your reader what the work is about (not what happens, but what the happenings add up to).
3. Whether you are writing about character or plot or meter or anything else, you will probably be telling your reader something about *how* the work functions—that is, how it develops. The stages by which a work advances may sometimes be marked fairly clearly. For instance, a poem of two stanzas may ask a question in the first and give an answer in the second, or it may express a hope in the first and reveal a doubt in the second. Novels are customarily divided into chapters, and even a short story may be printed with numbered parts. Virtually all works are built from parts, whether or not the parts are labeled.
4. In telling the reader how each part leads to the next, or how each part arises from what has come before, you will probably be commenting on such things as (in a story) changes in a character's state of mind—marked perhaps by a change in the setting—or (in a poem) changes in the speaker's tone of voice—for instance, from eager to resigned, or from cautious to enthusiastic. Probably you will not only be describing the development of character or of tone or of plot, but also (and more important) you will be advancing your own thesis by offering evidence that supports the thesis.

A Note on Technical Terminology

Literature—like the law, medicine, the dance, and for that matter, cooking and baseball—has given rise to technical terminology. A cookbook will tell you to boil, or bake, or blend, and it will speak of a "slow" oven (300 degrees), a "moderate" oven (350 degrees), or a "hot" oven (450 degrees). These are technical terms in the world of cookery. In watching a baseball game we find ourselves saying, "I think the hit-and-run is on," or "He'll probably bunt." We use these terms because they convey a good deal in a few words; they are clear and precise. Further, although we don't use them in order to impress our hearer, in fact they do indicate that we have more than a superficial acquaintance with the game. That is, the better we know our subject, the more likely we are to use the technical language of the subject. Why? *Because such language enables us to talk precisely and in considerable depth about the subject.* Technical language, unlike jargon (pretentious diction that needlessly complicates or obscures), is illuminating—provided that the reader is familiar with the terms.

In writing about literature you will, for the most part, use the same language that you use in your other courses, and you will not needlessly introduce the technical vocabulary of literary study—but you *will* use this vocabulary when it enables you to be clear, concise, and accurate.

A Lyric Poem and a Student's Argument

APHRA BEHN

Aphra Behn (1640–1689) is regarded as the first English woman to have made a living by writing. Not much is known of her life, but she seems to have married a London merchant of Dutch descent, and after his death to have served as a spy in the Dutch Wars (1665–1667). After her return to England she took up playwriting, and she gained fame with The Rover *(1677). Behn also wrote novels, the most important of which is* Oroonoko, or The Royal Slave *(1688), which is among the first works in English to express pity for enslaved Africans.*

Song: Love Armed

Love in fantastic triumph sate,
    Whilst bleeding hearts around him flowed,
For whom fresh pains he did create,
    And strange tyrannic power he showed:
From thy bright eyes he took his fire,
    Which round about in sport he hurled;
But 'twas from mine he took desire,
    Enough to undo the amorous world.
From me he took his sighs and tears:
    From thee, his pride and cruelty;
From me, his languishments and fears;
    And every killing dart from thee.
Thus thou and I the god have armed
    And set him up a deity;
But my poor heart alone is harmed,
    Whilst thine the victor is, and free.

[1676]

Joining the Conversation: Critical Thinking and Writing

1. The speaker (a man, although the author is a woman) talks of the suffering he is undergoing. Can we nevertheless feel that he enjoys his plight? *Why*, by the way, do we often enjoy songs of unhappy love?
2. The woman ("thee") is said to exhibit "pride and cruelty" (line 10). Is the poem sexist? Is it therefore offensive?
3. Do you suppose that men can enjoy the poem more than women? Set forth your response in a detailed argument.

Journal Entries

The subject is Aphra Behn's "song." We begin with two entries in a journal, kept by a first-year student, Geoffrey Sullivan, and we follow these entries with Sullivan's completed essay.

October 10. The title "Love Armed" puzzled me at first; funny, I somehow was thinking of the expression "strong-armed" and at first I didn't understand that "Love" in this poem is a human—no, not a human, but the god Cupid, who has a human form—and that he is shown as armed, with darts and so forth.

October 13. This god of "Love" is Cupid, and so he is something like what is on a valentine card—Cupid with his bow and arrow. But valentine cards just show cute little Cupids, and in this poem Cupid is a real menace. He causes lots of pain ("bleeding hearts," "tears," "killing dart," etc.). So what is Aphra Behn telling us about the god of love, or love? That love hurts? And she is singing about it! But we do sing songs about how hard life is. But do we sing them when we are really hurting, or only when we are pretty well off and just thinking about being hurt?

When you love someone and they don't return your love, it hurts, but even when love isn't returned it still gives some intense pleasure. Strange, but I think true. I wouldn't say that love always has this two-sided nature, but I do see the idea that love can have two sides, pleasure and pain. And love takes two kinds of people, male and female. Well, for most people, anyway. Maybe there's also something to the idea that "opposites attract." Anyway, Aphra Behn seems to be talking about men vs. women, pain vs. pleasure, power vs. weakness, etc. Pairs, opposites. And in two stanzas (a pair of stanzas?).

A Sample Essay by a Student: "The Double Nature of Love"

The final essay makes use of some, but not of all, of the preliminary jottings, and it includes much that Sullivan did not think of until he reread his jottings, reread the poem, and began drafting the essay.

Sullivan 1

Geoffrey Sullivan

Professor Morawski

English 2G

15 October 2009

The Double Nature of Love

Aphra Behn's "Love Armed" is in two stanzas, and it is about two people, "me" and "thee," that is, you and I, the lover and the woman he loves. I think the speaker is a man, since according to

Sullivan 2

the usual code men are supposed to be the active lovers and women are the (relatively) passive people who are loved. In this poem, the beloved—the woman, I think—has "bright eyes" (line 5) that provide the god of Love with fire, and she also provides the god with "pride and cruelty" (10). This of course is the way the man sees it if a woman does not respond to him; if she does not love him in return, she is (he thinks) arrogant and cruel. What does the man give to Love? He provides "desire" (7), "sighs and tears" (9), "languishments and fears" (11). None of this sounds very manly, but the joke is that the god of love—which means love—can turn a strong man into a crybaby when a woman does not respond to him.

Although both stanzas are clever *descriptions* of the god of love, the poem is not just a description. Of course there is not a plot in the way that a short story has a plot, but there is a sort of a switch at the end, giving the story something of a plot. The poem is, say, ninety percent expression of feeling and description of love, but during the course of expressing feelings and describing love something happens, so there is a tiny *story*. The first stanza sets the scene ("Love in fantastic triumph sate" [1]) and tells of some of the things that the speaker and the woman contributed to the god of Love. The woman's eyes provided Love with fire, and the man's feelings provided Love with "desire" (7). The second stanza goes on to mention other things that Love got from the speaker ("sighs and tears," etc. [9]), and other things

Sullivan 3

that Love got from the beloved ("pride and cruelty," etc. [10]), and in line 13 the poet says, "Thus thou and I the god have armed," so the two humans share something. They have both given Love his weapons. But—and this is the story I spoke of—the poem ends by emphasizing their difference: Only the man is "harmed," and the woman is the "victor" because her heart is not captured, as the man's heart is. In the battle that Love presides over, the woman is the winner; the man's heart has fallen for the woman, but, according to the last line, the woman's heart remains "free."

We have all seen the god of Love on valentine cards, a cute little Cupid armed with a bow and arrow. But despite the bow and arrow that the Valentine Day Cupid carries, I think that until I read Aphra Behn's "Love Armed" I had never really thought about Cupid as *powerful* and as capable of causing real pain. On valentine cards, he is just cute, but when I think about it, I realize the truth of Aphra Behn's concept of love. Love *is* (or can be) two-sided, whereas the valentine cards show only the sweet side.

I think it is interesting to notice that although the poem is about the destructive power of love, it is fun to read. I am not bothered by the fact that the lover is miserable. Why? I think I enjoy the poem, rather than am bothered by it, because *he is enjoying his misery*. After all, he is singing about it, sort of singing in the rain, telling anyone who will listen about how miserable he is, and he is having a very good time doing it.

[New page]

Sullivan 4

Work Cited

Behn, Aphra. "Love Armed." *Literature and Composition*. Ed. Sylvan Barnet, William Burto, and William E. Cain. 9th ed. New York: Longman, 2010. 152. Print.

Joining the Conversation: Critical Thinking and Writing

1. What do you think of the title? Is it sufficiently interesting and focused?
2. What are the writer's chief points? Are they clear, and are they adequately developed?
3. Do you think the writer is too concerned with himself, and that he loses sight of the poem? Or do you find it interesting that he connects the poem with life?
4. Focus on the writer's use of quotations. Does he effectively introduce and examine quoted lines and phrases?
5. What grade would you give the essay? What evidence can you offer to support your evaluation?

CHECKLIST: *Editing a Draft*

- Is the title of my essay interesting?
- Do I identify the subject of my essay (author and title) early?
- What is my thesis? Do I state it soon enough (perhaps even in the title) and keep it in view?
- Is the organization reasonable? Does each point lead into the next without irrelevancies and without anticlimaxes?
- Is each paragraph unified by a topic sentence or a topic idea? Are there adequate transitions from one paragraph to the next?
- Are generalizations supported by appropriate evidence, especially by brief quotations from the text?
- Is the opening paragraph interesting and, by its end, focused on the topic? Is the final paragraph conclusive without being repetitive?
- Is the tone appropriate? No sarcasm, no apologies, no condescension?
- If there is a summary, is it as brief as possible, given its purpose?
- Are the quotations adequately introduced, and are they accurate? Do they provide evidence and let the reader hear the author's voice, or do they merely add words to the essay?

- Is the present tense used to describe the author's work and the action of the work ("Shakespeare *shows*," "Hamlet *dies*")?
- Have I kept in mind the needs of my audience, for instance, by defining unfamiliar terms or by briefly summarizing works or opinions with which the reader may be unfamiliar?
- Is documentation provided where necessary?
- Are the spelling and punctuation correct? Are other mechanical matters (such as margins, spacing, and citations) in correct form? Have I proofread carefully?
- Is the paper properly identified—author's name, instructor's name, course number, and date?

Your Turn: Short Stories and Poems for Analysis

EDGAR ALLAN POE

Edgar Allan Poe (1809–1849) was the son of traveling actors. His father abandoned the family almost immediately, and his mother died when he was 2. The child was adopted—though never legally—by a prosperous merchant and his wife in Richmond. The tensions were great, aggravated by Poe's drinking and heavy gambling, and in 1827 Poe left Richmond for Boston. He wrote, served briefly in the army, attended West Point but left within a year, and became an editor for the remaining eighteen years of his life. It was during these years, too, that he wrote the poems, essays, and fiction—especially detective stories and horror stories—that have made him famous.

The Cask of Amontillado

The thousand injuries of Fortunato I had borne as I best could, but when he ventured upon insult, I vowed revenge. You, who so well know the nature of my soul, will not suppose, however, that I gave utterance to a threat. At *length* I would be avenged; this was a point definitely settled—but the very definitiveness with which it was resolved precluded the idea of risk. I must not only punish, but punish with impunity. A wrong is unredressed when retribution overtakes its redresser. It is equally unredressed when the avenger fails to make himself felt as such to him who has done the wrong.

It must be understood that neither by word nor deed had I given Fortunato cause to doubt my good will. I continued, as was my wont, to smile in his face, and he did not perceive that my smile *now* was at the thought of his immolation.

He had a weak point—this Fortunato—although in other regards he was a man to be respected and even feared. He prided himself on his connoisseurship in wine. Few Italians have the true virtuoso spirit. For the most part their enthusiasm is adopted to suit the time and opportunity to practice imposture upon the British and Austrian *millionaires.* In painting and gemmary Fortunato, like his countrymen, was a quack, but in the matter of old wines he was sincere. In this respect I did not differ from him materially;—I was skillful in the Italian vintages myself, and bought largely whenever I could.

It was about dusk, one evening during the supreme madness of the carnival season, that I encountered my friend. He accosted me with excessive warmth, for he had been drinking much. The man wore motley. He had on a tight-fitting parti-striped dress, and his head was surmounted by the conical cap and bells. I was so pleased to see him, that I thought I should never have done wringing his hand.

I said to him—"My dear Fortunato, you are luckily met. How remarkably well you are looking to-day! But I have received a pipe[1] of what passes for Amontillado, and I have my doubts."

"How?" said he, "Amontillado? A pipe? Impossible! And in the middle of the carnival?"

"I have my doubts," I replied; "and I was silly enough to pay the full Amontillado price without consulting you in the matter. You were not to be found, and I was fearful of losing a bargain."

"Amontillado!"

"I have my doubts."

"Amontillado!"

"And I must satisfy them."

"Amontillado!"

"As you are engaged, I am on my way to Luchesi. If any one has a critical turn, it is he. He will tell me—"

"Luchesi cannot tell Amontillado from Sherry."

"And yet some fools will have it that his taste is a match for your own."

"Come, let us go."

"Whither?"

"To your vaults."

"My friend, no; I will not impose upon your good nature. I perceive you have an engagement. Luchesi—"

"I have no engagement; come."

"My friend, no. It is not the engagement, but the severe cold with which I perceive you are afflicted. The vaults are insufferably damp. They are encrusted with nitre."

"Let us go, nevertheless. The cold is merely nothing. Amontillado! You have been imposed upon; and as for Luchesi, he cannot distinguish Sherry from Amontillado."

Thus speaking, Fortunato possessed himself of my arm. Putting on a mask of black silk, and drawing a *roquelaure*[2] closely about my person, I suffered him to hurry me to my palazzo.

There were no attendants at home; they had absconded to make merry in honor of the time. I had told them that I should not return until the morning, and had given them explicit orders not to stir from the house. These orders were sufficient, I well knew, to insure their immediate disappearance, one and all, as soon as my back was turned.

I took from their sconces two flambeaux, and giving one to Fortunato, bowed him through several suites of rooms to the archway that led into the vaults. I passed down a long and winding staircase, requesting him to be cautious as he followed. We came at length to the foot of the descent, and stood together on the damp ground of the catacombs of the Montresors.

The gait of my friend was unsteady, and the bells upon his cap jingled as he strode.

[1]**pipe** wine cask. [2] ***roquelaure*** short cloak.

"The pipe," said he.

"It is farther on," said I; "but observe the white web-work which gleams from these cavern walls."

He turned towards me, and looked into my eyes with two filmy orbs that distilled the rheum of intoxication.

"Nitre?" he asked, at length.

"Nitre," I replied. "How long have you had that cough?"

"Ugh! ugh! ugh!—ugh! ugh! ugh!—ugh! ugh! ugh!—ugh! ugh! ugh!—ugh! ugh! ugh!"

My poor friend found it impossible to reply for many minutes.

"It is nothing," he said, at last.

"Come," I said, with decision, "we will go back; your health is precious. You are rich, respected, admired, beloved; you are happy, as once I was. You are a man to be missed. For me it is no matter. We will go back; you will be ill, and I cannot be responsible. Besides, there is Luchesi—"

"Enough," he said; "the cough is a mere nothing: it will not kill me. I shall not die of a cough."

"True—true," I replied; "and, indeed, I had no intention of alarming you unnecessarily—but you should use all proper caution. A draught of this Medoc will defend us from the damps."

Here I knocked off the neck of a bottle which I drew from a long row of its fellows that lay upon the mould.

"Drink," I said, presenting him the wine.

He raised it to his lips with a leer: He paused and nodded to me familiarly, while his bells jingled.

"I drink," he said, "to the buried that repose around us."

"And I to your long life."

He again took my arm, and we proceeded.

"These vaults," he said, "are extensive."

"The Montresors," I replied, "were a great and numerous family."

"I forget your arms."

"A huge human foot d'or, in a field azure; the foot crushes a serpent rampant whose fangs are imbedded in the heel."

"And the motto?"

"*Nemo me impune lacessit.*"[3]

"Good!" he said.

The wine sparkled in his eyes and the bells jingled. My own fancy grew warm with the Medoc. We had passed through walls of piled bones, with casks and puncheons intermingling, into the inmost recesses of the catacombs. I paused again, and this time I made bold to seize Fortunato by an arm above the elbow.

"The nitre!" I said; "see, it increases. It hangs like moss upon the vaults. We are below the river's bed. The drops of moisture tickle among the bones. Come, we will go back ere it is too late. Your cough—"

"It is nothing," he said; "let us go on. But first, another draught of the Medoc."

I broke and reached him a flagon of De Grâve. He emptied it at a breath. His eyes flashed with a fierce light. He laughed and threw the bottle upwards with a gesticulation I did not understand.

I looked at him in surprise. He repeated the movement—a grotesque one.

[3]***Nemo me impune lacessit*** No one dare attack me with impunity (the motto of Scotland).

"You do not comprehend?" he said.

"Not I," I replied.

"Then you are not of the brotherhood."

"How?"

60 "You are not of the masons."[4]

"Yes, yes," I said, "yes, yes."

"You? Impossible! A mason?"

"A mason," I replied.

"A sign," he said.

65 "It is this," I answered, producing a trowel from beneath the folds of my *roquelaure.*

"You jest," he exclaimed, recoiling a few paces. "But let us proceed to the Amontillado."

"Be it so," I said, replacing the tool beneath the cloak, and again offering him my arm. He leaned upon it heavily. We continued our route in search of the Amontillado. We passed through a range of low arches, descended, passed on, and descending again, arrived at a deep crypt, in which the foulness of the air caused our flambeaux rather to glow than flame.

At the most remote end of the crypt there appeared another less spacious. Its walls had been lined with human remains piled to the vault overhead, in the fashion of the great catacombs of Paris. Three sides of this interior crypt were still ornamented in this manner. From the fourth the bones had been thrown down, and lay promiscuously upon the earth, forming at one point a mound of some size. Within the wall thus exposed by the displacing of the bones, we perceived a still interior recess, in depth about four feet, in width three, in height six or seven. It seemed to have been constructed for no especial use within itself, but formed merely the interval between two of the colossal supports of the roof of the catacombs, and was backed by one of their circumscribing walls of solid granite.

It was in vain that Fortunato, uplifting his dull torch, endeavored to pry into the depths of the recess. Its termination the feeble light did not enable us to see.

70 "Proceed," I said; "herein is the Amontillado. As for Luchesi—"

"He is an ignoramus," interrupted my friend, as he stepped unsteadily forward, while I followed immediately at his heels. In an instant he had reached the extremity of the niche, and finding his progress arrested by the rock, stood stupidly bewildered. A moment more and I had fettered him to the granite. In its surface were two iron staples, distant from each other about two feet, horizontally. From one of these depended a short chain, from the other a padlock. Throwing the links about his waist, it was but the work of a few seconds to secure it. He was too much astounded to resist. Withdrawing the key I stepped back from the recess.

"Pass your hand," I said, "over the wall; you cannot help feeling the nitre. Indeed it is very damp. Once more let me *implore* you to return. No? Then I must positively leave you. But I must first render you all the little attentions in my power."

"The Amontillado!" ejaculated my friend, not yet recovered from his astonishment.

"True," I replied; "the Amontillado."

75 As I said these words I busied myself among the pile of bones of which I have before spoken. Throwing them aside, I soon uncovered a quantity of building-stone and mortar. With these materials and with the aid of my trowel, I began vigorously to wall up the entrance of the niche.

[4]**of the masons** i.e., a member of the Freemasons, an international secret fraternity.

I had scarcely laid the first tier of masonry when I discovered that the intoxication of Fortunato had in a great measure worn off. The earliest indication I had of this was a low moaning cry from the depth of the recess. It was *not* the cry of a drunken man. There was then a long and obstinate silence. I laid the second tier, and the third, and the fourth; and then I heard the furious vibrations of the chain. The noise lasted for several minutes, during which, that I might hearken to it with the more satisfaction, I ceased my labors and sat down upon the bones. When at last the clanking subsided, I resumed the trowel, and finished without interruption the fifth, the sixth, and the seventh tier. The wall was now nearly upon a level with my breast. I again paused, and holding the flambeaux over the masonwork, threw a few feeble rays upon the figure within.

A succession of loud and shrill screams, bursting suddenly from the throat of the chained form, seemed to thrust me violently back. For a brief moment I hesitated—I trembled. Unsheathing my rapier, I began to grope with it about the recess; but the thought of an instant reassured me. I placed my hand upon the solid fabric of the catacombs, and felt satisfied. I reapproached the wall. I replied to the yells of him who clamored. I re-echoed—I aided—I surpassed them in volume and in strength. I did this, and the clamorer grew still.

It was now midnight, and my task was drawing to a close. I had completed the eighth, the ninth, and the tenth tier. I had finished a portion of the last and the eleventh; there remained but a single stone to be fitted and plastered in. I struggled with its weight; I placed it partially in its destined position. But now there came from out the niche a low laugh that erected the hairs upon my head. It was succeeded by a sad voice, which I had difficulty in recognizing as that of the noble Fortunato. The voice said—

"Ha! ha! ha!—he! he! he!—a very good joke indeed—an excellent jest. We will have many a rich laugh about it at the palazzo—he! he! he!—over our wine—he! he! he!"

"The Amontillado!" I said.

"He! he! he!—he! he! he!—yes, the Amontillado. But is it not getting late? Will not they be awaiting us at the palazzo, the Lady Fortunato and the rest? Let us be gone."

"Yes," I said, "let us be gone."

"For the love of God, Montresor!"

"Yes," I said, "for the love of God!"

But to these words I hearkened in vain for a reply. I grew impatient. I called aloud;

"Fortunato!"

No answer. I called again;

"Fortunato!"

No answer still, I thrust a torch through the remaining aperture and let it fall within. There came forth in return only a jingling of the bells. My heart grew sick—on account of the dampness of the catacombs. I hastened to make an end of my labor. I forced the last stone into its position; I plastered it up. Against the new masonry I reerected the old rampart of bones. For the half of a century no mortal has disturbed them. *In pace requiescat!*[5]

[1846]

[5]***In pace requiescat!*** May he rest in peace!

Joining the Conversation: Critical Thinking and Writing

1. To whom does Montresor tell his story? The story he tells happened fifty years earlier. Do we have any clues as to why he tells it now?
2. At the end of the story we learn that the murder occurred fifty years ago. Would the story be equally effective if Poe had had Montresor reveal this fact at the outset? Why, or why not?
3. Poe sets Montresor's story at dusk, "during the supreme madness of the carnival season." What is the "carnival season"? (If you are uncertain as to the meaning of "carnival," consult a dictionary.) What details of the story derive from the setting?
4. In the first line Montresor declares. "The thousand injuries of Fortunato I had borne as I best could, but when he ventured upon insult, I vowed revenge." Do we ever learn what those injuries and that insult were? What do we learn about Montresor from this declaration?
5. How does Montresor characterize Fortunato? What details of his portrait unwittingly enlist our sympathy for Fortunato? Does Montresor betray any sympathy for his victim?
6. "The Cask of Amontillado" is sometimes referred to as a "horror tale." Do you think it has anything in common with horror movies? If so, what? (You might begin by making a list of the characteristics of horror movies.) Why do people take pleasure in horror movies? Does this story offer any of the same sorts of pleasure? In any case, why might a reader take pleasure in this story? Set forth your response in an argument of 250–500 words.
7. Construct a definition of madness (you may want to do a little research, but if you make use of your findings, be sure to give credit to your sources) and write an essay of 500–750 words arguing whether or not Montresor is mad. (*Note:* You may want to distinguish between Montresor at the time of the killing and Montresor at the present.)

KATHERINE ANNE PORTER

Katherine Anne Porter (1890–1980) had the curious habit of inventing details in her life, but it is true that she was born in a log cabin in Indian Creek, Texas, that she was originally named Callie Russell Porter, that her mother died when the child was 2 years old, and that Callie was brought up by her maternal grandmother in Kyle, Texas. She was sent to convent schools, where, in her words, she received a "strangely useless and ornamental education." When she was 16 she left school, married (and soon divorced), and worked as a reporter, first in Texas and later in Denver and Chicago. She moved around a good deal, both within the United States and abroad; she lived for a while in Mexico, Belgium, Switzerland, France, and Germany.

*Even as a child she was interested in writing, but she did not publish her first story until she was 33. She wrote essays and one novel (*Ship of Fools*), but she is best known for her stories. Porter's* Collected Stories *won the Pulitzer Prize and the National Book Award in 1965.*

The Jilting of Granny Weatherall

She flicked her wrist neatly out of Doctor Harry's pudgy careful fingers and pulled the sheet up to her chin. The brat ought to be in knee breeches. Doctoring around the country with spectacles on his nose! "Get along now, take your schoolbooks and go. There's nothing wrong with me."

Doctor Harry spread a warm paw like a cushion on her forehead where the forked green vein danced and made her eyelids twitch. "Now, now, be a good girl, and we'll have you up in no time."

"That's no way to speak to a woman nearly eighty years old just because she's down. I'd have you respect your elders, young man."

"Well, Missy, excuse me." Doctor Harry patted her cheek. "But I've got to warn you, haven't I? You're a marvel, but you must be careful or you're going to be good and sorry."

5 "Don't tell me what I'm going to be. I'm on my feet now, morally speaking. It's Cornelia. I had to go to bed to get rid of her."

Her bones felt loose, and floated around in her skin, and Doctor Harry floated like a balloon around the foot of the bed. He floated and pulled down his waistcoat and swung his glasses on a cord. "Well, stay where you are, it certainly can't hurt you."

"Get along and doctor your sick," said Granny Weatherall. "Leave a well woman alone. I'll call for you when I want you. . . . Where were you forty years ago when I pulled through milk-leg and double pneumonia? You weren't even born. Don't let Cornelia lead you on," she shouted, because Doctor Harry appeared to float up to the ceiling and out. "I pay my own bills, and I don't throw my money away on nonsense!"

She meant to wave good-by, but it was too much trouble. Her eyes closed of themselves, it was like a dark curtain drawn around the bed. The pillow rose and floated under her, pleasant as a hammock in a light wind. She listened to the leaves rustling outside the window. No, somebody was swishing newspapers: no, Cornelia and Doctor Harry were whispering together. She leaped broad awake, thinking they whispered in her ear.

"She was *never* like this, never like this!" "Well, what can we expect?" "Yes, eighty years old. . . ."

10 Well, and what if she was? She still had ears. It was like Cornelia to whisper around doors. She always kept things secret in such a public way. She was always being tactful and kind. Cornelia was dutiful; that was the trouble with her. Dutiful and good: "So good and dutiful," said Granny, "that I'd like to spank her." She saw herself spanking Cornelia and making a fine job of it.

"What'd you say, Mother?"

Granny felt her face tying up in hard knots.

"Can't a body think, I'd like to know?"

"I thought you might want something."

15 "I do. I want a lot of things. First off, go away and don't whisper."

She lay and drowsed, hoping in her sleep that the children would keep out and let her rest a minute. It had been a long day. Not that she was tired. It was always pleasant to snatch a minute now and then. There was always so much to be done, let me see: tomorrow.

Tomorrow was far away and there was nothing to trouble about. Things were finished somehow when the time came; thank God there was always a little margin over for peace: then a person could spread out the plan of life and tuck in the edges orderly. It was good to have everything clean and folded away, with the hair brushes and tonic bottles sitting straight on the white embroidered linen: the day started without fuss and the pantry shelves laid out with rows of jelly glasses and brown jugs and white stone-china jars with blue whirligigs and words painted on them: coffee, tea, sugar, ginger, cinnamon, allspice: and the bronze clock with the lion on top nicely dusted off. The dust that lion could collect in twenty-four hours! The box in the attic with all those letters tied up, well, she'd have to go through that tomorrow. All those letters—George's letters and John's letters and her letters to them both—lying around for the children to find afterwards made her uneasy. Yes, that would be tomorrow's business. No use to let them know how silly she had been once.

While she was rummaging around she found death in her mind and it felt clammy and unfamiliar. She had spent so much time preparing for death there was no need for bringing it up again. Let it take care of itself now. When she was sixty she had felt very old, finished, and went around making farewell trips to see her children and grandchildren, with a secret in her mind: This is the very last of your mother, children! Then she made her will and came down with a long fever. That was all just a notion like a lot of other things, but it was lucky too, for she had once for all got over the idea of dying for a long time. Now she couldn't be worried. She hoped she had better sense now. Her father had lived to be one hundred and two years old and had drunk a noggin of strong hot toddy on his last birthday. He told the reporters it was his daily habit, and he owed his long life to that. He had made quite a scandal and was very pleased about it. She believed she'd just plague Cornelia a little.

"Cornelia! Cornelia!" No footsteps, but a sudden hand on her cheek. "Bless you, where have you been?"

20 "Here, Mother."

"Well, Cornelia, I want a noggin of hot toddy."

"Are you cold, darling?"

"I'm chilly, Cornelia. Lying in bed stops the circulation. I must have told you that a thousand times."

Well, she could just hear Cornelia telling her husband that Mother was getting a little childish and they'd have to humor her. The thing that most annoyed her was that Cornelia thought she was deaf, dumb, and blind. Little hasty glances and tiny gestures tossed around her and over her head saying, "Don't cross her, let her have her way, she's eighty years old," and she sitting there as if she lived in a thin glass cage. Sometimes Granny almost made up her mind to pack up and move back to her own house where nobody could remind her every minute that she was old. Wait, wait, Cornelia, till your own children whisper behind your back!

25 In her day she had kept a better house and had got more work done. She wasn't too old yet for Lydia to be driving eighty miles for advice when one of the children jumped the track, and Jimmy still dropped in and talked things over: "Now, Mammy, you've a good business head, I want to know what you think of this? . . ." Old. Cornelia couldn't change the furniture around without asking. Little things, little things! They had been so sweet when they were little. Granny wished the old days were back again with the children young and everything to be done over. It had been a hard pull, but not too much for her. When she thought of all the food she had cooked, and all the clothes she had cut and sewed, and all the gardens she had made—well, the children showed it. There they were, made out of her, and they couldn't get away from that. Sometimes she wanted to see John again and point to them and say, Well, I didn't do so badly,

did I? But that would have to wait. That was for tomorrow. She used to think of him as a man, but now all the children were older than their father, and he would be a child beside her if she saw him now. It seemed strange and there was something wrong in the idea. Why, he couldn't possibly recognize her. She had fenced in a hundred acres once, digging the post holes herself and clamping the wires with just a negro boy to help. That changed a woman. John would be looking for a young woman with the peaked Spanish comb in her hair and the painted fan. Digging post holes changed a woman. Riding country roads in the winter when women had their babies was another thing: sitting up nights with sick horses and sick negroes and sick children and hardly ever losing one. John, I hardly ever lost one of them! John would see that in a minute, that would be something he could understand, she wouldn't have to explain anything!

It made her feel like rolling up her sleeves and putting the whole place to rights again. No matter if Cornelia was determined to be everywhere at once, there were a great many things left undone on this place. She would start tomorrow and do them. It was good to be strong enough for everything, even if all you made melted and changed and slipped under your hands, so that by the time you finished you almost forgot what you were working for. What was it I set out to do? she asked herself intently, but she could not remember. A fog rose over the valley, she saw it marching across the creek swallowing the trees and moving up the hill like an army of ghosts. Soon it would be at the near edge of the orchard, and then it was time to go in and light the lamps. Come in, children, don't stay out in the night air.

Lighting the lamps had been beautiful. The children huddled up to her and breathed like little calves waiting at the bars in the twilight. Their eyes followed the match and watched the flame rise and settle in a blue curve, then they moved away from her. The lamp was lit, they didn't have to be scared and hang on to mother any more. Never, never, never more. God, for all my life I thank Thee. Without Thee, my God, I could never have done it. Hail, Mary, full of grace.

I want you to pick all the fruit this year and see that nothing is wasted. There's always someone who can use it. Don't let good things rot for want of using. You waste life when you waste good food. Don't let things get lost. It's bitter to lose things. Now, don't let me get to thinking, not when I am tired and taking a little nap before supper. . . .

The pillow rose about her shoulders and pressed against her heart and the memory was being squeezed out of it: oh, push down that pillow, somebody: it would smother her if she tried to hold it. Such a fresh breeze blowing and such a green day with no threats in it. But he had not come, just the same. What does a woman do when she has put on the white veil and set out the white cake for a man and he doesn't come? She tried to remember. No, I swear he never harmed me but in that. He never harmed me but in that . . . and what if he did? There was the day, the day, but a whirl of dark smoke rose and covered it, crept up and over into the bright field where everything was planted so carefully in orderly rows. That was hell, she knew hell when she saw it. For sixty years she had prayed against remembering him and against losing her soul in the deep pit of hell, and now the two things were mingled in one and the thought of him was a smoky cloud from hell that moved and crept in her head when she had just got rid of Doctor Harry and was trying to rest a minute. Wounded vanity, Ellen, said a sharp voice in the top of her mind. Don't let your wounded vanity get the upper hand of you. Plenty of girls get jilted. You were jilted, weren't you? Then stand up to it. Her eyelids wavered and let in streamers of blue-gray light like tissue paper over her eyes. She must get up and pull the shades down or she'd never sleep. She was in bed again and the shades were not down. How could that happen? Better turn over, hide from the light, sleeping in the light gave you nightmares. "Mother, how do you feel now?" and a stinging wetness on her forehead. But I don't like having my face washed in cold water!

30 Hapsy? George? Lydia? Jimmy? No, Cornelia, and her features were swollen and full of little puddles. "They're coming, darling, they'll all be here soon." Go wash your face, child, you look funny.

Instead of obeying, Cornelia knelt down and put her head on the pillow. She seemed to be talking but there was no sound. "Well, are you tongue-tied? Whose birthday is it? Are you going to give a party?"

Cornelia's mouth moved urgently in strange shapes. "Don't do that, you bother me, daughter."

"Oh, no, Mother. Oh, no. . . ."

Nonsense. It was strange about children. They disputed your every word. "No what, Cornelia?"

35 "Here's Doctor Harry."

"I won't see that boy again. He just left five minutes ago."

"That was this morning, Mother. It's night now. Here's the nurse."

"This is Doctor Harry, Mrs. Weatherall. I never saw you look so young and happy!"

"Ah, I'll never be young again—but I'd be happy if they'd let me lie in peace and get rested."

40 She thought she spoke up loudly, but no one answered. A warm weight on her forehead, a warm bracelet on her wrist, and a breeze went on whispering, trying to tell her something. A shuffle of leaves in the everlasting hand of God. He blew on them and they danced and rattled. "Mother, don't mind, we're going to give you a little hypodermic." "Look here, daughter, how do ants get in this bed? I saw sugar ants yesterday." Did you send for Hapsy too?

It was Hapsy she really wanted. She had to go a long way back through a great many rooms to find Hapsy standing with a baby on her arm. She seemed to herself to be Hapsy also, and the baby on Hapsy's arm was Hapsy and himself and herself, all at once, and there was no surprise in the meeting. Then Hapsy melted from within and turned flimsy as gray gauze and the baby was a gauzy shadow, and Hapsy came up close and said, "I thought you'd never come," and looked at her very searchingly and said, "You haven't changed a bit!" They leaned forward to kiss, when Cornelia began whispering from a long way off, "Oh, is there anything you want to tell me? Is there anything I can do for you?"

Yes, she had changed her mind after sixty years and she would like to see George. I want you to find George. Find him and be sure to tell him I forgot him. I want him to know I had my husband just the same and my children and my house like any other woman. A good house too and a good husband that I loved and fine children out of him. Better than I hoped for even. Tell him I was given back everything he took away and more. Oh, no, oh, God, no, there was something else besides the house and the man and the children. Oh, surely they were not all? What was it? Something not given back. . . . Her breath crowded down under her ribs and grew into a monstrous frightening shape with cutting edges; it bored up into her head, and the agony was unbelievable: Yes, John, get the doctor now, no more talk, my time has come.

When this one was born it should be the last. The last. It should have been born first, for it was the one she had truly wanted. Everything came in good time.

Nothing left out, left over. She was strong, in three days she would be as well as ever. Better. A woman needed milk in her to have her full health.

"Mother, do you hear me?"

"I've been telling you—"

"Mother, Father Connolly's here."

"I went to Holy Communion only last week. Tell him I'm not so sinful as all that."

"Father just wants to speak to you."

He could speak as much as he pleased. It was like him to drop in and inquire about her soul as if it were a teething baby, and then stay on for a cup of tea and a round of cards and gossip. He always had a funny story of some sort, usually about an Irishman who made his little mistakes and confessed them, and the point lay in some absurd thing he would blurt out in the confessional showing his struggles between native piety and original sin. Granny felt easy about her soul. Cornelia, where are your manners? Give Father Connolly a chair. She had her secret comfortable understanding with a few favorite saints who cleared a straight road to God for her. All as surely signed and sealed as the papers for the new Forty Acres. Forever . . . heirs and assigns forever. Since the day the wedding cake was not cut, but thrown out and wasted. The whole bottom dropped out of the world, and there she was blind and sweating with nothing under her feet and the walls falling away. His hand had caught her under the breast, she had not fallen, there was the freshly polished floor with the green rug on it, just as before. He had cursed like a sailor's parrot and said, "I'll kill him for you." Don't lay a hand on him, for my sake leave something to God. "Now, Ellen, you must believe what I tell you. . . ."

So there was nothing, nothing to worry about any more, except sometimes in the night one of the children screamed in a nightmare, and they both hustled out shaking and hunting for the matches and calling, "There, wait a minute, here we are!" John, get the doctor now, Hapsy's time has come. But there was Hapsy standing by the bed in a white cap. "Cornelia, tell Hapsy to take off her cap. I can't see her plain."

Her eyes opened very wide and the room stood out like a picture she had seen somewhere. Dark colors with the shadows rising toward the ceiling in long angles. The tall black dresser gleamed with nothing on it but John's picture, enlarged from a little one, with John's eyes very black when they should have been blue. You never saw him, so how do you know how he looked? But the man insisted the copy was perfect, it was very rich and handsome. For a picture, yes, but it's not my husband. The table by the bed had a linen cover and a candle and a crucifix. The light was blue from Cornelia's silk lampshades. No sort of light at all, just frippery. You had to live forty years with kerosene lamps to appreciate honest electricity. She felt very strong and she saw Doctor Harry with a rosy nimbus around him.

"You look like a saint, Doctor Harry, and I vow that's as near as you'll ever come to it."

"She's saying something."

"I heard you, Cornelia. What's all this carrying on?"

"Father Connolly's saying—"

Cornelia's voice staggered and bumped like a cart in a bad road. It rounded corners and turned back again and arrived nowhere. Granny stepped up in the cart very lightly and reached for the reins, but a man sat beside her and she knew him by his hands, driving the cart. She did not look in his face, for she knew without seeing, but looked instead down the road where the trees leaned over and bowed to each other and a thousand birds were singing a Mass. She felt like singing too, but she put her hand in the bosom of her dress and pulled out a rosary, and Father Connolly murmured Latin in a very solemn voice and tickled her feet. My God, will you stop that nonsense? I'm a married woman. What if he did run away and leave me to face the priest by myself? I found another a whole world better. I wouldn't have exchanged my husband for anybody except St. Michael himself, and you may tell him that for me with a thank you in the bargain.

Light flashed on her closed eyelids, and a deep roaring shook her. Cornelia, is that lightning? I hear thunder. There's going to be a storm. Close all the windows. Call the children in. . . . "Mother, here we are, all of us." "Is that you, Hapsy?" "Oh, no, I'm Lydia. We drove as fast as we could." Their faces drifted above her, drifted away. The rosary fell out of her hands and Lydia put it back. Jimmy tried to help, their hands fumbled together, and Granny closed two fingers around Jimmy's thumb. Beads wouldn't do, it must be something alive. She was so amazed her thoughts ran round and round. So, my dear Lord, this is my death and I wasn't even thinking about it. My children have come to see me die. But I can't, it's not time. Oh, I always hated surprises. I wanted to give Cornelia the amethyst set—Cornelia, you're to have the amethyst set, but Hapsy's to wear it when she wants, and, Doctor Harry, do shut up. Nobody sent for you. Oh, my dear Lord, do wait a minute. I meant to do something about the Forty Acres, Jimmy doesn't need it and Lydia will later on, with that worthless husband of hers. I meant to finish the altar cloth and send six bottles of wine to Sister Borgia for her dyspepsia. I want to send six bottles of wine to Sister Borgia, Father Connolly, now don't let me forget.

Cornelia's voice made short turns and tilted over and crashed. "Oh, Mother, oh, Mother, oh, Mother. . . ."

"I'm not going, Cornelia. I'm taken by surprise. I can't go."

You'll see Hapsy again. What about her? "I thought you'd never come." Granny made a long journey outward, looking for Hapsy. What if I don't find her? What then? Her heart sank down and down, there was no bottom to death, she couldn't come to the end of it. The blue light from Cornelia's lampshade drew into a tiny point in the center of her brain, it flickered and winked like an eye, quietly it fluttered and dwindled. Granny lay curled down within herself, amazed and watchful, starting at the point of light that was herself; her body was now only a deeper mass of shadow in an endless darkness and this darkness would curl around the light and swallow it up. God, give a sign!

For the second time there was no sign. Again no bridegroom and the priest in the house. She could not remember any other sorrow because this grief wiped them all away. Oh, no, there's nothing more cruel than this—I'll never forgive it. She stretched herself with a deep breath and blew out the light.

[1929]

Joining the Conversation: Critical Thinking and Writing

1. In a paragraph characterize Granny Weatherall. In another paragraph evaluate her claim that the anguish of the jilting has been compensated for by her subsequent life. Be sure to offer evidence to support your assertions.
2. The final paragraph alludes to Christ's parable of the bridegroom (Matthew 25:1–13). With this allusion in mind, write a paragraph explaining the title of the story.

José Armas

Born in 1944, José Armas has been a teacher (at the University of New Mexico and at the University of Albuquerque), publisher, critic, and community organizer. His interest in community affairs won him a fellowship, which in 1974–1975 brought him into association with the Urban Planning Department at the Massachusetts Institute of Technology. In 1980 he was awarded a writing fellowship by the National Endowment for the Arts, and he now writes a column on Hispanic affairs for The Albuquerque Journal.

El Tonto del Barrio[1]

Romero Estrado was called "El Cotorro"[2] because he was always whistling and singing. He made nice music even though his songs were spontaneous compositions made up of words with sounds that he liked but which seldom made any sense. But that didn't seem to bother either Romero or anyone else in the Golden Heights Centro where he lived. Not even the kids made fun of him. It just was not permitted.

Romero had a ritual that he followed almost every day. After breakfast he would get his broom and go up and down the main street of the Golden Heights Centro whistling and singing and sweeping the sidewalks for all the businesses. He would sweep in front of the Tortillería America,[3] the XXX Liquor Store, the Tres Milpas[4] Bar run by Tino Gabaldon, Barelas' Barber Shop, the used furniture store owned by Goldstein, El Centro Market of the Avila family, the Model Cities Office, and Lourdes Printing Store. Then, in the afternoons, he would come back and sit in Barelas' Barber Shop and spend the day looking at magazines and watching and waving to the passing people as he sang and composed his songs without a care in the world.

When business was slow, Barelas would let him sit in the barber's chair. Romero loved it. It was a routine that Romero kept every day except Sundays and Mondays when Barelas' Barber Shop was closed. After a period of years, people in the barrio got used to seeing Romero do his little task of sweeping the sidewalks and sitting in Barelas' Barber Shop. If he didn't show up one day someone assumed the responsibility to go to his house to see if he was ill. People would stop to say hello to Romero on the street and although he never initiated a conversation while he was sober, he always smiled and responded cheerfully to everyone. People passing the barber shop in the afternoons made it a point to wave even though they couldn't see him; they knew he was in there and was expecting some salutation.

When he was feeling real good, Romero would sweep in front of the houses on both sides of the block also. He took his job seriously and took great care to sweep cleanly, between the cracks and even between the sides of buildings. The dirt and small scraps went into the gutter. The bottles and bigger pieces of litter were put carefully in cardboard boxes, ready for the garbage man.

5 If he did it the way he wanted, the work took him the whole morning. And always cheerful—always with some song.

[1]**El Tonto del Barrio** the barrio dummy (in the United States, a barrio is a Spanish-speaking community) [all notes are by the editors]. [2]**El Cotorro** The Parrot. [3]**Tortillería America** Tortilla Factory. [4]**Tres Milpas** Three Cornfields.

Only once did someone call attention to his work. Frank Avila told him in jest that Romero had forgotten to pick up an empty bottle of wine from his door. Romero was so offended and made such a commotion that it got around very quickly that no one should criticize his work. There was, in fact, no reason to.

Although it had been long acknowledged that Romero was a little "touched," he fit very well into the community. He was a respected citizen.

He could be found at the Tres Milpas Bar drinking his occasional beer in the evenings. Romero had a rivalry going with the Ranchera songs on the jukebox. He would try to outsing the songs using the same melody but inserting his own selection of random words. Sometimes, like all people, he would "bust out" and get drunk.

One could always tell when Romero was getting drunk because he would begin telling everyone that he loved them.

"I looov youuu," he would sing to someone and offer to compose them a song.

"Ta bueno, Romero. Ta bueno, ya bete,"[5] they would tell him.

Sometimes when he got too drunk he would crap in his pants and then Tino would make him go home.

Romero received some money from Social Security but it wasn't much. None of the merchants gave him any credit because he would always forget to pay his bills. He didn't do it on purpose, he just forgot and spent his money on something else. So instead, the businessmen preferred to do little things for him occasionally. Barelas would trim his hair when things were slow. The Tortillería America would give him menudo[6] and fresh-made tortillas at noon when he was finished with his sweeping. El Centro Market would give him the overripe fruit and broken boxes of food that no one else would buy. Although it was unspoken and unwritten, there was an agreement that existed between Romero and the Golden Heights Centro. Romero kept the sidewalks clean and the barrio looked after him. It was a contract that worked well for a long time.

Then, when Seferino, Barelas' oldest son, graduated from high school he went to work in the barber shop for the summer. Seferino was a conscientious and sensitive young man and it wasn't long before he took notice of Romero and came to feel sorry for him.

One day when Romero was in the shop Seferino decided to act.

"Mira, Romero. Yo te doy 50 centavos por cada día que me barres la banqueta. Fifty cents for every day you sweep the sidewalk for us. Qué te parece?"[7]

Romero thought about it carefully.

"Hecho! Done!" he exclaimed. He started for home right away to get his broom.

"Why did you do that for, m'ijo?"[8] asked Barelas.

"It don't seem right, Dad. The man works and no one pays him for his work. Everyone should get paid for what they do."

"He don't need no pay. Romero has everything he needs."

"It's not the same, Dad. How would you like to do what he does and be treated the same way? It's degrading the way he has to go around getting scraps and handouts."

[5]**Ta bueno, ya bete** OK, now go away. [6]**menudo** tripe soup. [7]**Qué te parece?** How does that strike you? [8]**m'ijo** (mi hijo) my son.

"I'm not Romero. Besides you don't know about these things, m'ijo. Romero would be unhappy if his schedule was upset. Right now everyone likes him and takes care of him. He sweeps the sidewalks because he wants something to do, not because he wants money."

"I'll pay him out of my money, don't worry about it then."

"The money is not the point. The point is that money will not help Romero. Don't you understand that?"

"Look, Dad. Just put yourself in his place. Would you do it? Would you cut hair for nothing?"

Barelas just knew his son was putting something over on him but he didn't know how to answer. It seemed to make sense the way Seferino explained it. But it still went against his "instinct." On the other hand, Seferino had gone and finished high school. He must know something. There were few kids who had finished high school in the barrio, and fewer who had gone to college. Barelas knew them all. He noted (with some pride) that Seferino was going to be enrolled at Harvard University this year. That must count for something, he thought. Barelas himself had never gone to school. So maybe his son had something there. On the other hand . . . it upset Barelas that he wasn't able to get Seferino to see the issue. How can we be so far apart on something so simple, he thought. But he decided not to say anything else about it.

Romero came back right away and swept the front of Barelas' shop again and put what little dirt he found into the curb. He swept up the gutter, put the trash in a shoe box and threw it in a garbage can.

Seferino watched with pride as Romero went about his job and when he was finished he went outside and shook Romero's hand. Seferino told him he had done a good job. Romero beamed.

Manolo was coming into the shop to get his hair cut as Seferino was giving Romero his wages. He noticed Romero with his broom.

"What's going on?" he asked. Barelas shrugged his shoulders. "Qué tiene Romero?[9] Is he sick or something?"

"No, he's not sick," explained Seferino, who had now come inside. He told Manolo the story.

"We're going to make Romero a businessman," said Seferino. "Do you realize how much money Romero would make if everyone paid him just fifty cents a day? Like my dad says, 'Everyone should be able to keep his dignity, no matter how poor.' And he does a job, you know."

"Well, it makes sense," said Manolo.

"Hey, maybe I'll ask people to do that," said Seferino. "That way the poor old man could make a decent wage. Do you want to help, Manolo? You can go with me to ask people to pay him."

"Well," said Manolo as he glanced at Barelas, "I'm not too good at asking people for money."

This did not discourage Seferino. He went out and contacted all the businesses on his own, but no one else wanted to contribute. This didn't discourage Seferino either. He went on giving Romero fifty cents a day.

After a while, Seferino heard that Romero had asked for credit at the grocery store. "See, Dad. What did I tell you? Things are getting better for him already. He's becoming his own man. And look. It's only been a couple of weeks." Barelas did not reply.

[9]**Qué tiene Romero?** What's with Romero?

But then the next week Romero did not show up to sweep any sidewalks. He was around but he didn't do any work for anybody the entire week. He walked around Golden Heights Centro in his best gray work pants and his slouch hat, looking important and making it a point to walk right past the barber shop every little while.

Of course, the people in the Golden Heights Centro noticed the change immediately, and since they saw Romero in the street, they knew he wasn't ill. But the change was clearly disturbing the community. They discussed him in the Tortillería America where people got together for coffee, and at the Tres Milpas Bar. Everywhere the topic of conversation was the great change that had come over Romero. Only Barelas did not talk about it.

The following week Romero came into the barber shop and asked to talk with Seferino in private. Barelas knew immediately something was wrong. Romero never initiated a conversation unless he was drunk.

They went into the back room where Barelas could not hear and then Romero informed Seferino, "I want a raise."

"What? What do you mean, a raise? You haven't been around for a week. You only worked a few weeks and now you want a raise?" Seferino was clearly angry but Romero was calm and insistent.

Romero correctly pointed out that he had been sweeping the sidewalks for a long time. Even before Seferino finished high school.

"I deserve a raise," he repeated after an eloquent presentation.

Seferino looked coldly at Romero. It was clearly a stand-off.

Then Seferino said, "Look, maybe we should forget the whole thing. I was just trying to help you out and look at what you do."

Romero held his ground. "I helped you out too. No one told me to do it and I did it anyway. I helped you many years."

"Well, let's forget about the whole thing then," said Seferino.

"I quit then," said Romero.

"Quit?" exclaimed Seferino as he laughed at Romero.

"Quit! I quit!" said Romero as he walked out the front of the shop past Barelas, who was cutting a customer's hair.

Seferino came out shaking his head and laughing.

"Can you imagine that old guy?"

Barelas did not seem too amused. He felt he could have predicted that something bad like this would happen.

Romero began sweeping the sidewalks again the next day with the exception that when he came to the barber shop he would go around it and continue sweeping the rest of the sidewalks. He did this for the rest of the week. And the following Tuesday he began sweeping the sidewalk all the way up to the shop and then pushing the trash to the sidewalk in front of the barber shop. Romero then stopped coming to the barber shop in the afternoon.

The barrio buzzed with fact and rumor about Romero. Tino commented that Romero was not singing anymore. Even if someone offered to buy him a beer he wouldn't sing. Frank Avila said the neighbors were complaining because he was leaving his TV on loud the whole day and night. He still greeted people but seldom smiled. He had run up a big bill at the liquor store and when the manager stopped his credit, he caught Romero stealing bottles of whiskey. He was also getting careless about his dress. He didn't shave and clean like he used to. Women complained that he walked around in soiled pants, that he smelled bad. Even one of the little kids complained that Romero had kicked his puppy, but that seemed hard to believe.

Barelas felt terrible. He felt responsible. But he couldn't convince Seferino that what he had done was wrong. Barelas himself stopped going to the Tres Milpas Bar after work to avoid hearing about Romero. Once he came across Romero on the street and Barelas said hello but with a sense of guilt. Romero responded, avoiding Barelas' eyes and moving past him awkwardly and quickly. Romero's behavior continued to get erratic and some people started talking about having Romero committed.

"You can't do that," said Barelas when he was presented with a petition.

"He's flipped," said Tino, who made up part of the delegation circulating the petition. "No one likes Romero more than I do, you know that Barelas."

"But he's really crazy," said Frank Avila.

"He was crazy before. No one noticed," pleaded Barelas.

"But it was a crazy we could depend on. Now he just wants to sit on the curb and pull up the women's skirts. It's terrible. The women are going crazy. He's also running into the street stopping the traffic. You see how he is. What choice do we have?"

"It's for his own good," put in one of the workers from the Model Cities Office. Barelas dismissed them as outsiders. Seferino was there and wanted to say something but a look from Barelas stopped him.

"We just can't do that," insisted Barelas. "Let's wait. Maybe he's just going through a cycle. Look. We've had a full moon recently, qué no?[10] That must be it. You know how the moon affects people in his condition."

"I don't know," said Tino. "What if he hurts. . . ."

"He's not going to hurt anyone," cut in Barelas.

"No, Barelas. I was going to say, what if he hurts himself. He has no one at home. I'd say, let him come home with me for a while but you know how stubborn he is. You can't even talk to him any more."

"He gives everyone the finger when they try to pull him out of the traffic," said Frank Avila. "The cops have missed him, but it won't be long before they see him doing some of his antics and arrest him. Then what? Then the poor guy is in real trouble."

"Well, look," said Barelas. "How many names you got on the list?"

Tino responded slowly, "Well, we sort of wanted you to start off the list."

"Let's wait a while longer," said Barelas. "I just know that Romero will come around. Let's wait just a while, okay?"

No one had the heart to fight the issue and so they postponed the petition.

There was no dramatic change in Romero even though the full moon had completed its cycle. Still, no one initiated the petition again and then in the middle of August Seferino left for Cambridge to look for housing and to register early for school. Suddenly everything began to change again. One day Romero began sweeping the entire sidewalk again. His spirits began to pick up and his strange antics began to disappear.

At the Tortillería America the original committee met for coffee and the talk turned to Romero.

"He's going to be all right now," said a jubilant Barelas. "I guarantee it."

"Well, don't hold your breath yet," said Tino. "The full moon is coming up again."

"Yeah," said Frank Avila dejectedly.

[10]**qué no?** right?

When the next full moon was in force the group was together again drinking coffee and Tino asked, "Well, how's Romero doing?"

Barelas smiled and said, "Well. Singing songs like crazy."

[1982]

Joining the Conversation: Critical Thinking and Writing

1. What sort of man do you think Barelas is? In your response take account of the fact that the townspeople "sort of want" Barelas "to start off the list" of petitioners seeking to commit Romero.
2. The narrator, introducing the reader to Seferino, tells us that "Seferino was a conscientious and sensitive young man." Do you agree? Why, or why not? Be sure to support your position with evidence.
3. What do you make of the last line of the story?
4. Do you think this story could take place in almost any community? If you did not grow up in a barrio, could it take place in your community?

LESLIE MARMON SILKO

Leslie Marmon Silko was born in 1948 in Albuquerque, New Mexico, and grew up on the Laguna Pueblo Reservation some fifty miles to the west. Of her family she says,

> *We are mixed blood—Laguna, Mexican, white. . . . All those languages, all those ways of living are combined, and we live somewhere on the fringes of all three. But I don't apologize for this any more—not to whites, not to full bloods—our origin is unlike any other. My poetry, my storytelling rise out of this source.*

After graduating from the University of New Mexico in 1969, Silko entered law school but soon left to become a writer. She taught for two years at Navajo Community College at Many Farms, Arizona, and then went to Alaska for two years where she studied Eskimo-Aleut culture and worked on a novel, Ceremony. *After returning to the Southwest, she taught at the University of Arizona and then at the University of New Mexico.*

In addition to writing stories, a novel, and poems, Silko has written the screenplay for Marlon Brando's film Black Elk. *In 1981 she was awarded one of the so-called "genius grants" from the MacArthur Foundation, which supports "exceptionally talented individuals."*

The Man to Send Rain Clouds

One

They found him under a big cottonwood tree. His Levi jacket and pants were faded light-blue so that he had been easy to find. The big cottonwood tree stood apart from a small grove of winterbare cottonwoods which grew in the wide, sandy arroyo. He had been dead for a day or more, and the sheep had wandered and scattered up and down the arroyo. Leon and his brother-in-law, Ken, gathered the sheep and left them in the pen at the sheep camp before they returned to the cottonwood tree. Leon waited under the tree while Ken drove the truck through the deep sand to the edge of the arroyo. He squinted up at the sun and unzipped his jacket—it sure was hot for this time of year. But high and northwest the blue mountains were still deep in snow. Ken came sliding down the low, crumbling bank about fifty yards down, and he was bringing the red blanket.

Before they wrapped the old man, Leon took a piece of string out of his pocket and tied a small gray feather in the old man's long white hair. Ken gave him the paint. Across the brown wrinkled forehead he drew a streak of white and along the high cheekbones he drew a strip of blue paint. He paused and watched Ken throw pinches of corn meal and pollen into the wind that fluttered the small gray feather. Then Leon painted with yellow under the old man's broad nose, and finally, when he had painted green across the chin, he smiled.

"Send us rain clouds, Grandfather." They laid the bundle in the back of the pickup and covered it with a heavy tarp before they started back to the pueblo.

They turned off the highway onto the sandy pueblo road. Not long after they passed the store and post office they saw Father Paul's car coming toward them. When he recognized their faces he slowed his car and waved for them to stop. The young priest rolled down the car window.

5 "Did you find old Teofilo?" he asked loudly.

Leon stopped the truck. "Good morning, Father. We were just out to the sheep camp. Everything is O.K. now."

"Thank God for that. Teofilo is a very old man. You really shouldn't allow him to stay at the sheep camp alone."

"No, he won't do that any more now."

"Well, I'm glad you understand. I hope I'll be seeing you at Mass this week—we missed you last Sunday. See if you can get old Teofilo to come with you." The priest smiled and waved at them as they drove away.

Two

10 Louise and Teresa were waiting. The table was set for lunch, and the coffee was boiling on the black iron stove. Leon looked at Louise and then at Teresa.

"We found him under a cottonwood tree in the big arroyo near sheep camp. I guess he sat down to rest in the shade and never got up again." Leon walked toward the old man's head. The red plaid shawl had been shaken and spread carefully over the bed, and a new brown flannel shirt and pair of stiff new Levis were arranged neatly beside the pillow. Louise held the screen door open while Leon and Ken carried in the red blanket. He looked small and shriveled, and after they dressed him in the new shirt and pants he seemed more shrunken.

It was noontime now because the church bells rang the Angelus.[1] They ate the beans with hot bread, and nobody said anything until after Teresa poured the coffee.

Ken stood up and put on his jacket. "I'll see about the grave-diggers. Only the top layer of soil is frozen. I think it can be ready before dark."

Leon nodded his head and finished his coffee. After Ken had been gone for a while, the neighbors and clanspeople came quietly to embrace Teofilo's family and to leave food on the table because the grave-diggers would come to eat when they were finished.

[1]**Angelus** a devotional prayer commemorating the Annunciation (the angel Gabriel's announcement delivered to Mary of the Incarnation of God in the human form of Jesus).

Three

15 The sky in the west was full of pale-yellow light. Louise stood outside with her hands in the pockets of Leon's green army jacket that was too big for her. The funeral was over, and the old men had taken their candles and medicine bags and were gone. She waited until the body was laid into the pickup before she said anything to Leon. She touched his arm, and he noticed that her hands were still dusty from the corn meal that she had sprinkled around the old man. When she spoke, Leon could not hear her.

"What did you say? I didn't hear you."

"I said that I had been thinking about something."

"About what?"

"About the priest sprinkling holy water for Grandpa. So he won't be thirsty."

20 Leon stared at the new moccasins that Teofilo had made for the ceremonial dances in the summer. They were nearly hidden by the red blanket. It was getting colder, and the wind pushed gray dust down the narrow pueblo road. The sun was approaching the long mesa where it disappeared during the winter. Louise stood there shivering and watching his face. Then he zipped up his jacket and opened the truck door. "I'll see if he's there."

Ken stopped the pickup at the church, and Leon got out; and then Ken drove down the hill to the graveyard where people were waiting. Leon knocked at the old carved door with its symbols of the Lamb. While he waited he looked up at the twin bells from the king of Spain with the last sunlight pouring around them in their tower.

The priest opened the door and smiled when he saw who it was. "Come in! What brings you here this evening?"

The priest walked toward the kitchen, and Leon stood with his cap in his hand, playing with the earflaps and examining the living room—the brown sofa, the green armchair, and the brass lamp that hung down from the ceiling by links of chain. The priest dragged a chair out of the kitchen and offered it to Leon.

"No thank you, Father. I only came to ask you if you would bring your holy water to the graveyard."

25 The priest turned away from Leon and looked out the window at the patio full of shadows and the dining-room windows of the nuns' cloister across the patio. The curtains were heavy, and the light from within faintly penetrated; it was impossible to see the nuns inside eating supper. "Why didn't you tell me he was dead? I could have brought the Last Rites anyway."

Leon smiled. "It wasn't necessary, Father."

The priest stared down at his scuffed brown loafers and the worn hem of his cassock. "For a Christian burial it was necessary."

His voice was distant, and Leon thought that his blue eyes looked tired.

"It's O.K., Father, we just want him to have plenty of water."

30 The priest sank down in the green chair and picked up a glossy missionary magazine. He turned the colored pages full of lepers and pagans without looking at them.

"You know I can't do that, Leon. There should have been the Last Rites and a funeral Mass at the very least."

Leon put on his green cap and pulled the flaps down over his ears. "It's getting late, Father. I've got to go."

When Leon opened the door Father Paul stood up and said, "Wait." He left the room and came back wearing a long brown overcoat. He followed Leon out the door and across the dim churchyard to the adobe steps in front of the church.

They both stooped to fit through the low adobe entrance. And when they started down the hill to the graveyard only half of the sun was visible above the mesa.

The priest approached the grave slowly, wondering how they had managed to dig into the frozen ground, and then he remembered that this was New Mexico, and saw the pile of cold loose sand beside the hole. The people stood close to each other with little clouds of steam puffing from their faces. The priest looked at them and saw a pile of jackets, gloves, and scarves in the yellow, dry tumbleweeds that grew in the graveyard. He looked at the red blanket, not sure that Teofilo was so small, wondering if it wasn't some perverse Indian trick—something they did in March to ensure a good harvest—wondering if maybe old Teofilo was actually at sheep camp corraling the sheep for the night. But there he was, facing into a cold dry wind and squinting at the last sunlight, ready to bury a red wool blanket while the faces of the parishioners were in shadow with the last warmth of the sun on their backs.

His fingers were stiff, and it took them a long time to twist the lid off the holy water. Drops of water fell on the red blanket and soaked into dark icy spots. He sprinkled the grave and the water disappeared almost before it touched the dim, cold sand; it reminded him of something—he tried to remember what it was, because he thought if he could remember he might understand this. He sprinkled more water; he shook the container until it was empty, and the water fell through the light from sundown like August rain that fell while the sun was still shining, almost evaporating before it touched the wilted squash flowers.

The wind pulled at the priest's brown Franciscan robe and swirled away the corn meal and pollen that had been sprinkled on the blanket. They lowered the bundle into the ground, and they didn't bother to untie the stiff pieces of new rope that were tied around the ends of the blanket. The sun was gone, and over on the highway the eastbound lane was full of headlights. The priest walked away slowly. Leon watched him climb the hill, and when he had disappeared within the tall, thick walls, Leon turned to look up at the high blue mountains in the deep snow that reflected a faint red light from the west. He felt good because it was finished, and he was happy about the sprinkling of the holy water, now the old man could send them big thunderclouds for sure.

[1969]

Joining the Conversation: Critical Thinking and Writing

1. How would you describe the response of Leon, Ken, Louise, and Teresa to Teofilo's death? To what degree does it resemble or differ from responses to death that you are familiar with?
2. How do the funeral rites resemble or differ from those of your community?
3. How well does Leon understand the priest? How well does the priest understand Leon?
4. At the end of the story we are told that Leon "felt good." Do you assume that the priest also felt good? What evidence supports your view?
5. From what point of view is the story told? Mark the passages where the narrator enters a character's mind, and then explain what, in your opinion, Silko gains (or loses) by doing so.

Billy Collins

Born in New York City in 1941, Collins is a professor of English at Lehman College of the City University of New York. He is the author of several books of poetry and the recipient of numerous awards, including one from the National Endowment for the Arts. Collins's Sailing Alone Around the Room: New and Selected Poems *was published in 2001; in the same year, he was appointed poet laureate of the United States.*

Introduction to Poetry

I ask them to take a poem
and hold it up to the light
like a color slide

or press an ear against its hive.

I say drop a mouse into a poem
and watch him probe his way out,

or walk inside the poem's room
and feel the walls for a light switch.

I want them to waterski
across the surface of a poem
waving at the author's name on the shore.

But all they want to do
is tie the poem to a chair with rope
and torture a confession out of it.

They begin beating it with a hose
to find out what it really means.

[1988]

Joining the Conversation: Critical Thinking and Writing

1. Billy Collins has said about this poem, "It's about the teaching of poetry to students." What is Collins recommending? What is he objecting to?
2. One critic has said that "Introduction to Poetry" is a "good poem," but that lines 9–16 "should have come first"—that Collins should first have stated the bad way in which students often react and then he could have come forward with the right way. Prepare an argument in which you agree with this critic's comment, and then prepare an argument in which you disagree. Which of these two arguments do you find more convincing?
3. Which image in the poem do you think is the most effective? Is there an image that you think is not effective?—that is confusing or awkward, that you cannot understand?
4. Are the final two stanzas disturbing? Too disturbing? In their tone, are these stanzas similar to or different from the preceding stanzas?
5. If someone asked you, "What's the best way to teach poetry?," what would be your answer?

6. This is a relatively short poem, just sixteen lines. Please try to memorize it. Is this hard or easy for you? Does memorizing poems help you to enjoy poetry more? A lot, or a little? Not at all?

ROBERT FROST

Robert Frost (1874–1963) was born in California. After his father's death in 1885, Frost's mother brought the family to New England, where she taught in high schools in Massachusetts and New Hampshire. Frost studied for part of one term at Dartmouth College in New Hampshire, then did various jobs (including teaching), and from 1897 to 1899 was enrolled as a special student at Harvard. He later farmed in New Hampshire, published a few poems in local newspapers, left the farm and taught again, and in 1912 left for England, where he hoped to achieve more popular success as a writer. By 1915 he had won a considerable reputation, and he returned to the United States, settling on a farm in New Hampshire and cultivating the image of the country-wise farmer-poet. In fact he was well read in the classics, in the Bible, and in English and American literature.

Among Frost's many comments about literature, here are three: "Writing is unboring to the extent that it is dramatic"; "Every poem is . . . a figure of the will braving alien entanglements"; and, finally, a poem "begins in delight and ends in wisdom. . . . It runs a course of lucky events, and ends in a clarification of life—not necessarily a great clarification, such as sects and cults are founded on, but in a momentary stay against confusion."

The Road Not Taken

Two roads diverged in a yellow wood,
And sorry I could not travel both
And be one traveler, long I stood
And looked down one as far as I could
To where it bent in the undergrowth;

Then took the other, as just as fair,
And having perhaps the better claim,
Because it was grassy and wanted wear;
Though as for that the passing there
Had worn them really about the same,

And both that morning equally lay
In leaves no step had trodden black.
Oh, I kept the first for another day!
Yet knowing how way leads on to way,
I doubted if I should ever come back.

I shall be telling this with a sigh
Somewhere ages and ages hence:
Two roads diverged in a wood, and I—
I took the one less traveled by,
And that has made all the difference.

[1916]

Joining the Conversation: Critical Thinking and Writing

1. If the poem consisted of only the first and last stanzas, we probably would feel that Frost is talking about a clear-cut choice between two distinctive ways of life—for instance the life of a poet or the life of a farmer. The poem does not consist only of the first and last stanzas, however. What do the two middle stanzas do? Do they interestingly complicate the poem? Or do they make a muddle of it? Please explain.
2. The poem is often interpreted as Frost's statement that he chose the life of a poet. Yet Frost on several occasions said that he was spoofing the indecisiveness of a friend and fellow-poet, Edward Thomas. Given the fact that the middle stanzas suggest that the two roads are pretty much the same, and given the fact that the speaker in the last stanza does seem to playfully mock himself ("I shall be telling this with a sigh / Somewhere ages and ages hence"), do you think that we should or should not take the poem as a serious statement about the decisions we must make? Please explain.

ROBERT HERRICK

Robert Herrick (1591–1674) was born in London, the son of a goldsmith. After taking a master's degree at Cambridge, he was ordained in the Church of England, and later he was sent to the country parish of Dean Prior in Devonshire, where he wrote most of this poetry. A loyal supporter of the king, he was expelled in 1647 from his parish by the Puritans, though in 1662 he was restored to Dean Prior.

To the Virgins, to Make Much of Time

Gather ye rosebuds while ye may,
    Old Time is still a-flying;
And this same flower that smiles today,
    Tomorrow will be dying.

The glorious lamp of heaven, the sun,
    The higher he's a-getting,
The sooner will his race be run,
    And nearer he's to setting.

That age is best which is the first,
    When youth and blood are warmer;
But being spent, the worse, and worst
    Times still succeed the former.

Then be not coy, but use your time;
    And while ye may, go marry;
For having lost but once your prime,
    You may for ever tarry.

[1648]

Joining the Conversation: Critical Thinking and Writing

1. Why "rosebuds" rather than "roses" in the first line?
2. What sort of person seems to be speaking? Young or old? How do you know?
3. Doubtless this advice has something to commend it but it is not the whole truth. Does the value of this poem depend on the soundness of its advice? Explain.
4. Does the poem offer an argument? If so, how is the argument supported? Is it convincing?

MARTÍN ESPADA

Martín Espada was born in Brooklyn in 1957. He received a bachelor's degree from the University of Wisconsin and a law degree from Northeastern University. A poet who publishes regularly, Espada teaches creative writing at the University of Massachusetts–Amherst.

Bully

Boston, Massachusetts, 1987

In the school auditorium,
the Theodore Roosevelt statue;
is nostalgic
for the Spanish-American War,
each fist lonely for a saber,
or the reins of anguish-eyed horses,
or a podium to clatter with speeches
glorying in the malaria of conquest.

But now the Roosevelt school
is pronounced *Hernández.*
Puerto Rico has invaded Roosevelt
with its army of Spanish-singing children
in the hallways,
brown children devouring
the stockpiles of the cafeteria,
children painting *Taíno* ancestors
that leap naked across murals.

Roosevelt is surrounded
by all the faces
he ever shoved in eugenic spite
and cursed as mongrels, skin of one race,
hair and cheekbones of another.

Once Marines tramped
from the newsreel of his imagination;
now children plot to spray graffiti
in parrot-brilliant colors across the Victorian mustache
and monocle.

[1990]

Joining the Conversation: Critical Thinking and Writing

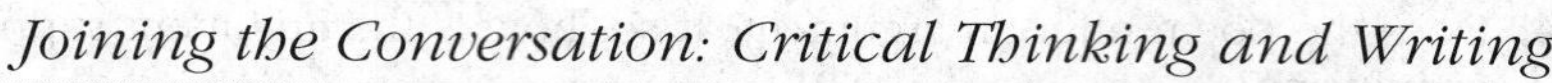

1. If you are not sure what Theodore Roosevelt was famous for, consult an encyclopedia. What *was* he famous for? In the first stanza, what words best express Espada's attitude toward him?
2. In the second stanza, what does Espada means when he says "Puerto Rico has invaded Roosevelt"? What does he mean by an "*army* of Spanish-singing children"? What are the *Taíno?*
3. What does "bully" mean as a noun? As an adjective?
4. Roosevelt was a great believer in America as a "melting pot." What is this theory? Do you think there is a great deal to it, something to it, or nothing to it? Why?
5. Here is a quotation from one of Roosevelt's speeches:

   > Every immigrant who comes here should be required within five years to learn English or leave the country.

   What do you think of this idea? Why? Suppose that for some reason (perhaps political, perhaps economic) you decided to spend the rest of your life in, say, Argentina, or Germany, or Israel, or Nigeria. Do you think the government might reasonably require you to learn the language? Support your response with reasons.

CHAPTER 7

Arguing an Interpretation

In Chapter 2 we discussed arguing about meanings or interpretations, and in Chapter 3 we discussed arguing with yourself as a way of developing ideas. In Chapter 11 we will discuss supporting arguments with evidence, but in the present chapter and in the next two chapters we want to talk about interpretation, assumptions, and evidence.

Interpretation and Meaning

We can define **interpretation** as

- a setting forth of the meaning, or, better,
- a setting forth of one or more of the meanings of a work of literature.

This question of *meaning* versus *meanings* deserves a brief explanation. Although some critics believe that a work of literature has a single meaning, the meaning it had for the author, most critics hold that a work has several meanings—for instance, the meaning it had for the author, the meaning(s) it had for its first readers (or viewers, if the work is a drama), the meaning(s) it had for later readers, and the meaning(s) it has for us today.

Take *Hamlet* (1600–1601), for example. Perhaps this play about a man who has lost his father had a very special meaning for Shakespeare, who had recently lost his own father. Further, Shakespeare had earlier lost a son named Hamnet, a variant spelling of Hamlet. The play, then, may have had important psychological meanings for Shakespeare—but the audience could not have shared (or even known) these meanings.

What *did* the play mean to Shakespeare's audience? Perhaps the original audience of *Hamlet*—people living in a monarchy, presided over by Queen Elizabeth I—were especially concerned with the issue (specifically raised in *Hamlet*) of whether a monarch's subjects ever have the right to overthrow the monarch. But obviously for twenty-first-century Americans the interest in the play lies elsewhere, and the play must mean something else. If we are familiar with Freud, we may see in the play a young man who subconsciously lusts after his mother and seeks to kill his father (in the form of Claudius, Hamlet's uncle). Or we may see the play as largely about an alienated young man in a bourgeois society. Or—but the interpretations are countless.

Is the Author's Intention a Guide to Meaning?

Shouldn't we be concerned, you might ask, with the *intention* of the author? The question is reasonable, but there are difficulties, as the members of the Supreme Court find when they try to base their decisions on the original intent of the writers of the Constitution. First, for older works we almost never know what the intention is. Authors did not leave comments about their intentions. We have *Hamlet*, but we do not have any statement of Shakespeare's intention concerning this or any other play. It might be argued that we can deduce Shakespeare's intention from the play itself, but to argue that we should study the play in the light of Shakespeare's intention, and that we can know his intention by studying the play, is to argue in a circle. We can say that Shakespeare must have intended to write a tragedy (if he intended to write a comedy he failed), but we cannot go much further in talking about his intention.

Even if an author has gone on record expressing an intention, we may think twice before accepting the statement as decisive. The author may be speaking facetiously, deceptively, mistakenly, or unconvincingly. For instance, Thomas Mann said, probably sincerely and accurately, that he wrote one of his novels merely in order to entertain his family—but we may nevertheless take the book seriously and find it profound.

What Characterizes a Sound Interpretation?

Even the most vigorous advocates of the idea that meaning is indeterminate do not believe that all interpretations are equally significant. Rather, they believe that an interpretive essay is offered against a background of ideas, shared by essayist and reader, as to what constitutes a *persuasive argument*. Thus, an essay (even if it is characterized as "interpretive free play" or "creative engagement") will have to be

- coherent,
- plausible, and
- rhetorically effective.

The *presentation*—the rhetoric—as well as the interpretation is significant. This means (to repeat a point made in Chapter 3) that the essayist cannot merely set down random expressions of feeling or unsupported opinions. The essayist must, on the contrary, convincingly *argue* a thesis—must point to evidence so that the reader will not only know what the essayist believes but will also understand why he or she believes it.

There are lots of ways of making sense (and even more ways of making nonsense), but one important way of helping readers to see things from your point of view is to do your best to face all of the complexities of the work. Put it this way: Some interpretations strike a reader as better than others because they are *more inclusive*, that is, because they *account for more of the details of the work*. The less satisfactory interpretations leave a reader pointing to some aspects of the work—to some parts of the whole—and saying, "Yes, but your explanation doesn't take account of . . ."

This does not mean, of course, that a reader must feel that a persuasive interpretation says the last word about the work. We always realize that the work—if we value it highly—is richer than the discussion; but, again, for us to value an interpretation we must find the interpretation plausible and inclusive.

Interpretation often depends not only on making connections among various elements of the work (for instance, among the characters in a story or among the images in a poem), and among the work and other works by the author, but also on making connections between the particular work and a cultural context. The cultural context usually includes other writers and specific works of literature, since a given literary work participates in a tradition. That is, if a work looks toward life, it also looks toward other works. A sonnet is about human experience, but it is also part of a tradition of sonnet writing. The more works of literature you are familiar with, the better equipped you are to interpret any particular work. Here is the way Robert Frost put it, in the preface to *Aforesaid,* a book of verse published in 1954:

> A poem is best read in the light of all the other poems ever written. We read A the better to read B (we have to start somewhere; we may get very little out of A). We read B the better to read C, C the better to read D, D the better to go back and get something more out of A. Progress is not the aim, but circulation. The thing is to get among the poems where they hold each other apart in their places as the stars do.

An Example: Interpreting Pat Mora's "Immigrants"

Let's think about interpreting a short poem by a contemporary poet, Pat Mora.

Immigrants

wrap their babies in the American flag,
feed them mashed hot dogs and apple pie,
name them Bill and Daisy,
buy them blonde dolls that blink
blue eyes or a football and tiny cleats
before the baby can even walk,
speak to them in thick English,
    hallo, babee, hallo.
whisper in Spanish or Polish
when the babies sleep, whisper
in a dark parent bed, that dark
parent fear, "Will they like
our boy, our girl, our fine american
boy, our fine american girl?"

[1986]

Perhaps most readers will agree that the poem expresses or dramatizes a desire, attributed to "immigrants," that their child grow up in an Anglo mode. (Mora is not saying that *all* immigrants have this desire; she has simply invented one speaker who says such-and-such. *We* may say that Mora says all immigrants have this desire, but that is our interpretation.) For this reason the parents call their children Bill and Daisy (rather than, say, José and Juanita) and give them blonde dolls and a football (rather than dark-haired dolls and a soccer ball). Up to this point, the parents seem a bit silly in their mimicking of Anglo ways. But the second part of the poem gives the reader a more interior view of the parents, brings out the fear and hope and worried concern that lies behind the behavior: Some unspecified "they" may not "like / our boy, our girl." Who are "they"? Most readers probably will agree that "they" refers to native-born citizens, especially the blond, blue-eyed "all-American" Anglo types that until recently constituted the establishment in the United States.

We can raise further questions about the interpretation of the poem.

- Exactly what does the poet mean when she says that immigrants "wrap their babies in the American flag"? Are we to take this literally?
- If not, how are we to take it?
- And why in the last two lines is the word "american" not capitalized? Is Mora imitating the non-native speaker's uncertain grasp of English punctuation? (But if so, why does Mora capitalize "American" in the first line and "Spanish" and "Polish" later in the poem?) Or is she perhaps implying some mild reservation about becoming 100 percent American, some suggestion that in changing from Spanish or Polish to "american" there is some sort of loss?

A reader might seek out Mora and ask her why she didn't capitalize "american" in the last line, but Mora might not be willing to answer, or she might not give a straight answer, or she might say that she doesn't really know why—it just seemed right when she wrote the poem. Most authors do in fact take this last approach. When they are working as writers, they work by a kind of instinct, a kind of feel for the material. Later they can look critically at their writing, but that's another sort of experience.

To return to our basic question: What characterizes a good interpretation? The short answer is, *Evidence,* and especially evidence that seems to cover all relevant issues. In an essay it is not enough merely to assert an interpretation. Your readers don't expect you to make an airtight case, but because you are trying to help readers to understand a work—to see a work the way you do—you are obliged to

- offer reasonable supporting evidence, and
- take account of what might be set forth as counterevidence to your thesis.

Of course your essay may originate in an intuition or an emotional response, a sense that the work is about such-and-such, but this intuition or emotion must then be examined, and it must stand a test of reasonableness. (It is usually a good idea to jot down in a journal your first responses to a work, and in later entries to reflect on them.) It is not enough in an essay merely to set forth your response. Your readers will expect you to *demonstrate* that the response is something that they can to a large degree share. They may not be convinced that the interpretation is right or true, but they must feel that the interpretation is plausible and in accord with the details of the work, rather than, say, highly eccentric and irreconcilable with some details.

This book includes several case studies, some of which include essays by critics advancing interpretations. When you read these interpretations, think about *why* you find some interpretations more convincing than others.

Thinking Critically about Responses to Literature

Usually you will begin with a strong *response* to your reading—interest, boredom, bafflement, annoyance, shock, pleasure, or whatever. Then, if you are going to think critically about the work, you will go on to *examine* your response in order to understand it, or to deepen it, or to change it.

How can you change a response? Critical thinking involves seeing an issue from all sides, to as great a degree as possible. As you know, in ordinary language *to criticize* usually means to find fault, but in literary studies the term does not have a negative connotation. Rather, it means "to examine carefully." (The word *criticism* comes from a Greek verb meaning "to distinguish," "to decide," "to judge.") Nevertheless, in one sense the term *critical thinking* does approach the usual meaning, since critical thinking requires you to take a skeptical view of your response. You will, so to speak, argue with yourself, seeing if your response can stand up to doubts.

Let's say that you have found a story implausible. Question yourself:

- Exactly what is implausible in it?
- Is implausibility always a fault?
- If so, exactly why?

Your answers may deepen your response. Usually, you will find supporting evidence for your response, but in your effort to distinguish and to decide and to judge, try also (if only as an exercise) to find counterevidence. See what can be said against your position. (The best lawyers, it is said, prepare two cases—their own, and the other side's.) As you consider the counterevidence you will sometimes find that it requires you to adjust your thesis. You may even find yourself developing an entirely different response. That's fine, though of course the paper that you ultimately hand in should clearly argue a thesis.

In short, **critical thinking** means examining or exploring one's own responses, by questioning and testing them. Critical thinking is not so much a skill (though it does involve the ability to understand a text) as it is a *habit of mind,* or, rather, several habits, including

- Open-mindedness
- Intellectual curiosity
- Willingness to work

It may involve, too, a willingness to discuss the issues with others and to do research, a topic that will be treated separately in Chapter 9, on writing a research paper.

Two Interpretations by Students

Robert Frost, "Stopping by Woods on a Snowy Evening"

Read Frost's "Stopping by Woods on a Snowy Evening," and then read the first interpretation, written by a first-year student. This interpretation is followed by a discussion that is devoted chiefly to two questions:

- What is the essayist's thesis?
- Does the essayist offer convincing evidence to support the thesis?

A second essay by another first-year student, offering a different interpretation of the poem, provides further material for you to analyze critically.

Robert Frost

Robert Frost (1874–1963) was born in California. After his father's death in 1885 Frost's mother brought the family to New England, where she taught in high schools in Massachusetts and New Hampshire. Frost studied for part of one term at Dartmouth College in New Hampshire, then did various jobs (including teaching), and from 1897 to 1899 was enrolled as a special student at Harvard. He then farmed in New Hampshire, published a few poems in local newspapers, left the farm and taught again, and in 1912 left for England, where he hoped to achieve more popular success as a writer. By 1915 he had won a considerable reputation, and he returned to the United States, settling on a farm in New Hampshire and cultivating the image of the country-wise farmer-poet. In fact he was well read in the classics, the Bible, and English and American literature.

Stopping by Woods on a Snowy Evening

Whose woods these are I think I know.
His house is in the village though;
He will not see me stopping here
To watch his woods fill up with snow.

My little horse must think it queer
To stop without a farmhouse near
Between the woods and frozen lake
The darkest evening of the year.

He gives his harness bells a shake
To ask if there is some mistake.
The only other sound's the sweep
Of easy wind and downy flake.

The woods are lovely, dark and deep.
But I have promises to keep,
And miles to go before I sleep,
And miles to go before I sleep.

[1923]

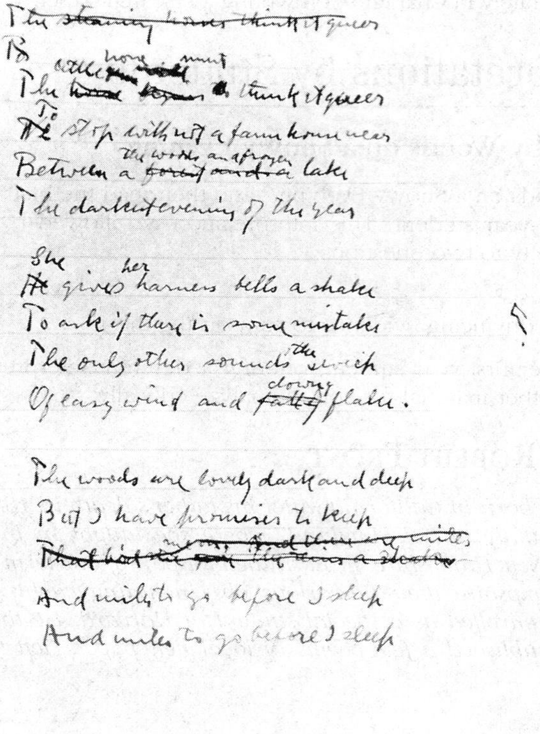

Manuscript version of Frost's "Stopping by Woods on a Snowy Evening." The first part is lost. (Courtesy of the Jones Library, Inc., Amherst, Mass.)

Sample Essay by a Student: "Stopping by Woods—and Going On"

MacDonald 1

Darrel MacDonald

Professor Conner

English 1102

4 October 2009

Stopping by Woods—and Going On

Robert Frost's "Stopping by Woods on a Snowy Evening" is about what the title says it is. It is also about something more than the title says.

When I say it is about what the title says, I mean that the poem really does give us the thoughts of a person who pauses (that is, a person who is "stopping") by woods on a snowy evening. (This person probably is a man, since Robert Frost wrote the poem and nothing in the poem clearly indicates that the speaker is not a man. But, and this point will be important, the speaker perhaps feels that he is not a very masculine man. As we will see, the word "queer" appears in the poem, and, also, the speaker uses the word "lovely," which sounds more like the word a woman would use than a man.) In line 3 the speaker says he is "stopping here," and it is clear that "here" is by woods, since "woods" is mentioned not only in the title but also in the first line of the poem, and again in the second stanza, and still again in the last stanza. It is equally clear that, as the title says, there is snow, and that the time is evening. The speaker mentions "snow" and "downy flake," and he says this is "The darkest evening of the year."

But in what sense is the poem about *more* than the title? The title does not tell us anything about the man who is "stopping by woods," but the poem—the man's meditation—tells us a lot about him. In the first stanza he reveals that he is uneasy at the thought that the owner of the woods may see him stopping by the woods. Maybe he is uneasy because he is trespassing, but the poem does not actually say that he has illegally entered someone else's property. More likely, he feels uneasy, almost ashamed, of watching the "woods fill up with snow." That is, he would not want anyone to see that he actually is enjoying a beautiful aspect of nature and is not hurrying about whatever his real business is in thrifty Yankee style.

The second stanza gives more evidence that he feels guilty about enjoying beauty. He feels so guilty that he even thinks the horse thinks there is something odd about him. In fact, he says that the horse thinks he is "queer," which of course may just mean "odd," but also (as is shown by *The American Heritage Dictionary*) it can mean "gay," "homosexual." A real man, he sort of suggests, would not spend time looking at snow in the woods.

So far, then, the speaker in two ways has indicated that he feels insecure, though perhaps he does not realize that he has given himself away. First, he expresses uneasiness that someone might see him watching the woods fill up with snow. Second, he expresses uneasiness when he suggests that even the horse

MacDonald 3

thinks he is strange, maybe even "queer" or unmanly, or at least unbusinesslike. And so in the last stanza, even though he finds the woods beautiful, he decides *not* to stop and to see the woods fill up with snow. And his description of the woods as "lovely"—a woman's word—sounds as though he may be something less than a he-man. He seems to feel ashamed of himself for enjoying the sight of the snowy woods and for seeing them as "lovely," and so he tells himself that he has spent enough time looking at the woods and that he must go on about his business. In fact, he tells himself *twice* that he has business to attend to. Why? Perhaps he is insisting too much. Just as we saw that he was excessively nervous in the first stanza, afraid that someone might see him trespassing and enjoying the beautiful spectacle, now at the end he is again afraid that someone might see him loitering, and so he very firmly, using repetition as a form of emphasis, tries to reassure himself that he is not too much attracted by beauty and is a man of business who keeps his promises.

Frost gives us, then, a man who indeed is seen "stopping by woods on a snowy evening," but a man who, afraid of what society will think of him, is also afraid to "stop" long enough to fully enjoy the sight that attracts him, because he is driven by a sense that he may be seen to be trespassing and also may be thought to be unmanly. So after only a brief stop in the woods he forces himself to go on, a victim (though he probably doesn't know it) of the work ethic and of an over-simple idea of manliness.

[New page]

MacDonald 4

Work Cited

Frost, Robert. "Stopping by Woods on a Snowy Evening." *Literature for Composition*. Ed. Sylvan Barnet, William Burto, and William E. Cain. 9th ed. New York: Longman, 2010. 188. Print.

Let's examine this essay briefly.

The **title** is interesting. It gives the reader a good idea of which literary work will be discussed ("Stopping by Woods") and it arouses interest, in this case by a sort of wordplay ("Stopping . . . Going On"). A title of this sort is preferable to a title that merely announces the topic, such as "An Analysis of Frost's 'Stopping by Woods'" or "On a Poem by Robert Frost."

The **opening paragraph** helpfully names the exact topic (Robert Frost's poem) and arouses interest by asserting that the poem is about something more than its title. The writer's thesis presumably will be a fairly specific assertion concerning what else the poem is "about."

The **body of the essay,** beginning with the second paragraph, begins to develop the thesis. (The **thesis** perhaps can be summarized thus: "The speaker, insecure of his masculinity, feels ashamed that he responds with pleasure to the sight of the snowy woods.") The writer's evidence in the second paragraph is that the word "queer" (a word sometimes used of homosexuals) appears, and that the word "lovely" is "more like the word a woman would use than a man." Readers of MacDonald's essay may at this point be unconvinced by this evidence, but probably they suspend judgment. In any case, he has offered what he considers to be evidence in support of his thesis.

The next paragraph dwells on what is said to be the speaker's uneasiness, and the following paragraph returns to the word "queer," which, MacDonald correctly says, can mean "gay, homosexual." The question of course is whether *here,* in this poem, the word has this meaning. Do we agree with MacDonald's assertion, in the last sentence of this paragraph, that Frost is suggesting that "A real man . . . wouldn't spend time looking at snow in the woods"?

Clearly this is the way MacDonald takes the poem—but is his response to these lines reasonable? After all, what Frost says is this: "My little horse must think it queer / To stop without a farmhouse near." Is it reasonable to see a reference to homosexuality (rather than merely to oddness) in *this* use of the word "queer"? Hasn't MacDonald offered a response that, so to speak, is private? It is *his* response—but are we likely to share it, to agree that we see it in Frost's poem?

The next paragraph, amplifying the point that the speaker is insecure, offers as evidence the argument that "lovely" is more often a woman's word than a man's. Probably most readers will agree on this point, though many or all might deny that only a gay man would use the word "lovely." And what do you think of MacDonald's assertions that the speaker of the poem "was excessively nervous in the first stanza" and is now "afraid that someone might see him loitering"? In your opinion, does the text lend much support to MacDonald's view?

The **concluding paragraph** effectively reasserts and clarifies MacDonald's thesis, saying that the speaker hesitates to stop and enjoy the woods because "he is driven by a sense that he may be seen to be trespassing and also may be thought to be unmanly."

The big questions, then, are these:

- Is the thesis *argued* rather than merely asserted, and
- Is it argued *convincingly?*

Or, to put it another way,

- Is the evidence adequate?

MacDonald certainly does argue (offer reasons) rather than merely assert, but does he offer enough evidence to make you think that his response is one that you can share? Has he helped you to enjoy the poem by seeing things that you may not have noticed—or has he said things that, however interesting, seem to you not to be in close contact with the poem as you see it?

Here is another interpretation of the same poem.

Sample Essay by a Student: "'Stopping by Woods on a Snowy Evening' as a Short Story"

Fong 1

Sara Fong

Professor Patel

English 102

3 December 2006

"Stopping by Woods on a Snowy Evening" as a Short Story

Robert Frost's "Stopping by Woods on a Snowy Evening" can be read as a poem about a man who pauses to observe the beauty of nature, and it can also be read as a poem about a man with a death wish, a man who seems to long to give himself up completely to nature and thus escape his responsibilities as a citizen. Much depends, apparently, on what a reader wants to emphasize. For instance, a reader can emphasize especially appealing lines about the beauty of nature: "The only other sound's the sweep / Of easy wind and downy flake," and "The woods are lovely, dark and deep." On the other hand, a reader can emphasize lines that show the speaker is fully aware of the responsibilities that most of us agree we have. For instance, at the very start of the poem he recognizes that the woods are not his but are owned by someone else, and at the end of the poem he recognizes that he has "promises to keep" and that before he sleeps (dies?) he must accomplish many things (go for "miles").

Does a reader have to choose between these two interpretations? I do not think so; to the contrary, I think it makes sense to read the poem as a kind of very short story, with a character whose developing thoughts make up a plot with four stages. In the first stage, the central figure is an ordinary person with rather ordinary thoughts. His very first thought is of the owner of the woods. He knows who the owner is, and since the owner lives in the village, the poet feels safe in trespassing, or at least in watching the woods "fill up with snow." Then, very subtly, the poet begins to tell us that although this seems to be an ordinary person thinking ordinary thoughts, he is a somewhat special person in a special situation. First of all, the horse thinks something is strange. He shakes his bells, wondering why the driver doesn't keep moving, as presumably ordinary drivers would. Second, we are told that this is "The darkest evening of the year." Frost could simply have said that the evening is dark, but he goes out of his way to make the evening a special evening.

Fong 3

We are now through with the first ten lines, and only six lines remain, yet in these six lines the story goes through two additional phases. The first three of these lines ("The only other sound's the sweep / Of easy wind and downy flake" and "The woods are lovely, dark and deep") are probably the most beautiful lines, in the sense that they are the ones that make us say, "I wish I were there," or "I'd love to experience this." We feel that the poet has moved from the ordinary thoughts of the first stanza, about such businesslike things as who owns the woods and where the owner's house is, to less materialistic thoughts, thoughts about the beauty of the nonhuman world of nature. And now, with the three final lines, we get the fourth stage of the story, the return to the ordinary world of people, the world of "promises." But this world that we get at the end is not exactly the same as the world we got at the beginning. The world at the beginning of the poem is a world of property (who owns the woods, and where the house is), but the world at the end of the poem is a world of unspecified and rather mysterious responsibilities ("promises to keep," "miles to go before I sleep"). It is almost as though the poet's experience of the beauty of nature—a beauty that for a moment made him forget the world of property—has in fact served to sharpen his sense that human beings have responsibilities. He clearly sees that "The woods are lovely, dark and deep," and then he says (I add the italics), "*But* I have promises to keep." The "but" would be logical if after saying that the woods are lovely, dark and deep, he had said something like "But in the daylight they look different," or "But one can freeze to death in them." The logic of what Frost says, however, is not at all clear: "The woods are lovely, dark and deep, / But I have promises to keep." What is the logical connection? We have to supply one, something like "but, *because we are human beings we have responsibilities;* we can refresh ourselves by perceiving the beauties of nature, and we can even for a moment get so caught up that we seem to enter an enchanted forest ('the woods are lovely, dark and deep'), but we cannot forget our responsibilities."

My point is not that Frost ends with an important moral, and it is also not that we have to choose between saying it is a poem about nature or a poem about a man with a death wish. Rather, my point is that the poem takes us through several stages and that, although the poem begins and ends with the speaker in the woods, the speaker has undergone mental experiences—has, we might say, gone through a plot with a conflict (the appeal of the snowy woods versus the call to return to the human world). It is not a matter of good versus evil and of one side winning. Frost in no way suggests that it is wrong to feel the beauty of nature—even to the momentary exclusion of all other thoughts. But the poem is certainly not simply a praise of the beauty of nature. Frost shows us, in this mini-story or mini-drama, one character who sees the woods as property, then sees them as a place of almost overwhelming beauty, and then

Fong 5

(maybe refreshed by this experience) rejoins the world of chores and responsibilities.

[New page]

Fong 6

Work Cited

Frost, Robert. "Stopping by Woods on a Snowy Evening." *Literature for Composition*. Ed. Sylvan Barnet, William Burto, and William E. Cain. 9th ed. New York: Longman, 2010. 188. Print.

Joining the Conversation: Critical Thinking and Writing

1. What is the thesis of the essay?
2. Does the essayist offer convincing evidence to support the thesis?
3. Do you consider the essay to be well written, poorly written, or something in between? On what evidence do you base your opinion?

Your Turn: Poems for Interpretation

ROBERT FROST

For a biographical note on Robert Frost, see page 98. For additional poems by Frost, see pages 99, 103, 178, and 187.

Mending Wall

Something there is that doesn't love a wall,
That sends the frozen-ground-swell under it,
And spills the upper boulders in the sun;
And makes gaps even two can pass abreast.
The work of hunters is another thing:
I have come after them and made repair

Where they have left not one stone on a stone,
But they would have the rabbit out of hiding,
To please the yelping dogs. The gaps I mean,
No one has seen them made or heard them made,
But at spring mending-time we find them there.
I let my neighbor know beyond the hill;
And on a day we meet to walk the line
And set the wall between us once again.
We keep the wall between us as we go.
To each the boulders that have fallen to each.
And some are loaves and some so nearly balls
We have to use a spell to make them balance:
"Stay where you are until our backs are turned!"
We wear our fingers rough with handling them.
Oh, just another kind of outdoor game,
One on a side. It comes to little more:
There where it is we do not need the wall:
He is all pine and I am apple orchard.
My apple trees will never get across
And eat the cones under his pines, I tell him.
He only says, "Good fences make good neighbors."
Spring is the mischief in me, and I wonder
If I could put a notion in his head:
"*Why* do they make good neighbors? Isn't it
Where there are cows? But here there are no cows.
Before I built a wall I'd ask to know
What I was walling in or walling out,
And to whom I was like to give offense.
Something there is that doesn't love a wall,
That wants it down." I could say "Elves" to him,
But it's not elves exactly, and I'd rather
He said it for himself. I see him there
Bringing a stone grasped firmly by the top
In each hand, like an old-stone savage armed.
He moves in darkness as it seems to me,
Not of woods only and the shade of trees.
He will not go behind his father's saying,
And he likes having thought of it so well
He says again, "Good fences make good neighbors."

[1914]

Joining the Conversation: Critical Thinking and Writing

1. The poem includes a scene, or action, in which the speaker and a neighbor are engaged. Briefly summarize the scene. What indicates that the scene has been enacted before and will be again?
2. Compare and contrast the speaker and the neighbor.

3. Notice that the speaker, not the neighbor, initiates the business of repairing the wall (line 12). Why do you think he does this?

4. Both the speaker and the neighbor repeat themselves; they each make one point twice in identical language. What do they say? And why does Frost allow the neighbor to have the last word?

5. "Something there is that doesn't love a wall" adds up to "Something doesn't love a wall." Or does it? Within the context of the poem, what is the difference between the two statements?

6. Write an essay of 500 words, telling of an experience in which you came to conclude that "good fences make good neighbors." Or tell of an experience that led you to conclude that fences (they can be figurative fences, of course) are "like to give offense" (see lines 32–34).

T. S. Eliot

Thomas Stearns Eliot (1888–1965) was born into a New England family that had moved to St. Louis. He attended a private school in Massachusetts, then graduated from Harvard and did further study in literature and philosophy in France, Germany, and England. In 1914 he began working for Lloyd's Bank in London, and three years later he published his first book of poems (it included "Prufrock"). In 1925 he joined a publishing firm, and in 1927 he became a British citizen and a member of the Church of England. Much of his later poetry, unlike "The Love Song of J. Alfred Prufrock," is highly religious. In 1948 Eliot received the Nobel Prize in Literature.

The Love Song of J. Alfred Prufrock

S'io credesse che mia risposta fosse
A persona che mai tornasse al mondo,
Questa fiamma staria senza piu scosse.
Ma perciocche giammai di questo fondo
Non torno vivo alcun, s'i' odo il vero,
*Senza tema d'infama ti rispondo.**

Let us go then, you and I,
When the evening is spread out against the sky
Like a patient etherized upon a table;
Let us go, through certain half-deserted streets,
The muttering retreats
Of restless nights in one-night cheap hotels
And sawdust restaurants with oyster-shells:
Streets that follow like a tedious argument

*In Dante's *Inferno* 27.61–66, a damned soul who had sought absolution before committing a crime addresses Dante, thinking that his words will never reach the Earth: "If I believed that my answer were to a person who could ever return to the world, this flame would no longer quiver. But because no one ever returned from this depth, if what I hear is true without fear of infamy, I answer you."

Of insidious intent
To lead you to an overwhelming question . . .
Oh, do not ask, "What is it?"
Let us go and make our visit.

In the room the women come and go
Talking of Michelangelo.

The yellow fog that rubs its back upon the window-panes,
The yellow smoke that rubs its muzzle on the window-panes
Licked its tongue into the corners of the evening,
Lingered upon the pools that stand in drains,
Let fall upon its back the soot that falls from chimneys,
Slipped by the terrace, made a sudden leap,
And seeing that it was a soft October night,
Curled once about the house, and fell asleep.

And indeed there will be time
For the yellow smoke that slides along the street,
Rubbing its back upon the window-panes;
There will be time, there will be time
To prepare a face to meet the faces that you meet;
There will be time to murder and create,
And time for all the works and days° of hands
That lift and drop a question on your plate;
Time for you and time for me,
And time yet for a hundred indecisions,
And for a hundred visions and revisions,
Before the taking of a toast and tea.
In the room the women come and go
Talking of Michelangelo.

And indeed there will be time
To wonder, "Do I dare?" and, "Do I dare?"
Time to turn back and descend the stair,
With a bald spot in the middle of my hair—
[They will say: "How his hair is growing thin!"]
My morning coat, my collar mounting firmly to the chin,
My necktie rich and modest, but asserted by a simple pin—
[They will say: "But how his arms and legs are thin!"]
Do I dare
Disturb the universe?
In a minute there is time
For decisions and revisions which a minute will reverse.

For I have known them all already, known them all:—
Have known the evenings, mornings, afternoons,
I have measured out my life with coffee spoons;
I know the voices dying with a dying fall°
Beneath the music from a farther room.
So how should I presume?

29 works and days "Works and Days" is the title of a poem on farm life by Hesiod (eighth century B.C.E.). **52 dying fall** This line echoes Shakespeare's *Twelfth Night* 1.1.4.

And I have known the eyes already, known them all—
The eyes that fix you in a formulated phrase,
And when I am formulated, sprawling on a pin,
When I am pinned and wriggling on the wall,
Then how should I begin
To spit out all the butt-ends of my days and ways?
  And how should I presume?

And I have known the arms already, known them all—
Arms that are braceleted and white and bare
[But in the lamplight, downed with light brown hair!]

Is it perfume from a dress
That makes me so digress?
Arms that lie along a table, or wrap about a shawl.
  And should I then presume?
  And how should I begin?

. . .

Shall I say, I have gone at dusk through narrow streets
And watched the smoke that rises from the pipes
Of lonely men in shirt-sleeves, leaning out of windows? . . .

I should have been a pair of ragged claws
Scuttling across the floors of silent seas.

. . .

And the afternoon, the evening, sleeps so peacefully!
Smoothed by long fingers,
Asleep . . . tired . . . or it malingers,
Stretched on the floor, here beside you and me.
Should I, after tea and cakes and ices,
Have the strength to force the moment to its crisis?
But though I have wept and fasted, wept and prayed,
Though I have seen my head [grown slightly bald]
  brought in upon a platter,°
I am no prophet—and here's no great matter;
And I have seen the moment of my greatness flicker,
And I have seen the eternal Footman hold my coat, and snicker,
And in short, I was afraid.

And would it have been worth it, after all,
After the cups, the marmalade, the tea,
Among the porcelain, among some talk of you and me,
Would it have been worth while,
To have bitten off the matter with a smile,
To have squeezed the universe into a ball°
To roll it toward some overwhelming question,
To say: "I am Lazarus,° come from the dead,
Come back to tell you all, I shall tell you all"—

81–83 But . . . platter These lines allude to John the Baptist (see Matthew 14:1–11). **92 To have . . . ball** This line echoes lines 41–42 of Marvell's "To His Coy Mistress" (see page 726). **94 Lazarus** See Luke 16 and John 11.

If one, settling a pillow by her head,
    Should say: "That is not what I meant at all.
    That is not it, at all."

And would it have been worth it, after all,
Would it have been worth while,
After the sunsets and the dooryards and the sprinkled streets,
After the novels, after the teacups, after the skirts that trail along the floor—
And this, and so much more?—
It is impossible to say just what I mean!
But as if a magic lantern threw the nerves in patterns on a screen:
Would it have been worth while
If one, settling a pillow or throwing off a shawl,
And turning toward the window, should say:
    "That is not it at all,
    That is not what I meant at all."

No! I am not Prince Hamlet, nor was meant to be;
Am an attendant lord, one that will do
To swell a progress, start a scene or two,
Advise the prince; no doubt, an easy tool,
Deferential, glad to be of use,
Politic, cautious, and meticulous;
Full of high sentence,° but a bit obtuse;°
At times, indeed, almost ridiculous—
Almost, at times, the Fool.
I grow old . . . I grow old . . .
I shall wear the bottoms of my trousers rolled.

Shall I part my hair behind? Do I dare to eat a peach?
I shall wear white flannel trousers, and walk upon the beach.
I have heard the mermaids singing, each to each.
I do not think that they will sing to me.

I have seen them riding seaward on the waves
Combing the white hair of the waves blown back
When the wind blows the water white and black.

We have lingered in the chambers of the sea
By sea-girls wreathed with seaweed red and brown
Till human voices wake us, and we drown.

[1910–11]

117 full of high sentence See Chaucer's description of the Clerk of Oxford in the *Canterbury Tales*. **112–117 Am . . . obtuse** These lines allude to Polonius and perhaps other figures in *Hamlet*.

Joining the Conversation: Critical Thinking and Writing

1. How does the speaker's name help to characterize him? What suggestions—of class, race, personality—do you find in it? Does the title of this poem strike you as ironic? If so, how or why?

2. What qualities of big-city life are suggested in the poem? How are these qualities linked to the speaker's mood? What other details of the setting—the weather, the time of day—express or reflect his mood? What images do you find especially striking?

3. The speaker's thoughts are represented in a stream-of-consciousness monologue, that is, in what appears to be an unedited flow of thought. Nevertheless, they reveal a story. What is the story?

4. In a paragraph, characterize Prufrock as he might be characterized by one of the women in the poem, and then, in a paragraph or two, offer your own characterization of him.

5. Consider the possibility that the "you" whom Prufrock is addressing is not a listener but is one aspect of Prufrock, and the "I" is another. Given this possibility, in a paragraph characterize the "you," and in another paragraph characterize the "I."

6. Prufrock has gone to a therapist, a psychiatrist, or a member of the clergy for help. Write a 500-word transcript of their session.

JOHN KEATS

John Keats (1795–1821), son of a London stablekeeper, was taken out of school when he was 15 and apprenticed to a surgeon and apothecary. In 1816 he was licensed to practice as an apothecary-surgeon, but he almost immediately abandoned medicine and decided to make a career as a poet. His progress was amazing: he published books of poems—to mixed reviews—in 1817, 1818, and 1820, before dying of tuberculosis at the age of 25. Today he is esteemed as one of England's greatest poets.

Ode on a Grecian Urn

I

Thou still unravished bride of quietness,
  Thou foster-child of silence and slow time,
Sylvan historian, who canst thus express
  A flowery tale more sweetly than our rhyme:
What leaf-fringed legend haunts about thy shape
  Of deities or mortals, or of both,
    In Tempe or the dales of Arcady?
  What men or gods are these? What maidens loth?
What mad pursuit? What struggle to escape?
  What pipes and timbrels? What wild ecstasy?

II

Heard melodies are sweet, but those unheard
  Are sweeter; therefore, ye soft pipes, play on;
Not to the sensual° ear, but, more endeared,
  Pipe to the spirit ditties of no tone:

13 sensual sensuous.

Fair youth, beneath the trees, thou canst not leave
  Thy song, nor ever can those trees be bare;
    Bold Lover, never, never canst thou kiss,
Though winning near the goal—yet, do not grieve;
    She cannot fade, though thou hast not thy bliss,
  For ever wilt thou love, and she be fair!

III

Ah, happy, happy boughs! that cannot shed
  Your leaves, nor ever bid the Spring adieu;
And, happy melodist, unwearied,
  For ever piping songs for ever new;
More happy love! more happy, happy love!
  For ever warm and still to be enjoyed,
    For ever panting, and for ever young;
All breathing human passion far above,
  That leaves a heart high-sorrowful and cloyed,
    A burning forehead, and a parching tongue.

IV

Who are these coming to the sacrifice?
  To what green altar, O mysterious priest,
Lead'st thou that heifer lowing at the skies,
  And all her silken flanks with garlands drest?
What little town by river or sea shore,
  Or mountain-built with peaceful citadel,
    Is emptied of this folk, this pious morn?
And, little town, thy streets for evermore
  Will silent be; and not a soul to tell
    Why thou art desolate can e'er return.

V

O Attic shape! Fair attitude! with brede°
  Of marble men and maidens overwrought,
With forest branches and the trodden weed;
  Thou, silent form, dost tease us out of thought
As doth eternity: Cold Pastoral!
When old age shall this generation waste,
    Thou shalt remain, in midst of other woe
  Than ours, a friend to man, to whom thou say'st,
"Beauty is truth, truth beauty,"—that is all
  Ye know on earth, and all ye need to know.

[1820]

41 brede design.

Joining the Conversation: Critical Thinking and Writing

1. In the first stanza Keats calls the urn an "unravished bride of quietness," a "foster-child of silence and slow time," and a "Sylvan historian." Paraphrase each of these terms.
2. How much sense does it make to say that "Heard melodies are sweet, but those unheard / Are sweeter" (lines 11–12)?
3. In the second stanza Keats says that the youth will forever sing, the trees will forever have their foliage, and the woman will forever be beautiful. But what words in the stanza suggest that this scene is not entirely happy? Where else in the poem is it suggested that there are painful aspects to the images on the urn?
4. What arguments can you offer to support the view that "Beauty is truth, truth beauty"?
5. There is much uncertainty about whether everything in the last two lines should be enclosed within quotation marks, or only "Beauty is truth, truth beauty." If only these five words from line 49 should be enclosed within quotation marks, does the speaker address the rest of line 49 and the whole of line 50 to the urn, or to the reader of the poem?

THOMAS HARDY

Thomas Hardy (1840–1928) was born in Dorset, England, the son of a stonemason. Despite great obstacles he studied the classics and architecture, and in 1862 he moved to London to study and practice as an architect. Ill health forced him to return to Dorset, where he continued to work as an architect and to write. Best known for his novels, Hardy ceased writing fiction after the hostile reception of Jude the Obscure *in 1896 and turned to writing lyric poetry.*

The Man He Killed

"Had he and I but met
By some old ancient inn,
We should have sat us down to wet
Right many a nipperkin!°

"But ranged as infantry,
And staring face to face,
I shot at him as he at me,
And killed him in his place.

"I shot him dead because—
Because he was my foe,
Just so: my foe of course he was;
That's clear enough; although

4 nipperkin cup.

"He thought he'd 'list, perhaps,
Off-hand—just as I—
Was out of work—had sold his traps°—
No other reason why.

"Yes; quaint and curious war is!
You shoot a fellow down
You'd treat if met where any bar is,
Or help to half-a-crown."

[1902]

15 traps personal belongings.

Joining the Conversation: Critical Thinking and Writing

1. What do we learn about the speaker's life before he enlisted in the infantry? How does his diction characterize him?
2. What is the effect of the series of monosyllables in lines 7 and 8?
3. Consider the punctuation of the third and fourth stanzas. Why are the heavy, frequent pauses appropriate? What question is the speaker trying to answer?
4. In the last stanza, what attitudes toward war does the speaker express? What, from the evidence of this poem, would you infer Hardy's attitude toward war to be? Cite evidence to support your argument.

GWENDOLYN BROOKS

*Gwendolyn Brooks (1917–2000) was born in Topeka, Kansas, but was raised in Chicago's South Side, where she spent most of her life. Brooks taught in several colleges and universities and she wrote a novel (*Maud Martha*, 1953) and a memoir (*Report from Part One*, 1972), but she is best known as a poet. In 1950, when she won the Pulitzer Prize for Poetry, she became the first African American writer to win a Pulitzer Prize. In 1985 Brooks became consultant in Poetry to the Library of Congress. Brooks died in Chicago in December, 2000.*

The Mother

Abortions will not let you forget.
You remember the children you got that you did not get,
The damp small pulps with a little or with no hair,
The singers and workers that never handled the air.
You will never neglect or beat
Them, or silence or buy with a sweet.
You will never wind up the sucking-thumb
of scuttle off ghosts that come.
You will never leave them, controlling your luscious sign,
Return for a snack of them, with gobbling mother-eye.

I have heard in the voices of the wind the voices of my dim killed children.
I have contracted. I have eased
My dim dears at the breasts they could never suck.
I have said, Sweets, if I sinned, if I seized
Your luck
And your lives form your unfinished reach,
If I stole your births and your names,
Your straight baby tears and your games,
Your stilted or lovely loves, your tumults, your marriages, aches, and your
deaths,
If I poisoned the beginnings of your breaths,
Believe that even in my deliberateness I was not deliberate,
Though why should I whine,
Whine that the crime was other than mine?—
Since anyhow you are dead
Or rather, or instead,
You were never made,
But that too, I am afraid,
Is faulty: oh, what shall I say, how is the truth to be said?
You were born, you had body, you died.
It is just that you never giggled or planned or cried.

Believe me, I loved you all.
Believe me, I knew you, though faintly, and I loved, I loved you
All.

[1945]

Joining the Conversation: Critical Thinking and Writing

1. The first ten lines sound like a chant. What gives them that quality? What makes them nonetheless serious?
2. In lines 20–23 the mother attempts to deny the "crime" but cannot. What is her reasoning here?
3. Do you find the last lines convincing? Explain.

Stories for Interpretation

EDGAR ALLAN POE

For a biographical note on Edgar Allan Poe, see page 157.

The Masque of the Red Death

The "Red Death" had long devastated the country. No pestilence had ever been so fatal, or so hideous. Blood was its Avatar[1] and its seal—the redness and the horror of blood. There were sharp pains, and sudden dizziness, and then profuse bleeding at the pores, with dissolution. The scarlet stains upon the body and especially

[1]**Avatar** incarnation of Hindu deity; embodiment of something.

upon the face of the victim, were the pest ban which shut him out from the aid and from the sympathy of his fellow-men. And the whole seizure, progress and termination of the disease, were the incidents of half an hour.

But the Prince Prospero was happy and dauntless and sagacious. When his dominions were half depopulated, he summoned to his presence a thousand hale and light-hearted friends from among the knights and dames of his court, and with these retired to the deep seclusion of one of his castellated abbeys. This was an extensive and magnificent structure, the creation of the prince's own eccentric yet august taste. A strong and lofty wall girdled it in. This wall had gates of iron. The courtiers, having entered, brought furnaces and massy hammers and welded the bolts. They resolved to leave means neither of ingress nor egress to the sudden impulses of despair or of frenzy from within. The abbey was amply provisioned. With such precautions the courtiers might bid defiance to contagion. The external world could take care of itself. In the meantime it was folly to grieve, or to think. The prince had provided all the appliances of pleasure. There were buffoons, there were improvisatori, there were ballet-dancers, there were musicians, there was Beauty, there was wine. All these and security were within. Without was the "Red Death."

It was toward the close of the fifth or sixth month of his seclusion, and while the pestilence raged most furiously abroad, that the Prince Prospero entertained his thousand friends at a masked ball of the most unusual magnificence.

It was a voluptuous scene, that masquerade. But first let me tell of the rooms in which it was held. There were seven—an imperial suite. In many palaces, however, such suites form a long and straight vista, while the folding doors slide back nearly to the walls on either hand, so that the view of the whole extent is scarcely impeded. Here the case was very different; as might have been expected from the duke's love of the *bizarre*. The apartments were so irregularly disposed that the vision embraced but little more than one at a time. There was a sharp turn at every twenty or thirty yards, and at each turn a novel effect. To the right and left, in the middle of each wall, a tall and narrow Gothic window looked out upon a closed corridor which pursued the windings of the suite. These windows were of stained glass whose color varied in accordance with the prevailing hue of the decorations of the chamber into which it opened. That at the eastern extremity was hung, for example, in blue—and vividly blue went its windows. The second chamber was purple in its ornaments and tapestries, and here the panes were purple. The third was green throughout, and so were the casements. The fourth was furnished and lighted with orange—the fifth with white—the sixth with violet. The seventh apartment was closely shrouded in black velvet tapestries that hung all over the ceiling and down the walls, falling in heavy folds upon a carpet of the same material and hue. But in this chamber only, the color of the windows failed to correspond with the decorations. The panes here were scarlet—a deep blood color. Now in no one of the seven apartments was there any lamp or candelabrum, amid the profusion of golden ornaments that lay scattered to and fro or depended from the roof. There was no light of any kind emanating from lamp or candle within the suite of chambers. But in the corridors that followed the suite, there stood, opposite to each window, a heavy tripod, bearing a brazier of fire that projected its rays through the tinted glass and so glaringly illumined the room. And thus were produced a multitude of gaudy and fantastic appearances. But in the western or black chamber the effect of the fire-light that streamed upon the dark hangings through the blood-tinted panes was ghastly in the extreme, and produced so wild a look upon the countenances of those who entered, that there were few of the company bold enough to set foot within its precincts at all.

5 It was in this apartment, also, that there stood against the western wall, a gigantic clock of ebony. Its pendulum swung to and fro with a dull, heavy, monotonous clang; and when the minute-hand made the circuit of the face, and the hour was to be stricken, there came from the brazen lungs of the clock a sound which was clear and loud and deep and exceedingly musical, but of so peculiar a note and emphasis that, at each lapse of an hour, the musicians of the orchestra were constrained to pause, momentarily, in their performance, to hearken to the sound; and a brief disconcert of the whole gay company; and, while the chimes of the clock yet rang, it was observed that the giddiest grew pale, and the more aged and sedate passed their hands over their brows as if in confused reverie or meditation. But when the echoes had fully ceased, a light laughter at once pervaded the assembly; the musicians looked at each other and smiled as if at their own nervousness and folly, and made whispering vows, each to the other, that the next chiming of the clock should produce in them no similar emotion: and then, after the lapse of sixty minutes (which embrace three thousand and six hundred seconds of the Time that flies) there came yet another chiming of the clock, and then were the same disconcert and tremulousness and meditation as before.

But, in spite of these things, it was a gay and magnificent revel. The tastes of the duke were peculiar. He had a fine eye for colors and effects. He disregarded the *decora* of mere fashion. His plans were bold and fiery, and his conceptions glowed with barbaric lustre. There are some who would have thought him mad. His followers felt that he was not. It was necessary to hear and see and touch him to be *sure* that he was not.

He had directed, in great part, the moveable embellishments of the seven chambers, upon occasion of this great *fête;* and it was his own guiding taste which had given character to the masqueraders. Be sure they were grotesque. There were much glare and glitter and piquancy and phantasm—much of what has been since seen in *Hernani.*[2] There were arabesque figures with unsuited limbs and appointments. There were delirious fancies such as the madman fashions. There were much of the beautiful, much of the wanton, much of the *bizarre,* something of the terrible, and not a little of that which might have excited disgust. To and fro in the seven chambers there stalked, in fact, a multitude of dreams. And these—the dreams—writhed in and about, taking hue from the rooms, and causing the wild music of the orchestra to seem as the echo of their steps. And, anon, there strikes the ebony clock which stands in the hall of the velvet. And then, for a moment, all is still, and all is silent save the voice of the clock. The dreams are stiff-frozen as they stand. But the echoes of the chime die away—they have endured but an instant—and a light, half-subdued laughter floats after them as they depart. And now again the music swells, and the dreams live, and writhe to and fro more merrily than ever, taking hue from the many-tinted windows through which stream the rays from the tripods. But to the chamber which lies most westwardly of the seven, there are now none of the maskers who venture: for the night is waning away; and there flows a ruddier light through the blood-colored panes; and the blackness of the sable drapery appalls: and to him whose foot falls upon the sable carpet, there comes from the near clock of ebony a muffled peal more solemnly emphatic than any which reaches *their* ears who indulge in the more remote gaieties of the other apartments.

[2]***Hernani*** a play by Victor Hugo (1802–1885, presented in 1830).

But these other apartments were densely crowded, and in them beat feverishly the heart of life. And the revel went whirlingly on, until at length there commenced the sounding of midnight upon the clock. And then the music ceased, as I have told: and the evolutions of the waltzers were quieted: and there was an uneasy cessation of all things as before. But now there were twelve strokes to be sounded by the bell of the clock: and thus it happened, perhaps, that more of thought crept, with more of time, into the meditations of the thoughtful among those who revelled. And thus, too, it happened, perhaps, that before the last echoes of the last chime had utterly sunk into silence, there were many individuals in the crowd who had found leisure to become aware of the presence of a masked figure which had arrested the attention of no single individual before. And the rumor of this new presence having spread itself whisperingly around, there arose at length from the whole company a buzz, finally of terror, of horror and of disgust.

In an assembly of phantasms such as I have painted, it may well be supposed that no ordinary appearance could have excited such sensation. In truth the masquerade license of the night was nearly unlimited: but the figure in question had out-Heroded Herod[3], and gone beyond the bounds of even the prince's indefinite decorum. There are chords in the hearts of the most reckless which cannot be touched without emotion. Even with the utterly lost, to whom life and death are equally jests, there are matters of which no jest can be made. The whole company, indeed, seemed now deeply to feel that in the costume and bearing of the stranger neither wit nor propriety existed. The figure was tall and gaunt, and shrouded from head to foot in the habiliments of the grave. The mask which concealed the visage was made so nearly to resemble the countenance of a stiffened corpse that the closest scrutiny must have had difficulty in detecting the cheat. And yet all this might have been endured, if not approved, by the mad revellers around. But the mummer had gone so far as to assume the type of the Red Death. His vesture was dabbled in *blood*—and his broad brow, with all the features of the face, was besprinkled with the scarlet horror.

10 When the eyes of Prince Prospero fell upon this spectral image (which with a slow and solemn movement, as if more fully to sustain its *rôle,* stalked to and fro among the waltzers) he was seen to be convulsed, in the first moment with a strong shudder either of terror or distaste; but, in the next, his brow reddened with rage.

"Who dares?" he demanded hoarsely of the courtiers who stood near him—"who dares insult us with this blasphemous mockery? Seize him and unmask him—that we may know whom we have to hang at sunrise, from the battlements!"

It was in the eastern or blue chamber in which stood the Prince Prospero as he uttered these words. They rang throughout the seven rooms loudly and clearly—for the prince was a bold and robust man, and the music had become hushed at the waving of his hand.

It was in the blue room where stood the prince, with a group of pale courtiers by his side. At first, as he spoke, there was a slight rushing movement of this group in the direction of the intruder, who at the moment was also near at hand, and now, with deliberate and stately step, made closer approach to the speaker. But from a certain nameless awe with which the mad assumptions of the mummer had inspired the whole party, there were found none who put forth hand to seize him; so that, unimpeded, he passed within a yard of the prince's person; and, while the vast assembly, as if with one impulse, shrank from the

[3]**Herod** for the story of Herod, Salome, and John the Baptist, see Mark 6:14-29.

centers of the rooms to the walls, he made his way uninterruptedly, but with the same solemn and measured step which had distinguished him from the first, through the blue chamber to the purple—through the purple to the green—through the green to the orange—through this again to the white—and even thence to the violet, ere a decided movement had been made to arrest him. It was then, however, that the Prince Prospero, maddening with rage and the shame of his own momentary cowardice, rushed hurriedly through the six chambers, while none followed him on account of a deadly terror that had seized upon all. He bore aloft a drawn dagger, and had approached, in rapid impetuosity, to within three or four feet of the retreating figure, when the latter, having attained the extremity of the velvet apartment, turned suddenly and confronted his pursuer. There was a sharp cry—and the dagger dropped gleaming upon the sable carpet, upon which, instantly afterwards, fell prostrate in death the Prince Prospero. Then, summoning the wild courage of despair, a throng of the revellers at once threw themselves into the black apartment, and, seizing the mummer, whose tall figure stood erect and motionless within the shadow of the ebony clock, gasped in unutterable horror at finding the grave-cerements and corpse-like mask which they handled with so violent a rudeness, untenanted by any tangible form.

And now was acknowledged the presence of the Red Death. He had come like a thief in the night. And one by one dropped the revellers in the blood-bedewed halls of their revel, and died each in the despairing posture of his fall. And the life of the ebony clock went out with that of the last of the gay. And the flames of the tripods expired. And Darkness and Decay and the Red Death held illimitable dominion over all.

[1842]

Joining the Conversation: Critical Thinking and Writing

1. Why, in perilous circumstances, do the Prince and his followers engage in merrymaking?
2. Does Poe indicate, or even faintly imply, disapproval of Prince Prospero for shutting out the suffering external world?
3. Why does the striking of the clock cause such nervousness?
4. If the prince is concerned with forgetting the presence of death, why is the seventh room black, with "blood-colored panes"?
5. In a paragraph describe the prince's emotion(s) when he sees the mysterious masked figure, and orders him to be seized. In your paragraph you may occasionally quote a word or phrase from the text, but most of the writing should be your own.
6. Do you think Poe meant anything by specifying seven rooms, of which the first is the easternmost, and the seventh is the westernmost? What do you make out of the statement that the arrangement, unlike that of some other palaces, prevents a person from seeing from one end to the other?
7. In 500 words discuss and evaluate the idea that "The Masque of the Red Death" suggests that life itself is sickness.

WILLA CATHER

Willa Cather (1873–1947) was born in Gore, Virginia, but when she was nine her family moved to rural Nebraska. While an undergraduate at the University of Nebraska she published short stories and served as a drama critic for the Nebraska State Journal. *From 1895 to 1906 she lived in Pittsburgh, working first as a journalist and later as a teacher. In 1906 she went to New York to work for* McClure's Magazine; *in 1911 she left the magazine in order to devote all of her time to writing. "Paul's Case," written in 1904, is a relatively early work. Her most widely known novels were written later:* O Pioneers *(1913),* The Song of the Lark *(1915),* My Antonia *(1918),* A Lost Lady *(1923), and* Death Comes for the Archbishop *(1927).*

Paul's Case

It was Paul's afternoon to appear before the faculty of the Pittsburgh High School to account for his various misdemeanors. He had been suspended a week ago, and his father had called at the Principal's office and confessed his perplexity about his son. Paul entered the faculty room suave and smiling. His clothes were a trifle outgrown and the tan velvet on the collar of his open overcoat was frayed and worn; but for all that there was something of the dandy about him, and he wore an opal pin in his neatly knotted black four-in-hand, and a red carnation in his buttonhole. This latter adornment the faculty somehow felt was not properly significant of the contrite spirit befitting a boy under the ban of suspension.

Paul was tall for his age and very thin, with high, cramped shoulders and a narrow chest. His eyes were remarkable for a certain hysterical brilliancy and he continually used them in a conscious, theatrical sort of way, peculiarly offensive in a boy. The pupils were abnormally large, as though he were addicted to belladonna, but there was a glassy glitter about them which that drug does not produce.

When questioned by the Principal as to why he was there, Paul stated, politely enough, that he wanted to come back to school. This was a lie, but Paul was quite accustomed to lying; found it, indeed, indispensable for overcoming friction. His teachers were asked to state their respective charges against him, which they did with such a rancor and aggrievedness as evinced that this was not a usual case. Disorder and impertinence were among the offenses named, yet each of his instructors felt that it was scarcely possible to put into words the real cause of the trouble, which lay in a sort of hysterically defiant manner of the boy's; in the contempt which they all knew he felt for them, and which he seemingly made not the least effort to conceal. Once, when he had been making a synopsis of a paragraph at the blackboard, his English teacher had stepped to his side and attempted to guide his hand. Paul had started back with a shudder and thrust his hands violently behind him. The astonished woman could scarcely have been more hurt and embarrassed had he struck at her. The insult was so involuntary and definitely personal as to be unforgettable. In one way and another, he had made all his teachers, men and women alike, conscious of the same feeling of physical aversion. In one class he habitually sat with his hand shading his eyes; in another he always looked out of the window during the recitation; in another he made a running commentary on the lecture, with humorous intention.

His teachers felt this afternoon that his whole attitude was symbolized by his shrug and his flippantly red carnation flower, and they fell upon him without mercy, his English teacher leading the pack. He stood through it smiling, his pale lips parted over his white teeth. (His lips were continually twitching, and he had a habit of raising his eyebrows that was contemptuous and irritating to the last degree.) Older boys than Paul had broken down and shed tears under that baptism of fire, but his set smile did not once desert him, and his only sign of discomfort was the nervous trembling of the fingers that toyed with the buttons of his overcoat, and an occasional jerking of the other hand that held his hat. Paul was always smiling, always glancing about him, seeming to feel that people might be watching him and trying to detect something. This conscious expression, since it was as far as possible from boyish mirthfulness, was usually attributed to insolence or "smartness."

5 As the inquisition proceeded, one of his instructors repeated an impertinent remark of the boy's, and the Principal asked him whether he thought that a courteous speech to have made a woman. Paul shrugged his shoulders slightly and his eyebrows twitched.

"I don't know," he replied. "I didn't mean to be polite or impolite, either. I guess it's a sort of way I have of saying things regardless."

The Principal, who was a sympathetic man, asked him whether he didn't think that a way it would be well to get rid of. Paul grinned and said he guessed so. When he was told that he could go, he bowed gracefully and went out. His bow was but a repetition of the scandalous red carnation.

His teachers were in despair, and his drawing master voiced the feeling of them all when he declared there was something about the boy which none of them understood. He added: "I don't really believe that smile of his comes altogether from insolence; there's something sort of haunted about it. The boy is not strong, for one thing. I happen to know that he was born in Colorado, only a few months before his mother died out there of a long illness. There is something wrong about the fellow."

The drawing master had come to realize that, in looking at Paul, one saw only his white teeth and the forced animation of his eyes. One warm afternoon the boy had gone to sleep at his drawing-board, and his master had noted with amazement what a white, blue-veined face it was; drawn and wrinkled like an old man's about the eyes, the lips twitching even in his sleep, and stiff with a nervous tension that drew them back from his teeth.

10 His teachers left the building dissatisfied and unhappy; humiliated to have felt so vindictive toward a mere boy, to have uttered this feeling in cutting terms, and to have set each other on, as it were, in the gruesome game of intemperate reproach. Some of them remembered having seen a miserable street cat set at bay by a ring of tormentors.

As for Paul, he ran down the hill whistling the Soldiers' Chorus from *Faust*[1] looking wildly behind him now and then to see whether some of his teachers were not there to writhe under his light-heartedness. As it was now late in the afternoon and Paul was on duty that evening as usher at Carnegie Hall, he decided that he would not go home to supper. When he reached the concert hall the doors were not yet open and, as it was chilly outside, he decided to go up into the picture gallery—always deserted at this hour—where there were some of Raffaelli's gay studies of Paris streets and an airy blue Venetian scene or two that always exhilarated him. He was delighted to find no one in the gallery but the old guard, who sat in one corner, a newspaper on his knee, a black patch over one eye and the other closed. Paul possessed himself of the place and walked confidently up and down, whistling under his breath. After a while he sat down before

[1]***Faust*** an opera by Charles Gounod (1818–1893).

a blue Rico and lost himself. When he bethought him to look at his watch, it was after seven o'clock, and he rose with a start and ran downstairs, making a face at Augustus, peering out from the cast-room, and an evil gesture at the Venus of Milo as he passed her on the stairway.

When Paul reached the ushers' dressing-room half-a-dozen boys were there already, and he began excitedly to tumble into his uniform. It was one of the few that at all approached fitting, and Paul thought it very becoming—though he knew that the tight, straight coat accentuated his narrow chest, about which he was exceedingly sensitive. He was always considerably excited while he dressed, twanging all over to the tuning of the strings and the preliminary flourishes of the horns in the music-room; but tonight he seemed quite beside himself, and he teased and plagued the boys until, telling him that he was crazy, they put him down on the floor and sat on him.

Somewhat calmed by his suppression, Paul dashed out to the front of the house to seat the early comers. He was a model usher; gracious and smiling he ran up and down the aisles; nothing was too much trouble for him; he carried messages and brought programmes as though it were his greatest pleasure in life, and all the people in his section thought him a charming boy, feeling that he remembered and admired them. As the house filled, he grew more and more vivacious and animated, and the color came to his cheeks and lips. It was very much as though this were a great reception and Paul were the host. Just as the musicians came out to take their places, his English teacher arrived with checks for the seats which a prominent manufacturer had taken for the season. She betrayed some embarrassment when she handed Paul the tickets, and a *hauteur* which subsequently made her feel very foolish. Paul was startled for a moment, and had the feeling of wanting to put her out; what business had she here among all these fine people and gay colors? He looked her over and decided that she was not appropriately dressed and must be a fool to sit downstairs in such togs. The tickets had probably been sent her out of kindness, he reflected as he put down a seat for her, and she had about as much right to sit there as he had.

When the symphony began Paul sank into one of the rear seats with a long sigh of relief, and lost himself as he had done before the Rico. It was not that symphonies, as such, meant anything in particular to Paul, but the first sigh of the instruments seemed to free some hilarious and potent spirit within him; something that struggled there like the Genius in the bottle found by the Arab fisherman. He felt a sudden zest of life; the lights danced before his eyes and the concert hall blazed into unimaginable splendor. When the soprano soloist came on, Paul forgot even the nastiness of his teacher's being there and gave himself up to the peculiar stimulus such personages always had for him. The soloist chanced to be a German woman, by no means in her first youth, and the mother of many children; but she wore an elaborate gown and a tiara, and above all she had that indefinable air of achievement, that world-shine upon her, which, in Paul's eyes, made her a veritable queen of Romance.

15 After a concert was over Paul was always irritable and wretched until he got to sleep, and tonight he was even more than usually restless. He had the feeling of not being able to let down, of its being impossible to give up this delicious excitement which was the only thing that could be called living at all. During the last number he withdrew and, after hastily changing his clothes in the dressing-room, slipped out to the side door where the soprano's carriage stood. Here he began pacing rapidly up and down the walk, waiting to see her come out.

Over yonder the Schenley, in its vacant stretch, loomed big and square through the fine rain, the windows of its twelve stories glowing like those of a lighted cardboard house under a Christmas tree. All the actors and singers of the better class stayed there when they were in the city, and a number of the big manufacturers of the place lived there in the winter. Paul had often hung about the hotel, watching the people go in and out, longing to enter and leave schoolmasters and dull care behind him forever.

At last the singer came out, accompanied by the conductor, who helped her into her carriage and closed the door with a cordial *auf wiedersehen*[2] which set Paul to wondering whether she were not an old sweetheart of his. Paul followed the carriage over to the hotel, walking so rapidly as not to be far from the entrance when the singer alighted and disappeared behind the swinging glass doors that were opened by a negro in a tall hat and a long coat. In the moment that the door was ajar it seemed to Paul that he, too, entered. He seemed to feel himself go after her up the steps, into the warm, lighted building, into an exotic, a tropical world of shiny, glistening surfaces and basking ease. He reflected upon the mysterious dishes that were brought into the dining-room, the green bottles in buckets of ice, as he had seen them in the supper party pictures of the *Sunday World* supplement. A quick gust of wind brought the rain down with sudden vehemence, and Paul was startled to find that he was still outside in the slush of the gravel driveway; that his boots were letting in the water and his scanty overcoat was clinging wet about him; that the lights in front of the concert hall were out, and that the rain was driving in sheets between him and the orange glow of the windows above him. There it was, what he wanted—tangibly before him, like the fairy world of a Christmas pantomime, but mocking spirits stood guard at the doors, and, as the rain beat in his face, Paul wondered whether he were destined always to shiver in the black night outside, looking up at it.

He turned and walked reluctantly toward the car tracks. The end had to come sometime; his father in his night-clothes at the top of the stairs, explanations that did not explain, hastily improvised fictions that were forever tripping him up, his upstairs room and its horrible yellow wall-paper, the creaking bureau with the greasy plush collar-box, and over his painted wooden bed the pictures of George Washington and John Calvin, and the framed motto, "Feed my Lambs," which had been worked in red worsted by his mother.

Half an hour later, Paul alighted from his car and went slowly down one of the side streets off the main thoroughfare. It was a highly respectable street, where all the houses were exactly alike, and where businessmen of moderate means begot and reared large families of children, all of whom went to Sabbath-school and learned the shorter catechism, and were interested in arithmetic; all of whom were as exactly alike as their homes, and of a piece with the monotony in which they lived. Paul never went up Cordelia Street without a shudder of loathing. His home was next to the house of the Cumberland minister. He approached it tonight with the nerveless sense of defeat, the hopeless feeling of sinking back forever into ugliness and commonness that he had always had when he came home. The moment he turned into Cordelia Street he felt the waters close above his head. After each of these orgies of living, he experienced all the physical depression which follows a debauch; the loathing of respectable beds, of common food, of a house penetrated by kitchen odors; a shuddering repulsion for the flavorless, colorless mass of everyday existence; a morbid desire for cool things and soft lights and fresh flowers.

[2]***auf wiedersehen*** farewell.

20 The nearer he approached the house, the more absolutely unequal Paul felt to the sight of it all; his ugly sleeping chamber; the cold bathroom with the grimy zinc tub, the cracked mirror, the dripping spigots; his father, at the top of the stairs, his hairy legs sticking out from his night-shirt, his feet thrust into carpet slippers. He was so much later than usual that there would certainly be inquiries and reproaches. Paul stopped short before the door. He felt that he could not be accosted by his father tonight; that he could not toss again on that miserable bed. He would not go in. He would tell his father that he had no car fare, and it was raining so hard he had gone home with one of the boys and stayed all night.

Meanwhile, he was wet and cold. He went around to the back of the house and tried one of the basement windows, found it open, raised it cautiously, and scrambled down the cellar wall to the floor. There he stood, holding his breath, terrified by the noise he had made, but the floor above him was silent, and there was no creak on the stairs. He found a soap-box, and carried it over to the soft ring of light that streamed from the furnace door, and sat down. He was horribly afraid of rats, so he did not try to sleep, but sat looking distrustfully at the dark, still terrified lest he might have awakened his father. In such reactions, after one of the experiences which made days and nights out of the dreary blanks of the calendar, when his senses were deadened, Paul's head was always singularly clear. Suppose his father had heard him getting in at the window and had come down and shot him for a burglar? Then, again, suppose his father had come down, pistol in hand, and he had cried out in time to save himself, and his father had been horrified to think how nearly he had killed him? Then, again, suppose a day should come when his father would remember that night, and wish there had been no warning cry to stay his hand? With this last supposition Paul entertained himself until daybreak.

The following Sunday was fine; the sodden November chill was broken by the last flash of autumnal summer. In the morning Paul had to go to church and Sabbath-school, as always. On seasonable Sunday afternoons the burghers of Cordelia Street always sat out on their front "stoops," and talked to their neighbors on the next stoop, or called to those across the street in neighborly fashion. The men usually sat on gay cushions placed upon the steps that led down to the sidewalk, while the women, in their Sunday "waists," sat in rockers on the cramped porches, pretending to be greatly at their ease. The children played in the streets; there were so many of them that the place resembled the recreation grounds of a kindergarten. The men on the steps—all in their shirt sleeves, their vests unbuttoned—sat with their legs well apart, their stomachs comfortably protruding, and talked of the prices of things, or told anecdotes of the sagacity of their various chiefs and overlords. They occasionally looked over the multitude of squabbling children, listened affectionately to their high-pitched, nasal voices, smiling to see their own proclivities reproduced in their offspring, and interspersed their legends of the iron kings with remarks about their sons' progress at school, their grades in arithmetic, and the amounts they had saved in their toy banks.

On this last Sunday of November, Paul sat all the afternoon on the lowest step of his "stoop," staring into the street, while his sisters, in their rockers, were talking to the minister's daughters next door about how many shirt-waists they had made in the last week, and how many waffles some one had eaten at the last church supper. When the weather was warm, and his father was in a particularly jovial frame of mind, the girls made lemonade, which was always brought out in a red-glass pitcher, ornamented with forget-me-nots in blue enamel. This the girls thought very fine, and the neighbors always joked about the suspicious color of the pitcher.

Today Paul's father sat on the top step, talking to a young man who shifted a restless baby from knee to knee. He happened to be the young man who was daily held up to Paul as a model, and after whom it was his father's dearest hope that he would pattern. This young man was of a ruddy complexion, with a compressed, red mouth, and faded, near-sighted eyes, over which he wore thick spectacles, with gold bows that curved about his ears. He was clerk to one of the magnates of a great steel corporation, and was looked upon in Cordelia Street as a young man with a future. There was a story that, some five years ago—he was now barely twenty-six—he had been a trifle dissipated but in order to curb his appetites and save the loss of time and strength that a sowing of wild oats might have entailed, he had taken his chief's advice, oft reiterated to his employees, and at twenty-one had married the first woman whom he could persuade to share his fortunes. She happened to be an angular school-mistress, much older than he, who also wore thick glasses, and who had now borne him four children, all near-sighted, like herself.

The young man was relating how his chief, now cruising in the Mediterranean, kept in touch with all the details of the business, arranging his office hours on his yacht just as though he were at home, and "knocking off work enough to keep two stenographers busy." His father told, in turn, the plan his corporation was considering, of putting in an electric railway plant at Cairo. Paul snapped his teeth; he had an awful apprehension that they might spoil it all before he got there. Yet he rather liked to hear these legends of the iron kings, that were told and retold on Sundays and holidays; these stories of palaces in Venice, yachts on the Mediterranean, and high play at Monte Carlo appealed to his fancy, and he was interested in the triumphs of these cash boys who had become famous, though he had no mind for the cash-boy stage.

After supper was over, and he had helped to dry the dishes, Paul nervously asked his father whether he could go to George's to get some help in his geometry, and still more nervously asked for car fare. This latter request he had to repeat, as his father, on principle, did not like to hear requests for money, whether much or little. He asked Paul whether he could not go to some boy who lived nearer, and told him that he ought not to leave his school work until Sunday; but he gave him the dime. He was not a poor man, but he had a worthy ambition to come up in the world. His only reason for allowing Paul to usher was, that he thought a boy ought to be earning a little.

Paul bounded upstairs, scrubbed the greasy odor of the dish-water from his hands with the ill-smelling soap he hated, and then shook over his fingers a few drops of violet water from the bottle he kept hidden in his drawer. He left the house with his geometry conspicuously under his arm, and the moment he got out of Cordelia Street and boarded a downtown car, he shook off the lethargy of two deadening days, and began to live again.

The leading juvenile of the permanent stock company which played at one of the downtown theatres was an acquaintance of Paul's, and the boy had been invited to drop in at the Sunday-night rehearsals whenever he could. For more than a year Paul had spent every available moment loitering about Charley Edwards's dressing-room. He had won a place among Edwards's following not only because the young actor, who could not afford to employ a dresser, often found him useful, but because he recognized in Paul something akin to what churchmen term "vocation."

It was at the theatre and at Carnegie Hall that Paul really lived; the rest was but a sleep and a forgetting. This was Paul's fairy tale, and it had for him all the allurement of a secret love. The moment he inhaled the gassy, painty, dusty odor behind the scenes, he breathed like a prisoner set free, and felt within him the possibility of doing or saying splendid, brilliant, poetic things. The moment the cracked orchestra beat out the overture from *Martha,* or jerked at the serenade from *Rigoletto,* all stupid and ugly things slid from him, and his senses were deliciously, yet delicately fired.

Perhaps it was because, in Paul's world, the natural nearly always wore the guise of ugliness, that a certain element of artificiality seemed to him necessary in beauty. Perhaps it was because his experience of life elsewhere was so full of Sabbath-school picnics, petty economies, wholesome advice as to how to succeed in life, and the unescapable odors of cooking, that he found this existence so alluring, these smartly-clad men and women so attractive, that he was so moved by these starry apple orchards that bloomed perennially under the lime-light.

It would be difficult to put it strongly enough how convincingly the stage entrance of that theatre was for Paul the actual portal of Romance. Certainly none of the company ever suspected it, least of all Charley Edwards. It was very like the old stories that used to float about London of fabulously rich Jews, who had subterranean halls there, with palms, and fountains, and soft lamps and richly apparelled women who never saw the disenchanting light of London day. So, in the midst of that smoke-palled city, enamored of figures and grimy toil, Paul had his secret temple, his wishing carpet, his bit of blue-and-white Mediterranean shore bathed in perpetual sunshine.

Several of Paul's teachers had a theory that his imagination had been perverted by garish fiction, but the truth was that he scarcely ever read at all. The books at home were not such as would either tempt or corrupt a youthful mind, and as for reading the novels that some of his friends urged upon him—well, he got what he wanted much more quickly from music; any sort of music, from an orchestra to a barrel organ. He needed only the spark, the indescribable thrill that made his imagination master of his senses, and he could make plots and pictures enough of his own. It was equally true that he was not stage struck—not, at any rate, in the usual acceptation of that expression. He had no desire to become an actor, any more than he had to become a musician. He felt no necessity to do any of these things; what he wanted was to see, to be in the atmosphere, float on the wave of it, to be carried out, blue league after blue league, away from everything.

After a night behind the scenes, Paul found the school-room more than ever repulsive; the bare floors and naked walls; the prosy men who never wore frock coats, or violets in their buttonholes; the women with their dull gowns, shrill voices, and pitiful seriousness about prepositions that govern the dative. He could not bear to have the other pupils think, for a moment, that he took these people seriously; he must convey to them that he considered it all trivial, and was there only by way of a jest, anyway. He had autographed pictures of all the members of the stock company which he showed his classmates, telling them the most incredible stories of his familiarity with these people, of his acquaintance with the soloists who came to Carnegie Hall, his suppers with them and the flowers he sent them. When these stories lost their effect, and his audience grew listless, he became desperate and would bid all the boys good-bye, announcing that he was going to travel for a while; going to Naples, to Venice, to Egypt. Then, next Monday, he would slip back, conscious and nervously smiling; his sister was ill, and he should have to defer his voyage until spring.

Matters went steadily worse with Paul at school. In the itch to let his instructors know how heartily he despised them and their homilies, and how thoroughly he was appreciated elsewhere, he mentioned once or twice that he had no time to fool with theorems; adding—with a twitch of the eyebrows and a touch of that nervous bravado which so perplexed them—that he was helping the people down at the stock company; they were old friends of his.

35 The upshot of the matter was that the Principal went to Paul's father, and Paul was taken out of school and put to work. The manager at Carnegie Hall was told to get another usher in his stead; the door-keeper at the theatre was warned not to admit him to the house; and Charley Edwards remorsefully promised the boy's father not to see him again.

The members of the stock company were vastly amused when some of Paul's stories reached them—especially the women. They were hard working women, most of them supporting indigent husbands or brothers, and they laughed rather bitterly at having stirred the boy to such fervid and florid inventions. They agreed with the faculty and with his father that Paul's was a bad case.

The east-bound train was ploughing through a January snow-storm; the dull dawn was beginning to show grey when the engine whistled a mile out of Newark. Paul started up from the seat where he had lain curled in uneasy slumber, rubbed the breath-misted window glass with his hand, and peered out. The snow was whirling in curling eddies above the white bottom lands, and the drifts lay already deep in the fields and along the fences, while here and there the long dead grass and dried weed stalks protruded black above it. Lights shone from the scattered houses, and a gang of laborers who stood beside the track waved their lanterns.

Paul had slept very little, and he felt grimy and uncomfortable. He had made the all-night journey in a day coach, partly because he was ashamed, dressed as he was, to go into a Pullman, and partly because he was afraid of being seen there by some Pittsburgh businessman, who might have noticed him in Denny & Carson's office. When the whistle awoke him, he clutched quickly at his breast pocket, glancing about him with an uncertain smile. But the little, clay-bespattered Italians were still sleeping, the slatternly women across the aisle were in open-mouthed oblivion, and even the crumby, crying babies were for the nonce stilled. Paul settled back to struggle with his impatience as best as he could.

When he arrived at the Jersey City station, he hurried through his breakfast, manifestly ill at ease and keeping a sharp eye about him. After he reached the Twenty-third Street station, he consulted a cabman, and had himself driven to a men's furnishing establishment that was just opening for the day. He spent upward of two hours there, buying with endless reconsidering and great care. His new street suit he put on in the fitting-room; the frock coat and dress clothes he had bundled into the cab with his linen. Then he drove to a hatter's and a shoe house. His next errand was at Tiffany's, where he selected his silver and a new scarf-pin. He would not wait to have his silver marked, he said. Lastly, he stopped at a trunk shop on Broadway, and had his purchases packed into various traveling bags.

40 It was a little after one-o'clock when he drove up to the Waldorf, and after settling with the cabman, went into the office. He registered from Washington; said his mother and father had been abroad, and that he had come down to await the arrival of their steamer. He told his story plausibly and had no trouble, since he volunteered to pay for them in advance, in engaging his rooms; a sleeping-room, sitting-room and bath.

Not once, but a hundred times Paul had planned this entry into New York. He had gone over every detail of it with Charley Edwards, and in his scrap book at home there were pages of description about New York hotels, cut from the Sunday papers. When he was shown to his sitting-room on the eighth floor, he saw at a glance that everything was as it should be; there was but one detail in his mental picture that the place did not realize, so he rang for the bell boy and sent him down for flowers. He moved about nervously until the boy returned, putting away his new linen and fingering it delightedly as he did so. When the flowers came, he put them hastily into water, and then tumbled into a hot bath. Presently he came out of his white bath-room, resplendent in his new silk underwear, and playing with the tassels of his red robe. The snow was whirling so fiercely outside his windows that he could scarcely see across the street, but within the air was deliciously soft and fragrant. He put the violets and jonquils on the taboret beside the couch, and threw himself down, with a long sigh, covering himself with a Roman blanket. He was thoroughly tired; he had been in such haste, he had stood up to such a strain, covered so much ground in the last twenty-four hours, that he wanted to think how it had all come about. Lulled by the sound of the wind, the warm air, and the cool fragrance of the flowers, he sank into deep, drowsy retrospection.

It had been wonderfully simple; when they had shut him out of the theatre and concert hall, when they had taken away his bone, the whole thing was virtually determined. The rest was a mere matter of opportunity. The only thing that at all surprised him was his own courage—for he realized well enough that he had always been tormented by fear, a sort of apprehensive dread that, of late years, as the meshes of the lies he had told closed about him, had been pulling the muscles of his body tighter and tighter. Until now, he could not remember the time when he had not been dreading something. Even when he was a little boy, it was always there—behind him, or before, or on either side. There had always been the shadowed corner, the dark place into which he dared not look, but from which something seemed always to be watching him—and Paul had done things that were not pretty to watch, he knew.

But now he had a curious sense of relief, as though he had at last thrown down the gauntlet to the thing in the corner.

Yet it was but a day since he had been sulking in the traces; but yesterday afternoon that he had been sent to the bank with Denny & Carson's deposit, as usual—but this time he was instructed to leave the book to be balanced. There was above two thousand dollars in checks, and nearly a thousand in the bank notes which he had taken from the book and quietly transferred to his pocket. At the bank he had made out a new deposit slip. His nerves had been steady enough to permit of his returning to the office, where he had finished his work and asked for a full day's holiday tomorrow, Saturday, giving a perfectly reasonable pretext. The bank book, he knew, would not be returned before Monday or Tuesday, and his father would be out of town for the next week. From the time he slipped the bank notes into his pocket until he boarded the night train for New York, he had not known a moment's hesitation. It was not the first time Paul had steered through treacherous waters.

How astonishingly easy it had all been; here he was, the thing done; and this time there would be no awakening, no figure at the top of the stairs. He watched the snow flakes whirling by his window until he fell asleep.

When he awoke, it was three o'clock in the afternoon. He bounded up with a start; half of one of his precious days gone already! He spent more than an hour in dressing, watching every stage of his toilet carefully in the mirror. Everything was quite perfect; he was exactly the kind of boy he had always wanted to be.

When he went downstairs, Paul took a carriage and drove up Fifth Avenue toward the Park. The snow had somewhat abated; carriages and tradesmen's wagons were hurrying soundlessly to and fro in the winter twilight; boys in woollen mufflers were shovelling off the doorsteps; the avenue stages made fine spots of color against the white street. Here and there on the corners were stands, with whole flower gardens blooming under glass cases, against the sides of which the snow flakes stuck and melted; violets, roses, carnations, lilies of the valley—somewhat vastly more lovely and alluring that they blossomed thus unnaturally in the snow. The Park itself was a wonderful stage winterpiece.

When he returned, the pause of the twilight had ceased, and the tune of the streets had changed. The snow was falling faster, lights streamed from the hotels that reared their dozen stories fearlessly up into the storm, defying the raging Atlantic winds. A long, black stream of carriages poured down the avenue, intersected here and there by other streams, tending horizontally. There were a score of cabs about the entrance of his hotel, and his driver had to wait. Boys in livery were running in and out of the awning stretched across the sidewalk, up and down the red velvet carpet laid from the door to the street. Above, about, within it all was the rumble and roar, the hurry and toss of thousands of human beings as hot for pleasure as himself, and on every side of him towered the glaring affirmation of the omnipotence of wealth.

The boy set his teeth and drew his shoulders together in a spasm of realization: the plot of all dramas, the text of all romances, the nerve-stuff of all sensations was whirling about him like the snow flakes. He burnt like a faggot in a tempest.

When Paul went down to dinner, the music of the orchestra came floating up the elevator shaft to greet him. His head whirled as he stepped into the thronged corridor, and he sank back into one of the chairs against the wall to get his breath. The lights, the chatter, the perfumes, the bewildering medley of color—he had, for a moment, the feeling of not being able to stand it. But only for a moment; these were his own people, he told himself. He went slowly about the corridors, through the writing-rooms, smoking-rooms, reception-rooms, as though he were exploring the chambers of an enchanted palace, built and peopled for him alone.

When he reached the dining-room he sat down at a table near a window. The flowers, the white linen, the many-colored wine glasses, the gay toilettes of the women, the low popping of corks, the undulating repetitions of the *Blue Danube*[3] from the orchestra, all flooded Paul's dream with bewildering radiance. When the roseate tinge of his champagne was added—that cold, precious, bubbling stuff that creamed and foamed in his glass—Paul wondered that there were honest men in the world at all. This was what all the world was fighting for, he reflected; this was what all the struggle was about. He doubted the reality of his past. Had he ever known a place called Cordelia Street, a place where fagged-looking businessmen got on the early car; mere rivets in a machine they seemed to Paul—sickening men, with combings of children's hair always hanging to their coats, and the smell of cooking in their clothes. Cordelia Street—Ah! that belonged to another time and country; had he not always been thus, had he not sat here night after night, from as far back as he could remember, looking pensively over just such shimmering textures, and slowly twirling the stem of a glass like this one between his thumb and middle finger? He rather thought he had.

He was not in the least abashed or lonely. He had no especial desire to meet or to know any of these people; all he demanded was the right to look on and conjecture, to watch the pageant. The mere stage properties were all he contended for. Nor was he lonely later in the evening, in his loge at the Metropolitan. He was now entirely rid of his nervous misgivings, of his forced aggressiveness, of the imperative desire to show himself different from his surroundings. He felt now

[3]***Blue Danube*** a waltz (1866), by Johann Strauss.

that his surroundings explained him. Nobody questioned the purple; he had only to wear it passively. He had only to glance down at his attire to reassure himself that here it would be impossible for anyone to humiliate him.

He found it hard to leave his beautiful sitting-room to go to bed that night, and sat long watching the raging storm from his turret window. When he went to sleep it was with the lights turned on in his bedroom; partly because of his old timidity, and partly so that, if he should wake in the night, there would be no wretched moment of doubt, no horrible suspicion of yellow wall-paper, or of Washington and Calvin above his bed.

Sunday morning the city was practically snow-bound. Paul breakfasted late, and in the afternoon he fell in with a wild San Francisco boy, a freshman at Yale, who said he had run down for a "little flyer" over Sunday. The young man offered to show Paul the night side of the town, and the two boys went out together after dinner, not returning to the hotel until seven o'clock the next morning. They had started out in the confiding warmth of a champagne friendship, but their parting in the elevator was singularly cool. The freshman pulled himself together to make his train, and Paul went to bed. He awoke at two o'clock in the afternoon, very thirsty and dizzy, and rang for ice-water, coffee, and the Pittsburgh papers.

On the part of the hotel management, Paul excited no suspicion. There was this to be said for him, that he wore his spoils with dignity and in no way made himself conspicuous. Even under the glow of his wine he was never boisterous, though he found the stuff like a magician's wand for wonder-building. His chief greediness lay in his ears and eyes, and his excesses were not offensive ones. His dearest pleasures were the grey winter twilights in his sitting-room; his quiet enjoyment of his flowers, his clothes, his wide divan, his cigarette, and his sense of power. He could not remember a time when he had felt so at peace with himself. The mere release from the necessity of petty lying, lying every day and every day, restored his self-respect. He had never lied for pleasure, even at school; but to be noticed and admired, to assert his difference from other Cordelia Street boys; and he felt a good deal more manly, more honest, even, now that he had no need for boastful pretensions, now that he could, as his actor friends used to say, "dress the part." It was characteristic that remorse did not occur to him. His golden days went by without a shadow, and he made each as perfect as he could.

On the the eighth day after his arrival in New York, he found the whole affair exploited in the Pittsburgh papers, exploited with a wealth of detail which indicated that local news of a sensational nature was at a low ebb. The firm of Denny & Carson announced that the boy's father had refunded the full amount of the theft, and that they had no intention of prosecuting. The Cumberland minister had been interviewed, and expressed his hope of yet reclaiming the motherless lad, and his Sabbath-school teacher declared that she would spare no effort to that end. The rumor had reached Pittsburgh that the boy had been seen in a New York hotel, and his father had gone East to find him and bring him home.

Paul had just come in to dress for dinner; he sank into a chair, weak to the knees, and clasped his head in his hands. It was to be worse than jail, even; the tepid waters of Cordelia Street were to close over him finally and forever. The grey monotony stretched before him in hopeless, unrelieved years; Sabbath-school, Young People's Meeting, the yellow-papered room, the damp dish-towels; it all rushed back upon him with a sickening vividness. He had the old feeling that the orchestra had suddenly stopped, the sinking sensation that the play was over. The sweat broke out on his face, and he sprang to his feet, looked about him with his white, conscious smile, and winked at himself in the mirror. With something of the old childish belief in miracles with which he had so often gone to class, all his lessons unlearned, Paul dressed and dashed whistling down the corridor to the elevator.

He had no sooner entered the dining-room and caught the measure of the music than his remembrance was lightened by his old elastic power of claiming the moment, mounting with it, and finding it all sufficient. The glare and glitter about him, the mere scenic accessories had again, and for the last time, their old potency. He would show himself that he was game, he would finish the thing splendidly. He doubted, more than ever, the existence of Cordelia Street, and for the first time he drank his wine recklessly. Was he not, after all, one of those fortunate beings born to the purple, was he not still himself and in his own place? He drummed a nervous accompaniment to the Pagliacci music and looked about him, telling himself over and over that it had paid.

He reflected drowsily, to the swell of the music and the chill sweetness of his wine, that he might have done it more wisely. He might have caught an outboard steamer and been well out of their clutches before now. But the other side of the world had seemed too far away and too uncertain then; he could not have waited for it; his need had been too sharp. If he had to choose over again, he would do the same thing tomorrow. He looked affectionately about the dining-room, now gilded with a soft mist. Ah, it had paid indeed!

60 Paul was awakened next morning by a painful throbbing in his head and feet. He had thrown himself across the bed without undressing, and had slept with his shoes on. His limbs and hands were lead heavy, and his tongue and throat were parched and burnt. There came upon him one of those fateful attacks of clear-headedness that never occurred except when he was physically exhausted and his nerves hung loose. He lay still and closed his eyes and let the tide of things wash over him.

His father was in New York; "stopping at some joint or other," he told himself. The memory of successive summers on the front stoop fell upon him like a weight of black water. He had not a hundred dollars left; and he knew now, more than ever, that money was everything, the wall that stood between all he loathed and all he wanted. The thing was winding itself up; he had thought of that on his first glorious day in New York, and had even provided a way to snap the thread. It lay on his dressing-table now; he had got it out last night when he came blindly up from dinner, but the shiny metal hurt his eyes, and he disliked the looks of it.

He rose and moved about with a painful effort, succumbing now and again to attacks of nausea. It was the old depression exaggerated; all the world had become Cordelia Street. Yet somehow he was not afraid of anything, was absolutely calm; perhaps because he had looked into the dark corner at last and knew. It was bad enough, what he saw there, but somehow not so bad as his long fear of it had been. He saw everything clearly now. He had a feeling that he had made the best of it, that he had lived the sort of life he was meant to live, and for half an hour he sat staring at the revolver. But he told himself that was not the way, so he went downstairs and took a cab to the ferry.

When Paul arrived at Newark, he got off the train and took another cab, directing the driver to follow the Pennsylvania tracks out of the town. The snow lay heavy on the roadways and had drifted deep in the open fields. Only here and there the dead grass or dried weed stalks projected, singularly black, above it. Once well into the country, Paul dismissed the carriage and walked, floundering along the tracks, his mind a medley of irrelevant things. He seemed to hold in his brain an actual picture of everything he had seen that morning. He remembered every feature of both his drivers, of the toothless old woman from whom he had bought the red flowers in his coat, the agent from whom he had got his ticket, and all of his fellow-passengers on the ferry. His mind, unable to cope with vital matters near at hand, worked feverishly and deftly at sorting and grouping these images. They made for him a part of the ugliness of the world, of the ache in his head, and the bitter burning on his tongue. He stooped and put a handful of snow into his mouth as he walked, but that, too, seemed hot. When he reached a little hillside, where the tracks ran through a cut some twenty feet below him, he stopped and sat down.

The carnations in his coat were drooping with the cold, he noticed; their red glory all over. It occurred to him that all the flowers he had seen in the glass cases that first night must have gone the same way, long before this. It was only one splendid breath they had, in spite of their brave mockery at the winter outside the glass; and it was a losing game in the end, it seemed, this revolt against the homilies by which the world is run. Paul took one of the blossoms carefully from his coat and scooped a little hole in the snow, where he covered it up. Then he dozed a while, from his weak condition, seemingly insensible to the cold.

65 The sound of an approaching train awoke him, and he started to his feet, remembering only his resolution, and afraid lest he should be too late. He stood watching the approaching locomotive, his teeth chattering, his lips drawn away from them in a frightened smile; once or twice he glanced nervously sidewise, as though he were being watched. When the right moment came, he jumped. As he fell, the folly of his haste occurred to him with merciless clearness, the vastness of what he had left undone. There flashed through his brain, clearer than ever before, the blue of Adriatic water, the yellow of Algerian sands.

He felt something strike his chest, and that his body was being thrown swiftly through the air, on and on, immeasurably far and fast, while his limbs were gently relaxed. Then, because the picture-making mechanism was crushed, the disturbing visions flashed into black, and Paul dropped back into the immense design of things.

[1904]

Joining the Conversation: Critical Thinking and Writing

1. Characterize Paul. In your response, try to indicate in what ways (if any) he is made sympathetic and in what ways (if any) he is made unsympathetic.
2. What values do the arts have for Paul? Does Cather suggest that Paul is "artistic"? Is the story about the difficulties of a refined sensibility in a crude world?
3. Whom do you blame (if anyone) for Paul's character and for what happens to him—Paul, or the people and the conditions surrounding him? How does your sorting out of blame help you to settle on the meaning of the story?
4. Cather uses an omniscient point of view, rather than a third-person limited omniscient point of view with Paul as the central intelligence. (See "central intelligence" in the glossary.) Why do you suppose she chose an omniscient point of view? How would the meaning of the story be different if it were told from the point of view of Paul's father or of the young man with whom Paul spends an evening?

Joyce Carol Oates

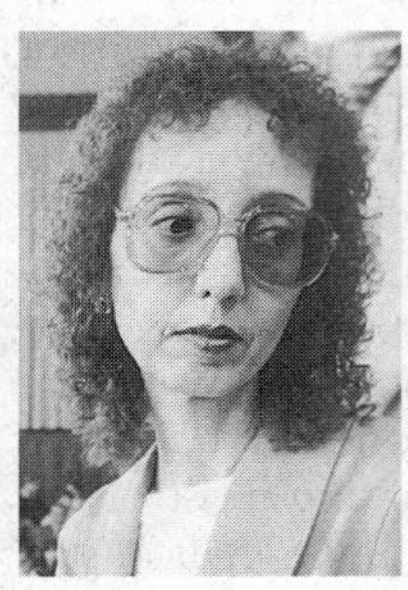

Joyce Carol Oates was born in 1938 in Millerport, New York. She won a scholarship to Syracuse University, from which she graduated (Phi Beta Kappa and valedictorian) in 1960. She then did graduate work in English, first at the University of Wisconsin and then at Rice University, but she withdrew from Rice in order to be able to devote more time to writing. Her first collection of stories, By the North Gate, *was published in 1963; since then she has published many books—stories, poems, essays, and novels. She has received many awards, has been elected to the American Academy and Institute of Arts and Letters, and now teaches creative writing at Princeton University.*

Where Are You Going, Where Have You Been?

For Bob Dylan

Her name was Connie. She was fifteen and she had a quick nervous giggling habit of craning her neck to glance into mirrors or checking other people's faces to make sure her own was all right. Her mother, who noticed everything and knew everything and who hadn't much reason any longer to look at her own face, always scolded Connie about it. "Stop gawking at yourself, who are you? You think you're so pretty?" she would say. Connie would raise her eyebrows at these familiar complaints and look right through her mother, into a shadowy vision of herself as she was right at that moment: she knew she was pretty and that was everything. Her mother had been pretty once too, if you could believe those old snapshots in the album, but now her looks were gone and that was why she was always after Connie.

"Why don't you keep your room clean like your sister? How've you got your hair fixed—what the hell stinks? Hair spray? You don't see your sister using that junk."

Her sister June was twenty-four and still lived at home. She was a secretary in the high school Connie attended, and if that wasn't bad enough—with her in the same building—she was so plain and chunky and steady that Connie had to hear her praised all the time by her mother and her mother's sisters. June did this, June did that, she saved money and helped clean the house and cooked and Connie couldn't do a thing, her mind was all filled with trashy daydreams. Their father was away at work most of the time and when he came home he wanted supper and he read the newspaper at supper and after supper he went to bed. He didn't bother talking much to them, but around his bent head Connie's mother kept picking at her until Connie wished her mother was dead and she herself was dead and it was all over. "She makes me want to throw up sometimes," she complained to her friends. She had a high, breathless, amused voice which made everything she said sound a little forced, whether it was sincere or not.

There was one good thing: June went places with girlfriends of hers, girls who were just as plain and steady as she, and so when Connie wanted to do that her mother had no objections. The father of Connie's best girlfriend drove the girls the three miles to town and left them off at a shopping plaza, so that they could walk through the stores or go to a movie, and when he came to pick them up again at eleven he never bothered to ask what they had done.

5 They must have been familiar sights, walking around that shopping plaza in their shorts and flat ballerina slippers that always scuffed the sidewalk, with charm bracelets jingling on their thin wrists; they would lean together to whisper and laugh secretly if someone passed by who amused or interested them. Connie had long dark blond hair that drew anyone's eye to it, and she wore part of it pulled up on her head and puffed out and the rest of it she let fall down her back. She wore a pull-over jersey blouse that looked one way when she was at home and another way when she was away from home. Everything about her had two sides to it, one for home and one for anywhere that was not home: her walk that could be childlike and bobbing, or languid enough to make anyone think she was hearing music in her head, her mouth which was pale and smirking most of the time, but bright and pink on these evenings out, her laugh which was cynical and drawling at home—"Ha, ha, very funny"—but high-pitched and nervous anywhere else, like the jingling of the charms on her bracelet.

Sometimes they did go shopping or to a movie, but sometimes they went across the highway, ducking fast across the busy road, to a drive-in restaurant where older kids hung out. The restaurant was shaped like a big bottle, though squatter than a real bottle, and on its cap was a revolving figure of a grinning boy who held a hamburger aloft. One night in midsummer they ran across, breathless with daring, and right away someone leaned out a car window and invited them over, but it was just a boy from high school they didn't like. It made them feel good to be able to ignore him. They went up through the maze of parked and cruising cars to the bright-lit, fly-infested restaurant, their faces pleased and expectant as if they were entering a sacred building that loomed out of the night to give them what haven and what blessing they yearned for. They sat at the counter and crossed their legs at the ankles, their thin shoulders rigid with excitement, and listened to the music that made everything so good: the music was always in the background like music at a church service, it was something to depend upon.

A boy named Eddie came in to talk with them. He sat backward on his stool, turning himself jerkily around in semicircles and then stopping and turning again, and after a while he asked Connie if she would like something to eat. She said she did and so she tapped her friend's arm on her way out—her friend pulled her face up into a brave droll look—and Connie said she would meet her at eleven, across the way. "I just hate to leave her like that," Connie said earnestly, but the boy said that she wouldn't be alone for long. So they went out to his car and on the way Connie couldn't help but let her eyes wander over the windshields and faces all around her, her face gleaming with a joy that had nothing to do with Eddie or even this place; it might have been the music. She drew her shoulders up and sucked in her breath with the pure pleasure of being alive, and just at that moment she happened to glance at a face just a few feet from hers. It was a boy with shaggy black hair, in a convertible jalopy painted gold. He stared at her and then his lips widened into a grin. Connie slit her eyes at him and turned away, but she couldn't help glancing back and there he was still watching her. He wagged a finger and laughed and said, "Gonna get you, baby," and Connie turned away again without Eddie noticing anything.

She spent three hours with him, at the restaurant where they ate hamburgers and drank Cokes in wax cups that were always sweating, and then down an alley a mile or so away, and when he left her off at five to eleven only the movie house was still open at the plaza. Her girlfriend was there, talking with a boy. When Connie came up the two girls smiled at each other and Connie said, "How was the movie?" and the girl said, "*You* should know." They rode off with the girl's father, sleepy and pleased, and Connie couldn't help but look at the darkened shopping plaza with its big empty parking lot and its signs that were faded and ghostly now, and over at the drive-in restaurant where cars were still circling tirelessly. She couldn't hear the music at this distance.

Next morning June asked her how the movie was and Connie said, "So-so."

10 She and that girl and occasionally another girl went out several times a week that way, and the rest of the time Connie spent around the house—it was summer vacation—getting in her mother's way and thinking, dreaming, about the boys she met. But all the boys fell back and dissolved into a single face that was not even a face, but an idea, a feeling, mixed up with the urgent insistent pounding of the music and the humid night air of July. Connie's mother kept dragging her back to the daylight by finding things for her to do or saying, suddenly, "What's this about the Pettinger girl?"

And Connie would say nervously, "Oh, her. That dope." She always drew thick clear lines between herself and such girls, and her mother was simple and kindly enough to believe her. Her mother was so simple, Connie thought, that it was maybe cruel to fool her so much. Her mother went scuffling around the house in old bedroom slippers and complained over the telephone to one sister about the other, then the other called up and the two of them complained about the third one. If June's name was mentioned her mother's tone was approving, and if Connie's name was mentioned it was disapproving. This did not really mean she disliked Connie and actually Connie thought that her mother preferred her to June because she was prettier, but the two of them kept up a pretense of exasperation, a sense that they were tugging and struggling over something of little value to either of them. Sometimes, over coffee, they were almost friends, but something would come up—some vexation that was like a fly buzzing suddenly around their heads—and their faces went hard with contempt.

One Sunday Connie got up at eleven—none of them bothered with church—and washed her hair so that it could dry all day long, in the sun. Her parents and sister were going to a barbecue at an aunt's house and Connie said no, she wasn't interested, rolling her eyes to let her mother know just what she thought of it. "Stay home alone then," her mother said sharply. Connie sat out back in a lawn chair and watched them drive away, her father quiet and bald, hunched around so that he could back the car out, her mother with a look that was still angry and not at all softened through the windshield, and in the back seat poor old June all dressed up as if she didn't know what a barbecue was, with all the running yelling kids and the flies. Connie sat with her eyes closed in the sun, dreaming and dazed with the warmth about her as if this were a kind of love, the caresses of love, and her mind slipped over onto thoughts of the boy she had been with the night before and how nice he had been, how sweet it always was, not the way someone like June would suppose but sweet, gentle, the way it was in movies and promised in songs; and when she opened her eyes she hardly knew where she was, the back yard ran off into weeds and a fence line of trees and behind it the sky was perfectly blue and still. The asbestos "ranch house" that was now three years old startled her—it looked small. She shook her head as if to get awake.

It was too hot. She went inside the house and turned on the radio to drown out the quiet. She sat on the edge of her bed, barefoot, and listened for an hour and a half to a program called XYZ Sunday Jamboree, record after record of hard, fast, shrieking songs she sang along with, interspersed by exclamations from "Bobby King": "An' look here you girls at Napoleon's—Son and Charley want you to pay real close attention to this song coming up!"

And Connie paid close attention herself, bathed in a glow of slow-pulsed joy that seemed to rise mysteriously out of the music itself and lay languidly about the airless little room, breathed in and breathed out with each gentle rise and fall of her chest.

15 After a while she heard a car coming up the drive. She sat up at once, startled, because it couldn't be her father so soon. The gravel kept crunching all the way in from the road—the driveway was long—and Connie ran to the window. It was a car she didn't know. It was an open jalopy, painted a bright gold that caught the sunlight opaquely. Her heart began to pound and her fingers snatched at her hair, checking it, and she whispered "Christ, Christ," wondering how bad she looked. The car came to a stop at the side door and the horn sounded four short taps as if this were a signal Connie knew.

She went into the kitchen and approached the door slowly, then hung out the screen door, her bare toes curling down off the step. There were two boys in the car and now she recognized the driver: he had shaggy, shabby black hair that looked crazy as a wig and he was grinning at her.

"I ain't late, am I?" he said.

"Who the hell do you think you are?" Connie said.

"Toldja I'd be out, didn't I?"

20 "I don't even know who you are."

She spoke sullenly, careful to show no interest or pleasure, and he spoke in a fast bright monotone. Connie looked past him to the other boy, taking her time. He had fair brown hair, with a lock that fell onto his forehead. His sideburns gave him a fierce, embarrassed look, but so far he hadn't even bothered to glance at her. Both boys wore sunglasses. The driver's glasses were metallic and mirrored everything in miniature.

"You wanta come for a ride?" he said.

Connie smirked and let her hair fall loose over one shoulder.

"Don'tcha like my car? New paint job," he said. "Hey."

25 "What?"

"You're cute."

She pretended to fidget, chasing flies away from the door.

"Don'tcha believe me, or what?" he said.

"Look, I don't even know who you are," Connie said in disgust.

30 "Hey, Ellie's got a radio, see. Mine's broke down." He lifted his friend's arm and showed her the little transistor the boy was holding, and now Connie began to hear the music. It was the same program that was playing inside the house.

"Bobby King?" she said.

"I listen to him all the time. I think he's great."

"He's kind of great." Connie said reluctantly.

"Listen, that guy's *great*. He knows where the action is."

35 Connie blushed a little, because the glasses made it impossible for her to see just what this boy was looking at. She couldn't decide if she liked him or if he was just a jerk, and so she dawdled in the doorway and wouldn't come down or go back inside. She said, "What's all that stuff painted on your car?"

"Can'tcha read it?" He opened the door very carefully, as if he was afraid it might fall off. He slid out just as carefully, planting his feet firmly on the ground, the tiny metallic world in his glasses slowing down like gelatine hardening and in the midst of it Connie's bright green blouse. "This here is my name, to begin with," he said. ARNOLD FRIEND was written in tarlike black letters on the side, with a drawing of a round grinning face that reminded Connie of a pumpkin, except it wore sunglasses. "I wanta introduce myself, I'm Arnold Friend and that's my real name and I'm gonna be your friend, honey, and inside the car's Ellie Oscar, he's kinda shy." Ellie brought his transistor radio up to his shoulder and balanced it there. "Now these numbers are a secret code, honey," Arnold Friend explained. He read off the numbers 33, 19, 17 and raised his eyebrows at her to see what she thought of that, but she didn't think much of it. The left rear fender had been smashed and around it was written, on the gleaming gold background: DONE BY CRAZY WOMAN DRIVER. Connie had to laugh at that. Arnold Friend was pleased at her laughter and looked up at her. "Around the other side's a lot more—you wanta come and see them?"

"No."

"Why not?"

"Why should I?"

"Don'tcha wanta see what's on the car? Don'tcha wanta go for a ride?"

"I don't know."

"Why not?"

"I got things to do."

"Like what?"

"Things."

He laughed as if she had said something funny. He slapped his thighs. He was standing in a strange way, leaning back against the car as if he were balancing himself. He wasn't tall, only an inch or so taller than she would be if she came down to him. Connie liked the way he was dressed, which was the way all of them dressed: tight faded jeans stuffed into black, scuffed boots, a belt that pulled his waist in and showed how lean he was, and a white pullover shirt that was a little soiled and showed the hard small muscles of his arms and shoulders. He looked as if he probably did hard work, lifting and carrying things. Even his neck looked muscular. And his face was a familiar face, somehow: the jaw and chin and cheeks slightly darkened, because he hadn't shaved for a day or two, and the nose long and hawklike, sniffing as if she were a treat he was going to gobble up and it was all a joke.

"Connie, you ain't telling the truth. This is your day set aside for a ride with me and you know it," he said, still laughing. The way he straightened and recovered from his fit of laughing showed that it had been all fake.

"How do you know what my name is?" she said suspiciously.

"It's Connie."

"Maybe and maybe not."

"I know my Connie," he said, wagging his finger. Now she remembered him even better, back at the restaurant, and her cheeks warmed at the thought of how she sucked in her breath just at the moment she passed him—how she must have looked to him. And he had remembered her. "Ellie and I come out here especially for you," he said. "Ellie can sit in back. How about it?"

"Where?"

"Where what?"

"Where're we going?"

He looked at her. He took off the sunglasses and she saw how pale the skin around his eyes was, like holes that were not in shadow but instead in light. His eyes were like chips of broken glass that catch the light in an amiable way. He smiled. It was as if the idea of going for a ride somewhere, to some place, was a new idea to him.

"Just for a ride, Connie sweetheart."

"I never said my name was Connie," she said.

"But I know what it is. I know your name and all about you, lots of things," Arnold Friend said. He had not moved yet but stood still leaning back against the side of his jalopy. "I took a special interest in you, such a pretty girl, and found out all about you like I know your parents and sister are gone somewheres and I know where and how long they're going to be gone, and I know who you were with last night, and your best girlfriend's name is Betty. Right?"

He spoke in a simple lilting voice, exactly as if he were reciting the words to a song. His smile assured her that everything was fine. In the car Ellie turned up the volume on his radio and did not bother to look around at them.

"Ellie can sit in the back seat," Arnold Friend said. He indicated his friend with a casual jerk of his chin, as if Ellie did not count and she should not bother with him.

"How'd you find out all that stuff?" Connie said.

"Listen: Betty Schultz and Tony Fitch and Jimmy Pettinger and Nancy Pettinger," he said, in a chant. "Raymond Stanley and Bob Hutter—"

"Do you know all those kids?"

"I know everybody."

"Look, you're kidding. You're not from around here."

"Sure."

"But—how come we never saw you before?"

"Sure you saw me before," he said. He looked down at his boots, as if he were a little offended. "You just don't remember."

"I guess I'd remember you," Connie said.

"Yeah?" He looked up at this, beaming. He was pleased. He began to mark time with the music from Ellie's radio, tapping his fists lightly together. Connie looked away from his smile to the car, which was painted so bright it almost hurt her eyes to look at it. She looked at that name, ARNOLD FRIEND. And up at the front fender was an expression that was familiar—MAN THE FLYING SAUCERS. It was an expression kids had used the year before, but didn't use this year. She looked at it for a while as if the words meant something to her that she did not yet know.

"What're you thinking about? Huh?" Arnold Friend demanded. "Not worried about your hair blowing around in the car, are you?"

"No."

"Think I maybe can't drive good?"

"How do I know?"

"You're a hard girl to handle. How come?" he said. "Don't you know I'm your friend? Didn't you see me put my sign in the air when you walked by?"

"What sign?"

"My sign." And he drew an X in the air, leaning out toward her. They were maybe ten feet apart. After his hand fell back to his side the X was still in the air, almost visible. Connie let the screen door close and stood perfectly still inside it, listening to the music from her radio and the boy's blend together. She stared at Arnold Friend. He stood there so stiffly relaxed, pretending to be relaxed, with one hand idly on the door handle as if he were keeping himself up that way and had no intention of ever moving again. She recognized most things about him, the tight jeans that showed his thighs and buttocks and the greasy leather boots and the tight shirt, and even that slippery friendly smile of his, that sleepy dreamy smile that all the boys used to get across ideas they didn't want to put into words. She recognized all this and also the singsong way he talked, slightly mocking, kidding, but serious and a little melancholy, and she recognized the way he tapped one fist against the other in homage to the perpetual music behind him. But all these things did not come together.

She said suddenly, "Hey, how old are you?"

His smile faded. She could see then that he wasn't a kid, he was much older—thirty, maybe more. At this knowledge her heart began to pound faster.

80 "That's a crazy thing to ask. Can'tcha see I'm your own age?"

"Like hell you are."

"Or maybe a coupla years older, I'm eighteen."

"Eighteen?" she said doubtfully.

He grinned to reassure her and lines appeared at the corners of his mouth. His teeth were big and white. He grinned so broadly his eyes became slits and she saw how thick the lashes were, thick and black as if painted with a black tar-like material. Then he seemed to become embarrassed, abruptly, and looked over his shoulder at Ellie. "*Him,* he's crazy," he said. "Ain't he a riot, he's a nut, a real character." Ellie was still listening to the music. His sunglasses told nothing about what he was thinking. He wore a bright orange shirt unbuttoned halfway to show his chest, which was a pale, bluish chest and not muscular like Arnold Friend's. His shirt collar was turned up all around and the very tips of the collar pointed out past his chin as if they were protecting him. He was pressing the transistor radio up against his ear and sat there in a kind of daze, right in the sun.

85 "He's kinda strange," Connie said.

"Hey, she says you're kinda strange! Kinda strange!" Arnold Friend cried. He pounded on the car to get Ellie's attention. Ellie turned for the first time and Connie saw with shock that he wasn't a kid either—he had a fair, hairless face, cheeks reddened slightly as if the veins grew too close to the surface of his skin, the face of a forty-year-old baby. Connie felt a wave of dizziness rise in her at this sight and she stared at him as if waiting for something to change the shock of the moment, make it all right again. Ellie's lips kept shaping words, mumbling along, with the words blasting in his ear.

"Maybe you two better go away," Connie said faintly.

"What? How come?" Arnold Friend cried. "We come out here to take you for a ride. It's Sunday." He had the voice of the man on the radio now. It was the same voice, Connie thought. "Don'tcha know it's Sunday all day and honey, no matter who you were with last night today you're with Arnold Friend and don't you forget it!—Maybe you better step out here," he said, and this last was in a different voice. It was a little flatter, as if the heat was finally getting to him.

"No. I got things to do."

90 "Hey."

"You two better leave."

"We ain't leaving until you come with us."

"Like hell I am—"

"Connie, don't fool around with me. I mean, I mean, don't fool *around,*" he said, shaking his head. He laughed incredulously. He placed his sunglasses on top of his head, carefully, as if he were indeed wearing a wig, and brought the stems down behind his ears. Connie stared at him, another wave of dizziness and fear rising in her so that for a moment he wasn't even in focus but was just a blur, standing there against his gold car, and she had the idea that he had driven up the driveway all right but had come from nowhere before that and belonged nowhere and that everything about him and even about the music that was so familiar to her was only half real.

95 "If my father comes and sees you—"

"He ain't coming. He's at a barbecue."

"How do you know that?"

"Aunt Tillie's. Right now they're—uh—they're drinking. Sitting around," he said vaguely, squinting as if he were staring all the way to town and over to Aunt Tillie's back yard. Then the vision seemed to get clear and he nodded energetically. "Yeah. Sitting around. There's your sister in a blue dress, huh? And high heels, the poor sad bitch—nothing like you, sweetheart! And your mother's helping some fat woman with the corn, they're cleaning the corn—husking the corn—"

"What fat woman?" Connie cried.

100 "How do I know what fat woman. I don't know every goddam fat woman in the world!" Arnold Friend laughed.

"Oh, that's Mrs. Hornby. . . . Who invited her?" Connie said. She felt a little light-headed. Her breath was coming quickly.

"She's too fat. I don't like them fat. I like them the way you are, honey," he said, smiling sleepily at her. They stared at each other for a while, through the screen door. He said softly, "Now what you're going to do is this: you're going to come out that door. You're going to sit up front with me and Ellie's going to sit in the back, the hell with Ellie, right? This isn't Ellie's date. You're my date. I'm your lover, honey."

"What? You're crazy—"

"Yes, I'm your lover. You don't know what that is but you will," he said. "I know that too. I know all about you. But look: it's real nice and you couldn't ask for nobody better than me, or more polite. I always keep my word. I'll tell you how it is, I'm always nice at first, the first time. I'll hold you so tight you won't think you have to try to get away or pretend anything because you'll know you can't. And I'll come inside you where it's all secret and you'll give in to me and you'll love me—"

105 "Shut up! You're crazy!" Connie said. She backed away from the door. She put her hands against her ears as if she'd heard something terrible, something not meant for her. "People don't talk like that, you're crazy," she muttered. Her heart was almost too big now for her chest and its pumping made sweat break out all over her. She looked out to see Arnold Friend pause and then take a step toward the porch lurching. He almost fell. But, like a clever drunken man, he managed to catch his balance. He wobbled in his high boots and grabbed hold of one of the porch posts.

"Honey?" he said. "You still listening?"

"Get the hell out of here!"

"Be nice, honey. Listen."

"I'm going to call the police—"

110 He wobbled again and out of the side of his mouth came a fast spat curse, an aside not meant for her to hear. But even this "Christ!" sounded forced. Then he began to smile again. She watched this smile come, awkward as if he were smiling from inside a mask. His whole face was a mask, she thought wildly, tanned down onto his throat but then running out as if he had plastered makeup on his face but had forgotten about his throat.

"Honey—? Listen, here's how it is. I always tell the truth and I promise you this: I ain't coming in that house after you."

"You better not! I'm going to call the police if you—if you don't—"

"Honey," he said, talking right through her voice, "honey, I'm not coming in there but you are coming out here. You know why?"

She was panting. The kitchen looked like a place she had never seen before, some room she had run inside but which wasn't good enough, wasn't going to help her. The kitchen window had never had a curtain, after three years, and there were dishes in the sink for her to do—probably—and if you ran your hand across the table you'd probably feel something sticky there.

115 "You listening, honey? Hey?"

"—going to call the police—"

"Soon as you touch the phone I don't need to keep my promise and can come inside. You won't want that."

She rushed forward and tried to lock the door. Her fingers were shaking. "But why lock it," Arnold Friend said gently, talking right into her face. "It's just a screen door. It's just nothing." One of his boots was at a strange angle, as if his foot wasn't in it. It pointed out to the left, bent at the ankle. "I mean, anybody can break through a screen door and glass and wood and iron or anything else if he needs to, anybody at all and specially Arnold Friend. If the place got lit up with a fire honey you'd come runnin' out into my arms, right into my arms an' safe at home—like you knew I was your lover and'd stopped fooling around. I don't mind a nice shy girl but I don't like no fooling around." Part of those words were spoken with a slight rhythmic lilt, and Connie somehow recognized them—the echo of a song from last year, about a girl rushing into her boyfriend's arms and coming home again—

Connie stood barefoot on the linoleum floor, staring at him. "What do you want?" she whispered.

120 "I want you," he said.

"What?"

"Seen you that night and thought, that's the one, yes sir. I never needed to look any more."

"But my father's coming back. He's coming to get me. I had to wash my hair first—" She spoke in a dry, rapid voice, hardly raising it for him to hear.

"No, your Daddy is not coming and yes, you had to wash your hair and you washed it for me. It's nice and shining and all for me, I thank you, sweetheart," he said, with a mock bow, but again he almost lost his balance. He had to bend and adjust his boots. Evidently his feet did not go all the way down; the boots must have been stuffed with something so that he would seem taller. Connie stared out at him and behind him Ellie in the car, who seemed to be looking off toward Connie's right into nothing. This Ellie said, pulling the words out of the air one after another as if he were just discovering them, "You want me to pull out the phone?"

125 "Shut your mouth and keep it shut," Arnold Friend said, his face red from bending over or maybe from embarrassment because Connie had seen his boots. "This ain't none of your business."

"What—what are you doing? What do you want?" Connie said. "If I call the police they'll get you, they'll arrest you—"

"Promise was not to come in unless you touch that phone, and I'll keep that promise," he said. He resumed his erect position and tried to force his shoulders back. He sounded like a hero in a movie, declaring something important. He spoke too loudly and it was as if he were speaking to someone behind Connie. "I ain't made plans for coming in that house where I don't belong but just for you to come out to me, the way you should. Don't you know who I am?"

"You're crazy," she whispered. She backed away from the door but did not want to go into another part of the house, as if this would give him permission to come through the door. "What do you . . . You're crazy, you . . ."

"Huh? What're you saying, honey?"

130 Her eyes darted everywhere in the kitchen. She could not remember what it was, this room.

"This is how it is, honey: you come out and we'll drive away, have a nice ride. But if you don't come out we're gonna wait till your people come home and then they're all going to get it."

"You want that telephone pulled out?" Ellie said. He held the radio away from his ear and grimaced, as if without the radio the air was too much for him.

"I toldja shut up, Ellie," Arnold Friend said, "you're deaf, get a hearing aid, right? Fix yourself up. This little girl's no trouble and's gonna be nice to me, so Ellie keep to yourself, this ain't your date—right? Don't hem in on me. Don't hog. Don't crush. Don't bird dog. Don't trail me," he said in a rapid meaningless voice, as if he were running through all the expressions he'd learned but was no longer sure which one of them was in style, then rushing on to new ones, making them up with his eyes closed, "Don't crawl under my fence, don't squeeze in my chipmunk hole, don't sniff my glue, suck my popsicle, keep your own greasy fingers on yourself!" He shaded his eyes and peered in at Connie, who was backed against the kitchen table. "Don't mind him honey he's just a creep. He's a dope. Right? I'm the boy for you and like I said you come out here nice like a lady and give me your hand, and nobody else gets hurt, I mean, your nice old bald-headed daddy and your mummy and your sister in her high heels. Because listen: why bring them in this?"

"Leave me alone," Connie whispered.

135 "Hey, you know that old woman down the road, the one with the chickens and stuff—you know her?"

"She's dead!"

"Dead? What? You know her?" Arnold Friend said.

"She's dead—"

"Don't you like her?"

140 "She's dead—she's—she isn't here any more—"

"But don't you like her, I mean, you got something against her? Some grudge or something?" Then his voice dipped as if he were conscious of a rudeness. He touched the sunglasses perched on top of his head as if to make sure they were still there. "Now you be a good girl."

"What are you going to do?"

"Just two things, or maybe three," Arnold Friend said. "But I promise it won't last long and you'll like me the way you get to like people you're close to. You will. It's all over for you here, so come on out. You don't want your people in any trouble, do you?"

She turned and bumped against a chair or something, hurting her leg, but she ran into the back room and picked up the telephone. Something roared in her ear, a tiny roaring, and she was so sick with fear that she could do nothing but listen to it—the telephone was clammy and very heavy and her fingers groped down to the dial but were too weak to touch it. She began to scream into the phone, into the roaring. She cried out, she cried for her mother, she felt her breath start jerking back and forth in her lungs as if it were something Arnold Friend were stabbing her with again and again with no tenderness. A noisy sorrowful wailing rose all about her and she was locked inside it the way she was locked inside the house.

145 After a while she could hear again. She was sitting on the floor with her wet back against the wall.

Arnold Friend was saying from the door, "That's a good girl. Put the phone back."

She kicked the phone away from her.

"No, honey. Pick it up. Put it back right."

She picked it up and put it back. The dial tone stopped.

150 "That's a good girl. Now come outside."

She was hollow with what had been fear, but what was now just an emptiness. All that screaming had blasted it out of her. She sat, one leg cramped under her, and deep inside her brain was something like a pinpoint of light that kept going and would not let her relax. She thought, I'm not going to see my mother again. She thought, I'm not going to sleep in my bed again. Her bright green blouse was all wet.

Arnold Friend said, in a gentle-loud voice that was like a stage voice, "The place where you came from ain't there any more, and where you had in mind to go is canceled out. This place you are now—inside your daddy's house—is nothing but a cardboard box I can knock down any time. You know that and always did know it. You hear me?"

She thought, I have got to think. I have to know what to do.

"We'll go out to a nice field, out in the country here where it smells so nice and it's sunny," Arnold Friend said. "I'll have my arms tight around you so you won't need to try to get away and I'll show you what love is like, what it does. The hell with this house! It looks solid all right," he said. He ran a fingernail down the screen and the noise did not make Connie shiver, as it would have the day before. "Now put your hand on your heart, honey. Feel that? That feels solid too but we know better, be nice to me, be sweet like you can because what else is there for a girl like you but to be sweet and pretty and give in?—and get away before her people come back?"

155 She felt her pounding heart. Her hand seemed to enclose it. She thought for the first time in her life that it was nothing that was hers, that belonged to her, but just a pounding, living thing inside this body that wasn't really hers either.

"You don't want them to get hurt," Arnold Friend went on. "Now get up, honey. Get up all by yourself."

She stood up.

"Now turn this way. That's right. Come over here to me—Ellie, put that away, didn't I tell you? You dope. You miserable creepy dope," Arnold Friend said. His words were not angry but only part of an incantation. The incantation was kindly. "Now come out through the kitchen to me honey, and let's see a smile, try it, you're a brave sweet little girl and now they're eating corn and hot dogs cooked to bursting over an outdoor fire, and they don't know one thing about you and never did and honey you're better than them because not a one of them would have done this for you."

Connie felt the linoleum under her feet; it was cool. She brushed her hair back out of her eyes. Arnold Friend let go of the post tentatively and opened his arms for her, his elbows pointing in toward each other and his wrists limp, to show that this was an embarrassed embrace and a little mocking, he didn't want to make her self-conscious.

160 She put out her hand against the screen. She watched herself push the door slowly open as if she were safe back somewhere in the other doorway, watching

this body and this head of long hair moving out into the sunlight where Arnold Friend waited.

"My sweet little blue-eyed girl," he said, in a half-sung sigh that had nothing to do with her brown eyes but was taken up just the same by the vast sunlit reaches of the land behind him and on all sides of him, so much land that Connie had never seen before and did not recognize except to know that she was going to it.

[1966]

Joining the Conversation: Critical Thinking and Writing

1. Characterize Connie. Do you think the early characterization of Connie prepares us for her later behavior?
2. Construct an argument in response to this question: Is Arnold Friend clairvoyant—definitely, definitely not, maybe?
3. Evaluate the view that Arnold's friend is both Satan and the incarnation of Connie's erotic desires.
4. What do you make of the fact that Oates dedicated the story to Bob Dylan? Is she perhaps contrasting Dylan's music with the escapist (or in some other way unwholesome) music of other popular singers?
5. If you have read Flannery O'Connor's "A Good Man Is Hard to Find" (page 404), compare and contrast Arnold Friend and the Misfit.

Thinking Critically: Case Study on William Faulkner's "A Rose for Emily"

Overview of the Case Study

1. In this case study we offer Faulkner's story with the illustrations by Weldon Bailey (1905–1945) that accompanied it when it was first published, in 1930, in *Forum* magazine. To the best of our knowledge, these illustrations have never been reproduced after their publication in 1930.
2. We also reproduce four pages of the pre-publication typescript of Faulkner's story. Three of these pages include material that does *not* appear in the published version. The fourth page (in this book on page 249), showing the final paragraph of the story, is rather different from the published version, so it allows the reader to see what is in effect a draft for the published final paragraph.
3. Faulkner served as writer-in-residence at the University of Virginia from 1957 to 1958. In the course of lectures and discussions he occasionally commented on "A Rose for Emily." We reproduce the relevant passages.
4. We include two interpretive essays by first-year students, each accompanied by an outline. These essays are not offered as models to emulate; rather, they are offered as material that can be discussed and evaluated in class.

William Faulkner

William Faulkner (1897–1962) was brought up in Oxford, Mississippi. His great-grandfather had been a Civil War hero, and his father was treasurer of the University of Mississippi in Oxford; the family was no longer rich, but it was still respected. In 1918 he enrolled in the Royal Canadian Air Force, though he never saw overseas service. After the war he returned to Mississippi and went to the university for two years. He then moved to New Orleans, where he became friendly with Sherwood Anderson, who was already an established writer. In New Orleans Faulkner worked for the Times-Picayune; *still later, even after he had established himself as a major novelist with* The Sound and the Fury *(1929), he had to do some work in Hollywood in order to make ends meet. In 1950 he was awarded the Nobel Prize in Literature.*

A Rose for Emily

I

When Miss Emily Grierson died, our whole town went to her funeral: the men through a sort of respectful affection for a fallen monument, the women mostly out of curiosity to see the inside of her house, which no one save an old Negro manservant—a combined gardener and cook—had seen in at least ten years.

It was a big, squarish, frame house that had once been white, decorated with cupolas and spires and scrolled balconies in the heavily lightsome style of the seventies, set on what had once been our most select street. But garages and cotton gins had encroached and obliterated even the august names of that neighborhood; only Miss Emily's house was left, lifting its stubborn and coquettish decay above the cotton wagons and the gasoline pumps—an eyesore among eyesores. And now Miss Emily had gone to join the representatives of those august names where they lay in the cedar-bemused cemetery among the ranked and anonymous graves of Union and Confederate soldiers who fell at the battle of Jefferson.

Alive, Miss Emily had been a tradition, a duty, and a care; a sort of hereditary obligation upon the town, dating from that day in 1894 when Colonel Sartoris, the mayor—he who fathered the edict that no Negro woman should appear on the streets without an apron—remitted her taxes, the dispensation dating from the death of her father on into perpetuity. Not that Miss Emily would have accepted charity. Colonel Sartoris invented an involved tale to the effect that Miss Emily's father had loaned money to the town, which the town, as a matter of business, preferred this way of repaying. Only a man of Colonel Sartoris' generation and thought could have invented it, and only a woman could have believed it.

When the next generation, with its more modern ideas, became mayors and aldermen, this arrangement created some little dissatisfaction. On the first of the year they mailed her a tax notice. February came, and there was no reply. They wrote her a formal letter, asking her to call at the sheriff's office at her convenience. A week later the mayor wrote her himself, offering to call or to send his car for her, and received in reply a note on paper of an archaic shape, in a thin, flowing calligraphy in faded ink, to the effect that she no longer went out at all. The tax notice was also enclosed, without comment.

5 They called a special meeting of the Board of Aldermen. A deputation waited upon her, knocked at the door through which no visitor had passed since she ceased giving china-painting lessons eight or ten years earlier. They were admitted by the old Negro into a dim hall from which a stairway mounted into still more shadow. It smelled of dust and disuse—a close, dank smell. The Negro led them into the parlor. It was furnished in heavy, leather-covered furniture. When the Negro opened the blinds of one window, they could see that the leather was cracked; and when they sat down, a faint dust rose sluggishly about their thighs, spinning with slow motes in the single sun-ray. On a tarnished gilt easel before the fireplace stood a crayon portrait of Miss Emily's father.

They rose when she entered—a small, fat woman in black, with a thin gold chain descending to her waist and vanishing into her belt, leaning on an ebony cane with a tarnished gold head. Her skeleton was small and spare; perhaps that was why what would have been merely plumpness in another was obesity in her. She looked bloated, like a body long submerged in motionless water, and of that pallid hue. Her eyes, lost in the fatty ridges of her face, looked like two small pieces of coal pressed into a lump of dough as they moved from one face to another while the visitors stated their errand.

She did not ask them to sit. She just stood in the door and listened quietly until the spokesman came to a stumbling halt. Then they could hear the invisible watch ticking at the end of the gold chain.

Her voice was dry and cold. "I have no taxes in Jefferson. Colonel Sartoris explained it to me. Perhaps one of you can gain access to the city records and satisfy yourselves."

"But we have. We are the city authorities, Miss Emily. Didn't you get a notice from the sheriff, signed by him?"

10 "I received a paper, yes," Miss Emily said. "Perhaps he considers himself the sheriff. . . . I have no taxes in Jefferson."

"But there is nothing on the books to show that, you see. We must go by the—"

"See Colonel Sartoris. I have no taxes in Jefferson."

"But, Miss Emily—"

"See Colonel Sartoris." (Colonel Sartoris had been dead almost ten years.) "I have no taxes in Jefferson. Tobe!" The Negro appeared. "Show these gentlemen out."

II

15 So she vanquished them, horse and foot, just as she had vanquished their fathers thirty years before about the smell. That was two years after her father's death and a short time after her sweetheart—the one we believed would marry her—had deserted her. After her father's death she went out very little; after her sweetheart went away, people hardly saw her at all. A few of the ladies had the temerity to call, but were not received, and the only sign of life about the place was the Negro man—a young man then—going in and out with a market basket.

"Just as if a man—any man—could keep a kitchen properly," the ladies said; so they were not surprised when the smell developed. It was another link between the gross, teeming world and the high and mighty Griersons.

A neighbor, a woman, complained to the mayor, Judge Stevens, eighty years old.

"But what will you have me do about it, madam?" he said.

"Why, send her word to stop it," the woman said. "Isn't there a law?"

20 "I'm sure that won't be necessary," Judge Stevens said. "It's probably just a snake or a rat that nigger of hers killed in the yard. I'll speak to him about it."

The next day he received two more complaints, one from a man who came in diffident deprecation. "We really must do something about it, Judge. I'd be the last one in the world to bother Miss Emily, but we've got to do something." That night the Board of Aldermen met—three graybeards and one younger man, a member of the rising generation.

"It's simple enough," he said. "Send her word to have her place cleaned up. Give her a certain time to do it in, and if she don't . . ."

"Dammit, sir," Judge Stevens said, "will you accuse a lady to her face of smelling bad?"

So the next night, after midnight, four men crossed Miss Emily's lawn and slunk about the house like burglars, sniffing along the base of the brickwork and at the cellar openings while one of them performed a regular sowing motion with his hand out of a sack slung from his shoulder. They broke open the cellar door and sprinkled lime there, and in all the outbuildings. As they recrossed the lawn, a window that had been dark was lighted and Miss Emily sat in it, the light behind her, and her upright torso motionlesss as that of an idol. They crept quietly across the lawn and into the shadow of the locusts that lined the street. After a week or two the smell went away.

25 That was when people had begun to feel really sorry for her. People in our town, remembering how old lady Wyatt, her great-aunt, had gone completely crazy at last, believed that the Griersons held themselves a little too high for what they really were. None of the young men were quite good enough for Miss Emily and such. We had long thought of them as a tableau, Miss Emily a slender figure in white in the background, her father a spraddled silhouette in the foreground, his back to her and clutching a horsewhip, the two of them framed by the back-flung front door. So when she got to be thirty and was still single, we were not pleased exactly, but vindicated; even with insanity in the family she wouldn't have turned down all of her chances if they had really materialized.

When her father died, it got about that the house was all that was left to her; and in a way, people were glad. At last they could pity Miss Emily. Being left alone, and a pauper, she had become humanized. Now she too would know the old thrill and the old despair of a penny more or less.

The day after his death all the ladies prepared to call at the house and offer condolence and aid, as is our custom. Miss Emily met them at the door, dressed as usual and with no trace of grief on her face. She told them that her father was not dead. She did that for three days, with the ministers calling on her, and the doctors, trying to persuade her to let them dispose of the body. Just as they were about to resort to law and force, she broke down, and they buried her father quickly.

We did not say she was crazy then. We believed she had to do that. We remembered all the young men her father had driven away, and we knew that with nothing left, she would have to cling to that which had robbed her, as people will.

III

She was sick for a long time. When we saw her again, her hair was cut short, making her look like a girl, with a vague resemblance to those angels in colored church windows—sort of tragic and serene.

30 The town had just let the contracts for paving the sidewalks, and in the summer after her father's death they began the work. The construction company came with niggers and mules and machinery, and a foreman named Homer Barron, a Yankee—a big, dark, ready man, with a big voice and eyes lighter than his face. The little boys would follow in groups to hear him cuss the niggers, and the niggers singing in time to the rise and fall of picks. Pretty soon he knew everybody in town. Whenever you heard a lot of laughing anywhere about the square, Homer Barron would be in the center of the group. Presently we began to see him and Miss Emily on Sunday afternoons driving in the yellow-wheeled buggy and the matched team of bays from the livery stable.

At first we were glad that Miss Emily would have an interest, because the ladies all said, "Of course a Grierson would not think seriously of a Northerner, a day laborer." But there were still others, older people, who said that even grief could not cause a real lady to forget *noblesse oblige*—without calling it *noblesse oblige*. They just said, "Poor Emily. Her kinfolks should come to her." She had some kin in Alabama; but years ago her father had fallen out with them over the estate of old lady Wyatt, the crazy woman, and there was no communication between the two families. They had not even been represented at the funeral.

And as soon as the old people said, "Poor Emily," the whispering began. "Do you suppose it's really so?" they said to one another. "Of course it is. What else could . . ." This behind their hands; rustling of craned silk and satin behind jalousies closed upon the sun of Sunday afternoon as the thin, swift clop-clop-clop of the matched team passed: "Poor Emily."

She carried her head high enough—even when we believed that she was fallen. It was as if she demanded more than ever the recognition of her dignity as the last Grierson; as if it had wanted that touch of earthiness to reaffirm her imperviousness. Like when she bought the rat poison, the arsenic. That was over a year after they had begun to say "Poor Emily," and while the two female cousins were visiting her.

"I want some poison," she said to the druggist. She was over thirty then, still a slight woman, though thinner than usual, with cold, haughty black eyes in a face the flesh of which was strained across the temples and about the eye-sockets as you imagine a lighthouse-keeper's face ought to look. "I want some poison," she said.

35 "Yes, Miss Emily. What kind? For rats and such? I'd recom—"

"I want the best you have. I don't care what kind."

The druggist named several. "They'll kill anything up to an elephant. But what you want is—"

"Arsenic," Miss Emily said. "Is that a good one?"

"Is . . . arsenic? Yes, ma'am. But what you want—"

40 "I want arsenic."

The druggist looked down at her. She looked back at him, erect, her face like a strained flag. "Why, of course," the druggist said. "If that's what you want. But the law requires you to tell what you are going to use it for."

Miss Emily just stared at him, her head tilted back in order to look him eye to eye, until he looked away and went and got the arsenic and wrapped it up. The Negro delivery boy brought her the package; the druggist didn't come back. When she opened the package at home there was written on the box, under the skull and bones: "For rats."

IV

So the next day we all said, "She will kill herself"; and we said it would be the best thing. When she had first begun to be seen with Homer Barron, we had said, "She will marry him." Then we said, "She will persuade him yet," because Homer himself had remarked—he liked men, and it was known that he drank with the younger men in the Elks' Club—that he was not a marrying man. Later we said, "Poor Emily" behind the jalousies as they passed on Sunday afternoon in the glittering buggy, Miss Emily with her head high and Homer Barron with his hat cocked and a cigar in his teeth, reins and whip in a yellow glove.

Then some of the ladies began to say that it was a disgrace to the town and a bad example to the young people. The men did not want to interfere, but at last the ladies forced the Baptist minister—Miss Emily's people were Episcopal—to call upon her. He would never divulge what happened during that interview, but he refused to go back again. The next Sunday they again drove about the streets, and the following day the minister's wife wrote to Miss Emily's relations in Alabama.

So she had blood-kin under her roof again and we sat back to watch developments. At first nothing happened. Then we were sure that they were to be married. We learned that Miss Emily had been to the jeweler's and ordered a man's toilet set in silver, with the letters H. B. on each piece. Two days later we learned that she had bought a complete outfit of men's clothing, including a nightshirt, and we said, "They are married." We were really glad. We were glad because the two female cousins were even more Grierson than Miss Emily had ever been.

So we were not surprised when Homer Barron—the streets had been finished some time since—was gone. We were a little disappointed that there was not a public blowing-off, but we believed that he had gone on to prepare for Miss Emily's coming, or to give her a chance to get rid of the cousins. (By that time it was a cabal, and we were all Miss Emily's allies to help circumvent the cousins.) Sure enough, after another week they departed. And, as we had expected all along, within three days Homer Barron was back in town. A neighbor saw the Negro man admit him at the kitchen door at dusk one evening.

And that was the last we saw of Homer Barron. And of Miss Emily for some time. The Negro man went in and out with the market basket, but the front door remained closed. Now and then we would see her at a window for a moment, as the men did that night when they sprinkled the lime, but for almost six months she did not appear on the streets. Then we knew that this was to be expected too; as if that quality of her father which had thwarted her woman's life so many times had been too virulent and too furious to die.

When we next saw Miss Emily, she had grown fat and her hair was turning gray. During the next few years it grew grayer and grayer until it attained an even pepper-and-salt iron gray, when it ceased turning. Up to the day of her death at seventy-four it was still that vigorous iron-gray, like the hair of an active man.

From that time on her front door remained closed, save for a period of six or seven years, when she was about forty, during which she gave lessons in china-painting. She fitted up a studio in one of the downstairs rooms, where the daughters and grand-daughters of Colonel Sartoris' contemporaries were sent to her with the same regularity and in the same spirit that they were sent to church on Sundays with a twenty-five cent piece for the collection plate. Meanwhile her taxes had been remitted.

50 Then the newer generation became the backbone and the spirit of the town, and the painting pupils grew up and fell away and did not send their children to her with boxes of color and tedious brushes and pictures cut from the ladies' magazines. The front door closed upon the last one and remained closed for good. When the town got free postal delivery, Miss Emily alone refused to let them fasten the metal numbers above her door and attach a mailbox to it. She would not listen to them.

Daily, monthly, yearly we watched the Negro grow grayer and more stooped, going in and out with the market basket. Each December we sent her a tax notice, which would be returned by the post office a week later, unclaimed. Now and then we would see her in one of the downstairs windows—she had evidently shut up the top floor of the house—like the carven torso of an idol in a niche, looking or not looking at us, we could never tell which. Thus she passed from generation to generation—dear, inescapable, impervious, tranquil, and perverse.

And so she died. Fell ill in the house filled with dust and shadows, with only a doddering Negro man to wait on her. We did not even know she was sick; we had long since given up trying to get any information from the Negro. He talked to no one, probably not even to her, for his voice had grown harsh and rusty, as if from disuse.

She died in one of the downstairs rooms, in a heavy walnut bed with a curtain, her gray head propped on a pillow yellow and moldy with age and lack of sunlight.

V

The Negro met the first of the ladies at the front door and let them in, with their hushed, sibilant voices and their quick, curious glances, and then he disappeared. He walked right through the house and out the back and was not seen again.

55 The two female cousins came at once. They held the funeral on the second day, with the town coming to look at Miss Emily beneath a mass of bought flowers, with the crayon face of her father musing profoundly above the bier and the ladies sibilant and macabre; and the very old men—some in their brushed Confederate uniforms—on the porch and the lawn, talking of Miss Emily as if she had been a contemporary of theirs, believing that they had danced with her and courted her perhaps, confusing time with its mathematical progression, as the old do, to whom all the past is not a diminishing road but, instead, a huge meadow which no winter ever quite touches, divided from the now by the narrow bottleneck of the most recent decade of years.

Already we knew that there was one room in that region above stairs which no one had seen in forty years, and which would have to be forced. They waited until Miss Emily was decently in the ground before they opened it.

The violence of breaking down the door seemed to fill this room with pervading dust. A thin, acrid pall as of the tomb seemed to lie everywhere upon this room decked and furnished as for a bridal: upon the valance curtains of faded rose color, upon the rose-shaded lights, upon the dressing table, upon the delicate array of crystal and the man's toilet things backed with tarnished silver, silver so tarnished that the monogram was obscured. Among them lay a collar and tie, as if they had just been removed, which, lifted, left upon the surface a pale crescent in the dust. Upon a chair hung the suit, carefully folded; beneath it the two mute shoes and the discarded socks.

The man himself lay in the bed.

For a long while we just stood there, looking down at the profound and fleshless grin. The body had apparently once lain in the attitude of an embrace, but now the long sleep that outlasts love, that conquers even the grimace of love, had cuckolded him. What was left of him, rotted beneath what was left of the nightshirt, had become inextricable from the bed in which he lay; and upon him and upon the pillow beside him lay that even coating of the patient and biding dust.

Then we noticed that in the second pillow was the indentation of a head. One of us lifted something from it, and leaning forward, that faint and invisible dust dry and acrid in the nostrils, we saw a long strand of iron-gray hair.

Joining the Conversation: Critical Thinking and Writing

1. Why does the narrator begin with what is almost the end of the story—the death of Miss Emily—rather than save this information for later? What devices does Faulkner use to hold the reader's interest throughout?
2. In a paragraph, offer a conjecture about Miss Emily's attitudes toward Homer Barron after he was last seen alive.
3. In a paragraph or two, characterize Miss Emily, calling attention not only to her eccentricities or even craziness, but also to what you conjecture to be her moral values.
4. In paragraph 44 we are told that the Baptist minister "would never divulge what happened" during the interview with Miss Emily. Why do you suppose Faulkner does not narrate or describe the interview? Let's assume that in his first draft of the story he *did* give a paragraph of narration or a short dramatic scene. Write such an episode.
5. Suppose that Homer Barron's remains had been discovered before Miss Emily died, and that she was arrested and charged with murder. You are the prosecutor and you are running for a statewide political office. In 500 words, set forth your argument that—despite the fact that she is a public monument—she should be convicted. Or: You are the defense attorney, also running for office. In 500 words, set forth your defense.
6. Assume that Miss Emily kept a journal—perhaps even from her days as a young girl. Write some entries for the journal, giving her thoughts about some of the episodes reported in Faulkner's story.
7. Does "A Rose for Emily" make you want to read more stories by Faulkner? Be as specific as you can in explaining your response.

Typescript Showing Material Deleted from the Published Version

The University of Virginia possesses a pre-publication typescript of "A Rose for Emily." The typescript is of special importance because it includes a passage—omitted from the published version—of extended dialogue between Miss Emily and the African American servant. If you look at paragraph 53 of the published version—it consists of only a single sentence—and compare it with the paragraph just above the middle of the first page that we reprint form the typed version, you will notice that the typescript includes a few additional words at the end of the sentence, and then goes on to give substantial material that Faulkner decided not to publish. This material is on the original typescript pages numbered 13, 14, and 15.

We also print an unnumbered page of the typescript, showing the very end of the story. The final paragraph of the typed version is, in the published version, reworded and made into two paragraphs.

dust and shadows, with only a doddering negro man to wait on her. We did not even know she was sick; we had long since given up trying to get any information from the negro. He talked to no one, probably not even to her, for his voice had grown ~~rusty~~ harsh and ~~ras~~ rusty, as though with disuse; the sparse words which he did speak sounded as though he had learned them that morning by rote---just enough of them to carry him through the day.

She died in one of the downstairs rooms, in a heavy walnut bed with a curtain, her gray head propped on a pillow yellow and moldy with age and lack of sunlight, her voice cold and strong to the last.

"But not till I'm gone," she said. "Dont you let a soul in until I'm gone, do you hear?" Standing beside the bed, his head in the dim light nimbused by a faint halo of napped, perfectly white hair, the negro made a brief gesture with his hand. Miss Emily lay with her eyes open, gazing into the opposite shadows of the room. Upon the coverlet her hands lay on her breast, gnarled, blue with age, motionless. "Hah," she said. "Then they can. Let 'em go up there and see what's in that room. ~~And you wont be the last one, either~~ Fools. ~~And~~ Let 'em. ~~And you wont be the last one~~ Satisfy their minds that I am crazy. Do you think I am?" The negro made no reply, no movement. He stood above the bed, ~~stooped, haloed like an angel~~ motionless, musing: a secret and unfathomable soul behind the death-mask of an ape and haloed like an angel. "Let 'em go up there and open that door. And you wont be the last one,

13.

either. Will you?"

"I wont have to," the negro said. "I know what's in that room. I dont have to see."

"Hah," Miss Emily said. "You do, do you. How long have you known?" Again he made that brief sign with his hand. Miss Emily had not turned her head. She stared into the shadows where the high ceiling was lost. "You should be glad. Now you can go to Chicago, like you've been talking about for thirty years. And with what you'll get for the house and furniture.... Colonel Sartoris has the will. He'll see they dont rob you."

"I dont want any house," the negro said.

"You cant help yourself. It's signed and sealed thirty-five years ago. Wasn't that our agreement when I found I couldn't pay you any wages? that you were to have everything that was left if you outlived me, and I was to bury you ~~with~~ in a coffin with your name on a gold plate if I outlived you?" He said nothing. "Wasn't it?" Miss Emily said.

"I was young then. Wanted to be rich. But now I dont want any house."

"Not when you have wanted to go to Chicago for thirty years?" Their breathing was alike: each that harsh, rasping breath of the old, the short inhalations that do not reach the bottom of the lungs: tireless, precarious, on the verge of cessation for all time, as if anything might suffice: a word, a look. "What are you going to do, then?"

"Going to the poorhouse."

"The poorhouse? When I'm trying to fix you so you'll

14.

have neither to worry nor lift your hand as long as you live?

"I dont want nothing," the negro said. "I'm going to the poorhouse. I already told them."

"Well," Miss Emily said. She had not moved her head, not moved at all. "Do you mind telling me why you want to go to the poorhouse?"

Again he mused. The room was still save for their breaing: it was as though they had both quitted all living and all dying; all the travail of mortality and of breath. "So I can set on that hill in the sun all day and watch them trains pass. See them at night too, with the engine puffing and lights in all the windows.

"Oh," Miss Emily said. Motionless, her knotted hands lying on the yellowed coverlet beneath her chin and her chin resting upon her breast, she appeared to muse intently, as though she were listening to dissolution setting up within her. "Hah," she said.

Then she died, and the negro met the first of the ladies at the front door and let them in, with their hushed sibilant voices and their quick curious glances, and he went on to the back and disappeared. He walked right through the house and out the back and was not seen again.

The two female cousins came at once. They held the funeral on the second day, with the town coming to look at Miss Emily beneath a mass of bought flowers, with the crayon face of her father musing profoundly above the bier and the la-grin cemented into what had once been a pillow by a substance like hardened sealing-wax. One side of the covers was flung back, as though he were preparing to rise; we lifted the covers completely away, liberating still another sluggish cloud of infinitesimal dust, invisible and tainted. The body had apparently once lain in the attitude of an embrace, but now the long sleep that outlasts love, that conquers even the grimace of love, had cuckolded him: what was left of him lay beneath what was left of the nightshirt, become inextricable with the bed in which he lay, and upon him and upon the pillow beside him lay that even coating of the patient and biding dust. /p/ Then we noticed that in the second pillow was the indentation of a head; one of us lifted something from it, and leaning forward, that faint and invisible dust lean and acrid in the nostrils, we saw a long strand of iron-gray hair.

William Faulkner

Comments on the Story

The following remarks, made on various occasions during Faulkner's stay at the University of Virginia 1957 and 1958 are derived from *Faulkner at the University: Class Conferences at the University of Virginia 1957–58,* ed. Frederick Gwynn and Joseph Blotner.

Q. Sir, in "A Rose for Emily" is it possible to take Homer Barron and Emily and sort of show that one represents the South and the North? Is there anything on your part there trying to show the North and the South in sort of a battle, maybe Miss Emily representing the South coming out victorious in the rather odd way that she did?

A. That would be only incidental. I think that the writer is too busy trying to create flesh-and-blood people that will stand up and cast a shadow to have time to be conscious of all the symbolism that he may put into what he does or what people may read into it. That if he had time to—that is, if one individual could write the authentic, credible, flesh-and-blood character and at the same time deliver the message, maybe he would, but I don't believe any writer is capable of doing both, that he's got to choose one of the two: either he is delivering a message or he's trying to create flesh-and-blood, living, suffering, anguishing human beings. And as any man works out of his past, since any man—no man is himself, he's the sum of his past, and in a way, if you can accept the term, of his future too. And this struggle between the South and the North could have been a part of my background, my experience, without me knowing it.

[March 11, 1957]

Q. Sir, it has been argued that "A Rose for Emily" is a criticism of the North, and others have argued saying that it is a criticism of the South. Now, could this story, shall we say, be more properly classified as a criticism of the times?

A. Now that I don't know, because I was simply trying to write about people. The writer uses environment—what he knows—and if there's a symbolism in which the lover represented the North and the woman who murdered him represents the South, I don't say that's not valid and not there, but it was no intention of the writer to say, Now let's see, I'm going to write a piece in which I will use a symbolism for the North and another symbol for the South, that he was simply writing about people, a story which he thought was tragic and true, because it came out of the human heart, the human aspiration, the human—the conflict of conscience with glands, with the Old Adam. It was a conflict not between the North and the South so much as between, well you might say, God and Satan.

Q. Sir, just a little more on that thing. You say it's a conflict between God and Satan. Well, I don't quite understand what you mean. Who is—did one represent the—

A. The conflict was in Miss Emily, that she knew that you do not murder people. She had been trained that you do not take a lover. You marry, you don't take a lover. She had broken all the laws of her tradition, her background, and she had finally broken the law of God too, which says you do not take human life. And she knew she was doing wrong, and that's why her own life was wrecked. Instead of murdering one lover, and then to go on and take another and when she used him up to murder him, she was expiating her crime.

Q. . . . She did do all the things that she had been taught not to do, and being a sensitive sort of a woman, it was sure to have told on her, but do you think it's fair to feel pity for her, because in a way she made her adjustment, and it seems to have wound up in a happy sort of a way—certainly tragic, but maybe it suited her just fine.

A. Yes, it may have, but then I don't think that one should withhold pity simply because the subject of the pity, object of pity, is pleased and satisfied. I think the pity is in the human striving against its own nature, against its own conscience. That's what deserves the pity. It's not the state of the individual, it's man in conflict with his heart, or with his fellows, or with his environment—that's what deserves the pity. It's not that the man suffered, or that he fell off the house, or was run over by the train. It's that he was—that man is trying to do the best he can with his desires and impulses against his own moral conscience, and the conscience of, the social conscience of his time and his place—the little town he must live in, the family he's a part of.

[March 13, 1957]

Q. What is the meaning of the title "A Rose for Emily"?

A. Oh, it's simply the poor woman had had no life at all. Her father had kept her more or less locked up and then she had a lover who was about to quit her, she had to murder him. It was just "A Rose for Emily"—that's all.

[April 15, 1957]

Q. I was wondering, one of your short stories, "A Rose for Emily," what ever inspired you to write this story . . . ?

A. That to me was another sad and tragic manifestation of man's condition in which he dreams and hopes, in which he is in conflict with himself or with his environment or with others. In this case there was the young girl with a young girl's normal aspirations to find love and then a husband and a family, who was browbeaten and kept down by her father, a selfish man who didn't want her to leave home because he wanted a housekeeper, and it was a natural instinct of—repressed which—you can't repress it—you can mash it down but it comes up somewhere else and very likely in a tragic form, and that was simply another manifestation of man's injustice to man, of the poor tragic human being struggling with its own heart, with others, with its environment, for the simple things which all human beings want. In that case it was a young girl that just wanted to be loved and to love and to have a husband and a family.

Q. And that purely came from your imagination?

A. Well, the story did but the condition is there. It exists. I didn't invent that condition, I didn't invent the fact that young girls dream of someone to love and children and a home, but the story of what her own particular tragedy was was invented, yes. . . .

[May 20, 1957]

Q. Is "A Rose for Emily" all fiction?

A. Yes sir. Yes sir, that's all fiction, for the reason I said, too. If any time a writer writes anything that seems at all familiar to anybody anywhere, he gets a letter about it, and if they think he's got enough money, he's sued, too, so he's awful careful not to write anything he ever saw himself, or anybody ever told him.

[May 30, 1957]

Two Interpretations by Students, with Notes/Outlines

Here we give two essays by students. Each essay is prefaced by some brief notes that the students used as an outline, but you will see that although the notes provided much guidance and doubtless helped the students to get started, in the course of drafting and revising and revising yet again, each writer did not hesitate to depart from the outline.

The point: Most writers jot down notes, as ideas occur to them, then they organize the notes into what seems to be a reasonable pattern, and from these organized notes they produce a first draft. But even as they write this first draft, fresh ideas will occur. The organized notes are a help in getting started, but they should not become a straitjacket. After the first draft has been written, writers revise it, and then revise the revision, often in the light of comments made by peer reviewers.

Why did Emily Grierson Kill Homer Barron?
  Emily must have a motive; she is like a real person, not a symbol (quote Faulkner)
classroom discussion:
  she needs a man (substitute for father)
  she feels guilty for having had sex with HB (I kept my mouth shut, but I think my point—that HB is gay, and she kills him when she finds out he has been using her as a cover for his gay life-style—makes better sense
Evidence:
  "he linked men"
  Homer = homo
  Barron = barren, sterile
  advantage of this interpretation:
  clear and simple; no phoney psychologizing

Freer 1

Sally Freer

Professor Hwang

English 102

22 October 2009

Why Miss Emily Grierson Killed Homer Barron

Classroom discussion of William Faulkner's "A Rose for Emily" concentrated on two topics: "What is the psychological nature of the woman who murders Homer Barron?" and "Is the

Freer 2

story really about Emily or is it about the Old South versus the New South, or perhaps about the South versus the North?" Many years ago someone at the University of Virginia raised this second issue when he or she asked Faulkner if it is "possible to take Homer Barron and Emily and sort of show that one represents the South and the North." Faulkner replied:

> That would be only incidental. I think that the writer is too busy trying to create flesh-and-blood people that will stand up and cast a shadow to have time to be conscious of all the symbolism that he may put into what he does or what people may read into it. (250)

Faulkner is not saying that interpretations concerning symbolism are wrong, only that they were not part of his conscious intention, and that he was much more concerned with a story about people than with saying something about the South, Old or New, or about the South and the North. This essay will concentrate on one person, Miss Emily Grierson, not as a symbol but as a, to use Faulkner's own words, "flesh-and-blood" person, and it will offer a reason as to why she killed Homer Barron.

The classroom psychological discussion of why Emily Grierson murdered Homer Barron emphasized Emily's need for a man in her life. In her early years, her father is that man—he has driven away any possible lovers—and when he dies, she tries to retain him by denying that he is dead. She cannot persist in this insane belief, but the need for a man, a substitute for her father, does persist. A man, Homer Barron, arrives, and as we know,

Freer 3

Emily kills him and holds on to him by keeping the corpse in a room in her house. Another psychological explanation for the murder claimed that Emily felt guilty for fornicating with Homer Barron, and therefore she murdered the man who led her into sin. The sociological explanations considered the pressures of the Southern code of chivalry, and they were concerned with explaining the story in terms of the Old South (Colonel Sartoris, and Emily) versus the New South (the townspeople), and with the culture of the South (represented by Colonel Sartoris and Emily) versus the North (Homer Barron). As we have seen, Faulkner indicated that these social differences were not obviously in his mind, though of course it is possible that they were in his subconscious mind.

This essay will concentrate on Miss Emily's reason for murdering Homer Barron. The reason is not that she had some sort of psychological complex, and not that she felt guilty because she had sinned by having sex and it is not related to any sort of cultural differences between the North and the South. The essay will offer a simple explanation that seems obvious to me but it was never raised in class. I will argue, and I will support my thesis with evidence, that Emily kills Homer Barron when she finds out that he is gay, when she finds out he is using her only as a cover for his sexual interest which is in young men, not in women. I am not justifying the murder, but am merely explaining, without turning to psychology or to some sort of allegory about the South and the North, *why* she murders him.

Freer 4

What evidence supports the argument that Homer Barron is gay? When I first read the story, I was immediately struck by this passage: "Homer himself had remarked—he liked men, and it was known that he drank with the younger men in the Elks' Club—that he was not a marrying man" (242). These words seemed to me to mean exactly what they say: Homer liked young men and was not the marrying kind, which is to say that he is gay. Why, then, on Sunday afternoons was he driving around in a yellow-wheeled buggy with Miss Emily? Because, I argue, he wanted people to think he was straight. He wanted some sort of cover for his sexual activity with young men. In the days when Faulkner wrote his stories, unlike today, a person could not be openly gay. A gay man had to seem to be sexually interested in women. If he secretly had relationships with other men, he would cover up his sexual orientation by dating women.

Another passage in the story also provides evidence that Homer Barron is gay.

> The construction company came with niggers and mules and machinery, and a foreman named Homer Barron, a Yankee. . . . (241)

First of all, notice the foreman's name, Homer Barren. Let's begin with his surname, Barron. The word, in another context, might suggest a member of the aristocracy, a baron, but in the context of the story Homer Barron clearly is not an aristocrat. Faulkner is certainly not suggesting that Homer Barron is in anyway noble. "Barron" suggests "barren," not "baron." As a gay man, a man sexually interested in other men, Homer is not going to have children; he is barren. Second, and this point is less obvious but I think it is significant, Homer in this sentence is associated with "mules" and with "machinery," again with things that are not fertile. (Mules, the offspring of female horses and male donkeys, are sterile, infertile.) Finally, though I am less confident about this point, I think that Homer Barron's given name, Homer, perhaps suggests "homosexual." I think that maybe it was commonly pronounced something like "Home uh," which wouldn't be too far from "homo."

If we accept the view that Miss Emily was shocked when she somehow found out that Homer Barron was using her as a cover for his sexual interest in men, we can understand her fury and her motive for murdering him. Faulkner himself said, when he was at the University of Virginia, that Emily "was a young girl that just wanted to be loved and to love and to have a husband and a family" (251). Imagine the shock when she discovered that the man she was going with would not marry her and would never help her to have children. I am not justifying her criminal action, but I do think this interpretation explains Emily's behavior without getting into guesses about her psychologically seeing Homer as a substitute for her father, and without getting into far-fetched interpretations—which Faulkner was not enthusiastic about—that see the story as some sort of allegory of the South and the North rather than a story about "flesh-and-blood people" that Faulkner says he wanted to create.

[New page]

Freer 6

Work Cited

Faulkner, William. "A Rose for Emily." *Literature for Composition.* Ed. Sylvan Barnet, William Burto, and William E. Cain. 9th ed. New York: Longman, 2010. 237–44. Print.

Joining the Conversation: Critical Thinking and Writing

1. What is Sally Freer's thesis?
2. What evidence does Freer offer in support of her thesis?
3. How convincing do you find the evidence? Please explain.
4. Putting aside the matter of whether the essay is convincing, did you find it clear and interesting? Please explain.
5. What grade would you give the essay? Why?

Here is the second essay, this one not concerned with Emily Grierson's motives but with a technique used by Faulkner. The student in effect asks the question "Who narrates the story of Emily Grierson?" Of course Faulkner *wrote* the story, but he invents a narrator who tells it. The student examines the effects that Faulkner gains by using the particular narrator that he does. (On kinds of narrators, see page 363.)

We begin with the notes that the student used as an outline.

Who tells story of Emily's life? A man?? A woman? Everyone in the town?
Faulkner says the men were "respectful," the women were moved by "curiosity." Sexist?
Druggist had written "for rats." How could narrator know this, if he isn't druggist?
Maybe it doesn't matter! Reader doesn't notice!
Character of narrator:
  sexist?
  decent guy otherwise?
    but sort of glad when he hears she is poor. That's bit nasty—or just human?
    "WE were glad." so, not just him!
Still, he seems understanding
WE UNDERSTAND, THROUGH HIM; we are grateful to him
Does he know TOO MUCH? Is he unpleasantly nosey?
No, or maybe just a bit yes; chiefly, he is pretty much a typical person
The rose is his tribute to Emily

John Daremo

Prof. Washington

English 100B

12 October 2009

Insight into Horror: The Role of the Narrator in "A Rose for Emily"

Who tells the reader the story of Miss Emily Grierson's life? Not the author William Faulkner, but a narrator whom the author invents. Faulkner's invented narrator is a member of the community in which Emily lived. This much is evident from the first sentence of the story:

> When Miss Emily Grierson died, our whole town went to her funeral: the men through a sort of respectful affection for a fallen monument, the women mostly out of curiosity to see the inside of her house, which no one save an old Negro manservant—a combined gardner and cook—had seen in at least ten years. (Faulkner 237)

The words "our whole town" identify the speaker as a member of Miss Emily's community. True, they do not identify the speaker as anyone very specific—for instance, a relative or a next-door neighbor or a local clergyman or the druggist who sold Miss Emily the poison—but they do identify the speaker as someone knowledgeable about the community. I will argue that the narrator is not just a character in the story but is essential to *the reader's* understanding of the story.

Before continuing to examine the speaker as a member of the community and also as a guide to the reader, it must be

Daremo 2

pointed out that the story includes a very few passages that such a narrator could not in fact report. After all, only Emily herself or possibly the African American servant Tobe could authoritatively report, "When she opened the package at home there was written on the box, under the skull and bones; 'For rats.'" Here we have the voice of an omniscient narrator, not the voice of a townsman. And the narrator could know about the handwriting and the ink of the letter Miss Emily wrote to the mayor only if the mayor told him, or showed him the letter—actions not mentioned by the narrator, so, again, the information about the writing and the ink reveals an omniscient narrator—a departure from the narrator who tells 99% of the story. But I think readers do not notice these very few passages unless they are re-reading the story and looking very closely to characterize the narrator. Significantly, Faulkner omits from the published version a long passage of dialogue, found in the type-written version (246–48), between the African American servant (Tobe) and Miss Emily. As Hans H. Skei points out (153) in *Reading Faulkner's Best Short Stories,* one reason Faulkner probably omitted this passage from the published version is that the man who narrates most of the story could not possibly have been present at this episode. Obviously Faulkner intended the story to be told by a narrator who is *not* omniscient, and although a very few details are given (such as about Miss Emily reading the label, and about her handwriting), a reader probably does not notice that they are inconsistent with a first-person point of view. On the

Daremo 3

other hand, a whole scene would certainly be noticed, and such a scene would violate our sense that a member of the town is narrating the story.

Although one scholar, Michael I. Burdock, says that the narrator is a woman, Burdock really offers no convincing evidence, and I think the first sentence of the story, with its explanation of the difference between the concern of the men ("respectful affection") and the concern of the women ("curiosity to see the inside of her house") is the sort of put-down of women that too often characterizes male thinking. One other passage seems to me to clearly indicate that the speaker is a male. In the third paragraph Faulkner tells us, through the narrator, that

> Colonel Sartoris invented an involved tale to the effect that Miss Emily's father had loaned money to the town, which the town, as a matter of business, preferred this way of repaying. Only a man of Colonel Sartoris' generation and thought could have invented it, and only a woman could have believed it. (238)

Still, even if we sometimes do hear the voice of a male rather than a female, we can still say that the narrator is more or less the voice of the community as a whole, or in these instances at least the voice of the males of the community, rather than a highly individualized specific character.

What else can we say about the narrator beyond saying that he is a member of the community? In the second paragraph the narrator describes Miss Emily's house, built in a fashionable style

Daremo 4

in the 1870s on what once was "our most select street" but now "an eyesore among eyesores" (237). The narrator certainly does not hesitate to express opinions, but here the opinion probably reflects the view of the entire community. Certainly we do not say that these words show that the narrator is a specialist in architecture, or that he is abnormally sensitive to beauty and to ugliness.

Throughout the story we get passages such as (to take some examples almost at random) "Thus she passed from generation to generation—dear, inescapable, impervious, tranquil, and perverse" (243), and "Two days later we learned that she had bought a complete outfit of men's clothing, including a nightshirt, and we said, 'They are married.' We were really glad" (242). Words such as "dear" and "We were really glad" are enough to disprove Kenneth Payson Kempton's comment that the narrator is an objective reporter (30–31), but we can agree with Kempton's point that the narrator serves chiefly as a reporter rather than as a highly defined character within the story. That is, these personal comments do not give the narrator a unique or distinct personality.

Notice, in fact, that the narrator does not say, "I was glad"; rather, he says, "We were . . . glad." That is, he speaks not as an individual but in his role as the voice of the community. Another passage in which he expresses strong partiality, but, again, as the representative of the entire town, is when he tells us that when Emily denied for three days that her father was dead,

Daremo 5

> We did not say she was crazy then. We believed she had to do that. We remembered all the young men her father had driven away, and we knew that with nothing left, she would have to cling to that which had robbed her, as people will. (240)

Here the narrator is very understanding, but in a few passages he—the community—is not highly sympathetic to Miss Emily. For example, he says, "So when she got to be thirty and was still single, we were not pleased exactly, but vindicated; even with insanity in the family she wouldn't have turned down all of her chances if they had really materialized" (240). We can say that the attitude here is not high-minded, but, again, it probably represents a wide-spread view rather than an individual view. A passage that closely follows this one similarly expresses a somewhat unpleasant but common view:

> When her father died, it got about that the house was all that was left to her; and in a way, people were glad. At last they could pity Miss Emily. Being left alone, and a pauper, she had become humanized. Now she too would know the old thrill and the old despair of a penny more or less. (240)

But even though it is hardly nice to be "glad" that someone has become a pauper, we can in this instance understand the narrator's feeling, and we can even admire his understanding of *why* he and the rest of the community felt this way. And perhaps, as readers, we recognize that *we* might feel pretty much what the community feels.

One objection to the narrator's behavior, not just in this last passage but throughout the story, is voiced especially strongly by the critic Ruth Sullivan. Sullivan argues that the narrator knows *too much* about Miss Emily, that the narrator is in effect a spy concerned with other people's sexuality. Sullivan, who apparently is a Freudian critic, says that the narrator reveals "unsavory qualities" (162). Sullivan speaks of the narrator's "aggression and sadism" (171), and she goes so far as to say that the story is "about types of perversion—Miss Emily's necrophilia and the narrator's voyeurism—that are motivated by frustrated sexual needs and by fears about loss of the loved object" (175). True, Faulkner does have the narrator say such things as "Daily, monthly, yearly, we watched," but surely it is going too far to see this interest in an eccentric as a "perversion," especially as a perversion comparable to necrophilia. And it is going too far to say that the story is *about* the narrator as well as about Emily. After all, this story is not at all like, say, Edgar Alan Poe's "The Cask of Amontillado" which certainly *is* about the narrator at least as much as it is about the nominal subject, a man named Fortunato.

My point thus far is simply this: Although the story is told by a first-person narrator, the reader's interest is chiefly in the *tale* the narrator tells—the story about Miss Emily—not in the narrator himself. Further, the narrator represents the voice of the community, and though on rare occasions he displays a somewhat unpleasant trait, as when he (and the rest of the community) is pleased that Miss Emily now knows the importance of every penny, on the whole (despite Ruth K. Sullivan's view that the narrator is a perverse voyeur) this narrative voice is chiefly sympathetic to Miss Emily. Even more important, and indeed the reason that this narrative voice is essential to the story, is the fact that Miss Emily's behavior—murdering Homer Barron and at least once laying next to the corpse—would be horrifying if it were not that the narrator has, by his intelligent and (for the most part) sympathetic comments, helped us to see her as an intelligible, believable character. Faulkner's story is not like, for instance, a ghost story, where the interest is entirely in fantastic happenings, and not in the personality of the central figure. Nor is it—even though the story is partly about a murder and a hidden corpse—is it like a detective story, where, again, the interest is entirely in the plot: Who did it, and how will the mystery be unraveled? Nor is Miss Emily some sort of stock figure out of a horror story, someone whose strange actions hold our attention primarily because they are strange, freakish. The story is *not* just a shocker, a meaningless tale with a surprise ending, a story that can be read only once, for its plot, and then, because the ending is known, cannot interest a reader a second or a third time. On the contrary, the story becomes *more* interesting each time one reads it, *more* a revelation of understandable human behavior.

Nor (except in the most literal sense) are the last words in the final paragraph the last word in the story. At the end,

Daremo 8

probably many readers briefly wonder why it is called "A Rose for Emily." Faulkner himself, when asked in 1955 in an interview in Japan what the significance of the title was, said that it was "a salute, just as if you were to make a gesture, a salute to anyone; to a woman you would hand a rose, as you would lift a cup of *sake* to a man" (71). The telling of this tale is itself the rose, the community's tribute. And because the narrator helps *us* to see Emily's humanity beneath her weirdness, *we* become part of the narrator's community. By the end of the story, when the narrator says "we," readers can include themselves in the "we." We, with the narrator's help, see the humanity in a woman whose behavior might seem monstrous to us if the narrator had not guided us.

[New page]

Daremo 9

Works Cited

Barnet, Sylvan, William Burto and William E. Cain, ed. *Literature for Composition*, 9th ed. New York: Longman, 2010. Print.

Burdock, Michael I. "Another View of Faulkner's Narrator in 'A Rose for Emily.'" *University of Mississippi Studies in English*, n.s. 8 (1990): 209–11. Print.

Faulkner, William. "A. Rose for Emily," Barnet, Burto, and Cain. 237–44. Print.

Daremo 10

Jelliffe, Robert A., ed. *Faulkner at Nagano.* Tokyo: Kenkyusha, 1956. Print.

Kempton, Kenneth. *The Short Story* Cambridge, Mass: Harvard UP, 1948. Print.

Skei, Hans H. *Reading Faulkner's Best Short Stories.* Columbia: U of South Carolina P, 1999. Print.

Sullivan, Ruth K. "The Narrator in 'A Rose for Emily.'" *Journal of Narrative Technique* 1 (1971): 159–78. Print.

Joining the Conversation: Critical Thinking and Writing

1. What is Daremo's thesis?
2. What evidence does Daremo offer in support of his thesis?
3. How convincing do you find the evidence? Please explain.
4. Putting aside the matter of whether the essay is convincing, did you find it clear and interesting? Please explain.
5. What grade would you give the essay? Why?

CHAPTER 8

Arguing an Evaluation

Criticism and Evaluation

Although, as previously noted, in ordinary usage *criticism* implies finding fault, and therefore implies evaluation—"This story is weak"—in fact most literary criticism is *not* concerned with evaluation. Rather, it is chiefly concerned with *interpretation* (the setting forth of meaning) and with *analysis* (examination of relationships among the parts, or of causes and effects).

For instance, an interpretation may argue that in *Death of a Salesman* Willy Loman is the victim of a cruel capitalistic economy, and an analysis may show how the symbolic setting of the play (a stage direction tells us that "towering, angular shapes" surround the salesman's house) contributes to the meaning.

In Chapter 5 we asked the question "What is literature?" We saw that an analysis of Robert Frost's "The Span of Life" (page 103) called attention to the contrast between the meter of the first line (relatively uneven or irregular, with an exceptional number of heavy stresses) and the meter of the second (relatively even and jingling). The analysis also called attention to the contrast between the content of the first line (the old dog) and the second (the speaker's memory of a young dog):

> The old dog barks backward without getting up.
> I can remember when he was a pup.

In our discussion we did not worry about whether this poem deserves an A, B, or C, nor did we consider whether it was better or worse than some other poem by Frost, or by some other writer. And, to repeat, if you read books and journals devoted to literary study, you find chiefly discussions of meaning. For the most part, critics assume that the works they are writing about have value and are good enough to merit attention, so critics largely concern themselves with other matters.

Still, some critical writing is indeed concerned with evaluation—with saying that works are good or bad, dated or classic, major or minor. (The language need not be as explicit as these words are: Evaluation can also be conveyed through words like *moving, successful, effective, important,* or, on the other hand, *tedious, unsuccessful, weak,* and *trivial.*) In reviews of plays, books, musical and dance performances, and films, professional critics usually devote much of their space to evaluating the work or the performance, or both. The reviewer seeks, finally, to tell readers whether to buy a book or a ticket—or to save their money and their time.

In short, although in our independent reading we read what we like, and we need not argue that one work is better than another, the issue of evaluation is evident all around us.

Are There Critical Standards?

One approach to evaluating a work of literature, or, indeed, to evaluating anything at all, is to rely on personal taste. This approach is evident in a statement such as "I don't know anything about modern art, but I know what I like." The idea is old, at least as old as the Roman saying *De gustibus non est disputandum* ("There is no disputing tastes").

If we say "This is a good work" or "This book is greater than that book," are we saying anything beyond "I like this" and "I like this better than that"? Are all expressions of evaluation really nothing more than expressions of taste? Most people believe that if there are such things as works of art, or works of literature, there must be standards by which they can be evaluated, just as most other things are evaluated by standards. The standards for evaluating a scissors, for instance, are perfectly clear: It ought to cut cleanly, it ought not to need frequent sharpening, and it ought to feel comfortable in the hand. We may also want it to look nice (perhaps to be painted—or on the contrary to reveal its stainless steel), and to be inexpensive, rustproof, and so on, but in any case we can easily state our standards. Similarly, there are agreed-upon standards for evaluating figure skating, gymnastics, fluency in language, and so on.

But what are the standards for evaluating literature? In earlier pages we have implied one standard: In a good work of literature, all of the parts contribute to the whole, making a unified work. Some people would add that mere unity is not enough; a work of high quality needs not only to be unified but also to be complex. The writer offers a "performance in words" (Frost's words, again), and when we read, we can see if the writer has successfully kept all of the Indian clubs in the air. If, for instance, the stated content of the poem is mournful, yet the meter jingles, we can probably say that the performance is unsuccessful; at least one of the juggler's Indian clubs is clattering on the floor.

Here are some of the standards commonly set forth:

- Moral content
- Truth, realism
- Personal taste
- Esthetic qualities, for instance unity

Let's look at some of these in detail.

Morality and Truth as Standards

"It is always a writer's duty to make the world better." Thus wrote Samuel Johnson, in 1765, in his "Preface to Shakespeare." In this view, morality plays a large role: A story that sympathetically treats lesbian or gay love is, from a traditional Judeo-Christian perspective, probably regarded as a bad story, or at least not as worthy as a story that celebrates heterosexual married love. On the other hand, a gay or lesbian critic, or anyone not committed to Judeo-Christian values, might regard the story highly because, in such a reader's view, it helps to educate readers and thereby does something "to make the world better."

But there are obvious problems. For one thing, a gay or lesbian story might strike even a reader with traditional values as a work that is effectively told, with believable and memorable characters, whereas a story of heterosexual married love might be unbelievable, awkwardly told, trite, sentimental. (More about sentimentality in a moment.) How much value should we give to the ostensible content of the story, the obvious moral or morality, and how much value should we give to the artistry exhibited in telling the story?

People differ greatly about moral (and religious) issues. Edward Fitzgerald's 1859 translation of *The Rubáiyát of Omar Khayyám* (a twelfth-century Persian poem) suggests that God does not exist, or—perhaps worse—if He does exist,

He doesn't care about us. That God does not exist is a view held by many moral people; it is also a view opposed by many moral people. The issue then may become a matter of **truth.** Does the value of the poem depend on which view is right? In fact, does a reader have to subscribe to Fitzgerald's view to enjoy (and to evaluate highly) the following stanza from the poem, in which Fitzgerald suggests that the pleasures of this world are the only paradise that we can experience?

> A book of verses underneath the bough,
> A jug of wine, a loaf of bread—and thou
>   Beside me singing in the wilderness—
> Oh, wilderness were paradise enow!

Some critics can give high value to a literary work only if they share its beliefs, if they think that the work corresponds to reality. They measure the work against their vision of the truth.

Other critics highly value a work of literature that expresses ideas they do not believe, arguing that literature does not require us to believe in its views. Rather, this theory claims, literature gives a reader a strong sense of *what it feels like* to hold certain views—even though the reader does not share those views. Take, for instance, a lyric poem in which Christina Rossetti (1830–1894), a devout Anglican, expresses both spiritual numbness and spiritual hope. Here is one stanza from "A Better Resurrection":

> My life is like a broken bowl.
>   A broken bowl that cannot hold
> One drop of water for my soul
>   Or cordial in the searching cold:
> Cast in the fire the perished thing:
>   Melt and remould it, till it be
> A royal cup for Him, my King:
>   O Jesus, drink of me.

One need not be an Anglican suffering a crisis to find this poem of considerable interest. It offers insight into a state of mind, and the truth or falsity of religious belief is not at issue. Similarly, we can argue that although *The Divine Comedy* by Dante Alighieri (1265–1321) is deeply a Roman Catholic work, the non-Catholic reader can read it with interest and pleasure because of (for example) its rich portrayal of a wide range of characters, the most famous of whom perhaps are the pathetic lovers Paolo and Francesca. In Dante's view, they are eternally damned because they were unrepentant adulterers, but a reader need not share this belief.

Other Ways of Thinking about Truth and Realism

Other solutions to the problem of whether a reader must share a writer's beliefs have been offered. One extreme view says that beliefs are irrelevant, since literature has nothing to do with truth. In this view, a work of art does not correspond to anything "outside" itself, that is, to anything in the real world. If a work of art has any "truth," it is only in the sense of being internally consistent. Thus Shakespeare's *Macbeth,* like, say, the lullaby "Rock-a-bye Baby," isn't making assertions about reality. *Macbeth* has nothing to do with the history of Scotland, just as (in this view) Shakespeare's *Julius Caesar* has nothing to do with the history of Rome, although Shakespeare borrowed some of his material from history books. These tragedies, like lullabies, are worlds in themselves—not to be judged against historical accounts of Scotland or Rome—and we are interested in the characters in the plays only as they exist *in the plays.* We may require, for instance, that the characters be consistent, believable, and engaging, but we cannot require that they correspond to historical figures.

Literary works are neither true nor false; they are only (when successful) coherent and interesting. The poet William Butler Yeats (1865–1939) perhaps had in mind something along these lines when he said that you can refute a philosopher, but you cannot refute the song of sixpence. And indeed "Sing a song of sixpence, / Pocket full of rye" has endured for a couple of centuries, perhaps partly because it has nothing to do with truth or falsity; it has created its own engaging world.

And yet it's possible to object, offering a commonsense response: Surely when we see a play, or read an engaging work of literature, whether it is old or new, we feel that somehow the work says something about the life around us, the real world. True, some of what we read—let's say, detective fiction—is chiefly fanciful: We read it to test our wits, or to escape, or to kill time. But most literature seems to be connected to life. This commonsense view, that literature is related to life, has an ancient history, and in fact almost everyone in the Western world believed it from the time of the ancient Greeks until the nineteenth century. And many people—including authors and highly skilled readers—still believe it today.

Certainly a good deal of literature, most notably the realistic short story and the novel, is devoted to giving a detailed picture that at least *looks like* the real world. One reason we read the fiction of Kate Chopin is to find out what "the real world" of Creole New Orleans in the late nineteenth century was like—as seen through Chopin's eyes, of course. (You need not be a Marxist to believe, with Karl Marx, that you can learn more about industrial England from the novels of Dickens and Elizabeth Gaskell than from economic treatises.) Writers of stories, novels, and plays are concerned to give plausible, indeed precise and insightful, images of the relationships between people. Writers of lyric poems presumably are specialists in presenting human feelings—the experience of love, for instance, or of the loss of faith. Presumably we are invited to compare the writer's created world to the world that we live in, perhaps to be reminded that our own lives can be richer than they are.

Even when a writer describes an earlier time, the implication is that the description is accurate, and especially that people *did* behave the way the writer says they did—and the way our own daily experience shows us that people do behave. Here is George Eliot at the beginning of her novel *Adam Bede* (1859):

> With a single drop of ink for a mirror, the Egyptian sorcerer undertook to reveal to any chance comer far-reaching visions of the past. This is what I undertake to do for you, reader. With this drop of ink at the end of my pen, I will show you the roomy workshop of Jonathan Burge, carpenter and builder in the village of Hayslope, as it appeared on the 18th of June, in the year of Our Lord, 1799.

Why do novelists like George Eliot give us detailed pictures, and cause us to become deeply involved in the lives of their characters? Another novelist, D. H. Lawrence, offers a relevant comment in the ninth chapter of *Lady Chatterley's Lover* (1928):

> It is the way our sympathy flows and recoils that really determines our lives. And here lies the vast importance of the novel, properly handled. It can inform and lead into new places the flow of our sympathetic consciousness, and it can lead our sympathy away in recoil from things gone dead. Therefore, the novel, properly handled, can reveal the most secret places of life.

In Lawrence's view, we can evaluate a novel in terms of its moral effect on the reader: The good novel, Lawrence claims, leads us into worlds—human relationships—that deserve our attention, and leads us away from "things gone dead," presumably relationships and values—whether political, moral, or religious—that no longer deserve to survive. To be blunt, Lawrence claims that good books improve us. His comment is similar to a more violent comment, quoted earlier, by Franz Kafka: "A book must be an ice-axe to break the frozen sea inside us."

Realism is not the writer's only tool. In *Gulliver's Travels* Swift gives us a world of Lilliputians, people about six inches tall. Is his book pure fancy, unrelated to life? Not at all. We perceive that the Lilliputians are (except for their size) pretty much like ourselves, and we realize that their tiny stature is an image of human pettiness, an *un*realistic device that helps us to see the real world more clearly.

The view that we have been talking about—that writers do connect us to the world—does not require realism, but it does assume that writers see, understand, and, through the medium of their writings, give us knowledge, deepen our understanding, and even perhaps improve our character. If, the argument goes, a work distorts reality—let's say because the author sees women superficially—the work is inferior. Some such assumption is found, for instance, in a comment by Elaine Savory Fido, who says that the work of Derek Walcott, a Caribbean poet and dramatist, is successful when Walcott deals with racism and with colonialism but is unsuccessful when he deals with women. "His treatment of women," Fido says in an essay in *Journal of Commonwealth Literature* (1986),

> is full of clichés, stereotypes and negativity. I shall seek to show how some of his worst writing is associated with these portraits of women, which sometimes lead him to the brink of losing verbal control, or give rise to a retreat into abstract, conventional terms which prevent any real treatment of the subject. (109)

We need not here be concerned with whether Fido's evaluations of Walcott's works about women and about colonialism are convincing: What concerns us is her assumption that works can be—should be—evaluated in terms of the keenness of the writer's perception of reality.

Although we need not be concerned with an evaluation, we may wish to be concerned with it—and if so, we will probably find, perhaps to our surprise, that in the very process of arguing our evaluation (perhaps only to ourselves) we are also interpreting and reinterpreting. That is, we find ourselves observing passages closely, from a new point of view, and we may therefore find ourselves seeing them differently, finding new meanings in them.

Your Turn: Poems and Stories for Evaluation

SARAH N. CLEGHORN

Sarah N. Cleghorn (1876–1959) was born in Manchester, Vermont. A Quaker, she was active in pacifist, anti-vivisectionist, and women's suffrage movements. Among her many books are The True Ballad of Glorious Harriet Tubman *(1933) and an autobiography,* Threescore *(1936).*

The Golf Links

The golf links lie so near the mill
    That almost every day
The laboring children can look out
    And see the men at play.

[1917]

Joining the Conversation: Critical Thinking and Writing

1. Check the meanings of "ironic," "satiric," and "sarcastic" in a dictionary, and decide which if any of these words applies well to Cleghorn's poem.

2. The poem was published in 1917, when child labor was common. (Children as young as ten worked as much as fifteen hours a day in mills. In 1916—a year before the poem was published—Congress had passed the Child Labor Act, but in 1918 the Supreme Court struck down the act, arguing that Congress did not have the right to control labor within a state.) Today, however, child labor in the United States is virtually nonexistent. Is there any point, then, in reading this poem? Set forth your response in a brief argument, perhaps of two paragraphs.

WILFRED OWEN

Wilfred Owen (1893–1918) was born in the county of Shropshire in western England, and he studied at London University. He enlisted in the army at the outbreak of World War I and fought in the Battle of the Somme (Jul.–Nov., 1916) until he was hospitalized with shell shock. After his recuperation in England, he returned to the front only to be killed in action one week before the end of the war (Nov. 11, 1918). His collected poems were published posthumously (Dec. 1, 1920).

*Dulce et Decorum Est**

Bent double, like old beggars under sacks,
Knock-kneed, coughing like hags, we cursed through sludge,
Till on the haunting flares we turned our backs
And towards our distant rest began to trudge.
Men marched asleep. Many had lost their boots
But limped on, blood-shod. All went lame; all blind;
Drunk with fatigue; deaf even to the hoots
Of tired, outstripped Five-Nines° that dropped behind.

Gas! Gas! Quick, boys! — An ecstasy of fumbling,
Fitting the clumsy helmets just in time;
But someone still was yelling out and stumbling
And flound'ring like a man in fire or lime . . .
Dim, through the misty panes and thick green light,

*__Dulce et Decorum Est__ From the Latin poet Horace's *Odes* (III:2.13): *Dulce et decorum est pro patria mori*—"It is sweet and honorable to die for your country." **8 Five-Nines** shells containing poison gas.

As under a green sea, I saw him drowning.
In all my dreams, before my helpless sight,
He plunges at me, guttering, choking, drowning.

If in some smothering dreams you too could pace
Behind the wagon that we flung him in,
And watch the white eyes writhing in his face,
His hanging face, like a devil's sick of sin;
If you could hear, at every jolt, the blood
Come gargling from the froth-corrupted lungs,
Obscene as cancer, bitter as the cud
Of vile, incurable sores on innocent tongues,—
My friend,° you would not tell with such high zest
To children ardent for some desperate glory,
The old Lie: Dulce et decorum est
Pro patria mori.

[1917]

25 My friend Jessie Pope, author of patriotic verse.

Joining the Conversation: Critical Thinking and Writing

How highly do you rate this poem? Why? Does your knowledge of the fact that Owen died in World War I affect your response toward the poem, especially your sense of its value?

Anthem for Doomed Youth

What passing-bells for these who die as cattle?
Only the monstrous anger of the guns.
Only the stuttering rifles' rapid rattle
Can patter out their hasty orisons.
No mockeries for them from prayers or bells,
Nor any voice of mourning save the choirs—
The shrill, demented choirs of wailing shells;
And bugles calling for them from sad shires.

What candles may be held to speed° them all?
Not in the hands of boys, but in their eyes
Shall shine the holy glimmers of good-byes.
The pallor of girls' brows shall be their pall;
Their flowers the tenderness of patient minds,
And each slow dusk a drawing-down of blinds.

[1920]

9 speed aid.

Joining the Conversation: Critical Thinking and Writing

1. What is an anthem? What are some of the words or phrases in this poem that might be found in a traditional anthem? What are some of the words or phrases that you would not expect in an anthem?
2. How would you characterize the speaker's state of mind? (Your response probably will require more than one word.)

HENRY REED

Born in Birmingham, England, Henry Reed (1914–1986) served in the British army during World War II. Later, in civilian life, he had a distinguished career as a journalist, a translator of French and Italian literature, a writer of radio plays, and a poet.

"Naming of Parts" draws on his experience as a military recruit.

Naming of Parts

Today we have naming of parts. Yesterday,
We had daily cleaning. And tomorrow morning,
We shall have what to do after firing. But today,
Today we have naming of parts. Japonica
Glistens like coral in all of the neighboring gardens,
And today we have naming of parts.

This is the lower sling swivel. And this
Is the upper sling swivel, whose use you will see,
When you are given your slings. And this is the piling swivel,
Which in your case you have not got. The branches
Hold in the gardens their silent, eloquent gestures,
Which in our case we have not got.

This is the safety-catch, which is always released
With an easy flick of the thumb. And please do not let me
See anyone using his finger. You can do it quite easy
If you have any strength in your thumb. The blossoms
Are fragile and motionless, never letting anyone see
Any of them using their finger.

And this you can see is the bolt. The purpose of this
Is to open the breech, as you see. We can slide it
Rapidly backwards and forwards: we call this
Easing the spring. And rapidly backwards and forwards
The early bees are assaulting and fumbling the flowers:
They call it easing the Spring.

They call it easing the Spring: it is perfectly easy
If you have any strength in your thumb: like the bolt,
And the breech, and the cocking-piece, and the point of balance,
Which in our case we have not got; and the almond-blossom
Silent in all of the gardens and the bees going backwards and forwards,
    For today we have naming of parts.

[1946]

Joining the Conversation: Critical Thinking and Writing

1. How many speakers do you hear in the poem? How would you characterize each of them?
2. Would you argue that this poem is a better poem than one or the other of the two preceding poems? Or is it poorer? Or can't one argue such a topic? Explain.

KATHERINE MANSFIELD

Katherine Mansfield (1888–1923), née Kathleen Mansfield Beauchamp, was born in New Zealand. In 1902 she went to London for schooling; in 1906 she returned to New Zealand, but dissatisfied with its provincialism, she returned in 1908 to London to become a writer. After a disastrous marriage and a love affair, she went to Germany, where she wrote stories; in 1910 she returned to London, published a book of stories in 1911, and in 1912 met and began living with the writer John Middleton Murry. In 1918, after her first husband at last divorced her, she married Murry. She died of tuberculosis in 1923, a few months after her thirty-fourth birthday.

Mansfield published about seventy stories, and left some others unpublished. An early admirer of Chekhov, she read his works in German translations before they were translated into English.

Miss Brill

Although it was so brilliantly fine—the blue sky powdered with gold and great spots of light like white wine splashed over the Jardins Publiques[1]—Miss Brill was glad that she had decided on her fur. The air was motionless, but when you opened your mouth there was just a faint chill, like a chill from a glass of iced water before you sip, and now and again a leaf came drifting—from nowhere, from the sky. Miss Brill put up her hand and touched her fur. Dear little thing! It was nice to feel it again. She had taken it out of its box that afternoon, shaken out the moth-powder, given it a good brush, and rubbed the life back into the dim little eyes. "What has been happening to me?" said the sad little eyes. Oh, how sweet it was to see them snap at her again from the red eiderdown! . . . But the nose, which was of some black composition, wasn't at all firm. It must have had a knock, somehow. Never mind—a little dab of black sealing-wax when the time came—when it was absolutely necessary. . . . Little rogue! Yes, she really felt like that about it. Little rogue biting its tail just by her left ear. She could have taken it off

[1]**Jardins Publiques** Public Gardens (French).

and laid it on her lap and stroked it. She felt a tingling in her hands and arms, but that came from walking, she supposed. And when she breathed, something light and sad—no, not sad, exactly—something gentle seemed to move in her bosom.

There were a number of people out this afternoon, far more than last Sunday. And the band sounded louder and gayer. That was because the Season had begun. For although the band played all year round on Sundays, out of season it was never the same. It was like some one playing with only the family to listen; it didn't care how it played if there weren't any strangers present. Wasn't the conductor wearing a new coat, too? She was sure it was new. He scraped with his foot and flapped his arms like a rooster about to crow, and the bandsmen sitting in the green rotunda blew out their cheeks and glared at the music. Now there came a little "flutey" bit—very pretty!—a little chain of bright drops. She was sure it would be repeated. It was; she lifted her head and smiled.

Only two people shared her "special" seat: a fine old man in a velvet coat, his hands clasped over a huge carved walking-stick, and a big old woman, sitting upright, with a roll of knitting on her embroidered apron. They did not speak. This was disappointing, for Miss Brill always looked forward to the conversation. She had become really quite expert, she thought, at listening as though she didn't listen, at sitting in other people's lives just for a minute while they talked round her.

She glanced, sideways, at the old couple. Perhaps they would go soon. Last Sunday, too, hadn't been as interesting as usual. An Englishman and his wife, he wearing a dreadful Panama hat and she button boots. And she'd gone on the whole time about how she ought to wear spectacles; she knew she needed them; but that it was no good getting any; they'd be sure to break and they'd never keep on. And he'd been so patient. He'd suggested everything—gold rims, the kind that curved round your ears, little pads inside the bridge. No, nothing would please her. "They'll always be sliding down my nose!" Miss Brill had wanted to shake her.

5 The old people sat on the bench, still as statues. Never mind, there was always the crowd to watch. To and fro, in front of the flower-beds and the band rotunda, the couples and groups paraded, stopped to talk, to greet, to buy a handful of flowers from the old beggar who had his tray fixed to the railings. Little children ran among them, swooping and laughing; little boys with big white silk bows under their chins, little girls, little French dolls, dressed up in velvet and lace. And sometimes a tiny staggerer came suddenly rocking into the open from under the trees, stopped, stared, as suddenly sat down "flop," until its small high-stepping mother, like a young hen, rushed scolding to its rescue. Other people sat on the benches and green chairs, but they were nearly always the same, Sunday after Sunday, and—Miss Brill had often noticed—there was something funny about nearly all of them. They were odd, silent, nearly all old, and from the way they stared they looked as though they'd just come from dark little rooms or even—even cupboards!

Behind the rotunda the slender trees with yellow leaves down drooping, and through them just a line of sea, and beyond the blue sky with gold-veined clouds.

Tum-tum-tum tiddle-um! tiddle-um! tum tiddley-um tum ta! blew the band.

Two young girls in red came by and two young soldiers in blue met them, and they laughed and paired and went off arm-in-arm. Two peasant women with funny straw hats passed, gravely, leading beautiful smoke-colored donkeys. A cold, pale nun hurried by. A beautiful woman came along and dropped her bunch of violets, and a little boy ran after to hand them to her, and she took them and threw them away as if they'd been poisoned. Dear me! Miss Brill didn't know whether to admire that or not! And now an ermine toque[2] and a gentleman in

[2]**toque** a brimless, close-fitting woman's hat.

grey met just in front of her. He was tall, stiff, dignified, and she was wearing the ermine toque she'd bought when her hair was yellow. Now everything, her hair, her face, even her eyes, was the same color as the shabby ermine, and her hand, in its cleaned glove, lifted to dab her lips, was a tiny yellowish paw. Oh, she was so pleased to see him—delighted! She rather thought they were going to meet that afternoon. She described where she'd been—everywhere, here, there, along by the sea. The day was so charming—didn't he agree? And wouldn't he, perhaps? . . . But he shook his head, lighted a cigarette, slowly breathed a great deep puff into her face, and, even while she was still talking and laughing, flicked the match away and walked on. The ermine toque was alone; she smiled more brightly than ever. But even the band seemed to know what she was feeling and played more softly, played tenderly, and the drum beat, "The Brute! The Brute!" over and over. What would she do? What was going to happen now? But as Miss Brill wondered, the ermine toque turned, raised her hand as though she'd seen some one else, much nicer, just over there, and pattered away. And the band changed again and played more quickly, more gaily than ever, and the old couple on Miss Brill's seat got up and marched away, and such a funny old man with long whiskers hobbled along in time to the music and was nearly knocked over by four girls walking abreast.

Oh, how fascinating it was! How she enjoyed it! How she loved sitting here, watching it all! It was like a play. It was exactly like a play. Who could believe the sky at the back wasn't painted? But it wasn't till a little brown dog trotted on solemn and then slowly trotted off, like a little "theatre" dog, a little dog that had been drugged, that Miss Brill discovered what it was that made it so exciting. They were all on the stage. They weren't only the audience, not only looking on; they were acting. Even she had a part and came every Sunday. No doubt somebody would have noticed if she hadn't been there; she was part of the performance after all. How strange she'd never thought of it like that before! And yet it explained why she made such a point of starting from home at just the same time each week—so as not to be late for the performance—and it also explained why she had quite a queer, shy feeling at telling her English pupils how she spent her Sunday afternoons. No wonder! Miss Brill nearly laughed out loud. She was on the stage. She thought of the old invalid gentleman to whom she read the newspaper four afternoons a week while he slept in the garden. She had got quite used to the frail head on the cotton pillow, the hollowed eyes, the open mouth and the high pinched nose. If he'd been dead she mightn't have noticed for weeks; she wouldn't have minded. But suddenly he knew he was having the paper read to him by an actress! "An actress!" The old head lifted; two points of light quivered in the old eyes. "An actress—are ye?" And Miss Brill smoothed the newspaper as though it were the manuscript of her part and said gently: "Yes, I have been an actress for a long time."

10 The band had been having a rest. Now they started again. And what they played was warm, sunny, yet there was just a faint chill—a something, what was it?—not sadness—no, not sadness—a something that made you want to sing. The tune lifted, lifted, the light shone; and it seemed to Miss Brill that in another moment all of them, all the whole company, would begin singing. The young ones, the laughing ones who were moving together, they would begin, and the men's voices, very resolute and brave, would join them. And then she too, she too, and the others on the benches—they would come in with a kind of accompaniment—something low, that scarcely rose or fell, something so beautiful—moving. . . . And Miss Brill's eyes filled with tears and she looked smiling at all the other members of the company. Yes, we understand, we understand, she thought—though what they understood she didn't know.

Just at that moment a boy and a girl came and sat down where the old couple had been. They were beautifully dressed; they were in love. The hero and heroine, of course, just arrived from his father's yacht. And still soundlessly singing, still with that trembling smile, Miss Brill prepared to listen.

"No, not now," said the girl. "Not here, I can't."

"But why? Because of that stupid old thing at the end there?" asked the boy. "Why does she come here at all—who wants her? Why doesn't she keep her silly old mug at home?"

"It's her fu-fur which is so funny," giggled the girl. "It's exactly like a fried whiting."[3]

"Ah, be off with you!" said the boy in an angry whisper. Then: "Tell me, my petite chère[4]—"

"No, not here," said the girl. "Not *yet*."

On her way home she usually bought a slice of honey-cake at the baker's. It was her Sunday treat. Sometimes there was an almond in her slice, sometimes not. It made a great difference. If there was an almond it was like carrying home a tiny present—a surprise—something that might very well not have been there. She hurried on the almond Sundays and struck the match for the kettle in quite a dashing way.

But today she passed the baker's by, climbed the stairs, went into the little dark room—her room like a cupboard—and sat down on the red eiderdown. She sat there for a long time. The box that the fur came out of was on the bed. She unclasped the necklet quickly; quickly, without looking, laid it inside. But when she put the lid on she thought she heard something crying.

[1920]

[3]**whiting** a kind of fish. [4]***petite chère*** darling.

Joining the Conversation: Critical Thinking and Writing

1. Why do you think Mansfield did not give Miss Brill a first name?
2. What would be lost (or gained?) if the first paragraph were omitted?
3. Suppose someone said that the story is about a woman who is justly punished for her pride. What might be your response?

W. Somerset Maugham

W(illiam) Somerset Maugham (1874–1965), born in Paris but of English origin, grew up in England, where he was trained as a physician, but he never practiced medicine. Rather, he preferred to make his living as a novelist, playwright, and writer of short stories. His best-known novel is Of Human Bondage *(1915). The following story is in fact a speech uttered by a character in one of Maugham's plays,* Sheppey *(1933).*

The Appointment in Samarra

Death speaks: There was a merchant in Bagdad who sent his servant to market to buy provisions and in a little while the servant came back, white and trembling, and said, Master, just now when I was in the marketplace I was jostled by a woman in the crowd and when I turned I saw it was Death that jostled me. She looked at me and made a threatening gesture, now, lend me your horse, and I will ride away from the city and avoid my fate. I will go to Samarra and there Death will not find me. The merchant lent him his horse, and the servant mounted it, and he dug his spurs in its flanks and as fast as the horse could gallop he went. Then the merchant went down to the marketplace and he saw me standing in the crowd and he came to me and said, Why did you make a threatening gesture to my servant when you saw him this morning? That was not a threatening gesture, I said, it was only a start of surprise. I was astonished to see him in Bagdad, for I had an appointment with him tonight in Samarra.

[1933]

Joining the Conversation: Critical Thinking and Writing

1. What would you say the thesis or point or moral of the story is? Do you share this belief?
2. If you don't hold the view expressed in the story, can you still enjoy the story, or at least agree that it is an effectively told story? Offer a short argument explaining your position.

O. HENRY

O. Henry is the pen name of William Sydney Porter (1862–1910). Born in Greensboro, North Carolina, Porter dropped out of school when he was fifteen (not at all unusual in this period, when only a small minority of the population graduated from high school), did odd jobs including some work as a reporter, was convicted of embezzling, spent three years in prison (1898–1901), and while in prison he began to write short stories. His stories became immensely popular, but in his last years he was often in financial difficulties, largely because of heavy drinking. He died of cirrhosis of the liver.

The Ransom of Red Chief

It looked like a good thing: but wait till I tell you. We were down South, in Alabama—Bill Driscoll and myself—when this kidnapping idea struck us. It was, as Bill afterward expressed it, "during a moment of temporary mental apparition"; but we didn't find that out till later.

There was a town down there, as flat as a flannel-cake, and called Summit, of course. It contained inhabitants of as undeleterious and self-satisfied a class of peasantry as ever clustered around a Maypole.

Bill and me had a joint capital of about six hundred dollars, and we needed just two thousand dollars more to pull off a fraudulent town-lot scheme in Western Illinois with. We talked it over on the front steps of the hotel. Philoprogenitiveness,[1] says we, is strong in semi-rural communities therefore, and for other reasons, a kidnapping project ought to do better there than in the radius of newspapers that send

[1]**Philoprogenitiveness** producing many offspring, loving children.

reporters out in plain clothes to stir up talk about such things. We knew that Summit couldn't get after us with anything stronger than constables and, maybe, some lackadaisical bloodhounds and a diatribe or two in the *Weekly Farmers' Budget*. So, it looked good.

We selected for our victim the only child of a prominent citizen named Ebenezer Dorset. The father was respectable and tight, a mortgage fancier and a stern, upright collection-plate passer and forecloser. The kid was a boy of ten, with bas-relief freckles, and hair the colour of the cover of the magazine you buy at the news-stand when you want to catch a train. Bill and me figured that Ebenezer would melt down for a ransom of two thousand dollars to a cent. But wait till I tell you.

5 About two miles from Summit was a little mountain, covered with a dense cedar brake. On the rear elevation of this mountain was a cave. There we stored provisions.

One evening after sundown, we drove in a buggy past old Dorset's house. The kid was in the street, throwing rocks at a kitten on the opposite fence.

"Hey, little boy!" says Bill, "would you like to have a bag of candy and a nice ride?"

The boy catches Bill neatly in the eye with a piece of brick.

"That will cost the old man an extra five hundred dollars," says Bill, climbing over the wheel.

10 That boy put up a fight like a welter-weight cinnamon bear; but, at last, we got him down in the bottom of the buggy and drove away. We took him up to the cave, and I hitched the horse in the cedar brake. After dark I drove the buggy to the little village, three miles away, where we had hired it, and walked back to the mountain.

Bill was pasting court-plaster over the scratches and bruises on his features. There was a fire burning behind the big rock at the entrance of the cave, and the boy was watching a pot of boiling coffee, with two buzzard tailfeathers stuck in his red hair. He points a stick at me when I come up, and says:

"Ha! cursed paleface, do you dare to enter the camp of Red Chief, the terror of the plains?"

"He's all right now," says Bill, rolling up his trousers and examining some bruises on his shins. "We're playing Indian. We're making Buffalo Bill's show look like magic-lantern views of Palestine in the town hall. I'm Old Hank, the Trapper, Red Chief's captive, and I'm to be scalped at daybreak. By Geronimo! that kid can kick hard."

Yes, sir, that boy seemed to be having the time of his life. The fun of camping out in a cave had made him forget that he was a captive himself. He immediately christened me Snake-eye, the Spy, and announced that, when his braves returned from the warpath, I was to be broiled at the stake at the rising of the sun.

15 Then we had supper; and he filled his mouth full of bacon and bread and gravy, and began to talk. He made a during-dinner speech something like this:

"I like this fine. I never camped out before; but I had a pet 'possum once, and I was nine last birthday. I hate to go to school. Rats ate up sixteen of Jimmy Talbot's aunt's speckled hen's eggs. Are there any real Indians in these woods? I want some more gravy. Does the trees moving make the wind blow? We had five puppies. What makes your nose so red, Hank? My father has lots of money. Are the stars hot? I whipped Ed Walker twice, Saturday. I don't like girls. You dassent catch toads unless with a string. Do oxen make any noise? Why are oranges round? Have you got beds to sleep on in this cave? Amos Murray has got six toes.

A parrot can talk, but a monkey or a fish can't. How many does it take to make twelve?"

Every few minutes he would remember that he was a pesky redskin, and pick up his stick rifle and tiptoe to the mouth of the cave to rubber for the scouts of the hated paleface. Now and then he would let out a warwhoop that made Old Hank the Trapper, shiver. That boy had Bill terrorized from the start.

"Red Chief," says I to the kid, "would you like to go home?"

"Aw, what for?" says he. "I don't have any fun at home. I hate to go to school. I like to camp out. You won't take me back home again, Snake-eye, will you?"

20 "Not right away," says I. "We'll stay here in the cave a while."

"All right!" says he. "That'll be fine. I never had such fun in all my life."

We went to bed about eleven o'clock. We spread down some wide blankets and quilts and put Red Chief between us. We weren't afraid he'd run away. He kept us awake for three hours, jumping up and reaching for his rifle and screeching: "Hist! pard," in mine and Bill's ears, as the fancied crackle of a twig or the rustle of a leaf revealed to his young imagination the stealthy approach of the outlaw band. At last, I fell into a troubled sleep, and dreamed that I had been kidnapped and chained to a tree by a ferocious pirate with red hair.

Just at daybreak, I was awakened by a series of awful screams from Bill. They weren't yells, or howls, or shouts, or whoops, or yawps, such as you'd expect from a manly set of vocal organs—they were simply indecent, terrifying, humiliating screams, such as women emit when they see ghosts or caterpillars. It's an awful thing to hear a strong, desperate, fat man scream incontinently in a cave at daybreak.

I jumped up to see what the matter was. Red Chief was sitting on Bill's chest, with one hand twined in Bill's hair. In the other he had the sharp case-knife we used for slicing bacon; and he was industriously and realistically trying to take Bill's scalp, according to the sentence that had been pronounced upon him the evening before.

25 I got the knife away from the kid and made him lie down again. But, from that moment, Bill's spirit was broken. He laid down on his side of the bed, but he never closed an eye again in sleep as long as that boy was with us. I dozed off for a while, but along toward sun-up I remembered that Red Chief had said I was to be burned at the stake at the rising of the sun. I wasn't nervous or afraid; but I sat up and lit my pipe and leaned against a rock.

"What you getting up so soon for, Sam?" asked Bill.

"Me?" says I. "Oh, I got a kind of a pain in my shoulder. I thought sitting up would rest it."

"You're a liar!" says Bill. "You're afraid. You was to be burned at sunrise, and you was afraid he'd do it. And he would, too, if he could find a match. Ain't it awful, Sam? Do you think anybody will pay out money to get a little imp like that back home?"

"Sure," said I. "A rowdy kid like that is just the kind that parents dote on. Now, you and the Chief get up and cook breakfast, while I go up on the top of this mountain and reconnoitre."

30 I went up on the peak of the little mountain and ran my eye over the contiguous vicinity. Over toward Summit I expected to see the sturdy yeomanry of the village armed with scythes and pitchforks beating the countryside for the dastardly kidnappers. But what I saw was a peaceful landscape dotted with one man ploughing with a dun mule. Nobody was dragging the creek; no couriers dashed hither and yon, bringing tidings of no news to the distracted parents. There was a

sylvan attitude of somnolent sleepiness pervading that section of the external outward surface of Alabama that lay exposed to my view. "Perhaps," says I to myself, "it has not yet been discovered that the wolves have borne away the tender lambkin from the fold. Heaven help the wolves!" says I, and I went down the mountain to breakfast.

When I got to the cave I found Bill backed up against the side of it, breathing hard, and the boy threatening to smash him with a rock half as big as a cocoanut.

"He put a red-hot boiled potato down my back," explained Bill, "and then mashed it with his foot; and I boxed his ears. Have you got a gun about you, Sam?"

I took the rock away from the boy and kind of patched up the argument. "I'll fix you," says the kid to Bill. "No man ever yet struck the Red Chief but what he got paid for it. You better beware!"

After breakfast the kid takes a piece of leather with strings wrapped around it out of his pocket and goes outside the cave unwinding it.

"What's he up to now?" says Bill, anxiously. "You don't think he'll run away, do you, Sam?"

"No fear of it," says I. "He don't seem to be much of a home body. But we've got to fix up some plan about the ransom. There don't seem to be much excitement around Summit on account of his disappearance; but maybe they haven't realized yet that he's gone. His folks may think he's spending the night with Aunt Jane or one of the neighbors. Anyhow, he'll be missed to-day. To-night we must get a message to his father demanding the two thousand dollars for his return."

Just then we heard a kind of war-whoop, such as David might have emitted when he knocked out the champion Goliath. It was a sling that Red Chief had pulled out of his pocket, and he was whirling it around his head.

I dodged, and heard a heavy thud and a kind of a sigh from Bill, like a horse gives out when you take his saddle off. A niggerhead rock the size of an egg had caught Bill just behind his left ear. He loosened himself all over and fell in the fire across the frying pan of hot water for washing the dishes. I dragged him out and poured cold water on his head for half an hour.

By and by, Bill sits up and feels behind his ear and says: "Sam, do you know who my favourite Biblical character is?"

"Take it easy," says I. "You'll come to your senses presently."

"King Herod," says he. "You won't go away and leave me here alone, will you, Sam?"

I went out and caught that boy and shook him until his freckles rattled.

"If you don't behave," says I, "I'll take you straight home. Now, are you going to be good, or not?"

"I was only funning," says he sullenly. "I didn't mean to hurt Old Hank. But what did he hit me for? I'll behave, Snake-eye, if you won't send me home, and if you'll let me play the Black Scout to-day."

"I don't know the game," says I. "That's for you and Mr. Bill to decide. He's your playmate for the day. I'm going away for a while, on business. Now, you come in and make friends with him and say you are sorry for hurting him, or home you go, at once."

I made him and Bill shake hands, and then I took Bill aside and told him I was going to Poplar Cove, a little village three miles from the cave, and find out what I could about how the kidnapping had been regarded in Summit. Also, I thought it best to send a peremptory letter to old man Dorset that day, demanding the ransom and dictating how it should be paid.

"You know, Sam," says Bill, "I've stood by you without batting an eye in earthquakes, fire and flood—in poker games, dynamite outrages, police raids, train robberies and cyclones. I never lost my nerve yet till we kidnapped that two-legged skyrocket of a kid. He's got me going. You won't leave me long with him, will you, Sam?"

"I'll be back some time this afternoon," says I. "You must keep the boy amused and quiet till I return. And now we'll write the letter to old Dorset."

Bill and I got paper and pencil and worked on the letter while Red Chief, with a blanket wrapped around him, strutted up and down, guarding the mouth of the cave. Bill begged me tearfully to make the ransom fifteen hundred dollars instead of two thousand. "I ain't attempting," says he, "to decry the celebrated moral aspect of parental affection, but we're dealing with humans, and it ain't human for anybody to give up two thousand dollars for that forty-pound chunk of freckled wildcat. I'm willing to take a chance at fifteen hundred dollars. You can charge the difference up to me."

50 So, to relieve Bill, I acceded, and we collaborated a letter that ran this way:

Ebenezer Dorset, Esq.:

We have your boy concealed in a place far from Summit. It is useless for you or the most skilful detectives to attempt to find him. Absolutely, the only terms on which you can have him restored to you are these: We demand fifteen hundred dollars in large bills for his return; the money to be left at midnight to-night at the same spot and in the same box as your reply—as hereinafter described. If you agree to these terms, send your answer in writing by a solitary messenger to-night at half-past eight o'clock. After crossing Owl Creek, on the road to Poplar Cove, there are three large trees about a hundred yards apart, close to the fence of the wheat field on the right-hand side. At the bottom of the fence-post, opposite the third tree, will be found a small pasteboard box.

The messenger will place the answer in this box and return immediately to Summit.

If you attempt any treachery or fail to comply with our demand as stated, you will never see your boy again.

If you pay the money as demanded, he will be returned to you safe and well within three hours. These terms are final, and if you do not accede to them no further communication will be attempted.

TWO DESPERATE MEN.

I addressed this letter to Dorset, and put it in my pocket. As I was about to start, the kid comes up to me and says:

"Aw, Snake-eye, you said I could play the Black Scout while you was gone."

"Play it, of course," says I. "Mr. Bill will play with you. What kind of a game is it?"

"I'm the Black Scout," says Red Chief, "and I have to ride to the stockade to warn the settlers that the Indians are coming. I'm tired of playing Indian myself. I want to be the Black Scout."

55 "All right," says I. "It sounds harmless to me. I guess Mr. Bill will help you foil the pesky savages."

"What am I to do?" asks Bill, looking at the kid suspiciously.

"You are the hoss," says Black Scout. "Get down on your hands and knees. How can I ride to the stockade without a hoss?"

"You'd better keep him interested," said I, "till we get the scheme going. Loosen up."

Bill gets down on his all fours, and a look comes in his eye like a rabbit's when you catch it in a trap.

60 "How far is it to the stockade, kid?" he asks, in a husky manner of voice.

"Ninety miles," says the Black Scout. "And you have to hump yourself to get there on time. Whoa, now!"

The Black Scout jumps on Bill's back and digs his heels in his side.

"For Heaven's sake," says Bill, "hurry back, Sam, as soon as you can. I wish we hadn't made the ransom more than a thousand. Say, you quit kicking me or I'll get up and warm you good."

I walked over to Poplar Cove and sat around the postoffice and store, talking with the chawbacons that came in to trade. One whiskerando says that he hears Summit is all upset on account of Elder Ebenezer Dorset's boy having been lost or stolen. That was all I wanted to know. I bought some smoking tobacco, referred casually to the price of black-eyed peas, posted my letter surreptitiously and came away. The postmaster said the mail-carrier would come by in an hour to take the mail on to Summit.

65 When I got back to the cave Bill and the boy were not to be found. I explored the vicinity of the cave, and risked a yodel or two, but there was no response.

So I lighted my pipe and sat down on a mossy bank to await developments.

In about half an hour I heard the bushes rustle, and Bill wabbled out into the little glade in front of the cave. Behind him was the kid, stepping softly like a scout, with a broad grin on his face. Bill stopped, took off his hat and wiped his face with a red handkerchief. The kid stopped about eight feet behind him.

"Sam," says Bill, "I suppose you'll think I'm a renegade, but I couldn't help it. I'm a grown person with masculine proclivities and habits of self-defence, but there is a time when all systems of egotism and predominance fail. The boy is gone. I have sent him home. All is off. There was martyrs in old times," goes on Bill, "that suffered death rather than give up the particular graft they enjoyed. None of 'em ever was subjugated to such supernatural tortures as I have been. I tried to be faithful to our articles of depredation; but there came a limit."

"What's the trouble, Bill?" I asks him.

70 "I was rode," says Bill, "the ninety miles to the stockade, not barring an inch. Then, when the settlers was rescued, I was given oats. Sand ain't a palatable substitute. And then, for an hour I had to try to explain to him why there was nothin' in holes, how a road can run both ways and what makes the grass green. I tell you, Sam, a human can only stand so much. I takes him by the neck of his clothes and drags him down the mountain. On the way he kicks my legs black-and-blue from the knees down; and I've got two or three bites on my thumb and hand cauterized.

"But he's gone"—continues Bill—"gone home. I showed him the road to Summit and kicked him about eight feet nearer there at one kick. I'm sorry we lose the ransom; but it was either that or Bill Driscoll to the madhouse."

Bill is puffing and blowing, but there is a look of ineffable peace and growing content on his rose-pink features.

"Bill," says I, "there isn't any heart disease in your family, is there?"

"No," says Bill, "nothing chronic except malaria and accidents. Why?"

75 "Then you might turn around," says I, "and have a look behind you."

Bill turns and sees the boy, and loses his complexion and sits down plump on the ground and begins to pluck aimlessly at grass and little sticks. For an hour I was afraid for his mind. And then I told him that my scheme was to put the whole job through immediately and that we would get the ransom and be off with it by midnight if old Dorset fell in with our proposition. So Bill braced up enough to give the kid a weak sort of a smile and a promise to play the Russian in a Japanese war[2] with him as soon as he felt a little better.

I had a scheme for collecting that ransom without danger of being caught by counterplots that ought to commend itself to professional kidnappers. The tree under which the answer was to be left—and the money later on—was close to the road fence with big, bare fields on all sides. If a gang of constables should be watching for anyone to come for the note they could see him a long way off crossing the fields or in the road. But no, sirree! At half-past eight I was up in that tree as well hidden as a tree toad, waiting for the messenger to arrive.

Exactly on time, a half-grown boy rides up the road on a bicycle, locates the pasteboard box at the foot of the fencepost, slips a folded piece of paper into it and pedals away again back toward Summit.

I waited an hour and then concluded the thing was square. I slid down the tree, got the note, slipped along the fence till I struck the woods, and was back at the cave in another half an hour. I opened the note, got near the lantern and read it to Bill. It was written with a pen in a crabbed hand, and the sum and substance of it was this:

> Two Desperate Men.
>
> Gentlemen: I received your letter to-day by post, in regard to the ransom you ask for the return of my son. I think you are a little high in your demands, and I hereby make you a counter-proposition, which I am inclined to believe you will accept. You bring Johnny home and pay me two hundred and fifty dollars in cash, and I agree to take him off your hands. You had better come at night, for the neighbors believe he is lost, and I couldn't be responsible for what they would do to anybody they saw bringing him back.
>
> Very respectfully,
> EBENEZER DORSET.

"Great pirates of Penzance!"[3] says I; "of all the impudent—"

But I glanced at Bill, and hesitated. He had the most appealing look in his eyes I ever saw on the face of a dumb or a talking brute.

"Sam," says he, "what's two hundred and fifty dollars, after all? We've got the money. One more night of this kid will send me to a bed in Bedlam.[4] Besides being a thorough gentleman, I think Mr. Dorset is a spendthrift for making us such a liberal offer. You ain't going to let the chance go, are you?"

"Tell you the truth, Bill," says I, "this little he ewe lamb has somewhat got on my nerves too. We'll take him home, pay the ransom and make our get-away."

We took him home that night. We got him to go by telling him that his father had bought a silver-mounted rifle and a pair of moccasins for him, and we were going to hunt bears the next day.

[2]**play . . . war** Japan defeated Russia in a war fought in 1904–1905. [3]**Pirates of Penzance** comic opera (1879) by Gilbert and Sullivan. [4]**Bedlam** insane asylum.

85 It was just twelve o'clock when we knocked at Ebenezer's front door. Just at the moment when I should have been abstracting the fifteen hundred dollars from the box under the tree, according to the original proposition, Bill was counting out two hundred and fifty dollars into Dorset's hand.

When the kid found out we were going to leave him at home he started up a howl like a calliope and fastened himself as tight as a leech to Bill's leg. His father peeled him away gradually, like a porous plaster.

"How long can you hold him?" asks Bill.

"I'm not as strong as I used to be," says old Dorset, "but I think I can promise you ten minutes."

"Enough," says Bill. "In ten minutes I shall cross the Central, Southern, and Middle Western States, and be legging it trippingly for the Canadian border."

90 And, as dark as it was, and as fat as Bill was, and as good a runner as I am, he was a good mile and a half out of Summit before I could catch up with him.

[1910]

Joining the Conversation: Critical Thinking and Writing

1. Do you think that O. Henry chose a good title? Please explain why or why not.
2. Choose a title or your own, and argue why you think it is better.
3. How do we know, as the story begins, that this story about kidnapping—which is a serious crime—will have a comic quality? Please point to details in the language to explain your sense of its tone and meaning.
4. Do you find the story to be funny? Does it have a serious point?
5. If you were one of the kidnappers, what would you have done to control the boy?
6. Are the references to Native Americans upsetting, even offensive, to readers today? How would you respond to someone who says, "But those references should not bother us; after all, the story was published in 1910, when things were very different than they are now"?

AMBROSE BIERCE

Ambrose Bierce (1842–1914?) was born in Horse Creek, Ohio, but soon his family moved to Indiana, where at the age of nineteen he enlisted in the Union Army. In the next four years he fought in several of the bloodiest battles of the Civil War, was wounded twice, and rose to the rank of lieutenant. After the war he worked as a journalist in San Francisco, England, and again in San Francisco. In 1912 he went to Mexico to cover the Mexican Revolution, but he disappeared there and it is assumed that he died in 1914.

Bierce's literary reputation rests chiefly on one story, reprinted here, but he wrote other stories of interest—some about the supernatural—as well as a witty, cynical book called The Devil's Dictionary. *Sample definition:* "Marriage. *The state or condition of a community consisting of a master, a mistress, and two slaves, making in all, two."*

An Occurrence at Owl Creek Bridge

1

A man stood upon a railroad bridge in northern Alabama, looking down into the swift water twenty feet below. The man's hands were behind his back, the wrists bound with a cord. A rope closely encircled his neck. It was attached to a stout cross-timber above his head and the slack fell to the level of his knees. Some loose boards laid upon the sleepers[1] supporting the metals of the railway supplied a footing for him and his executioners—two private soldiers of the Federal army, directed by a sergeant who in civil life may have been a deputy sheriff. At a short remove upon the same temporary platform was an officer in the uniform of his rank, armed. He was a captain. A sentinel at each end of the bridge stood with his rifle in the position known as "support," that is to say, vertical in front of the left shoulder, the hammer resting on the forearm thrown straight across the chest—a formal and unnatural position, enforcing an erect carriage of the body. It did not appear to be the duty of these two men to know what was occurring at the center of the bridge; they merely blockaded the two ends of the foot planking that traversed it.

Beyond one of the sentinels nobody was in sight; the railroad ran straight away into a forest for a hundred yards, then, curving, was lost to view. Doubtless there was an outpost farther along. The other bank of the stream was open ground—a gentle acclivity topped with a stockade of vertical tree trunks, loopholed for rifles, with a single embrasure through which protruded the muzzle of a brass cannon commanding the bridge. Midway of the slope between bridge and fort were the spectators—a single company of infantry in line, at "parade rest," the butts of the rifles on the ground, the barrels inclining slightly backward against the right shoulder, the hands crossed upon the stock. A lieutenant stood at the right of the line, the point of his sword upon the ground, his left hand resting upon his right. Excepting the group of four at the center of the bridge, not a man moved. The company faced the bridge, staring stonily, motionless. The sentinels, facing the banks of the stream, might have been statues to adorn the bridge. The captain stood with folded arms, silent, observing the work of his subordinates, but making no sign. Death is a dignitary who when he comes announced is to be received with formal manifestations of respect, even by those most familiar with him. In the code of military etiquette silence and fixity are forms of deference.

The man who was engaged in being hanged was apparently about thirty-five years of age. He was a civilian, if one might judge from his habit, which was that of a planter. His features were good—a straight nose, firm mouth, broad forehead, from which his long, dark hair was combed straight back, falling behind his ears to the collar of his well-fitting frock-coat. He wore a mustache and pointed beard, but no whiskers; his eyes were large and dark gray, and had a kindly expression which one would hardly have expected in one whose neck was in the hemp. Evidently this was no vulgar assassin. The liberal military code makes provision for hanging many kinds of persons, and gentlemen are not excluded.

The preparations being complete, the two private soldiers stepped aside and each drew away the plank upon which he had been standing. The sergeant turned to the captain, saluted and placed himself immediately behind that officer,

[1]**sleepers** railroad crossties.

who in turn moved apart one pace. These movements left the condemned man and the sergeant standing on the two ends of the same plank, which spanned three of the crossties of the bridge. The end upon which the civilian stood almost, but not quite, reached a fourth. This plank had been held in place by the weight of the captain; it was now held by that of the sergeant. At a signal from the former the latter would step aside, the plank would tilt and the condemned man go down between two ties. The arrangement commended itself to his judgment as simple and effective. His face had not been covered nor his eyes bandaged. He looked a moment at his "unsteadfast footing," then let his gaze wander to the swirling water of the stream racing madly beneath his feet. A piece of dancing driftwood caught his attention and his eyes followed it down the current. How slowly it appeared to move! What a sluggish stream!

5 He closed his eyes in order to fix his last thoughts upon his wife and children. The water, touched to gold by the early sun, the brooding mists under the banks at some distance down the stream, the fort, the soldiers, the piece of drift—all had distracted him. And now he became conscious of a new disturbance. Striking through the thought of his dear ones was a sound which he would neither ignore nor understand, a sharp, distinct, metallic percussion like the stroke of a blacksmith's hammer upon the anvil; it had the same ringing quality. He wondered what it was, and whether immeasurably distant or near by—it seemed both. Its recurrence was regular, but as slow as the tolling of a death knell. He awaited each stroke with impatience and—he knew not why—apprehension. The intervals of silence grew progressively longer; the delays became maddening. With their greater infrequency the sounds increased in strength and sharpness. They hurt his ear like the thrust of a knife; he feared he would shriek. What he heard was the ticking of his watch.

He unclosed his eyes and saw again the water below him. "If I could free my hands," he thought, "I might throw off the noose and spring into the stream. By diving I could evade the bullets and, swimming vigorously, reach the bank, take to the woods and get away home. My home, thank God, is as yet outside their lines; my wife and little ones are still beyond the invader's farthest advance."

As these thoughts, which have here to be set down in words, were flashed into the doomed man's brain rather than evolved from it the captain nodded to the sergeant. The sergeant stepped aside.

2

Peyton Farquhar was a well-to-do planter, of an old and highly respected Alabama family. Being a slave owner and like other slave owners a politician he was naturally an original secessionist and ardently devoted to the Southern cause. Circumstances of an imperious nature, which it is unnecessary to relate here, had prevented him from taking service with the gallant army that had fought the disastrous campaigns ending with the fall of Corinth,[2] and he chafed under the inglorious restraint, longing for the release of his energies, the larger life of the soldier, the opportunity for distinction. That opportunity, he felt, would come, as it comes to all in war time. Meanwhile he did what he could. No service was too humble for him to perform in aid of the South, no adventure too perilous for him to undertake if consistent with the character of a civilian who was at heart a soldier, and who in good faith and without too much qualification assented to at least a part of the frankly villainous dictum that all is fair in love and war.

[2]**Corinth** Corinth, Mississippi, where Confederate Forces were defeated, October 3–4, 1862.

One evening while Farquhar and his wife were sitting on a rustic bench near the entrance to his grounds, a gray-clad soldier rode up to the gate and asked for a drink of water. Mrs. Farquhar was only too happy to serve him with her own white hands. While she was fetching the water her husband approached the dusty horseman and inquired eagerly for news from the front.

"The Yanks are repairing the railroads," said the man, "and are getting ready for another advance. They have reached the Owl Creek bridge, put it in order and built a stockade on the north bank. The commandant has issued an order, which is posted everywhere, declaring that any civilian caught interfering with the railroad, its bridges, tunnels or trains will be summarily hanged. I saw the order."

"How far is it to the Owl Creek bridge?" Farquhar asked.

"About thirty miles."

"Is there no force on this side the creek?"

"Only a picket post half a mile out, on the railroad, and a single sentinel at this end of the bridge."

"Suppose a man—a civilian and student of hanging—should elude the picket post and perhaps get the better of the sentinel," said Farquhar, smiling, "what could he accomplish?"

The soldier reflected. "I was there a month ago," he replied, "I observed that the flood of last winter had lodged a great quantity of driftwood against the wooden pier at this end of the bridge. It is now dry and would burn like tow."

The lady had now brought the water, which the soldier drank. He thanked her ceremoniously, bowed to her husband and rode away. An hour later, after nightfall, he repassed the plantation, going northward in the direction from which he had come. He was a Federal scout.

3

As Peyton Farquhar fell straight downward through the bridge he lost consciousness and was as one already dead. From this state he was awakened—ages later, it seemed to him—by the pain of a sharp pressure upon his throat, followed by a sense of suffocation. Keen, poignant agonies seemed to shoot from his neck downward through every fiber of his body and limbs. These pains appeared to flash along well-defined lines of ramification and to beat with an inconceivably rapid periodicity. They seemed like streams of pulsating fire heating him to an intolerable temperature. As to his head, he was conscious of nothing but a feeling of fulness—of congestion. These sensations were unaccompanied by thought. The intellectual part of his nature was already effaced; he had power only to feel, and feeling was torment. He was conscious of motion. Encompassed in a luminous cloud, of which he was now merely the fiery heart, without material substance, he swung through unthinkable arcs of oscillation, like a vast pendulum. Then all at once, with terrible suddenness, the light about him shot upward with the noise of a loud plash; a frightful roaring was in his ears, and all was cold and dark. The power of thought was restored; he knew that the rope had broken and he had fallen into the stream. There was no additional strangulation; the noose about his neck was already suffocating him and kept the water from his lungs. To die of hanging at the bottom of a river!—the idea seemed to him ludicrous. He opened his eyes in the darkness and saw above him a gleam of light, but how distant, how inaccessible! He was still sinking, for the light became fainter and fainter until it was a mere glimmer. Then it began to grow and brighten, and he knew that he was rising toward the surface—knew it with reluctance, for he was now very comfortable. "To be hanged and drowned," he thought, "that is not so bad; but I do not wish to be shot. No; I will not be shot; that is not fair."

He was not conscious of an effort, but a sharp pain in his wrist apprised him that he was trying to free his hands. He gave the struggle his attention, as an idler might observe the feat of a juggler, without interest in the outcome. What splendid effort!—what magnificent, what superhuman strength! Ah, that was a fine endeavor! Bravo! The cord fell away; his arms parted and floated upward; the hands dimly seen on each side in the growing light. He watched them with new interest as first one and then the other pounced upon the noose at his neck. They tore it away and thrust it fiercely aside, its undulations resembling those of a water-snake. "Put it back, put it back!" He thought he shouted these words to his hands, for the undoing of the noose had been succeeded by the direst pang that he had yet experienced. His neck ached horribly; his brain was on fire; his heart, which had been fluttering faintly, gave a great leap, trying to force itself out at his mouth. His whole body was racked and wrenched with an insupportable anguish! But his disobedient hands gave no heed to the command. They beat the water vigorously with quick, downward strokes, forcing him to the surface. He felt his head emerge; his eyes were blinded by the sunlight; his chest expanded convulsively, and with a supreme and crowning agony his lungs engulfed a great draught of air, which instantly he expelled in a shriek!

He was now in full possession of his physical senses. They were, indeed, preternaturally keen and alert. Something in the awful disturbance of his organic system had so exalted and refined them that they made record of things never before perceived. He felt the ripples upon his face and heard their separate sounds as they struck. He looked at the forest on the bank of the stream, saw the individual trees, the leaves and the veining of each leaf—saw the very insects upon them: the locusts, the brilliant-bodied flies, the gray spiders stretching their webs from twig to twig. He noted the prismatic colors in all the dewdrops upon a million blades of grass. The humming of the gnats that danced above the eddies of the stream, the beating of the dragon-flies' wings, the strokes of water-spider's legs, like oars which had lifted their boat—all these made audible music. A fish slid along beneath his eyes and he heard the rush of its body parting the water.

He had come to the surface facing down the stream; in a moment the visible world seemed to wheel slowly round, himself the pivotal point, and he saw the bridge, the fort, the soldiers upon the bridge, the captain, the sergeant, the two privates, his executioners. They were in silhouette against the blue sky. They shouted and gesticulated, pointing at him. The captain had drawn his pistol, but did not fire; the others were unarmed. Their movements were grotesque and horrible, their forms gigantic.

Suddenly he heard a sharp report and something struck the water smartly within a few inches of his head, spattering his face with spray. He heard a second report, and saw one of the sentinels with his rifle at his shoulder, a light cloud of blue smoke rising from the muzzle. The man in the water saw the eye of the man on the bridge gazing into his own through the sights of the rifle. He observed that it was a gray eye and remembered having read that gray eyes were keenest, and that all famous marksmen had them. Nevertheless, this one had missed.

A counter-swirl had caught Farquhar and turned him half round; he was again looking into the forest on the bank opposite the fort. The sound of a clear, high voice in a monotonous singsong now rang out behind him and came across the water with a distinctness that pierced and subdued all other sounds, even the beating of the ripples in his ears. Although no soldier, he had frequented camps enough to know the dread significance of that deliberate, drawling, aspirated chant; the lieutenant on shore was taking a part in the morning's work. How coldly and pitilessly—with what an even, calm intonation, presaging, and enforcing tranquility in the men—with what accurately measured intervals fell those cruel words:

"Attention, company! . . . Shoulder arms! . . . Ready! . . . Aim! . . . Fire!"

Farquhar dived—dived as deeply as he could. The water roared in his ears like the voice of Niagara, yet he heard the dulled thunder of the volley and, rising again toward the surface, met shining bits of metal, singularly flattened, oscillating slowly downward. Some of them touched him on the face and hands, then fell away, continuing their descent. One lodged between his collar and neck; it was uncomfortably warm and he snatched it out.

As he rose to the surface, gasping for breath, he saw that he had been a long time under water; he was perceptibly farther down stream—nearer to safety. The soldiers had almost finished reloading; the metal ramrods flashed all at once in the sunshine as they were drawn from the barrels, turned in the air, and thrust into their sockets. The two sentinels fired again, independently and ineffectually.

The hunted man saw all this over his shoulder; he was now swimming vigorously with the current. His brain was as energetic as his arms and legs; he thought with the rapidity of lightning.

"The officer," he reasoned, "will not make that martinet's error a second time. It is as easy to dodge a volley as a single shot. He has probably already given the command to fire at will. God help me, I cannot dodge them all!"

An appalling plash within two yards of him was followed by a loud, rushing sound, *diminuendo*,[3] which seemed to travel back through the air to the fort and died in an explosion which stirred the very river to its deeps! A rising sheet of water curved over him, fell down upon him, blinded him, strangled him! The cannon had taken a hand in the game. As he shook his head free from the commotion of the smitten water he heard the deflected shot humming through the air ahead, and in an instant it was cracking and smashing the branches in the forest beyond.

"They will not do that again," he thought; "the next time they will use a charge of grape.[4] I must keep my eye upon the gun; the smoke will apprise me—the report arrives too late; it lags behind the missile. That is a good gun."

Suddenly he felt himself whirled round and round—spinning like a top. The water, the banks, the forests, the now distant bridge, fort and men—all were commingled and blurred. Objects were represented by their colors only; circular horizontal streaks of color—that was all he saw. He had been caught in a vortex and was being whirled on with a velocity of advance and gyration that made him giddy and sick. In a few moments he was flung upon the gravel at the foot of the left bank of the stream—the southern bank—and behind a projecting point which concealed him from his enemies. The sudden arrest of his motion, the abrasion of one of his hands on the gravel, restored him, and he wept with delight. He dug his fingers into the sand, threw it over himself in handfuls and audibly blessed it. It looked like diamonds, rubies, emeralds; he could think of nothing beautiful which it did not resemble. The trees upon the bank were giant garden plants; he noted a definite order in their arrangement, inhaled the fragrance of their blooms. A strange, roseate light shone through the spaces among their trunks and the wind made in their branches the music of aeolian harps. He had no wish to perfect his escape—was content to remain in that enchanting spot until retaken.

[3]***Diminuendo*** decreasing in loudness.

[4]**grapeshot:** a cluster of small iron balls fired from a cannon.

A whiz and rattle of grapeshot among the branches high above his head roused him from his dream. The baffled cannoneer had fired him a random farewell. He sprang to his feet, rushed up the sloping bank, and plunged into the forest.

All that day he traveled, laying his course by the rounding sun. The forest seemed interminable; nowhere did he discover a break in it, not even a woodman's road. He had not known that he lived in so wild a region. There was something uncanny in the revelation.

By nightfall he was fatigued, footsore, famishing. The thought of his wife and children urged him on. At last he found a road which led him in what he knew to be the right direction. It was as wide and straight as a city street, yet it seemed untraveled. No fields bordered it, no dwelling anywhere. Not so much as the barking of a dog suggested human habitation. The black bodies of the trees formed a straight wall on both sides, terminating on the horizon in a point, like a diagram in a lesson in perspective. Overhead, as he looked up through this rift in the wood, shone great golden stars looking unfamiliar and grouped in strange constellations. He was sure they were arranged in some order which had a secret and malign significance. The wood on either side was full of singular noises, among which—once, twice, and again—he distinctly heard whispers in an unknown tongue.

35 His neck was in pain and lifting his hand to it he found it horribly swollen. He knew that it had a circle of black where the rope had bruised it. His eyes felt congested; he could no longer close them. His tongue was swollen with thirst; he relieved its fever by thrusting it forward from between his teeth into the cold air. How softly the turf had carpeted the untraveled avenue—he could no longer feel the roadway beneath his feet!

Doubtless, despite his suffering, he had fallen asleep while walking, for now he sees another scene—perhaps he has merely recovered from a delirium. He stands at the gate of his own home. All is as he left it, and all bright and beautiful in the morning sunshine. He must have traveled the entire night. As he pushes open the gate and passes up the wide white walk, he sees a flutter of female garments; his wife, looking fresh and cool and sweet, steps down from the veranda to meet him. At the bottom of the steps she stands waiting, with a smile of ineffable joy, an attitude of matchless grace and dignity. Ah, how beautiful she is! He springs forward with extended arms. As he is about to clasp her he feels a stunning blow upon the back of the neck; a blinding white light blazes all about him with a sound like the shock of a cannon—then all is darkness and silence!

Peyton Farquhar was dead; his body, with a broken neck, swung gently from side to side beneath the timbers of the Owl Creek bridge.

[1891]

Joining the Conversation: Critical Thinking and Writing

1. Characterize Peyton Farquhar. If you think Bierce makes him sympathetic, consider the *ways* in which Bierce does so.
2. Early in the story the narrator says, "The liberal military code makes provision for hanging many kinds of people, and gentlemen are not excluded." How would you characterize the tone of this sentence? What, if anything, does the sentence contribute to the story?

3. Do you think that Bierce takes sides, suggesting that the North—or the South—is morally superior? What evidence can you offer to support your view?
4. Is the ending a complete surprise? Do some passages in the story suggest—at least on rereading—that perhaps Farquhar has not escaped? If so, point out a few.
5. What do you think of the title of the story? How does it compare with, for example, "Peyton Farquhar," or "Peyton Farquhar's Escape," or "The Hanging at Owl Creek Bridge"?

Isabel Allende

Isabel Allende was born in Lima, Peru, in 1942, where her father was stationed as a Chilean diplomat, but she grew up in Chile. When her father's brother, the socialist president of Chile, was murdered in September 1973, Isabel was forced into exile, and she now lives in Marin County, California. In addition to writing several novels, including one called Eva Luna *(1988), about a half-European and half-Indian orphan who is a storyteller, Allende has written a collection of short fiction,* The Stories of Eva Luna *(1991), from which the following story is reprinted.*

If You Touched My Heart

Translated by Margaret Sayers Peden

Amadeo Peralta was raised in the midst of his father's gang and, like all the men of his family, grew up to be a ruffian. His father believed that school was for cissies; you don't need books to get ahead in life, he always said, just balls and quick wits, and that was why he trained his boys to be rough and ready. With time, nevertheless, he realized that the world was changing very rapidly and that his business affairs needed to be more firmly anchored. The era of undisguised plunder had been replaced by one of corruption and bribery; it was time to administer his wealth by using modern criteria, and to improve his image. He called his sons together and assigned them the task of establishing friendships with influential persons and of learning the legal tricks that would allow them to continue to prosper without danger of losing their impunity. He also encouraged them to find sweethearts among the old-line families and in this way see whether they could cleanse the Peralta name of all its stains of mud and blood. By then Amadeo was thirty-two years old; the habit of seducing girls and then abandoning them was deeply ingrained; the idea of marriage was not at all to his liking but he did not dare disobey his father. He began to court the daughter of a wealthy landowner whose family had lived in the same place for six generations. Despite her suitor's murky reputation, the girl accepted, for she was not very attractive and was afraid of ending up an old maid. Then began one of those tedious provincial engagements. Wretched in a white linen suit and polished boots, Amadeo came every day to visit his fiancée beneath the hawk-like eye of his future mother-in-law or some aunt, and while the young lady served coffee and *guayaba* sweets he would peek at his watch, calculating the earliest moment to make his departure.

A few weeks before the wedding, Amadeo Peralta had to make a business trip through the provinces and found himself in Agua Santa, one of those towns where nobody stays and whose name travellers rarely recall. He was walking down a narrow street at the hour of the siesta, cursing the heat and the oppressive, cloying odour of mango marmalade in the air, when he heard a crystalline sound like water purling between stones; it was coming from a modest house with paint flaked by the sun and rain like most of the houses in that town. Through the ornamental iron grille he glimpsed an entryway of dark paving stones and white-washed walls, then a patio and, beyond, the surprising vision of a young girl sitting cross-legged on the ground and cradling a blond wood psaltery on her knees. For a while he stood and watched her.

"Come here, sweet thing," he called, finally. She looked up, and despite the distance he could see the startled eyes and uncertain smile in a still-childish face. "Come with me," Amadeo asked—implored—in a hoarse voice.

She hesitated. The last notes lingered like a question in the air of the patio. Peralta called again. The girl stood up and walked towards him; he slipped his hand through the iron grille, shot the bolt, opened the gate, and seized her hand, all the white reciting his entire repertoire of seduction: he swore that he had seen her in his dreams, that he had been looking for her all his life, that he could not let her go, and that she was the woman fate had meant for him—all of which he could have omitted because the girl was simple and even though she may have been enchanted by the tone of his voice she did not understand the meaning of his words. Hortensia was her name and she had just turned fifteen, her body was turned for its first embrace, though she was unable to put a name to the restlessness and tremors that shook it. It was so easy for Peralta to lead her to his car and drive to a nearby clearing that an hour later he had completely forgotten her. He did not recognize her even when a week later she suddenly appeared at his house, one hundred and forty kilometres away, wearing a simple yellow cotton dress and canvas espadrilles, her psaltery under her arm, and inflamed with the fever of love.

5 Forty-seven years later, when Hortensia was rescued from the pit in which she had been entombed and newspapermen travelled from every corner of the nation to photograph her, not even she could remember her name or how she had got there.

The reporters accosted Amadeo Peralta: "Why did you keep her locked up like a miserable beast?"

"Because I felt like it," he replied calmly. By then he was eighty, and as lucid as ever; he could not understand this belated outcry over something that did happened so long ago.

He was not inclined to offer explanations. He was a man of authority, a patriarch, a great-grandfather, no one dared look him in the eye; even priests greeted him with bowed head. During the course of his long life he had multiplied the fortune he inherited from his father; he had become the owner of all the land from the ruins of the Spanish fort to the state line, and then had launched himself on a political career that made him the most powerful cacique[1] in the territory. He had married the landowner's ugly daughter and sired nine legitimate descendants with her and an indefinite number of bastards with other women, none of whom he remembered since he had a heart hardened to love. The only woman he could not entirely discard was Hortensia; she stuck in his consciousness like a persistent nightmare. After the brief encounter in the tall grass of an empty lot, he had returned to his home, his work, and his insipid, well-bred fiancée. It was Hortensia who had searched until she found *him;* it was she who had planted herself before

[1]**cacique** political boss.

him and clung to his shirt with the terrifying submission of a slave. This is a fine kettle of fish, he had thought; here I am about to get married with all this hoopla and to-do, and now this idiot girl turns up on my doorstep. He wanted to get rid of her, and yet when he saw her in her yellow dress, with those entreating eyes, it seemed a waste not to take advantage of the opportunity, and he decided to hide her while he found a solution.

And so, by carelessness, really, Hortensia ended up in the cellar of an old sugar mill that belonged to the Peraltas, where she was to remain for a lifetime. It was a large room, dank, and dark, suffocating in summer and in the dry season often cold at night, furnished with a few sticks of furniture and a straw pallet. Amadeo Peralta never took time to make her more comfortable, despite his occasionally feeding a fantasy of making the girl a concubine from an oriental tale, clad in gauzy robes and surrounded with peacock feathers, brocade tented ceilings, stained-glass lamps, gilded furniture with spiral feet, and thick rugs where he could walk barefoot. He might actually have done it had Hortensia reminded him of his promises, but she was like a wild bird, one of these blind guacharos that live in the depths of caves: all she needed was a little food and water. The yellow dress rotted away and she was left naked.

10 "He loves me; he has always loved me," she declared when she was rescued by neighbours. After being locked up for so many years she had lost the use of words and her voice came out in spurts like the croak of a woman on her deathbed.

For a few weeks, Amadeo had spent a lot of time in the cellar with her, satisfying an appetite he thought insatiable. Fearing that she would be discovered, and jealous even of his own eyes, he did not want to expose her to daylight and allowed only a pale ray to enter through the tiny hole that provided ventilation. In the darkness, they coupled frenziedly, their skin burning and their hearts impatient as carnivorous crabs. In that cavern all odours and tastes were heightened to the extreme. When they touched, each entered the other's being and sank into the other's most secret desires. There, voices resounded in repeated echoes; the walls returned amplified murmurs and kisses. The cellar became a sealed flask in which they wallowed like playful twins swimming in amniotic fluid, two swollen, stupefied foetuses. For days they were lost in an absolute intimacy they confused with love.

When Hortensia fell asleep, her lover went out to look for food and before she awakened returned with renewed energy to resume the cycle of caresses. They should have made love to each other until they died of desire; they should have devoured one another or flamed like mirrored torches, but that was not to be. What happened instead was more predictable and ordinary, much less grandiose. Before a month had passed, Amadeo Peralta tired of the games, which they were beginning to repeat; he sensed the dampness eating into his joints, and he began to feel the attraction of things outside the walls of that grotto. It was time to return to the world of the living and to pick up the reins of his destiny.

"You wait for me here. I'm going out and get very rich. I'll bring you gifts and dresses and jewels fit for a queen," he told her as he said goodbye.

"I want children," said Hortensia.

15 "Children, no; but you shall have dolls."

In the months that followed, Peralta forgot about the dresses, the jewels, and the dolls. He visited Hortensia when he thought of her, not always to make love, sometimes merely to hear her play some old melody on the psaltery; he liked to watch her bent over the instrument, strumming chords. Sometimes he was in such a rush that he did not even speak; he filled her water jugs, left her a sack filled with provisions, and departed. Once he forgot about her for nine days, and found her on the verge of death; he realized then the need to find someone to help care for his prisoner, because his family, his travels, his business, and his social engagements occupied all his time. He chose a tight-mouthed Indian woman to fill that role. She kept the key to the padlock, and regularly came to clean the cell and scrape away the lichens growing on Hortensia's body like pale delicate flowers almost invisible to the naked eye and redolent of tilled soil and neglected things.

"Weren't you ever sorry for that poor woman?" they asked when they arrested her as well, charging her with complicity in the kidnapping. She refused to answer but stared straight ahead with expressionless eyes and spat a black stream of tobacco.

No, she had felt no pity for her; she believed the woman had a calling to be a slave and was happy being one, or else had been born an idiot and like others in her situation was better locked up than exposed to the jeers and perils of the street. Hortensia had done nothing to change her jailer's opinion; she never exhibited any curiosity about the world, she made no attempt to be outside for fresh air, and she complained about nothing. She never seemed bored; her mind had stopped at some moment in her childhood, and solitude in no way disturbed her. She was, in fact, turning into a subterranean creature. There in her tomb her senses grew sharp and she learned to see the invisible; she was surrounded by hallucinatory spirits who led her by the hand to other universes. She left behind a body huddled in a corner and travelled through starry space like a messenger particle, living in a dark land beyond reason. Had she had a mirror, she would have been terrified by her appearance; as she could not see herself, however, she was not witness to her deterioration: she was unaware of the scales sprouting from her skin, or the silkworms that had spun a nest in her long, tangled hair, or the lead-coloured clouds covering eyes already dead from peering into shadows. She did not feel her ears growing to capture external sounds, even the faintest and most distant, like the laughter of children at school recess, the ice-cream vendor's bell, birds in flight, or the murmuring river. Nor did she realize that her legs, once graceful and firm, were growing twisted as they adjusted to moving in that confined space, to crawling, nor that her toenails were thickening like an animal's hooves, her bones changing into tubes of glass, her belly caving in, and a hump forming on her back. Only her hands, forever occupied with the psaltery, maintained their shape and size, although her fingers had forgotten the melodies they had once known and now extracted from the instrument the unvoiced sob trapped in her breast. From a distance, Hortensia resembled a tragic circus monkey; on closer view, she inspired infinite pity. She was totally ignorant of the malignant transformations taking place; in her mind she held intact the image of herself as the young girl she had last seen reflected in the window of Amadeo Peralta's automobile the day he had driven her to this lair. She believed she was as pretty as ever, and continued to act as if she were; the memory of beauty crouched deep inside her and only if someone approached very close would he have glimpsed it beneath the external façade of a prehistoric dwarf.

All the while, Amadeo Peralta, rich and feared, cast the net of his power across the region. Every Sunday he sat at the head of a long table occupied by his sons and nephews, cronies, and accomplices, and special guests such as politicians and generals whom he treated with a hearty cordiality tinged with sufficient arrogance to remind everyone who was master here. Behind his back, people whispered about his victims, about how many he had ruined or caused to disappear, about bribes to authorities; there was talk that he had made half his fortune from smuggling, but no one was disposed to seek the proof of his transgressions. It was also rumoured that Peralta kept a woman prisoner in a cellar. That aspect of his black deeds was repeated with more conviction even than stories of his crooked dealings; in fact, many people knew about it, and with time it became an open secret.

One afternoon on a very hot day, three young boys played hookey from school to swim in the river. They spent a couple of hours splashing around on the muddy bank and then wandered off towards the old Peralta sugar mill that had been closed two generations earlier when cane ceased to be a profitable crop. The mill had the reputation of being haunted; people said you could hear sounds of devils, and many had seen a dishevelled old witch invoking the spirits of dead slaves. Excited by their adventure, the boys crept onto the property and approached the mill. Soon they were daring enough to enter the ruins; they ran through large rooms with thick adobe walls and termite-riddled beams; they picked their way through weeds growing from the floor, mounds of rubbish and dog shit, rotted roof tiles, and snakes' nests. Making jokes to work up their courage, egging each other on, they came to the huge roofless room that contained the ruined sugar presses; here rain and sun had created an impossible garden, and the boys thought they could detect a lingering scent of sugar and sweat. Just as they were growing bolder they heard, clear as a bell, the notes of a monstrous song. Trembling, they almost retreated, but the lure of horror was stronger than their fear, and they huddled there, listening, as the last note drilled into their foreheads. Gradually, they were released from their paralysis; their fear evaporated and they began looking for the source of those weird sounds so different from any music they had even known. They discovered a small trap door in the floor, closed with a lock they could not open. They rattled the wood planks that sealed the entrance and were struck in the face by an indescribable odour that reminded them of a caged beast. They called but no one answered; they heard only a hoarse panting on the other side. Finally they ran home to shout the news that they had discovered the door to hell.

The children's uproar could not be stilled, and thus the neighbours finally proved what they had suspected for decades. First the boys' mothers came to peer through the cracks in the trap door; they, too, heard the terrible notes of the psaltery, so different from the banal melody that had attracted Amadeo Peralta the day he had paused in a small alley in Agua Santa to dry the sweat from his forehead. The mothers were followed by throngs of curious and, last of all, after a crowd had already gathered, came the police and firemen, who chopped open the door and descended into the hole with their lamps and equipment. In the cave they found a naked creature with flaccid skin hanging in pallid folds; this apparition had tangled grey hair that dragged the floor, and moaned in terror of the noise and light. It was Hortensia, glowing with a mother-of-pearl phosphorescence under the steady beams of the firefighter' lanterns; she was nearly blind, her teeth had rotted away, and her legs were so weak she could barely stand. The only sign of her human origins was the ancient psaltery clasped to her breast.

The news stirred indignation throughout the country. Television screens and newspapers displayed pictures of the woman rescued from the hole where she had spent her life, now, at least, half-clothed in a cloak someone had tossed around her shoulders. In only a few hours, the indifference that had surrounded the prisoner for almost half a century was converted into a passion to avenge and succour her. Neighbors improvised lynch parties for Amadeo Peralta; they stormed his house, dragged him out, and had the Guard not arrived in time, would have torn him limb from limb in the plaza. To assuage their guilt for having ignored Hortensia for so many years, everyone wanted to do something for her. They collected money to provide her a pension, they gathered tons of clothing and medicine she did not need, and several welfare organizations were given the task of scraping the filth from her body, cutting her hair, and outfitting her from head to toe, so she looked like an ordinary old lady. The nuns offered her a bed in a shelter for indigents, and for several months kept her tied up to prevent her from running back to her cellar, until finally she grew accustomed to day-light and resigned to living with other human beings.

Taking advantage of the public furor fanned by the press, Amadeo Peralta's numerous enemies finally gathered courage to launch an attack against him. Authorities who for years had overlooked his abuses fell upon him with the full fury of the law. The story occupied everyone's attention long enough to see the former caudillo[2] in prison, and then faded and died away. Rejected by family and friends, a symbol of all that is abominable and abject, harassed by both jailers and companions-in-misfortune, Peralta spent the rest of his days in prison. He remained in his cell, never venturing into the courtyard with the other inmates. From there, he could hear the sounds from the street.

Every day at ten in the morning, Hortensia, with the faltering step of a madwoman, tottered down to the prison where she handed the guard at the gate a warm saucepan for the prisoner.

25 "He almost never left me hungry," she would tell the guard in an apologetic tone. Then she would sit in the street to play her psaltery, wresting from it moans of agony impossible to bear. In the hope of distracting her or silencing her, some passers-by gave her money.

Crouched on the other side of the wall, Amadeo Peralta heard those sounds that seemed to issue from the depths of the earth and course through every nerve in his body. This daily castigation must mean something, but he could not remember what. From time to time he felt something like a stab of guilt, but immediately his memory failed and images of the past evaporated in a dense mist. He did not know why he was in that tomb, and gradually he forgot the world of light and lost himself in his misfortune.

[1991]

[2]**caudillo** dictator.

Joining the Conversation: Critical Thinking and Writing

1. Imagine that you are coming to this story for the first time. What is your response to the opening paragraph?
2. Now that you have completed your reading of the story, please reread the opening paragraph. What is your response to it?
3. If you were assigned to lead a class discussion of Allende's story and were told by your teacher to focus on a single paragraph, which one would you select and why?
4. A literary scholar has praised "If You Touched My Heart" for its "powerful use of symbolism." Do you agree?

5. Please describe the style of this story. Cite examples from the text to support your response.
6. Sometimes it is said that a good short story has a strong "takeaway point"—that is, that it leaves us with an important insight about or perspective on human experience. In your view, what is the takeaway point of this story?

HELENA MARIA VIRAMONTES

Helena Maria Viramontes was born in East Los Angeles in 1954. After completing her undergraduate studies at Immaculate Heart College, she did graduate work at California State University, Los Angeles, and further work (1979–1981) in the MFA Creative Writing Program at the University of California, Irvine. Viramontes has won first prize in several fiction contests, including the Irvine Chicano Literary Contest. In 1989, the year in which she was awarded a Creative Writing Fellowship from the National Endowment for the Arts, she participated in a "Storytelling for Film" workshop at the Sundance Film Institute.

Viramontes writes chiefly about women whose lives are circumscribed by a patriarchal Latino society. Eight of her stories have been collected in "The Moths" and Other Stories *(1985).*

The Moths

I was fourteen years old when Abuelita[1] requested my help. And it seemed only fair. Abuelita had pulled me through the rages of scarlet fever by placing, removing and replacing potato slices on the temples of my forehead; she had seen me through several whippings, an arm broken by a dare jump off Tío Enrique's toolshed, puberty, and my first lie. Really, I told Amá, it was only fair.

Not that I was her favorite granddaughter or anything special. I wasn't even pretty or nice like my older sisters and I just couldn't do the girl things they could do. My hands were too big to handle the fineries of crocheting or embroidery and I always pricked my fingers or knotted my colored threads time and time again while my sisters laughed and called me bull hands with their cute waterlike voices. So I began keeping a piece of jagged brick in my sock to bash my sisters or anyone who called me bull hands. Once, while we all sat in the bedroom, I hit Teresa on the forehead, right above her eyebrow and she ran to Amá with her mouth open, her hand over her eye while blood seeped between her fingers. I was used to the whippings by then.

I wasn't respectful either. I even went so far as to doubt the power of Abuelita's slices, the slices she said absorbed my fever. "You're still alive, aren't you?" Abuelita snapped back, her pasty gray eye beaming at me and burning holes in my suspicions. Regretful that I had let secret questions drop out of my mouth, I couldn't look into her eyes. My hands began to fan out, grow like a liar's nose until they hung by my side like low weights. Abuelita made a balm out of dried moth wings and Vicks and rubbed my hands, shaped them back to size and it was the strangest feeling. Like bones melting. Like sun shining through the darkness of your eyelids. I didn't mind helping Abuelita after that, so Amá would always send me over to her.

[1]**Abuelita** Grandma (Spanish); other Spanish words for relatives mentioned in the story are *Tío,* Uncle, *Amá,* Mother, and *Apá,* Dad.

In the early afternoon Amá would push her hair back, hand me my sweater and shoes, and tell me to go to Mama Luna's. This was to avoid another fight and another whipping, I knew. I would deliver one last direct shot on Marisela's arm and jump out of our house, the slam of the screen door burying her cries of anger, and I'd gladly go help Abuelita plant her wild lilies or jasmine or heliotrope or cilantro or hierbabuena in red Hills Brothers coffee cans. Abuelita would wait for me at the top step of her porch holding a hammer and nail and empty coffee cans. And although we hardly spoke, hardly looked at each other as we worked over root transplants, I always felt her gray eye on me. It made me feel, in a strange sort of way, safe and guarded and not alone. Like God was supposed to make you feel.

5 On Abuelita's porch, I would puncture holes in the bottom of the coffee cans with a nail and a precise hit of a hammer. This completed, my job was to fill them with red clay mud from beneath her rose bushes, packing it softly, then making a perfect hole, four fingers round, to nest a sprouting avocado pit, or the spidery sweet potatoes that Abuelita rooted in mayonnaise jars with toothpicks and daily water, or prickly chayotes[2] that produced vines that twisted and wound all over her porch pillars, crawling to the roof, up and over the roof, and down the other side, making her small brick house look like it was cradled within the vines that grew pear-shaped squashes ready for the pick, ready to be steamed with onions and cheese and butter. The roots would burst out of the rusted coffee cans and search for a place to connect. I would then feed the seedlings with water.

But this was a different kind of help, Amá said, because Abuelita was dying. Looking into her gray eye, then into her brown one, the doctor said it was just a matter of days. And so it seemed only fair that these hands she had melted and formed found use in rubbing her caving body with alcohol and marihuana, rubbing her arms and legs, turning her face to the window so that she could watch the Bird of Paradise blooming or smell the scent of clove in the air. I toweled her face frequently and held her hand for hours. Her gray wiry hair hung over the mattress. Since I could remember, she'd kept her long hair in braids. Her mouth was vacant and when she slept, her eyelids never closed all the way. Up close, you could see her gray eye beaming out the window, staring hard as if to remember everything. I never kissed her. I left the window open when I went to the market.

Across the street from Jay's Market there was a chapel. I never knew its denomination, but I went in just the same to search for candles. I sat down on one of the pews because there were none. After I cleaned my fingernails, I looked up at the high ceiling. I had forgotten the vastness of these places, the coolness of the marble pillars and the frozen statues with blank eyes. I was alone. I knew why I had never returned.

That was one of Apá's biggest complaints. He would pound his hands on the table, rocking the sugar dish or spilling a cup of coffee and scream that if I didn't go to mass every Sunday to save my goddamn sinning soul, then I had no reason to go out of the house, period. Punto final.[3] He would grab my arm and dig his nails into me to make sure I understood the importance of catechism. Did he make himself clear? Then he strategically directed his anger at Amá for her lousy ways of bringing up daughters, being disrespectful and unbelieving, and my older sisters would pull me aside and tell me if I didn't get to mass right this minute,

[2]**chayotes** squashlike fruit. [3]**Punto final** period.

they were all going to kick the holy shit out of me. Why am I so selfish? Can't you see what it's doing to Amá, you idiot? So I would wash my feet and stuff them in my black Easter shoes that shone with Vaseline, grab a missal and veil, and wave good-bye to Amá.

I would walk slowly down Lorena to First to Evergreen, counting the cracks on the cement. On Evergreen I would turn left and walk to Abuelita's. I liked her porch because it was shielded by the vines of the chayotes and I could get a good look at the people and car traffic on Evergreen without them knowing. I would jump up the porch steps, knock on the screen door as I wiped my feet and call Abuelita? mi Abuelita? As I opened the door and stuck my head in, I would catch the gagging scent of toasting chile on the placa.[4] When I entered the sala,[5] she would greet me from the kitchen, wringing her hands in her apron. I'd sit at the corner of the table to keep from being in her way. The chiles made my eyes water. Am I crying? No, Mama Luna, I'm sure not crying. I don't like going to mass, but my eyes watered anyway, the tears dropping on the tablecloth like candle wax. Abuelita lifted the burnt chiles from the fire and sprinkled water on them until the skins began to separate. Placing them in front of me, she turned to check the menudo.[6] I peeled the skins off and put the flimsy, limp looking green and yellow chiles in the molcajete[7] and began to crush and crush and twist and crush the heart out of the tomato, the clove of garlic, the stupid chiles that made me cry, crushed them until they turned into liquid under my bull hand. With a wooden spoon, I scraped hard to destroy the guilt, and my tears were gone. I put the bowl of chile next to a vase filled with freshly cut roses. Abuelita touched my hand and pointed to the bowl of menudo that steamed in front of me. I spooned some chile into the menudo and rolled a corn tortilla thin with the palms of my hands. As I ate, a fine Sunday breeze entered the kitchen and a rose petal calmly feathered down to the table.

10 I left the chapel without blessing myself and walked to Jay's. Most of the time Jay didn't have much of anything. The tomatoes were always soft and the cans of Campbell soups had rusted spots on them. There was dust on the tops of cereal boxes. I picked up what I needed: rubbing alcohol, five cans of chicken broth, a big bottle of Pine Sol. At first Jay got mad because I thought I had forgotten the money. But it was there all the time, in my back pocket.

When I returned from the market, I heard Amá crying in Abuelita's kitchen. She looked up at me with puffy eyes. I placed the bags of groceries on the table and began putting the cans of soup away. Amá sobbed quietly. I never kissed her. After a while, I patted her on the back for comfort. Finally: "¿Y mi Amá?"[8] she asked in a whisper, then choked again and cried into her apron.

Abuelita fell off the bed twice yesterday, I said, knowing that I shouldn't have said it and wondering why I wanted to say it because it only made Amá cry harder. I guess I became angry and just so tired of the quarrels and beatings and unanswered prayers and my hands just there hanging helplessly by my side. Amá looked at me again, confused, angry, and her eyes were filled with sorrow. I went outside and sat on the porch swing and watched the people pass. I sat there until she left. I dozed off repeating the words to myself like rosary prayers: when do you stop giving when do you start giving when do you . . . and when my hands fell from my lap, I awoke to catch them. The sun was setting, an orange glow, and I knew Abuelita was hungry.

[4]**placa** round cast-iron griddle. [5]**sala** living room. [6]**menudo** tripe soup. [7]**molcajete** mixing vessel, mortar. [8]**¿Y mi Amá?** And my Mother?

There comes a time when the sun is defiant. Just about the time when moods change, inevitable seasons of a day, transitions from one color to another, that hour or minute or second when the sun is finally defeated, finally sinks into the realization that it cannot with all its power to heal or burn, exist forever, there comes an illumination where the sun and earth meet, a final burst of burning red orange fury reminding us that although endings are inevitable, they are necessary for rebirths, and when that time came, just when I switched on the light in the kitchen to open Abuelita's can of soup, it was probably then that she died.

The room smelled of Pine Sol and vomit and Abuelita had defecated the remains of her cancerous stomach. She had turned to the window and tried to speak, but her mouth remained open and speechless. I heard you, Abuelita, I said, stroking her cheek, I heard you. I opened the windows of the house and let the soup simmer and overboil on the stove. I turned the stove off and poured the soup down the sink. From the cabinet I got a tin basin, filled it with lukewarm water and carried it carefully to the room. I went to the linen closet and took out some modest bleached white towels. With the sacredness of a priest preparing his vestments, I unfolded the towels one by one on my shoulders. I removed the sheets and blankets from her bed and peeled off her thick flannel nightgown. I toweled her puzzled face, stretching out the wrinkles, removing the coils of her neck, toweled her shoulders and breasts. Then I changed the water. I returned to towel the creases of her stretch-marked stomach, her sporadic vaginal hairs, and her sagging thighs. I removed the lint from between her toes and noticed a mapped birthmark on the fold of her buttock. The scars on her back which were as thin as the life lines on the palms of her hands made me realize how little I really knew of Abuelita. I covered her with a thin blanket and went into the bathroom. I washed my hands, and turned on the tub faucets and watched the water pour into the tub with vitality and steam. When it was full, I turned off the water and undressed. Then, I went to get Abuelita.

15 She was not as heavy as I thought and when I carried her in my arms, her body fell into a V, and yet my legs were tired, shaky, and I felt as if the distance between the bedroom and bathroom was miles and years away. Amá, where are you?

I stepped into the bathtub one leg first, then the other. I bent my knees slowly to descend into the water slowly so I wouldn't scald her skin. There, there, Abuelita, I said, cradling her, smoothing her as we descended, I heard you. Her hair fell back and spread across the water like eagle's wings. The water in the tub overflowed and poured onto the tile of the floor. Then the moths came. Small, gray ones that came from her soul and out through her mouth fluttering to light, circling the single dull light bulb of the bathroom. Dying is lonely and I wanted to go to where the moths were, stay with her and plant chayotes whose vines would crawl up her fingers and into the clouds; I wanted to rest my head on her chest with her stroking my hair, telling me about the moths that lay within the soul and slowly eat the spirit up; I wanted to return to the waters of the womb with her so that we would never be alone again. I wanted. I wanted my Amá. I removed a few strands of hair from Abuelita's face and held her small light head within the hollow of my neck. The bathroom was filled with moths, and for the first time in a long time I cried, rocking us, crying for her, for me, for Amá, the sobs emerging from the depths of anguish, the misery of feeling half born, sobbing until finally the sobs rippled into circles and circles of sadness and relief. There, there, I said to Abuelita, rocking us gently, there, there.

[1982]

Joining the Conversation: Critical Thinking and Writing

1. The narrator says that she was not "pretty or nice," could not "do . . . girl things," and was not "respectful." But what *can* she do, and what *is* she? How, in short, would you characterize her?
2. Elements of the fantastic are evident, notably in the moths at the end. What efforts, if any, does the author exert in order to make the fantastic elements plausible or at least partly acceptable?
3. Why do you suppose the author included the rather extended passages about the sprouting plants and (later) the sun?
4. We can say, on the basis of the description of the bathing of Abuelita in the final paragraph, that the narrator is loving, caring, and grief-stricken. What else, if anything, does this paragraph reveal about the narrator?

ARTHUR C. CLARKE

Arthur C. Clarke (1917–2008), English writer of science fiction, is most widely known for his novel, 2001: A Space Odyssey, *written with the film director Stanley Kubrick.*

During World War II, Clarke served in the Royal Air Force as a radar technician and instructor. After the war, he earned a bachelor's degree, with honors, in mathematics and physics at King's College, London. In addition to writing science fiction, Clarke wrote several nonfiction books concerning rocketry and space flight, as well as a semiautobiographical novel, Glide Path *(1963). In 1958 he emigrated to Sri Lanka, apparently to pursue his interest in scuba diving. He lived the rest of his life there.*

The Nine Billion Names of God

"This is a slightly unusual request," said Dr. Wagner, with what he hoped was commendable restraint. "As far as I know, it's the first time anyone's been asked to supply a Tibetan monastery with an automatic sequence computer. I don't wish to be inquisitive, but I should hardly thought that your—ah—establishment had much use for such a machine. Could you explain just what you intend to do with it?"

"Gladly," replied the lama, readjusting his silk robe and carefully putting away the slide rule he had been using for currency conversions. "Your Mark V computer can carry out any routine mathematical operation involving up to ten digits. However, for our work we are interested in letters, not numbers. As we wish you to modify the output circuits, the machine will be printing words, not columns of figures."

"I don't understand . . ."

"This is a project on which we have been working for the last three centuries—since the lamasery was founded, in fact. It is somewhat alien to your way of thought, so I hope you will listen with an open mind while I explain it."

5 "Naturally."

"It is really quite simple. We have been compiling a list which shall contain all the possible names of God."

"I beg your pardon?"

"We have reason to believe," continued the lama imperturbably, "that all such names can be written with not more than nine letters in an alphabet we have devised."

"And you have been doing this for three centuries?"

10 "Yes. We expected it would take us about fifteen thousand years to complete the task."

"Oh." Dr. Wagner looked a little dazed. "Now I see why you wanted to hire one of our machines. But exactly what is the purpose of this project?"

The lama hesitated for a fraction of a second, and Wagner wondered if he had offended him. If so, there was no trace of annoyance in the reply.

"Call it ritual, if you like, but it's a fundamental part of our belief. All the many names of the Supreme Being—God, Jehovah, Allah, and so on—they are only man-made labels. There is a philosophical problem of some difficulty here, which I do not propose to discuss, but somewhere among all the possible combinations of letters, which can occur, are what one may call the real names of God. By systematic permutation of letters, we have been trying to list them all."

"I see. You've been starting at AAAAAAAA . . . and working up to ZZZZZZZZZ. . . ."

15 "Exactly—though we use a special alphabet of our own. Modifying the electromatic typewriters to deal with this is, of course, trivial. A rather more interesting problem is that of devising suitable circuits to eliminate ridiculous combinations. For example, no letter must occur more than three times in succession."

"Three? Surely you mean two."

"Three is correct. I am afraid it would take too long to explain why, even if you understood our language."

"I'm sure it would," said Wagner hastily. "Go on."

"Luckily it will be a simple matter to adapt your automatic sequence computer for this work, since once it has been programmed properly it will permute each letter in turn and print the result. What would have taken us fifteen thousand years it will be able to do in a thousand days."

20 Dr. Wagner was scarcely conscious of the faint sounds from the Manhattan streets far below. He was in a different world, a world of natural, not man-made, mountains. High up in their remote aeries these monks had been patiently at work, generation after generation, compiling their lists of meaningless words. Was there any limit to the follies of mankind? Still, he must give no hint of his inner thoughts. The customer was always right . . .

"There's no doubt," replied the doctor, "that we can modify the Mark V to print lists of this nature. I'm much more worried about the problem of installation and maintenance. Getting out to Tibet, in these days, is not going to be easy."

"We can arrange that. The components are small enough to travel by air—that is one reason why we chose your machine. If you can get them to India, we will provide transport from there."

"And you want to hire two of our engineers?"

"Yes, for the three months which the project should occupy."

25 "I've no doubt that Personnel can manage that." Dr. Wagner scribbled a note on his desk pad. "There are just two other points—"

Before he could finish the sentence, the lama had produced a small slip of paper.

"This is my certified credit balance at the Asiatic Bank."

"Thank you. It appears to be—ah—adequate. The second matter is so trivial that I hesitate to mention it—but it's surprising how often the obvious gets overlooked. What source of electrical energy have you?"

"A diesel generator providing 50 kilowatts at 110 volts. It was installed about five years ago and is quite reliable. It's made life at the lamasery much more comfortable, but of course it was really installed to provide power for the motors driving the prayer wheels."

"Of course," echoed Dr. Wagner. "I should have thought of that."

The view from the parapet was vertiginous, but in time one gets used to anything. After three months George Hanley was not impressed by the two-thousand-foot swoop into the abyss or the remote checkerboard of fields in the valley below. He was leaning against the wind-smoothed stones and staring morosely at the distant mountains whose names he had never bothered to discover.

This, thought George, was the craziest thing that had ever happened to him. "Project Shangri-La," some wit at the labs had christened it. For weeks now, Mark V had been churning out acres of sheets covered with gibberish. Patiently, inexorably, the computer had been rearranging letters in all their possible combinations, exhausting each class before going on to the next. As the sheets had emerged from the electromatic typewriters, the monks had carefully cut them up and pasted them into enormous books. In another week, heaven be praised, they would have finished. Just what obscure calculations had convinced the monks that they needn't bother to go on to words of ten, twenty, or a hundred letters, George didn't know. One of his recurring nightmares was that there would be some change of plan and that the High Lama (whom they'd naturally called Sam Jaffe,[1] though he didn't look a bit like him) would suddenly announce that the project would be extended to approximately 2060 A.D. They were quite capable of it.

George heard the heavy wooden door slam in the wind as Chuck came out onto the parapet beside him. As usual, Chuck was smoking one of the cigars that made him so popular with the monks—who, it seemed, were quite willing to embrace all the minor and most of the major pleasures of life. That was one thing in their favor: they might be crazy, but they weren't bluenoses. Those frequent trips they took down to the village, for instance . . ." "Listen, George," said Chuck urgently. "I've learned something that means trouble."

"What's wrong? Isn't the machine behaving?" That was the worst contingency George could imagine. It might delay his return, than which nothing could be more horrible. The way he felt now, even the sight of a TV commercial would seem like manna from heaven. At least it would be some link from home.

"No—it's nothing like that." Chuck settled himself on the parapet, which was unusual, because normally he was scared of the drop.

"I've just found out what all this is about."

"What d'ya mean—I thought we knew."

"Sure—we know what the monks are trying to do. But we didn't know why. It's the craziest thing—"

"Tell me something new," growled George.

". . . but old Sam's just come clean with me. You know the way he drops in every afternoon to watch the sheets roll out. Well, this time he seemed rather excited, or at least as near as he'll ever get to it. When I told him we were on the last

[1]**Sam Jaffe** American film actor (1891–1984) who played the role of the High Lama in *Lost Horizon* (1937), a film set in the Himalayas.

cycle he asked me, in that cute English accent of his, if I'd ever wondered what they were trying to do. I said, 'Sure'—and he told me."

"Go on, I'll buy it."

"Well, they believe that when they have listed all His names—and they reckon that there are about nine billion of them—God's purpose will have been achieved. The human race will have finished what it was created to do, and there won't be any point in carrying on. Indeed, the very idea is something like blasphemy."

"Then what do they expect us to do? Commit suicide?"

"There's no need for that. When the list's completed, God steps in and simply winds things up . . . . bingo!"

"Oh, I get it. When we finish our job, it will be the end of the world."

Chuck gave a nervous little laugh.

"That's just what I said to Sam. And do you know what happened? He looked at me in a very queer way, like I'd been stupid in class, and said, 'It's nothing as trivial as that.'"

George thought this over for a moment.

"That's what I call taking the Wide View," he said presently.

"But what d'ya suppose we should do about it? I don't see that it makes the slightest difference to us. After all, we already knew that they were crazy."

"Yes—but don't you see what may happen? When the list's complete and the Last Trump doesn't blow—or whatever it is that they expect—we may get the blame. It's our machine they've been using. I don't like the situation one little bit."

"I see," said George slowly. "You've got a point there. But this sort of thing's happened here before, you know. When I was a kid down in Louisiana we had a crackpot preacher who said the world was going to end next Sunday. Hundreds of people believed him—even sold their homes. Yet nothing happened; they didn't turn nasty, as you'd expect. They just decided that he'd made a mistake in his calculations and went right on believing. I guess some of them still do."

"Well, this isn't Louisiana, in case you hadn't noticed. There are just two of us and hundreds of these monks. I like them, and I'll be sorry for old Sam when his lifework backfires on him. But all the same, I wish I was somewhere else."

"I've been wishing that for weeks. But there's nothing we can do until the contract's finished and the transport arrives to fly us out."

"Of course," said Chuck thoughtfully, "we could always try a bit of sabotage."

"Like hell we could! That would make things worse."

"Not the way I meant. Look at it like this. The machine will finish its run four days from now, on the present twenty-hours-a-day basis. The transport calls in a week. O.K., then all we need to do is to find something that wants replacing during one of the overhaul periods—something that will hold up the works for a couple of days. We'll fix it, of course, but not too quickly. If we time matters properly, we can be down at the airfield when the last name pops out of the register. They won't be able to catch us then."

"I don't like it," said George. "It will be the first time I ever walked out on a job. Besides, it would make them suspicious. No, I'll sit tight and take what comes."

"I still don't like it," he said seven days later, as the tough little mountain ponies carried them down the winding road. "And don't you think I'm running away because I'm afraid. I'm just sorry for those poor old guys up there, and I don't want to be around when they find what suckers they've been. Wonder how Sam will take it?"

"It's funny," replied Chuck, "but when I said goodbye I got the idea he knew we were walking out on him—and that he didn't care because he knew the machine was running smoothly and that the job would soon be finished. After that—well, of course, for him there just isn't any After That . . ."

George turned in his saddle and stared back up the mountain road. This was the last place from which one could get a clear view of the lamasery. The squat, angular buildings were silhouetted against the afterglow of the sunset; here and there lights gleamed like portholes in the sides of an ocean liner. Electric lights, of course, sharing the same circuit as the Mark V. How much longer would they share it? wondered George. Would the monks smash up the computer in their rage and disappointment? Or would they just sit down quietly and begin their calculations all over again?

He knew exactly what was happening up on the mountain at this very moment. The High Lama and his assistants would be sitting in their silk robes, inspecting the sheets as the junior monks carried them away from the typewriters and pasted them into the great volumes. No one would be saying anything. The only sound would be the incessant patter, the never-ending rainstorm, of the keys hitting the paper, for the Mark V itself was utterly silent as it flashed through its thousands of calculations a second. Three months of this, thought George, was enough to start anyone climbing up the wall.

"There she is!" called Chuck, pointing down into the valley. "Ain't she beautiful!"

She certainly was, thought George. The battered old DC-3 lay at the end of the runway like a tiny silver cross. In two hours she would be bearing them away to freedom and sanity. It was a thought worth savoring like a fine liqueur. George let it roll around in his mind as the pony trudged patiently down the slope.

The swift night of the high Himalayas was now almost upon them. Fortunately the road was very good, as roads went in this region, and they were both carrying torches. There was not the slightest danger, only a certain discomfort from the bitter cold. The sky overhead was perfectly clear and ablaze with the familiar, friendly stars. At least there would be no risk, thought George, of the pilot being unable to take off because of weather conditions. That had been his only remaining worry.

He began to sing but gave it up after a while. This vast arena of mountains, gleaming like whitely hooded ghosts on every side, did not encourage such ebullience. Presently George glanced at his watch.

"Should be there in an hour," he called back over his shoulder to Chuck. Then he added, in an afterthought, "Wonder if the computer's finished its run? It was due about now."

Chuck didn't reply, so George swung round in his saddle. He could just see Chuck's face, a white oval turned toward the sky.

"Look," whispered Chuck, and George lifted his eyes to heaven. (There is always a last time for everything.)

Overhead, without any fuss, the stars were going out.

[1953]

Joining the Conversation: Critical Thinking and Writing

1. How would you characterize the Caucasians whom we meet—Dr. Wagner, George Hanley, and Chuck? How would you characterize the lama?
2. Not until paragraphs 40–44 do we learn *why* the monks are engaged in the project. Do you think the story would have been more interesting if we had been told earlier? Why, or why not?
3. The lama explains that words such as "Supreme Being," "God," "Jehovah," and "Allah" are "only man-made labels," and they are *not* "the real names of God." Does this make sense to you? Please explain.
4. Many cultures have taboos on uttering or writing the name of God. Why do you suppose this is so?

CHAPTER 9

Research: Writing with Sources

A problem adequately stated is a problem on its way to being solved.

R. BUCKMINSTER FULLER

What Research Is, and What Research Is Not

Because a research paper requires its writer to collect and interpret evidence usually including the opinions of earlier investigators, it is sometimes said that a research paper, unlike a critical essay, is not the expression of personal opinion. But such a view is unjust both to criticism and to research. A critical essay is not a mere expression of personal opinions; if it is any good, as we have implied in all of our earlier chapters (and expressly indicated in Chapters 7 and 8, on interpretation and evaluation), it is an *argument,* offering evidence that supports the opinions and thus persuades the reader of their objective rightness. And a research paper is in the final analysis largely personal, because the author continuously uses his or her own judgment to evaluate the evidence, deciding what is relevant and convincing. A research paper is not the mere presentation of what a dozen scholars have already said about a topic; it is a thoughtful evaluation of the available evidence, and so it is, finally, an expression of what the author thinks the evidence adds up to.

The literary critic Kenneth Burke said that when we read and write, we are participating in what he calls a "conversation" that has been going on for a long time. A playwright or poet or story-teller wrote a work—a work that itself was a sort of response to life around the author—and then, in the following days or decades or centuries other people have commented on the work. And now you have read it: In Burke's term, you are joining the conversation. Your responses (pleasure, bafflement, anger, whatever) are your first comments; then you begin to think seriously about it, perhaps discussing it with your classmates and the instructor, or with friends and family at home, and now you are going to write about it. In writing about it you will be putting words down onto paper, perhaps in the margin of the book, or keyboarding words onto a screen, and the very act of writing will require you to comment on your own comments—that is, you will revise your words as you go along and after you read each draft.

Your responses are chiefly to the literary works you are writing about, but you are also responding to what you may have read *about* literature in this book and to what your instructor and your classmates have said, and—this is especially important—you are responding to *your own* second and third and even fourth thoughts in this unending conversation that you hold with a book and with yourself. The English philosopher John Locke nicely summarizes the relationship between reading and thinking:

> Reading furnishes our mind only with materials of knowledge; it is thinking [that] makes what we read ours.

> ***Note:*** This chapter is concerned with the use of sources, *not* with the format in which you will document your use of them. For details about *citing* sources—for instance, in footnotes and in a bibliography—consult Appendix B, pages 1366–78. For information about plagiarism, see Appendix C, pages 1379–85

Primary and Secondary Materials

The materials of literary research can be conveniently divided into two sorts, primary and secondary. The *primary materials,* or sources, are the real subject of study; the *secondary materials* are critical and historical accounts already written about these primary materials. For example, Langston Hughes wrote poems, stories, plays, and essays. For a student of Hughes, these works are the primary materials. (We include several of his works in this book.) If you want to study his ways of representing African American speech, or his representations of whites, or his collaboration with Zora Neale Hurston, you will read the primary material—his own writings (and Hurston's, in the case of the collaborative work). But in an effort to reach a thoughtful understanding of some aspect of his work, you will also want to look at later biographical and critical studies of his works and perhaps also at scholarly writing on such topics as Black English. You may even find yourself looking at essays on Black English that do not specifically mention Hughes but that nevertheless may prove helpful.

Similarly, if you are writing about Charlotte Perkins Gilman (we include one of her stories), the primary material includes not only other stories but also her social and political writing. If you are writing about her views of medical treatment of women, you will want to look not only at the story we reprint ("The Yellow Wallpaper") but also at her autobiography. Further, you will also want to look at some secondary material, such as recent scholarly books and articles on medical treatment of women in the late nineteenth and early twentieth centuries.

Locating Materials: First Steps

This chapter is devoted to traditional resources. Consult Appendix B for a detailed introduction to electronic resources.

The easiest way to locate articles and books on literature written in a modern language—that is, on a topic other than literature of the ancient world—is to consult the

> *MLA International Bibliography of Books and Articles in the Modern Languages and Literatures* (1922–),

which until 1969 was published as part of *PMLA* (*Publications of the Modern Language Association*) and since 1969 has been published separately. Many college and university libraries also now offer the *MLA International Bibliography* as part of their package of online resources for research, and it is even more up-to-date.

MLA International Bibliography lists scholarly studies—books as well as articles in academic journals—published in a given year. Because of the great number of items listed, the print version of the bibliography runs to more than one volume, but material on writing in English (including, for instance, South African authors who write in English) is in one volume. To see what has been published on Langston Hughes in a given year, then, in this volume you turn to the section on American literature (as opposed to British, Canadian, Irish, and so forth), and then to the subsection labeled 1900–1999, to see if anything that sounds relevant is listed.

Because your time is limited, you probably cannot read everything published on your topic. At least for the moment, therefore, you will use only the last five or ten years of this bibliography. Presumably, any important earlier material will have been incorporated into some of the recent studies listed. If, when you come to read these recent studies, you find references to an article of, say, 1975 that sounds essential, of course you will read that article too.

Although *MLA International Bibliography* includes works on American literature, if you are doing research on an aspect of American literature you may want to begin with

American Literary Scholarship (1965–).

This annual publication is noted for its broad coverage of articles and books on major and minor American writers, and is especially valuable for its frank comments on the material that it lists.

On some recent topics—for instance, the arguments for and against dropping *Huckleberry Finn* from high school curricula—there may be few or no books, and there may not even be material in the scholarly journals indexed in *MLA International Bibliography*. Popular magazines, however, such as *Atlantic, Ebony,* and *Newsweek*—unlisted in *MLA*—may include some useful material. These magazines, and about 200 others, are indexed in

Readers' Guide to Periodical Literature (1900–).

If you want to write a research paper on the controversy over *Huckleberry Finn*—Mark Twain uses the "N-word"—or on the popular reception given to Kenneth Branagh's films of Shakespeare's *Henry V, Much Ado about Nothing,* and *Hamlet,* you can locate material (for instance, reviews of Branagh's films) through *Readers' Guide*. For that matter, you can also locate reviews of older films, let's say Olivier's films of Shakespeare's plays, by consulting the volumes for the years in which the films were released.

On many campuses *Readers' Guide* has been supplanted by

InfoTrac (1985–)

on CD-ROM. The CD is preinstalled in a microcomputer that can be accessed from a computer terminal. This index to authors and subjects in popular and scholarly magazines and in newspapers provides access to several database indexes, including

- The *General Periodicals Index*, available in the Academic Library Edition (about 1,100 general and scholarly periodicals) and in the Public Library Edition (about 1,100 popular magazines)
- The *Academic Index* (400 general-interest publications, all of which are also available in the Academic Library Edition of the *General Periodicals Index*)
- The *Magazine Index Plus* (the four most recent years of the *New York Times*, the two most recent months of the *Wall Street Journal*, and 400 popular magazines, all of which are included in the Public Library Edition of the *General Periodicals Index*)
- The *National Newspaper Index* (the four most recent years of the *New York Times*, the *Christian Science Monitor*, the *Washington Post*, and the *Los Angeles Times*)

Once again, many college and university libraries are now making available online versions of these and similar resources for research. Some students (and faculty) prefer to use the books on the shelf, but the electronic editions have significant advantages. Often, it is easier to perform "searches" using them; and in many cases they are updated well before the next print editions are published.

Other Bibliographic Aids

There are hundreds of guides to publications and to reference works. *The Oxford Companion to African American Literature* (1997), edited by William L. Andrews, Frances Smith Foster, and Trudier Harris, provides detailed entries on authors, literary works, and many literary, historical, and cultural topics and terms, as well as suggestions for further reading. *Reader's Guide to Literature in English* (1996), edited by Mark Hawkins-Dady, is a massive work (nearly 1,000 pages) that gives thorough summaries of recent critical and scholarly writing on English and American authors.

How do you find such books? Two invaluable guides to reference works (that is, to bibliographies and to such helpful compilations as handbooks of mythology, place names, and critical terms) are

> James L. Harner, *Literary Research Guide: A Guide to Reference Sources for the Study of Literatures in English and Related Topics,* 5th ed. (2008)

and

> Michael J. Marcuse, *A Reference Guide for English Studies* (1990).

And there are guides to these guides: reference librarians. If you don't know where to turn to find something, turn to the librarian.

Electronic Sources

Encyclopedias: Print and Electronic Versions

Encyclopedias can give you the basics about a subject, but like all resources, they have limitations. An encyclopedia may not cover the subject that you are researching or not cover it in adequate depth. Knowledge expands rapidly, and because it does, even a good encyclopedia lags somewhat behind current scholarship. A number of encyclopedias are now online. Many such encyclopedias are linked to the World Wide Web, or exist entirely in WWW form, where updated information and links to reference and research resources are listed. Be sure to check with the librarians at your school; they can tell you about the kinds of resources that are available. If your library offers a tutorial on the use of electronic and Internet resources, we recommend that you sign up for it. We take such tutorials ourselves with our students every year and are always surprised by the new resources we learn about.

It is helpful to have updated information and links, but only when they are reliable. Remember to be a critical user of reference materials. Not everything is of equal value, and we must make good judgments about the sources we consult—and whether or not we can depend on them for reliable, accurate information. More on this point in a moment.

The Internet/World Wide Web

Because of the ease of using the Internet, with its access to e-mail, newsgroups, mailing lists, and, especially, sites and links on the World Wide Web, many students now make it their first—and, unfortunately, too often their *only*—resource for research.

As we noted a moment ago, all of us must be *critical* users of the materials we find on the WWW. The WWW is up-to-date *and* out-of-date, helpful *and* disappointing. It can be a researcher's dream come true, but also a source of errors and a time-waster.

Keeping this point in mind, we recommend to students that for each WWW site they consult, they should consult at least two print sources.

Evaluating Sources on the World Wide Web

For sources on the World Wide Web, as with print sources, you must evaluate what you have located and gauge how much or how little it will contribute to your literary analysis and argument. In the words of one reference librarian, Joan Stockard (formerly of Wellesley College), "The most serious mistake students make when they use the Internet for research is to assume everything is of equal (and acceptable) quality. They need to establish who wrote the material, the qualifications of the author to write on the topic, whether any bias is likely, how current the information is, and how other resources compare."

What Does Your Own Institution Offer?

We'll mention again that many colleges and universities now offer as part of their resources for research a wide range of electronic materials and databases.

At Wellesley College, for example, the library offers a detailed list of research resources, and there is another listing arranged according to department and interdisciplinary program. Some of these are open or free sites, available to anyone with a connection to the WWW. But others are by "subscription only," which means that only members of this academic community can access them.

Sign up for a library tutorial at your own school, and browse in and examine both the library's home page and the online catalog's options and directories.

One of the best research sites, to which many libraries subscribe, is the *FirstSearch* commercial database service.

FirstSearch enables you to find books, articles, theses, films, computer software, and other types of material for just about any field, subject, or topic. Its categories include

Arts and Humanities
Business and Economics
Conferences and Proceedings
Consumer Affairs and People
Education
Engineering and Technology
General and Reference
General Science
Life Sciences
Medicine and Health
News and Current Events
Public Affairs and Law
Social Sciences

Within these categories, you will find a number of useful databases and resources. Make your "search" as focused as possible: Look for materials that bear on the topic that you are writing about, and, even more, that show a connection to the thesis that you are working to develop and demonstrate. Learn from what you find, but approach it critically: Is this source a good one? What are its strengths, and what are (or might be) its limitations? Keep in mind too that you engage in the process of selecting good sources in order to strengthen *your* topic and thesis. The quotations you give from the sources are there to support your ideas and insights. Above all your reader is interested in what *you* have to say.

A good choice of secondary sources can help you to develop your analysis of a literary work, but remember that it is your point of view that counts. Use sources to help present your own interpretation more effectively.

✓ CHECKLIST: *Using the World Wide Web*

Focus the topic of your research as precisely as you can before you embark on a WWW search. Lots of surfing and browsing can sometimes turn up good material, but using the WWW without a focus can prove distracting and unproductive. It takes you away from library research (where the results might be better) and from the actual planning and writing of the paper.

Ask the following questions:

- ☐ Does this site or page look like it can help me in my assignment?
- ☐ Whose site or page is this?
- ☐ Who is the intended audience?
- ☐ What is the point of view? Are there signs of a specific slant or bias?
- ☐ How good is the detail, depth, and quality of the material presented?
- ☐ Is the site well constructed and well organized?

- Is the text well written?
- Can the information be corroborated or supported by print sources?
- When was the site or page made available? Has it been recently revised or updated?
- Can the person or institution, company, or agency responsible for this site or page receive e-mail comments, questions, and criticisms?

Taking Notes

Let's assume now that you have checked some bibliographies and that you have a fair number of references you must read to have a substantial knowledge of the evidence and the common interpretations of the evidence. Most researchers find it convenient, when examining bibliographies and the library catalog, to write down each reference on a 3″ × 5″ index card—one title per card. On the card, put the author's full name (last name first), the exact title of the book or article, and the name of the journal (with dates and pages). Titles of books and periodicals (publications issued periodically—for example, monthly or four times a year) are underlined; titles of articles and of essays in books are enclosed in quotation marks. It's also a good idea to put the library catalog number on the card to save time if you need to get the item for a second look.

Next, start reading or scanning the materials whose titles you have collected. Some of these items will prove irrelevant or silly; others will prove valuable in themselves and also in the leads they give you to further references, which you should duly record in your computer or on note cards.

Two Mechanical Aids: The Photocopier and the Computer

Use the **photocopier** to make copies of material from the library (including material that does not circulate) that you know you need, or that you might want to refer to later. But remember that sometimes it is even more efficient to

- read the material in the library,
- select carefully what pertains to the purpose of your research, and
- take your notes on it.

The **computer** is useful not only in the final stage, to produce a neat copy, but also in the early stages of research, when you are getting ideas and taking notes. With the help of the computer, you can brainstorm ideas, make connections, organize and reorganize material; develop (and change) outlines. This file can be a kind of creative "work space" for your research paper.

A Guide to Note-Taking

Some students use note cards but most write their notes on a computer, and then organize and rearrange this body of material by copying and pasting, moving the notes into a coherent order. (We advise you not to delete material that, when you reread your notes, strikes you as irrelevant. It *probably* is irrelevant; but on the other hand, it may turn out to be valuable after all. Just put unwanted material into a file called "rejects," or some such thing, until you have completed the paper.)

Whichever method you prefer, keep in mind the following:

- **For everything you consult or read in detail, always specify the source,** so that you know exactly from where you have taken a key point or a quotation.
- **Write summaries (abridgments), not paraphrases (restatements).** (See pages 126–28).
- **Quote sparingly.** Remember that this is *your* paper—it will present your thesis, not the thesis and arguments and analyses of someone else. Quote directly only those passages that are particularly effective, or crucial, or memorable. In your finished paper these quotations will provide authority and emphasis.
- **Quote accurately.** After copying a quotation, check your note against the original, correct any misquotation, and then put a checkmark after your quotation to indicate that it is accurate. Verify the page number also, and then put a checkmark on your note after the page number. If a quotation runs from the bottom of, say, page 306 to the top of 307, on your note put a distinguishing mark (for instance two parallel vertical lines after the last word of the first page), so that if you later use only part of the quotation, you will know the page on which it appeared.

  Use ellipses (three spaced periods) to indicate the omission of any words within a sentence. If the omitted words are at the end of the quoted sentence, put a period where you end the sentence, and then add three spaced periods to indicate the omission:

  > If the . . . words were at the end of the quoted sentence, put a
  >
  > period where you end. . . .

  Use square brackets to indicate your additions to the quotation. Here is an example:

  > Here is an [uninteresting] example.

- **Never copy a passage by changing an occasional word,** under the impression that you are thereby putting it into your own words. Notes of this sort may find their way into your paper, your reader will sense a style other than yours, and suspicions of plagiarism may follow. (For a detailed discussion of plagiarism, see pages 316–19 and Appendix C.)
- **Comment on your notes** as you do your work, and later as you reflect on what you have jotted down from the sources. Make a special mark—we recommend using double parentheses ((. . .)) or a different-colored pen to write, for example, "Jones seriously misreads the passage," or "Smith makes a good point but fails to see its implications." As you work, consider it your obligation to *think* about the material, evaluating it and using it as a stimulus to further thought.
- **In the upper corner of each note card, write a brief key**—for example, "Swordplay in *Hamlet*"—so that later you can tell at a glance what is on the note.

Drafting the Paper

The difficult job of writing up your findings remains, but if you have taken good notes and have put useful headings on each note, you are well on your way.

- **Read through the notes and organize them** into packets of related material. Remove all notes that you now see are irrelevant to your paper. (Do not destroy them, however; you may want them later.) Go through the notes again and again, sorting and resorting, putting together what belongs together.
- Probably you will find that you have to do a little **additional research**—somehow you aren't quite clear about this or that—but after you have done this additional research, you should be able to arrange the packets into a reasonable and consistent sequence. You now have a kind of first draft, or at least a tentative organization for your paper.
- **Beware of the compulsion to include every note in your essay;** that is, beware of telling the reader, "A says . . . ; B says . . . ; C says . . ."
- **You must have a point, a thesis.** Make sure that you state it early, and that you keep it evident to your readers.
- **Make sure that the organization is evident to the reader.** When you were doing your research, and even perhaps when you were arranging your notes, you were not entirely sure where you where going; but by now, with your notes arranged into what seems to you to be the right sequence, you think you know what everything adds up to. Doubtless in the process of drafting you will make important changes in your focus, but do not abandon a draft until you think it not only says what you want to say, but says it in what seems to you to be a reasonable order. The final version of the paper should be a finished piece of work, without the inconsistencies, detours, and occasional dead ends of an early draft. Your readers should feel that they are moving toward a conclusion (by means of your thoughtful evaluation of the evidence) rather than merely reading an anthology of commentary on the topic. And so we should get some such structure as "There are three common views on. . . . The first two are represented by A and B; the third, and by far the most reasonable, is C's view that. . . . A argues . . . but. . . . The second view, B's, is based on . . . but. . . . Although the third view, C's, is not conclusive, still. . . . Moreover, C's point can be strengthened when we consider a piece of evidence that she does not make use of. . . ."
- **Preface all or almost all quotations with a lead-in,** such as "X concisely states the common view" or "Z, without offering any proof, asserts that . . ." Let the reader know where you are going, or, to put it a little differently, **let the reader know *how* the quotation fits into your argument.**

Quotations and summaries, in short, are accompanied by judicious analyses of your own. By the end of the paper, your readers have not only read a neatly typed paper (see page 1347) and gained an idea of what previous writers have said but also are persuaded that under your guidance they have seen the evidence, heard the arguments justly summarized, and reached a sound conclusion.

A bibliography or list of works consulted (see pages 1366–78) is usually appended to a research paper so that readers may easily look further into the primary and secondary material if they wish; but if you have done your job well, readers will be content to leave the subject where you left it, grateful that you have set matters straight.

Focus on Primary Sources

Remember that your paper should highlight *primary* sources, the materials that are your real subject (as opposed to the secondary sources, the critical and historical discussion of these primary materials). **The paper should be, above all, *your* paper,** a paper in which you present a thesis that you have developed about the literary work or works that you have chosen to examine. By using secondary sources, you can enrich your analysis, as you place yourself in the midst of the scholarly community interested in this author or authors and you make your contribution to the ongoing conversation. But keep a judicious proportion between primary sources, which should receive the greater emphasis, and secondary sources, which should be used selectively.

To help you succeed in this balancing act, when you review your draft, mark with a red pen the quotations from and references to primary sources, and then with a blue pen do the same marking for secondary sources. If, when you scan the pages of your paper-in-progress, you see a lot more blue than red, you should change the emphasis, the proportion, to what it should be. Guard against the tendency to rely heavily on the secondary sources you have compiled. **The point of view that really counts is your own.**

Avoiding Plagiarism

Honesty requires that you acknowledge your indebtedness for material, not only when you quote directly from a work but also when you appropriate an idea that is not common knowledge. Not to acknowledge such borrowing is plagiarism. If in doubt whether to give credit, give credit.

You ought, however, to develop a sense of what is considered **common knowledge.** Definitions in a dictionary can be considered common knowledge, so there is no need to say, "According to Webster, a novel is . . ." (This is weak in three ways: It's unnecessary, it's uninteresting, and it's unclear, since "Webster" appears in the titles of several dictionaries, some good and some bad.) Similarly, the date of first publication of *The Scarlet Letter* (1850) can be considered common knowledge. Few can give it when asked, but it can be found out from innumerable sources, and no one need get the credit for providing you with the date. The idea that Hamlet delays is also a matter of common knowledge. But if you are impressed by so-and-so's argument that Claudius has been much maligned, you should give credit to so-and-so.

Suppose that in the course of your research for a paper on Langston Hughes you happen to come across Arnold Rampersad's statement, in an essay in *Voices and Visions* (ed. Helen Vendler), that

> books alone could not save Hughes from loneliness, let alone give him the strength to be a writer. At least one other factor was essential in priming him for creative obsession. In the place in his heart, or psychology, vacated by his parents entered the black masses. (355)

This is an interesting idea, and in the last sentence the shift from heart to psychology is perhaps especially interesting. You certainly *cannot* say—with the implication that the idea and the words are your own—something like

> Hughes let enter into his heart, or his psychology—a place vacated by his parents—the black masses.

The writer is simply lifting Rampersad's ideas and making only tiny changes in the wording. But even a larger change in the wording is unacceptable unless Rampersad is given credit. Here is a restatement that is an example of plagiarism even though the words differ from Rampersad's:

> Hughes took into himself ordinary black people, thus filling the gap created by his mother and father.

In this version, the writer presents Rampersad's idea as if it were the writer's own—and presents it less effectively than Rampersad.

What to do? Give Rampersad credit, perhaps along these lines:

> As Arnold Rampersad has said, "in the place in his heart, or his psychology" where his parents had once been, Hughes now substituted ordinary black people (355).

You can use another writer's ideas, and even some of the very words, but you *must* give credit, and you *must* use quotation marks when you quote.

You can

- give credit and quote directly, or
- give credit and summarize the writer's point, or
- give credit and summarize the point but include—within quotation marks—some phrase you think is especially interesting

Reminder: For review of and guidance in the process of selecting and citing sources, please consult the quiz on plagiarism that we reprint in Appendix C (pages 1379–80).

Part II

Up Close

Thinking Critically about Literary Works and Literary Forms

CHAPTER 10

Critical Thinking: Arguing with Oneself, Asking Questions, and Making Comparisons

What Is Critical Thinking?

The verb *to think* has several meanings, such as *to imagine* ("Think how he'll hit the ceiling when you tell him this"), *to expect or hope* ("I think I'll get the job"), and—the meaning we will chiefly be concerned with—*to consider closely, especially by exercising one's powers of reason* ("I've been thinking about why she did it, and I've come to some conclusions").

When we engage in critical thinking as close consideration, we are keenly aware of what we are doing. We are, for instance, studying an effect and are searching for its causes. "This story bores me, but exactly *why* does it bore me?" Is the plot too familiar? Are the characters unrealistic? Is the language trite? Or so technical that I can't follow it? Does the author use too many words to say too little? Or: "I loved the book but hated the movie. Why?" And again we start to consider the problem closely, probably (again) by examining the parts that make up the whole. And here we are at the heart of *critical thinking*.

The words *critic, critical,* and *criticism* come from a Greek word *krinein,* meaning "to separate." In ordinary talk, *to criticize* is to find fault or to judge severely. But in the sense we are concerned with here, *to criticize* is to examine and to judge, not necessarily to find fault.

> Having said that critical thinking does not necessarily involve fault-finding, we want to modify this statement. There is one writer whose work you should indeed judge severely. The writer is you. When you read a draft of your work, adopt a skeptical spirit. As you read the draft, ask yourself if assertions are supported with sufficient evidence, and ask if other interpretations of the evidence might reasonably be offered. If you engage in this process, you are engaged in critical thinking.

Asking and Answering Questions

Critical thinking is a matter of separating the whole into parts, in order to see relationships. If you ask yourself questions about a work—whether the work is something reprinted in this book or is something that you have just drafted—you will almost surely set yourself thinking about how the parts relate to each other and to the whole, their context. Here are some typical questions:

- What expectations does the title arouse in a reader?
- Does the middle drag?
- Do certain characters or settings seem to be symbolic, suggesting more than themselves?
- Is the end satisfactory, and if so, why? Because it is surprising? Because, on the contrary, foreshadowing caused us to anticipate it, and it therefore fulfills our expectations?

When you ask yourself questions such as these, you will find that you are deepening your understanding of how a work (perhaps an essay, story, poem, or play in this book, perhaps an essay of your own) works.

Because thinking about questions is an excellent way to deepen your understanding, we include questions along with most of the literature in this book. And we include numerous checklists—in effect, lists of questions for you to ask yourself when you are writing—in order to help you think about your own productions.

A process that in effect is synonymous with critical thinking is **analysis;** this word also comes from a Greek word, meaning *to separate into parts.* And because the point of analysis is to understand how things connect, how things work, and because the point of writing an analysis is to share your understanding with your readers, your essay normally will include a **synthesis,** "a putting together." It can almost be said that essays based on critical thinking will propose a **thesis,** and will support the thesis by giving **reasons,** that is, by giving evidence: "X is so, *because* . . ."

You probably will find, like almost everyone else, that your best arguments come to you when you start to put them into writing, whether with pencil and paper or with a keyboard and a computer. Although our main concern in this book is with writing about literature, and in a moment we will look at a short poem, let's start indirectly by thinking analytically, thinking critically, about a photograph. (Our method will be in accord with Polonius's advice in *Hamlet,* "By indirections find directions out.")

Comparing and Contrasting

The photograph we will focus on here is of Sitting Bull and Buffalo Bill, taken by a Canadian photographer, William Notman (1826–1891). Buffalo Bill—William F. Cody—got his name from his activities as a supplier of buffalo meat for workers on the Kansas Pacific Railway, but his fame came chiefly from his exploits as an army scout and a fighter against the Sioux Indians, and later from Buffalo Bill's Wild West. Buffalo Bill's Wild West was a show (though he never used this word because he insisted that the exhibition recreated recent Western history) consisting of mock battles with Indians, an attack on a stagecoach, and feats of horsemanship and sharpshooting. Sitting Bull, a Sioux chief, had defeated Custer at the Battle of Little Bighorn ten years before this picture was taken, but he had fled to Canada soon after the battle. In 1879 he was granted amnesty and returned to the United States, and in 1885 he appeared in Buffalo Bill's Wild West. The photograph, entitled *Foes in '76, Friends in '85,* was used to publicize the show.

William Notman, *Foes in '76, Friends in '85.* The Sioux chief appeared for one season in William F. Cody's show, which was called *Buffalo Bill's Wild West.* Souvenir cards with this picture were sold. (Buffalo Bill Historical Center, Cody, WY [P.69.2125])

In Chapter 3 we talked about writing a comparison (pages 129–31), but we now want to add a few things. The writer Howard Nemerov once said, "If you really want to see something, look at something else." He was talking about the power of comparison to illuminate. We compare X and Y, not for the sake of making lists of similarities and differences, but for the sake of seeing X (or Y) more clearly. This book offers material for you to read with pleasure, and one source of pleasure is understanding. Your understanding of one work may be heightened by thinking about it in comparison with another work. We offer several *case studies* that present a writer *in depth.* For example, we give three stories by Raymond Carver—in fact, we give two versions of one of the stories so thinking about one story in comparison with another, or within this context, will enrich your understanding. Similarly, we offer several thematic chapters, for instance a chapter on "Love and Hate," where, again, works invite comparison.

Suppose we want to think about the picture of Sitting Bull and Buffalo Bill, in order to deepen our understanding of it and to share our understanding with others. To say that the photograph's dimensions are such-and-such or even to say that it shows two people is merely to *describe* it, not to do anything that can be called thinking. But if we look more closely, and compare the two figures, our mind is energized. (Strictly speaking, **to compare** is to take note of similarities, and **to contrast** is to take note of differences, but in ordinary usage *compare* covers both activities.) Comparing greatly stimulates the mind; by comparing X with Y, we notice things that we might otherwise pass over. Suppose we ask these questions:

- What resemblances and differences do we see in the clothes of the two figures?
- What about their facial expressions?
- How do their poses compare?
- Is the setting significant?

If we try to answer these and other questions that come to mind, we may find ourselves jotting down phrases and sentences along these lines:

> Buffalo Bill is in fancy clothing (shiny boots, a mammoth buckle, a decorated jacket)
>
> BB is striking a pose-very theatrical, his right hand on his heart, his head tilted slightly back, his eyes looking off as though he is gazing into the future. He seems to be working hard to present a grand image of himself.
>
> Sitting Bull simply stands there, apparently looking downward. One feels that he is going along with what is expected of him-after all, he had joined the show-but he refuses to make a fool of himself.
>
> Sitting Bull lets BB have upper hand (literally-on gun)
>
> BB in effect surrounds SB (Bill's right shoulder is behind Sitting Bull and Bill's left leg is in front of him).

Analyzing and Evaluating Evidence

If we continue to look closely, we probably notice that the landscape is fake—not the great outdoors but a set, a painted backdrop and probably a fake grass mat. If we see these things, we may formulate the thesis that Buffalo Bill here is all show biz, and that Sitting Bull retains his dignity. And if in our essay we support these assertions by pointing to **evidence,** we are demonstrating critical thinking.

Here, in fact, is the final paragraph from an essay that a student wrote on this picture:

> Buffalo Bill is obviously the dominant figure in this photograph, but he is not the outstanding one. His efforts to appear great only serve to make him appear small. His attempt to outshine Sitting Bull strikes us as faintly ridiculous. We do not need nor want to know any more about Buffalo Bill's personality; it is spread before us in the picture. Sitting Bull's inwardness and

dignity make him more interesting than Buffalo Bill, and make us wish to prove our intuition and to ascertain that this proud Sioux was a great chief.

We think this analysis is excellent, but when we did some of our own research on Buffalo Bill we found that he was more complicated and more interesting than we at first thought. But this is to get ahead of the story.

Thinking Critically: Arguing with Oneself, Asking Questions, and Comparing—E. E. Cummings's "Buffalo Bill 's"

Let's look now at a short poem by E. E. Cummings, probably written in 1917, the year Buffalo Bill died, but not published until 1920. Cummings did not give it a title, but included it in a group of poems called "Portraits." (In line 6, *pigeons* are clay targets used in skeet shooting or in exhibitions of marksmanship.)

Buffalo Bill 's
defunct
        who used to
        ride a watersmooth-silver
                                                        stallion
and break onetwothreefourfive pigeonsjustlikethat
                                                                                  Jesus
he was a handsome man
                                             and what i want to know is
how do you like your blueeyed boy
Mister Death

Read the poem, preferably aloud, at least two or three times, and with as open a mind as possible. *Don't* assume that because the photograph shows us a man for whom we probably would not want to work, this poem necessarily conveys the same attitude.

Ultimately you will want to ask your own questions about the poem and about your responses, but for a start you may find it useful to put down tentative answers to some or all of these questions. We say "tentative" answers because you will, when you think about them, almost surely begin to question them and thus improve your responses.

1. What is the speaker's attitude toward Buffalo Bill? (How do you know? What *evidence* can you point to?)
2. In line 6, why do you suppose the poet ran the words together?
3. Why do you think Cummings spaced the poem as he does? One student suggested that the lines form an arrowhead pointing to the right. Do you find merit in this suggestion? If not, what better explanation(s) can you offer?

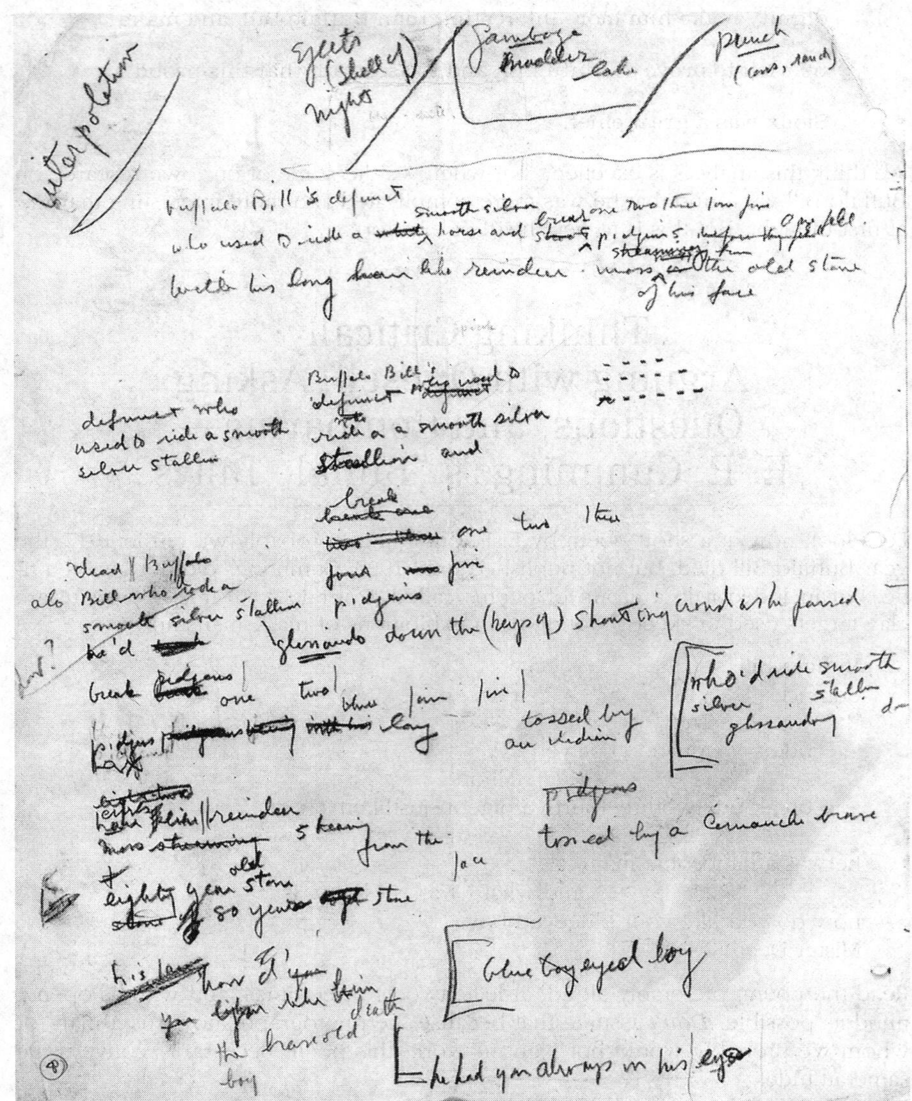

Manuscript of the draft of E. E. Cummings's poem (the final version is printed on page 327). (By permission of the Houghton Library, Harvard University. MS Am 1823.7 [21])

4. What do you make out of the address to "Mister Death"? Why "Mister Death" rather than "Mr. Death" or "Death"? If Mister Death could speak, what answer do you think he might give to the speaker's question?
5. What do you make of the use of "defunct" (as opposed to "dead") in line 2?
6. What do you make of "Jesus" in line 7? What is the effect of placing the word on a line by itself? Is Cummings being blasphemous? Is he inviting us to compare Buffalo Bill with Jesus? Again, support your response with *evidence*.

buffalo Bill [~~is~~]'s defunct
smooth silver break one two three four five one fell.
who used to ride a ~~white~~^horse and ~~shoot~~^pidgens ~~before they fell~~.
streaming from
xxxx
with his long hair like reindeer moss^~~in~~ the old stone
of his face

Buffalo Bill's - - - -
who used to
defunct who defunct ~~defunct~~ - - - - -
used to ride a smooth ~~who~~
silver stallion ride a a smooth silver r - - - - -
[~~horse~~] stallion and

break
~~break one~~
dead ‖Buffalo ~~two three~~ one two three
'd
alo Bill who rode a four ~~xxxx~~ five
smooth silver stallion pidgens
he'd ~~break~~
how? pidgens glissando down the (hapy) shouting crowd as he passed
break ~~break~~
one two
three four five who'd ride smooth
silver ' stallion
pidgens ~~pidgens being with his~~ long tossed by glissandoing do
ax an indian
~~eighty two~~
curls
hair like ‖ reindeer ~~pidgens~~
streaming
moss ~~streaming~~ from the tossed by a Comanche brave
face
~~x~~ old
~~xxx~~ eighty year stone
stone ~~xx~~ 80 years ~~xxx~~ stone
his ~~long~~
how d'~~you~~
~~you~~ [~~like~~] you like [~~it~~] him blue ~~boy~~ eye[~~s~~]d boy
death
the brave old
boy
he had you always in his | ey[~~es~~]e |

Modern transcription of the draft reproduced on page 328. (By permission of the Houghton Library, Harvard University. MS Am 1823.7 [80])

7. Compare the published poem with the manuscript draft. In the manuscript (see page 328, and for a scholar's transcription of it, see above) you will notice that Cummings wrote, near the start, "with his long hair like reindeer moss streaming from the old stone of his face." These words do not appear in the final version. Do you think Cummings showed good judgment in deleting the line? Explain.
8. Some readers say that Cummings is satirizing Buffalo Bill, others that he is satirizing death. Do you agree with either of these views? Why? (In a sentence or two define *satire*—feel free to consult a dictionary—and perhaps give a clear example. By the way, it's possible to satirize the common human

fear of death, but can death be satirized? How might that be done? And what would be the point?)

You may want to discuss some or all of these questions, and others that you generate for yourself, with classmates and with your instructor. It will be interesting to see whether at least some differences of opinion can be resolved by discussion, by pointing to evidence.

Finally, after you have thought about the preceding questions, and any questions that you may initiate, consider these two opinions, from published discussions of the poem:

1. Buffalo Bill, in the poem, functions as a destroyer, an agent of death.
2. The picture of Buffalo Bill on his "watersmooth-silver stallion," riding to the center of the tent to accept the adulation of the crowd before his demonstration of crack marksmanship is, I think, acidly ironic.

Do you agree with either, or with both? What evidence in the poem can you point to, in order to support or rebut these assertions?

Buffalo Bill on a favorite horse, around 1910. (Buffalo Bill Historical Center, Cody, WY [P.69.862])

A Short-Short Story and Its Revised Version

Consider now two versions of a very short story by Raymond Carver. In 1977 he published the first version, called "Mine." In 1981 he published a revised version with a new title, "Popular Mechanics," and in 1986 he published the same revised version but under yet another title, "Little Things."

Read "Mine," then read "Little Things," and then go back over both, marking differences and jotting down your own responses. To take an obvious point, you may want to jot down your responses to the titles: Do you think the new title is better, or not? Why? Or consider the sentences that end the first paragraph in each version: "It was getting dark, outside and inside," and "But it was getting dark on the inside too." Do you think Carver improved the end of the first paragraph? Why, or why not?

Raymond Carver

For a biographical note on Raymond Carver, see page 709.

Mine

During the day the sun had come out and the snow melted into dirty water. Streaks of water ran down from the little, shoulder-high window that faced the back yard. Cars slushed by on the street outside. It was getting dark, outside and inside.

He was in the bedroom pushing clothes into a suitcase when she came to the door.

I'm glad you're leaving. I'm glad you're leaving! she said. Do you hear?

He kept on putting his things into the suitcase and didn't look up.

5 Sonofabitch! I'm so glad you're leaving! She began to cry. You can't even look me in the face, can you? Then she noticed the baby's picture on the bed and picked it up.

He looked at her and she wiped her eyes and stared at him before turning and going back to the living room.

Bring that back.

Just get your things and get out, she said.

He did not answer. He fastened the suitcase, put on his coat, and looked at the bedroom before turning off the light. Then he went out to the living room. She stood in the doorway of the little kitchen, holding the baby.

10 I want the baby, he said.

Are you crazy?

Little Things

Early that day the weather turned and the snow was melting into dirty water. Streaks of it ran down from the little shoulder-high window that faced the backyard. Cars slushed by on the street outside, where it was getting dark. But it was getting dark on the inside too.

He was in the bedroom pushing clothes into a suitcase when she came to the door.

I'm glad you're leaving! I'm glad you're leaving! she said. Do you hear?

He kept on putting his things into the suitcase.

5 Son a bitch! I'm so glad you're leaving! She began to cry. You can't even look me in the face, can you?

Then she noticed the baby's picture on the bed and picked it up.

He looked at her and she wiped her eyes and stared at him before turning and going back to the living room.

Bring that back, he said.

Just get your things and get out, she said.

10 He did not answer. He fastened the suitcase, put on his coat, looked around the bedroom before turning off the light. Then he went out to the living room.

She stood in the doorway of the little kitchen, holding the baby.

No, but I want the baby. I'll get someone to come by for his things.

You can go to hell! You're not touching this baby.

The baby had begun to cry and she uncovered the blanket from around its head.

Oh, oh, she said, looking at the baby.

He moved towards her.

For God's sake! she said. She took a step back into the kitchen.

I want the baby.

Get out of here!

She turned and tried to hold the baby over in a corner behind the stove as he came up.

He reached across the stove and tightened his hands on the baby.

Let go of him, he said.

Get away, get away! she cried.

The baby was red-faced and screaming. In the scuffle they knocked down a little flower pot that hung behind the stove.

He crowded her into the wall then, trying to break her grip, holding onto the baby and pushing his weight against her arm.

Let go of him, he said.

Don't, she said, you're hurting him!

He didn't talk again. The kitchen window gave no light. In the near dark he worked on her fisted fingers with one hand and with the other hand he gripped the screaming baby up under an arm near the shoulder.

She felt her fingers being forced open and the baby going from her. No, she said, just as her hands came loose. She would have it, this baby whose chubby face gazed up at them from the picture on the table. She grabbed for the baby's other arm. She caught the baby around the wrist and leaned back.

He would not give. He felt the baby going out of his hands and he pulled back hard. He pulled back very hard.

I want the baby, he said.

Are you crazy?

No, but I want the baby. I'll get someone to come by for his things.

You're not touching this baby, she said.

The baby had begun to cry and she uncovered the blanket from around his head.

Oh, oh, she said, looking at the baby.

He moved toward her.

For God's sake! she said. She took a step back into the kitchen.

I want the baby.

Get out of here!

She turned and tried to hold the baby over in a corner behind the stove.

But he came up. He reached across the stove and tightened his hands on the baby.

Let go of him, he said.

Get away, get away! she cried.

The baby was red-faced and screaming. In the scuffle they knocked down a flowerpot that hung behind the stove.

He crowded her into the wall then, trying to break her grip. He held on to the baby and pushed with all his weight.

Let go of him, he said.

Don't, she said. You're hurting the baby, she said.

I'm not hurting the baby, he said.

The kitchen window gave no light. In the near-dark he worked on her fisted fingers with one hand and with the other hand he gripped the screaming baby up under an arm near the shoulder.

She felt her fingers being forced open. She felt the baby going from her.

No! she screamed just as her hands came loose.

She would have it, this baby. She grabbed for the baby's other arm. She caught the baby around the wrist and leaned back.

In this manner they decided the issue.

[1977]

But he would not let go. He felt the baby slipping out of his hands and he pulled back very hard.

In this manner, the issue was decided.

[1981]

Your Turn: Writing an Argument about Carver's Two Stories

After annotating the two stories, and thinking about your annotations, write a short essay arguing that, on balance, one version is superior to the other. You do not of course have to believe that every change was an improvement (or a worsening); in fact, you may want to argue that in some ways the earlier version is better, and in some ways the later version is better, but in any case formulate a thesis sentence—a sentence that tells the reader the gist of your point—and then in 250–500 words support the thesis.

CHAPTER 11

A Brief Guide: Writing about Literature

What can be said at all can be said clearly.

LUDWIG WITTGENSTEIN

Other chapters in this book offer fuller discussions of the points that we make here, but right now a concise version of what composition teachers call "the writing process"—especially as it relates to writing arguments—may be welcome. Because no single process works for all writers—indeed, most writers use different processes for different kinds of assignments—the following advice may help you to get going, especially on a short paper that draws chiefly on your own responses to a work.

Standing Back: Kinds of Writing

Most writing about literature seeks to do one or both of two things:

- **to inform** ("This play was written only five years ago"; "The images of night suggest death.")
- **to persuade** ("This early story is one of her best"; "Despite the widespread view that the images of night suggest death, I will argue that here they do nothing more than indicate a time of day.")

Whether you are primarily concerned with informing or with persuading (and the two purposes are often indistinguishable because writers usually want to persuade readers that the information is significant), you ought to be prompted by a strong interest in a work or a body of work. This interest usually is a highly favorable response to the material (essentially, "That's terrific"), but an unfavorable response ("Awful!") or a sense of bafflement ("Why would anyone care for that?") may also motivate writing. In any case, stimulated by a work, you put words onto paper, perhaps first by jotting down observations in no particular sequence. Later you will organize them for the benefit of an imagined reader, offering what D. H. Lawrence calls "a reasoned account of the feelings" produced by a work. Don't be embarrassed if a work produces strong feelings in you, pleasant or unpleasant.

Most academic writing about literature is chiefly explanatory, or, we can say, *analytic*: It is concerned with examining the relationships (for instance, of the parts to the whole within a work, or of historical causes and effects), and indeed your instructors probably will ask you to write papers that are largely analytic. Writing about literature includes a range of kinds of writing:

- **description** ("The story is unusually brief, only a page long"; "The poem consists of four stanzas each of four lines; within each stanza, the first and third lines rhyme, and the second and fourth lines rhyme with a different sound. The rhyme scheme can thus be indicated as *abab*.")

- **analysis** or **explanation of the internal relationships—the structure—of the work** ("The second scene in this play has at least three functions.")
- **personal report,** or what might be called "confession," a report of one's immediate response and perhaps of later responses ("The story reminds me of an experience I had when I was about the age of the central character"). Personal report often implies **evaluation** ("The story is shocking," or, on the contrary, "There is simply nothing here that holds our interest"). In Appendix A we discuss some critical principles that underlie evaluation. Here it is enough to say that the two most common sources for judging are
  1. a spontaneous personal response ("The death of a child is deeply disturbing") and
  2. a principle alleged to be widely held ("A story ought to be unified.")

Although personal responses can hardly be argued about in rational terms, they can and must be set forth clearly and interestingly, so that the reader understands—because the writer points to things in the literary work that evoke the responses—*why* the writer experiences these responses and *why* the writer evaluates the work as he or she does.

- **argument**—writing that offers reasons (and the reasons will be supported by *evidence,* notably references to passages from the literary works you are discussing) and
- **evaluation** ("The story is the best that I have read thus far.")

Again, your instructors will probably ask you to write papers that are chiefly analytic, though some description, personal report, and evaluation almost surely will be implicit (if not explicit) in your analyses.

Getting Close: Drafting the Essay

Generating Ideas

1. **Consider the writing situation.** Is the specific topic assigned, or do you choose your own topic?
   - If the choice is yours, choose a work you like, but
   - allow plenty of time (you may find, once you get to work, that you want to change your topic).

   How long will the essay be? (Allow an appropriate amount of time.)

   What kinds of sources are you expected to use?
   - Only your own insights, supplemented by conversations with friends, and perhaps familiarity with your textbooks?
   - Some research?
   - Substantial research?

   Again, allow the appropriate amount of time.

   Who is the audience?
   - Classmates?
   - The general public (e.g., readers of weekly newsmagazines)? Awareness of the audience—your imagined readers—will help you to determine the amount of detail you need to provide. Unless you are told otherwise,

assume that your classmates are your audience; they are intelligent adults, but they have not thought as deeply as you have about the particular topic you are writing about. (More about the audience in a moment.)

When is the essay due? Allow time

- to write, type, and revise the draft several times,
- to proofread, and
- to check any sources.

2. **Jot down at least a few ideas *before* you write a first draft.** Key phrases will do—and you probably will find that these jottings, this mixture of assertions and questions, will engender further ideas. You can immediately generate some ideas by thinking about the impact the work makes on you.
   - *Why* does it please, displease, or even anger you?
   - What relevant assertions have you heard in lectures or read in books—for instance, concerning tragedy or characterization, or concerning the criteria for judging a poem?
   - How convincing *are* these ideas? Now that you are looking closely at a particular work or works, do these criteria really apply without modification? What modifications now suggest themselves? (In your final version, be sure to give credit for any ideas that you borrow.) Writing at this stage is not only the setting forth of ideas; it is largely the *discovering* of ideas you didn't know were in you.
3. **Rearrange these jottings into an outline (i.e., a tentative plan for a draft).** A list of a few phrases indicating the topics you plan to address (e.g., "historical context," "metaphor") and the sequence will help you to get going. Such an outline may follow this pattern:
   - The first paragraph will probably name the writer or writers and the works and will specify the general approach (e.g., biographical or comparative) or scope (an early and a late work by a story-writer) of the paper.
   - Additional jottings, in sequence, will indicate the gist of each paragraph.
4. **Start writing without worrying about mechanical errors.** Yes, you have been putting down words, but those preliminary jottings were what composition instructors call "prewriting." Now you are writing a draft—not yet a first draft but a zero draft, so don't worry about mechanical matters such as spelling and punctuation and stylistic elegance. Such things will be important when you revise and edit, but at the moment you are trying to find out what your ideas are and how much sense they make. Don't be afraid to set forth your hunches. As E. M. Forster put it, "How do I know what I think until I see what I say?" Write in a spirit of confidence, and if you are using a computer, be sure to save your material.

   If you have jotted down an outline, begin by following the outline, but remember, the outline is a helpful guide to get you going; it is not a road map that must be followed. Write freely and get your ideas down on paper or up on the screen. At this stage, you are still wrestling with ideas, trying things out, clarifying things *for yourself,* engaging in a search and discovery operation.

Later, of course, you will read and reread with a critical (skeptical) mind what you have said, and you will want to make sure that assertions are supported by evidence. But for now, follow your instincts.

Revising a Draft

1. **Reread and revise your material.** This should preferably happen after an interval of a few hours or even a day. You are now prepared to write a serious draft. Your tentative or working thesis has now evolved into a point in which you have confidence. Revisions will be of two sorts:
   - global (large scale, such as reorganization) and
   - local (the substitution of a precise word for an imprecise one or a spelling correction).

   Generally speaking, try to begin by making the necessary global revisions. You may, for instance, decide that introductory background material is or is not needed, or that background material should be distributed throughout the essay rather than given all at once at the start, or that you are too colloquial, too chatty (or, on the other hand, too formal, too stuffy). But, of course, if you spot a spelling error, or realize that a particular word is not the best word, there is no harm in pausing to make such a correction when you first see the need.

   Now is the time to keep asking yourself key questions:
   - What will my audience—my readers—make of this paragraph, this sentence, this word?
   - Does this word need to be defined?
   - Do I offer adequate support for this generalization?
   - Is my point clear, and is it expressed effectively?

   Put yourself in your readers' shoes; ask yourself if they will be aware of where they are going. That is, ask yourself if you have provided transitions or signposts such as "moreover," "on the other hand," and "for example." Yes, your instructor or your section leader is in fact your reader, but do *not* write for this specific person. Invent (imagine) a friendly but skeptical reader; if you write for this imagined reader, you will have created a silent but helpful collaborator, someone who will tell you that you need a transition or a definition or a concrete example.
2. **Reread and revise the draft again.** Ask yourself what your reader will make out of each sentence.
3. **Make certain that the mechanics are according to specifications.** Here you are acting not so much as an author but as an *editor.*
   - It is appropriate for an author, in the heat of drafting material, to be indifferent to mechanical details, but
   - it is appropriate for an editor to be cool, detached, finicky—in short, for the editor to tell the author to come down to earth and to package the essay neatly, correctly.
   - Margins, spacing, page numbering, and labeling of illustrations should follow the instructor's requirements.
   - Documentation should be according to the *MLA Handbook for Writers of Research Papers,* 7th edition, guidelines given in Appendix B.
4. **If possible, get a classmate or a friend to read your essay and to make suggestions.** This representative of your audience should not, of course, rewrite the essay for you, but he or she can call your attention to
   - paragraphs that need development,
   - unclear organization,

- unconvincing arguments,
- awkward sentences, and
- errors in punctuation and spelling.

5. **Consider your reader's suggestions and revise where you think necessary.** If your reader finds some terms obscure or an argument unsubstantiated, you will almost surely want to revise, clarifying the terms and providing evidence for the argument. As before, in the process of revising, try to imagine yourself as your hypothetical reader.
6. **Print out a hard copy of the revised draft, read it, and revise again—and again—as needed.**

It all adds up to *seeing* and *saying,* to seeing (discovering) in the works of literature things that you will then want to communicate to your reader (this is a matter of getting ideas) and to saying effectively the things you want to say. Chapter 2 offers suggestions about getting ideas, about finding things that, once found, you will want to communicate to others, and Chapters 5 and 9 offer suggestions about the art of writing, from developing effective opening and concluding paragraphs to technical matters such as using the accepted forms in documenting print and electronic sources.

✓ CHECKLIST: *Reviewing the Basics*

- ☐ Is my title engaging?
- ☐ Does the introduction provide essential information (author, work, topic, or approach of the essay)?
- ☐ Does the paper have a thesis, a point?
- ☐ Do I support my argument with sufficient persuasive detail?
- ☐ Have I kept the needs of my audience in mind—for instance, have I defined unfamiliar terms? Have I recognized possible objections to my thesis, and have I offered adequate counterarguments to these objections
- ☐ Is the paper organized, and is the organization clear to the reader?
- ☐ Have I set forth my views effectively and yet not talked too much about myself?
- ☐ Does the essay fulfill the assignment (length, scope)?

CHAPTER 12

Reading and Writing about Essays

The word *essay* entered the English language in 1597, when Francis Bacon called a small book of ten short prose pieces *Essays*. Bacon borrowed the word from Michel de Montaigne, a French writer who in 1580 had published some short prose pieces under the title *Essais*—that is, "testings," or "attempts," from the French verb *essayer*, "to try." Montaigne's title indicated that his graceful and personal jottings—the fruit of pleasant study and meditation—were not fully thought-out treatises but rather sketches that could be amplified and amended.

If you keep a journal, you are working in Montaigne's tradition. You jot down your tentative thoughts, perhaps your responses to a work of literature, partly to find out what you think and how you feel. Montaigne said, in the preface to his book, "I am myself the subject of my book," and in all probability you are the real subject of your journal. Your entries—your responses to other writers and your reflections on those responses—require you to examine yourself.

Types of Essays

If you have already taken a course in composition (or even if you haven't), you are probably familiar with the chief kinds of essays. Essays are usually classified—roughly, of course—along the following lines: meditation (or speculation or reflection), argument (or persuasion), exposition (or information), narration, and description.

Of these, the **meditative** (or **speculative** or **reflective**) **essay** is the closest to Montaigne. In a meditative essay, the writer is chiefly concerned with exploring an idea or a feeling. The organization usually seems casual, not a careful and evident structure but a free flow of thought—what the Japanese (who wrote with brush and ink) called "following the brush." The essayist is thinking, but he or she is not especially concerned with arguing a case, or even with being logical. We think along with the essayist, chiefly because we find the writer's tentative thoughts engaging. The writer may in the long run be pressing a point, advancing an argument, but the emphasis is on the free play of mind, not on an orderly and logical analysis.

In the **argumentative** (or **persuasive**) **essay,** the organization probably is apparent, and it is reasonable: The essay may announce a problem, define some terms, present and refute solutions that the writer considers to be inadequate, and then, by way of a knockdown ending, offer what the writer considers to be the correct solution.

The **expository essay,** in which the writer is concerned with giving information (for instance, on how to annotate a text, or how to read a poem, or how to use a computer), ordinarily has an equally clear organization. A clear organization is necessary in such an essay because the reader is reading not in order to come into contact with an interesting mind that may keep doubling back on its thinking (as in a meditative essay), and not in order to come to a decision about some controversial issue (as in an argumentative essay), but in order to gain information.

Narrative and **descriptive essays** are usually meditative essays. For instance, a narrative essay may recount some happening—often a bit of autobiography—partly to allow the writer and the reader to meditate on it. Similarly, a description, let's say of a spider spinning a web or of children playing in the street, usually turns out to be offered not so much as information—it thus is unlike the account of how to annotate a text—but rather as something for the writer and reader to enjoy in itself, and perhaps to think further about.

Most essays are not pure specimens. An informative essay, let's say on how to use a computer, may begin with a paragraph that seeks to persuade you to use this particular software. Or it might begin with a very brief narrative, an anecdote of a student who switched from program X to program Y, again in order to persuade the reader to use this software (Y, of course). Similarly, an argument—and probably most of the essays that you write in English courses will be arguments advancing a thesis concerning the meaning or structure of a literary work—may include some exposition—for instance, a very brief summary to remind the reader of the work you will be arguing about.

The Essayist's Persona

Many of the essays that give readers the most pleasure are, like entries in a journal, reflective. An essay of this kind sets forth the writer's attitudes or states of mind—the writer's **persona**—and the reader's interest in the essay is almost entirely in the way the writer sees things. It's not so much *what* the writers see and say as *how* they say what they see. Even in essays that are narrative—that is, in essays that recount events, such as a bit of biography—our interest is more in the essayists' *responses* to the events than in the events themselves. When we read an essay, we almost say, "So that's how it feels to be you," and "Tell me more about the way you see things." The bit of history is less important than the memorable presence of the writer.

Voice

When you read an essay in this chapter or in a later one, try to imagine the kind of person who wrote it, the kind of person who seems to be speaking it. Then slowly reread the essay, noticing *how* the writer conveyed this personality or persona or "**voice**" (even while he or she was writing about a topic "out there"). The writer's persona may be revealed by common or uncommon words, for example, by short or long sentences, by literal or figurative language, or by familiar or erudite examples.

Let's take a simple, familiar example of words that establish a persona. Lincoln begins the Gettysburg Address with "Four score and seven years ago . . ." He might have said "Eighty-seven years ago"—but the language would have lacked the biblical echo, and the persona would thus have been that of an ordinary person rather than that of a man who has about him something of the tone of an Old Testament prophet. This religious tone of "four score and seven years" is entirely fitting, since

- President Lincoln was speaking at the dedication of a cemetery for "these hallowed dead" and
- he was urging the members of his audience to give all of their energies to ensure that the dead men had not died in vain.

By such devices as the choice of words, the length of sentences, and the sorts of evidence offered, an author sounds to the reader solemn or agitated or witty or genial or severe. If you are familiar with Martin Luther King's "I Have a Dream," you may recall that he begins the piece (originally it was a speech, delivered at the Lincoln Memorial on the one-hundredth anniversary of Lincoln's Emancipation Proclamation) with these words: "Five score years ago . . . ." King is deliberately echoing Lincoln's words, partly in tribute to Lincoln, but also to help establish himself as the spiritual descendant of Lincoln and, further back, of the founders of the Judeo-Christian tradition.

Tone

Only by reading closely can we hear in the mind's ear the writer's **tone**—friendly, or bitter, or indignant, or ironic (characterized by wry understatement or overstatement). Perhaps you have heard the line from Owen Wister's novel *The Virginian* (1902): "When you call me that, smile!" Words spoken with a smile mean something different from the same words forced through clenched teeth. But while speakers can communicate—or, we might say, can guide the responses of their audience—by body language and by gestures, by facial expressions and by changes in tone of voice, writers have only words in ink on paper.

As a writer, you are learning control of tone as you learn to take pains in your choice of words, in the way you arrange sentences, and even in the punctuation marks you may find yourself changing in your final draft. These skills will pay off doubly if you apply them to your reading, by putting yourself in the place of the writer whose work you are reading.

As a reader, you must make some effort to "hear" the writer's tone as part of the meaning the words communicate. Skimming is not adequate to that task. Thinking carefully about the works in this book means, first of all, reading them carefully, listening for the sound of the speaking voice, so that you can respond to the persona—the personality or character the author presents in the essay.

Consider the following paragraph from the middle of "Black Men and Public Space," a short essay by Brent Staples. Staples is talking about growing up in a tough neighborhood. Of course the paragraph is only a small example; the tone depends, finally, on the entire essay, which will follow in a moment.

> As a boy, I saw countless tough guys locked away; I have since buried several, too. They were babies, really—a teenage cousin, a brother of twenty-two, a childhood friend in his mid-twenties—all gone down in episodes of bravado played out in the streets. I came to doubt the virtues of intimidation early on. I chose, perhaps unconsciously, to remain a shadow—timid, but a survivor.

Judging only from these few lines, what sense of Staples do we get? Perhaps you will agree that we can probably say something along these lines:

- He is relatively quiet and gentle. We sense this not simply because he tells us that he was "timid" but because (at least in this passage) he does not raise his voice either in a denunciation of white society for creating a system that produces black violence or in a denunciation of those blacks of his youth who engaged in violence.

- He is perceptive; he sees that the "tough guys," despite the fact that some were in their twenties, were babies; their bravado was infantile and destructive.
- He speaks with authority; he is giving a firsthand report.
- He doesn't claim to be especially shrewd; he modestly says that he may have "unconsciously" adopted the behavior that enabled him to survive.
- In saying that he is a "survivor" he displays a bit of wry humor. The usual image of a survivor is a guy in a Banana Republic outfit, gripping a knife, someone who survived a dog-eat-dog world by being tougher than the others. But Staples almost comically says he is a "survivor" who is "timid."

If your responses to the paragraph are somewhat different, jot them down and in a few sentences try to explain them.

Prewriting: Identifying the Topic and Thesis

Although we have emphasized the importance of the essayist's personality, essayists also make a point. They have a thesis or argument, and an argument implies taking a specific viewpoint toward a topic. In reading an essay, then, try to identify the topic. The topic of "Do-It-Yourself Brain Surgery" cannot really be brain surgery; it must be do-it-yourself books, and the attitude probably will be amused contempt for such books. Even an essay that is largely narrative, like Brent Staples's, recounting a personal experience or a bit of history, probably will include an attitude toward the event that is being narrated. It is that attitude—the interpretation of the event rather than the event itself—that may be the real topic of the essay.

It's time to look at Staples's essay. (Following the essay you will find a student's outline of it and another student's version of its thesis.)

BRENT STAPLES

Brent Staples, born in 1951 in Chester, Pennsylvania, received a bachelor's degree from Widener University in Chester, Pennsylvania, and a PhD from the University of Chicago. After working as a journalist in Chicago, he joined the New York Times *in 1985, and he is now on the newspaper's editorial board, where he writes on politics and culture. His essay was first published in* Ms. *magazine in 1986 and reprinted in a slightly revised form—the form we give here—in* Harper's *in 1987.*

Black Men and Public Space

My first victim was a woman—white, well dressed, probably in her late twenties. I came upon her late one evening on a deserted street in Hyde Park, a relatively affluent neighborhood in an otherwise mean, impoverished section of Chicago. As I swung onto the avenue behind her, there seemed to be a discreet, uninflammatory distance between us. Not so. She cast back a worried glance. To her, the youngish black man—a broad six feet two inches with a beard and billowing hair, both hands shoved into the pockets of a bulky military jacket—seemed menacingly close. After a few more quick glimpses, she picked up her pace and was soon running in earnest. Within seconds, she disappeared into a cross street.

That was more than a decade ago. I was twenty-two years old, a graduate student newly arrived at the University of Chicago. It was in the echo of that terrified woman's footfalls that I first began to know the unwieldy inheritance I'd come into—the ability to alter public space in ugly ways. It was clear that she thought herself the quarry of a mugger, a rapist, or worse. Suffering a bout of insomnia, however, I was stalking sleep, not defenseless wayfarers. As a softy who is scarcely able to take a knife to a raw chicken—let alone hold one to a person's throat—I was surprised, embarrassed, and dismayed all at once. Her flight made me feel like an accomplice in tyranny. It also made it clear that I was indistinguishable from the muggers who occasionally seeped into the area from the surrounding ghetto. That first encounter, and those that followed, signified that a vast, unnerving gulf lay between nighttime pedestrians—particularly women—and me. And I soon gathered that being perceived as dangerous is a hazard in itself. I only needed to turn a corner into a dicey situation, or crowd some frightened, armed person in a foyer somewhere, or make an errant move after being pulled over by a policeman. Where fear and weapons meet—and they often do in urban America—there is always the possibility of death.

In that first year, my first away from my hometown, I was to become thoroughly familiar with the language of fear. At dark, shadowy intersections, I could cross in front of a car stopped at a traffic light and elicit the *thunk*, thunk, thunk, thunk of the driver—black, white, male, or female—hammering down the door locks. On less traveled streets after dark, I grew accustomed to but never comfortable with people crossing to the other side of the street rather than pass me. Then there were the standard unpleasantries with policemen, doormen, bouncers, cabdrivers, and others whose business it is to screen out troublesome individuals *before* there is any nastiness.

I moved to New York nearly two years ago and I have remained an avid night walker. In central Manhattan, the near-constant crowd cover minimizes tense one-on-one street encounters. Elsewhere—in SoHo, for example, where sidewalks are narrow and tightly spaced buildings shut out the sky—things can get very taut indeed.

5 After dark, on the warrenlike streets of Brooklyn where I live, I often see women who fear the worst from me. They seem to have set their faces on neutral, and with their purse straps strung across their chests bandolier-style, they forge ahead as though bracing themselves against being tackled. I understand, of course, that the danger they perceive is not a hallucination. Women are particularly vulnerable to street violence, and young black males are drastically overrepresented among the perpetrators of that violence. Yet these truths are no solace against the kind of alienation that comes of being ever the suspect, a fearsome entity with whom pedestrians avoid making eye contact.

It is not altogether clear to me how I reached the ripe old age of twenty-two without being conscious of the lethality nighttime pedestrians attributed to me. Perhaps it was because in Chester, Pennsylvania, the small, angry industrial town where I came of age in the 1960s, I was scarcely noticeable against a backdrop of gang warfare, street knifings, and murders. I grew up one of the good boys, had perhaps a half-dozen fistfights. In retrospect, my shyness of combat has clear sources.

As a boy, I saw countless tough guys locked away; I have since buried several, too. They were babies, really—a teenage cousin, a brother of twenty-two, a childhood friend in his mid-twenties—all gone down in episodes of bravado played out in the streets. I came to doubt the virtues of intimidation early on. I chose, perhaps unconsciously, to remain a shadow—timid, but a survivor.

The fearsomeness mistakenly attributed to me in public places often has a perilous flavor. The most frightening of these confusions occurred in the late 1970s and early 1980s, when I worked as a journalist in Chicago. One day, rushing into the office of a magazine I was writing for with a deadline story in hand, I was mistaken for a burglar. The office manager called security and, with an ad hoc posse, pursued me through the labyrinthine halls, nearly to my editor's door. I had no way of proving who I was. I could only move briskly toward the company of someone who knew me.

Another time I was on assignment for a local paper and killing time before an interview. I entered a jewelry store on the city's affluent Near North Side. The proprietor excused herself and returned with an enormous red Doberman pinscher straining at the end of a leash. She stood, the dog extended toward me, silent to my questions, her eyes bulging nearly out of her head. I took a cursory look around, nodded, and bade her good night.

10 Relatively speaking, however, I never fared as badly as another black male journalist. He went to nearby Waukegan, Illinois, a couple of summers ago to work on a story about a murderer who was born there. Mistaking the reporter for the killer, police officers hauled him from his car at gunpoint and but for his press credentials would probably have tried to book him. Such episodes are not uncommon. Black men trade tales like this all the time.

Over the years, I learned to smother the rage I felt at so often being taken for a criminal. Not to do so would surely have led to madness. I now take precautions to make myself less threatening. I move about with care, particularly late in the evening. I give a wide berth to nervous people on subway platforms during the wee hours, particularly when I have exchanged business clothes for jeans. If I happen to be entering a building behind some people who appear skittish, I may walk by, letting them clear the lobby before I return, so as not to seem to be following them. I have been calm and extremely congenial on those rare occasions when I've been pulled over by the police.

And on late-evening constitutionals I employ what has proved to be an excellent tension-reducing measure: I whistle melodies from Beethoven and Vivaldi and the more popular classical composers. Even steely New Yorkers hunching toward nighttime destinations seem to relax, and occasionally they even join in the tune. Virtually everybody seems to sense that a mugger wouldn't be warbling bright, sunny selections from Vivaldi's *Four Seasons.* It is my equivalent of the cowbell that hikers wear when they know they are in bear country.

[1986]

Summary and Analysis

A summary is a condensation or abridgment; it briefly gives the reader the gist of a longer work. It boils down the longer work, resembling the longer work as a bouillon cube resembles a bowl of soup. A summary of Staples's "Black Men and Public Space" will reduce the essay, perhaps to a paragraph or two or even to a sentence. It will not call attention to Staples's various strategies, and it will not evaluate his views or his skill as a writer; it will merely present the gist of what he says.

If, then, you are asked to write an analysis of something you have read, you should not hand in a summary. On the other hand, a very brief summary may appropriately appear within an analytic essay. Usually, in fact, the reader needs some information, and the writer of the essay will briefly summarize this information. For example, a student who wrote about Staples's essay is *summarizing* when she writes

> Staples says that he is aware that his presence frightens many whites, especially women.

She is summarizing because she is reporting, without personal comment, what Staples said. On the other hand, she is *analyzing* when she writes

> By saying at the outset, "My first victim was a woman—white, well dressed, probably in her late twenties," Staples immediately catches the reader's attention and sets up expectations that will be undermined in the next paragraph.

In this sentence the writer is not reporting *what* Staples said but is explaining *how* he achieved an effect.

In Chapter 6 we discussed a few principles that govern summaries (see the list on pages 126–27). Here is a summary of our comments on "summary":

> A summary is a condensation or abridgment. Its chief characteristics are that (1) it is rarely more than one-fourth as long as the original; (2) its brevity is usually achieved by leaving out most of the concrete details of the original; (3) it is accurate; (4) it may rearrange the organization of the original, especially if a rearrangement will make things clearer; (5) it normally is in the present tense; and (6) quoted words need not be enclosed in quotation marks.

Preparing a Summary

If you are summarizing an essay, you may find that the essay includes its own summary, perhaps at the start or more likely near the end. If it does, you're in luck.

If it doesn't, we suggest that on rereading you jot down, after reading each paragraph, a sentence summarizing the gist of the paragraph. (A very long or poorly unified paragraph may require two sentences, but make every effort to boil the paragraph down to a dozen or so words.) Of course if a paragraph consists merely of a transitional sentence or two ("We will now turn to another example") you will lump it with the next paragraph. Similarly, if for some reason you encounter a series of very short paragraphs—for instance, three examples, each briefly stated, and all illustrating the same point—you probably will find that you can cover them with a single sentence. But if a paragraph runs to half a page or more of print, it's probably worth its own sentence of summary. In fact, your author may summarize the paragraph in the paragraph's opening sentence or in its final sentence.

Here is a student's paragraph-by-paragraph summary of Staples's "Black Men and Public Space." The numbers refer to Staples's paragraphs.

1. "First victim" was a white woman in Chicago, who hurried away.
2. Age 22, he realized—to his surprise and embarrassment—that he (a "youngish black man") could be perceived by strangers as a mugger. And, since his presence created fear, he was in a dangerous situation.

3,4,5. At intersections he heard drivers of cars lock their doors, and elsewhere he sensed hostility of bouncers and others. In NY, lots of tension on narrow sidewalks. Women are esp. afraid of him; he knows why, but that's "no solace."

6. He's not sure why it took him 22 years to see that others fear him, but prob. because in his hometown of Chester, Pa., there was lots of adolescent violence, though he stayed clear of it.

7. As a boy, he saw young toughs killed, and he kept clear, "timid, but a survivor."

8,9,10. Though he is gentle, he looks fearsome. Once, working as a journalist, he was mistaken for a burglar. Another time, in a jewelry store, the clerk brought out a guard dog. Another black journalist was covering a crime, but the police thought the journalist was the killer. Many blacks have had such experiences.

11. He has learned to smother his rage—and he keeps away from nervous people.

12. Walking late at night, he whistles familiar classical music, trying to reassure others that he is not a mugger.

When you have written your sentence summarizing the last paragraph, you may have done enough if the summary was intended simply for your own private use—for example, to help you review material for an examination. But if you are going to use it as the basis of a summary within an essay you are writing, you probably won't want to include a summary longer than three or four sentences, so your job will be to reduce and combine the sentences you have jotted down. Indeed, you may even want to reduce the summary to a single sentence.

Joining the Conversation: Critical Thinking and Writing

1. Assuming that you find the sentences summarizing "Black Men and Public Space" acceptable, reduce them to a summary no longer than four readable sentences. Then compare your version with the versions of two other students and, working as a group, produce a summary.

Stating the Thesis of an Essay

Summarizing each stage of the essay (we discuss summarizing on page 347) forces a reader to be attentive and can assist the reader to formulate a **thesis sentence,** a sentence that (in the reader's opinion) sets forth the writer's central point. If an essay is essentially an argument—for example, a defense of (or an argument against) capital punishment—it will probably include one or more sentences that directly assert the thesis. "Black Men and Public Space," chiefly a narrative essay, is much less evidently an argument, but it does have a point, and some of its sentences come pretty close to summarizing the point. Here are three of those sentences:

> And I soon gathered that being perceived as dangerous is a hazard in itself. (2)
> The fearsomeness mistakenly attributed to me in public places often has a perilous flavor. (8)
> I now take precautions to make myself less threatening. (11)

We asked our students to formulate their own thesis sentence for Staples's essay. One student came up with the following sentence after first drafting a couple of tentative versions and then rereading the essay in order to modify them:

> In "Black Men and Public Space" Staples recognizes that because many whites fear a young black man and therefore may do violence to him, he may do well to try to cool the situation by making himself unthreatening.

Notice, again, that a thesis sentence states the *point* of the work. Don't confuse a thesis sentence with a summary of a narrative, such as "Staples at the age of twenty-two came to realize that his presence was threatening to whites, and he has since taken measures to make himself less threatening." This sentence, though true, doesn't clearly get at the point of the essay, the generalization that can be drawn from Staples's example.

Look again at the student's formulation of a thesis sentence (*not* the narrative summary sentence that we have just given). If you don't think that it fairly represents Staples's point, you may (if you are writing an essay about Staples's essay) want to come up with a sentence that seems more precise to you.

Whether you use the sentence we have quoted or a sentence that you formulate for yourself, you can in any case of course disagree very strongly with what you take to be Staples's point. Your version of Staples's thesis should accurately reflect your understanding of Staples's point, but you need not agree with the point. You may think that Staples is hypersensitive or (to mention only one other possibility) that he is playing the Uncle Tom.

A thesis sentence—whether the words are your own or the author's—is thus a very brief summary of the argument (not of the narrative) of the work. If you are writing an essay about an essay, you'll probably want to offer a sentence that reminds your reader of the point of the work you are discussing or gives the reader the basis of an unfamiliar work:

> Black males, however harmless, are in a perilous situation because whites, especially white women, perceive them as threatening.

Or:

> In "Black Men and Public Space" Brent Staples recognizes that because many whites fear young black men and may therefore do violence to them, black men may do well to try to cool the situation by making themselves nonthreatening.

Drafting a Summary

Sometimes, however, a fuller statement may be useful. For instance, if you are writing about a complex essay that makes six points, you may help your reader if you briefly restate all six. The length of your summary will depend on your purpose and the needs of your audience.

The following principles may help you to write your summary:

1. After having written sentences that summarize each paragraph or group of paragraphs, formulate the essay's thesis sentence. Formulating the sentence in writing will help you to stay with what you take to be the writer's main point.

2. Write a first draft by turning your summaries of the paragraphs into fewer and better sentences. The student who wrote the paragraph-by-paragraph summary (pages 345–46) of Staples's essay turned her first five sentences (on Staples's first paragraphs) into this:

   Staples's "first victim" was a white woman in Chicago. When she hurried away from him, he realized—to his surprise and embarrassment—that because he was large and black and young he seemed to her to be a mugger. And since his presence created fear, *he* was in a dangerous situation. Other experiences, such as hearing drivers lock their cars when they were waiting at an intersection, have made him aware of the hostility of others. Women are especially afraid of him, and although he knows why, this knowledge is "no solace."

   The student turned the remaining sentences of the outline into the following summary:

   Oddly, it took him twenty-two years to see that others fear him. Perhaps it took this long because he grew up in a violent neighborhood, though he kept clear, "timid, but a survivor." Because he is black and large, whites regard him as fearsome and treat him accordingly (once a clerk in a jewelry store brought out a guard dog), but other blacks have been treated worse. He has learned to smother his rage, and in order to cool things he tries to reassure nervous people by keeping away from them and (when he is walking late at night) by whistling classical music.

3. Write a lead-in sentence, probably incorporating the thesis sentence. Here is an example:

   Brent Staples, in "Black Men and Public Space," tells how his awareness that many white people regarded him as dangerous caused him to realize that *he* was in danger. His implicitly recommended solution is to try to cool the anxiety by adopting nonthreatening behavior.

   After writing a lead-in, revise the draft of your summary, eliminating needless repetition, providing transitions, and adding whatever you think may be needed to clarify the work for someone who is unfamiliar with it. You may rearrange the points if you think the rearrangement will clarify matters.

4. Edit your draft for errors in grammar, punctuation, and spelling. Read it aloud to test it once more for readability. Sometimes only by reading aloud do writers detect needless repetition or confusing phrases.

Joining the Conversation: Critical Thinking and Writing

1. In a paragraph or two, set forth what you take to be Staples's *purpose.* Do you think he was writing chiefly to clarify some ideas for himself—for instance, to

explore how he came to discover the "alienation that comes of being ever the suspect"? Or writing to assist blacks? Or to assist whites? Or what? (You may of course conclude that none of these suggestions, or all, are relevant.)

2. If you think the essay is effective, in a paragraph or two addressed to your classmates try to account for its effectiveness. Do certain examples strike you as particularly forceful? If so, why? Do certain sentences seem especially memorable? Again, why? For example, if the opening and concluding paragraphs strike you as effective, explain why. On the other hand, if you are unimpressed by part or all of the essay, explain why.
3. The success of a narrative as a piece of writing often depends on the reader's willingness to identify with the narrator. From an examination of "Black Men and Public Space," what explanations can you give for your willingness (or unwillingness) to identify yourself with Staples? (Probably you will want to say something about his persona as you sense it from the essay.) In the course of a 500-word essay explaining your position, very briefly summarize Staples's essay and state his thesis.
4. Have *you* ever unintentionally altered public space? You might recall an experience in which, as a child, your mere presence caused adults to alter their behavior—for instance, to stop quarreling.

   After a session of brainstorming, in which you produce some possible topics, you'll want to try to settle on one. After you have chosen a topic and produced a first draft, if you are not satisfied with your first paragraph—if you feel that it is not likely to get and hold the reader's attention—you may want to imitate the strategy that Staples adopted for his first paragraph.
5. If you have ever been in the position of one of Staples's "victims," that is, if you have ever shown fear or suspicion of someone who, it turned out, meant you no harm (or if you can imagine being in that position), write an essay from the "victim's" point of view. Explain what happened, what you did and thought. Did you think at the time about the feelings of the person you avoided or fled from? Has reading Staples's essay prompted further reflections on your experience? (Suggested length: 750 words.)

CHECKLIST: *Getting Ideas for Writing about Essays*

Persona and Tone

- What sort of *persona* does the writer create? Authoritative? Tentative? Wise-guy? Or what?
- How does the writer create this persona? (Does the writer use colloquial language or formal language or technical language? Short sentences or long ones? Personal anecdotes? Quotations from authorities?)
- What is the *tone* of the essay? Is it, for example, solemn, or playful? Is the tone consistent? If not, how do the shifts affect your understanding of the writer's point or your identification of the writer's persona? Who is the *audience*?

(*continued*)

Getting Ideas for Writing about Essays (continued)

Kind of Essay

- What kind of essay is it? Is it chiefly a presentation of facts (an exposition, a report, a history)? A meditation? Or is it chiefly an argument? If it is an argument, what persuasive devices does the writer use? Logic? Appeals to the emotion? (Probably the essay draws on several kinds of writing, but which kind is it primarily? How are the other kinds related to the main kind?) What is the overall *purpose* of the essay?
- What does it seem to add up to? If the essay is chiefly meditative or speculative, how much emphasis is placed on the persona? That is, if the essay is a sort of thinking-out-loud, is your interest chiefly in the announced or ostensible topic, or in the writer's mood and personality? If the essay is chiefly a presentation of facts, does it also have a larger implication? If it narrates a happening (history), does the reader draw an inference—find a meaning—in the happening? If the essay is chiefly an argument, what is the thesis? How is the thesis supported? (Is it supported, for example, by induction, deduction, analogy, or emotional appeal?) Do you accept the assumptions (explicit and implicit)?

Structure

- Is the title appropriate? Propose a better title, if possible.
- Did the opening paragraph interest you? Why, or why not? Did the essay continue more or less as expected, or did it turn out to be rather different from what you anticipated?
- Prepare an outline of the essay. What effect does the writer seem to be aiming at by using this structure?

Value

- What is especially good (or bad) about the essay? Is it logically persuasive? Or entertaining? Or does it introduce an engaging persona? Or (if it is a narrative) does it tell a story effectively, using (where appropriate) description, dialogue, and commentary, and somehow make you feel that this story is worth reporting?
- Does the writer seem to hold values that you share? Or cannot share? Explain.
- Do you think that most readers will share your response, or do you think that for some reason—for example, your age, or your cultural background—your responses are unusual? Explain.

Your Turn: Essays for Analysis

LANGSTON HUGHES

Langston Hughes (1902–1967) was born in Joplin, Missouri. He lived part of his youth in Mexico, spent a year at Columbia University, served as a merchant seaman, and worked in a Paris nightclub, where he showed some of his poems to Alain Locke, a strong advocate of African American literature. After returning to the United States, Hughes went on to publish poetry, fiction, plays, essays, and biographies.

Salvation

I was saved from sin when I was going on thirteen. But not really saved. It happened like this. There was a big revival at my Auntie Reed's church. Every night for weeks there had been much preaching, singing, praying, and shouting, and some very hardened sinners had been brought to Christ, and the membership of the church had grown by leaps and bounds. Then just before the revival ended, they held a special meeting for children, "to bring the young lambs to the fold." My aunt spoke of it for days ahead. That night I was escorted to the front row and placed on the mourners' bench with all the other young sinners, who had not yet been brought to Jesus.

My aunt told me that when you were saved you saw a light, and something happened to you inside! And Jesus came into your life! And God was with you from then on! She said you could see and hear and feel Jesus in your soul. I believed her. I had heard a great many old people say the same thing and it seemed to me they ought to know. So I sat there calmly in the hot, crowded church, waiting for Jesus to come to me.

The preacher preached a wonderful rhythmical sermon, all moans and shouts and lonely cries and dire pictures of hell, and then he sang a song about the ninety and nine safe in the fold, but one little lamb was left out in the cold. Then he said: "Won't you come? Won't you come to Jesus? Young lambs, won't you come?" And he held out his arms to all us young sinners there on the mourners' bench. And the little girls cried. And some of them jumped up and went to Jesus right away. But most of us just sat there.

A great many old people came and knelt around us and prayed, old women with jet-black faces and braided hair, old men with work-gnarled hands. And the church sang a song about the lower lights are burning, some poor sinners to be saved. And the whole building rocked with prayer and song.

5 Still I kept waiting to *see* Jesus.

Finally all the young people had gone to the altar and were saved, but one boy and me. He was a rounder's son named Westley. Westley and I were surrounded by sisters and deacons praying. It was very hot in the church, and getting late now. Finally Westley said to me in a whisper: "God damn! I'm tired o' sitting here. Let's get up and be saved." So he got up and was saved.

Then I was left all alone on the mourners' bench. My aunt came and knelt at my knees and cried, while prayers and songs swirled all around me in the little church. The whole congregation prayed for me alone, in a mighty wail of moans and voices. And I kept waiting serenely for Jesus, waiting, waiting—but he didn't come. I wanted to see him, but nothing happened to me. Nothing! I wanted something to happen to me, but nothing happened.

I heard the songs and the minister saying: "Why don't you come? My dear child, why don't you come to Jesus? Jesus is waiting for you. He wants you. Why don't you come? Sister Reed, what is this child's name?"

"Langston," my aunt sobbed.

10 "Langston, why don't you come? Why don't you come and be saved? Oh, Lamb of God! Why don't you come?"

Now it was really getting late. I began to be ashamed of myself, holding everything up so long. I began to wonder what God thought about Westley, who certainly hadn't seen Jesus either, but who was now sitting proudly on the platform, swinging his knickerbockered legs and grinning down at me, surrounded by deacons and old women on their knees praying. God had not struck Westley dead for taking his name in vain or for lying in the temple. So I decided that maybe to save further trouble, I'd better lie, too, and say that Jesus had come, and get up and be saved.

So I got up.

Suddenly the whole room broke into a sea of shouting, as they saw me rise. Waves of rejoicing swept the place. Women leaped in the air. My aunt threw her arms around me. The minister took me by the hand and led me to the platform.

When things quieted down, in a hushed silence, punctuated by a few ecstatic "Amens," all the new young lambs were blessed in the name of God. Then joyous singing filled the room.

15 That night, for the last time in my life but one—for I was a big boy twelve years old—I cried. I cried, in bed alone, and couldn't stop. I buried my head under the quilts, but my aunt heard me. She woke up and told my uncle I was crying because the Holy Ghost had come into my life, and because I had seen Jesus. But I was really crying because I couldn't bear to tell her that I had lied, that I had deceived everybody in the church, and I hadn't seen Jesus, and that now I didn't believe there was a Jesus any more, since he didn't come to help me.

[1940]

Joining the Conversation: Critical Thinking and Writing

1. Do you find the piece amusing, or serious, or both? Explain.
2. How would you characterize the style or voice of the first three sentences? Childlike, or sophisticated, or what? How would you characterize the final sentence? How can you explain the change in style or tone?
3. Why does Hughes bother to tell us, in paragraph 11, that Westley was "swinging his knickerbockered legs and grinning"? Do you think that Westley too may have cried that night? Give your reasons.
4. Is the episode told from the point of view of someone "going on thirteen," or from the point of view of a mature man? Cite evidence to support your position.
5. One of the golden rules of narrative writing is "Show, don't tell." In about 500 words, report an experience—for instance, a death in the family, or a severe (perhaps unjust) punishment, or the first day in a new school—that produced strong

feelings. Like Hughes, you may want to draw on an experience in which you were subjected to group pressure. Do not explicitly state what the feelings were; rather, let the reader understand the feelings chiefly through concretely detailed actions. But, like Hughes, you might state your thesis or basic position in your first paragraph and then indicate when and where the experience took place.

LAURA VANDERKAM

Laura Vanderkam wrote this essay a few months after graduating from Princeton University. At the time that it was published she was working as a Collegiate Network intern with the editorial board of USA Today. *She is a member of* USA Today's *Board of Contributors, and her work has appeared in* Scientific American, Wired, *and other publications.*

Hookups Starve the Soul

The scene: my college dorm's basement bathroom on a Sunday morning early in my freshman year. As hungover girls crowded around the sinks, I caught a friend's eye in the mirror. What happened when she left last night's party with a boy neither of us had ever seen before?

"Oh," she said with a knowing look, "we hooked up."

No, not planes refueling in midair. Hookups are when a guy and girl get together for a physical encounter and don't expect anything else. They've all but replaced dating at most colleges, according to a study being released today by the Institute on American Values, a non-partisan family issues think tank. Only half of the women interviewed had been on six or more dates during college; a third had been on no more than two.

As a new college graduate, I can attest to this. I've had as many dates in my first 2 months in the real world as I had during my whole college career.

5 Lest you think college students are all libertines, hooking up doesn't mean having sex, although it can. The term includes all of the bases, and the ambiguity is intentional. Modest types can imply that less happened than did, and braggarts can hint at hitting a home run. Hookups are defined by alcohol, physical attraction and a lack of expectations in the morning.

While the study found that only 40% of the women interviewed admitted to hooking up, the practice pervades college culture. Dates and, for the most part, love affairs, are passé. Why bother asking someone to dinner when you can meet at a party, down a few drinks and go home together?

I hear the traditionalists clucking. Sex without commitment. Sounds like a male plot, right? But women are going along.

Some blame the sexual revolution. Some blame co-ed dorms and alcohol abuse. I blame something else. Hookups are part of a larger cultural picture. Today's college kids are the first generation to have had their entire childhoods scheduled. To them, dating is simply not a productive use of time.

Author David Brooks used the phrase "Organization Kid" in April's *Atlantic Monthly* to describe what he discovered at my alma mater, Princeton. After a lifetime of shuffling from soccer practice to scout meetings and piano lessons, today's college kids no longer want to spend hours debating the nature of good and evil, he noted. Once obsessed with getting into increasingly selective colleges—and now obsessed with getting great grades and even greater jobs—they no longer have hours to spend wooing a lover.

10 "I was amazed to learn how little dating goes on," Brooks wrote in the magazine. "Students go out in groups, and there is certainly a fair bit of partying on campus, but as one told me, 'People don't have time or energy to put into real relationships.'"

But 20-year-olds still have hormones, so they hook up instead. They stumble home together late Saturday night, roll around in bed, then pass out. The next morning, it's as if nothing happened.

Hookups do satisfy biology, but the emotional detachment doesn't satisfy the soul. And that's the real problem—not the promiscuity, but the lack of meaning.

People who don't bother with love affairs cut themselves off from life's headier emotions. What about Scarlett O'Hara's passion, or Juliet's? What about the mad jealousy of Dostoevsky's Dmitry Karamazov or even the illicit pleasures of Lady Chatterley and her lover? No great art will be inspired by the muse of Milwaukee's Best or a tryst that both parties are trying to forget.

In the same way, the Organization Kid's lack of soul-searching doesn't bode well for future poets and philosophers. Dostoevsky's Ivan wouldn't have had time to dream up the Grand Inquisitor if he spent his youth being carted from one sport to another and his early 20s obsessed with the perfect lab report.

15 Parents want the best for their kids—but some also want the perfect kid. Somewhere along the way to achieving these perfect children through structured activities, overachieving parents stunt the growth of their children's souls. Too much supervision creates kids who'd rather hook up than fall in love, who'd rather get the right answers on tests than ask the larger questions.

It's too late to bring back the dormitory mothers, curfews and traditional morals that forced courtships in the past. But the Organization Kid culture can be changed. If parents stop rigidly scheduling their children's lives, and if they no longer teach that life is only a series of concrete goals to be met and then exceeded, then there will be more real lovers and truth-seekers in the future—and fewer hookups.

[2001]

Joining the Conversation: Critical Thinking and Writing

1. Vanderkam's opening words—"The scene"—is unusual, since it sounds like the opening of a play. What other rhetorical devices does Vanderkam use in order to make her essay interesting?
2. In a sentence or two, state Vanderkam's thesis. (Please do not confuse a statement of the thesis—the point, the argument—with a summary of the essay.) Do you agree with her thesis? In whole, in part, or not at all? Whether you agree or disagree, write your own 500-word essay on hookups, or, alternatively, on a related topic, such as college dating.

Chapter 13

Reading and Writing about Stories

Stories True and False

The word *story* comes from *history;* the stories that historians, biographers, and journalists narrate are supposed to be true accounts of what happened. The stories of novelists and short-story writers, however, are admittedly untrue; they are "fiction," things made up, imagined, manufactured. As readers, we come to a supposedly true story with expectations different from those we bring to fiction.

Consider the difference between reading a narrative in a newspaper and one in a book of short stories. If, while reading a newspaper, we come across a story of, say, a subway accident, we assume that the account is true, and we read it for the information about a relatively unusual event. Anyone hurt? What sort of people? In our neighborhood? Whose fault? When we read a book of fiction, however, we do not expect to encounter literal truths; we read novels and short stories not for facts but for pleasure and for some insight or for a sense of what an aspect of life means to the writer. Consider the following short story by Grace Paley.

Grace Paley

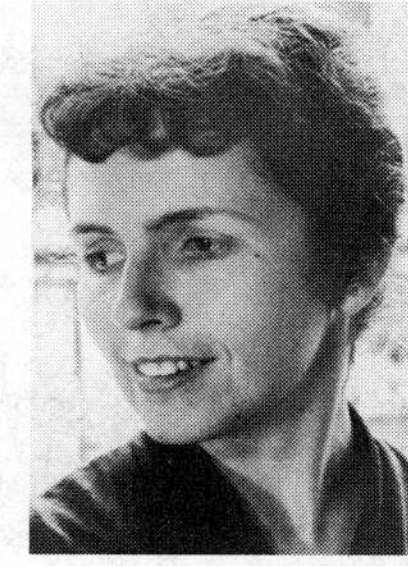

Born in New York City, Grace Paley (1922–2007) attended Hunter College and New York University but left without a degree. While raising two children she wrote poetry and then, in the 1950s, turned to writing fiction. Her publications include Collected Stories *(1994).*

Paley's chief subject was the life of little people struggling in the Big City. Of life she said, "How daily life is lived is a mystery to me. You write about what's mysterious to you. What is it like? Why do people do this?" Of the short story she said, "It can be just telling a little tale, or writing a complicated philosophical story. It can be a song, almost."

Samuel

Some boys are very tough. They're afraid of nothing. They are the ones who climb a wall and take a bow at the top. Not only are they brave on the roof, but they make a lot of noise in the darkest part of the cellar where even the super hates to go. They also jiggle and hop on the platform between the locked doors of the subway cars.

Four boys are jiggling on the swaying platform. Their names are Alfred, Calvin, Samuel, and Tom. The men and the women in the cars on either side watch them. They don't like them to jiggle or jump but don't want to interfere.

Of course some of the men in the cars were once brave boys like these. One of them had ridden the tail of a speeding truck from New York to Rockaway Beach without getting off, without his sore fingers losing hold. Nothing happened to him then or later. He had made a compact with other boys who preferred to watch: Starting at Eighth Avenue and Fifteenth Street, he would get to some specified place, maybe Twenty-third and the river, by hopping the tops of the moving trucks. This was hard to do when one truck turned a corner in the wrong direction and the nearest truck was a couple of feet too high. He made three or four starts before succeeding. He had gotten his idea from a film at school called *The Romance of Logging.* He had finished high school, married a good friend, was in a responsible job and going to night school.

These two men and others looked at the four boys jumping and jiggling on the platform and thought, It must be fun to ride that way, especially now the weather is nice and we're out of the tunnel and way high over the Bronx. Then they thought, These kids do seem to be acting sort of stupid. They *are* little. Then they thought of some of the brave things they had done when they were boys and jiggling didn't seem so risky.

The ladies in the car became very angry when they looked at the four boys. Most of them brought their brows together and hoped the boys could see their extreme disapproval. One of the ladies wanted to get up and say, Be careful you dumb kids, get off that platform or I'll call a cop. But three of the boys were Negroes and the fourth was something else she couldn't tell for sure. She was afraid they'd be fresh and laugh at her and embarrass her. She wasn't afraid they'd hit her, but she was afraid of embarrassment. Another lady thought, Their mothers never know where they are. It wasn't true in this particular case. Their mothers all knew that they had gone to see the missile exhibit on Fourteenth Street.

5 Out on the platform, whenever the train accelerated, the boys would raise their hands and point them up to the sky to act like rockets going off, then they rat-tat-tatted the shatterproof glass pane like machine guns, although no machine guns had been exhibited.

For some reason known only to the motorman, the train began a sudden slowdown. The lady who was afraid of embarrassment saw the boys jerk forward and backward and grab the swinging guard chains. She had her own boy at home. She stood up with determination and went to the door. She slid it open and said, "You boys will be hurt. You'll be killed. I'm going to call the conductor if you don't just go into the next car and sit down and be quiet."

Two of the boys said, "Yes'm," and acted as though they were about to go. Two of them blinked their eyes a couple of times and pressed their lips together. The train resumed its speed. The door slid shut, parting the lady and the boys. She leaned against the side door because she had to get off at the next stop.

The boys opened their eyes wide at each other and laughed. The lady blushed. The boys looked at her and laughed harder. They began to pound each other's back. Samuel laughed the hardest and pounded Alfred's back until Alfred coughed and the tears came. Alfred held tight to the chain hook. Samuel pounded him even harder when he saw the tears. He said, "Why you bawling? You a baby, huh?" and laughed. One of the men whose boyhood had been more watchful than brave became angry. He stood up straight and looked at the boys for a couple of seconds. Then he walked in a citizenly way to the end of the car, where he pulled the emergency cord. Almost at once, with a terrible hiss, the pressure of air abandoned the brakes and the wheels were caught and held.

People standing in the most secure places fell forward, then backward. Samuel had let go of his hold on the chain so he could pound Tom as well as Alfred. All the passengers in the cars whipped back and forth, but he pitched only forward and fell head first to be crushed and killed between the cars.

10 The train had stopped hard, halfway into the station, and the conductor called at once for the trainmen who knew about this kind of death and how to take the body from the wheels and brakes. There was silence except for passengers from other cars who asked, What happened! What happened! The ladies waited around wondering if he might be an only child. The men recalled other afternoons with very bad endings. The little boys stayed close to each other, leaning and touching shoulders and arms and legs.

When the policeman knocked at the door and told her about it, Samuel's mother began to scream. She screamed all day and moaned all night, though the doctors tried to quiet her with pills.

Oh, oh, she hopelessly cried. She did not know how she could ever find another boy like that one. However, she was a young woman and she became pregnant. Then for a few months she was hopeful. The child born to her was a boy. They brought him to be seen and nursed. She smiled. But immediately she saw that this baby wasn't Samuel. She and her husband together have had other children, but never again will a boy exactly like Samuel be known.

[1968]

Joining the Conversation: Critical Thinking and Writing

1. Paley wrote the story, but an unspecified person *tells* it. Describe the voice of this narrator in the first paragraph. Is the voice neutral and objective, or do you hear some sort of attitude, a point of view? If you do hear an attitude, what words or phrases in the story indicate it?
2. What do you know about the setting—the locale—of "Samuel"? What can you infer about the neighborhood?
3. In the fourth paragraph we are told that "three of the boys were Negroes and the fourth was something else." Is race important in this story? Is Samuel "Negro" or "something else"? Does it matter? Respond to these questions in a short argumentative essay.
4. Exactly *why* did a man walk "in a citizenly way to the end of the car, where he pulled the emergency cord"? Do you think the author blames him? What evidence can you offer to support your view? Do *you* blame him? Or do you blame the boys? Or anyone? Explain.
5. The story is called "Samuel," and it is, surely, about him. But what happens after Samuel dies? (You might want to list the events.) What else is the story about? (You might want to comment on why you believe the items in your list are important.)
6. Can you generalize about what the men think of the jigglers and about what the women think? Is Paley saying something about the sexes? About the attitudes of onlookers in a big city?

Elements of Fiction

You might think about the ways in which "Samuel" differs from a newspaper story of an accident in a subway. (You might even want to write a newspaper version of the happening.) In some ways, Paley's story somewhat resembles an account that might appear in a newspaper. Journalists are taught to give information about

- who,
- what,
- when,
- where, and
- why,

and Paley does provide this material. Thus, the **characters** (Samuel and others) are the journalist's Who; the **plot** (the boys were jiggling on the platform, and when a man pulled the emergency cord one of them was killed) is the What; the **setting** (the subway, presumably in modern times) is the When and the Where; the **motivation** (the irritation of the man who pulls the emergency cord) is the Why.

To write about fiction you would think about these elements of fiction, asking yourself questions about each, both separately and how they work together. Much of the rest of this chapter will be devoted to examining such words as *character* and *plot,* but before you read those pages notice the questions we've posed about "Samuel" and try responding to them. Your responses will teach you a good deal about what fiction is, and some of the ways in which it works.

Plot and Character

In some stories, such as adventure stories, the emphasis is on physical action—wanderings and strange encounters. In Paley's "Samuel," however, although there is a violent death in the subway, the emphasis is less on an unusual happening than on other things: for instance, the contrast between some of the adults, the contrast between uptight adults and energetic children, and the impact of the death on Samuel's mother.

The novelist E. M. Forster, in a short critical study entitled *Aspects of the Novel* (1927), introduced a distinction between **flat characters** and **round characters.** A *flat character* is relatively simple and usually has only one trait: loving wife (or jealous wife), tyrannical husband (or meek husband), braggart, pedant, hypocrite, or whatever. Thus, in "Samuel" we are told about a man "whose boyhood had been more watchful than brave." This man walks "in a citizenly way" to the end of the subway car, where he pulls the emergency cord. He is, so to speak, the conventional solid citizen. He is flat, or uncomplicated, but that is probably part of what the author is getting at. A *round character,* on the other hand, embodies several or even many traits that cohere to form a complex personality. In a story as short as "Samuel" we can hardly expect to find fully rounded characters, but we can say that, at least by comparison with the "citizenly" man, the man who had once been a wild kid, had gone to night school, and now holds a "responsible job" is relatively round. Paley's story asserts rather than shows the development of the character, but much fiction does show such a development.

Whereas a flat character is usually *static* (at the end of the story the character is pretty much what he or she was at the start), a round character is likely to be *dynamic,* changing considerably as the story progresses.

A frequent assignment in writing courses is to set forth a character sketch, describing some person in the story or novel. In preparing such a sketch, take these points into consideration:

- what the character says (but consider that what he or she says need not be taken at face value; the character may be hypocritical, or self-deceived, or biased—you will have to detect this from the context),
- what the character does,
- what other characters say about the character, and
- what others *do.* (A character who serves as a contrast to another character is called a **foil.**)

A character sketch can be complex and demanding, but usually you will want to do more than write a character sketch. You will probably discuss the character's function, or trace the development of his or her personality, or contrast the character with another. (One of the most difficult topics, the narrator's personality, is discussed later in this chapter under the heading "Narrative Point of View.") In writing on one of these topics you will probably still want to keep in mind the four suggestions for getting at a character, but you will also want to go further, relating your findings to additional matters that we discuss later.

Most discussions of fiction are concerned with happenings and with *why* they happen. Why does Samuel die? Because (to put it too simply) his youthful high spirits clash with the values of a "citizenly" adult. Paley never explicitly says anything like this, but a reader of the story tries to make sense out of the details, filling in the gaps.

Things happen, in most good fiction, partly because the people have certain personalities or character traits (moral, intellectual, and emotional qualities) and, given their natures, because they respond plausibly to other personalities. What their names are and what they look like may help you to understand them, but probably the best guide to characters is what they do and what they say. As we get to know more about their drives and goals—and especially about the choices they make—we enjoy seeing the writer complete the portraits, finally presenting us with a coherent and credible picture of people in action.

In this view, plot and character are inseparable. Plot is not simply a series of happenings, but happenings that come out of character, that reveal character, and that influence character. The novelist Henry James put it thus in his essay, "The Art of Fiction" (1884): "What is character but the determination of incident? What is incident but the illustration of character?" James goes on: "It is an incident for a woman to stand up with her hand resting on a table and look out at you in a certain way."

Foreshadowing

Although some stories depend heavily on a plot with a surprise ending, other stories prepare the reader for the outcome, to some degree. The **foreshadowing** that would eliminate surprise, or greatly reduce it, and destroy a story that has nothing else to offer, is a powerful tool in the hands of a writer of serious fiction. In "Samuel," the reader perhaps senses even in the first paragraph that these "tough" boys who "jiggle and hop on the platform" may be vulnerable, may come to an unfortunate end. When a woman says, "You'll be killed," the reader doesn't yet know if she is right, but a seed has been planted.

Even in such a story as Faulkner's "A Rose for Emily" (page 237), where we are surprised to learn near the end that Miss Emily has slept beside the decaying corpse of her dead lover, from the outset we expect something strange; that is, we are not surprised by the surprise, only by its precise nature. The first sentence of the story tells us that after Miss Emily's funeral (the narrator begins at the end) the townspeople cross her threshold "out of curiosity to see the inside of her house, which no one save an old manservant . . . had seen in at least ten years." As the story progresses, we see Miss Emily prohibiting people from entering the house, we hear that after a certain point no one ever sees Homer Barron again, that "the front door remained closed," and (a few paragraphs before the end of the story) that the townspeople "knew that there was one room in that region above the stairs which no one had seen in forty years." The paragraph preceding the revelation that "the man himself lay in the bed" is devoted to a description of Homer's dust-covered clothing and toilet articles. In short, however much we are unprepared for the precise revelation, we are prepared for some strange thing in the house; and, given Miss Emily's purchase of poison and Homer's disappearance, we have some idea of what will be revealed.

The full meaning of a passage will not become apparent until you have read the entire story. In a sense, a story has at least three lives:

- when we read the story sentence by sentence, trying to turn the sequence of sentences into a consistent whole,
- when we have finished reading the story and we think back on it as a whole, even if we think no more than "That was a waste of time,"
- when we reread a story, knowing already even as we read the first line how it will turn out at the end.

Setting and Atmosphere

Foreshadowing normally makes use of **setting.** The setting or environment is not mere geography, not mere locale: It provides an **atmosphere,** an air that the characters breathe, a world in which they move. Narrowly speaking, the setting is the physical surroundings—the furniture, the architecture, the landscape, the climate—and these often are highly appropriate to the characters who are associated with them. Thus, in Emily Brontë's *Wuthering Heights* (1847) the passionate Earnshaw family is associated with Wuthering Heights, the storm-exposed moorland, whereas the mild Linton family is associated with Thrushcross Grange in the sheltered valley below.

Broadly speaking, setting includes not only the physical surroundings but also a point (or several points) in time. The background against which we see the characters and the happenings may be specified as morning or evening, spring or fall. In a good story, this temporal setting will probably be highly relevant; it will probably be part of the story's meaning, perhaps providing an ironic contrast to or exerting an influence on the characters.

Symbolism

When we read, we may feel that certain characters and certain things in the story stand for more than themselves, or hint at larger meanings. We feel, that is, that they are **symbolic.** But here we must be careful. How does a reader know that this or that figure or place is symbolic? In Hemingway's "Cat in the Rain" (page 684), is the cat symbolic? Is the innkeeper? Is the rain? Reasonable people may differ in their answers. Again, in Chopin's "The Story of an Hour" (page 45), is the railroad accident a symbol? Is Josephine a symbol? Is the season (springtime) a symbol? And again, reasonable people may differ in their responses.

Let's assume for the moment, however, that if writers use symbols, they want readers to perceive—at least faintly—that certain characters or places or seasons or happenings have rich implications, stand for something more than what they are on the surface. How do writers help us to perceive these things? By emphasizing them—for instance, by describing them at some length, or by introducing them at times when they might not seem strictly necessary, or by calling attention to them repeatedly.

Consider Chopin's treatment of the season in which "The Story of an Hour" takes place. The story has to take place at *some* time, but Chopin does not simply say, "On a spring day," or an autumn day, and let things go at that. Rather, she tells us about the sky, the trees, the rain, the twittering sparrows—and all of this in an extremely short story where we might think there is no time for talk about the setting. After all, none of this material is strictly necessary to a story about a woman who has heard that her husband was killed in an accident, who grieves, then recovers, and then dies when he suddenly reappears.

Why, then, does Chopin give such emphasis to the season? Because, we think, she is using the season symbolically. In this story, the spring is not just a bit of detail added for realism. It is rich with suggestions of renewal, of the new life that Louise achieves for a moment. But here, a caution. We think that the spring in this story is symbolic, but this is not to say that whenever spring appears in a story, it always stands for renewal, any more than whenever winter appears it always symbolizes death. Nor does it mean that since spring recurs, Louise will be reborn. In short, in *this* story Chopin uses the season to convey specific implications.

Is the railroad accident in "The Story of an Hour" also a symbol? Our answer is no—though we don't expect all readers to agree with us. We think that the railroad accident in "The Story of an Hour" is just a railroad accident. It's our sense that Chopin is *not* using this event to say something about modern travel, or about industrialism. The steam-propelled railroad train could be used, symbolically, to say something about industrialism displacing an agrarian economy, but does Chopin give her train any such suggestion? We don't think so. Had she wished to do so, she would probably have talked about the enormous power of the train, the shriek of its whistle, the smoke pouring out of the smokestack, the intense fire burning in the engine, its indifference as it charged through the countryside, and so forth. Had she done so, the story would be a different story. Or she might have made the train a symbol of fate overriding human desires. But, again in our opinion, Chopin does not endow her train with such suggestions. She gives virtually no emphasis to the train, and so we believe it has virtually no significance for the reader.

What of Chopin's "Ripe Figs" (page 11)? Maman-Nainaine tells Babette that when the figs are ripe Babette can visit her cousins. Maman may merely be setting an arbitrary date, but as we read the story we probably feel—because of the emphasis on the *ripening* of the figs, which occurs in the spring or early summer—that the ripening of the figs in some way suggests the maturing of Babette. If we do get such ideas, we will in effect be saying that the story is not simply an anecdote about an old woman whose behavior is odd. True, the narrator of the story, after telling us of Maman-Nainaine's promise, adds, "Not that the ripening of figs had the least thing to do with it, but that is the way Maman-Nainaine was." The narrator sees nothing special—merely Maman-Nainaine's eccentricity—in the connection between the ripening of the figs and Babette's visit to her cousins. Readers, however, may see more than the narrator sees or says. They may see in Babette a young girl maturing; they may see in Maman-Nainaine an older woman who, almost collaborating with nature, helps Babette to mature.

And here, as we talk about symbolism we are getting into the theme of the story. An apparently inconsequential and even puzzling action, such as is set forth in "Ripe Figs," may cast a long shadow. As Robert Frost once said,

> There is no story written that has any value at all, however straightforward it looks and free from doubleness, double entendre, that you'd value at all if it didn't have intimations of something more than itself.

The stranger, the more mysterious the story, the more likely we are to suspect some sort of significance, but even realistic stories such as Chopin's "The Storm" and "The Story of an Hour" may be rich in suggestions. This is not to say, however, that the suggestions (rather than the details of the surface) are what count. A reader does not discard the richly detailed, highly specific narrative (Mrs. Mallard learned that her husband was dead and reacted in such-and-such a way) in favor of some supposedly universal message or theme that it implies. We do not throw away the specific narrative—the memorable characters or the interesting things that happen in the story—and move on to some "higher truth." Robert Frost went on to say, "The anecdote, the parable, the surface meaning has got to be good and got to be sufficient in itself."

Narrative Point of View

An author must choose a **point of view** (or sometimes, several points of view) from which he or she will narrate the story. The choice will contribute to the total effect of the story.

Narrative points of view can be divided into two sorts: **participant** (or **first-person**) and **nonparticipant** (or **third-person**). That is, the narrator may or may not be a character who participates in the story. Each of these two divisions can be subdivided:

- **I.** Participant (first-person narrative)
  - **A.** Narrator as a major character
  - **B.** Narrator as a minor character
- **II.** Nonparticipant (third-person narrative)
  - **A.** Omniscient
  - **B.** Selective omniscient
  - **C.** Objective

Participant Points of View Toni Bambara's "The Lesson" (page 638) begins:

> Back in the days when everyone was old and stupid or young and foolish and me and Sugar were the only ones just right, this lady moved on our block with nappy hair and proper speech and no makeup.

In this story, the narrator is a major character. Bambara is the author, but the narrator—the person who tells us the story—is a young girl who speaks of "me and Sugar," and the story is chiefly about the narrator. We can say, then, that Bambara uses a first-person (or participant) point of view. She has invented a young girl who tells us about the impact a woman in the neighborhood had on her: "[Sugar] can run if she want to and even run faster. But ain't nobody gonna beat me at nuthin." The narrator is a major character. She, and not Bambara, tells the story.

Sometimes a first-person narrator tells a story that focuses on someone other than the narrator; he or she is a minor character, a peripheral witness, for example, to a story about Sally Jones, and we get the story of Sally filtered through, say, the eyes of her friend or brother or cat.

Whether a major or a minor character, a first-person narrator is a particular character, seeing things in a particular way. The reader should not assume that the speaker is necessarily a reliable source. Some, in fact, are notably **unreliable narrators**—for instance young children, mentally impaired adults, and psychopaths. A story told by an unreliable narrator, let's say by a man consumed with vengeful thoughts, depends largely on the reader's perception of the gap between what the narrator says and what the facts presumably are.

Nonparticipant Points of View In a nonparticipant (third-person) point of view, the teller of the tale does not introduce himself or herself as a character. If the point of view is **omniscient,** the narrator relates what he or she wants to relate about the thoughts as well as the deeds of all the characters. The omniscient teller can enter the mind of any character; the first-person narrator can only say, "I was angry" or "Jack seemed angry," but the omniscient teller can say, "Jack was inwardly angry but gave no sign; Jill continued chatting, but she sensed his anger." Thus, in Paley's "Samuel," the narrator tells us that Samuel's mother was "hopeful," but when the new baby was born "immediately she saw that this baby wasn't Samuel."

Furthermore, a distinction can be made between **neutral omniscience** (the narrator recounts deeds and thoughts but does not judge) and **editorial omniscience** (the narrator not only recounts but also judges). An editorially omniscient narrator knows what goes on in the minds of all the characters and might comment approvingly or disapprovingly: "He closed the book, having finished the story, but, poor fellow, he had missed the meaning."

Because a short story can scarcely hope to develop a picture of several minds effectively, authors may prefer to limit their omniscience to the minds of a few of their characters, or even to that of only one of the characters; that is, they may use **selective omniscience** as the point of view. Selective omniscience provides a focus, especially if it is limited to a single character. When thus limited, the author sees one character from both outside and inside, but sees the other characters only from the outside and from the impact they have on the mind of this selected receptor. When selective omniscience attempts to record mental activity ranging from consciousness to the unconscious, from clear perceptions to confused longings, it is sometimes labeled the **stream-of-consciousness** point of view.

Finally, sometimes a third-person narrator does not enter even a single mind but records only what crosses an apparently dispassionate eye and ear. Such a point of view is **objective** (sometimes called the **camera** or **fly-on-the-wall point of view**). The absence of editorializing and of dissection of the mind often produces the effect of a play; we see and hear the characters in action. Much of Chekhov's

"Misery" (page 83) is objective, consisting of bits of dialogue that make the story look like a play:

> "My head aches," says one of the tall ones. "At the Dukmasovs' yesterday Vaska and I drank four bottles of brandy between us."
>
> "I can't make out why you talk such stuff," says the other tall one angrily. "You lie like a brute."
>
> "Strike me dead, it's the truth! . . ."
>
> "It's about as true as that a louse coughs."

Style and Point of View

A story told by a first-person narrator will have a distinctive style—let's say the voice of an adolescent boy, or an elderly widow, or a madman. The voice of a third-person narrator—especially the voice of a supposedly objective narrator—will be much less distinctive, but if, especially on rereading, you listen carefully, you will probably hear a distinctive tone. (Look, for instance, at the first paragraph of Grace Paley's "Samuel.") Put it this way: Even a supposedly objective point of view is not purely objective, since it represents the writer's choice of a style, a way of reporting material with an apparently dispassionate voice.

After reading a story, you may want to think about what the story might be like if told from a different point of view. You may find it instructive, for instance, to rewrite "Samuel" from the "citizenly" man's point of view, or "Ripe Figs" from Babette's.

Theme

First, we can distinguish between story (or plot) and theme in fiction. *Story* is concerned with "How does it turn out? What happens?" But **theme** is concerned with "What is it about? What does it add up to? What motif holds the happenings together? What does it make of life, and, perhaps, what wisdom does it offer?" In a good work of fiction, the details add up, or, to use Flannery O'Connor's words, they are "controlled by some overall purpose."

In F. Scott Fitzgerald's *The Great Gatsby,* for example, there are many references to popular music, especially to jazz. These references contribute to our sense of the reality of Fitzgerald's depiction of America in the 1920s, but they do more: They help to comment on the shallowness of the white middle-class characters, and they sometimes (very gently) remind us of an alternative culture. A reader might study Fitzgerald's references to music with an eye toward getting a deeper understanding of what the novel is about.

Suppose we think for a moment about the theme of Paley's "Samuel." Do we sense an "overall purpose" that holds the story together? Different readers inevitably will come up with different readings, that is, with different views of what the story is about. Here is one student's version:

> Whites cannot understand the feelings of blacks.

This statement gets at an important element in the story—the conflict between the sober-minded adults and the jiggling boys—but it assumes that all of the adults are white, an inference that cannot be supported by pointing to evidence in the story. Further, we cannot be certain that Samuel is black. And, finally, even if Samuel and his mother are black, surely white readers *do understand his youthful enthusiasm and his mother's inconsolable grief.*

Here is a second statement:

> One should not interfere with the actions of others.

Does the story really offer such specific advice? This version of the theme seems to us to reduce the story to a too-simple code of action, a heartless rule of behavior, a rule that seems at odds with the writer's awareness of the mother's enduring grief.

A third version:

> Middle-class adults, acting from what seem to them to be the best of motives, may cause irreparable harm and grief.

This last statement seems to us to be one that can be fully supported by checking it against the story, but other equally valid statements can probably be made. How would you put it?

✓ CHECKLIST: *Getting Ideas for Writing about Stories*

Here are some questions that may help to stimulate ideas about stories. Not every question is relevant to every story; but if after reading a story and thinking about it, you then run your eye over these questions, you will find some questions that will help you to think further about the story—in short, that will help you to get ideas.

As we have said in earlier chapters, it's best to do your thinking with a pen or pencil in hand. If some of the following questions seem to you to be especially relevant to the story you will be writing about, jot down your initial responses, interrupting your writing only to glance again at the story when you feel the need to check the evidence.

Plot

- ☐ Does the plot grow out of the characters, or does it depend on chance or coincidence? Did something at first strike you as irrelevant that later you perceived as relevant? Do some parts continue to strike you as irrelevant?
- ☐ Does surprise play an important role, or does foreshadowing? If surprise is very important, can the story be read a second time with any interest? If so, what gives it this further interest?
- ☐ What conflicts does the story include? Conflicts of one character against another? Of one character against the setting, or against society? Conflicts within a single character?
- ☐ Are certain episodes narrated out of chronological order? If so, were you puzzled? Annoyed? On reflection, does the arrangement of episodes seem effective? Why, or why not? Are certain situations repeated? If so, what do you make out of the repetitions?

(*continued*)

Getting Ideas for Writing about Stories (continued)

Character

- Which character chiefly engages your interest? Why?
- What purposes do minor characters serve? Do you find some who by their similarities and differences help to define each other or help to define the major character? How else is a particular character defined—by his or her words, actions (including thoughts and emotions), dress, setting, narrative point of view? Do certain characters act differently in the same, or in a similar, situation?
- How does the author reveal character? By explicit authorial (editorial) comment, for instance, or, on the other hand, by revelation through dialogue? Through depicted action? Through the actions of other characters? How are the author's methods especially suited to the whole of the story?
- Is the behavior plausible—that is, are the characters well motivated?
- If a character changes, why and how does he or she change? (You may want to jot down each event that influences a change.) Or did you change your attitude toward a character not because the character changes but because you came to know the character better?
- Are the characters round or flat? Are they complex, or, on the other hand, highly typical (for instance, one-dimensional representatives of a social class or age)? Are you chiefly interested in a character's psychology, or does the character strike you as standing for something, such as honesty or the arrogance of power?
- How has the author caused you to sympathize with certain characters? How does your response—your sympathy or lack of sympathy—contribute to your judgment of the conflict?

Point of View

- Who tells the story? How much does the narrator know? Does the narrator strike you as reliable? What effect is gained by using this narrator?
- How does the point of view help shape the theme? After all, the basic story of "Little Red Riding Hood"—what happens—remains unchanged whether told from the wolf's point of view or the girl's, but if we hear the story from the wolf's point of view, we may feel that the story is about terrifying yet pathetic compulsive behavior; if from the girl's point of view, about terrified innocence.
- It is sometimes said that the best writers are subversive, forcing readers to see something they do not want to see—something that is true but that violates their comfortable conventional ideas. Does this story oppose comfortable conventional views?
- Does the narrator's language help you to construct a picture of the narrator's character, class, attitude, strengths, and limitations? (Jot down some evidence, such as colloquial or—on the other hand—formal expressions, ironic comments, figures of speech.) How far can you trust the narrator? Why?

Setting

- Do you have a strong sense of the time and place? Is the story very much about, say, New England Puritanism, or race relations in the South in the late nineteenth century, or midwestern urban versus small-town life? If time and place are important, how and at what points in the story has the author conveyed this sense? If you do not strongly feel the setting, do you think the author should have made it more evident?

- What is the relation of the setting to the plot and the characters? (For instance, do houses or rooms or their furnishings say something about their residents?) Would anything be lost if the descriptions of the setting were deleted from the story or the setting were changed?

Symbolism

- Do certain characters seem to you to stand for something in addition to themselves? Does the setting—whether a house, a farm, a landscape, a town, a period—have an extra dimension?
- If you do believe that the story has symbolic elements, do you think they are adequately integrated within the story, or do they strike you as being too obviously stuck in?

Style

- How has the point of view shaped or determined the style?
- How would you characterize the style? Simple? Understated? Figurative? Or what, and why?
- Do you think that the style is consistent? If it isn't—for instance, if there are shifts from simple sentences to highly complex ones—what do you make of the shifts?

Theme

- Is the title informative? What does it mean or suggest? Did the meaning seem to change after you read the story? Does the title help you to formulate a theme? If you had written the story, what title would you use?
- Do certain passages—dialogue or description—seem to you to point especially toward the theme? Do you find certain repetitions of words or pairs of incidents highly suggestive and helpful in directing your thoughts toward stating a theme? Flannery O'Connor, in *Mystery and Manners* (1969), says, "In good fiction, certain of the details will tend to accumulate meaning from the action of the story itself, and when that happens, they become symbolic in the way they work." Does this story work that way?
- Is the meaning of the story embodied in the whole story, or does it seem stuck in—for example in certain passages of editorializing?
- Suppose someone asked you to state the point—the theme—of the story. Could you? And if you could, would you say that the theme of a particular story reinforces values you hold, or does it to some degree challenge them? Or is the concept of a theme irrelevant to this story?

Your Turn: Stories for Analysis

LOUISE ERDRICH

Louise Erdrich, born in 1954 in Little Falls, Minnesota, grew up in North Dakota, a member of the Turtle Mountain Band of Chippewa. Her father had been born in Germany; her mother was French Ojibwe; both parents taught at the Bureau of Indian Affairs School. After graduating from Dartmouth College (with a major in anthropology) in 1976, Erdrich returned briefly to North Dakota to teach in the Poetry in the Schools Program, and went to Johns Hopkins University, where she earned a master's degree in creative writing. She now lives in Minneapolis, Minnesota.

Erdrich has published two books of poems and several novels, one of which, Love Medicine *(1986), won the National Book Critics Circle Award. "The Red Convertible" is a self-contained story, but it is also part of* Love Medicine, *which consists of narratives about life on a North Dakota reservation.*

The Red Convertible

Lyman Lamartine

I was the first one to drive a convertible on my reservation. And of course it was red, a red Olds. I owned that car along with my brother Henry Junior. We owned it together until his boots filled with water on a windy night and he bought out my share. Now Henry owns the whole car, and his youngest brother Lyman (that's myself), Lyman walks everywhere he goes.

How did I earn enough money to buy my share in the first place? My own talent was I could always make money. I had a touch for it, unusual in a Chippewa. From the first I was different that way, and everyone recognized it. I was the only kid they let in the American Legion Hall to shine shoes, for example, and one Christmas I sold spiritual bouquets for the mission door to door. The nuns let me keep a percentage. Once I started, it seemed the more money I made the easier the money came. Everyone encouraged it. When I was fifteen I got a job washing dishes at the Joliet Café, and that was where my first big break happened.

It wasn't long before I was promoted to bussing tables, and then the short-order cook quit and I was hired to take her place. No sooner than you know it I was managing the Joliet. The rest is history. I went on managing. I soon became part owner, and of course there was no stopping me then. It wasn't long before the whole thing was mine.

After I'd owned the Joliet for one year, it blew over in the worst tornado ever seen around here. The whole operation was smashed to bits. A total loss. The fryalator was up in a tree, the grill torn in half like it was paper. I was only sixteen. I had it all in my mother's name, and I lost it quick, but before I lost it I had every one of my relatives, and their relatives, to dinner, and I also bought that red Olds I mentioned, along with Henry.

5 The first time we saw it! I'll tell you when we first saw it. We had gotten a ride up to Winnipeg, and both of us had money. Don't ask me why, because we never mentioned a car or anything, we just had all our money. Mine was cash, a big bankroll from the Joliet's insurance. Henry had two checks—a week's extra pay for being laid off, and his regular check from the Jewel Bearing Plant.

We were walking down Portage anyway, seeing the sights, when we saw it. There it was, parked, large as life. Really as *if* it was alive. I thought of the word *repose*, because the car wasn't simply stopped, parked, or whatever. That car reposed, calm and gleaming, a FOR SALE sign in its left front window. Then, before we had thought it over at all, the car belonged to us and our pockets were empty. We had just enough money for gas back home.

We went places in that car, me and Henry. We took off driving all one whole summer. We started off toward the Little Knife River and Mandaree in Fort Berthold and then we found ourselves down in Wakpala somehow, and then suddenly we were over in Montana on the Rocky Boys, and yet the summer was not even half over. Some people hang on to details when they travel, but we didn't let them bother us and just lived our everyday lives here to there.

I do remember this one place with willows. I remember I laid under those trees and it was comfortable. So comfortable. The branches bent down all around me like a tent or a stable. And quiet, it was quiet, even though there was a powwow close enough so I could see it going on. The air was not too still, not too windy either. When the dust rises up and hangs in the air around the dancers like that, I feel good. Henry was asleep with his arms thrown wide. Later on, he woke up and we started driving again. We were somewhere in Montana, or maybe on the Blood Reserve—it could have been anywhere. Anyway it was where we met the girl.

All her hair was in buns around her ears, that's the first thing I noticed about her. She was posed alongside the road with her arm out, so we stopped. That girl was short, so short her lumber shirt looked comical on her, like a nightgown. She had jeans on and fancy moccasins and she carried a little suitcase.

"Hop on in," says Henry. So she climbs in between us.

"We'll take you home," I says. "Where do you live?"

"Chicken," she says.

"Where the hell's that?" I ask her.

"Alaska."

"Okay," says Henry, and we drive.

We got up there and never wanted to leave. The sun doesn't truly set there in summer, and the night is more a soft dusk. You might doze off, sometimes, but before you know it you're up again, like an animal in nature. You never feel like you have to sleep hard or put away the world. And things would grow up there. One day just dirt or moss, the next day flowers and long grass. The girl's name was Susy. Her family really took to us. They fed us and put us up. We had our own tent to live in by their house, and the kids would be in and out of there all day and night. They couldn't get over me and Henry being brothers, we looked so different. We told them we knew we had the same mother, anyway.

One night Susy came in to visit us. We sat around in the tent talking of this thing and that. The season was changing. It was getting darker by that time, and the cold was even getting just a little mean. I told her it was time for us to go. She stood up on a chair.

"You never seen my hair," Susy said.

That was true. She was standing on a chair, but still, when she unclipped her buns the hair reached all the way to the ground. Our eyes opened. You couldn't tell how much hair she had when it was rolled up so neatly. Then my brother Henry did something funny. He went up to the chair and said, "Jump on my shoulders." So she did that, and her hair reached down past his waist, and he started twirling, this way and that, so her hair was flung out from side to side.

20 "I always wondered what it was like to have long pretty hair," Henry says. Well we laughed. It was a funny sight, the way he did it. The next morning we got up and took leave of those people.

On to greener pastures, as they say. It was down through Spokane and across Idaho then Montana and very soon we were racing the weather right along under the Canadian border through Columbus, Des Lacs, and then we were in Bottineau County and soon home. We'd made most of the trip, that summer, without putting up the car hood at all. We got home just in time, it turned out, for the army to remember Henry had signed up to join it.

I don't wonder that the army was so glad to get my brother that they turned him into a Marine. He was built like a brick outhouse anyway. We liked to tease him that they really wanted him for his Indian nose. He had a nose big and sharp as a hatchet, like the nose on Red Tomahawk, the Indian who killed Sitting Bull, whose profile is on signs all along the North Dakota highways. Henry went off to training camp, came home once during Christmas, then the next thing you know we got an overseas letter from him. It was 1970, and he said he was stationed up in the northern hill country. Whereabouts I did not know. He wasn't such a hot letter writer, and only got off two before the enemy caught him. I could never keep it straight, which direction those good Vietnam soldiers were from.

I wrote him back several times, even though I didn't know if those letters would get through. I kept him informed all about the car. Most of the time I had it up on blocks in the yard or half taken apart, because that long trip did a hard job on it under the hood.

I always had good luck with numbers, and never worried about the draft myself. I never even had to think about what my number was. But Henry was never lucky in the same way as me. It was at least three years before Henry came home. By then I guess the whole war was solved in the government's mind, but for him it would keep on going. In those years I'd put his car into almost perfect shape. I always thought of it as his car while he was gone, even though when he left he said, "Now it's yours," and threw me his key.

25 "Thanks for the extra key," I'd say. "I'll put it up in your drawer just in case I need it." He laughed.

When he came home, though, Henry was very different, and I'll say this: the change was no good. You could hardly expect him to change for the better, I know. But he was quiet, so quiet, and never comfortable sitting still anywhere but always up and moving around. I thought back to times we'd sat still for whole afternoons, never moving a muscle, just shifting our weight along the ground, talking to whoever sat with us, watching things. He'd always had a joke, then, too, and now you couldn't get him to laugh, or when he did it was more the sound of a man choking, a sound that stopped up the throats of other people around him. They got to leaving him alone most of the time, and I didn't blame them. It was a fact: Henry was jumpy and mean.

I'd bought a color TV set for my mom and the rest of us while Henry was away. Money still came very easy. I was sorry I'd ever bought it though, because of Henry. I was also sorry I'd bought color, because with black-and-white the pictures seem older and farther away. But what are you going to do? He sat in front of it, watching it, and that was the only time he was completely still. But it was the kind of stillness that you see in a rabbit when it freezes and before it will bolt. He was not easy. He sat in his chair gripping the armrests with all his might, as if the chair itself was moving at a high speed and if he let go at all he would rocket forward and maybe crash right through the set.

Once I was in the room watching TV with Henry and I heard his teeth click at something. I looked over, and he'd bitten through his lip. Blood was going down his chin. I tell you right then I wanted to smash that tube to pieces. I went over to it but Henry must have known what I was up to. He rushed from his chair and shoved me out of the way, against the wall. I told myself he didn't know what he was doing.

My mom came in, turned the set off real quiet, and told us she had made something for supper. So we went and sat down. There was still blood going down Henry's chin, but he didn't notice it and no one said anything, even though every time he took a bit of his bread his blood fell onto it until he was eating his own blood mixed in with the food.

30 While Henry was not around we talked about what was going to happen to him. There were no Indian doctors on the reservation, and my mom was afraid of trusting Old Man Pillager because he courted her long ago and was jealous of her husbands. He might take revenge through her son. We were afraid that if we brought Henry to a regular hospital they would keep him.

"They don't fix them in those places," Mom said; "they just give them drugs."

"We wouldn't get him there in the first place," I agreed, "so let's just forget about it."

Then I thought about the car.

Henry had not even looked at the car since he'd gotten home, though like I said, it was in tip-top condition and ready to drive. I thought the car might bring the old Henry back somehow. So I bided my time and waited for my chance to interest him in the vehicle.

35 One night Henry was off somewhere. I took myself a hammer. I went out to that car and I did a number on its underside. Whacked it up. Bent the tail pipe double. Ripped the muffler loose. By the time I was done with the car it looked worse than any typical Indian car that has been driven all its life on reservation roads, which they always say are like government promises—full of holes. It just about hurt me, I'll tell you that! I threw dirt in the carburetor and I ripped all the electric tape off the seats. I made it look just as beat up as I could. Then I sat back and waited for Henry to find it.

Still, it took him over a month. That was all right, because it was just getting warm enough, not melting, but warm enough to work outside.

"Lyman," he says, walking in one day, "that red car looks like shit."

"Well it's old," I says. "You got to expect that."

"No way!" says Henry. "That car's a classic! But you went and ran the piss right out of it, Lyman, and you know it don't deserve that. I kept that car in A-one shape. You don't remember. You're too young. But when I left, that car was running like a watch. Now I don't even know if I can get it to start again, let alone get it anywhere near its old condition."

40 "Well you try," I said, like I was getting mad, "but I say it's a piece of junk."

Then I walked out before he could realize I knew he'd strung together more than six words at once.

After that I thought he'd freeze himself to death working on that car. He was out there all day, and at night he rigged up a little lamp, ran a cord out the window, and had himself some light to see by while he worked. He was better than he had been before, but that's still not saying much. It was easier for him to do the things the rest of us did. He ate more slowly and didn't jump up and down during the meal to get this or that or look out the window. I put my hand in the back of the TV set, I admit, and fiddled around with it good, so that it was almost impossible now to get a clear picture. He didn't look at it very often anyway. He was always out with that car or going off to get parts for it. By the time it was really melting outside, he had it fixed.

I had been feeling down in the dumps about Henry around this time. We had always been together before. Henry and Lyman. But he was such a loner now that I didn't know how to take it. So I jumped at the chance one day when Henry seemed friendly. It's not that he smiled or anything. He just said, "Let's take that old shitbox for a spin." Just the way he said it made me think he could be coming around.

We went out to the car. It was spring. The sun was shining very bright. My only sister, Bonita, who was just eleven years old, came out and made us stand together for a picture. Henry leaned his elbow on the red car's windshield, and he took his other arm and put it over my shoulder, very carefully, as though it was heavy for him to lift and he didn't want to bring the weight down all at once.

"Smile," Bonita said, and he did.

That picture, I never look at it anymore. A few months ago, I don't know why, I got his picture out and tacked it on the wall. I felt good about Henry at the time, close to him. I felt good having his picture on the wall, until one night when I was looking at television. I was a little drunk and stoned. I looked up at the wall and Henry was staring at me. I don't know what it was, but his smile had changed, or maybe it was gone. All I know is I couldn't stay in the same room with that picture. I was shaking. I got up, closed the door, and went into the kitchen. A little later my friend Ray came over and we both went back into that room. We put the picture in a brown bag, folded the bag over and over tightly, then put it way back in a closet.

I still see that picture now, as if it tugs at me, whenever I pass that closet door. The picture is very clear in my mind. It was so sunny that day Henry had to squint against the glare. Or maybe the camera Bonita held flashed like a mirror, blinding him, before she snapped the picture. My face is right out in the sun, big and round. But he might have drawn back, because the shadows on his face are deep as holes. There are two shadows curved like little hooks around the ends of his smile, as if to frame it and try to keep it there—that one, first smile that looked like it might have hurt his face. He has his field jacket on and the worn-in clothes he'd come back in and kept wearing ever since. After Bonita took the picture, she went into the house and we got into the car. There was a full cooler in the trunk. We started off, east, toward Pembina and the Red River because Henry said he wanted to see the high water.

The trip over there was beautiful. When everything starts changing, drying up, clearing off, you feel like your whole life is starting. Henry felt it, too. The top was down and the car hummed like a top. He'd really put it back in shape, even the tape on the seats was very carefully put down and glued back in layers. It's not that he smiled again or even joked, but his face looked to me as if it was clear, more peaceful. It looked as though he wasn't thinking of anything in particular except the bare fields and windbreaks and houses we were passing.

The river was high and full of winter trash when we got there. The sun was still out, but it was colder by the river. There were still little clumps of dirty snow here and there on the banks. The water hadn't gone over the banks yet, but it would, you could tell. It was just at its limit, hard swollen glossy like an old gray scar. We made ourselves a fire, and we sat down and watched the current go. As I watched it I felt something squeezing inside me and tightening and trying to let go all at the same time. I knew I was not just feeling it myself; I knew I was feeling what Henry was going through at that moment. Except that I couldn't stand it, the closing and opening. I jumped to my feet. I took Henry by the shoulders and I started shaking him. "Wake up," I says, "wake up, wake up, wake up!" I didn't know what had come over me. I sat down beside him again.

50 His face was totally white and hard. Then it broke, like stones break all of a sudden when water boils up inside them.

"I know it," he says. "I know it. I can't help it. It's no use."

We start talking. He said he knew what I'd done with the car. It was obvious it had been whacked out of shape and not just neglected. He said he wanted to give the car to me for good now, it was no use. He said he'd fixed it just to give it back and I should take it.

"No way," I says, "I don't want it."

"That's okay," he says, "you take it."

55 "I don't want it, though," I says back to him, and then to emphasize, just to emphasize, you understand, I touch his shoulder. He slaps my hand off.

"Take that car," he says.

"No," I say, "make me," I say, and then he grabs my jacket and rips the arm loose. That jacket is a class act, suede with tags and zippers. I push Henry backwards, off the log. He jumps up and bowls me over. We go down in a clinch and come up swinging hard, for all we're worth, with our fists. He socks my jaw so hard I feel like it swings loose. Then I'm at his ribcage and land a good one under his chin so his head snaps back. He's dazzled. He looks at me and I look at him and then his eyes are full of tears and blood and at first I think he's crying. But no, he's laughing. "Ha! Ha!" he says. "Ha! Ha! Take good care of it."

"Okay," I says, "okay, no problem. Ha! Ha!"

I can't help it, and I start laughing, too. My face feels fat and strange, and after a while I get a beer from the cooler in the trunk, and when I hand it to Henry he takes his shirt and wipes my germs off. "Hoof-and-mouth disease," he says. For some reason this cracks me up, and so we're really laughing for a while, and then we drink all the rest of the beers one by one and throw them in the river and see how far, how fast, the current takes them before they fill up and sink.

60 "You want to go on back?" I ask after a while. "Maybe we could snag a couple nice Kashpaw girls."

He says nothing. But I can tell his mood is turning again.

"They're all crazy, the girls up here, every damn one of them."

"You're crazy too," I say, to jolly him up. "Crazy Lamartine boys!"

He looks as though he will take this wrong at first. His face twists, then clears, and he jumps up on his feet. "That's right!" he says. "Crazier 'n hell. Crazy Indians!"

65 I think it's the old Henry again. He throws off his jacket and starts swinging his legs out from the knees like a fancy dancer. He's down doing something between a grouse dance and a bunny hop, no kind of dance I ever saw before, but neither has anyone else on all this green growing earth. He's wild. He wants to pitch whoopee! He's up and at me and all over. All this time I'm laughing so hard, so hard my belly is getting tied up in a knot.

"Got to cool me off!" he shouts all of a sudden. Then he runs over to the river and jumps in.

There's boards and other things in the current. It's so high. No sound comes from the river after the splash he makes, so I run right over. I look around.

It's getting dark. I see he's halfway across the water already, and I know he didn't swim there but the current took him. It's far. I hear his voice, though, very clearly across it.

"My boots are filling," he says.

He says this in a normal voice, like he just noticed and he doesn't know what to think of it. Then he's gone. A branch comes by. Another branch. And I go in.

By the time I get out of the river, off the snag I pulled myself onto, the sun is down. I walk back to the car, turn on the high beams, and drive it up the bank. I put it in first gear and then I take my foot off the clutch. I get out, close the door, and watch it plow softly into the water. The headlights reach in as they go down, searching, still lighted even after the water swirls over the back end. I wait. The wires short out. It is all finally dark. And then there is only the water, the sound of it going and running and going and running and running.

[1984]

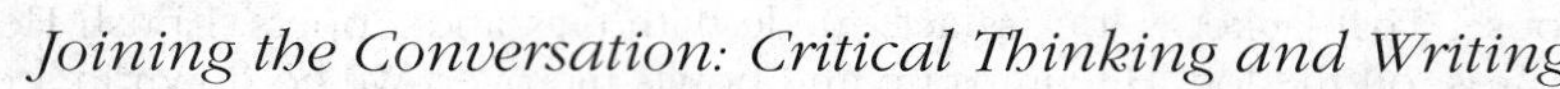

Joining the Conversation: Critical Thinking and Writing

1. Characterize the narrator. Is he someone you'd like to know? Please explain.
2. What is Henry like when he returns home?
3. One critic has said that the red convertible is a "powerful symbol." In your view, what does it symbolize? Please point to details in the text that support your analysis and argument.
4. What is the effect on the reader of the final paragraph?
5. Prepare an argument in which you claim that the final paragraph is exactly right for the story, and then prepare a second argument in which you claim it is not needed—that the story would end more effectively with the sentence, "And I go in." Which of these arguments is more convincing to you?
6. Is this an anti-war story? What leads you to say that?

Oscar Casares

Oscar Casares, born and raised in Brownsville, Texas, and now a resident of San Antonio, is a graduate of the Iowa Writers' Workshop. He has published widely and received numerous prizes, including the James Michener Award. We reprint a story from his collection, Brownsville Stories *(2003).*

Yolanda

When I can't sleep at night I think of Yolanda Castro. She was a woman who lived next door to us one summer when I was growing up. I've never told Maggie about her because it's not something she'd appreciate knowing. Trust me. Tonight, like most nights, she fell asleep before I was even done brushing my teeth. And now all I can hear are little snores. Sometimes she even talks to herself, shouts out other people's names, and then in the morning says she can't remember any of it. Either way, I let her go on sleeping. She's over on her side of the bed. It's right where she ought to be. This thing with Yolanda doesn't really concern her.

I was only twelve years old when Frank and Yolanda Castro moved into the beige house with green trim. Frank pulled up on our street in a U-Haul he'd driven all the way from California to Texas. I remember it being a different neighborhood back then. Everybody knew everybody, and people left their doors unlocked at night. You didn't worry about people stealing shit you didn't lock up. I'm talking about more than twenty years ago now. I'm talking about before some drunk spent all afternoon in one of the cantinas on Fourteenth Street, then drove his car straight into the Rivas front yard and ran over the Baby Jesus that was still lying in the manger because Lonny Rivas was too flojo[1] to put it away a month after Christmas, and then the guy tried to run, but fell down, asleep, in our yard, and when the cops were handcuffing him all he could say was *ma-ri-juan-a,* which even then, at the age of fifteen, I knew wasn't a good thing to say when you were being arrested. This was before Pete Zuniga was riding his brand-new ten-speed from Western Auto and, next to the Friendship Garden, saw a white dude who'd been knifed a couple of dozen times and was floating in the green water of the resaca.[2] Before some crazy woman hired a curandera[3] to put a spell on her daughter's ex-boyfriend, which really meant hiring a couple of hit men from Matamoros to do a drive-by. Before the cops ever had to show up at El Disco de Oro Tortillería. Like holding up a 7-Eleven was getting old, right? You know, when you could sit at the Brownsville Coffee Shop #1 and not worry about getting it in the back while you ate your menudo.[4] When you didn't have to put an alarm *and* the Club on your car so it wouldn't end up in Reynosa. Before my father had to put iron bars on the windows and doors because some future convict from the junior high was always breaking into the house. And before my father had to put a fence in the front because, in his words, I'm sick and tired of all those damn dogs making poo in my yard. I guess what I'm trying to say is, things were different back then.

Frank Castro was an older man, in his fifties by that point, and Yolanda couldn't have been more than thirty, if that. My mother got along with Yolanda okay and even helped her get a job at the HEB store where she had worked since before I was born. You could say that was where the problems started, because Frank Castro didn't want his wife working at HEB, or any other place for that matter. You have no business being in that grocery store, I heard him yell one night when I was trying to fall asleep. I could hear almost everything Frank yelled that summer. Our houses were only a few yards apart, and my window was the closest to the action. My father's bougainvilleas were the dividing line between the two properties. I heard Yolanda beg Frank to please let her take the job. I heard Frank yell something in Spanish about how no woman in his family had ever worked behind a cosmetics counter, selling lipstick. I heard her promise she'd only work part-time, and she'd quit if they ever scheduled her on nights or weekends. I heard her tell him how much she loved him and how she'd never take a job that would keep them apart. Francisco, tú eres mi vida,[5] she said to him. I heard him get real quiet. Then I heard Frank and Yolanda Castro making love. I didn't know what making love sounded like back then, but I can tell you now that's what it was.

If you saw what Yolanda looked like, you might not have blamed Frank for not wanting her to leave the house. It also wouldn't have been a big mystery to you how she went into the store applying for a job in the meat department and ended up getting one in cosmetics. The only girl I'd ever seen that even came close to being as

[1]**flojo** weak-willed. [2]**resaca** dry streambed. [3]**curandera** midwife. [4]**menudo** tripe soup.
[5]**tú . . . vida** You are my life.

beautiful as Yolanda was in a *Playboy* I found under my parents' bed the summer before. The girl in the magazine had the same long black hair, light brown skin, and green eyes that Yolanda did, only she was sitting bareback on an Appaloosa.

5 The thing I remember most about Frank was his huge forearms. They were like Popeye's, except with a lot more black and gray hair mixed in. But the hair on his arms was just the beginning. There wasn't a time I saw the guy that he didn't look like he could've used a good shave. And it didn't help that his thick eyebrows were connected into one long eyebrow that stretched across the bottom of his forehead like a piece of electrical tape. He was average size, but he looked short and squatty when he stood next to Yolanda. Frank was a mechanic at the airport and, according to my father, probably made good money. I was with my father the first time he met Frank. He always made it a point to meet any new neighbors and then come back to the house and give a full report to my mother, who would later meet the neighbors herself and say he was exaggerating about how shifty so-and-so's eyes were or how rich he thought another neighbor might be because he had one of those new foreign cars in the driveway, un carro extranjero,[6] a Toyota or a Honda. Frank was beginning to mow his front yard when we walked up. My father introduced me as his boy, and I shook our neighbor's sweaty hand. I've lived thirty-six years on this earth and never shaken hands with a bear, but I have a good idea that it wouldn't be much different from shaking Frank Castro's hand. Even his fingers needed a haircut. Frank stood there answering a couple of my father's questions about whether he liked the neighborhood (he liked it) and how long he had lived in California before moving back to Texas (ten years—he held up both hands to show us exactly how many). Suddenly, my father nodded and said we had to go. He turned around and walked off, then looked over his shoulder and yelled at me to hurry up. This whole time, Frank had not shut off his mower. My father was forced to stand there and shout over the sound of the engine. The report on Frank wasn't pretty when we got back to the house. From that point on, my father would only refer to him as El Burro.

It wasn't just my father. Nobody liked Frank. He had this thing about his yard where he didn't want anybody getting near it. We found this out one day when Lonny and I were throwing the football around in the street. Lonny was showing off and he threw the ball over my head, way over, and it landed in Frank's yard. When I was getting the ball, Frank opened the front door and yelled something about it being private property. Then he went over, turned on the hose, and started watering his yard and half the street in front of his yard. He did this every afternoon from that day on. The hose with a spray gun in his right hand, and a Schlitz tallboy in his left. Lonny thought we should steal the hose when Frank wasn't home, or maybe poke a few holes in it, just to teach the fucker a lesson. One Saturday morning we even saw him turn the hose on some Jehovahs who were walking up the street towards his house. A skinny man wearing a tie and short-sleeve shirt kept trying to give him a pamphlet, but Frank wasn't listening.

My mother gave Yolanda a ride to work every day. In the afternoons, Yolanda got off work early enough to be waiting for Frank to pull up in his car and drive her back to the house. My mother told us at home that Yolanda had asked Frank to teach her how to drive when they first got married but that Frank had said she was his princesa now and any place she needed to go, he'd take her. One morning, when both my mother and Yolanda had the day off, my mother asked

[6]**carro extranjero** foreign car.

her if she wanted to learn how to drive. They drove out by the port, and my mother pulled over so Yolanda could take the wheel. I was hanging out at the Jiffy-Mart, down the street, when I saw Yolanda driving my mother's car. Yolanda honked the horn, and they both waved at me as they turned the corner.

That night—like a lot of nights that summer—I listened to Frank and Yolanda Castro. What they said went something like this:

"I can show you."

"I don't wanna see."

"Why not?"

"Because you have *no* business driving a car around town."

"But this way you don't have to pick me up every day. You can come straight home, and I'll be here already, waiting."

"I don't care. I'm talking about you learning to drive."

"Frank, it's nothing."

"You don't even have a car. What do you want with a license?"

"I can buy one."

"With what?"

"I've been getting bonuses. The companies gives us a little extra if we sell more of their makeup."

"Is that right?"

"It isn't that much, Frank."

"And then?"

"Well, maybe I can buy a used one."

"It's because of that store."

"What's wrong with the store?"

"It's putting ideas in your head."

"Frank, what ideas?"

"Ideas! Is there some place I haven't taken you?"

"No."

"Well, then?"

"Francisco."

"Don't 'Francisco' me."

"Baby . . ."

"¡Qué no!"[7]

They were beginning to remind me of one of my mother's novellas, which she was probably watching in the living room at that very moment. Things like that usually made me want to laugh—and I did a little, into my pillow, but it was only because I couldn't believe I was actually hearing it, and I could see Frank Castro pounding me into the ground with his big forearms if he ever found out.

"No! I said."

"I'm not Trini."

"I never said . . ."

"Then stop treating me like her. ¿No sabes qué tanto te quiero, Francisco?"[8]

It got quiet for a while after that. Then there was the sound of something hitting the floor, the sound of two bodies dropping on a bed with springs that had seen better days (and nights), the sound of Yolanda saying, *Ay, Diosito,*[9] over and over and over again—just like my tía[10] Hilda did the day her son, my cousin Rudy, almost drowned in the swimming pool at the Civic Center—then the sound of the

[7]**¡Qué no!** Why not! [8]**¿No . . . Francisco?** Don't you know how much I love you, Francisco?
[9]**Ay, Diosito** Oh, God. [10]**tía** aunt.

bed springs making their own crazy music, and the sound of what I imagine a bear is like when he's trying to make little bears.

Yolanda kept getting a ride to work with my mother, and Frank kept bringing her home in the afternoons. My mother had offered to drive Yolanda to the DPS office and let her borrow our car for the driving part of the test, but Yolanda said she'd changed her mind and didn't want to talk about it. I heard my mother telling my father what she'd said, and they agreed it probably had something to do with Frank. El Burro, my father let out when they didn't have anything else to say.

It was the Fourth of July when I got sick that summer. I remember my mother wouldn't let me go outside with Lonny. He kept yelling at me from the street that night to stop being a baby and come out of the house so I could pop some firecrackers. We'd been talking all week about shooting some bottle rockets in the direction of Frank's house. It didn't feel like anything at first, just a fever, but the next morning we knew it was the chicken pox. My mother had to miss a few days of work, staying home with me until I got over the worst part. After that, Yolanda volunteered to come look in on me when she wasn't working. But I told my mother I didn't want her coming over when I still looked like those dead people in that *Night of the Living Dead* movie. My mother said Yolanda would understand I was sick, and if she didn't, that's what I'd get for watching those kinds of movies. So for about a week she came over in the mornings and we watched *The Price Is Right* together. Yolanda was great at guessing the prices of things, and she said it was from working in a grocery store and having a good memory. I told her I thought she should go on the show. She laughed and said she probably wouldn't win anything, since she'd be too nervous. What I meant to say was that she should go on the show and be one of the girls who stands next to the car, smiling. She was prettier than any of them, but I never told her that, because I got embarrassed whenever I thought about saying it.

If Yolanda came over in the afternoon, we'd watch *General Hospital* together. She said she'd been watching it for years. There wasn't anything else on at that hour, so I didn't really care. Once, she brought over some lime sherbert, and we played Chinese checkers in my room until she had to get home to Frank Castro. Each time she left she'd reach down and give me a little kiss on the cheek, and each time her hair smelled like a different fruit. Sometimes like a pear, sometimes like a strawberry, sometimes like an apple. The strawberry was my favorite.

This was about the time when Frank said that from now on, he would take Yolanda to work in the morning—no matter how out of the way it was for him, or the fact that he and my mother were always pulling out of the driveway at the same time. A week or two went by, and then my mother told my father that Frank had started showing up at the store in the middle of the day, usually during his lunch hour, but sometimes also at two or three in the afternoon. He wouldn't talk to Yolanda, but instead just hung out by the magazine rack, pretending to read a wrestling magazine. Yolanda tried to ignore him. My mother said she had talked to her in the break room, but Yolanda kept saying it was nothing, that Frank's hours had changed at the airport.

45 There was one Saturday when he was off from work, and as usual, he spent it in his front yard, sitting in a green lawn chair, drinking tallboys. He had turned on the sprinkler and was watching his grass and half the street get a good watering. Lonny and I were throwing the football around. Frank sat in that stupid chair all afternoon. He only went in to grab another beer and, I guess, take a piss. Each time he got up and turned around, we shot him the finger.

That night, I heard Frank's voice loud and clear. He wanted answers. Something about a phone number. Something about a customer he'd seen Yolanda talking to a couple of days earlier. Did she think he was blind? What the hell was so funny when the two of them were talking? How many times? he wanted to know. ¡Desgraciado![11] Where? Goddammit! he wanted to know. What game show? ¡El sanavabiche! Something shattered against the wall and then a few seconds later Yolanda screamed. I sat up. I didn't know if I could form words if I had to. What the hell were you doing listening anyway? they would ask me. There was another scream and then the sound of the back door slamming. I looked out my window and saw Frank Castro chase Yolanda into their backyard. She was wearing a nightgown that came down to her knees. Frank had on the same khakis and muscle shirt he'd worn that afternoon. He only ran a few feet down from the back steps before his head hit the clothesline, and he fell to the ground, hard. Yolanda didn't turn to look back and ran around the right side of their house. I thought she'd gone back inside to call the police. Then I heard footsteps and a tapping on my window. It was Yolanda whispering, Open it, open it.

I didn't say anything for a long time. Yolanda had climbed in and let down the blinds. We were lying on the bed, facing the window. She was behind me, holding me tight. I finally asked her if she wanted a glass of water or some Kool-Aid. I made it myself, I told her. It's the orange kind, I said. I didn't know what else to talk about. She said no, and then she told me to be quiet. I kept thinking, This has to be a dream and any minute now my mother's going to walk in and tell me the barbacoa[12] is sitting on the table and to come eat because we're going to eleven o'clock mass and don't even think about putting on those blue jeans with the patches in the knees ¿me entiendes?[13] But that wasn't happening, and something told me then that no matter what happened after tonight, this was something I'd never forget. There would always be a time *before* Yolanda crawled into my bed and a time *after*. As she held me, I could feel her heart beating. Then I felt her chiches[14] pressed against my back. And even though I couldn't see them, I knew they were perfect like the rest of her. I knew that they'd fit right in the palms of my hands, if only I had enough guts to turn around. Just turn around, that's all I had to do. I thought back to when she was tapping on the window, and I was sure she wasn't wearing a bra. I was sure there was nothing but Yolanda underneath her nightgown. I could have sworn I'd seen even more. I'd been close to a woman's body before. But this wasn't like when my tía Gloria came into town and couldn't believe how much I'd grown, and then she squeezed me so hard my head got lost in her huge and heavily perfumed chiches. And it wasn't anything like the Sears catalog where the girls had a tiny rose at the top of their panties. No, this was Yolanda and she was in my bed, pressed up against my back, like it was the only place in the world for us to be.

I could go on and tell you the rest of the details—how I never turned around and always regretted it, how we stayed there and listened to Frank crying in his backyard, how Lonny's dad finally called the cops on his ass, how Yolanda had a cousin pick her up the next morning, how she ended up leaving Frank for a man who worked for one of the shampoo companies, how it didn't matter because she'd also been seeing an assistant manager and would be having his baby soon enough, and how it really didn't matter because the assistant manager was already married and wasn't about to leave his wife and kids, and how, actually, none of it mattered because she'd been taking money out of the register and was about to be caught—but that's not the part of the story I like to remember.

[11]**¡Desgraciado!** Disgraceful! [12]**barbacoa** baked lamb or goat. [13]**¿me entiendes?** Do you understand me? [14]**chiches** breasts.

In that bed of mine, the one with the Dallas Cowboy pillows and covers, Yolanda and I were safe. We were safe from Frank Castro and safe from anybody else that might try to hurt us. And it was safe for me to fall asleep in Yolanda's arms, with her warm, beautiful body pressed against mine, and dream that we were riding off to some faraway place on an Appaloosa.

[2003]

Joining the Conversation: Critical Thinking and Writing

1. Characterize the narrator. Characterize Frank.
2. In the next-to-last paragraph we learn that Yolanda has been "taking money out of the register." Did this statement surprise you? Why do you think the author included it?
3. An exercise in constructing an argument: Do you think that the narrator is or was in love with Yolanda? Explain.

GABRIEL GARCÍA MÁRQUEZ

Gabriel García Márquez was born in 1927 in Aracataca, a small village in Colombia. After being educated in Bogota, where he studied journalism and law, he worked as a journalist in Latin America, Europe, and the United States. He began writing fiction when he was in Paris, and at twenty-seven he published his first novel, La hojarasca *(*Leaf Storm*, 1955). During most of the 1960s he lived in Mexico, where he wrote film scripts and the novel that made him famous:* Cien años de soledad *(1967, translated in 1970 as* A Hundred Years of Solitude*). In 1982 Márquez was awarded the Nobel Prize in Literature.*

In addition to writing stories and novels—often set in Macondo, a town modeled on Aracataca—Márquez has written screenplays. A socialist, he now lives in Mexico because his presence is not welcome in Colombia.

A Very Old Man with Enormous Wings: A Tale for Children

Translated by Gregory Rabassa

On the third day of rain they had killed so many crabs inside the house that Pelayo had to cross his drenched courtyard and throw them into the sea, because the newborn child had a temperature all night and they thought it was due to the stench. The world had been sad since Tuesday. Sea and sky were a single ash-gray thing and the sands of the beach, which on March nights glimmered like powdered light, had become a stew of mud and rotten shellfish. The light was so weak at noon that when Pelayo was coming back to the house after throwing away the crabs, it was hard for him to see what it was that was moving and groaning in the rear of the courtyard. He had to go very close to see that it was an old man, a very old man, lying face down in the mud, who, in spite of his tremendous efforts, couldn't get up, impeded by his enormous wings.

Frightened by that nightmare, Pelayo ran to get Elisenda, his wife, who was putting compresses on the sick child, and he took her to the rear of the courtyard. They both looked at the fallen body with mute stupor. He was dressed like a ragpicker. There were only a few faded hairs left on his bald skull and very few teeth in his mouth, and his pitiful condition of a drenched great-grandfather had taken away any sense of grandeur he might have had. His huge buzzard wings, dirty and half-plucked, were forever entangled in the mud. They looked at him so long and so closely that Pelayo and Elisenda very soon overcame their surprise and in the end found him familiar. Then they dared speak to him, and he answered in an incomprehensible dialect with a strong sailor's voice. That was how they skipped over the inconvenience of the wings and quite intelligently concluded that he was a lonely castaway from some foreign ship wrecked by the storm. And yet, they called in a neighbor woman who knew everything about life and death to see him, and all she needed was one look to show them their mistake.

"He's an angel," she told them. "He must have been coming for the child, but the poor fellow is so old that the rain knocked him down."

On the following day everyone knew that a flesh-and-blood angel was held captive in Pelayo's house. Against the judgment of the wise neighbor woman, for whom angels in those times were the fugitive survivors of a celestial conspiracy, they did not have the heart to club him to death. Pelayo watched over him all afternoon from the kitchen, armed with his bailiff's club, and before going to bed he dragged him out of the mud and locked him up with the hens in the wire chicken coop. In the middle of the night, when the rain stopped, Pelayo and Elisenda were still killing crabs. A short time afterward the child woke up without a fever and with a desire to eat. Then they felt magnanimous and decided to put the angel on a raft with fresh water and provisions for three days and leave him to his fate on the high seas. But when they went out into the courtyard with the first light of dawn, they found the whole neighborhood in front of the chicken coop having fun with the angel, without the slightest reverence, tossing him things to eat through the openings in the wire as if he weren't a supernatural creature but a circus animal.

5 Father Gonzaga arrived before seven o'clock, alarmed at the strange news. By that time onlookers less frivolous than those at dawn had already arrived and they were making all kinds of conjectures concerning the captive's future. The simplest among them thought that he should be named mayor of the world. Others of sterner mind felt that he should be promoted to the rank of five-star general in order to win all wars. Some visionaries hoped that he could be put to stud in order to implant on earth a race of winged wise men who could take charge of the universe. But Father Gonzaga, before becoming a priest, had been a robust woodcutter. Standing by the wire, he reviewed his catechism in an instant and asked them to open the door so that he could take a close look at that pitiful man who looked more like a huge decrepit hen among the fascinated chickens. He was lying in a corner drying his open wings in the sunlight among the fruit peels and breakfast leftovers that the early risers had thrown him. Alien to the impertinences of the world, he only lifted his antiquarian eyes and murmured something in his dialect when Father Gonzaga went into the chicken coop and said good morning to him in Latin. The parish priest had his first suspicion of an imposter when he saw that he did not understand the language of God or know how to greet His ministers. Then he noticed that seen close up he was much too human: he had an unbearable

smell of the outdoors, the back side of his wings was strewn with parasites and his main feathers had been mistreated by terrestrial winds, and nothing about him measured up to the proud dignity of angels. Then he came out of the chicken coop and in a brief sermon warned the curious against the risks of being ingenuous. He reminded them that the devil had the bad habit of making use of carnival tricks in order to confuse the unwary. He argued that if wings were not the essential element in determining the difference between a hawk and an airplane, they were even less so in the recognition of angels. Nevertheless, he promised to write a letter to his bishop so that the latter would write to his primate so that the latter would write to the Supreme Pontiff in order to get the final verdict from the highest courts.

His prudence fell on sterile hearts. The news of the captive angel spread with such rapidity that after a few hours the courtyard had the bustle of a marketplace and they had to call in troops with fixed bayonets to disperse the mob that was about to knock the house down. Elisenda, her spine all twisted from sweeping up so much marketplace trash, then got the idea of fencing in the yard and charging five cents admission to see the angel.

The curious came from far away. A traveling carnival arrived with a flying acrobat who buzzed over the crowd several times, but no one paid any attention to him because his wings were not those of an angel but, rather, those of a sidereal bat. The most unfortunate invalids on earth came in search of health: a poor woman who since childhood had been counting her heartbeats and had run out of numbers; a Portuguese man who couldn't sleep because the noise of the stars disturbed him; a sleepwalker who got up at night to undo the things he had done while awake; and many others with less serious ailments. In the midst of that shipwreck disorder that made the earth tremble, Pelayo and Elisenda were happy with fatigue, for in less than a week they had crammed their rooms with money and the line of pilgrims waiting their turn to enter still reached beyond the horizon.

The angel was the only one who took no part in his own act. He spent his time trying to get comfortable in his borrowed nest, befuddled by the hellish heat of the oil lamps and sacramental candles that had been placed along the wire. At first they tried to make him eat some mothballs, which, according to the wisdom of the wise neighbor woman, were the food prescribed for angels. But he turned them down, just as he turned down the papal lunches that the penitents brought him, and they never found out whether it was because he was an angel or because he was an old man that in the end he ate nothing but eggplant mush. His only supernatural virtue seemed to be patience. Especially during the first days, when the hens pecked at him, searching for the stellar parasites that proliferated in his wings, and the cripples pulled out feathers to touch their defective parts with, and even the most merciful threw stones at him, trying to get him to rise so they could see him standing. The only time they succeeded in arousing him was when they burned his side with an iron for branding steers, for he had been motionless for so many hours that they thought he was dead. He awoke with a start, ranting in his hermetic language and with tears in his eyes, and he flapped his wings a couple of times, which brought on a whirlwind of chicken dung and lunar dust and a gale of panic that did not seem to be of this world. Although many thought that his reaction had been one not of rage but of pain, from then on they were careful not to annoy him, because the majority understood that his passivity was not that of a hero taking his ease but that of a cataclysm in repose.

Father Gonzaga held back the crowd's frivolity with formulas of maidservant inspiration while awaiting the arrival of a final judgment on the nature of the captive. But the mail from Rome showed no sense of urgency. They spent their time finding out if the prisoner had a navel, if his dialect had any connection with Aramaic, how many times he could fit on the head of a pin, or whether he wasn't just a Norwegian with wings. Those meager letters might have come and gone until the end of time if a providential event had not put an end to the priest's tribulations.

10 It so happened that during those days, among so many other carnival attractions, there arrived in town the traveling show of the woman who had been changed into a spider for having disobeyed her parents. The admission to see her was not only less than the admission to see the angel, but people were permitted to ask her all manner of questions about her absurd state and to examine her up and down so that no one would ever doubt the truth of her horror. She was a frightful tarantula the size of a ram and with the head of a sad maiden. What was most heart-rending, however, was not her outlandish shape but the sincere affliction with which she recounted the details of her misfortune. While still practically a child she had sneaked out of her parents' house to go to a dance, and while she was coming back through the woods after having danced all night without permission, a fearful thunderclap rent the sky in two and through the crack came the lightning bolt of brimstone that changed her into a spider. Her only nourishment came from the meatballs that charitable souls chose to toss into her mouth. A spectacle like that, full of so much human truth and with such a fearful lesson, was bound to defeat without even trying that of a haughty angel who scarcely deigned to look at mortals. Besides, the few miracles attributed to the angel showed a certain mental disorder, like the blind man who didn't recover his sight but grew three new teeth, or the paralytic who didn't get to walk but almost won the lottery, and the leper whose sores sprouted sunflowers. Those consolation miracles, which were more like mocking fun, had already ruined the angel's reputation when the woman who had been changed into a spider finally crushed him completely. That was how Father Gonzaga was cured forever of his insomnia and Pelayo's courtyard went back to being as empty as during the time it had rained for three days and crabs walked through the bedrooms.

The owners of the house had no reason to lament. With the money they saved they built a two-story mansion with balconies and gardens and high netting so that crabs wouldn't get in during the winter, and with iron bars on the windows so that angels couldn't get in. Pelayo also set up a rabbit warren close to town and gave up his job as bailiff for good, and Elisenda bought some satin pumps with high heels and many dresses of iridescent silk, the kind worn on Sunday by the most desirable women in those times. The chicken coop was the only thing that didn't receive any attention. If they washed it down with creolin and burned tears of myrrh inside it every so often, it was not in homage to the angel but to drive away the dungheap stench that still hung everywhere like a ghost and was turning the new house into an old one. At first, when the child learned to walk, they were careful that he not get too close to the chicken coop. But then they began to lose their fears and got used to the smell, and before the child got his second teeth he'd gone inside the chicken coop to play, where the wires were falling apart. The angel was no less standoffish with him than with other mortals, but he tolerated the most ingenious infamies with the patience of a dog who had no illusions. They both came down with chicken pox at the same time. The doctor who took care of the child couldn't resist the temptation to listen to the angel's heart, and he found so much whistling in the heart and so many sounds in his kidneys that it seemed impossible for him to be alive. What surprised him most, however, was the logic of his wings. They seemed so natural on that completely human organism that he couldn't understand why other men didn't have them too.

When the child began school it had been some time since the sun and rain had caused the collapse of the chicken coop. The angel went dragging himself about here and there like a stray dying man. They would drive him out of the bedroom with a broom and a moment later find him in the kitchen. He seemed to be in so many places at the same time that they grew to think that he'd been duplicated, that he was reproducing himself all through the house, and the exasperated and unhinged Elisenda shouted that it was awful living in that hell full of angels. He could scarcely eat and his antiquarian eyes had also become so foggy that he went about bumping into posts. All he had left were the bare cannulae of his last feathers. Pelayo threw a blanket over him and extended him the charity of letting him sleep in the shed, and only then did they notice that he had a temperature at night, and was delirious with the tongue twisters of an old Norwegian. That was one of the few times they became alarmed, for they thought he was going to die and not even the wise neighbor woman had been able to tell them what to do with dead angels.

And yet he not only survived his worst winter, but seemed improved with the first sunny days. He remained motionless for several days in the farthest corner of the courtyard, where no one would see him, and at the beginning of December some large, stiff feathers began to grow on his wings, the feathers of a scarecrow, which looked more like another misfortune of decrepitude. But he must have known the reason for those changes, for he was quite careful that no one should notice them, that no one should hear the sea chanteys that he sometimes sang under the stars. One morning Elisenda was cutting some bunches of onions for lunch when a wind that seemed to come from the high seas blew into the kitchen. Then she went to the window and caught the angel in his first attempts at flight. They were so clumsy that his fingernails opened a furrow in the vegetable patch and he was on the point of knocking the shed down with the ungainly flapping that slipped on the light and couldn't get a grip on the air. But he did manage to gain altitude. Elisenda let out a sigh of relief, for herself and for him, when she saw him pass over the last houses, holding himself up in some way with the risky flapping of a senile vulture. She kept watching him even when she was through cutting the onions and she kept on watching until it was no longer possible for her to see him, because then he was no longer an annoyance in her life but an imaginary dot on the horizon of the sea.

[1968]

Joining the Conversation: Critical Thinking and Writing

1. The subtitle is "A Tale for Children." Do you think that the story is more suited to children than to adults? What in the story do you think children would especially like, or dislike?
2. Is the story chiefly about the inability of adults to perceive and respect the miraculous world?
3. Characterize the narrator of the story.
4. Characterize Pelayo, Elisenda, their son, and the man with wings.

John Updike

John Updike (1932–2009) grew up in Shillington, Pennsylvania, where his father was a teacher and his mother a writer. After receiving a BA degree in 1954 from Harvard, where he edited the Harvard Lampoon *(for which he both wrote and drew), he studied drawing at Oxford for a year, but an offer from* The New Yorker *brought him back to the United States. He was hired as a reporter for the magazine but soon began contributing poetry, essays, and fiction. In 1957 he left the* New Yorker *in order to write independently full-time, though his stories and book reviews appear regularly in it.*

In 1959 Updike published his first book of stories (The Same Door) *and also his first novel* (The Poorhouse Fair); *the next year he published* Rabbit, Run, *a highly successful novel whose protagonist, "Rabbit" Angstrom, has reappeared in three later novels:* Rabbit Redux *(1971),* Rabbit Is Rich *(1981), and* Rabbit at Rest *(1990). The first and the last Rabbit books each won a Pulitzer Prize.*

A & P

In walks these three girls in nothing but bathing suits. I'm in the third checkout slot, with my back to the door, so I don't see them until they're over by the bread. The one that caught my eye first was the one in the plaid green two-piece. She was a chunky kid, with a good tan and a sweet broad soft-looking can with those two crescents of white just under it, where the sun never seems to hit, at the top of the backs of her legs. I stood there with my hand on a box of HiHo crackers trying to remember if I rang it up or not. I ring it up again and the customer starts giving me hell. She's one of these cash-register-watchers, a witch about fifty with rouge on her cheekbones and no eyebrows, and I know it made her day to trip me up. She'd been watching cash registers for fifty years and probably never seen a mistake before.

By the time I got her feathers smoothed and her goodies into a bag—she gives me a little snort in passing, if she'd been born at the right time they would have burned her over in Salem—by the time I get her on her way the girls had circled around the bread and were coming back, without a pushcart, back my way along the counters, in the aisle between the checkouts and the Special bins. They didn't even have shoes on. There was this chunky one, with the two-piece—it was bright green and the seams of the bra were still sharp and her belly was still pretty pale so I guessed she just got it (the suit)—there was this one, with one of those chubby berry-faces, the lips all bunched together under her nose, this one, and a tall one, with black hair that hadn't quite frizzed right, and one of these sunburns right across under the eyes, and a chin that was way too long—you know, the kind of girl other girls think is very "striking" and "attractive" but never quite makes it, as they very well know, which is why they like her so much—and then the third one, that wasn't quite so tall. She was the queen. She kind of led them, the other two peeking around and making their shoulders round. She didn't look around, not this queen, she just walked straight on slowly, on these long white prima-donna legs. She came down a little hard on her heels, as if she didn't walk in her bare feet that much, putting down her heels and then letting the weight move along to her toes as if she was testing the floor with every step, putting a little deliberate extra action into it. You never know for sure how girls' minds work (do they really think it's a mind in there or just a little buzz like a bee in a glass jar?) but you got the idea she had talked the other two into coming in here with her, and now she was showing them how to do it, walk slow and hold yourself straight.

She had on a kind of dirty pink—beige maybe, I don't know—bathing suit with a little nubble all over it and, what got me, the straps were down. They were off her shoulders looped loose around the cool tops of her arms, and I guess as a result the suit had slipped on her, so all around the top of the cloth there was this shining rim. If it hadn't been there you wouldn't have known there could have been anything whiter than those shoulders. With the straps pushed off, there was nothing between the top of the suit and the top of her head except just *her*, this clean bare plane of the top of her chest down from the shoulder bones like a dented sheet of metal tilted in the light. I mean, it was more than pretty.

She had sort of oaky hair that the sun and salt had bleached, done up in a bun that was unravelling, and a kind of prim face. Walking into the A & P with your straps down, I suppose it's the only kind of face you *can* have. She held her head so high her neck, coming up out of those white shoulders, looked kind of stretched, but I didn't mind. The longer her neck was, the more of her there was.

5 She must have felt in the corner of her eye me and over my shoulder Stokesie in the second slot watching, but she didn't tip. Not this queen. She kept her eyes moving across the racks, and stopped, and turned so slow it made my stomach rub the inside of my apron, and buzzed to the other two, who kind of huddled against her for relief, and then they all three of them went up the cat and dog food-breakfast cereal-macaroni-rice-raisins-seasonings-spreads-spaghetti-soft drinks-crackers-and-cookies aisle. From the third slot I look straight up this aisle to the meat counter, and I watched them all the way. The fat one with the tan sort of fumbled with the cookies, but on second thought she put the package back. The sheep pushing their carts down the aisle—the girls were walking against the usual traffic (not that we have one-way signs or anything)—were pretty hilarious. You could see them, when Queenie's white shoulders dawned on them, kind of jerk, or hop, or hiccup, but their eyes snapped back to their own baskets and on they pushed. I bet you could set off dynamite in the A & P and the people would by and large keep reaching and checking oatmeal off their lists and muttering "Let me see, there was a third thing, began with A, asparagus, no, ah, yes, applesauce!" or whatever it is they do mutter. But there was no doubt, this jiggled them. A few house slaves in pin curlers even look around after pushing their carts past to make sure what they had seen was correct.

You know, it's one thing to have a girl in a bathing suit down on the beach, where what with the glare nobody can look at each other much anyway, and another thing in the cool of the A & P, under the fluorescent lights, against all those stacked packages, with her feet paddling along naked over our checker-board green-and-cream, rubber-tile floor.

"Oh, Daddy," Stokesie said beside me. "I feel so faint."

"Darling," I said. "Hold me tight." Stokesie's married, with two babies chalked up on his fuselage already, but as far as I can tell that's the only difference. He's twenty-two, and I was nineteen this April.

"Is it done?" he asks, the responsible married man finding his voice. I forgot to say he thinks he's going to be a manager some sunny day, maybe in 1990 when it's called the Great Alexandrov and Petrooshki Tea Company or something.

10 What he meant was, our town is five miles from a beach, with a big summer colony out on the Point, but we're right in the middle of town, and the women generally put on a shirt or shorts or something before they get out of the car into

the street. And anyway these are usually women with six children and varicose veins mapping their legs and nobody, including them, could care less. As I say, we're right in the middle of town, and if you stand at our front doors you can see two banks and the Congregational church and the newspaper store and three real estate offices and about twenty-seven old freeloaders tearing up Central Street because the sewer broke again. It's not as if we're on the Cape; we're north of Boston and there's people in this town haven't seen the ocean for twenty years.

The girls had reached the meat counter and were asking McMahon something. He pointed, they pointed, and they shuffled out of sight behind a pyramid of Diet Delight peaches. All that was left for us to see was old McMahon patting his mouth and looking after them sizing up their joints. Poor kids, I began to feel sorry for them, they couldn't help it.

Now here comes the sad part of the story, at least my family says it's sad, but I don't think it's so sad myself. The store's pretty empty, it being Thursday afternoon, so there was nothing much to do except lean on the register and wait for the girls to show up again. The whole store was like a pinball machine and I didn't know which tunnel they'd come out of. After a while they come around out of the far aisle, around the light bulbs, records at discount of the Caribbean Six or Tony Martin Sings or some such gunk you wonder they waste the wax on, six-packs of candy bars, and plastic toys done up in cellophane that fall apart when a kid looks at them anyway. Around they come, Queenie still leading the way, and holding a little gray jar in her hand. Slots Three through Seven are unmanned and I could see her wondering between Stokes and me, but Stokesie with his usual luck draws an old party in baggy gray pants who stumbles up with four giant cans of pineapple juice (what do these bums *do* with all that pineapple juice? I've often asked myself) so the girls come to me. Queenie puts down the jar and I take it into my fingers icy cold. Kingfish Fancy Herring Snacks in Pure Sour Cream: 49¢. Now her hands are empty, not a ring or a bracelet, bare as God made them, and I wonder where the money's coming from. Still with the prim look she lifts a folded dollar bill out of the hollow at the center of her nubbled pink top. The jar went heavy in my hand. Really, I thought that was so cute.

Then everybody's luck begins to run out. Lengel comes in from haggling with a truck full of cabbages on the lot and is about to scuttle into the door marked MANAGER behind which he hides all day when the girls touch his eye. Lengel's pretty dreary, teaches Sunday school and the rest, but he doesn't miss that much. He comes over and says, "Girls, this isn't the beach."

Queenie blushes, though maybe it's just a brush of sunburn I was noticing for the first time, now that she was so close. "My mother asked me to pick up a jar of herring snacks." Her voice kind of startled me, the way voices do when you see the people first, coming out so flat and dumb yet kind of tony, too, the way it ticked over "pick up" and "snacks." All of a sudden I slid right down her voice into her living room. Her father and the other men were standing around in ice-cream coats and bow ties and the women were in sandals picking up herring snacks on toothpicks off a big glass plate and they were all holding drinks the color of water with olives and sprigs of mint in them. When my parents have somebody over they get lemonade and if it's a real racy affair Schlitz in tall glasses with "They'll Do It Every Time" cartoons stencilled on.

15 "That's all right," Lengel said. "But this isn't the beach." His repeating this struck me as funny, as if it had just occurred to him, and he had been thinking all these years the A & P was a great big dune and he was the head lifeguard. He didn't like my smiling—as I say he doesn't miss much—but he concentrates on giving the girls that sad Sunday-school-superintendent stare.

Queenie's blush was no sunburn now, and the plump one in plaid, that I liked better from the back—a really sweet can—pipes up, "We weren't doing any shopping. We just came in for the one thing."

"That makes no difference," Lengel tells her, and I could see from the way his eyes went that he hadn't noticed she was wearing at two-piece before. "We want you decently dressed when you come in here."

"We *are* decent," Queenie says suddenly, her lower lip pushing, getting sore now that she remembers her place, a place from which the crowd that runs the A & P must look pretty crummy. Fancy Herring Snacks flashed in her very blue eyes.

"Girls, I don't want to argue with you. After this come in here with your shoulders covered. It's our policy." He turns his back. That's policy for you. Policy is what the kingpins want. What the others want is juvenile delinquency.

20 All this while, the customers had been showing up with their carts but, you know, sheep, seeing a scene, they had all bunched up on Stokesie, who shook open a paper bag as gently as peeling a peach, not wanting to miss a word. I could feel in the silence everybody getting nervous, most of all Lengel, who asks me, "Sammy, have you rung up this purchase?"

I thought and said "No" but it wasn't about that I was thinking. I go through the punches, 4, 9, GROC, TOT—it's more complicated than you think and after you do it often enough, it begins to make a little song, that you hear words to, in my case "Hello (*bing*) there, you (*gung*) hap-py *pee*pul (*splat*)!"—the *splat* being the drawer flying out. I uncrease the bill, tenderly as you may imagine, it just having come from between the two smoothest scoops of vanilla I had ever known were there, and pass a half and a penny into her narrow pink palm and nestle the herrings in a bag and twist its neck and hand it over, all the time thinking.

The girls, and who'd blame them, are in a hurry to get out, so I say "I quit" to Lengel quick enough for them to hear, hoping they'll stop and watch me, their unsuspected hero. They keep right on going, into the electric eye; the door flies open and they flicker across the lot to their car, Queenie and Plaid and Big Tall Goony-Goony (not that as raw material she was so bad), leaving me with Lengel and a kink in his eyebrow.

"Did you say something, Sammy?"

"I said I quit."

25 "I thought you did."

"You didn't have to embarrass them."

"It was they who were embarrassing us."

I started to say something that came out "Fiddle-de-doo." It's a saying of my grandmother's, and I know she would have been pleased.

"I don't think you know what you're saying," Lengel said.

30 "I know you don't," I said. "But I do." I pull the bow at the back of my apron and start shrugging it off my shoulders. A couple customers that had been heading for my slot begin to knock against each other, like scared pigs in a chute.

Lengel sighs and begins to look very patient and old and gray. He's been a friend of my parents for years. "Sammy, you don't want to do this to your Mom and Dad," he tells me. It's true, I don't. But it seems to me that once you begin a gesture it's fatal not to go through with it. I fold the apron, "Sammy" stitched in red on the pocket, and put it on the counter, and drop the bow tie on top of it. The bow tie is theirs, if you've ever wondered. "You'll feel this for the rest of your life," Lengel says, and I know that's true, too, but remembering how he made that pretty girl blush makes me so scrunchy inside I punch the No Sale tab and the machine whirs "pee-pul" and the drawer splats out. One advantage to this scene taking place in summer, I can follow this up with a clean exit, there's no fumbling around getting your coat and galoshes, I just saunter into the electric eye in my white shirt that my mother ironed the night before, and the door heaves itself open, and outside the sunshine is skating round on the asphalt.

I look around for my girls, but they're gone, of course. There wasn't anybody but some young married screaming with her children about some candy they didn't get by the door of a powder-blue Falcon station wagon. Looking back in the big windows, over the bags of peat moss and aluminum lawn furniture stacked on the pavement, I could see Lengel in my place in the slot, checking the sheep through. His face was dark gray and his back stiff, as if he'd just had an injection of iron, and my stomach kind of fell as I felt how hard the world was going to be to me hereafter.

[1962]

Joining the Conversation: Critical Thinking and Writing

1. In what sort of community is this A & P located? To what extent does this community resemble yours?
2. Do you think Sammy is a male chauvinist pig? Why, or why not? And if you think he is, do you find the story offensive? Again, why or why not? Present your response in the form of a detailed argument.
3. In the last line of the story Sammy says, "I felt how hard the world was going to be to me hereafter." Do you think the world is going to be hard to Sammy? Why, or why not? And if it is hard to him, is this because of a virtue or a weakness in Sammy?
4. Write Lengel's version of the story (500–1000 words) as he might narrate it to his wife during dinner. Or write the story from Queenie's point of view.
5. In speaking of contemporary fiction, Updike said:

    > I want stories to startle and engage me within the first few sentences, and in their middle to widen or deepen or sharpen my knowledge of human activity, and to end by giving me a sensation of completed statement.

    Let's assume that you share Updike's view of what a story should do. To what extent do you think "A & P" fulfills these demands? (You may want to put your response in the form of a letter to Updike.)

DIANA CHANG

Diana Chang, author of several novels and books of poems, taught creative writing at Barnard College. She identifies herself as an American writer whose background is mostly Chinese.

The Oriental Contingent

Connie couldn't remember whose party it was, whose house. She had an impression of kerosene lamps on brown wicker tables, of shapes talking in doorways. It was summer, almost the only time Connie has run into her since, too, and someone was saying, "You must know Lisa Mallory."

"I don't think so."

"She's here. You must know her."

Later in the evening, it was someone else who introduced her to a figure perched on the balustrade of the steps leading to the lawn where more shapes milled. In stretching out a hand to shake Connie's, the figure almost fell off sideways. Connie pushed her back upright onto her perch and, peering, took in the fact that Lisa Mallory had a Chinese face. For a long instant, she felt nonplussed, and was rendered speechless.

5 But Lisa Mallory was filling in the silence. "Well, now, Connie Sung," she said, not enthusiastically but with a kind of sophisticated interest. "I'm not in music myself, but Paul Wu's my cousin. Guilt by association!" She laughed. "No-tone music, I call his. He studied with John Cage, Varèse,[1] and so forth."

Surprised that Lisa knew she was a violinist, Connie murmured something friendly, wondering if she should simply ask outright, "I'm sure I should know, but what do you do?" but she hesitated, taking in her appearance instead, while Lisa went on with, "It's world class composing. Nothing's wrong with the level. But it's hard going for the layman, believe me."

Lisa Mallory wore a one-of-a-kind kimono dress, but it didn't make her look Japanese at all, and her hair was drawn back tightly in a braid which stood out from close to the top of her head horizontally. You could probably lift her off her feet by grasping it, like the handle of a pot.

"You should give a concert here, Connie," she said, using her first name right away, Connie noticed, like any American. "Lots of culturati around." Even when she wasn't actually speaking, she pursued her own line of thought actively and seemed to find herself mildly amusing.

"I'm new to the area," Connie said, deprecatingly. "I've just been a weekend guest, actually, till a month ago."

10 "It's easy to be part of it. Nothing to it. I should know. You'll see."

"I wish it weren't so dark," Connie found herself saying, waving her hand in front of her eyes as if the night were a veil to brush aside. She recognized in herself that intense need to see, to see into fellow Orientals, to fathom them. So far, Lisa Mallory had not given her enough clues, and the darkness itself seemed to be interfering.

Lisa dropped off her perch. "It's important to be true to oneself," she said. "Keep the modern stuff out of your repertory. Be romantic. Don't look like that! You're best at the romantics. Anyhow, take it from me. I know. And *I* like what I like."

Released by her outspokenness, Connie laughed and asked, "I'm sure I should know, but what is it that you do?" She was certain Lisa would say something like, "I'm with a public relations firm." "I'm in city services."

But she replied, "What do all Chinese excel at?" Not as if she'd asked a rhetorical question, she waited, then answered herself. "Well, aren't we all physicists, musicians, architects, or in software?"

15 At that point a voice broke in, followed by a large body which put his arms around both women, "The Oriental contingent! I've got to break this up."

Turning, Lisa kissed him roundly, and said over her shoulder to Connie, "I'll take him away before he tells us we look alike!"

They melted into the steps below, and Connie, feeling put off balance and somehow slow-witted, was left to think over her new acquaintance.

* * *

[1]**John Cage** (1912–1992) and **Edgard Varèse** (1883–1965) were important and controversial avante-garde composers.

"Hello, Lisa Mallory," Connie Sung always said on the infrequent occasions when they ran into one another. She always said "Hello, Lisa Mallory," with a shyness she did not understand in herself. It was strange, but they had no mutual friends except for Paul Wu, and Connie had not seen him in ages. Connie had no one of whom to ask her questions. But sometime soon, she'd be told Lisa's maiden name. Sometime she'd simply call her Lisa. Sometime what Lisa did with her life would be answered.

Three, four years passed, with their running into one another at receptions and openings, and still Lisa Mallory remained an enigma. Mildly amused herself, Connie wondered if other people, as well, found her inscrutable. But none of her American friends (though, of course, Lisa and she were Americans, too, she had to remind herself), none of their Caucasian friends seemed curious about backgrounds. In their accepting way, they did not wonder about Lisa's background, or about Connie's or Paul Wu's. Perhaps they assumed they were all cut from the same cloth. But to Connie, the Orientals she met were unread books, books she never had the right occasion or time to fully pursue.

She didn't even see the humor in her situation—it was such an issue with her. The fact was she felt less, much less, sure of herself when she was with real Chinese.

As she was realizing this, the truth suddenly dawned on her. Lisa Mallory never referred to her own background because it was more Chinese than Connie's, and therefore of a higher order. She was tact incarnate. All along, she had been going out of her way not to embarrass Connie. Yes, yes. Her assurance was definitely uppercrust (perhaps her father had been in the diplomatic service), and her offhand didacticness, her lack of self-doubt, was indeed characteristically Chinese-Chinese. Connie was not only impressed by these traits, but also put on the defensive because of them.

Connie let out a sigh—a sigh that follows the solution to a nagging problem . . . Lisa's mysteriousness. But now Connie knew only too clearly that her own background made her decidedly inferior. Her father was a second-generation gynecologist who spoke hardly any Chinese. Yes, inferior and totally without recourse.

Of course, at one of the gatherings, Connie met Bill Mallory, too. He was simply American, maybe Catholic, possibly lapsed. She was not put off balance by him at all. But most of the time he was away on business, and Lisa cropped up at functions as single as Connie.

Then one day, Lisa had a man in tow—wiry and tall, he looked Chinese from the Shantung area, or perhaps from Beijing, and his styled hair made him appear vaguely artistic.

"Connie," I'd like you to meet Eric Li. He got out at the beginning of the *detente,* went to Berkeley, and is assimilating a mile-a-minute," Lisa said, with her usual irony. "Bill found him and is grooming him, though he came with his own charisma."

Eric waved her remark aside. "Lisa has missed her calling. She was born to be in PR," he said, with an accent.

"Is that what she does?" Connie put in at once, looking only at him. "Is that her profession?"

"You don't know?" he asked, with surprise.

Though she was greeting someone else, Lisa turned and answered, "I'm a fabrics tycoon, I think I can say without immodesty." She moved away and continued her conversation with the other friend.

30 Behind his hand, he said, playfully, as though letting Connie in on a secret, "Factories in Hongkong and Taipei, and now he's—Bill, that is—is exploring them on the mainland."

"With her fabulous contacts over there!" Connie exclaimed, now seeing it all. "Of course, what a wonderful business combination they must make."

Eric was about to utter something, but stopped, and said flatly, "I have all the mainland contacts, even though I was only twenty when I left, but my parents . . ."

"How interesting," Connie murmured lamely. "I see," preoccupied as she was with trying to put two and two together.

Lisa was back and said without an introduction, continuing her line of thought, "You two look good together, if I have to say so myself. Why don't you ask him to one of your concerts? And you, Eric, you're in America now, so don't stand on ceremony, or you'll be out in left field." She walked away with someone for another drink.

35 Looking uncomfortable, but recovering himself with a smile, Eric said, "Lisa makes me feel more Chinese than I am becoming—it is her directness, I suspect. In China, we'd say she is too much like a man."

At which Connie found herself saying, "She makes me feel *less* Chinese."

"Less!"

"Less Chinese than she is."

"That is not possible," Eric said, with a shade of contempt—for whom? Lisa or Connie? He barely suppressed a laugh, cold as Chinese laughter could be.

40 Connie blurted out, "I'm a failed Chinese. Yes, and it's to you that I need to say it." She paused and repeated emphatically, "I am a failed Chinese." Her heart was beating quicker, but she was glad to have got that out, a confession and a definition that might begin to free her. "Do you know you make me feel that, too? You've been here only about ten years, right?"

"Right, and I'm thirty-one."

"You know what I think? I think it's harder for a Chinese to do two things."

At that moment, an American moved in closer, looking pleased somehow to be with them.

She continued, "It's harder for us to become American than, say, for a German, and it's also harder not to remain residually Chinese, even if you are third generation."

45 Eric said blandly, "Don't take yourself so seriously. You can't help being an American product."

Trying to be comforting, the American interjected with, "The young lady is not a product, an object. She is a human being, and there is no difference among peoples that I can see."

"I judge myself both as a Chinese and as an American," Connie said.

"You worry too much," Eric said, impatiently. Then he looked around and though she wasn't in sight, he lowered his voice. "She is what she is. I know what she is. But she avoids going to Hongkong. She avoids it."

Connie felt turned around. "Avoids it?"

50 "Bill's in Beijing right now. She's here. How come?"

"I don't know," Connie replied, as though an answer had been required of her.

"She makes up many excuses, reasons. Ask her. Ask her yourself," he said, pointedly.

"Oh, I couldn't do that. By the way, I'm going on a concert tour next year in three cities—Shanghai, Beijing and Nanking," Connie said. "It'll be my first time in China."

"Really! You must be very talented to be touring at your age," he said, genuinely interested for the first time. Because she was going to China, or because she now came across as an over-achiever, even though Chinese American?

"I'm just about your age," she said, realizing then that maybe Lisa Mallory had left them alone purposely.

"You could both pass as teenagers!" the American exclaimed.

Two months later, she ran into Lisa again. As usual, Lisa began in the middle of her own thoughts. "Did he call?"

"Who? Oh. No, no."

"Well, it's true he's been in China the last three weeks with Bill. They'll be back this weekend."

Connie saw her opportunity. "Are you planning to go to China yourself?"

For the first time, Lisa seemed at a loss for words. She raised her shoulders, than let them drop. Too airily, she said, "You know, there's always Paris. I can't bear not to go to Paris, if I'm to take a trip."

"But you're Chinese. You *have* been to China, you came from China originally, didn't you?"

"I could go to Paris twice a year, I love it so," Lisa said. "And then there's London, Florence, Venice."

"But—but your business contacts?"

"*My* contacts? Bill, he's the businessman who makes the contacts. Always has. I take care of the New York office, which is a considerable job. We have a staff of eighty-five."

Connie said, "I told Eric I'll be giving a tour in China. I'm taking Chinese lessons right now."

Lisa Mallory laughed, "Save your time. They'll still be disdainful over there. See, *they* don't care," and she waved her hand at the crowd. "Some of them have been born in Buffalo, too! It's the Chinese you can't fool. They know you're not the genuine article—you and I."

Her face was suddenly heightened in color, and she was breathing as if ready to flee from something. "Yes, you heard right. I was born in Buffalo."

"You were!" Connie exclaimed before she could control her amazement.

"Well, what about you?" Lisa retorted. She was actually shaking and trying to hide it by making sudden gestures.

"Westchester."

"But your parents at least were Chinese."

"Well, so were, so are, yours!"

"I was adopted by Americans. My full name is Lisa Warren Mallory."

Incredulous, Connie said, "I'm more Chinese than you!"

"Who isn't?" She laughed, unhappily. "Having Chinese parents makes all the difference. We're worlds apart."

"And all the time I thought . . . never mind what I thought."

"You have it over me. It's written all over you. I could tell even in the dark that night."

"Oh, Lisa," Connie said to comfort her, "none of this matters to anybody except us. Really and truly. They're too busy with their own problems."

"The only time I feel Chinese is when I'm embarrassed I'm not more Chinese—which is a totally Chinese reflex I'd give anything to be rid of!"

"I know what you mean."

"And as for Eric looking down his nose at me, he's knocking himself out to be so American, *but as a secure Chinese!* What's so genuine about that article?"

Both of them struck their heads laughing, but their eyes were not merry.

"Say it again," Connie asked of her, "say it again that my being more Chinese is written all over me."

"Consider it said," Lisa said. "My natural mother happened to be there at the time—I can't help being born in Buffalo."

"I know, I know," Connie said with feeling. "If only you had had some say in the matter."

"It's only Orientals who haunt me!" Lisa stamped her foot. "Only them!"

"I'm so sorry," Connie Sung said, for all of them. "It's all so turned around."

"So I'm made in America, so there!" Lisa Mallory declared, making a sniffing sound, and seemed to be recovering her sangfroid.

Connie felt tired—as if she'd traveled—but a lot had been settled on the way.

[1989]

Joining the Conversation: Critical Thinking and Writing

1. In an interview published in 1995, Diana Chang says of "The Oriental Contingent": "[This story] is about two Chinese-American women who meet, each trying to hide from the other that she feels inadequate as a Chinese, not as an American." Please present an argument in support of Chang's comment.
2. One scholar who has written about "The Oriental Contingent" maintains that in it Chang "challenges the myth of authentic Asian-American identity." Another scholar says, to the contrary, that it does not. Construct a good argument for your own interpretation.
3. In her 1995 interview, Chang mentions in passing that as a writer she is interested in the "emotion of thought." What do you think this phrase means? Do you perceive examples of emotion of thought in this story?

GISH JEN

Gish Jen, born in 1955 in Yonkers, New York, and the daughter of Chinese immigrants, was named Lillian Jen by her parents. She disliked the name Lillian, and her school friends created a new name for her, derived from the name of a famous actress of the silent screen—Lillian Gish. Jen graduated from Harvard and then, in accordance with her parents' wishes, went to Stanford Business School (MBA, 1980). Then, following her own wishes, Jen went to the University of Iowa, where in 1983 she earned an M.F.A. in the writing program. She has published three novels and a book of short stories, Who's Irish? *We reprint the title story.*

Who's Irish?

In China, people say mixed children are supposed to be smart, and definitely my granddaughter Sophie is smart. But Sophie is wild, Sophie is not like my daughter Natalie, or like me. I am work hard my whole life, and fierce besides. My husband always used to say he is afraid of me, and in our restaurant, busboys and cooks all afraid of me too. Even the gang members come for protection money, they try to talk to my husband. When I am there, they stay away. If they come by mistake, they pretend they are come to eat. They hide behind the menu, they order a lot of food. They talk about their mothers. Oh, my mother have some arthritis, need to take herbal medicine, they say. Oh, my mother getting old, her hair all white now.

I say, Your mother's hair used to be white, but since she dye it, it become black again. Why don't you go home once in a while and take a look? I tell them, Confucius[1] say a filial son knows what color his mother's hair is.

My daughter is fierce too, she is vice president in the bank now. Her new house is big enough for everybody to have their own room, including me. But Sophie take after Natalie's husband's family, their name is Shea. Irish. I always thought Irish people are like Chinese people, work so hard on the railroad, but now I know why the Chinese beat the Irish. Of course, not all Irish are like the Shea family, of course not. My daughter tell me I should not say Irish this, Irish that.

How do you like it when people say the Chinese this, the Chinese that, she say.

5 You know, the British call the Irish heathen, just like they call the Chinese, she say.

You think the Opium War[2] was bad, how would you like to live right next door to the British, she say.

And that is that. My daughter have a funny habit when she win an argument, she take a sip of something and look away, so the other person is not embarrassed. So I am not embarrassed. I do not call anybody anything either. I just happen to mention about the Shea family, an interesting fact: four brothers in the family, and not one of them work. The mother, Bess, have a job before she got sick, she was executive secretary in a big company. She is handle everything for a big shot, you would be surprised how complicated her job is, not just type this, type that. Now she is a nice woman with a clean house. But her boys, every one of them is on welfare, or so-called severance pay, or so-called disability pay. Something. They say they cannot find work, this is not the economy of the fifties, but I say, Even the black people doing better these days, some of them live so fancy, you'd be surprised. Why the Shea family have so much trouble? They are white people, they speak English. When I come to this country, I have no money and do not speak English. But my husband and I own our restaurant before he die. Free and clear, no mortgage. Of course, I understand I am just lucky, come from a country where the food is popular all over the world. I understand it is not the Shea family's fault they come from a country where everything is boiled. Still, I say.

She's right, we should broaden our horizons, say one brother, Jim, at Thanksgiving. Forget about the car business. Think about egg rolls.

Pad thai, say another brother, Mike. I'm going to make my fortune in pad thai. It's going to be the new pizza.

10 I say, You people too picky about what you sell. Selling egg rolls not good enough for you, but at least my husband and I can say, We made it. What can you say? Tell me. What can you say?

Everybody chew their tough turkey.

I especially cannot understand my daughter's husband John, who has no job but cannot take care of Sophie either. Because he is a man, he say, and that's the end of the sentence.

[1]**Confucius** Chinese religious leader and philosopher (551–479 B.C.E.). [2]**Opium War** conflicts, 1839–1842 and 1856–1860, between China and Great Britain involving the opium trade.

Plain boiled food, plain boiled thinking. Even his name is plain boiled: John. Maybe because I grew up with black bean sauce and hoisin sauce and garlic sauce, I always feel something is missing when my son-in-law talk.

But, okay: so my son-in-law can be man, I am baby-sitter. Six hours a day, same as the old sitter, crazy Amy, who quit. This is not so easy, now that I am sixty-eight, Chinese age almost seventy. Still, I try. In China, daughter take care of mother. Here it is the other way around. Mother help daughter, mother ask, Anything else I can do? Otherwise daughter complain mother is not supportive. I tell daughter, We do not have this word in Chinese, *supportive.* But my daughter too busy to listen, she has to go to meeting, she has to write memo while her husband go to the gym to be a man. My daughter say otherwise he will be depressed. Seems like all his life he has this trouble, depression.

No one wants to hire someone who is depressed, she say. It is important for him to keep his spirits up.

Beautiful wife, beautiful daughter, beautiful house, oven can clean itself automatically. No money left over, because only one income, but lucky enough, got the baby-sitter for free. If John lived in China, he would be very happy. But he is not happy. Even at the gym things go wrong. One day, he pull a muscle. Another day, weight room too crowded. Always something.

Until finally, hooray, he has a job. Then he feel pressure.

I need to concentrate, he say. I need to focus.

He is going to work for insurance company. Salesman job. A paycheck, he say, and at least he will wear clothes instead of gym shorts. My daughter buy him some special candy bars from the health-food store. They say THINK! on them, and are supposed to help John think.

John is a good-looking boy, you have to say that, especially now that he shave so you can see his face.

I am an old man in a young man's game, say John.

I will need a new suit, say John.

This time I am not going to shoot myself in the foot, say John.

Good, I say.

She means to be supportive, my daughter say. Don't start the send her back to China thing, because we can't.

Sophie is three years old American age, but already I see her nice Chinese side swallowed up by her wild Shea side. She looks like mostly Chinese. Beautiful black hair, beautiful black eyes. Nose perfect size, not so flat looks like something fell down, not so large looks like some big deal got stuck in wrong face. Everything just right, only her skin is a brown surprise to John's family. So brown, they say. Even John say it. She never goes in the sun, still she is that color, he say. Brown. They say, Nothing the matter with brown. They are just surprised. So brown. Nattie is not that brown, they say. They say, It seems like Sophie should be a color in between Nattie and John. Seems funny, a girl named Sophie Shea be brown. But she is brown, maybe her name should be Sophie Brown. She never go in the sun, still she is that color, they say. Nothing the matter with brown. They are just surprised.

The Shea family talk is like this sometimes, going around and around like a Christmas-tree train.

Maybe John is not her father, I say one day, to stop the train. And sure enough, train wreck. None of the brothers ever say the word *brown* to me again.

Instead, John's mother, Bess, say, I hope you are not offended.

30 She say, I did my best on those boys. But raising four boys with no father is no picnic.

You have a beautiful family, I say.

I'm getting old, she say.

You deserve a rest, I say. Too many boys make you old.

I never had a daughter, she say. You have a daughter.

35 I have a daughter, I say. Chinese people don't think a daughter is so great, but you're right. I have a daughter.

I was never against the marriage, you know, she say. I never thought John was marrying down. I always thought Nattie was just as good as white.

I was never against the marriage either, I say. I just wonder if they look at the whole problem.

Of course you pointed out the problem, you are a mother, she say. And now we both have a granddaughter. A little brown granddaughter, she is so precious to me.

I laugh. A little brown granddaughter, I say. To tell you the truth, I don't know how she came out so brown.

40 We laugh some more. These days Bess need a walker to walk. She take so many pills, she need two glasses of water to get them all down. Her favorite TV show is about bloopers, and she love her bird feeder. All day long, she can watch that bird feeder, like a cat.

I can't wait for her to grow up, Bess say. I could use some female company.

Too many boys, I say.

Boys are fine, she say. But they do surround you after a while.

You should take a break, come live with us, I say. Lots of girls at our house.

45 Be careful what you offer, say Bess with a wink. Where I come from, people mean for you to move in when they say a thing like that.

Nothing the matter with Sophie's outside, that's the truth. It is inside that she is like not any Chinese girl I ever see. We go to the park, and this is what she does. She stand up in the stroller. She take off all her clothes and throw them in the fountain.

Sophie! I say. Stop!

But she just laugh like a crazy person. Before I take over as baby-sitter, Sophie has that crazy-person sitter, Amy the guitar player. My daughter thought this Amy very creative—another word we do not talk about in China. In China, we talk about whether we have difficulty or no difficulty. We talk about whether life is bitter or not bitter. In America, all day long, people talk about creative. Never mind that I cannot even look at this Amy, with her shirt so short that her belly button showing. This Amy think Sophie should love her body. So when Sophie take off her diaper, Amy laugh. When Sophie run around naked, Amy say she wouldn't want to wear a diaper either. When Sophie go *shu-shu* in her lap, Amy laugh and say there are no germs in pee. When Sophie take off her shoes, Amy say bare feet is best, even the pediatrician say so. That is why Sophie now walk around with no shoes like a beggar child. Also why Sophie love to take off her clothes.

Turn around! say the boys in the park. Let's see that ass!

50 Of course, Sophie does not understand. Sophie clap her hands, I am the only one to say, No! This is not a game.

It has nothing to do with John's family, my daughter say. Amy was too permissive, that's all.

But I think if Sophie was not wild inside, she would not take off her shoes and clothes to begin with.

You never take off your clothes when you were little, I say. All my Chinese friends had babies, I never saw one of them act wild like that.

Look, my daughter say. I have a big presentation tomorrow.

John and my daughter agree Sophie is a problem, but they don't know what to do.

You spank her, she'll stop, I say another day.

But they say, Oh no.

In America, parents not supposed to spank the child.

It gives them low self-esteem, my daughter say. And that leads to problems later, as I happen to know.

My daughter never have big presentation the next day when the subject of spanking come up.

I don't want you to touch Sophie, she say. No spanking, period.

Don't tell me what to do, I say.

I'm not telling you what to do, say my daughter. I'm telling you how I feel.

I am not your servant, I say. Don't you dare talk to me like that.

My daughter have another funny habit when she lose an argument. She spread out all her fingers and look at them, as if she like to make sure they are still there.

My daughter is fierce like me, but she and John think it is better to explain to Sophie that clothes are a good idea. This is not so hard in the cold weather. In the warm weather, it is very hard.

Use your words, my daughter say. That's what we tell Sophie. How about if you set a good example.

As if good example mean anything to Sophie. I am so fierce, the gang members who used to come to the restaurant all afraid of me, but Sophie is not afraid.

I say, Sophie, if you take off your clothes, no snack.

I say, Sophie, if you take off your clothes, no lunch.

I say, Sophie, if you take off your clothes, no park.

Pretty soon we are stay home all day, and by the end of six hours she still did not have one thing to eat. You never saw a child stubborn like that.

I'm hungry! she cry when my daughter come home.

What's the matter, doesn't your grandmother feed you? My daughter laugh.

No! Sophie say. She doesn't feed me anything!

My daughter laugh again. Here you go, she say.

She say to John, Sophie must be growing.

Growing like a weed, I say.

Still Sophie take off her clothes, until one day I spank her. Not too hard, but she cry and cry, and when I tell her if she doesn't put her clothes back on I'll spank her again, she put her clothes back on. Then I tell her she is good girl, and give her some food to eat. The next day we go to the park and, like a nice Chinese girl, she does not take off her clothes.

She stop taking off her clothes, I report. Finally!

How did you do it? my daughter ask.

After twenty-eight years experience with you, I guess I learn something, I say.

It must have been a phase, John say, and his voice is suddenly like an expert.

His voice is like an expert about everything these days, now that he carry a leather briefcase, and wear shiny shoes, and can go shopping for a new car. On the company, he say. The company will pay for it, but he will be able to drive it whenever he want.

A free car, he say. How do you like that.

It's good to see you in the saddle again, my daughter say. Some of your family patterns are scary.

At least I don't drink, he say. He say, And I'm not the only one with scary family patterns.

That's for sure, say my daughter.

Everyone is happy. Even I am happy, because there is more trouble with Sophie, but now I think I can help her Chinese side fight against her wild side. I teach her to eat food with fork or spoon or chopsticks, she cannot just grab into the middle of a bowl of noodles. I teach her not to play with garbage cans. Sometimes I spank her, but not too often, and not too hard.

90 Still, there are problems. Sophie like to climb everything. If there is a railing, she is never next to it. Always she is on top of it. Also, Sophie like to hit the mommies of her friends. She learn this from her playground best friend, Sinbad, who is four. Sinbad wear army clothes every day and like to ambush his mommy. He is the one who dug a big hole under the play structure, a foxhole he call it, all by himself. Very hardworking. Now he wait in the foxhole with a shovel full of wet sand. When his mommy come, he throw it right at her.

Oh, it's all right, his mommy say. You can't get rid of war games, it's part of their imaginative play. All the boys go through it.

Also, he like to kick his mommy, and one day he tell Sophie to kick his mommy too.

I wish this story is not true.

Kick her, kick her! Sinbad say.

95 Sophie kick her. A little kick, as if she just so happened was swinging her little leg and didn't realize that big mommy leg was in the way. Still I spank Sophie and make Sophie say sorry, and what does the mommy say?

Really, it's all right, she say. It didn't hurt.

After that, Sophie learn she can attack mommies in the playground, and some will say, Stop, but others will say, Oh, she didn't mean it, especially if they realize Sophie will be punished.

This is how, one day, bigger trouble come. The bigger trouble start when Sophie hide in the foxhole with that shovel full of sand. She wait, and when I come look for her, she throw it at me. All over my nice clean clothes.

Did you ever see a Chinese girl act this way?

100 Sophie! I say. Come out of there, say you're sorry.

But she does not come out. Instead, she laugh. Naaah, naah-na, naaa-naaa, she say.

I am not exaggerate: millions of children in China, not one act like this.

Sophie! I say. Now! Come out now!

But she know she is in big trouble. She know if she come out, what will happen next. So she does not come out. I am sixty-eight, Chinese age almost seventy, how can I crawl under there to catch her? Impossible. So I yell, yell, yell, and what happen? Nothing. A Chinese mother would help, but American mothers, they look at you, they shake their head, they go home. And, of course, a Chinese child would give up, but not Sophie.

105 I hate you! she yell. I hate you, Meanie!

Meanie is my new name these days.

Long time this goes on, long long time. The foxhole is deep, you cannot see too much, you don't know where is the bottom. You cannot hear too much either.

If she does not yell, you cannot even know she is still there or not. After a while, getting cold out, getting dark out. No one left in the playground, only us.

Sophie, I say. How did you become stubborn like this? I am go home without you now.

I try to use a stick, chase her out of there, and once or twice I hit her, but still she does not come out. So finally I leave. I go outside the gate.

Bye-bye! I say. I'm go home now.

But still she does not come out and does not come out. Now it is dinnertime, the sky is black. I think I should maybe go get help, but how can I leave a little girl by herself in the playground? A bad man could come. A rat could come. I go back in to see what is happen to Sophie. What if she have a shovel and is making a tunnel to escape?

Sophie! I say.

No answer.

Sophie!

I don't know if she is alive. I don't know if she is fall asleep down there. If she is crying, I cannot hear her.

So I take the stick and poke.

Sophie! I say. I promise I no hit you. If you come out, I give you a lollipop.

No answer. By now I worried. What to do, what to do, what to do? I poke some more, even harder, so that I am poking and poking when my daughter and John suddenly appear.

What are you doing? What is going on? say my daughter.

Put down that stick? say my daughter.

You are crazy! say my daughter.

John wiggle under the structure, into the foxhole, to rescue Sophie.

She fell asleep, say John the expert. She's okay. That is one big hole.

Now Sophie is crying and crying.

Sophie, my daughter say, hugging her. Are you okay, peanut? Are you okay?

She's just scared, say John.

Are you okay? I say too. I don't know what happen, I say.

She's okay, say John. He is not like my daughter, full of questions. He is full of answers until we get home and can see by the lamplight.

Will you look at her? he yell then. What the hell happened?

Bruises all over her brown skin, and a swollen-up eye.

You are crazy! say my daughter. Look at what you did! You are crazy!

I try very hard, I say.

How could you use a stick? I told you to use your words!

She is hard to handle, I say.

She's three years old! You cannot use a stick! say my daughter.

She is not like any Chinese girl I ever saw, I say.

I brush some sand off my clothes. Sophie's clothes are dirty too, but at least she has her clothes on.

Has she done this before? ask my daughter. Has she hit you before?

She hits me all the time, Sophie say, eating ice cream.

Your family, say John.

Believe me, say my daughter.

A daughter I have, a beautiful daughter. I took care of her when she could not hold her head up. I took care of her before she could argue with me, when she was a little girl with two pigtails, one of them always crooked. I took care of her when we have to escape from China, I took care of her when suddenly we live in a country with cars everywhere, if you are not careful your little girl get run over. When my husband die, I promise him I will keep the family together, even though it was just two of us, hardly a family at all.

But now my daughter take me around to look at apartments. After all, I can cook, I can clean, there's no reason I cannot live by myself, all I need is a telephone. Of course, she is sorry. Sometimes she cry, I am the one to say everything will be okay. She say she have no choice, she doesn't want to end up divorced. I say divorce is terrible, I don't know who invented this terrible idea. Instead of live with a telephone, though, surprise, I come to live with Bess. Imagine that. Bess make an offer and, sure enough, where she come from, people mean for you to move in when they say things like that. A crazy idea, go to live with someone else's family, but she like to have some female company, not like my daughter, who does not believe in company. These days when my daughter visit, she does not bring Sophie. Bess say we should give Nattie time, we will see Sophie again soon. But seems like my daughter have more presentation than ever before, every time she come she have to leave.

I have a family to support, she say, and her voice is heavy, as if soaking wet. I have a young daughter and a depressed husband and no one to turn to.

When she say no one to turn to, she mean me.

These days my beautiful daughter is so tired she can just sit there in a chair and fall asleep. John lost his job again, already, but still they rather hire a baby-sitter than ask me to help, even they can't afford it. Of course, the new baby-sitter is much younger, can run around. I don't know if Sophie these days is wild or not wild. She call me Meanie, but she like to kiss me too, sometimes. I remember that every time I see a child on TV. Sophie like to grab my hair, a fistful in each hand, and then kiss me smack on the nose. I never see any other child kiss that way.

The satellite TV has so many channels, more channels than I can count, including a Chinese channel from the Mainland and a Chinese channel from Taiwan, but most of the time I watch bloopers with Bess. Also, I watch the bird feeder—so many, many kinds of birds come. The Shea sons hang around all the time, asking when will I go home, but Bess tell them, Get lost.

She's a permanent resident, say Bess. She isn't going anywhere.

Then she wink at me, and switch the channel with the remote control.

Of course, I shouldn't say Irish this, Irish that, especially now I am become honorary Irish myself, according to Bess. Me! Who's Irish? I say, and she laugh. All the same, if I could mention one thing about some of the Irish, not all of them of course, I like to mention this: Their talk just stick. I don't know how Bess Shea learn to use her words, but sometimes I hear what she say a long time later. *Permanent resident. Not going anywhere.* Over and over I hear it, the voice of Bess.

[1998]

Joining the Conversation: Critical Thinking and Writing

1. The word "fierce" is used several times in "Who's Irish?" Please look up the definition of "fierce" in a good dictionary, and explain its significance for your understanding of the story.
2. Does the narrator change as a result of the experiences she describes?

3. Imagine that you have been assigned to teach "Who's Irish?" in a course on creative writing. What are the features of its style and structure that you would highlight for your students?
4. Now that you have read and studied "Who's Irish?," what is your response to Jen's choice of title? If the author asked you to suggest an alternate title, what would it be? Explain in detail why you feel that your title would be a good one.
5. Does this story help you to perceive something new about "diversity"? Do you think that "diversity" is an overused term? Why or why not?
6. How would you describe the differences between the generations as these are expressed in Jen's story? Do you think in general that there are significant differences between members of older and younger generations, or would you say that these are exaggerated?
7. Do you believe that sometimes these are good reasons for classifying people by race and ethnicity? What are these reasons? Do you find them convincing? How should we classify "mixed race" persons?

Chapter 14

Thinking Critically: A Case Study about Flannery O'Connor

In this case study we give two short stories and several comments of O'Connor's on literature:

1. "A Good Man Is Hard to Find"
2. "Revelation"
3. Passages from five essays about fiction and a letter on "A Good Man Is Hard to Find"

We also include a page from the manuscript of "A Good Man Is Hard to Find," showing O'Connor's revisions.

Flannery O'Connor (1925–1964)—her first name was Mary but she did not use it—was born in Savannah, Georgia, but spent most of her life in Milledgeville, Georgia, where her family moved when she was 12. She was educated in parochial schools and at the local college and then went to the School for Writers at the University of Iowa, where she earned an MFA in 1946. For a few months she lived at a writers' colony in Saratoga Springs, New York, and then for a few weeks she lived in New York City, but most of her life was spent back in Milledgeville, where she tended her peacocks and wrote stories, novels, essays (posthumously published as Mystery and Manners *[1970]), and letters (posthumously published under the title* The Habit of Being *[1979]).*

In 1951, when she was 25, Flannery O'Connor discovered that she was a victim of lupus erythematosus, an incurable autoimmune disease that had crippled and then killed her father ten years before. She died at the age of 39. O'Connor faced her illness with stoic courage, Christian fortitude—and tough humor. Here is a glimpse, from one of her letters, of how she dealt with those who pitied her:

> *An old lady got on the elevator behind me and as soon as I turned around she fixed me with a moist gleaming eye and said in a loud voice, "Bless you, darling!" I felt exactly like the Misfit [in "A Good Man Is Hard to Find"] and I gave her a weakly lethal look, whereupon greatly encouraged she grabbed my arm and whispered (very loud) in my ear, "Remember what they said to John at the gate, darling!" It was not my floor but I got off and I suppose the old lady was astounded at how quick I could get away on crutches. I have a one-legged friend and I asked her what they said to John at the gate. She said she reckoned they said, "The lame shall enter first." This may be because the lame will be able to knock everybody else aside with their crutches.*

A devout Catholic, O'Connor forthrightly summarized the relation between her belief and her writing:

> *I see from the standpoint of Christian orthodoxy. This means that for me the meaning of life is centered in our Redemption by Christ and what I see in the world I see in its relation to that.*

A Good Man Is Hard to Find

The grandmother didn't want to go to Florida. She wanted to visit some of her connections in east Tennessee and she was seizing every chance to change Bailey's mind. Bailey was the son she lived with, her only boy. He was sitting on the edge of his chair at the table, bent over the orange sports section of the *Journal.* "Now look here, Bailey," she said, "see here, read this," and she stood with one hand on her thin hip and the other rattling the newspaper at his bald head. "Here this fellow that calls himself The Misfit is aloose from the Federal Pen and headed toward Florida and you read here what it says he did to these people. Just you read it. I wouldn't take my children in any direction with a criminal like that aloose in it. I couldn't answer to my conscience if I did."

Bailey didn't look up from his reading so she wheeled around then and faced the children's mother, a young woman in slacks, whose face was as broad and innocent as a cabbage and was tied around with a green headkerchief that had two points on the top like rabbit's ears. She was sitting on the sofa, feeding the baby his apricots out of a jar. "The children have been to Florida before," the old lady said. "You all ought to take them somewhere else for a change so they would see different parts of the world and be broad. They never have been to east Tennessee."

The children's mother didn't seem to hear her, but the eight-year-old boy, John Wesley, a stocky child with glasses, said. "If you don't want to go to Florida, why dontcha stay at home?" He and the little girl, June Star, were reading the funny papers on the floor.

"She wouldn't stay at home to be queen for a day," June Star said without raising her yellow head.

5 "Yes, and what would you do if this fellow, The Misfit, caught you?" the grandmother said.

"I'd smack his face," John Wesley said.

"She wouldn't stay at home for a million bucks," June Star said. "Afraid she'd miss something. She has to go everywhere we go."

"All right, Miss," the grandmother said. "Just remember that the next time you want me to curl your hair."

June Star said her hair was naturally curly.

10 The next morning the grandmother was the first one in the car, ready to go. She had her big black valise that looked like the head of a hippopotamus in one corner, and underneath it she was hiding a basket with Pitty Sing, the cat, in it. She didn't intend for the cat to be left alone in the house for three days because he would miss her too much and she was afraid he might brush against one of the gas burners and accidentally asphyxiate himself. Her son, Bailey, didn't like to arrive at a motel with a cat.

She sat in the middle of the back seat with John Wesley and June Star on either side of her. Bailey and the children's mother and the baby sat in front and they left Atlanta at eight forty-five with the mileage on the car at 55890. The

2

She was the first one ready to load up the next morning at six o'clock. She had Baby Brother's bucking bronco and what she called her "valise" and Pitty Sing, the cat, packed in the car before Boatwrite had a chance to get the rest of the luggage out of the hall. They got off at seven-thirty, Boatwrite and the children's mother in the front and Granny, John Wesley, Baby Brother, Little Sister Mary Ann, Pitty Sing, and the bucking bronco in the back.

"Why the hell did you bring that goddam rocking horse?" Boatwrite asked because as soon as they were out of the city, Baby Brother began to squall to get on the bucking bronco. "He can't get on that thing in this car and that's final," his father who was a stern man said.

"Can we open the lunch now?" Little Sister asked. "It'll shut Baby Brother up. Mamma, can we open up the lunch?"

"No," their grandmother said. It's only eight-thirty.

Their mother was reading SCREEN MOTHERS AND THEIR CHILDREN. "Yeah, sure," she said without looking up. She was all dressed up today. She had on a purple silk dress and a hat and a choker of pink beads and a new pocket book, and high heel pumps.

"Let's go through Georgia quick so we won't have to look at it much," John Wesley said.

"You should see Tennessee," his grandmother said. "Now there is a beautiful state."

"Like hell," John Wesley said. "That's just a hillbilly dumping ground."

"Haw," his mother said, and nudged Boatwrite. "Didjer hear that?" She was from Arkansas.

They ate their lunch and got along fine for a while until Pitty Sing who had been asleep jumped into the front of the car and caused Boatwrite to swerve to the right into a ditch. Pitty Sing was a large grey-striped cat with a yellow hind leg and a big soiled white face. Granny thought that she was the only person in the world that he really loved but the truth was he had never looked farther than her middle and he didn't even like other cats. He jumped snarling into the front seat and Boatwrite's shoulders

Typescript page from "A Good Man Is Hard to Find" with O'Connor's handwritten changes.

grandmother wrote this down because she thought it would be interesting to say how many miles they had been when they got back. It took them twenty minutes to reach the outskirts of the city.

The old lady settled herself comfortably, removing her white cotton gloves and putting them up with her purse on the shelf in front of the back window. The children's mother still had on slacks and still had her head tied up in a green kerchief, but the grandmother had on a navy blue straw sailor hat with a bunch of white violets on the brim and a navy blue dress with a small white dot in the print. Her collars and cuffs were white organdy trimmed with lace and at her neckline she had pinned a purple spray of cloth violets containing a sachet. In case of an accident, anyone seeing her dead on the highway would know at once that she was a lady.

She said she thought it was going to be a good day for driving, neither too hot nor too cold, and she cautioned Bailey that the speed limit was fifty-five miles an hour and that the patrolmen hid themselves behind bill-boards and small clumps of trees and sped out after you before you had a chance to slow down. She pointed out interesting details of the scenery: Stone Mountain; the blue granite that in some places came up to both sides of the highway; the brilliant red clay banks slightly streaked with purple; and the various crops that made rows of green lace-work on the ground. The trees were full of silver-white sunlight and the meanest of them sparkled. The children were reading comic magazines and their mother had gone back to sleep.

"Let's go through Georgia fast so we won't have to look at it much," John Wesley said.

15 "If I were a little boy," said the grandmother, "I wouldn't talk about my native state that way. Tennessee has the mountains and Georgia has the hills."

"Tennessee is just a hillbilly dumping ground," John Wesley said, "and Georgia is a lousy state too."

"You said it," June Star said.

"In my time," said the grandmother, folding her thin veined fingers, "children were more respectful of their native states and their parents and everything else. People did right then. Oh look at the cute little pickaninny!" she said and pointed to a Negro child standing in the door of a shack. "Wouldn't that make a picture, now?" she asked and they all turned and looked at the little Negro out of the back window. He waved.

"He didn't have any britches on," June Star said.

20 "He probably didn't have any," the grandmother explained. "Little niggers in the country don't have things like we do. If I could paint, I'd paint that picture," she said.

The children exchanged comic books.

The grandmother offered to hold the baby and the children's mother passed him over the front seat to her. She set him on her knee and bounced him and told him about the things they were passing. She rolled her eyes and screwed up her mouth and stuck her leathery thin face into his smooth bland one. Occasionally he gave her a faraway smile. They passed a large cotton field with five or six graves fenced in the middle of it, like a small island. "Look at the graveyard!" the grandmother said, pointing it out. "That was the old family burying ground. That belonged to the plantation."

"Where's the plantation?" John Wesley asked.

"Gone With the Wind,"[1] said the grandmother. "Ha. Ha."

25 When the children finished all the comic books they had brought, they opened the lunch and ate it. The grandmother ate a peanut butter sandwich and an olive and would not let the children throw the box and the paper napkins out the window. When there was nothing else to do they played a game by choosing a cloud and making the other two guess what shape it suggested. John Wesley took one the shape of a cow and June Star guessed a cow and John Wesley said, no, an automobile, and June Star said he didn't play fair, and they began to slap each other over the grandmother.

The grandmother said she would tell them a story if they would keep quiet. When she told a story, she rolled her eyes and waved her head and was very

[1]***Gone With the Wind*** a 1939 film about the plantation South and the Civil War that was adapted from Margaret Mitchell's 1936 novel of the same name.

dramatic. She said once when she was a maiden lady she had been courted by a Mr. Edgar Atkins Teagarden from Jasper, Georgia. She said he was a very good-looking man and a gentleman and that he brought her a watermelon every Saturday afternoon with his initials cut in it, E.A.T. Well, one Saturday, she said, Mr. Teagarden brought the watermelon and there was nobody at home and he left it on the front porch and returned in his buggy to Jasper, but she never got the watermelon, she said, because a nigger boy ate it when he saw the initials, E.A.T.! This story tickled John Wesley's funny bone and he giggled and giggled but June Star didn't think it was any good. She said she wouldn't marry a man that just brought her a watermelon on Saturday. The grandmother said she would have done well to marry Mr. Teagarden because he was a gentleman and had bought Coca-Cola stock when it first came out and that he had died only a few years ago, a very wealthy man.

They stopped at The Tower for barbecued sandwiches. The Tower was a part-stucco and part-wood filling station and dance hall set in a clearing outside of Timothy. A fat man named Red Sammy Butts ran it and there were signs stuck here and there on the building and for miles up and down the highway saying, TRY RED SAMMY'S FAMOUS BARBECUE. NONE LIKE FAMOUS RED SAMMY'S! RED SAM! THE FAT BOY WITH THE HAPPY LAUGH. A VETERAN! RED SAMMY'S YOUR MAN!

Red Sammy was lying on the bare ground outside The Tower with his head under a truck while a gray monkey about a foot high, chained to a small chinaberry tree, chattered nearby. The monkey sprang back into the tree and got on the highest limb as soon as he saw the children jump out of the car and run toward him.

Inside, The Tower was a long dark room with a counter at one end and tables at the other and dancing space in the middle. They all sat down at a broad table next to the nickelodeon and Red Sam's wife, a tall burnt-brown woman with hair and eyes lighter than her skin, came and took their order. The children's mother put a dime in the machine and played "The Tennessee Waltz," and the grandmother said that tune always made her want to dance. She asked Bailey if he would like to dance but he only glared at her. He didn't have a naturally sunny disposition like she did and trips made him nervous. The grandmother's brown eyes were very bright. She swayed her head from side to side and pretended she was dancing in her chair. June Star said play something she could tap to so the children's mother put in another dime and played a fast number and June Star stepped out onto the dance floor and did her tap routine.

"Ain't she cute?" Red Sam's wife said, leaning over the counter. "Would you like to come be my little girl?"

"No, I certainly wouldn't," June Star said. "I wouldn't live in a broken-down place like this for a million bucks!" and she ran back to the table.

"Ain't she cute?" the woman repeated, stretching her mouth politely.

"Aren't you ashamed?" hissed the grandmother.

Red Sam came in and told his wife to quit lounging on the counter and hurry with these people's order. His khaki trousers reached just to his hip bones and his stomach hung over them like a sack of meal swaying under his shirt. He came over and sat down at a table nearby and let out a combination sigh and yodel. "You can't win," he said. "You can't win," and he wiped his sweating red face off with a gray handkerchief. "These days you don't know who to trust," he said. "Ain't that the truth?"

"People are certainly not nice like they used to be," said the grandmother.

"Two fellers come in here last week," Red Sammy said, "driving a Chrysler. It was an old beat-up car but it was a good one and these boys looked all right to me. Said they worked at the mill and you know I let them fellers charge the gas they bought? Now why did I do that?"

"Because you're a good man!" the grandmother said at once.

"Yes'm, I suppose so," Red Sam said as if he were struck with this answer.

His wife brought the orders, carrying the five plates all at once without a tray, two in each hand and one balanced on her arm. "It isn't a soul in this green world of God's that you can trust," she said. "And I don't count nobody out of that, not nobody," she repeated, looking at Red Sammy.

40 "Did you read about that criminal, The Misfit, that's escaped?" asked the grandmother.

"I wouldn't be a bit surprised if he didn't attack this place right here," said the woman. "If he hears about it being here, I wouldn't be none surprised to see him. If he hears it's two cent in the cash register, I wouldn't be a tall surprised if he . . ."

"That'll do," Red Sam said. "Go bring these people their Co'Colas," and the woman went off to get the rest of the order.

"A good man is hard to find," Red Sammy said. "Everything is getting terrible. I remember the day you could go off and leave your screen door unlatched. Not no more."

He and the grandmother discussed better times. The old lady said that in her opinion Europe was entirely to blame for the way things were now. She said the way Europe acted you would think we were made of money and Red Sam said it was no use talking about it, she was exactly right. The children ran outside into the white sunlight and looked at the monkey in the lacy chinaberry tree. He was busy catching fleas on himself and biting each one carefully between his teeth as if it were a delicacy.

45 They drove off again into the hot afternoon. The grandmother took cat naps and woke up every five minutes with her own snoring. Outside of Toombsboro she woke up and recalled an old plantation that she had visited in this neighborhood once when she was a young lady. She said the house had six white columns across the front and that there was an avenue of oaks leading up to it and two little wooden trellis arbors on either side in front where you sat down with your suitor after a stroll in the garden. She recalled exactly which road to turn off to get to it. She knew that Bailey would not be willing to lose any time looking at an old house, but the more she talked about it, the more she wanted to see it once again and find out if the little twin arbors were still standing. "There was a secret panel in this house," she said craftily, not telling the truth but wishing that she were, "and the story went that all the family silver was hidden in it when Sherman came through but it was never found . . ."

"Hey!" John Wesley said. "Let's go see it! We'll find it! We'll poke all the woodwork and find it! Who lives there? Where do you turn off at? Hey, Pop, can't we turn off there?"

"We never have seen a house with a secret panel!" June Star shrieked. "Let's go to the house with the secret panel! Hey, Pop, can't we go see the house with the secret panel!"

"It's not far from here, I know," the grandmother said. "It wouldn't take over twenty minutes."

Bailey was looking straight ahead. His jaw was as rigid as a horseshoe. "No," he said.

50 The children began to yell and scream that they wanted to see the house with the secret panel. John Wesley kicked the back of the front seat and June Star hung over her mother's shoulder and whined desperately into her ear that they never

had any fun even on their vacation, that they could never do what THEY wanted to do. The baby began to scream and John Wesley kicked the back of the seat so hard that his father could feel the blows in his kidney.

"All right!" he shouted and drew the car to a stop at the side of the road. "Will you all shut up? Will you all just shut up for one second? If you don't shut up, we won't go anywhere."

"It would be very educational for them," the grandmother murmured.

"All right," Bailey said, "but get this. This is the only time we're going to stop for anything like this. This is the one and only time."

"The dirt road that you have to turn down is about a mile back," the grandmother directed. "I marked it when we passed."

55 "A dirt road," Bailey groaned.

After they had turned around and were headed toward the dirt road, the grandmother recalled other points about the house, the beautiful glass over the front doorway and the candle lamp in the hall. John Wesley said that the secret panel was probably in the fireplace.

"You can't go inside this house," Bailey said. "You don't know who lives there."

"While you all talk to the people in front, I'll run around behind and get in a window," John Wesley suggested.

"We'll all stay in the car," his mother said.

60 They turned onto the dirt road and the car raced roughly along in a swirl of pink dust. The grandmother recalled the times when there were no paved roads and thirty miles was a day's journey. The dirt road was hilly and there were sudden washes in it and sharp curves on dangerous embankments. All at once they would be on a hill, looking down over the blue tops of trees for miles around, then the next minute, they would be in a red depression with the dust-coated trees looking down on them.

"This place had better turn up in a minute," Bailey said, "or I'm going to turn around."

The road looked as if no one had traveled on it in months.

"It's not much farther," the grandmother said and just as she said it, a horrible thought came to her. The thought was so embarrassing that she turned red in the face and her eyes dilated and her feet jumped up, upsetting her valise in the corner. The instant the valise moved, the newspaper top she had over the basket under it rose with a snarl and Pitty Sing, the cat, sprang onto Bailey's shoulder.

The children were thrown to the floor and their mother, clutching the baby, was thrown out the door onto the ground; the old lady was thrown into the front seat. The car turned over once and landed right-side-up in a gulch on the side of the road. Bailey remained in the driver's seat with the cat—gray-striped with a broad white face and an orange nose—clinging to his neck like a caterpillar.

65 As soon as the children saw they could move their arms and legs, they scrambled out of the car, shouting, "We've had an ACCIDENT!" The grandmother was curled up under the dashboard, hoping she was injured so that Bailey's wrath would not come down on her all at once. The horrible thought she had had before the accident was that the house she had remembered so vividly was not in Georgia but in Tennessee.

Bailey removed the cat from his neck with both hands and flung it out the window against the side of a pine tree. Then he got out of the car and started looking for the children's mother. She was sitting against the side of the red gutted ditch, holding the screaming baby, but she only had a cut down her face and a broken shoulder. "We've had an ACCIDENT!" the children screamed in a frenzy of delight.

"But nobody's killed," June Star said with disappointment as the grandmother limped out of the car, her hat still pinned to her head but the broken front brim standing up at a jaunty angle and the violet spray hanging off the side. They all sat down in the ditch, except the children, to recover from the shock. They were all shaking.

"Maybe a car will come along," said the children's mother hoarsely.

"I believe I have injured an organ," said the grandmother, pressing her side, but no one answered her. Bailey's teeth were clattering. He had on a yellow sport shirt with bright blue parrots designed in it and his face was as yellow as the shirt. The grandmother decided that she would not mention that the house was in Tennessee.

70 The road was about ten feet above and they could see only the tops of the trees on the other side of it. Behind the ditch they were sitting in there were more woods, tall and dark and deep. In a few minutes they saw a car some distance away on top of a hill, coming slowly as if the occupants were watching them. The grandmother stood up and waved both arms dramatically to attract their attention. The car continued to come on slowly, disappeared around a bend and appeared again, moving even slower on top of the hill they had gone over. It was a big black battered hearselike automobile. There were three men in it.

It came to a stop just over them and for some minutes, the driver looked down with a steady expressionless gaze to where they were sitting, and didn't speak. Then he turned his head and muttered something to the other two and they got out. One was a fat boy in black trousers and a red sweat shirt with a silver stallion embossed on the front of it. He moved around on the right side of them and stood staring, his mouth partly open in a kind of loose grin. The other had on khaki pants and a blue striped coat and a gray hat pulled down very low, hiding most of his face. He came around slowly on the left side. Neither spoke.

The driver got out of the car and stood by the side of it, looking down at them. He was an older man than the other two. His hair was just beginning to gray and he wore silver-rimmed spectacles that gave him a scholarly look. He had a long creased face and didn't have on any shirt or undershirt. He had on blue jeans that were too tight for him and was holding a black hat and a gun. The two boys also had guns.

"We've had an ACCIDENT!" the children screamed.

The grandmother had the peculiar feeling that the bespectacled man was someone she knew. His face was as familiar to her as if she had known him all her life but she could not recall who he was. He moved away from the car and began to come down the embankment, placing his feet carefully so that he wouldn't slip. He had on tan and white shoes and no socks, and his ankles were red and thin. "Good afternoon," he said. "I see you all had you a little spill."

75 "We turned over twice!" said the grandmother.

"Oncet," he corrected. "We seen it happen. Try their car and see will it run, Hiram," he said quietly to the boy with the gray hat.

"What you got that gun for?" John Wesley asked. "Whatcha gonna do with that gun?"

"Lady," the man said to the children's mother, "would you mind calling them children to sit down by you? Children make me nervous. I want all you to sit down right together there where you're at."

"What are you telling us what to do for?" June Star asked.

80 Behind them the line of woods gaped like a dark open mouth. "Come here," said their mother.

"Look here now," Bailey began suddenly, "we're in a predicament! We're in . . ."

The grandmother shrieked. She scrambled to her feet and stood staring. "You're The Misfit!" she said. "I recognized you at once!"

"Yes'm," the man said, smiling slightly as if he were pleased in spite of himself to be known, "but it would have been better for all of you, lady, if you hadn't of reckernized me."

Bailey turned his head sharply and said something to his mother that shocked even the children. The old lady began to cry and The Misfit reddened.

85 "Lady," he said, "don't you get upset. Sometimes a man says things he don't mean. I don't reckon he meant to talk to you thataway."

"You wouldn't shoot a lady, would you?" the grandmother said and removed a clean handkerchief from her cuff and began to slap at her eyes with it.

The Misfit pointed the toe of his shoe into the ground and made a little hole and then covered it up again. "I would hate to have to," he said.

"Listen," the grandmother almost screamed, "I know you're a good man. You don't look a bit like you have common blood. I know you must come from nice people!"

"Yes ma'm," he said, "finest people in the world." When he smiled he showed a row of strong white teeth. "God never made a finer woman than my mother and my daddy's heart was pure gold," he said. The boy with the red sweat shirt had come around behind them and was standing with his gun at his hip. The Misfit squatted down on the ground. "Watch them children, Bobby Lee," he said. "You know they make me nervous." He looked at the six of them huddled together in front of him and he seemed to be embarrassed as if he couldn't think of anything to say. "Ain't a cloud in the sky," he remarked, looking up at it. "Don't see no sun but don't see no cloud neither."

90 "Yes, it's a beautiful day," said the grandmother. "Listen," she said, "you shouldn't call yourself The Misfit because I know you're a good man at heart. I can just look at you and tell."

"Hush!" Bailey yelled, "Hush! Everybody shut up and let me handle this!" He was squatting in the position of a runner about to sprint forward but he didn't move.

"I pre-chate that, lady," The Misfit said and drew a little circle in the ground with the butt of his gun.

"It'll take a half a hour to fix this here car," Hiram called, looking over the raised hood of it.

"Well, first you and Bobby Lee get him and that little boy to step over yonder with you," The Misfit said, pointing to Bailey and John Wesley. "The boys want to ask you something," he said to Bailey. "Would you mind stepping back in them woods there with them?"

95 "Listen," Bailey began, "we're in a terrible predicament! Nobody realizes what this is," and his voice cracked. His eyes were as blue and intense as the parrots in his shirt and he remained perfectly still.

The grandmother reached up to adjust her hat brim as if she were going to the woods with him but it came off in her hand. She stood staring at it and after a second she let it fall on the ground. Hiram pulled Bailey up by the arm as if he were assisting an old man. John Wesley caught hold of his father's hand and Bobby Lee followed. They went off toward the woods and just as they reached the dark edge, Bailey turned and supporting himself against a gray naked pine trunk, he shouted, "I'll be back in a minute, Mamma, wait on me!"

"Come back this instant!" his mother shrilled but they all disappeared into the woods.

"Bailey Boy!" the grandmother called in a tragic voice but she found she was looking at The Misfit squatting on the ground in front of her. "I just know you're a good man," she said desperately. "You're not a bit common!"

"Nome, I ain't a good man," The Misfit said after a second as if he had considered her statement carefully, "but I ain't the worst in the world neither. My daddy said I was a different breed of dog from my brothers and sisters. 'You know,' Daddy said, 'It's some that can live their whole life without asking about it and it's others has to know why it is, and this boy is one of the latters. He's going to be into everything!'" He put on his black hat and looked up suddenly and then away deep into the woods as if he were embarrassed again. "I'm sorry I don't have on a shirt before you ladies," he said, hunching his shoulders slightly. "We buried our clothes that we had on when we escaped and we're just making do until we can get better. We borrowed these from some folks we met," he explained.

100 "That's perfectly all right," the grandmother said. "Maybe Bailey has an extra shirt in his suitcase."

"I'll look and see terrectly," The Misfit said.

"Where are they taking him?" the children's mother screamed.

"Daddy was a card himself," The Misfit said. "You couldn't put anything over on him. He never got in trouble with the Authorities though. Just had the knack of handling them."

"You could be honest too if you'd only try," said the grandmother. "Think how wonderful it would be to settle down and live a comfortable life and not have to think about somebody chasing you all the time."

105 The Misfit kept scratching in the ground with the butt of his gun as if he were thinking about it. "Yes'm, somebody is always after you," he murmured.

The grandmother noticed how thin his shoulder blades were just behind his hat because she was standing up looking down on him. "Do you ever pray?" she asked.

He shook his head. All she saw was the black hat wiggle between his shoulder blades. "Nome," he said.

There was a pistol shot from the woods, followed closely by another. Then silence. The old lady's head jerked around. She could hear the wind move through the tree tops like a long satisfied insuck of breath. "Bailey Boy!" she called.

"I was a gospel singer for a while," The Misfit said. "I been most everything. Been in the arm service, both land and sea, at home and abroad, been twict married, been an undertaker, been with the railroads, plowed Mother Earth, been in a tornado, seen a man burnt alive oncet," and he looked up at the children's mother and the little girl who were sitting close together, their faces white and their eyes glassy; "I even seen a woman flogged," he said.

110 "Pray, pray," the grandmother began, "pray, pray. . . ."

"I never was a bad boy that I remember of," The Misfit said in an almost dreamy voice, "but somewheres along the line I done something wrong and got sent to the penitentiary. I was buried alive," and he looked up and held her attention to him by a steady stare.

"That's when you should have started to pray," she said. "What did you do to get sent up to the penitentiary that first time?"

"Turn to the right, it was a wall," The Misfit said, looking up again at the cloudless sky. "Turn to the left, it was a wall. Look up it was a ceiling, look down it was a floor. I forget what I done, lady. I set there and set there, trying to remember what it was I done and I ain't recalled it to this day. Oncet in a while, I would think it was coming to me, but it never come."

"Maybe they put you in by mistake," the old lady said vaguely.

115 "Nome," he said. "It wasn't no mistake. They had the papers on me."

"You must have stolen something," she said.

The Misfit sneered slightly. "Nobody had nothing I wanted," he said. "It was a head-doctor at the penitentiary said what I had done was kill my daddy but I known that for a lie. My daddy died in nineteen ought nineteen of the epidemic flu and I never had a thing to do with it. He was buried in the Mount Hopewell Baptist churchyard and you can go there and see for yourself."

"If you would pray," the old lady said, "Jesus would help you."

"That's right," The Misfit said.

120 "Well then, why don't you pray?" she asked trembling with delight suddenly.

"I don't want no hep," he said. "I'm doing all right by myself."

Bobby Lee and Hiram came ambling back from the woods. Bobby Lee was dragging a yellow shirt with bright blue parrots on it.

"Throw me that shirt, Bobby Lee," The Misfit said. The shirt came flying at him and landed on his shoulder and he put it on. The grandmother couldn't name what the shirt reminded her of. "No, lady," The Misfit said while he was buttoning it up, "I found out the crime don't matter. You can do one thing or you can do another, kill a man or take a tire off his car, because sooner or later you're going to forget what it was you done and just be punished for it."

The children's mother had begun to make heaving noises as if she couldn't get her breath. "Lady," he asked, "would you and that little girl like to step off yonder with Bobby Lee and Hiram and join your husband?"

125 "Yes, thank you," the mother said faintly. Her left arm dangled helplessly and she was holding the baby, who had gone to sleep, in the other. "Hep that lady up, Hiram," The Misfit said as she struggled to climb out of the ditch, "and Bobby Lee, you hold onto that little girl's hand."

"I don't want to hold hands with him," June Star said. "He reminds me of a pig."

The fat boy blushed and laughed and caught her by the arm and pulled her off into the woods after Hiram and her mother.

Alone with The Misfit, the grandmother found that she had lost her voice. There was not a cloud in the sky nor any sun. There was nothing around her but woods. She wanted to tell him that he must pray. She opened and closed her mouth several times before anything came out. Finally she found herself saying, "Jesus, Jesus," meaning, Jesus will help you, but the way she was saying it, it sounded as if she might be cursing.

"Yes'm," The Misfit said as if he agreed. "Jesus thown everything off balance. It was the same case with Him as with me except He hadn't committed any crime and they could prove I had committed one because they had the papers on me. Of course," he said, "they never shown me my papers. That's why I sign myself now. I said long ago, you get you a signature and sign everything you do and keep a copy of it. Then you'll know what you done and you can hold up the crime to the punishment and see do they match and in the end you'll have something to prove you ain't been treated right. I call myself The Misfit," he said, "because I can't make what all I done wrong fit what all I gone through in punishment."

130 There was a piercing scream from the woods, followed closely by a pistol report. "Does it seem right to you, lady, that one is punished a heap and another ain't punished at all?"

"Jesus!" the old lady cried. "You've got good blood! I know you wouldn't shoot a lady! I know you come from nice people! Pray! Jesus, you ought not to shoot a lady. I'll give you all the money I've got!"

"Lady," The Misfit said, looking beyond her far into the woods, "there never was a body that give the undertaker a tip."

There were two more pistol reports and the grandmother raised her head like a parched old turkey hen crying for water and called, "Bailey Boy, Bailey Boy!" as if her heart would break.

"Jesus was the only One that ever raised the dead," The Misfit continued, "and He shouldn't have done it. He thown everything off balance. If He did what He said, then it's nothing for you to do but thow away everything and follow Him, and if He didn't, then it's nothing for you to do but enjoy the few minutes you got left the best way you can—by killing somebody or burning down his house or doing some other meanness to him. No pleasure but meanness," he said and his voice had become almost a snarl.

135 "Maybe He didn't raise the dead," the old lady mumbled, not knowing what she was saying and feeling so dizzy that she sank down in the ditch with her legs twisted under her.

"I wasn't there so I can't say He didn't," The Misfit said. "I wisht I had of been there," he said, hitting the ground with his fist. "It ain't right I wasn't there because if I had of been there I would of known. Listen lady," he said in a high voice, "if I had of been there I would of known and I wouldn't be like I am now." His voice seemed about to crack and the grandmother's head cleared for an instant. She saw the man's face twisted close to her own as if he were going to cry and she murmured, "Why you're one of my babies. You're one of my own children!" She reached out and touched him on the shoulder. The Misfit sprang back as if a snake had bitten him and shot her three times through the chest. Then he put his gun down on the ground and took off his glasses and began to clean them.

Hiram and Bobby Lee returned from the woods and stood over the ditch, looking down at the grandmother who half sat and half lay in a puddle of blood with her legs crossed under her like a child's and her face smiling up at the cloudless sky.

Without his glasses, The Misfit's eyes were red-rimmed and pale and defenseless-looking. "Take her off and thow her where you thown the others," he said, picking up the cat that was rubbing itself against his leg.

"She was a talker, wasn't she?" Bobby Lee said, sliding down the ditch with a yodel.

140 "She would of been a good woman," The Misfit said, "if it had been somebody there to shoot her every minute of her life."

"Some fun!" Bobby Lee said.

"Shut up, Bobby Lee," The Misfit said. "It's no real pleasure in life."

[1953]

Revelation

The doctor's waiting room, which was very small, was almost full when the Turpins entered and Mrs. Turpin, who was very large, made it look even smaller by her presence. She stood looming at the head of the magazine table set in the center of it, a living demonstration that the room was inadequate and ridiculous. Her little bright black eyes took in all the patients as she sized up the seating situation. There was one vacant chair and a place on a sofa occupied by a blond child in a dirty blue romper who should have been told to move over and make room for the lady. He was five or six, but Mrs. Turpin saw at once that no one was going to tell him to move over. He was slumped down in the seat, his arms idle at his sides and his eyes idle in his head; his nose ran unchecked.

Mrs. Turpin put a firm hand on Claud's shoulder and said in a voice that included anyone who wanted to listen, "Claud, you sit in that chair there," and gave him a push down into the vacant one. Claud was florid and bald and sturdy, somewhat shorter than Mrs. Turpin, but he sat down as if he were accustomed to doing what she told him to.

Mrs. Turpin remained standing. The only man in the room besides Claud was a lean stringy old fellow with a rusty hand spread out on each knee, whose eyes were closed as if he were asleep or dead or pretending to be so as not to get up and offer her his seat. Her gaze settled agreeably on a well-dressed grey-haired lady whose eyes met hers and whose expression said: If that child belonged to me, he would have some manners and move over—there's plenty of room there for you and him too.

Claud looked up with a sigh and made as if to rise.

"Sit down," Mrs. Turpin said. "You know you're not supposed to stand on that leg. He has an ulcer on his leg," she explained.

Claud lifted his foot onto the magazine table and rolled his trouser leg up to reveal a purple swelling on a plump marble-white calf.

"My!" the pleasant lady said. "How did you do that?"

"A cow kicked him," Mrs. Turpin said.

"Goodness!" said the lady.

Claud rolled his trouser leg down.

"Maybe the little boy would move over," the lady suggested, but the child did not stir.

"Somebody will be leaving in a minute," Mrs. Turpin said. She could not understand why a doctor—with as much money as they made charging five dollars a day to just stick their head in the hospital door and look at you—couldn't afford a decent-sized waiting room. This one was hardly bigger than a garage. The table was cluttered with limp-looking magazines and at one end of it there was a big green glass ash tray full of cigaret butts and cotton wads with little blood spots on them. If she had had anything to do with the running of the place, that would have been emptied every so often. There were no chairs against the wall at the head of the room. It had a rectangular-shaped panel in it that permitted a view of the office where the nurse came and went and the secretary listened to the radio. A plastic fern in a gold pot sat in the opening and trailed its fronds down almost to the floor. The radio was softly playing gospel music.

Just then the inner door opened and a nurse with the highest stack of yellow hair Mrs. Turpin had ever seen put her face in the crack and called for the next patient. The woman sitting beside Claud grasped the two arms of her chair and hoisted herself up; she pulled her dress free from her legs and lumbered through the door where the nurse had disappeared.

Mrs. Turpin eased into the vacant chair, which held her tight as a corset. "I wish I could reduce," she said, and rolled her eyes and gave a comic sigh.

"Oh, *you* aren't fat," the stylish lady said.

"Ooooo I am too," Mrs. Turpin said. "Claud he eats all he wants to and never weighs over one hundred and seventy-five pounds, but me I just look at something good to eat and I gain some weight," and her stomach and shoulders shook with laughter. "You can eat all you want to, can't you, Claud?" she asked, turning to him.

Claud only grinned.

"Well, as long as you have such a good disposition," the stylish lady said, "I don't think it makes a bit of difference what size you are. You just can't beat a good disposition."

Next to her was a fat girl of eighteen or nineteen, scowling into a thick blue book which Mrs. Turpin saw was entitled *Human Development.* The girl raised her head and directed her scowl at Mrs. Turpin as if she did not like her looks. She appeared annoyed that anyone should speak while she tried to read. The poor girl's face was blue with acne and Mrs. Turpin thought how pitiful it was to have a face like that at that age. She gave the girl a friendly smile but the girl only scowled the harder. Mrs. Turpin herself was fat but she had always had good skin, and, though she was forty-seven years old, there was not a wrinkle in her face except around her eyes from laughing too much.

20 Next to the ugly girl was the child, still in exactly the same position, and next to him was a thin leathery old woman in a cotton print dress. She and Claud had three sacks of chicken feed in their pump house that was in the same print. She had seen from the first that the child belonged with the old woman. She could tell by the way they sat—kind of vacant and white-trashy, as if they would sit there until Doomsday if nobody called and told them to get up. And at right angles but next to the well-dressed pleasant lady was a lank-faced woman who was certainly the child's mother. She had on a yellow sweat shirt and wine-colored slacks, both gritty-looking, and the rims of her lips were stained with snuff. Her dirty yellow hair was tied behind with a little piece of red paper ribbon. Worse than niggers any day, Mrs. Turpin thought.

The gospel hymn playing was, "When I looked up and He looked down," and Mrs. Turpin, who knew it, supplied the last line mentally, "And wona these days I know I'll we-era crown."

Without appearing to, Mrs. Turpin always noticed people's feet. The well-dressed lady had on red and grey suede shoes to match her dress. Mrs. Turpin had on her good black patent leather pumps. The ugly girl had on Girl Scout shoes and heavy socks. The old woman had on tennis shoes and the white-trashy mother had on what appeared to be bedroom slippers, black straw with gold braid threaded through them—exactly what you would have expected her to have on.

Sometimes at night when she couldn't go to sleep, Mrs. Turpin would occupy herself with the question of who she would have chosen to be if she couldn't have been herself. If Jesus had said to her before he made her, "There's only two places available for you. You can either be a nigger or white-trash," what would she have said? "Please, Jesus, please," she would have said, "just let me wait until there's another place available," and he would have said, "No, you have to go right now and I have only those two places so make up your mind." She would have wiggled and squirmed and begged and pleaded but it would have been no use and finally she would have said, "All right, make me a nigger then—but that don't mean a trashy one." And he would have made her a neat clean respectable Negro-woman, herself but black.

Next to the child's mother was a red-headed youngish woman, reading one of the magazines and working a piece of chewing gum, hell for leather, as Claud would say. Mrs. Turpin could not see the woman's feet. She was not white-trash, just common. Sometimes Mrs. Turpin occupied herself at night naming the classes of people. On the bottom of the heap were most colored people, not the kind she would have been if she had been one, but most of them; then next to them—not above, just away from—were the white-trash; then above them were the homeowners, and above them the home-and-land owners, to which she and Claud belonged. Above she and Claud were people with a lot of money and much bigger houses and much more land. But here the complexity of it would begin to bear in on her, for some of the people with a lot of money were common and ought to be below she and Claud and some of the people who had good blood had lost their money and had to rent and then there were colored people who owned their homes and land as well. There was a colored dentist in town who had two red Lincolns and a swimming pool and a farm with registered white-face cattle on it. Usually by the time she had fallen asleep all the classes of people were moiling and roiling around in her head, and she would dream they were all crammed in together in a box car, being ridden off to be put in a gas oven.

25 "That's a beautiful clock," she said and nodded to her right. It was a big wall clock, the face encased in a brass sunburst.

"Yes, it's very pretty," the stylish lady said agreeably. "And right on the dot too," she added, glancing at her watch.

The ugly girl beside her cast an eye upward at the clock, smirked, then looked directly at Mrs. Turpin and smirked again. Then she returned her eyes to her book. She was obviously the lady's daughter because, although they didn't look anything alike as to disposition, they both had the same shape of face and the same blue eyes. On the lady they sparkled pleasantly but in the girl's seared face they appeared alternately to smolder and to blaze.

What if Jesus had said, "All right, you can be white-trash or a nigger or ugly"!

Mrs. Turpin felt an awful pity for the girl, though she thought it was one thing to be ugly and another to act ugly.

30 The woman with the snuff-stained lips turned around in her chair and looked up at the clock. Then she turned back and appeared to look a little to the side of Mrs. Turpin. There was a cast in one of her eyes. "You want to know wher you can get one of themther clocks?" she asked in a loud voice.

"No, I already have a nice clock," Mrs. Turpin said. Once somebody like her got a leg in the conversation, she would be all over it.

"You can get you one with green stamps," the woman said. "That's most likely wher he got hisn. Save you up enough, you can get you most anything. I got me some joo'ry."

Ought to have got you a wash rag and some soap, Mrs. Turpin thought.

"I get contour sheets with mine," the pleasant lady said.

35 The daughter slammed her book shut. She looked straight in front of her, directly through Mrs. Turpin and on through the yellow curtain and the plate glass window which made the wall behind her. The girl's eyes seemed lit all of a sudden with a peculiar light, an unnatural light like night road signs give. Mrs. Turpin turned her head to see if there was anything going on outside that she should see, but she could not see anything. Figures passing cast only a pale shadow through the curtain. There was no reason the girl should single her out for her ugly looks.

"Miss Finley," the nurse said, cracking the door. The gum chewing woman got up and passed in front of her and Claud and went into the office. She had on red high-heeled shoes.

Directly across the table, the ugly girl's eyes were fixed on Mrs. Turpin as if she had some very special reason for disliking her.

"This is wonderful weather, isn't it?" the girl's mother said.

"It's good weather for cotton if you can get the niggers to pick it," Mrs. Turpin said, "but niggers don't want to pick cotton any more. You can't get the white folks to pick it and now you can't get the niggers—because they got to be right up there with the white folks."

40 "They gonna *try* anyways," the white-trash woman said, leaning forward.

"Do you have one of those cotton-picking machines?" the pleasant lady asked.

"No," Mrs. Turpin said, "they leave half the cotton in the field. We don't have much cotton anyway. If you want to make it farming now, you have to have a little of everything. We got a couple of acres of cotton and a few hogs and chickens and just enough white-face that Claud can look after them himself."

"One thang I don't want," the white-trash woman said, wiping her mouth with the back of her hand. "Hogs. Nasty stinking things, a-gruntin and a-rootin all over the place."

Mrs. Turpin gave her the merest edge of her attention. "Our hogs are not dirty and they don't stink," she said. "They're cleaner than some children I've seen. Their feet never touch the ground. We have a pig-parlor—that's where you raise them on concrete," she explained to the pleasant lady, "and Claud scoots them down with the hose every afternoon and washes off the floor." Cleaner by far than that child right there, she thought. Poor nasty little thing. He had not moved except to put the thumb of his dirty hand into his mouth.

45 The woman turned her face away from Mrs. Turpin. "I know I wouldn't scoot down no hog with no hose," she said to the wall.

You wouldn't have no hog to scoot down, Mrs. Turpin said to herself.

"A-gruntin and a-rootin and a-groanin," the woman muttered.

"We got a little of everything," Mrs. Turpin said to the pleasant lady. "It's no use in having more than you can handle yourself with help like it is. We found enough niggers to pick our cotton this year but Claud he has to go after them and take them home again in the evening. They can't walk that half a mile. No they can't. I tell you," she said and laughed merrily, "I sure am tired of buttering up niggers, but you got to love em if you want em to work for you. When they come in the morning, I run out and I say, 'Hi yawl this morning?' and when Claud drives them off to the field I just wave to beat the band and they just wave back." And she waved her hand rapidly to illustrate.

"Like you read out of the same book," the lady said, showing she understood perfectly.

50 "Child, yes," Mrs. Turpin said. "And when they come in from the field, I run out with a bucket of icewater. That's the way it's going to be from now on," she said. "You may as well face it."

"One thang I know," the white-trash woman said. "Two thangs I ain't going to do: love no niggers or scoot down no hog with no hose." And she let out a bark of contempt.

The look that Mrs. Turpin and the pleasant lady exchanged indicated they both understood that you had to *have* certain things before you could *know* certain things. But every time Mrs. Turpin exchanged a look with the lady, she was aware that the ugly girl's peculiar eyes were still on her, and she had trouble bringing her attention back to the conversation.

"When you got something," she said, "you got to look after it." And when you ain't got a thing but breath and britches, she added to herself, you can afford to come to town every morning and just sit on the Court House coping and spit.

A grotesque revolving shadow passed across the curtain behind her and was thrown palely on the opposite wall. Then a bicycle clattered down against the outside of the building. The door opened and a colored boy glided in with a tray from the drug store. It had two large red and white paper cups on it with tops on them. He was a tall, very black boy in discolored white pants and a green nylon shirt. He was chewing gum slowly as if to music. He set the tray down in the office opening next to the fern and stuck his head through to look for the secretary. She was not in there. He rested his arms on the ledge and waited, his narrow bottom stuck out, swaying slowly to the left and right. He raised a hand over his head and scratched the base of his skull.

55 "You see that button there, boy?" Mrs. Turpin said. "You can punch that and she'll come. She's probably in the back somewhere."

"Is that right?" the boy said agreeably, as if he had never seen the button before. He leaned to the right and put his finger on it. "She sometime out," he said and twisted around to face his audience, his elbows behind him on the counter. The nurse appeared and he twisted back again. She handed him a dollar and he rooted in his pocket and made the change and counted it out to her. She gave him fifteen cents for a tip and he went out with the empty tray. The heavy door swung to slowly and closed at length with the sound of suction. For a moment no one spoke.

"They ought to send all them niggers back to Africa," the white-trash woman said. "That's wher they come from in the first place."

"Oh, I couldn't do without my good colored friends," the pleasant lady said.

"There's a heap of things worse than a nigger," Mrs. Turpin agreed. "It's all kinds of them just like it's all kinds of us."

60 "Yes, and it takes all kinds to make the world go round," the lady said in her musical voice.

As she said it, the raw-complexioned girl snapped her teeth together. Her lower lip turned downwards and inside out, revealing the pale pink inside of her mouth. After a second it rolled back up. It was the ugliest face Mrs. Turpin had ever seen anyone make and for a moment she was certain that the girl had made it at her. She was looking at her as if she had known and disliked her all her life—all of Mrs. Turpin's life, it seemed too, not just all the girl's life. Why, girl, I don't even know you, Mrs. Turpin said silently.

She forced her attention back to the discussion. "It wouldn't be practical to send them back to Africa," she said. "They wouldn't want to go. They got it too good here."

"Wouldn't be what they wanted—if I had anythang to do with it," the woman said.

"It wouldn't be a way in the world you could get all the niggers back over there," Mrs. Turpin said. "They'd be hiding out and lying down and turning sick on you and wailing and hollering and raring and pitching. It wouldn't be a way in the world to get them over there."

65 "They got over here," the trashy woman said. "Get back like they got over."

"It wasn't so many of them then," Mrs. Turpin explained.

The woman looked at Mrs. Turpin as if here was an idiot indeed but Mrs. Turpin was not bothered by the look, considering where it came from.

"Nooo," she said, "they're going to stay here where they can go to New York and marry white folks and improve their color. That's what they all want to do, every one of them, improve their color."

"You know what comes of that, don't you?" Claud asked.

70 "No, Claud, what?" Mrs. Turpin said.

Claud's eyes twinkled. "White-faced niggers," he said with never a smile.

Everybody in the office laughed except the white-trash and the ugly girl. The girl gripped the book in her lap with white fingers. The trashy woman looked around her from face to face as if she thought they were all idiots. The old woman in the feed sack dress continued to gaze expressionless across the floor at the high-top shoes of the man opposite her, the one who had been pretending to be asleep when the Turpins came in. He was laughing heartily, his hands still spread out on his knees. The child had fallen to the side and was lying now almost face down in the old woman's lap.

While they recovered from their laughter, the nasal chorus on the radio kept the room from silence.

You go to blank blank
And I'll go to mine
But we'll all blank along
To-geth-ther,
And all along the blank
We'll hep each other out
Smile-ling in any kind of
Weath-ther!

Mrs. Turpin didn't catch every word but she caught enough to agree with the spirit of the song and it turned her thoughts sober. To help anybody out that needed it was her philosophy of life. She never spared herself when she found somebody in need, whether they were white or black, trash or decent. And of all she had to be thankful for, she was most thankful that this was so. If Jesus had said, "You can be high society and have all the money you want and be thin and svelte-like, but you can't be a good woman with it," she would have had to say, "Well don't make me that then. Make me a good woman and it don't matter what else, how fat or how ugly or how poor!" Her heart rose. He had not made her a nigger or white-trash or ugly! He had made her herself and given her a little of everything. Jesus, thank you! she said. Thank you thank you thank you! Whenever she counted her blessings she felt as buoyant as if she weighed one hundred and twenty-five pounds instead of one hundred and eighty.

"What's wrong with your little boy?" the pleasant lady asked the white-trashy woman.

"He has a ulcer," the woman said proudly. "He ain't give me a minute's peace since he was born. Him and her are just alike," she said, nodding at the old woman, who was running her leathery fingers through the child's pale hair. "Look like I can't get nothing down them two but Co'Cola and candy."

That's all you try to get down em, Mrs. Turpin said to herself. Too lazy to light the fire. There was nothing you could tell her about people like them that she didn't know already. And it was not just that they didn't have anything. Because if you gave them everything, in two weeks it would all be broken or filthy or they would have chopped it up for lightwood. She knew all this from her own experience. Help them you must, but help them you couldn't.

All at once the ugly girl turned her lips inside out again. Her eyes were fixed like two drills on Mrs. Turpin. This time there was no mistaking that there was something urgent behind them.

Girl, Mrs. Turpin exclaimed silently, I haven't done a thing to you! The girl might be confusing her with somebody else. There was no need to sit by and let herself be intimidated. "You must be in college," she said boldly, looking directly at the girl. "I see you reading a book there."

The girl continued to stare and pointedly did not answer.

Her mother blushed at this rudeness. "The lady asked you a question, Mary Grace," she said under her breath.

"I have ears," Mary Grace said.

The poor mother blushed again. "Mary Grace goes to Wellesley College," she explained. She twisted one of the buttons on her dress. "In Massachusetts," she added with a grimace. "And in the summer she just keeps right on studying. Just reads all the time, a real book worm. She's done real well at Wellesley; she's taking English and Math and History and Psychology and Social Studies," she rattled on, "and I think it's too much. I think she ought to get out and have fun."

The girl looked as if she would like to hurl them all through the plate glass window.

85 "Way up north," Mrs. Turpin murmured and thought, well, it hasn't done much for her manners.

"I'd almost rather to have him sick," the white-trash woman said, wrenching the attention back to herself. "He's so mean when he ain't. Look like some children just take natural to meanness. It's some gets bad when they get sick but he was the opposite. Took sick and turned good. He don't give me no trouble now. It's me waitin to see the doctor," she said.

If I was going to send anybody back to Africa, Mrs. Turpin thought, it would be your kind, woman. "Yes, indeed," she said aloud, but looking up at the ceiling, "it's a heap of things worse than a nigger." And dirtier than a hog, she added to herself.

"I think people with bad dispositions are more to be pitied than anyone on earth," the pleasant lady said in a voice that was decidedly thin.

"I thank the Lord he has blessed me with a good one," Mrs. Turpin said. "The day has never dawned that I couldn't find something to laugh at."

90 "Not since she married me anyways," Claud said with a comical straight face.

Everybody laughed except the girl and the white-trash.

Mrs. Turpin's stomach shook. "He's such a caution," she said, "that I can't help but laugh at him."

The girl made a loud ugly noise through her teeth.

Her mother's mouth grew thin and tight. "I think the worst thing in the world," she said, "is an ungrateful person. To have everything and not appreciate it. I know a girl," she said, "who has parents who would give her anything, a little brother who loves her dearly, who is getting a good education, who wears the best clothes, but who can never say a kind word to anyone, who never smiles, who just criticizes and complains all day long."

95 "Is she too old to paddle?" Claud asked.

The girl's face was almost purple.

"Yes," the lady said. "I'm afraid there's nothing to do but leave her to her folly. Some day she'll wake up and it'll be too late."

"It never hurt anyone to smile," Mrs. Turpin said. "It just makes you feel better all over."

"Of course," the lady said sadly, "but there are just some people you can't tell anything to. They can't take criticism."

100 "If it's one thing I am," Mrs. Turpin said with feeling, "it's grateful. When I think who all I could have been besides myself and what all I got, a little of everything, and a good disposition besides, I just feel like shouting, 'Thank you, Jesus, for making everything the way it is!' It could have been different!" For one thing, somebody else could have got Claud. At the thought of this, she was flooded with gratitude and a terrible pang of joy ran through her. "Oh thank you, Jesus, Jesus, thank you!" she cried aloud.

The book struck her directly over her left eye. It struck almost at the same instant that she realized the girl was about to hurl it. Before she could utter a sound, the raw face came crashing across the table toward her, howling. The girl's fingers sank like clamps into the soft flesh of her neck. She heard the mother cry out and Claud shout, "Whoa!" There was an instant when she was certain that she was about to be in an earthquake.

All at once her vision narrowed and she saw everything as if it were happening in a small room far away, or as if she were looking at it through the wrong end of a telescope. Claud's face crumpled and fell out of sight. The nurse ran in, then out, then in again. Then the gangling figure of the doctor rushed out of the inner door. Magazines flew this way and that as the table turned over. The girl fell with a thud and Mrs. Turpin's vision suddenly reversed itself and she saw everything large instead of small. The eyes of the white-trashy woman were staring hugely at the floor. There the girl, held down on one side by the nurse and on the other by her mother, was wrenching and turning in their grasp. The doctor was kneeling astride her, trying to hold her arm down. He managed after a second to sink a long needle into it.

Mrs. Turpin felt entirely hollow except for her heart which swung from side to side as if it were agitated in a great empty drum of flesh.

"Somebody that's not busy call for the ambulance," the doctor said in the offhand voice young doctors adopt for terrible occasions.

105 Mrs. Turpin could not have moved a finger. The old man who had been sitting next to her skipped nimbly into the office and made the call, for the secretary still seemed to be gone.

"Claud!" Mrs. Turpin called.

He was not in his chair. She knew she must jump up and find him but she felt like someone trying to catch a train in a dream, when everything moves in slow motion and the faster you try to run the slower you go.

"Here I am," a suffocated voice, very unlike Claud's, said.

He was doubled up in the corner on the floor, pale as paper, holding his leg. She wanted to get up and go to him but she could not move. Instead, her gaze was drawn slowly downward to the churning face on the floor, which she could see over the doctor's shoulder.

110 The girl's eyes stopped rolling and focused on her. They seemed a much lighter blue than before, as if a door that had been tightly closed behind them was now open to admit light and air.

Mrs. Turpin's head cleared and her power of motion returned. She leaned forward until she was looking directly into the fierce brilliant eyes. There was no doubt in her mind that the girl did know her, knew her in some intense and personal way, beyond time and place and condition. "What you got to say to me?" she asked hoarsely and held her breath, waiting, as for a revelation.

The girl raised her head. Her gaze locked with Mrs. Turpin's. "Go back to hell where you came from, you old wart hog," she whispered. Her voice was low but clear. Her eyes burned for a moment as if she saw with pleasure that her message had struck its target.

Mrs. Turpin sank back in her chair.

After a moment the girl's eyes closed and she turned her head wearily to the side.

115 The doctor rose and handed the nurse the empty syringe. He leaned over and put both hands for a moment on the mother's shoulders, which were shaking. She was sitting on the floor, her lips pressed together, holding Mary Grace's hand in her lap. The girl's fingers were gripped like a baby's around her thumb. "Go on to the hospital," he said. "I'll call and make the arrangements."

"Now let's see that neck," he said in a jovial voice to Mrs. Turpin. He began to inspect her neck with his first two fingers. Two little moonshaped lines like pink fish bones were indented over her windpipe. There was the beginning of an angry red swelling above her eye. His fingers passed over this also.

"Lea' me be," she said thickly and shook him off. "See about Claud. She kicked him."

"I'll see about him in a minute," he said and felt her pulse. He was a thin gray-haired man, given to pleasantries. "Go home and have yourself a vacation the rest of the day," he said and patted her on the shoulder.

Quit your pattin me, Mrs. Turpin growled to herself.

120 "And put an ice pack over that eye," he said. Then he went and squatted down beside Claud and looked at his leg. After a moment he pulled him up and Claud limped after him into the office.

Until the ambulance came, the only sounds in the room were the tremulous moans of the girl's mother, who continued to sit on the floor. The white-trash woman did not take her eyes off the girl. Mrs. Turpin looked straight ahead at nothing. Presently the ambulance drew up, a long dark shadow, behind the curtain. The attendants came in and set the stretcher down beside the girl and lifted her expertly onto it and carried her out. The nurse helped the mother gather up her things. The shadow of the ambulance moved silently away and the nurse came back in the office.

"That ther girl is going to be a lunatic, ain't she?" the white-trash woman asked the nurse, but the nurse kept on to the back and never answered her.

"Yes, she's going to be a lunatic," the white-trash woman said to the rest of them.

"Po' critter," the old woman murmured. The child's face was still in her lap. His eyes looked idly out over her knees. He had not moved during the disturbance except to draw one leg up under him.

125 "I thank Gawd," the white-trash woman said fervently, "I ain't a lunatic."

Claud came limping out and the Turpins went home.

As their pick-up truck turned into their own dirt road and made the crest of the hill, Mrs. Turpin gripped the window ledge and looked out suspiciously. The land sloped gracefully down through a field dotted with lavender weeds and at the start of the rise their small yellow frame house, with its little flower beds spread out around it like a fancy apron, sat primly in its accustomed place between two giant hickory trees. She would not have been startled to see a burnt wound between two blackened chimneys.

Neither of them felt like eating so they put on their house clothes and lowered the shade in the bedroom and lay down, Claud with his leg on a pillow and herself with a damp washcloth over her eye. The instant she was flat on her back, the image of a razor-backed hog with warts on its face and horns coming out behind its ears snorted into her head. She moaned, a low quiet moan.

"I am not," she said tearfully, "a wart hog. From hell." But the denial had no force. The girl's eyes and her words, even the tone of her voice, low but clear, directed only to her, brooked no repudiation. She had been singled out for the message, though there was trash in the room to whom it might justly have been applied. The full force of this fact struck her only now. There was a woman there who was neglecting her own child but she had been overlooked. The message had been given to Ruby Turpin, a respectable, hard-working, church-going woman. The tears dried. Her eyes began to burn instead with wrath.

130 She rose on her elbow and the washcloth fell into her hand. Claud was lying on his back, snoring. She wanted to tell him what the girl had said. At the same time she did not wish to put the image of herself as a wart hog from hell into his mind.

"Hey, Claud," she muttered and pushed his shoulder.

Claud opened one pale baby blue eye.

She looked into it warily. He did not think about anything. He just went his way.

"Wha, whasit?" he said and closed the eye again.

135 "Nothing," she said. "Does your leg pain you?"

"Hurts like hell," Claud said.

"It'll quit terreckly," she said and lay back down. In a moment Claud was snoring again. For the rest of the afternoon they lay there. Claud slept. She scowled at the ceiling. Occasionally she raised her fist and made a small stabbing motion over her chest as if she was defending her innocence to invisible guests who were like the comforters of Job, reasonable-seeming but wrong.

About five-thirty Claud stirred. "Got to go after those niggers," he sighed, not moving.

She was looking straight up as if there were unintelligible handwriting on the ceiling. The protuberance over her eye had turned a greenish-blue. "Listen here," she said.

140 "What"?

"Kiss me."

Claud leaned over and kissed her loudly on the mouth. He pinched her side and their hands interlocked. Her expression of ferocious concentration did not change. Claud got up, groaning and growling, and limped off. She continued to study the ceiling.

She did not get up until she heard the pick-up truck coming back with the Negroes. Then she rose and thrust her feet in her brown oxfords, which she did not bother to lace, and stumped out onto the back porch and got her red plastic bucket. She emptied a tray of ice cubes into it and filled it half full of water and went out into the back yard. Every afternoon after Claud brought the hands in, one of the boys helped him put out hay and the rest waited in the back of the truck until he was ready to take them home. The truck was parked in the shade under one one of the hickory trees.

"Hi yawl this evening?" Mrs. Turpin asked grimly, appearing with the bucket and the dipper. There were three women and a boy in the truck.

145 "Us doin nicely," the oldest woman said. "Hi you doin?" and her gaze stuck immediately on the dark lump on Mrs. Turpin's forehead. "You done fell down, ain't you?" she asked in a solicitous voice. The old woman was dark and almost toothless. She had on an old felt hat of Claud's set back on her head. The other two women were younger and lighter and they both had new bright green sun hats. One of them had hers on her head; the other had taken hers off and the boy was grinning beneath it.

Mrs. Turpin set the bucket down on the floor of the truck. "Yawl hep yourselves," she said. She looked around to make sure Claud had gone. "No. I didn't fall down," she said, folding her arms. "It was something worse than that."

"Ain't nothing bad happen to you!" the old woman said. She said it as if they all knew Mrs. Turpin was protected in some special way by Divine Providence. "You just had you a little fall."

"We were in town at the doctor's office for where the cow kicked Mr. Turpin," Mrs. Turpin said in a flat tone that indicated they could leave off their foolishness. "And there was this girl there. A big fat girl with her face all broke out. I could look at that girl and tell she was peculiar but I couldn't tell how. And me and her mama were just talking and going along and all of a sudden WHAM! She throws this big book she was reading at me and . . ."

"Naw!" the old woman cried out.

"And then she jumps over the table and commences to choke me."

"Naw!" they all exclaimed, "naw!"

"Hi come she do that?" the old woman asked. "What ail her?"

Mrs. Turpin only glared in front of her.

"Somethin ail her," the old woman said.

"They carried her off in an ambulance," Mrs. Turpin continued, "but before she went she was rolling on the floor and they were trying to hold her down to give her a shot and she said something to me." She paused. "You know what she said to me?"

"What she say?" they asked.

"She said," Mrs. Turpin began, and stopped, her face very dark and heavy. The sun was getting whiter and whiter, blanching the sky overhead so that the leaves of the hickory tree were black in the face of it. She could not bring forth the words. "Something real ugly," she muttered.

"She sho shouldn't said nothin ugly to you," the old woman said. "You so sweet. You the sweetest lady I know."

"She pretty too," the one with the hat on said.

"And stout," the other one said. "I never knowed no sweeter white lady."

"That's the truth befo' Jesus," the old woman said. "Amen! You des as sweet and pretty as you can be."

Mrs. Turpin knew just exactly how much Negro flattery was worth and it added to her rage. "She said," she began again and finished this time with a fierce rush of breath, "that I was an old wart hog from hell."

There was an astounded silence.

"Where she at?" the youngest woman cried in a piercing voice.

"Lemme see her. I'll kill her!"

"I'll kill her with you!" the other one cried.

"She b'long in the sylum," the old woman said emphatically. "You the sweetest white lady I know."

"She pretty too," the other two said. "Stout as she can be and sweet. Jesus satisfied with her!"

"Deed he is," the old woman declared.

Idiots! Mrs. Turpin growled to herself. You could never say anything intelligent to a nigger. You could talk at them but not with them. "Yawl ain't drunk your water," she said shortly. "Leave the bucket in the truck when you're finished with it. I got more to do than just stand around and pass the time of day," and she moved off and into the house.

She stood for a moment in the middle of the kitchen. The dark protuberance over her eye looked like a miniature tornado cloud which might any moment sweep across the horizon of her brow. Her lower lip protruded dangerously. She squared her massive shoulders. Then she marched into the front of the house and out the side door and started down the road to the pig parlor. She had the look of a woman going single-handed, weaponless, into battle.

The sun was a deep yellow now like a harvest moon and was riding westward very fast over the far tree line as if it meant to reach the hogs before she did. The road was rutted and she kicked several good-sized stones out of her path as she strode along. The pig parlor was on a little knoll at the end of a lane that ran off from the side of the barn. It was a square of concrete as large as a small room, with a board fence about four feet high around it. The concrete floor sloped slightly so that the hog wash could drain off into a trench where it was carried to the field for fertilizer. Claud was standing on the outside, on the edge of the concrete, hanging onto the top board, hosing down the floor inside. The hose was connected to the faucet of a water trough nearby.

Mrs. Turpin climbed up beside him and glowered down at the hogs inside. There were seven long-snouted bristly shoats in it—tan with liver-colored spots—and an old sow a few weeks off from farrowing. She was lying on her side grunting. The shoats were running about shaking themselves like idiot children, their little slit pig eyes searching the floor for anything left. She had read that pigs were the most intelligent animal. She doubted it. They were supposed to be smarter than dogs. There had even been a pig astronaut. He had performed his assignment perfectly but died of a heart attack afterwards because they left him in his electric suit, sitting upright throughout his examination when naturally a hog should be on all fours.

A-gruntin and a-rootin and a-groanin.

175 "Gimme that hose," she said, yanking it away from Claud. "Go on and carry them niggers home and then get off that leg."

"You look like you might have swallowed a mad dog," Claud observed, but he got down and limped off. He paid no attention to her humors.

Until he was out of earshot, Mrs. Turpin stood on the side of the pen, holding the hose and pointing the stream of water at the hind quarter of any shoat that looked as if it might try to lie down. When he had had time to get over the hill, she turned her head slightly and her wrathful eyes scanned the path. He was nowhere in sight. She turned back again and seemed to gather herself up. Her shoulders rose and she drew in her breath.

"What do you send me a message like that for?" she said in a low fierce voice, barely above a whisper but with the force of a shout in its concentrated fury. "How am I a hog and me both? How am I saved and from hell too?" Her free fist was knotted and with the other she gripped the hose, blindly pointing the stream of water in and out of the eye of the old sow whose outraged squeal she did not hear.

The pig parlor commanded a view of the back pasture where their twenty beef cows were gathered around the hay-bales Claud and the boy had put out. The freshly cut pasture sloped down to the highway. Across it was their cotton field and beyond that a dark green dusty wood which they owned as well. The sun was behind the wood, very red, looking over the paling of trees like a farmer inspecting his own hogs.

180 "Why me?" she rumbled. "It's no trash around here, black or white, that I haven't given to. And break my back to the bone every day working. And do for the church."

She appeared to be the right size woman to command the arena before her. "How am I a hog?" she demanded. "Exactly how am I like them?" and she jabbed the stream of water at the shoats. "There was plenty of trash there. It didn't have to be me."

"If you like trash better, go get yourself some trash then," she railed. "You could have made me trash. Or a nigger. If trash is what you wanted why didn't you make me trash?" She shook her fist with the hose in it and a watery snake appeared momentarily in the air. "I could quit working and take it easy and be filthy," she growled. "Lounge about the sidewalks all day drinking root beer. Dip snuff and spit in every puddle and have it all over my face. I could be nasty."

"Or you could have made me a nigger. It's too late for me to be a nigger," she said with deep sarcasm, "but I could act like one. Lay down in the middle of the road and stop traffic. Roll on the ground."

In the deepening light everything was taking on a mysterious hue. The pasture was growing a peculiar glassy green and the streak of highway had turned lavender. She braced herself for a final assault and this time her voice rolled out over the pasture. "Go on," she yelled, "call me a hog! Call me a hog again. From hell. Call me a wart hog from hell. Put that bottom rail on top. There'll still be a top and bottom!"

185 A garbled echo returned to her.

A final surge of fury shook her and she roared, "Who do you think you are?"

The color of everything, field and crimson sky, burned for a moment with a transparent intensity. The question carried over the pasture and across the highway and the cotton field and returned to her clearly like an answer from beyond the wood.

She opened her mouth but no sound came out of it.

A tiny truck, Claud's, appeared on the highway, heading rapidly out of sight. Its gears scraped thinly. It looked like a child's toy. At any moment a bigger truck might smash into it and scatter Claud's and the niggers' brains all over the road.

190 Mrs. Turpin stood there, her gaze fixed on the highway, all her muscles rigid, until in five or six minutes the truck reappeared, returning. She waited until it had had time to turn into their own road. Then like a monumental statue coming to life, she bent her head slowly and gazed, as if through the very heart of the mystery, down into the pig parlor at the hogs. They had settled all in one corner around the old sow who was grunting softly. A red glow suffused them. They appeared to pant with a secret life.

Until the sun slipped finally behind the tree line, Mrs. Turpin remained there with her gaze bent to them as if she were absorbing some abysmal life-giving knowledge. At last she lifted her head. There was only a purple streak in the sky, cutting through a field of crimson and leading, like an extension of the highway, into the descending dusk. She raised her hands from the side of the pen in a gesture hieratic and profound. A visionary light settled in her eyes. She saw the streak as a vast swinging bridge extending upward from the earth through a field of living fire. Upon it a vast horde of souls were rumbling toward heaven. There were whole companies of white-trash, clean for the first time in their lives, and bands of black niggers in white robes, and battalions of freaks and lunatics shouting and clapping and leaping like frogs. And bringing up the end of the procession was a tribe of people whom she recognized at once as those who, like herself and Claud, had always had a little of everything and the God-given wit to use it right. She leaned forward to observe them closer. They were marching behind the others with great dignity, accountable as they had always been for good order and common sense and respectable behavior. They alone were on key. Yet she could see by their shocked and altered faces that even their virtues were being burned away. She lowered her hands and gripped the rail of the hog pen, her eyes small but fixed unblinkingly on what lay ahead. In a moment the vision faded but she remained where she was, immobile.

At length she got down and turned off the faucet and made her slow way on the darkening path to the house. In the woods around her the invisible cricket choruses had struck up, but what she heard were the voices of the souls climbing upward into the starry field and shouting hallelujah.

[1964]

Remarks from Essays and Letters

From "The Fiction Writer and His Country"

In the greatest fiction, the writer's moral sense coincides with his dramatic sense, and I see no way for it to do this unless his moral judgment is part of the very act of seeing, and he is free to use it. I have heard it said that belief in Christian dogma is a hindrance to the writer, but I myself have found nothing further from the truth. Actually, it frees the storyteller to observe. It is not a set of rules which fixes what he sees in the world. It affects his writing primarily by guaranteeing his respect for mystery. . . .

When I look at stories I have written I find that they are, for the most part, about people who are poor, who are afflicted in both mind and body, who have little—or at best a distorted—sense of spiritual purpose, and whose actions do not apparently give the reader a great assurance of the joy of life.

Yet how is this? For I am no disbeliever in spiritual purpose and no vague believer. I see from the standpoint of Christian orthodoxy. This means that for me the meaning of life is centered in our Redemption by Christ and what I see in the world I see in its relation to that. . . .

The novelist with Christian concerns will find in modern life distortions which are repugnant to him, and his problem will be to make these appear as distortions to an audience which is used to seeing them as natural; and he may well be forced to take ever more violent means to get his vision across to this hostile audience. When you can assume that your audience holds the same beliefs you do, you can relax a little and use more normal means of talking to it; when you have to assume that it does not, then you have to make your vision apparent by shock—to the hard of hearing you shout, and for the almost-blind you draw large and startling figures.

From "Some Aspects of the Grotesque in Southern Fiction"

If the writer believes that our life is and will remain essentially mysterious, if he looks upon us as beings existing in a created order to whose laws we freely respond, then what he sees on the surface will be of interest to him only as he can go through it into an experience of mystery itself. His kind of fiction will always be pushing its own limits outward toward the limits of mystery, because for this kind of writer, the meaning of a story does not begin except at a depth where adequate motivation and adequate psychology and the various determinations have been exhausted. Such a writer will be interested in what we don't understand rather than in what we do. He will be interested in possibility rather than in probability. He will be interested in characters who are forced out to meet evil and grace and who act on a trust beyond themselves—whether they know very clearly what it is they act upon or not. To the modern mind, this kind of character, and his creator, are typical Don Quixotes, tilting at[1] what is not there.

From "The Nature and Aim of Fiction"

The novel works by a slower accumulation of detail than the short story does. The short story requires more drastic procedures than the novel because more has to

[1]**tilting at** "tilting at windmills" is a popular expression that derives from Cervantes's novel *Don Quixote,* published in 1604/5.

be accomplished in less space. The details have to carry more immediate weight. In good fiction, certain of the details will tend to accumulate meaning from the story itself, and when this happens, they become symbolic in their action.

Now the word *symbol* scares a good many people off, just as the word *art* does. They seem to feel that a symbol is some mysterious thing put in arbitrarily by the writer to frighten the common reader—sort of a literary Masonic grip that is only for the initiated. They seem to think that it is a way of saying something that you aren't actually saying, and so if they can be got to read a reputedly symbolic work at all, they approach it as if it were a problem in algebra. Find *x*. And when they do find or think they find this abstraction, *x,* then they go off with an elaborate sense of satisfaction and the notion that they have "understood" the story. Many students confuse the *process* of understanding a thing with understanding it.

I think that for the fiction writer himself, symbols are something he uses simply as a matter of course. You might say that these are details that, while having their essential place in the literal level of the story, operate in depth as well as on the surface, increasing the story in every direction. . . .

People have a habit of saying, "What is the theme of your story?" and they expect you to give them a statement: "The theme of my story is the economic pressure of the machine on the middle class"—or some such absurdity. And when they've got a statement like that, they go off happy and feel it is no longer necessary to read the story.

Some people have the notion that you read the story and then climb out of it into the meaning, but for the fiction writer himself the whole story is the meaning, because it is an experience, not an abstraction.

From "Writing Short Stories"

Being short does not mean being slight. A short story should be long in depth and should give us an experience of meaning. . . .

Meaning is what keeps the short story from being short. I prefer to talk about the meaning in a story rather than the theme of a story. People talk about the theme of a story as if the theme were like the string that a sack of chicken feed is tied with. They think that if you can pick out the theme, the way you pick the right thread in the chicken-feed sack, you can rip the story open and feed the chickens. But this is not the way meaning works in fiction.

When you can state the theme of a story, when you can separate it from the story itself, then you can be sure the story is not a very good one. The meaning of a story has to be embodied in it, has to be made concrete in it. A story is a way to say something that can't be said any other way, and it takes every word in the story to say what the meaning is. You tell a story because a statement would be inadequate. When anybody asks what a story is about, the only proper thing is to tell him to read the story. The meaning of fiction is not abstract meaning but experienced meaning, and the purpose of making statements about the meaning of a story is only to help you to experience that meaning more fully.

On Interpreting "A Good Man Is Hard to Find"

A professor of English had sent O'Connor the following letter: "I am writing as spokesman for three members of our department and some ninety university students in three classes who for a week now have been discussing your story 'A Good Man Is Hard to Find.' We have debated at length several possible interpretations, none of which fully satisfies us. In general we believe that the appearance of the Misfit is not 'real' in the same sense that the incidents of the first half of the story are real. Bailey, we believe, imagines the appearance of the Misfit, whose activities have been called to his attention on the night before the trip and again during the stopover at the roadside restaurant. Bailey, we further believe, identifies himself with the Misfit and so plays two roles in the imaginary last half of the story. But we cannot, after great effort, determine the point at which reality fades into illusion or reverie. Does the accident literally occur, or is it a part of Bailey's dream? Please believe me when I say we are not seeking an easy way out of our difficulty. We admire your story and have examined it with great care, but we are convinced that we are missing something important which you intended for us to grasp. We will all be very grateful if you comment on the interpretation which I have outlined above and if you will give us further comments about your intention in writing 'A Good Man Is Hard to Find.'" She replied:

To a Professor of English

28 March 61

The interpretation of your ninety students and three teachers is fantastic and about as far from my intentions as it could get to be. If it were a legitimate interpretation, the story would be little more than a trick and its interest would be simply for abnormal psychology. I am not interested in abnormal psychology.

There is a change of tension from the first part of the story to the second where the Misfit enters, but this is no lessening of reality. This story is, of course, not meant to be realistic in the sense that it portrays the everyday doings of people in Georgia. It is stylized and its conventions are comic even though its meaning is serious.

Bailey's only importance is as the Grandmother's boy and the driver of the car. It is the Grandmother who first recognizes the Misfit and who is most concerned with him throughout. The story is a duel of sorts between the Grandmother and her superficial beliefs and the Misfit's more profoundly felt involvement with Christ's action which set the world off balance for him.

The meaning of a story should go on expanding for the reader the more he thinks about it, but meaning cannot be captured in an interpretation. If teachers are in the habit of approaching a story as if it were a research problem for which any answer is believable so long as it is not obvious, then I think students will never learn to enjoy fiction. Too much interpretation is certainly worse than too little and where feeling for a story is absent, theory will not supply it.

My tone is not meant to be obnoxious. I am in a state of shock.

"A Reasonable Use of the Unreasonable"

Last fall I received a letter from a student who said she would be "graciously appreciative" if I would tell her "just what enlightenment" I expected her to get from each of my stories. I suspect she had a paper to write. I wrote her back to forget about the enlightenment and just try to enjoy them. I knew that was the most unsatisfactory answer I could have given because, of course, she didn't want to enjoy them, she just wanted to figure them out.

In most English classes the short story has become a kind of literary specimen to be dissected. Every time a story of mine appears in a Freshman anthology, I have a vision of it, with its little organs laid open, like a frog in a bottle.

I realize that a certain amount of this what-is-the-significance has to go on, but I think something has gone wrong in the process when, for so many students, the story becomes simply a problem to be solved, something which you evaporate to get Instant Enlightenment.

A story really isn't any good unless it successfully resists paraphrase, unless it hangs on and expands in the mind. Properly, you analyze to enjoy, but it's equally true that to analyze with any discrimination, you have to have enjoyed already, and I think that the best reason to hear a story read is that it should stimulate that primary enjoyment.

I don't have any pretensions to being an Aeschylus or Sophocles and providing you in this story with a cathartic experience out of your mythic background, though this story I'm going to read certainly calls up a good deal of the South's mythic background, and it should elicit from you a degree of pity and terror, even though its way of being serious is a comic one. I do think, though, that like the Greeks you should know what is going to happen in this story so that any element of suspense in it will be transferred from its surface to its interior.

I would be most happy if you have already read it, happier still if you knew it well, but since experience has taught me to keep my expectations along these lines modest, I'll tell you that this is the story of a family of six which, on its way driving to Florida, gets wiped out by an escaped convict who calls himself the Misfit. The family is made up of the Grandmother and her son, Bailey, and his children, John Wesley and June Star and the baby, and there is also the cat and the children's mother. The cat is named Pitty Sing, and the Grandmother is taking him with them, hidden in a basket.

Now I think it behooves me to try to establish with you the basis on which reason operates in this story. Much of my fiction takes its character from a reasonable use of the unreasonable, though the reasonableness of my use of it may not always be apparent. The assumptions that underlie this use of it, however, are those of the central Christian mysteries. These are assumptions to which a large part of the modern audience takes exception. About this I can only say that there are perhaps other ways than my own in which this story could be read, but none other by which it could have been written. Belief, in my own case anyway, is the engine that makes perception operate.

The heroine of this story, the Grandmother, is in the most significant position life offers the Christian. She is facing death. And to all appearances she, like the rest of us, is not too well prepared for it. She would like to see the event postponed. Indefinitely.

I've talked to a number of teachers who use this story in class and who tell their students that the Grandmother is evil, that in fact, she's a witch, even down to the cat. One of these teachers told me that his students, and particularly his Southern students, resisted this interpretation with a certain bemused vigor, and he didn't understand why. I had to tell him that they resisted it because they all had grandmothers or great-aunts just like her at home, and they knew, from personal experience, that the old lady lacked comprehension, but that she had a good heart. The Southerner is usually tolerant of those weaknesses that proceed from innocence, and he knows that a taste for self-preservation can be readily combined with the missionary spirit.

This same teacher was telling his students that morally the Misfit was several cuts above the Grandmother. He had a really sentimental attachment to the Misfit. But then a prophet gone wrong is almost always more interesting than your grandmother, and you have to let people take their pleasures where they find them.

It is true that the old lady is a hypocritical old soul; her wits are no match for the Misfit's, nor is her capacity for grace equal to his; yet I think the unprejudiced reader will feel that the Grandmother has a special kind of triumph in this story which instinctively we do not allow to someone altogether bad.

I often ask myself what makes a story work, and what makes it hold up as a story, and I have decided that it is probably some action, some gesture of a character that is unlike any other in the story, one which indicates where the real heart of the story lies. This would have to be an action or a gesture which was both totally right and totally unexpected; it would have to be one that was both in character and beyond character; it would have to suggest both the world and eternity. The action or gesture I'm talking about would have to be on the anagogical level, that is, the level which has to do with the Divine life and our participation in it. It would be a gesture that transcended any neat allegory that might have been intended or any pat moral categories a reader could make. It would be a gesture which somehow made contact with mystery.

There is a point in this story where such a gesture occurs. The Grandmother is at last alone, facing the Misfit. Her head clears for an instant and she realizes, even in her limited way, that she is responsible for the man before her and joined to him by ties of kinship which have their roots deep in the mystery she has been merely prattling about so far. And at this point, she does the right thing, she makes the right gesture.

I find that students are often puzzled by what she says and does here, but I think myself that if I took out this gesture and what she says with it, I would have no story. What was left would not be worth your attention. Our age not only does not have a very sharp eye for the almost imperceptible intrusions of grace, it no longer has much feeling for the nature of the violences which precede and follow them. The devil's greatest wile, Baudelaire has said, is to convince us that he does not exist.

I suppose the reasons for the use of so much violence in modern fiction will differ with each writer who uses it, but in my own stories I have found that violence is strangely capable of returning my characters to reality and preparing them to accept their moment of grace. Their heads are so hard that almost nothing else will do the work. This idea, that reality is something to which we must be returned at considerable cost, is one which is seldom understood by the casual reader, but it is one which is implicit in the Christian view of the world.

I don't want to equate the Misfit with the devil. I prefer to think that, however unlikely this may seem, the old lady's gesture, like the mustard-seed, will grow to be a great crow-filled tree in the Misfit's heart, and will be enough of a pain to him there to turn him into the prophet he was meant to become. But that's another story.

This story has been called grotesque, but I prefer to call it literal. A good story is literal in the same sense that a child's drawing is literal. When a child draws, he doesn't intend to distort but to set down exactly what he sees, and as his gaze is direct, he sees the lines that create motion. Now the lines of motion that interest the writer are usually invisible. They are lines of spiritual motion. And in this story you should be on the lookout for such things as the action of grace in the Grandmother's soul, and not for the dead bodies.

We hear many complaints about the prevalence of violence in modern fiction, and it is always assumed that this violence is a bad thing and meant to be an end in itself. With the serious writer, violence is never an end in itself. It is the extreme situation that best reveals what we are essentially, and I believe these are times when writers are more interested in what we are essentially than in the tenor of our daily lives. Violence is a force which can be used for good or evil, and among other things taken by it is the kingdom of heaven. But regardless of what can be taken by it, the man in the violent situation reveals those qualities least dispensable in his personality, those qualities which are all he will have to take into eternity with him; and since the characters in this story are all on the verge of eternity, it is appropriate to think of what they take with them. In any case, I hope that if you consider these points in connection with the story, you will come to see it as something more than an account of a family murdered on the way to Florida.

[1957]

CHAPTER 15

Reading and Writing about Plays

Types of Plays

Most of the world's great plays written before the twentieth century may be regarded as one of two kinds: **tragedy** or **comedy.** Roughly speaking, tragedy dramatizes the conflict between the vitality of the individual life and the laws or limits of life. The tragic hero reaches a height, going beyond the experience of others but at the cost of his or her life. Comedy, on the other hand, dramatizes the vitality of the laws of social life. In comedy, the good life is seen to reside in the shedding of an individualism that isolates, in favor of a union with a genial and enlightened society. These points must be amplified a bit before we go on to the further point that, of course, any important play does much more than can be put into such crude formulas.

Tragedy

Tragic heroes usually go beyond the standards to which reasonable people adhere; they do some fearful deed which ultimately destroys them. This deed is often said to be an act of **hubris,** a Greek word meaning something like "overweening pride." It may involve, for instance, violating a taboo, such as that against taking life. But if the hubristic act ultimately destroys the man or woman who performs it, it also shows that person (paradoxically) to be in some way more fully a living being—a person who has experienced life more fully, whether by heroic action or by capacity for enduring suffering—than the other characters in the play. (If the tragic hero does not die, he or she is usually left in some deathlike state, as is the blind Oedipus in *Oedipus the King*.) In tragedy we see humanity pushed to an extreme; the hero enters a world unknown to most and reveals magnificence. After the hero's departure from the stage, we are left in a world of smaller people.

What has just been said may (or may not) be true of most tragedies, but it is not true of all. If you are writing about a tragedy, you might consider whether the points just made are illustrated in your play. Is the hero guilty of hubris? Does the hero seem a greater person than the others in the play? An essay examining such questions probably requires not only a character sketch but also comparison with other characters.

Tragedy commonly involves **irony** of two sorts: unconsciously ironic deeds and unconsciously ironic speeches. Ironic deeds have some consequence more or less the reverse of what the doer intends. Macbeth thinks that by killing Duncan he will gain happiness, but he finds that his deed brings him sleepless nights. Brutus thinks that by killing Caesar he will bring liberty to Rome, but he brings tyranny. In an unconsciously ironic speech, the words mean one thing to the speaker but something more significant to the audience, as when King Duncan, baffled by Cawdor's treason, says:

There's no art
To find the mind's construction in the face:
He was a gentleman on whom I built
An absolute trust.

At this moment Macbeth, whom we have already heard meditating the murder of Duncan, enters. Duncan's words are true, but he does not apply them to Macbeth, as the audience does. A few moments later Duncan praises Macbeth as "a peerless kinsman." Soon Macbeth will indeed become peerless, when he kills Duncan and ascends to the throne.[1] Sophocles' use of ironic deeds and speeches is so pervasive, especially in *Oedipus Rex,* that **Sophoclean irony** has become a critical term.

When the deed backfires or has a reverse effect, such as Macbeth's effort to gain happiness has, we have what Aristotle (the first—and still the greatest—drama critic) called a **peripeteia,** or a **reversal.** A character who comes to perceive what has happened (Macbeth's "I have lived long enough: my way of life / Is fall'n into the sere, the yellow leaf") experiences (in Aristotle's language) an **anagnorisis,** or **recognition.** Strictly speaking, for Aristotle the recognition was a matter of literal identification—for example, the recognition that Oedipus was the son of a man he killed. In *Macbeth,* the recognition in this sense is that Macduff, "from his mother's womb / Untimely ripped," is the man who fits the prophecy that Macbeth can be conquered only by someone not "of woman born."

In his analysis of drama, Aristotle says that the tragic hero comes to grief through his **hamartia,** a term sometimes translated as **tragic flaw** but perhaps better translated as **tragic error,** since *flaw* implies a moral fault. Thus it is a great error for Hamlet not to inspect the foils at the start of the deadly fencing match with Laertes; had he done so, he would have seen that one of the foils was blunt and one pointed. If we hold to the translation *flaw,* we begin to hunt for a fault in the tragic hero's character; and we say, for instance, that Hamlet is gullible, or some such thing. In doing this, we may diminish or even overlook the hero's grandeur.

Comedy

Although in tragedy the hero usually seems to embody certain values that are superior to those of the surrounding society, in comedy the fullest life is seen to reside *within* enlightened social norms: At the beginning of a comedy we find banished dukes, unhappy lovers, crabby parents, jealous husbands, and harsh laws; but at the end we usually have a unified and genial society, often symbolized by a marriage feast to which everyone, or almost everyone, is invited. Early in *A Midsummer Night's Dream,* for instance, we meet quarreling young lovers and a father who demands that his daughter either marry a man she does not love or enter a convent. Such is the Athenian law. At the end of the play the lovers are properly matched, to everyone's satisfaction.

[1]**Dramatic irony** (ironic deeds, or happenings, and unconsciously ironic speeches) must be distinguished from **verbal irony,** which is produced when the speaker is *conscious* that his words mean something different from what they say. In *Macbeth* Lennox says, "The gracious Duncan / Was pitied of Macbeth. Marry, he was dead! / And the right valiant Banquo walked too late. / . . . / Men must not walk too late." He *says* nothing about Macbeth having killed Duncan and Banquo, but he *means* that Macbeth has killed them.

Speaking broadly, most comedies fall into one of two classes: **satiric comedy** or **romantic comedy.** In satiric comedy, the emphasis is on the obstructionists—the irate fathers, hardheaded businessmen, and other members of the establishment who at the beginning of the play seem to hold all the cards, preventing joy from reigning. They are held up to ridicule because they are repressive monomaniacs enslaved to themselves, acting mechanistically (always irate, always hardheaded) instead of responding genially to the ups and downs of life. The outwitting of these obstructionists, usually by the younger generation, often provides the resolution of the plot. Ben Jonson, Molière, and George Bernard Shaw are in this tradition; their comedy, according to an ancient Roman formula, "chastens morals with ridicule"—that is, it reforms folly or vice by laughing at it. On the other hand, in romantic comedy (think of Shakespeare's *A Midsummer Night's Dream, As You Like It,* and *Twelfth Night*) the emphasis is on a pair or pairs of delightful people who engage our sympathies as they run their obstacle race to the altar. There are obstructionists here too, but the emphasis is on festivity.

In writing about comedy you may be concerned with the function of one scene or character. But whatever your topic, you may find it helpful to begin by trying to decide whether the play is primarily romantic or primarily satiric (or something else). One way of getting at this is to ask yourself to what degree you sympathize with the characters. Do you laugh *with* them, sympathetically, or on the other hand do you laugh *at* them, regarding them as at least somewhat contemptible?

Elements of Drama

Theme

If we have read or seen a drama thoughtfully, we ought to be able to formulate its **theme,** its underlying idea—and perhaps we can even go so far as to say its moral attitudes, its view of life, its wisdom. Some critics, it is true, have argued that the concept of theme is meaningless. They hold that *Macbeth,* for example, gives us only an extremely detailed history of one imaginary man. In this view, *Macbeth* says nothing to you or me; it only says what happened to some imaginary man. Even *Julius Caesar* says nothing about the historical Julius Caesar or about the nature of Roman politics. Here we can agree; no one would offer Shakespeare's play as evidence of what the historical Caesar said or did. But surely the view that the concept of theme is meaningless, and that a work tells us only about imaginary creatures, is a desperate one. We *can* say that we see in *Julius Caesar* the fall of power, or (if we are thinking of Brutus) the vulnerability of idealism, or some such thing.

To the reply that these are mere truisms, we can counter: Yes, but the truisms are presented in such a way that they take on life and become a part of us rather than remain things of which we say, "I've heard it said, and I guess it's so." The play offers instruction, in a pleasant and persuasive way. And surely we are in no danger of equating the play with the theme that we sense underlies it. We recognize that the play presents the theme with such detail that our statement is only a wedge to help us enter into the play.

Some critics (influenced by Aristotle's statement that a drama is an imitation of an action) use **action** in a sense equivalent to theme. In this sense, the action is the underlying happening—the inner happening—for example, "the enlightenment of a character," or "the coming of unhappiness to a character," or "the finding of the self by self-surrender." It might be said that the theme of *Macbeth,* is embodied in some words that Macbeth himself utters: "Blood will have blood." This is not to say that these words and no other words embody the theme or the action; it is only to say that these words seem to the writer (and, if the essay is effective, to the reader) to bring us close to the center of the play.

Plot

Plot is variously defined, sometimes as equivalent to *story* (in this sense a synopsis of *Julius Caesar* has the same plot as *Julius Caesar*), but more often, and more usefully, as the dramatist's particular *arrangement of the story.* Thus, because Shakespeare's *Julius Caesar* begins with a scene dramatizing an encounter between plebeians and tribunes, its plot is different from that of a play on Julius Caesar in which such a scene (not necessary to the story) is omitted.

Handbooks on drama often suggest that a plot (arrangement of happenings) should have a **rising action,** a **climax,** and a **falling action.** This sort of plot can be diagrammed as a pyramid: The tension rises through complications or **crises** to a climax, at which point the climax is the apex, and the tension allegedly slackens as we witness the **dénouement** (literally, *unknotting*). Shakespeare sometimes used a pyramidal structure, placing his climax neatly in the middle of what seems to us to be the third of five acts. In *Hamlet,* the protagonist proves to his own satisfaction Claudius's guilt in 3.2, with the play within the play; but almost immediately he begins to worsen his position, by failing to kill Claudius when he is an easy target (3.3) and by contaminating himself with the murder of Polonius (3.4). In *Romeo and Juliet,* the first half shows Romeo winning Juliet; but when in 3.1 he kills her cousin Tybalt, Romeo sets in motion the second half of the play, the losing of Juliet and of his own life.

Of course, no law demands such a structure, and a hunt for the pyramid usually causes the hunter to overlook all the crises but the middle one. William Butler Yeats once suggestively diagrammed a good plot not as a pyramid but as a line moving diagonally upward, punctuated by several crises. Perhaps it is sufficient to say that a good plot has its moments of tension, but the location of these will vary with the play. They are the product of **conflict,** but it should be noted that not all conflict produces tension; there is conflict but little tension in a ball game when the home team is ahead 10–0 and the visiting pitcher comes to bat in the ninth inning with two out and none on base.

Regardless of how a plot is diagramed, the **exposition** is that part that tells the audience what it has to know about the past, the **antecedent action.** Two gossiping servants who tell each other that after a year away in Paris the young master is coming home tomorrow with a new wife are giving the audience the exposition. But the exposition may also extend far into the play, being given in small, explosive revelations.

Exposition has been discussed as though it consists simply of informing the audience about events, but exposition can do much more. It can give us an understanding of the characters who themselves are talking about other characters, it can evoke a mood, and it can generate tension. When we summarize the opening act, and treat it as "mere exposition," we are probably losing what is dramatic in it.

In fact, exposition usually includes **foreshadowing.** Details given in the exposition, which we may at first take as mere background, often turn out to be highly relevant to later developments. For instance, in the very short first scene of

Macbeth the witches introduce the name of Macbeth, but in such words as "Fair is foul" and "when the battle's lost and won" they also give glimpses of what will happen: Macbeth will become foul, and though he will seem to win (he becomes king) he will lose the most important battle. Similarly, during the exposition in the second scene we learn that Macbeth has loyally defeated Cawdor, who betrayed King Duncan, and Macbeth has been given Cawdor's title. Later we will find that, like Cawdor, Macbeth betrays Duncan. That is, in giving us the background about Cawdor, the exposition is also telling us (though we don't know it, when we first see or read the play) something about what will happen to Macbeth.

In writing about an aspect of plot, you may want to consider one of the following topics:

- Is the plot improbable? If so, is the play therefore weak?
- Does a scene that might at first glance seem unimportant or even irrelevant serve an important function?
- If certain actions that could be shown onstage take place offstage, is there a reason? In *Macbeth,* for instance, why do you suppose the murder of Duncan takes place offstage, whereas Banquo and Macduff's family are murdered onstage? Why, then, might Shakespeare have preferred not to show us the murder of Duncan? What has he gained? (A good way to approach this sort of question is to think of what your own reaction would be if the action were shown on the stage.)
- If there are several conflicts—for example, between pairs of lovers or between parents and their children and also between the parents themselves—how are these conflicts related? Are they parallel? Or contrasting?
- Does the arrangement of scenes have a structure? For instance, do the scenes depict a rise and then a fall?
- Does the plot seem satisfactorily concluded? Are there loose threads? If so, is the apparent lack of a complete resolution a weakness in the play? Or does it serve a function?

Gestures

The language of a play, broadly conceived, includes the **gestures** that the characters make and the settings in which they make them. As Ezra Pound says, "The medium of drama is not words, but persons moving about on a stage using words." Because plays are meant to be seen, make every effort to visualize the action when you read a play. Ibsen is getting at something important when he tells us in a stage direction that Nora "walks cautiously over to the door to the study and listens." Her silent actions tell us as much about her as many of her speeches do.

Gesture can be interpreted even more broadly: The mere fact that a character enters, leaves, or does not enter may be highly significant. John Russell Brown comments on the actions and the absence of certain words that in *Hamlet* convey the growing separation between King Claudius and his wife, Gertrude:

> Their first appearance together with a public celebration of marriage is a large and simple visual effect, and Gertrude's close concern for her son suggests a simple, and perhaps unremarkable modification. . . . But Claudius enters without Gertrude for his "Prayer Scene" (3.2) and, for the first time, Gertrude enters without him for the Closet Scene (3.4) and is left alone, again for the first time, when Polonius hides behind the arras. Thereafter earlier accord is revalued by an increasing separation, often poignantly silent and unexpected.

When Claudius calls Gertrude to leave with him after Hamlet has dragged off Polonius' body, she makes no reply; twice more he urges her and she is still silent. But he does not remonstrate or question; rather he speaks of his own immediate concerns and, far from supporting her with assurances, becomes more aware of his own fears:

O, come away!
My soul is full of discord and dismay. (4.1.44–45)

Emotion has been so heightened that it is remarkable that they leave together without further words. The audience has been aware of a new distance between Gertrude and Claudius, of her immobility and silence, and of his self-concern, haste, and insistence.[2]

Setting

Drama of the nineteenth and early twentieth centuries (for example, the plays of Henrik Ibsen, Anton Chekhov, and George Bernard Shaw) is often thought to be "realistic," but even a realistic playwright or stage designer selects from among many available materials. A **realistic setting** (indication of the **locale**), then, can say a great deal, and can even serve as a symbol. Over and over again in Ibsen we find the realistic setting of a nineteenth-century drawing room, with its heavy draperies and its bulky furniture, helping to convey his vision of a bourgeois world that oppresses the individual who struggles to affirm other values.

Twentieth-century dramatists are often explicit about the symbolic qualities of the setting. Here is an example from Eugene O'Neill's *Desire Under the Elms;* only a part of the initial stage direction is given:

The house is in good condition but in need of paint. Its walls are a sickly grayish, the green of the shutters faded. Two enormous elms are on each side of the house. They bend their trailing branches down over the roof. They appear to protect and at the same time subdue. There is a sinister maternity in their aspect, a crushing, jealous absorption. . . . They are like exhausted women resting their sagging breasts and hands and hair on its roof.

Not surprisingly, the action in the play includes deeds of "sinister maternity" (a mother kills her infant) and "jealous absorption."

In *The Glass Menagerie* Tennessee Williams tells us that

the apartment faces an alley and is entered by a fire-escape, a structure whose name is a touch of accidental poetic truth, for all of these huge buildings are always burning with the slow and implacable fires of human desperation.

Characterization and Motivation

Characterization, or personality, is defined, as in fiction (see pages 358–59), by what the characters do (a stage direction tells us that "Nora dances more and more wildly"), by what they say (she asks her husband to play the piano), by what others say about them, and by the setting in which they move. The characters are also defined in part by other characters whom they in some degree resemble or from whom they in some degree differ. Hamlet, Laertes, and Fortinbras have each lost their fathers, but Hamlet spares the praying King Claudius, whereas

[2]John Russell Brown, *Shakespeare's Plays in Performance* (New York: St. Martin's, 1967), p. 139.

Laertes, seeking vengeance on Hamlet for murdering Laertes's father, says he would cut Hamlet's throat in church; Hamlet meditates about the nature of action, but Fortinbras leads the Norwegians in a military campaign and ultimately acquires Denmark.

Other plays also provide examples of such **foils,** or characters who set one another off. Macbeth and Banquo both hear prophecies, but they act and react differently; Brutus is one kind of assassin, Cassius another, and Casca still another. Any analysis of a character, then, will probably have to take into account, in some degree, the other characters who help to show what he or she is, and who thus help to set forth his or her **motivation** (grounds for action, inner drives, goals).

Organizing an Analysis of a Character

As you read and reread, you'll annotate the text and will jot down (in whatever order they come to you) your thoughts about the character you are studying. Reading, with a view toward writing, you'll want to

1. jot down traits as they come to mind ("kind," "forgetful," "enthusiastic");
2. look back at the text, searching for supporting evidence (characteristic actions, brief supporting quotations);
3. and you will also look for counterevidence so that you may modify your earlier impressions.

Brainstorming leads to an evaluation of your ideas and to a shaping of them. Evaluating and shaping lead to a tentative outline, and a tentative outline leads to the search for supporting evidence—the material that will constitute the body of your essay.

When you set out to write a first draft, review your annotations and notes and see if you can summarize your view of the character in one or two sentences:

X is . . . ,

or

Although X is . . . , she is also. . . .

That is, try to formulate a thesis sentence or a thesis paragraph, a proposition that you will go on to support.

You want to let your reader know early, probably in your first sentence—and almost certainly by the end of your first paragraph—which character you are writing about and what your overall thesis is.

First Draft

Here is the first draft of an **opening paragraph** that identifies the character and sets forth a thesis:

> Romeo is a very interesting character, I think. In the beginning of the play Romeo is very adolescent. Romeo is smitten with puppy love for a woman named Rosaline. He desires to show

all of his friends that he knows how a lover is supposed to act. When he sees Juliet he experiences true love. From the point when he sees Juliet he experiences true love, and from this point he steadily matures in *Romeo and Juliet.* He moves from a self-centered man to a man who lives not for himself but only for Juliet.

Revised Draft

Later the student edited the draft. We reprint the original, with the additional editing in handwriting:

> Romeo ~~is a very interesting character, I think. In the beginning of the play Romeo is very~~ *begins as an* adolescent, ~~Romeo is~~ smitten with puppy love for ~~a woman named~~ Rosaline, *and a desire* ~~He desires~~ to show all of his friends that he knows how a lover is supposed to act. When he sees Juliet, *however,* he experiences true love, *and* ~~F~~from ~~the~~ *this* point ~~when he sees Juliet he experiences true love, and from this point~~ he steadily matures, ~~in *Romeo and Juliet*. He moves~~ *moving* from a self-centered ~~man~~ *adolescent* to a man who lives ~~not for himself but~~ only for Juliet.

Here is a revised version of another effective opening paragraph, effective partly because it identifies the character and offers a thesis:

> In the last speech of *Macbeth*, Malcolm characterizes Lady Macbeth as "fiend-like," and indeed she invokes evil spirits and prompts her husband to commit murder. But despite her bold pose, her role in the murder, and her belief that she will be untroubled by guilt, she has a conscience that torments her and that finally drives her to suicide. She is not a mere heartless villain; she is a human being who is less strong—and more moral—than she thinks she is.

Notice that

- the paragraph quotes a word ("fiend-like") from the text. It happens that the writer goes on to argue that this word is *not* a totally accurate description, but the quotation nevertheless helps to bring the reader into close contact with the subject of the essay.

- in writing about literature we do not ordinarily introduce the thesis formally. We do not, that is, say "In this paper it is my intention to prove that . . ." Such a sentence may be perfectly appropriate in a paper in political science, but in a paper on literature it sounds too stiff.

The body of your essay will be devoted to supporting your thesis. If you have asserted that although Lady Macbeth is cruel and domineering she nevertheless is endowed with a conscience, you will go on in your essay to support those assertions with references to passages that demonstrate them. This does *not* mean that you tell the plot of the whole work; an essay on a character is by no means the same as a summary of the plot. But since you must support your generalizations, you will have to make brief references to specific episodes that reveal her personality, and almost surely you will quote an occasional word or passage.

There are many possible **ways to organize** an essay on a character. Much will depend, of course, on your purpose and thesis. For instance,

- you may want to show how the character develops—gains knowledge, or matures, or disintegrates. Or, again,
- you may want to show what the character contributes to the story or play as a whole. Or, to give yet another example,
- you may want to show that the character is unbelievable.

Still, although no single organization is always right, two methods are common and effective. One is to let the organization of your essay follow closely the sequence of the literary work; that is, you might devote a paragraph to Lady Macbeth as we perceive her in the first act, and then in subsequent paragraphs go on to show that her character is later seen to be more complex than it at first appears. Such an essay may trace your changing responses. This does not mean that you need to write five paragraphs, one on her character in each of the five acts. But it does mean that you might begin with Lady Macbeth as you perceive her in, say, the first act, and then go on to the additional revelations of the rest of the play.

A second effective way of organizing an essay on a character is to set forth, early in the essay, the character's chief traits—let's say the chief strengths and two or three weaknesses—and then go on to study each trait you have listed. Here the organization would (to maintain the reader's interest) probably begin with the most obvious points and then move on to the less obvious, subtler points. The body of your essay, in any case, is devoted to offering evidence that supports your generalizations about the character.

What about a **concluding paragraph?** The concluding paragraph ought *not* to begin with the obviousness of "Thus we see," or "In conclusion," or "I recommend this play because . . ." In fact, after you have given what you consider a sound sketch of the character, it may be appropriate simply to quit. Especially if your essay has moved from the obvious traits to the more subtle and more important traits, and if your essay is fairly short (say, fewer than 500 words), a reader may not need a conclusion. Further, there probably is no reason to blunt what you have just said by adding an unnecessary and merely repetitive summary. But if you do feel that a conclusion is necessary, you may find it effective to write a summary of the character, somewhat as you did in your opening. For the conclusion, relate the character's character to the entire drama—that is, try to give the reader a sense of the role that the character plays.

CHECKLIST: *Getting Ideas for Writing Arguments about Plays*

Plot and Conflict

- Does the **exposition** introduce elements that will be ironically fulfilled? During the exposition do you perceive things differently from the way the characters perceive them?
- **Are certain happenings or situations recurrent?** If so, what significance do you attach to them?
- **If there is more than one plot,** do the plots seem to you to be related? Is one plot clearly the main plot and another plot a sort of subplot, a minor variation on the theme?
- **Do any scenes strike you as irrelevant?**
- **Are certain scenes so strongly foreshadowed that you anticipated them?** If so, did the happenings in these scenes merely fulfill your expectations, or did they also surprise you?
- What kinds of **conflict** are there? One character against another, one group against another, one part of a personality against another part in the same person?
- **How is the conflict resolved?** By an unambiguous triumph of one side or by a triumph that is also in some degree a loss for the triumphant side? Do you find the resolution satisfying, or unsettling, or what? Why?

Character

- A dramatic character is not likely to be thoroughly realistic, a copy of someone we might know. Still, **we can ask if the character is consistent and coherent.** We can also ask if the character is complex or is, on the other hand, a rather simple representative of some human type.
- **How is the character defined?** Consider what the character says and does and what others say about him or her and do to him or her. Also consider other characters who more or less resemble the character in question, because the similarities—and the differences—may be significant.
- **How trustworthy are the characters when they characterize themselves? When they characterize others?**
- **Do characters change** as the play goes on, or do we simply know them better at the end?
- What do you make of the **minor characters?** Are they merely necessary to the plot, or are they foils to other characters? Or do they serve some other functions?
- If **a character is tragic,** does the tragedy seem to you to proceed from a moral flaw, from an intellectual error, from the malice of others, from sheer chance, or from some combination of these?
- **What are the character's goals?** To what degree do you sympathize with them? If a character is comic, do you laugh *with* or *at* the character?
- **Do you think the characters are adequately motivated?**

(*continued*)

Getting Ideas for Writing Arguments about Plays (continued)

- Is a given character so meditative that you feel he or she is engaged less in a dialogue with others than in a dialogue with the self? If so, do you feel that this character is in large degree a **spokesperson for the author,** commenting not only on the world of the play but also on the outside world?

Nonverbal Language

- If the playwright does not provide full stage directions, **try to imagine for at least one scene what gestures and tones might accompany each speech.** (The first scene is usually a good one to try your hand at.)
- **What do you make of the setting?** Does it help to reveal character? Do changes of scene strike you as symbolic? If so, symbolic of what?

Reviewing a Dramatic Production

A review requires analytic skill, but it is not identical with an analysis. First of all, a reviewer normally assumes that the reader is unfamiliar with the production being reviewed, and unfamiliar with the play if the play is not a classic. Thus, the first paragraph usually provides a helpful introduction, along these lines:

> Marsha Norman's recent play, *'night, Mother,* a tragedy with only two actors and one set, shows us a woman's preparation for suicide. Jesse has concluded that she no longer wishes to live, and so she tries to put her affairs into order, which chiefly means preparing her rather uncomprehending mother to get along without her.

Inevitably some retelling of the plot is necessary if the play is new, and a summary of a sentence or two is acceptable even for a familiar play, but the review will chiefly be concerned with

1. describing,
2. analyzing, and, especially,
3. evaluating.

By the way, don't confuse description with analysis. Description tells what something—for instance, the set or the costumes—looks like; analysis tells us how it works, what it adds up to, what it contributes to the total effect.) If the play is new, much of the evaluation may center on the play itself, but if the play is a classic, the evaluation probably will be devoted chiefly to the acting, the set, and the direction.

Other points:

1. **Save the playbill.** It will give you the names of the actors, and perhaps a brief biography of the author, a synopsis of the plot, and a photograph of the set, all of which may be helpful.
2. **Draft your review as soon as possible,** while the performance is still fresh in your mind. If you can't draft it immediately after seeing the play, at least jot down some notes about the setting and the staging, the acting, and the audience's responses.
3. **Read the play** if possible—ideally, before the performance and again after it.

4. **In your first draft, don't worry about limitations of space.** Write as long a review as you can, putting down everything that comes to mind. Later you can cut it to the required length, retaining only the chief points and the necessary supporting details. But in your first draft try to produce a fairly full record of the performance and your response to it, so that a day or two later, when you revise, you won't have to trust a fading memory for details.

A Sample Review by a Student: "An Effective *Macbeth*"

If you read reviews of plays in *Time, Newsweek,* or a newspaper, you will soon develop a sense of what reviews do. The following example, an undergraduate's review of a college production of *Macbeth,* is typical except in one respect: Reviews of new plays, as we have already suggested, include a few sentences summarizing the plot and classifying the play (a tragedy, a farce, a rock musical, or whatever), perhaps briefly putting it in the context of the author's other works. Because *Macbeth* is so widely known, however, the writer of this review chose not to risk offending her readers by telling them that *Macbeth* is a tragedy by Shakespeare.

PRELIMINARY JOTTINGS During the two intermissions and immediately after the end of the performance, the reviewer made a few jottings, which the next day she rewrote:

Compare with last year's *Midsummer Night's Dream*
occasionally exciting production, strong visual effects
  Useful?
witches: powerful, not funny
stage: battlefield? barren land?
  costume: earth-colored rags
  they seduce—even caress—Mac.
Macbeth
  ~~witches caress him~~
  strong; also gentle (with Lady M)
Lady Macb.
  sexy in speech about unsexing her
  too attractive? Prob. ok
Banquo's ghost: naturalistic; covered with blood
Duncan: terrible; worst actor except for Lady Macduff's boy
costumes: leather, metal; only Duncan in robes
pipe framework used for D, and murder of Lady Macduff
forest; branches unrealistic; stylized? or cheesy?

THE FINISHED VERSION The published review appears below, accompanied by some marginal notes in which we comment on its strengths.

Title implies thesis

An Effective *Macbeth*

Opening paragraph is informative, letting the reader know the reviewer's overall attitude

Macbeth at the University Theater is a thoughtful and occasionally exciting production, partly because the director, Mark Urice, has trusted Shakespeare and has not imposed a gimmick on the play. The characters do not wear cowboy costumes as they did in last year's production of *A Midsummer Night's Dream.*

Reviewer promptly turns to a major issue

Probably the chief problem confronting a director of *Macbeth* is how to present the witches so that they are powerful supernatural forces and not silly things that look as though they came from a Halloween party. Urice gives us ugly but not absurdly grotesque witches, and he introduces them most effectively. The stage seems to be a bombed-out battlefield littered with rocks and great chunks of earth, but some of these begin to stir—the earth seems to come alive—and the clods move, unfold, and become the witches, dressed in brown and dark gray rags. The suggestion is that the witches are a part of nature, elemental forces that can hardly be escaped. This effect is increased by the moans and creaking noises that they make, all of which could be comic but which in this production are impressive.

First sentence of this paragraph provides an effective transition

The witches' power over Macbeth is further emphasized by their actions. When the witches first meet Macbeth, they encircle him, touch him, caress him, even embrace him, and he seems helpless, almost their plaything. Moreover, in the scene in which he imagines that he sees a dagger, the director has arranged for one of the witches to appear, stand near Macbeth, and guide his hand toward the invisible dagger. This is, of course, not in the text, but the interpretation is reasonable rather than intrusive. Finally, near the end of the play, just before Macduff kills Macbeth, a witch appears and laughs at Macbeth as Macduff explains that he was not "born of woman." There is no doubt that throughout the tragedy Macbeth has been a puppet of the witches.

Paragraph begins with a broad assertion and then offers supporting details

Stephen Beers (Macbeth) and Tina Peters (Lady Macbeth) are excellent. Beers is sufficiently brawny to be convincing as a battlefield hero, but he also speaks the lines sensitively, so the audience feels that in addition to being a hero, he is a man of gentleness. One can believe Lady Macbeth when she says that she fears he is "too full o' the milk of human kindness" to murder Duncan. Lady Macbeth is especially effective in the scene in which she asks the spirits to "unsex her." During this speech she is reclining on a bed and as she delivers the lines she becomes increasingly sexual in her bodily motions, deriving excitement from her own stimulating words. Her attachment to Macbeth is strongly sexual, and so is his attraction to her. The scene when she persuades him to kill Duncan ends with their passionately embracing. The strong attraction of each for the other, so evident in the early part

Reference to a particular scene

of the play, disappears after the murder, when Macbeth keeps his distance from Lady Macbeth and does not allow her to touch him. The acting of the other performers is effective, except for John Berens (Duncan), who recites the lines mechanically and seems not to take much account of their meaning.

Description, but also analysis

The set consists of a barren plot, at the rear of which stands a spidery framework of piping of the sort used by construction companies, supporting a catwalk. This framework fits with the costumes (lots of armor, leather, heavy boots), suggesting a sort of elemental, primitive, and somewhat sadistic world. The catwalk, though effectively used when Macbeth goes off to murder Duncan (whose room is presumably upstairs and offstage), is not much used in later scenes. For the most part it is an interesting piece of scenery but not otherwise helpful. For instance, there is no reason why the scene with Macduff's wife and children is staged on it. The costumes are not in any way Scottish—no plaids—but in several scenes the sound of a bagpipe is heard, adding another weird or primitive tone to the production.

Concrete details to support evaluation

Summary

This *Macbeth* appeals to the eye, the ear, and the mind. The director has given us a unified production that makes sense and that is faithful to the spirit of Shakespeare's play.

Work Cited

Documentation

Macbeth. By William Shakespeare. Dir. Mark Urice. Perf. Stephen Beers, Tina Peters, and John Berens. University Theater, Medford, MA. 3 Mar. 1998.

The Review Reviewed

The marginal notes call attention to certain qualities in the review, but three additional points should be made:

1. The reviewer's feelings and evaluations are clearly expressed, not in such expressions as "furthermore I feel," and "it is also my opinion," but in such expressions as "a thoughtful and occasionally exciting production," "excellent," and "appeals to the eye, the ear, and the mind."
2. The evaluations are supported by details. For instance, the evaluation that the witches are effectively presented is supported by a brief description of their appearance.
3. The reviewer is courteous, even when (as in the discussion of the catwalk, in the next-to-last paragraph) she is talking about aspects of the production she doesn't care for.

Note: Another review by a student (of a film version of *Hamlet*) appears in Chapter 22, which includes a case study on *Hamlet*.

Thinking about a Filmed Version of a Play

Although one might at first think that a film-version of a play is pretty much the play caught on film, as soon as one realizes that movies use such techniques as close-ups and high and low angle shots (the action is seen from above or below), one realizes that the filmed version of a play can be very different from the version on the stage, even though in both forms a story is told by means of actors. In Laurence Olivier's *Hamlet* (1944), dreamlike dissolves (the shot fades into the background while a new shot appears to emerge from beneath it) suggest the prince's irresoluteness. Or consider the use of black-and-white versus color film; Olivier made Shakespeare's *Henry V* (1944) in color but *Hamlet* in black-and-white because, in Olivier's view, color conveyed a splendor appropriate to England's heroic history, whereas black-and-white seemed more suited to somber tragedy.

Filmmakers customarily "open out" plays, giving us scenes of skies, beaches, city streets, and so forth. In Olivier's *Hamlet* we get shots of the sea and the sky. The camera descends from a great height just before Hamlet delivers his first soliloquy, and when the Ghost leaves at 1.5.96 the camera soars into the air, as though with the Ghost, and then, from above the camera shows Hamlet fainting at the battlements. Even when the camera shows us scenes within the palace it in effect opens the play by panning and traveling through long empty corridors and over staircases, suggesting Hamlet's irresolute mind. (Kenneth Branagh's film version of *Hamlet* [1996] is very different; for a student's discussion of this film, see the essay by Will Saretta that we reprint in our casebook on *Hamlet,* page 1024.)

The 1987 film version of *The Glass Menagerie,* directed by Paul Newman, may suffer in part because the camera is not adventurous enough. Much of the play is shot close-up, with the result that this film of Williams's "Memory Play" has a realism, an in-your-face quality that is at odds with the dreaminess and fragility of the play. A stage production—usually set within a proscenium and making use of evidently theatrical lighting—has an illusionary or unrealistic quality appropriate to Williams's play, in which a narrator (Tom) conjures up scenes. Newman gives us almost all of Williams's dialogue, but he loses almost all of the magic of the play.

Getting Ready to Write

Mastery of terminology does not make anyone a perceptive film critic, but it helps writers communicate their perceptions to their readers. Probably an essay on a film will not be primarily about the use of establishing shots or of wipes or of any such matters; rather, it will be about the reasons why a particular film pleases or displeases, succeeds or fails, seems significant or insignificant, and in discussing these large matters it is sometimes necessary (or at least economical) to use common technical terms. Large matters are often determined in part by such seemingly small matters as the distance of the camera from its subject or the way in which transitions are made, and one may as well use the conventional terms. But it is also true that a filmmaker's technique and technology alone cannot make a first-rate film. An idea, a personal vision, a theme must be embodied in all that is flashed on the screen.

Writing an essay about a new film—one not yet available for study on DVD—presents difficulties not encountered in writing about stories, plays, or poems. Because we experience film in a darkened room, we cannot easily take notes, and because the film may be shown only once, we cannot always take another look at passages that puzzle us. But some brief notes can be taken even in the dark; it is best to amplify them as soon as light is available, while you still know what the scrawls mean. If you can see the film more than once, do so, and, of course, if the script has been published, study it. Draft your paper as soon as possible after your first viewing, and then see the film again. You can sometimes check hazy memories of certain scenes and techniques with fellow viewers. But even with multiple viewings and the aid of friends, it is almost impossible to get all of the details right; it is best for the writer to be humble and for the reader to be tolerant.

Reminder: For a sample essay by a student, see the essay on Kenneth Branagh's *Hamlet,* printed on page 1024.

CHECKLIST: *Writing about a Filmed Play*

Preliminaries

- ☐ Is the title of the film the same as the title of the play? If not, what is implied?

Dramatic Adaptations

- ☐ **Does the film closely follow its original** and neglect the potentialities of the camera? Or does it so revel in cinematic devices that it distorts the original?
- ☐ **Does the film do violence to the theme of the original?** Is the film better than its source? Are the additions or omissions due to the medium or to a crude or faulty interpretation of the original?

Plot and Character

- ☐ **Can film deal as effectively with inner action**—mental processes—as with external, physical action? In a given film, how is the inner action conveyed? Olivier used voice-over for parts of Hamlet's soliloquies—that is, we hear Hamlet's voice but his lips do not move.
- ☐ **Are shots and sequences adequately developed,** or do they seem jerky? (A shot may be jerky by being extremely brief or at an odd angle; a sequence may be jerky by using discontinuous images or fast cuts. Sometimes, of course, jerkiness may be desirable.) If such cinematic techniques as wipes, dissolves, and slow motion are used, are they meaningful and effective?
- ☐ **Are the characters believable?**
- ☐ **Are the actors appropriately cast?**

Sound Track

- ☐ Does the sound track offer **more than realistic dialogue?** Is the music appropriate and functional? (Music may, among other things, imitate natural sounds, give a sense of locale or of ethnic group, suggest states of mind, provide ironic commentary, or—by repeated melodies—help establish connections.) Are volume, tempo, and pitch—whether of music or of such sounds as the wind blowing or cars moving—used to stimulate emotions?

Your Turn: Plays for Analysis

David Ives

David Ives, born in Chicago in 1950, was educated at Northwestern University and at the Yale Drama School. Sure Thing *was first publicly staged in 1988, and later was staged with six other one-act plays, grouped under the title* All in the Timing.

Sure Thing

This play is for Jason Buzas

BETTY, *a woman in her late twenties, is reading at a café table. An empty chair is opposite her.* BILL, *same age, enters.*

BILL: Excuse me. Is this chair taken?
BETTY: Excuse me?
BILL: Is this taken?
BETTY: Yes it is.
BILL: Oh. Sorry.
BETTY: Sure thing.

[*A bell rings softly.*]

BILL: Excuse me. Is this chair taken?
BETTY: Excuse me?
BILL: Is this taken?
BETTY: No, but I'm expecting somebody in a minute.
BILL: Oh. Thanks anyway.
BETTY: Sure thing.

[*A bell rings softly.*]

BILL: Excuse me. Is this chair taken?
BETTY: No, but I'm expecting somebody very shortly.
BILL: Would you mind if I sit here till he or she or it comes?
BETTY [*glances at her watch*]: They do seem to be pretty late. . . .
BILL: You never know who you might be turning down.
BETTY: Sorry. Nice try, though.
BILL: Sure thing.

[*Bell.*]

Is this seat taken?
BETTY: No it's not.
BILL: Would you mind if I sit here?
BETTY: Yes I would.
BILL: Oh.

[*Bell.*]

Is this chair taken?
BETTY: No it's not.
BILL: Would you mind if I sit here?
BETTY: No. Go ahead.
BILL: Thanks. [*He sits. She continues reading.*] Everyplace else seems to be taken.
BETTY: Mm-hm.

BILL: Great place.
BETTY: Mm-hm.
BILL: What's the book?
BETTY: I just wanted to read in quiet, if you don't mind.
BILL: No. Sure thing.

[*Bell.*]

BILL: Everyplace else seems to be taken.
BETTY: Mm-hm.
BILL: Great place for reading.
BETTY: Yes, I like it.
BILL: What's the book?
BETTY: *The Sound and the Fury.*
BILL: Oh. Hemingway.

[*Bell.*]

What's the book?
BETTY: *The Sound and the Fury.*
BILL: Oh. Faulkner.
BETTY: Have you read it?
BILL: Not . . . actually. I've sure read *about* it, though. It's supposed to be great.
BETTY: It is great.
BILL: I hear it's great. [*Small pause.*] Waiter?

[*Bell.*]

What's the book?
BETTY: *The Sound and the Fury.*
BILL: Oh. Faulkner.
BETTY: Have you read it?
BILL: I'm a Mets fan, myself.

[*Bell.*]

BETTY: Have you read it?
BILL: Yeah, I read it in college.
BETTY: Where was college?
BILL: I went to Oral Roberts University.

[*Bell.*]

BETTY: Where was college?
BILL: I was lying. I never really went to college. I just like to party.

[*Bell.*]

BETTY: Where was college?
BILL: Harvard.
BETTY: Do you like Faulkner?
BILL: I love Faulkner. I spent a whole winter reading him once.
BETTY: I've just started.
BILL: I was so excited after ten pages that I went out and bought everything else he wrote. One of the greatest reading experiences of my life. I mean, all that incredible psychological understanding. Page after page of gorgeous prose. His profound grasp of the mystery of time and human existence. The smells of the earth . . . What do you think?
BETTY: I think it's pretty boring.

[*Bell.*]

BILL: What's the book?
BETTY: *The Sound and the Fury.*
BILL: Oh! Faulkner!
BETTY: Do you like Faulkner?
BILL: I love Faulkner.
BETTY: He's incredible.
BILL: I spent a whole winter reading him once.
BETTY: I was so excited after ten pages that I went out and bought everything else he wrote.
BILL: All that incredible psychological understanding.
BETTY: And the prose is so gorgeous.
BILL: And the way he's grasped the mystery of time—
BETTY: —and human existence. I can't believe I've waited this long to read him.
BILL: You never know. You might not have liked him before.
BETTY: That's true.
BILL: You might not have been ready for him. You have to hit these things at the right moment or it's no good.
BETTY: That's happened to me.
BILL: It's all in the timing. [*Small pause.*] My name's Bill, by the way.
BETTY: I'm Betty.
BILL: Hi.
BETTY: Hi. [*Small pause.*]
BILL: Yes I thought reading Faulkner was . . . a great experience.
BETTY: Yes. [*Small pause.*]
BILL: *The Sound and the Fury* . . . [*Another small pause.*]
BETTY: Well. Onwards and upwards. [*She goes back to her book.*]
BILL: Waiter—?

[*Bell.*]

You have to hit these things at the right moment or it's no good.
BETTY: That's happened to me.
BILL: It's all in the timing. My name's Bill, by the way.
BETTY: I'm Betty.
BILL: Hi.
BETTY: Hi.
BILL: Do you come in here a lot?
BETTY: Actually I'm just in town for two days from Pakistan.
BILL: Oh. Pakistan.

[*Bell.*]

My name's Bill, by the way.
BETTY: I'm Betty.
BILL: Hi.
BETTY: Hi.
BILL: Do you come in here a lot?
BETTY: Every once in a while. Do you?
BILL: Not so much anymore. Not as much as I used to. Before my nervous breakdown.

[*Bell.*]

Do you come in here a lot?
BETTY: Why are you asking?

BILL: Just interested.

BETTY: Are you really interested, or do you just want to pick me up?

BILL: No, I'm really interested.

BETTY: Why would you be interested in whether I come in here a lot?

BILL: I'm just . . . getting acquainted.

BETTY: Maybe you're only interested for the sake of making small talk long enough to ask me back to your place to listen to some music, or because you've just rented this great tape for your VCR, or because you've got some terrific unknown Django Reinhardt record, only all you really want to do is fuck—which you won't do very well—after which you'll go into the bathroom and pee very loudly, then pad into the kitchen and get yourself a beer from the refrigerator without asking me whether I'd like anything, and then you'll proceed to lie back down beside me and confess that you've got a girlfriend named Stephanie who's away at medical school in Belgium for a year, and that you've been involved with her—*off and on*—in what you'll call a very "intricate" relationship, for the past *seven* YEARS. None of which *interests* me, mister!

BILL: Okay.

[*Bell.*]

Do you come in here a lot?

BETTY: Every other day, I think.

BILL: I come in here quite a lot and I don't remember seeing you.

BETTY: I guess we must be on different schedules.

BILL: Missed connections.

BETTY: Yes. Different time zones.

BILL: Amazing how you can live right next door to somebody in this town and never even know it.

BETTY: I know.

BILL: City life.

BETTY: It's crazy.

BILL: We probably pass each other in the street every day. Right in front of this place, probably.

BETTY: Yep.

BILL [*looks around*]: Well the waiters here sure seem to be in some different time zone. I can't seem to locate one anywhere. . . . Waiter! [*He looks back.*] So what do you—[*He sees that she's gone back to her book.*]

BETTY: I beg pardon?

BILL: Nothing. Sorry.

[*Bell.*]

BETTY: I guess we must be on different schedules.

BILL: Missed connections.

BETTY: Yes. Different time zones.

BILL: Amazing how you can live right next door to somebody in this town and never even know it.

BETTY: I know.

BILL: City life.

BETTY: It's crazy.

BILL: You weren't waiting for somebody when I came in, were you?

BETTY: Actually I was.

BILL: Oh. Boyfriend?

BETTY: Sort of.

BILL: What's a sort-of boyfriend?

BETTY: My husband.

BILL: Ah-ha.

[*Bell.*]

You weren't waiting for somebody when I came in, were you?

BETTY: Actually I was.

BILL: Oh. Boyfriend?

BETTY: Sort of.

BILL: What's a sort-of boyfriend?

BETTY: We were meeting here to break up.

BILL: Mm-hm . . .

[*Bell.*]

What's a sort-of boyfriend?

BETTY: My lover. Here she comes right now!

[*Bell.*]

BILL: You weren't waiting for somebody when I came in, were you?

BETTY: No, just reading.

BILL: Sort of a sad occupation for a Friday night, isn't it? Reading here, all by yourself?

BETTY: Do you think so?

BILL: Well sure. I mean, what's a good-looking woman like you doing out alone on a Friday night?

BETTY: Trying to keep away from lines like that.

BILL: No, listen—

[*Bell.*]

You weren't waiting for somebody when I came in, were you?

BETTY: No, just reading.

BILL: Sort of a sad occupation for a Friday night, isn't it? Reading here all by yourself?

BETTY: I guess it is, in a way.

BILL: What's a good-looking woman like you doing out alone on a Friday night anyway? No offense, but . . .

BETTY: I'm out alone on a Friday night for the first time in a very long time.

BILL: Oh.

BETTY: You see, I just recently ended a relationship.

BILL: Oh.

BETTY: Of rather long standing.

BILL: I'm sorry. [*Small pause.*] Well listen, since reading by yourself is such a sad occupation for a Friday night, would you like to go elsewhere?

BETTY: No . . .

BILL: Do something else?

BETTY: No thanks.

BILL: I was headed out to the movies in a while anyway.

BETTY: I don't think so.

BILL: Big chance to let Faulkner catch his breath. All those long sentences get him pretty tired.

BETTY: Thanks anyway.

BILL: Okay.

BETTY: I appreciate the invitation.

BILL: Sure thing.

[*Bell.*]

You weren't waiting for somebody when I came in, were you?

BETTY: No, just reading.

BILL: Sort of a sad occupation for a Friday night, isn't it? Reading here all by yourself?

BETTY: I guess I was trying to think of it as existentially romantic. You know—cappuccino, great literature, rainy night . . .

BILL: That only works in Paris. We *could* hop the late plane to Paris. Get on a Concorde. Find a café . . .

BETTY: I'm a little short on plane fare tonight.

BILL: Darn it, so am I.

BETTY: To tell you the truth, I was headed to the movies after I finished this section. Would you like to come along? Since you can't locate a waiter?

BILL: That's a very nice offer, but . . .

BETTY: Uh-huh. Girlfriend?

BILL: Two, actually. One of them's pregnant, and Stephanie—

[*Bell.*]

BETTY: Girlfriend?

BILL: No, I don't have a girlfriend. Not if you mean the castrating bitch I dumped last night.

[*Bell.*]

BETTY: Girlfriend?

BILL: Sort of. Sort of.

BETTY: What's a sort-of girlfriend?

BILL: My mother.

[*Bell.*]

I just ended a relationship, actually.

BETTY: Oh.

BILL: Of rather long standing.

BETTY: I'm sorry to hear it.

BILL: This is my first night out alone in a long time. I feel a little bit at sea, to tell you the truth.

BETTY: So you didn't stop to talk because you're a Moonie, or you have some weird political affiliation—?

BILL: Nope. Straight-down-the-ticket Republican.

[*Bell.*]

Straight-down-the-ticket Democrat.

[*Bell.*]

Can I tell you something about politics?

[*Bell.*]

I like to think of myself as a citizen of the universe.

[*Bell.*]

I'm unaffiliated.

BETTY: That's a relief. So am I.

BILL: I vote my beliefs.

BETTY: Labels are not important.

BILL: Labels are not important, exactly. Take me, for example. I mean, what does it matter if I had a two-point at—

[*Bell.*]

three-point at—

[*Bell.*]

four-point at college? Or if I did come from Pittsburgh—

[*Bell.*]

Cleveland—

[*Bell.*]

Westchester County?

BETTY: Sure.

BILL: I believe that a man is what he is.

[*Bell.*]

A person is what he is.

[*Bell.*]

A person is . . . what they are.

BETTY: I think so too.

BILL: So what if I admire Trotsky?

[*Bell.*]

So what if I once had a total-body liposuction?

[*Bell.*]

So what if I don't have a penis?

[*Bell.*]

So what if I spent a year in the Peace Corps? I was acting on my convictions.

BETTY: Sure.

BILL: You just can't hang a sign on a person.

BETTY: Absolutely. I'll bet you're a Scorpio.

[*Many bells ring.*]

Listen, I was headed to the movies after I finished this section. Would you like to come along?

BILL: That sounds like fun. What's playing?

BETTY: A couple of the really early Woody Allen movies.

BILL: Oh.

BETTY: You don't like Woody Allen?

BILL: Sure. I like Woody Allen.

BETTY: But you're not crazy about Woody Allen.

BILL: Those early ones kind of get on my nerves.

BETTY: Uh-huh.

[*Bell.*]

BILL: Y'know I was headed to the—

BETTY [*simultaneously*]: I was thinking about—

BILL: I'm sorry.
BETTY: No, go ahead.
BILL: I was going to say that I was headed to the movies in a little while, and . . .
BETTY: So was I.
BILL: The Woody Allen festival?
BETTY: Just up the street.
BILL: Do you like the early ones?
BETTY: I think anybody who doesn't ought to be run off the planet.
BILL: How many times have you seen *Bananas*?
BETTY: Eight times.
BILL: Twelve. So are you still interested [*Long pause.*]
BETTY: Do you like Entenmann's crumb cake . . . ?
BILL: Last night I went out at two in the morning to get one. Did you have an Etch-a-Sketch as a child?
BETTY: Yes! And do you like Brussels sprouts? [*Pause.*]
BILL: No, I think they're disgusting.
BETTY: They *are* disgusting!
BILL: Do you still believe in marriage in spite of current sentiments against it?
BETTY: Yes.
BILL: And children?
BETTY: Three of them.
BILL: Two girls and a boy.
BETTY: Harvard, Vassar, and Brown.
BILL: And will you love me?
BETTY: Yes.
BILL: And cherish me forever?
BETTY: Yes.
BILL: Do you still want to go to the movies?
BETTY: Sure thing.
BILL AND BETTY [*together*]: *Waiter!*
BLACKOUT

[1988]

Joining the Conversation: Critical Thinking and Writing

1. Does the play have a plot? Does it follow the traditional formula of a beginning, a middle, and an end? (The conventional advice to playwrights is, "Get your guy up a tree, throw rocks at him, and get him down.") Is there an ending, a resolution, or do you think the play could go on and on? Please explain.
2. Ives's opening stage direction tells us that the play is set in a café, but no details are given. If you were staging the play, would you provide more than a table and two chairs? Some sort of atmosphere? Why, or why not?
3. Ives's text calls at the end for a blackout—a sudden darkening of the stage. Do you think this ending is preferable to a gradual fading of the lights, or a gradual closing of the curtain? Or, for that matter, why shouldn't the two characters leave some money on the table and walk out together? In short, staying with Ives's dialogue, evaluate other possible endings and present an argument for

which one you believe is most effective. Ask yourself, "What kind of evidence do I need to make my argument as convincing as possible?"

4. If someone were to say to you that the play shows the need for people to keep revising their personalities, to (so to speak) keep reinventing themselves if they wish to function efficiently in the world, what might you reply? What does it mean to say that someone is "reinventing" himself or herself? Is that a desirable thing to do?
5. If someone asked you, "What is the meaning of *Sure Thing?*" how would you reply? Is there one meaning, or more than one? What is your evidence? Please present your view, and the evidence for it, in the form of a good argument.
6. Imagine and write up a scene that Ives neglected to include in *Sure Thing*. How does your new scene change the play? In your view, does it make the play better?
7. Prepare an essay of 1–2 pages, which you might imagine being sent to Ives, in which you argue why his play would benefit from the addition of your new scene.

A Note on Greek Tragedy

Little or nothing is known for certain about the origin of Greek tragedy. The most common hypothesis holds that it developed from improvised speeches during choral dances honoring Dionysus, a Greek nature god associated with spring, fertility, and wine. Thespis (who perhaps never existed) is said to have introduced an actor into these choral performances in the sixth century B.C.E. Aeschylus (525–456 B.C.E.), Greece's first great writer of tragedies, added the second actor, and Sophocles (496?–406 B.C.E.) added the third actor and fixed the size of the chorus at fifteen. (Because the chorus leader often functioned as an additional actor, and because the actors sometimes doubled in their parts, a Greek tragedy could have more characters than might at first be thought.)

All of the extant great Greek tragedy is of the fifth century B.C.E. It was performed at religious festivals in the winter and early spring, in large outdoor amphitheaters built on hillsides. Some of these theaters were enormous; the one at Epidaurus held about fifteen thousand people. The audience sat in tiers, looking down on the *orchestra* (a dancing place), with the acting area behind it and the *skene* (the scene building) yet farther back. The scene building served as dressing room, background (suggesting a palace or temple), and place for occasional entrances and exits.

Furthermore, this building helped to provide good acoustics, for speech travels well if there is a solid barrier behind the speaker and a hard, smooth surface in front of him, and if the audience sits in tiers. The wall of the scene building provided the barrier; the orchestra provided the surface in front of the actors; and the seats on the hillside fulfilled the third requirement. Moreover, the acoustics were somewhat improved by slightly elevating the actors above the orchestra, but it is not known exactly when this platform was first constructed in front of the scene building.

A tragedy commonly begins with a *prologos* (prologue), during which the exposition is given. Next comes the *párodos*, the chorus's ode of entrance, sung while the chorus marches into the theater, through the side aisles, and

The theater at Epidaurus, Greece. (©Frederick Ayers/Photo Researchers)

onto the orchestra. The *epeisodion* (episode) is the ensuing scene; it is followed by a *stasimon* (choral song, ode). Usually there are four or five *epeisodia,* alternating with *stasima*. Each of these choral odes has a *strophe* (lines presumably sung while the chorus dances in one direction) and an *antistrophe* (lines presumably sung while the chorus retraces its steps). Sometimes a third part, an *epode,* concludes an ode. (In addition to odes that are *stasima,* there can be odes within episodes; the fourth episode of *Antigonê* contains an ode complete with *epode*.) After the last part of the last ode comes the *exodos,* the epilogue or final scene.

The actors (all male) wore masks, and they seem to have chanted much of the play. Perhaps the total result of combining speech with music and dancing was a sort of music-drama roughly akin to opera with some spoken dialogue, like Mozart's *The Magic Flute* (1791).

Jane Lapotaire in *Antigonê*. National Theatre, London, 1984. (Donald Cooper/Photostage)

SOPHOCLES

One of the three great writers of tragedies in ancient Greece, Sophocles (496?–406 B.C.E.) was born in Colonus, near Athens, into a well-to-do family. Well educated, he first won public acclaim as a tragic poet at the age of 27, in 468 B.C.E., when he defeated Aeschylus in a competition for writing a tragic play. He is said to have written some 120 plays, but only seven tragedies are extant; among them are Oedipus the King, Antigonê, *and* Oedipus at Colonus. *He died, much honored, in his ninetieth year, in Athens, where he had lived his entire life.*

Antigonê

Translated by Dudley Fitts and Robert Fitzgerald

CHARACTERS

ANTIGONÊ
ISMENÊ
EURYDICÊ
CREON
HAIMON
TEIRESIAS
A SENTRY
A MESSENGER
CHORUS

SCENE: *Before the palace of* CREON, *King of Thebes. A central double door, and two lateral doors. A platform extends the length of the façade, and from this platform three steps lead down into the "orchestra," or chorus-ground.*

TIME: *Dawn of the day after the repulse of the Argive army from the assault on Thebes.*

Prologue

ANTIGONÊ *and* ISMENÊ *enter from the central door of the palace.*

ANTIGONÊ: Ismenê, dear sister,
You would think that we had already suffered enough
For the curse on Oedipus:°
I cannot imagine any grief
That you and I have not gone through. And now—
Have they told you of the new decree of our King Creon?

ISMENÊ: I have heard nothing: I know
That two sisters lost two brothers, a double death
In a single hour; and I know that the Argive army
Fled in the night; but beyond this, nothing.

ANTIGONÊ: I thought so. And that is why I wanted you
To come out here with me. There is something we must do.

ISMENÊ: Why do you speak so strangely?

ANTIGONÊ: Listen, Ismenê:
Creon buried our brother Eteoclês
With military honors, gave him a soldier's funeral,
And it was right that he should; but Polyneicês,
Who fought as bravely and died as miserably,—
They say that Creon has sworn
No one shall bury him, no one mourn for him,
But his body must lie in the fields, a sweet treasure
For carrion birds to find as they search for food.
That is what they say, and our good Creon is coming here
To announce it publicly; and the penalty—
Stoning to death in the public square!
There it is,
And now you can prove what you are:
A true sister, or a traitor to your family.

ISMENÊ: Antigonê, you are mad! What could I possibly do?

ANTIGONÊ: You must decide whether you will help me or not.

ISMENÊ: I do not understand you. Help you in what?

ANTIGONÊ: Ismenê, I am going to bury him. Will you come?

ISMENÊ: Bury him! You have just said the new law forbids it.

ANTIGONÊ: He is my brother. And he is your brother, too.

ISMENÊ: But think of the danger! Think what Creon will do!

ANTIGONÊ: Creon is not strong enough to stand in my way.

ISMENÊ: Ah sister!
Oedipus died, everyone hating him
For what his own search brought to light, his eyes
Ripped out by his own hand; and Iocastê died,
His mother and wife at once: she twisted the cords

3 Oedipus Once King of Thebes, Oedipus was the father of Antigonê and Ismenê, and of their brothers Polyneicês and Eteoclês. Oedipus unwittingly killed his father, Laïos, and married his own mother Iocaste. When he learned what he had done, he blinded himself and left Thebes. Eteoclês and Polyneicês quarreled; Polyneicês was driven out but returned to assault Thebes. In the battle each brother killed the other; Creon became king and ordered that Polyneicês be left to rot unburied on the battlefield as a traitor.

That strangled her life; and our two brothers died,
Each killed by the other's sword. And we are left:
But oh, Antigonê,
Think how much more terrible than these
Our own death would be if we should go against Creon
And do what he has forbidden! We are only women,
We cannot fight with men, Antigonê!
The law is strong, we must give in to the law
In this thing, and in worse. I beg the Dead
To forgive me, but I am helpless: I must yield
To those in authority. And I think it is dangerous business
To be always meddling.

ANTIGONÊ: If that is what you think,
I should not want you, even if you asked to come.
You have made your choice, you can be what you want to be.
But I will bury him; and if I must die,
I say that this crime is holy: I shall lie down
With him in death, and I shall be as dear
To him as he to me.
It is the dead,
Not the living, who make the longest demands:
We die for ever . . .
You may do as you like,
Since apparently the laws of the gods mean nothing to you.

ISMENÊ: They mean a great deal to me; but I have no strength
To break laws that were made for the public good.

ANTIGONÊ: That must be your excuse, I suppose. But as for me,
I will bury the brother I love.

ISMENÊ: Antigonê,
I am so afraid for you!

ANTIGONÊ: You need not be:
You have yourself to consider, after all.

ISMENÊ: But no one must hear of this, you must tell no one!
I will keep it a secret, I promise!

ANTIGONÊ: O tell it! Tell everyone!
Think how they'll hate you when it all comes out
If they learn that you knew about it all the time!

ISMENÊ: So fiery! You should be cold with fear.

ANTIGONÊ: Perhaps. But I am doing only what I must.

ISMENÊ: But you can do it? I say that you cannot.

ANTIGONÊ: Very well: when my strength gives out, I shall do no more.

ISMENÊ: Impossible things should not be tried at all.

ANTIGONÊ: Go away, Ismenê:
I shall be hating you soon, and the dead will too,
For your words are hateful. Leave me my foolish plan:
I am not afraid of the danger; if it means death,
It will not be the worst of deaths—death without honor.

ISMENÊ: Go then, if you feel that you must.
You are unwise,
But a loyal friend indeed to those who love you.

Exit into the palace. ANTIGONÊ *goes off, left. Enter the* CHORUS.

Párodos

Strophe 1

CHORUS: Now the long blade of the sun, lying
Level east to west, touches with glory
Thebes of the Seven Gates. Open, unlidded
Eye of golden day! O marching light
Across the eddy and rush of Dircê's stream,°
Striking the white shields of the enemy
Thrown headlong backward from the blaze of morning!

CHORAGOS: Polyneicês their commander
Roused them with windy phrases,
He the wild eagle screaming
Insults above our land,
His wings their shields of snow,
His crest their marshalled helms.

Antistrophe 1

CHORUS: Against our seven gates in a yawning ring
The famished spears came onward in the night;
But before his jaws were sated with our blood,
Or pinefire took the garland of our towers,
He was thrown back; and as he turned, great Thebes—
No tender victim for his noisy power—
Rose like a dragon behind him, shouting war.

CHORAGOS: For God hates utterly
The bray of bragging tongues;
And when he beheld their smiling,
Their swagger of golden helms,
The frown of his thunder blasted
Their first man from our walls.

Strophe 2

CHORUS: We heard his shout of triumph high in the air
Turn to a scream; far out in a flaming arc
He fell with his windy torch, and the earth struck him.
And others storming in fury no less than his
Found shock of death in the dusty joy of battle.

CHORAGOS: Seven captains at seven gates
Yielded their clanging arms to the god
That bends the battle-line and breaks it.
These two only, brothers in blood,
Face to face in matchless rage,
Mirroring each the other's death,
Clashed in long combat.

Antistrophe 2

CHORUS: But now in the beautiful morning of victory
Let Thebes of the many chariots sing for joy!

5 Dircê's stream a stream west of Thebes.

With hearts for dancing we'll take leave of war:
Our temples shall be sweet with hymns of praise,
And the long night shall echo with our chorus.

Scene I

CHORAGOS: But now at last our new King is coming:
Creon of Thebes, Menoikeus' son.
In this auspicious dawn of his reign
What are the new complexities
That shifting Fate has woven for him?
What is his counsel? Why has he summoned
The old men to hear him?

Enter CREON *from the palace, center. He addresses the* CREON *from the top step.*

CREON: Gentlemen: I have the honor to inform you that our Ship of State, which recent storms have threatened to destroy, has come safely to harbor at last, guided by the merciful wisdom of Heaven. I have summoned you here this morning because I know that I can depend upon you: your devotion to King Laïos was absolute; you never hesitated in your duty to our late ruler Oedipus; and when Oedipus died, your loyalty was transferred to his children. Unfortunately, as you know, his two sons, the princes Eteoclês and Polyneicês, have killed each other in battle; and I, as the next in blood, have succeeded to the full power of the throne.

I am aware, of course, that no Ruler can expect complete loyalty from his subjects until he has been tested in office. Nevertheless, I say to you at the very outset that I have nothing but contempt for the kind of Governor who is afraid, for whatever reason, to follow the course that he knows is best for the State; and as for the man who sets private friendship above the public welfare,—I have no use for him, either. I call God to witness that if I saw my country headed for ruin, I should not be afraid to speak out plainly; and I need hardly remind you that I would never have any dealings with an enemy of the people. No one values friendship more highly than I; but we must remember that friends made at the risk of wrecking our Ship are not real friends at all.

These are my principles, at any rate, and that is why I have made the following decision concerning the sons of Oedipus: Eteoclês, who died as a man should die, fighting for his country, is to be buried with full military honors, with all the ceremony that is usual when the greatest heroes die; but his brother Polyneicês, who broke his exile to come back with fire and sword against his native city and the shrines of his fathers' gods, whose one idea was to spill the blood of his blood and sell his own people into slavery—Polyneicês, I say, is to have no burial: no man is to touch him or say the least prayer for him; he shall lie on the plain, unburied; and the birds and the scavenging dogs can do with him whatever they like.

This is my command, and you can see the wisdom behind it. As long as I am King, no traitor is going to be honored with the loyal man. But whoever shows by word and deed that he is on the side of the State,—he shall have my respect while he is living, and my reverence when he is dead.

CHORAGOS: If that is your will, Creon son of Menoikeus,
You have the right to enforce it: we are yours.

CREON: That is my will. Take care that you do your part.

CHORAGOS: We are old men: let the younger ones carry it out.
CREON: I do not mean that: the sentries have been appointed.
CHORAGOS: Then what is it that you would have us do?
CREON: You will give no support to whoever breaks this law.
CHORAGOS: Only a crazy man is in love with death!
CREON: And death it is, yet money talks, and the wisest
Have sometimes been known to count a few coins too many.

Enter SENTRY *from left.*

SENTRY: I'll not say that I'm out of breath from running, King, because every time I stopped to think about what I have to tell you, I felt like going back. And all the time a voice kept saying, "You fool, don't you know you're walking straight into trouble?"; and then another voice: "Yes, but if you let somebody else get the news to Creon first, it will be even worse than that for you!" But good sense won out, at least I hope it was good sense, and here I am with a story that makes no sense at all; but I'll tell it anyhow, because, as they say, what's going to happen's going to happen and—

CREON: Come to the point. What have you to say?

SENTRY: I did not do it. I did not see who did it. You must not punish me for what someone else has done.

CREON: A comprehensive defense! More effective, perhaps,
If I knew its purpose. Come: what is it?
SENTRY: A dreadful thing . . . I don't know how to put it—
CREON: Out with it!
SENTRY: Well, then;
The dead man—
Polyneicês—

Pause. The SENTRY *is overcome, fumbles for words.* CREON *waits impassively.*

out there—
someone,—
New dust on the slimy flesh!

Pause. No sign from CREON.

Someone has given it burial that way, and
Gone . . .

Long pause. CREON *finally speaks with deadly control.*

CREON: And the man who dared do this?
SENTRY: I swear I
Do not know! You must believe me!
Listen:
The ground was dry, not a sign of digging, no,
Not a wheeltrack in the dust, no trace of anyone.
It was when they relieved us this morning: and one of them,
The corporal, pointed to it.
There it was,
The strangest—
Look:
The body, just mounded over with light dust: you see?
Not buried really, but as if they'd covered it
Just enough for the ghost's peace. And no sign
Of dogs or any wild animal that had been there.

And then what a scene there was! Every man of us
Accusing the other: we all proved the other man did it,
We all had proof that we could not have done it.
We were ready to take hot iron in our hands,
Walk through fire, swear by all the gods,
It was not I!
I do not know who it was, but it was not I!

CREON*'s rage has been mounting steadily, but the* SENTRY *is too intent upon his story to notice it.*

And then, when this came to nothing, someone said
A thing that silenced us and made us stare
Down at the ground: you had to be told the news,
And one of us had to do it! We threw the dice,
And the bad luck fell to me. So here I am,
No happier to be here than you are to have me:
Nobody likes the man who brings bad news.

CHORAGOS: I have been wondering, King: can it be that the gods have done this?

CREON [*furiously*]: Stop!
Must you doddering wrecks
Go out of your heads entirely? "The gods!"
Intolerable!
The gods favor this corpse? Why? How had he served them?
Tried to loot their temples, burn their images,
Yes, and the whole State, and its laws with it!
Is it your senile opinion that the gods love to honor bad men?
A pious thought!—
No, from the very beginning
There have been those who have whispered together,
Stiff-necked anarchists, putting their heads together,
Scheming against me in alleys. These are the men,
And they have bribed my own guard to do this thing.

[*Sententiously.*] Money!
There's nothing in the world so demoralizing as money.
Down go your cities,
Homes gone, men gone, honest hearts corrupted,
Crookedness of all kinds, and all for money!
[*To* SENTRY.] But you—!
I swear by God and by the throne of God,
The man who has done this thing shall pay for it!
Find that man, bring him here to me, or your death
Will be the least of your problems: I'll string you up
Alive, and there will be certain ways to make you
Discover your employer before you die;
And the process may teach you a lesson you seem to have missed:
The dearest profit is sometimes all too dear:
That depends on the source. Do you understand me?
A fortune won is often misfortune.

SENTRY: King, may I speak?

CREON: Your very voice distresses me.

SENTRY: Are you sure that it is my voice, and not your conscience?

CREON: By God, he wants to analyze me now!
SENTRY: It is not what I say, but what has been done, that hurts you.
CREON: You talk too much.
SENTRY: Maybe; but I've done nothing.
CREON: Sold your soul for some silver: that's all you've done.
SENTRY: How dreadful it is when the right judge judges wrong!
CREON: Your figures of speech
May entertain you now; but unless you bring me the man,
You will get little profit from them in the end.

Exit CREON *into the palace.*

SENTRY: "Bring me the man"—!
I'd like nothing better than bringing him the man!
But bring him or not, you have seen the last of me here.
At any rate, I am safe!

Exit SENTRY.

Ode I°

Strophe 1

CHORUS: Numberless are the world's wonders, but none
More wonderful than man; the stormgray sea
Yields to his prows, the huge crests bear him high;
Earth, holy and inexhaustible, is graven
With shining furrows where his plows have gone
Year after year, the timeless labor of stallions.

Antistrophe 1

The lightboned birds and beasts that cling to cover,
The lithe fish lighting their reaches of dim water,
All are taken, tamed in the net of his mind;
The lion on the hill, the wild horse windy-maned,
Resign to him; and his blunt yoke has broken
The sultry shoulders of the mountain bull.

Strophe 2

Words also, and thought as rapid as air,
He fashions to his good use; statecraft is his,
And his the skill that deflects the arrows of snow,
The spears of winter rain: from every wind
He has made himself secure—from all but one:
In the late wind of death he cannot stand.

Antistrophe 2

O clear intelligence, force beyond all measure!
O fate of man, working both good and evil!
When the laws are kept, how proudly his city stands!
When the laws are broken, what of his city then?
Never may the anárchic man find rest at my hearth,
Never be it said that my thoughts are his thoughts.

°**Ode I** First song sung by the Chorus, who at the same time danced. Here again, as in the párodos, *strophe* and *antistrophe* probably divide the song into two movements of the dance: right to left, then left to right.

Scene II

Re-enter SENTRY *leading* ANTIGONÊ.

CHORAGOS: What does this mean? Surely this captive woman
Is the Princess, Antigonê. Why should she be taken?

SENTRY: Here is the one who did it! We caught her
In the very act of burying him.—Where is Creon?

CHORAGOS: Just coming from the house.

Enter CREON, *center.*

CREON: What has happened?
Why have you come back so soon?

SENTRY [*expansively*]: O King,
A man should never be too sure of anything:
I would have sworn
That you'd not see me here again: your anger
Frightened me so, and the things you threatened me with;
But how could I tell then
That I'd be able to solve the case so soon?

No dice-throwing this time: I was only too glad to come!

Here is this woman. She is the guilty one:
We found her trying to bury him.
Take her, then; question her; judge her as you will.
I am through with the whole thing now, and glad of it.

CREON: But this is Antigonê! Why have you brought her here?

SENTRY: She was burying him, I tell you!

CREON [*severely*]: Is this the truth?

SENTRY: I saw her with my own eyes. Can I say more?

CREON: The details: come, tell me quickly!

SENTRY: It was like this:
After those terrible threats of yours, King,
We went back and brushed the dust away from the body.
The flesh was soft by now, and stinking,
So we sat on a hill to windward and kept guard.
No napping this time! We kept each other awake.
But nothing happened until the white round sun
Whirled in the center of the round sky over us:
Then, suddenly,
A storm of dust roared up from the earth, and the sky
Went out, the plain vanished with all its trees
In the stinging dark. We closed our eyes and endured it.
The whirlwind lasted a long time, but it passed;
And then we looked, and there was Antigonê!
I have seen
A mother bird come back to a stripped nest, heard
Her crying bitterly a broken note or two
For the young ones stolen. Just so, when this girl
Found the bare corpse, and all her love's work wasted,
She wept, and cried on heaven to damn the hands
That had done this thing.
And then she brought more dust
And sprinkled wine three times for her brother's ghost.

We ran and took her at once. She was not afraid,
Not even when we charged her with what she had done.
She denied nothing.
And this was a comfort to me,
And some uneasiness: for it is a good thing
To escape from death, but it is no great pleasure
To bring death to a friend.
Yet I always say
There is nothing so comfortable as your own safe skin!

CREON [*slowly, dangerously*]: And you, Antigonê,
You with your head hanging,—do you confess this thing?

ANTIGONÊ: I do. I deny nothing.

CREON [*to* SENTRY]: You may go.

Exit SENTRY.

[*To* ANTIGONÊ.] Tell me, tell me briefly:
Had you heard my proclamation touching this matter?

ANTIGONÊ: It was public. Could I help hearing it?

CREON: And yet you dared defy the law.

ANTIGONÊ: I dared.
It was not God's proclamation. That final Justice
That rules the world below makes no such laws.

Your edict, King, was strong,
But all your strength is weakness itself against
The immortal unrecorded laws of God.
They are not merely now: they were, and shall be,
Operative for ever, beyond man utterly.

I knew I must die, even without your decree:
I am only mortal. And if I must die
Now, before it is my time to die,
Surely this is no hardship: can anyone
Living, as I live, with evil all about me,
Think Death less than a friend? This death of mine
Is of no importance; but if I had left my brother
Lying in death unburied, I should have suffered.
Now I do not.
You smile at me. Ah Creon,
Think me a fool, if you like; but it may well be
That a fool convicts me of folly.

CHORAGOS: Like father, like daughter: both headstrong, deaf to reason!
She has never learned to yield.

CREON: She has much to learn.
The inflexible heart breaks first, the toughest iron
Cracks first, and the wildest horses bend their necks
At the pull of the smallest curb.
Pride? In a slave?
This girl is guilty of a double insolence,
Breaking the given laws and boasting of it.
Who is the man here,
She or I, if this crime goes unpunished?
Sister's child, or more than sister's child,

Or closer yet in blood—she and her sister
Win bitter death for this!
[*To* SERVANTS.] Go, some of you,
Arrest Ismenê. I accuse her equally.
Bring her: you will find her sniffling in the house there.

Her mind's a traitor: crimes kept in the dark
Cry for light, and the guardian brain shudders;
But how much worse than this
Is brazen boasting of barefaced anarchy!

ANTIGONÊ: Creon, what more do you want than my death?
CREON: Nothing.
That gives me everything.
ANTIGONÊ: Then I beg you: kill me.
This talking is a great weariness: your words
Are distasteful to me, and I am sure that mine
Seem so to you. And yet they should not seem so:
I should have praise and honor for what I have done.
All these men here would praise me
Were their lips not frozen shut with fear of you.
[*Bitterly.*] Ah the good fortune of kings,
Licensed to say and do whatever they please!
CREON: You are alone here in that opinion.
ANTIGONÊ: No, they are with me. But they keep their tongues in leash.
CREON: Maybe. But you are guilty, and they are not.
ANTIGONÊ: There is no guilt in reverence for the dead.
CREON: But Eteoclês—was he not your brother too?
ANTIGONÊ: My brother too.
CREON: And you insult his memory?
ANTIGONÊ [*softly*]: The dead man would not say that I insult it.
CREON: He would: for you honor a traitor as much as him.
ANTIGONÊ: His own brother, traitor or not, and equal in blood.
CREON: He made war on his country. Eteoclês defended it.
ANTIGONÊ: Nevertheless, there are honors due all the dead.
CREON: But not the same for the wicked as for the just.
ANTIGONÊ: Ah Creon, Creon,
Which of us can say what the gods hold wicked?
CREON: An enemy is an enemy, even dead.
ANTIGONÊ: It is my nature to join in love, not hate.
CREON [*finally losing patience*]: Go join them, then; if you must have your love,
Find it in hell!
CHORAGOS: But see, Ismenê comes:

Enter ISMENÊ, *guarded.*

Those tears are sisterly, the cloud
That shadows her eyes rains down gentle sorrow.
CREON: You too, Ismenê,
Snake in my ordered house, sucking my blood
Stealthily—and all the time I never knew
That these two sisters were aiming at my throne!
Ismenê,

Do you confess your share in this crime, or deny it?
Answer me.

ISMENÊ: Yes, if she will let me say so. I am guilty.

ANTIGONÊ [*coldly*]: No, Ismenê. You have no right to say so.
You would not help me, and I will not have you help me.

ISMENÊ: But now I know what you meant; and I am here
To join you, to take my share of punishment.

ANTIGONÊ: The dead man and the gods who rule the dead
Know whose act this was. Words are not friends.

ISMENÊ: Do you refuse me, Antigonê? I want to die with you:
I too have a duty that I must discharge to the dead.

ANTIGONÊ: You shall not lessen my death by sharing it.

ISMENÊ: What do I care for life when you are dead?

ANTIGONÊ: Ask Creon. You're always hanging on his opinions.

ISMENÊ: You are laughing at me. Why, Antigonê?

ANTIGONÊ: It's a joyless laughter, Ismenê.

ISMENÊ: But can I do nothing?

ANTIGONÊ: Yes. Save yourself. I shall not envy you.
There are those who will praise you; I shall have honor, too.

ISMENÊ: But we are equally guilty!

ANTIGONÊ: No more, Ismenê.
You are alive, but I belong to Death.

CREON [*to the* CHORUS]: Gentlemen, I beg you to observe these girls:
One has just now lost her mind; the other,
It seems, has never had a mind at all.

ISMENÊ: Grief teaches the steadiest minds to waver, King.

CREON: Yours certainly did, when you assumed guilt with the guilty!

ISMENÊ: But how could I go on living without her?

CREON: You are.
She is already dead.

ISMENÊ: But your own son's bride!

CREON: There are places enough for him to push his plow.
I want no wicked women for my sons!

ISMENÊ: O dearest Haimon, how your father wrongs you!

CREON: I've had enough of your childish talk of marriage!

CHORAGOS: Do you really intend to steal this girl from your son?

CREON: No; Death will do that for me.

CHORAGOS: Then she must die?

CREON [*ironically*]: You dazzle me.
—But enough of this talk!
[*To* GUARDS.] You, there, take them away and guard them well:
For they are but women, and even brave men run
When they see Death coming.

Exeunt ISMENÊ, ANTIGONÊ, *and* GUARDS.

Ode II

Strophe 1

CHORUS: Fortunate is the man who has never tasted God's vengeance!
Where once the anger of heaven has struck, that house is shaken
For ever: damnation rises behind each child

Like a wave cresting out of the black northeast,
When the long darkness under sea roars up
And bursts drumming death upon the windwhipped sand.

Antistrophe 1

I have seen this gathering sorrow from time long past
Loom upon Oedipus' children: generation from generation
Takes the compulsive rage of the enemy god.
So lately this last flower of Oedipus' line
Drank the sunlight! but now a passionate word
And a handful of dust have closed up all its beauty.

Strophe 2

What mortal arrogance
Transcends the wrath of Zeus?
Sleep cannot lull him nor the effortless long months
Of the timeless gods: but he is young for ever,
And his house is the shining day of high Olympos.
All that is and shall be,
And all the past, is his.
No pride on earth is free of the curse of heaven.

Antistrophe 2

The straying dreams of men
May bring them ghosts of joy:
But as they drowse, the waking embers burn them;
Or they walk with fixed eyes, as blind men walk.
But the ancient wisdom speaks for our own time:
Fate works most for woe
With Folly's fairest show.
Man's little pleasure is the spring of sorrow.

Scene III

CHORAGOS: But here is Haimon, King, the last of all your sons.
Is it grief for Antigonê that brings him here,
And bitterness at being robbed of his bride?

Enter HAIMON.

CREON: We shall soon see, and no need of diviners.
—Son,
You have heard my final judgment on that girl:
Have you come here hating me, or have you come
With deference and with love, whatever I do?
HAIMON: I am your son, father. You are my guide.
You make things clear for me, and I obey you.
No marriage means more to me than your continuing wisdom.
CREON: Good. That is the way to behave: subordinate
Everything else, my son, to your father's will.
This is what a man prays for, that he may get
Sons attentive and dutiful in his house,
Each one hating his father's enemies,
Honoring his father's friends. But if his sons
Fail him, if they turn out unprofitably,

What has he fathered but trouble for himself
And amusement for the malicious?
So you are right
Not to lose your head over this woman.
Your pleasure with her would soon grow cold, Haimon,
And then you'd have a hellcat in bed and elsewhere.
Let her find her husband in Hell!
Of all the people in this city, only she
Has had contempt for my law and broken it.

Do you want me to show myself weak before the people?
Or to break my sworn word? No, and I will not.
The woman dies.
I suppose she'll plead "family ties." Well, let her.
If I permit my own family to rebel,
How shall I earn the world's obedience?
Show me the man who keeps his house in hand,
He's fit for public authority.
I'll have no dealings
With law-breakers, critics of the government:
Whoever is chosen to govern should be obeyed—
Must be obeyed, in all things, great and small,
Just and unjust! O Haimon,
The man who knows how to obey, and that man only,
Knows how to give commands when the time comes.
You can depend on him, no matter how fast
The spears come: he's a good soldier, he'll stick it out.

Anarchy, anarchy! Show me a greater evil!
This is why cities tumble and the great houses rain down,
This is what scatters armies!

No, no: good lives are made so by discipline.
We keep the laws then, and the lawmakers,
And no woman shall seduce us. If we must lose,
Let's lose to a man, at least! Is a woman stronger than we?

CHORAGOS: Unless time has rusted my wits,
What you say, King, is said with point and dignity.

HAIMON [*boyishly earnest*]: Father:
Reason is God's crowning gift to man, and you are right
To warn me against losing mine. I cannot say—
I hope that I shall never want to say!—that you
Have reasoned badly. Yet there are other men
Who can reason, too; and their opinions might be helpful.
You are not in a position to know everything
That people say or do, or what they feel:
Your temper terrifies them—everyone
Will tell you only what you like to hear.
But I, at any rate, can listen; and I have heard them
Muttering and whispering in the dark about this girl.
They say no woman has ever, so unreasonably,

Died so shameful a death for a generous act:
"She covered her brother's body. Is this indecent?
She kept him from dogs and vultures. Is this a crime?
Death?—She should have all the honor that we can give her!"

This is the way they talk out there in the city.

You must believe me:
Nothing is closer to me than your happiness.
What could be closer? Must not any son
Value his father's fortune as his father does his?
I beg you, do not be unchangeable:
Do not believe that you alone can be right.
The man who thinks that,
The man who maintains that only he has the power
To reason correctly, the gift to speak, the soul—
A man like that, when you know him, turns out empty.

It is not reason never to yield to reason!

In flood time you can see how some trees bend,
And because they bend, even their twigs are safe,
While stubborn trees are torn up, roots and all.
And the same thing happens in sailing:
Make your sheet fast, never slacken,—and over you go,
Head over heels and under: and there's your voyage.
Forget you are angry! Let yourself be moved!
I know I am young; but please let me say this:
The ideal condition
Would be, I admit, that men should be right by instinct;
But since we are all too likely to go astray,
The reasonable thing is to learn from those who can teach.

CHORAGOS: You will do well to listen to him, King,
If what he says is sensible. And you, Haimon,
Must listen to your father.—Both speak well.

CREON: You consider it right for a man of my years and experience
To go to school to a boy?

HAIMON: It is not right,
If I am wrong. But if I am young, and right,
What does my age matter?

CREON: You think it right to stand up for an anarchist?

HAIMON: Not at all. I pay no respect to criminals.

CREON: Then she is not a criminal?

HAIMON: The City would deny it, to a man.

CREON: And the City proposes to teach me how to rule?

HAIMON: Ah. Who is it that's talking like a boy now?

CREON: My voice is the one voice giving orders in this City!

HAIMON: It is no City if it takes orders from one voice.

CREON: The State is the King!

HAIMON: Yes, if the State is a desert.

Pause.

CREON: This boy, it seems, has sold out to a woman.

HAIMON: If you are a woman: my concern is only for you.
CREON: So? Your "concern"! In a public brawl with your father!
HAIMON: How about you, in a public brawl with justice?
CREON: With justice, when all that I do is within my rights?
HAIMON: You have no right to trample on God's right.
CREON [*completely out of control*]: Fool, adolescent fool! Taken in by a woman!
HAIMON: You'll never see me taken in by anything vile.
CREON: Every word you say is for her!
HAIMON [*quietly, darkly*]: And for you.
And for me. And for the gods under the earth.
CREON: You'll never marry her while she lives.
HAIMON: Then she must die.—But her death will cause another.
CREON: Another?
Have you lost your senses? Is this an open threat?
HAIMON: There is no threat in speaking to emptiness.
CREON: I swear you'll regret this superior tone of yours!
You are the empty one!
HAIMON: If you were not my father,
I'd say you were perverse.
CREON: You girl-struck fool, don't play at words with me!
HAIMON: I am sorry. You prefer silence.
CREON: Now, by God—!
I swear, by all the gods in heaven above us,
You'll watch it, I swear you shall!
[*To the* SERVANTS.] Bring her out!
Bring the woman out! Let her die before his eyes!
Here, this instant, with her bridegroom beside her!
HAIMON: Not here, no; she will not die here, King.
And you will never see my face again.
Go on raving as long as you've a friend to endure you.

Exit HAIMON.

CHORAGOS: Gone, gone.
Creon, a young man in a rage is dangerous!
CREON: Let him do, or dream to do, more than a man can.
He shall not save these girls from death.
CHORAGOS: These girls?
You have sentenced them both?
CREON: No, you are right.
I will not kill the one whose hands are clean.
CHORAGOS: But Antigonê?
CREON [*somberly*]: I will carry her far away
Out there in the wilderness, and lock her
Living in a vault of stone. She shall have food,
As the custom is, to absolve the State of her death.
And there let her pray to the gods of hell:
They are her only gods:
Perhaps they will show her an escape from death,
Or she may learn,
though late,
That piety shown the dead is pity in vain.

Exit CREON.

Ode III

Strophe

CHORUS: Love, unconquerable
Waster of rich men, keeper
Of warm lights and all-night vigil
In the soft face of a girl:
Sea-wanderer, forest-visitor!
Even the pure Immortals cannot escape you,
And mortal man, in his one day's dusk,
Trembles before your glory.

Antistrophe

Surely you swerve upon ruin
The just man's consenting heart,
As here you have made bright anger
Strike between father and son—
And none has conquered but Love!
A girl's glánce wórking the will of heaven:
Pleasure to her alone who mocks us,
Merciless Aphroditê.°

Scene IV

CHORAGOS [*as* ANTIGONÊ *enters guarded*]:
But I can no longer stand in awe of this,
Nor, seeing what I see, keep back my tears.
Here is Antigonê, passing to that chamber
Where all find sleep at last.

Strophe 1

ANTIGONÊ: Look upon me, friends, and pity me
Turning back at the night's edge to say
Good-by to the sun that shines for me no longer;
Now sleepy Death
Summons me down to Acheron,° that cold shore:
There is no bridesong there, nor any music.

CHORUS: Yet not unpraised, not without a kind of honor,
You walk at last into the underworld;
Untouched by sickness, broken by no sword.
What woman has ever found your way to death?

Antistrophe 1

ANTIGONÊ: How often I have heard the story of Niobê,°
Tantalos' wretched daughter, how the stone
Clung fast about her, ivy-close: and they say
The rain falls endlessly
And sifting soft snow; her tears are never done.
I feel the loneliness of her death in mine.

16 Aphroditê goddess of love. **9 Acheron** a river of the underworld, which was ruled by Hades. **15 Niobê** Niobê boasted of her numerous children, provoking Leto, the mother of Apollo to destroy them. Niobê wept profusely, and finally was turned to stone on Mount Sipylos, whose streams are her tears.

CHORUS: But she was born of heaven, and you
Are woman, woman-born. If her death is yours,
A mortal woman's, is this not for you
Glory in our world and in the world beyond?

Strophe 2

ANTIGONÊ: You laugh at me. Ah, friends, friends,
Can you not wait until I am dead? O Thebes,
O men many-charioted, in love with Fortune,
Dear springs of Dircê, sacred Theban grove,
Be witnesses for me, denied all pity,
Unjustly judged! and think a word of love
For her whose path turns
Under dark earth, where there are no more tears.

CHORUS: You have passed beyond human daring and come at last
Into a place of stone where Justice sits.
I cannot tell
What shape of your father's guilt appears in this.

Antistrophe 2

ANTIGONÊ: You have touched it at last: that bridal bed
Unspeakable, horror of son and mother mingling:
Their crime, infection of all our family!
O Oedipus, father and brother!
Your marriage strikes from the grave to murder mine.
I have been a stranger here in my own land:
All my life
The blasphemy of my birth has followed me.

CHORUS: Reverence is a virtue, but strength
Lives in established law: that must prevail.
You have made your choice,
Your death is the doing of your conscious hand.

Epode

ANTIGONÊ: Then let me go, since all your words are bitter,
And the very light of the sun is cold to me.
Lead me to my vigil, where I must have
Neither love nor lamentation; no song, but silence.

CREON *interrupts impatiently.*

CREON: If dirges and planned lamentations could put off death,
Men would be singing for ever.
[*To the* SERVANTS.] Take her, go!
You know your orders: take her to the vault
And leave her alone there. And if she lives or dies,
That's her affair, not ours: our hands are clean.

ANTIGONÊ: O tomb, vaulted bride-bed in eternal rock,
Soon I shall be with my own again
Where Persephonê° welcomes the thin ghosts underground:
And I shall see my father again, and you, mother,
And dearest Polyneicês—
dearest indeed

60 Persephonê queen of the underworld.

To me, since it was my hand
That washed him clean and poured the ritual wine:
And my reward is death before my time!

And yet, as men's hearts know, I have done no wrong,
I have not sinned before God. Or if I have,
I shall know the truth in death. But if the guilt
Lies upon Creon who judged me, then, I pray,
May his punishment equal my own.

CHORAGOS: O passionate heart,
Unyielding, tormented still by the same winds!

CREON: Her guards shall have good cause to regret their delaying.

ANTIGONÊ: Ah! That voice is like the voice of death!

CREON: I can give you no reason to think you are mistaken.

ANTIGONÊ: Thebes, and you my fathers' gods,
And rulers of Thebes, you see me now, the last
Unhappy daughter of a line of kings,
Your kings, led away to death. You will remember
What things I suffer, and at what men's hands,
Because I would not transgress the laws of heaven.
[*To the* GUARDS, *simply*.] Come: let us wait no longer.

Exit ANTIGONÊ, *left, guarded.*

Ode IV

Strophe 1

CHORUS: All Danaê's beauty was locked away
In a brazen cell where the sunlight could not come:
A small room still as any grave, enclosed her.
Yet she was a princess too,
And Zeus in a rain of gold poured love upon her.
O child, child,
No power in wealth or war
Or tough sea-blackened ships
Can prevail against untiring Destiny!

Antistrophe 1

And Dryas' son° also, that furious king,
Bore the god's prisoning anger for his pride:
Sealed up by Dionysos in deaf stone,
His madness died among echoes.
So at the last he learned what dreadful power
His tongue had mocked:
For he had profaned the revels,
And fired the wrath of the nine
Implacable Sisters that love the sound of the flute.

10 Dryas' son Lycurgus, King of Thrace.

Strophe 2

And old men tell a half-remembered tale
Of horror where a dark ledge splits the sea
And a double surf beats on the gráy shóres:
How a king's new woman,° sick
With hatred for the queen he had imprisoned,
Ripped out his two sons' eyes with her bloody hands
While grinning Arês° watched the shuttle plunge
Four times: four blind wounds crying for revenge,

Antistrophe 2

Crying, tears and blood mingled.—Piteously born,
Those sons whose mother was of heavenly birth!
Her father was the god of the North Wind
And she was cradled by gales,
She raced with young colts on the glittering hills
And walked untrammeled in the open light:
But in her marriage deathless Fate found means
To build a tomb like yours for all her joy.

Scene V

Enter blind TEIRESIAS, *led by a boy. The opening speeches of* TEIRESIAS *should be in singsong contrast to the realistic lines of* CREON.

TEIRESIAS: This is the way the blind man comes, Princes, Princes,
Lockstep, two heads lit by the eyes of one.
CREON: What new thing have you to tell us, old Teiresias?
TEIRESIAS: I have much to tell you: listen to the prophet, Creon.
CREON: I am not aware that I have ever failed to listen.
TEIRESIAS: Then you have done wisely, King, and ruled well.
CREON: I admit my debt to you. But what have you to say?
TEIRESIAS: This, Creon: you stand once more on the edge of fate.
CREON: What do you mean? Your words are a kind of dread.
TEIRESIAS: Listen Creon:
I was sitting in my chair of augury, at the place
Where the birds gather about me. They were all a-chatter,
As is their habit, when suddenly I heard
A strange note in their jangling, a scream, a
Whirring fury; I knew that they were fighting,
Tearing each other, dying
In a whirlwind of wings clashing. And I was afraid.
I began the rites of burnt-offering at the altar,
But Hephaistos° failed me: instead of bright flame,
There was only the sputtering slime of the fat thigh-flesh
Melting: the entrails dissolved in gray smoke,
The bare bone burst from the welter. And no blaze!

22 king's new woman Eidothea, second wife of King Phineus, blinded her stepsons. Their mother, Cleopatra had been imprisoned in a cave. Phineus was the son of a king, and Cleopatra, his first wife, was the daughter of Boreas, the North wind, but this illustrious ancestry could not protect his sons from violence and darkness **25 Arês** god of war. **19 Hephaistos** god of fire.

This was a sign from heaven. My boy described it,
Seeing for me as I see for others.

I tell you, Creon, you yourself have brought
This new calamity upon us. Our hearths and altars
Are stained with the corruption of dogs and carrion birds
That glut themselves on the corpse of Oedipus' son.
The gods are deaf when we pray to them, their fire
Recoils from our offering, their birds of omen
Have no cry of comfort, for they are gorged
With the thick blood of the dead.
O my son,
These are no trifles! Think: all men make mistakes,
But a good man yields when he knows his course is wrong,
And repairs the evil. The only crime is pride.

Give in to the dead man, then: do not fight with a corpse—
What glory is it to kill a man who is dead?
Think, I beg you:
It is for your own good that I speak as I do.
You should be able to yield for your own good.

CREON: It seems that prophets have made me their especial province.
All my life long
I have been a kind of butt for the dull arrows
Of doddering fortune-tellers!
No, Teiresias:
If your birds—if the great eagles of God himself
Should carry him stinking bit by bit to heaven,
I would not yield. I am not afraid of pollution:
No man can defile the gods.
Do what you will,
Go into business, make money, speculate
In India gold or that synthetic gold from Sardis,
Get rich otherwise than by my consent to bury him.
Teiresias, it is a sorry thing when a wise man
Sells his wisdom, lets out his words for hire!

TEIRESIAS: Ah Creon! Is there no man left in the world—

CREON: To do what?—Come, let's have the aphorism!

TEIRESIAS: No man who knows that wisdom outweighs any wealth?

CREON: As surely as bribes are baser than any baseness.

TEIRESIAS: You are sick, Creon! You are deathly sick!

CREON: As you say: it is not my place to challenge a prophet.

TEIRESIAS: Yet you have said my prophecy is for sale.

CREON: The generation of prophets has always loved gold.

TEIRESIAS: The generation of kings has always loved brass.

CREON: You forget yourself! You are speaking to your King.

TEIRESIAS: I know it. You are a king because of me.

CREON: You have a certain skill; but you have sold out.

TEIRESIAS: King, you will drive me to words that—

CREON: Say them, say them!
Only remember: I will not pay you for them.

TEIRESIAS: No, you will find them too costly.

CREON: No doubt. Speak:
Whatever you say, you will not change my will.

TEIRESIAS: Then take this, and take it to heart!
The time is not far off when you shall pay back
Corpse for corpse, flesh of your own flesh.
You have thrust the child of this world into living night,
You have kept from the gods below the child that is theirs:
The one in a grave before her death, the other,
Dead, denied the grave. This is your crime:
And the Furies and the dark gods of Hell
Are swift with terrible punishment for you.

Do you want to buy me now, Creon?
Not many days,
And your house will be full of men and women weeping,
And curses will be hurled at you from far
Cities grieving for sons unburied, left to rot
Before the walls of Thebes.

These are my arrows, Creon: they are all for you.
[*To* BOY.] But come, child: lead me home.
Let him waste his fine anger upon younger men.
Maybe he will learn at last
To control a wiser tongue in a better head.

Exit TEIRESIAS.

CHORAGOS: The old man has gone, King, but his words
Remain to plague us. I am old, too,
But I cannot remember that he was ever false.

CREON: That is true . . . . It troubles me.
Oh it is hard to give in! but it is worse
To risk everything for stubborn pride.

CHORAGOS: Creon: take my advice.

CREON: What shall I do?

CHORAGOS: Go quickly: free Antigonê from her vault
And build a tomb for the body of Polyneicês.

CREON: You would have me do this!

CHORAGOS: Creon, yes!
And it must be done at once: God moves
Swiftly to cancel the folly of stubborn men.

CREON: It is hard to deny the heart! But I
Will do it: I will not fight with destiny.

CHORAGOS: You must go yourself, you cannot leave it to others.

CREON: I will go.
—Bring axes, servants:
Come with me to the tomb. I buried her, I
Will set her free.
Oh quickly!
My mind misgives—
The laws of the gods are mighty, and a man must serve them
To the last day of his life!

Exit CREON.

Paean°

Strophe 1

CHORAGOS: God of many names
CHORUS: O Iacchos
son
of Kadmeian Sémelê
O born of the Thunder!
Guardian of the West
Regent
of Eleusis' plain
O Prince of maenad Thebes
and the Dragon Field by rippling Ismenós:°

Antistrophe 1

CHORAGOS: God of many names
CHORUS: the flame of torches
flares on our hills
the nymphs of Iacchos
dance at the spring of Castalia:°
from the vine-close mountain
come ah come in ivy:
Evohé evohé! sings through the streets of Thebes

Strophe 2

CHORAGOS: God of many names
CHORUS: Iacchos of Thebes
heavenly Child
of Sémelê bride of the Thunderer!
The shadow of plague is upon us:
come
with clement feet
oh come from Parnassos
down the long slopes
across the lamenting water

Antistrophe 2

CHORAGOS: Iô Fire! Chorister of the throbbing stars!
O purest among the voices of the night!
Thou son of God, blaze for us!
CHORUS: Come with choric rapture of circling Maenads
Who cry *Iô Iacche!*
God of many names!

Éxodos

Enter MESSENGER *from left.*

MESSENGER: Men of the line of Kadmos,° you who live
Near Amphion's citadel:°
I cannot say

°**Paean** a hymn (here dedicated to Iacchos, also called Dionysos. His father was Zeus, his mother was Sémelê, daughter of Kadmos. Iacchos's worshipers were the Maenads, whose cry was "Evohé evohé"). **5 Ismenós** a river east of Thebes (from a dragon's teeth sown near the river, there sprang men who became the ancestors of the Theban nobility. **8 Castalia** a spring on Mount Parnassos. **1 Kadmos** The founder of Thebes, best known for sowing the dragon's teeth. **2 Amphion's citadel** Amphion played so sweetly on his lyre that he charmed stones to form a wall around Thebes.

Of any condition of human life "This is fixed,
This is clearly good, or bad." Fate raises up,
And Fate casts down the happy and unhappy alike:
No man can foretell his Fate.
Take the case of Creon:
Creon was happy once, as I count happiness:
Victorious in battle, sole governor of the land,
Fortunate father of children nobly born.
And now it has all gone from him! Who can say
That a man is still alive when his life's joy fails?
He is a walking dead man. Grant him rich,
Let him live like a king in his great house:
If his pleasure is gone, I would not give
So much as the shadow of smoke for all he owns.

CHORAGOS: Your words hint at sorrow: what is your news for us?

MESSENGER: They are dead. The living are guilty of their death.

CHORAGOS: Who is guilty? Who is dead? Speak!

MESSENGER: Haimon.
Haimon is dead; and the hand that killed him
Is his own hand.

CHORAGOS: His father's? or his own?

MESSENGER: His own, driven mad by the murder his father had done.

CHORAGOS: Teiresias, Teiresias, how clearly you saw it all!

MESSENGER: This is my news: you must draw what conclusions you can from it.

CHORAGOS: But look: Eurydicê, our Queen:
Has she overheard us?

Enter EURYDICÊ *from the palace, center.*

EURYDICÊ: I have heard something, friends:
As I was unlocking the gate of Pallas'° shrine,
For I needed her help today, I heard a voice
Telling of some new sorrow. And I fainted
There at the temple with all my maidens about me.
But speak again: whatever it is, I can bear it:
Grief and I are no strangers.

MESSENGER: Dearest Lady.
I will tell you plainly all that I have seen.
I shall not try to comfort you: what is the use,
Since comfort could lie only in what is not true?
The truth is always best.
I went with Creon
To the outer plain where Polyneicês was lying,
No friend to pity him, his body shredded by dogs.
We made our prayers in that place to Hecatê
And Pluto,° that they would be merciful. And we bathed
The corpse with holy water, and we brought
Fresh-broken branches to burn what was left of it,

27 Pallas Pallas Athene, goddess of wisdom. **39–40 Hecatê and Pluto** Hecatê and Pluto (also known as Hades) were deities of the underworld.

And upon the urn we heaped up a towering barrow
Of the earth of his own land.
When we were done, we ran
To the vault where Antigonê lay on her couch of stone.
One of the servants had gone ahead,
And while he was yet far off he heard a voice
Grieving within the chamber, and he came back
And told Creon. And as the King went closer,
The air was full of wailing, the words lost,
And he begged us to make all haste. "Am I a prophet?"
He said, weeping, "And must I walk this road,
The saddest of all that I have gone before?
My son's voice calls me on. Oh quickly, quickly!
Look through the crevice there, and tell me
If it is Haimon, or some deception of the gods!"

We obeyed; and in the cavern's farthest corner
We saw her lying:
She had made a noose of her fine linen veil
And hanged herself. Haimon lay beside her,
His arms about her waist, lamenting her,
His love lost under ground, crying out
That his father had stolen her away from him.

When Creon saw him the tears rushed to his eyes
And he called to him: "What have you done, child? Speak to me.
What are you thinking that makes your eyes so strange?
O my son, my son, I come to you on my knees!"
But Haimon spat in his face. He said not a word,
Staring—
And suddenly drew his sword
And lunged. Creon shrank back, the blade missed; and the boy,
Desperate against himself, drove it half its length
Into his own side, and fell. And as he died
He gathered Antigonê close in his arms again,
Choking, his blood bright red on her white cheek.
And now he lies dead with the dead, and she is his
At last, his bride in the houses of the dead.

Exit EURYDICÊ *into the palace.*

CHORAGOS: She has left us without a word. What can this mean?
MESSENGER: It troubles me, too; yet she knows what is best,
Her grief is too great for public lamentation,
And doubtless she has gone to her chamber to weep
For her dead son, leading her maidens in his dirge.
CHORAGOS: It may be so: but I fear this deep silence.

Pause.

MESSENGER: I will see what she is doing. I will go in.

Exit MESSENGER *into the palace.*

Enter CREON *with attendants, bearing* HAIMON*'s body.*

CHORAGOS: But here is the king himself: oh look at him,
Bearing his own damnation in his arms.

CREON: Nothing you say can touch me any more.
My own blind heart has brought me
From darkness to final darkness. Here you see
The father murdering, the murdered son—
And all my civic wisdom!

Haimon my son, so young, so young to die,
I was the fool, not you; and you died for me.
CHORAGOS: That is the truth; but you were late in learning it.
CREON: This truth is hard to bear. Surely a god
Has crushed me beneath the hugest weight of heaven,
And driven me headlong a barbaric way
To trample out the thing I held most dear.

The pains that men will take to come to pain!

Enter MESSENGER *from the palace.*

MESSENGER: The burden you carry in your hands is heavy,
But it is not all: you will find more in your house.
CREON: What burden worse than this shall I find there?
MESSENGER: The Queen is dead.
CREON: O port of death, deaf world,
Is there no pity for me? And you, Angel of evil,
I was dead, and your words are death again.
Is it true, boy? Can it be true?
Is my wife dead? Has death bred death?
MESSENGER: You can see for yourself.

The doors are opened and the body of EURYDICÊ *is disclosed within.*

CREON: Oh pity!
All true, all true, and more than I can bear!
O my wife, my son!
MESSENGER: She stood before the altar, and her heart
Welcomed the knife her own hand guided,
And a great cry burst from her lips for Megareus° dead,
And for Haimon dead, her sons; and her last breath
Was a curse for their father, the murderer of her sons.
And she fell, and the dark flowed in through her closing eyes.
CREON: O God, I am sick with fear.
Are there no swords here? Has no one a blow for me?
MESSENGER: Her curse is upon you for the deaths of both.
CREON: It is right that it should be. I alone am guilty.
I know it, and I say it. Lead me in,
Quickly, friends.
I have neither life nor substance. Lead me in.
CHORAGOS: You are right, if there can be right in so much wrong.
The briefest way is best in a world of sorrow.
CREON: Let it come,
Let death come quickly, and be kind to me.
I would not ever see the sun again.

114 Megareus The brother of Haimon, Megareus had died in the assault on Thebes.

CHORAGOS: All that will come when it will; but we, meanwhile,
Have much to do. Leave the future to itself.
CREON: All my heart was in that prayer!
CHORAGOS: Then do not pray any more: the sky is deaf.
CREON: Lead me away. I have been rash and foolish.
I have killed my son and my wife.
I look for comfort; my comfort lies here dead.
Whatever my hands have touched has come to nothing.
Fate has brought all my pride to a thought of dust.

As CREON *is being led into the house, the* CHORAGOS *advances and speaks directly to the audience.*

CHORAGOS: There is no happiness where there is no wisdom;
No wisdom but in submission to the gods.
Big words are always punished,
And proud men in old age learn to be wise.

[441 B.C.E.]

Joining the Conversation: Critical Thinking and Writing

1. Would you argue that masks should be used for some (or all) of the characters? If so, would they be masks that fully cover the face, Greek style, or some sort of half-masks? (A full mask enlarges the face, and conceivably the mouthpiece can amplify the voice, but only an exceptionally large theater might require such help. Perhaps half-masks are enough if the aim is chiefly to distance the actors from the audience and from daily reality, and to force the actors to develop resources other than facial gestures. One director, arguing in favor of half-masks, has said that an actor who wears even a half-mask learns to act not with his eyes but with his neck.)
2. How would you costume the players? Would you dress them as the Greeks might have? Why? One argument sometimes used by those who hold the modern productions of Greek drama should use classical costumes is that Greek drama *ought* to be remote and ritualistic. Evaluate this view. What sort of modern dress might be effective?
3. If you were directing a college production of *Antigonê,* how large a chorus would you use? (Sophocles is said to have used a chorus of fifteen.) Would you have the chorus recite (or chant) the odes in unison, or would you assign lines to single speakers?
4. Although Sophocles called his play *Antigonê,* many critics say that Creon is the real tragic hero, pointing out that Antigonê is absent from the last third of the play. Argue for or against this view.
5. In some Greek tragedies, fate plays a great role in bringing about the downfall of the tragic hero. Though there are references to the curse on the House of Oedipus in *Antigonê,* do we feel that Antigonê goes to her death as a result of the workings of fate? Do we feel that fate is responsible for Creon's fall? Are both Antigonê and Creon the creators of their own tragedy?
6. Are the words *hubris* (page 434) and *hamartia* (page 435) relevant to Antigonê? To Creon? Argue your position.

7. Why does Creon, contrary to the Chorus's advice, bury the body of Polyneicês before he releases Antigonê? Does his action show a zeal for piety as short-sighted as his earlier zeal for law? Is his action plausible, in view of the facts that Teiresias has dwelt on the wrong done to Polyneicês and that Antigonê has ritual food to sustain her? Or are we not to worry about Creon's motive?
8. A *foil* is a character who, by contrast, sets off or helps define another character. To what extent is Ismenê a foil to Antigonê? Is she entirely without courage?
9. What function does Eurydicê serve? How deeply do we feel about her fate?

CHAPTER 16

Reading and Writing about Poems

Elements of Poetry

The Speaker and the Poet

The **speaker,** or **voice,** or **mask,** or **persona** (Latin for *mask*) that speaks a poem is not usually identical with the poet who writes it. The author assumes a role, or counterfeits the speech of a person in a particular situation. The nineteenth-century English poet Robert Browning, for instance, in "My Last Duchess" invented a Renaissance Italian duke who, in his palace, talks about his first wife and his art collection with an emissary from a count who is negotiating to offer his daughter in marriage to the duke.

In reading a poem, then, the first and most important question to ask yourself is this: Who is speaking? If an audience and a setting are suggested, keep them in mind, too, although these are not always indicated in a poem. Consider, for example, the following poem.

EMILY DICKINSON

I'm Nobody! Who are you?
Are you—Nobody—too?
Then there's a pair of us!
Don't tell! they'd banish us—you know!

How dreary—to be—Somebody!
How public—like a Frog—
To tell your name—the livelong June—
To an admiring Bog!

[1861?]

We cannot quite say that the speaker is Emily Dickinson, though if we have read a fair number of her poems we can say that the voice in this poem is familiar, and perhaps here we *can* talk of Dickinson rather than of "the speaker of the poem," since this speaker (unlike Browning's Renaissance duke) clearly is not a figure utterly remote from the poet.

Let's consider the sort of person we hear in "I'm Nobody! Who are you?" (Read it aloud, to see if you agree with what we say. In fact, you should test each of our assertions by reading the poem aloud.)

- The voice in the first line is rather like that of a child playing a game with a friend.
- In the second and third lines the speaker sees the reader as a fellow spirit ("Are you—Nobody—too?") and invites the reader to join her ("Then there's a pair of us!"), to form a conspiracy of silence against outsiders ("Don't tell!").

In "they'd banish us," however, we hear a word that a child would not be likely to use, and we probably feel that the speaker is a shy but (with the right companion) playful adult, who here is speaking to an intimate friend, the reader. By means of "banish," a word that brings to mind images of a king's court, the speaker almost comically inflates and thereby makes fun of the "they" who are opposed to "us."

In the second stanza, or we might better say in the space between the two stanzas, the speaker puts aside the childlike manner. In "How dreary," the first words of the second stanza, we hear a sophisticated voice, one might even say a world-weary voice or a voice perhaps with more than a touch of condescension. But since by now we are paired with the speaker in a conspiracy against outsiders, we enjoy the contrast that the speaker makes between the Nobodies and the Somebodies. Who are these Somebodies, these people who would imperiously "banish" the speaker and the friend? What are the Somebodies like?

How dreary—to be—Somebody!
How public—like a Frog—
To tell your name—the livelong June—
To an admiring Bog!

The last two lines do at least two things:

- They amusingly explain to the speaker's new friend (the reader) in what way a Somebody is public (it proclaims its presence all day), and
- they indicate the absurdity of the Somebody-Frog's behavior (the audience is "an admiring Bog").

By the end of the poem we are convinced that it is better to be a Nobody (like Dickinson and the reader?) than a Somebody (a loudmouth).

Dickinson did not always speak in this persona, however. In another poem, "Wild Nights," probably written in the same year as "I'm Nobody! Who are you?", Dickinson speaks as an impassioned lover, but we need not assume that the beloved is actually in the presence of the lover. Since the second line says, "Were I with Thee," the reader must assume that the person addressed is *not* present. The poem represents a state of mind—a sort of talking to oneself—rather than an address to another person.

Wild Nights—Wild Nights,
Were I with Thee
Wild Nights should be
Our luxury

Futile—the Winds
To a Heart in port—
Done with the Compass—
Done with the Chart!

Rowing in Eden—
Ah, the Sea!
Might I but moor—Tonight—
In Thee.

[c. 1861]

This speaker is passionately in love. The following questions invite you to look more closely at how the speaker of "Wild Nights" is characterized.

Joining the Conversation: Critical Thinking and Writing

1. How does this poem communicate the speaker's state of mind? For example, in the first stanza (lines 1–4), what—beyond the meaning of the words—is communicated by the repetition of "Wild Nights"? In the last stanza (lines 9–12), what is the tone of "Ah, the Sea!"? ("Tone" means something like emotional coloring, as for instance a "businesslike tone," a "bitter tone," or an "eager tone.")
2. Paraphrase (that is, put into your own words) the second stanza. What does this stanza communicate about the speaker's love for the beloved? Compare your paraphrase and the original. What does the form of the original sentences (the *omission*, for instance, of the verbs of lines 5 and 6 and of the subject in lines 7 and 8) communicate?
3. Paraphrase the last stanza. How does "Ah, the Sea!" fit into your paraphrase? If you had trouble fitting it in, do you think the poem would be better off without it? If not, why not?

The voice speaking a poem may have the ring of the author's own voice, and to make a distinction between speaker and author may at times seem perverse. Some poetry (especially contemporary American poetry) is highly autobiographical. Still, even in autobiographical poems it may be convenient to distinguish between author and speaker. The speaker of a given poem is, let's say, Sylvia Plath in her role as parent, or Sylvia Plath in her role as daughter, not simply Sylvia Plath the poet.

The Language of Poetry: Diction and Tone

How is a voice or mask or persona created? From the whole of language, the author consciously or unconsciously selects certain words and grammatical constructions; this selection constitutes the persona's diction. It is, then, partly by the diction that we come to know the speaker of a poem. Just as in life there is a difference between people who speak of a "belly button," a "navel," or an "umbilicus," so in poetry there is a difference between speakers who use one word rather than another. Of course it is also possible that all three of these words are part of a given speaker's vocabulary, and the speaker's choice among the three would depend on the situation. That is, in addressing a child, the speaker would probably use the word "belly button"; in addressing an adult other than a family member or close friend, the speaker might be more likely to use "navel"; and if the speaker is a physician addressing an audience of physicians, he or she might be most likely to use "umbilicus." But this is only to say, again, that the dramatic situation in which you find yourself helps to define yourself, helps to establish the particular role that you are playing.

Some words are used in virtually all poems: *I, see, and,* and the like. Still, the grammatical constructions in which they appear may help to define the speaker. In Dickinson's "Wild Nights," for instance, expressions such as "Were I with Thee" and "Might I" indicate a speaker of an earlier century than ours, and probably an educated speaker.

Speakers have attitudes toward

- themselves,
- their subjects, and
- their audiences,

and, consciously or unconsciously, they choose their words, pitch, and modulation accordingly; all these add up to their tone. In written literature, tone must be detected without the aid of the ear, although it's a good idea to read poetry aloud, trying to find the appropriate tone of voice. The reader must understand by the selection and sequence of words the way the words are meant to sound—playful, angry, confidential, or ironic, for example. The reader must catch what Frost calls "the speaking tone of voice somehow entangled in the words and fastened to the page for the ear of the imagination."

William Shakespeare

William Shakespeare (1564–1616), born in Stratford-upon-Avon in England, is chiefly known as a playwright, but he also wrote nondramatic poetry. In 1609 a volume of 154 of his sonnets was published, apparently without his permission. Probably he chose to keep his sonnets unpublished not because he thought that they were of little value, but because it was more prestigious to be an amateur poet (unpublished) than a professional (published). Although the sonnets were published in 1609, they were probably written in the mid-1590s, when there was a vogue for sonneteering. A contemporary writer in 1598 said that Shakespeare's "sugred Sonnets [circulate] among his private friends."

We print other sonnets on pages 115, 723, and 724.

Sonnet 146

Poor soul, the center of my sinful earth,
[My sinful earth] these rebel pow'rs that thee array,
Why dost thou pine within and suffer dearth,
Painting thy outward walls so costly gay?
Why so large cost,° having so short a lease,
Dost thou upon thy fading mansion spend?
Shall worms, inheritors of this excess,
Eat up thy charge? Is this thy body's end?
Then, soul, live thou upon thy servant's loss,
And let that pine to aggravate thy store;
Buy terms divine° in selling hours of dross;
Within be fed, without be rich no more.
    So shalt thou feed on Death, that feeds on men,
    And death once dead, there's no more dying then.

[1609]

5 cost expense. **11 buy terms divine** buy ages of immortality.

Joining the Conversation: Critical Thinking and Writing

1. "My sinful earth," in line 2, is doubtless an error made by the printer of the first edition (1609), who mistakenly repeated the end of the first line. Among suggested replacements are "Thrall to," "Fooled by," "Rebuke," "Leagued with," and "Feeding." If you wish, suggest your own corrections. Which do you prefer?
2. In what tone of voice would you speak the first line? The last line? Trace the speaker's shifts in emotion throughout the poem.
3. Is the speaker presenting an argument? What is the argument (if you think there is one)? How does the speaker support it?

Writing about the Speaker

Robert Frost once said:

> Everything written is as good as it is dramatic. . . . [A poem is] heard as sung or spoken by a person in a scene—in a character, in a setting. By whom, where and when is the question. By the dreamer of a better world out in a storm in autumn; by a lover under a window at night.

Suppose, in reading the poem by Frost we reprint below, we try to establish "by whom, where and when" it is spoken. We may not be able to answer all three questions in great detail, but let's see what the poem suggests. As you read it, you'll notice—alerted by the quotation marks—that there are *two* speakers; the poem is a tiny drama. Thus, the closing quotation marks at the end of line 9 signal to us that the first speech is finished.

Robert Frost

The Telephone

"When I was just as far as I could walk
From here today
There was an hour
All still
When leaning with my head against a flower
I heard you talk.
Don't say I didn't, for I heard you say—
You spoke from that flower on the window sill—
Do you remember what it was you said?"

"First tell me what it was you thought you heard."

"Having found the flower and driven a bee away,
I leaned my head,
And holding by the stalk,
I listened and I thought I caught the word—
What was it? Did you call me by my name?
Or did you say—
Someone said 'Come'—I heard it as I bowed."

"I may have thought as much, but not aloud."
"Well, so I came."

[1916]

Suppose we ask: Who are these two speakers? What is their relationship? What's going on between them? Where are they? We don't think that these questions can be answered with absolute certainty, but we do think some answers are more probable than others. For instance, line 8 ("You spoke from that flower on the window sill") tells us that the speakers are in a room, probably of a home—rather than, say, in a railroad station—but we cannot say whether the home is a farmhouse, or a house in a village, town, or city, or an apartment.

Let's put the questions (even if they may turn out to be unanswerable) into a more specific form.

Joining the Conversation: Critical Thinking and Writing

1. One speaker speaks lines 1–9, 11–17, and 19. The other speaks lines 10 and 18. Do you think you can tell the gender of each speaker? For sure, probably, or not at all? On what do you base your answer?
2. Try to visualize this miniature drama. In line 7 the first speaker says, "Don't say I didn't, . . ." What happens—what do you see in your mind's eye—after line 6 that causes the speaker to say this?
3. Why do you suppose the speaker of lines 10 and 18 says so little? How would you characterize the tone of these two lines? What sort of relationship do you think exists between the two speakers?
4. How would you characterize the tone of lines 11–17? Of the last line of the poem?

If you haven't jotted down your responses, we suggest that you do so before reading what follows.

Journal Entries

Given questions somewhat like the preceding ones, students were asked to try to identify the speakers by sex, to speculate on their relationship, and then to add whatever they wished to say. One student recorded the following thoughts:

> These two people care about each other—maybe husband and wife, or lovers—and a man is doing most of the talking, though I can't prove it. He has walked as far as possible—that is, as far as possible and still get back on the same day—and he seemed to hear the other person call him. He claims that she spoke to him "from that flower on the window sill," and that's why I think the second person is a woman. She's at home, near the window. Somehow I even imagine she was at the window near the kitchen sink, maybe working while he was out on this long walk.
>
> Then she speaks one line; she won't say if she did or didn't speak. She is very cautious, or suspicious: "First tell me what it was you thought you heard." Maybe she doesn't want to say something and then have her husband embarrass her by saying, "No, that's not what I thought." Or maybe she just doesn't feel like talking. Then he claims that he heard her speaking through a flower, as though the flower was a telephone, just as though it was hooked up to the flower on the window sill. But at first he

> won't say what he supposedly heard, or "thought" he heard. Instead, he says that maybe it was someone else: "*Someone* said 'Come.'" Is he teasing her? Pretending that she may have a rival?
>
> Then she speaks—again just one line, saying, "I may have thought as much, but not aloud." She won't admit that she *did* think this thought. And then the man says, "Well, so I came." Just like that; short and sweet. No more fancy talk about flowers as telephones. He somehow (through telepathy?) got the message, and so here he is. He seems like a sensitive guy, playful (the stuff about the flowers as telephones), but also he knows when to stop kidding around.

Another student also identified the couple as a man and woman and thought that this dialogue occurs after a quarrel:

> As the poem goes on, we learn that the man wants to be with the woman, but it starts by telling us that he walked as far away from her as he could. He doesn't say why, but I think from the way the woman speaks later in the poem, they had a fight and he walked out. Then, when he stopped to rest, he thought he heard her voice. He really means that he was thinking of her and he was hoping she was thinking of him. So he returns, and he tells her he heard her calling him, but he pretends he heard her call him through a flower on their window sill. He can't admit that *he* was thinking about her. This seems very realistic to me; when someone feels a bit ashamed, it's sometimes hard to admit that you were wrong, and you want the other person to tell you that things are OK anyhow. And judging from line 7, when he says "Don't say I didn't," it seems that she is going to interrupt him by denying it. She is still angry, or maybe she doesn't want to make up too quickly. But he wants to pretend that *she* called him back. So when he says, "Do you remember what it was you said?" she won't admit that she *was* thinking of him, and she says, "First tell me what it was you thought you heard." She's testing him a little. So he goes on, with the business about flowers as telephones, and he says "someone" called him. He understands that she doesn't want to be pushed into forgiving him, so he backs off. Then she is willing to admit that she did think about him, but still she doesn't quite admit it. She is too proud to say openly that she wants him back but she does say, "I *may* have thought as much, . . ." And then, since they both have preserved their dignity, and also both have admitted that they care about the other, he can say, "Well, so I came."

Joining the Conversation: Critical Thinking and Writing

1. In a paragraph or two, *evaluate* one of these two entries recorded by students. Do you think the comments are weak, plausible, or convincing, and *why* do you think so? Can you offer additional supporting evidence or, on the other hand, counterevidence? You may want to set forth your own scenario.
2. Two small questions: In a sentence or two, offer a suggestion as to why in line 11 Frost wrote, "and driven a bee away." After all, the bee plays no role in the

poem. Second, in line 17 Frost has the speaker say, "I heard it as I bowed." "Bowed" rhymes with "aloud," but let's assume that the need for a rhyme did not dictate the choice of this word. Do you think "I heard it as I bowed" is better than, say, "I heard it as I waited," or "I heard it as I listened"? Why?

3. Write an essay of 500 words either about an uncanny experience of your own or about a quarrel or disagreement that was resolved in a way you had not expected.

Figurative Language

Robert Frost has said, "Poetry provides the one permissible way of saying one thing and meaning another." This is an exaggeration, but it shrewdly suggests the importance of figurative language—saying one thing in terms of something else. Words have their literal meanings, but they can also be used so that something other than the literal meaning is implied. "My love is a rose" is, literally, nonsense, for a person is not a five-petaled, many-stamened plant with a spiny stem. But the suggestions of *rose* (at least for Robert Burns, who compared his beloved to a rose in the line "My love is like a red, red rose"), include "delicate beauty," "soft," and "perfumed," and thus the word *rose* can be meaningfully applied—figuratively rather than literally—to "my love." The girl is fragrant; her skin is perhaps like a rose in texture and (in some measure) color; she will not keep her beauty long. The poet, that is, has communicated his perception very precisely.

People who write about poetry have found it convenient to name the various kinds of figurative language. Just as the student of geology employs such special terms as *kames* and *eskers,* the student of literature employs special terms to name things as accurately as possible. The following paragraphs discuss the most common terms.

In a **simile,** items from different classes are explicitly compared by a connective such as *like, as,* or *than,* or by a verb such as *appears* or *seems.* (If the objects compared are from the same class, for example, "Tokyo is like Los Angeles," no simile is present.)

Float like a butterfly, sting like a bee.

—Muhammad Ali

It is a beauteous evening, calm and free.
The holy time is quiet as a Nun,
Breathless with adoration.

—William Wordsworth

All of our thoughts will be fairer than doves.

—Elizabeth Bishop

Seems he a dove? His feathers are but borrowed.

—Shakespeare

A **metaphor** asserts the identity, without a connective such as *like* or a verb such as *appears,* of terms that are literally incompatible.

Umbrellas clothe the beach in every hue.

—Elizabeth Bishop

whirlwind fife-and-drum of the storm bends the salt
marsh grass

—Marianne Moore

Two common types of metaphor have Greek names. In **synecdoche** the whole is replaced by the part, or the part by the whole. For example, *bread* in "Give us this day our daily bread" replaces all sorts of food. In **metonymy** something is named that replaces something closely related to it. For example, James Shirley names certain objects, using them to replace social classes (royalty and the peasantry) to which they are related:

> Scepter and crown must tumble down
> And in the dust be equal made
> With the poor crooked scythe and spade.

The attribution of human feelings or characteristics or abstractions to inanimate objects is called **personification.**

> Memory,
> that exquisite blunderer.
>
> —Amy Clampitt

> There's Wrath who has learnt every trick of guerilla warfare,
> The shamming dead, the night-raid, the feinted retreat.
>
> —W. H. Auden

> Hope, thou bold taster of delight.
>
> —Richard Crashaw

Crashaw's personification, "Hope, thou bold taster of delight," is also an example of the figure called **apostrophe,** an address to a person or thing not literally listening. Wordsworth begins a sonnet by apostrophizing Milton:

> Milton, thou shouldst be living at this hour.

What conclusions can we draw about figurative language? First, figurative language, with its literally incompatible terms, forces the reader to attend to the **connotations** (suggestions, associations) rather than to the **denotations** (dictionary definitions) of one of the terms. Second, although figurative language is said to differ from ordinary speech, it is found in ordinary speech as well as in poetry and other literary forms. "It rained cats and dogs," "War is hell," "Don't be a pig," "Mr. Know-it-all," and other tired figures are part of our daily utterances. But through repeated use, these, and most of the figures we use, have lost whatever impact they once had and are only a shade removed from expressions which, though once figurative, have become literal: the *eye* of a needle, a *branch* office, the *face* of a clock. Third, good figurative language is usually concrete, condensed, and interesting.

We should mention, too, that figurative language is not limited to literary writers; it is used by scientists and social scientists—by almost everyone who is concerned with effective expression. Take, for instance, R. H. Tawney's *Religion and the Rise of Capitalism* (1926), a classic of economics. Among the titles of Tawney's chapters are "The Economic Revolution," "The Puritan Movement," and "The New Medicine for Poverty," all of which include metaphors. (To take only the last: Poverty is seen as a sick person or a disease.) Or take this sentence from Tawney (almost any sentence will serve equally well to reveal his bent for metaphor): "By the end of the sixteenth century the divorce between religious theory and economic realities had long been evident."

Figures are not a fancy way of speaking. Quite the opposite: Writers use figures because they are forceful and exact. Literal language would not only be less interesting, it would also be less precise.

We have already printed two sonnets by Shakespeare; here is a third, but before you read it we might mention that if you have read the other sonnets you may recall that they abound with figurative language. For instance, in Sonnet 73 (page 115), the speaker says that he is aging not by telling us how old he is but by saying

he is like a tree with "yellow leaves" (we might say, again using a figure of speech, that he is in the autumn of his life),
he is in his "twilight," and
he is like a fire that now is merely embers lying on a bed of ashes.

In Sonnet 146 (p. 491) he compares his body to "earth" and to a "fading mansion," and he says that the body is the "servant" of the soul—expressions that are figurative, not literal. But in the following poem we see that Shakespeare can also laugh at figurative comparisons. His contemporaries wrote countless sonnets in which they compared their beloved's eyes to the sun, the redness of her lips to coral, her blonde hair to fine gold wire, her red and white complexion to damask roses (or perhaps to a silk called damask—mixed red and white), her breath to perfume, her speech to music, and her gait to that of a goddess (goddesses were said to walk on air, not on earth). Now see how Shakespeare describes his mistress. But first, two cautions: In line 8, "reeks," in "the breath that from my mistress reeks," in Shakespeare's day did not have the strong negative suggestion that it has today; rather, it meant something like "emanates." Second, in the final line, "any she belied with false compare" means "any woman misrepresented by false comparisons."

Sonnet 130

My mistress' eyes are nothing like the sun;
Coral is far more red than her lips' red;
If snow be white, why then her breasts are dun;
If hairs be wires, black wires grow on her head.
I have seen roses damasked, red and white,
But no such roses see I in her cheeks;
And in some perfumes is there more delight
Than in the breath that from my mistress reeks.
I love to hear her speak, yet well I know
That music hath a far more pleasing sound;
I grant I never saw a goddess go;
My mistress, when she walks, treads on the ground.
And yet, by heaven, I think my love as rare
As any she belied with false compare.

[1609]

Joining the Conversation: Critical Thinking and Writing

Shakespeare here seems to ridicule figurative language, yet he uses figurative language in his sonnets and his plays. How can this be explained?

Dana Gioia

Dana Gioia (pronounced "JOY uh"), born in 1950, is a poet and the author of several books on literature. He has also been a successful businessman and served as Chairman for the National Endowment for the Arts from 2004 to 2009.

Money

Money is a kind of poetry.

—Wallace Stevens

Money, the long green,
cash, stash, rhino, jack
or just plain dough.

Chock it up, fork it over,
shell it out. Watch it
burn holes through pockets.

To be made of it! To have it
to burn! Greenbacks, double eagles,
megabucks and Ginnie Maes.

It greases the palm, feathers a nest,
holds heads above water,
makes both ends meet.

Money breeds money.
Gathering interest, compounding daily.
Always in circulation

Money. You don't know where it's been,
but you put it where your mouth is.
And it talks.

[1991]

Joining the Conversation: Critical Thinking and Writing

1. Are any of the terms in the poem unfamiliar to you? If so, check a dictionary, and if you don't find an explanation in a dictionary, turn to other resources—the Internet, and friends and classmates. Do some of the terms come from particular worlds of discourse, for instance banking, or gambling, or drug-dealing?
2. Suppose the last stanza had been placed first. Would the poem be better? Or worse? Why? Argue your case.
3. Write a somewhat comparable poem on a topic of your choice, for instance students, teachers, athletes, or work.

Although one is almost tempted to say that figurative language is essential to literature, in fact some literature, even some poetry, is not figurative. Consider this short piece.

Robert Frost

The Hardship of Accounting

Never ask of money spent
Where the spender thinks it went.
Nobody was ever meant
To remember or invent
What he did with every cent.

[1936]

Joining the Conversation: Critical Thinking and Writing

Do you consider Frost's lines to be a poem? Why, or why not? The lines rhyme, but most people agree that not everything that rhymes is a poem. Consider:

Thirty days hath September,
April, June, and November;
February has twenty-eight alone,
All the rest have thirty-one,
Excepting leap year, that's the time
When February's days are twenty-nine.

Most teachers of literature would agree that although "Thirty days" is verse, it is not poetry. Why? And if "Thirty days" is not poetry, is Frost's "The Hardship of Accounting" poetry? Why or why not?

Imagery and Symbolism

When we read *rose* we may more or less call to mind a picture of a rose, or perhaps we are reminded of the odor or texture of a rose. Whatever in a poem appeals to any of our senses (including sensations of heat as well as of sight, smell, taste, touch, sound) is an image. In short, images are the sensory content of a work, whether literal or figurative. When a poet says "My rose" and is speaking about a rose, we have no figure of speech—though we still have an image. If, however, "My rose" is a shortened form of "My love is a rose," some would say that the poet is using a metaphor; but others would say that because the first term is omitted ("My love is"), the rose is a symbol. A poem about the transience of a rose might compel the reader to feel that the transience of female beauty is the larger theme even though it is never explicitly stated.

Some symbols are **conventional symbols**—people have agreed to accept them as standing for something other than their literal meanings: A poem about the cross would probably be about Christianity; similarly, the rose has long been a symbol for love. In Virginia Woolf's novel *Mrs. Dalloway,* the husband communicates his love by proffering this conventional symbol: "He was holding out flowers—roses, red and white roses. (But he could not bring himself to say he loved her; not in so many words.)" Here is a poem that uses the conventional symbol of the rose.

EDMUND WALLER

Edmund Waller (1606–1687), born into a country family of wealth in Buckinghamshire in England, attended Eton and Cambridge before spending most of his life as a Member of Parliament. When the Puritans came to power, he was imprisoned and eventually banished to France, although he was soon allowed to return to England. When the monarchy was restored to the throne, he returned to Parliament.

Song

Go, lovely rose,
Tell her that wastes her time and me,
That now she knows,
When I resemble her to thee,
How sweet and fair she seems to be.

Tell her that's young,
And shuns to have her graces spied,
That hadst thou sprung
In deserts where no men abide,
Thou must have uncommended died.

Small is the worth
Of beauty from the light retired:
Bid her come forth,
Suffer her self to be desired,
And not blush so to be admired.

Then die, that she
The common fate of all things rare
May read in thee,
How small a part of time they share,
That are so wondrous sweet and fair.

[1645]

Joining the Conversation: Critical Thinking and Writing

1. In the first stanza the poet says that the resemblance between the rose and the woman is that both are "sweet and fair," words that reappear at the end of the poem. In between these two passages, what additional resemblances does the poet say they are?

2. The poem contains a narrative of the brief life and the imminent death of a rose. In the third stanza, however, the rose is momentarily forgotten while the poet meditates and speaks directly about the woman. If you agree that this third stanza could conceivably stand as an independent poem, explain why it becomes a better poem when placed within the context of the address to the rose.

Let's now look at yet another poem that speaks of a rose, but in a much less traditional way.

William Blake

The Sick Rose

O rose, thou art sick!
The invisible worm
That flies in the night,
In the howling storm,

Has found out thy bed
Of crimson joy,
And his dark secret love

Does thy life destroy.

[1794]

A reader might perhaps argue that the worm is invisible (line 2) merely because it is hidden within the rose, but an "invisible worm / That flies in the night" is more than a long, slender, soft-bodied, creeping animal; and a rose that has, or is, a "bed / Of crimson joy" is more than a gardener's rose. Blake's worm and rose suggest things beyond themselves—a stranger, more vibrant world than the world we are usually aware of. They are, in short, symbolic, though readers will doubtless differ in their interpretations. Perhaps we find ourselves half thinking, for example, that the worm is male, the rose female, and that the poem is about the violation of virginity. Or that the poem is about the destruction of beauty: Woman's beauty, rooted in joy, is destroyed by a power that feeds on her.

But these interpretations are not fully satisfying: The poem presents a worm and a rose, and yet it is not merely about a worm and a rose. These objects resonate, stimulating our thoughts toward something else, but the something else is elusive. This is not to say, however, that symbols mean whatever any reader says they mean. A reader could scarcely support, we imagine, an interpretation arguing that the poem is about the need to love all aspects of nature. All interpretations are not equally valid; it's the writer's job to offer a reasonably persuasive interpretation.

A symbol, then, is an image so loaded with significance that it is not simply literal, and it does not simply stand for something else; it is both itself *and* something else that it richly suggests, a manifestation of something too complex or too elusive to be otherwise revealed. Blake's poem is about a blighted rose and at the same time about much more. In a symbol, as the nineteenth-century Scottish essayist and historian Thomas Carlyle wrote, "the Infinite is made to blend with the Finite, to stand visible, and as it were, attainable there."

Linda Pastan

Linda Pastan was born in New York City in 1932. The author of many books of poems, she has won numerous prizes and has received grants from the National Endowment for the Arts. In the following poem she wittily plays with repetitions and with pauses.

Jump Cabling

When our cars touched
When you lifted the hood of mine

To see the intimate workings underneath,
When we were bound together
By a pulse of pure energy,
When my car like the princess
In the tale woke with a start,
I thought why not ride the rest of the way together?

[1984]

Joining the Conversation: Critical Thinking and Writing

1. Suppose someone argued that this is merely prose broken up into arbitrary units. Would you agree? Explain.
2. As you read the poem aloud, think about the spacing that Pastan designed for it. What is the effect of the space between the first and second parts of the first seven lines? Why does she do something different for the final line?

Verbal Irony and Paradox

Among the most common devices in poems is **verbal irony.** The speaker's words mean more or less the opposite of what they seem to say. Sometimes verbal irony takes the form of **overstatement,** or **hyperbole,** as when Lady Macbeth says, while sleepwalking, "All the perfumes of Arabia will not sweeten this little hand." Sometimes it takes the form of **understatement,** as when Andrew Marvell's speaker in "To His Coy Mistress" remarks with cautious wryness, "The grave's a fine and private place, / But none, I think, do there embrace," or when Sylvia Plath sees an intended suicide as "the big strip tease." Speaking broadly, intensely emotional contemporary poems like those of Plath often use irony to undercut—and thus make acceptable—the emotion presented.

Another common device in poems is **paradox:** the assertion of an apparent contradiction, as in Marvell's "am'rous birds of prey" in "To His Coy Mistress." Normally we think of amorous birds as gentle—doves, for example—and not as birds of prey, such as hawks. Another example of an apparent contradiction: In "Auld Lang Syne" there is the paradox that the remembrance of joy evokes sadness.

Structure

The arrangement of the parts, the organization of the entire poem, is its **structure.** Sometimes the poem is divided into blocks of, say, four lines each, but even if the poem is printed as a solid block it probably has some principle of organization. It may move, for example, from sorrow in the first two lines to joy in the next two or from a question in the first three lines to an answer in the last line.

Consider this short poem by an English poet of the seventeenth century.

ROBERT HERRICK

Upon Julia's Clothes

Whenas in silks my Julia goes,
Then, then, methinks, how sweetly flows
That liquefaction of her clothes.

Next, when I cast mine eyes, and see
That brave° vibration, each way free,
O how that glittering taketh me!

[1648]

5 brave splendid.

A Sample Essay by a Student: "Herrick's Julia, Julia's Herrick"

One student, Stan Wylie, began thinking about this poem by copying it, double-spaced, and by making the following notes on his copy:

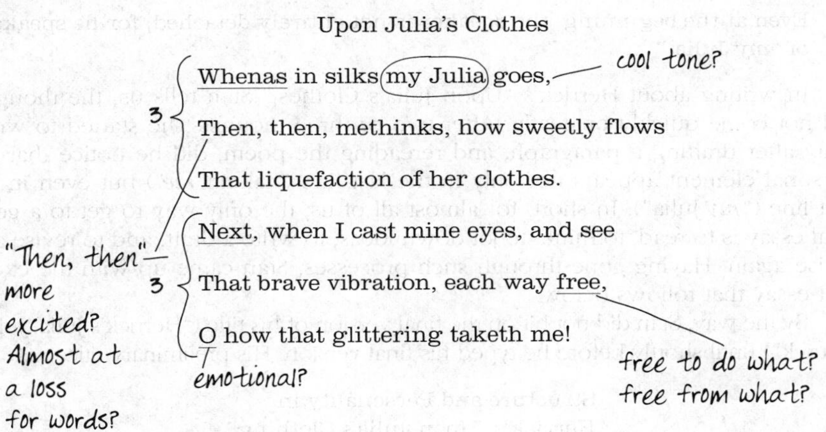

Stan got some further ideas by thinking about several of the questions that, in the checklist on pages 519–20, we suggest you ask yourself while rereading a poem. Among the questions are these:

- Does the poem proceed in a straightforward way, or at some point or points does the speaker reverse course, altering his or her tone or perception?
- What is the effect on you of the form?

With such questions in mind, Stan was stimulated to see if there is some sort of reversal or change in Herrick's poem, and if there is, how it is related to the structure. After rereading the poem several times, thinking about it in the light of these questions and perhaps others that came to mind, he produced the following notes:

> Two stanzas, each of three lines, with the same structure
> Basic structure of first stanza: When X (one line), then Y (two lines)
> Basic structure of second stanza: Next (one line), then Z (two lines)

When he marked the text, after reading the poem a few times, Stan noticed that the last line—an exclamation of delight ("O how that glittering taketh me!")—is much more personal than the rest of the poem. A little further thought enabled him to refine this last perception:

> Although the pattern of stanzas is repeated, the somewhat analytic, detached tone of the beginning ("Whenas," "Then," "Next") changes to an open, enthusiastic confession of delight in what the poet sees.

Further thinking led to this:

> Although the title is "Upon Julia's Clothes," and the first five lines describe Julia's silken dress, the poem finally is not only about Julia's clothing but about the effect of Julia (moving in silk that liquefies or seems to become a liquid) on the poet.

This is a nice observation, but when Stan looked again at the poem the next day, and started to write about it, he found that he was able to refine his observation.

> Even at the beginning, the speaker is not entirely detached, for he speaks of "*my* Julia."

In writing about Herrick's "Upon Julia's Clothes," Stan tells us, the thoughts did not come quickly or neatly. After two or three thoughts, he started to write. Only after drafting a paragraph, and rereading the poem, did he notice that the personal element appears not only in the last line ("taketh *me*") but even in the first line ("*my* Julia"). In short, for almost all of us, the only way to get to a good final essay is to read, to think, to jot down ideas, to write a draft, and to revise and revise again. Having gone through such processes, Stan came up with the excellent essay that follows below.

By the way, Stan did not hit on the final version of his title ("Herrick's Julia, Julia's Herrick") until shortly before he typed his final version. His preliminary title was

Structure and Personality in
Herrick's "Upon Julia's Clothing"

That's a bit heavy-handed but at least it is focused, as opposed to such an uninformative title as "On a Poem." He soon revised his tentative title to

Julia, Julia's Clothing, and Julia's Poet

That's a good title: It is neat, and it is appropriate, since it moves (as the poem and the essay do) from Julia and her clothing to the poet. Of course it doesn't tell the reader exactly what the essay will be about, but it does stimulate the reader's interest. The essayist's final title, however, is even better:

Herrick's Julia, Julia's Herrick

Again, it is neat (the balanced structure, and structure is part of the student's topic), and it moves (as the poem itself moves) from Julia to the poet.

Wiley 1

Stan Wiley

Professor Lloyd

English 112

19 April 2009

Herrick's Julia, Julia's Herrick

Robert Herrick's "Upon Julia's Clothes" begins as a description of Julia's clothing and ends as an expression of the poet's response not just to Julia's clothing but to Julia herself. Despite the apparently objective or detached tone of the first stanza and the first two lines of the second stanza, the poem finally conveys a strong sense of the speaker's excitement.

The first stanza seems to say, "Whenas" X (one line), "Then" Y (two lines). The second stanza repeats this basic structure of one line of assertion and two lines describing the consequence: "Next" (one line), "then" (two lines). But the logic or coolness of "Whenas," "Then," and "Next," and of such rather scientific language as "liquefaction" (a more technical-sounding word than "melting") and "vibration," is undercut by the breathlessness or excitement of "Then, then" (that is very different from a simple "Then"). It is also worth mentioning that although there is a personal rather than a fully detached note even in the first line, in "*my* Julia," this expression scarcely reveals much feeling. In fact, it reveals a touch of male chauvinism, a suggestion that the woman is a possession of the speaker's. Not until the last line does the speaker reveal that, far from Julia being his possession, he is possessed by Julia: "O how that glittering taketh me!" If he

Wiley 2

begins coolly, objectively, and somewhat complacently, and uses a structure that suggests a somewhat detached mind, in the exclamatory "O" he nevertheless at last confesses (to our delight) that he is enraptured by Julia.

[New page]

Wiley 3

Work Cited

Herrick, Robert. "Upon Julia's Clothes." *Literature for Composition*. Ed. Sylvan Barnet, William Burto, and William E. Cain. 9th ed. New York: Longman, 2010. 503. Print.

The Argument Analyzed

Other things might be said about this poem. For instance, the writer says nothing about the changes in the basic iambic meter and their contributions to the poem. We have in mind not so much the trochees (a trochee is a metrical foot with a stressed syllable followed by an unstressed one) at the beginning of some lines, which is a fairly routine variation, but the spondees (two consecutive stresses) in "Then, then" and "O how" and the almost-spondees in "Next, when," "each way free," and "that glittering." Also of interest are the two run-on lines (line 2 runs into 3, and 4 runs into 5) introducing related expressions, "That liquefaction" and "that brave vibration."

He also doesn't comment on the *s* and *z* sounds (*Whenas, silk, goes, thinks, sweetly flows*), which presumably imitate the sound of a silk gown in motion, a sound that can be said to resemble the sound of liquid, hence *liquefaction*—though the dress in motion also visually resembles flowing liquid. But the present essay seems excellent to us, and the neglected topics—sound effects in the poem—might be material for another essay.

CHRISTINA ROSSETTI

In an Artist's Studio

One face looks out from all his canvases,
   One selfsame figure sits or walks or leans:
   We found her hidden just behind those screens,

That mirror gave back all her loveliness.
A queen in opal or in ruby dress,
  A nameless girl in freshest summer-greens
  A saint, an angel—every canvas means
The same one meaning, neither more nor less.
He feeds upon her face by day and night,
  And she with true kind eyes looks back on him,
Fair as the moon and joyful as the light:
  Not wan with waiting, not with sorrow dim;
Not as she is, but was when hope shone bright;
  Not as she is, but as she fills his dream.

[1856]

This poem is a sonnet. We discuss the form later, on page 517, but if you study the rhymes here you will notice that the first eight lines are united by rhymes, and the next six by different rhymes. A reader might, for a start at least, think about whether what is said has any relation to these units. The first eight lines are about the model, but are the next six equally about her or about someone else?

Joining the Conversation: Critical Thinking and Writing

1. What do we know about the model in the first eight lines? What do we know about her in the last two lines?
2. How are the contrasts (between then and now, between model and painter) communicated by the repetition of "Not as she is," in lines 13 and 14?

Explication

As we said in Chapter 5, a line-by-line commentary on a text is an explication (literally, unfolding, or spreading out). Although your explication will for the most part move steadily from the beginning to the end of the selection, try to avoid writing along these lines (or, we might say, along this one line): "In the first line. . . . In the second line. . . . In the third line. . . ." That is, don't hesitate to write such things as

> The poem begins. . . . In the next line. . . . The speaker immediately adds. . . . He then introduces. . . . The next stanza begins by complicating the tone. . . .

And you can discuss the second line before the first if that seems the best way of handling the passage.

An explication is not a paraphrase (a rewording, a sort of translation)—though it may include paraphrase if a passage in the original seems unclear, perhaps because of an unusual word or an unfamiliar expression. On the whole, however, an explication goes beyond paraphrase, seeking to make explicit what the reader perceives as implicit in the work. It is chiefly concerned with

- connotations of words—for instance, "look" versus "behold";

- implications of syntax—for instance, whether it is notably complex (thereby implying one sort of speaker) or notably simple (implying a very different sort of speaker);
- implications of rhyme—for instance, the implied connection in meaning between "throne" and "alone";
- patterns of imagery—for instance, commercial imagery in a love poem.

As we said in Chapters 5 and 6, explication and analysis are not clearly distinct from each other; it is reasonable to think of explication as a kind of analysis operating on the level of verbal details.

An Example

Let's look at a short poem by the Irish poet William Butler Yeats. The "balloon" in the second line is a dirigible, a blimp.

William Butler Yeats

The Balloon of the Mind

Hands, do what you're bid:
Bring the balloon of the mind
That bellies and drags in the wind
Into its narrow shed.

[1917]

Annotations and Journal Entries

A student, Tina Washington, began thinking about Yeats's poem by copying it, double-spaced. Then she jotted down her first thoughts:

sounds abrupt

Hands, do what you're bid: —balloon imagined by the mind? Or a mind like a balloon?

Bring the balloon of the mind

That bellies and drags in the wind no real rhymes?

Into its narrow shed. line seems to drag—it's so long!

Later she wrote some notes in a journal:

> I'm still puzzled about the meaning of the words "The balloon of the mind." Does "balloon of the mind" mean a balloon that belongs to the mind, sort of like "a disease of the heart"? If so, it means a balloon that the mind has, a balloon that the mind possesses, I guess by imagining it. Or does it mean that the mind is like a balloon, as when you say "he's a pig of a man," meaning he is like a pig, he is a pig? Can it mean both? What's a balloon that the mind imagines? Something like dreams of fame, wealth? Castles in Spain.

Is Yeats saying that the "hands" have to work hard to make dreams a reality? Maybe. But maybe the idea really is that the mind is like a balloon—hard to keep under control, floating around. Very hard to keep the mind on the job. If the mind is like a balloon, it's hard to get it into the hangar (shed).

"Bellies." Is there such a verb? In this poem it seems to mean something like "puffs out" or "flops around in the wind." Just checked The American Heritage Dictionary, and it says "belly" can be a verb, "to swell out," "to bulge." Well, you learn something every day.

A later entry:

OK; I think the poem is about a writer trying to keep his balloon-like mind from floating around, trying to keep the mind under control, trying to keep it working at the job of writing something, maybe writing something with the "clarity, unity, and coherence" I keep hearing about in this course.

A Sample Essay by a Student: "Explication of W. B. Yeats's 'The Balloon of the Mind'"

Here is Tina Washington's final version of the explication:

Washington 1

Tina Washington

Professor Chase

English 102

2 November 2009

Explication of W. B. Yeats's "The Balloon of the Mind"

Yeats's "Balloon of the Mind" is about writing poetry, specifically about the difficulty of getting one's floating thoughts down in lines on the page. The first line, a short, stern, heavily stressed command to the speaker's hands, perhaps implies by its severe or impatient tone that these hands will be disobedient or inept or careless if not watched closely: the poor bumbling body so often fails to achieve the goals of the mind. The bluntness of the command in the first line is emphasized by the fact that all

Washington 2

the subsequent lines have more syllables. Furthermore, the first line is a grammatically complete sentence, whereas the thought of line 2 spills over into the next lines, implying the difficulty of fitting ideas into confining spaces, that is, of getting one's thoughts into order, especially into a coherent poem.

Lines 2 and 3 amplify the metaphor already stated in the title (the product of the mind is an airy but unwieldy balloon), and they also contain a second command, "Bring." Alliteration ties this command, "Bring," to the earlier "bid"; it also ties both of these verbs to their object, "balloon," and to the verb that most effectively describes the balloon, "bellies." In comparison with the abrupt first line of the poem, lines 2 and 3 themselves seem almost swollen, bellying and dragging, an effect aided by using adjacent unstressed syllables ("of the," "[bell]ies and," "in the") and by using an eye rhyme ("mind" and "wind") rather than an exact rhyme. And then comes the short last line: almost before we could expect it, the cumbersome balloon—here, the idea that is to be packed into the stanza—is successfully lodged in its "narrow shed." Aside from the relatively colorless "into," the only words of more than one syllable in the poem are "balloon," "bellies," and "narrow," and all three emphasize the difficulty of the task. But after "narrow"—the word itself almost looks long and narrow, in this context like a hangar—we get the simplicity of the monosyllable "shed." The difficult job is done, the thought is safely packed away, the poem is completed—but again with an off-rhyme ("bid" and "shed"), for neatness can go only so far when hands and mind and a balloon are involved.

[New page]

Washington 3

Work Cited

Yeats, W. B. "The Balloon of the Mind." *Literature for Composition*. Ed. Sylvan Barnet, William Burto, and William E. Cain. 9th ed. New York: Longman, 2010. 508. Print.

The reader of an explication needs to see the text, and because the explicated text is usually short, it is advisable to quote it all. (Remember, your imagined audience probably consists of your classmates; even if they have already read the work you are explicating, they have not memorized it, and so you helpfully remind them of the work by quoting it.) You can quote the entire text at the outset, or you can quote the first unit (for example, a stanza), then explicate that unit, and then quote the next unit, and so on. And if the poem or passage of prose is longer than, say, six lines, you might number each line at the right for easy reference.

✓ CHECKLIST: *Explication*

On page 113 we provided a Checklist on explication. We repeat some of the key points again here, for convenience.

Overall Considerations

- ☐ Does the poem imply a story of some sort—for instance, the speaker's report of a love affair, or of a response to nature? If so, what is its beginning, middle, and end?
- ☐ If you detect a story in the speaker's mind, a change of mood—for instance, a shift from bitterness that a love affair has ended to hope for its renewal—is this change communicated in part by the connotations of certain words? By syntax? By metrical shifts?

Detailed Considerations

- ☐ If the poem has a title other than the first line, what are the implications of the title?
- ☐ Are there clusters or patterns of imagery—for instance, religious images, economic images, or images drawn from nature? If so, how do they contribute to the meaning of the poem?
- ☐ Is irony (understatement or overstatement) used? To what effect?
- ☐ How do the connotations of certain words (for instance, "dad" rather than "father") help to establish the meaning?
- ☐ What are the implications of the syntax—for instance, of notably simple or notably complex sentences? What do such sentences tell us about the speaker?

(*continued*)

Explication (continued)

- Do metrical variations occur, and if so, what is their significance?
- Do rhyming words have some meaningful connection, as in the clichés "moon" and "June," "dove" and "love"?
- What are the implications of the appearance of the poem on the page—for example, of an indented line, or of the stanzaic pattern? (For instance, if the poem consists of two stanzas of four lines each, does the second stanza offer a reversal of the first?)

Rhythm and Versification: A Glossary for Reference

Rhythm (most simply, in English poetry, stresses at regular intervals) has a power of its own. A highly pronounced rhythm is common in such forms of poetry as charms, college yells, and lullabies; all of them are aimed at inducing a special effect magically. It is not surprising that *carmen,* the Latin word for poem or song, is also the Latin word for *charm* and the word from which our word *charm* is derived.

In much poetry, rhythm is only half heard, but its presence is suggested by the way poetry is printed. Prose (from Latin *prorsus,* "forward," "straight on") keeps running across the paper until the right-hand margin is reached; then, merely because the paper has given out, the writer or printer starts again at the left, with a small letter. But verse (Latin *versus,* "a turning") often ends well short of the right-hand margin. The next line begins at the left—usually with a capital—not because paper has run out but because the rhythmic pattern begins again. Lines of poetry are continually reminding us that they have a pattern.

Note that a mechanical, unvarying rhythm may be good to put the baby to sleep, but it can be deadly to readers who want to stay awake. Poets vary their rhythm according to their purposes; they ought not to be so regular that they are (in W. H. Auden's words) "accentual pests." In competent hands, rhythm contributes to meaning; it says something. Ezra Pound had a relevant comment: "Rhythm *must* have meaning. It cannot be merely a careless dash off, with no grip and no real hold to the words and sense, a tumty tum tumty tum tum ta."

Consider this description of Hell from John Milton's *Paradise Lost* (stressed syllables are marked by ´, unstressed syllables by ˘:

> Rócks, cáves, lákes, féns, bógs, déns, ăňd shádes ŏf déath.

The normal line in *Paradise Lost* is written in iambic feet—alternate unstressed and stressed syllables—but in this line Milton immediately follows one heavy stress with another, helping to communicate the "meaning"—the oppressive monotony of Hell. As a second example, consider the function of the rhythm in two lines by Alexander Pope:

> Wȟen Ájăx stríves soḿe róck's vást wéight t̆o thrów,
> T̆he líne tóo lábŏrs, aňd t̆he wórds móve slów.

The stressed syllables do not merely alternate with the unstressed ones; rather the great weight of the rock is suggested by three consecutive stressed words, "rock's vast weight," and the great effort involved in moving it is suggested by another three consecutive stresses, "line too labors," and by yet another three, "words move slow." Note also the abundant pauses within the lines. In the first line, for example, unless one's speech is slovenly, one must pause at least slightly after "Ajax," "strives," "rock's," "vast," "weight," and "throw." The grating sounds in "Ajax" and "rock's" do their work, too, and so do the explosive *t*'s.

When Pope wishes to suggest lightness, he reverses his procedure, and he groups *un*stressed syllables:

> Not so, when swift Camilla scours the plain,
> Fliés o'ĕr th' ŭnbénding córn, ańd sḱims ălŏng tȟe máin.

This last line has twelve syllables and is thus longer than the line about Ajax, but the addition of *along* helps to communicate lightness and swiftness because in this line (it can be argued) neither syllable of *along* is strongly stressed. If *along* is omitted, the line still makes grammatical sense and becomes more "regular," but it also becomes less imitative of lightness.

The very regularity of a line may be meaningful too. Shakespeare begins a sonnet thus:

> Wȟen Í dŏ cóunt tȟe clóck tȟat téllṡ tȟe tíme.

This line about a mechanism runs with appropriate regularity. (It is worth noting, too, that "*c*ount the *c*lock" and "*t*ells the *t*ime" emphasize the regularity by the repetition of sounds and syntax.) But notice what Shakespeare does in the middle of the next line:

> Ańd sée tȟe bráve dáy súnk ĭn hídeŏus níght.

The technical vocabulary of **prosody** (the study of the principles of verse structure, including meter, rhyme and other sound effects, and stanzaic patterns) is large. An understanding of these terms will not turn you into a poet, but it will enable you to write about some aspects of poetry more efficiently. The chief terms of prosody presented in the sections ahead will provide a good base.

Meter

Most poetry written in English has a pattern of stressed (accented) sounds. This pattern is the **meter** (from the Greek word for "measure"). Strictly speaking, we really should not talk of "unstressed" or "unaccented" syllables, since to utter a syllable—however lightly—is to give it some stress. It is a matter of *relative* stress, but the fact is that "unstressed" or "unaccented" are parts of the established terminology of versification.

In a line of poetry, the **foot** is the basic unit of measurement. It is on rare occasions a single stressed syllable; but generally a foot consists of two or three syllables, one of which is stressed. The repetition of feet, then, produces a pattern of stresses throughout the poem.

Two cautions:

- A poem will seldom contain only one kind of foot throughout; significant variations usually occur, but one kind of foot is dominant.
- When reading a poem, we chiefly pay attention to the sense, not to presupposed metrical pattern. By paying attention to the sense, we often find (reading aloud is a great help) that the stress falls on a word that according

to the metrical pattern would be unstressed. Or a word that according to the pattern would be stressed may be seen to be unstressed. Furthermore, by reading for sense we find that not all stresses are equally heavy; some are almost as light as unstressed syllables, and sometimes there is a **hovering stress**—that is, the stress is equally distributed over two adjacent syllables. To repeat: We read for sense, allowing the syntax to help indicate the stresses.

METRICAL FEET There are six common types of metrical feet in English poetry:

- **Iamb** (adjective: **iambic**): one unstressed syllable followed by one stressed syllable. The iamb, said to be the most common pattern in English speech, is surely the most common in English poetry. The following example has four iambic feet:

  M̆y héart ĭs líke ă síngĭng bírd.

  —Christina Rossetti

- **Trochee (trochaic):** one stressed syllable followed by one unstressed.

  Wé w̆ere véry̆ tírĕd, wé w̆ere véry̆ mérry̆

  —Edna St. Vincent Millay

- **Anapest (anapestic):** two unstressed syllables followed by one stressed.

  T̆here ăre mány̆ w̆ho sáy t̆hat ă dóg h̆as h̆is dáy.

  —Dylan Thomas

- **Dactyl (dactylic):** one stressed syllable followed by two unstressed. This trisyllabic foot, like the anapest, is common in light verse or verse suggesting joy, but its use is not limited to such material, as Longfellow's *Evangeline* shows. Thomas Hood's sentimental "The Bridge of Sighs" begins

  Táke hĕr ŭp tén̆derl̆y.

- **Spondee (spondaic):** two stressed syllables; most often used as a substitute for an iamb or trochee.

  Smárt lád, t̆o sĺip b̆etímes ăwáy.

  —A. E. Housman

- **Pyrrhic:** two unstressed syllables; it is often not considered a legitimate foot in English.

METRICAL LINES A metrical line consists of one or more feet and is named for the number of feet in it. The following names are used:

- **monometer:** one foot
- **dimeter:** two feet
- **trimeter:** three feet
- **tetrameter:** four feet
- **pentameter:** five feet
- **hexameter:** six feet
- **heptameter:** seven feet

A line is scanned for the kind and number of feet in it, and the **scansion** tells you if it is, say, anapestic trimeter (three anapests):

Ăs Ĭ cáme t̆o t̆he édge ŏf t̆he wóods.

—Robert Frost

Or, in another example, iambic pentameter:

> Thĕ súmmĕr thúndĕr, líke ă wóodĕn bĕll
>
> —Louise Bogan

A line ending with a stress has a **masculine ending;** a line ending with an extra unstressed syllable has a **feminine ending.** The **caesura** (usually indicated by the symbol / /) is a slight pause within the line. It need not be indicated by punctuation (notice the fourth and fifth lines in the following quotation), and it does not affect the metrical count:

> Awake, my St. John! / / leave all meaner things
> To low ambition, / / and the pride of kings.
> Let us / / (since Life can little more supply
> Than just to look about us / / and to die)
> Expatiate free / / o'er all this scene of Man;
> A mighty maze! / / but not without a plan;
> A wild, / / where weeds and flowers promiscuous shoot;
> Or garden, / / tempting with forbidden fruit.
>
> —Alexander Pope

The varying position of the caesura helps to give Pope's lines an informality that plays against the formality of the pairs of rhyming lines.

An **end-stopped line** concludes with a distinct syntactical pause, but a **run-on line** has its sense carried over into the next line without syntactical pause. (The running-on of a line is called **enjambment.**) In the following passage, only the first is a run-on line:

> Yet if we look more closely we shall find
> Most have the seeds of judgment in their mind:
> Nature affords at least a glimmering light;
> The lines, though touched but faintly, are drawn right.
>
> —Alexander Pope

Meter produces **rhythm,** recurrences at equal intervals, but rhythm (from a Greek word meaning "flow") is usually applied to larger units than feet. Often it depends most obviously on pauses. Thus, a poem with run-on lines will have a different rhythm from a poem with end-stopped lines, even though both are in the same meter. And prose, though it is unmetrical, can have rhythm, too.

In addition to being affected by syntactical pause, rhythm is affected by pauses attributable to consonant clusters and to the length of words. Polysyllabic words establish a different rhythm from monosyllabic words, even in metrically identical lines. We can say, then, that rhythm is altered by shifts in meter, syntax, and the length and ease of pronunciation. But even with no such shift, even if a line is repeated verbatim, a reader may sense a change in rhythm. The rhythm of the final line of a poem, for example, may well differ from that of the line before, even though in all other respects the lines are identical, as in Frost's "Stopping by Woods on a Snowy Evening" (page 188), which concludes by repeating "And miles to go before I sleep." The reader may simply sense that this final line ought to be spoken, say, more slowly and with more stress on "miles."

Patterns of Sound

Though rhythm is basic to poetry, **rhyme**—the repetition of identical or similar stressed sound or sounds—is not. Rhyme is, presumably, pleasant in itself; it suggests order; and it also may be related to meaning, for it brings two words sharply together, often implying a relationship, as in the now trite *dove* and *love*, or in the more imaginative *throne* and *alone*.

The commonest patterns are:

- **Perfect rhyme** (or **exact rhyme**): differing consonant sounds followed by identical stressed vowel sounds. The following sounds, if any, are identical (*foe—toe; meet—fleet; buffer—rougher*). Notice that perfect rhyme involves identity of sound, not of spelling. *Fix* and *sticks*, like *buffer* and *rougher*, are perfect rhymes.
- **Half-rhyme** (or **off-rhyme**): rhymes in which only the final consonant sounds of the words are identical; the stressed vowel sounds as well as the initial consonant sounds, if any, differ (*soul—oil; mirth—forth; trolley—bully*).
- **Eye rhyme:** sounds that do not in fact rhyme but look as though they would rhyme (*cough—bough*).
- **Masculine rhyme:** Final syllables that are stressed and, after their differing initial consonant sounds, are identical in sound (*stark—mark; support—retort*).
- **Feminine rhyme** (or **double rhyme**): stressed rhyming syllables followed by identical unstressed syllables (*revival—arrival; flatter—batter*). **Triple rhyme** is a kind of feminine rhyme in which identical stressed vowel sounds are followed by two identical unstressed syllables (*machinery—scenery; tenderly—slenderly*).
- **End rhyme** (or **terminal rhyme**): Rhyming words that occur at the ends of the lines.
- **Internal rhyme:** a type of rhyme in which at least one of the rhyming words occurs within the line (Oscar Wilde's "Each narrow *cell* in which we *dwell*").
- **Alliteration:** sometimes defined as the repetition of initial sounds ("*A*ll the *a*wful *a*uguries," or "*B*ring me my *b*ow of *b*urning gold"), and sometimes as the prominent repetition of a consonant ("a*f*ter li*f*e's *f*it*f*ul *f*ever").
- **Assonance:** the repetition, in words of proximity, of identical vowel sounds preceded and followed by differing consonant sounds. Whereas *tide* and *hide* are rhymes, *tide* and *mine* are assonantal.
- **Consonance:** the repetition of identical consonant sounds and differing vowel sounds in words in proximity (*fail—feel; rough—roof; pitter—patter*). Sometimes consonance is more loosely defined merely as the repetition of a consonant (*fail—peel*).
- **Onomatopoeia:** the use of words that imitate sounds, such as *hiss* and *buzz*. There is a mistaken tendency to see onomatopoeia everywhere—for example, in *thunder* and *horror*. Many words sometimes thought to be onomatopoeic are not clearly imitative of the thing they refer to; they merely contain some sounds that, when we know what the word means, seem to have some resemblance to the thing they denote. Tennyson's lines from "Come down, O maid" are usually cited as an example of onomatopoeia:

  The moan of doves in immemorial elms
  And murmuring of innumerable bees.

Stanzaic Patterns

Lines of poetry are commonly arranged in a rhythmical unit called a **stanza** (from an Italian word meaning "room" or "stopping-place"). Usually all the stanzas in a poem have the same rhyme pattern. A stanza is sometimes called a **verse**, though *verse* may also mean a single line of poetry. (In discussing stanzas, rhymes are indicated by identical letters. Thus, *abab* indicates that the first and third lines rhyme with each other, while the second and fourth lines are linked by a different rhyme. An unrhymed line is denoted by *x*.) Common stanzaic forms in English poetry are the following:

- **Couplet:** a stanza of two lines, usually, but not necessarily, with end-rhymes. *Couplet* is also used for a pair of rhyming lines. The **octosyllabic couplet** is iambic or trochaic tetrameter:

    Had we but world enough, and time,
    This coyness, lady, were no crime.

    —Andrew Marvell

- **Heroic couplet:** a rhyming couplet of iambic pentameter, often "closed"—that is, containing a complete thought, with a fairly heavy pause at the end of the first line and a still heavier one at the end of the second. Commonly, there is a parallel or an *antithesis* (contrast) within a line or between the two lines. It is called heroic because in England, especially in the eighteenth century, it was much used for heroic (epic) poems.

    Some foreign writers, some our own despise;
    The ancients only, or the moderns, prize.

    —Alexander Pope

- **Triplet** (or **tercet**): a three-line stanza, usually with one rhyme:

    Whenas in silks my Julia goes
    Then, then (methinks) how sweetly flows
    That liquefaction of her clothes.

    —Robert Herrick

- **Quatrain:** a four-line stanza, rhymed or unrhymed. The **heroic** (or **elegiac**) **quatrain** is iambic pentameter, rhyming *abab*. That is, the first and third lines rhyme (so they are designated *a*), and the second and fourth lines rhyme (so they are designated *b*).
- **Sonnet:** a fourteen-line poem, predominantly in iambic pentameter. The rhyme is usually according to one of two schemes. The **Italian** (or **Petrarchan**[1]) **sonnet** has two divisions: The first eight lines (rhyming *abba abba*) are the **octave,** and the last six (rhyming *cd cd cd*, or a variant) are the **sestet.** The second kind of sonnet, the **English** (or **Shakespearean**) **sonnet,** is usually arranged into three quatrains and a couplet, rhyming *abab cdcd efef gg*. (For examples, see pages 115, 491, and 497.) In many sonnets there is a marked correspondence between the rhyme scheme and the development of the thought. Thus an Italian sonnet may state a generalization in the octave and a specific example in the sestet. Or an English sonnet may give three examples—one in each quatrain—and draw a conclusion in the couplet.

[1]So called after Francesco Petrarch (1304–1374), the Italian poet who perfected and popularized the form.

BILLY COLLINS

Born in New York City in 1941, Collins is a professor of English at Lehman College of the City University of New York. He is the author of many books of poetry and the recipient of numerous awards, including one from the National Endowment for the Arts. Collins's Sailing Alone Around the Room: New and Selected Poems *was published in 2001; in the same year, he was appointed poet laureate of the United States.*

The following sonnet uses the Petrarchan form, which consists of an octave and a sestet. Petrarch is additionally present in the poem by the allusion in line 3 to "a little ship on love's storm-tossed seas," because Petrarch compared the hapless lover, denied the favor of his mistress, to a ship in a storm: The lover cannot guide his ship because the North Star is hidden (Petrarch's beloved Laura averts her eyes), and the sails of the ship are agitated by the lover's pitiful sighs. As you will see, Petrarch and Laura explicitly enter the poem in the last three lines.

In line 8 Collins refers to the stations of the cross. In Roman Catholicism, one of the devotions consists of prayers and meditations before each of fourteen crosses or images set up along a path that commemorates the fourteen places at which Jesus halted when, just before the Crucifixion, he was making his way in Jerusalem to Golgotha.

Sonnet

All we need is fourteen lines, well, thirteen now,
and after this next one just a dozen
to launch a little ship on love's storm-tossed seas,
then only ten more left like rows of beans.
How easily it goes unless you get Elizabethan
and insist the iambic bongos must be played
and rhymes positioned at the ends of lines,
one for every station of the cross.
But hang on here while we make the turn
into the final six where all will be resolved,
where longing and heartache will find an end,
where Laura will tell Petrarch to put down his pen,
take off those crazy medieval tights,
blow out the lights, and come at last to bed.

[1999]

Joining the Conversation: Critical Thinking and Writing

1. The headnote explains the stations of the cross (line 8), but what is the point of introducing this image into a sonnet?
2. Normally the "turn" (*volta*) in an Italian sonnet occurs at the beginning of the ninth line; the first eight lines (the octave) establish some sort of problem, and the final six lines (the sestet) respond—for instance—by answering a question, or by introducing a contrasting emotion. In your view, how satisfactorily does Collins handle this form? Support your evaluation with reasons.

Blank Verse and Free Verse

A good deal of English poetry is unrhymed, much of it in **blank verse,** that is, unrhymed iambic pentameter. Introduced into English poetry by Henry Howard, Earl of Surrey, in the middle of the sixteenth century, late in the century it became the standard medium (especially in the hands of Christopher Marlowe and Shakespeare) of English drama. In the seventeenth century, Milton used blank verse for *Paradise Lost,* and it has continued to be used in both dramatic and nondramatic literature. For an example, see the first scene of *Hamlet* (page 908), until the Ghost appears.

The second kind of unrhymed poetry fairly common in English, especially in the twentieth century, is **free verse** (or **vers libre**): rhythmical lines varying in length, adhering to no fixed metrical pattern and usually unrhymed. The pattern is often largely based on repetition and parallel grammatical structure. For an example, see T. S. Eliot's "The Love Song of J. Alfred Prufrock" (page 199).

✓ CHECKLIST: *Getting Ideas for Writing Arguments about Poems*

If you are going to write about a short poem (say, under thirty lines), it's not a bad idea to copy out the poem, writing or typing it double-spaced. By writing it out you will be forced to notice details, down to the punctuation. After you have copied the poem, proofread it carefully against the original. Catching an error—even the addition or omission of a comma—may help you to notice a detail in the original that you might otherwise have overlooked. And of course, now that you have the poem with ample space between the lines, you have a worksheet with room for jottings.

A good essay is based on a genuine response to a poem; a response may be stimulated in part by first reading the poem aloud and then considering the following questions.

First Response

- ☐ **What was your response to the poem on first reading?** Did some parts especially please or displease you, or puzzle you? After some study—perhaps checking the meanings of some of the words in a dictionary and reading the poem several times—did you modify your initial response to the parts and to the whole?

Speaker and Tone

- ☐ **Who is the speaker?** (Consider age, sex, personality, frame of mind, and tone of voice.) Is the speaker defined precisely (for instance, an older woman speaking to a child), or is the speaker simply a voice meditating? (Jot down your first impressions, then reread the poem and make further jottings, if necessary.)
- ☐ **Do you think the speaker is fully aware of what he or she is saying,** or does the speaker unconsciously reveal his or her personality and values? What is your attitude toward this speaker?

(*continued*)

Getting Ideas for Writing Arguments about Poems (continued)

- Is the speaker **narrating or reflecting** on an earlier experience or attitude? If so, does he or she convey a sense of new awareness, such as of regret for innocence lost?

Audience

- **To whom is the speaker speaking?** What is the situation (including time and place)? (In some poems, a listener is strongly implied, but in others, especially those in which the speaker is meditating, there may be no audience other than the reader, who "overhears" the speaker.)

Structure and Form

- **Does the poem proceed in a straightforward way,** or at some point or points does the speaker reverse course, altering his or her tone or perception? If there is a shift, what do you make of it?
- **Is the poem organized into sections?** If so, what are these sections—stanzas, for instance—and how does each section (characterized, perhaps, by a certain tone of voice, or a group of rhymes) grow out of what precedes it?
- **What is the effect on you of the form**—say, quatrains (stanzas of four lines) or blank verse (unrhymed lines of ten syllables)? If the sense overflows the form, running without pause from (for example) one quatrain into the next, what effect is created?

Center of Interest and Theme

- **What is the poem about?** Is the interest chiefly in a distinctive character, or in meditation? That is, is the poem chiefly psychological or chiefly philosophical?
- **Is the theme stated explicitly (directly) or implicitly?** How might you state the theme in a sentence?

Diction

- **Do certain words have rich and relevant associations** that relate to other words and help to define the speaker or the theme or both?
- **What is the role of figurative language, if any?** Does it help to define the speaker or the theme?
- **What do you think is to be taken figuratively or symbolically, and what literally?**

Sound Effects

- **What is the role of sound effects,** including repetitions of sound (for instance, alliteration) and of entire words, and shifts in versification?
- **If there are off-rhymes** (for instance "dizzy" and "easy," or "home" and "come"), what effect do they have on you? Do they, for instance, add a note of tentativeness or uncertainty?
- **If there are unexpected stresses or pauses,** what do they communicate about the speaker's experience? How do they affect you?

Your Turn: Poems about People

Robert Browning

Born in a suburb of London into a middle-class family, Robert Browning (1812–1889) was educated primarily at home, where he read widely. For a while he wrote for the stage, and in 1846 he married Elizabeth Barrett—herself a poet—and lived with her in Italy until her death in 1861. He then returned to England and settled in London with their son. Regarded as one of the most distinguished poets of the Victorian period, he is buried in Westminster Abbey.

My Last Duchess

Ferrara°

That's my last Duchess painted on the wall,
Looking as if she were alive. I call
That piece a wonder, now; Frà Pandolf's° hands
Worked busily a day, and there she stands.
Will't please you sit and look at her? I said
"Frà Pandolf" by design, for never read
Strangers like you that pictured countenance,
The depth and passion of its earnest glance,
But to myself they turned (since none puts by
The curtain I have drawn for you, but I)
And seemed as they would ask me, if they durst,
How such a glance came there; so, not the first
Are you to turn and ask thus. Sir, 'twas not
Her husband's presence only, called that spot
Of joy into the Duchess' cheek; perhaps
Frà Pandolf chanced to say "Her mantle laps
Over my lady's wrist too much," or, "Paint
Must never hope to reproduce the faint
Half-flush that dies along her throat." Such stuff
Was courtesy, she thought, and cause enough
For calling up that spot of joy. She had
A heart—how shall I say?—too soon made glad,
Too easily impressed; she liked whate'er
She looked on, and her looks went everywhere.
Sir, 'twas all one! My favor at her breast,
The dropping of the daylight in the west,
The bough of cherries some officious fool
Broke in the orchard for her, the white mule
She rode with round the terrace—all and each
Would draw from her alike the approving speech,
Or blush, at least. She thanked men—good! but thanked
Somehow—I know not how—as if she ranked
My gift of a nine-hundred-years-old name

°**Ferrara** a town in Italy. **3 Frà Pandolf** a fictitious painter.

With anybody's gift. Who'd stoop to blame
This sort of trifling? Even had you skill
In speech—(which I have not)—to make your will
Quite clear to such an one, and say, "Just this
Or that in you disgusts me; here you miss,
Or there exceed the mark"—and if she let
Herself be lessoned so, nor plainly set
Her wits to yours, forsooth, and made excuse,
—E'en then would be some stooping; and I choose
Never to stoop. Oh, Sir, she smiled, no doubt,
Whene'er I passed her; but who passed without
Much the same smile? This grew; I gave commands;
Then all smiles stopped together. There she stands
As if alive. Will't please you rise? We'll meet
The company below, then. I repeat,
The Count your master's known munificence
Is ample warrant that no just pretense
Of mine for dowry will be disallowed;
Though his fair daughter's self, as I avowed
At starting, is my object. Nay, we'll go
Together down, Sir. Notice Neptune, though,
Taming a sea-horse, thought a rarity,
Which Claus of Innsbruck° cast in bronze for me!

[1842]

56 Claus of Innsbruck a fictitious sculptor.

Joining the Conversation: Critical Thinking and Writing

1. Who is speaking to whom? On what occasion?
2. What words or lines especially convey the speaker's arrogance? What is our attitude toward the speaker? Loathing? Fascination? Respect? Explain.
3. The time and place are Renaissance Italy; how do they affect our attitude toward the duke? What would be the effect if the poem were set in the twentieth century?
4. Years after writing this poem, Browning explained that the duke's "commands" (line 45) were "that she should be put to death, or he might have had her shut up in a convent." Should the poem have been more explicit? Does Browning's later uncertainty indicate that the poem is badly thought out? Suppose we did not have Browning's comment on line 45; could the line then mean only that he commanded her to stop smiling and that she obeyed? Explain.
5. Elizabeth Barrett (not yet Mrs. Browning) wrote to Robert Browning that it was not "by the dramatic medium that poets teach most impressively. . . . It is too difficult for the common reader to analyze, and to discern between the vivid and the earnest." She went on, urging him to teach "in the directest and most impressive way, the mask thrown off." What teaching, if any, is in this poem? If there is any teaching here, would it be more impressive if Browning had not used the mask of a Renaissance duke? Explain.

6. You are the envoy, writing to the count, your master, a 500-word report of your interview with the duke. What do you write?
7. You are the envoy, writing to the count, advising—as diplomatically as possible—for or against this marriage. Notice that this exercise, unlike the previous exercise, which calls for a *report*, calls for an *argument*.

E. E. CUMMINGS

E. E. Cummings was the pen name of Edwin Estlin Cummings (1894–1962), who grew up in Cambridge, Massachusetts, and was graduated from Harvard, where he became interested in modern literature and art, especially in the movements called Cubism and Futurism. His father, a conservative clergyman and a professor at Harvard, seems to have been baffled by the youth's interests, but Cummings's mother encouraged his artistic activities, including his use of unconventional punctuation and capitalization.

Politically liberal in his youth, Cummings became more conservative after a visit to Russia in 1931, but early and late his work emphasizes individuality and freedom of expression.

anyone lived in a pretty how town

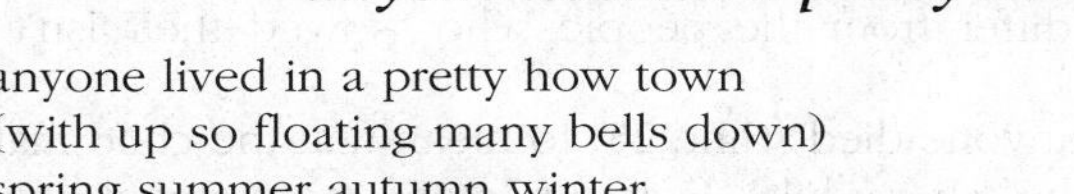

anyone lived in a pretty how town
(with up so floating many bells down)
spring summer autumn winter
he sang his didn't he danced his did.

Women and men (both little and small)
cared for anyone not at all
they sowed their isn't they reaped their same
sun moon stars rain

children guessed (but only a few
and down they forgot as up they grew
autumn winter spring summer)
that noone loved him more by more

when by now and tree by leaf
she laughed his joy she cried his grief
bird by snow and stir by still
anyone's any was all to her

someones married their everyones
laughed their cryings and did their dance
(sleep wake hope and then) they
said their nevers they slept their dream

stars rain sun moon
(and only the snow can begin to explain
how children are apt to forget to remember
with up so floating many bells down)

one day anyone died i guess
(and noone stooped to kiss his face)
busy folk buried them side by side
little by little and was by was

all by all and deep by deep
and more by more they dream their sleep
noone and anyone earth by april
wish by spirit and if by yes.

Women and men(both dong and ding)
summer autumn winter spring
reaped their sowing and went their came
sun moon stars rain

[1940]

Joining the Conversation: Critical Thinking and Writing

1. Put into normal order (as far as possible) the words of the first two stanzas and then compare your version with Cummings's. What does Cummings gain—or lose?
2. Characterize the "anyone" who "sang his didn't" and "danced his did." In your opinion, how does he differ from the people who "sowed their isn't they reaped their same"?
3. Some readers interpret "anyone died" (line 25) to mean that the child matured and became as dead as the other adults. How, in an argument, might you support or refute this interpretation?

SYLVIA PLATH

Sylvia Plath (1932–1963) was born in Boston, the daughter of German immigrants. While still an undergraduate at Smith College, she published in Seventeen *and* Mademoiselle, *but her years at college, like her later years, were marked by manic-depressive periods. After graduating from college she went to England to study at Cambridge University, where she met the English poet Ted Hughes, whom she married in 1956. The marriage was unsuccessful, and they separated. One day she committed suicide by turning on the kitchen gas.*

Plath was a talented painter; one of her paintings appears on the cover of this book.

Daddy

You do not do, you do not do
Any more, black shoe
In which I have lived like a foot
For thirty years, poor and white,
Barely daring to breathe or Achoo.

Daddy, I have had to kill you.
You died before I had time—
Marble-heavy, a bag full of God,
Ghastly statue with one gray toe
Big as a Frisco seal

And a head in the freakish Atlantic
Where it pours bean green over blue
In the waters off beautiful Nauset.
I used to pray to recover you.
Ach, du.°

In the German tongue, in the Polish town
Scraped flat by the roller
Of wars, wars, wars.
But the name of the town is common.
My Polack friend

Says there are a dozen or two.
So I never could tell where you
Put your foot, your root,
I never could talk to you.
The tongue stuck in my jaw.

It stuck in a barb wire snare.
Ich, ich, ich, ich,°
I could hardly speak.
I thought every German was you.
And the language obscene

An engine, an engine
Chuffing me off like a Jew.
A Jew to Dachau, Auschwitz, Belsen.°
I began to talk like a Jew.
I think I may well be a Jew.

The snows of the Tyrol, the clear beer of Vienna
Are not very pure or true.
With my gypsy ancestress and my weird luck
And my Taroc pack and my Taroc pack
I may be a bit of a Jew.

I have always been scared of you,
With your Luftwaffe,° your gobbledygoo.
And your neat moustache
And your Aryan eye, bright blue,
Panzer-man,° panzer-man, O You—

15 Ach, du O, you (German). **27 Ich, ich, ich, ich** I, I, I, I. **33 Dachau, Auschwitz, Belsen** concentration camps. **42 Luftwaffe** German air force. **45 Panzer-man** member of a tank crew.

Not God but a swastika
So black no sky could squeak through.
Every woman adores a Fascist,
The boot in the face, the brute
Brute heart of a brute like you.

You stand at the blackboard, daddy,
In the picture I have of you,
A cleft in your chin instead of your foot
But no less a devil for that, no not
Any less the black man who

Bit my pretty red heart in two.
I was ten when they buried you.
At twenty I tried to die
And get back, back, back to you.
I thought even the bones would do

But they pulled me out of the sack,
And they stuck me together with glue,
And then I knew what to do.
I made a model of you,
A man in black with a Meinkampf° look

And a love of the rack and the screw.
And I said I do, I do.
So daddy, I'm finally through.
The black telephone's off at the root,
The voices just can't worm through.

If I've killed one man, I've killed two—
The vampire who said he was you
And drank my blood for a year,
Seven years, if you want to know.
Daddy, you can lie back now.

There's a stake in your fat black heart
And the villagers never liked you.
They are dancing and stamping on you.
They always *knew* it was you.
Daddy, daddy, you bastard, I'm through.

[1965]

65 Mein Kampf *My Struggle* (title of Hitler's autobiography).

Joining the Conversation: Critical Thinking and Writing

1. Many readers find in this poem something that reminds them of nursery rhymes. If you are among these readers, specify the resemblance(s).
2. Some critics have called parts of the poem "surrealistic." Check a college dictionary, and then argue in a paragraph or two why the word is or is not appropriate.
3. Is this a poem whose experience a reader can share? Explain.

Gwendolyn Brooks

For a biographical note on Gwendolyn Brooks, see page 206.

We Real Cool

The Pool Players.
Seven at the Golden Shovel.

We real cool. We
Left school. We

Lurk late. We
Strike straight. We

Sing sin. We
Thin gin. We

Jazz June. We
Die soon.

[1960]

Joining the Conversation: Critical Thinking and Writing

1. What does it mean for the pool players to say that they are "cool," and not just "cool," but "real cool"?
2. Why does Brooks give seven speakers? Why not simply one, as in "I real cool" and so on? Would that have been more focused and thus more effective?
3. The stanzas could have been written:

   We real cool.
   We left school.

   We lurk late.
   We strike straight.

   And so on. What does Brooks gain by organizing the lines as she does?
4. Brooks presents the poem in a first-person plural voice, "we." If someone claimed that Brooks would have made the poem more objective, and hence better, if she had presented it in third-personal plural, "they," what would be your argument in response?
5. One commentary we consulted says that this poem describes "pool-playing gang members at a bar called The Golden Shovel on the South Side of Chicago." Does this specific information add to or detract from your experience of the poem?
6. Is it accurate—or is it misleading—to say that this poem presents an argument?

ETHERIDGE KNIGHT

Etheridge Knight, born in Corinth, Mississippi, in 1931, dropped out of school in the eighth grade. He served in the U.S. Army from 1947 to 1951, but after his discharge became addicted to drugs and soon was involved in a life of crime. Arrested for robbery in 1960, Knight began to write poetry while in prison, encouraged by the African American poets Dudley Randall, Sonia Sanchez, and Gwendolyn Brooks. His first book, Poems from Prison, *was published in 1968 by Randall's Broadside Press. Knight was a leading figure in the Black Arts movement of the 1960s and 1970s, a form of radical cultural activity (related to the broader Black Power movement) that promoted "social engagement" as a crucial feature of literary practice. His* Belly Song and Other Poems *(1973) was one of the most influential books of the period for African American writers and critics. Knight died in 1985.*

The following poem was written a year after the assassination of the charismatic African American militant, writer, and orator Malcolm X (nicknamed "Red"). Born in Omaha, Nebraska, in 1925, Malcolm Little moved to Boston in the early 1940s, and there and in New York City, he was a drug dealer and a thief. He was arrested in 1946 for armed robbery and spent the next six years in prisons in Massachusetts. While still in prison, he became acquainted with the teachings of Elijah Muhammed, the leader of the Nation of Islam, and he embarked upon an intensive program of self-education, especially in history. Upon his release from prison, Malcolm Little changed his name to Malcolm X, the "X" signifying the name, unknown to him, of his African ancestors who had been sold into slavery. He broke with Elijah Muhammed in 1963 and formed a rival organization, the Muslim Mosque, Inc. He then made a pilgrimage to Mecca, converted to orthodox Islam, and, while remaining a militant black nationalist, stated that he was no longer a racial separatist. In the Audubon Ballroom in Harlem, on February 21, 1965, Malcolm X was murdered by members of the Nation of Islam, though controversy still surrounds the conspiracy that led to his death. Malcolm X's writings and speeches are included in his Autobiography *(as told to Alex Haley, 1964) and* Malcolm X Speaks *(1965).*

For Malcolm, a Year After

Compose for Red a proper verse;
Adhere to foot and strict iamb;
Control the burst of angry words
Or they might boil and break the dam.
Or they might boil and overflow
And drench me, drown me, drive me mad.
So swear no oath, so shed no tear,
And sing no song blue Baptist sad.
Evoke no image, stir no flame,
And spin no yarn across the air.
Make empty anglo tea lace words—
Make them dead and white and dry bone bare.

Compose a verse for Malcolm man,
And make it rime and make it prim.
The verse will die—as all men do—
But not the memory of him!

Death might come singing sweet like C,
Or knocking like the old folk say,
The moon and stars may pass away,
But not the anger of that day.

[1966]

Joining the Conversation: Critical Thinking and Writing

1. Knight's poem is both about Malcolm X and about the writing of a poem about him. Why might Knight have wanted to connect the subject of this poem to the act of writing the poem in the first place? Do you think that Knight should have presented a more straightforward tribute?
2. Explain the meaning of line 8. And of line 11. Which line is more effective? Are these lines more or less effective than other lines in the poem?
3. Are the first two lines of the second stanza puzzling? Why the word "prim"?
4. What is the relationship of the fourth line of the second stanza to the final line of the poem?
5. Do you think that Knight's poem remains powerful today? How does a poem keyed to a specific historical event or person retain its power decades after the event or after the person's death? Or is it the case, in your view, that the passing of time always diminishes the impact of a poem like this one?

ANNE SEXTON

Anne Sexton (1928–1974) was born in Newton, Massachusetts. She was a member of a well-educated New England family but did not attend college. After the birth of her second child she suffered a mental breakdown, and for much of the rest of her life she was under psychiatric care. Indeed, a psychiatrist encouraged her to write poetry, and she was soon able to publish in national journals such as the New Yorker. *Despite her success, she continued to suffer mentally, and in 1974 she committed suicide.*

Her Kind

I have gone out, a possessed witch,
haunting the black air, braver at night;
dreaming evil, I have done my hitch
over the plain houses, light by light;
lonely thing, twelve-fingered, out of mind.
A woman like that is not a woman, quite.
I have been her kind.

I have found the warm caves in the woods,
filled them with skillets, carvings, shelves,
closets, silks, innumerable goods;
fixed the suppers for the worms and the elves:
whining, rearranging the disaligned.
A woman like that is misunderstood.
I have been her kind.

I have ridden in your cart, driver,
waved my nude arms at villages going by,
learning the last bright routes, survivor
where your flames still bite my thigh
and my ribs crack where your wheels wind.
A woman like that is not ashamed to die.
I have been her kind.

[1960]

Joining the Conversation: Critical Thinking and Writing

Whether you are male or female, can you categorically say that you are *not* "her kind"? Explain.

JAMES WRIGHT

James Wright (1927–1980) was born in Martins Ferry, Ohio, which provided him with the locale for many of his poems. He is often thought of as a poet of the Midwest, but (as in the example that we give) his poems move beyond the scenery. Wright was educated at Kenyon College in Ohio and at the University of Washington. He wrote several books of poetry and published many translations of European and Latin American poetry.

Lying in a Hammock at William Duffy's Farm in Pine Island, Minnesota

Over my head, I see the bronze butterfly,
Asleep on the black trunk,
Blowing like a leaf in green shadow.
Down the ravine behind the empty house,
The cowbells follow one another
Into the distances of the afternoon.
To my right,
In a field of sunlight between two pines,
The droppings of last year's horses
Blaze up into golden stones.
I lean back, as the evening darkens and comes on.
A chicken hawk floats over, looking for home.
I have wasted my life.

[1963]

Joining the Conversation: Critical Thinking and Writing

1. How important is it that the poet is "lying in a hammock"? That he is at some place other than his own home?
2. Do you take the last line as a severe self-criticism, or as a joking remark, or as something in between, or what?
3. Imagine yourself lying in a hammock—perhaps you can recall an actual moment in a hammock—or lying in bed, your eye taking in the surroundings. Write a description ending with some sort of judgment or concluding comment, as Wright does. You may want to parody Wright's poem, but you need not. (Keep in mind that the best parodies are written by people who regard the original with affection.)

CHAPTER 17

Thinking Critically about Poems: Two Case Studies

A Case Study about Emily Dickinson

In this case study, we give the texts of ten poems and an essay by a student that focuses on Emily Dickinson's religious poetry.

Dickinson is one of the most important and influential American poets, with an amazing gift for vivid, piercing language and an extraordinary ability to suggest and represent complex movements of thought and feeling. Dickinson is highly engaging and accessible in some poems, and difficult and demanding in many others. She is difficult in large measure because she is unique: No one wrote like this before her, and no one has written like this since. Spending time with Dickinson means rising to a special challenge, and at first this may strike you as a chore or a burden. But in truth it is an intellectual opportunity. Give this poet a chance, and you'll be amply rewarded.

For isn't this, after all, central to our interest in and love of literature? We want to be pushed, provoked, tested, and challenged. When we read Dickinson, it's true that we are often made uncomfortable: She gives immediate kinds of pleasure but also causes in us struggle and strain. She makes us reach and stretch. This is precisely what Dickinson—so innovative and complex and electrifyingly *alive*—sought to achieve in her verse and this is why we value her. She compels us to think and feel in ways we had not imagined possible.

Yet one of the ironies of Dickinson as a poet, and one of her sources of fascination for us, is that for all her impact, very few of her contemporaries were even aware that she wrote poetry, as the following brief biography indicates.

Amherst College Library, Archives and Special Collection

Except for brief trips in her youth to Boston, Worcester, and Cambridge, a longer visit to Washington and Philadelphia in 1855, and a few weeks in Cambridge in 1864 for treatment of an eye disorder, Emily Dickinson (1830–1886) spent her entire life in Amherst, Massachusetts. She was capable of warmth, affection, and playful humor, but, especially as she became older, Dickinson made sure that she alone established (and secured) the terms for interacting with other people. She had no desire for any kind of public life or career; she had no interest in politics or reform movements; and, however fervent her feelings for both men and women may have been, she had no sexual relationship or sustained romance with anyone. She rigorously maintained her privacy in the family home; she dressed in white all the time and only allowed a doctor to examine her as she walked by a door that was open a crack in an adjoining room.

Self-sentenced to confinement in her Amherst house, Dickinson baked bread, spent time in the garden, made brief appearances in this or that room or hallway and then vanished through a door or up a stairway. She sent many heightened, exuberant, often mirthful, and sometimes enigmatic notes and letters, above all to her sister-in-law Sue Gilbert, who lived next door.

Dickinson was complicatedly connected to the members of her family and to a few friends. There was, for example, her ambitious, aloof father, Edward Dickinson, who was an attorney, treasurer of Amherst College, and a one-term U.S. congressman, and her melancholy, detached, but wryly humorous mother, Emily Norcross. There was also the young lawyer B. F. Newton (who gave her a copy of Emerson's poems); the literary journalists and editors Josiah Holland and Samuel Bowles; Charles Wadsworth, a married Presbyterian minister and almost certainly the man, addressed as "Master," to whom Dickinson wrote passionate letters; the radical reformer and essayist Thomas Wentworth Higginson, with whom Dickinson corresponded about her poetry, and who visited her in 1870 (he told his wife, "I never was with anyone who drained my nerve power so much"); and Otis Phillips Lord, a crusty Whig politician and Massachusetts judge, two decades older than Dickinson, with whom she exchanged ardent letters late in her life.

Emotionally and intellectually (she felt special kinship with Shakespeare, Charlotte Brontë, Elizabeth Barrett Browning, and George Eliot), Dickinson was supercharged, as the nearly 1,800 poems she composed—many of which she neatly sewed into booklets and hid away in the drawers of her bureau—demonstrate with a stunning, even shocking, thematic brilliance and technical daring. Extremely condensed in syntax and structure, idiosyncratic in punctuation, and breathtaking in imagery and phrasing, Dickinson's poems (and many of her letters, too) catch our attention immediately.

Only a handful of poems by Dickinson were published in her lifetime, all of them anonymously and probably without her consent. Through her father's friends and acquaintances, and familiar as she was with literary journals and papers, she could have published more, and in her own name, if publication had been a goal. But perhaps Dickinson understood poetry as writing to be done first and foremost for oneself and then in certain instances to be shared with friends and family members, as was the case with the poems she bestowed upon Sue Gilbert. Dickinson saved her poems and assembled many of them into bundles, but, her biographer Alfred Habegger acknowledges, there is not a single "explicit statement as to what the massive project meant to her."

Dickinson made her sister and brother promise that after her death they would burn all of her papers. As instructed, Lavinia proceeded to destroy all of the letters that Dickinson had saved. The poems, which were a revelation to her, she preserved, and many of them were published in the 1890s and in subsequent decades, though in editions that often revised and tampered with the wording and structure of the texts. Modern scholars, led by Thomas H. Johnson and R. W. Franklin, have restored the poems to the versions that Dickinson herself composed.

It is unnerving to realize that we know (and now can read in correct form) Dickinson's thrilling poems because of a broken promise. Possessed as she was with a fierce, ironic intelligence, Dickinson would have understood deeply both the love and betrayal that her sister's act displayed.

As you read the poems below, feel the excitement of, and take delight in, Dickinson's organizations of language as she explores her major themes and subjects, which include the meaning of death, the nature of identity, the beauty and mystery of nature, the anguish and ecstasy of love, and the majesty of God. But seek too, from poem to poem, to draw and develop for yourself a poetic portrait of Dickinson: What does she sound like? How does her mind work? What makes her so distinctive, so special?

I heard a Fly buzz—when I died—

I heard a Fly buzz—when I died—
The Stillness in the Room
Was like the Stillness in the Air—
Between the Heaves of Storm—

The Eyes around—had wrung them dry—
And Breaths were gathering firm
For the last Onset—when the King
Be witnessed—in the Room—

I willed my Keepsakes—Signed away
What portion of me be
Assignable—and then it was
There interposed a Fly—

With Blue—uncertain stumbling Buzz—
Between the light—and me—
And then the Windows failed—and then
I could not see to see—

[c. 1862]

The Soul selects her own Society

The Soul selects her own Society—
Then—shuts the Door—
To her divine Majority—
Present no more—

Unmoved—she notes the Chariots—pausing—
At her low Gate—
Unmoved—an Emperor be kneeling
Upon her Mat—

I've known her—from an ample nation—
Choose One—
Then—close the Valves° of her attention—
Like Stone—

[1862]

11 Valves the two halves of a hinged door, such as is now found on old telephone booths. Possibly also an allusion to a bivalve, such as an oyster or a clam, having a shell consisting of two hinged parts.

These are the days when Birds come back

These are the days when Birds come back—
A very few—a Bird or two—
To take a backward look.

These are days when skies resume
The old—old sophistries° of June—
A blue and gold mistake.

O fraud that cannot cheat the Bee—
Almost thy plausibility
Induces my belief.

Till ranks of seeds their witness bear—
And softly thro' the altered air
Hurries a timid leaf.

Oh Sacrament of summer days,
Oh Last Communion in the Haze—
Permit a child to join.

Thy sacred emblems to partake—
Thy consecrated bread to take
And thine immortal wine!

[1859]

5 sophistries deceptively subtle arguments.

Papa above!

Papa above!
Regard a Mouse
O'erpowered by the Cat!
Reserve within thy kingdom
A "Mansion" for the Rat!

Snug in seraphic Cupboards
To nibble all the day,
While unsuspecting Cycles°
Wheel solemnly away!

[c. 1859]

8 Cycles long periods, eons.

There's a certain Slant of light

There's a certain Slant of light,
Winter Afternoons—
That oppresses, like the Heft°
Of Cathedral Tunes—

3 Heft weight.

Heavenly Hurt, it gives us—
We can find no scar,
But internal difference,
Where the Meanings, are—

None may teach it—Any—
'Tis the Seal Despair—
An imperial affliction
Sent us of the Air—

When it comes, the Landscape listens—
Shadows—hold their breath—
When it goes, 'tis like the Distance
On the look of Death—

[c. 1861]

This World is not Conclusion

This World is not Conclusion.
A Species stands beyond—
Invisible, as Music—
But positive, as Sound—
It beckons, and it baffles—
Philosophy—dont know—
And through a Riddle, at the last—
Sagacity, must go—
To guess it, puzzles scholars—
To gain it, Men have borne
Contempt of Generations
And Crucifixion, shown—
Faith slips—and laughs, and rallies—
Blushes, if any see—
Plucks at a twig of Evidence—
And asks a Vane, the way—
Much Gesture, from the Pulpit—
Strong Hallelujahs roll—
Narcotics cannot still the Tooth
That nibbles at the soul—

[c. 1862]

I got so I could hear his name—

I got so I could hear his name—
Without—Tremendous gain—
That Stop-sensation—on my Soul—
And Thunder—in the Room—

I got so I could walk across
That Angle in the floor,
Where he turned so, and I turned—how—
And all our Sinew tore—

I got so I could stir the Box—
In which his letters grew
Without that forcing, in my breath—
As Staples—driven through—

Could dimly recollect a Grace—
I think, they call it "God"—
Renowned to ease Extremity—
When Formula, had failed—

And shape my Hands—
Petition's way,
Tho' ignorant of a word
That Ordination°—utters—

My Business, with the Cloud,
If any Power behind it, be,
Not subject to Despair—

It care, in some remoter way,
For so minute affair
As Misery—
Itself, too great, for interrupting—more—

[1861]

20 Ordination the ministry.

Those—dying, then

Those—dying, then
Knew where they went
They went to God's Right Hand—
The Hand is amputated now
And God cannot be found—

The abdication of Belief
Makes the Behavior small—
Better an ignis fatuus°
Than no illume at all—

[1882]

8 ignis fatuus a phosphorescent light that hovers over swampy ground, hence something deceptive.

Apparently with no surprise

Apparently with no surprise
To any happy Flower
The Frost beheads it at its play—
In accidental power—
The blonde Assassin passes on—
The Sun proceeds unmoved
To measure off another Day
For an Approving God.

[c. 1884]

Tell all the Truth but tell it slant

Tell all the Truth but tell it slant—
Success in Circuit lies
Too bright for our infirm Delight
The Truth's superb surprise

As Lightning to the Children eased
With explanation kind
The Truth must dazzle gradually
Or every man be blind—

[c. 1868]

A Sample Argument by a Student: "Religion and Religious Imagery in Emily Dickinson"

Gottsegen 1

Peter Gottsegen

Professor Diaz

English 150G

12 April 2009

Religion and Religious Imagery in Emily Dickinson

Emily Dickinson was not a preacher but a poet, so if we read her poetry about God we should not be surprised if we do not find a simple, consistent view, or even a clear development from one view—for instance, belief—to another—for instance, loss of faith. Rather, judging from some examples of her poetry, she explored various views, and we should not try to convert this variety into unity.

We can begin by looking at extreme views, first two poems of faith, and then a poem of doubt. One of the poems of faith, "Papa above!" (535), begins with a childlike or almost playful version of

Gottsegen 2

the Lord's Prayer. (In Matthew 6:9 Jesus begins a prayer by saying, "Our Father who art in heaven.") I think this poem says that God will see to it that even a mouse or rat will get into heaven, and will remain there for eternity. But Dickinson's God is not always concerned for all of the creatures of the world. In another poem that expresses belief in the existence of God, "Apparently with no surprise" (537), Dickinson describes the frost as beheading a flower—that is, beauty perishes—and she goes on to make the point that this occurs under the eyes of "an Approving God." Here she seems to be saying that evil takes place, and God approves of it. It is important to realize that in this poem Dickinson still says that God exists, even if he is indifferent to suffering.

In another poem, "Those—dying, then" (537), Dickinson expresses doubt that God exists. In olden days, she says, people mistakenly thought that God would protect them, but now, she says, "God cannot be found." She uses a particularly terrifying image to convey the loss of God. In the past, Dickinson says, the faithful went to "God's Right Hand," but, she goes on to say, "The Hand is amputated now. . . ." The faith in God that earlier people had was an illusion, but it was something, and it was "better" than the nothingness we now experience. This nothingness, or something not much more than nothingness, is the subject of "I heard a Fly buzz—when I died" (534). In this poem, the speaker expects "the King" (God) to appear to her as she dies, but all she

Gottsegen 3

sees is a fly, and then she hears its buzz. God ("the King") never appears.

Even these few poems show that Dickinson held a variety of views about God and religion, and it is difficult or perhaps impossible for us to say exactly what her religious beliefs were. But what is certain is that religious ideas were so important to her, so much a part of her mind, that even when she was not explicitly writing about the existence of a benevolent God or the absence of God, she used religious imagery—for instance, to describe impressive things in the natural world around her. In "These are the days when Birds come back" (535), she talks about what we call Indian summer, fall days that are like summer days. But the poem is filled with religious words: "belief," "Sacrament," "Communion," "consecrated bread," "immortal wine." The fifth stanza goes like this:

> Oh Sacrament of summer days,
> Oh Last Communion in the Haze—
> Permit a child to join.

I do not think Dickinson is really talking about traditional religion here. Instead, she is using religious imagery to talk about a particular precious moment in the seasons. As a second example of her use of religious imagery in a poem that is about nature and not about God, we might look at "There's a certain Slant of light" (535). In this poem she says that on "Winter Afternoons" this particular light has "the Heft / Of Cathedral

Gottsegen 4

Tunes." That is, the winter light has the solidity, the feel, the "heft" of religious music. When we see this light, Dickinson says, we are moved, in a way that we are moved by music in church. She is not saying anything here about whether God is benevolent or not, or whether he exists or not. Rather, she is drawing on experiences in church—probably experiences shared by many people even today—to help us to see nature more effectively.

Speaking as someone who was brought up with traditional religious beliefs but who does not go to church now, I can say that Dickinson effectively represents the ideas of a believer and also of a nonbeliever. But what I think is especially impressive is that she sees that someone who no longer is a believer can't help but still think in religious terms when he or she sees something exceptionally beautiful, for instance on a winter day "a certain Slant of light."

[New page]

Gottsegen 5

Works Cited

Barnet, Sylvan, William Burto, and William E. Cain. *Literature for Composition*. 9th ed. New York: Longman. 2010. Print.

Dickinson, Emily. "Apparently with no surprise." Barnet, Burto, and Cain 537.

Gottsegen 6

———. "I heard a Fly buzz—when I died." Barnet, Burto, and Cain 534.

———. "Papa above!" Barnet, Burto, and Cain 535.

———. "There's a certain Slant of light." Barnet, Burto, and Cain 535–36.

———. "Those—dying, then." Barnet, Burto, and Cain 537.

Joining the Conversation: Critical Thinking and Writing

1. In this essay Gottsegen comments on the following poems: "Papa above!" "Apparently with no surprise," "Those—dying, then," "I heard a Fly buzz—when I died," "These are the days when Birds come back," and "There's a certain Slant of light." Read or reread each of these poems to see if you agree with Gottsegen's interpretations.
2. Are there other poems in the case study that you think Gottsegen could have used with better effect than some that he did use? Explain.
3. Reread the concluding paragraph. Do you think it is effective? Explain.

A Case Study on Comparing Poems and Pictures

Despite Mallarmé's witty remark that poems are not made with ideas but with words, and despite Archibald MacLeish's assertion that "A poem should not mean / But be," poems do include ideas, and they do have meanings. When you read the poems that accompany the paintings in the color insert section (pages 544–66) think about some of the following questions:

- What is your own first response to the painting? In interpreting the painting, consider the subject matter, the composition (for instance, balanced masses, as opposed to an apparent lack of equilibrium), the technique (for instance, vigorous brush strokes of thick paint, as opposed to thinly applied strokes that leave no trace of the artist's hand), the color, and the title.
- After having read the poem, do you see the painting in a somewhat different way?
- To what extent does the poem illustrate the painting, and to what extent does it depart from the painting and make a very different statement?
- If the painting is based on a poem (see Demuth's painting on page 546), to what extent does the painting capture the poem?
- Beyond the subject matter, what (if anything) do the two works have in common?

Word and Image

Poetry is a speaking picture, painting is silent poetry.

—Simonides

Vincent van Gogh. *Vincent's Bed in Arles.* (Oil on canvas, 72 × 90 cm. Vincent van Gogh Foundation/Van Gogh Museum, Amsterdam.)

Jane Flanders

Jane Flanders, born in Waynesboro, Pennsylvania, in 1940 and educated at Bryn Mawr College and Columbia University, is the author of three books of poems. Among her awards are poetry fellowships from the National Endowment for the Arts and the New York Foundation for the Arts.

Van Gogh's Bed

is orange,
like Cinderella's coach, like
the sun when he looked it
straight in the eye.

is narrow,
he slept alone, tossing
between two pillows, while it carried him
bumpily to the ball.

is clumsy,
but friendly. A peasant
built the frame; an old wife beat
the mattress till it rose like meringue.

is empty,
morning light pours in
like wine, melody, fragrance,
the memory of happiness

[1985]

Joining the Conversation: Critical Thinking and Writing

Jane Flanders tells us that the poem is indebted not only to the painting but also to two comments in letters that van Gogh wrote to his brother, Theo:

> I can tell you that for my part I will try to keep a straight course, and will paint the most simple, the most common things.
>
> [December 1884]

> My eyes are still tired, but then I had a new idea in my head and here is the sketch of it. . . . It's just simply my bedroom, only here color is to do everything, and giving by its simplification a grander style to things, is to be suggestive here of *rest* or of sleep in general. In a word, to look at the picture ought to rest the brain or rather the imagination.
>
> [September 1888]

1. Does the painting convey "rest" to you? If not, has van Gogh failed to paint a picture of interest? What *does* the picture convey to you?
2. In an earlier version, the last stanza of the poem went thus:

> empty,
> morning light pours in
> like wine; the sheets are what they are,
> casting no shadows.

Which version do you prefer? In an argument of one page, explain why.

Charles Demuth. *I Saw the Figure 5 in Gold.* 1928. (Oil on composition board, 36 × 29¾ in. The Metropolitan Museum of Art, Alfred Stieglitz Collection, 1949. [49.59.1] Photograph © 1986 The Metropolitan Museum of Art.)

William Carlos Williams

William Carlos Williams (1883–1963) was the son of an English traveling salesman and a Basque-Jewish woman. The couple met in Puerto Rico and settled in Rutherford, New Jersey, where Williams was born. He spent his life there, practicing as a pediatrician and writing poems in the moments between seeing patients who were visiting his office.

In his Autobiography *Williams gives an account of the origin of this poem. He was walking in New York City, on his way to visit a friend:*

> *As I approached his number I heard a great clatter of bells and the roar of a fire engine passing the end of the street down Ninth Avenue. I turned just in time to see a golden 5 on a red background flash by. The impression*

was so sudden and forceful that I took a piece of paper out of my pocket and wrote a short poem about it.

Several years later his friend Charles Demuth (1883–1939), an American painter who has been called a cubist-realist, painted this picture, inspired by the poem. The picture is one of a series of paintings about Demuth's friends.

The Great Figure

Among the rain
and lights
I saw the figure 5
in gold
on a red
fire truck
moving
tense
unheeded
to gong clangs
siren howls
and wheels rumbling
through the dark city

[1920]

Joining the Conversation: Critical Thinking and Writing

Williams's draft for the poem runs thus:

Among the rain
and lights
I saw the figure 5
gold on red
moving
to gong clangs
siren howls
and wheels rumbling
tense
unheeded
through the dark city

Do you think the final version is better in all respects, some respects, or no respect? Please present a good argument for your view.

Edwin Romanzo Elmer. *Mourning Picture.* 1890. (Oil on canvas, 28 × 36 in. Smith College Museum of Art, Northampton, Massachusetts [purchase, 1953].)

Adrienne Rich

Adrienne Rich's most recent books of poetry include Telephone Ringing in the Labyrinth: Poems 2004–2006 *and* The School Among the Ruins: 2000–2004. *A selection of her essays,* Arts of the Possible: Essays and Conversations, *appeared in 2001. She edited Muriel Rukeyser's* Selected Poems *for the Library of America. In Spring 2009, Norton published* A Human Eye: Essays on Art in Society. *She is a recipient of the National Book Foundation's 2006 Medal for Distinguished Contribution to American Letters, among other honors. She lives in California.*

Mourning Picture

(The picture was painted by Edwin Romanzo Elmer (1850–1923) as a memorial to his daughter Effie. In the poem, it is the dead girl who speaks.)

They have carried the mahogany chair and the cane rocker
out under the lilac bush,

and my father and mother darkly sit there, in black clothes.
Our clapboard house stands fast on its hill,
my doll lies in her wicker pram
gazing at western Massachusetts.
This was our world.
I could remake each shaft of grass
feeling its rasp on my fingers,
draw out the map of every lilac leaf
or the net of veins on my father's
grief-tranced hand.

Out of my head, half-bursting,
still filling, the dream condenses—
shadows, crystals, ceilings, meadows, globes of dew.
Under the dull green of the lilacs, out in the light
carving each spoke of the pram, the turned porch-pillars,
under high early-summer clouds,
I am Effie, visible and invisible,
remembering and remembered.

They will move from the house,
give the toys and pets away.
Mute and rigid with loss my mother
will ride the train to Baptist Corner,
the silk-spool will run bare.
I tell you, the thread that bound us lies
faint as a web in the dew.
Should I make you, world, again,
could I give back the leaf its skeleton, the air
its early-summer cloud, the house
its noonday presence, shadowless,
and leave *this* out? I am Effie, you were my dream.

[1965]

Kitagawa Utamaro.* *Two Women Dressing Their Hair.* (1974–1975. New York Public Library/Art Resource, NY.)

Cathy Song

Cathy Song was born in Honolulu in 1952 of a Chinese mother and a Korean father. She holds a bachelor's degree from Wellesley College and a master's degree in creative writing from Boston University. A manuscript that she submitted to the Yale Series of Younger Poets was chosen as the winner and in 1983 was published under the title of Picture Bride.

*Kitagawa Utamaro (1754–1806) lived in Edo (now called Tokyo). He specialized in designing pictures of courtesans and actors that were then used to make woodblock prints. Brothels and the theater were important parts of what was called the Floating World, that is, the world of transient pleasure.

Beauty and Sadness

for Kitagawa Utamaro

He drew hundreds of women
in studies unfolding
like flowers from a fan.
Teahouse waitresses, actresses,
geishas, courtesans and maids.
They arranged themselves
before this quick, nimble man
whose invisible presence
one feels in these prints
is as delicate
as the skinlike paper
he used to transfer
and retain their fleeting loveliness.

Crouching like cats,
they purred amid the layers of
kimono
swirling around them
as though they were bathing
in a mountain pool with irises
growing in the silken sunlit water.
Or poised like porcelain vases,
slender, erect and tall; their heavy
brocaded hair was piled high
with sandalwood combs and blossom
sprigs
poking out like antennae.
They resembled beautiful iridescent
insects,
creatures from a floating world.

Utamaro absorbed these women of
Edo
in their moments of melancholy
He captured the wisp of shadows,
the half-draped body
emerging from a bath; whatever
skin was exposed
was powdered white as snow.
A private space disclosed.
Portraying another girl
catching a glimpse of her own
vulnerable
face in the mirror, he transposed
the trembling plum lips
like a drop of blood
soaking up the white expanse of
paper.

At times, indifferent to his
inconsolable
eye, the women drifted
through the soft gray feathered light,
maintaining stillness, the moments in
between.
Like the dusty ash-winged moths
that cling to the screens in summer
and that the Japanese venerate
as ancestors reincarnated;
Utamaro graced these women with
immortality
in the thousand sheaves of prints
fluttering into the reverent hands of
keepers:
the dwarfed and bespectacled painter
holding up to a square of sunlight
what he had carried home beneath
his coat
one afternoon in winter.

[1983]

Joining the Conversation: Critical Thinking and Writing

1. In the first stanza the women in Utamaro's prints possess a "fleeting loveliness." What does "fleeting" suggest here? What are Utamaro's characteristics in this stanza?
2. In the second stanza would you say that the women are beautiful, or not? And in the third stanza? What do they look like in each stanza?
3. In the last stanza, in the last few lines, we learn that Utamaro was a "dwarfed and bespectacled painter." We might have learned this earlier in the poem, or not at all. Why does Song wait until this late in the poem to tell us?

Sandro Botticelli. *The Birth of Venus*. c. 1480. (Uffizi Gallery, Florence.)

Mary Jo Salter

Mary Jo Salter, born in 1954 in Grand Rapids, Michigan, was raised in Detroit and Baltimore and educated at Harvard and at Cambridge University. The author of several books of poetry, Salter has received numerous awards, including a fellowship from the National Endowment for the Arts.

The Rebirth of Venus

He's knelt to fish her face up from the sidewalk
all morning, and at last some shoppers gather
to see it drawn—wide-eyed, and dry as chalk—
whole from the sea of dreams. It's she. None other

than the other one who's copied in the book
he copies from, that woman men divined
ages before a painter let them look
into the eyes their eyes had had in mind.

Love's called him too, today, though she has taught
him in her beauty to love best
the one who first had formed her from a thought.
One square of pavement, like a headstone (lest

anyone mistake where credit lies),
reads BOTTICELLI, but the long-closed dates
suggest, instead, a view of centuries
coming unbracketed, as if the gates

might swing wide to admit, here, in the sun,
one humble man into the pantheon
older and more exalted than her own.
    Slow gods of Art, late into afternoon

let there be light: a few of us drop the wish
into his glinting coinbox like a well,
remembering the forecast. Yet he won't rush
her finish, though it means she'll have no shell

to harbor in; it's clear enough the rain
will swamp her like a tide, and lion-hearted
he'll set off, black umbrella sprung again,
envisioning faces where the streets have parted.

[1989]

Joining the Conversation: Critical Thinking and Writing

1. In the first stanza, what words suggest that Venus, whose portrait is being drawn on the sidewalk, is born in the sea? What medium is the artist using?
2. What do you think Salter means when she says (lines 6–8) that the sidewalk artist's picture is of "that woman men divined / ages before a painter let them look / into the eyes their eyes had had in mind"?
3. According to the Hebrew Bible, "Let there be light" (line 21) is what God said in Genesis 1:3. In the context of Salter's poem, what do the words mean? Does the poet expect her wish (in line 21) to be granted?
4. If you agree that the poem is lighthearted, what makes it so?
5. Botticelli's painting is a great favorite. Why do you suppose it is so popular?

Vincent van Gogh. *The Starry Night*. 1889. (Oil on canvas, 29 × 36¼ in. Museum of Modern Art, New York. Acquired through the Lillie P. Bliss Bequest. [472.19].)

ANNE SEXTON

Anne Sexton (1928–1975) was born in Newton, Massachusetts. She attended Garland Junior College, married at 20, and began a life as a housewife. After a mental breakdown at the age of 28, she took up writing poetry on the suggestion of a therapist. She published eight books of poetry, the third of which won a Pulitzer Prize. Despite her literary success, her life was deeply troubled, and she attempted suicide on several occasions. At last she succeeded, by carbon monoxide poisoning.

The Starry Night

That does not keep me from having a terrible need of—shall I say the word—religion. Then I go out at night to paint the stars.
—Vincent van Gogh in a letter to his brother

The town does not exist
except where one black-haired tree slips
up like a drowned woman into the hot sky.
The town is silent. The night boils with eleven stars
Oh starry night! This is how
I want to die.

It moves. They are all alive.
Even the moon bulges in its orange irons
to push children, like a god, from its eye.
The old unseen serpent swallows up the stars.
Oh starry night! This is how
I want to die:

into that rushing beast of the night,
sucked up by that great dragon, to split
from my life with no flag,
no belly,
no cry.

[1961]

Joining the Conversation: Critical Thinking and Writing

1. Sexton calls her poem "The Starry Night" and uses an epigraph from van Gogh. In what ways does her poem not describe or evoke van Gogh's painting? In what ways *does* it describe the painting?
2. Does Sexton's poem require a familiarity with Van Gogh's painting in order to be effective? Please argue first that it does, and then that it does not.

Pieter Brueghel the Elder. *Landscape with the Fall of Icarus.* (Musée d'Art Ancien, Musées Royaux des Beaux–Arts, Brussels, Belgium.)

W. H. Auden

Wystan Hugh Auden (1907–1973) was born in York, England, and educated at Oxford. In the 1930s his left-wing poetry earned him wide acclaim as the leading poet of his generation. He went to Spain during the Spanish Civil War, intending to serve as an ambulance driver for the Republicans in their struggle against fascism, but he was so distressed by the violence of the Republicans that he almost immediately returned to England. In 1939 he came to America, and in 1946 he became a citizen of the United States, though he spent his last years in England. Much of his poetry is characterized by a combination of colloquial diction and technical dexterity.

In the following poem, Auden offers a meditation triggered by a painting in the Museum of Fine Arts in Brussels. The painting, by Pieter Brueghel (c. 1525–1569), is based on the legend of Icarus, told by the Roman poet Ovid (43 B.C.E.–17 C.E.) in his Metamorphoses. *The story goes thus: Daedalus, father of Icarus, was confined with his son on the island of Crete. To escape, Daedalus made wings for himself and Icarus by fastening feathers together with wax; but Icarus flew too near the sun, the wax melted, and Icarus fell into the sea. According to Ovid, the event—a boy falling through the sky—was witnessed with amazement by a plowman, a shepherd, and an angler. In the painting, however, these figures seem to pay no attention to Icarus, who is represented not falling through the sky but already in the water (in the lower right corner, near the ship), with only his lower legs still visible.*

Musée des Beaux Arts

About suffering they were never wrong,
The Old Masters: how well they understood
Its human position; how it takes place
While someone else is eating or opening a window or just walking dully along;
How, when the aged are reverently, passionately waiting
For the miraculous birth, there always must be
Children who did not specially want it to happen, skating
On a pond at the edge of the wood:
They never forgot
That even the dreadful martyrdom must run its course
Anyhow in a corner, some untidy spot
Where the dogs go on with their doggy life and the torturer's horse
Scratches its innocent behind on a tree.

In Brueghel's *Icarus*, for instance: how everything turns away
Quite leisurely from the disaster; the ploughman may
Have heard the splash, the forsaken cry,
But for him it was not an important failure; the sun shone
As it had to on the white legs disappearing into the green
Water; and the expensive delicate ship that must have seen
Something amazing, a boy falling out of the sky,
Had somewhere to get to and sailed calmly on.

[1938]

Joining the Conversation: Critical Thinking and Writing

1. In your own words sum up what, according to the speaker (in lines 1–13), the Old Masters understood about human suffering. (The Old Masters were the great European painters who worked from about 1500 to about 1750.)

2. Suppose the first lines read:

> The Old Masters were never wrong about suffering.
> They understood its human position well.

What (beside the particular rhymes) would change or be lost?

3. Reread the poem a number of times, jotting down your chief responses after each reading. Then, in connection with a final reading, study your notes, and write an essay of 500 words setting forth the history of your final response to the poem. For example, you may want to report that certain difficulties soon were clarified and that your enjoyment increased. Or, conversely, you may want to report that the poem became less interesting (for reasons you will set forth) the more you studied it. Probably your history will be somewhat more complicated than these simple examples. Try to find a chief pattern in your experience, and shape it into a thesis.

4. Consider a picture, either in a local museum or reproduced in a book, and write a 500-word reflection on it. If the picture is not well known, include a reproduction (a postcard from the museum or a photocopy of a page of a book).

Marcel Duchamp. *Nude Descending a Staircase, No. 2.* 1912. (Oil on canvas, 58 × 35 in. Philadelphia Museum of Art. The Louise and Walter Arensberg Collection [Acc. No. 1950-134-59]. © 2004 Artists Rights Society [ARS], New York/ADAGP, Paris/Sucession of Marcel Duchamp.)

X. J. KENNEDY

X. J. Kennedy was born in New Jersey in 1929. For many years, he taught at Tufts University and is the author of several books of poems, books for children, and college textbooks.

Marcel Duchamp's Nude Descending a Staircase, No. 2 *(1912) was exhibited in 1913 in the Armory Show, an international exhibition held at an armory in New York, and later in Chicago and Boston. The Armory Show gave America its first good look at contemporary European art, for instance, cubism, which had influenced Duchamp's painting.*

Nude Descending a Staircase

Toe upon toe, a snowing flesh,
A gold of lemon, root and rind,
She sifts in sunlight down the stairs
With nothing on. Nor on her mind.

We spy beneath the banister
A constant thresh of thigh on thigh—
Her lips imprint the swinging air
That parts to let her parts go by
One-woman waterfall, she wears
Her slow descent like a long cape
And pausing, on the final stair
Collects her motions into shape.

[1961]

Joining the Conversation: Critical Thinking and Writing

1. To what extent does the poem describe the painting? To what extent does it do something else?
2. Some viewers have found Duchamp's painting strange and confusing. Does Kennedy's poem help you to understand Duchamp's style of art? Explain.

John James Audubon. *Greater Flamingo, American Flamingo*. c. 1830. (Courtesy William S. Reese.)

Greg Pape

Greg Pape was born in 1947 in Eureka, California, and educated at Fresno State College (now California State University, Fresno) and the University of Arizona. The author of several books of poems, he has served as writer-in-residence at several colleges and universities, and now teaches at Northern Arizona University, in Flagstaff.

American Flamingo

I know he shot them to know them.
I did not know the eyes of the flamingo
are blue, a deep live blue.

And the tongue is lined with many small
tongues, thirteen, in the sketch
by Audubon,° to function as a sieve.

I knew the long rose-pink neck,
the heavy tricolored down-sweeping bill,
the black primaries.

But I did not know the blue eye
drawn so passionately by Audubon
it seems to look out, wary, intense,

6 Audubon John James Audubon, American ornithologist and artist (1785–1851), author of the multivolume *Birds of America* (1827–1938).

from the paper it is printed on.
                                        —*what*
Is man but his passion?

asked Robert Penn Warren.° In the background
of this sketch, tenderly subtitled *Old Male,*
beneath the over-draping feathered

monument of the body, between the long
flexible neck and the long bony legs
covered with pink plates of flesh,

Audubon has given us eight postures,
eight stunning movements in the ongoing
dance of the flamingos.

Once at Hialeah° in late afternoon
I watched the satin figures of the jockeys
perched like bright beetles on the backs

of horses pounding down the home
stretch, a few crops whipping
the lathering flanks, the loud flat

metallic voice of the announcer fading
as the flamingos, grazing the pond water
at the far end of the infield, rose

in a feathery blush, only a few feet
off the ground, and flew one long
clipped-winged ritual lap

in the heavy Miami light, a great
slow swirl of grace from the old world
that made tickets fall from hands,

stilled horses, and drew toasts from the stands
as they settled down again
like a rose-colored fog on the pond.

[1998]

16 Robert Penn Warren American poet, novelist, and literary critic (1905–1989).
25 Hialeah city in southeast Florida, site of Hialeah Park racetrack.

Joining the Conversation: Critical Thinking and Writing

1. Why is the speaker preoccupied with the flamingo's eyes?
2. A transition occurs in lines 14–15, with the italicized quotation from Robert Penn Warren. What is the relationship of this to the description of the flamingo (and the speaker's reflections) that precede it?
3. From line 25 to the end, the speaker carefully describes a scene at Hialeah. Take note of the specific details and terms that the speaker presents, and explain how these make the poem both a vivid description and something more than that.

Edouard Manet. *Luncheon on the Grass (Déjeuner sur l'herbe)*. 1863. (Musée d'Orsay, Paris, France.)

CARL PHILLIPS

Carl Phillips was born in 1959 in Everett, Washington, and was educated at Harvard and at Boston University. African American, gay, a scholar of classical Greek and Latin, and the author of numerous books of poetry, he has taught creative writing at Harvard, and he now teaches English and African American studies at Washington University in St. Louis.

Luncheon on the Grass

They're a curious lot. Manet's scandalous
lunch partners. The two men, lost
in cant and full dress, their legs sprawled
subway-style, as men's legs invariably are, seem
remarkably unruffled, all but oblivious to their nude
female companion. Her nudity is puzzling and
correct; clothes for her are surely only needed
to shrug a shoulder out of. She herself appears
baldly there-for-the-ride; her eyes, moving out
toward the viewer, are wide with the most banal,
detached surprise, as if to say, "where's
the *real* party?"

Now, in a comparable state of outdoor
undress, I'm beginning to have a fair idea
of what's going on in that scene. Watching
you, in clothes, remove one boot to work your
finger toward an itch in your athletic sock,
I look for any similarities between art
and our afternoon here on abandoned
property. The bather in the painting's
background, presumably there for a certain
balance of composition, is for us an ungainly,
rusted green dumpster, rising from overgrown
weeds that provide a contrast only remotely
pastoral. We are two to Manet's main group
of three, but the hum of the odd car or truck
on the highway below us offers a transient third.
Like the nude, I don't seem especially hungry,
partly because it's difficult eating naked when
everyone else is clothed, partly because
you didn't remember I hate chicken salad.
The beer you opened for me sits untouched,
going flat in the sun. I stroke the wet bottle
fitfully, to remind myself just how far
we've come or more probably have always been
from the shape of romance. My dear,
this is not art; we're not anywhere close
to Arcadia.°

[1993]

38 Arcadia an ancient region in Greece, traditionally associated in art and literature with the simple, pastoral life, a Golden Age of unfailing romantic love.

Joining the Conversation: Critical Thinking and Writing

1. The author is openly gay. Does knowledge of his sexual orientation affect the way in which you read the poem? Explain.
2. Do you agree that the speaker and the partner are "not anywhere close / to Arcadia"? Support your argument with evidence.

Pablo Picasso. *Girl Before a Mirror.* 1932. (Museum of Modern Art, New York. Gift of Mrs. Simon Guggenheim [2.1938].

JOHN UPDIKE

John Updike (1932–2009), grew up in Shillington, Pennsylvania, where his father was a teacher and his mother was a writer. After receiving a B.A. degree from Harvard he studied drawing at Oxford for a year, but an offer from the New Yorker *magazine brought him back to the United States. He at first served as a reporter for the magazine, but soon began contributing poetry, essays, and fiction. He was one of America's most prolific and well-known writers.*

Before the Mirror

How many of us still remember
when Picasso's *Girl Before a Mirror* hung
at the turning of the stairs in the pre-
expansion Museum of Modern Art?

Millions of us, maybe, but we form
a dwindling population. Garish
and brush-slashed and yet as balanced
as a cardboard queen in a deck of giant cards,
the painting proclaimed, *Enter here*
and abandon preconception. She bounced
the erotic balls of herself back and forth
between reflection and reality.

Now I discover, in the recent retro-
spective at the same establishment,
that the dazzling painting dates
from March of 1932,
the very month in which I first saw light,
squinting in quick nostalgia for the womb.
Inspecting, I bend closer. The blacks,
the stripy cyanide greens are still uncracked,
I note with satisfaction; the cherry reds
and lemon yellows full of childish juice.
No sag, no wrinkle. Fresh as paint. *Back then,*
I reflect, *they knew just how to lay it on.*

[1996]

Joining the Conversation: Critical Thinking and Writing

1. The painting shows a young woman looking into a mirror. In viewing a picture with this subject, what associations might reasonably come to mind? Vanity? Mortality? Or what?
2. The woman (at the left) has two faces, one in profile. Do you think Picasso is showing us two views of the same face, or perhaps two stages in the woman's life? And what of the face in the mirror? Do you think it shows either or both of the faces at the left, or a third face or stage?
3. Why do you suppose the woman is reaching out toward the mirror? (There cannot be any way of proving whatever you or anyone else might offer as an answer, but *why* do you offer the explanation that you do offer?)
4. What do you think the poem is chiefly about? The distinctiveness of modern art (meaning the age of Picasso)? The excellent condition of the picture? The speaker's response to the picture? Explain.
5. The first twelve lines of this poem describe the speaker's thoughts "then," when he first saw *Girl Before a Mirror;* the last twelve lines describe his ideas and feelings "now." In two paragraphs, or in one extended paragraph, write a "Then and Now," describing a picture or a song or a scene—a lake, a house, a kitchen—or a person, then and now.

Pieter Brueghel the Elder. *Two Chained Monkeys.* c.1525–1592. (Oil on wood. Gemäldegalerie, Staaliche Museen zu Berlin, Berlin, Germany.)

Wislawa Szymborska

Wislawa Szymborska (pronounced "Vislawa Zimborska"), born 1923, is one of Poland's leading poets. Her first book published in 1952, she has published seven later volumes. Some of her work is available in English, in Sounds, Feelings, Thoughts *(1981). In 1996 she was awarded the Nobel Prize in Literature.*

*Brueghel's Two Monkeys**

This is what I see in my dream about final exams:
two monkeys, chained to the floor, sit on the windowsill,
the sky behind them flutters,
the sea is taking its bath.

The exam is History of Mankind.
I stammer and hedge.

One monkey stares and listens with mocking disdain,
the other seems to be dreaming away—
but when it's clear I don't know what to say
he prompts me with a gentle
clinking of his chain.

[1983]

*Translated, from the Polish, by Stanislaw Baranczak and Clare Cavanagh.

Joining the Conversation: Critical Thinking and Writing

1. What do we know, or guess, about the speaker from the poem's first line? Are we willing to listen to him (or her)?
2. We are not likely to be examined on "History of Mankind." Why do you suppose the speaker is being quizzed on it? What does the speaker do? (Paraphrase line 6.)
3. In the third stanza the speaker again does not know what to say. Do we know what the question is? Does the prompting (line 10) help?
4. Write a comment, in prose or verse, on Brueghel's painting.

A Sample Argument by a Student

Read (preferably aloud) Anne Sexton's "The Starry Night" (page 555) which was inspired by van Gogh's painting of the same name. Then read the following essay.

Myers 1

Lisa Myers

Professor Peres

English 10G

12 November 2009

Two Ways of Looking at a Starry Night

About a hundred years ago Vincent van Gogh looked up into the sky at night and painted what he saw, or what he felt. We know that he was a very religious man, but even if we had not heard this in an art course or read it in a book we would know it from his painting *The Starry Night* (554), which shows a glorious heaven, with stars so bright that they all have halos. Furthermore, almost in the lower center of the picture is a church, with its steeple rising above the hills and pointing to the heavens.

Anne Sexton's poem is about this painting, and also (we know from the line she quotes above the poem) about van Gogh's religious vision of the stars. But her poem is not about the heavenly comfort that the starry night offered van Gogh. It is a poem about her wish to die. As I understand the poem, she wants to die in a blaze of light, and to become extinct. She says, in the last line of the poem, that she wants to disappear with "no cry," but this seems to me to be very different from anything van Gogh is saying. His picture is about the glorious heavens, not about

Myers 2

himself. Or if it is about himself, it is about how wonderful he feels when he sees God's marvelous creation. Van Gogh is concerned with praising God as God expresses himself in nature; Anne Sexton is concerned with expressing her anguish and with her hope that she can find extinction. Sexton's world is not ruled by a benevolent God but is ruled by an "old unseen serpent." The night is a "rushing beast," presided over by a "great dragon."

Sexton has responded to the painting in a highly unique way. She is not trying to put van Gogh's picture into words that he might approve of. Rather, she has boldly used the picture as a point of departure for her own word-picture.

[New page]

Myers 3

Work Cited

Sexton, Anne. "The Starry Night." *Literature for Composition*. Ed. Sylvan Barnet, William Burto, and William E. Cain. 9th ed. New York: Longman, 2010. 554–55. Print.

Van Gogh, Vincent. *The Starry Night. Literature for Composition*. Ed. Sylvan Barnet, William Burto, and William E. Cain. 9th ed. New York: Longman, 2010. 554. Print.

Joining the Conversation: Critical Thinking and Writing

1. Do you agree with Lisa Myers's analysis, especially her interpretation of Sexton's poem?
2. Has Myers cited and examined passages from the poem in a convincing way?
3. A general question: Do you think poets are obliged to be faithful to the paintings that they write about, or do poets enjoy the freedom—a kind of poetic license—to interpret a painting just as they choose, doing with it whatever the purpose of the poem requires?

Part III

Standing Back

A Thematic Anthology

Chapter 18

The World Around Us

Short Views

We cannot command nature except by obeying her.
Francis Bacon

Study nature, love nature, stay close to nature. It will never fail you.
Frank Lloyd Wright

If a man walks in the woods for love of them half of each day, he is in danger of being regarded as a loafer. But if he spends his days as a speculator, shearing off those woods and making the earth bald before her time, he is deemed an industrious and enterprising citizen.
Henry David Thoreau

A weed is no more than a flower in disguise.
James Russell Lowell

Nature teaches more than she preaches. There are no sermons in stones. It is easier to get a spark out of a stone than a moral.
John Burroughs

Cats are intended to teach us that not everything in nature has a function.
Joseph Wood Krutch

It is a wholesome and necessary thing for us to turn again to the earth and in the contemplation of her beauties to know of wonder and humility.
Rachel Carson

In nature, nothing is perfect and everything is perfect. Trees can be contorted, bent in weird ways, and they're still beautiful.
Alice Walker

What I see in Nature is a magnificent structure that we can comprehend only very imperfectly, and that must fill a thinking person with a feeling of humility. This is a genuinely religious feeling that has nothing to do with mysticism.
Albert Einstein

We cannot remember too often that when we observe nature, and especially the ordering of nature, it is always ourselves alone that we are observing.
G. C. Lichtenberg

We abuse land because we regard it as a commodity belonging to us. When we see land as a community to which we belong, we may begin to use it with love and respect.
Aldo Leopold

Some keep the Sabbath going to Church,
I keep it staying at Home—
With a bobolink for a Chorister,
And an Orchard, for a Dome.
Emily Dickinson

Nature, red in tooth and claw.
Alfred, Lord Tennyson

If people think nature is their friend, then they sure don't need an enemy.
Kurt Vonnegut Jr.

Now, nature, as I am only too well aware, has her enthusiasts, but on the whole, I am not to be counted among them. To put it rather bluntly, I am not the type who wants to go back to the land—I am the type who wants to go back to the hotel.
Fran Lebowitz

Joining the Conversation: Critical Thinking and Writing

1. Select a quotation that especially appeals to you, and make it the focus of an essay of about 500 words.
2. Take two of the passages—perhaps one that you especially like and one that you think is wrongheaded—and write a dialogue of about 500 words in which the two authors converse or argue. They may each try to convince the other, or they may find that to some degree they share views and they may then work out a statement that both can accept. If you do take the first position—that one writer is on the correct track but the other is utterly mistaken—try to be fair to the view that you think is mistaken. (As an experiment in critical thinking, imagine that you accept it, and make the best case for it that you possibly can.)

ESSAYS

HENRY DAVID THOREAU

The author of "Civil Disobedience" (1849) and Walden *(1854), Henry David Thoreau (1817–1862) was born in Concord, Massachusetts. After his graduation from Harvard, he worked intermittently as a teacher, a handyman, and an assistant to Ralph Waldo Emerson. Thoreau held no full-time job and never married; he was, above all, an observer of nature and a prolific writer of books, essays, poems, and journal entries—his journals alone fill twenty volumes.*

The selection below is taken from Walden, *Thoreau's account of his two years' residence in a cabin by the shores of Walden Pond in Concord. Some readers have said that in "The Battle of the Ants" Thoreau is emphasizing, with keen attention to detail, a vivid scene of conflict and struggle in the natural world. Others, taking note of his references to classical myth and American and European history, have proposed that Thoreau's focus is less on nature than on the horrors of war, government, and imperialism.*

The Battle of the Ants[1]

One day when I went out to my wood-pile, or rather my pile of stumps, I observed two large ants, the one red, the other much larger, nearly half an inch long, and black, fiercely contending with one another. Having once got hold they never let go, but struggled and wrestled and rolled on the chips incessantly. Looking farther, I was surprised to find that the chips were covered with such combatants, that it was not a *duellum,* but a *bellum,*[2] a war between two races of ants, the red always pitted against the black, and frequently two red ones to one black. The legions of these Myrmidons[3] covered all the hills and vales in my wood-yard, and the ground was already strewn with the dead and dying, both red and black. It was the only battle which I have ever witnessed, the only battle-field I ever trod while the battle was raging; internecine war; the red republicans on the one hand, and the black imperialists on the other. On every side they were engaged in deadly combat, yet without any noise that I could hear, and human soldiers never fought so resolutely. I watched a couple that were fast locked in each other's embraces, in a little sunny valley amid the chips, now at noonday prepared to fight till the sun went down, or life went out. The smaller red champion had fastened himself like a vice to his adversary's front, and through all the tumblings on that field never for an instant ceased to gnaw at one of his feelers near the root, having already caused the other to go by the board; while the stronger black one dashed him from side to side, and, as I saw on looking nearer, had already divested him of several of his members. They fought with more pertinacity than bulldogs. Neither manifested the least disposition to retreat. It was evident that their battle-cry was "Conquer or die." In the meanwhile there came along a single red ant on the hillside of this valley, evidently full of excitement, who either had despatched his foe, or had not yet taken part in the battle; probably the latter, for he had lost none of his limbs; whose mother had charged him to return with his shield or upon it. Or perchance

[1]All notes are by the editors. [2]**duellum . . . bellum** Latin words for, respectively, a combat of two persons and a war. [3]**Myrmidons** Zeus is said to have created the Myrmidons, legendary warriors in Homer's *Iliad,* out of ants.

he was some Achilles, who had nourished his wrath apart, and had now come to avenge or rescue his Patroclus.[4] He saw this unequal combat from afar—for the blacks were nearly twice the size of the red—he drew near with rapid pace till he stood on his guard within half an inch of the combatants; then, watching his opportunity, he sprang upon the black warrior, and commenced his operations near the root of his right fore leg, leaving the foe to select among his own members; and so there were three united for life, as if a new kind of attraction had been invented which put all other locks and cements to shame. I should not have wondered by this time to find that they had their respective musical bands stationed on some eminent chip, and playing their national airs the while, to excite the slow and cheer the dying combatants. I was myself excited somewhat even as if they had been men. The more you think of it, the less the difference. And certainly there is not the fight recorded in Concord history, at least, if in the history of America, that will bear a moment's comparison with this, whether for the numbers engaged in it, or for the patriotism and heroism displayed. For numbers and for carnage it was an Austerlitz or Dresden.[5] Concord Fight! Two killed on the patriots' side, and Luther Blanchard wounded! Why here every ant was a Buttrick—"Fire! for God's sake fire!"—and thousands shared the fate of Davis and Hosmer. There was not one hireling there. I have no doubt that it was a principle they fought for, as much as our ancestors, and not to avoid a three-penny tax on their tea; and the results of this battle will be as important and memorable to those whom it concerns as those of the battle of Bunker Hill, at least.

I took up the chip on which the three I have particularly described were struggling, carried it into my house, and placed it under a tumbler on my window-sill, in order to see the issue. Holding a microscope to the first-mentioned red ant, I saw that, though he was assiduously gnawing at the near fore leg of his enemy, having severed his remaining feeler, his own breast was all torn away, exposing what vitals he had there to the jaws of the black warrior, whose breastplate was apparently too thick for him to pierce; and the dark carbuncles of the sufferer's eyes shone with ferocity such as war only could excite. They struggled half an hour longer under the tumbler, and when I looked again the black soldier had severed the heads of his foes from their bodies, and the still living heads were hanging on either side of him like ghastly trophies at his saddle-bow, still apparently as firmly fastened as ever, and he was endeavoring with feeble struggles, being without feelers, and with only the remnant of a leg, and I know not how many other wounds, to divest himself of them, which at length, after half an hour more, he accomplished. I raised the glass, and he went off over the window-sill in that crippled state. Whether he finally survived that combat, and spent the remainder of his days in some Hôtel des Invalides[6], I do not know; but I thought that his industry would not be worth much thereafter. I never learned which party was victorious, nor the cause of the war, but I felt for the rest of that day as if I had my feelings excited and harrowed by witnessing the struggle, the ferocity and carnage, of a human battle before my door.

Kirby and Spence tell us that the battles of ants have long been celebrated and the date of them recorded, though they say that Huber[7] is the only modern author

[4]**Patroclus** In the *Iliad*, Achilles avenges the death of his friend Patroclus. [5]**Austerlitz or Dresden** battles during the Napoleonic wars, 1803–1815. [6]**Hôtel des Invalides** the complex of buildings in Paris that includes the burial place of Napoleon Bonaparte. [7]**Kirby and Spence . . . Huber** Kirby and Spence were nineteenth-century American entomologists; Huber was a Swiss entomologist.

who appears to have witnessed them. "Aeneas Sylvius," say they, "after giving a very circumstantial account of one contested with great obstinacy by a great and small species on the trunk of a pear tree," adds that "'this action was fought in the pontificate of Eugenius the Fourth, in the presence of Nicholas Pistoriensis, an eminent lawyer, who related the whole history of the battle with the greatest fidelity.' A similar engagement between great and small ants is recorded by Olaus Magnus, in which the small ones, being victorious, are said to have buried the bodies of their own soldiers, but left those of their giant enemies a prey to the birds. This event happened previous to the expulsion of the tyrant Christiern [*sic*] the Second from Sweden." The battle which I witnessed took place in the Presidency of Polk, five years before the passage of Webster's Fugitive-Slave Bill.

[1854]

Joining the Conversation: Critical Thinking and Writing

1. The final sentence refers to Daniel Webster's Fugitive-Slave Bill. What is the relevance of this sentence to Thoreau's essay?
2. We trust you will agree that the essay has a point, that it is not mere description. Are the metaphors of war serious or playful, or both? Do they glorify ants? Trivialize human beings? Or what? What is Thoreau's attitude toward his material—that is, toward ants, human beings, and war? In a paragraph or two, describe Thoreau's persona here—his voice, his presentation of himself. Support your characterization with concrete references to the essay. (On persona, see page 340.) To what degree does Thoreau express his feelings directly? In what ways does he express them indirectly? Support your thesis with evidence.
3. Thoreau says, "I have no doubt that it was a principle they fought for." Does this statement make sense? Can we learn anything about human life—about how we ought to behave—by observing ants?
4. In a paragraph, set forth your interpretation of Thoreau's essay. You may want to consider if the essay has a point, or if it is mere description.
5. In 500–750 words describe some aspect of animal behavior that you have witnessed—for instance, a family of skunks feeding, or a fly buzzing in a windowpane—in such a way that you give an accurate report and at the same time suggest a larger world of nature or of society.

BILL MCKIBBEN

Bill McKibben, born in California in 1960 and educated at Harvard, became a staff writer for the New Yorker, *and then became a freelance writer, publishing in numerous magazines including the* New York Review of Books, Rolling Stone, *and the* New Republic. *Among his many books are* The End of Nature *(1989),* The Age of Missing Information *(1992), and* A Year of Living Strenuously *(2000).*

Now or Never

When global warming first emerged as a potential crisis in the late '80s, one academic analyst called it "the public policy problem from hell." The years since have only proven him more astute—15 years into our understanding of climate change, we have yet to figure out how we're going to tackle it. And environmentalists are just as clueless as anyone else: Do we need to work on lifestyles or on lobbying, on politics or on photovoltaics? And is there a difference? How well we handle global warming will determine what kind of century we inhabit—and indeed what kind of planet we leave behind to everyone and everything that follows us down into geologic time. It is *the* environmental question, the one that cuts closest to home and also floats off most easily into the abstract. So far it has been the ultimate "can't get there from here" problem, but the time has come to draw a roadmap—one that may help us deal with the handful of other issues on the list of real, world-shattering problems.

The first thing to know about global warming is this: The science is sound. In 1988, when scientists first testified before Congress about the potential for rapid and destabilizing climate change, they were still describing a hypothesis. It went like this: Every time human beings burn coal, gas, oil, wood or any other carbon-based fuel, they emit large quantities of carbon dioxide. (A car emits its own weight in carbon annually if you drive it the average American distance.) This carbon dioxide accumulates in the atmosphere. It's not a normal pollutant—it doesn't poison you, or change the color of the sunset. But it does have one interesting property: Its molecular structure traps heat near the surface of the planet that would otherwise radiate back out to space. It acts like the panes of glass on a greenhouse.

The hypothesis was that we were putting enough carbon dioxide into the atmosphere to make a difference. The doubters said no—that the earth would compensate for any extra carbon by forming extra clouds and cooling the planet, or through some other feedback mechanism. And so, as scientists will, they went at it. For five years—lavishly funded by governments that wanted to fund research instead of making politically unpopular changes—scientists produced paper after paper. They studied glacial cores and tree rings and old pollen sediments in lake beds to understand past climates; they took temperature measurements on the surface and from space; they refined their computer models and ran them backward in time to see if they worked. By 1995 they had reached a conclusion. That year the Intergovernmental Panel on Climate Change (IPCC), a group of all the world's climatologists assembled under the auspices of the United Nations, announced that human beings were indeed heating up the planet.

The scientists kept up the pace of their research for the next five years, and in the past five months have published a series of massive updates to their findings. These results are uniformly grimmer than even five years before. They include:

- The prediction that humans will likely heat the planet 4 to 6 degrees Fahrenheit in this century, twice as much as earlier forecast, taking global temperatures to a level not seen in millions of years, and never before in human history.
- The worst-case possibility that we will raise the temperature by as much as 11 degrees Fahrenheit, a true science-fiction scenario that no one had seriously envisaged before.
- The near certainty that these temperature increases will lead to rises in sea level of at least a couple of feet.
- The well-documented fear that disease will spread quickly as vectors like mosquitoes expand their range to places that used to be too cool for their survival.

5 But it isn't just the scientists who are hard at work on this issue. For the past five years, it's almost as if the planet itself has been peer-reviewing their work. We've had the warmest years on record—including 1998, which was warmer than any year for which records exist. And those hot years have shown what even

small changes in temperature—barely a degree Fahrenheit averaged globally—can do to the earth's systems.

Consider hydrology, for instance. Warm air holds more water vapor than cold air, so there is an increase in evaporation in dry areas, and hence more drought—something that has been documented on every continent. Once that water is in the atmosphere, it's going to come down somewhere—and indeed we have seen the most dramatic flooding ever recorded in recent years. In 1998, 300 million humans, one in 20 of us, had to leave their homes for a week, a month, a year, forever because of rising waters.

Or look at the planet's cryosphere, its frozen places. Every alpine glacier is in retreat; the snows of Kilimanjaro will have vanished by 2015; and the Arctic ice cap is thinning fast—data collected by U.S. and Soviet nuclear submarines show that it is almost half gone compared with just four decades ago.

In other words, human beings are changing the planet more fundamentally in the course of a couple of decades than in all the time since we climbed down from the trees and began making clever use of our opposable thumbs. There's never been anything like this.

Yet to judge from the political response, this issue ranks well below, say, the estate tax as a cause for alarm and worry. In 1988, there was enough public outcry that George Bush the Elder promised to combat "the greenhouse effect with the White House effect." In 1992, Bill Clinton promised that Americans would emit no more carbon dioxide by 2000 than they had in 1990—and that his administration would do the work of starting to turn around our ocean liner of an economy, laying the foundation for the transition to a world of renewable energy.

10 That didn't happen, of course. Fixated on the economy, Clinton and Gore presided over a decade when Americans, who already emitted a quarter of the world's carbon dioxide, actually managed to increase their total output by 12 percent. Now we have a president who seems unsure whether global warming is real, and far more concerned with increasing power production than with worrying about trifles like the collapse of the globe's terrestrial systems. In November, the hope of global controls on carbon dioxide production essentially collapsed at an international conference in the Hague, when the United States refused to make even modest concessions on its use of fossil fuels, and the rest of the world finally walked away from the table in disgust.

In the face of all this, what is an environmentalist to do? The normal answer, when you're mounting a campaign, is to look for self-interest, to scare people by saying what will happen to us if we don't do something: all the birds will die, the canyon will disappear beneath a reservoir, we will choke to death on smog.

But in the case of global warming, those kind of answers don't exactly do the trick, at least in the time frame we're discussing. At this latitude, climate change will creep up on us. Severe storms have already grown more frequent and more damaging. The seasons are less steady in their progression. Some agriculture is less reliable. But face it: Our economy is so enormous that it handles those kinds of changes in stride. Economists who work on this stuff talk about how it will shave a percentage or two off GNP over the next few decades—not enough to notice in the kind of generalized economic boom they describe. And most of us live lives so divorced from the natural world that we hardly notice the changes anyway. Hotter? Turn up the air conditioning. Stormier? Well, an enormous percentage of Americans commute from remote-controlled garage to office parking garage—they may have gone the last year without getting good and wet in a rainstorm. By the time the magnitude of the change is truly in our faces, it well be too late to do much about it: There's such a lag time with carbon dioxide in the atmosphere that we need to be making the switch to solar and wind and hydrogen right about now. Yesterday, in fact.

So maybe we should think of global warming in a different way—as the great moral crisis of our moment, the equivalent in our time of the civil rights movement of the '60s.

Why a moral question? In the first place, because we've never figured out a more effective way to screw the marginalized and poor of this planet. Having taken their dignity, their resources and their freedom under a variety of other schemes, we now are taking the very physical stability on which they depend for the most bottom-line of existences.

Our economy can absorb these changes for a while, but for a moment consider Bangladesh. A river delta that houses 130 million souls in an area the size of Wisconsin, Bangladesh actually manages food self-sufficiency most years. But in 1998, the sea level in the Bay of Bengal was higher than normal, just the sort of thing we can expect to become more frequent and severe. The waters sweeping down the Ganges and the Brahmaputra from the Himalayas could not drain easily into the ocean—they backed up across the country, forcing most of its inhabitants to spend three months in thigh-deep water. The fall rice crop didn't get planted. We've seen this same kind of disaster in the last few years in Mozambique or Honduras or Venezuela or any of a dozen other wretched spots.

And a moral crisis, too, if you place any value on the rest of creation. Coral reef researchers indicate that these spectacularly intricate ecosystems are also spectacularly vulnerable—rising water temperatures will likely bleach them to extinction by mid-century. In the Arctic, polar bears are 20 percent scrawnier than they were a decade ago: As pack ice melts, so does the opportunity for hunting seals. All in all, this century seems poised to see extinctions at a rate not observed since the last big asteroid slammed into the planet. But this time the asteroid is us.

A moral question, finally, if you think we owe any debt to the future. No one ever has figured out a more thorough-going way to stripmine the present and degrade what comes after. Forget the seventh generation—we're talking 70th generation, and 700th. All the people that will ever be related to you. Ever. No generation yet to come will ever forget us—we are the ones present at the moment when the temperature starts to spike, and so far we have not reacted. If it had been done to us, we would loathe the generation that did it, precisely as we will one day be loathed.

But trying to make a moral campaign is no easy task. In most moral crises, there is a villain—some person or class or institution that must be overcome. Once they're identified, the battle can commence. But you can't really get angry at carbon dioxide, and the people responsible for its production are, well, us. So perhaps we need some symbols to get us started, some places to sharpen the debate and rally ourselves to action. There are plenty to choose from: our taste for ever bigger houses and the heating and cooling bills that come with them; our penchant for jumping on airplanes at the drop of a hat; and so on. But if you wanted one glaring example of our lack of balance, you could do worse than point the finger at sport utility vehicles.

SUVs are more than mere symbol. They are a major part of the problem—one reason we emit so much more carbon dioxide now than we did a decade ago is because our fleet of cars and trucks actually has gotten steadily less fuel efficient for the past 10 years. If you switched today from the average American car to a big SUV, and drove it for just one year, the difference in carbon dioxide that you produced would be the equivalent of opening your refrigerator door and then forgetting to close it for six years. SUVs essentially are machines for burning fossil fuel that just happen to also move you and your stuff around.

20 But what makes them such a perfect symbol is the brute fact that they are simply unnecessary. Go to the parking lot of the nearest suburban supermarket and look around: the only conclusion you can draw is that to reach the grocery, people must drive through three or four raging rivers and up the side of a trackless canyon. These are semi-military machines (some, like the Hummer, are not semi at all), Brinks trucks on a slight diet. They don't keep their occupants safer, they do wreck whatever they plow into—they are the perfect metaphor for a heedless, supersized society. And a gullible one, which has been sold on these vast vehicles partly by the promise that they somehow allow us to commune with nature.

That's why we need a much broader politics than the White House–lobbying that's occupied the big enviros for the past decade, or the mass-market mailing that has been their stock in trade for the past quarter century. We need to take all the brilliant and energetic strategies of local grassroots groups fighting dumps and cleaning up rivers, and we need to make those tactics national and international. So that's why some pastors are starting to talk with their congregations about what car they're going to buy, and why some college seniors are passing around petitions pledging to stay away from the Ford Explorers and Excursions and Extraneouses, and why some few auto dealers have begun to notice informational picketers outside on Saturday mornings urging their customers to think about gas mileage when they go inside.

The point is not that by themselves such actions—any individual actions—will make any real dent in the production of carbon dioxide pouring into our atmosphere. Even if you got 10 percent of Americans really committed to changing energy use, their solar homes wouldn't make much of a dent in our national totals. But 10 percent would be enough to change the politics of the issue, to insure the passage of the laws that would cause us all to shift our habits. And so we need to begin to take an issue that is now the province of technicians and turn it into a political issue—just as bus boycotts began to take the issue of race and make it public, forcing the system to respond. That response is likely to be ugly—there are huge companies with a lot to lose, and many people so tied in to their current ways of life that advocating change smacks of subversion. But this has to become a political issue—and fast. The only way that may happen, short of a hideous drought or monster flood, is if it becomes a personal issue first.

[2001]

Joining the Conversation: Critical Thinking and Writing

1. McKibben argues that global warming constitutes "a moral crisis" (paragraph 13). What reasons does he offer?
2. In paragraphs 19–20 McKibben talks about SUVs, saying that "they are simply unnecessary." Do you agree? If you don't, explain why. And if you do agree, explain why SUVs are popular.

3. What *persona* does McKibben convey in this essay? (On *persona,* see pages 340–42.) Thoughtful? Belligerent? Hysterical? Concerned but eccentric? Support your answer with evidence.
4. McKibben often varies the length of his sentences, sometimes perhaps surprisingly. For instance, in the first paragraph the first sentence contains 24 words, the second 29 words, the third 24, but the fourth—a question—contains only 5 words. What effect does he gain? Take another passage in his essay where there is a sharp contrast, and explain the effect.
5. Now that you have read McKibben's essay, and thought further about it, do you plan to change your behavior in any way? Explain.

STORIES

AESOP

In ancient Greece and Rome many fables were attributed to Aesop, said to have been a Greek slave who lived in the sixth century B.C.E. *We gave one fable, "The City Mouse and the Country Mouse," in Chapter 4. Here are two additional ones. In the first of these two, English versions speak of a grasshopper but in Greek the insect is a cicada.*

The Ant and the Grasshopper

One cold winter day an ant was dragging out a grain which he had buried during the winter. A hungry grasshopper asked for a bit of the grain.

"What did you do all summer?" asked the ant.

"I was busy all summer long, singing," replied the grasshopper.

"Well," said the ant, "since you sang all summer, now dance all winter."

The Moral: Negligence leads to hardship.

Joining the Conversation: Critical Thinking and Writing

1. Let's rewrite the ant's final remark, thus: "Well, since you spent the whole summer singing, I guess you'll dance now in the winter." We assume you agree that the original version is more effective. Exactly what makes the original better?
2. Do you think we can draw lessons from nature about how we should behave? Is a significant part of the argument (so to speak) of an Aesop fable that it is "natural," that it shows us "nature's way"? Think of some other fables that draw upon the nonhuman world, such as "The City Mouse and the Country Mouse" (page 94) and "The Fox and the Grapes." (The gist of "The Fox and the Grapes" is this: "A starving fox, seeing bunches of grapes hanging from a vine, but out of reach, went away saying, "Those grapes aren't ripe, they're sour.") What do such fables gain by being set in the nonhuman world? Why not just say, "A starving man, seeing bunches of grapes that were out of reach . . ."? Again, what, if anything, is gained by using talking animals? Is the moral enforced by nature?

The North Wind and the Sun

The North Wind and the Sun once got into an argument about which of the two was the most powerful. They agreed that whichever could make a certain traveler take off his overcoat would be declared the winner.

The North Wind was the first to try: He blew as hard as he could, but the harder he blew, the more the traveler buttoned up his coat and held it close to his body by folding his arms across his chest. The wind blew and blew, but finally he was out of breath.

Then it was the Sun's turn. The Sun smiled, sending beams of light that drove away the fog and the mist. He smiled a bit more, and the man unbuttoned his coat and after a little while, feeling pleasantly warm, took off the coat.

The North Wind agreed that the Sun was the winner.

The Moral: Gentleness is more persuasive than violence.

Joining the Conversation: Critical Thinking and Writing

1. Do you think the moral can reasonably be drawn from the story? Do you think the moral is true?

2. Do you think nature can teach us anything about moral behavior? If so, what sorts of things? Be as specific as possible. You may want to cite concrete instances. If you think it cannot teach us anything about morality, explain why you hold this view.

JACK LONDON

Jack London (1876–1916) was born in San Francisco and educated in Oakland High School and the University of California, Berkeley, but his formal education was intermittent. At thirteen or fourteen he was a pirate raiding oyster beds in San Francisco Bay; a little later he worked in a cannery, and at seventeen he joined a sealing expedition to Japan and Siberia. Back in the United States he worked at odd jobs, became a socialist, finished high school in 1895, spent one semester at the University of California, and then was off to the Klondike (age twenty-one) looking—unsuccessfully, it turned out—for gold. He published his first story in 1899, his first collection of stories (The Son of the Wolf) *in 1900, and his first novel* (The Call of the Wild) *in 1903. The novel was an immediate hit. London continued to write, both fiction and journalism, earning over a million dollars from his writing—at that time an astounding amount, and especially for a writer.*

To Build a Fire

Day had broken cold and gray, exceedingly cold and gray, when the man turned aside from the main Yukon trail and climbed the high earth-bank, where a dim and little-travelled trail led eastward through the fat spruce timberland. It was a steep bank, and he paused for breath at the top, excusing the act to himself by looking at his watch. It was nine o'clock. There was no sun nor hint of sun, though there was not a cloud in the sky. It was a clear day, and yet there seemed an intangible pall over the face of things, a subtle gloom that made the day dark, and that was due to the absence of sun. This fact did not worry the man. He was used to the lack of sun. It had been days since he had seen the sun, and he knew that a few more days must pass before that cheerful orb, due south, should just peep above the sky line and dip immediately from view.

The man flung a look back along the way he had come. The Yukon[1] lay a mile wide and hidden under three feet of ice. On top of this ice were as many feet of snow. It was all pure white, rolling in gentle undulations where the ice jams of the freeze-up had formed. North and south, as far as his eye could see, it was unbroken white, save for a dark hairline that curved and twisted from around the spruce-covered island to the south, and that curved and twisted away into the north, where it disappeared behind another spruce-covered island. This dark hairline was the trail—the main trail—that led south five hundred miles to the Chilcoot Pass, Dyea, and salt water; and that led north seventy miles to Dawson, and still on to the north a thousand miles to Nulato, and finally to St. Michael, on Bering Sea, a thousand miles and a half a thousand more.

Bull all this—the mysterious, fair-reaching hairline trail, the absence of sun from the sky, the tremendous cold, and the strangeness and weirdness of it all—made no impression on the man. It was not because he was long used to it. He was a newcomer in the land, a *chechaquo,* and this was his first winter. The trouble with him was that he was without imagination. He was quick and alert in the things of life, but only in the things, and not in the significances. Fifty degrees below zero meant eighty-odd degrees of frost. Such fact impressed him as being cold and uncomfortable, and that was all. It did not lead him to meditate upon his frailty as a creature of temperature, and upon man's frailty in general, able only to live within certain narrow limits of heat and cold; and from there on it did not lead him to the conjectural field of immortality and man's place in the universe. Fifty degrees below zero stood for a bite of frost that hurt and that must be guarded against by the use of mittens, ear flaps, warm moccasins, and thick socks. Fifty degrees below zero was to him just precisely fifty degrees below zero. That there should be anything more to it than that was a thought that never entered his head.

As he turned to go on, he spat speculatively. There was a sharp, explosive crackle that startled him. He spat again. And again, in the air, before it could fall to the snow, the spittle crackled. He knew that at fifty below spittle crackled on the snow, but this spittle had crackled in the air. Undoubtedly it was colder than fifty below—how much colder he did not know. But the temperature did not matter. He was bound for the old claim on the left fork of Henderson Creek, where the boys were already. They had come over across the divide from the Indian Creek country, while he had come the roundabout way to take a look at the possibilities of getting out logs in the spring from the islands in the Yukon. He would be in to camp by six o'clock; a bit after dark, it was true, but the boys would be there, a fire would be going, and a hot supper would be ready. As for lunch, he pressed his hand against the protruding bundle under his jacket. It was also under his shirt, wrapped up in a handkerchief and lying against the naked skin. It was the only way to keep the biscuits from freezing. He smiled agreeably to himself as he thought of those biscuits, each cut open and sopped in bacon grease, and each enclosing a generous slice of fried bacon.

5 He plunged in among the big spruce trees. The trail was faint. A foot of snow had fallen since the last sled had passed over, and he was glad he was without a sled, traveling light. In fact, he carried nothing but the lunch wrapped in the handkerchief. He was surprised, however, at the cold. It certainly was cold, he

[1]**Yukon** a major river in Alaska and western Canada.

concluded, as he rubbed his numb nose and cheekbones with his mittened hand. He was a warm-whiskered man, but the hair on his face did not protect the high cheekbones and the eager nose that thrust itself aggressively into the frosty air.

At the man's heels trotted a dog, a big native husky, the proper wolf dog, gray-coated and without any visible or temperamental difference from its brother, the wild wolf. The animal was depressed by the tremendous cold. It knew that it was not time for traveling. Its instinct told it a truer tale than was told to the man by the man's judgment. In reality, it was not merely colder than fifty below zero; it was colder than sixty below, than seventy below. It was seventy-five below zero. Since the freezing point is thirty-two above zero, it meant that one hundred and seven degrees of frost obtained. The dog did not know anything about thermometers. Possibly in its brain there was no sharp consciousness of a condition of very cold such as was in the man's brain. But the brute had its instinct. It experienced a vague but menacing apprehension that subdued it and made it slink along at the man's heels, and that made it question eagerly every unwonted movement of the man as if expecting him to go into camp or to seek shelter somewhere and build a fire. The dog had learned fire, and it wanted fire, or else to burrow under the snow and cuddle its warmth away from the air.

The frozen moisture of its breathing had settled on its fur in a fine powder of frost, and especially were its jowls, muzzle, and eyelashes whitened by its crystalled breath. The man's red beard and mustache were likewise frosted, but more solidly, the deposit taking the form of ice and increasing with every warm, moist breath he exhaled. Also, the man was chewing tobacco, and the muzzle of ice held his lips so rigidly that he was unable to clear his chin when he expelled the juice. The result was that a crystal beard of the color and solidity of amber was increasing its length on his chin. If he fell down it would shatter itself, like glass, into brittle fragments. But he did not mind the appendage. It was the penalty all tobacco chewers paid in that country, and he had been out before in two cold snaps. They had not been so cold as this, he knew, but by the spirit thermometer at Sixty Mile he knew they had been registered at fifty below and at fifty-five.

He held on through the level stretch of woods for several miles, crossed a wide flat of nigger heads, and dropped down a bank to the frozen bed of a small stream. This was Henderson Creek, and he knew he was ten miles from the forks. He looked at his watch. It was ten o'clock. He was making four miles an hour, and he calculated that he would arrive at the forks at half-past twelve. He decided to celebrate that event by eating his lunch there.

The dog dropped in again at his heels, with a tail drooping discouragement, as the man swung along the creek bed. The furrow of the old sled trail was plainly visible, but a dozen inches of snow covered the marks of the last runners. In a month no man had come up or down that silent creek. The man held steadily on. He was not much given to thinking, and just then particularly he had nothing to think about save that he would eat lunch at the forks and that at six o'clock he would be in camp with the boys. There was nobody to talk to; and, had there been, speech would have been impossible because of the ice muzzle on his mouth. So he continued monotonously to chew tobacco and to increase the length of his amber beard.

10 Once in a while the thought reiterated itself that it was very cold and that he had never experienced such cold. As he walked along he rubbed his cheekbones and nose with the back of his mittened hand. He did this automatically, now and again changing hands. But, rub as he would, the instant he stopped his cheekbones went numb, and the following instant the end of his nose went numb. He was sure to frost his cheeks; he knew that, and experienced a pang of regret that

he had not devised a nose strap of the sort Bud wore in cold snaps. Such a strap passed across the cheeks, as well, and saved them. But it didn't matter much, after all. What were frosted cheeks? A bit painful, that was all; they were never serious.

Empty as the man's mind was of thoughts, he was keenly observant, and he noticed the changes in the creek, the curves and bends and timber jams, and always he sharply noted where he placed his feet. Once, coming around a bend, he shied abruptly, like a startled horse, curved away from the place where he had been walking, and retreated several paces back along the trail. The creek he knew was frozen clear to the bottom—no creek could contain water in that arctic winter—but he knew also that there were springs that bubbled out from the hillsides and ran along under the snow and on top the ice of the creek. He knew that the coldest snaps never froze these springs, and he knew likewise their danger. They were traps. They hid pools of water under the snow that might be three inches deep, or three feet. Sometimes a skin of ice half an inch thick covered them, and in turn was covered by the snow. Sometimes there were alternate layers of water and ice skin, so that when one broke through he kept on breaking through for a while, sometimes wetting himself to the waist.

That was why he had shied in such panic. He had felt the give under his feet and heard the crackle of a snow-hidden ice skin. And to get his feet wet in such a temperature meant trouble and danger. At the very least it meant delay, for he would be forced to stop and build a fire, and under its protection to bare his feet while he dried his socks and moccasins. He stood and studied the creek bed and its banks, and decided that the flow of water came from the right. He reflected awhile, rubbing his nose and cheeks, then skirted to the left, stepping gingerly and testing the footing for each step. Once clear of the danger, he took a fresh chew of tobacco and swung along at his four-mile gait.

In the course of the next two hours he came upon several similar traps. Usually the snow above the hidden pools had a sunken, candied appearance that advertised the danger. Once again, however, he had a close call; and once, suspecting danger, he compelled the dog to go on in front. The dog did not want to go. It hung back until the man shoved it forward, and then it went quickly across the white, unbroken surface. Suddenly it broke through, floundered to one side, and got away to firmer footing. It had wet its forefeet and legs, and almost immediately the water that clung to it turned to ice. It made quick efforts to lick the ice off its legs, then dropped down in the snow and began to bite out the ice that had formed between the toes. This was a matter of instinct. To permit the ice to remain would mean sore feet. It did not know this. It merely obeyed the mysterious prompting that arose from the deep crypts of its being. But the man knew, having achieved a judgment on the subject, and he removed the mitten from his right hand and helped tear out the ice particles. He did not expose his fingers more than a minute, and was astonished at the swift numbness that smote them. It certainly was cold. He pulled on the mitten hastily, and beat the hand savagely across his chest.

At twelve o'clock the day was at its brightest. Yet the sun was too far south on its winter journey to clear the horizon. The bulge of the earth intervened between it and Henderson Creek, where the man walked under a clear sky at noon and cast no shadow. At half-past twelve, to the minute, he arrived at the forks of the creek. He was pleased at the speed he had made. If he kept it up, he would certainly be with the boys by six. He unbuttoned his jacket and shirt and drew forth his lunch. The action consumed no more than a quarter of a minute, yet in that brief moment the numbness laid hold of the exposed fingers. He did not put the mitten on, but, instead, struck the fingers a dozen sharp smashes against his leg.

Then he sat down on a snow-covered log to eat. The sting that followed upon the striking of his fingers against his leg ceased so quickly that he was startled. He had had no chance to take a bite of biscuit. He struck the fingers repeatedly and returned them to the mitten, baring the other hand for the purpose of eating. He tried to take a mouthful, but the ice muzzle prevented. He had forgotten to build a fire and thaw out. He chuckled at his foolishness, and as he chuckled he noted the numbness creeping into the exposed fingers. Also, he noted that the stinging which had first come to his toes when he sat down was already passing away. He wondered whether the toes were warm or numb. He moved them inside the moccasins and decided that they were numb.

He pulled the mitten on hurriedly and stood up. He was a bit frightened. He stamped up and down until the stinging returned into the feet. It certainly was cold, was his thought. That man from Sulphur Creek had spoken the truth when telling how cold it sometimes got in the country. And he had laughed at him at the time! That showed one must not be too sure of things. There was no mistake about it, it *was* cold. He strode up and down, stamping his feet and threshing his arms, until reassured by the returning warmth. Then he got out matches and proceeded to make a fire. From the undergrowth, where high water of the previous spring had lodged a supply of seasoned twigs, he got his firewood. Working carefully from a small beginning, he soon had a roaring fire, over which he thawed the ice from his face and in the protection of which he ate his biscuits. For the moment the cold of space was outwitted. The dog took satisfaction in the fire, stretching out close enough for warmth and far enough away to escape being singed.

When the man had finished, he filled his pipe and took his comfortable time over a smoke. Then he pulled on his mittens, settled the ear flaps of his cap firmly about his ears, and took the creek trail up the left fork. The dog was disappointed and yearned back toward the fire. This man did not know cold. Possibly all the generations of his ancestry had been ignorant of cold, of real cold, of cold one hundred and seven degrees below freezing point. But the dog knew; all its ancestry knew, and it had inherited the knowledge. And it knew that it was not good to walk abroad in such fearful cold. It was the time to lie snug in a hole in the snow and wait for a curtain of cloud to be drawn across the face of outer space whence this cold came. On the other hand, there was no keen intimacy between the dog and the man. The one was the toil slave of the other, and the only caresses it had ever received were the caresses of the whip lash and of harsh and menacing throat sounds that threatened the whip lash. So the dog made no effort to communicate its apprehension to the man. It was not concerned in the welfare of the man; it was for its own sake that it yearned back toward the fire. But the man whistled, and spoke to it with the sound of whip lashes, and the dog swung in at the man's heels and followed after.

The man took a chew of tobacco and proceeded to start a new amber beard. Also, his moist breath quickly powdered with white his mustache, eyebrows, and lashes. There did not seem to be so many springs on the left fork of the Henderson, and for half an hour the man saw no signs of any. And then it happened. At a place where there were no signs, where the soft, unbroken snow seemed to advertise solidity beneath, the man broke through. It was not deep. He wet himself halfway to the knees before he floundered out to the firm crust.

He was angry, and cursed his luck aloud. He had hoped to get into camp with the boys at six o'clock, and this would delay him an hour, for he would have to build a fire and dry out his footgear. This was imperative at that low temperature—he knew that much; and he turned aside to the bank, which he climbed. On top, tangled in the underbrush about the trunks of several small spruce trees, was a highwater deposit of dry firewood—sticks and twigs, principally, but also larger portions of seasoned branches and fine dry last year's grasses. He threw down several large pieces on top of the snow. This served for a foundation and prevented the young flame from drowning itself in the snow it otherwise would melt. The flame he got by touching a match to a small shred of birch bark that he took from his pocket. This burned even more readily than paper. Placing it on the foundation, he fed the young flame with wisps of dry grass and with the tiniest dry twigs.

He worked slowly and carefully, keenly aware of his danger. Gradually, as the flame grew stronger, he increased the size of the twigs with which he fed it. He squatted in the snow, pulling the twigs out from their entanglement in the brush and feeding directly to the flame. He knew there must be no failure. When it is seventy-five below zero, a man must not fail in his first attempt to build a fire—that is, if his feet are wet. If his feet are dry, and he fails, he can run along the trail for half a mile and restore his circulation. But the circulation of wet and freezing feet cannot be restored by running when it is seventy-five below. No matter how fast he runs, the wet feet will freeze the harder.

All this the man knew. The old-timer on Sulphur Creek had told him about it the previous fall, and now he was appreciating the advice. Already all sensation had gone out of his feet. To build the fire he had been forced to remove his mittens, and the fingers had quickly gone numb. His pace of four miles an hour had kept his heart pumping blood to the surface of his body and to all the extremities. But the instant he stopped, the action of the pump eased down. The cold of space smote the unprotected tip of the planet, and he, being on that unprotected tip, received the full force of the blow. The blood of his body recoiled before it. The blood was alive, like the dog, and like the dog it wanted to hide away and cover itself up from the fearful cold. So long as he walked four miles an hour, he pumped that blood, willy-nilly, to the surface; but now it ebbed away and sank down into the recesses of his body. The extremities were the first to feel its absence. His wet feet froze the faster, and his exposed fingers numbed the faster, though they had not yet begun to freeze. Nose and cheeks were already freezing, while the skin of all his body chilled as it lost its blood.

But he was safe. Toes and nose and cheeks would be only touched by the frost, for the fire was beginning to burn with strength. He was feeding it with twigs the size of his finger. In another minute he would be able to feed it with branches the size of his wrist, and then he could remove his wet footgear, and, while it dried, he could keep his naked feet warm by the fire, rubbing them at first, of course, with snow. The fire was a success. He was safe. He remembered the advice of the old-timer on Sulphur Creek, and smiled. The old-timer had been very serious in laying down the law that no man must travel alone in the Klondike after fifty below. Well, here he was; he had had the accident; he was alone; and he had saved himself. Those old-timers were rather womanish, some of them, he thought. All a man had to do was to keep his head, and he was all right. Any man who was a man could travel alone. But it was surprising, the rapidity with which his cheeks and nose were freezing. And he had not thought his fingers could go lifeless in so short a time. Lifeless they were, for he could scarcely make them move together to grip a twig, and they seemed remote from his body and from him. When he touched a twig, he had to look and see whether or not he had hold of it. The wires were pretty well down between him and his finger ends.

All of which counted for little. There was the fire, snapping and crackling and promising life with every dancing flame. He started to untie his moccasins. They were coated with ice; the thick German socks were like sheaths of iron halfway to the knees; and the moccasin strings were like rods of steel all twisted and knotted as by some conflagration. For a moment he tugged with his numb fingers, then, realizing the folly of it, he drew his sheath knife.

But before he could cut the strings, it happened. It was his own fault or, rather, his mistake. He should not have built the fire under the spruce tree. He should have built it in the open. But it had been easier to pull the twigs from the brush and drop them directly on the fire. Now the tree under which he had done this carried a weight of snow on its boughs. No wind had blown for weeks, and each bough was fully freighted. Each time he had pulled a twig he had communicated a slight agitation to the tree—an imperceptible agitation, so far as he was concerned, but an agitation sufficient to bring about the disaster. High up in the tree one bough capsized its load of snow. This fell on the boughs beneath, capsizing them. This process continued, spreading out and involving the whole tree. It grew like an avalanche, and it descended without warning upon the man and the fire, and the fire was blotted out! Where it had burned was a mantle of fresh and disordered snow.

The man was shocked. It was as though he had just heard his own sentence of death. For a moment he sat and stared at the spot where the fire had been. Then he grew very calm. Perhaps the old-timer on Sulphur Creek was right. If he had only had a trail mate he would have been in no danger now. The trail mate could have built the fire. Well, it was up to him to build the fire over again, and this second time there must be no failure. Even if he succeeded, he would most likely lose some toes. His feet must be badly frozen by now, and there would be some time before the second fire was ready.

Such were his thoughts, but he did not sit and think them. He was busy all the time they were passing through his mind. He made a new foundation for a fire, this time in the open, where no treacherous tree could blot it out. Next he gathered dry grasses and tiny twigs from the high-water flotsam. He could not bring his fingers together to pull them out, but he was able to gather them by the handful. In this way he got many rotten twigs and bits of green moss that were undesirable, but it was the best he could do. He worked methodically, even collecting an armful of the larger branches to be used later when the fire gathered strength. And all the while the dog sat and watched him, a certain yearning wistfulness in its eyes, for it looked upon him as the fire provider, and the fire was slow in coming.

When all was ready, the man reached in his pocket for a second piece of birch bark. He knew the bark was there, and, though he could not feel it with his fingers, he could hear its crisp rustling as he fumbled for it. Try as he would, he could not clutch hold of it. And all the time, in his consciousness, was the knowledge that each instant his feet were freezing. This thought tended to put him in a panic, but he fought against it and kept calm. He pulled on his mittens with his teeth, and threshed his arms back and forth, beating his hands with all his might against his sides. He did this sitting down, and he stood up to do it; and all the while the dog sat in the snow, its wolf brush of a tail curled around warmly over its forefeet, its sharp wolf ears pricked forward intently as it watched the man. And the man, as he beat and threshed with his arms and hands, felt a great surge of envy as he regarded the creature that was warm and secure in its natural covering.

After a time he was aware of the first faraway signals of sensation in his beaten fingers. The faint tingling grew stronger till it evolved into a stinging ache that was excruciating, but which the man hailed with satisfaction. He stripped the mitten from his right hand and fetched forth the birch bark. The exposed fingers were quickly going numb again. Next he brought out his bunch of sulphur matches. But the tremendous cold had already driven the life out of his fingers. In his effort to separate one match from the others, the whole bunch fell in the snow. He tried to pick it out of the snow, but failed. The dead fingers could neither touch nor clutch. He was very careful. He drove the thought of his freezing feet, and nose, and cheeks, out of his mind, devoting his whole soul to the matches. He watched, using the sense of vision in place of that of touch, and when he saw his fingers on each side the bunch, he closed them—that is he willed to close them, for the wires were down, and the fingers did not obey. He pulled the mitten on the right hand, and beat it fiercely against his knee. Then, with both mittened hands, he scooped the bunch of matches, along with much snow, into his lap. Yet he was no better off.

After some manipulation he managed to get the bunch between the heels of his mittened hands. In this fashion he carried it to his mouth. The ice crackled and snapped when by a violent effort he opened his mouth. He drew the lower jaw in, curled the upper lip out of the way, scraped the bunch with his upper teeth in order to separate a match. He succeeded in getting one, which he dropped on his lap. He was no better off. He could not pick it up. Then he devised a way. He picked it up in his teeth and scratched it on his leg. Twenty times he scratched before he succeeded in lighting it. As it flamed he held it with his teeth to the birch bark. But the burning brimstone went up his nostrils and into his lungs, causing him to cough spasmodically. The match fell into the snow and went out.

The old-timer on Sulphur Creek was right, he thought in the moment of controlled despair that ensued: after fifty below, a man should travel with a partner. He beat his hands, but failed in exciting any sensation. Suddenly he bared both hands, removing the mittens with his teeth. He caught the whole bunch between the heels of his hands. His arm muscles not being frozen enabled him to press the hand heels tightly against the matches. Then he scratched the bunch along his leg. It flared into flame, seventy sulphur matches at once! There was no wind to blow them out. He kept his head to one side to escape the strangling fumes, and held the blazing bunch to the birch bark. As he so held it, he became aware of sensation in his hand. His flesh was burning. He could smell it. Deep down below the surface he could feel it. The sensation developed into pain that grew acute. And still he endured it, holding the flame of the matches clumsily to the bark that would not light readily because his own burning hands were in the way, absorbing most of the flame.

At last, when he could endure no more, he jerked his hands apart. The blazing matches fell sizzling into the snow, but the birch bark was alight. He began laying dry grasses and the tiniest twigs on the flame. He could not pick and choose, for he had to lift the fuel between the heels of his hands. Small pieces of rotten wood and green moss clung to the twigs, and he bit them off as well as he could with his teeth. He cherished the flame carefully and awkwardly. It meant life, and it must not perish. The withdrawal of blood from the surface of his body now made him begin to shiver, and he grew more awkward. A large piece of green moss fell squarely on the little fire. He tried to poke it out with his fingers, but his shivering frame made him poke too far, and he disrupted the nucleus of the little fire, the burning grasses and tiny twigs separating and scattering. He tried to poke them together again, but in spite of the tenseness of the effort, his shivering got away with him, and the twigs were hopelessly scattered. Each twig gushed a puff of smoke and went out. The fire provider had failed. As he looked apathetically about him, his eyes chanced on the dog, sitting across the ruins of the fire from him, in the snow, making restless, hunching, movements, slightly lifting one forefoot and then the other, shifting its weight back and forth on them with wistful eagerness.

The sight of the dog put a wild idea into his head. He remembered the tale of the man, caught in a blizzard, who killed a steer and crawled inside the carcass, and so was saved. He would kill the dog and bury his hands in the warm body until the numbness went out of them. Then he could build another fire. He spoke to the dog, calling it to him; but in his voice was a strange note of fear that frightened the animal, who had never known the man to speak in such way before. Something was the matter, and its suspicious nature sensed danger—it knew not what danger, but somewhere, somehow, in its brain arose an apprehension of the man. It flattened its ears down at the sound of the man's voice, and its restless, hunching movements and the liftings and shiftings of its forefeet became more pronounced; but it would not come to the man. He got on his hands and knees and crawled toward the dog. This unusual posture again excited suspicion, and the animal sidled mincingly away.

The man sat up in the snow for a moment and struggled for calmness. Then he pulled on his mittens, by means of his teeth, and got upon his feet. He glanced down at first in order to assure himself that he was really standing up, for the absence of sensation in his feet left him unrelated to the earth. His erect position in itself started to drive the webs of suspicion from the dog's mind; and when he spoke peremptorily, with the sound of whip lashes in his voice, the dog rendered its customary allegiance and came to him. As it came within reaching distance the man lost his control. His arms flashed out to the dog, and he experienced genuine surprise when he discovered that his hands could not clutch, that there was neither bend nor feeling in the fingers. He had forgotten for the moment that they were frozen and that they were freezing more and more. All this happened quickly, and before the animal could get away, he encircled its body with his arms. He sat down in the snow, and in this fashion held the dog, while it snarled and whined and struggled.

But it was all he could do, hold its body encircled in his arms and sit there. He realized that he could not kill the dog. There was no way to do it. With his helpless hands he could neither draw nor hold his sheath knife nor throttle the animal. He released it, and it plunged wildly away, with tail between its legs, and still snarling. It halted forty feet away and surveyed him curiously, with ears sharply pricked forward.

The man looked down at his hands in order to locate them, and found them hanging on the ends of his arms. It struck him as curious that one should have to use his eyes in order to find out where his hands were. He began threshing his arms back and forth, beating the mittened hands against his sides. He did this for five minutes, violently, and his heart pumped enough blood up to the surface to put a stop to his shivering. But no sensation was aroused in the hands. He had an impression that they hung like weights on the ends of his arms, but when he tried to run the impression down, he could not find it.

35 A certain fear of death, dull and oppressive, came to him. This fear quickly became poignant as he realized that it was no longer a mere matter of freezing his fingers and toes, or of losing his hands and feet, but that it was a matter of life and death with the chances against him. This threw him into a panic, and he turned and ran up the creek bed along the old, dim trail. The dog joined in behind and kept up with him. He ran blindly, without intention, in fear such as he had never known in his life. Slowly, as he plowed and floundered through the snow, he began to see things again—the banks of the creek, the old timber

jams, the leafless aspens, and the sky. The running made him feel better. He did not shiver. Maybe, if he ran on, his feet would thaw out; and, anyway, if he ran far enough, he would reach camp and the boys. Without doubt he would lose some fingers and toes and some of his face; but the boys would take care of him, and save the rest of him when he got there. And at the same time there was another thought in his mind that said he would never get to the camp and the boys; that it was too many miles away, that the freezing had too great a start on him, and that he would soon be stiff and dead. This thought he kept in the background and refused to consider. Sometimes it pushed itself forward and demanded to be heard, but he thrust it back and strove to think of other things.

It struck him as curious that he could run at all on feet so frozen that he could not feel them when they struck the earth and took the weight of his body. He seemed to himself to skim along above the surface, and to have no connection with the earth. Somewhere he had once seen a winged Mercury,[2] and he wondered if Mercury felt as he felt when skimming over the earth.

His theory of running until he reached camp and the boys had one flaw in it: he lacked the endurance. Several times he stumbled, and finally he tottered, crumpled up, and fell. When he tried to rise, he failed. He must sit and rest, he decided, and next time he would merely walk and keep on going. As he sat and regained his breath, he noted that he was feeling quite warm and comfortable. He was not shivering, and it even seemed that a warm glow had come to this chest and trunk. And yet, when he touched his nose or cheeks, there was no sensation. Running would not thaw them out. Nor would it thaw out his hands and feet. Then the thought came to him that the frozen portions of his body must be extending. He tried to keep this thought down, to forget it, to think of something else; he was aware of the panicky feeling that it caused, and he was afraid of the panic. But the thought asserted itself, and persisted, until it produced a vision of his body totally frozen. This was too much, and he made another wild run along the trail. Once he slowed down to a walk, but the thought of the freezing extending itself made him run again.

And all the time the dog ran with him, at his heels. When he fell down a second time, it curled its tail over its forefeet and sat in front of him, facing him, curiously eager and intent. The warmth and security of the animal angered him, and he cursed it till it flattened down its ears appeasingly. This time the shivering came more quickly upon the man. He was losing his battle with the frost. It was creeping into his body from all sides. The thought of it drove him on, but he ran no more than a hundred feet, when he staggered and pitched headlong. It was his last panic. When he had recovered his breath and control, he sat up and entertained in his mind the conception of meeting death with dignity. However, the conception did not come to him in such terms. His idea of it was that he had been making a fool of himself, running around like a chicken with its head cut off—such was the simile that occurred to him. Well, he was bound to freeze anyway, and he might as well take it decently. With this new-found peace of mind came the first glimmerings of drowsiness. A good idea, he thought, to sleep off to death. It was like taking an anesthetic. Freezing was not so bad as people thought. There were lots worse ways to die.

He pictured the boys finding his body next day. Suddenly he found himself with them, coming along the trail and looking for himself. And, still with them, he

[2]**winged Mercury** the winged messenger of Roman mythology.

came around a turn in the trail and found himself lying in the snow. He did not belong with himself any more, for even then he was out of himself, standing with the boys and looking at himself in the snow. It certainly was cold, was his thought. When he got back to the States he could tell the folks what real cold was. He drifted on from this to a vision of the old-timer on Sulphur Creek. He
40 could see him quite clearly, warm and comfortable, and smoking a pipe.

"You were right, old hoss; you were right," the man mumbled to the old-timer of Sulphur Creek.

Then the man drowsed off into what seemed to him the most comfortable and satisfying sleep he had ever known. The dog sat facing him and waiting. The brief day drew to a close in a long, slow twilight. There were no signs of a fire to be made, and, besides, never in the dog's experience had it known a man to sit like that in the snow and make no fire. As the twilight drew on, its eager yearning for the fire mastered it, and with a great lifting and shifting of forefeet, it whined softly, then flattened its ears down in anticipation of being chidden by the man. But the man remained silent. Later the dog whined loudly. And still later it crept close to the man and caught the scent of death. This made the animal bristle and back away. A little longer it delayed, howling under the stars that leaped and danced and shone brightly in the cold sky. Then it turned and trotted up the trail in the direction of the camp it knew, where were the other food providers and fire providers.

[1908]

Joining the Conversation: Critical Thinking and Writing

1. In a paragraph, explain the significance of the sentence, "The trouble with him was that he was without imagination" (paragraph 3).
2. In a letter to a young writer, London said; "Don't you tell the reader. . . . But HAVE YOUR CHARACTERS TELL IT BY THEIR DEEDS, ACTIONS, TALK, ETC. . . . The reader . . . doesn't want your dissertations on the subject, . . . your ideas—BUT PUT ALL THOSE THINGS WHICH ARE YOURS INTO THE STORIES." Good advice for a storyteller. Judging from this story, what do you suppose London's "ideas" were? Write a short dissertation—about 250 words—setting forth what you assume was London's view of man and nature.

SARAH ORNE JEWETT

Sarah Orne Jewett (1849–1909) was born and raised in South Berwick, Maine. A sickly girl, Jewett received little formal education, but her father, a doctor, introduced her to British and American fiction. Inspired by the writings of Harriet Beecher Stowe, in her teens Jewett determined to become a writer and began writing sketches and stories about the rural people of her native region. (Although South Berwick in Jewett's day was beginning to become industrialized, it had once been a busy port in a rural setting; Jewett's grandfather had been a sea captain and a leading owner of ships.) When she was twenty, she published her first story in the Atlantic Monthly, *and she continued to publish in national magazines stories about the vanishing era of her childhood.*

A White Heron

I

The woods were already filled with shadows one June evening, just before eight o'clock, though a bright sunset still glimmered faintly among the trunks of the trees. A little girl was driving home her cow, a plodding, dilatory, provoking creature in her behavior, but a valued companion for all that. They were going away from whatever light there was, and striking deep into the woods, but their feet were familiar with the path, and it was no matter whether their eyes could see it or not.

There was hardly a night the summer through when the old cow could be found waiting at the pasture bars; on the contrary, it was her greatest pleasure to hide herself away among the huckleberry bushes, and though she wore a loud bell she had made the discovery that if one stood perfectly still it would not ring. So Sylvia had to hunt for her until she found her, and call Co'! Co'! with never an answering Moo, until her childish patience was quite spent. If the creature had not given good milk and plenty of it, the case would have seemed very different to her owners. Besides, Sylvia had all the time there was, and very little use to make of it. Sometimes in pleasant weather it was a consolation to look upon the cow's pranks as an intelligent attempt to play hide and seek, and as the child had no playmates she lent herself to this amusement with a good deal of zest. Though this chase had been so long that the wary animal herself had given an unusual signal of her whereabouts, Sylvia had only laughed when she came upon Mistress Moolly at the swamp-side, and urged her affectionately homeward with a twig of birch leaves. The old cow was not inclined to wander farther, she even turned in the right direction for once as they left the pasture, and stepped along the road at a good pace. She was quite ready to be milked now, and seldom stopped to browse. Sylvia wondered what her grandmother would say because they were so late. It was a great while since she had let home at half-past five o'clock, but everybody knew the difficulty of making this errand a short one. Mrs. Tilley had chased the hornéd torment too many summer evenings herself to blame any one else for lingering, and was only thankful as she waited that she had Sylvia, nowadays, to give such valuable assistance. The good woman suspected that Sylvia loitered occasionally on her own account; there never was such a child for straying about out-of-doors since the world was made! Everybody said that it was a good change for a little maid who had tried to grow for eight years in a crowded manufacturing town, but as for Sylvia herself, it seemed as if she never had been alive at all before she came to live at the farm. She thought often with wistful compassion of a wretched geranium that belonged to a town neighbor.

"'Afraid of folks,'" old Mrs. Tilley said to herself, with a smile, after she had made the unlikely choice of Sylvia from her daughter's houseful of children, and was returning to the farm. "'Afraid of folks,' they said! I guess she won't be troubled no great with 'em up to the old place!" When they reached the door of the lonely house and stopped to unlock it, and the cat came to purr loudly, and rub against them, a deserted pussy, indeed, but fat with young robins, Sylvia whispered that this was a beautiful place to live in, and she never should wish to go home.

The companions followed the shady woodroad, the cow taking slow steps and the child very fast ones. The cow stopped long at the brook to drink, as if the pasture were not half a swamp, and Sylvia stood still and waited, letting her bare feet cool themselves in the shoal water, while the great twilight moths struck softly against her. She waded on through the brook as the cow moved away, and listened to the thrushes with a heart that beat fast with pleasure. There was a stirring in the great boughs overhead. They were full of little birds and beasts that seemed to be wide awake, and going about their world, or else saying goodnight to each other in sleepy twitters. Sylvia herself felt sleepy as she walked along. However, it was not much farther to the house, and the air was soft and sweet. She was not often in the woods so late as this, and it made her feel as if she were a part of the gray shadows and the moving leaves. She was just thinking how long it seemed since she first came to the farm a year ago, and wondering if everything went on in the noisy town just the same as when she was there; the thought of the great red-faced boy who used to chase and frighten her made her hurry along the path to escape from the shadow of the trees.

5 Suddenly this little woods-girl is horror-stricken to hear a clear whistle not very far away. Not a bird's-whistle, which would have a sort of friendliness, but a boy's whistle, determined, and somewhat aggressive. Sylvia left the cow to whatever sad fate might await her, and stepped discreetly aside into the brushes, but she was just too late. The enemy had discovered her, and called out in a very cheerful and persuasive tone, "Halloa, little girl, how far is it to the road?" and trembling Sylvia answered almost inaudibly, "A good ways."

She did not dare to look boldly at the tall young man, who carried a gun over his shoulder, but she came out of her bush and again followed the cow, while he walked alongside.

"I have been hunting for some birds," the stranger said kindly, "and I have lost my way, and need a friend very much. Don't be afraid," he added gallantly. "Speak up and tell me what your name is, and whether you think I can spend the night at your house, and go out gunning early in the morning."

Sylvia was more alarmed than before. Would not her grandmother consider her much to blame? But who could have foreseen such an accident as this? It did not seem to be her fault, and she hung her head as if the stem of it were broken, but managed to answer "Sylvy," with much effort when her companion again asked her name.

Mrs. Tilley was standing in the doorway when the trio came into view. The cow gave a loud moo by way of explanation.

10 "Yes, you'd better speak up for yourself, you old trial! Where'd she tucked herself away this time, Sylvy?" But Sylvia kept an awed silence; she knew by instinct that her grandmother did not comprehend the gravity of the situation. She must be mistaking the stranger for one of the farmer-lads of the region.

The young man stood his gun beside the door, and dropped a lumpy game-bag beside it; then he bade Mrs. Tilley good-evening, and repeated his wayfarer's story, and asked if he could have a night's lodging.

"Put me anywhere you like," he said. "I must be off early in the morning, before day; but I am very hungry indeed. You can give me some milk at any rate, that's plain."

"Dear sakes, yes," responded the hostess, whose long slumbering hospitality seemed to be easily awakened. "You might fare better if you went out to the main road a mile or so, but you're welcome to what we've got. I'll milk right off, and you make yourself at home. You can sleep on husks or feathers," she proffered graciously. "I raised them all myself. There's good pasturing for geese just below here towards the ma'sh. Now step round and set a plate for the gentleman, Sylvy!" And Sylvia promptly stepped. She was glad to have something to do, and she was hungry herself.

It was a surprise to find so clean and comfortable a little dwelling in this New England wilderness. The young man had known the horrors of its most primitive housekeeping, and the dreary squalor of that level of society which does not rebel at the companionship of hens. This was the best thrift of an old-fashioned farmstead, though on such a small scale that it seemed like a hermitage. He listened eagerly to the old woman's quaint talk, he watched Sylvia's pale face and shining gray eyes with ever growing enthusiasm, and insisted that this was the best supper he had eaten for a month, and afterward the new-made friends sat down in the door-way together while the moon came up.

Soon it would be berry-time, and Sylvia was a great help at picking. The cow was a good milker, though a plaguy thing to keep track of, the hostess gossiped frankly, adding presently that she had buried four children, so Sylvia's mother, and a son (who might be dead) in California were all the children she had left. "Dan, my boy, was a great hand to go gunning," she explained sadly. "I never wanted for pa'tridges or gray squer'ls while he was to home. He's been a great wand'rer, I expect, and he's no hand to write letters. There, I don't blame him, I'd ha' seen the world myself if it had been so I could."

"Sylvy takes after him," the grandmother continued affectionately, after a minute's pause. "There ain't a foot o' ground she don't know her way over, and the wild creaturs counts her one o' themselves. Squer'ls she'll tame to come an' feed right out o' her hands, and all sorts o' birds. Last winter she got the jaybirds to bangeing here, and I believe she'd 'a' scanted herself of her own meals to have plenty to throw out amongst 'em, if I hadn't kep' watch. Anything but crows, I tell her, I'm willin' to help support—though Dan he had a tamed one o' them that did seem to have reason same as folks. It was round here a good spell after he went away. Dan an' his father they didn't hitch,—but the never held up his head ag'in after Dan had dared him an' gone off."

The guest did not notice this hint of family sorrows in his eager interest in something else.

"So Sylvy knows all about birds, does she?" he exclaimed, as he looked round at the little girl who sat, very demure but increasingly sleepy, in the moonlight. "I am making a collection of birds myself. I have been at it every since I was a boy." (Mrs. Tilley smiled.) "There are two or three very rare ones I have been hunting for these five years. I mean to get them on my own ground if they can be found."

"Do you cage 'em up?" asked Mrs. Tilley doubtfully, in response to this enthusiastic announcement.

"Oh no, they're stuffed and preserved, dozens and dozens of them," said the ornithologist, "and I have shot or snared every one myself. I caught a glimpse of a white heron a few miles from here on Saturday, and I have followed it in this direction. They have never been found in this district at all. The little white heron, it is," and he turned again to look at Sylvia with the hope of discovering that the rare bird was one of her acquaintances.

But Sylvia was watching a hop-toad in the narrow footpath.

"You would know the heron if you saw it," the stranger continued eagerly. "A queer tall white bird with soft feathers and long thin legs. And it would have a nest perhaps in the top of a high tree, made of sticks, something like a hawk's nest."

Sylvia's heart gave a wild beat; she knew that strange white bird, and had once stolen softly near where it stood in some bright green swamp grass, away over at the other side of the woods. There was an open place where the sunshine always seemed strangely yellow and hot, where tall, nodding rushes grew, and her grandmother had warned her that she might sink in the soft black mud underneath and never be heard of more. Not far beyond were the salt marshes just this side the sea itself, which Sylvia wondered and dreamed much about, but never had seen, whose great voice could sometimes be heard above the noise of the woods on stormy nights.

"I can't think of anything I should like so much as to find that heron's nest," the handsome stranger was saying. "I would give ten dollars to anybody who could show it to me," he added desperately, "and I mean to spend my whole vacation hunting for it if need be. Perhaps it was only migrating, or had been chased out of its own region by some bird of prey."

Mrs. Tilley gave amazed attention to all this, but Sylvia still watched the toad, not divining, as she might have done at some calmer time, that the creature wished to get to its hole under the door-step, and was much hindered by the unusual spectators at that hour of the evening. No amount of thought, that night, could decide how many wished-for treasures the ten dollars, so lightly spoken of, would buy.

The next day the young sportsman hovered about the woods, and Sylvia kept him company, having lost her first fear of the friendly lad, who proved to be most kind and sympathetic. He told her many things about the birds and what they knew and where they lived and what they did with themselves. And he gave her a jack-knife, which she thought as great a treasure as if she were a desert-islander. All day long he did not once make her troubled or afraid except when he brought down some unsuspecting singing creature from its bough. Sylvia would have liked him vastly better without his gun: she could not understand why he killed the very birds he seemed to like so much. But as the day waned, Sylvia still watched the young man with loving admiration. She had never seen anybody so charming and delightful; the woman's heart, asleep in the child, was vaguely thrilled by a dream of love. Some premonition of that great power stirred and swayed these young creatures who traversed the solemn woodlands with soft-footed silent care. They stopped to listen to a bird's song; they pressed forward again eagerly, parting the branches—speaking to each other rarely and in whispers; the young man going first and Sylvia following, fascinated, a few steps behind, with her gray eyes dark with excitement.

She grieved because the longed-for white heron was elusive, but she did not lead the guest, she only followed, and there was no such thing as speaking first. The sound of her own unquestioned voice would have terrified her—it was hard enough to answer yes or no when there was need of that. At last evening began to fall, and they drove the cow home together, and Sylvia smiled with pleasure when they came to the place where she heard the whistle and was afraid only the night before.

II

Half a mile from home, at the farther edge of the woods, where the land was highest, a great pine-tree stood, the last of its generation. Whether it was left for a boundary mark, or for what reason, no one could say; the woodchoppers who had felled its mates were dead and gone long ago, and a whole forest of sturdy trees, pines and oaks and maples, had grown again. But the stately head of this old pine towered above them all and made a landmark for sea and shore miles and miles away. Sylvia knew it well. She had always believed that whoever climbed to the top of it could see the ocean; and the little girl had often laid her hand on the great rough trunk and looked up wistfully at those dark boughs that the wind always stirred, no matter how hot and still the air might be below. Now she thought of the tree with a new excitement, for why, if one climbed it at break of day could not one see all the world, and easily discover from whence the white heron flew, and mark the place, and find the hidden nest?

What a spirit of adventure, what wild ambition! What fancied triumph and delight and glory for the later morning when she could make known the secret! It was almost too real and too great for the childish heart to bear.

All night the door of the little house stood open and the whippoorwills came and sang upon the very step. The young sportsman and his old hostess were sound asleep, but Sylvia's great design kept her broad awake and watching. She forgot to think of sleep. The short summer night seemed as long as the winter darkness, and at last when the whippoorwills ceased, and she was afraid the morning would after all come too soon, she stole out of the house and followed the pasture path through the woods, hastening toward the open ground beyond, listening with a sense of comfort and companionship to the drowsy twitter of a half-awakened bird, whose perch she had jarred in passing. Alas, if the great wave of human interest which flooded for the first time this dull little life should sweep away the satisfactions of an existence heart to heart with nature and the dumb life of the forest!

There was the huge tree asleep yet in the paling moonlight, and small and silly Sylvia began with utmost bravery to mount to the top of it, with tingling, eager blood coursing the channels of her whole frame, with her bare feet and fingers, that pinched and held like bird's claws to the monstrous ladder reaching up, up, almost to the sky itself. First she must mount the white oak tree that grew alongside, where she was almost lost among the dark branches and the green leaves heavy and wet with dew; a bird fluttered off its nest, and a red squirrel ran to and fro and scolded pettishly at the harmless housebreaker. Sylvia felt her way easily. She had often climbed there, and knew hat higher still one of the oak's upper branches chafed against the pine trunk, just where its lower boughs were set close together. There, when she made the dangerous pass from one tree to the other, the great enterprise would really begin.

She crept out along the swaying oak limb at last, and took the daring step across into the old pine-tree. The way was harder than she thought; she must reach far and hold fast, the sharp dry twigs caught and held her and scratched her like angry talons, the pitch made her thin little fingers clumsy and stiff as she went round and round the tree's great stem, higher and higher upward. The sparrows and robins in the woods below were beginning to wake and twitter to the dawn, yet it seemed much lighter there aloft in the pine-tree, and the child knew she must hurry if her project were to be of any use.

The tree seemed to lengthen itself out as she went up, and to reach farther and farther upward. It was like a great main-mast to the voyaging earth; it must truly have been amazed that morning through all its ponderous frame as it felt this determined spark of human spirit wending its way from higher branch to branch. Who knows how steadily the least twigs held themselves to advantage this light, weak creature on her way! The old pine must have loved his new dependent. More than all the hawks, and bats, and moths, and even the sweet voiced thrushes, was the brave, beating heart of the solitary gray-eyed child. And the tree stood still and frowned away the winds that June morning while the dawn grew bright in the east.

Sylvia's face was like a pale star, if one had seen it from the ground, when the last thorny bough was past, and she stood trembling and tired but wholly triumphant, high in the treetop. Yes, there was the sea with the dawning sun making a golden dazzle over it, and toward that glorious east flew two hawks with slow-moving pinions. How low they looked in the air from that height when one had only seen them before far up, and dark against the blue sky. Their gray feathers were as soft as moths; they seemed only a little way from the tree, and Sylvia felt as if she too could go flying away among the clouds. Westward, the woodlands and farms reached miles and miles into the distance; here and there were church steeples, and white villages, truly it was a vast and awesome world!

35 The birds sang louder and louder. At last, the sun came up bewilderingly bright. Sylvia could see the white sails of ships out at sea, and the clouds that were purple and rose-colored and yellow at first began to fade away. Where was the white heron's nest in the sea of green branches, and was this wonderful sight and pageant of the world the only reward for having climbed to such a giddy height? Now look down again, Sylvia, where the green marsh is set among the shining birches and dark hemlocks; there where you saw the white heron once you will see him again; look, look! a white spot of him like a single floating feather comes up from the dead hemlock and grows larger, and rises, and comes close at last, and goes by the landmark pine with steady sweep of wing and outstretched slender neck and crested head. And wait! wait! do not move a foot or a finger, little girl, do not send an arrow of light and consciousness from your two eager eyes, for the heron has perched on a pine bough not far beyond yours, and cries back to his mate on the nest and plumes his feathers for the new day!

The child gives a long sigh a minute later when a company of shouting catbirds comes also to the tree, and vexed by their fluttering and lawlessness the solemn heron goes away. She knows his secret now, the wild, light, slender bird that floats and wavers, and goes back like an arrow presently to his home in the green world beneath. Then Sylvia, well satisfied, makes her perilous way down again, not daring to look far below the branch she stands on, ready to cry sometimes because her fingers ache and her lamed feet slip. Wondering over and over again what the stranger would say to her, and what he would think when she told him how to find his way straight to the heron's nest.

"Sylvy, Sylvy!" called the busy old grandmother again and again, but nobody answered, and the small husk bed was empty and Sylvia had disappeared.

The guest waked from a dream, and remembering his day's pleasure hurried to dress himself that might it sooner begin. He was sure from the way the shy little girl looked once or twice yesterday that she had at least seen the white heron, and now she must really be made to tell. Here she comes now, paler than ever, and her worn old frock is torn and tattered, and smeared with pine pitch. The grandmother and the sportsman stand in the door together and question her, and the splendid moment has come to speak of the dead hemlock-tree by the green marsh.

But Sylvia does not speak after all, though the old grandmother fretfully rebukes her, and the young man's kind, appealing eyes are looking straight in her own. He can make them rich with money; he has promised it, and they are poor now. He is so well worth making happy, and he waits to hear the story she can tell.

40 No, she must keep silence! What is it that suddenly forbids her and makes her dumb? Has she been nine years growing and now, when the great world for the first time puts out a hand to her, must she thrust it aside for a bird's sake? The murmur of the pine's green branches is in her ears, she remembers how the white

heron came flying through the golden air and how they watched the sea and the morning together, and Sylvia cannot speak; she cannot tell the heron's secret and give its life away.

Dear loyalty, that suffered a sharp pang as the guest went away disappointed later in the day, that could have served and followed him and loved him as a dog loves! Many a night Sylvia heard the echo of his whistle haunting the pasture path as she came home with the loitering cow. She forgot even her sorrow at the sharp report of his gun and the sight of thrushes and sparrows dropping silent to the ground, their songs hushed and their pretty feathers stained and wet with blood. Were the birds better friends than their hunter might have been,—who can tell? Whatever treasures were lost to her, woodlands and summer-time, remember! Bring your gifts and graces and tell your secrets to this lonely country child!

[1886]

Joining the Conversation: Critical Thinking and Writing

1. What does the name "Sylvia" mean? Why is this name appropriate to the central figure and to the theme of the story?
2. Why does Jewett include the passage about the grandmother's son, Dan? To what extent does Sylvia take after Dan?
3. In 250 words or so, discuss whether or not the final paragraph of "A White Heron" is appropriate and effective.
4. Many fairy tales tell of a hero or heroine who strays (usually into a wood), encounters a villain who seems friendly, passes a test, enters a new world, escapes from the villain, and returns safely home. If you can think of such a fairy tale, perhaps "Little Red Riding Hood" or "Jack and the Beanstalk," write an essay of 750 to 1,000 words, set down its framework, and then see to what extent it corresponds to the framework of "A White Heron."

POEMS

MATTHEW ARNOLD

Matthew Arnold (1822–1888) is a central figure in nineteenth century English literature. After his graduation from Oxford University in 1844, he became an inspector of schools, a post he held nearly his entire life. He is admired both for his poetry and for his influential essays on culture and literature.

In the title of the following sonnet, "Nature" apparently means the world of things other than human beings, a world without human morality.

In Harmony with Nature

To a Preacher

"In Harmony with Nature?" Restless fool,
Who with such heat dost preach what were to thee,
When true, the last impossibility—
To be like Nature strong, like Nature cool!

Know, man hath all which Nature hath, but more,
And in that *more* lie all his hopes of good.
Nature is cruel, man is sick of blood;
Nature is stubborn, man would fain adore;

Nature is fickle, man hath need of rest;
Nature forgives no debt, and fears no grave;
Man would be mild, and with safe conscience blest.

Man must begin, know this, where Nature ends;
Nature and man can never be fast friends.
Fool, if thou canst not pass her, rest her slave!

[1849]

Joining the Conversation: Critical Thinking and Writing

1. In the first stanza, the speaker is replying to someone, perhaps a preacher, who has espoused the goal of being "in harmony with Nature." Nature is said (line 4) to be "strong" and "cool." Do these adjectives make sense?
2. Having said that nature is strong and cool, Arnold goes on, in lines 5–8, to say that nature is "cruel" and "stubborn." Is the speaker contradicting himself? Please explain how the first two stanzas do, or do not, fit together.
3. In the remainder of the poem, the speaker objects to the idea of living "in harmony with nature." Exactly what are the grounds of his objection?
4. Please make your way through the poem, line by line, stating in your own words what the speaker is saying about Nature, and about man. What is the speaker's overall argument?
5. In line 10 Arnold says "Nature forgives no debt." What do you think this means? Do you think that Arnold is establishing a contrast between an amoral nature and the morality that Jesus preached when he said, in the Lord's Prayer, "Forgive us our debts, as we forgive our debtors" (Matthew 6:12).
6. What does "harmony" mean? Do you believe we can live "in harmony with nature"? How would you define "nature"?
7. Read Whitman's "A Noiseless Patient Spider" (page 605) and then respond to the fourth question that follows Whitman's poem.

THOMAS HARDY

Thomas Hardy (1840–1928) was born near Dorchester, in southwest England, where at 15 he was apprenticed to an architect. At the age of 21 he went to London to practice as an architect, but he soon turned to writing fiction and poetry. Between 1872 and 1896 he achieved fame as a novelist; among his novels are The Return of the Native *(1878) and* Tess of the D'Urbervilles *(1891). With the hostile reception of* Jude the Obscure *(1896) he abandoned writing fiction and concentrated on writing poetry.*

Transformations

Portion of this yew
Is a man my grandsire knew,
Bosomed here at its foot:
This branch may be his wife,
A ruddy human life
Now turned to a green shoot.

These grasses must be made
Of her who often prayed,
Last century, for repose;
And the fair girl long ago
Whom I often tried to know
May be entering the rose.

So, they are not underground,
But as nerves and veins abound
In the growths of upper air,
And they feel the sun and rain,
And the energy again
That made them what they were!

[1917]

Joining the Conversation: Critical Thinking and Writing

1. What is your sense of the speaker's tone in the first stanza? In the last? In lines 7–8 the speaker conjectures that "These grasses must be made / Of her who often prayed." What sort of visual connection is suggested between the grasses and the woman?
2. How might the speaker know that someone "often prayed, / Last century, for repose"?
3. At what stage of life is the speaker? How do you know?
4. What do you think Hardy means by "the energy . . . / That made them what they were"?
5. Do you find the poem far-fetched, or do you feel that the poet has made his assertions plausible? Explain.

JOHN KEATS

John Keats (1795–1821), son of a London stable keeper, was taken out of school when he was 15 and apprenticed to a surgeon and apothecary. In 1816 he was licensed to practice as an apothecary-surgeon, but he almost immediately abandoned medicine and decided to make a career as a poet. His progress was amazing; he quickly moved from routine verse to major accomplishments, publishing books of poems in 1817, 1818, and 1820, before dying of tuberculosis at the age of 25. Today he is esteemed as one of England's greatest poets.

To Autumn

I

Season of mists and mellow fruitfulness,
  Close bosom-friend of the maturing sun;
Conspiring with him how to load and bless
  With fruit the vines that round the thatch-eaves run;
To bend with apples the mossed cottage trees,
  And fill all fruit with ripeness to the core;
    To swell the gourd, and plump the hazel shells
With a sweet kernel; to set budding more,
  And still more, later flowers for the bees,
  Until they think warm days will never cease,
    For summer has o'er-brimmed their clammy cells.

II

Who hath not seen thee oft amid thy store?
  Sometimes whoever seeks abroad may find
Thee sitting careless on a granary floor,
  Thy hair soft-lifted by the winnowing wind;
Or on a half-reaped furrow sound asleep,
  Drowsed with the fume of poppies, while thy hook
    Spares the next swath and all its twined flowers:
And sometime like a gleaner thou dost keep
  Steady thy laden head across a brook;
  Or by a cider-press, with patient look,
    Thou watchest the last oozings hours by hours.

III

Where are the songs of Spring? Ay, where are they?
  Think not of them, thou hast thy music too,—
While barred clouds bloom the soft-dying day,
  And touch the stubble-plains with rosy hue;
Then in a wailful choir the small gnats mourn
  Among the river sallows, borne aloft
    Or sinking as the light wind lives or dies;
And full-grown lambs loud bleat from hilly bourn;
  Hedge-crickets sing; and now with treble soft
  The red-breast whistles from a garden-croft;
    And gathering swallows twitter in the skies.

[1819]

Joining the Conversation: Critical Thinking and Writing

1. Please summarize what the speaker is saying in each stanza.

2. A critic who admires Keats has nonetheless said about "To Autumn" that while the poem is "full of gorgeous language," it "lacks a clear point." Do you agree or disagree with this claim?

3. Select a favorite line or lines in "To Autumn." Please explain your choice, and explain how this line or lines fit in the structure of the poem as a whole.
4. If you were assigned to write a poem about one of the four seasons, which one would you choose? Why? Which one offers the most possibilities for poetry?

GERARD MANLEY HOPKINS

Gerard Manley Hopkins (1844–1889) was born near London and was educated at Oxford, where he studied the classics. A convert from Anglicanism to Roman Catholicism, he was ordained a Jesuit priest in 1877. After serving as a parish priest and teacher, he was appointed professor of Greek at the Catholic University of Ireland in Dublin.

Hopkins published only a few poems during his lifetime, partly because he believed that the pursuit of literary fame was incompatible with his vocation as a priest, and partly because he was aware that his highly individual style might puzzle readers.

God's Grandeur

The world is charged with the grandeur of God.
It will flame out, like shining from shook foil;
It gathers to a greatness, like the ooze of oil
Crushed. Why do men then now not reck his rod?
Generations have trod, have trod, have trod;
And all is seared with trade; bleared, smeared with toil;
And wears man's smudge and shares man's smell: the soil
Is bare now, nor can foot feel, being shod.

And for all this, nature is never spent;
There lives the dearest freshness deep down things;
And though the last lights off the black West went
Oh, morning, at the brown brink eastward, springs—
Because the Holy Ghost over the bent
World broods with warm breast and with ah! bright wings.

[1877]

Joining the Conversation: Critical Thinking and Writing

1. How would you define "charged" in the first line? How does the meaning connect with "flame out," in the next line? The Judeo-Christian tradition, unlike some ancient religions, insists that there are no thunder gods, lightning gods, river gods, and so forth; God is independent of nature, and therefore nature is not to be worshipped. Taking the poem as a whole, do you think Hopkins has slipped into nature-worship? Explain.
2. Hopkins in a letter explained "foil" in the second line thus: "I mean foil in its sense of leaf or tinsel. . . . Shaken goldfoil gives off broad glares like sheet lightning and also, and this is true of nothing else, owing to its zigzag dints and creasings and network of small many cornered facets, a sort of fork lightning

too." Suppose Hopkins had not explained it, and a reader thought that "foil" referred to a fencing sword. Might the meaning of the passage—the concept of nature that the line conveys—be equally interesting? How would you characterize Hopkins's view of nature, based on the first two sentences of the poem? ("The ooze of oil / Crushed" probably evokes an image of oil crushed from olives or from seed.)

3. Hopkins was a Roman Catholic priest. Does it therefore make sense to say that in line 6 "man's smudge" probably refers not only to a polluted environment (for instance, from factory smoke) but also to the doctrine of original sin? (If you are unfamiliar with this doctrine, begin by looking up "original sin" in a dictionary.)
4. The poem is a sonnet (14 lines), and, like many (but not all) sonnets, it is constructed with a unit of eight lines (the octave) followed by a unit of six lines (the sestet). What change in voice, in tone, do you hear at the beginning of the sestet? A writing assignment: Is the second part of the sonnet (lines 9–14) more unified or less unified than the first? Probably after writing a first draft you will be able to form a thesis that describes an overall pattern. As you revise your drafts, make sure (a) that the thesis is clear to the reader, and (b) that it is adequately supported by quotations that provide evidence.
5. The Holy Ghost (line 13) is described in Luke 3:22 as descending in the form of a dove. Given this information, explicate the final two lines of the poem.
6. Do you think that a reader has to be a Roman Catholic (as Hopkins was), or at least some sort of believer in the Judeo-Christian God in order to find the poem meaningful? Explain.

Walt Whitman

Walt Whitman (1819–1892) was born on Long Island, the son of a farmer. The young Whitman taught school and worked as a carpenter, a printer, a newspaper editor, and, during the Civil War, as a volunteer nurse on the Union side. After the war he supported himself by doing secretarial jobs. In Whitman's own day his poetry was highly controversial because of its unusual form (formlessness, many people said) and (though not in the following poem) its abundant erotic implications.

A Noiseless Patient Spider

A noiseless patient spider,
I mark'd where on a little promontory it stood isolated,
Mark'd how to explore the vacant vast surrounding,
It launch'd forth filament, filament, filament, out of itself,
Ever unreeling them, ever tirelessly speeding them.

And you O my soul where you stand,
Surrounded, detached, in measureless oceans of space,
Ceaselessly musing, venturing, throwing, seeking the spheres to connect them,
Till the bridge you will need be form'd, till the ductile anchor hold,
Till the gossamer thread you fling catch somewhere, O my soul.

[1862–1863]

Joining the Conversation: Critical Thinking and Writing

1. How are the suggestions in "launch'd" (line 4) and "unreeling" (line 5) continued in the second stanza?
2. How are the varying lengths of lines 1, 4, and 8 relevant to their ideas?
3. The second stanza is not a complete sentence. Why? The poem is unrhymed. What effect does the near-rhyme (*bold—soul*) in the last two lines have on you?
4. Whitman apparently thinks we can learn something about ourselves by observing nature. Read Matthew Arnold's "In Harmony with Nature" (pages 600–01) and then write a dialogue of about 500 words in which Arnold and Whitman talk about nature.

EDNA ST. VINCENT MILLAY

Edna St. Vincent Millay (1892–1950) was born in Rockland, Maine. Even as a child she wrote poetry, and by the time she graduated from Vassar College (1917) she had achieved some notice as a poet. Millay settled for a while in Greenwich Village, a center of bohemian activity in New York City, where she wrote, performed in plays, and engaged in feminist causes. In 1923, the year she married, she became the first woman to win the Pulitzer Prize for Poetry. Numerous other awards followed. Though she is best known as a lyric poet—especially as a writer of sonnets—she also wrote political poetry and nature poetry as well as short stories, plays, and a libretto for an opera.

Mindful of you the sodden earth in spring

Mindful of you the sodden earth in spring,
And all the flowers that in the springtime grow,
And dusty roads, and thistles, and the slow
Rising of the round moon, all throats that sing
The summer through, and each departing wing,
And all the nests that the bared branches show,
And all winds that in any weather blow,
And all the storms that the four seasons bring.
You go no more on your exultant feet
Up paths that only mist and morning knew,
Or watch the wind, or listen to the beat
Of a bird's wings too high in air to view,—
But you were something more than young and sweet
And fair,—and the long year remembers you.

[1917]

Joining the Conversation: Critical Thinking and Writing

1. Notice that the title of this poem is its first line—it does not have a separate title. Please come up with three or four possible titles, and explain which one you think is the best.
2. How many sentences does this poem contain? Please paraphrase them.
3. Decades ago, a scholar said, "Even if we did not know that Millay wrote this poem, we nonetheless would be able to tell that it was written by a woman." Is there evidence for such a claim? Is there evidence that you could cite in order to refute it?
4. From the speaker's account, what do we know about the "you" of this poem?
5. What kind of feeling does Millay's poem leave you with? Please explain how the poem created this feeling.

EMILY DICKINSON

For a biographical note on Emily Dickinson, see page 532.

"Nature" is what we see

"Nature" is what we see—
The Hill—the Afternoon—
Squirrel—Eclipse—the Bumble bee—
Nay—Nature is Heaven—
Nature is what we hear—
The Bobolink—the Sea—
Thunder—the Cricket—
Nay—Nature is Harmony—
Nature is what we know—
Yet have no art to say—
So impotent Our Wisdom is
To her Simplicity.

[1863]

Joining the Conversation: Critical Thinking and Writing

1. Why does Dickinson place the word "Nature" in quotation marks?
2. What is the effect of the word "Nay," which Dickinson uses twice?
3. What is the meaning of lines 9–10?
4. What is the meaning of lines 11–12, and what is their relation to the two lines that precede them?
5. The critic Margaret Homans has said: "[The poem] exposes the futility of efforts to master nature by finding linguistic equivalencies for it." Please explain and provide evidence for this interpretation. Do you agree with it?

EMILY DICKINSON

A narrow Fellow in the Grass

A narrow Fellow in the Grass
Occasionally rides—
You may have met Him—did you not
His notice sudden is—

The Grass divides as with a Comb—
A spotted shaft is seen—
And then it closes at your feet
And opens further on—

He likes a Boggy Acre
A Floor too cool for Corn—
Yet when a Boy, and Barefoot—
I more than once at Noon
Have passed, I thought, a Whip lash
Unbraiding in the Sun
When stopping to secure it
It wrinkled, and was gone—

Several of Nature's People
I know, and they know me—
I feel for them a transport
Of cordiality—

But never met this Fellow
Attended, or alone
Without a tighter breathing
And Zero at the Bone—

[c. 1865]

Joining the Conversation: Critical Thinking and Writing

1. What sorts of things is Dickinson implying by referring to the snake as "a narrow fellow"?
2. Why does she address the reader in line 3, and then again in line 7? Do you like this effect?
3. How would you reply to someone who says, "I find it confusing that Dickinson presents herself here as a boy."
4. Is this a serious poem, or a humorous one? Please point to evidence in the text to support your view.
5. Please rewrite this poem in prose, and punctuate it as you see fit. What is your response to this prose version?

Thinking Critically: Case Study about Robert Frost

Robert Frost

Robert Frost (1874–1963) was born in California. After his father's death in 1885, Frost's mother brought the family to New England, where she taught in high schools in Massachusetts and New Hampshire. Frost studied for part of one term at Dartmouth College in New Hampshire, then did odd jobs (including teaching), and from 1897 to 1899 was enrolled as a special student at Harvard. He then farmed in New Hampshire, published a few poems in local newspapers, left the farm and taught again, and in 1912 left for England, where he hoped to achieve more popular success as a writer. By 1915 he had won a considerable reputation, and he returned to the United States, settling on a farm in New Hampshire and cultivating the image of the country-wise farmer-poet. In fact he was well read in the classics, the Bible, and English and American literature.

Among Frost's many comments about literature, here are three: "Writing is unboring to the extent that it is dramatic"; "Every poem is . . . a figure of the will braving alien entanglements"; and, finally, a poem "begins in delight and ends in wisdom. . . . It runs a course of lucky events, and ends in a clarification of life—not necessarily a great clarification, such as sects and cults are founded on, but in a momentary stay against confusion."

Here is Frost, in a letter, writing about his own work:

> *You get more credit for thinking if you restate formulae or cite cases that fall in easily under formulae, but all the fun is outside[,] saying things that suggest formulae that won't formulate—that almost but don't quite formulate. I should like to be so subtle at this game as to seem to the casual person altogether obvious. The casual person would assume I meant nothing or else I came near enough meaning something he was familiar with to mean it for all practical purposes. Well, well, well.*

We give six of Frost's poems, arranged in chronological order, and we follow these poems with an essay by Frost on poetry. The first poem, "The Pasture," is one that Frost customarily put at the beginning of his collected poems. The last words of each stanza, "You come too," are an invitation to the reader to join him.

The Pasture

I'm going out to clean the pasture spring;
I'll only stop to rake the leaves away
(And wait to watch the water clear, I may):
I shan't be gone long.—You come too.

I'm going out to fetch the little calf
That's standing by the mother. It's so young,
It totters when she licks it with her tongue.
I shan't be gone long.—You come too.

[1913]

Joining the Conversation: Critical Thinking and Writing

1. Would the poem be just as good—maybe better?—if it consisted of only one stanza, either the first or second? Explain.
2. Although Frost had already published books of poems, after he wrote "The Pasture" he always placed this poem first in any collected edition of his poems. Why do you suppose he did this?

Mowing

There was never a sound beside the wood but one,
And that was my long scythe whispering to the ground.
What was it it whispered? I knew not well myself;
Perhaps it was something about the heat of the sun,
Something, perhaps, about the lack of sound—
And that was why it whispered and did not speak.
It was no dream of the gift of idle hours,
Or easy gold at the hand of fay or elf:
Anything more than the truth would have seemed too weak
To the earnest love that laid the swale in rows,
Not without feeble-pointed spikes of flowers
(Pale orchises), and scared a bright green snake.
The fact is the sweetest dream that labor knows.
My long scythe whispered and left the hay to make.

[1913]

Joining the Conversation: Critical Thinking and Writing

1. What associations come to mind from the title?
2. Please explain the distinction that Frost's speaker makes between whispering and speaking.
3. What is the speaker saying in lines 7–8?
4. Line 13 is well known to many readers. What does it mean? How is this line connected to the meaning of the poem as a whole?
5. Frost was keenly interested in tones of voice—in getting these tones into his poetry. How would you describe the tone or tones of voice in this poem?
6. Frost is a very popular poet, widely read and studied both inside and outside college classrooms. Is this a poem that you like? Please explain.
7. Could you imagine learning "Mowing" by heart? Why might someone want to memorize this poem?

The Wood-Pile

Out walking in the frozen swamp one grey day,
I paused and said, "I will turn back from here.
No, I will go on farther—and we shall see."
The hard snow held me, save where now and then
One foot went through. The view was all in lines
Straight up and down of tall slim trees
Too much alike to mark or name a place by
So as to say for certain I was here
Or somewhere else: I was just far from home.
A small bird flew before me. He was careful
To put a tree between us when he lighted,
And say no word to tell me who he was
Who was so foolish as to think what *he* thought.
He thought that I was after him for a feather—
The white one in his tail; like one who takes
Everything said as personal to himself.
One flight out sideways would have undeceived him.
And then there was a pile of wood for which
I forgot him and let his little fear
Carry him off the way I might have gone,
Without so much as wishing him good-night.
He went behind it to make his last stand.
It was a cord of maple, cut and split
And piled—and measured, four by four by eight.
And not another like it could I see.
No runner tracks in this year's snow looped near it.
And it was older sure than this year's cutting,
Or even last year's or the year's before.
The wood was grey and the bark warping off it
And the pile somewhat sunken. Clematis
Had wound strings round and round it like a bundle.
What held it though on one side was a tree
Still growing, and on one a stake and prop,
These latter about to fall. I thought that only
Someone who lived in turning to fresh tasks
Could so forget his handiwork on which
He spent himself, the labour of his axe,
And leave it there far from a useful fireplace
To warm the frozen swamps as best it could
With the slow smokeless burning of decay.

[1914]

Joining the Conversation: Critical Thinking and Writing

1. What is the contrast that Frost makes between human beings and nature?
2. What does he say about the relationship between human beings and nature?

The Oven Bird

There is a singer everyone has heard,
Loud, a mid-summer and a mid-wood bird,
Who makes the solid tree trunks sound again.
He says that leaves are old and that for flowers
Mid-summer is to spring as one to ten.
He says the early petal-fall is past
When pear and cherry bloom went down in showers
On sunny days a moment overcast;
And comes that other fall we name the fall.
He says the highway dust is over all.
The bird would cease and be as other birds
But that he knows in singing not to sing.
The question that he frames in all but words
Is what to make of a diminished thing.

[1916]

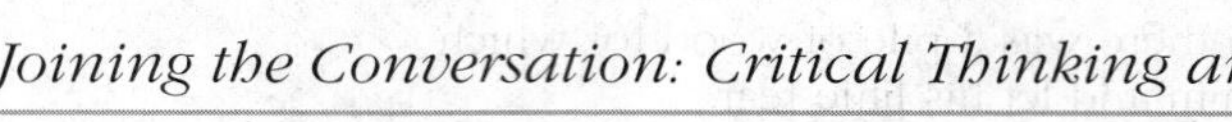

Joining the Conversation: Critical Thinking and Writing

1. Does the poem offer anything to a reader who has *not* heard an oven bird? If so, what?
2. Do you have an answer to "The question" raised in the last two lines? If so, what is the answer?

The Need of Being Versed in Country Things

The house had gone to bring again
To the midnight sky a sunset glow.
Now the chimney was all of the house that stood,
Like a pistil after the petals go.

The barn opposed across the way,
That would have joined the house in flame
Had it been the will of the wind, was left
To bear forsaken the place's name.

No more it opened with all one end
For teams that came by the stony road
To drum on the floor with scurrying hoofs
And brush the mow with the summer load.

The birds that came to it through the air
At broken windows flew out and in,
Their murmur more like the sigh we sigh
From too much dwelling on what has been.

Yet for them the lilac renewed its leaf,
And the aged elm, though touched with fire;
And the dry pump flung up an awkward arm;
And the fence post carried a strand of wire.

For them there was really nothing sad.
But though they rejoiced in the nest they kept,
One had to be versed in country things
Not to believe the phoebes wept.

[1923]

Joining the Conversation: Critical Thinking and Writing

1. By the end of the second stanza the reader understands that the farmhouse has been destroyed by a fire. Why do you suppose (putting aside the matter of rhyme) in line 2 Frost wrote "a sunset glow" instead of (say) "a burst of flame"? And what is the effect of the simile in line 4? That is, what do these comparisons contribute to the poem? (If you are unsure of the meaning of "pistil," check a dictionary.)
2. In the fifth stanza Frost uses personifications: "the lilac renewed its leaf," and the "pump flung up an awkward arm," and "the fence post carried a strand of wire." What other personifications do you find in the poem? What effect do these personifications have on you? And why do you suppose there are no personifications in the last two lines of the poem?
3. In a sentence or two or three, characterize the speaker. (You can probably characterize him or her by means of an adjective or two or three; use the rest of the allotment to provide evidence, such as brief quotations.)
4. Much of the poem describes a scene, but the speaker also interprets the scene. How would you summarize the interpretation? How might you paraphrase the title? Does the speaker convince you of the "need" to be "versed in country things"?
5. Do you think the poem is sentimental? Or, on the other hand, cynical? Explain.
6. Suppose you were to write a parody of "The Need of Being Versed in Country Things." What scene might you use, or what objects might you personify? (A parody is an amusing imitation of the style of another work, often with an inappropriate subject. Thus, one might parody a sports writer by imitating his or her style, but the subject would not be an athletic event but, say, students engaged in peer review.) Suggestion: consider the possibility of using your neighborhood or your workplace as a subject.

The Most of It

He thought he kept the universe alone;
For all the voice in answer he could wake
Was but the mocking echo of his own
From some tree-hidden cliff across the lake.
Some morning from the boulder-broken beach
He would cry out on life, that what it wants
Is not its own love back in copy speech,
But counter-love, original response.
And nothing ever came of what he cried
Unless it was the embodiment that crashed
In the cliff's talus on the other side,
And then in the far distant water splashed,

But after a time allowed for it to swim,
Instead of proving human when it neared
And someone else additional to him,
As a great buck it powerfully appeared,
Pushing the crumpled water up ahead,
And landed pouring like a waterfall,
And stumbled through the rocks with horny tread,
And forced the underbrush—and that was all.

[1942]

Joining the Conversation: Critical Thinking and Writing

1. How would you characterize the "He" of the first line?
2. Frost does *not* say "a great buck powerfully appeared." Rather, he says, "As a great buck it powerfully appeared." What is going on here?

ROBERT FROST ON POETRY

The Figure a Poem Makes

Abstraction is an old story with the philosophers, but it has been like a new toy in the hands of the artists of our day. Why can't we have any one quality of poetry we choose by itself? We can have in thought. Then it will go hard if we can't in practice. Our lives for it.

Granted no one but a humanist much cares how sound a poem is if it is only *a* sound. The sound is the gold in the ore. Then we will have the sound out alone and dispense with the inessential. We do till we make the discovery that the object in writing poetry is to make all poems sound as different as possible from each other, and the resources for that of vowels, consonants, punctuation, syntax, words, sentences, meter are not enough. We need the help of context—meaning—subject matter. That is the greatest help towards variety. All that can be done with words is soon told. So also with meters—particularly in our language where there are virtually but two, strict iambic and loose iambic. The ancients with many were still poor if they depended on meters for all tune. It is painful to watch our sprung-rhythmists straining at the point of omitting one short from a foot for relief from monotony. The possibilities for tune from the dramatic tones of meaning struck across the rigidity of a limited meter are endless. And we are back in poetry as merely one more art of having something to say, sound or unsound. Probably better if sound, because deeper and from wider experience.

Then there is this wildness whereof it is spoken. Granted again that it has an equal claim with sound to being a poem's better half. If it is a wild tune, it is a poem. Our problem then is, as modern abstractionists, to have the wildness pure: to be wild with nothing to be wild about. We bring up as aberrationists, giving way to undirected associations and kicking ourselves from one chance suggestion to another in all directions as of a hot afternoon in the life of a grasshopper. Theme alone can steady us down. Just as the first mystery was how a poem could have a tune in such a straightness as meter, so the second mystery is how a poem can have wildness and at the same time a subject that shall be fulfilled.

It should be of the pleasure of a poem itself to tell how it can. The figure a poem makes. It begins in delight and ends in wisdom. The figure is the same as for love. No one can really hold that the ecstasy should be static and stand still in one place. It begins in delight, it inclines to the impulse, it assumes direction with the first line laid down, it runs a course of lucky events, and ends in a clarification of life—not necessarily a great clarification, such as sects and cults are founded on, but in a momentary stay against confusion. It has denouement. It has an outcome that though unforeseen was predestined from the first image of the original mood—and indeed from the very mood. It is but a trick poem and no poem at all if the best of it was thought of first and saved for the last. It finds its own name as it goes and discovers the best waiting for it in some final phrase at once wise and sad—the happy-sad blend of the drinking song.

5 No tears in the writer, no tears in the reader. No surprise for the writer, no surprise for the reader. For me the initial delight is in the surprise of remembering something I didn't know I knew. I am in a place, in a situation, as if I had materialized from cloud or risen out of the ground. There is a glad recognition of the long lost and the rest follows. Step by step the wonder of unexpected supply keeps growing. The impressions most useful to my purpose seem always those I was unaware of and so made no note of at the time when taken, and the conclusion is come to that like giants we are always hurling experience ahead of us to pave the future with against the day when we may want to strike a line of purpose across it for somewhere. The line will have the more charm for not being mechanically straight. We enjoy the straight crookedness of a good walking stick. Modern instruments of precision are being used to make things crooked as if by eye and hand in the old days.

I tell how there may be a better wildness of logic than of inconsequence. But the logic is backward, in retrospect, after the act. It must be more felt than seen ahead like prophecy. It must be a revelation, or a series of revelations, as much for the poet as for the reader. For it to be that there must have been the greatest freedom of the material to move about in it and to establish relations in it regardless of time and space, previous relation, and everything but affinity. We prate of freedom. We call our schools free because we are not free to stay away from them till we are sixteen years of age. I have given up my democratic prejudices and now willingly set the lower classes free to be completely taken care of by the upper classes. Political freedom is nothing to me. I bestow it right and left. All I would keep for myself is the freedom of my material—the condition of body and mind now and then to summons aptly from the vast chaos of all I have lived through.

Scholars and artists thrown together are often annoyed at the puzzle of where they differ. Both work from knowledge; but I suspect they differ most importantly in the way their knowledge is come by. Scholars get theirs with conscientious thoroughness along projected lines of logic; poets theirs cavalierly and it happens in and out of books. They stick to nothing deliberately, but let what will stick to them like burrs where they walk in the fields. No acquirement is on assignment, or even self-assignment. Knowledge of the second kind is much more available in the wild free ways of wit and art. A school boy may be defined as one who can tell you what he knows in the order in which he learned it. The artist must value himself as he snatches a thing from some previous order in time and space into a new order with not so much as a ligature clinging to it of the old place where it was organic.

More than once I should have lost my soul to radicalism if it had been the originality it was mistaken for by young converts. Originality and initiative are what I ask for my country. For myself the originality need be no more than the freshness of a poem run in the way I have described: from delight to wisdom. The figure is the same as for love. Like a piece of ice on a hot stove the poem must ride on its own melting. A poem may be worked over once it is in being, but may not be worried into being. Its most precious quality will remain its having run itself and carried away the poet with it. Read it a hundred times: it will forever keep its freshness as a metal keeps its fragrance. It can never lose its sense of a meaning that once unfolded by surprise as it went.

[1939]

Chapter Overview: Looking Backward/Looking Forward

1. Does it make sense for hunters and fishers to say that their activity shows they are lovers of nature? Whatever your personal view, write two essays, each of 500 words, one essay taking one side and the other essay taking the other side.
2. Do you "love nature"? What does it mean to say such a thing?
3. When someone says, "you should take more interest in the world around you," what does this person mean?
4. Could a person live a good life without paying any attention to nature?
5. A well-known contemporary writer who lives in New York City has said, "I hate nature." Please compose a letter of 500–750 words, in which you explain to this writer why she is wrong to feel this way.
6. Would you enjoy living on a farm and making your living from the crops you grew and the animals you raised and cared for?
7. Please describe your most rewarding experience of living or traveling in an unusual natural setting, here or abroad—a setting that you found very different from where you live most of the time.

Chapter 19

Journeys

Short Views

Here are some brief comments about journeys—inner and outer. Read them carefully, and then write on one of the topics that appear after the last quotation.

If you don't know where you want to go, any road will take you there.
Lewis Carroll

They change their clime, not their disposition, who run across the sea.
Horace

Travel makes a wise man better, but a fool worse.
Thomas Fuller

Why do you wonder that globe-trotting does not help you, seeing that you always take yourself with you? The reason which set you wandering is ever at your heels.
Seneca, attributing the line to Socrates

Worth seeing, yes; but not worth going to see.
Samuel Johnson

We shall not cease from exploration
And the end of all our exploring
Will be to arrive where we started
And know the place for the first time.
T. S. Eliot

It is easier to sail many thousand miles through cold and storm and cannibals, in a government ship, with five hundred men and boys to assist one, than it is to explore the private sea, the Atlantic and Pacific Ocean of one's being alone. . .
Henry David Thoreau

I have traveled a good deal in Concord.
Henry David Thoreau

I am not much an advocate for traveling. Who are you that have no task to keep you at home?

Ralph Waldo Emerson

The whole object of travel is not to set foot on foreign land; it is at last to set foot on one's own country as a foreign land.

G. K. Chesterton

Before taking steps the wise man knows the object and end of his journey.

W. E. B. Du Bois

Without stirring abroad
One can know the whole world;
Without looking out of the window
One can see the way of heaven
The further one goes
The less one knows

Lao-Tzu, trans. D. C. Lau

For my part, I travel not to go anywhere, but to go. I travel for travel's sake. The great affair is to move; to feel the needs and hitches of our life more nearly; to come down off this featherbed of civilization, and find the globe granite underfoot and strewn with cutting flints.

Robert Louis Stevenson

I always think that the most delightful thing about traveling is to always be running into Americans and to always feel at home.

Anita Loos

Travel spins us round in two ways at once: It shows us the sights and values and issues that we might ordinarily ignore; but it also, and more deeply, shows us all the parts of ourselves that might otherwise grow rusty. For in traveling to a truly foreign place, we inevitably travel to moods and states of mind and hidden inward passages that we'd otherwise seldom have cause to visit. . . . Travel, then is a voyage into that famously subjective zone, the imagination, and what the traveler brings back is—and has to be—an ineffable compound of himself and the place, what's really there and what's only in him.

Pico Iyer

Because it was there.

George Mallory (answering the question why he wanted to climb Mt. Everest)

Like love, travel makes you innocent again.

Diane Ackerman

Getting there is half the fun.
Proverbial

All the way to Heaven is Heaven.
St. Catherine of Siena

Joining the Conversation: Critical Thinking and Writing

1. Select a quotation that especially appeals to you, and make it the focus of an essay of about 500 words.
2. Take two of the passages—perhaps one that you especially like and one that you think is wrongheaded—and write a dialogue of about 500 words in which the two authors converse or argue. They may each try to convince the other, or they may find that to some degree they share views and they may then work out a statement that both can accept. If you do take the first position—that one writer is on the correct track but the other is utterly mistaken—try to be fair to the view that you think is mistaken. (As an experiment in critical thinking, imagine that you accept it, and make the best case for it that you possibly can.)
3. Emerson says, above, that he is "not much [of] an advocate for traveling." Imagine that you are an advocate *for* traveling, and that Emerson is your reader. List the key points of your argument. Then, working from this list, write an essay of two pages.
4. According to W. E. B. Du Bois, above, before a person travels, he or she should know "the object and end" of the journey. What is Du Bois saying? Do you agree? If Du Bois is right, then why is it said so often that a person should always travel "with an open mind"?
5. Once again, consider Du Bois's observation about travel. Have you ever traveled somewhere when you have known from the start "the object and end"? Please describe this experience. Have you ever traveled somewhere without knowing "the object and end"? Now, describe this experience.
6. Diane Ackerman suggests that travel restores a person's "innocence." What does this mean? Do you believe it? She also connects the experience of travel and love. What is her point? How would her point about travel change if the phrase "like love" were deleted?

ESSAYS

JOAN DIDION

Joan Didion was born in Sacramento in 1934, and she was educated at the University of California, Berkeley. She has written essays, stories, screenplays, and novels.

On Going Home

I am home for my daughter's first birthday. By "home" I do not mean the house in Los Angeles where my husband and I and the baby live, but the place where my family is, in the Central Valley of California. It is a vital although troublesome distinction.

My husband likes my family but is uneasy in their house, because once there I fall into their ways, which are difficult, oblique, deliberately inarticulate, not my husband's ways. We live in dusty houses ("D-U-S-T," he once wrote with his finger on surfaces all over the house, but no one noticed it) filled with mementos quite without value to him (what could the Canton dessert plates mean to him? How could he have known about the assay scales, why should he care if he did know?), and we appear to talk exclusively about people we know who have been committed to mental hospitals, about people we know who have been booked on drunk-driving charges, and about property, particularly about property, land, price per acre and C-2 zoning and assessments, and freeway access. My brother does not understand my husband's inability to perceive the advantage in the rather common real-estate transaction known as "sale-leaseback," and my husband in turn does not understand why so many of the people he hears about in my father's house have recently been committed to mental hospitals or booked on drunk-driving charges. Nor does he understand that when we talk about sale-leasebacks and right-of-way condemnations we are talking in code about the things we like best, the yellow fields and the cottonwoods and the rivers rising and falling and the mountain roads closing when the heavy snow comes in. We miss each other's points, have another drink and regard the fire. My brother refers to my husband, in his presence, as "Joan's husband." Marriage is the classic betrayal.

Or perhaps it is not any more. Sometimes I think that those of us who are now in our thirties were born into the last generation to carry the burden of "home," to find in family life the source of all tension and drama. I had by all objective accounts a "normal" and a "happy" family situation, and yet I was almost thirty years old before I could talk to my family on the telephone without crying after I had hung up. We did not fight. Nothing was wrong. And yet some nameless anxiety colored the emotional charges between me and the place that I came from. The question of whether or not you could go home again was a very real part of the sentimental and largely literary baggage with which we left home in the fifties; I suspect that it is irrelevant to the children born of the fragmentation after World War II. A few weeks ago in a San Francisco bar I saw a pretty young girl on crystal take off her clothes and dance for the cash prize in an "amateur-topless" contest. There was no particular sense of moment about this, none of the effect of romantic degradation, of "dark journey," for which my generation strived so assiduously. What sense could that girl possibly make of, say, *Long Day's Journey into Night*? Who is beside the point?

That I am trapped in this particular irrelevancy is never more apparent to me than when I am home. Paralyzed by the neurotic lassitude engendered by meeting one's past at every turn, around every corner, inside every cupboard, I go aimlessly from room to room. I decide to meet it head-on and clean out a drawer, and I spread the contents on the bed. A bathing suit I wore the summer I was seventeen. A letter of rejection from *The Nation*, an aerial photograph of the site for a shopping center my father did not build in 1954. Three teacups hand-painted with cabbage roses and signed "E.M.," my grandmother's initials. There is no final solution for letters of rejection from *The Nation* and teacups hand-painted in 1900. Nor is there any answer to snapshots of one's grandfather as a young man on skis, surveying around Donner Pass in the year 1910. I smooth out the snapshot and look into his face, and do and do not see my own. I close the drawer, and have another cup of coffee with my mother. We get along very well, veterans of a guerilla war we never understood.

Days pass. I see no one. I come to dread my husband's evening call, not only because he is full of news of what by now seems to me our remote life in Los Angeles, people he has seen, letters which require attention, but because he asks what I have been doing, suggests uneasily that I get out, drive to San Francisco or Berkeley. Instead I drive across the river to a family graveyard. It has been vandalized since my last visit and the monuments are broken, overturned in the dry grass. Because I once saw a rattlesnake in the grass I stay in the car and listen to a country-and-Western station. Later I drive with my father to a ranch he has in the foothills. The man who runs his cattle on it asks us to the roundup, a week from Sunday, and although I know I will be in Los Angeles I say, in the oblique way my family talks, that I will come. Once home I mention the broken monuments in the graveyard. My mother shrugs.

5 I go to visit my great-aunts. A few of them think now that I am my cousin, or their daughter who died young. We recall an anecdote about a relative last seen in 1948, and they ask if I still like living in New York City. I have lived in Los Angeles for three years, but I say that I do. The baby is offered a horehound drop, and I am slipped a dollar bill "to buy a treat." Questions trail off, answers are abandoned, the baby plays with the dust motes in a shaft of afternoon sun.

It is time for the baby's birthday party: a white cake, strawberry-marshmellow ice cream, a bottle of champagne saved from another party. In the evening, after she has gone to sleep, I kneel beside the crib and touch her face, where it is pressed against the slats, with mine. She is an open and trusting child, unprepared for and unaccustomed to the ambushes of family life, and perhaps it is just as well that I can offer her a little of that life. I would like to give her more. I would like to promise her that she will grow up with a sense of her cousins and of rivers and of her great-grandmother's teacups, would like to pledge her a picnic on a river with fried chicken and her hair uncombed, would like to give her *home* for her birthday, but we live differently now and I can promise her nothing like that. I give her a xylophone and a sundress from Madeira, and promise to tell her a funny story.

[1968]

Joining the Conversation: Critical Thinking and Writing

1. Didion reveals that members of her family are difficult, inarticulate, poor housekeepers, and so forth. Do you find these revelations about her family distasteful? Would you mind seeing in print similarly unflattering things you had written about your own family? How might such revelations be justified? Are they justified in this essay?
2. Summarize the point of the second paragraph. Do you find Didion's speculations about the difference between her generation and succeeding generations meaningful? Are they accurate for your generation?
3. Do you think that growing up necessarily involves estrangement from one's family? Support your thesis with reasons.

Montesquieu (Charles de Secondat, Baron de la Brède et de Montesquieu)

Montesquieu (1689–1755), French jurist, political philosopher, and writer, was born at La Brède, near Bordeaux. Today he is known chiefly for The Spirit of Laws *(1748), a study of three kinds of government (republic, monarchy, despotism), but he achieved fame in his own day with his* Persian Letters *(1721), letters supposedly written by two Persians (and their correspondents) traveling in Europe. Through the device of using narrators who are unsophisticated in European ways—innocent eyes, so to speak—he was able to satirize European social, political, religious, and literary customs. (If you are familiar with the fable of the emperor's clothes, in which a child sees that the emperor is naked, you are familiar with the device of using an innocent to tell the truth.)*

Persian Letters

Translated by J. Robert Loy

Letter 24: Rica to Ibben in Smyrna

We have been in Paris for a month and have been continually in motion. It takes much doing to find a place to live, to meet people to whom you are recommended, and to provide yourself with necessities all at the same time.

Paris is as large as Ispahan. The houses here are so high that you would swear they were all inhabited by astrologers. You can readily understand that a city built up in the air, with six or seven houses built one on top of the other, is an extremely populous city, and that when everyone is down in the streets, there is great confusion.

Perhaps you will not believe this, but for the month I have been here, I have seen nobody walking. There are no people in the world who get so much out of their carcasses as the French: they run; they fly. The slow carriages of Asia, the regular pace of our camels, would make them swoon. As for myself, I am not built that way, and when I go walking, as I do often, without changing my pace, I sometimes fume and rage like a Christian. For, passing over the fact that I am splashed from head to foot, still I cannot forgive the elbowings in my ribs that I collect regularly and periodically. A man walking behind me, passes me and turns me half-around; then another, coming toward me from the opposite direction, briskly puts me back into the position where the first fellow hit me. I have barely made a hundred paces before I am more bruised than if I had gone ten leagues.

Do not expect me to be able just now to talk to you seriously about European usages and customs. I have only a faint idea of them myself and have barely had time to be amazed by them.

5 The King of France is the most powerful prince of Europe. Unlike his neighbor the King of Spain, he has no gold mines. Yet he possesses greater riches, for he draws from the vanity of his subjects a wealth more inexhaustible than mines. He has been known to undertake and wage great wars with no other funds than honorary titles to sell, and by reason of this miracle of human pride, his troops are paid, his fortresses armed, and his navies fitted out.

Moreover, this king is a great magician. He exercises his empire over the very minds of his subjects and makes them think as he likes. If he has only one million crowns in his treasury and he needs two million, he has only to convince them that one crown equals two, and they believe him. If he is involved in a war that is difficult in the waging and finds himself short of money, he has only to put into their heads the notion that a slip of paper is money, and they are immediately convinced. He even goes so far as to make them believe that he can cure them of all manner of disease by touching them, so great is his strength and dominion over their minds. . . .

I shall continue to write to you, and I shall teach you things far removed from Persian character and spirit. It is certainly the same earth carrying both countries, but the men of this country where I am and those of the country where you are are quite different.

From Paris, the 4th of the Moon of Rebiab II, 1712

[1721]

Joining the Conversation: Critical Thinking and Writing

1. In the third paragraph Montesquieu's narrator says of his stay in Paris, "I have seen nobody walking. . . . [T]hey run; they fly." He is writing in the eighteenth century, so "they fly" is a figure of speech. (A European friend of ours, visiting Los Angeles, wrote to us that he was the only person walking; everyone else was jogging or roller-blading.) Write your own Persian letter to a fellow-Persian, reporting (as an innocent eye) on the strange behavior that surrounds you in the classroom, the streets, or (drawing on the newspapers and television) the nation. Or you may prefer to take on the persona of some other alleged innocent—for instance, a creature from Mars or an eighteenth-century person, who via a time machine, finds himself or herself in the twenty-first century.

2. Voltaire, Montesquieu's contemporary, said that *Persian Letters* was "a book which anybody might have written easily." Perhaps his thinking was along the lines of Samuel Johnson, who said of Jonathan Swift's *Gulliver's Travels* that once you thought of little people and big people, the rest was easy. If you have written your own Persian letter, evaluate Voltaire's comment.

STORIES

NATHANIEL HAWTHORNE

Nathaniel Hawthorne (1804–1864) was born in Salem, Massachusetts, the son of a sea captain. Two of his ancestors were judges; one had persecuted Quakers, and another had served at the Salem witch trials. After graduating from Bowdoin College in Maine, Hawthorne went back to Salem in order to write in relative seclusion. In 1835 he published one of his best stories, "Young Goodman Brown."

From 1839 to 1841 Hawthorne worked in the Boston Customs House and then spent a few months as a member of a communal society, Brook Farm. In 1842 he married and settled with his wife in Concord, Massachusetts, where they became friendly with Emerson and Thoreau. From 1846 to 1849 he was a surveyor at the Salem Customs House; from 1849 to 1850 he wrote The Scarlet Letter, *the book that made him famous. From 1853 to 1857 he served as American consul in Liverpool, England, a plum awarded him in exchange for writing a campaign biography of a former college classmate, President Franklin Pierce. In 1860, after living in England and Italy, he returned to the United States, settling in Concord, Massachusetts.*

In his stories and novels Hawthorne keeps returning to the Puritan past, studying guilt, sin, and isolation.

Young Goodman Brown

Young Goodman Brown came forth at sunset into the street at Salem village; but put his head back, after crossing the threshold, to exchange a parting kiss with his young wife. And Faith, as the wife was aptly named, thrust her own pretty head into the street, letting the wind play with the pink ribbons of her cap while she called to Goodman Brown.

"Dearest heart," whispered she, softly and rather sadly, when her lips were close to his ear, "prithee put off your journey until sunrise and sleep in your own bed to-night. A lone woman is troubled with such dreams and such thoughts that she's afeared of herself sometimes. Pray tarry with me this night, dear husband, of all nights in the year."

"My love and my Faith," replied young Goodman Brown, "of all nights in the year, this one night must I tarry away from thee. My journey, as thou callest it, forth and back again, must needs be done 'twixt now and sunrise. What, my sweet, pretty wife, dost thou doubt me already, and we but three months married?"

"Then God bless you!" said Faith, with the pink ribbons; "and may you find all well when you come back."

5 "Amen!" cried Goodman Brown. "Say thy prayers, dear Faith, and go to bed at dusk, and no harm will come to thee."

So they parted; and the young man pursued his way until, being about to turn the corner by the meeting-house, he looked back and saw the head of Faith still peeping after him with a melancholy air, in spite of her pink ribbons.

"Poor little Faith!" thought he, for his heart smote him. "What a wretch am I to leave her on such an errand! She talks of dreams, too. Methought as she spoke there was trouble in her face, as if a dream had warned her what work is to be done to-night. But no, no; 'twould kill her to think it. Well, she's a blessed angel on earth; and after this one night I'll cling to her skirts and follow her to heaven."

With this excellent resolve for the future, Goodman Brown felt himself justified in making more haste on his present evil purpose. He had taken a dreary road, darkened by all the gloomiest trees of the forest, which barely stood aside to let the narrow path creep through, and closed immediately behind. It was all as lonely as could be; and there is this peculiarity in such a solitude, that the traveler knows not who may be concealed by the innumerable trunks and the thick boughs overhead; so that with lonely footsteps he may yet be passing through an unseen multitude.

"There may be a devilish Indian behind every tree," said Goodman Brown to himself; and he glanced fearfully behind him as he added, "What if the devil himself should be at my very elbow!"

10 His head being turned back, he passed a crook of the road, and, looking forward again, beheld the figure of a man, in grave and decent attire, seated at the

foot of an old tree. He arose at Goodman Brown's approach and walked onward side by side with him.

"You are late, Goodman Brown," said he. "The clock of the Old South was striking as I came through Boston, and that is full fifteen minutes agone."

"Faith kept me back a while," replied the young man, with a tremor in his voice, caused by the sudden appearance of his companion, though not wholly unexpected.

It was now deep dusk in the forest, and deepest in that part of it where these two were journeying. As nearly as could be discerned, the second traveller was about fifty years old, apparently in the same rank of life as Goodman Brown, and bearing a considerable resemblance to him, though perhaps more in expression than features. Still they might have been taken for father and son. And yet, though the elder person was as simply clad as the younger, and as simple in manner too, he had an indescribable air of one who knew the world, and who would not have felt abashed at the governor's dinner table or in King William's court,[1] were it possible that his affairs should call him thither. But the only thing about him that could be fixed upon as remarkable was his staff, which bore the likeness of a great black snake, so curiously wrought that it might almost be seen to twist and wriggle itself like a living serpent. This, of course, must have been an ocular deception, assisted by the uncertain light.

"Come, Goodman Brown," cried his fellow-traveller, "this is a dull pace for the beginning of a journey. Take my staff, if you are so soon weary."

15 "Friend," said the other, exchanging his slow pace for a full stop, "Having kept covenant by meeting thee here, it is my purpose now to return whence I came. I have scruples touching the matter thou wot'st of."

"Sayest thou so?" replied he of the serpent, smiling apart. "Let us walk on, nevertheless, reasoning as we go; and if I convince thee not thou shalt turn back. We are but a little way in the forest yet."

"Too far! too far!" exclaimed the goodman, unconsciously resuming his walk. "My father never went into the woods on such an errand, not his father before him. We have been a race of honest men and good Christians since the days of the martyrs; and shall I be the first of the name of Brown that ever took this path and kept—"

"Such company, thou wouldst say," observed the elder person, interpreting his pause. "Well said, Goodman Brown! I have been as well acquainted with your family as with ever a one among the Puritans; and that's no trifle to say. I helped your grandfather, the constable, when he lashed the Quaker woman so smartly through the streets of Salem; and it was I that brought your father a pitch-pine knot, kindled at my own hearth, to set fire to an Indian village, in King Philip's war. They were my good friends, both; and many a pleasant walk have we had along this path, and returned merrily after midnight. I would fain be friends with you for their sake."

"If it be as thou sayest," replied Goodman Brown, "I marvel they never spoke of these matters; or, verily, I marvel not, seeing that the least rumor of the sort would have driven them from New England. We are a people of prayer, and good works to boot, and abide no such wickedness."

20 "Wickedness or not," said the traveller with the twisted staff, "I have a very general acquaintance here in New England. The deacons of many a church have drunk the communion wine with me; the selectmen of divers towns make me their chairman; and a majority of the Great and General Court are firm supporters of my interest. The governor and I, too—But these are state secrets."

[1]**King William's court** refers to the English king who ruled from 1688 to 1694.

"Can this be so?" cried Goodman Brown, with a stare of amazement at his undisturbed companion. "Howbeit, I have nothing to do with the governor and council; they have their own ways, and are no rule for a simple husbandman like me. But, were I to go on with thee, how should I meet the eye of that good old man, our minister, at Salem village? Oh, his voice would make me tremble both Sabbath day and lecture day."

Thus far the elder traveller had listened with due gravity; but now burst into a fit of irrepressible mirth, shaking himself so violently that his snake-like staff actually seemed to wriggle in sympathy.

"Ha! ha! ha!" shouted he again and again; then composing himself, "Well, go on, Goodman Brown, go on; but, prithee, don't kill me with laughing."

"Well, then, to end the matter at once," said Goodman Brown, considerably nettled, "there is my wife, Faith. It would break her dear little heart; and I'd rather break my own."

25 "Nay, if that be the case," answered the other, "e'en go thy ways, Goodman Brown. I would not for twenty old women like the one hobbling before us that Faith should come to any harm."

As he spoke he pointed his staff at a female figure on the path, in whom Goodman Brown recognized a very pious and exemplary dame, who had taught him his catechism in youth, and was still his moral and spiritual adviser, jointly with the minister and Deacon Gookin.

"A marvel, truly, that Goody Cloyse should be so far in the wilderness at nightfall," said he. "But with your leave, friend, I shall take a cut through the woods until we have left this Christian woman behind. Being a stranger to you, she might ask whom I was consorting with and whither I was going."

"Be it so," said his fellow-traveller. "Betake you the woods, and let me keep the path."

Accordingly the young man turned aside, but took care to watch his companion, who advanced softly along the road until he had come within a staff's length of the old dame. She, meanwhile, was making the best of her way, with singular speed for so aged a woman, and mumbling some indistinct words—a prayer, doubtless—as she went. The traveller put forth his staff and touched her withered neck with what seemed the serpent's tail.

30 "The devil!" screamed the pious old lady.

"Then Goody Cloyse knows her old friend?" observed the traveller, confronting her and leaning on his writhing stick.

"Ah, forsooth, and is it your worship indeed?" cried the good dame. "Yea, truly is it, and in the very image of my old gossip, Goodman Brown, the grandfather of the silly fellow that now is. But—would your worship believe it?—my broomstick hath strangely disappeared, stolen, as I suspect, by that unhanged witch, Goody Cory, and that, too, when I was all anointed with the juice of smallage, and cinquefoil, and wolf's bane—"

"Mingled with fine wheat and the fat of a new-born babe," said the shape of old Goodman Brown.

"Ah, your worship knows the recipe," cried the old lady, cackling aloud. "So, as I was saying, being all ready for the meeting, and no horse to ride on, I made up my mind to foot it; for they tell me there is a nice young man to be taken into communion to-night. But now your good worship will lend me your arm, and we shall be there in a twinkling."

35 "That can hardly be," answered her friend. "I may not spare you my arm, Goody Cloyse; but here is my staff, if you will."

So saying, he threw it down at her feet, where, perhaps, it assumed life, being one of the rods which its owner had formerly lent to the Egyptian magi. Of this fact, however, Goodman Brown could not take cognizance. He had cast up his eyes in astonishment, and, looking down again, beheld neither Goody Cloyse nor the serpentine staff, but his fellow-traveller alone, who waited for him as calmly as if nothing had happened.

"That old woman taught me my catechism," said the young man; and there was a world of meaning in this simple comment.

They continued to walk onward, while the elder traveller exhorted his companion to make good speed and persevere in the path, discoursing so aptly that his arguments seemed rather to spring up in the bosom of his auditor than to be suggested by himself. As they went, he plucked a branch of maple to serve for a walking stick, and began to strip it of the twigs and the little boughs, which were wet with evening dew. The moment his fingers touched them they became strangely withered and dried up as with a week's sunshine. Thus the pair proceeded, at a good free pace, until suddenly, in a gloomy hollow of the road, Goodman Brown sat himself down on the stump of a tree and refused to go any farther.

"Friend," said he, stubbornly, "my mind is made up. Not another step will I budge on this errand. What if a wretched old woman do choose to go to the devil when I thought she was going to heaven: is that any reason why I should quit my dear Faith and go after her?"

40 "You will think better of this by and by," said his acquaintance, composedly. "Sit here and rest yourself a while; and when you feel like moving again, there is my staff to help you along."

Without more words, he threw his companion the maple stick, and was as speedily out of sight as if he had vanished into the deepening gloom. The young man sat a few moments by the roadside, applauding himself greatly, and thinking with how clear a conscience he should meet the minister in his morning walk, nor shrink from the eye of good old Deacon Gookin. And what calm sleep would be his that very night, which was to have been spent so wickedly, but so purely and sweetly now, in the arms of Faith! Amidst these pleasant and praiseworthy meditations, Goodman Brown heard the tramp of horses along the road, and deemed it advisable to conceal himself within the verge of the forest, conscious of the guilty purpose that had brought him thither, though now so happily turned from it.

On came the hoof tramps and the voices of the riders, two grave old voices, conversing soberly as they drew near. These mingled sounds appeared to pass along the road, within a few yards of the young man's hiding-place; but, owing doubtless to the depth of the gloom at that particular spot, neither the travellers nor their steeds were visible. Though their figures brushed the small boughs by the wayside, it could not be seen that they intercepted, even for a moment, the faint gleam from the strip of bright sky athwart which they must have passed. Goodman Brown alternately crouched and stood on tiptoe, pulling aside the branches and thrusting forth his head as far as he durst without discerning so much as a shadow. It vexed him the more, because he could have sworn, were such a thing possible, that he recognized the voices of the minister and Deacon Gookin, jogging along quietly, as they were wont to do, when bound to some ordination or ecclesiastical council. While yet within hearing, one of the riders stopped to pluck a switch.

"Of the two, reverend sir," said the voice like the deacon's, "I had rather miss an ordination dinner than to-night's meeting. They tell me that some of our community are to be here from Falmouth and beyond, and others from Connecticut and Rhode Island, besides several of the Indian powwows, who, after their fashion, know almost as much deviltry as the best of us. Moreover, there is a goodly young woman to be taken into communion."

"Mighty well, Deacon Gookin!" replied the solemn old tones of the minister. "Spur up, or we shall be late. Nothing can be done, you know, until I get on the ground."

The hoofs clattered again; and the voices, talking so strangely in the empty air, passed on through the forest, where no church had ever been gathered or solitary Christian prayed. Whither, then, could these holy men be journeying so deep into the heathen wilderness? Young Goodman Brown caught hold of a tree for support, being ready to sink down on the ground, faint and overburdened with the heavy sickness of his heart. He looked up to the sky, doubting whether there really was a heaven above him. Yet there was the blue arch, and the stars brightening in it.

"With heaven above and Faith below, I will yet stand firm against the devil!" cried Goodman Brown.

While he still gazed upward into the deep arch of the firmament and had lifted his hands to pray, a cloud, though no wind was stirring, hurried across the zenith and hid the brightening stars. The blue sky was still visible, except directly overhead, where this black mass of cloud was sweeping swiftly northward. Aloft in the air, as if from the depths of the cloud, came a confused and doubtful sound of voices. Once the listener fancied that he could distinguish the accents of townspeople of his own, men and women, both pious and ungodly, many of whom he had met at the communion table, and had seen others rioting at the tavern. The next moment, so indistinct were the sounds, he doubted whether he had heard aught but the murmur of the old forest, whispering without a wind. Then came a stronger swell of those familiar tones, heard daily in the sunshine at Salem village, but never until now from a cloud of night. There was one voice, of a young woman, uttering lamentations, yet with an uncertain sorrow, and entreating for some favor, which, perhaps, it would grieve her to obtain; and all the unseen multitude, both saints and sinners, seemed to encourage her onward.

"Faith!" shouted Goodman Brown, in a voice of agony and desperation; and the echoes of the forest mocked him, crying, "Faith! Faith!" as if bewildered wretches were seeking her all through the wilderness.

The cry of grief, rage, and terror was yet piercing the night, when the unhappy husband held his breath for a response. There was a scream, drowned immediately in a louder murmur of voices, fading into far-off laughter, as the dark cloud swept away, leaving the clear and silent sky above Goodman Brown. But something fluttered lightly down through the air and caught on the branch of a tree. The young man seized it, and beheld a pink ribbon.

"My Faith is gone!" cried he, after one stupefied moment. "There is no good on earth; and sin is but a name. Come, devil; for to thee is this world given."

And, maddened with despair, so that he laughed loud and long, did Goodman Brown grasp his staff and set forth again, at such a rate that he seemed to fly along the forest path rather than to walk or run. The road grew wilder and drearier and more faintly traced, and vanished at length, leaving him in the heart of the dark wilderness, still rushing onward with the instinct that guides mortal man to evil. The whole forest was peopled with frightful sounds—the creaking of the trees, the howling of wild beasts, and the yell of Indians; while sometimes the wind tolled like a distant church bell, and sometimes gave a broad roar around the traveller, as if all Nature were laughing him to scorn. But he was himself the chief horror of the scene, and shrank not from its other horrors.

"Ha! ha! ha!" roared Goodman Brown when the wind laughed at him. "Let us hear which will laugh loudest. Think not to frighten me with your deviltry. Come witch, come wizard, come Indian powwow, come devil himself, and here comes Goodman Brown. You may as well fear him as he fear you."

In truth, all through the haunted forest there could be nothing more frightful than the figure of Goodman Brown. On he flew among the black pines, brandishing his staff with frenzied gestures, now giving vent to an inspiration of horrid blasphemy, and now shouting forth such laughter as set all the echoes of the forest laughing like demons around him. The fiend in his own shape is less hideous than when he rages in the breast of man. Thus sped the demoniac on his course, until, quivering among the trees, he saw a red light before him, as when the felled trunks and branches of a clearing have been set on fire, and throw up their lurid blaze against the sky, at the hour of midnight. He paused, in a lull of the tempest that had driven him onward, and heard the swell of what seemed a hymn, rolling solemnly from a distance with the weight of many voices. He knew the tune; it was a familiar one in the choir of the village meeting-house. The verse died heavily away, and was lengthened by a chorus, not of human voices, but of all the sounds of the benighted wilderness pealing in awful harmony together. Goodman Brown cried out, and his cry was lost to his own ear by its unison with the cry of the desert.

In the interval of silence he stole forward until the light glared full upon his eyes. At one extremity of an open space, hemmed in by the dark wall of the forest, arose a rock, bearing some rude, natural resemblance either to an altar or a pulpit, and surrounded by four blazing pines, their tops aflame, their stems untouched, like candles at an evening meeting. The mass of foliage that had overgrown the summit of the rock was all on fire, blazing high into the night and fitfully illuminating the whole field. Each pendent twig and leafy festoon was in a blaze. As the red light arose and fell, a numerous congregation alternately shone forth, then disappeared in shadow, and again grew, as it were, out of the darkness, peopling the heart of the solitary woods at once.

"A grave and dark-clad company," quoth Goodman Brown.

In truth they were such. Among them, quivering to and fro between gloom and splendor, appeared faces that would be seen next day at the council board of the province, and others which, Sabbath after Sabbath, looked devoutly heavenward, and benignantly over the crowded pews, from the holiest pulpits in the land. Some affirm that the lady of the governor was there. At least three were high dames well known to her, and wives of honored husbands, and widows, a great multitude, and ancient maidens, all of excellent repute, and fair young girls, who trembled lest their mothers should espy them. Either the sudden gleams of light flashing over the obscure field bedazzled Goodman Brown, or he recognized a score of the church members of Salem village famous for their especial sanctity. Good old Deacon Gookin had arrived, and waited at the skirts of that venerable saint, his revered pastor. But, irreverently consorting with these grave, reputable, and pious people, these elders of the church, these chaste dames and dewy virgins, there were men of dissolute lives and women of spotted fame, wretches given over to all mean and filthy vice, and suspected even of horrid crimes. It was strange to see that the good shrank not from the wicked, nor were the sinners abashed by the saints. Scattered also among their pale-faced enemies were the Indian priests, or powwows, who had often scared their native forest with more hideous incantations than any known to English witchcraft.

"But where is Faith?" thought Goodman Brown; and, as hope came into his heart, he trembled.

Another verse of the hymn arose, a slow and mournful strain, such as the pious love, but joined to words which expressed all that our nature can conceive of sin, and darkly hinted at far more. Unfathomable to mere mortals is the lore of fiends. Verse after verse was sung; and still the chorus of the desert swelled between like the deepest tone of a mighty organ; and with the final peal of that dreadful anthem there came a sound, as if the roaring wind, the rushing streams, the howling beasts, and every other voice of the unconcerted wilderness were mingling and according with the voice of guilty man in homage to the prince of all. The four blazing pines threw up a loftier flame, and obscurely discovered shapes and visages of horror on the smoke wreaths above the impious assembly. At the same moment the fire on the rock shot redly forth and formed a glowing arch above its base, where now appeared a figure. With reverence be it spoken, the figure bore no slight similitude, both in garb and manner, to some grave divine of the New England churches.

"Bring forth the converts!" cried a voice that echoed through the field and rolled into the forest.

60 At the word, Goodman Brown stepped forth from the shadow of the trees and approached the congregation, with whom he felt a loathful brotherhood by the sympathy of all that was wicked in his heart. He could have well-nigh sworn that the shape of his own dead father beckoned him to advance, looking downward from a smoke wreath, while a woman, with dim features of despair, threw out her hand to warn him back. Was it his mother? But he had no power to retreat one step, nor to resist, even in thought, when the minister and good old Deacon Gookin seized his arms and led him to the blazing rock. Thither came also the slender form of a veiled female, led between Goody Cloyse, that pious teacher of the catechism, and Martha Carrier, who had received the devil's promise to be queen of hell. A rampant hag was she. And there stood the proselytes beneath the canopy of fire.

"Welcome, my children," said the dark figure, "to the communion of your race. Ye have found thus young your nature and your destiny. My children, look behind you!"

They turned; and flashing forth, as it were, in a sheet of flame, the fiend worshippers were seen; the smile of welcome gleamed darkly on every visage.

"There," resumed the sable form, "are all whom ye have reverenced from youth. Ye deemed them holier than yourselves, and shrank from your own sin, contrasting it with their lives of righteousness and prayerful aspirations heavenward. Yet here are they all in my worshipping assembly. This night it shall be granted you to know their secret deeds: how hoary-bearded elders of the church have whispered wanton words to the young maids of their households; how many a woman, eager for widows' weeds, has given her husband a drink at bedtime and let him sleep his last sleep in her bosom; how beardless youths have made haste to inherit their fathers' wealth; and how fair damsels—blush not, sweet ones—have dug little graves in the garden, and bidden me, the sole guest, to an infant's funeral. By the sympathy of your human hearts for sin ye shall scent out all the places—whether in church, bedchamber, street, field, or forest—where crime has been committed, and shall exult to behold the whole earth one stain of guilt, one mighty blood spot. Far more than this. It shall be yours to penetrate, in every bosom, the deep mystery of sin, the fountain of all wicked arts, and which inexhaustibly supplies more evil impulses than human power—than my power at its utmost—can make manifest in deeds. And now, my children, look upon each other."

They did so; and, by the blaze of the hell-kindled torches, the wretched man beheld his Faith, and the wife her husband, trembling before that unhallowed altar.

"Lo, there ye stand, my children," said the figure, in a deep and solemn tone, almost sad with its despairing awfulness, as if his once angelic nature could yet mourn for our miserable race. "Depending upon one another's hearts, ye had still hoped that virtue were not all a dream. Now are ye undeceived. Evil is the nature of mankind. Evil must be your only happiness. Welcome again, my children, to the communion of your race."

"Welcome," repeated the fiend worshippers, in one cry of despair and triumph.

And there they stood, the only pair, as it seemed, who were yet hesitating on the verge of wickedness in this dark world. A basin was hollowed, naturally, in the rock. Did it contain water, reddened by the lurid light? or was it blood? or, perchance, a liquid flame? Herein did the shape of evil dip his hand and prepare to lay the mark of baptism upon their foreheads, that they might be partakers of the mystery of sin, more conscious of the secret guilt of others, both in deed and thought, than they could now be of their own. The husband cast one look at his pale wife, and Faith at him. What polluted wretches would the next glance show them to each other, shuddering alike at what they disclosed and what they saw!

"Faith! Faith!" cried the husband, "look up to heaven, and resist the wicked one."

Whether Faith obeyed he knew not. Hardly had he spoken when he found himself amid calm night and solitude, listening to a roar of the wind which died heavily away through the forest. He staggered against the rock, and felt it chill and damp; while a hanging twig, that had been all on fire, besprinkled his cheek with the coldest dew.

The next morning young Goodman Brown came slowly into the street of Salem village, staring around him like a bewildered man. The good old minister was taking a walk along the graveyard to get an appetite for breakfast and meditate his sermon, and bestowed a blessing, as he passed, on Goodman Brown. He shrank from the venerable saint as if to avoid an anathema. Old Deacon Gookin was at domestic worship, and the holy words of his prayer were heard through the open window. "What God doth the wizard pray to?" quoth Goodman Brown. Goody Cloyse, that excellent old Christian, stood in the early sunshine at her own lattice, catechizing a little girl who had brought her a pint of morning's milk. Goodman Brown snatched away the child as from the grasp of the fiend himself. Turning the corner by the meeting-house, he spied the head of Faith, with the pink ribbons, gazing anxiously forth, and bursting into such joy at sight of him that she skipped along the street and almost kissed her husband before the whole village. But Goodman Brown looked sternly and sadly into her face, and passed on without a greeting.

Had Goodman Brown fallen asleep in the forest and only dreamed a wild dream of a witch-meeting?

Be it so if you will; but alas! it was a dream of evil omen for young Goodman Brown. A stern, a sad, a darkly meditative, a distrustful, if not a desperate man did he become from the night of that fearful dream. On the Sabbath day, when the congregation were singing a holy psalm, he could not listen because an anthem of sin rushed loudly upon his ear and drowned all the blessed strain. When the minister spoke from the pulpit with power and fervid eloquence, and, with his hand on the open Bible, of the sacred truths of our religion, and of saint-like lives and triumphant deaths, and of future bliss or misery unutterable, then did

Goodman Brown turn pale, dreading lest the roof should thunder down upon the gray blasphemer and his hearers. Often, awaking suddenly at midnight, he shrank from the bosom of Faith; and at morning or eventide, when the family knelt down at prayer, he scowled and muttered to himself, and gazed sternly at his wife, and turned away. And when he had lived long, and was borne to his grave a hoary corpse, followed by Faith, an aged woman, and children and grandchildren, a goodly procession, besides neighbors not a few, they carved no hopeful verse upon his tombstone, for his dying hour was gloom.

[1835]

Joining the Conversation: Critical Thinking and Writing

1. What do you think Hawthorne gains (or loses) by the last sentence?
2. Evaluate the view that when young Goodman Brown enters the dark forest he is really entering his own evil mind. Why, by the way, does he go into the forest at night? (Hawthorne gives no explicit reason, but you may want to offer a conjecture.)
3. In a sentence or two summarize the plot, and then in another sentence or two state the theme of the story. (On theme, see pages 364–65.)
4. If you have undergone a religious experience, write an essay discussing your condition before, during, and after the experience.

EUDORA WELTY

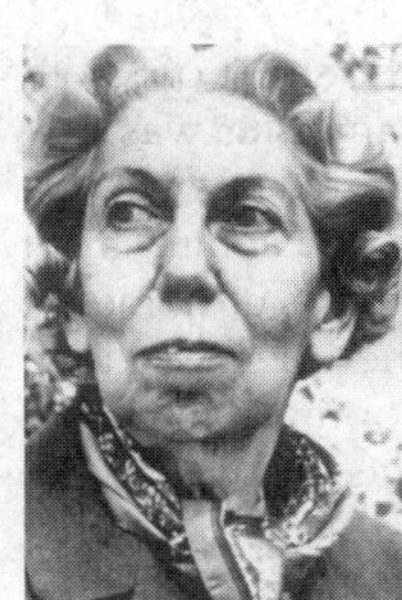

Eudora Welty (1909–2001) was born in Jackson, Mississippi. Although she earned a bachelor's degree at the University of Wisconsin, and she spent a year studying advertising in New York City at the Columbia University Graduate School of Business, she lived almost all of her life in Jackson.

In the preface to her Collected Stories *she says:*

> *I have been told, both in approval and in accusation, that I seem to love all my characters. What I do in writing of any character is to try to enter into the mind, heart and skin of a human being who is not myself. Whether this happens to be a man or a woman, old or young, with skin black or white, the primary challenge lies in making the jump itself. It is the act of a writer's imagination that I set most high.*

In addition to writing stories and novels, Welty wrote a book about fiction, The Eye of the Story *(1977), and a memoir,* One Writer's Beginnings *(1984).*

A Worn Path

It was December—a bright frozen day in the early morning. Far out in the country there was an old Negro woman with her head tied in a red rag, coming along a path through the pinewoods. Her name was Phoenix Jackson. She was very old and small and she walked slowly in the dark pine shadows, moving a little from side to side in her steps, with the balanced heaviness and lightness of a pendulum in a grandfather clock. She carried a thin, small cane made from an umbrella, and with this she kept tapping the frozen earth in front of her. This made a grave and persistent noise in the still air, that seemed meditative like the chirping of a solitary little bird.

She wore a dark striped dress reaching down to her shoe tops, and an equally long apron of bleached sugar sacks, with a full pocket: all neat and tidy, but every time she took a step she might have fallen over her shoelaces, which dragged from her unlaced shoes. She looked straight ahead. Her eyes were blue with age. Her skin had a pattern all its own of numberless branching wrinkles and as though a whole little tree stood in the middle of her forehead, but a golden color ran underneath, and the two knobs of her cheeks were illuminated by a yellow burning under the dark. Under the red rag her hair came down on her neck in the frailest of ringlets, still black, and with an odor like copper.

Now and then there was a quivering in the thicket. Old Phoenix said, "Out of my way, all you foxes, owls, beetles, jack rabbits, coons, and wild animals! . . . Keep out from under these feet, little bob-whites. . . . Keep the big wild hogs out of my path. Don't let none of those come running my direction. I got a long way." Under her small black-freckled hand her cane, limber as a buggy whip, would switch at the brush as if to rouse up any hiding things.

On she went. The woods were deep and still. The sun made the pine needles almost too bright to look at, up where the wind rocked. The cones dropped as light as feathers. Down in the hollow was the mourning dove—it was not too late for him.

5 The path ran up a hill. "Seem like there is chains about my feet, time I get this far," she said, in the voice of argument old people keep to use with themselves. "Something always take a hold of me on this hill—pleads I should stay."

After she got to the top she turned and gave a full, severe look behind her where she had come. "Up through pines," she said at length. "Now down through oaks."

Her eyes opened their widest, and she started down gently. But before she got to the bottom of the hill a bush caught her dress.

Her fingers were busy and intent, but her skirts were full and long, so that before she could pull them free in one place they were caught in another. It was not possible to allow the dress to tear. "I in the thorny bush," she said. "Thorns, you doing your appointed work. Never want to let folks pass—no sir. Old eyes thought you was a pretty little *green* bush."

Finally, trembling all over, she stood free, and after a moment dared to stoop for her cane.

10 "Sun so high!" she cried, leaning back and looking, while the thick tears went over her eyes. "The time getting all gone here."

At the foot of this hill was a place where a log was laid across the creek.

"Now comes the trial," said Phoenix.

Putting her right foot out, she mounted the log and shut her eyes. Lifting her skirt, levelling her cane fiercely before her, like a festival figure in some parade, she began to march across. Then she opened her eyes and she was safe on the other side.

"I wasn't as old as I thought," she said.

15 But she sat down to rest. She spread her skirts on the bank around her and folded her hands over her knees. Up above her was a tree in a pearly cloud of mistletoe. She did not dare to close her eyes, and when a little boy brought her a little plate with a slice of marble-cake on it she spoke to him. "That would be

acceptable," she said. But when she went to take it there was just her own hand in the air.

So she left that tree, and had to go through a barbed-wire fence. There she had to creep and crawl, spreading her knees and stretching her fingers like a baby trying to climb the steps. But she talked loudly to herself: she could not let her dress be torn now, so late in the day, and she could not pay for having her arm or leg sawed off if she got caught fast where she was.

At last she was safe through the fence and risen up out in the clearing. Big dead trees, like black men with one arm, were standing in the purple stalks of the withered cotton field. There sat a buzzard.

"Who you watching?"

In the furrow she made her way along.

"Glad this not the season for bulls," she said, looking sideways, "and the good Lord made his snakes to curl up and sleep in the winter. A pleasure I don't see no two-headed snake coming around that tree, where it come once. It took a while to get by him, back in the summer."

She passed through the old cotton and went into a field of dead corn. It whispered and shook and was taller than her head. "Through the maze now," she said, for there was no path.

Then there was something tall, black, and skinny there, moving before her.

At first she took it for a man. It could have been a man dancing in the field. But she stood still and listened, and it did not make a sound. It was as silent as a ghost.

"Ghost," she said sharply, "who be you the ghost of? For I have heard of nary death close by."

But there was no answer—only the ragged dancing in the wind.

She shut her eyes, reached out her hand, and touched a sleeve. She found a coat and inside that an emptiness, cold as ice.

"You scarecrow," she said. Her face lighted. "I ought to be shut up for good," she said with laughter. "My senses is gone, I too old. I the oldest people I ever know. Dance, old scarecrow," she said, "while I dancing with you."

She kicked her foot over the furrow, and with mouth drawn down, shook her head once or twice in a little strutting way. Some husks blew down and whirled in streamers about her skirts.

Then she went on, parting her way from side to side with the cane, through the whispering field. At last she came to the end, to a wagon track where the silver grass blew between the red ruts. The quail were walking around like pullets, seeming all dainty and unseen.

"Walk pretty," she said. "This the easy place. This the easy going."

She followed the track, swaying through the quiet bare fields, through the little strings of trees silver in their dead leaves, past cabins silver from weather, with the doors and windows boarded shut, all like old women under a spell sitting there. "I walking in their sleep," she said, nodding her head vigorously.

In a ravine she went where a spring was silently flowing through a hollow log. Old Phoenix bent and drank. "Sweet-gum makes the water sweet," she said, and drank more. "Nobody know who made this well, for it was here when I was born."

The track crossed a swampy part where the moss hung as white as lace from every limb. "Sleep on, alligators, and blow your bubbles." Then the track went into the road.

Deep, deep the road went down between the high green-colored banks. Overhead the live-oaks met, and it was as dark as a cave.

35 A black dog with a lolling tongue came up out of the weeds by the ditch. She was meditating, and not ready, and when he came at her she only hit him a little with her cane. Over she went in the ditch, like a little puff of milk-weed.

Down there, her senses drifted away. A dream visited her, and she reached her hand up, but nothing reached down and gave her a pull. So she lay there and presently went to talking. "Old woman," she said to herself, "that black dog come up out of the weeds to stall you off, and now there he sitting on his fine tail, smiling at you."

A white man finally came along and found her—a hunter, a young man, with his dog on a chain.

"Well, Granny!" he laughed. "What are you doing there?"

"Lying on my back like a June-bug waiting to be turned over, mister," she said, reaching up her hand.

40 He lifted her up, gave her a swing in the air, and set her down. "Anything broken, Granny?"

"No sir, them old dead weeds is springy enough," said Phoenix, when she had got her breath. "I thank you for your trouble."

"Where do you live, Granny?" he asked, while the two dogs were growling at each other.

"Away back yonder, sir, behind the ridge. You can't even see it from here."

"On your way home?"

45 "No, sir, I going to town."

"Why, that's too far! That's as far as I walk when I come out myself, and I get something for my trouble." He patted the stuffed bag he carried, and there hung down a little closed claw. It was one of the bob-whites, with its beak hooked bitterly to show it was dead. "Now you go on home, Granny!"

"I bound to go to town, mister," said Phoenix. "The time come around."

He gave another laugh, filling the whole landscape. "I know you old colored people! Wouldn't miss going to town to see Santa Claus!"

But something held Old Phoenix very still. The deep lines in her face went into a fierce and different radiation. Without warning, she had seen with her own eyes a flashing nickel fall out of the man's pocket onto the ground.

50 "How old are you, Granny?" he was saying.

"There is no telling, mister," she said, "no telling."

Then she gave a little cry and clapped her hands and said, "Git on away from here, dog! Look! Look at that dog!" She laughed as if in admiration. "He ain't scared of nobody. He a big black dog." She whispered, "Sic him!"

"Watch me get rid of that cur," said the man. "Sic him, Pete! Sic him!"

Phoenix heard the dogs fighting, and heard the man running and throwing sticks. She even heard a gunshot. But she was slowly bending forward by that time, further and further forward, the lids stretched down over her eyes, as if she were doing this in her sleep. Her chin was lowered almost to her knees. The yellow palm of her hand came out from the fold of her apron. Her fingers slid down and along the ground under the piece of money with the grace and care they would have in lifting an egg from under a sitting hen. Then she slowly straightened up, she stood erect, and the nickel was in her apron pocket. A bird flew by. Her lips moved. "God watching me the whole time. I come to stealing."

55 The man came back, and his own dog panted about them. "Well, I scared him off that time," he said, and then he laughed and lifted his gun and pointed it at Phoenix.

She stood straight and faced him.

"Doesn't the gun scare you?" he said, still pointing it.

"No, sir, I seen plenty go off closer by, in my day, and for less than what I done," she said, holding utterly still.

He smiled, and shouldered the gun. "Well, Granny," he said, "you must be a hundred years old, and scared of nothing. I'd give you a dime if I had any money with me. But you take my advice and stay home, and nothing will happen to you."

"I bound to go on my way, mister," said Phoenix. She inclined her head in the red rag. Then they went in different directions, but she could hear the gun shooting again and again over the hill.

She walked on. The shadows hung from the oak trees to the road like curtains. Then she smelled wood-smoke, and smelled the river, and she saw a steeple and the cabins on their steep steps. Dozens of little black children whirled around her. There ahead was Natchez shining. Bells were ringing. She walked on.

In the paved city it was Christmas time. There were red and green electric lights strung and crisscrossed everywhere, and all turned on in the daytime. Old Phoenix would have been lost if she had not distrusted her eyesight and depended on her feet to know where to take her.

She paused quietly on the sidewalk where people were passing by. A lady came along in the crowd, carrying an armful of red-, green-, and silver-wrapped presents; she gave off perfume like the red roses in hot summer, and Phoenix stopped her.

"Please, missy, will you lace up my shoe?" She held up her foot.

"What do you want, Grandma?"

"See my shoe," said Phoenix. "Do all right for out in the country, but wouldn't look right to go in a big building."

"Stand still then, Grandma," said the lady. She put her packages down on the sidewalk beside her and laced and tied both shoes tightly.

"Can't lace 'em with a cane," said Phoenix. "Thank you, missy. I doesn't mind asking a nice lady to tie up my shoe, when I gets out on the street."

Moving slowly and from side to side, she went into the big building and into a tower of steps, where she walked up and around and around until her feet knew to stop.

She entered a door, and there she saw nailed up on the wall the document that had been stamped with the gold seal and framed in the gold frame, which matched the dream that was hung up in her head.

"Here I be," she said. There was a fixed and ceremonial stiffness over her body.

"A charity case, I suppose," said an attendant who sat at the desk before her.

But Phoenix only looked above her head. There was sweat on her face, the wrinkles in her skin shone like a bright net.

"Speak up, Grandma," the woman said. "What's your name? We must have your history, you know. Have you been here before? What seems to be the trouble with you?"

Old Phoenix only gave a twitch to her face as if a fly were bothering her.

"Are you deaf?" cried the attendant.

But then the nurse came in.

"Oh, that's just old Aunt Phoenix," she said. "She doesn't come for herself—she has a little grandson. She makes these trips just as regular as clockwork. She lives away back off the old Natchez Trace." She bent down. "Well, Aunt Phoenix, why don't you just take a seat? We won't keep you standing after your long trip." She pointed.

The old woman sat down, bolt upright in the chair.

80 "Now, how is the boy?" asked the nurse.

Old Phoenix did not speak.

"I said, how is the boy?"

But Phoenix only waited and stared straight ahead, her face very solemn and withdrawn into rigidity.

"Is his throat any better?" asked the nurse. "Aunt Phoenix, don't you hear me? Is your grandson's throat any better since the last time you came for the medicine?"

85 With her hands on her knees, the old woman waited, silent, erect and motionless, just as if she were in armor.

"You mustn't take up our time this way, Aunt Phoenix," the nurse said. "Tell us quickly about your grandson, and get it over. He isn't dead, is he?"

At last there came a flicker and then a flame of comprehension across her face, and she spoke.

"My grandson. It was my memory had left me. There I sat and forgot why I made my long trip."

"Forgot?" The nurse frowned. "After you came so far?"

90 Then Phoenix was like an old woman begging a dignified forgiveness for waking up frightened in the night. "I never did go to school, I was too old at the Surrender," she said in a soft voice. "I'm an old woman without an education. It was my memory fail me. My little grandson, he is just the same, and I forgot it in the coming."

"Throat never heals, does it?" said the nurse, speaking in a loud, sure voice to Old Phoenix. By now she had a card with something written on it, a little list. "Yes. Swallowed lye. When was it—January—two-three years ago—"

Phoenix spoke unasked now. "No, missy, he not dead, he just the same. Every little while his throat begin to close up again, and he not able to swallow. He not get his breath. He not able to help himself. So the time come around, and I go on another trip for the soothing medicine."

"All right. The doctor said as long as you came to get it, you could have it," said the nurse. "But it's an obstinate case."

"My little grandson, he sit up there in the house all wrapped up, waiting by himself," Phoenix went on. "We is the only two left in the world. He suffer and it don't seem to put him back at all. He got a sweet look. He going to last. He wear a little patch quilt and peep out holding his mouth open like a little bird. I remembers so plain now. I not going to forget him again, no, the whole enduring time. I could tell him from all the others in creation."

95 "All right." The nurse was trying to hush her now. She brought her a bottle of medicine. "Charity," she said, making a check mark in a book.

Old Phoenix held the bottle close to her eyes and then carefully put it into her pocket.

"I thank you," she said.

"It's Christmas time, Grandma," said the attendant. "Could I give you a few pennies out of my purse?"

"Five pennies is a nickel," said Phoenix stiffly.

100 "Here's a nickel," said the attendant.

Phoenix rose carefully and held out her hand. She received the nickel and then fished the other nickel out of her pocket and laid it beside the new one. She stared at her palm closely, with her head on one side.

Then she gave a tap with her cane on the floor.

"This is what come to me to do," she said. "I going to the store and buy my child a little windmill they sells, made out of paper. He going to find it hard to believe there such a thing in the world. I'll march myself back where he waiting, holding it straight up in his hand."

She lifted her free hand, gave a little nod, turned round, and walked out of the doctor's office. Then her slow step began on the stairs, going down.

[1941]

Joining the Conversation: Critical Thinking and Writing

1. If you do not know the legend of the phoenix, look it up in a dictionary or, better, in an encyclopedia. Then carefully reread the story, to learn whether the story in any way connects with the legend.
2. What do you think of the hunter?
3. What would be lost if the episode (with all of its dialogue) of Phoenix falling into the ditch and being helped out of it by the hunter were omitted?
4. Is Christmas a particularly appropriate time in which to set the story? Why or why not?
5. In an argument of no more than one page, explain the significance of the story's title.

TONI CADE BAMBARA

Toni Cade Bambara (1939–1995), was born in New York City and grew up in various African American neighborhoods of the city. After studying at the University of Florence in Italy and at City College in New York, where she received a master's degree, she worked for a while as a case investigator for the New York State Welfare Department. Later she directed a recreation program for hospital patients. After her literary reputation became established, she spent most of her time writing, though she also served as writer in residence at Spelman College in Atlanta.

The Lesson

Back in the days when everyone was old and stupid or young and foolish and me and Sugar were the only ones just right, this lady moved on our block with nappy hair and proper speech and no makeup. And quite naturally we laughed at her, laughed the way we did at the junk man who went about his business like he was some big-time president and his sorry-ass horse his secretary. And we kinda hated her too, hated the way we did the winos who cluttered up our parks and pissed on our handball walls and stank up our hallways and stairs so you couldn't halfway play hide-and-seek without a goddamn gas mask. Miss Moore was her name. The only woman on the block with no first name. And she was black as hell, cept for her feet, which were fish-white and spooky. And she was always planning these boring-ass things for us to do, us being my cousin, mostly, who lived on the block cause we all moved North the same time and to the same apartment then spread out gradual to breathe. And our parents would yank our heads into some kinda shape and crisp up our clothes so we'd be presentable for travel with Miss Moore, who always looked like she was going to church, though she never did. Which is just one of the things the grownups talked about when they talked behind her back like a dog. But when she came calling with some sachet she'd sewed up or some gingerbread she'd made or some book, why then they'd all be too embarrassed to turn her down and we'd get handed over all spruced up. She'd been to college and said it was only right that she should take responsibility for the young ones' education, and she not even related by marriage or blood. So they'd go for it. Specially Aunt Gretchen. She was the main gofer in the family. You got some ole dumb shit foolishness you want somebody to go for, you send for Aunt Gretchen. She been screwed into the go-along for so long, it's a blood-deep natural thing with her. Which is how she got saddled with me and Sugar and Junior in the first place while our mothers were in a la-de-da apartment up the block having a good ole time.

So this one day Miss Moore rounds us all up at the mailbox and it's puredee hot and she's knockin herself out about arithmetic. And school suppose to let up in summer I heard, but she don't never let up. And the starch in my pinafore scratching the shit outta me and I'm really hating this nappy-head bitch and her goddamn college degree. I'd much rather go to the pool or to the show where it's cool. So me and Sugar leaning on the mailbox being surly, which is a Miss Moore word. And Flyboy checking out what everybody brought for lunch. And Fat Butt already wasting his peanut-butter-and-jelly sandwich like the pig he is. And Junebug punchin on Q.T.'s arm for potato chips. And Rosie Giraffe shifting from one hip to the other waiting for somebody to step on her foot or ask her if she from Georgia so she can kick ass, preferably Mercedes'. And Miss Moore asking us do we know what money is, like we a bunch of retards. I mean real money, she say, like it's only poker chips or monopoly papers we lay on the grocer. So right away I'm tired of this and say so. And would much rather snatch Sugar and go to the Sunset and terrorize the West Indian kids and take their hair ribbons and their money too. And Miss Moore files that remark away for next week's lesson on brotherhood, I can tell. And finally I say we oughta get to the subway cause it's cooler and besides we might meet some cute boys. Sugar done swiped her mama's lipstick, so we ready.

So we heading down the street and she's boring us silly about what things cost and what our parents make and how much goes for rent and how money ain't divided up right in this country. And then she gets to the part about we all poor and live in the slums, which I don't feature. And I'm ready to speak on that, but she steps out in the street and hails two cabs just like that. Then she hustles half the crew in with her and hands me a five-dollar bill and tells me to calculate 10 percent tip for the driver. And we're off. Me and Sugar and Junebug and Flyboy hangin out the window and hollering to everybody, putting lipstick on each other cause Flyboy a faggot anyway, and making farts with our sweaty armpits. But I'm mostly trying to figure how to spend this money. But they all fascinated with the meter ticking and Junebug starts laying bets to how much it'll read when Flyboy can't hold his breath no more. Then Sugar lays bets as to how much it'll be when we get there. So I'm stuck. Don't nobody want to go for my plan, which is to jump out at the next light and run off to the first bar-b-que we can find. Then the driver tells us to get the hell out cause we there already. And the meter reads eighty-five cents. And I'm stalling to figure out the tip and Sugar say give him a dime. And I decide he don't need it as bad as I do, so later for him. But then he tries to take off with Junebug foot still in the door so we talk about his mama something ferocious. Then we check out that we on Fifth Avenue and everybody dressed up in stockings. One lady in a fur coat, hot as it is. White folks crazy.

"This is the place," Miss Moore say, presenting it to us in the voice she uses at the museum. "Let's look in the windows before we go in."

"Can we steal?" Sugar asks very serious like she's getting the ground rules squared away before she plays. "I beg your pardon," say Miss Moore, and we fall out. So she leads us around the windows of the toy store and me and Sugar screamin, "This is mine, that's mine, I gotta have that, that was made for me, I was born for that," till Big Butt drowns us out.

"Hey, I'm goin to buy that there."

"That there? You don't even know what it is, stupid."

"I do so," he say punchin on Rosie Giraffe. "It's a microscope."

"Whatcha gonna do with a microscope, fool?"

"Look at things."

"Like what, Ronald?" ask Miss Moore. And Big Butt ain't got the first notion. So here go Miss Moore gabbing about the thousands of bacteria in a drop of water and the somethinorother in a speck of blood and the million and one living things in the air around us is invisible to the naked eye. And what she say that for? Junebug go to town on that "naked" and we rolling. Then Miss Moore ask what it cost. So we all jam into the window smudgin it up and the price tag say $300. So then she ask how long'd take for Big Butt and Junebug to save up their allowances. "Too long," I say. "Yeh," adds Sugar, "outgrown it by that time." And Miss Moore say no, you never outgrow learning instruments. "Why, even medical students and interns and," blah, blah, blah. And we ready to choke Big Butt for bringing it up in the first damn place.

"This here costs four hundred eighty dollars," say Rosie Giraffe. So we pile up all over her to see what she pointin out. My eyes tell me it's a chunk of glass cracked with something heavy, and different-color inks dripped into the splits, then the whole thing put into a oven or something. But for $480 it don't make sense.

"That's a paperweight made of semi-precious stones fused together under tremendous pressure," she explains slowly, and her hands doing the mining and all the factory work.

"So what's a paperweight?" asks Rosie Giraffe.

"To weigh paper with, dumbbell," say Flyboy, the wise man from the East.

"Not exactly," say Miss Moore, which is what she say when you warm or way off too. "It's to weigh paper down so it won't scatter and make your desk untidy." So right away me and Sugar curtsy to each other and then to Mercedes who is more the tidy type.

"We don't keep paper on top of the desk in my class," say Junebug, figuring Miss Moore crazy or lyin one.

"At home, then," she say. "Don't you have a calendar and a pencil case and a blotter and a letter-opener on your desk at home where you do your homework?" And she know damn well what our homes look like cause she nosys around in them every chance she gets.

"I don't even have a desk," say Junebug. "Do we?"

"No. And I don't get no homework neither," says Big Butt.

"And I don't even have a home," say Flyboy like he do at school to keep the white folks off his back and sorry for him. Send this poor kid to camp posters, is his specialty.

"I do," says Mercedes. "I have a box of stationery on my desk and a picture of my cat. My godmother bought the stationery and the desk. There's a big rose on each sheet and the envelopes smell like roses."

"Who wants to know about your smelly-ass stationery," say Rosie Giraffe fore I can get my two cents in.

"It's important to have a work area all your own so that . . ."

"Will you look at this sailboat, please," say Flyboy, cuttin her off and pointin to the thing like it was his. So once again we tumble all over each other to gaze at this magnificent thing in the toy store which is just big enough to maybe sail two kittens across the pond if you strap them to the posts tight. We all start reciting the price tag like we in assembly. "Handcrafted sailboat of fiberglass at one thousand one hundred ninety-five dollars."

"Unbelievable," I hear myself say and am really stunned. I read it again for myself just in case the group recitation put me in a trance. Same thing. For some reason this pisses me off. We look at Miss Moore and she lookin at us, waiting for I dunno what.

"Who'd pay all that when you can buy a sailboat set for a quarter at Pop's, a tube of glue for a dime, and a ball of string for eight cents? It must have a motor and a whole lot else besides," I say. "My sailboat cost me about fifty cents."

"But will it take water?" say Mercedes with her smart ass.

"Took mine to Alley Pond Park once," say Flyboy. "String broke. Lost it. Pity."

"Sailed mine in Central Park and it keeled over and sank. Had to ask my father for another dollar."

"And you got the strap," laugh Big Butt. "The jerk didn't even have a string on it. My old man wailed on his behind."

Little Q.T. was staring hard at the sailboat and you could see he wanted it bad. But he too little and somebody'd just take it from him. So what the hell. "This boat for kids, Miss Moore?"

"Parents silly to buy something like that just to get all broke up," say Rosie Giraffe.

"That much money it should last forever," I figure.

"My father'd buy it for me if I wanted it."

"Your father, my ass," say Rosie Giraffe getting a chance to finally push Mercedes.

"Must be rich people shop here," say Q.T.

"You are a very bright boy," say Flyboy. "What was your first clue?" And he rap him on the head with the back of his knuckles, since Q.T. the only one he could get away with. Though Q.T. liable to come up behind you years later and get his licks in when you half expect it.

"What I want to know is," I says to Miss Moore though I never talk to her, I wouldn't give the bitch that satisfaction, "is how much a real boat costs? I figure a thousand'd get you a yacht any day."

"Why don't you check that out," she says, "and report back to the group?" Which really pains my ass. If you gonna mess up a perfectly good swim day least you could do is have some answers. "Let's go in," she say like she got something up her sleeve. Only she don't lead the way. So me and Sugar turn the corner to where the entrance is, but when we get there I kinda hang back. Not that I'm scared, what's there to be afraid of, just a toy store. But I feel funny, shame. But what I got to be shamed about? Got as much right to go in as anybody. But somehow I can't seem to get hold of the door, so I step away for Sugar to lead. But she hangs back too. And I look at her and she looks at me and this is ridiculous. I mean, damn,

I have never ever been shy about doing nothing or going nowhere. But then Mercedes steps up and then Rosie Giraffe and Big Butt crowd in behind and shove, and next thing we all stuffed into the doorway with only Mercedes squeezing past us, smoothing out her jumper and walking right down the aisle. Then the rest of us tumble in like a glued-together jigsaw done all wrong. And people lookin at us. And it's like the time me and Sugar crashed into the Catholic church on a dare. But once we got in there and everything so hushed and holy and the candles and the bowin and the handkerchiefs on all the drooping heads, I just couldn't go through with the plan. Which was for me to run up to the altar and do a tap dance while Sugar played the nose flute and messed around in the holy water. And Sugar kept givin me the elbow. Then later teased me so bad I tied her up in the shower and turned it on and locked her in. And she'd be there till this day if Aunt Gretchen hadn't finally figured I was lyin about the boarder takin a shower.

Same thing in the store. We all walkin on tiptoe and hardly touchin the games and puzzles and things. And I watched Miss Moore who is steady watchin us like she waitin for a sign. Like Mama Drewery watches the sky and sniffs the air and takes note of just how much slant is in the bird formation. Then me and Sugar bump smack into each other, so busy gazing at the toys, 'specially the sailboat. But we don't laugh and go into our fat-lady bumpstomach routine. We just stare at that price tag. Then Sugar run a finger over the whole boat. And I'm jealous and want to hit her. Maybe not her, but I sure want to punch somebody in the mouth.

"Whatcha bring us here for, Miss Moore?"

"You sound angry, Sylvia. Are you mad about something?" Givin me one of them grins like she tellin a grown-up joke that never turns out to be funny. And she's lookin very closely at me like maybe she plannin to do my portrait from memory. I'm mad, but I won't give her that satisfaction. So I slouch around the store bein very bored and say, "Let's go."

Me and Sugar at the back of the train watchin the tracks whizzin by large then small then gettin gobbled up in the dark. I'm thinkin about this tricky toy I saw in the store. A clown that somersaults on a bar then does chin-ups just cause you yank lightly at his leg. Cost $35. I could see me askin my mother for a $35 birthday clown. "You wanna who that costs what?" she'd say, cocking her head to the side to get a better view of the hole in my head. Thirty-five dollars could buy new bunk beds for Junior and Gretchen's boy. Thirty-five dollars and the whole household could go visit Granddaddy Nelson in the country. Thirty-five dollars would pay for the rent and the piano bill too. Who are these people that spend that much for performing clowns and $1000 for toy sailboats? What kinda work they do and how they live and how come we ain't in on it? Where we are is who we are, Miss Moore always pointin out. But it don't necessarily have to be that way, she always adds then waits for somebody to say that poor people have to wake up and demand their share of the pie and don't none of us know what kind of pie she talkin about in the first damn place. But she ain't so smart cause I still got her four dollars from the taxi and she sure ain't gettin it. Messin up my day with this shit. Sugar nudges me in my pocket and winks.

45 Miss Moore lines us up in front of the mailbox where we started from, seem like years ago, and I got a headache for thinkin so hard. And we lean all over each other so we can hold up under the draggy-ass lecture she always finishes us off with at the end before we thank her for borin us to tears. But she just looks at us like she readin tea leaves. Finally she say, "Well, what do you think of F. A. O. Schwarz?"

Rosie Giraffe mumbles, "White folks crazy."

"I'd like to go there again when I get my birthday money," says Mercedes, and we shove her out the pack so she has to lean on the mailbox by herself.

"I'd like a shower. Tiring day," say Flyboy.

Then Sugar surprises me by sayin, "You know, Miss Moore, I don't think all of us here put together eat in a year what that sailboat costs." And Miss Moore lights up like somebody goosed her. "And?" she say, urging Sugar on. Only I'm standin on her foot so she don't continue.

50 "Imagine for a minute what kind of society it is in which some people can spend on a toy what it would cost to feed a family of six or seven. What do you think?"

"I think," say Sugar pushing me off her feet like she never done before, cause I whip her ass in a minute, "that this is not much of a democracy if you ask me. Equal chance to pursue happiness means an equal crack at the dough, don't it?" Miss Moore is besides herself and I am disgusted with Sugar's treachery. So I stand on her foot one more time to see if she'll shove me. She shuts up, and Miss Moore looks at me, sorrowfully I'm thinkin. And somethin weird is goin on, I can feel it in my chest.

"Anybody else learn anything today?" lookin dead at me. I walk away and Sugar has to run to catch up and don't even seem to notice when I shrug her arm off my shoulder.

"Well, we got four dollars anyway," she says.

"Uh hunh."

55 "We could go to Hascombs and get half a chocolate layer and then go to the Sunset and still have plenty money for potato chips and ice cream sodas."

"Uh hunh."

"Race you to Hascombs," she say.

We start down the block and she gets ahead which is O.K. by me cause I'm going to the West End and then over to the Drive to think this day through. She can run if she want to and even run faster. But ain't nobody gonna beat me at nuthin.

[1972]

Joining the Conversation: Critical Thinking and Writing

1. What is the point of Miss Moore's lesson? Why does Sylvia resist it?
2. Describe the relationship between Sugar and Sylvia. What is Sugar's function in the story?
3. What does the last line of the story suggest?
4. In a paragraph or two, characterize the narrator. Do not summarize the story—assume that your reader is familiar with it—but support your characterization by some references to episodes in the story and perhaps by a few brief quotations.

AMY HEMPEL

Amy Hempel was born in Chicago in 1951. She was educated in California and at Columbia University, and now lives in New York City, where she writes fiction and teaches creative writing at Brooklyn College.

Today Will Be a Quiet Day

"I think it's the other way around," the boy said. "I think if the quake hit now the *bridge* would collapse and the *ramps* would be left."

He looked at his sister with satisfaction.

"You are just trying to scare your sister," the father said. "You know that is not true."

"No, really," the boy insisted, "and I heard birds in the middle of the night. Isn't that a warning?"

5 The girl gave her brother a toxic look and ate a handful of Raisinets. The three of them were stalled in traffic on the Golden Gate Bridge.

That morning, before waking his children, the father had canceled their music lessons and decided to make a day of it. He wanted to know how they were, is all. Just—how were they. He thought his kids were as self-contained as one of those dogs you sometimes see carrying home its own leash. But you could read things wrong.

Could you ever.

The boy had a friend who jumped from a floor of Langley Porter. The friend had been there for two weeks, mostly playing Ping-Pong. All the friend said the day the boy visited and lost every game was never play Ping-Pong with a mental patient because it's all we do and we'll kill you. That night the friend had cut the red belt he wore in two and left the other half on his bed. That was this time last year when the boy was twelve years old.

You think you're safe, the father thought, but it's thinking you're invisible because you closed your eyes.

10 This day they were headed for Petaluma–the chicken, egg, and arm-wrestling capital of the nation—for lunch. The father had offered to take them to the men's arm-wrestling semifinals. But it was said that arm wrestling wasn't so interesting since the new safety precautions, that hardly anyone broke an arm or a wrist anymore. The best anyone could hope to see would be dislocation, so they said they would rather go to Pete's. Pete's was a gas station turned into a place to eat. The hamburgers there were named after cars, and the gas pumps in front still pumped gas.

"Can I have one?" the boy asked, meaning the Raisinets.

"No," his sister said.

"Can I have two?"

"Neither of you should be eating candy before lunch," the father said. He said it with the good sport of a father who enjoys his kids and gets a kick our of saying Dad things.

15 "You mean dinner," said the girl. "It will be dinner before we get to Pete's."

Only the northbound lanes were stopped. Southbound traffic flashed past at the normal speed.

"Check it out," the boy said from the back seat. "Did you see the bumper sticker on that Porsche? 'If you don't like the way I drive, stay off the sidewalk.'"

He spoke directly to his sister. "I've just solved my Christmas shopping."

"I got the highest score in my class in Driver's Ed," she said.

20 "I thought I would let your sister drive home today," the father said.

From the back seat came sirens, screams for help, and then a dirge.

The girl spoke to her father in a voice rich with complicity. "Don't people make you want to give up?"

"Don't the two of you know any jokes? I haven't laughed all day," the father said.

"Did I tell you the guillotine joke?" the girl said.

"He hasn't laughed all day, so you must've," her brother said.

The girl gave her brother a look you could iron clothes with. Then her gaze dropped down. "Oh-oh," she said, "Johnny's out of jail."

Her brother zipped his pants back up. He said, "Tell the joke."

"Two Frenchmen and a Belgian were about to be beheaded," the girl began. "The first Frenchman was led to the block and blindfolded. The executioner let the blade go. But it stopped a quarter inch above the Frenchman's neck. So he was allowed to go free, and ran off shouting 'C'est un miracle! 'C'est un miracle!' "

"It's a miracle," the father said.

"Then the second Frenchman was led to the block, and same thing—the blade stopped just before cutting off his head. So *he* got to go free, and ran off shouting, 'C'est un miracle!'

"Finally the Belgian was led to the block. But before they could blindfold him, he looked up, pointed to the top of the guillotine, and cried, 'Voila la difficulté!' "

She doubled over.

"Maybe *I* would be wetting *my* pants if I knew what that meant," the boy said.

"You can't explain after the punch line," the girl said, "and have it still be funny."

"There's the problem," said the father.

The waitress handed out menus to the party of three seated in the corner booth of what used to be the lube bay. She told them the specialty of the day was Moroccan chicken.

"That's what I want," the boy said. "Morerotten chicken."

But he changed his order to a Studeburger and fries after his father and sister had ordered.

"So," the father said, "who misses music lessons?"

"I'm serious about what I asked you last week," the girl said. "About switching to piano? My teacher says a real flutist only breathes with the stomach, and I can't."

"The real reason she wants to change," said the boy, "is her waist will get two inches bigger when she learns to stomach-breathe. That's what *else* her teacher said."

The boy buttered a piece of sourdough bread and flipped a chunk of cold butter onto his sister's sleeve.

"Jeezo-beezo," the girl said, "why don't they skip the knife and fork and just set his place with a slingshot!"

"Who will ever adopt you if you don't mind your manners?" the father said. "Maybe we could try a little quiet today."

"You sound like your tombstone," the girl said. "Remember what you wanted it to say?"

Her brother joined in with his mouth full: "Today will be a quiet day."

"Because it never is with us around," the boy said.

"You guys," said the father.

The waitress brought plates. The father passed sugar to the boy and salt to the girl without being asked. He watched the girl shake out salt onto the fries.

"If I had a sore throat, I would gargle with those," he said.

"Looks like she's trying to melt a driveway," the boy offered.

The father watched his children eat. They ate fast. They called it Hoovering. He finished while they sucked at straws in empty drinks.

"Funny," he said thoughtfully, "I'm not hungry anymore."

Every meal ended this way. It was his benediction, one of the Dad things they expected him to say.

"That reminds me," the girl said. "Did you feed Rocky before we left?"

"Uh-uh," her brother said. "I fed him yesterday."

"*I* fed him yesterday!" the girl said.

"Okay, we'll compromise," the boy said. "We won't feed the cat today."

"I'd say you are out of bounds on that one," the father said.

He meant you could not tease her about animals. Once, during dinner, that cat ran into the dining room shot from guns. He ran around the table at top speed, then spun out on the parquet floor into a leg of the table. He fell over onto his side and made short coughing sounds. "Isn't he smart?" the girl had crooned, kneeling beside him. "He knows he's hurt."

For years, her father had to say that the animals seen on shoulders of roads were napping.

"He never would have not fed Homer," she said to her father.

"Homer was a dog," the boy said. "If I forgot to feed him, he could just go into the hills and bite a deer."

"Or a Campfire Girl selling mints at the front door," their father reminded them.

"Homer," the girl sighed. "I hope he likes chasing sheep on that ranch in the mountains."

The boy looked at her, incredulous.

"You *believed* that? You actually *believed* that?"

In her head, a clumsy magician yanked the cloth and the dishes all crashed to the floor. She took air into her lungs until they filled, and then she filled her stomach, too.

"I thought she knew," the boy said.

The dog was five years ago.

"The girl's parents insisted," the father said. "It's the law in California."

"Then I hate California," she said. "I hate its guts."

The boy said he would wait for them in the car, and left the table.

"What would help?" the father asked.

"For Homer to be alive," she said.

"What would help?"

"Nothing."

"Help."

She pinched a trail of salt on her plate.

"A ride," she said. "I'll drive."

The girl started the car and screamed, "Goddammit."

With the power off, the boy had tuned in the Spanish station. Mariachis exploded on ignition.

"Dammit isn't God's last name," the boy said, quoting another bumper sticker.

"Don't people make you want to give up?" the father said.

"No talking," the girl said to the rearview mirror, and put the car in gear.

She drove for hours. Through groves of eucalyptus with their damp peeling bark, past acacia bushes with yellow flowers pulsing off their stems. She cut over to the coast route and the stony gray-green tones of Inverness.

"What you'd call scenic," the boy tried.

Otherwise they were quiet.

No one said anything else until the sky started to close, and then it was the boy again, asking shouldn't they be going home.

90 "No, no," the father said, and made a show of looking out the window, up at the sky and back at his watch. "No," he said, "keep driving—it's getting earlier."

But the sky spilled rain, and the girl headed south toward the bridge. She turned on the headlights and the dashboard lit up green. She read off the odometer on the way home: "Twenty-six thousand, three hundred eighty three and eight-tenths miles."

"Today?" the boy said.

The boy got to Rocky first. "Let's play the cat," he said, and carried the Siamese to the upright piano. He sat on the bench holding the cat in his lap and pressed its paws to the keys. Rocky played "Born Free." He tried to twist away.

"Come on, Rocky, ten more minutes and we'll break."

95 "Give him to me," the girl said.

She puckered up and gave the cat a five-lipper.

"Bring the Rock upstairs," the father called. "Bring sleeping bags, too."

Pretty soon three sleeping bags formed a triangle in the master bedroom. The father was the hypotenuse. The girl asked him to brush out her hair, which he did while the boy ate a tangerine, peeling it up close to his face, inhaling the mist. Then he held each segment to the light to find seeds. In his lap, cat paws fluttered like dreaming eyes.

"What are you thinking?" the father asked.

100 "Me?" the girl said. "Fifty-seven T-bird, white with red interior, convertible. I drive it to Texas and wear skirts with rick-rack. I'm changing my name to Ruby," she said, "or else Easy."

The father considered her dream of a checkered future.

"Early ripe, early rot," he warned.

A wet wind slammed the window in its warped sash, and the boy jumped.

"I hate rain," he said. "I hate its guts."

105 The father got up and closed the window tighter against the storm. "It's a real frog-choker," he said.

In darkness, lying still, it was no less camp-like than if they had been under the stars, singing to a stone-ringed fire burned down to embers.

They had already said good-night some minutes earlier when the boy and girl heard their father's voice in the dark.

"Kids, I just remembered—I have some good news and some bad news. Which do you want first?"

It was his daughter who spoke. "Let's get it over with," she said. "Let's get the bad news over with."

110 The father smiled. They are all right, he decided. My kids are as right as this rain. He smiled at the exact spots he knew their heads were turned to his, and doubted he would ever feel—not better, but *more* than he did now.

"I lied," he said. "There is no bad news."

Joining the Conversation: Critical Thinking and Writing

1. The story begins with characters in a car on a bridge, talking about the possibility of the bridge collapsing during an earthquake. A few lines later we read about a boy who committed suicide. Moreover, we are told that the father somehow fears that he may not really know his children. When you began reading the story, did these ominous touches seem to you to be foreshadowing? That is, did they suggest to you that the story might end unhappily? Or, on the contrary, did you somehow feel, despite these threats, that the story would not end unhappily? Explain.
2. At the beginning of the story, the father says that the boy is trying to "scare" the sister. How would you characterize the relationship between the two children?
3. The mother is never mentioned. Should we have been told if she is dead, or if she has abandoned the family, or whatever? Why do you hold the view that you hold?
4. We are told in paragraph 14 that the father "gets a kick out of saying Dad things" to his children. Try your hand at inventing some "Dad things" that he might have said in this story.
5. The point of the joke about the guillotine is that it doesn't pay to point out the source of difficulties. How does this joke help you to make sense of the story?

BOBBIE ANN MASON

Bobbie Ann Mason, born in 1940 in rural western Kentucky and a graduate of the University of Kentucky, now lives in Pennsylvania. She earned a master's degree at the State University of New York at Binghamton, and a PhD at the University of Connecticut, writing a dissertation on a novel by Vladimir Nabokov. Between graduate degrees she worked for various magazines, including T.V. Star Parade. *In 1974 she published her first book—the dissertation on Nabokov—and in 1975 she published her second,* The Girl Sleuth: A Guide to the Bobbsey Twins, Nancy Drew and Their Sisters. *She is, however, most widely known for her fiction, which usually deals with blue-collar people in rural Kentucky. "I write," she says, "about people trapped in circumstances. . . . I identify with people who are ambivalent about their situation. And I guess in my stories, I'm in a way imagining myself as I would have felt if I had not gotten away and gotten a different perspective on things—if, for example, I had gotten pregnant in high school and had to marry a truck driver as the woman did in my story 'Shiloh'."*

Shiloh

Leroy Moffitt's wife, Norma Jean, is working on her pectorals. She lifts three-pound dumbbells to warm up, then progresses to a twenty-pound barbell. Standing with her legs apart, she reminds Leroy of Wonder Woman.

"I'd give anything if I could just get these muscles to where they're real hard," says Norma Jean. "Feel this arm. It's not as hard as the other one."

"That's cause you're right-handed," says Leroy, dodging as she swings the barbell in an arc.

"Do you think so?"

"Sure."

Leroy is a truckdriver. He injured his leg in a highway accident four months ago, and his physical therapy, which involves weights and a pulley, prompted Norma Jean to try building herself up. Now she is attending a body-building class. Leroy has been collecting temporary disability since his tractor-trailer jackknifed in Missouri, badly twisting his left leg in its socket. He has a steel pin in his hip. He will probably not be able to drive his rig again. It sits in the backyard, like a gigantic bird that has flown home to roost. Leroy has been home in Kentucky for three months, and his leg is almost healed, but the accident frightened him and he does not want to drive any more long hauls. He is not sure what to do next. In the meantime, he makes things from craft kits. He started by building a miniature log cabin from notched Popsicle sticks. He varnished it and placed it on the TV set, where it remains. It reminds him of a rustic Nativity scene. Then he tried string art (sailing ships on black velvet), a macramé owl kit, a snap-together B-17 Flying Fortress, and a lamp made out of a model truck, with a light fixture screwed in the top of the cab. At first the kits were diversions, something to kill time, but now he is thinking about building a full-scale log house from a kit. It would be considerably cheaper than building a regular house, and besides, Leroy has grown to appreciate how things are put together. He has begun to realize that in all the years he was on the road he never took time to examine anything. He was always flying past scenery.

"They won't let you build a log cabin in any of the new subdivisions," Norma Jean tells him.

"They will if I tell them it's for you," he says, teasing her. Ever since they were married, he has promised Norma Jean he would build her a new home one day. They have always rented, and the house they live in is small and nondescript. It does not even feel like a home, Leroy realizes now.

Norma Jean works at the Rexall drugstore, and she has acquired an amazing amount of information about cosmetics. When she explains to Leroy the three stages of complexion care, involving creams, toners, and moisturizers, he thinks happily of other petroleum products—axle grease, diesel fuel. This is a connection between him and Norma Jean. Since he has been home, he has felt unusually tender about his wife and guilty over his long absences. But he can't tell what she feels about him. Norma Jean has never complained about his traveling; she has never made hurt remarks, like calling his truck a "widow-maker." He is reasonably certain she has been faithful to him, but he wishes she would celebrate his permanent home-coming more happily. Norma Jean is often startled to find Leroy at home, and he thinks she seems a little disappointed about it. Perhaps he reminds her too much of the early days of their marriage, before he went on the road. They had a child who died as an infant, years ago. They never speak about their memories of Randy, which have almost faded, but now that Leroy is home all the time, they sometimes feel awkward around each other, and Leroy wonders if one of them should mention the child. He has the feeling that they are waking up out of a dream together—that they must create a new marriage, start afresh. They are lucky they are still married. Leroy has read that for most people losing a child destroys the marriage—or else he heard this on *Donahue*.[1] He can't always remember where he learns things anymore.

[1]***Donahue*** popular television talk show of the 1980s and 1990s.

10 At Christmas, Leroy bought an electric organ for Norma Jean. She used to play the piano when she was in high school. "It don't leave you," she told him once. "It's like riding a bicycle."

The new instrument had so many keys and buttons that she was bewildered by it at first. She touched the keys tentatively, pushed some buttons, then pecked out "Chopsticks." It came out in an amplified fox-trot rhythm, with marimba sounds.

"It's an orchestra!" she cried.

The organ had a pecan-look finish and eighteen preset chords, with optional flute, violin, trumpet, clarinet, and banjo accompaniments. Norma Jean mastered the organ almost immediately. At first she played Christmas songs. Then she bought *The Sixties Songbook* and learned every tune in it, adding variations to each with the rows of brightly colored buttons.

"I didn't like these old songs back then," she said. "But I have this crazy feeling I missed something."

15 "You didn't miss a thing," said Leroy.

Leroy likes to lie on the couch and smoke a joint and listen to Norma Jean play "Can't Take My Eyes Off You" and "I'll Be Back." He is back again. After fifteen years on the road, he is finally settling down with the woman he loves. She is still pretty. Her skin is flawless. Her frosted curls resemble pencil trimmings.

Now that Leroy has come home to stay, he notices how much the town has changed. Subdivisions are spreading across western Kentucky like an oil slick. The sign at the edge of town says "Pop: 11,500"—only seven hundred more than it said twenty years before. Leroy can't figure out who is living in all the new houses. The farmers who used to gather around the courthouse square on Saturday afternoons to play checkers and spit tobacco juice have gone. It has been years since Leroy has thought about the farmers, and they have disappeared without his noticing.

Leroy meets a kid named Stevie Hamilton in the parking lot at the new shopping center. While they pretend to be strangers meeting over a stalled car, Stevie tosses an ounce of marijuana under the front seat of Leroy's car. Stevie is wearing orange jogging shoes and a T-shirt that says CHATTAHOOCHEE SUPER-RAT. His father is a prominent doctor who lives in one of the expensive subdivisions in a new white-columned brick house that looks like a funeral parlor. In the phone book under his name there is a separate number, with the listing "Teenagers."

"Where do you get this stuff?" asks Leroy. "From your pappy?"

20 "That's for me to know and you to find out," Stevie says. He is slit-eyed and skinny.

"What else you got?"

"What you interested in?"

"Nothing special. Just wondered."

Leroy used to take speed on the road. Now he has to go slowly. He needs to be mellow. He leans back against the car and says, "I'm aiming to build me a log house, soon as I get time. My wife, though, I don't think she likes the idea."

25 "Well, let me know when you want me again," Stevie says. He has a cigarette in his cupped palm, as though sheltering it from the wind. He takes a long drag, then stomps it on the asphalt and slouches away.

Stevie's father was two years ahead of Leroy in high school. Leroy is thirty-four. He married Norma Jean when they were both eighteen, and their child Randy was born a few months later, but he died at the age of four months and three days. He would be about Stevie's age now. Norma Jean and Leroy were at the drive-in, watching a double feature (*Dr. Strangelove* and *Lover Come Back*), and the baby was sleeping in the back seat. When the first movie ended, the baby was dead. It was the sudden infant death syndrome. Leroy remembers handing Randy to a nurse at the emergency room, as though he were offering her a large doll as a present. A dead baby feels like a sack of flour. "It just happens sometimes," said the doctor, in what Leroy always recalls as a nonchalant tone. Leroy can hardly remember the child anymore, but he still sees vividly a scene from *Dr. Strangelove* in which the President of the United States was talking in a folksy voice on the hot line to the Soviet premier about the bomber accidentally headed toward Russia. He was in the War Room, and the world map was lit up. Leroy remembers Norma Jean standing catatonically beside him in the hospital and himself thinking: Who is this strange girl? He had forgotten who she was. Now scientists are saying that crib death is caused by a virus. Nobody knows anything, Leroy thinks. The answers are always changing.

When Leroy gets home from the shopping center, Norma Jean's mother, Mabel Beasley, is there. Until this year, Leroy has not realized how much time she spends with Norma Jean. When she visits, she inspects the closets and then the plants, informing Norma Jean when a plant is droopy or yellow. Mabel calls the plants "flowers," although there are never any blooms. She also notices if Norma Jean's laundry is piling up. Mabel is a short, overweight woman whose tight, brown-dyed curls look more like a wig than the actual wig she sometimes wears. Today she has brought Norma Jean an off-white dust ruffle she made for the bed; Mabel works in a custom-upholstery shop.

"This is the tenth one I made this year," Mabel says. "I got started and couldn't stop."

"It's real pretty," says Norma Jean.

30 "Now we can hide things under the bed," says Leroy, who gets along with his mother-in-law primarily by joking with her. Mabel has never really forgiven him for disgracing her by getting Norma Jean pregnant. When the baby died, she said that fate was mocking her.

"What's that thing?" Mabel says to Leroy in a loud voice, pointing to a tangle of yarn on a piece of canvas.

Leroy holds it up for Mabel to see. "It's my needlepoint," he explains. "This is a *Star Trek* pillow cover."

"That's what a woman would do," says Mabel. "Great day in the morning!"

"All the big football players on TV do it," he says.

35 "Why, Leroy, you're always trying to fool me. I don't believe you for one minute. You don't know what to do with yourself—that's the whole trouble. Sewing!"

"I'm aiming to build us a log house," says Leroy. "Soon as my plans come."

"Like *heck* you are," says Norma Jean. She takes Leroy's needlepoint and shoves it into a drawer. "You have to find a job first. Nobody can afford to build now anyway."

Mabel straightens her girdle and says, "I still think before you get tied down y'all ought to take a little run to Shiloh."

"One of these days, Mama," Norma Jean says impatiently.

40 Mabel is talking about Shiloh, Tennessee. For the past few years, she has been urging Leroy and Norma Jean to visit the Civil War battleground there. Mabel went there on her honeymoon—the only real trip she ever took. Her husband

died of a perforated ulcer when Norma Jean was ten, but Mabel, who was accepted into the United Daughters of the Confederacy in 1975, is still preoccupied with going back to Shiloh.

"I've been to kingdom come and back in that truck out yonder," Leroy says to Mabel, "but we never yet set foot in that battleground. Ain't that something? How did I miss it?"

"It's not even that far," Mabel says.

After Mabel leaves, Norma Jean reads to Leroy from a list she has made. "Things you could do," she announces. "You could get a job as a guard at Union Carbide, where they'd let you set on a stool. You could get on at the lumberyard. You could do a little carpenter work, if you want to build so bad. You could—"

"I can't do something where I'd have to stand up all day."

"You ought to try standing up all day behind a cosmetics counter. It's amazing that I have strong feet, coming from two parents that never had strong feet at all." At the moment Norma Jean is holding on to the kitchen counter, raising her knees one at a time as she talks. She is wearing two-pound ankle weights.

"Don't worry," says Leroy. "I'll do something."

"You could truck calves to slaughter for somebody. You wouldn't have to drive any big old truck for that."

"I'm going to build you this house," says Leroy. "I want to make you a real home."

"I don't want to live in any log cabin."

"It's not a cabin. It's a house."

"I don't care. It looks like a cabin."

"You and me together could lift those logs. It's just like lifting weights."

Norma Jean doesn't answer. Under her breath, she is counting. Now she is marching through the kitchen. She is doing goose steps.

Before his accident, when Leroy came home he used to stay in the house with Norma Jean, watching TV in bed and playing cards. She would cook fried chicken, picnic ham, chocolate pie—all his favorites. Now he is home alone much of the time. In the mornings, Norma Jean disappears, leaving a cooling place in the bed. She eats a cereal called Body Buddies, and she leaves the bowl on the table, with the soggy tan balls floating in a milk puddle. He sees things about Norma Jean that he never realized before. When she chops onions, she stares off into a corner, as if she can't bear to look. She puts on her house slippers almost precisely at nine o'clock every evening and nudges her jogging shoes under the couch. She saves bread heels for the birds. Leroy watches the birds at the feeder. He notices the peculiar way goldfinches fly past the window. They close their wings, then fall, then spread their wings to catch and lift themselves. He wonders if they close their eyes when they fall. Norma Jean closes her eyes when they are in bed. She wants the lights turned out. Even then, he is sure she closes her eyes.

He goes for long drives around town. He tends to drive a car rather carelessly. Power steering and an automatic shift make a car feel so small and inconsequential that his body is hardly involved in the driving process. His injured leg stretches out comfortably. Once or twice he has almost hit something, but even the prospect of an accident seems minor in a car. He cruises the new subdivisions, feeling like a criminal rehearsing for a robbery. Norma Jean is probably right about a log house being inappropriate here in the new subdivision. All the houses look grand and complicated. They depress him.

One day when Leroy comes home from a drive he finds Norma Jean in tears. She is in the kitchen making a potato and mushroom-soup casserole, with grated cheese topping. She is crying because her mother caught her smoking.

"I didn't hear her coming. I was standing here puffing away pretty as you please," Norma Jean says, wiping her eyes.

"I knew it would happen sooner or later," says Leroy, putting his arm around her.

"She don't know the meaning of the word 'knock,'" says Norma Jean. "It's a wonder she hadn't caught me years ago."

60 "Think of it this way," Leroy says. "What if she caught me with a joint?"

"You better not let her!" Norma Jean shrieks. "I'm warning you, Leroy Moffitt!"

"I'm just kidding. Here, play me a tune. That'll help you relax."

Norma Jean puts the casserole in the oven and sets the timer. Then she plays a ragtime tune, with horns and banjo, as Leroy lights up a joint and lies on the couch, laughing to himself about Mabel's catching him at it. He thinks of Stevie Hamilton—a doctor's son pushing grass. Everything is funny. The whole town seems crazy and small. He is reminded of Virgil Mathis, a boastful policeman Leroy used to shoot pool with. Virgil recently led a drug bust in a back room at a bowling alley, where he seized ten thousand dollars' worth of marijuana. The newspaper had a picture of him holding up the bags of grass and grinning widely. Right now, Leroy can imagine Virgil breaking down the door and arresting him with a lungful of smoke. Virgil would probably have been alerted to the scene because of all the racket Norma Jean is making. Now she sounds like a hard-rock band. Norma Jean is terrific. When she switches to a Latin-rhythm version of "Sunshine Superman," Leroy hums along. Norma Jean's foot goes up and down, up and down.

"Well, what do you think?" Leroy says, when Norma Jean pauses to search through her music.

65 "What do I think about what?"

His mind has gone blank. Then he says, "I'll sell my rig and build us a house." That wasn't what he wanted to say. He wanted to know what she thought—what she *really* thought—about them.

"Don't start in on that again," says Norma Jean. She begins playing "Who'll Be the Next in Line?"

Leroy used to tell hitchhikers his whole life story—about his travels, his hometown, the baby. He would end with a question: "Well, what do you think?" It was just a rhetorical question. In time, he had the feeling that he'd been telling the same story over and over to the same hitchhikers. He quit talking to hitchhikers when he realized how his voice sounded—whining and self-pitying, like some teenage-tragedy song. Now Leroy has the sudden impulse to tell Norma Jean about himself, as if he had just met her. They have known each other so long they have forgotten a lot about each other. They could become reacquainted. But when the oven timer goes off and she runs to the kitchen, he forgets why he wants to do this.

The next day, Mabel drops by. It is Saturday and Norma Jean is cleaning. Leroy is studying the plans of his log house, which have finally come in the mail. He has them spread out on the table—big sheets of stiff blue paper, with diagrams and numbers printed in white. While Norma Jean runs the vacuum, Mabel drinks coffee. She sets her coffee cup on a blueprint.

70 "I'm just waiting for time to pass," she says to Leroy, drumming her fingers on the table.

As soon as Norma Jean switches off the vacuum, Mabel says in a loud voice, "Did you hear about the datsun dog that killed the baby?"

Norma Jean says, "The word is 'dachshund.'"

"They put the dog on trial. It chewed the baby's legs off. The mother was in the next room all the time." She raises her voice. "They thought it was neglect."

Norma Jean is holding her ears. Leroy manages to open the refrigerator and get some Diet Pepsi to offer Mabel. Mabel still has some coffee and she waves away the Pepsi.

75 "Datsuns are like that," Mabel says. "They're jealous dogs. They'll tear a place to pieces if you don't keep an eye on them."

"You better watch out what you're saying, Mabel," says Leroy.

"Well, facts is facts."

Leroy looks out the window at his rig. It is like a huge piece of furniture gathering dust in the backyard. Pretty soon it will be an antique. He hears the vacuum cleaner. Norma Jean seems to be cleaning the living room rug again.

Later, she says to Leroy, "She just said that about the baby because she caught me smoking. She's trying to pay me back."

80 "What are you talking about?" Leroy says, nervously shuffling blueprints.

"You know good and well," Norma Jean says. She is sitting in a kitchen chair with her feet up and her arms wrapped around her knees. She looks small and helpless. She says, "The very idea, her bringing up a subject like that! Saying it was neglect."

"She didn't mean that," Leroy says.

"She might not have *thought* she meant it. She always says things like that. You don't know how she goes on."

"But she didn't really mean it. She was just talking."

85 Leroy opens a king-sized bottle of beer and pours it into two glasses, dividing it carefully. He hands a glass to Norma Jean and she takes it from him mechanically. For a long time, they sit by the kitchen window watching the birds at the feeder.

Something is happening. Norma Jean is going to night school. She has graduated from her six-week body-building course and now she is taking an adult-education course in composition at Paducah Community College. She spends her evenings outlining paragraphs.

"First, you have a topic sentence," she explains to Leroy. "Then you divide it up. Your secondary topic has to be connected to your primary topic."

To Leroy, this sounds intimidating. "I never was any good in English," he says.

"It makes a lot of sense."

90 "What are you doing this for, anyhow?"

She shrugs. "It's something to do." She stands up and lifts her dumbbells a few times.

"Driving a rig, nobody cared about my English."

"I'm not criticizing your English."

Norma Jean used to say, "If I lose ten minutes' sleep, I just drag all day." Now she stays up late, writing compositions. She got a B on her first paper—a how-to theme on soup-based casseroles. Recently Norma Jean has been cooking unusual foods—tacos, lasagna, Bombay chicken. She doesn't play the organ anymore, though her second paper was called "Why Music Is Important to Me." She sits at the kitchen table, concentrating on her outlines, while Leroy plays with his log house plans, practicing with a set of Lincoln Logs. The thought of getting a truckload of notched, numbered logs scares him, and he wants to be prepared. As he and Norma Jean work together at the kitchen table, Leroy has the hopeful thought that they are sharing something, but he knows he is a fool to think this. Norma Jean is miles away. He knows he is going to lose her. Like Mabel, he is just waiting for time to pass.

95 One day, Mabel is there before Norma Jean gets home from work, and Leroy finds himself confiding in her. Mabel, he realizes, must know Norma Jean better than he does.

"I don't know what's got into that girl," Mabel says. "She used to go to bed with the chickens. Now you say she's up all hours. Plus her a-smoking. I like to died."

"I want to make her this beautiful home," Leroy says, indicating the Lincoln Logs. "I don't think she even wants it. Maybe she was happier with me gone."

"She don't know what to make of you, coming home like this."

"Is that it?"

100 Mabel takes the roof off his Lincoln Log cabin. "You couldn't get *me* in a log cabin," she says. "I was raised in one. It's no picnic, let me tell you."

"They're different now," says Leroy.

"I tell you what," Mabel says, smiling oddly at Leroy.

"What?"

"Take her on down to Shiloh. Y'all need to get out together, stir a little. Her brain's all balled up over them books."

105 Leroy can see traces of Norma Jean's features in her mother's face. Mabel's worn face has the texture of crinkled cotton, but suddenly she looks pretty. It occurs to Leroy that Mabel has been hinting all along that she wants them to take her with them to Shiloh.

"Let's all go to Shiloh," he says. "You and me and her. Come Sunday."

Mabel throws up her hand in protest. "Oh, no, not me. Young folks want to be by theirselves."

When Norma Jean comes in with groceries, Leroy says excitedly, "Your mama here's been dying to go to Shiloh for thirty-five years. It's about time we went, don't you think?"

"I'm not going to butt in on anybody's second honeymoon," Mabel says.

110 "Who's going on a honeymoon, for Christ's sake?" Norma Jean says loudly.

"I never raised no daughter of mine to talk that-a-way," Mabel says.

"You ain't seen nothing yet," says Norma Jean. She starts putting away boxes and cans, slamming cabinet doors.

"There's a log cabin at Shiloh," Mabel says. "It was there during the battle. There's bullet holes in it."

"When are you going to *shut up* about Shiloh, Mama?" asks Norma Jean.

115 "I always thought Shiloh was the prettiest place, so full of history," Mabel goes on. "I just hoped y'all could see it once before I die, so you could tell me about it." Later, she whispers to Leroy, "You do what I said. A little change is what she needs."

"Your name means 'the king,'" Norma Jean says to Leroy that evening. He is trying to get her to go to Shiloh, and she is reading a book about another century.

"Well, I reckon I ought to be right proud."

"I guess so."

"Am I still king around here?"

Norma Jean flexes her biceps and feels them for hardness. "I'm not fooling around with anybody, if that's what you mean," she says.

"Would you tell me if you were?"

"I don't know."

"What does *your* name mean?"

"It was Marilyn Monroe's real name."

"No kidding!"

"Norma comes from the Normans. They were invaders," she says. She closes her book and looks hard at Leroy. "I'll go to Shiloh with you if you'll stop staring at me."

On Sunday, Norma Jean packs a picnic and they go to Shiloh. To Leroy's relief Mabel says she does not want to come with them. Norma Jean drives, and Leroy, sitting beside her, feels like some boring hitchhiker she has picked up. He tries some conversation, but she answers him in monosyllables. At Shiloh, she drives aimlessly through the park, past bluffs and trails and steep ravines. Shiloh is an immense place, and Leroy cannot see it as a battleground. It is not what he expected. He thought it would look like a golf course. Monuments are everywhere, showing through the thick clusters of trees. Norma Jean passes the log cabin Mabel mentioned. It is surrounded by tourists looking for bullet holes.

"That's not the kind of log house I've got in mind," says Leroy apologetically.

"I know *that*."

"This is a pretty place. Your mama was right."

"It's O.K.," says Norma Jean. "Well, we've seen it. I hope she's satisfied."

They burst out laughing together.

At the park museum, a movie on Shiloh is shown every half hour, but they decide that they don't want to see it. They buy a souvenir Confederate flag for Mabel, and then they find a picnic spot near the cemetery. Norma Jean has brought a picnic cooler, with pimento sandwiches, soft drinks, and Yodels. Leroy eats a sandwich and then smokes a joint, hiding it behind the picnic cooler. Norma Jean has quit smoking altogether. She is picking cake crumbs from the cellophane wrapper, like a fussy bird.

Leroy says, "So the boys in gray ended up in Corinth. The Union soldiers zapped 'em finally. April 7, 1862."

They both know that he doesn't know any history. He is just talking about some of the historical plaques they have read. He feels awkward, like a boy on a date with an older girl. They are still just making conversation.

"Corinth is where Mama eloped to," says Norma Jean.

They sit in silence and stare at the cemetery for the Union dead and, beyond, at a tall cluster of trees. Campers are parked nearby, bumper to bumper, and small children in bright clothing are cavorting and squealing. Norma Jean wads up the cake wrapper and squeezes it tightly in her hand. Without looking at Leroy, she says, "I want to leave you."

Leroy takes a bottle of Coke out of the cooler and flips off the cap. He holds the bottle poised near his mouth but cannot remember to take a drink. Finally he says, "No, you don't."

"Yes, I do."

"I won't let you."

"You can't stop me."

"Don't do me that way."

Leroy knows Norma Jean will have her own way. "Didn't I promise to be home from now on?" he says.

"In some ways, a woman prefers a man who wanders," says Norma Jean. "That sounds crazy, I know."

"You're not crazy."

Leroy remembers to drink from his Coke. Then he says, "Yes, you *are* crazy. You and me could start all over again. Right back at the beginning."

"We *have* started all over again," says Norma Jean. "And this is how it turned out."

"What did I do wrong?"

"Nothing."

"Is this one of those women's lib things?" Leroy asks.

"Don't be funny."

The cemetery, a green slope dotted with white markers, looks like a subdivision site. Leroy is trying to comprehend that his marriage is breaking up, but for some reason he is wondering about white slabs in a graveyard.

"Everything was fine till Mama caught me smoking." says Norma Jean, standing up. "That set something off."

"What are you talking about?"

"She won't leave me alone—*you* won't leave me alone." Norma Jean seems to be crying, but she is looking away from him. "I feel eighteen again. I can't face that all over again." She starts walking away. "No, it *wasn't* fine. I don't know what I'm saying. Forget it."

Leroy takes a lungful of smoke and closes his eyes as Norma Jean's words sink in. He tries to focus on the fact that thirty-five hundred soldiers died on the grounds around him. He can only think of that war as a board game with plastic soldiers. Leroy almost smiles, as he compares the Confederates' daring attack on the Union camps and Virgil Mathis's raid on the bowling alley. General Grant, drunk and furious, shoved the Southerners back to Corinth, where Mabel and Jet Beasley were married years later, when Mabel was still thin and good-looking. The next day, Mabel and Jet visited the battleground, and then Norma Jean was born, and then she married Leroy and they had a baby, which they lost, and now Leroy and Norma Jean are here at the same battleground. Leroy knows he is leaving out a lot. He is leaving out the insides of history. History was always just names and dates to him. It occurs to him that building a house of logs is similarly empty—too simple. And the real inner workings of a marriage, like most of history, have escaped him. Now he sees that building a log house is the dumbest idea he could have had. It was clumsy of him to think Norma Jean would want a log house. It was a crazy idea. He'll have to think of something else, quickly. He will wad the blueprints into tight balls and fling them into the lake. Then he'll get moving again. He opens his eyes. Norma Jean has moved away and is walking through the cemetery, following a serpentine brick path.

Leroy gets up to follow his wife, but his good leg is asleep and his bad leg still hurts him. Norma Jean is far away, walking rapidly toward the bluff by the river, and he tries to hobble toward her. Some children run past him, screaming noisily. Norma Jean has reached the bluff, and she is looking out over the Tennessee River. Now she turns toward Leroy and waves her arms. Is she beckoning to him? She seems to be doing an exercise for her chest muscles. The sky is unusually pale—the color of the dust ruffle Mabel made for their bed.

[1982]

Joining the Conversation: Critical Thinking and Writing

1. Whose feelings—Leroy's or Norma Jean's—are more fully presented in the story? Do we know exactly what Norma Jean wants? Do you think that she herself knows?
2. The story is written in the present tense—for instance "Leroy Moffitt's wife, Norma Jean, is working on her pectorals," rather than (as would be more common in fiction) ". . . was working on her pectorals." What is gained by using the present in this story?
3. Why is Leroy preoccupied with kits, and why is Norma Jean so eagerly attempting to improve her body and her mind?
4. When we first meet Mabel, Norma Jean's mother, we learn that she has made "an off-white dust ruffle for the bed." Leroy jokes about it, and Mason refers to it in the last line of the story, a place of great emphasis. Why this business about a dust ruffle for a bed?
5. Do you think "Shiloh" is a good title? Why?

James Joyce

James Joyce (1882–1941) was born into a middle-class family in Dublin, Ireland. His father drank, became increasingly irresponsible and unemployable, and the family sank in the social order. Still, Joyce received a strong classical education at excellent Jesuit schools and at University College, Dublin, where he studied modern languages. In 1902, at the age of 20, he left Ireland so that he might spend the rest of his life writing about life in Ireland. ("The shortest way to Tara," he said, "is via Holyhead," i.e., the shortest way to the heart of Ireland is to take ship away.) In Trieste, Zurich, and Paris he supported his family in a variety of ways, sometimes teaching English in a Berlitz language school. His fifteen stories, collected under the title of Dubliners, *were written between 1904 and 1907, but he could not get them published until 1914. (The story we present here "Eveline," comes from* Dubliners*) Next came a highly autobiographical novel,* A Portrait of the Artist as a Young Man *(1916).* Ulysses *(1922), a complex novel covering eighteen hours in Dublin, was for some years banned by the United States Post Office, though few if any readers today find it offensive. Joyce spent most of the rest of his life working on* Finnegans Wake *(1939).*

Nine years before he succeeded in getting Dubliners *published, Joyce described the manuscript in these terms:*

> *My intention was to write a chapter of the moral history of my country and I chose Dublin for the scene because that city seemed to me the centre of paralysis. . . . I have written it for the most part in a style of scrupulous meanness and with the conviction that he is a very bold man who dares to alter in the presentment, still more to deform, whatever he has seen and heard.*

Eveline

She sat at the window watching the evening invade the avenue. Her head was leaned against the window curtains and in her nostrils was the odor of dusty cretonne. She was tired.

Few people passed. The man out of the last house passed on his way home; she heard his footsteps clacking along the concrete pavement and afterwards crunching on the cinder path before the new red houses. One time there used to be a field there in which they used to play every evening with other people's children. Then a man from Belfast[1] bought the field and built houses in it—not like their little brown houses but bright brick houses with shining roofs. The children of the avenue used to play together in that field—the Devines, the Waters, the Dunns, little Keogh the cripple, she and her brothers and sisters. Ernest, however, never played: he was too grown up. Her father used often to hunt them in out of the field with his blackthorn stick; but usually little Keogh used to keep *nix*[2] and call out when he saw her father coming. Still they seemed to have been rather happy then. Her father was not so bad then; and besides, her mother was alive. That was a long time ago; she and her brothers and sisters were all grown up; her mother was dead. Tizzie Dunn was dead, too, and the Waters had gone back to England. Everything changes. Now she was going to go away like the others, to leave her home.

Home! She looked around the room, reviewing all its familiar objects which she had dusted once a week for so many years, wondering where on earth all the dust came from. Perhaps she would never see again those familiar objects from which she had never dreamed of being divided. And yet during all those years she had never found out the name of the priest whose yellowing photograph hung on the wall above the broken harmonium beside the colored print of the promises made to Blessed Margaret Mary Alacoque. He had been a school friend of her father. Whenever he showed the photograph to a visitor her father used to pass it with a casual word:

"He is in Melbourne now."

5 She had consented to go away, to leave her home. Was that wise? She tried to weigh each side of the question. In her home anyway she had shelter and food; she had those whom she had known all her life about her. Of course she had to work hard both in the house and at business. What would they say of her in the Stores when they found out that she had run away with a fellow? Say she was a fool, perhaps; and her place would be filled up by advertisement. Miss Gavan would be glad. She had always had an edge on her, especially whenever there were people listening.

"Miss Hill, don't you see these ladies are waiting?"

"Look lively, Miss Hill, please."

She would not cry many tears at leaving the Stores.

But in her new home, in a distant unknown country, it would not be like that. Then she would be married—she, Eveline. People would treat her with respect then. She would not be treated as her mother had been. Even now, though she was over nineteen, she sometimes felt herself in danger of her father's violence. She knew it was that that had given her the palpitations. When they were growing up he had never gone for her, like he used to go for Harry and Ernest, because

[1]**a man from Belfast** i.e. a Protestant.

[2]**to keep *nix*** to stand guard.

she was a girl; but latterly he had begun to threaten her and say what he would do to her only for her dead mother's sake. And now she had nobody to protect her. Ernest was dead and Harry, who was in the church decorating business, was nearly always down somewhere in the country. Besides, the invariable squabble for money on Saturday nights had begun to weary her unspeakably. She always gave her entire wages—seven shillings—and Harry always sent up what he could but the trouble was to get any money from her father. He said she used to squander the money, that she had no head, that he wasn't going to give her his hard-earned money to throw about the streets, and much more, for he was usually fairly bad of a Saturday night. In the end he would give her the money and ask her had she any intention of buying Sunday dinner. Then she had to rush out as quickly as she could and do her marketing, holding her black leather purse tightly in her hand as she elbowed her way through the crowds and returning home late under her load of provisions. She had hard work to keep the house together and to see that the two young children, who had been left to her charge went to school regularly and got their meals regularly. It was hard work—a hard life—but now that she was about to leave it she did not find it a wholly undesirable life.

10 She was about to explore another life with Frank. Frank was very kind, manly, open-hearted. She was to go away with him by the night-boat to be his wife and to live with him in Buenos Aires where he had a home waiting for her. How well she remembered the first time she had seen him; he was lodging in a house on the main road where she used to visit. It seemed a few weeks ago. He was standing at the gate, his peaked cap pushed back on his head and his hair tumbled forward over a face of bronze. Then they had come to know each other. He used to meet her outside the Stores every evening and see her home. He took her to see *The Bohemian Girl* and she felt elated as she sat in an unaccustomed part of the theater with him. He was awfully fond of music and sang a little. People knew that they were courting and, when he sang about the lass that loves a sailor, she always felt pleasantly confused. He used to call her Poppens out of fun. First of all it had been an excitement for her to have a fellow and then she had begun to like him. He had tales of distant countries. He had started as a deck boy at a pound a month on a ship of the Allan Line going out to Canada. He told her the names of the ships he had been on and the names of the different services. He had sailed through the Straits of Magellan and he told her stories of the terrible Patagonians. He had fallen on his feet in Buenos Aires, he said, and had come over to the old country just for a holiday. Of course, her father had found out the affair and had forbidden her to have anything to say to him.

"I know these sailor chaps," he said.

One day he had quarreled with Frank and after that she had to meet her lover secretly.

The evening deepened in the avenue. The white of two letters in her lap grew indistinct. One was to Harry; the other was to her father. Ernest had been her favorite but she liked Harry too. Her father was becoming old lately, she noticed; he would miss her. Sometimes he could be very nice. Not long before, when she had been laid up for a day, he had read her out a ghost story and made toast for her at the fire. Another day, when their mother was alive, they had all gone for a picnic to the Hill of Howth. She remembered her father putting on her mother's bonnet to make the children laugh.

Her time was running out but she continued to sit by the window, leaning her head against the window curtain, inhaling the odor of dusty cretonne. Down far in the avenue she could hear a street organ playing. She knew the air. Strange that it should come that very night to remind her of the promise to her mother, her promise to keep the home together as long as she could. She remembered the last night of her mother's illness; she was again in the close dark room at the other side of the hall and outside she heard a melancholy air of Italy. The organ player had been ordered to go away and given sixpence. She remembered her father strutting back into the sickroom saying:

"Damned Italians! coming over here!"

As she mused the pitiful vision of her mother's life laid its spell on the very quick of her being—that life of commonplace sacrifices closing in final craziness. She trembled as she heard again her mother's voice saying constantly with foolish insistence:

"Derevaun Seraun! Derevaun Seraun!"[3]

She stood up in a sudden impulse of terror. Escape! She must escape! Frank would save her. He would give her life, perhaps love, too. But she wanted to live. Why should she be unhappy? She had a right to happiness. Frank would take her in his arms, fold her in his arms. He would save her.

She stood among the swaying crowd in the station at the North Wall. He held her hand and she knew that he was speaking to her, saying something about the passage over and over again. The station was full of soldiers with brown baggages. Through the wide doors of the sheds she caught a glimpse of the black mass of the boat, lying in beside the quay wall, with illumined portholes. She answered nothing. She felt her cheek pale and cold and, out of a maze of distress, she prayed to God to direct her, to show her what was her duty. The boat blew a long mournful whistle into the mist. If she went, tomorrow she would be on the sea with Frank, steaming towards Buenos Aires. Their passage had been booked. Could she still draw back after all he had done for her? Her distress awoke a nausea in her body and she kept moving her lips in silent, fervent prayer.

A bell clanged upon her heart. She felt him seize her hand:

"Come!"

All the seas of the world tumbled about her heart. He was drawing her into them: he would drown her. She gripped with both hands at the iron railing.

"Come!"

No! No! No! It was impossible. Her hands clutched the iron in frenzy. Amid the seas she sent a cry of anguish!

"Eveline! Evvy!"

He rushed beyond the barrier and called to her to follow. He was shouted at to go on but he still called to her. She set her white face to him, passive, like a helpless animal. Her eyes gave him no sign of love or farewell or recognition.

[1914]

Joining the Conversation: Critical Thinking and Writing

1. Why, in your opinion, does Eveline not join Frank?
2. What do you think are Eveline's virtues and what are her weaknesses? How sympathetic are you to Eveline?

[3]**Derevaun Seraun** possibly a garbled version of Gaelic for "The end of pleasure is pain," but perhaps meaningless syllables uttered by the dying woman.

3. In paragraph 18 Eveline tells herself that "She had a right to happiness." Do we have a right to happiness? If so, where does this right come from? Does it make sense for us to speak of such a right?
4. You are a friend of Eveline's. Write her a letter (500 words) in which you urge her to leave—or to stay.

POEMS

JOHN KEATS

John Keats (1795–1821), son of a London stable keeper, was taken out of school when he was 15 and was apprenticed to a surgeon and apothecary. In 1816 he was licensed to practice as an apothecary-surgeon, but he almost immediately abandoned medicine and decided to make a career as a poet. His progress was amazing; he quickly moved from routine verse to major accomplishments, publishing books of poems in 1817, 1818, and 1820, before dying of tuberculosis at the age of 25.

On First Looking into Chapman's Homer°

Much have I traveled in the realms of gold,
And many goodly states and kingdoms seen;
Round many western islands have I been
Which bards in fealty to Apollo° hold.
Oft of one wide expanse have I been told
That deep-browed Homer ruled as his demesne;°
Yet did I never breathe its pure serene°
Till I heard Chapman speak out loud and bold;
Then felt I like some watcher of the skies
When a new planet swims into his ken;
Or like stout Cortez when with eagle eyes
He stared at the Pacific—and all his men
Looked at each other with a wild surmise—
Silent, upon a peak in Darien.

[1816]

°**Chapman's Homer** George Chapman (1559–1634?), Shakespeare's contemporary, is chiefly known for his translations (from the Greek) of Homer's *Odyssey* and *Iliad*. In lines 11–14 Keats mistakenly says that Cortés was the first European to see the Pacific, from the heights of Darien, in Panama. In fact, Balboa was the first. **4 Apollo** god of poetry. **6 demesne** domain. **7 serene** open space.

Joining the Conversation: Critical Thinking and Writing

1. In line 1, what do you think "realms of gold" stands for? Chapman was an Elizabethan; how does this fact add relevance to the metaphor in the first line.
2. Does line 9 introduce a totally new idea, or can you somehow connect it to the opening metaphor?
3. Do you like this poem? As specifically as you can, please explain why or why not.

PERCY BYSSHE SHELLEY

Percy Bysshe Shelley (1792–1822) was born in Sussex in England, the son of a prosperous country squire. Educated at Eton, he went on to Oxford but was expelled for having written a pamphlet supporting a belief in atheism. Like John Keats he was a member of the second generation of English romantic poets. (The first generation included Wordsworth and Coleridge.) And like Keats, Shelley died young; he was drowned during a violent storm off the western coast of Italy while sailing with a friend.

Ozymandias

I met a traveler from an antique land
Who said: Two vast and trunkless legs of stone
Stand in the desert . . . Near them, on the sand,
Half sunk, a shattered visage lies, whose frown,
And wrinkled lip, and sneer of cold command,
Tell that its sculptor well those passions read
Which yet survive, stamped on these lifeless things,
The hand that mocked them, and the heart that fed:
And on the pedestal these words appear:
"My name is Ozymandias, king of kings:
Look on my works, ye Mighty, and despair!"
Nothing beside remains. Round the decay
Of that colossal wreck, boundless and bare
The lone and level sands stretch far away.

[1817]

Lines 4–8 are somewhat obscure, but the point is that the passions—still evident in the "shattered visage"—survive the sculptor's hand that "mocked"—that is, (1) imitated or copied, (2) derided—them, and the passions also survive the king's heart that had nourished them.

Joining the Conversation: Critical Thinking and Writing

There is an irony of plot here: Ozymandias believed that he created enduring works, but his intentions came to nothing. However, another irony is also present: How are his words, in a way he did not intend, true?

ALFRED, LORD TENNYSON

Alfred, Lord Tennyson (1809–1892), the son of an English clergyman, was born in Lincolnshire, where he began writing verse at age 5. Educated at Cambridge, he had to leave without a degree when his father died and Alfred had to accept responsibility for bringing up his brothers and sisters. In fact, the family had inherited ample funds, but for some years the money was tied up by litigation. Following Wordsworth's death in 1850, Tennyson was made poet laureate. With his government pension he moved with his family to the Isle of Wight, where he lived in comfort until his death.

Ulysses°

It little profits that an idle king,
By this still hearth, among these barren crags,
Matched with an aged wife, I mete and dole
Unequal laws unto a savage race,
That hoard, and sleep, and feed, and know not me.
I cannot rest from travel; I will drink
Life to the lees. All times I have enjoyed
Greatly, have suffered greatly, both with those
That loved me, and alone; on shore, and when
Thro' scudding drifts the rainy Hyades
Vext the dim sea. I am become a name;
For always roaming with a hungry heart
Much have I seen and known,—cities of men
And manners, climates, councils, governments,
Myself not least, but honored of them all,—
And drunk delight of battle with my peers,
Far on the ringing plains of windy Troy.
I am a part of all that I have met
Yet all experience is an arch wherethro'
Gleams that untravelled world whose margin fades
For ever and for ever when I move.
How dull it is to pause, to make an end,
To rust unburnished, not to shine in use!
As tho' to breathe were life! Life piled on life
Were all too little, and of one to me
Little remains; but every hour is saved
From that eternal silence, something more,
A bringer of new things; and vile it were
For some three suns to store and hoard myself,
And this gray spirit yearning in desire
To follow knowledge like a sinking star
Beyond the utmost bound of human thought.

This is my son, mine own Telemachus,
To whom I leave the scepter and the isle,—
Well-loved of me, discerning to fulfill
This labor, by slow prudence to make mild
A rugged people, and thro' soft degrees
Subdue them to the useful and the good.
Most blameless is he, centered in the sphere
Of common duties, decent not to fail
In offices of tenderness, and pay
Meet adoration to my household gods,
When I am gone. He works his work, I mine.

°**Ulysses** Odysseus, King of Ithaca, a leader of the Greeks in the Trojan War, famous for his ten years of journeying to remote places.

There lies the port; the vessel puffs her sail;
There gloom the dark, broad seas. My mariners,
Souls that have toiled, and wrought, and thought with me,—
That ever with a frolic welcome took
The thunder and the sunshine, and opposed
Free hearts, free foreheads,—you and I are old;
Old age hath yet his honor and his toil.
Death closes all; but something ere the end,
Some work of noble note, may yet be done,
Not unbecoming men that strove with Gods.
The lights begin to twinkle from the rocks;
The long day wanes; the slow moon climbs; the deep
Moans round with many voices. Come, my friends.
'Tis not too late to seek a newer world.
Push off, and sitting well in order smite
The sounding furrows; for my purpose holds
To sail beyond the sunset, and the baths
Of all the western stars, until I die.
It may be that the gulfs will wash us down;
It may be we shall touch the Happy Isles,
And see the great Achilles, whom we knew.
Tho' much is taken, much abides; and tho'
We are not now that strength which in old days
Moved earth and heaven, that which we are, we are.
One equal temper of heroic hearts,
Made weak by time and fate, but strong in will
To strive, to seek, to find, and not to yield.

[1833]

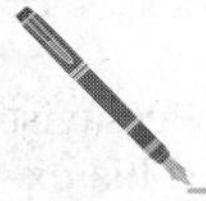

Joining the Conversation: Critical Thinking and Writing

1. Given the fact that Ulysses is a king and therefore a person with great responsibilities, does such a line as "I cannot rest from travel" (line 6) strike you as irresponsible? Explain.
2. It has been said that although at first glance the poem seems optimistic and highly positive—the final line is "To strive, to seek, to find, and not to yield"—the poem in fact is melancholy and filled with suggestions of death. Your view?
3. Is Tennyson presenting an argument here for how we should live? If so, what is your response?

Countee Cullen

Countee Cullen (1903–1946) was born Countee Porter in New York City, raised by his grandmother, and then adopted by the Reverend Frederick A Cullen, a Methodist minister in Harlem. Cullen received a bachelor's degree from New York University (Phi Beta Kappa) and a master's degree from Harvard. He earned his living as a high school teacher of French, but his literary gifts were recognized in his own day.

Incident

(For Eric Walrond)

Once riding in old Baltimore,
   Heart-filled, head-filled with glee,
I saw a Baltimorean
   Keep looking straight at me.

Now I was eight and very small,
   And he was no whit bigger,
And so I smiled, but he poked out
   His tongue, and called me, "Nigger."

I saw the whole of Baltimore
   From May until December;
Of all the things that happened there
   That's all that I remember.

[1925]

Joining the Conversation: Critical Thinking and Writing

1. How would you define an "incident"? A serious occurrence? A minor occurrence, or what? Think about the word, and then think about Cullen's use of it as a title for the event recorded in this poem. Test out one or two other possible titles as a way of helping yourself to see the strengths or weaknesses of Cullen's title.
2. The dedicatee, Eric Walrond (1898–1966), was an African American essayist and writer of fiction, who in an essay, "On Being Black," had described his experiences of racial prejudice. How does the presence of the dedication bear on our response to Cullen's account of the "incident"?
3. What is the tone of the poem? Indifferent? Angry? Or what? What do you think is the speaker's attitude toward the "incident"? What is your attitude?
4. Ezra Pound, poet and critic, once defined literature as "news that *stays* news." What do you think he meant by this? Do you think that the definition fits Cullen's poem?

WILLIAM STAFFORD

William Stafford (1914–1993) was born in Hutchinson, Kansas, and was educated at the University of Kansas and the State University of Iowa. A conscientious objector during World War II, he worked for the Brethren Service and the Church World Service. After the war he taught at several universities and then settled at Lewis and Clark College in Portland, Oregon. In addition to writing several books of poems, Stafford wrote Down in My Heart *(1947), an account of his experiences as a conscientious objector.*

Traveling Through the Dark

Traveling through the dark I found a deer
dead on the edge of the Wilson River road.
It is usually best to roll them into the canyon:
the road is narrow; to swerve might make more dead.

By glow of the tail-light I stumbled back of the car
and stood by the heap, a doe, a recent killing;
she had stiffened already, almost cold.
I dragged her off; she was large in the belly.

My fingers touching her side brought me the reason—
her side was warm; her fawn lay there waiting,
alive, still, never to be born.
Beside that mountain road I hesitated.

The car aimed ahead its lowered parking lights;
under the hood purred the steady engine.
I stood in the glare of the warm exhaust turning red;
around our group I could hear the wilderness listen.

I thought hard for us all—my only swerving—
Then pushed her over the edge into the river.

[1960]

Joining the Conversation: Critical Thinking and Writing

1. Look at the first sentence (the first two lines) and try to recall what your impression of the speaker was, based only on these two lines, or pretend that you have not read the entire poem, and characterize him merely on these two lines. Then take the entire poem into consideration and characterize him.
2. What do you make of the title? Do you think it is a good title for this poem? Explain.

ADRIENNE RICH

For a biographical note on Adrienne Rich (b. 1929), see page 548.

Diving into the Wreck

First having read the book of myths,
and loaded the camera,
and checked the edge of the knife-blade,

I put on
the body-armor of black rubber
the absurd flippers
the grave and awkward mask.
I am having to do this
not like Cousteau° with his
assiduous team
aboard the sun-flooded schooner
but here alone.

There is a ladder.
The ladder is always there
hanging innocently
close to the side of the schooner.
We know what it is for,
we who have used it.
Otherwise
it's a piece of maritime floss
some sundry equipment.

I go down.
Rung after rung and still
the oxygen immerses me
the blue light
the clear atoms
of our human air.
I go down.
My flippers cripple me,
I crawl like an insect down the ladder
and there is no one
to tell me when the ocean
will begin.

First the air is blue and then
it is bluer and then green and then
black I am blacking out and yet
my mask is powerful
it pumps my blood with power
the sea is another story
the sea is not a question of power
I have to learn alone
to turn my body without force
in the deep element.

And now: it is easy to forget
what I came for
among so many who have always
lived here
swaying their crenellated fans
between the reefs

9 Cousteau Jacques Cousteau (1910–1997), French underwater explorer.

and besides
you breathe differently down here.

I came to explore the wreck.
The words are purposes.
The words are maps.
I came to see the damage that was done
and the treasures that prevail.
I stroke the beam of my lamp
slowly along the flank
of something more permanent
than fish or weed

the thing I came for:
the wreck and not the story of the wreck
the thing itself and not the myth
the drowned face always staring
toward the sun
the evidence of damage
worn by salt and sway into this threadbare beauty
the ribs of the disaster
curving their assertion
among the tentative haunters.

This is the place.
And I am here, the mermaid whose dark hair
streams black, the merman in his armored body
We circle silently
about the wreck
we dive into the hold.
I am she: I am he

whose drowned face sleeps with open eyes
whose breasts still bear the stress
whose silver, copper, vermeil cargo lies
obscurely inside barrels
half-wedged and left to rot
we are the half-destroyed instruments
that once held to a course
the water-eaten log
the fouled compass

We are, I am, you are
by cowardice or courage
the one who find our way
back to this scene
carrying a knife, a camera
a book of myths
in which
our names do not appear.

[1972]

DEREK WALCOTT

Derek Walcott, born in 1930 on the Caribbean island of St. Lucia, was awarded the Nobel Prize in Literature in 1992. Although in the United States he is known chiefly as a poet, Walcott is also an important playwright and director of plays. Much of his work is concerned with his mixed heritage—a black writer from the Caribbean, whose language is English and who lives part of the year in Massachusetts, where he teaches in the Creative Writing Program at Boston University. Walcott's books include Collected Poems *(1986) and* Omeros *(1989), a Caribbean epic that echoes Homer's* Iliad *and* Odyssey *as it explores the Caribbean's past and present.*

A Far Cry from Africa

A wind is ruffling the tawny pelt
Of Africa. Kikuyu,° quick as flies,
Batten upon the bloodstreams of the veldt.°
Corpses are scattered through a paradise.
Only the worm, colonel of carrion, cries:
"Waste no compassion on these separate dead!"
Statistics justify and scholars seize
The salients of colonial policy.
What is that to the white child hacked in bed?
To savages, expendable as Jews?

Threshed out by beaters, the long rushes break
In a white dust of ibises whose cries
Have wheeled since civilization's dawn
From the parched river or beast-teeming plain.
The violence of beast on beast is read
As natural law, but upright man
Seeks his divinity by inflicting pain.
Delirious as these worried beasts, his wars
Dance to the tightened carcass of a drum,
While he calls courage still that native dread
Of the white peace contracted by the dead.

Again brutish necessity wipes its hands
Upon the napkins of a dirty cause, again
A waste of our compassion, as with Spain,°
The gorilla wrestles with the superman.

I who am poisoned with the blood of both,
Where shall I turn, divided to the vein?
I who have cursed
The drunken officer of British rule, how choose
Between this Africa and the English tongue I love?
Betray them both, or give back what they give?
How can I face such slaughter and be cool?
How can I turn from Africa and live?

[1962]

2 Kikuyu an African tribe that fought against British colonialists. **3 veldt** grassland in southern Africa. **24 Spain** a reference to the triumph of fascism in Spain after the civil war of 1936–1939.

Joining the Conversation: Critical Thinking and Writing

1. Now that you have read the poem, explain the meaning of the title.
2. Do you find the first stanza hard to understand? Why, or why not?
3. Focus on lines 15–17: What is Walcott saying here? Do you think that the poem might be even more effective if these lines were placed at the beginning? Or do they belong exactly where they are?
4. Imagine that Walcott sent this poem to you with a letter that asked for your response. In a letter ("Dear Mr. Walcott . . .") of one page in length, give your response to the poem.
5. What is the meaning of line 25?
6. Walcott uses the first-person "I" in the final stanza. How would you answer each of the questions he asks in it? Or do you think the point is that these questions cannot be answered?
7. What is your own experience of Africa? Have you lived or traveled there? Would you like to? Has Walcott given you a new perspective on Africa, its history and culture?

SHERMAN ALEXIE

Sherman Alexie, born in 1966 in Spokane, Washington, holds a BA from Washington State University. Author of novels, stories, and poems, and author and director of the highly praised film Smoke Signals *(1998), Alexie has been awarded a grant from the National Endowment for the Arts. Of his life and his work he says, "I am a Spokane Coeur d'Alene Indian. . . . I live on the Spokane Indian Reservation. Everything I do now, writing and otherwise, has its origin in that."*

On the Amtrak from Boston to New York City

The white woman across the aisle from me says, "Look,
look at all the history, that house
on the hill there is over two hundred years old,"
as she points out the window past me

into what she has been taught. I have learned
little more about American history during my few days
back East than what I expected and far less
of what we should all know of the tribal stories

whose architecture is 15,000 years older
than the corners of the house that sits
museumed on the hill. "Walden Pond,"°
the woman on the train asks, "Did you see Walden Pond?"

and I don't have a cruel enough heart to break
her own by telling her there are five Walden Ponds
on my little reservation out West
and at least a hundred more surrounding Spokane,

the city I pretend to call my home. "Listen,"
I could have told her. "I don't give a shit
about Walden. I know the Indians were living stories
around that pond before Walden's grandparents were born

and before his grandparents' grandparents were born.
I'm tired of hearing about Don-fucking-Henley° saving it, too,
because that's redundant. If Don Henley's brothers and sisters
and mothers and fathers hadn't come here in the first place

then nothing would need to be saved."
But I didn't say a word to the woman about Walden
Pond because she smiled so much and seemed delighted
that I thought to bring her an orange juice

back from the food car. I respect elders
of every color. All I really did was eat
my tasteless sandwich, drink my Diet Pepsi
and nod my head whenever the woman pointed out

another little piece of her country's history
while I, as all Indians have done
since this war began, made plans
for what I would do and say the next time

somebody from the enemy thought I was one of their own.

[1993]

11 Walden Pond site in Massachusetts where Henry David Thoreau (1817–1862) lived from 4 July 1845 to 6 September 1847, and about which he wrote in his most famous book, *Walden* (1854).
22 Don Henley rock singer who was active in preserving Walden from building developers.

Joining the Conversation: Critical Thinking and Writing

1. Characterize the speaker.
2. Take the common idea that "Columbus discovered America." What attitude toward the history of this land and toward Indians is implicit in these words?

WILLIAM BUTLER YEATS

William Butler Yeats (1865–1939) was born in Dublin, Ireland. The early Yeats was much interested in highly lyrical, romantic poetry, often drawing on Irish mythology. The later poems, from about 1910 (and especially after Yeats met Ezra Pound in 1911), are often more colloquial. Although these later poems often employ mythological references too, many believe that the poems are more down-to-earth. Yeats was awarded the Nobel Prize in Literature in 1923.

In the seventh century B.C.E. *the ancient Greeks founded the city of Byzantium in Thrace, where Istanbul, Turkey, now stands. (Constantine, the first Christian ruler of the Roman Empire, built a new city there in 330* C.E. *Named Constantinople, the city served as the capital of the Roman Empire until 1453, when the Turks captured it. In 1930 the name was officially changed to Istanbul.) The capital of the Roman Empire and the "holy city" of the Greek Orthodox Church, Byzantium had two golden ages. The first, in its early centuries, continued the traditions of the antique Greco-Roman world. The second, which is what Yeats had in mind, extended from the mid-ninth to the mid-thirteenth century and was a distinctive blend of classical, Christian, Slavic, and even Islamic culture. This period is noted for mysticism, for the preservation of ancient learning, and for exquisitely refined symbolic art. In short, Byzantium (as Yeats saw it) was wise and passionless. In* A Vision, *his prose treatment of his complex mystical system, Yeats says:*

> *I think that in early Byzantium, maybe never before or since in recorded history, religious, aesthetic and practical life were one, that architect and artificers—though not, it may be, poets, for language has been the instrument of controversy and must have grown abstract—spoke to the multitude and the few alike. The painter, the mosaic worker, the worker in gold and silver, the illuminator of sacred books, were almost impersonal, almost perhaps without the consciousness of individual design, absorbed in their subject matter and that the vision of the whole people. They could copy out of old Gospel books those pictures that seemed as sacred as the text, and yet weave all into a vast design, the work of many that seemed the work of one, that made building, picture, pattern, metal-work of rail and lamp, seem but a single image.*

Sailing to Byzantium

I

That is no country for old men. The young
In one another's arms, birds in the trees
—Those dying generations—at their song,
The salmon-falls, the mackerel-crowded seas,
Fish, flesh, or fowl, commend all summer long
Whatever is begotten, born, and dies.
Caught in that sensual music all neglect
Monuments of unaging intellect.

II

An aged man is but a paltry thing,
A tattered coat upon a stick, unless
Soul clap its hands and sing, and louder sing
For every tatter in its mortal dress.
Nor is there singing school but studying
Monuments of its own magnificence;
And therefore I have sailed the seas and come
To the holy city of Byzantium.

III

O sages standing in God's holy fire
As in the gold mosaic of a wall,
Come from the holy fire, perne° in a gyre,
And be the singing-masters of my soul.
Consume my heart away; sick with desire
And fastened to a dying animal
It knows not what it is; and gather me
Into the artifice of eternity.

IV

Once out of nature I shall never take
My bodily form from any natural thing,
But such a form as Grecian goldsmiths make
Of hammered gold and gold enameling
To keep a drowsy Emperor awake;
Or set upon a golden bough to sing
To lords and ladies of Byzantium
Of what is past, or passing, or to come.

[1926]

19 perne whirl down.

Joining the Conversation: Critical Thinking and Writing

1. What is "that . . . country," mentioned in the first line?
2. By the end of the first stanza, the speaker seems to be dismissing the natural world. Do you agree that even in this stanza, however, he sounds attracted to it?
3. The poem is filled with oppositions—for instance, "old men" versus "the young" (both in line 1), and "birds in the trees" (line 2) versus the mechanical bird in the final stanza. List as many opposites as you see in the poem, and then explain what Yeats is getting at.
4. The first stanza speaks of "monuments of unaging intellect." What might be some examples of these?
5. After reading and rereading this poem, do you think you will—even if only briefly—*act* differently, redirect any of your choices? Support your response with reasons.
6. Have you ever visited any place—perhaps the place where you or your parents or grandparents were born, or perhaps a house of worship, or perhaps a college campus—that you have come to see symbolically, standing for a way of life or for some aspect of life? If so, describe the place and the significance that you give it.

Christina Rossetti

Christina Rossetti (1830–1894) was the daughter of an exiled Italian patriot who lived in London and the sister of the poet and painter Dante Gabriel Rossetti. After her father became an invalid, she led an extremely ascetic life, devoting most of her life to doing charitable work. Her first and best-known volume of poetry, Goblin Market and Other Poems, *was published in 1862.*

Uphill

Does the road wind uphill all the way?
  Yes, to the very end.
Will the day's journey take the whole long day?
  From morn to night, my friend.

But is there for the night a resting-place?
  A roof for when the slow dark hours begin.
May not the darkness hide it from my face?
  You cannot miss that inn.

Shall I meet other wayfarers at night?
  Those who have gone before.
Then must I knock, or call when just in sight?
  They will not keep you standing at that door.

Shall I find comfort, travel-sore and weak?
  Of labor you shall find the sum.
Will there be beds for me and all who seek?
  Yea, beds for all who come.

[1858]

Joining the Conversation: Critical Thinking and Writing

1. Suppose that someone told you this poem is about a person preparing to go on a hike. The person is supposedly making inquiries about the road and the possible hotel arrangements. What would you reply?
2. Who is the questioner? A woman? A man? All human beings collectively? "Uphill" does not use quotation marks to distinguish between two speakers. Can one say that in "Uphill" the questioner and the answerer are the same person?
3. Are the answers unambiguously comforting? Or can it, for instance, be argued that the "roof" is (perhaps among other things) the lid of a coffin—hence the questioner will certainly not be kept "standing at that door"? If the poem can be read along these lines, is it chilling rather than comforting?

Emily Dickinson

For a biographical note on Emily Dickinson, see page 532.

Because I could not stop for Death

Because I could not stop for Death—
He kindly stopped for me—
The Carriage held but just Ourselves—
And Immortality.

We slowly drove—He knew no haste
And I had put away
My labor and my leisure too,
For His Civility—

We passed the School, where Children strove
At Recess—in the Ring—
We passed the Fields of Gazing Grain—
We passed the Setting Sun—

Or rather—He passed Us—
The Dews drew quivering and chill—
For only Gossamer, my Gown—
My Tippet°—only Tulle°—

We paused before a House that seemed
A Swelling of the Ground—
The Roof was scarcely visible—
The Cornice—in the Ground—

Since then—'tis Centuries—and yet
Feels shorter than the Day
I first surmised the Horses' Heads
Were toward Eternity—

[c. 1863]

16 Tippet shawl; **Tulle** net of silk.

Joining the Conversation: Critical Thinking and Writing

1. Characterize death as it appears in lines 1–8.
2. What is the significance of the details and their arrangement in the third stanza? Why "strove" rather than "played" (line 9)? What meanings does "Ring" (line 10) have? Is "Gazing Grain" better than "Golden Grain"?
3. The "House" in the fifth stanza is a sort of riddle. What is the answer? Does this stanza introduce an aspect of death not present—or present only very faintly—in the rest of the poem? Explain.
4. Evaluate this statement about the poem (from the literary critic Yvor Winters's *In Defense of Reason*): "In so far as it concentrates on the life that is being left behind, it is wholly successful; in so far as it attempts to experience the death to come, it is fraudulent, however exquisitely."

Chapter Overview: Looking Backward/Looking Forward

1. In a single paragraph, summarize the best, or the worst, consequence of travel. Next, try to do the same in just a single sentence.
2. Review the essay that you wrote for the first topic, in defense of travel. What are the strengths and weaknesses of your argument? Do you see any weaknesses? How might you revise this essay to make it more effective? Do you think you should introduce counterarguments into your essay—arguments "on the other side" that you could address and try to answer? Or would this prove confusing to your reader?
3. When someone says to you that he or she "hates to travel," what is your response? Do you think that such a position can really be defended? If you had to argue that traveling is a bad idea, what would be the main points you would make? Do you think you would cite any of the quotations given at the beginning of this chapter? Which ones? What would you gain from such a citation? What, if anything, might you lose?
4. If someone surprised you with the gift of a free trip, which destination would excite you the most? Which one would excite you the least?
5. Do you spend much time exploring your own thoughts and feelings? Do you set aside a specific time for this? Is there a specific place where it occurs? Is this an activity you undertake by yourself, or with someone else, or with some group? Describe an occasion when you explored your thoughts and feelings, and explain what happened next.

Chapter 20

Love and Hate

Short Views

Love is a great beautifier.
Louisa May Alcott

I do not think that what is called Love at first sight *is so great an absurdity as it is sometimes imagined to be. We generally make up our minds beforehand to the sort of person we should like, grave or gay, black, brown, or fair; with golden tresses or raven locks—and when we meet with a complete example of the qualities we admire, the bargain is soon struck.*
William Hazlitt

For what is love itself, for the one we love best?—an enfolding of immeasurable cares which yet are better than any joys outside our love.
George Eliot

We've got this gift of love, but love is like a precious plant. You can't just accept it and leave it in the cupboard or just think it's going to get on by itself. You've got to keep watering it. You've got to really look after it and nurture it.
John Lennon

Lovers should also have their days off.
Natalie Clifford Barney

In love, there is always one who kisses and one who offers the cheek.
French proverb

Love is the word used to label the sexual excitement of the young, the habituation of the middle-aged, and the mutual dependence of the old.
John Ciardi

A man falls in love through his eyes, a woman through her ears. What is said to [women] and what they believe about a man's status is usually more important than the superficiality of good looks.
Woodrow Wyatt

Now hatred is by far the longest pleasure,
Men love in haste, but they detest at leisure.
Lord Byron

Men hate more steadily than they love.
Samuel Johnson

The price of hating other human beings is loving oneself less.
Eldridge Cleaver

In hatred as in love, we grow like the thing we brood upon. What we loathe, we graft into our very soul.
Mary Renault

I tell you, there is such a thing as creative hate.
Willa Cather

Never in this world can hatred be stilled by hatred; it will be stilled only by non-hatred: This is the law Eternal.
Buddha

Joining the Conversation: Critical Thinking and Writing

1. Select a quotation that especially appeals to you, and make it the focus of an essay of about 500 words.
2. Take two of the passages—perhaps one that you especially like and one that you think is wrongheaded—and write a dialogue of about 500 words in which the two authors converse or argue. They may each try to convince the other, or they may find that to some degree they share views and they may then work out a statement that both can accept. If you do take the first position—that one writer is on the correct track but the other is utterly mistaken—try to be fair to the view that you think is mistaken. (As an experiment in critical thinking, imagine that you accept it, and make the best case for it that you possibly can.)

Essay

Judith Ortiz Cofer

Born in Puerto Rico in 1952 of a Puerto Rican mother and a United States mainland father who served in the Navy, Judith Ortiz Cofer was educated both in Puerto Rico and on the mainland. After earning a bachelor's and a master's degree in English, she did further graduate work at Oxford and then taught English in Florida. Her publications include books of poetry, a novel, and collections of stories and essays. She is now a professor of English and creative writing at the University of Georgia.

The following selection comes from an autobiography, Silent Dancing *(1990).*

I Fell in Love, or My Hormones Awakened

I fell in love, or my hormones awakened from their long slumber in my body, and suddenly the goal of my days was focused on one thing: to catch a glimpse of my secret love. And it had to remain secret, because I had, of course, in the great tradition of tragic romance, chosen to love a boy who was totally out of my reach. He was not Puerto Rican; he was Italian and rich. He was also an older man. He was a senior at the high school when I came in as a freshman. I first saw him in the hall, leaning casually on a wall that was the border line between girlside and boyside for underclassmen. He looked extraordinarily like a young Marlon Brando—down to the ironic little smile. The total of what I knew about the boy who starred in every one of my awkward fantasies was this: that he was the nephew of the man who owned the supermarket on my block; that he often had parties at his parents' beautiful home in the suburbs which I would hear about; that his family had money (which came to our school in many ways)—and this fact made my knees weak: and that he worked at the store near my apartment building on weekends and in the summer.

My mother could not understand why I became so eager to be the one sent out on her endless errands. I pounced on every opportunity from Friday to late Saturday afternoon to go after eggs, cigarettes, milk (I tried to drink as much of it as possible, although I hated the stuff)—the staple items that she would order from the "American" store.

Week after week I wandered up and down the aisles, taking furtive glances at the stock room in the back, breathlessly hoping to see my prince. Not that I had a plan. I felt like a pilgrim waiting for a glimpse of Mecca. I did not expect him to notice me. It was sweet agony.

One day I did see him. Dressed in a white outfit like a surgeon: white pants and shirt, white cap, and (gross sight, but not to my love-glazed eyes) blood-smeared butcher's apron. He was helping to drag a side of beef into the freezer storage area of the store. I must have stood there like an idiot, because I remember that he did see me, he even spoke to me! I could have died. I think he said, "Excuse me," and smiled vaguely in my direction.

5 After that, I *willed* occasions to go to the supermarket. I watched my mother's pack of cigarettes empty ever so slowly. I wanted her to smoke them fast. I drank

milk and forced it on my brother (although a second glass for him had to be bought with my share of Fig Newton cookies which we both liked, but we were restricted to one row each). I gave my cookies up for love, and watched my mother smoke her L&M's with so little enthusiasm that I thought (God, no!) that she might be cutting down on her smoking or maybe even giving up the habit. At this crucial time!

I thought I had kept my lonely romance a secret. Often I cried hot tears on my pillow for the things that kept us apart. In my mind there was no doubt that he would never notice me (and that is why I felt free to stare at him—I was invisible). He could not see me because I was a skinny Puerto Rican girl, a freshman who did not belong to any group he associated with.

At the end of the year I found out that I had not been invisible. I learned one little lesson about human nature—adulation leaves a scent, one that we are all equipped to recognize, and no matter how insignificant the source, we seek it.

In June the nuns at our school would always arrange for some cultural extravaganza. In my freshman year it was a Roman banquet. We had been studying Greek drama (as a prelude to church history—it was at a fast clip that we galloped through Sophocles and Euripedes toward the early Christian martyrs), and our young, energetic Sister Agnes was in the mood for spectacle. She ordered the entire student body (it was a small group of under 300 students) to have our mothers make us togas out of sheets. She handed out a pattern on mimeo pages fresh out of the machine. I remember the intense smell of the alcohol on the sheets of paper, and how almost everyone in the auditorium brought theirs to their noses and inhaled deeply—mimeographed handouts were the school-day buzz that the new Xerox generation of kids is missing out on. Then, as the last couple of weeks of school dragged on, the city of Paterson becoming a concrete oven, and us wilting in our uncomfortable uniforms, we labored like frantic Roman slaves to build a splendid banquet hall in our small auditorium. Sister Agnes wanted a raised dais where the host and hostess would be regally enthroned.

She had already chosen our Senator and Lady from among our ranks. The Lady was to be a beautiful new student named Sophia, a recent Polish immigrant, whose English was still practically unintelligible, but whose features, classically perfect without a trace of makeup, enthralled us. Everyone talked about her gold hair cascading past her waist, and her voice which could carry a note right up to heaven in choir. The nuns wanted her for God. They kept saying that she had vocation. We just looked at her in awe, and the boys seemed afraid of her. She just smiled and did as she was told. I don't know what she thought of it all. The main privilege of beauty is that others will do almost everything for you, including thinking.

10 Her partner was to be our best basketball player, a tall, red-haired senior whose family sent its many offspring to our school. Together, Sophia and her senator looked like the best combination of immigrant genes our community could produce. It did not occur to me to ask then whether anything but their physical beauty qualified them for the starring roles in our production. I had the highest average in the church history class, but I was given the part of one of many "Roman Citizens." I was to sit in front of the plastic fruit and recite a greeting in Latin along with the rest of the school when our hosts came into the hall and took their places on their throne.

On the night of our banquet, my father escorted me in my toga to the door of our school. I felt foolish in my awkwardly draped sheet (blouse and skirt required underneath). My mother had no great skill as a seamstress. The best she could do was hem a skirt or a pair of pants. That night I would have traded her for a peasant woman with a golden needle. I saw other Roman ladies emerging from their parents' cars looking authentic in sheets of material that folded over their bodies like the garments on a statue by Michelangelo. How did they do it? How was it that I always got it just slightly wrong, and worse, I believed that other people were just too polite to mention it. "The poor little Puerto Rican girl," I could hear them thinking. But in reality, I must have been my worst critic, self-conscious as I was.

Soon, we were all sitting at our circle of tables joined together around the dais. Sophia glittered like a golden statue. Her smile was beatific: a perfect, silent Roman lady. Her "senator" looked uncomfortable, glancing around at his buddies, perhaps waiting for the ridicule that he would surely get in the locker room later. The nuns in their black habits stood in the background watching us. What were they supposed to be, the Fates? Nubian slaves? The dancing girls did their modest little dance to tinny music from their finger cymbals, then the speeches were made. Then the grape juice "wine" was raised in a toast to the Roman Empire we all knew would fall within the week—before finals anyway.

All during the program I had been in a state of controlled hysteria. My secret love sat across the room from me looking supremely bored. I watched his every move, taking him in gluttonously. I relished the shadow of his eyelashes on his ruddy cheeks, his pouty lips smirking sarcastically at the ridiculous sight of our little play. Once he slumped down on his chair, and our sergeant-at-arms nun came over and tapped him sharply on his shoulder. He drew himself up slowly, with disdain. I loved his rebellious spirit. I believed myself still invisible to him in my "nothing" status as I looked upon my beloved. But toward the end of the evening, as we stood chanting our farewells in Latin, he looked straight across the room and into my eyes! How did I survive the killing power of those dark pupils? I trembled in a new way. I was not cold—I was burning! Yet I shook from the inside out, feeling light-headed, dizzy.

The room began to empty and I headed for the girls' lavatory. I wanted to relish the miracle in silence. I did not think for a minute that anything more would follow. I was satisfied with the enormous favor of a look from my beloved. I took my time, knowing that my father would be waiting outside for me, impatient, perhaps glowing in the dark in his phosphorescent white Navy uniform. The others would ride home. I would walk home with my father, both of us in costume. I wanted as few witnesses as possible. When I could no longer hear the crowds in the hallway, I emerged from the bathroom, still under the spell of those mesmerizing eyes.

15 The lights had been turned off in the hallway and all I could see was the lighted stairwell, at the bottom of which a nun would be stationed. My father would be waiting just outside. I nearly screamed when I felt someone grab me by the waist. But my mouth was quickly covered by someone else's mouth. I was being kissed. My first kiss and I could not even tell who it was. I pulled away to see that face not two inches away from mine. It was he. He smiled down at me. Did I have a silly expression on my face? My glasses felt crooked on my nose. I was unable to move or to speak. More gently, he lifted my chin and touched his lips to mine. This time I did not forget to enjoy it. Then, like the phantom lover that he was, he walked away into the darkened corridor and disappeared.

I don't know how long I stood there. My body was changing right there in the hallway of a Catholic school. My cells were tuning up like musicians in an orchestra, and my heart was a chorus. It was an opera I was composing, and I wanted to stand very still and just listen. But, of course, I heard my father's voice talking to the nun. I was in trouble if he had had to ask about me. I hurried down the stairs making up a story on the way about feeling sick. That would explain my flushed face and it would buy me a little privacy when I got home.

The next day Father announced at the breakfast table that he was leaving on a six month tour of Europe with the Navy in a few weeks and that at the end of the school year my mother, my brother, and I would be sent to Puerto Rico to stay for half a year at Mamá's (my mother's mother) house. I was devastated. This was the usual routine for us. We had always gone to Mamá's to stay when Father was away for long periods. But this year it was different for me. I was in love, and . . . my heart knocked against my bony chest at this thought . . . he loved me too? I broke into sobs and left the table.

In the next week I discovered the inexorable truth about parents. They can actually carry on with their plans right through tears, threats, and the awful spectacle of a teenager's broken heart. My father left me to my mother who impassively packed while I explained over and over that I was at a crucial time in my studies and that if I left my entire life would be ruined. All she would say was, "You are an intelligent girl, you'll catch up." Her head was filled with visions of *casa*[1] and family reunions, long gossip sessions with her mamá and sisters. What did she care that I was losing my one chance at true love?

In the meantime I tried desperately to see him. I thought he would look for me too. But the few times I saw him in the hallway, he was always rushing away. It would be long weeks of confusion and pain before I realized that the kiss was nothing but a little trophy for his ego. He had no interest in me other than as his adorer. He was flattered by my silent worship of him, and he had *bestowed* a kiss on me to please himself, and to fan the flames. I learned a lesson about the battle of the sexes then that I have never forgotten: the object is not always to win, but most times simply to keep your opponent (synonymous at times with "the loved one") guessing.

20 But this is too cynical a view to sustain in the face of that overwhelming rush of emotion that is first love. And in thinking back about my own experience with it, I can be objective only to the point where I recall how sweet the anguish was, how caught up in the moment I felt, and how every nerve in my body was involved in this salute to life. Later, much later, after what seemed like an eternity of dragging the weight of unrequited love around with me, I learned to make myself visible and to relish the little battles required to win the greatest prize of all. And much later, I read and understood Camus'[2] statement about the subject that concerns both adolescent and philosopher alike: if love were easy, life would be too simple.

[1990]

[1]*casa* home. [2]**Albert Camus** (1913–1960), French novelist and philosopher.

Joining the Conversation: Critical Thinking and Writing

1. If you agree with us that Cofer's essay is amusing, try to analyze the sources of its humor. Why are some passages funny?
2. In paragraph 9 Cofer says, "The main privilege of beauty is that others will do almost everything for you, including thinking." Do you agree that the beautiful are privileged? If so, draw on your experience (as one of the privileged or the

unprivileged) to recount an example or two. By the way, Cofer seems to imply (paragraph 10) that the academically gifted should be privileged, or at least should be recognized as candidates for leading roles (e.g., that of "a perfect, silent Roman lady") in school productions. Is it any fairer to privilege brains than to privilege beauty? Explain.

3. In her final paragraph Cofer speaks of the experience as a "salute to life." What do you think she means by that?
4. Cofer is describing a state that is (or used to be) called "puppy love." If you have experienced anything like what Cofer experienced, write your own autobiographical essay. (You can of course amplify or censor as you wish.) If you have experienced a love that you think is more serious, more lasting, write about *that*.

STORIES

ERNEST HEMINGWAY

Ernest Hemingway (1899–1961) was born in Oak Park, Illinois. After graduating from high school in 1917 he worked on the Kansas City Star, *but left to serve as a volunteer ambulance driver in Italy, where he was wounded in action. He returned home, married, and then served as European correspondent for the* Toronto Star, *but he soon focused on fiction. In 1922 he settled in Paris, where he moved in a circle of American expatriates that included Ezra Pound, Gertrude Stein, and F. Scott Fitzgerald. It was in Paris that he wrote stories and novels about what Gertrude Stein called a "lost generation" of rootless Americans in Europe. (For Hemingway's reminiscences of the Paris years, see his posthumously published* A Moveable Feast.*) He served as a journalist during the Spanish Civil War and during World War II, but he was also something of a private soldier.*

After World War II his reputation ebbed, though he was still active as a writer (for instance, he wrote The Old Man and the Sea *in 1952). In 1954 Hemingway was awarded the Nobel Prize in Literature, but in 1961, depressed by a sense of failing power, he took his own life.*

Cat in the Rain

There were only two Americans stopping at the hotel. They did not know any of the people they passed on the stairs on their way to and from their room. Their room was on the second floor facing the sea. It also faced the public garden and the war monument. There were big palms and green benches in the public garden. In the good weather there was always an artist with his easel. Artists liked the way the palms grew and the bright colors of the hotels facing the gardens and the sea. Italians came from a long way off to look up at the war monument. It was made of bronze and glistened in the rain. It was raining. The rain dripped from the palm trees. Water stood in pools on the gravel paths. The sea broke in a long line in the rain and slipped back down the beach to come up and break again in a long line in the rain. The motor cars were gone from the square by the war monument. Across the square in the doorway of the café a waiter stood looking out at the empty square.

The American wife stood at the window looking out. Outside right under their window a cat was crouched under one of the dripping green tables. The cat was trying to make herself so compact that she would not be dripped on.

"I'm going down and get that kitty," the American wife said.

"I'll do it," her husband offered from the bed.

"No, I'll get it. The poor kitty is out trying to keep dry under a table."

The husband went on reading, lying propped up with the two pillows at the foot of the bed.

"Don't get wet," he said.

The wife went downstairs and the hotel owner stood up and bowed to her as she passed the office. His desk was at the far end of the office. He was an old man and very tall.

"Il piove,"[1] the wife said. She liked the hotel-keeper.

"Si, si, Signora, brutto tempo. It is very bad weather."

He stood behind his desk in the far end of the dim room. The wife liked him. She liked the deadly serious way he received any complaints. She liked his dignity. She liked the way he wanted to serve her. She liked the way he felt about being a hotel-keeper. She liked his old, heavy face and big hands.

Liking him she opened the door and looked out. It was raining harder. A man in a rubber cape was crossing the empty square to the café. The cat would be around to the right. Perhaps she could go along under the eaves. As she stood in the doorway an umbrella opened behind her. It was the maid who looked after their room.

"You must not get wet," she smiled, speaking Italian. Of course, the hotel-keeper had sent her.

With the maid holding the umbrella over her, she walked along the gravel path until she was under their window. The table was there, washed bright green in the rain, but the cat was gone. She was suddenly disappointed. The maid looked up at her.

"Ha perduto qualque cosa, Signora?"[2]

"There was a cat," said the American girl.

"A cat?"

"Si, il gatto."

"A cat?" the maid laughed. "A cat in the rain?"

"Yes," she said, "under the table." Then. "Oh. I wanted it so much. I wanted a kitty."

When she talked English the maid's face tightened.

"Come, Signora," she said. "We must get back inside. You will be wet."

"I suppose so," said the American girl.

They went back along the gravel path and passed in the door. The maid stayed outside to close the umbrella. As the American girl passed the office, the padrone bowed from his desk. Something felt very small and tight inside the girl. The padrone made her feel very small and at the same time really important. She had a momentary feeling of being of supreme importance. She went on up the stairs. She opened the door of the room. George was on the bed, reading.

"Did you get the cat?" he asked, putting the book down.

[1]**Il piove** It's raining (Italian). [2]**Ha . . . Signora** Have you lost something, Madam?

"It was gone."

"Wonder where it went to," he said, resting his eyes from reading.

She sat down on the bed.

"I wanted it so much," she said. "I don't know why I wanted it so much. I wanted that poor kitty. It isn't any fun to be a poor kitty out in the rain."

George was reading again.

She went over and sat in front of the mirror of the dressing table looking at herself with the hand glass. She studied her profile, first one side and then the other. Then she studied the back of her head and her neck.

"Don't you think it would be a good idea if I let my hair grow out?" she asked, looking at her profile again.

George looked up and saw the back of her neck, clipped close like a boy's.

"I like it the way it is."

"I get so tired of it," she said. "I get so tired of looking like a boy."

George shifted his position in the bed. He hadn't looked away from her since she started to speak.

"You look pretty darn nice," he said.

She laid the mirror down on the dresser and went over to the window and looked out. It was getting dark.

"I want to pull my hair back tight and smooth and make a big knot at the back that I can feel," she said. "I want to have a kitty to sit on my lap and purr when I stroke her."

"Yeah?" George said from the bed.

"And I want to eat at a table with my own silver and I want candles. And I want it to be spring and I want to brush my hair out in front of a mirror and I want a kitty and I want some new clothes."

"Oh, shut up and get something to read," George said. He was reading again.

His wife was looking out of the window. It was quite dark now and still raining in the palm trees.

"Anyway, I want a cat," she said, "I want a cat. I want a cat now. If I can't have long hair or any fun, I can have a cat."

George was not listening. He was reading his book. His wife looked out of the window where the light had come on in the square.

Someone knocked at the door.

"Avanti,"[3] George said. He looked up from his book.

In the doorway stood the maid. She held a big tortoise-shell cat pressed tight against her and swung down against her body.

"Excuse me," she said, "the padrone asked me to bring this for the Signora."

[1925]

[3]**Avanti** Come in.

A Student's Notes and Journal Entries on "Cat in the Rain"

When you read a story—or, perhaps more accurately, when you reread a story before discussing it or writing about it—you'll find it helpful to jot an occasional note (for instance, a brief response or a question) in the margins and to underline or highlight passages that strike you as especially interesting. Here is part of the story, with the annotations of a student, Bill Yanagi.

The cat was trying to make herself so compact that she would not be dripped on.

"I'm going down and get that kitty," the American wife said.

"I'll do it," her husband offered from the bed.

He doesn't make a move

"No, I'll get it. The poor kitty is out trying to keep dry under a table."

The husband went on reading, lying propped up with the two pillows at the foot of the bed.

still doesn't move

"Don't get wet," he said.

Is he making a joke? Or maybe he just isn't even thinking about what he is saying?

The wife went downstairs and the hotel owner stood up and bowed to her as she passed the office. His desk was at the far end of the office. He was an old man and very tall.

contrast with the husband

"Il piove," the wife said. She liked the hotel-keeper.

"Si, si, Signora, brutto tempo. It is very bad weather."

He stood behind his desk in the far end of the dim room. The wife liked him. She liked the deadly serious way he received any complaints. She liked his dignity. She liked the way he wanted to serve her. She liked the way he felt about being a hotel-keeper. She liked his old, heavy face and big hands.

She respects him and she is pleased by the attention he shows

Liking him she opened the door and looked out. It was raining harder. A man in a rubber cape was crossing the empty square to the café. The cat would be around to the right.

to emphasize the bad weather??

Asking Questions about a Story

Everything in a story presumably is important, but having read the story once, probably something has especially interested (or puzzled) you, such as the relationship between two people, or the way the end of the story is connected to the beginning. On rereading, then, pen in hand, you'll find yourself noticing things that you missed or didn't find especially significant on your first reading. Now that you know the end of the story, you will read the beginning in a different way.

If your instructor asks you to think about certain questions, you'll keep these in mind while you reread, and you will find ideas coming to you. In "Cat in the Rain," suppose you are asked (or you ask yourself) if the story might just as well be about a dog in the rain. Would anything be lost?

Here are a few questions that you can ask of almost any story. (On pages 365–67, we give a fuller list.) After scanning the questions, you will want to reread the story, pen in hand, and then jot down your responses on a sheet of paper. As you write, it is helpful to go back and reread the story or at least parts of it.

1. *What happens?* In two or three sentences—say 25–50 words—summarize what happens in the story.

2. *What sorts of people are the chief characters?* In "Cat in the Rain" the chief characters are George, George's wife, and the innkeeper (the padrone). Jot down the traits that each seems to possess, and next to each trait briefly give some supporting evidence.
3. *What especially pleased or displeased you in the story?* Devote at least a sentence or two to the end of the story. Do you find the end satisfying? Why or why not?
4. *Have you any thoughts about the title?* If so, what are they? If the story did not have a title, what would you call it?

After you have made your own jottings, compare them with these responses by a student. No two readers will respond in exactly the same way, but all readers can examine their responses and try to account for them, at least in part. If your responses are substantially different, how do you account for the differences?

1. *A summary.* A young wife, stopping with her husband at an Italian hotel, from her room sees a cat in the rain. She goes to get it, but it is gone, and so she returns empty-handed. A moment later the maid knocks at the door, holding a tortoise-shell cat.
2. *The characters: The woman.*

kind-hearted (pities cat in rain)
appreciates innkeeper's courtesy ("liked the way he wanted to serve her") and admires him ("She liked his dignity")
unhappy (wants a cat, wants to change her hair, wants to eat at a table with her own silver)
The husband, George.
not willing to put himself out (says he'll go to garden to get cat but doesn't move)
doesn't seem very interested in wife (hardly talks to her—he's reading; tells her to "shut up")
but he does say he finds her attractive ("You look pretty darn nice")
The innkeeper.
serious, dignified ("She liked the deadly serious way he received any complaints. She liked his dignity")
courteous, helpful (sends maid with umbrella; at end sends maid with cat)
3. *Dislikes and likes.* "Dislikes" is too strong, but I was disappointed that more didn't happen at the end. What is the husband's reaction to the cat? Or his final reaction to his wife? I mean, what did he think about his wife when the maid brings the cat? And, for that matter, what is the wife's reaction? Is she satisfied? Or does she realize that the cat can't really make her happy? Now for the *likes.* (1) I guess I did like the way it turned out; it's sort of a happy ending, I think, since she wants the cat and gets it. (2) I also especially like the innkeeper. Maybe I like him partly because the wife likes him, and if she likes him he must be nice. And he *is* nice—very helpful. And I also like the way Hemingway shows the husband. I don't mean that I like the man himself, but I like the way Hemingway shows he is such a bastard—not getting off the bed to get the cat, telling his wife to shut up and read.

Another thing about him is that the one time he says something nice about her, it's about her hair, and she isn't keen on the way her hair is. She says it makes her look "like a boy," and she is "tired" of looking like a boy. There's something wrong with this marriage. George hardly pays attention to his wife, but he wants her to look like a boy. Maybe the idea is that this macho guy wants to keep her looking like an inferior (immature) version of himself. Anyway, he certainly doesn't seem interested in letting her fulfill herself as a woman.

I think my feelings add up to this: I like the way Hemingway shows us the relation between the husband and wife (even though the relation is pretty bad), and I like the innkeeper. Even if the relation with the couple ends unhappily, the story has a sort of happy ending, so far as it goes, since the innkeeper does what he can to please his guest: he sends the maid, with the cat. There's really nothing more that he can do.

More about the ending. The more I think about it, the more I feel that the ending is as happy as it can be. George is awful. When his wife says "I want a cat and I want a cat now," Hemingway tells us "George was not listening." And then, a moment later, almost like a good fairy the maid appears and grants the wife's wish.

4. *The title.* I don't suppose that I would have called it "Cat in the Rain," but I don't know what I would have called it. Maybe "An American Couple in Italy." Or maybe "The Innkeeper." I really do think that the innkeeper is very important, even though he only has a few lines. He's very impressive—not only to the girl, but to me (and maybe to all readers), since at the end of the story we see how careful the innkeeper is.

   But the more I think about Hemingway's title, the more I think that maybe it also refers to the girl. Like the "poor kitty" in the rain, the wife is in a pretty bad situation. "It isn't any fun to be a poor kitty out in the rain." Of course the woman is indoors, but her husband generates lots of unpleasant weather. She may as well be out in the rain. She says "I want to have a kitty to sit on my lap and purr when I stroke her." This shows that she wants to be affectionate and that she also wants to have someone respond to her affection. She *is* like a cat in the rain.

The responses of this student probably include statements that you want to take issue with. Or perhaps you feel that the student did not even mention some things that you think are important. You may want to jot down some notes and raise some questions in class.

A Sample Essay by a Student: "Hemingway's American Wife"

The responses that we have quoted were written by Bill Yanagi, who later wrote an essay developing one of them. Here is the essay.

Yanagi 1

Bill Yanagi

Professor Costello

English 10B

20 October 2010

Hemingway's American Wife

My title alludes not to any of the four women to whom Hemingway was married, but to "the American wife" who is twice called by this term in his short story "Cat in the Rain." We first meet her in the first sentence of the story ("There were only two Americans stopping at the hotel"), and the next time she is mentioned (apart from a reference to the wife and her husband as "they") it is as "the American wife," at the beginning of the second paragraph of the story. The term is used again at the end of the third paragraph.

She is, then, at least in the early part of this story, just an American or an American wife—someone identified only by her nationality and her marital status, but not at all by her personality, her individuality, her inner self. She first becomes something of an individual when she separates herself from her husband by leaving the hotel room and going to look for a cat that she has seen in the garden, in the rain. This act of separation, however, has not the slightest effect on her husband, who "went on reading" (685).

When she returns, without the cat, he puts down his book and speaks to her, but it is obvious that he has no interest in her, beyond as a physical object ("You look pretty darn nice"). This comment is produced when she says she is thinking of letting her hair grow out, because she is "so tired of looking like a boy" (686). Why, a reader wonders, does her husband, who has paid almost no attention to her up to now, assure her that she looks "pretty darn nice"? I think it is reasonable to conclude that he *wants* her to look like someone who is not truly a woman, in particular someone who is immature. That she does not feel she has much identity is evident when she continues to talk about letting her hair grow, and she says "I want to pull my hair back tight and smooth and make a big knot at the back that I can feel" (686). Long hair is, or at least was, the traditional sign of a woman; she wants long hair, and at the same time she wants to keep it under her control by tying it in a "big knot," a knot that she can feel, a knot whose presence reminds her, because she can feel it, of her feminine nature.

She goes on to say that she wants to brush her hair "in front of a mirror." That is, she wants to *see* and to feel her femininity, since her husband apparently—so far as we can see in the story, at least—scarcely recognizes it or her. Perhaps her desire for the cat ("I want a cat") is a veiled way of saying that she wants to express her animal nature, and not be simply a neglected woman who is made by her husband to look like a boy. Hemingway tells us, however, that when she looked for the cat in the garden she could not find it, a sign, I think, of her failure to break from the man.

Yanagi 3

At the end of the story the maid brings her the cat, but a woman cannot just be handed a new nature and accept it, just like that. She has to find it herself, and in herself, so I think the story ends with "the American wife" still nothing more than an American wife.

[New page]

Yanagi 4

Work Cited

Hemingway, Ernest, "Cat in the Rain." *Literature for Composition*. Ed. Sylvan Barnet, William Burto, and William E. Cain. 9th ed. New York: Longman, 2010. 684–86. Print.

A few comments and questions may be useful.

- Do you find the essay interesting? Explain your response.
- Do you find the essay well written? Explain.
- Do you find the argument convincing? Can you suggest ways of strengthening it, or do you think its argument is mistaken? Carefully reread "Cat in the Rain," taking note of passages that give further support to this student's argument, or that seem to challenge or qualify it.
- We often say that a good critical essay sends us back to the literary work with a fresh point of view. Our rereading differs from our earlier reading. Does this essay change your reading of Hemingway's story?

Joining the Conversation: Critical Thinking and Writing

1. Can we be certain that the cat at the end of the story is the cat that the woman saw in the rain? (When we first hear about the cat in the rain we are not told anything about its color, and at the end of the story we are not told that the tortoise-shell cat is wet.) Does it matter if there are two cats?
2. One student argued that the cat represents the child that the girl wants to have. Do you think there is something to this idea? How might you support or refute it?

3. Consider the following passage:

> As the American girl passed the office, the padrone bowed from his desk. Something felt very small and tight inside the girl. The padrone made her feel very small and at the same time really important. She had a momentary feeling of being of supreme importance.

Do you think there is anything sexual here? And if so, that the passage tells us something about her relations with her husband? Support your view.

4. What do you suppose Hemingway's attitude was toward each of the three chief characters? How might you support your hunch?

5. Hemingway wrote the story in Italy, when his wife Hadley was pregnant. In a letter to F. Scott Fitzgerald he said,

> Cat in the Rain wasn't about Hadley. . . . When I wrote that we were at Rapallo but Hadley was 4 months pregnant with Bumby. The Inn Keeper was the one at Cortina D'Ampezzo. . . . Hadley never made a speech in her life about wanting a baby because she had been told various things by her doctor and I'd—no use going into all that. (*Letters* 180)

According to some biographers, the story shows that Hemingway knew his marriage was going on the rocks (Hemingway and Hadley divorced). Does knowing that Hemingway's marriage turned out unhappily help you to understand the story? Does it make the story more interesting? And do you think that the story tells a biographer something about Hemingway's life?

6. It is sometimes said that a good short story does two things at once: It provides a believable picture of the surface of life, and it also illuminates some moral or psychological complexity that we feel is part of the essence of human life. This dual claim may not be true, but for the moment accept it. Do you think that Hemingway's story fulfills either or both of these specifications? Support your view.

A Second Example: An Essay Drawing on Related Material in the Chapter

Another student, Holly Klein, wrote about "Cat in the Rain," but she thought about it partly in terms of a familiar saying, "All the world loves a lover." She also draws on a less familiar quotation; it might have been better to have cited the source of the unfamiliar quotation, but since the words are attributed to an author and are given within quotation marks, there is no problem of plagiarism. Here are her first notes, and the essay that she developed from them.

Journal Entries

"All the world loves a lover? Not necessarily. In real life, few emotions are less sociable than romantic passion." Certainly there's not much romantic passion in this story. But are these people in love?

Is it true that love stories are about people who are happy in love, or are they mostly about people who are unhappy? Many lovers may suffer and some even die (Leonardo DiCaprio in *Titanic*), but aren't they happy anyway? They are happy in their unhappiness. (And Rose—Kate Winslet—survives, happy and unhappy in her love.)

Is "Cat" really a love story anyway? Yes, in the sense it is about people who must at least at some time in the past have been lovers—happy lovers—but who now seem stuck with each other. The wife still seems to be in love, or maybe she is trying to bring a dead love back to life.

Is there something to the idea (as Wilcox says), that "love is a mood" to men but is "life or death" to women? Does this add up to saying that for men, love is something of the moment, and is trivial, but for women it is enduring and important? And do men and women react differently to love stories? Someone in class—and there was plenty of agreement and almost no disagreement—said that *Titanic* is a "woman's picture." But Mark liked it as much as I did. Or at least he said so.

A Sample Essay by a Student: "Hemingway's Unhappy Lovers"

Here is the final version of Holly Klein's essay:

Klein 1

Holly Klein

Professor Chung

English 1102

30 January 2010

Hemingway's Unhappy Lovers

In class someone suggested that *Romeo and Juliet* is not so much about how happy two people are but about how unhappy they are. This statement, which at first I thought was ridiculous, now strikes me as true, or for the most part true. The lovers in *Romeo and Juliet*, *West Side Story*, and in the television drama *All My Children* (Haley, Mateo, Lisa, and several other young adults) would not give up being in love, but during most of the time they are unhappy. I have heard a saying, "Love means not ever having to say you are sorry," but some of these lovers, and other lovers in daytime television programs, are always saying they are sorry, and always feeling sorry for themselves. And we

Klein 2

feel sorry for them. Our interest in them is not in their happiness, but in their unhappiness.

Certainly in Ernest Hemingway's "Cat in the Rain" the woman is unhappy—and who would not be unhappy, with a husband like hers? She says she is going out into the rain to get the cat, and he says "Don't get wet" (685), and he goes right on reading, obviously uninterested in what his wife is doing, or in her needs. The wife never explicitly says she is unhappy, but it is obvious that she is. Her husband pays very little attention to her, and then, when he does—he goes so far as to say "You look pretty darn nice"—it is only after she tells him she wants to change her appearance: "I get so tired of looking like a boy." When she adds that she wants to change her hair, his response is, "Yeah?" And a moment later he says, "Oh, shut up and get something to read" (686). I felt like hitting him, and I suddenly realized that, at least for this story, lovers are unhappy. If Hemingway's lovers were happy and spent their time cooing at each other, the story probably would have been boring. What is interesting here is, paradoxically, the man's lack of interest in his wife—he is probably affectionate only when he wants sex—and the woman's basic unhappiness. Her unhappiness is revealed partly by her almost desperate attempt to give affection to the cat, and to receive some affection from it: "I want to have a kitty to sit on my lap and purr when I stroke her" (686). Ella Wheeler Wilcox may be overstating the matter, but, allowing for what is called poetic

Klein 3

license, there is something sound in her view that "love is a mood—no more—to man, / And love to a woman is life or death".

Many people probably do not make a distinction between the attitudes of men and women toward love, and they therefore do not distinguish between the responses of men and of women to love stories. I think it is probably true that most love stories are chiefly about unhappiness, but it is probably also true that women in love are more likely than men to express in words their unhappiness. (I think there are psychological or sociological studies that support this view.) In any case, in support of the idea that love stories are chiefly about unhappiness, I can say that "Cat in the Rain" interested me not because the lovers keep expressing their romantic passion but because the man does *not* express his love, and the woman expresses her frustration. In this story about lovers, the man is in bed—but he spends most of his time *reading* in bed, and (as I said) about the best he can say to the woman is that she looks "pretty darn nice". The wife holds our interest because she is unhappy, stuck with this guy, and she is so grateful for a kind word from the hotel-keeper. She does not explicitly say that she is desperately unhappy, but she does express very vigorously a desire for a life different from the one she is now living, and we do feel that (at least for her) love is not just a "mood," as it probably is for the man, but is a matter of "life or death." She is, so to speak, dying to be loved.

Klein 4

Work Cited

Hemingway, Ernest, "Cat in the Rain." *Literature for Composition.* Ed. Sylvan Barnet, William Burto, and William E. Cain. 9th ed. New York: Longman, 2010. 684–86. Print.

We can ask of this essay the same questions that we asked of an earlier essay:

- Do you find the essay interesting? Explain your response.
- Do you find the essay well written? Explain.
- Do you find the argument convincing? Can you suggest ways of strengthening it, or do you think its argument is mistaken? Carefully reread "Cat in the Rain," taking note of passages that give further support to this student's argument, or that seem to challenge or qualify it.
- We often say that a good critical essay sends us back to the literary work with a fresh point of view. Our rereading differs from our earlier reading. Does this essay change your reading of Hemingway's story?

We can also ask one additional question:

- Sometimes writers make their essays far too impersonal, removing every trace of the writer as an individual human being, a distinct person. Do you think that this writer goes too far in the other direction, making the essay too personal? If you think that she does, what advice would you give her, to help her strike the right balance?

ZORA NEALE HURSTON

Zora Neale Hurston (1891–1960) was brought up in Eatonville, Florida, a town said to be the first all-black self-governing town in the United States. Her mother died in 1904, and when Hurston's father remarried, Hurston felt out of place. In 1914, she joined a traveling theatrical group as a maid, hoping to save money for school. Later, by working at such jobs as manicurist and waitress, she put herself through college, entering Howard University in 1923. After receiving a scholarship, she transferred in 1926 to Barnard College in New York, where she was the first African American student in the college. After graduating from Barnard in 1928 she taught drama, worked as an editor, and studied anthropology. But when grant money ran out in 1932 she returned to Eatonville to edit the folk material that she had collected during four years of fieldwork, and to do some further writing. She steadily published from 1932 to 1938—stories, folklore, and two novels—but she gained very little money. Furthermore, although she played a large role in the Harlem Renaissance in the 1930s, she was criticized by Richard Wright and other influential black authors for

portraying blacks as stereotypes and for being politically conservative. To many in the 1950s her writing seemed reactionary, almost embarrassing in an age of black protest, and she herself—working as a domestic, a librarian, and a substitute teacher—was almost forgotten. Hurston died in a county welfare home in Florida and is buried in an unmarked grave. But literary scholars now judge her one of the major authors of her era and her work is widely read and taught.

Sweat

It was eleven o'clock of a Spring night in Florida. It was Sunday. Any other night, Delia Jones would have been in bed for two hours by this time. But she was a washwoman, and Monday morning meant a great deal to her. So she collected the soiled clothes on Saturday when she returned the clean things. Sunday night after church, she sorted them and put the white things to soak. It saved her almost a half day's start. A great hamper in the bedroom held the clothes that she brought home. It was so much neater than a number of bundles lying around.

She squatted in the kitchen floor beside the great pile of clothes, sorting them into small heaps according to color, and humming a song in a mournful key, but wondering through it all where Sykes, her husband, had gone with her horse and buckboard.[1]

Just then something long, round, limp and black fell upon her shoulders and slithered to the floor beside her. A great terror took hold of her. It softened her knees and dried her mouth so that it was a full minute before she could cry out or move. Then she saw that it was the big bull whip her husband liked to carry when he drove.

5 She lifted her eyes to the door and saw him standing there bent over with laughter at her fright. She screamed at him.

"Sykes, what you throw dat whip on me like dat? You know it would skeer me—looks just like a snake, an' you knows how skeered Ah is of snakes."

"Course Ah knowed it! That's how come Ah done it." He slapped his leg with his hand and almost rolled on the ground in his mirth. "If you such a big fool dat you got to have a fit over a earth worm or a string, Ah don't keer how bad Ah skeer you."

"You aint got no business doing it. Gawd knows it's a sin. Some day Ah'm gointuh drop dead from some of yo' foolishness. 'Nother thing, where you been wid mah rig? Ah feeds dat pony. He aint fuh you to be drivin' wid no bull whip."

"Yo sho is one aggravatin' nigger woman!" he declared and stepped into the room. She resumed her work and did not answer him at once. "Ah done tole you time and again to keep them white folks' clothes outa dis house."

He picked up the whip and glared down at her. Delia went on with her work. She went out into the yard and returned with a galvanized tub and set it on the washbench. She saw that Sykes had kicked all of the clothes together again, and
10 now stood in her way truculently, his whole manner hoping, *praying,* for an argument. But she walked calmly around him and commenced to re-sort the things.

"Next time, Ah'm gointer to kick 'em outdoors," he threatened as he struck a match along the leg of his corduroy breeches.

Delia never looked up from her work, and her thin, stooped shoulders sagged further.

"Ah aint for no fuss t'night Sykes. Ah just come from taking sacrament at the church house."

He snorted scornfully. "Yeah, you just come from de church house on a Sunday night, but heah you is gone to work on them clothes. You aint nothing

[1]**buckboard** an open wagon.

but a hypocrite. One of them amen-corner Christians—sing, whoop, shout, then come home and wash white folks clothes on the Sabbath."

He stepped roughly upon the whitest pile of things, kicking them helter-skelter as he crossed the room. His wife gave a little scream of dismay, and quickly gathered them together again.

"Sykes, you quit grindin' dirt into these clothes! How can Ah git through by Sat'day if Ah don't start on Sunday?"

"Ah don't keer if you never git through. Anyhow, Ah done promised Gawd and a couple of other men, Ah aint gointer have it in mah house. Don't gimme no lip neither, else Ah'll throw 'em out and put mah fist up side yo' head to boot."

Delia's habitual meekness seemed to slip from her shoulders like a blown scarf. She was on her feet; her poor little body, her bare knuckly hands bravely defying the strapping hulk before her.

"Looka heah, Sykes, you done gone too fur. Ah been married to you fur fifteen years, and Ah been takin' in washin' for fifteen years. Sweat, sweat, sweat! Work and sweat, cry and sweat, pray and sweat!"

"What's that got to do with me?" he asked brutally.

"What's it got to do with you, Sykes? Mah tub of suds is filled yo' belly with vittles more times than yo' hands is filled it. Mah sweat is done paid for this house and Ah reckon Ah kin keep on sweatin in it."

She seized the iron skillet from the stove and struck a defensive pose, which act surprised him greatly, coming from her. It cowed him and he did not strike her as he usually did.

"Naw you won't," she panted, "that ole snaggle-toothed black woman you runnin' with aint comin' heah to pile up on *mah* sweat and blood. You aint paid for nothin' on this place, and Ah'm gointer stay right heah till Ah'm toted out foot foremost."

"Well, you better quit gittin' me riled up, else they'll be totin' you out sooner than you expect. Ah'm so tired of you Ah don't know whut to do. Gawd! how Ah hates skinny wimmen!"

A little awed by this new Delia, he sidled out of the door and slammed the back gate after him. He did not say where he had gone, but she knew too well. She knew very well that he would not return until nearly daybreak also. Her work over, she went on to bed but not to sleep at once. Things had come to a pretty pass!

She lay awake, gazing upon the debris that cluttered their matrimonial trail. Not an image left standing along the way. Anything like flowers had long ago been drowned in the salty stream that had been pressed from her heart. Her tears, her sweat, her blood. She had brought love to the union and he had brought a longing for the flesh. Two months after the wedding, he had given her the first brutal beating. She had the memory of numerous trips to Orlando with all of his wages when he had returned to her penniless, even before the first year had passed. She was young and soft then, but now she thought of her knotty, muscled limbs, her harsh knuckly hands, and drew herself up into an unhappy little ball in the middle of the big feather bed. Too late now to hope for love, even if it were not Bertha it would be someone else. This case differed from the others only in that she was bolder than the others. Too late for everything except her little home. She had built it for her old days, and planted one by one the trees and flowers there. It was lovely to her, lovely.

Somehow before sleep came, she found herself saying aloud: "Oh well, whatever goes over the Devil's back, is got to come under his belly. Sometime or ruther, Sykes, like everybody else, is gointer reap his sowing." After that she was able to build a spiritual earthworks against her husband. His shells could no longer reach her. *Amen*. She went to sleep and slept until he announced his presence in bed by kicking her feet and rudely snatching the cover away.

"Gimme some kivah heah, an' git yo' damn foots over on yo' own side! Ah oughter mash you in yo' mouf fuh drawing dat skillet on me."

Delia went clear to the rail without answering him. A triumphant indifference to all that he was or did.

The week was as full of work for Delia as all other weeks, and Saturday found her behind her little pony, collecting and delivering clothes.

30 It was a hot, hot day near the end of July. The village men on Joe Clarke's porch even chewed cane listlessly. They did not hurl the cane-knots as usual. They let them dribble over the edge of the porch. Even conversation had collapsed under the heat.

"Heah comes Delia Jones," Jim Merchant said, as the shaggy pony came round the bend of the road toward them. The rusty buckboard was heaped with baskets of crisp, clean laundry.

"Yep," Joe Lindsay agreed, "Hot or col', rain or shine, jes ez reg'lar ez de weeks roll roun' Delia carries 'em an' fetches 'em on Sat'day."

"She better if she wanter eat," said Moss. "Syke Jones aint wuth de shot an' powder hit would tek tuh kill 'em. Not to *huh* he aint."

"He sho' aint," Walter Thomas chimed in. "It's too bad, too, cause she wuz a right pritty lil trick when he got huh. Ah'd uh mah'ied huh mahseft' it' he hadnter beat me to it."

35 Delia nodded briefly at the men as she drove past.

"Too much knockin will ruin *any* 'oman. He done beat huh nough tuh kill three women, let 'lone change they looks," said Elijah Mosely. "How Syke kin stommuck dat big black greasy Mogu[2] he's layin' roun' wid, gits me. Ah swear dat eightrock couldn't kiss a sardine can Ah done thowed out de back do' 'way las' yeah."

"Aw, she's fat, thass how come. He's allus been crazy 'bout fat women," put in Merchant. "He'd a' been tied up wid one long time ago if he could a' found one tuh have him. Did Ah tell yuh 'bout him come sidlin' roun *mah* 'wife—bringin' her a basket uh pee-cans outa his yard fuh a present? Yes-sir, mah wife! She tol' him tuh take 'em right straight back home, cause Delia works so hard ovah dat washtub she reckon everything en de place taste lak sweat an' soap-suds. Ah jus' wisht Ah'd a' caught 'im 'roun' dere! Ah'd a' made his hips ketch on fiah down dat shell road."

"Ah know he done it, too. Ah sees 'im grinnin' at every 'oman dat passes," Walter Thomas said. "But even so, he useter eat some mighty big hunks uh humble pie tuh git dat lil' 'oman he got. She wuz ez pritty ez a speckled pup! Dat wuz fifteen yeahs ago. He useter be so skeered uh losin' huh, she could make him do some parts of a husband's duty. Dey never wuz de same in de mind."

"There oughter be a law about him," said Lindsay. "He aint fit tuh carry guts tuh a bear."

40 Clarke spoke for the first time. "Taint no law on earth dat kin make a man be decent if it aint in 'im. There's plenty men dat takes a wife lak dey do a joint uh sugar-cane. It's round, juicy an' sweet when dey gits it. But dey squeeze an' grind, squeeze an' grind an' wring tell dey wring every drop uh pleasure dat's in 'em out. When dey's satisfied dat dey is wring dry, dey treats 'em jes lak dey do a

[2]**Mogu** big person.

cane-chew. Dey thows 'em away. Dey knows whut dey is doin' while dey is at it, an' hates theirselves fuh it but they keeps on hangin' after huh tell she's empty. Den dey hates huh fuh bein' a cane-chew an' in de way."

"We oughter take Syke an' dat stray 'oman uh his'n down in Lake Howell swamp an' lay on de rawhide till they cain't say 'Lawd a' mussy.' He allus wuz uh ovahbearin' niggah, but since dat white 'oman from up north done teached 'im how to run a automobile, he done got too biggety to live—an' we oughter kill 'im," Old Man Anderson advised.

A grunt of approval went around the porch. But the heat was melting their civic virtue and Elijah Moseley began to bait Joe Clarke.

"Come on, Joe, git a melon outa dere an' slice it up for yo' customers. We'se all sufferin' wid de heat. De bear's done got *me!*"

"Thass right. Joe, a watermelon is jes' whut Ah needs tuh cure de eppizudicks."[3] Walter Thomas joined forces with Moseley. "Come on dere, Joe. We all is steady customers an' you aint set us up in a long time. Ah chooses dat long, bow-legged Floridy favorite."

"A god, an' be dough. You all gimme twenty cents and slice away," Clarke retorted. "Ah needs a col' slice m'self. Heah, everybody chip in. Ah'll lend y'll mah meat knife."

The money was quickly subscribed and the huge melon brought forth. At that moment, Sykes and Bertha arrived. A determined silence fell on the porch and the melon was put away again.

Merchant snapped down the blade of his jackknife and moved toward the store door.

"Come on in, Joe, an' gimme a slab uh sow belly an' uh pound uh coffee—almost fuhgot 'twas Sat'day. Got to git on home." Most of the men left also.

Just then Delia drove past on her way home, as Sykes was ordering magnificently for Bertha. It pleased him for Delia to see.

"Git whutsoever yo' heart desires, Honey. Wait a minute, Joe. Give huh two bottles uh strawberry soda-water, uh quart uh parched groundpeas, an' a block uh chewin' gum."

With all this they left the store, with Sykes reminding Bertha that this was his town and she could have it if she wanted it.

The men returned soon after they left, and held their watermelon feast. "Where did Syke Jones git dat 'oman from nohow?" Lindsay asked.

"Ovah Apopka. Guess dey musta been cleanin' out de town when she lef. She don't look lak a thing but a hunk uh liver wid hair on it."

"Well, she sho' kin squall," Dave Carter contributed. "When she gits ready tuh laff, she jes' opens huh mouf an' latches it back tuh de las' notch. No ole grandpa alligator down in Lake Bell aint got nothin' on huh."

Bertha had been in town three months now. Sykes was still paying her room rent at Della Lewis'—the only house in town that would have taken her in. Sykes took her frequently to Winter Park to "stomps."[4] He still assured her that he was the swellest man in the state.

"Sho' you kin have dat lil' ole house soon's Ah kin git dat 'oman outa dere. Everything b'longs tuh me an' you sho' kin have it. Ah sho' 'bominates uh skinny 'oman. Lawdy, you sho' is got one portly shape on you! You kin git *anything* you wants. Dis is *mah* town an' you sho' kin have it.

[3]**eppizudicks** i.e., epizootic, an epidemic among animals. [4]**stomps** dances.

Delia's work-worn knees crawled over the earth in Gethsemane and on the rocks of Calvary[5] many, many times during these months. She avoided the villagers and meeting places in her effort to be blind and deaf. But Bertha nullified this to a degree, by coming to Delia's house to call Sykes out to her at the gate.

Delia and Sykes fought all the time now with no peaceful interludes. They slept and ate in silence. Two or three times Delia had attempted a timid friendliness, but she was repulsed each time. It was plain that the breaches must remain agape.

The sun had burned July to August. The heat streamed down like a million hot arrows, smiting all things living upon the earth. Grass withered, leaves browned, snakes went blind in shedding and men and dogs went mad. Dog days!

60 Delia came home one day and found Sykes there before her. She wondered, but started to go on into the house without speaking, even though he was standing in the kitchen door and she must either stoop under his arm or ask him to move. He made no room for her. She noticed a soap box beside the steps, but paid no particular attention to it, knowing that he must have brought it there. As she was stooping to pass under his outstretched arm, he suddenly pushed her backward, laughingly.

"Look in de box dere Delia. Ah done brung yuh somethin'!"

She nearly fell upon the box in her stumbling, and when she saw what it held, she all but fainted outright.

"Syke! Syke, mah Gawd! You take dat rattlesnake 'way from heah! You *gottuh*. Oh, Jesus, have mussy!"

"Ah aint gut tuh do nuthin' uh de kin'—fact is Ah aint got tuh do nothin' but die. Taint no use uh you puttin' on airs makin' out lak you sceered uh dat snake—he's gointer stay right heah tell he die. He wouldn't bite me cause Ah knows how tuh handle 'im. Nohow he wouldn't risk breakin' out his fangs 'gin *yo'* skinny laigs."

65 "Naw, now Syke, don't keep dat thing 'roun' heah tuh skeer me tuh death. You knows Ah'm even feared uh earth worms. Thass de biggest snake Ah evah did see. Kill 'im Syke, please."

"Doan ast me tuh do nothin 'fuh yuh. Goin' 'roun' tryin' to be so damn asterperious. Naw, Ah aint gonna kill it. Ah think uh damn sight mo' uh him dan you! Dat's a nice snake an' anybody doan lak 'im kin jes' hit de grit."

The village soon heard that Sykes had the snake, and came to see and ask questions.

"How de hen-fire did you ketch dat six-foot rattler, Syke?" Thomas asked.

"He's full uh frogs so he caint hardly move, thass how Ah eased up on 'm. But Ah'm a snake charmer an' knows how tuh handle 'em. Shux, dat aint nothin'. Ah could ketch one eve'y day if Ah so wanted tuh."

70 "Whut he needs is a heavy hick'ry club leaned real heavy on his head. Dat's de bes 'way tuh charm a rattlesnake."

"Naw, Walt, y'll jes' don't understand dese diamon' backs lak Ah do," said Sykes in a superior tone of voice.

The village agreed with Walter, but the snake stayed on. His box remained by the kitchen door with its screen wire covering. Two or three days later it had digested its meal of frogs and literally came to life. It rattled at every movement in

[5]**Gethsemane** the garden where Jesus prayed just before he was betrayed (Matthew 26:36–47); **Calvary** was the hill where he was crucified.

the kitchen or the yard. One day as Delia came down the kitchen steps she saw his chalky-white fangs curved like scimitars hung in the wire meshes. This time she did not run away with averted eyes as usual. She stood for a long time in the doorway in a red fury that grew bloodier for every second that she regarded the creature that was her torment.

That night she broached the subject as soon as Sykes sat down to the table.

"Syke, Ah wants you tuh take dat snake 'way fum heah. You done starved me an' Ah put up widcher, you done beat me an Ah took dat, but you done kilt all mah insides bringin' dat varmint heah."

75 Sykes poured out a saucer full of coffee and drank it deliberately before he answered her.

"A whole lot Ah keer 'bout how you feels inside uh out. Dat snake aint goin' no damn wheah till Ah gits ready fuh 'im tuh go. So fur as beatin' is concerned, yuh aint took near all dat you gointer take ef yuh stay 'roun' *me*."

Delia pushed back her plate and got up from the table. "Ah hates you. Sykes," she said calmly. "Ah hates you tuh de same degree dat Ah useter love yuh. Ah done took an' took till mah belly is full up tuh mah neck. Dat's de reason Ah got mah letter fum de church an' moved mah membership tuh Woodbridge—so Ah don't haftuh take no sacrament wid yuh. Ah don't wantuh see yuh, 'roun' me atall. Lay 'roun' wid dat 'oman all yuh wants tuh, but gwan 'way fum me an' mah house. Ah hates yuh lak uh suck-egg dog."

Sykes almost let the huge wad of corn bread and collard greens he was chewing fall out of his mouth in amazement. He had a hard time whipping himself to the proper fury to try to answer Delia.

"Well, Ah'm glad you does hate me. Ah'm sho' tiahed uh you hangin' ontuh me. Ah don't want yuh. Look at yuh stringey ole neck! Yo' raw-bony laigs an' arms is enough tuh cut uh man tuh death. You looks jes' lak de devvul's doll-baby tuh *me*. You cain't hate me no worse dan Ah hates you. Ah been hatin' *you* fuh years."

80 "Yo' ole black hide don't look lak nothin' tuh me, but uh passle uh wrinkled up rubber, wid yo' big ole yeahs flappin' on each side lak uh paih uh buzzard wings. Don't think Ah'm gointuh be run 'way fum mah house neither. Ah'm goin' tuh de white folks about *you,* mah young man, de very nex' time you lay yo' han's on me. Mah cup is done run ovah." Delia said this with no signs of fear and Sykes departed from the house, threatening her, but made not the slightest move to carry out any of them.

That night he did not return at all, and the next day being Sunday, Delia was glad that she did not have to quarrel before she hitched up her pony and drove the four miles to Woodbridge.

She stayed to the night service—"love feast"—which was very warm and full of spirit. In the emotional winds her domestic trials were borne far and wide so that she sang as she drove homeward.

"Jurden water,[6] black an' col'
Chills de body, not de soul
An' Ah wantah cross Jurden in uh calm time."

She came from the barn to the kitchen door and stopped.

"Whut's de mattah, ol' satan, you aint kickin' up yo' racket?" She addressed the snake's box. Complete silence. She went on into the house with a new hope

[6]**Jurden** the river Jordan, which the Israelites had to cross in order to reach the Promised Land.

in its birth struggles. Perhaps her threat to go to the white folks had frightened Sykes! Perhaps he was sorry! Fifteen years of misery and suppression had brought Delia to the place where she would hope *anything* that looked towards a way over or through her wall of inhibitions.

85 She felt in the match safe behind the stove at once for a match. There was only one there.

"Dat niggah wouldn't fetch nothin heah tuh save his rotten neck, but he kin run thew whut Ah brings quick enough. Now he done toted off nigh on tuh haff uh box uh matches. He done had dat 'oman heah in mah house, too."

Nobody but a woman could tell how she knew this even before she struck the match. But she did and it put her into a new fury.

Presently she brought in the tubs to put the white things to soak. This time she decided she need not bring the hamper out of the bedroom; she would go in there and do the sorting. She picked up the pot-bellied lamp and went in. The room was small and the hamper stood hard by the foot of the white iron bed. She could sit and reach through the bedposts—resting as she worked.

"Ah wantah cross Jurden in uh calm time." She was singing again. The mood of the "love feast" had returned. She threw back the lid of the basket almost gaily. Then, moved by both horror and terror, she sprang back toward the door. *There lay the snake in the basket!* He moved sluggishly at first, but even as she turned round and round, jumped up and down in an insanity of fear, he began to stir vigorously. She saw him pouring his awful beauty from the basket upon the bed, then she seized the lamp and ran as fast as she could to the kitchen. The wind from the open door blew out the light and the darkness added to her terror. She sped to the darkness of the yard, slamming the door after her before she thought to set down the lamp. She did not feel safe even on the ground, so she climbed up in the hay barn.

90 There for an hour or more she lay sprawled upon the hay a gibbering wreck.

Finally she grew quiet, and after that, coherent thought. With this, stalked through her a cold, bloody rage. Hours of this. A period of introspection, a space of retrospection, then a mixture of both. Out of this an awful calm.

"Well, Ah done de bes' Ah could. If things aint right, Gawd knows taint mah fault."

She went to sleep—a twitchy sleep—and woke up to a faint gray sky. There was a loud hollow sound below. She peered out. Sykes was at the wood-pile, demolishing a wire-covered box.

He hurried to the kitchen door, but hung outside there some minutes before he entered, and stood some minutes more inside before he closed it after him.

95 The gray in the sky was spreading. Delia descended without fear now, and crouched beneath the low bedroom window. The drawn shade shut out the dawn, shut in the night. But the thin walls held back no sound.

"Dat ol' scratch is woke up now!" She mused at the tremendous whirr inside, which every woodsman knows, is one of the sound illusions. The rattler is a ventriloquist. His whirr sounds to the right, to the left, straight ahead, behind, close under foot—everywhere but where it is. Woe to him who guesses wrong unless he is prepared to hold up his end of the argument! Sometimes he strikes without rattling at all.

Inside, Sykes heard nothing until he knocked a pot lid off the stove while trying to reach the match safe in the dark. He had emptied his pockets at Bertha's.

The snake seemed to wake up under the stove and Sykes made a quick leap into the bedroom. In spite of the gin he had had, his head was clearing now.

"Mah Gawd!" he chattered. "Ef Ah could only strack uh light!"

100 The rattling ceased for a moment as he stood paralyzed. He waited. It seemed that the snake waited also.

"Oh, fuh de light! Ah thought he'd be too sick"—Sykes was muttering to himself when the whirr began again, closer, right underfoot this time. Long before this, Sykes' ability to think had been flattened down to primitive instinct and he leaped—onto the bed.

Outside Delia heard a cry that might have come from a maddened chimpanzee, a stricken gorilla. All the terror, all the horror, all the rage that man possibly could express, without a recognizable human sound.

A tremendous stir inside there, another series of animal screams, the intermittent whirr of the reptile. The shade torn violently down from the window, letting in the red dawn, a huge brown hand seizing the window stick, great dull blows upon the wooden floor punctuating the gibberish of sound long after the rattle of the snake had abruptly subsided. All this Delia could see and hear from her place beneath the window, and it made her ill. She crept over to the four-o'clocks[7] and stretched herself on the cool earth to recover.

She lay there. "Delia, Delia!" She could hear Sykes calling in a most despairing tone as one who expected no answer. The sun crept on up, and he called. Delia could not move—her legs were gone flabby. She never moved, he called, and the sun kept rising.

105 "Mah Gawd!" She heard him moan. "Mah Gawd fum Heben!" She heard him stumbling about and got up from her flower-bed. The sun was growing warm. As she approached the door she heard him call out hopefully. "Delia, is dat you Ah heah?"

She saw him on his hands and knees as soon as she reached the door. He crept an inch or two toward her—all that he was able, and she saw his horribly swollen neck and his one open eye shining with hope. A surge of pity too strong to support bore her away from that eye that must, could not, fail to see the tubs. He would see the lamp. Orlando with its doctors was too far. She could scarcely reach the Chinaberry tree, where she waited in the growing heat while inside she knew the cold river was creeping up and up to extinguish that eye which must know by now that she knew.

[1926]

[7]**four-o'clocks** flowers that open in the late afternoon.

Joining the Conversation: Critical Thinking and Writing

1. Summarize the relationship of Delia and Sykes before the time of the story.
2. How do the men on Joe Clark's porch further your understanding of Delia and Sykes and of the relationship between the two?
3. To what extent is Delia responsible for Sykes's death? To what extent is Sykes responsible? Do you think that Delia's action (or inaction) at the end of the story is immoral? Why, or why not?
4. To what extent does the relationship between African Americans and whites play a role in the lives of the characters in "Sweat" and in the outcome of the story?

5. Are the African Americans in "Sweat" portrayed stereotypically, as some of Hurston's critics charged? (See the biographical note, page 697.) How, on the evidence available in this story, might Hurston's fiction be defended from that charge?

Bel Kaufman

Bel Kaufman, born in Berlin, Germany, came to the United States in her early years. She holds a bachelor's degree from Hunter College and a master's degree from Columbia University, and she has served as adjunct professor at the City University of New York.

In 1965 Kaufman won national fame with Up the Down Staircase, *a work of fiction that was later made into a popular film. She is also the author of another novel,* Love *(1979), and of essays and prize-winning short stories.*

Sunday in the Park

It was still warm in the late-afternoon sun, and the city noises came muffled through the trees in the park. She put her book down on the bench, removed her sunglasses, and sighed contentedly. Morton was reading the *Times Magazine* section, one arm flung around her shoulder; their three-year-old son, Larry, was playing in the sandbox: a faint breeze fanned her hair softly against her cheek. It was five-thirty of a Sunday afternoon, and the small playground, tucked away in a corner of the park, was all but deserted. The swings and seesaws stood motionless and abandoned, the slides were empty, and only in the sandbox two little boys squatted diligently side by side. *How good this is*, she thought, and almost smiled at her sense of well-being. They must go out in the sun more often; Morton was so city-pale, cooped up all week inside the gray factorylike university. She squeezed his arm affectionately and glanced at Larry, delighting in the pointed little face frowning in concentration over the tunnel he was digging. The other boy suddenly stood up and with a quick, deliberate swing of his chubby arm threw a spadeful of sand at Larry. It just missed his head. Larry continued digging; the boy remained standing, shovel raised, stolid and impassive.

"No, no, little boy." She shook her finger at him, her eyes searching for the child's mother or nurse. "We mustn't throw sand. It may get in someone's eyes and hurt. We must play nicely in the nice sandbox." The boy looked at her in unblinking expectancy. He was about Larry's age but perhaps ten pounds heavier, a husky little boy with none of Larry's quickness and sensitivity in his face. Where was his mother? The only other people left in the playground were two women and a little girl on roller skates leaving now through the gate, and a man on a bench a few feet away. He was a big man, and he seemed to be taking up the whole bench as he held the Sunday comics close to his face. She supposed he was the child's father. He did not look up from his comics, but spat once deftly out of the corner of his mouth. She turned her eyes away.

At that moment, as swiftly as before, the fat little boy threw another spadeful of sand at Larry. This time some of it landed on his hair and forehead. Larry looked up at his mother, his mouth tentative; her expression would tell him whether to cry or not.

Her first instinct was to rush to her son, brush the sand out of his hair, and punish the other child, but she controlled it. She always said that she wanted Larry to learn to fight his own battles.

5 "Don't *do* that, little boy," she said sharply, leaning forward on the bench. "You mustn't throw sand!"

The man on the bench moved his mouth as if to spit again, but instead he spoke. He did not look at her, but at the boy only.

"You go right ahead, Joe," he said loudly. "Throw all you want. This here is a *public* sandbox."

She felt a sudden weakness in her knees as she glanced at Morton. He had become aware of what was happening. He put his *Times* down carefully on his lap and turned his fine, lean face toward the man, smiling the shy, apologetic smile he might have offered a student in pointing out an error in his thinking. When he spoke to the man, it was with his usual reasonableness.

"You're quite right," he said pleasantly, "but just because this is a public place. . . ."

10 The man lowered his funnies and looked at Morton. He looked at him from head to foot, slowly and deliberately. "Yeah?" His insolent voice was edged with menace. "My kid's got just as good right here as yours, and if he feels like throwing sand, he'll throw it, and if you don't like it, you can take your kid the hell out of here."

The children were listening, their eyes and mouths wide open, their spades forgotten in small fists. She noticed the muscle in Morton's jaw tighten. He was rarely angry; he seldom lost his temper. She was suffused with a tenderness for her husband and an impotent rage against the man for involving him in a situation so alien and so distasteful to him.

"Now, just a minute," Morton said courteously, "you must realize. . . ."

"Aw, shut up," said the man.

Her heart began to pound. Morton half rose; the *Times* slid to the ground. Slowly the other man stood up. He took a couple of steps toward Morton, then stopped. He flexed his great arms, waiting. She pressed her trembling knees together. Would there be violence, fighting? How dreadful, how incredible. . . . She must do something, stop them, call for help. She wanted to put her hand on her husband's sleeve, to pull him down, but for some reason she didn't.

15 Morton adjusted his glasses. He was very pale. "This is ridiculous," he said unevenly. "I must ask you. . . ."

"Oh, yeah?" said the man. He stood with his legs spread apart, rocking a little, looking at Morton with utter scorn. "You and who else?"

For a moment the two men looked at each other nakedly. Then Morton turned his back on the man and said quietly, "Come on, let's get out of here." He walked awkwardly, almost limping with self-consciousness, to the sandbox. He stooped and lifted Larry and his shovel out.

At once Larry came to life; his face lost its rapt expression and he began to kick and cry. "I don't *want* to go home, I want to play better, I don't *want* any supper, I don't *like* supper. . . ." It became a chant as they walked, pulling their child between them, his feet dragging on the ground. In order to get to the exit gate they had to pass the bench where the man sat sprawling again. She was careful not to look at him. With all the dignity she could summon, she pulled Larry's sandy, perspiring little hand, while Morton pulled the other. Slowly and with head high she walked with her husband and child out of the playground.

Her first feeling was one of relief that a fight had been avoided, that no one was hurt. Yet beneath it there was a layer of something else, something heavy and inescapable. She sensed that it was more than just an unpleasant incident, more than defeat of reason by force. She felt dimly it had something to do with her and Morton, something acutely personal, familiar, and important.

20 Suddenly Morton spoke. "It wouldn't have proved anything."

"What?" she asked.

"A fight. It wouldn't have proved anything beyond the fact that he's bigger than I am."

"Of course," she said.

"The only possible outcome," he continued reasonably, "would have been—what? My glasses broken, perhaps a tooth or two replaced, a couple of days' work missed—and for what? For justice? For truth?"

25 "Of course," she repeated. She quickened her step. She wanted only to get home and to busy herself with her familiar tasks; perhaps then the feeling, glued like heavy plaster on her heart, would be gone. *Of all the stupid, despicable bullies,* she thought, pulling harder on Larry's hand. The child was still crying. Always before she had felt a tender pity for his defenseless little body, the frail arms, the narrow shoulders with sharp, winglike shoulder blades, the thin and unsure legs, but now her mouth tightened in resentment.

"Stop crying," she said sharply. "I'm ashamed of you!" She felt as if all three of them were tracking mud along the street. The child cried louder.

If there had been an issue involved, she thought, *if there had been something to fight for. . . . But what else could he possibly have done? Allow himself to be beaten? Attempt to educate the man? Call a policeman? "Officer, there's a man in the park who won't stop his child from throwing sand on mine. . . ."* The whole thing was as silly as that, and not worth thinking about.

"Can't you keep him quiet, for Pete's sake?" Morton asked irritably.

"What do you suppose I've been trying to do?" she said.

30 Larry pulled back, dragging his feet.

"If you can't discipline this child, I will," Morton snapped, making a move toward the boy.

But her voice stopped him. She was shocked to hear it, thin and cold and penetrating with contempt. "Indeed?" she heard herself say. "You and who else?"

[1985]

Joining the Conversation: Critical Thinking and Writing

1. When you first saw the title of this story, did it arouse any particular expectations? If so, of what sort?
2. Reread the first paragraph, in order to remind yourself of the way in which Bel Kaufman introduces the characters to the reader. How (after reading the first paragraph) did you feel about the woman and Morton?
3. What is the woman's attitude toward her husband at the end of the story? Is it appropriate? At the end of the story, what is your attitude toward Morton? Toward the woman? How do you account for these attitudes? Do you judge either character morally?

RAYMOND CARVER

Raymond Carver (1938–1988) was born in Clatskanie, a logging town in Oregon. In 1963 he graduated from Humboldt State College in northern California and then did further study at the University of Iowa.

His early years were not easy—he married while still in college, divorced a little later, and sometimes suffered from alcoholism. In his last years he found domestic happiness, but he died of cancer at the age of fifty.

As a young man he wrote poetry while working at odd jobs (janitor, deliveryman, etc.); later he turned to fiction, though he continued to write poetry. Most of Carver's fiction narrates stories about bewildered and sometimes exhausted men and women.

Cathedral

This blind man, an old friend of my wife's, he was on his way to spend the night. His wife had died. So he was visiting the dead wife's relatives in Connecticut. He called my wife from his in-laws'. Arrangements were made. He would come by train, a five-hour trip, and my wife would meet him at the station. She hadn't seen him since she worked for him one summer in Seattle ten years ago. But she and the blind man had kept in touch. They made tapes and mailed them back and forth. I wasn't enthusiastic about his visit. He was no one I knew. And his being blind bothered me. My idea of blindness came from the movies. In the movies, the blind moved slowly and never laughed. Sometimes they were led by seeing-eye dogs. A blind man in my house was not something I looked forward to.

That summer in Seattle she had needed a job. She didn't have any money. The man she was going to marry at the end of the summer was in officers' training school. He didn't have any money, either. But she was in love with the guy, and he was in love with her, etc. She'd seen something in the paper: HELP WANTED—*Reading to Blind Man,* and a telephone number. She phoned and went over, was hired on the spot. She'd worked with this blind man all summer. She read stuff to him, case studies, reports, that sort of thing. She helped him organize his little office in the county social-service department. They'd become good friends, my wife and the blind man. How do I know these things? She told me. And she told me something else. On her last day in the office, the blind man asked if he could touch her face. She agreed to this. She told me he touched his fingers to every part of her face, her nose—even her neck! She never forgot it. She even tried to write a poem about it. She was always trying to write a poem. She wrote a poem or two every year, usually after something really important had happened to her.

When we first started going out together, she showed me the poem. In the poem, she recalled his fingers and the way they had moved around over her face. In the poem, she talked about what she had felt at the time, about what went through her mind when the blind man touched her nose and lips. I can remember I didn't think much of the poem. Of course, I didn't tell her that. Maybe I just don't understand poetry. I admit it's not the first thing I reach for when I pick up something to read.

Anyway, this man who'd first enjoyed her favors, the officer-to-be, he'd been her childhood sweetheart. So okay. I'm saying that at the end of the summer she let the blind man run his hands over her face, said goodbye to him, married her childhood etc., who was now a commissioned officer, and she moved away from Seattle. But they'd kept in touch, she and the blind man. She made the first contact after a year or so. She called him up one night from an Air Force base in Alabama. She wanted to talk. They talked. He asked her to send a tape and tell him about her life. She did this. She sent the tape. On the tape, she told the blind man about her husband and about their life together in the military. She told the blind man she loved her husband but she didn't like it where they lived and she didn't like it that he was part of the military-industrial thing. She told the blind man she'd written a poem and he was in it. She told him that she was writing a poem about what it was like to be an Air Force officer's wife. The poem wasn't finished yet. She was still writing it. The blind man made a tape. He sent her the tape. She made a tape. This went on for years. My wife's officer was posted to one base and then another. She sent tapes from Moody AFB, McGuire, McConnell, and finally Travis, near Sacramento, where one night she got to feeling lonely and cut off from people she kept losing in that moving-around life. She got to feeling she couldn't go it another step. She went in and swallowed all the pills and capsules in the medicine chest and washed them down with a bottle of gin. Then she got into a hot bath and passed out.

5 But instead of dying, she got sick. She threw up. Her officer—why should he have a name? he was the childhood sweetheart, and what more does he want?—came home from somewhere, found her, and called the ambulance. In time, she put it all on a tape and sent the tape to the blind man. Over the years, she put all kinds of stuff on tapes and sent the tapes off lickety-split. Next to writing a poem every year, I think it was her chief means of recreation. On one tape, she told the blind man she'd decided to live away from her officer for a time. On another tape, she told him about her divorce. She and I began going out, and of course she told her blind man about it. She told him everything, or so it seemed to me. Once she asked me if I'd like to hear the latest tape from the blind man. This was a year ago. I was on the tape, she said. So I said okay, I'd listen to it. I got us drinks and we settled down in the living room. We made ready to listen. First she inserted the tape into the player and adjusted a couple of dials. Then she pushed a lever. The tape squeaked and someone began to talk in this loud voice. She lowered the volume. After a few minutes of harmless chitchat, I heard my own name in the mouth of this stranger, this blind man I didn't even know! And then this: "From all you've said about him, I can only conclude—" But we were interrupted, a knock at the door, something, and we didn't ever get back to the tape. Maybe it was just as well. I'd heard all I wanted to.

Now this same blind man was coming to sleep in my house.

"Maybe I could take him bowling," I said to my wife. She was at the draining board doing scalloped potatoes. She put down the knife she was using and turned around.

"If you love me," she said, "you can do this for me. If you don't love me, okay. But if you had a friend, any friend, and the friend came to visit, I'd make him feel comfortable." She wiped her hands with the dish towel.

"I don't have any blind friends," I said.

10 "You don't have *any* friends," she said. "Period. Besides," she said, "goddamn it, his wife's just died! Don't you understand that? The man's lost his wife!"

I didn't answer. She'd told me a little about the blind man's wife. Her name was Beulah. Beulah! That's a name for a colored woman.

"Was his wife a Negro?" I asked.

"Are you crazy?" my wife said. "Have you just flipped or something?" She picked up a potato. I saw it hit the floor, then roll under the stove. "What's wrong with you?" she said. "Are you drunk?"

"I'm just asking," I said.

15 Right then my wife filled me in with more detail than I cared to know. I made a drink and sat at the kitchen table to listen. Pieces of the story began to fall into place.

Beulah had gone to work for the blind man the summer after my wife had stopped working for him. Pretty soon Beulah and the blind man had themselves a church wedding. It was a little wedding—who'd want to go to such a wedding in the first place?—just the two of them, plus the minister and the minister's wife. But it was a church wedding just the same. It was what Beulah had wanted, he'd said. But even then Beulah must have been carrying the cancer in her glands. After they had been inseparable for eight years—my wife's word, *inseparable*—Beulah's health went into a rapid decline. She died in a Seattle hospital room, the blind man sitting beside the bed and holding on to her hand. They'd married, lived and worked together, slept together—had sex, sure—and then the blind man had to bury her. All this without his having ever seen what the goddamned woman looked like. It was beyond my understanding. Hearing this, I felt sorry for the blind man for a little bit. And then I found myself thinking what a pitiful life this woman must have led. Imagine a woman who could never see herself as she was seen in the eyes of her loved one. A woman who could go on day after day and never receive the smallest compliment from her beloved. A woman whose husband could never read the expression on her face, be it misery or something better. Someone who could wear makeup or not—what difference to him? She could, if she wanted, wear green eye-shadow around one eye, a straight pin in her nostril, yellow slacks, and purple shoes, no matter. And then to slip off into death, the blind man's hand on her hand, his blind eyes streaming tears—I'm imagining now—her last thought maybe this: that he never even knew what she looked like, and she on an express to the grave. Robert was left with a small insurance policy and a half of a twenty-peso Mexican coin. The other half of the coin went into the box with her. Pathetic.

So when the time rolled around, my wife went to the depot to pick him up. With nothing to do but wait—sure, I blamed him for that—I was having a drink and watching the TV when I heard the car pull into the drive. I got up from the sofa with my drink and went to the window to have a look.

I saw my wife laughing as she parked the car. I saw her get out of the car and shut the door. She was still wearing a smile. Just amazing. She went around to the other side of the car to where the blind man was already starting to get out. This blind man, feature this, he was wearing a full beard! A beard on a blind man! Too much, I say. The blind man reached into the back seat and dragged out a suitcase. My wife took his arm, shut the car door, and, talking all the way, moved him down the drive and then up the steps to the front porch. I turned off the TV. I finished my drink, rinsed the glass, dried my hands. Then I went to the door.

My wife said, "I want you to meet Robert. Robert, this is my husband. I've told you all about him." She was beaming. She had this blind man by his coat sleeve.

20 The blind man let go of his suitcase and up came his hand. I took it. He squeezed hard, held my hand, and then he let it go.

"I feel like we've already met," he boomed.

"Likewise," I said. I didn't know what else to say. Then I said, "Welcome. I've heard a lot about you." We began to move then, a little group, from the porch into the living room, my wife guiding him by the arm. The blind man was carrying his suitcase in his other hand. My wife said things like, "To your left here, Robert.

That's right. Now watch it, there's a chair. That's it. Sit down right here. This is the sofa. We just bought this sofa two weeks ago."

I started to say something about the old sofa. I'd liked that old sofa. But I didn't say anything. Then I wanted to say something else, small-talk, about the scenic ride along the Hudson. How going *to* New York, you should sit on the right-hand side of the train, and coming *from* New York, the left-hand side.

"Did you have a good train ride?" I said. "Which side of the train did you sit on, by the way?"

25 "What a question, which side!" my wife said. "What's it matter which side?" she said.

"I just asked," I said.

"Right side," the blind man said. "I hadn't been on a train in nearly forty years. Not since I was a kid. With my folks. That's been a long time. I'd nearly forgotten the sensation. I have winter in my beard now," he said. "So I've been told, anyway. Do I look distinguished, my dear?" the blind man said to my wife.

"You look distinguished, Robert," she said. "Robert," she said. "Robert, it's just so good to see you."

My wife finally took her eyes off the blind man and looked at me. I had the feeling she didn't like what she saw. I shrugged.

30 I've never met, or personally known, anyone who was blind. This blind man was late forties, a heavy-set, balding man with stooped shoulders, as if he carried a great weight there. He wore brown slacks, brown shoes, a light-brown shirt, a tie, a sports coat. Spiffy. He also had this full beard. But he didn't use a cane and he didn't wear dark glasses. I'd always thought dark glasses were a must for the blind. Fact was, I wished he had a pair. At first glance, his eyes looked like anyone else's eyes. But if you looked close, there was something different about them. Too much white in the iris, for one thing, and the pupils seemed to move around in the sockets without his knowing it or being able to stop it. Creepy. As I stared at his face, I saw the left pupil turn in toward his nose while the other made an effort to keep in one place. But it was only an effort, for that eye was on the roam without his knowing it or wanting it to be.

I said, "Let me get you a drink. What's your pleasure? We have a little of everything. It's one of our pastimes."

"Bub, I'm a Scotch man myself," he said fast enough in this big voice.

"Right," I said. Bub! "Sure you are. I knew it."

He let his fingers touch his suitcase, which was sitting alongside the sofa. He was taking his bearings. I didn't blame him for that.

35 "I'll move that up to your room," my wife said.

"No, that's fine," the blind man said loudly. "It can go up when I go up."

"A little water with the Scotch?" I said.

"Very little," he said.

"I knew it," I said.

40 He said, "Just a tad. The Irish actor, Barry Fitzgerald? I'm like that fellow. When I drink water, Fitzgerald said, I drink water. When I drink whiskey, I drink whiskey." My wife laughed. The blind man brought his hand up under his beard. He lifted his beard slowly and let it drop.

I did the drinks, three big glasses of Scotch with a splash of water in each. Then we made ourselves comfortable and talked about Robert's travels. First the long flight from the West Coast to Connecticut, we covered that. Then from Connecticut up here by train. We had another drink concerning that leg of the trip.

I remembered having read somewhere that the blind didn't smoke because, as speculation had it, they couldn't see the smoke they exhaled. I thought I knew that much and that much only about blind people. But this blind man smoked his cigarette down to the nubbin and then lit another one. This blind man filled his ashtray and my wife emptied it.

When we sat down at the table for dinner, we had another drink. My wife heaped Robert's plate with cube steak, scalloped potatoes, green beans. I buttered him up two slices of bread. I said, "Here's bread and butter for you." I swallowed some of my drink. "Now let us pray," I said, and the blind man lowered his head. My wife looked at me, her mouth agape. "Pray the phone won't ring and the food doesn't get cold," I said.

We dug in. We ate everything there was to eat on the table. We ate like there was no tomorrow. We didn't talk. We ate. We scarfed. We grazed that table. We were into serious eating. The blind man had right away located his foods, he knew just where everything was on his plate. I watched with admiration as he used his knife and fork on the meat. He'd cut two pieces of meat, fork the meat into his mouth, and then go all out for the scalloped potatoes, the beans next, and then he'd tear off a hunk of buttered bread and eat that. He'd follow this up with a big drink of milk. It didn't seem to bother him to use his fingers once in a while, either.

We finished everything, including half a strawberry pie. For a few moments, we sat as if stunned. Sweat beaded on our faces. Finally, we got up from the table and left the dirty plates. We didn't look back. We took ourselves into the living room and sank into our places again. Robert and my wife sat on the sofa. I took the big chair. We had us two or three more drinks while they talked about the major things that had come to pass for them in the past ten years. For the most part, I just listened. Now and then I joined in. I didn't want him to think I'd left the room, and I didn't want her to think I was feeling left out. They talked of things that had happened to them—to them!—these past ten years. I waited in vain to hear my name on my wife's sweet lips: "And then my dear husband came into my life"—something like that. But I heard nothing of the sort. More talk of Robert. Robert had done a little of everything, it seemed, a regular blind jack-of-all-trades. But most recently he and his wife had had an Amway distributorship, from which, I gathered, they'd earned their living, such as it was. The blind man was also a ham radio operator. He talked in his loud voice about conversations he'd had with fellow operators in Guam, in the Philippines, in Alaska, and even in Tahiti. He said he'd have a lot of friends there if he ever wanted to go visit those places. From time to time, he'd turn his blind face toward me, put his hand under his beard, ask me something. How long had I been in my present position? (Three years.) Did I like my work? (I didn't.) Was I going to stay with it? (What were the options?) Finally, when I thought he was beginning to run down, I got up and turned on the TV.

My wife looked at me with irritation. She was heading toward a boil. Then she looked at the blind man and said, "Robert, do you have a TV?"

The blind man said, "My dear, I have two TVs. I have a color set and a black-and-white thing, an old relic. It's funny, but if I turn the TV on, and I'm always turning it on, I turn on the color set. It's funny, don't you think?"

I didn't know what to say to that. I had absolutely nothing to say to that. No opinion. So I watched the news program and tried to listen to what the announcer was saying.

"This is a color TV," the blind man said. "Don't ask me how, but I can tell."

"We traded up a while ago," I said.

The blind man had another taste of his drink. He lifted his beard, sniffed it, and let it fall. He leaned forward on the sofa. He positioned his ashtray on the coffee table, then put the lighter to his cigarette. He leaned back on the sofa and crossed his legs at the ankles.

My wife covered her mouth, and then she yawned. She stretched. She said, "I think I'll go upstairs and put on my robe. I think I'll change into something else. Robert, you make yourself comfortable," she said.

"I'm comfortable," the blind man said.

"I want you to feel comfortable in this house," she said.

55 "I am comfortable," the blind man said.

After she'd left the room, he and I listened to the weather report and then to the sports roundup. By that time, she'd been gone so long I didn't know if she was going to come back. I thought she might have gone to bed. I wished she'd come back downstairs. I didn't want to be left alone with a blind man. I asked him if he wanted another drink, and he said sure. Then I asked if he wanted to smoke some dope with me. I said I'd just rolled a number. I hadn't, but I planned to do so in about two shakes.

"I'll try some with you," he said.

"Damn right," I said. "That's the stuff."

I got our drinks and sat down on the sofa with him. Then I rolled us two fat numbers. I lit one and passed it. I brought it to his fingers. He took it and inhaled.

60 "Hold it as long as you can," I said. I could tell he didn't know the first thing.

My wife came back downstairs wearing her pink robe and her pink slippers.

"What do I smell?" she said.

"We thought we'd have us some cannabis," I said.

My wife gave me a savage look. Then she looked at the blind man and said, "Robert, I didn't know you smoked."

65 He said, "I do now, my dear. There's a first time for everything. But I don't feel anything yet."

"This stuff is pretty mellow," I said. "This stuff is mild. It's dope you can reason with," I said. "It doesn't mess you up."

"Not much it doesn't, bub," he said, and laughed.

My wife sat on the sofa between the blind man and me. I passed her the number. She took it and toked and then passed it back to me. "Which way is this going?" she said. Then she said, "I shouldn't be smoking this. I can hardly keep my eyes open as it is. That dinner did me in. I shouldn't have eaten so much."

"It was the strawberry pie," the blind man said. "That's what did it," he said, and he laughed his big laugh. Then he shook his head.

70 "There's more strawberry pie," I said.

"Do you want some more, Robert?" my wife said.

"Maybe in a little while," he said.

We gave our attention to the TV. My wife yawned again. She said, "Your bed is made up when you feel like going to bed, Robert. I know you must have had a long day. When you're ready to go to bed, say so." She pulled his arm. "Robert?"

He came to and said, "I've had a real nice time. This beats tapes, doesn't it?"

75 I said, "Coming at you," and I put the number between his fingers. He inhaled, held the smoke, and then let it go. It was like he'd been doing it since he was nine years old.

"Thanks, bub," he said. "But I think this is all for me. I think I'm beginning to feel it," he said. He held the burning roach out for my wife.

"Same here," she said. "Ditto. Me, too." She took the roach and passed it to me. "I may just sit here for a while between you two guys with my eyes closed. But don't let me bother you, okay? Either one of you. If it bothers you, say so. Otherwise, I may just sit here with my eyes closed until you're ready to go to bed," she said. "Your bed's made up, Robert, when you're ready. It's right next to our room at the top of the stairs. We'll show you up when you're ready. You wake me up now, you guys, if I fall asleep." She said that and then she closed her eyes and went to sleep.

The news program ended. I got up and changed the channel. I sat back down on the sofa. I wished my wife hadn't pooped out. Her head lay across the back of the sofa, her mouth open. She'd turned so that her robe slipped away from her legs, exposing a juicy thigh. I reached to draw her robe back over her, and it was then that I glanced at the blind man. What the hell! I flipped the robe open again.

"You say when you want some strawberry pie," I said.

80 "I will," he said.

I said, "Are you tired? Do you want me to take you up to your bed? Are you ready to hit the hay?"

"Not yet," he said. "No, I'll stay up with you, bub. If that's all right. I'll stay up until you're ready to turn in. We haven't had a chance to talk. Know what I mean? I feel like me and her monopolized the evening." He lifted his beard and he let it fall. He picked up his cigarettes and his lighter.

"That's all right," I said. Then I said, "I'm glad for the company."

And I guess I was. Every night I smoked dope and stayed up as long as I could before I fell asleep. My wife and I hardly ever went to bed at the same time. When I did go to sleep, I had these dreams. Sometimes I'd wake up from one of them, my heart going crazy.

85 Something about the church and the Middle Ages was on the TV. Not your run-of-the-mill TV fare. I wanted to watch something else. I turned to the other channels. But there was nothing on them, either. So I turned back to the first channel and apologized.

"Bub, it's all right," the blind man said. "It's fine with me. Whatever you want to watch is okay. I'm always learning something. Learning never ends. It won't hurt me to learn something tonight. I got ears," he said.

We didn't say anything for a time. He was leaning forward with his head turned at me, his right ear aimed in the direction of the set. Very disconcerting. Now and then his eyelids drooped and then they snapped open again. Now and then he put his fingers into his beard and tugged, like he was thinking about something he was hearing on the television.

On the screen, a group of men wearing cowls was being set upon and tormented by men dressed in skeleton costumes and men dressed as devils. The men dressed as devils wore devil masks, horns, and long tails. This pageant was part of a procession. The Englishman who was narrating the thing said it took place in Spain once a year. I tried to explain to the blind man what was happening.

"Skeletons," he said. "I know about skeletons," he said, and he nodded.

90 The TV showed this one cathedral. Then there was a long, slow look at another one. Finally, the picture switched to the famous one in Paris, with its flying buttresses and its spires reaching up to the clouds. The camera pulled away to show the whole of the cathedral rising above the skyline.

There were times when the Englishman who was telling the thing would shut up, would simply let the camera move around the cathedrals. Or else the camera would tour the countryside, men in fields walking behind oxen. I waited as long as I could. Then I felt I had to say something. I said, "They're showing the outside of this cathedral now. Gargoyles. Little statues carved to look like monsters. Now I guess they're in Italy. Yeah, they're in Italy. There's paintings on the walls of this one church."

"Are those fresco paintings, bub?" he asked, and he sipped from his drink.

I reached for my glass. But it was empty. I tried to remember what I could remember. "You're asking me are those frescoes?" I said. "That's a good question. I don't know."

The camera moved to a cathedral outside Lisbon. The differences in the Portuguese cathedral compared with the French and Italian were not that great. But they were there. Mostly the interior stuff. Then something occurred to me, and I said, "Something has occurred to me. Do you have any idea what a cathedral is? What they look like, that is? Do you follow me? If somebody says cathedral to you, do you have any notion what they're talking about? Do you know the difference between that and a Baptist church, say?"

95 He let the smoke dribble from his mouth. "I know they took hundreds of workers fifty or a hundred years to build," he said. "I just heard the man say that, of course. I know generations of the same families worked on a cathedral. I heard him say that, too. The men who began their life's work on them, they never lived to see the completion of their work. In that wise, bub, they're no different from the rest of us, right?" He laughed. Then his eyelids drooped again. His head nodded. He seemed to be snoozing. Maybe he was imagining himself in Portugal. The TV was showing another cathedral now. This one was in Germany. The Englishman's voice droned on. "Cathedrals," the blind man said. He sat up and rolled his head back and forth. "If you want the truth, bub, that's about all I know. What I just said. What I heard him say. But maybe you could describe one to me? I wish you'd do it. I'd like that. If you want to know, I really don't have a good idea."

I stared hard at the shot of the cathedral on the TV. How could I even begin to describe it? But say my life depended on it. Say my life was being threatened by an insane guy who said I had to do it or else.

I stared some more at the cathedral before the picture flipped off into the countryside. There was no use. I turned to the blind man and said, "To begin with, they're very tall." I was looking around the room for clues. "They reach way up. Up and up. Toward the sky. They're so big, some of them, they have to have these supports. To help hold them up, so to speak. These supports are called buttresses. They remind me of viaducts, for some reason. But maybe you don't know viaducts, either? Sometimes the cathedrals have devils and such carved into the front. Sometimes lords and ladies. Don't ask me why this is," I said.

He was nodding. The whole upper part of his body seemed to be moving back and forth.

"I'm not doing so good, am I?" I said.

100 He stopped nodding and leaned forward on the edge of the sofa. As he listened to me, he was running his fingers through his beard. I wasn't getting through to him, I could see that. But he waited for me to go on just the same. He nodded, like he was trying to encourage me. I tried to think what else to say. "They're really big," I said. "They're massive. They're built of stone. Marble, too, sometimes. In those olden days, when they built cathedrals, men wanted to be close to God. In those olden days, God was an important part of everyone's life.

You could tell this from their cathedral-building. I'm sorry," I said, "but it looks like that's the best I can do for you. I'm just no good at it."

"That's all right, bub," the blind man said. "Hey, listen. I hope you don't mind my asking you. Can I ask you something? Let me ask you a simple question, yes or no. I'm just curious and there's no offense. You're my host. But let me ask if you are in any way religious? You don't mind my asking?"

I shook my head. He couldn't see that, though. A wink is the same as a nod to a blind man. "I guess I don't believe in it. In anything. Sometimes it's hard. You know what I'm saying?"

"Sure, I do," he said.

"Right," I said.

The Englishman was still holding forth. My wife sighed in her sleep. She drew a long breath and went on with her sleeping.

"You'll have to forgive me," I said. "But I can't tell you what a cathedral looks like. It just isn't in me to do it. I can't do any more than I've done."

The blind man sat very still, his head down, as he listened to me.

I said, "The truth is, cathedrals don't mean anything special to me. Nothing. Cathedrals. They're something to look at on late-night TV. That's all they are."

It was then that the blind man cleared his throat. He brought something up. He took a handkerchief from his back pocket. Then he said, "I get it, bub. It's okay. It happens. Don't worry about it," he said. "Hey, listen to me. Will you do me a favor? I got an idea. Why don't you find us some heavy paper? And a pen. We'll do something. We'll draw one together. Get us a pen and some heavy paper. Go on, bub, get the stuff," he said.

So I went upstairs. My legs felt like they didn't have any strength in them. They felt like they did after I'd done some running. In my wife's room, I looked around. I found some ballpoints in a little basket on her table. And then I tried to think where to look for the kind of paper he was talking about.

Downstairs, in the kitchen, I found a shopping bag with onion skins in the bottom of the bag. I emptied the bag and shook it. I brought it into the living room and sat down with it near his legs. I moved some things, smoothed the wrinkles from the bag, spread it out on the coffee table.

The blind man got down from the sofa and sat next to me on the carpet.

He ran his fingers over the paper. He went up and down the sides of the paper. The edges, even the edges. He fingered the corners.

"All right," he said. "All right, let's do her."

He found my hand, the hand with the pen. He closed his hand over my hand. "Go ahead, bub, draw," he said. "Draw. You'll see. I'll follow along with you. It'll be okay. Just begin now like I'm telling you. You'll see. Draw," the blind man said.

So I began. First I drew a box that looked like a house. It could have been the house I lived in. Then I put a roof on it. At either end of the roof, I drew spires. Crazy.

"Swell," he said. "Terrific. You're doing fine," he said. "Never thought anything like this could happen in your lifetime, did you, bub? Well, it's a strange life, we all know that. Go on now. Keep it up."

I put in windows with arches. I drew flying buttresses. I hung great doors. I couldn't stop. The TV station went off the air. I put down the pen and closed and opened my fingers. The blind man felt around over the paper. He moved the tips of his fingers over the paper, all over what I had drawn, and he nodded.

"Doing fine," the blind man said.

120 I took up the pen again, and he found my hand. I kept at it. I'm no artist. But I kept drawing just the same.

My wife opened up her eyes and gazed at us. She sat up on the sofa, her robe hanging open. She said, "What are you doing? Tell me, I want to know."

I didn't answer her.

The blind man said, "We're drawing a cathedral. Me and him are working on it. Press hard," he said to me. "That's right. That's good," he said. "Sure. You got it, bub, I can tell. You didn't think you could. But you can, can't you? You're cooking with gas now. You know what I'm saying? We're going to really have us something here in a minute. How's the old arm?" he said. "Put some people in there now. What's a cathedral without people?"

My wife said, "What's going on? Robert, what are you doing? What's going on?"

125 "It's all right," he said to her. "Close your eyes now," the blind man said to me.

I did it. I closed them just like he said.

"Are they closed?" he said. "Don't fudge."

"They're closed," I said.

"Keep them that way," he said. He said, "Don't stop now. Draw."

130 So we kept on with it. His fingers rode my fingers as my hand went over the paper. It was like nothing else in my life up to now.

Then he said, "I think that's it. I think you got it," he said. "Take a look. What do you think?"

But I had my eyes closed. I thought I'd keep them that way for a little longer. I thought it was something I ought to do.

"Well?" he said. "Are you looking?"

My eyes were still closed. I was in my house. I knew that. But I didn't feel like I was inside anything.

135 "It's really something," I said.

[1983]

Joining the Conversation: Critical Thinking and Writing

1. What was your impression of the narrator after reading the first five paragraphs?
2. Why does the narrator feel threatened by the blind man? Has he any reason to feel threatened?
3. What attitude does the narrator reveal in the following passage:

> She'd turned so that her robe slipped away from her legs, exposing a juicy thigh. I reached to draw her robe back over her and it was then that I glanced at the blind man. What the hell! I flipped the robe open again.

4. Why does the narrator not open his eyes at the end of the story?
5. The television program happens to be about cathedrals, but if the point is to get the narrator to draw something while the blind man's hand rests on the narrator's, the program could have been about some other topic—for example, about skyscrapers or about the Statue of Liberty. In a short argument (250 words) explain why you think that a cathedral is or is not a better choice, for Carver's purposes, than these other subjects.
6. In what ways does Carver prepare us for the narrator's final state of mind?

Poems

Anonymous

Western Wind

Westron° wind, when will thou blow?
The small rain down can rain.
Christ, that my love were in my arms,
And I in my bed again.

[c. 1500]

1 Westron western.

Joining the Conversation: Critical Thinking and Writing

1. In "Western Wind," what do you think is the tone of the speaker's voice in the first two lines? Angry? Impatient? Supplicating? Be as precise as possible. What is the tone in the next two lines?
2. In England, the west wind, warmed by the Gulf Stream, rises in the spring. What associations link the wind and rain of lines 1 and 2 with lines 3 and 4?
3. Should we have been told why the lovers are separated? Explain.

Christopher Marlowe

Christopher Marlowe (1564–1593), English poet and playwright, was born in the same year as Shakespeare. An early death, in a tavern brawl, cut short what might have been a brilliant career.

Marlowe's "The Passionate Shepherd to His Love" is a pastoral poem; it depicts shepherds and shepherdesses in an idyllic, timeless setting. This poem engendered many imitations and replies, two of which we reprint after Marlowe's.

The Passionate Shepherd to His Love

Come live with me and be my love,
And we will all the pleasures prove,
That valleys, groves, hills, and fields,
Woods or steepy mountain yields.

There we will sit upon the rocks,
And see the shepherds feed their flocks,
By shallow rivers to whose falls
Melodious birds sing madrigals.

And I will make thee beds of roses
With a thousand fragrant posies,
A cap of flowers, and a kirtle
Embroidered all with leaves of myrtle;

A gown made of the finest wool
Which from our pretty lambs we pull;
Fair lined slippers for the cold,
With buckles of the purest gold;

A belt of straw and ivy buds,
With coral clasps and amber studs:
And if these pleasures may thee move,
Come live with me and be my love.

The shepherds' swains shall dance and sing
For thy delight each May morning:
If these delights thy mind may move,
Then live with me and be my love.

[1599–1600]

Joining the Conversation: Critical Thinking and Writing

Read the poem two or three times, preferably aloud. Marlowe's poem is not to be taken seriously as a picture of the pastoral (shepherd) life, but if you have enjoyed the poem, exactly what have you enjoyed?

Sir Walter Raleigh

Walter Raleigh (1552–1618) is known chiefly as a soldier and a colonizer—he was the founder of the settlement in Virginia, and he introduced tobacco into Europe—but in his own day he was known also as a poet.

The Nymph's Reply to the Shepherd

If all the world and love were young,
And truth in every shepherd's tongue,
These pretty pleasures might me move,
To live with thee, and be thy love.

Time drives the flocks from field to fold,
When rivers rage, and rocks grow cold,
And Philomel° becometh dumb,
The rest complains of cares to come.

The flowers do fade, and wanton fields,
To wayward winter reckoning yields,
A honey tongue, a heart of gall,
Is fancy's spring, but sorrow's fall.

7 Philomel In Greek mythology, Philomela was a beautiful woman who was raped and later transformed into a chattering sparrow, but in most Roman versions she is transformed into the nightingale, noted for its beautiful song.

Thy gowns, thy shoes, thy beds of roses,
Thy cap, thy kirtle, and thy posies,
Soon break, soon wither, soon forgotten:
In folly ripe, in reason rotten.

Thy belt of straw and ivy buds,
Thy coral clasps and amber studs,
All these in me no means can move,
To come to thee, and be thy love.

But could youth last, and love still breed,
Had joys no date, nor age no need,
Then these delights my mind might move,
To live with thee and be thy love.

[c. 1600]

Joining the Conversation: Critical Thinking and Writing

1. What is the season in Marlowe's poem? What season(s) does Raleigh envision?
2. Some readers find puns in line 12, in "fancy's spring, but sorrow's fall." How do you paraphrase and interpret the line?
3. How would you describe the tone of the final stanza?
4. Now that you have read Raleigh's poem, reread Marlowe's. Do you now, in the context of Raleigh's poem, enjoy Marlowe's more than before, or less? Why? (You might think of it this way: Does Raleigh's refutation cause you to lose interest in Marlowe's poem?)

JOHN DONNE

John Donne (1572–1631) wrote religious poetry as well as love poetry. In the following lyric, he alters Marlowe's pastoral setting to a setting involving people engaged in fishing. The poem thus belongs to a type called piscatory lyric (Latin piscis, "fish"). For a fuller biographical note, and another poem, see page 116.

The Bait

Come live with me, and be my love,
And we will some new pleasures prove
Of golden sands, and crystal brooks,
With silken lines, and silver hooks.

There will the river whispering run
Warmed by thy eyes, more than the Sun.
And there th'enamored fish will stay,
Begging themselves they may betray.

When thou wilt swim in that live bath,
Each fish, which every channel hath,
Will amorously to thee swim,
Gladder to catch thee, than thou him.

If thou, to be so seen, beest loath,
By Sun, or Moon, thou darknest both,
And if my self have leave to see,
I need not their light, having thee.

Let others freeze with angling reeds,
And cut their legs, with shells and weeds,
Or treacherously poor fish beset,
With strangling snare, or windowy net:

Let coarse bold hands, from slimy nest
The bedded fish in banks out-wrest,
Or curious traitors, sleavesilk flies
Bewitch poor fishes' wandring eyes.

For thee, thou needst no such deceit,
For thou thy self art thine own bait;
That fish, that is not catched thereby,
Alas, is wiser far than I.

[1633]

Joining the Conversation: Critical Thinking and Writing

1. In Donne's first stanza, which words especially indicate that we are (as in Marlowe's poem) in an idealized world?
2. Which words later in Donne's poem indicate what (for Donne) the real world of fishing is?
3. Paraphrase the last stanza, making it as clear as possible.

WILLIAM SHAKESPEARE

Shakespeare (1564–1616) was born into a middle-class family in Stratford-upon-Avon. Although we have a fair number of records about his life—documents concerning marriage, the birth of children, the purchase of property, and so forth—it is not known exactly why and when he turned to the theater. What we do know, however, is important. He was an actor and a shareholder in a playhouse, and he did *write the plays that are attributed to him. The dates of some of the plays can be set precisely, but the dates of some others can be only roughly set.* Hamlet *was probably written between 1599 and 1600. Most of Shakespeare's 154 sonnets were probably written in the late 1590s, but they were not published until 1609.*

Sonnet 29

When, in disgrace with Fortune and men's eyes,
I all alone beweep my outcast state,
And trouble deaf heaven with my bootless° cries,
And look upon myself and curse my fate,
Wishing me like to one more rich in hope,
Featured like him, like him° with friends possessed,
Desiring this man's art and that man's scope,
With what I most enjoy contented least;
Yet in these thoughts myself almost despising,
Haply° I think on thee, and then my state,
Like to the lark at break of day arising
From sullen earth, sings hymns at heaven's gate;
　For thy sweet love rememb'red such wealth brings,
　That then I scorn to change my state with kings.

[c. 1600]

3 bootless useless. **6 like him, like him** like a second man, like a third man.
10 Haply perchance.

Joining the Conversation: Critical Thinking and Writing

1. Paraphrase the first eight lines. Then, in a sentence, summarize the speaker's state of mind to this point in the poem.
2. Summarize the speaker's state of mind in lines 9–12. What does "sullen earth" (line 12) suggest to you?
3. Notice that every line in the poem except line 11 ends with a comma or semicolon, indicating a pause. How does the lack of punctuation at the end of line 11 affect your reading of this line and your understanding of the speaker's emotion?
4. In the last two lines of a sonnet Shakespeare often summarizes the preceding lines. In this sonnet, how does the *structure* (the organization) of the summary differ from that of the statement in the first twelve lines? Why? Try reading the last lines as if they were reversed. Thus:

   For then I scorn to change my state with kings.
   Since thy sweet love rememb'red such wealth brings.

   Which version do you like better? What are your reasons?
5. The "thee" of this poem is almost certainly a man, not a woman. Is the "love" of the poem erotic love, or can it be taken as something like brotherly love or even as loving-kindness?
6. Write a paragraph (or a sonnet) describing how thinking of someone you love—or hate—changes your mood.

Sonnet 116

Let me not to the marriage of true minds
Admit impediments; love is not love
Which alters when it alteration finds,
Or bends with the remover to remove.
O, no, it is an ever-fixèd mark°
That looks on tempests and is never shaken;
It is the star° to every wand'ring bark,
Whose worth's unknown, although his height be taken.
Love's not Time's fool,° though rosy lips and cheeks
Within his bending sickle's compass° come;
Love alters not with his° brief hours and weeks
But bears° it out even to the edge of doom.°
  If this be error and upon° me proved,
  I never writ, nor no man ever loved.

[c. 1600]

5 ever-fixèd mark seamark, guide to mariners. **7 the star** the North Star. **9 fool** plaything. **10 compass** range, circle. **11 his** time's. **12 bears** survives; **doom** Judgment Day. **13 upon** against.

Joining the Conversation: Critical Thinking and Writing

1. Paraphrase (that is, put into your own words) "Let me not to the marriage of true minds / Admit impediments." Is there more than one appropriate meaning of "Admit"?
2. Notice that the poem celebrates "the marriage of true minds," not bodies. In a sentence or two, using only your own words, summarize Shakespeare's idea of the nature of such love, both what it is and what it is not.
3. Paraphrase lines 13–14. What is the speaker's tone here? Would you say that the tone is different from the tone in the rest of the poem?
4. Write a paragraph or a poem defining either love or hate?
5. Find a definition of love or hate in a popular song. Bring the lyrics to class. Why is this definition a good one?

JOHN DONNE

John Donne (1572–1631) was born into a Roman Catholic family in England, but in the 1590s he abandoned that faith. In 1615 he became an Anglican priest and soon was known as a great preacher. A hundred and sixty of his sermons survive, including one with the famous line "No man is an island, entire of itself; every man is a piece of the continent, a part of the main; if a clod be washed away by the sea, Europe is the less. . . ; and therefore never send to know for whom the bell tolls; it tolls for thee." From 1621 until his death Donne was dean of St. Paul's Cathedral in London. His love poems (often bawdy and cynical) are said to be his early work, and his "Holy Sonnets" (among the greatest religious poems written in English) his later work.

A Valediction: Forbidding Mourning

As virtuous men pass mildly away,
And whisper to their souls, to go,
Whilst some of their sad friends do say,
"The breath goes now," and some say, "No":

So let us melt, and make no noise,
No tear-floods, nor sigh-tempests move;
'Twere profanation of our joys
To tell the laity our love.

Moving of th' earth° brings harms and fears;
Men reckon what it did and meant;
But trepidation of the spheres,
Though greater far, is innocent.°

Dull sublunary° lovers' love
(Whose soul is sense) cannot admit
Absence, because it doth remove
Those things which elemented it.

But we, by a love so much refined
That our selves know not what it is,
Inter-assurèd of the mind,
Care less, eyes, lips, and hands to miss.

Our two souls therefore, which are one,
Though I must go, endure not yet
A breach, but an expansion,
Like gold to airy thinness beat.

If they be two, they are two so
As stiff twin compasses° are two:
Thy soul, the fixed foot, makes no show
To move, but doth, if the other do.

And though it in the center sit,
Yet when the other far doth roam,
It leans, and hearkens after it,
And grows erect as that comes home.

Such wilt thou be to me, who must,
Like the other foot, obliquely run;
Thy firmness makes my circle just,
And makes me end where I begun.

[1611]

9 Moving of th' earth an earthquake. **11–12 But trepidation . . . innocent** But the movement of the heavenly spheres (in Ptolemaic astronomy), though far greater, is harmless. **13 sublunary** under the moon, i.e., earthly. **26 compasses** i.e., a carpenter's compass.

Joining the Conversation: Critical Thinking and Writing

1. The first stanza describes the death of "virtuous men." To what is their death compared in the second stanza?

2. Who is the speaker of this poem? To whom does he speak, and what is the occasion? Explain the title.
3. What is the meaning of "laity" in line 8? What does it imply about the speaker and his beloved?
4. In the fourth stanza the speaker contrasts the love of "dull sublunary lovers" (i.e., ordinary mortals) with the love he and his beloved share. What is the difference?
5. In the figure of the carpenter's or draftsperson's compass (lines 25–36) the speaker offers reasons—some stated clearly, some not so clearly—why he will end where he began. In 250 words explain these reasons.
6. In line 35 Donne speaks of his voyage as a "circle." Explain in a paragraph why the circle is traditionally a symbol of perfection.
7. Write a farewell note—or poem—to someone you love (or hate).

ANDREW MARVELL

Born in 1621 near Hull in England, Andrew Marvell attended Trinity College, Cambridge, and graduated in 1638. During the Civil War he was tutor to the daughter of Sir Thomas Fairfax in Yorkshire at Nun Appleton House, where most of his best-known poems were written. In 1657 he was appointed assistant to John Milton, the Latin Secretary for the Commonwealth. After the Restoration of the monarchy in 1659 until his death, Marvell represented Hull as a member of Parliament. Most of his poems were not published until after his death in 1678.

To His Coy Mistress

Had we but world enough, and time.
This coyness, lady, were no crime.
We would sit down, and think which way
To walk, and pass our long love's day.
Thou by the Indian Ganges' side
Should'st rubies find: I by the tide
Of Humber° would complain.° I would
Love you ten years before the Flood,
And you should, if you please, refuse
Till the conversion of the Jews.°
My vegetable° love should grow
Vaster than empires, and more slow.
An hundred years should go to praise
Thine eyes, and on thy forehead gaze:
Two hundred to adore each breast:
But thirty thousand to the rest.
An age at least to every part,
And the last age should show your heart.
For, lady, you deserve this state,
Nor would I love at lower rate,

7 Humber river in England; **complain** write love poems. **10 conversion of the Jews** It was believed by Christians that the conversion of the Jews would occur just before the Last Judgment. **11 vegetable** slowly growing.

But at my back I always hear
Time's winged chariot hurrying near;
And yonder all before us lie
Deserts of vast eternity.
Thy beauty shall no more be found,
Nor in thy marble vault shall sound
My echoing song; then worms shall try
That long preserved virginity,
And your quaint honor turn to dust,
And into ashes all my lust.
The grave's a fine and private place,
But none, I think, do there embrace.
Now therefore, while the youthful hue
Sits on thy skin like morning dew,
And while thy willing soul transpires
At every pore with instant fires,
Now let us sport us while we may;
And now, like am'rous birds of prey,
Rather at once our time devour,
Than languish in his slow-chapt° power,
Let us roll all our strength, and all
Our sweetness, up into one ball;
And tear our pleasures with rough strife
Thorough° the iron gates of life.
Thus, though we cannot make our sun
Stand still, yet we will make him run.

[1641]

40 slow-chapt slowly devouring. **44 Thorough** through.

Joining the Conversation: Critical Thinking and Writing

1. What does "coy" mean in the title, and "coyness" in line 2?
2. Do you think that the speaker's claims in lines 1–20 are so inflated that we detect behind them a playfully ironic tone? Explain. Why does the speaker say in line 8 that he would love "ten years before the Flood," rather than merely "since the Flood"?
3. What do you make of lines 21–24? Why is time behind the speaker, and eternity in front of him? Is this "eternity" the same as the period discussed in lines 1–20? Discuss the change in the speaker's tone after line 20.

WILLIAM BLAKE

William Blake (1757–1827) was born in London and at 14 was apprenticed for seven years to an engraver. A Christian visionary poet, he made his living by giving drawing lessons and by illustrating books, including his own Songs of Innocence *(1789) and* Songs of Experience *(1794). These two books represent, he said, "two contrary states of the human soul." In 1809 Blake exhibited his art, but the show was a failure. Not until he was in his sixties, when he stopped writing poetry, did he achieve any public recognition—and then it was as a painter.*

The Garden of Love

I went to the Garden of Love,
And saw what I never had seen:
A Chapel was built in the midst,
Where I used to play on the green.

And the gates of this Chapel were shut,
And "Thou shalt not" writ over the door;
So I turn'd to the Garden of Love,
That so many sweet flowers bore,

And I saw it was filled with graves,
And tomb-stones where flowers should be;
And Priests in black gowns were walking their rounds,
And binding with briars my joys & desires.

[1794]

Joining the Conversation: Critical Thinking and Writing

1. What is the speaker's mood as he surveys "the Garden of Love"? What does he report?
2. Does the form of the poem contribute to the speaker's mood? Try taking out the *ands* wherever you can, consistent with the meaning of the sentences. There is a change in effect, but can you say what it is?
3. In a brief essay (500 words) compare Blake's "The Echoing Green" (page 890) with "The Garden of Love."

A Poison Tree

I was angry with my friend:
I told my wrath, my wrath did end.
I was angry with my foe:
I told it not, my wrath did grow.

And I watered it in fears,
Night and morning with my tears:
And I sunnèd it with smiles,
And with soft deceitful wiles.

And it grew both day and night,
Till it bore an apple bright.
And my foe beheld it shine,
And he knew that it was mine.

And into my garden stole
When the night had veiled the pole:
In the morning glad I see
My foe outstretched beneath the tree.

[1794]

"The Garden of Love" by William Blake, from *Songs of Experience*. (By kind permission of the Provost and Scholars of King's College, Cambridge.)

Joining the Conversation: Critical Thinking and Writing

1. In the first stanza, the speaker describes two actions. What is the difference between them? Does the poem indicate that we should choose one action over the other?
2. What reaction do you have to the speaker in stanza 2?

3. In stanzas 3 and 4, what does the "foe" do? Paraphrase line 14.
4. The poem ends, "In the morning glad I see / My foe outstretched beneath the tree." Does the reader share this gladness to any degree? Explain.
5. Like many of Blake's other poems, this one has a childlike tone. Does the tone enrich or does it impoverish the poem? Why?

EDNA ST. VINCENT MILLAY

For a biographical note on Edna St. Vincent Millay, see page 606.

Love Is Not All: It Is Not Meat nor Drink

Love is not all: it is not meat nor drink
Nor slumber nor a roof against the rain;
Nor yet a floating spar to men that sink
And rise and sink and rise and sink again;
Love can not fill the thickened lung with breath,
Nor clean the blood, nor set the fractured bone;
Yet many a man is making friends with death
Even as I speak, for lack of love alone.
It well may be that in a difficult hour,
Pinned down by pain and moaning for release,
Or nagged by want past resolution's power,
I might be driven to sell your love for peace,
Or trade the memory of this night for food.
It well may be. I do not think I would.

[1931]

Joining the Conversation: Critical Thinking and Writing

1. "Love Is Not All" is a sonnet. Using your own words, briefly summarize the argument of the octet (the first 8 lines). Next, paraphrase the sestet, line by line. On the whole, does the sestet repeat the idea of the octet, or does it add a new idea?
2. Whom did you imagine to be speaking the octet? What does the sestet add to your knowledge of the speaker and the occasion? (And how did you paraphrase line 11?)
3. The first and last lines of the poem consist of words of one syllable, and both lines have a distinct pause in the middle. Do you imagine the lines to be spoken in the same tone of voice? If not, can you describe the difference and account for it?
4. Lines 7 and 8 appear to mean that the absence of love can be a cause of death. To what degree do you believe that to be true?
5. Would you call "Love Is Not All" a love poem? Why or why not? Describe the kind of person who might include the poem in a love letter or valentine, or who would be happy to receive it.
6. One of our friends recited this poem at her wedding. What do you think of that idea?

ROBERT FROST

For a biographical note on Robert Frost, see page 609.

The Silken Tent

She is as in a field a silken tent
At midday when a sunny summer breeze
Has dried the dew and all its ropes relent,
So that in guys it gently sways at ease,
And its supporting central cedar pole,
That is its pinnacle to heavenward
And signifies the sureness of the soul,
Seems to owe naught to any single cord,
But strictly held by none, is loosely bound
By countless silken ties of love and thought
To everything on earth the compass round,
And only by one's going slightly taut
In the capriciousness of summer air
Is of the slightest bondage made aware.

[1943]

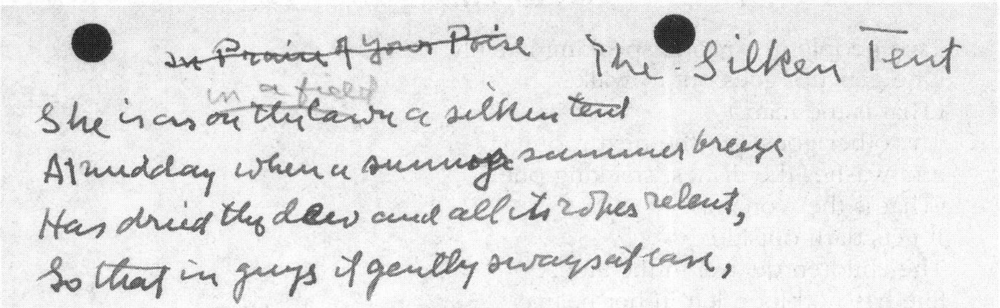
~~In Praise of Your Poise~~ The Silken Tent

She is as ~~on the lawn~~ in a field a silken tent
At midday when a ~~sunny~~ summer breeze
Has dried the dew and all its ropes relent,
So that in guys it gently sways at ease,
And its supporting central cedar pole,
That is its ~~summit pointing~~ pinnacle to heavenward
And signifies the sureness of the soul,
Seems to owe ~~nothing~~ naught to any single cord,
But strictly held by none, is loosely bound
By countless silken ties of love and thought
To everything on earth the compass round,
And only by one's going slightly taut
In the capriciousness of of summer air,
Is of the slightest bondage made aware.

Page from Frost's notebooks, showing "The Silken Tent." (Printed with the permission of The Poetry/Rare Books Collection, University Libraries, State University of New York at Buffalo.)

Joining the Conversation: Critical Thinking and Writing

1. The second line places the scene at "midday" in "summer." In addition to giving us the concreteness of a setting, do these words help to characterize the woman whom the speaker describes? If so, how?
2. The tent is supported by "guys" (not men, but the cords or "ties" of line 10) and by its "central cedar pole." What does Frost tell us about these ties? What does he tell us about the pole?
3. What do you make of lines 12–14?
4. Construct a simile that explains a relationship, and then, in a paragraph, explain how the simile works.

ADRIENNE RICH

For a biographical note on Adrienne Rich (b. 1929), see page 548.

Novella

Two people in a room, speaking harshly.
One gets up, goes out to walk.
(That is the man.)
The other goes into the next room
and washes the dishes, cracking one.
(That is the woman.)
It gets dark outside.
The children quarrel in the attic.
She has no blood left in her heart.
The man comes back to a dark house.
The only light is in the attic.
He has forgotten his key.
He rings at his own door
and hears sobbing on the stairs.
The lights go on in the house.
The door closes behind him.
Outside, separate as minds.
the stars too come alight.

[1967]

*XI.**

Every peak is a crater. This is the law of volcanoes,
making them eternally and visibly female.
No height without depth, without a burning core,
though our straw soles shred on the hardened lava.
I want to travel with you to every sacred mountain
smoking within like the sibyl stooped over her tripod,

*From *Twenty-One Love Poems.*

I want to reach for your hand as we scale the path,
to feel your arteries glowing in my clasp,
never failing to note the small, jewel-like flower
unfamiliar to us, nameless till we rename her,
that clings to the slowly altering rock—
that detail outside ourselves that brings us to ourselves,
was here before us, knew we would come, and sees beyond us.

[1978]

ROBERT PACK

Robert Pack, born in New York City in 1929, was educated at Dartmouth College and Columbia University. The author of many books, he is an emeritus professor at Middlebury College and currently teaches at the University of Montana.

The Frog Prince

(A Speculation on Grimm's Fairy Tale)

Imagine the princess' surprise!
Who would have thought a frog's cold frame
Could hold the sweet and gentle body
Of a prince? How can I name
The joy she must have felt to learn
His transformation was the wonder
Of her touch—that she too, in
Her way, had been transformed under
Those clean sheets? Such powers were
Like nothing she had ever read.
And in the morning when her mother
Came and saw them there in bed,
Heard how a frog became a prince;
What was it that her mother said?

[1980]

Joining the Conversation: Critical Thinking and Writing

1. Fairy-tale characters seldom have characteristics that go beyond the legend they are in. What characteristics does Pack give to the princess? How do you understand "she too, in / Her way, had been transformed" (lines 7–8)?
2. And "What was it that her mother said?"
3. Transform a fairy tale that you know by giving one character or two some realistic traits. Retell the story, or one scene from it.

Joseph Brodsky

The poet and critic Joseph Brodsky (1940–1996) was born in St. Petersburg (then Leningrad), Russia in 1940. Because of his resistance to Soviet authority, he was sentenced in the 1960s to a labor camp and later, in 1972, was expelled from the country. He emigrated to the United States, and taught and lectured at a number of colleges and universities. He received the Nobel Prize in Literature in 1987 and was named Poet Laureate by the Library of Congress in 1991. His books include a collection of poems, To Urania *(1988), and* Less Than One: Selected Essays *(1986).*

Love Song

If you were drowning, I'd come to the rescue,
    wrap you in my blanket and pour hot tea.
If I were a sheriff, I'd arrest you
    and keep you in the cell under lock and key.

If you were a bird, I'd cut a record
    and listen all night long to your high-pitched trill.
If I were a sergeant, you'd be my recruit,
    and boy I can assure you you'd love the drill.

If you were Chinese, I'd learn the language,
    burn a lot of incense, wear funny clothes.
If you were a mirror, I'd storm the Ladies,
    give you my red lipstick and puff your nose.

If you loved volcanoes, I'd be lava
    relentlessly erupting from my hidden source.
And if you were my wife, I'd be your lover
    because the church is firmly against divorce.

[1996]

Joining the Conversation: Critical Thinking and Writing

1. This poem is structurally simple: four stanzas long, it is based on a series of if/then sentences (although the "then" is only implied). Start with the first of these in lines 1–2. How does this scene portray the speaker and the person being addressed? Now move to the next, in lines 3–4, and explain as clearly as you can how this if/then differs in tone and emphasis from the one before. And so on through the poem as a whole.
2. Lines 15–16 bring the poem to a close with a line that begins with "And" rather than "If." Put the speaker's witty point here into your own words. Are these final lines comic or serious or both?

Nikki Giovanni

Nikki Giovanni was born in Knoxville, Tennessee, in 1943 and educated at Fisk University, the University of Pennsylvania School of Social Work, and Columbia University. She has taught at Queens College, Rutgers University, and Ohio State University, and she now teaches at Virginia Tech in Blacksburg, Virginia. Giovanni has published many books of poems, an autobiography (Gemini: An Extended Autobiographical Statement on My First Twenty-Five Years of Being a Black Poet), *a book of essays, and a book consisting of a conversation with James Baldwin (1972).*

Love in Place

I really don't remember falling in love all that much
I remember wanting to bake corn bread and boil a ham and I
certainly remember making lemon pie and when I used to smoke I
stopped in the middle of my day to contemplate

I know I must have fallen in love once because I quit biting
my cuticles and my hair is gray and that must indicate
something and I all of a sudden had a deeper appreciation
for Billie Holiday° and Billy Strayhorn° so if it wasn't love I don't
know what it was

I see the old photographs and I am smiling and I'm sure quite
happy but what I mostly see is me
through your eyes
and I am still young and slim and very much committed to the
love we still have

[1997]

8 **Billie Holiday** jazz singer (1915–1959); **Billy Strayhorn** jazz composer and musician (1915–1967).

Joining the Conversation: Critical Thinking and Writing

1. What reasons does the speaker offer for supposing that she once fell in love? How seriously does she expect us to take those reasons?
2. Read the poem again, but begin with the third stanza and then read the first and second stanzas. Does it make a difference? If so, what is the difference?
3. In line 14 we learn of the "love we still have." Does "still" refer to the present, or to the time of the "old photographs" (10), as the "still" in line 13 does?
4. Why do you suppose Giovanni puts extra space between the words?
5. What do you make of the title?

6. In the first line Giovanni speaks of "falling in love," and she returns to the idea in the fifth line. Judging from your own experience (which includes your knowledge of the people around you), is the term "falling in love" apt, or do people come to love one another in a more gradual fashion than "falling in love" implies? In an essay of 500 words, discuss the similarities and differences between "Love in Place" and the remark by the English essayist William Hazlitt (1778–1830), quoted on p. 678.

PLAY

TERRENCE MCNALLY

Terrence McNally, born in 1939 in St. Petersburg, Florida, grew up in Corpus Christi, Texas, and did his undergraduate work at Columbia University. "I'm a gay man who writes plays," he has said, and most of his work concerns gay people—or the responses of straight people to gay people.

We give the original script of Andre's Mother *(1988); McNally later amplified it for a 1990 television broadcast (running time is 58 minutes) that was awarded an Emmy.*

Andre's Mother

CHARACTERS

CAL, a young man
ARTHUR, his father
PENNY, his sister
ANDRE'S MOTHER
Time: *Now*
Place: *New York City, Central Park*

Four people— CAL, ARTHUR, PENNY, *and* ANDRE'S MOTHER*—enter: They are nicely dressed and each carries a white helium-filled balloon on a string.*

CAL: You know what's really terrible? I can't think of anything terrific to say. Goodbye. I love you. I'll miss you. And I'm supposed to be so great with words!

PENNY: What's that over there?

ARTHUR: Ask your brother.

CAL: It's a theatre. An outdoor theatre. They do plays there in the summer. Shakespeare's plays. [*To* ANDRE'S MOTHER.] God, how much he wanted to play Hamlet again. He would have gone to Timbuktu to have another go at that part. The summer he did it in Boston, he was so happy!

PENNY: Cal, I don't think she . . . ! It's not the time. Later.

ARTHUR: Your son was a . . . the Jews have a word for it . . .

PENNY [QUIETLY APPALLED]: Oh my God!

ARTHUR: Mensch, I believe it is, and I think I'm using it right. It means warm, solid, the real thing. Correct me if I'm wrong.

PENNY: Fine, Dad, fine. Just quit while you're ahead.

ARTHUR: I won't say he was like a son to me. Even my son isn't always like a son to me. I mean . . . ! In my clumsy way, I'm trying to say how much I liked Andre. And how much he helped me to know my own boy. Cal was always two handsful but Andre and I could talk about anything under the sun. My wife was very fond of him, too.

PENNY: Cal, I don't understand about the balloons.

CAL: They represent the soul. When you let go, it means you're letting his soul ascend to Heaven. That you're willing to let go. Breaking the last earthly ties.

PENNY: Does the Pope know about this?

ARTHUR: Penny!

PENNY: Andre loved my sense of humor. Listen, you can hear him laughing. [*She lets go of her white balloon.*] So long, you glorious, wonderful, I-know-what-Cal-means-about-words . . . *man!* God forgive me for wishing you were straight every time I laid eyes on you. But if any man was going to have you, I'm glad it was my brother! Look how fast it went up. I bet that means something. Something terrific.

ARTHUR [LETS HIS BALLOON GO]: Good-bye. God speed.

PENNY: Cal?

CAL: I'm not ready yet.

PENNY: Okay. We'll be over there. Come on, Pop, you can buy your little girl a Good Humor.

ARTHUR: They still make Good Humor?

PENNY: Only now they're called Dove Bars and they cost twelve dollars.

[PENNY TAKES ARTHUR OFF. CAL AND ANDRE'S MOTHER *stand with their balloons.*]

CAL: I wish I knew what you were thinking. I think it would help me. You know almost nothing about me and I only know what Andre told me about you. I'd always had it in my mind that one day we would be friends, you and me. But if you didn't know about Andre and me . . . If this hadn't happened, I wonder if he would have ever told you. When he was sick, if I asked him once I asked him a thousand times, tell her. She's your mother. She won't mind. But he was so afraid of hurting you and of your disapproval. I don't know which was worse. [*No response. He sighs.*] God, how many of us live in this city because we don't want to hurt our mothers and live in mortal terror of their disapproval. We lose ourselves here. Our lives aren't furtive, just our feelings toward people like you are! A city of fugitives from our parents' scorn or heartbreak. Sometimes he'd seem a little down and I'd say, "What's the matter, babe?" and this funny sweet, sad smile would cross his face and he'd say, "Just a little homesick, Cal, just a little bit." I always accused him of being a country boy just playing at being a hotshot, sophisticated New Yorker. [*He sighs.*]

It's bullshit. It's all bullshit. [*Still no response.*]

Do you remember the comic strip *Little Lulu*? Her mother had no name, she was so remote, so formidable to all the children. She was just Lulu's mother. "Hello, Lulu's Mother," Lulu's friends would say. She was almost anonymous in her remoteness. You remind me of her. Andre's Mother. Let me answer the questions you can't ask and then I'll leave you alone and you won't ever have to see me again. Andre died of AIDS. I don't know how he got it. I tested negative. He died bravely. You would have been proud of him. The only thing that frightened him was you. I'll have everything that was his sent to you. I'll pay for it. There isn't much. You should have come up the summer he played Hamlet. He was magnificent. Yes, I'm bitter. I'm bitter I've lost him. I'm bitter what's happening. I'm bitter even now, after all this, I can't reach you. I'm beginning to feel your disapproval and it's making me ill. [*He looks at his balloon*.] Sorry, old friend. I blew it. [*He lets go of the balloon*.]

Good night, sweet prince, and flights of angels sing thee to they rest![1] [*Beat*.]

Goodbye, Andre's Mother.

[*He goes.* ANDRE'S MOTHER *stands alone holding her white balloon. Her lips tremble. She looks on the verge of breaking down. She is about to let go of the balloon when she pulls it down to her. She looks at it awhile before she gently kisses it. She lets go of the balloon. She follows it with her eyes as it rises and rises. The lights are beginning to fade.* ANDRE'S MOTHER*'s eyes are still on the balloon. The lights fade*.]

[1988]

[1]**Good night . . . rest!** Cal is quoting lines that Hamlet's friend Horatio speaks (5.2.336–337) at the moment of Hamlet's death.

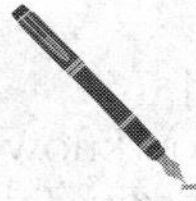

Joining the Conversation: Critical Thinking and Writing

1. Andre's Mother doesn't speak in the play, but we learn something about her through Cal's words, and something more through the description in the final stage direction. In a paragraph, characterize Andre's Mother.
2. Let's assume that you drafted this play, and now, on rereading it you decide that you want to give Andre's Mother one speech, and one speech only. Write the speech—it can go anywhere in the play that you think best—and then in a brief essay explain why you think the speech is effective.
3. Cal tells Penny that the balloons "represent the soul. When you let go, it means you're letting his soul ascend to Heaven." Is that exactly the way you see the balloons, or would see them if you attended a funeral where white balloons were distributed? Explain.

Chapter Overview: Looking Backward/Looking Forward

1. Do you think it is possible to love many people? Or is love so special that it can only be felt for a few people? Would you go further and say that love—real love, love in the deepest sense—can in truth only be felt for one person in your life?
2. How do we know when we have moved from "liking" someone to "loving" him or her? What are the signs? What is the evidence?

3. What does it mean to say that we have "fallen out of love" with someone? Is this change in us the result of something specific? Or does it, somehow, simply happen? Once you fall out of love, can you ever fall back in, or is that feeling lost forever?
4. Have you ever hated someone? How did this come about? Do you still hate the person, or have your feelings changed?
5. "Love" is a term that is often used in literature courses—love poetry, for instance, or love in the modern novel. What do you imagine a course in literature could teach you about love? Have you read a literary work that made you think and feel differently about love?
6. Do you find it hard to say, "I love you"? Why is that?
7. Do you think that it is a good experience to write about personal feelings, such as love and hate? Would you prefer not to? Would you like to do more of this kind of personal writing in your courses, or less?
8. Are you a religious person? Do you love God? How is this love felt and expressed in your life from day to day?

CHAPTER 21

Making Men and Women

SHORT VIEWS

The multitude will hardly believe the excessive force of education, and in the difference of modesty between men and women, ascribe that to nature which is altogether owing to early instruction. Miss is scarce three years old, but she's spoke to every day to hide her leg, and rebuked in good earnest if she shows it, whilst little Master at the same age is bid to take up his coats and piss like a man.

Bernard Mandeville

We are all androgynous, not only because we are all born of a woman impregnated by the seed of a man but because each of us, helplessly and forever, contains the other—male in female, female in male, white in black and black in white. We are a part of each other. Many of my countrymen appear to find this fact exceedingly inconvenient and even unfair, and so, very often, do I. But none of us can do anything about it.

James Baldwin

In the theory of gender I began from zero. There is no masculine power or privilege I did not covet. But slowly, step by step, decade by decade, I was forced to acknowledge that even a woman of abnormal will cannot escape her hormonal identity.

Camille Paglia

A woman simply is, but a man must become. Masculinity is risky and elusive. It is achieved by a revolt from woman, and it is confirmed only by other men.

Camille Paglia

One is not born, but rather becomes, a woman.

Simone de Beauvoir

There is no female mind. The brain is not an organ of sex. As well speak of a female liver.

Charlotte Perkins Gilman

Growing up female in America. What a liability! You grew up with your ears full of cosmetic ads, love songs, advice columns, whoreoscopes, Hollywood gossip, and moral dilemmas on the level of TV soap operas. What litanies the advertisers of the good life chanted at you! What curious catechisms.

Erica Jong

Men are not to be told anything they might find too painful; the secret depths of human nature, the sordid physicalities, might overwhelm or damage them. For instance, men often faint at the sight of their own blood, to which they are not accustomed. For this reason you should never stand behind one in the line at the Red Cross donor clinic.

Margaret Atwood

The true man wants two things: danger and play. For that reason he wants woman, as the most dangerous plaything.

Friedrich Nietzsche

Joining the Conversation: Critical Thinking and Writing

1. Select a quotation that especially appeals to you, and make it the focus of an essay of about 500 words.
2. Take two of the passages—perhaps one that you especially like and one that you think is wrongheaded—and write a dialogue of about 500 words in which the two authors converse or argue. They may each try to convince the other, or they may find that to some degree they share views and they may then work out a statement that both can accept. If you do take the first position—that one writer is on the correct track but the other is utterly mistaken—try to be fair to the view that you think is mistaken. (As an experiment in critical thinking, imagine that you accept it, and make the best case for it that you possibly can.)

ESSAYS

STEVEN DOLOFF

Steven Doloff, a professor of English and Humanities at Pratt Institute, has published essays on contemporary culture, education, and travel in numerous publications, including the New York Times, *the* Boston Globe, *and the* Philadelphia Inquirer.

The Opposite Sex

For just one day, imagine yourself a boy (wow!). A girl (ugh).

Having seen Dustin Hoffman's female impersonation in the movie, "Tootsie," I decided to give myself some reading over the Christmas recess by assigning in-class essays to my English composition students on how each would spend a day as a member of his or her respective opposite sex. From four classes I received approximately 100 essays. The sample, perhaps like the movie, proved both entertaining and annoying in its predictability.

The female students, as a group, took to the subject immediately and with obvious gusto, while the male students tended to wait a while (in several cases half the period), in something of a daze, before starting. The activities hypothetically engaged in by the women, whose ages averaged about 20, generally reflected two areas: envy of men's physical and social privileges, and curiosity regarding men's true feelings concerning women.

In their essays, women jauntily went places *alone,* and sometimes stayed out *all night.* They threw their clothes on the floor and left dishes in the sink. They hung out on the street and sweated happily in a variety of sports from football to weightlifting.

More than a third of them went out to cruise for dates. Appointing themselves in brand names of men's clothing and dousing themselves in men's cologne I have never heard of (I was instructed to read Gentleman's Quarterly magazine), they deliberately and aggressively accosted women, *many* women, on the street, in discos, in supermarkets. Others sought out the proverbial locker room for the kinds of bull sessions they hoped would reveal the real nitty-gritty masculine mind at work (on the subject of women).

5 At least two female students in each class spent chunks of their essays under the sheets with imaginary girlfriends, wives or strangers, finding out with a kind of scientific zeal what sex is like as a man.

Some, but not all of the women ended their essays with a formal, almost obligatory sounding statement of preference to be a female, and of gratitude in returning to their correct gender after a day as Mr. Hyde.

The male students, after their initial paralysis wore off, did not write as much as the females. They seemed envious of very little that was female, and curious about nothing. Three or four spent their day as women frantically seeking medical help to turn back into men more quickly. Those who accepted the assignment more seriously, if unenthusiastically, either stayed home and apathetically checked off a list of domestic chores or, more evasively, went off to work in an office and engaged in totally asexual business office routines.

A small percentage of the men ventured into the more feminine pursuits of putting on makeup and going to the beauty parlor. They agreed looking good was important.

If they stayed home as housewives, when their hypothetical husbands returned from work they ate dinner, watched some television and then went right to sleep. If they were businesswomen, they came directly home after work, ate some dinner, watched TV and went right to sleep. A handful actually went out on dates, had dinner in the most expensive restaurants they could cajole their escorts into taking them to, and then, after being taken home, very politely slammed the doors in their escorts' faces and went right to sleep. Not one male student let anybody lay a finger on him/her.

10 Finally, the sense of heartfelt relief at the end of the male students' essays, underscored by the much-repeated fervent anticipation of masculinity returning with the dawn, seemed equivalent to that of jumping up after having been forced to sit on a lit stove.

Granted, my flimsy statistical sample is nothing to go to the Ford Foundation with for research money. But on the other hand, do I really need to prove that young people even now are still burdened with sexist stereotypes and sexist self-images not nearly as vestigial as we would like to think? (One male student rhetorically crumpled up his paper after 10 minutes and growled, "You can't make me write this!") What does that imply about the rest of us? What would *you* do as a member of the opposite sex for a day? This last question is your essay assignment.

[1983]

Joining the Conversation: Critical Thinking and Writing

1. In paragraphs 2–4 Doloff summarizes the essays that the women wrote, and in paragraphs 7–10 the essays that the men wrote. Do you think you would have written something fairly close to the essays he attributes to the persons of your sex? Explain.
2. Do you think Doloff's assignment is a good one? Please argue why or why not.
3. Write an essay that fulfills Doloff's assignment and that honestly represents your thoughts, but that does *not* largely fit the pattern that Doloff finds.

GRETEL EHRLICH

Gretel Ehrlich, born in 1946, was educated at Bennington College, the UCLA Film School, and the New School for Social Research. She has written fiction and poetry, especially about open spaces (she has lived in Wyoming, Colorado, and Greenland), and has received numerous awards. The following selection comes from The Solace of Open Spaces *(1985).*

About Men

When I'm in New York but feeling lonely for Wyoming I look for the Marlboro ads in the subway. What I'm aching to see is horseflesh, the glint of a spur, a line of distant mountains, brimming creeks, and a reminder of the ranchers and cowboys I've ridden with for the last eight years. But the men I see in those posters with their stern, humorless looks remind me of no one I know here. In our hellbent earnestness to romanticize the cowboy we've ironically disesteemed his true character. If he's "strong and silent" it's because there's probably no one to talk to. If he "rides away into the sunset" it's because he's been on horseback since four in the morning moving cattle and he's trying, fifteen hours later, to get home to his family. If he's "a rugged individualist" he's also part of a team: ranch work is teamwork and even the glorified open-range cowboys of the 1880s rode up and down the Chisholm Trail in the company of twenty or thirty other riders. Instead of the macho, trigger-happy man our culture has perversely wanted him to be, the cowboy is more apt to be convivial, quirky, and softhearted. To be "tough" on a ranch has nothing to do with conquests and displays of power. More often than not, circumstances—like the colt he's riding or an unexpected blizzard—are overpowering him. It's not toughness but "toughing it out" that counts. In other words, this macho, cultural artifact the cowboy has become is simply a man who possesses resilience, patience, and an instinct for survival. "Cowboys are just like a pile of rocks—everything happens to them. They get climbed on, kicked, rained and snowed on, scuffed up by wind. Their job is 'just to take it,'" one old-timer told me.

A cowboy is someone who loves his work. Since the hours are long—ten to fifteen hours a day—and the pay is $30 he has to. What's required of him is an odd mixture of physical vigor and maternalism. His part of the beef-raising industry is to birth and nurture calves and take care of their mothers. For the most part his work is done on horseback and in a lifetime he sees and comes to know more animals than people. The iconic myth surrounding him is built on American notions of heroism: the index of a man's value as measured in physical courage. Such ideas have perverted manliness into a self-absorbed race for cheap thrills. In a rancher's world, courage has less to do with facing danger than with acting spontaneously—usually on behalf of an animal or another rider. If a cow is stuck in a boghole he throws a loop around her neck, takes his dally (a half hitch around the saddle horn), and pulls her out with horsepower. If a calf is born sick, he may take her home, warm her in front of the kitchen fire, and massage her legs until dawn. One friend, whose favorite horse was trying to swim a lake with hobbles on, dove under water and cut her legs loose with a knife, then swam her to shore, his arm around her neck lifeguard-style, and saved her from drowning. Because these incidents are usually linked to someone or something outside himself, the westerner's courage is selfless, a form of compassion.

The physical punishment that goes with cowboying is greatly underplayed. Once fear is dispensed with, the threshold of pain rises to meet the demands of the job. When Jane Fonda asked Robert Redford (in the film *Electric Horseman*) if he was sick as he struggled to his feet one morning, he replied, "No, just bent." For once the movies had it right. The cowboys I was sitting with laughed in agreement. Cowboys are rarely complainers; they show their stoicism laughing at themselves.

If a rancher or cowboy has been thought of as a "man's man"—laconic, hard-drinking, inscrutable—there's almost no place in which the balancing act between male and female, manliness and femininity, can be more natural. If he's gruff, handsome, and physically fit on the outside, he's androgynous at the core. Ranchers are midwives, hunters, nurturers, providers, and conservationists all at once. What we've interpreted as toughness—weathered skin, calloused hands, a squint in the eye and a growl in the voice—only masks the tenderness inside. "Now don't go telling me these lambs are cute," one rancher warned me the first day I walked into the football-field-sized lambing sheds. The next thing I knew he was holding a black lamb. "Ain't this little rat good-lookin'?"

5 So many of the men who came to the West were Southerners—men looking for work and a new life after the Civil War—that chivalrousness and strict codes of honor were soon thought of as western traits. There were very few women in Wyoming during territorial days, so when they did arrive (some as mail-order brides from places like Philadelphia) there was a standoffishness between the sexes and a formality that persists now. Ranchers still tip their hats and say, "Howdy, ma'am" instead of shaking hands with me.

Even young cowboys are often evasive with women. It's not that they're Jekyll and Hyde creatures—gentle with animals and rough on women—but rather, that they don't know how to bring their tenderness into the house and lack the vocabulary to express the complexity of what they feel. Dancing wildly all night becomes a metaphor for the explosive emotions pent up inside, and when these are, on occasion, released, they're so battery-charged and potent that one caress of the face or one "I love you" will peal for a long while.

The geographical vastness and the social isolation here make emotional evolution seem impossible. Those contradictions of the heart between respectability, logic, and convention on the one hand, and impulse, passion, and intuition on the other, played out wordlessly against the paradisiacal beauty of the West, give cowboys a wide-eyed but drawn look. Their lips pucker up, not with kisses but with immutability. They may want to break out, staying up all night with a lover just to talk, but they don't know how and can't imagine what the consequences will be. Those rare occasions when they do bare themselves result in confusion. "I feel as if I'd sprained my heart," one friend told me a month after such a meeting.

My friend Ted Hoagland wrote, "No one is as fragile as a woman but no one is as fragile as a man." For all the women here who use "fragileness" to avoid work or as a sexual ploy, there are men who try to hide theirs, all the while clinging to an adolescent dependency on women to cook their meals, wash their clothes, and keep the ranch house warm in winter. But there is true vulnerability in evidence here. Because these men work with animals, not machines or numbers, because they live outside in landscapes of torrential beauty, because they are confined to a place and a routine embellished with awesome variables, because calves die in the arms that pulled others into life, because they go to the mountains as if on a pilgrimage to find out what makes a herd of elk tick, their strength is also a softness, their toughness, a rare delicacy.

[1985]

Joining the Conversation: Critical Thinking and Writing

1. Early on, Ehrlich says: "In our hellbent earnestness to romanticize the cowboy we've ironically disesteemed his true character." What is she saying in this sentence? Do you find the sentence clear, or confusing? Please explain.
2. Later, Ehrlich says that cowboys are not like "Jekyll and Hyde." Identify and explain this reference. Where did you go to find this information?
3. In a paragraph of three or four sentences, summarize the main point that Ehrlich is making. Do you find it hard or easy to write this summary? What does your response suggest to you about Ehrlich's essay as a piece of writing?
4. Would you describe this essay as an "argument"? Or is it something different? After you read the essay, did your understanding of the topic change? In what way?

STORIES

CHARLOTTE PERKINS GILMAN

Charlotte Perkins Gilman (1860–1935), was born in Hartford, Connecticut. Her father deserted the family soon after Charlotte's birth; she was brought up by her mother, who found it difficult to make ends meet. For a while Charlotte worked as an artist and teacher of art, and in 1884, when she was 24, she married an artist. In 1885 she had a daughter, but soon after the birth of the girl Charlotte had a nervous breakdown. At her husband's urging she spent a month in the sanitarium of Dr. S. Weir Mitchell, a physician who specialized in treating women with nervous disorders. (Mitchell is specifically named in

"The Yellow Wallpaper.") Because the treatment—isolation and total rest—nearly drove her to insanity, she fled Mitchell and her husband. In California she began a career as a lecturer and writer on feminist topics. (She also supported herself by teaching school and by keeping a boardinghouse.) Among her books are Women and Economics *(1899) and* The Man-Made World *(1911), which have been revived by the feminist movement. In 1900 she married a cousin, George Gilman. From all available evidence, the marriage was successful. Certainly it did not restrict her activities as a feminist. In 1935, suffering from inoperable cancer, she took her own life.*

"The Yellow Wallpaper," written in 1892—that is, written after she had been treated by S. Weir Mitchell for her nervous breakdown—was at first interpreted either as a ghost story or as a Poe-like study of insanity. Only in recent years has it been seen as a feminist story. (One might ask oneself if these interpretations are mutually exclusive.)

The Yellow Wallpaper

It is very seldom that mere ordinary people like John and myself secure ancestral halls for the summer.

A colonial mansion, a hereditary estate. I would say a haunted house, and reach the height of romantic felicity—but that would be asking too much of fate!

Still I will proudly declare that there is something queer about it.

Else, why should it be let so cheaply? And why have stood so long untenanted?

John laughs at me, of course, but one expects that in marriage.

John is practical in the extreme. He has no patience with faith, an intense horror of superstition, and he scoffs openly at any talk of things not to be felt and seen and put down in figures.

John is a physician, and *perhaps*—(I would not say it to a living soul, of course, but this is dead paper and a great relief to my mind)—*perhaps* that is one reason I do not get well faster.

You see he does not believe I am sick!

And what can one do?

If a physician of high standing, and one's own husband, assures friends and relatives that there is really nothing the matter with one but temporary nervous depression—a slight hysterical tendency—what is one to do?

My brother is also a physician, and also of high standing, and he says the same thing.

So I take phosphates or phosphites—whichever it is, and tonics, and journeys, and air, and exercise, and am absolutely forbidden to "work" until I am well again.

Personally, I disagree with their ideas.

Personally, I believe that congenial work, with excitement and change, would do me good.

But what is one to do?

I did write for a while in spite of them: but it *does* exhaust me a good deal—having to be so sly about it, or else meet with heavy opposition.

I sometimes fancy that in my condition if I had less opposition and more society and stimulus—but John says the very worst thing I can do is to think about my condition, and I confess it always makes me feel bad.

So I will let it alone and talk about the house.

The most beautiful place! It is quite alone, standing well back from the road, quite three miles from the village. It makes me think of English places that you read about, for there are hedges and walls and gates that lock, and lots of separate little houses for the gardeners and people.

20 There is a *delicious* garden! I never saw such a garden—large and shady, full of box-bordered paths, and lined with long grapecovered arbors with seats under them.

There were greenhouses, too, but they are all broken now. There was some legal trouble. I believe, something about the heirs and coheirs: anyhow, the place has been empty for years.

That spoils my ghostliness. I am afraid, but I don't care—there is something strange about the house—I can feel it.

I even said so to John one moonlight evening, but he said what I felt was a *draught,* and shut the window.

I get unreasonably angry with John sometimes. I'm sure I never used to be so sensitive. I think it is due to this nervous condition.

25 But John says if I feel so, I shall neglect proper self-control: so I take pains to control myself—before him, at least, and that makes me very tired.

I don't like our room a bit. I wanted one downstairs that opened on the piazza and had roses all over the window, and such pretty old-fashioned chintz hangings! But John would not hear of it.

He said there was only one window and not room for two beds, and no near room for him if he took another.

He is very careful and loving, and hardly lets me stir without special direction.

I have a schedule prescription for each hour in the day: he takes all care from me, and so I feel basely ungrateful not to value it more.

30 He said we came here solely on my account, that I was to have perfect rest and all the air I could get. "Your exercise depends on your strength, my dear," said he, "and your food somewhat on your appetite; but air you can absorb all the time." So we took the nursery at the top of the house.

It is a big, airy room, the whole floor nearly, with windows that look all ways, and air and sunshine galore. It was nursery first and then playroom and gymnasium, I should judge; for the windows are barred for little children, and there are rings and things in the walls.

The paint and paper look as if a boys' school had used it. It is stripped off—the paper—in great patches all around the head of my bed, about as far as I can reach, and in a great place on the other side of the room low down. I never saw a worse paper in my life.

One of those sprawling flamboyant patterns committing every artistic sin.

It is dull enough to confuse the eye in following, pronounced enough to constantly irritate and provoke study, and when you follow the lame uncertain curves for a little distance they suddenly commit suicide—plunge off at outrageous angles, destroy themselves in unheard of contradictions.

35 The color is repellent, almost revolting: a smouldering unclean yellow, strangely faded by the slow-turning sunlight.

It is a dull yet lurid orange in some places, a sickly sulphur tint in others.

No wonder the children hated it! I should hate it myself if I had to live in this room long.

There comes John, and I must put this away,—he hates to have me write a word.

We have been here two weeks, and I haven't felt like writing before, since that first day.

I am sitting by the window now, up in this atrocious nursery, and there is nothing to hinder my writing as much as I please, save lack of strength.

John is away all day, and even some nights when his cases are serious.

I am glad my case is not serious!

But these nervous troubles are dreadfully depressing.

John does not know how much I really suffer. He knows there is no *reason* to suffer, and that satisfies him.

Of course it is only nervousness. It does weigh on me so not to do my duty in any way!

I meant to be such a help to John, such a real rest and comfort, and here I am a comparative burden already!

Nobody would believe what an effort it is to do what little I am able,—to dress and entertain, and order things.

It is fortunate Mary is so good with the baby. Such a dear baby!

And yet I *cannot* be with him, it makes me so nervous.

I suppose John never was nervous in his life. He laughs at me so about this wallpaper!

At first he meant to repaper the room, but afterwards he said that I was letting it get the better of me, and that nothing was worse for a nervous patient than to give way to such fancies.

He said that after the wallpaper was changed it would be the heavy bed-stead, and then the barred windows, and then that gate at the head of the stairs, and so on.

"You know the place is doing you good," he said, "and really, dear, I don't care to renovate the house just for a three months' rental."

"Then do let us go downstairs," I said, "there are such pretty rooms there."

Then he took me in his arms and called me a blessed little goose, and said he would go down to the cellar, if I wished, and have it whitewashed into the bargain.

But he is right enough about the beds and windows and things.

It is an airy and comfortable room as any one need wish, and, of course, I would not be so silly as to make him uncomfortable just for a whim.

I'm really getting quite fond of the big room, all but that horrid paper.

Out of one window I can see the garden, those mysterious deep-shaded arbors, the riotous old-fashioned flowers, and bushes and gnarly trees.

Out of another I get a lovely view of the bay and a little private wharf belonging to the estate. There is a beautiful shaded lane that runs down there from the house. I always fancy I see people walking in these numerous paths and arbors, but John has cautioned me not to give way to fancy in the least. He says that with my imaginative power and habit of story-making, a nervous weakness like mine is sure to lead to all manner of excited fancies, and that I ought to use my will and good sense to check the tendency. So I try.

I think sometimes that if I were only well enough to write a little it would relieve the press of ideas and rest me.

But I find I get pretty tired when I try.

It is so discouraging not to have any advice and companionship about my work. When I get really well, John says we will ask Cousin Henry and Julia down for a long visit; but he says he would as soon put fireworks in my pillow-case as to let me have those stimulating people about now.

I wish I could get well faster.

But I must not think about that. This paper looks to me as if it *knew* what a vicious influence it had!

There is a recurrent spot where the pattern lolls like a broken neck and two bulbous eyes stare at you upside down.

I get positively angry with the impertinence of it and the everlastingness. Up and down and sideways they crawl, and those absurd, unblinking eyes are everywhere. There is one place where two breadths didn't match, and the eyes go all up and down the line, one a little higher than the other.

I never saw so much expression in an inanimate thing before, and we all know how much expression they have! I used to lie awake as a child and get more entertainment and terror out of blank walls and plain furniture than most children could find in a toystore.

I remember what a kindly wink the knobs of our big, old bureau used to have, and there was one chair that always seemed like a strong friend.

I used to feel that if any of the other things looked too fierce I could always hop into that chair and be safe.

The furniture in this room is no worse than inharmonious, however, for we had to bring it all from downstairs. I suppose when this was used as a playroom they had to take the nursery things out, and no wonder! I never saw such ravages as the children have made here.

The wallpaper, as I said before, is torn off in spots, and it sticketh closer than a brother—they must have had perseverance as well as hatred.

Then the floor is scratched and gouged and splintered, the plaster itself is dug out here and there, and this great heavy bed which is all we found in the room, looks as if it had been through the wars.

But I don't mind it a bit—only the paper.

There comes John's sister. Such a dear girl as she is, and so careful of me! I must not let her find me writing.

She is a perfect and enthusiastic housekeeper, and hopes for no better profession. I verily believe she thinks it is the writing which made me sick!

But I can write when she is out, and see her a long way off from these windows.

There is one that commands the road, a lovely shaded winding road, and one that just looks off over the country. A lovely country, too, full of great elms and velvet meadows.

This wallpaper has a kind of sub-pattern in a different shade, a particularly irritating one, for you can only see it in certain lights, and not clearly then.

But in the places where it isn't faded and where the sun is just so—I can see a strange, provoking, formless sort of figure, that seems to skulk about behind that silly and conspicuous front design.

There's sister on the stairs!

Well, the Fourth of July is over! The people are all gone and I am tired out. John thought it might do me good to see a little company, so we just had mother and Nellie and the children down for a week.

Of course I didn't do a thing. Jennie sees to everything now. But it tired me all the same.

John says if I don't pick up faster he shall send me to Weir Mitchell in the fall.

But I don't want to go there at all. I had a friend who was in his hands once, and she says he is just like John and my brother, only more so!

Besides, it is such an undertaking to go so far.

I don't feel as if it was worth while to turn my hand over for anything, and I'm getting dreadfully fretful and querulous.

I cry at nothing, and cry most of the time.

Of course I don't when John is here, or anybody else, but when I am alone.

And I am alone a good deal just now. John is kept in town very often by serious cases, and Jennie is good and lets me alone when I want her to.

So I walk a little in the garden or down that lovely lane, sit on the porch under the roses, and lie down up here a good deal.

I'm getting really fond of the room in spite of the wallpaper. Perhaps *because* of the wallpaper.

It dwells in my mind so!

I lie here on this great immovable bed—it is nailed down, I believe—and follow that pattern about by the hour. It is as good as gymnastics, I assure you. I start, we'll say, at the bottom, down in the corner over there where it has not been touched, and I determine for the thousandth time that I *will* follow that pointless pattern to some sort of a conclusion.

I know a little of the principle of design, and I know this thing was not arranged on any laws of radiation, or alternation, or repetition, or symmetry, or anything else that I ever heard of.

It is repeated, of course, by the breadths, but not otherwise.

Looked at in one way each breadth stands alone, the bloated curves and flourishes—a kind of "debased Romanesque" with *delirium tremens*—go waddling up and down in isolated columns of fatuity.

But, on the other hand, they connect diagonally, and the sprawling outlines run off in great slanting waves of optic horror, like a lot of wallowing seaweeds in full chase.

The whole thing goes horizontally, too, at least it seems so, and I exhaust myself in trying to distinguish the order of its going in that direction.

They have used a horizontal breadth for a frieze, and that adds wonderfully to the confusion.

There is one end of the room where it is almost intact, and there, when the crosslights fade and the low sun shines directly upon it, I can almost fancy radiation after all,—the interminable grotesques seem to form around a common center and rush off in headlong plunges of equal distraction.

It makes me tired to follow it. I will take a nap I guess.

I don't know why I should write this.

I don't want to.

I don't feel able.

And I know John would think it absurd. But I *must* say what I feel and think in some way—it is such a relief.

But the effort is getting to be greater than the relief!

Half the time now I am awfully lazy, and lie down ever so much.

John says I mustn't lose my strength, and has me take cod liver oil and lots of tonics and things, to say nothing of ale and wine and rare meat.

Dear John! He loves me very dearly, and hates to have me sick. I tried to have a real earnest reasonable talk with him the other day, and tell him how I wish he would let me go and make a visit to Cousin Henry and Julia.

But he said I wasn't able to go, nor able to stand it after I got there: and I did not make out a very good case for myself, for I was crying before I had finished.

It is getting to be a great effort for me to think straight. Just this nervous weakness I suppose.

And dear John gathered me up in his arms, and just carried me upstairs and laid me on the bed, and sat by me and read to me till it tired my head.

He said I was his darling and his comfort and all he had, and that I must take care of myself for his sake, and keep well.

115 He says no one but myself can help me out of it, that I must use my will and self-control and not let any silly fancies run away with me.

There's one comfort, the baby is well and happy, and does not have to occupy this nursery with the horrid wallpaper.

If we had not used it, that blessed child would have! What a fortunate escape! Why, I wouldn't have a child of mine, an impressionable little thing, live in such a room for worlds.

I never thought of it before, but it is lucky that John kept me here after all. I can stand it so much easier than a baby, you see.

Of course I never mention it to them any more—I am too wise,—but I keep watch of it all the same.

120 There are things in that paper that nobody knows but me, or ever will.

Behind that outside pattern the dim shapes get clearer every day.

It is always the same shape, only very numerous.

And it is like a woman stooping down and creeping about behind that pattern. I don't like it a bit. I wonder—I begin to think—I wish John would take me away from here!

It is so hard to talk with John about my case, because he is so wise, and because he loves me so.

125 But I tried last night.

It was moonlight. The moon shines in all around just as the sun does.

I hate to see it sometimes, it creeps so slowly, and always comes in by one window or another.

John was asleep and I hated to waken him, so I kept still and watched the moonlight on that undulating wallpaper till I felt creepy.

The faint figure behind seemed to shake the pattern, just as if she wanted to get out.

130 I got up softly and went to feel and see if the paper *did* move, and when I came back John was awake.

"What is it, little girl?" he said. "Don't go walking about like that—you'll get cold."

I thought it was a good time to talk, so I told him that I really was not gaining here, and that I wished he would take me away.

"Why darling!" said he, "our lease will be up in three weeks, and I can't see how to leave before."

"The repairs are not done at home, and I cannot possibly leave town just now. Of course if you were in any danger, I could and would, but you really are better, dear, whether you can see it or not. I am a doctor, dear, and I know. You are gaining flesh and color, your appetite is better, I feel really much easier about you."

135 "I don't weigh a bit more," said I, "nor as much: and my appetite may be better in the evening when you are here, but it is worse in the morning when you are away!"

"Bless her little heart!" said he with a big hug, "she shall be as sick as she pleases! But now let's improve the shining hours by going to sleep, and talk about it in the morning!"

"And you won't go away?" I asked gloomily.

"Why, how can I, dear? It is only three weeks more and then we will take a nice little trip of a few days while Jennie is getting the house ready. Really dear you are better!"

"Better in body perhaps—" I began, and stopped short, for he sat up straight and looked at me with such a stern, reproachful look that I could not say another word.

"My darling," said he, "I beg of you, for my sake and for our child's sake, as well as for your own, that you will never for one instant let that idea enter your mind! There is nothing so dangerous, so fascinating, to a temperament like yours. It is a false and foolish fancy. Can you not trust me as a physician when I tell you so?"

So of course I said no more on that score, and we went to sleep before long. He thought I was asleep first, but I wasn't and lay there for hours trying to decide whether that front pattern and the back pattern really did move together or separately.

On a pattern like this, by daylight, there is a lack of sequence, a defiance of law, that is a constant irritant to a normal mind.

The color is hideous enough, and unreliable enough, and infuriating enough, but the pattern is torturing.

You think you have mastered it, but just as you get well underway in following, it turns a back-somersault and there you are. It slaps you in the face, knocks you down, and tramples upon you. It is like a bad dream.

The outside pattern is a florid arabesque, reminding one of a fungus. If you can imagine a toadstool in joints, an interminable string of toadstools, budding and sprouting in endless convolutions—why, that is something like it.

That is, sometimes!

There is one marked peculiarity about this paper, a thing nobody seems to notice but myself, and that is that it changes as the light changes.

When the sun shoots in through the east window—I always watch for that first long, straight ray—it changes so quickly that I never can quite believe it.

That is why I watch it always.

By moonlight—the moon shines in all night when there is a moon—I wouldn't know it was the same paper.

At night in any kind of light, in twilight, candle light, lamplight, and worst of all by moonlight, it becomes bars! The outside pattern I mean, and the woman behind it is as plain as can be.

I didn't realize for a long time what the thing was that showed behind, that dim sub-pattern, but now I am quite sure it is a woman.

By daylight she is subdued, quiet. I fancy it is the pattern that keeps her so still. It is so puzzling. It keeps me quiet by the hour.

I lie down ever so much now. John says it is good for me, and to sleep all I can.

Indeed he started the habit by making me lie down for an hour after each meal.

It is a very bad habit I am convinced, for you see I don't sleep.

And that cultivates deceit, for I don't tell them I'm awake—O no!

The fact is I am getting a little afraid of John.

He seems very queer sometimes, and even Jennie has an inexplicable look.

It strikes me occasionally, just as a scientific hypothesis—that perhaps it is the paper!

I have watched John when he did not know I was looking, and come into the room suddenly on the most innocent excuses, and I've caught him several times *looking at the paper!* And Jennie too. I caught Jennie with her hand on it once.

She didn't know I was in the room, and when I asked her in a quiet, a very quiet voice, with the most restrained manner possible, what she was doing with the paper—she turned around as if she had been caught stealing, and looked quite angry—asked me why I should frighten her so!

Then she said that the paper stained everything it touched, that she had found yellow smooches on all my clothes and John's, and she wished we would be more careful!

Did not that sound innocent? But I know she was studying that pattern, and I am determined that nobody shall find it out but myself!

Life is very much more exciting now than it used to be. You see I have something more to expect, to look forward to, to watch. I really do eat better, and am more quiet than I was.

John is so pleased to see me improve! He laughed a little the other day, and said I seemed to be flourishing in spite of my wallpaper.

I turned it off with a laugh. I had no intention of telling him it was *because* of the wallpaper—he would make fun of me. He might even want to take me away.

I don't want to leave now until I have found it out. There is a week more, and I think that will be enough.

I'm feeling ever so much better! I don't sleep much at night, for it is so interesting to watch developments, but I sleep a good deal in the daytime.

In the daytime it is tiresome and perplexing.

There are always new shoots on the fungus, and new shades of yellow all over it. I cannot keep count of them, though I have tried conscientiously.

It is the strangest yellow, that wallpaper! It makes me think of all the yellow things I ever saw—not beautiful ones like buttercups, but old foul, bad yellow things.

But there is something else about that paper—the smell! I noticed it the moment we came into the room, but with so much air and sun it was not bad. Now we have had a week of fog and rain, and whether the windows are open or not, the smell is here.

It creeps all over the house.

I find it hovering in the dining-room, skulking in the parlor, hiding in the hall, lying in wait for me on the stairs.

It gets into my hair.

Even when I go to ride, if I turn my head suddenly and surprise it—there is that smell!

Such a peculiar odor, too! I have spent hours in trying to analyze it, to find what it smelled like.

It is not bad—at first, and very gentle, but quite the subtlest, most enduring odor I ever met.

In this damp weather it is awful, I wake up in the night and find it hanging over me.

It used to disturb me at first. I thought seriously of burning the house—to reach the smell.

But now I am used to it. The only thing I can think of that it is like is the *color* of the paper! A yellow smell.

There is a very funny mark on this wall, low down, near the mopboard. A streak that runs round the room. It goes behind every piece of furniture, except the bed, a long, straight, even *smooch,* as if it had been rubbed over and over.

I wonder how it was done and who did it, and what they did it for. Round and round and round—round and round and round—it makes me dizzy!

I really have discovered something at last.

Through watching so much at night, when it changes so, I have finally found out.

The front pattern *does* move—and no wonder! The woman behind shakes it!

Sometimes I think there are a great many women behind, and sometimes only one, and she crawls around fast, and her crawling shakes it all over.

Then in the very bright spots she keeps still, and in the very shady spots she just takes hold of the bars and shakes them hard.

And she is all the time trying to climb through. But nobody could climb through that pattern—it strangles so: I think that is why it has so many heads.

They get through, and then the pattern strangles them off and turns them upside down, and makes their eyes white!

If those heads were covered or taken off it would not be half so bad.

I think that woman gets out in the daytime!

And I'll tell you why—privately—I've seen her!

I can see her out of every one of my windows!

It is the same woman, I know, for she is always creeping, and most women do not creep by daylight.

I see her on that long road under the trees, creeping along, and when a carriage comes she hides under the blackberry vines.

I don't blame her a bit. It must be very humiliating to be caught creeping by daylight!

I always lock the door when I creep by daylight. I can't do it at night, for I know John would suspect something at once.

And John is so queer now, that I don't want to irritate him. I wish he would take another room! Besides, I don't want anybody to get that woman out at night but myself.

I often wonder if I could see her out of all the windows at once.

But, turn as fast as I can, I can only see out of one at one time. And though I always see her, she *may* be able to creep faster than I can turn!

I have watched her sometimes away off in the open country, creeping as fast as a cloud shadow in a high wind.

If only that top pattern could be gotten off from the under one! I mean to try it, little by little.

I have found out another funny thing, but I shan't tell at this time! It does not do to trust people too much.

There are only two more days to get this paper off, and I believe John is beginning to notice. I don't like the look in his eyes.

And I heard him ask Jennie a lot of professional questions about me. She had a very good report to give.

She said I slept a good deal in the daytime.

John knows I don't sleep very well at night, for all I'm so quiet!

He asked me all sorts of questions, too, and pretended to be very loving and kind.

As if I couldn't see through him!

Still, I don't wonder he acts so, sleeping under this paper for three months.

It only interests me, but I feel sure John and Jennie are secretly affected by it.

Hurrah! This is the last day, but it is enough. John is to stay in town over night, and won't be out until this evening.

Jennie wanted to sleep with me—the sly thing! But I told her I should undoubtedly rest better for a night all alone.

That was clever, for really I wasn't alone a bit! As soon as it was moonlight and that poor thing began to crawl and shake the pattern, I got up and ran to help her.

I pulled and she shook, I shook and she pulled, and before morning we had peeled off yards of that paper.

A strip about as high as my head and half round the room. And then when the sun came and that awful pattern began to laugh at me, I declared I would finish it today!

We go away tomorrow, and they are moving all the furniture down again to leave things as they were before.

Jennie looked at the wall in amazement, but I told her merrily that I did it out of pure spite at the vicious thing.

She laughed and said she wouldn't mind doing it herself, but I must not get tired.

How she betrayed herself that time!

But I am here, and no person touches this paper but me—not *alive!*

She tried to get me out of the room—it was too patent! But I said it was so quiet and empty and clean now that I believed I would lie down again and sleep all I could; and not to wake me even for dinner—I would call when I woke.

So now she is gone, and the servants are gone, and the things are gone, and there is nothing left but that great bedstead nailed down, with the canvas mattress we found on it.

We shall sleep downstairs tonight, and take the boat home tomorrow.

I quite enjoy the room, now it is bare again.

How those children did tear about here!

This bedstead is fairly gnawed!

But I must get to work.

I have locked the door and thrown the key down into the front path.

I don't want to go out, and I don't want to have anybody come in, till John comes.

I want to astonish him.

I've got a rope up here that even Jennie did not find. If that woman does get out, and tries to get away, I can tie her!

But I forgot I could not reach far without anything to stand on! This bed will *not* move!

I tried to lift and push it until I was lame, and then I got so angry I bit off a little piece at one corner—but it hurt my teeth.

Then I peeled off all the paper I could reach standing on the floor. It sticks horribly and the pattern just enjoys it! All those strangled heads and bulbous eyes and waddling fungus growths just shriek with derision!

I am getting angry enough to do something desperate. To jump out of the window would be admirable exercise, but the bars are too strong even to try.

Besides I wouldn't do it. Of course not, I know well enough that a step like that is improper and might be misconstrued.

I don't like to *look* out of the windows even—there are so many of those creeping women, and they creep so fast.

I wonder if they all come out of that wallpaper as I did?

But I am securely fastened now by my well-hidden rope—you don't get *me* out in the road there!

I suppose I shall have to get back behind the pattern when it comes night, and that is hard!

It is so pleasant to be out in this great room and creep around as I please!

I don't want to go outside. I won't, even if Jennie asks me to.

For outside you have to creep on the ground, and everything is green instead of yellow.

But here I can creep smoothly on the floor, and my shoulder just fits in that long smooch around the wall, so I cannot lose my way.

Why there's John at the door!

It is no use, young man, you can't open it!

How he does call and pound!

Now he's crying for an axe.

It would be a shame to break down that beautiful door!

"John dear!" said I in the gentlest voice, "the key is down by the front steps, under a plantain leaf!"

That silenced him for a few moments.

Then he said—very quietly indeed, "Open the door, my darling!"

"I can't," said I. "The key is down by the front door under a plantain leaf!"

And then I said it again, several times, very gently and slowly, and said it so often that he had to go and see, and he got it of course, and came in. He stopped short by the door.

"What is the matter?" he cried. "For God's sake, what are you doing!"

I kept on creeping just the same, but I looked at him over my shoulder.

"I've got out at last," said I, "in spite of you and Jane. And I've pulled off most of the paper, so you can't put me back!"

Now why should that man have fainted? But he did, and right across my path by the wall, so that I had to creep over him every time!

[1892]

Joining the Conversation: Critical Thinking and Writing

1. Is the narrator insane at the start of the story, or does she become insane at some point during the narrative? Or can't we be sure? Support your view with evidence from the story.
2. How reliable do you think the narrator's characterization of her husband is? Support your answer with reasons.
3. The narrator says that she cannot get better because her husband is a physician. What do you take this to mean? Do you think the story is about a husband who deliberately drives his wife insane?
4. Is Gilman attacking men in this story? If so, is that a bad thing? If she is not, then what is she doing?

Richard Wright

Richard Wright (1908–1960), the grandson of a slave and the son of an impoverished sharecropper couple, was born on a cotton plantation near Natchez, Mississippi. When Richard was 5 his father deserted the family; five years later his mother suffered the first of a series of strokes that left her partly paralyzed. Richard was then brought up by relatives in Jackson, Mississippi, and Memphis, Tennessee. He dropped out of school after completing the ninth grade, took a variety of odd jobs, and in 1927 moved to Chicago, where he worked as a porter, dishwasher, burial-insurance salesman, and postal clerk. He also worked for the WPA, first as a writer of guidebooks and then as a director of the Federal Negro Theater. In 1932 he joined the John Reed Club, a left-wing organization. In 1937 he moved to New York, where he became the Harlem editor of The Daily Worker, *a Communist newspaper. In the following year he published his first book,* Uncle Tom's Children: Four Novellas. *In 1947 Wright and his family moved to Paris, where they lived until he suffered a fatal heart attack in 1960.*

With Native Son *(1940), a novel about a black man who murders a white woman, Wright became the first black writer to reach a white audience with a militant attack on racism. In the following year he wrote the text for* Twelve Million Black Voices, *a pictorial "folk history of the Negro in the United States." His next best-selling work was an autobiography,* Black Boy *(1945). Wright had already left the Communist Party in 1944, but material about his disillusionment with Communism was deleted from the manuscript of* Black Boy *and was first published in a posthumous book,* American Hunger *(1977). By the time he moved to France, then, Wright was strongly anti-Communist. He continued to write novels, though he also wrote nonfiction, including an account of a trip to the Gold Coast of West Africa.*

The Man Who Was Almost a Man

Dave struck out across the fields, looking homeward through paling light. Whut's the use talkin wid em niggers in the field? Anyhow, his mother was putting supper on the table. Them niggers can't understan nothing. One of these days he was going to get a gun and practice shooting, then they couldn't talk to him as though he were a little boy. He slowed, looking at the ground. Shucks, Ah ain scareda them even if they are biggern me! Aw, Ah know what Ahma do. Ahm going by ol Joe's sto n git that Sears Roebuck catlog n look at them guns. Mebbe Ma will lemme buy one when she gits mah pay from ol man Hawkins. Ahma beg her t gimme some money. Ahm ol ernough to hava gun. Ahm seventeen. Almost a man. He strode, feeling his long loose-jointed limbs. Shucks, a man oughta hava little gun aftah he done worked hard all day.

He came in sight of Joe's store. A yellow lantern glowed on the front porch. He mounted steps and went through the screen door, hearing it bang behind him. There was a strong smell of coal oil and mackerel fish. He felt very confident until he saw fat Joe walk in through the rear door, then his courage began to ooze.

"Howdy, Dave! Whutcha want?"

"How yuh, Mistah Joe? Aw, Ah don wanna buy nothing. Ah jus wanted t see ef yuhd lemme look at tha catlog erwhile."

5 "Sure! You wanna see it here?"

"Nawsuh. Ah wants t take it home wid me. Ah'll bring it back termorrow when Ah come in from the fiels."

"You plannin on buying something?"

"Yessuh."

"Your ma lettin you have your own money now?"

"Shucks. Mistah Joe, Ahm gittin t be a man like anybody else!"

Joe laughed and wiped his greasy white face with a red bandanna.

"Whut you plannin on buyin?"

Dave looked at the floor, scratched his head, scratched his thigh, and smiled. Then he looked up shyly.

"Ah'll tell yuh, Mistah Joe, ef yuh promise yuh won't tell."

"I promise."

"Waal, Ahma buy a gun."

"A gun? What you want with a gun?"

"Ah wanna keep it."

"You ain't nothing but a boy. You don't need a gun."

"Aw, lemme have the catlog, Mistah Joe. Ah'll bring it back."

Joe walked through the rear door. Dave was elated. He looked around at barrels of sugar and flour. He heard Joe coming back. He craned his neck to see if he were bringing the book. Yeah, he's got it. Gawddog, he's got it!

"Here, but be sure you bring it back. It's the only one I got."

"Sho, Mistah Joe."

"Say, if you wanna buy a gun, why don't you buy one from me? I gotta gun to sell."

"Will it shoot?"

"Sure it'll shoot."

"Whut kind is it?"

"Oh, it's kinda old . . . a left-hand Wheeler. A pistol. A big one."

"Is it got bullets in it?"

"It's loaded."

"Kin Ah see it?"

"Where's your money?"

"Whut yuh wan fer it?"

"I'll let you have it for two dollars."

"Just two dollahs? Shucks, Ah could buy tha when Ah git mah pay."

"I'll have it here when you want it."

"Awright, suh. Ah be in fer it."

He went through the door, hearing it slam again behind him. Ahma git some money from Ma n buy me a gun! Only two dollahs! He tucked the thick catalogue under his arm and hurried.

"Where yuh been, boy?" His mother held a steaming dish of blackeyed peas.

"Aw, Ma, Ah jus stopped down the road t talk wid the boys."

"Yuh know bettah t keep suppah waitin."

He sat down, resting the catalogue on the edge of the table.

"Yuh git up from there and git to the well n wash yosef! Ah ain feedin no hogs in mah house!"

She grabbed his shoulder and pushed him. He stumbled out of the room, then came back to get the catalogue.

"Whut this?"

"Aw, Ma, it's jusa catlog."

"Who yuh git it from?"

"From Joe, down at the sto."

"Waal, thas good. We kin use it in the outhouse."

50 "Naw, Ma." He grabbed for it. "Gimme ma catlog, Ma."

She held onto it and glared at him.

"Quit hollerin at me! Whut's wrong wid yuh? Yuh crazy?"

"But Ma, please. It ain mine! It's Joe's! He tol me t bring it back t im termorrow."

She gave up the book. He stumbled down the back steps, hugging the thick book under his arm. When he had splashed water on his face and hands, he groped back to the kitchen and fumbled in a corner for the towel. He bumped into a chair; it clattered to the floor. The catalogue sprawled at his feet. When he had dried his eyes he snatched up the book and held it again under his arm. His mother stood watching him.

55 "Now, ef yuh gonna act a fool over that ol book, Ah'll take it n burn it up."

"Naw, Ma, please."

"Waal, set down n be still!"

He sat down and drew the oil lamp close. He thumbed page after page, unaware of the food his mother set on the table. His father came in. Then his small brother.

"Whutcha got there, Dave?" his father asked.

60 "Jusa catlog," he answered, not looking up.

"Yeah, here they is!" His eyes glowed at blue-and-black revolvers. He glanced up, feeling sudden guilt. His father was watching him. He eased the book under the table and rested it on his knees. After the blessing was asked, he ate. He scooped up peas and swallowed fat meat without chewing. Buttermilk helped to wash it down. He did not want to mention money before his father. He would do much better by cornering his mother when she was alone. He looked at his father uneasily out of the edge of his eye.

"Boy, how come yuh don quit foolin wid tha book n eat yo suppah?"

"Yessuh."

"How you n ol man Hawkins gitten erlong?"

65 "Suh?"

"Can't yuh hear? Why don yuh lissen? Ah ast yu how wuz yuh n ol man Hawkins gittin erlong?"

"Oh, swell, Pa. Ah plows mo lan than anybody over there."

"Waal, yuh oughta keep you mind on what yuh doin."

"Yessuh."

70 He poured his plate full of molasses and sopped it up slowly with a chunk of cornbread. When his father and brother had left the kitchen, he still sat and looked again at the guns in the catalogue, longing to muster courage enough to present his case to his mother. Lawd, ef Ah only had tha pretty one! He could almost feel the slickness of the weapon with his fingers. If he had a gun like that he would polish it and keep it shining so it would never rust! N Ah'd keep it loaded, by Gawd!

"Ma?" His voice was hesitant.

"Hunh?"

"Ol man Hawkins give yuh mah money yit?"

"Yeah, but ain no usa yuh thinking bout throwin nona it erway. Ahm keeping tha money sos yuh kin have cloes t go to school this winter."

75 He rose and went to her side with the open catalogue in his palms. She was washing dishes, her head bent low over a pan. Shyly he raised the book. When he spoke, his voice was husky, faint.

"Ma, Gawd knows Ah wans one of these."

"One of whut?" she asked, not raising her eyes.

"One of these," he said again, not daring even to point. She glanced up at the page, then at him with wide eyes.

"Nigger, is yuh gone plumb crazy?"

"Aw, Ma—"

"Git outta here! Don yuh talk t me bout no gun! Yuh a fool!"

"Ma, Ah kin buy one fer two dollahs."

"Not ef Ah knows it, yuh ain!"

"But yuh promised me one—"

"Ah don care what Ah promised! Yuh ain nothing but a boy yit!"

"Ma, ef yuh lemme buy one Ah'll *never* ast yuh fer nothing no mo."

"Ah tol yuh t git outta here! Yuh ain gonna toucha penny of tha money fer no gun! Thas how come Ah has Mistah Hawkins t pay yo wages t me, cause Ah knows yuh ain got no sense."

"But, Ma, we needa gun. Pa ain got no gun. We needa gun in the house. Yuh kin never tell whut might happen."

"Now don yuh try to maka fool outta me, boy! Ef we did hava gun, yuh wouldn't have it!"

He laid the catalogue down and slipped his arm around her waist.

"Aw, Ma, Ah done worked hard alla summer n ain ast yuh fer nothing, is Ah, now?"

"Thas what yuh spose t do!"

"But Ma, Ah wans a gun. Yuh kin lemme have two dollahs outta mah money. Please, Ma. I kin give it to Pa. . . . Please, Ma! Ah loves yuh, Ma!"

When she spoke her voice came soft and low.

"What yu wan wida gun, Dave? Yuh don need no gun. Yuh'll git in trouble. N ef yo pa jus thought Ah let yuh have money t buy a gun he'd hava fit."

"Ah'll hide it, Ma. It ain but two dollahs."

"Lawd, chil, whut's wrong wid yuh?"

"Ain nothin wrong, Ma. Ahm almos a man now. Ah wans a gun."

"Who gonna sell yuh a gun?"

"Ol Joe at the sto."

"N it don cos but two dollahs?"

"Thas all, Ma. Jus two dollahs. Please, Ma."

She was stacking the plates away; her hands moved slowly, reflectively. Dave kept an anxious silence. Finally, she turned to him.

"Ah'll let yuh git tha gun if yuh promise me one thing."

"What's tha, Ma?"

"Yuh bring it straight back t me, yuh hear? It be fer Pa."

"Yessum! Lemme go now, Ma."

She stooped, turned slightly to one side, raised the hem of her dress, rolled down the top of her stocking, and came up with a slender wad of bills.

"Here," she said. "Lawd knows yuh don need no gun. But yer pa does. Yuh bring it right back t me, yuh hear? Ahma put it up. Now ef yuh don, Ahma have yuh pa lick yuh so hard yuh won fergit it."

"Yessum."

He took the money, ran down the steps, and across the yard.

"Dave! Yuuuuuh Daaaaave!"

He heard, but he was not going to stop now. "Naw, Lawd!"

The first movement he made the following morning was to reach under the pillow for the gun. In the gray light of dawn he held it loosely, feeling a sense of power. Could kill a man with a gun like this. Kill anybody, black or white. And if he were holding his gun in his hand, nobody could run over him; they would have to respect him. It was a big gun, with a long barrel and a heavy handle. He raised and lowered it in his hand, marveling at its weight.

115 He had not come straight home with it as his mother had asked; instead he had stayed out in the fields, holding the weapon in his hand, aiming it now and then at some imaginary foe. But he had not fired it; he had been afraid that his father might hear. Also he was not sure he knew how to fire it.

To avoid surrendering the pistol he had not come into the house until he knew that they were all asleep. When his mother had tiptoed to his bedside late that night and demanded the gun, he had first played possum; then he had told her that the gun was hidden outdoors, that he would bring it to her in the morning. Now he lay turning it slowly in his hands. He broke it, took out the cartridges, felt them, and then put them back.

He slid out of bed, got a long strip of old flannel from a trunk, wrapped the gun in it, and tied it to his naked thigh while it was still loaded. He did not go in to breakfast. Even though it was not yet daylight he started for Jim Hawkins' plantation. Just as the sun was rising he reached the barns where the mules and plows were kept.

"Hey! That you, Dave?"

He turned. Jim Hawkins stood eyeing him suspiciously.

"What're yuh doing here so early?"

120 "Ah didn't know Ah wuz gittin up so early, Mistah Hawkins. Ah was fixin t hitch up ol Jenny n take her t the fiels."

"Good. Since you're so early, how about plowing that stretch down by the woods?"

"Suits me, Mistah Hawkins."

"O.K. Go to it!"

125 He hitched Jenny to a plow and started across the fields. Hot dog! This was just what he wanted. If he could get down by the woods, he could shoot his gun and nobody would hear. He walked behind the plow, hearing the traces creaking, feeling the gun tied tight to his thigh.

When he reached the woods, he plowed two whole rows before he decided to take out the gun. Finally, he stopped, looked in all directions, then untied the gun and held it in his hand. He turned to the mule and smiled.

"Know whut this is, Jenny? Naw, yuh wouldn know! Yuhs jusa ol mule! Anyhow, this is a gun, n it kin shoot, by Gawd!"

He held the gun at arm's length. Whut t hell, Ahma shoot this thing! He looked at Jenny again.

"Lissen here, Jenny! When Ah pull this ol trigger, Ah don wan yuh t run n acka fool now!"

130 Jenny stood with head down, her short ears pricked straight. Dave walked off about twenty feet, held the gun far out from him at arm's length, and turned his head. Hell, he told himself, Ah ain afraid. The gun felt loose in his fingers; he waved it wildly for a moment. Then he shut his eyes and tightened his forefinger. Bloom! A report half deafened him and he thought his right hand was torn from his arm. He heard Jenny whinnying and galloping over the field, and he found himself on his knees, squeezing his fingers hard between his legs. His hand was numb; he jammed it into his mouth, trying to warm it, trying to stop the pain. The gun

lay at his feet. He did not quite know what had happened. He stood up and stared at the gun as though it were a living thing. He gritted his teeth and kicked the gun. Yuh almos broke mah arm! He turned to look for Jenny; she was far over the fields, tossing her head and kicking wildly.

"Hol on there, ol mule!"

When he caught up with her she stood trembling, walling her big white eyes at him. The plow was far away; the traces had broken. Then Dave stopped short, looking, not believing. Jenny was bleeding. Her left side was red and wet with blood. He went closer. Lawd, have mercy! Wondah did Ah shoot this mule? He grabbed for Jenny's mane. She flinched, snorted, whirled, tossing her head.

"Hol on now! Hol on."

Then he saw the hole in Jenny's side, right between the ribs. It was round, wet, red. A crimson stream streaked down the front leg, flowing fast. Good Gawd! Ah wuzn't shootin at tha mule. He felt panic. He knew he had to stop that blood, or Jenny would bleed to death. He had never seen so much blood in all his life. He chased the mule for half a mile, trying to catch her. Finally she stopped, breathing hard, stumpy tail half arched. He caught her mane and led her back to where the plow and gun lay. Then he stopped and grabbed handfuls of damp black earth and tried to plug the bullet hole. Jenny shuddered, whinnied, and broke from him.

"Hol on! Hol on now!"

He tried to plug it again, but blood came anyhow. His fingers were hot and sticky. He rubbed dirt into his palms, trying to dry them. Then again he attempted to plug the bullet hole, but Jenny shied away, kicking her heels high. He stood helpless. He had to do something. He ran at Jenny; she dodged him. He watched a red stream of blood flow down Jenny's leg and form a bright pool at her feet.

"Jenny . . . Jenny," he called weakly.

His lips trembled. She's bleeding t death! He looked in the direction of home, wanting to go back, wanting to get help. But he saw the pistol lying in the damp black clay. He had a queer feeling that if he only did something, this would not be; Jenny would not be there bleeding to death.

When he went to her this time, she did not move. She stood with sleepy, dreamy eyes; and when he touched her she gave a low-pitched whinny and knelt to the ground, her front knees slopping in blood.

"Jenny . . . Jenny . . ." he whispered.

For a long time she held her neck erect; then her head sank, slowly. Her ribs swelled with a mighty heave and she went over.

Dave's stomach felt empty, very empty. He picked up the gun and held it gingerly between his thumb and forefinger. He buried it at the foot of a tree. He took a stick and tried to cover the pool of blood with dirt—but what was the use? There was Jenny lying with her mouth open and her eyes walled and glassy. He could not tell Jim Hawkins he had shot his mule. But he had to tell something. Yeah, Ah'll tel'em Jenny started gittin wil n fell on the joint of the plow. . . . But that would hardly happen to a mule. He walked across the field slowly, head down.

It was sunset. Two of Jim Hawkins' men were over near the edge of the woods digging a hole in which to bury Jenny. Dave was surrounded by a knot of people all of whom were looking down at the dead mule.

"I don't see how in the world it happened," said Jim Hawkins for the tenth time.

The crowd parted and Dave's mother, father, and small brother pushed into the center.

"Where Dave?" his mother called.

"There he is," said Jim Hawkins.

His mother grabbed him.

"Whut happened, Dave? Whut yuh done?"

150 "Nothin."

"C mon, boy, talk," his father said.

Dave took a deep breath and told the story he knew nobody believed.

"Waal," he drawled. "Ah brung ol Jenny down here sos Ah could do mah plowin. Ah plowed bout two rows, just like yuh see." He stopped and pointed at the long rows of upturned earth. "Then somethin musta been wrong wid ol Jenny. She wouldn ack right a-tall. She started snortin n kickin her heels. Ah tried t hol her, but she pulled erway, tearin n goin in. Then when the point of the plow was stickin up in the air, she swung erroun n twisted herself back on it. . . . She stuck herself n started t bleed. N fo Ah could do anything, she wuz dead."

"Did you ever hear anything like that in all your life?" asked Jim Hawkins.

155 There were white and black standing in the crowd. They murmured. Dave's mother came close to him and looked hard into his face. "Tell the truth, Dave," she said.

"Looks like a bullet hole to me," said one man.

"Dave, whut yuh do wid the gun?" his mother asked.

The crowd surged in, looking at him. He jammed his hands into his pockets, shook his head slowly from left to right, and backed away. His eyes were wide and painful.

"Did he hava gun?" asked Jim Hawkins.

160 "By Gawd, Ah tol yuh tha wuz a gun wound," said a man, slapping his thigh.

His father caught his shoulders and shook him till his teeth rattled.

"Tell whut happened, yuh rascal! Tell whut. . . ."

Dave looked at Jenny's stiff legs and began to cry.

165 "Whut yuh do wid tha gun?" his mother asked.

"What wuz he doin wida gun?" his father asked.

"Come on and tell the truth," said Hawkins. "Ain't nobody going to hurt you. . . ."

His mother crowded close to him.

"Did yuh shoot tha mule, Dave?"

Dave cried, seeing blurred white and black faces.

170 "Ahh ddinn gggo tt sshooot hher. . . . Ah ssswear ffo Gawd Ahh ddin. . . . Ah wuz a-tryin t sssee ef the old gggun would sshoot—"

"Where yuh git the gun from?" his father asked.

"Ah got it from Joe, at the sto."

"Where yuh git the money?"

"Ma give it t me."

175 "He kept worryin me, Bob. Ah had t. Ah tol im t bring the gun right back t me. . . . It was fer yuh, the gun."

"But how yuh happen to shoot that mule?" asked Jim Hawkins.

"Ah wuzn shootin at the mule, Mistah Hawkins. The gun jumped when Ah pulled the trigger. . . . N fo Ah knowed anythin Jenny was there a-bleedin."

Somebody in the crowd laughed. Jim Hawkins walked close to Dave and looked into his face.

"Well, looks like you have bought you a mule, Dave."

180 "Ah swear fo Gawd, Ah didn go t kill the mule, Mistah Hawkins!"

"But you killed her!"

All the crowd was laughing now. They stood on tiptoe and poked heads over one another's shoulders.

"Well, boy, looks like yuh done bought a dead mule! Hahaha!"

"Ain tha ershame."

"Hohohohoho."

Dave stood, head down, twisting his feet in the dirt.

"Well, you needn't worry about it, Bob," said Jim Hawkins to Dave's father. "Just let the boy keep on working and pay me two dollars a month."

"Whut yuh wan fer yo mule, Mistah Hawkins?"

Jim Hawkins screwed up his eyes.

"Fifty dollars."

"Whut yuh do wid tha gun?" Dave's father demanded.

Dave said nothing.

"Yuh wan me t take a tree n beat yuh till yuh talk!"

"Nawsuh!"

"Whut yuh do wid it?"

"Ah throwed it erway."

"Where?"

"Ah . . . Ah throwed it in the creek."

"Waal, c mon home. N firs thing in the mawnin git to tha creek n fin tha gun."

"Yessuh."

"Whut yuh pay fer it?"

"Two dollahs."

"Take tha gun n git yo money back n carry it to Mistah Hawkins, yuh hear? N don fergit Ahma lam you black bottom good fer this! Now march yosef on home, suh!"

Dave turned and walked slowly. He heard people laughing. Dave glared, his eyes welling with tears. Hot anger bubbled in him. Then he swallowed and stumbled on.

That night Dave did not sleep. He was glad that he had gotten out of killing the mule so easily, but he was hurt. Something hot seemed to turn over inside him each time he remembered how they had laughed. He tossed on his bed, feeling his hard pillow. N Pa says he's gonna beat me. . . . He remembered other beatings, and his back quivered. Naw, naw, Ah sho don wan im t beat me tha way no mo. Dam em all! Nobody ever gave him anything. All he did was work. They treat me like a mule, n then they beat me. He gritted his teeth. N Ma had t tell on me.

Well, if he had to, he would take old man Hawkins that two dollars. But that meant selling the gun. And he wanted to keep that gun. Fifty dollars for a dead mule.

He turned over, thinking how he had fired the gun. He had an itch to fire it again. Ef other men kin shoota gun, by Gawd, Ah kin! He was still, listening. Mebbe they all sleepin now. The house was still. He heard the soft breathing of his brother. Yes, now! He would go down and get that gun and see if he could fire it. He eased out of bed and slipped into overalls.

The moon was bright. He ran almost all the way to the edge of the woods: He stumbled over the ground, looking for the spot where he had buried the gun. Yeah, here it is. Like a hungry dog scratching for a bone, he pawed it up. He puffed his black cheeks and blew dirt from the trigger and barrel. He broke it and found four cartridges unshot. He looked around; the fields were filled with silence and moonlight. He clutched the gun stiff and hard in his fingers. But, as soon as he wanted to pull the trigger, he shut his eyes and turned his head. Naw, Ah can't shoot wid mah eyes closed n mah head turned. With effort he held his eyes open: then he squeezed. *Blooooom!* He was stiff, not breathing. The gun was still in his hands. Dammit, he'd done it! He fired again. *Blooooom!* He smiled. *Blooooom! Blooooom! Click, click.* There! It was empty. If anybody could shoot a gun, he could. He put the gun into his hip pocket and started across the fields.

When he reached the top of a ridge he stood straight and proud in the moonlight, looking at Jim Hawkins' big white house, feeling the gun sagging in his pocket. Lawd, ef Ah had just one mo bullet Ah'd taka shot at tha house. Ah'd like t scare ol man Hawkins jusa little. . . . Jusa enough t let im know Dave Saunders is a man.

To his left the road curved, running to the tracks of the Illinois Central. He jerked his head, listening. From far off come a faint *hoooof-hoooof; hoooof-hoooof.* . . . He stood rigid. Two dollahs a mont. Les see now. . . . Tha means it'll take bout two years. Shucks! Ah'll be dam!

He started down the road, toward the tracks. Yeah, here she comes! He stood beside the track and held himself stiffly. Here she comes, erroun the ben. . . . C mon, yuh slow poke! C mon! He had his hand on his gun; something quivered in his stomach. Then the train thundered past, the gray and brown box cars tumbling and clinking. He gripped the gun tightly; then he jerked his hand out of his pocket. Ah betcha Bill wouldn't do it? Ah betcha. . . . The cars slid past, steel grinding upon steel. Ahm ridin yuh ternight, so hep me Gawd! He was hot all over. He hesitated just a moment; then he grabbed, pulled atop of a car, and lay flat. He felt his pocket; the gun was still there. Ahead the long rails were glinting in the moonlight, stretching away, away to somewhere, somewhere where he could be a man. . . .

[1940]

Joining the Conversation: Critical Thinking and Writing

1. Why does Dave place such emphasis on owning a gun?
2. Do you assume that at the end of the story Dave is a man, or that he is only an immature boy who may come to a sad end? Explain.
3. Does the title strike you as odd? Would "The Boy Who Was Almost a Man" be more appropriate?
4. Is race central to the meaning of this story? How would you reply to someone who said that race is not central to the story at all?

Gloria Naylor

Gloria Naylor (b. 1950), a native of New York City, holds a bachelor's degree from Brooklyn College and a master's degree in Afro-American Studies from Yale University. "The Two" comes from The Women of Brewster Place *(1982), a book that won the American Book Award for First Fiction.*

The Two

At first they seemed like such nice girls. No one could remember exactly when they had moved into Brewster. It was earlier in the year before Ben[1] was killed—of course, it had to be before Ben's death. But no one remembered if it was in the winter or spring of that year that the two had come. People often came and went on Brewster Place like a restless night's dream, moving in and out in the dark to avoid eviction notices or neighborhood bulletins about the dilapidated condition of their furnishings. So it wasn't until the two were clocked leaving in the mornings and returning in the evenings at regular intervals that it was quietly absorbed that they now claimed Brewster as home. And Brewster waited, cautiously prepared to claim them, because you never knew about young women, and obviously single at that. But when no wild music or drunken friends careened out of the corner building on weekends, and especially, when no slightly eager husbands were encouraged to linger around that first-floor apartment and run errands for them, a suspended sigh of relief floated around the two when they dumped their garbage, did their shopping, and headed for the morning bus.

The women of Brewster had readily accepted the lighter, skinny one. There wasn't much threat in her timid mincing walk and the slightly protruding teeth she seemed so eager to show everyone in her bell-like good mornings and evenings. Breaths were held a little longer in the direction of the short dark one—too pretty, and too much behind. And she insisted on wearing those thin Qiana dresses that the summer breeze molded against the maddening rhythm of the twenty pounds of rounded flesh that she swung steadily down the street. Through slitted eyes, the women watched their men watching her pass, knowing the bastards were praying for a wind. But since she seemed oblivious to whether these supplications went answered, their sighs settled around her shoulders too. Nice girls.

And so no one even cared to remember exactly when they had moved into Brewster Place, until the rumor started. It had first spread through the block like a sour odor that's only faintly perceptible and easily ignored until it starts growing in strength from the dozen mouths it had been lying in, among clammy gums and scum-coated teeth. And then it was everywhere—lining the mouths and whitening the lips of everyone as they wrinkled up their noses at its pervading smell, unable to pinpoint the source or time of its initial arrival. Sophie could—she had been there.

[1]**Ben** the custodian of Brewster Place.

It wasn't that the rumor had actually begun with Sophie. A rumor needs no true parent. It only needs a willing carrier, and it found one in Sophie. She had been there—on one of those August evenings when the sun's absence is a mockery because the heat leaves the air so heavy it presses the naked skin down on your body, to the point that a sheet becomes unbearable and sleep impossible. So most of Brewster was outside that night when the two had come in together, probably from one of those air-conditioned movies downtown, and had greeted the ones who were loitering around their building. And they had started up the steps when the skinny one tripped over a child's ball and the darker one had grabbed her by the arm and around the waist to break her fall. "Careful, don't wanna lose you now." And the two of them had laughed into each other's eyes and went into the building.

5 The smell had begun there. It outlined the image of the stumbling woman and the one who had broken her fall. Sophie and a few other women sniffed at the spot and then, perplexed, silently looked at each other. Where had they seen that before? They had often laughed and touched each other—held each other in joy or its dark twin—but where had they seen *that* before? It came to them as the scent drifted down the steps and entered their nostrils on the way to their inner mouths. They had seen that—done that—with their men. That shared moment of invisible communion reserved for two and hidden from the rest of the world behind laughter or tears or a touch. In the days before babies, miscarriages, and other broken dreams, after stolen caresses in barn stalls and cotton houses, after intimate walks from church and secret kisses with boys who were now long forgotten or permanently fixed in their lives—that was where. They could almost feel the odor moving about in their mouths, and they slowly knitted themselves together and let it out into the air like a yellow mist that began to cling to the bricks on Brewster.

So it got around that the two in 312 were *that* way. And they had seemed like such nice girls. Their regular exits and entrances to the block were viewed with a jaundiced eye. The quiet that rested around their door on the weekends hinted of all sorts of secret rituals, and their friendly indifference to the men on the street was an insult to the women as a brazen flaunting of unnatural ways.

Since Sophie's apartment windows faced theirs from across the air shaft, she became the official watchman for the block, and her opinions were deferred to whenever the two came up in conversation. Sophie took her position seriously and was constantly alert for any telltale signs that might creep out around their drawn shades, across from which she kept a religious vigil. An entire week of drawn shades was evidence enough to send her flying around with reports that as soon as it got dark they pulled their shades down and put on the lights. Heads nodded in knowing unison—a definite sign. If doubt was voiced with a "But I pull my shades down at night too," a whispered "Yeah, but you're not *that* way" was argument enough to win them over.

Sophie watched the lighter one dumping their garbage, and she went outside and opened the lid. Her eyes darted over the crushed tin cans, vegetable peelings, and empty chocolate chip cookie boxes. What do they do with all them chocolate chip cookies? It was surely a sign, but it would take some time to figure that one out. She saw Ben go into their apartment, and she waited and blocked his path as he came out, carrying his toolbox.

"What ya see?" She grabbed his arm and whispered wetly in his face.

10 Ben stared at her squinted eyes and drooping lips and shook his head slowly. "Uh, uh, uh, it was terrible."

"Yeah?" She moved in a little closer.

"Worst busted faucet I seen in my whole life." He shook her hand off his arm and left her standing in the middle of the block.

"You old sop bucket," she muttered, as she went back up on her stoop. A broken faucet, huh? Why did they need to use so much water?

Sophie had plenty to report that day. Ben had said it was terrible in there. No, she didn't know exactly what he had seen, but you can imagine—and they did. Confronted with the difference that had been thrust into their predictable world, they reached into their imaginations and, using an ancient pattern, weaved themselves a reason for its existence. Out of necessity they stitched all of their secret fears and lingering childhood nightmares into this existence, because even though it was deceptive enough to try and look as they looked, talk as they talked, and do as they did, it had to have some hidden stain to invalidate it—it was impossible for them both to be right. So they leaned back, supported by the sheer weight of their numbers and comforted by the woven barrier that kept them protected from the yellow mist that enshrouded the two as they came and went on Brewster Place.

15 Lorraine was the first to notice the change in the people on Brewster Place. She was a shy but naturally friendly woman who got up early, and had read the morning paper and done fifty sit-ups before it was time to leave for work. She came out of her apartment eager to start her day by greeting any of her neighbors who were outside. But she noticed that some of the people who had spoken to her before made a point of having something else to do with their eyes when she passed, although she could almost feel them staring at her back as she moved on. The ones who still spoke only did so after an uncomfortable pause, in which they seemed to be peering through her before they begrudged her a good morning or evening. She wondered if it was all in her mind and she thought about mentioning it to Theresa, but she didn't want to be accused of being too sensitive again. And how would Tee even notice anything like that anyway? She had a lousy attitude and hardly ever spoke to people. She stayed in that bed until the last moment and rushed out of the house fogged-up and grumpy, and she was used to being stared at—by men at least—because of her body.

Lorraine thought about these things as she came up the block from work, carrying a large paper bag. The group of women on her stoop parted silently and let her pass.

"Good evening," she said, as she climbed the steps.

Sophie was standing on the top step and tried to peek into the bag. "You been shopping, huh? What ya buy?" It was almost an accusation.

"Groceries." Lorraine shielded the top of the bag from view and squeezed past her with a confused frown. She saw Sophie throw a knowing glance to the others at the bottom of the stoop. What was wrong with this old woman? Was she crazy or something?

20 Lorraine went into her apartment. Theresa was sitting by the window, reading a copy of *Mademoiselle*. She glanced up from her magazine. "Did you get my chocolate chip cookies?"

"Why good evening to you, too, Tee. And how was my day? Just wonderful." She sat the bag down on the couch. "The little Baxter boy brought in a puppy for show-and-tell, and the damn thing pissed all over the floor and then proceeded to chew the heel off my shoe, but, yes, I managed to hobble to the store and bring you your chocolate chip cookies."

Oh, Jesus, Theresa thought, she's got a bug up her ass tonight.

"Well, you should speak to Mrs. Baxter. She ought to train her kid better than that." She didn't wait for Lorraine to stop laughing before she tried to stretch her good mood. "Here, I'll put those things away. Want me to make dinner so you can rest? I only worked half a day, and the most tragic thing that went down was a broken fingernail and that got caught in my typewriter."

Lorraine followed Theresa into the kitchen. "No, I'm not really tired, and fair's fair, you cooked last night. I didn't mean to tick off like that; it's just that . . . well, Tee, have you noticed that people aren't as nice as they used to be?"

Theresa stiffened. Oh, God, here she goes again. "What people, Lorraine? Nice in what way?"

"Well, the people in this building and on the street. No one hardly speaks anymore. I mean, I'll come in and say good evening—and just silence. It wasn't like that when we first moved in. I don't know, it just makes you wonder; that's all. What are they thinking?"

"I personally don't give a shit what they're thinking. And their good evenings don't put any bread on my table."

"Yeah, but you didn't see the way that woman looked at me out there. They must feel something or know something. They probably—"

"They, they, they!" Theresa exploded. "You know, I'm not starting up with this again, Lorraine. Who in the hell are they? And where in the hell are we? Living in some dump of a building in this God-forsaken part of town around a bunch of ignorant niggers with the cotton still under their fingernails because of you and your theys. They knew something in Linden Hills, so I gave up an apartment for you that I'd been in for the last four years. And then they knew in Park Heights, and you made me so miserable there we had to leave. Now these mysterious theys are on Brewster Place. Well, look out that window, kid. There's a big wall down that block, and this is the end of the line for me. I'm not moving anymore, so if that's what you're working yourself up to—save it!"

When Theresa became angry she was like a lump of smoldering coal, and her fierce bursts of temper always unsettled Lorraine.

"You see, that's why I didn't want to mention it." Lorraine began to pull at her fingers nervously. "You're always flying up and jumping to conclusions—no one said anything about moving. And I didn't know your life has been so miserable since you met me. I'm sorry about that," she finished tearfully.

Theresa looked at Lorraine, standing in the kitchen door like a wilted leaf, and she wanted to throw something at her. Why didn't she ever fight back? The very softness that had first attracted her to Lorraine was now a frequent cause for irritation. Smoked honey. That's what Lorraine had reminded her of, sitting in her office clutching that application. Dry autumn days in Georgia woods, thick bloated smoke under a beehive, and the first glimpse of amber honey just faintly darkened about the edges by the burning twigs. She had flowed just that heavily into Theresa's mind and had stuck there with a persistent sweetness.

But Theresa hadn't known then that this softness filled Lorraine up to the very middle and that she would bend at the slightest pressure, would be constantly seeking to surround herself with the comfort of everyone's goodwill, and would shrivel up at the least touch of disapproval. It was becoming a drain to be continually called upon for this nurturing and support that she just didn't understand. She had supplied it at first out of love for Lorraine, hoping that she would harden eventually, even as honey does when exposed to the cold. Theresa was growing tired of being clung to—of being the one who was leaned on. She didn't want a child—she wanted someone who could stand toe to toe with her and be willing to slug it out at times. If they practiced that way with each other, then they could turn back to back and beat the hell out of the world for trying to invade their territory.

But she had found no such sparring partner in Lorraine, and the strain of fighting alone was beginning to show on her.

"Well, if it was that miserable, I would have been gone a long time ago," she said, watching her words refresh Lorraine like a gentle shower.

35 "I guess you think I'm some sort of a sick paranoid, but I can't afford to have people calling my job or writing letters to my principal. You know I've already lost a position like that in Detroit. And teaching is my whole life, Tee."

"I know," she sighed, not really knowing at all. There was no danger of that ever happening on Brewster Place. Lorraine taught too far from this neighborhood for anyone here to recognize her in that school. No, it wasn't her job she feared losing this time, but their approval. She wanted to stand out there and chat and trade makeup secrets and cake recipes. She wanted to be secretary of their block association and be asked to mind their kids while they ran to the store. And none of that was going to happen if they couldn't even bring themselves to accept her good evenings.

Theresa silently finished unpacking the groceries. "Why did you buy cottage cheese? Who eats that stuff?"

"Well, I thought we should go on a diet."

"If *we* go on a diet, then you'll disappear. You've got nothing to lose but your hair."

40 "Oh, I don't know. I thought that we might want to try and reduce our hips or something." Lorraine shrugged playfully.

"No, thank you. We are very happy with our hips the way they are," Theresa said, as she shoved the cottage cheese to the back of the refrigerator. "And even when I lose weight, it never comes off there. My chest and arms just get smaller, and I start looking like a bottle of salad dressing."

The two women laughed, and Theresa sat down to watch Lorraine fix dinner. "You know, this behind has always been my downfall. When I was coming up in Georgia with my grandmother, the boys used to promise me penny candy if I would let them pat my behind. And I used to love those jawbreakers—you know, the kind that lasted all day and kept changing colors in your mouth. So I was glad to oblige them, because in one afternoon I could collect a whole week's worth of jawbreakers."

"Really. That's funny to you? Having some boy feeling all over you."

Theresa sucked her teeth. "We were only kids, Lorraine. You know, you remind me of my grandmother. That was one straight-laced old lady. She had a fit when my brother told her what I was doing. She called me into the smokehouse and told me in this real scary whisper that I could get pregnant from letting little boys pat my butt and that I'd end up like my cousin Willa. But Willa and I had been thick as fleas, and she had already given me a step-by-step summary of how she'd gotten into her predicament. But I sneaked around to her house that night just to double-check her story, since that old lady had seemed so earnest. 'Willa, are you sure?' I whispered through her bedroom window. 'I'm tellin' ya, Tee,' she said. 'Just keep both feet on the ground and you home free.' Much later I learned that advice wasn't too biologically sound, but it worked in Georgia because those country boys didn't have much imagination."

45 Theresa's laughter bounced off of Lorraine's silent, rigid back and died in her throat. She angrily tore open a pack of the chocolate chip cookies.

"Yeah," she said, staring at Lorraine's back and biting down hard into the cookie, "it wasn't until I came up north to college that I found out there's a whole lot of things that a dude with a little imagination can do to you even with both feet on the ground. You see, Willa forgot to tell me not to bend over or squat or—"

"Must you!" Lorraine turned around from the stove with her teeth clenched tightly together.

"Must I what, Lorraine? Must I talk about things that are as much a part of life as eating or breathing or growing old? Why are you always so uptight about sex or men?"

"I'm not uptight about anything. I just think its disgusting when you go on and on about—"

"There's nothing disgusting about it, Lorraine. You've never been with a man, but I've been with quite a few—some better than others. There were a couple who I still hope to this day will die a slow, painful death, but then there were some who were good to me—in and out of bed."

"If they were so great, then why are you with me?" Lorraine's lips were trembling.

"Because—" Theresa looked steadily into her eyes and then down at the cookie she was twirling on the table. "Because," she continued slowly, "you can take a chocolate chip cookie and put holes in it and attach it to your ears and call it an earring, or hang it around your neck on a silver chain and pretend it's a necklace—but it's still a cookie. See—you can toss it in the air and call it a Frisbee or even a flying saucer, if the mood hits you, and it's still just a cookie. Send it spinning on a table—like this—until it's a wonderful blur of amber and brown light that you can imagine to be a topaz or rusted gold or old crystal, but the law of gravity has got to come into play, sometime, and it's got to come to rest—sometime. Then all the spinning and pretending and hoopla is over with. And you know what you got?"

"A chocolate chip cookie," Lorraine said.

"Uh-huh." Theresa put the cookie in her mouth and winked. "A lesbian." She got up from the table. "Call me when dinner's ready. I'm going back to read." She stopped at the kitchen door. "Now, why are you putting gravy on that chicken, Lorraine? You know it's fattening."

[1982]

Joining the Conversation: Critical Thinking and Writing

1. The first sentence says, "At first they seemed like such nice girls." What do we know about the person who says it? What does it tell us (and imply) about the "nice girls"?
2. What is Sophie's role in the story?
3. In the second part of the story, who is the narrator? Does she or he know Theresa's thoughts, or Lorraine's, or both?
4. How does the story end? What do you think will happen between Lorraine and Theresa?
5. Try writing a page or less that is the *end* of a story about two people (men, women, children—but *people*) whose relationship is going to end soon, or is going to survive, because of, or despite, its difficulties.

Alice Munro

Alice Munro was born in 1931 in Wingham, Ontario, Canada, a relatively rural community and the sort of place in which she sets much of her fiction. She began publishing stories when she was an undergraduate at the University of Western Ontario. She left Western after two years, worked in a library and in a bookstore, then married, moved to Victoria, British Columbia, and founded a bookstore there. She continued to write while raising three children. She divorced and remarried; much of her fiction concerns marriage or divorce, which is to say it concerns shifting relationships in a baffling world.

Boys and Girls

My father was a fox farmer. That is, he raised silver foxes, in pens; and in the fall and early winter, when their fur was prime, he killed them and skinned them and sold their pelts to the Hudson's Bay Company or the Montreal Fur Traders. These companies supplied us with heroic calendars to hang, one on each side of the kitchen door. Against a background of cold blue sky and black pine forests and treacherous northern rivers, plumed adventurers planted the flags of England or of France: magnificent savages bent their backs to the portage.

For several weeks before Christmas, my father worked after supper in the cellar of our house. The cellar was whitewashed, and lit by a hundred-watt bulb over the worktable. My brother Laird and I sat on the top step and watched. My father removed the pelt inside-out from the body of the fox which looked surprisingly small, mean and rat-like, deprived of its arrogant weight of fur. The naked, slippery bodies were collected in a sack and buried at the dump. One time the hired man, Henry Bailey, had taken a swipe at me with this sack, saying, "Christmas present!" My mother thought that was not funny. In fact she disliked the whole pelting operation—that was what the killing, skinning, and preparation of the furs was called—and wished it did not have to take place in the house. There was the smell. After the pelt had been stretched inside-out on a long board my father scraped away delicately, removing the little clotted webs of blood vessels, the bubbles of fat; the smell of blood and animal fat, with the strong primitive odor of the fox itself, penetrated all parts of the house. I found it reassuringly seasonal, like the smell of oranges and pine needles.

Henry Bailey suffered from bronchial troubles. He would cough and cough until his narrow face turned scarlet, and his light blue, derisive eyes filled up with tears; then he took the lid off the stove, and, standing well back, shot out a great clot of phlegm—hsss—straight into the heart of the flames. We admired him for this performance and for his ability to make his stomach growl at will, and for his laughter, which was full of high whistlings and gurglings and involved the whole faulty machinery of his chest. It was sometimes hard to tell what he was laughing at, and always possible that it might be us.

After we had been sent to bed we could still smell fox and still hear Henry's laugh, but these things, reminders of the warm, safe, brightly lit downstairs world, seemed lost and diminished, floating on the stale cold air upstairs. We were afraid at night in the winter. We were not afraid of *outside* though this was the time of year when snowdrifts curled around our house like sleeping whales and the wind harassed us all night, coming up from the buried fields, the frozen swamp, with its old bugbear chorus of threats and misery. We were afraid of *inside*, the room where we slept. At this time the upstairs of our house was not finished. A brick chimney went up one wall. In the middle of the floor was a square hole, with a wooden railing around it; that was where the stairs came up. On the other side of the stairwell were the things that nobody had any use for any more—a soldiery roll of linoleum, standing on end, a wicker baby carriage, a fern basket, china jugs and basins with cracks in them, a picture of the Battle of Balaclava, very sad to look at. I had told Laird, as soon as he was old enough to understand such things, that bats and skeletons lived over there; whenever a man escaped from the county jail, twenty miles away, I imagined that he had somehow let himself in the window and was hiding behind the linoleum. But we had rules to keep us safe. When the light was on, we were safe as long as we did not step off the square of worn carpet which defined our bedroom-space; when the light was off no place was safe but the beds themselves. I had to turn out the light kneeling on the end of my bed, and stretching as far as I could to reach the cord.

5 In the dark we lay on our beds, our narrow life rafts, and fixed our eyes on the faint light coming up the stairwell, and sang songs. Laird sang "Jingle Bells," which he would sing any time, whether it was Christmas or not, and I sang "Danny Boy." I loved the sound of my own voice, frail and supplicating, rising in the dark. We could make out the tall frosted shapes of the windows now, gloomy and white. When I came to the part, *When I am dead, as dead I well may be*—a fit of shivering caused not by the cold sheets but by pleasurable emotion almost silenced me. *You'll kneel and say, an Ave there above me*—What was an Ave? Every day I forgot to find out.

Laird went straight from singing to sleep. I could hear his long, satisfied, bubbly breaths. Now for the time that remained to me, the most perfectly private and perhaps the best time of the whole day, I arranged myself tightly under the covers and went on with one of the stories I was telling myself from night to night. These stories were about myself, when I had grown a little older; they took place in a world that was recognizably mine, yet one that presented opportunities for courage, boldness and self-sacrifice, as mine never did. I rescued people from a bombed building (it discouraged me that the real war had gone on so far away from Jubilee). I shot two rabid wolves who were menacing the schoolyard (the teachers cowered terrified at my back). I rode a fine horse spiritedly down the main street of Jubilee, acknowledging the townspeople's gratitude for some yet-to-be-worked-out piece of heroism (nobody ever rode a horse there, except King Billy in the Orangemen's Day parade).[1] There was always riding and shooting in these stories, though I had only been on a horse twice—bareback because we did not own a saddle—and the second time I had slid right around and dropped under the horse's feet; it had stepped placidly over me. I really was learning to shoot, but I could not hit anything yet, not even tin cans on fence posts.

Alive, the foxes inhabited a world my father made for them. It was surrounded by a high guard fence, like a medieval town, with a gate that was padlocked at night. Along the streets of this town were ranged large, sturdy pens. Each of them had a real door that a man could go through, a wooden ramp along the wire, for the foxes to run up and down on, and a kennel—something like a clothes chest with airholes—where they slept and stayed in winter and had their young. There were feeding and watering dishes attached to the wire in such a way that they could

[1]**Orangemen's Day parade** The Orange Society is named for William of Orange, who, as King William III of England, defeated James II of England at the Battle of the Boyne on 12 July 1609. It sponsors an annual procession on 12 July. (All notes are by the editors.)

be emptied and cleaned from the outside. The dishes were made of old tin cans, and the ramps and kennels of odds and ends of old lumber. Everything was tidy and ingenious; my father was tirelessly inventive and his favorite book in the world was Robinson Crusoe. He had fitted a tin drum on a wheelbarrow, for bringing water to the pens. This was my job in summer, when the foxes had to have water twice a day. Between nine and ten o'clock in the morning, and again after supper, I filled the drum at the pump and trundled it down through the barnyard to the pens, where I parked it, and filled my watering can and went along the streets. Laird came too, with his little cream and green gardening can, filled too full and knocking against his legs and slopping water on his canvas shoes. I had the real watering can, my father's, though I could only carry it three-quarters full.

The foxes all had names, which were printed on a tin plate and hung beside their doors. They were not named when they were born, but when they survived the first year's pelting and were added to the breeding stock. Those my father had named were called names like Prince, Bob, Wally and Betty. Those I had named were called Star or Turk, or Maureen or Diana. Laird named one Maud after a hired girl we had when he was little, one Harold after a boy at school, and one Mexico, he did not say why.

Naming them did not make pets out of them, or anything like it. Nobody but my father ever went into the pens, and he had twice had blood-poisoning from bites. When I was bringing them their water they prowled up and down on the paths they had made inside their pens, barking seldom—they saved that for night-time, when they might get up a chorus of community frenzy—but always watching me, their eyes burning, clear gold, in their pointed, malevolent faces. They were beautiful for their delicate legs and heavy, aristocratic tails and the bright fur sprinkled on dark down their backs—which gave them their name—but especially for their faces, drawn exquisitely sharp in pure hostility, and their golden eyes.

10 Besides carrying water I helped my father when he cut the long grass, and the lamb's quarter and flowering money-musk, that grew between the pens. He cut with the scythe and I raked into piles. Then he took a pitchfork and threw fresh-cut grass all over the top of the pens to keep the foxes cooler and shade their coats, which were browned by too much sun. My father did not talk to me unless it was about the job we were doing. In this he was quite different from my mother, who, if she was feeling cheerful, would tell me all sorts of things—the name of a dog she had when she was a little girl, the names of boys she had gone out with later on when she was grown up, and what certain dresses of hers had looked like—she could not imagine now what had become of them. Whatever thoughts and stories my father had were private, and I was shy of him and would never ask him questions. Nevertheless I worked willingly under his eyes, and with a feeling of pride. One time a feed salesman came down into the pens to talk to him and my father said, "Like to have you meet my new hired man." I turned away and raked furiously, red in the face with pleasure.

"Could of fooled me," said the salesman. "I thought it was only a girl."

After the grass was cut, it seemed suddenly much later in the year. I walked on stubble in the earlier evening, aware of the reddening skies, the entering silences, of fall. When I wheeled the tank out of the gate and put the padlock on, it was almost dark. One night at this time I saw my mother and father standing on the little rise of ground we called the gangway, in front of the barn. My father had just come from the meathouse; he had his stiff bloody apron on, and a pail of cut-up meat in his hand.

It was an odd thing to see my mother down at the barn. She did not often come out of the house unless it was to do something—hang out the wash or dig potatoes in the garden. She looked out of place, with her bare lumpy legs, not touched by the sun, her apron still on and damp across the stomach from the supper dishes. Her hair was tied up in a kerchief, wisps of it falling out. She would tie her hair up like this in the morning, saying she did not have time to do it properly, and it would stay tied up all day. It was true, too; she really did not have time. These days our back porch was piled with baskets of peaches and grapes and pears, bought in town, and onions and tomatoes and cucumbers grown at home, all waiting to be made into jelly and jam and preserves, pickles and chili sauce. In the kitchen there was a fire in the stove all day, jars clinked in boiling water, sometimes a cheesecloth bag was strung on a pole between two chairs straining blue-black grape pulp for jelly. I was given jobs to do and I would sit at the table peeling peaches that had been soaked in the hot water, or cutting up onions, my eyes smarting and streaming. As soon as I was done I ran out of the house, trying to get out of earshot before my mother thought of what she wanted me to do next. I hated the hot dark kitchen in summer, the green blinds and the flypapers, the same old oilcloth table and wavy mirror and bumpy linoleum. My mother was too tired and preoccupied to talk to me, she had no heart to tell about the Normal School Graduation Dance; sweat trickled over her face and she was always counting under her breath, pointing at jars, dumping cups of sugar. It seemed to me that work in the house was endless, dreary and peculiarly depressing; work done out of doors, and in my father's service, was ritualistically important.

I wheeled the tank up to the barn, where it was kept, and I heard my mother saying, "Wait till Laird gets a little bigger, then you'll have a real help."

15 What my father said I did not hear. I was pleased by the way he stood listening, politely as he would to a salesman or a stranger, but with an air of wanting to get on with his real work. I felt my mother had no business down here and I wanted him to feel the same way. What did she mean about Laird? He was no help to anybody. Where was he now? Swinging himself sick on the swing, going around in circles, or trying to catch caterpillars. He never once stayed with me till I was finished.

"And then I can use her more in the house," I heard my mother say. She had a dead-quiet, regretful way of talking about me that always made me uneasy. "I just get my back turned and she runs off. It's not like I had a girl in the family at all."

I went and sat on a feed bag in the corner of the barn, not wanting to appear when this conversation was going on. My mother, I felt, was not to be trusted. She was kinder than my father and more easily fooled, but you could not depend on her, and the real reasons for the things she said and did were not to be known. She loved me, and she sat up late at night making a dress of the difficult style I wanted, for me to wear when school started, but she was also my enemy. She was always plotting. She was plotting now to get me to stay in the house more, although she knew I hated it (*because* she knew I hated it) and keep me from working for my father. It seemed to me she would do this simply out of perversity, and to try her power. It did not occur to me that she could be lonely, or jealous. No grown-up could be; they were too fortunate. I sat and kicked my heels monotonously against a feed bag, raising dust, and did not come out till she was gone.

At any rate, I did not expect my father to pay any attention to what she said. Who could imagine Laird doing my work—Laird remembering the padlock and cleaning out the watering dishes with a leaf on the end of a stick, or even wheeling the tank without it tumbling over? It showed how little my mother knew about the way things really were.

I have forgotten to say what the foxes were fed. My father's bloody apron reminded me. They were fed horsemeat. At this time most farmers still kept horses, and when a horse got too old to work, or broke a leg or got down and would not get up, as they sometimes did, the owner would call my father, and he and Henry went out to the farm in the truck. Usually they shot and butchered the horse there, paying the farmer from five to twelve dollars. If they had already too much meat on hand, they would bring the horse back alive, and keep it for a few days or weeks in our stable, until the meat was needed. After the war the farmers were buying tractors and gradually getting rid of horses altogether, so it sometimes happened that we got a good healthy horse, that there was just no use for any more. If this happened in the winter we might keep the horse in our stable till spring, for we had plenty of hay and if there was a lot of snow—and the plow did not always get our road cleared—it was convenient to be able to go to town with a horse and cutter.[2]

The winter I was eleven years old we had two horses in the stable. We did not know what names they had had before, so we called them Mack and Flora. Mack was an old black workhorse, sooty and indifferent. Flora was a sorrel mare, a driver. We took them both out in the cutter. Mack was slow and easy to handle. Flora was given to fits of violent alarm, veering at cars and even at other horses, but we loved her speed and high-stepping, her general air of gallantry and abandon. On Saturdays we went down to the stable and as soon as we opened the door on its cosy, animal-smelling darkness Flora threw up her head, rolled her eyes, whinnied despairingly and pulled herself through a crisis of nerves on the spot. It was not safe to go into her stall; she would kick.

This winter also I began to hear a great deal more on the theme my mother had sounded when she had been talking in front of the barn. I no longer felt safe. It seemed that in the minds of the people around me there was a steady undercurrent of thought, not to be deflected, on this one subject. The word *girl* had formerly seemed to me innocent and unburdened, like the word *child;* now it appeared that it was no such thing. A girl was not, as I had supposed, simply what I was; it was what I had to become. It was a definition, always touched with emphasis, with reproach and disappointment. Also it was a joke on me. Once Laird and I were fighting, and for the first time ever I had to use all my strength against him; even so, he caught and pinned my arm for a moment, really hurting me. Henry saw this, and laughed, saying, "Oh, that there Laird's gonna show you, one of these days!" Laird was getting a lot bigger. But I was getting bigger too.

My grandmother came to stay with us for a few weeks and I heard other things. "Girls don't slam doors like that." "Girls keep their knees together when they sit down." And worse still, when I asked some questions, "That's none of girls' business." I continued to slam the doors and sit as awkwardly as possible, thinking by such measures I kept myself free.

When spring came, the horses were let out in the barnyard. Mack stood against the barn wall trying to scratch his neck and haunches, but Flora trotted up and down and reared at the fences, clattering her hooves against the rails. Snow drifts dwindled quickly, revealing the hard gray and brown earth, the familiar rise and fall of the ground, plain and bare after the fantastic landscape of winter. There was a

[2]**cutter** a small sleigh.

great feeling of opening-out, of release. We just wore rubbers now, over our shoes; our feet felt ridiculously light. One Saturday we went to the stable and found all the doors open, letting in the unaccustomed sunlight and fresh air. Henry was there, just idling around looking at his collection of calendars which were tacked up behind the stalls in a part of the stable my mother had probably never seen.

"Come to say goodbye to your old friend Mack?" Henry said. "Here you give him a taste of oats." He poured some oats in Laird's cupped hands and Laird went to feed Mack. Mack's teeth were in bad shape. He ate very slowly, patiently shifting the oats around in his mouth, trying to find a stump of a molar to grind it on. "Poor old Mac," said Henry mournfully. "When a horse's teeth's gone, he's gone. That's about the way."

25 "Are you going to shoot him today?" I said. Mack and Flora had been in the stable so long I had almost forgotten they were going to be shot.

Henry didn't answer me. Instead he started to sing in a high, trembly, mocking-sorrowful voice. *Oh, there's no more work, for poor Uncle Ned, he's gone where the good darkies go.* Mack's thick, blackish tongue worked diligently at Laird's hand. I went out before the song was ended and sat down on the gangway.

I had never seen them shoot a horse, but I knew where it was done. Last summer Laird and I had come upon a horse's entrails before they were buried. We had thought it was a big black snake, coiled up in the sun. That was around in the field that ran up beside the barn. I thought that if we went inside the barn, and found a wide crack or a knothole to look through, we would be able to see them do it. It was not something I wanted to see; just the same, if a thing really happened, it was better to see, and know.

My father came down from the house, carrying the gun.

"What are you doing here?" he said.

30 "Nothing."

"Go on up and play around the house."

He sent Laird out of the stable. I said to Laird, "Do you want to see them shoot Mack?" and without waiting for an answer led him around to the front door of the barn, opened it carefully, and went in. "Be quiet or they'll hear us," I said. We could hear Henry and my father talking in the stable; then the heavy, shuffling steps of Mack being backed out of his stall.

In the loft it was cold and dark. Thin crisscrossed beams of sunlight fell through the cracks. The hay was low. It was a rolling country, hills and hollows, slipping under our feet. About four feet up was a beam going around the walls. We piled hay up in one corner and I boosted Laird up and hoisted myself. The beam was not very wide; we crept along it with our hands flat on the barn walls. There were plenty of knotholes, and I found one that gave me the view I wanted—a corner of the barnyard, the gate, part of the field. Laird did not have a knothole and began to complain.

I showed him a widened crack between two boards. "Be quiet and wait. If they hear you you'll get us in trouble."

35 My father came in sight carrying the gun. Henry was leading Mack by the halter. He dropped it and took out his cigarette papers and tobacco; he rolled cigarettes for my father and himself. While this was going on Mack nosed around in the old, dead grass along the fence. Then my father opened the gate and they took Mack through. Henry led Mack away from the path to a patch of ground and they talked together, not loud enough for us to hear. Mack again began searching for a mouthful of fresh grass, which was not to be found. My father walked away in a straight line, and stopped short a distance which seemed to suit him. Henry was

walking away from Mack too, but sideways, still negligently holding on to the halter. My father raised the gun and Mack looked up as if he had noticed something and my father shot him.

Mack did not collapse at once but swayed, lurched sideways and fell, first on his side; then he rolled over on his back and, amazingly, kicked his legs for a few seconds in the air. At this Henry laughed, as if Mack had done a trick for him. Laird, who had drawn a long, groaning breath of surprise when the shot was fired, said out loud, "He's not dead." And it seemed to me it might be true. But his legs stopped, he rolled on his side again, his muscles quivered and sank. The two men walked over and looked at him in a business-like way; they bent down and examined his forehead where the bullet had gone in, and now I saw his blood on the brown grass.

"Now they just skin him and cut him up," I said. "Let's go." My legs were a little shaky and I jumped gratefully down into the hay. "Now you've seen how they shoot a horse," I said in a congratulatory way, as if I had seen it many times before. "Let's see if any barn cat's had kittens in the hay." Laird jumped. He seemed young and obedient again. Suddenly I remembered how, when he was little, I had brought him into the barn and told him to climb the ladder to the top beam. That was in the spring, too, when the hay was low. I had done it out of a need for excitement, a desire for something to happen so that I could tell about it. He was wearing a little bulky brown and white checked coat, made down from one of mine. He went all the way up just as I told him, and sat down on the top beam with the hay far below him on one side, and the barn floor and some old machinery on the other. Then I ran screaming to my father. "Laird's up on the top beam!" My father came, my mother came, my father went up the ladder talking very quietly and brought Laird down under his arm, at which my mother leaned against the ladder and began to cry. They said to me, "Why weren't you watching him?" but nobody ever knew the truth. Laird did not know enough to tell. But whenever I saw the brown and white checked coat hanging in the closet, or at the bottom of the rag bag, which was where it ended up, I felt a weight in my stomach, the sadness of unexorcised guilt.

I looked at Laird, who did not even remember this, and I did not like the look on his thin, winter-pale face. His expression was not frightened or upset, but remote, concentrating. "Listen," I said, in an unusually bright and friendly voice, "you aren't going to tell, are you?"

"No," he said absently.

"Promise."

"Promise," he said. I grabbed the hand behind his back to make sure he was not crossing his fingers. Even so, he might have a nightmare; it might come out that way. I decided I had better work hard to get all thoughts of what he had seen out of his mind—which, it seemed to me, could not hold very many things at a time. I got some money I had saved and that afternoon we went into Jubilee and saw a show, with Judy Canova,[3] at which we both laughed a great deal. After that I thought it would be all right.

Two weeks later I knew they were going to shoot Flora. I knew from the night before, when I heard my mother ask if the hay was holding out all right, and my father said, "Well, after tomorrow there'll just be the cow, and we should be able to put her out to grass in another week." So I knew it was Flora's turn in the morning.

This time I didn't think of watching it. That was something to see just one time. I had not thought about it very often since, but sometimes when I was busy working at school, or standing in front of the mirror combing my hair and wondering if I would

[3] **Judy Canova** American comedian, popular in films in the 1940s.

be pretty when I grew up, the whole scene would flash into my mind: I would see the easy, practiced way my father raised the gun, and hear Henry laughing when Mack kicked his legs in the air. I did not have any great feeling of horror and opposition, such as a city child might have had; I was too used to seeing the death of animals as a necessity by which we lived. Yet I felt a little ashamed, and there was a new wariness, a sense of holding-off, in my attitude to my father and his work.

It was a fine day, and we were going around the yard picking up tree branches that had been torn off in winter storms. This was something we had been told to do, and also we wanted to use them to make a teepee. We heard Flora whinny, and then my father's voice and Henry's shouting, and we ran down to the barnyard to see what was going on.

The stable door was open. Henry had just brought Flora out, and she had broken away from him. She was running free in the barnyard, from one end to the other. We climbed up on the fence. It was exciting to see her running, whinnying, going up on her hind legs, prancing and threatening like a horse in a Western movie, an unbroken ranch horse, though she was just an old driver, an old sorrel mare. My father and Henry ran after her and tried to grab the dangling halter. They tried to work her into a corner, and they had almost succeeded when she made a run between them, wild-eyed, and disappeared around the corner of the barn. We heard the rail clatter down as she got over the fence, and Henry yelled. "She's into the field now!"

That meant she was in the long L-shaped field that ran up by the house. If she got around the center, heading toward the lane, the gate was open; the truck had been driven into the field this morning. My father shouted to me, because I was on the other side of the fence, nearest the lane. "Go shut the gate!"

I could run very fast. I ran across the garden, past the tree where our swing was hung, and jumped across a ditch into the lane. There was the open gate. She had not got out, I could not see her up the road; she must have run to the other end of the field. The gate was heavy. I lifted it out of the gravel and carried it across the roadway. I had it halfway across when she came in sight, galloping straight toward me. There was just time to get the chain on. Laird came scrambling through the ditch to help me.

Instead of shutting the gate, I opened it as wide as I could. I did not make any decision to do this, it was just what I did. Flora never slowed down; she galloped straight past me, and Laird jumped up and down, yelling "Shut it, shut it!" even after it was too late. My father and Henry appeared in the field a moment too late to see what I had done. They only saw Flora heading for the township road. They would think I had not got there in time.

They did not waste any time asking about it. They went back to the barn and got the gun and the knives they used, and put these in the truck; then they turned the truck around and came bouncing up the field toward us. Laird called to them. "Let me go too, let me go too!" and Henry stopped the truck and they took him in. I shut the gate after they were all gone.

I supposed Laird would tell. I wondered what would happen to me. I had never disobeyed my father before, and I could not understand why I had done it. Flora would not really get away. They would catch up with her in the truck. Or if they did not catch her this morning somebody would see her and telephone us this afternoon or tomorrow. There was no wild country here for her to run to, only farms. What was more, my father had paid for her, we needed the meat to feed the foxes, we needed the foxes to make our living. All I had done was make more work for my father who worked hard enough already. And when my father found out about it he was not going to trust me any more; he would know that

I was not entirely on his side. I was on Flora's side, and that made me no use to anybody, not even to her. Just the same, I did not regret it; when she came running at me and I held the gate open, that was the only thing I could do.

I went back to the house, and my mother said, "What's all the commotion?" I told her that Flora had kicked down the fence and got away. "Your poor father," she said, "now he'll have to go chasing over the countryside. Well, there isn't any use planning dinner before one." She put up the ironing board. I wanted to tell her, but thought better of it and went upstairs, and sat on my bed.

Lately I had been trying to make my part of the room fancy, spreading the bed with old lace curtains, and fixing myself a dressing table with some leftovers of cretonne for a skirt. I planned to put up some kind of barricade between my bed and Laird's, to keep my section separate from his. In the sunlight, the lace curtains were just dusty rags. We did not sing at night any more. One night when I was singing Laird said, "You sound silly," and I went right on but the next night I did not start. There was not so much need to anyway, we were no longer afraid. We knew it was just old furniture over there, old jumble and confusion. We did not keep to the rules. I still stayed awake after Laird was asleep and told myself stories, but even in these stories something different was happening, mysterious alterations took place. A story might start off in the old way, with a spectacular danger, a fire or wild animals, and for a while I might rescue people; then things would change around, and instead, somebody would be rescuing me. It might be a boy from our class at school, or even Mr. Campbell, our teacher, who tickled girls under the arms. And at this point the story concerned itself at great length with what I looked like—how long my hair was, and what kind of dress I had on; by the time I had these details worked out the real excitement of the story was lost.

It was later than one o'clock when the truck came back. The tarpaulin was over the back, which meant there was meat in it. My mother had to heat dinner up all over again. Henry and my father had changed from their bloody overalls into ordinary working overalls in the barn, and they washed their arms and necks and faces at the sink, and splashed water on their hair and combed it. Laird lifted his arm to show off a streak of blood. "We shot old Flora," he said, "and cut her up in fifty pieces."

"Well I don't want to hear about it," my mother said. "And don't come to my table like that."

55 My father made him go and wash the blood off.

We sat down and my father said grace and Henry pasted his chewing gum on the end of his fork, the way he always did; when he took it off he would have us admire the pattern. We began to pass the bowls of steaming, overcooked vegetables. Laird looked across the table at me and said proudly, distinctly, "Anyway it was her fault Flora got away."

"What?" my father said.

"She could of shut the gate and she didn't. She just open' it up and Flora run out."

"Is that right?" my father said.

60 Everybody at the table was looking at me. I nodded, swallowing food with great difficulty. To my shame, tears flooded my eyes.

My father made a curt sound of disgust. "What did you do that for?"

I did not answer. I put down my fork and waited to be sent from the table, still not looking up.

But this did not happen. For some time nobody said anything, then Laird said matter-of-factly, "She's crying."

"Never mind," my father said. He spoke with resignation, even good humor, the words which absolved and dismissed me for good. "She's only a girl," he said.

65 I didn't protest that, even in my heart. Maybe it was true.

[1968]

Joining the Conversation: Critical Thinking and Writing

1. Explain, in a paragraph, what the narrator means when she says (paragraph 21), "The word *girl* had formerly seemed to me innocent and unburdened, like the word *child;* now it appeared that it was no such thing. A girl was not, as I had supposed, simply what I was; it was what I had to become."

2. The narrator says that she "could not understand" why she disobeyed her father and allowed the horse to escape. Can you explain her action to her? If so, do so.

3. In a paragraph, characterize the mother.

POEMS

Anonymous Nursery Rhyme

Nursery rhymes are of course found in books, but they survive because children find them memorable and pass them on to their playmates and, when they become adults, to their children. Nursery rhymes include lullabies ("Rock-a-by baby, on the tree tops"), counting-out rhymes ("eeny, meeny, miny, mo," "One potato, two potato"), charms ("rain, rain, go away"), short narratives ("Jack and Jill," "Mary had a little lamb"), and they are marked by emphatic rhymes. Scholars believe that perhaps half of the best-loved nursery rhymes of today go back to the eighteenth century, and many to the seventeenth. The earliest printed collections are *Tommy Thumb's Pretty Song Book* (1744) and *Mother Goose's Melody: or Sonnets for the Cradle* (1781).

When you read the following nursery rhyme (or call to mind others that you know), ask yourself this question: Do nursery rhymes indoctrinate children—that is, do they engender or reinforce attitudes about age, gender, and class? If so, how? And what should be done about it? Explain, using as examples these rhymes or others that you know.

What Are Little Boys Made Of

What are little boys made of, made of?
What are little boys made of?
    Snips and snails
    And puppy-dogs' tails,
That's what little boys are made of.

What are little girls made of, made of?
What are little girls made of?
    Sugar and spice
    And all things nice,
That's what little girls are made of.

Joining the Conversation: Critical Thinking and Writing

1. Do you imagine that boys like the description of what boys are made of? Do girls like the description of what girls are made of? Or is it only grown-ups who like these descriptions? Explain.
2. A version in 1846 gives two additional stanzas: "What are young men made of? / Sighs and leers and crocodile tears," and "What are young women made of? / Ribbons and laces, and sweet pretty faces." To the best of our knowledge, these two verses are not nearly so widely known as the first two. Why do you think this is so?

ANONYMOUS

The following lines have been attributed to various writers, including the American philosopher William James (1842–1910), but to the best of our knowledge the author is unknown.

Higamus, Hogamus,
Woman's monogamous;
Hogamus, Higamus,
Man is polygamous.

Joining the Conversation: Critical Thinking and Writing

1. If you find these lines engaging, how do you account for their appeal? Does it make any difference—even a tiny difference—if the pairs are reversed; that is, if the first two lines are about men, and the second two about women?
2. The underlying idea largely coincides with the saying, "Men are from Mars, women are from Venus." But consider the four lines of verse: Do you agree that in the form we have just given them, they are more effective than "Men are from Mars, women are from Venus"? And how about "Women are from Venus, men are from Mars"? Admittedly the differences are small, but would you argue that one form is decidedly more effective than the others? How do you explain the greater effectiveness?

DOROTHY PARKER

Dorothy Parker (1893–1967) was born in West End, New Jersey, but brought up in New York City. From 1917 to 1920 she served as drama critic for the magazine Vanity Fair, *where her witty, satiric reviews gained her the reputation of being hard to please. She distinguished between wit and wisecracking: "Wit has truth in it; wisecracking is simply calisthenics with words."*

In addition to writing essays and stories, Parker also wrote light verse, especially about love.

General Review of the Sex Situation

Woman wants monogamy;
Man delights in novelty.
Love is woman's moon and sun;
Man has other forms of fun.

Woman lives but in her lord;
Count to ten, and man is bored.
With this the gist and sum of it,
What earthly good can come of it?

[1926]

Joining the Conversation: Critical Thinking and Writing

1. How would you characterize Parker's message? (For instance, is it sad, happy, pitiful?) How would you characterize her tone—her attitude, as you perceive it?
2. How much truth do you think there is in Parker's lines? (Remember: No poem, or, for that matter, no novel—however long—can tell the whole truth about life.) As for truth, how would you compare it with the following passage, from Barbara Dafoe Whitehead's review (*The Times Literary Supplement,* 9 June 1995) of two sociological studies, *The Social Organization of Sexuality: Sexual Practice in the U.S.* and *Sex in America:*

   > Men and women have different sexual interests, stakes and appetites, with men more oriented to the sex act and women more interested in sex as an expression of affiliative and romantic love.

LOUISE BOGAN

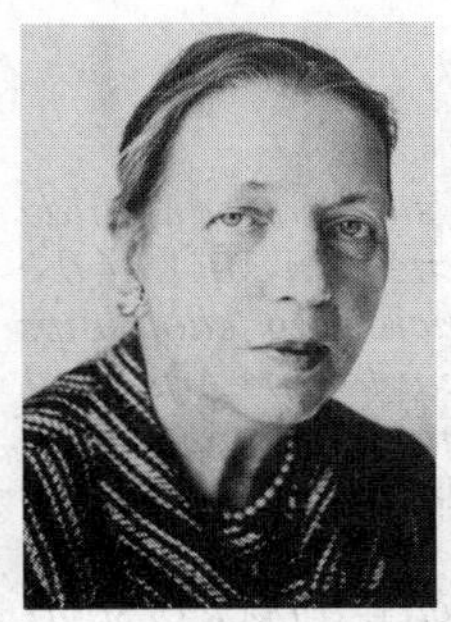

Louise Bogan (1897–1970) was born in Maine, but the family moved to Boston, where she attended Girls' Latin School, a school noted for its academic excellence. Here she began her career as a poet, publishing not only in school journals but also in the Boston Evening Transcript. *Bogan married early and had a child, but the marriage was unhappy and the couple separated. Her husband died soon after, when Bogan was only 23. She remarried, but this marriage ended in divorce. For most of her life she was an independent single woman, supporting herself by working in bookstores and libraries, and by writing reviews of poetry for magazines, including the* Atlantic Monthly *and the* New Yorker. *Most of her poems were written before 1940, and although she achieved considerable fame in her youth she was less visible as a poet in her later years. But today both her poetry and critical writing are widely admired.*

Women

Women have no wilderness in them,
They are provident instead,
Content in the tight hot cell of their hearts
To eat dusty bread.

They do not see cattle cropping red winter grass,
They do not hear
Snow water going down under culverts
Shallow and clear.

They wait, when they should turn to journeys,
They stiffen, when they should bend.
They use against themselves that benevolence
To which no man is friend.

They cannot think of so many crops to a field
Or of clean wood cleft by an axe.
Their love is an eager meaninglessness
Too tense, or too lax.

They hear in every whisper that speaks to them
A shout and a cry.
As like as not, when they take life over their door-sills
They should let it go by.

[1922]

Joining the Conversation: Critical Thinking and Writing

1. Bogan is much admired for her technical skills as a poet. What techniques do you observe in "Women," and how do they work?
2. Bogan writes of women as "they" rather than "we." Try substituting "we" in the poem. What is gained, or lost?
3. Write an imitation of "Women" called "Men." Observe as many of the structural features of the poem (line length, rhyme, metaphor) as you can. What did you learn from this exercise about poetry? About your feelings about men??

RITA DOVE

Rita Dove was born in 1952 in Akron, Ohio. After graduating summa cum laude and Phi Beta Kappa from Miami University (Ohio), Dove earned an MFA at the Iowa Writers' Workshop. She has received numerous awards, including fellowships from the Guggenheim Foundation and the National Endowment for the Arts, and a Pulitzer Prize for Poetry. In 1993–1995 she served as Poet Laureate of the United States and as Consultant to the Library of Congress, in 1996 she was awarded the National Humanities Medal, and in 2001 she was awarded the Duke Ellington Lifetime Achievement Award. The author of several books of poetry, a book of short stories, a novel, and a book of her laureate lectures, Dove is Commonwealth Professor of English at the University of Virginia in Charlottesville.

Daystar

She wanted a little room for thinking:
but she saw diapers steaming on the line,
a doll slumped behind the door.
So she lugged a chair behind the garage
to sit out the children's naps.

Sometimes there were things to watch—
the pinched armor of a vanished cricket,
a floating maple leaf. Other days
she stared until she was assured
when she closed her eyes
she'd see only her own vivid blood.

She had an hour, at best, before Liza appeared
pouting from the top of the stairs.
And just *what* was mother doing
out back with the field mice? Why,
building a palace. Later
that night when Thomas rolled over and
lurched into her, she would open her eyes
and think of the place that was hers
for an hour—where
she was nothing,
pure nothing, in the middle of the day.

[1986]

Joining the Conversation: Critical Thinking and Writing

1. How would you characterize the woman who is the subject of the poem?
2. What do you make of the title?
3. Do you think that women respond to this poem differently from the way that men do? What is your evidence for your view? How would you support it?

ROBERT HAYDEN

Robert Hayden (1913–1980) was born in Detroit, Michigan. His parents divorced when he was a child, and he was brought up by a neighboring family, whose name he adopted. In 1942, at the age of 29, he graduated from Detroit City College (now Wayne State University); he received a master's degree from the University of Michigan. He taught at Fisk University from 1946 to 1969 and after that, for the remainder of his life, at the University of Michigan. In 1979 he was appointed Consultant in Poetry to the Library of Congress, the first African American to hold the post.

Those Winter Sundays

Sundays too my father got up early
and put his clothes on in the blueblack cold,
then with cracked hands that ached
from labor in the weekday weather made
banked fires blaze. No one ever thanked him.

I'd wake and hear the cold splintering, breaking.
When the rooms were warm, he'd call,
and slowly I would rise and dress,
fearing the chronic angers of that house.

Speaking indifferently to him,
who had driven out the cold
and polished my good shoes as well.
What did I know, what did I know
of love's austere and lonely offices?

[1962]

Joining the Conversation: Critical Thinking and Writing

1. In line 1, what does the word *too* tell us about the father? What does it suggest about the speaker and the implied hearer of the poem?
2. How old do you believe the speaker was at the time he recalls in the second and third stanzas? What details suggest this age?
3. What is the meaning of *offices* in the last line? What does this word suggest that other words Hayden might have chosen do not?
4. What do you take to be the speaker's present attitude toward his father? What circumstances, do you imagine, prompted his memory of "Those Winter Sundays"?
5. In a page or two, try to get down the exact circumstances when you spoke "indifferently," or not at all, to someone who had deserved your gratitude.

THEODORE ROETHKE

Theodore Roethke (1908–1963) was born in Saginaw, Michigan, and educated at the University of Michigan and Harvard. From 1947 until his death he taught at the University of Washington in Seattle, where he exerted considerable influence on the next generation of poets. Many of Roethke's best poems are lyrical memories of his childhood.

My Papa's Waltz

The whiskey on your breath
Could make a small boy dizzy;
but I hung on like death:
Such waltzing was not easy.

We romped until the pans
Slid from the kitchen shelf;
My mother's countenance
Could not unfrown itself.

The hand that held my wrist
Was battered on one knuckle;
At every step you missed
My right ear scraped a buckle.

You beat time on my head
With a palm caked hard by dirt,
Then waltzed me off to bed
Still clinging to your shirt.

[1948]

Joining the Conversation: Critical Thinking and Writing

1. Do the syntactical pauses vary much from stanza to stanza? Be specific. Would you say that the rhythm suggests lightness? Why?
2. Does the rhythm parallel or ironically contrast with the episode described? Was the dance a graceful waltz? Explain.
3. What would you say is the function of the stresses in lines 13–14?
4. How different would the poem be if the speaker were a female, and "girl" instead of "boy" appeared in line 2?

SHARON OLDS

Sharon Olds, born in San Francisco in 1942 and educated at Stanford University and Columbia University, has published many volumes of poetry and has received major awards. Olds held the position of New York State Poet from 1998 to 2000, and currently teaches poetry workshops in the Graduate Creative Writing Program at New York University.

Rites of Passage

As the guests arrive at my son's party
They gather in the living room—
short men, men in first grade
with smooth jaws and chins.
Hands in pockets, they stand around
jostling, jockeying for place, small fights
breaking out and calming. One says to another
How old are you? Six. I'm seven. So?
They eye each other, seeing themselves
tiny in the other's pupils. They clear their
throats a lot, a room of small bankers,
they fold their arms and frown. *I could beat you*
up, a seven says to a six,
the dark cake, round and heavy as a

turret, behind them on the table. My son,
freckles like specks of nutmeg on his cheeks,
chest narrow as the balsa keel of a
model boat, long hands
cool and thin as the day they guided him
out of me, speaks up as a host
for the sake of the group.
We could easily kill a two-year-old,
he says in his clear voice. The other
men agree, they clear their throats
like Generals, they relax and get down to
playing war, celebrating my son's life.

[1983]

Joining the Conversation: Critical Thinking and Writing

1. Focus on the details that the speaker provides about the boys—how they look, how they speak. What do the details reveal about them?
2. Is the speaker's son the same as or different from the other boys?
3. Some readers find the ironies in this poem (e.g., "short men") to be somewhat comical, while others, noting such phrases as "kill a two-year-old" and "playing war," conclude that the poem as a whole is meant to be upsetting, even frightening. How would you describe the kinds of irony that Olds uses here?
4. An experiment in irony and point of view: Try writing a poem like this one, from the point of view of a father about the birthday party of his son, and then try writing another one, by either a father or mother about a daughter's party.

FRANK O'HARA

Frank O'Hara (1926–1966), was born in Baltimore, and died in a tragic accident—he was run over by a beach vehicle—on Fire Island, New York. O'Hara was not only a prolific writer of verse but also an astute critic of sculpture and painting who worked as an assistant curator at the Museum of Modern Art, in New York, and as an editor of Art News. *O'Hara's first volume of poetry was* A City Winter, and Other Poems *(1952);* Collected Poems *was issued in 1971, but it was not complete. It has been supplemented by two additional volumes,* Early Poems *(1977) and* Poems Retrieved *(1977).*

Homosexuality

So we are taking off our masks, are we, and keeping
our mouths shut? as if we'd been pierced by a glance!

The song of an old cow is not more full of judgment
than the vapors which escape one's soul when one is sick;

so I pull the shadows around me like a puff
and crinkle my eyes as if at the most exquisite moment

of a very long opera, and then we are off!
without reproach and without hope that our delicate feet

will touch the earth again, let alone "very soon."
It is the law of my own voice I shall investigate.

I start like ice, my finger to my ear, my ear
to my heart, that proud cur at the garbage can

in the rain. It's wonderful to admire oneself
with complete candor, tallying up the merits of each

of the latrines. 14th Street is drunken and credulous,
53rd tries to tremble but is too at rest. The good

love a park and the inept a railway station,
and there are the divine ones who drag themselves up

and down the lengthening shadow of an Abyssinian head
in the dust, trailing their long elegant heels of hot air

crying to confuse the brave "It's a summer day,
and I want to be wanted more than anything else in the world."

[1971]

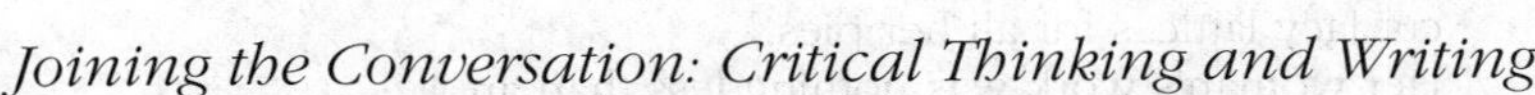

Joining the Conversation: Critical Thinking and Writing

1. Describe your response to the word that O'Hara chooses for his title. In what ways does the poem define and explore the meanings of this word and our responses to it?
2. Characterize the point of view and tone of the speaker. Who is or are the "we" named in line 1?
3. In line 1 the speaker declares that "we are taking off our masks," but then immediately seems to confuse or contradict his point when he says "we" are "keeping / our mouths shut." Explain as clearly as you can what the speaker is suggesting in this first stanza.
4. Some of the language in this poem is ugly or unpleasant—for example, the "cur at the garbage can," "the latrines." What is the purpose of such language? What is its place in the structure of the poem as a whole? Or can one argue that such language has no place in a decent poem?
5. Could O'Hara's poem be reasonably described as an argument on behalf of gays and lesbians? Please explain.

Julia Alvarez

The Latina author Julia Alvarez born in 1950 in New York of Dominican descent, has written fiction, poetry, and nonfictional prose. Her books include the novel How the Garcia Girls Lost Their Accents *(1991), which tells the story of four sisters and their parents who emigrate from the Dominican Republic to the United States;* Something to Declare: Essays *(1998); and* Homecoming: New and Collected Poems *(1996), which includes her first book,* Homecoming *(1984), as well as more recent work. The following poem is taken from that collection.*

Woman's Work

Who says a woman's work isn't high art?
She'd challenge as she scrubbed the bathroom tiles.
Keep house as if the address were your heart.

We'd clean the whole upstairs before we'd start
downstairs. I'd sigh, hearing my friends outside.
Doing her woman's work was a hard art

to practice when the summer sun would bar
the floor I swept till she was satisfied.
She kept me prisoner in her housebound heart.

She'd shine the tines of forks, the wheels of carts,
cut lacy lattices for all her pies.
Her woman's work was nothing less than art.

And, I, her masterpiece since I was smart,
was primed, praised, polished, scolded and advised
to keep a house much better than my heart.

I did not want to be her counterpart!
I struck out . . . but became my mother's child:
a woman working at home on her art,
housekeeping paper as if it were her heart.

[1996]

Joining the Conversation: Critical Thinking and Writing

1. The poet explores the relationship between mother and daughter through the work that each performs. Describe this work, and in particular the lessons that the mother teaches through what she does and how she does it.
2. What is the meaning of line 3?
3. How do you interpret the phrase "I struck out"?
4. Do you feel inclined to argue for or against Alvarez's conception of "woman's work"? Please explain, and cite evidence from the poem.

Marge Piercy

Marge Piercy, born in Detroit in 1936, was the first member of her family to attend college. After earning a bachelor's degree from the University of Michigan in 1957 and a master's degree from Northwestern University in 1958, she moved to Chicago. There she worked at odd jobs while writing novels (unpublished) and engaging in action on behalf of women and African Americans and against the war in Vietnam. In 1970—the year she moved to Wellfleet, Massachusetts, where she still lives—she published her first book, a novel. Since then she has published other novels, short stories, poems, and essays.

Barbie Doll

This girlchild was born as usual
and presented dolls that did pee-pee
and miniature GE stoves and irons
and wee lipsticks the color of cherry candy.
Then in the magic of puberty, a classmate said:
You have a great big nose and fat legs.

She was healthy, tested intelligent,
possessed strong arms and back,
abundant sexual drive and manual dexterity.
She went to and fro apologizing.
Everyone saw a fat nose on thick legs.

She was advised to play coy,
exhorted to come on hearty,
exercise, diet, smile and wheedle.
Her good nature wore out
like a fan belt.
So she cut off her nose and her legs
and offered them up.

In the casket displayed on satin she lay
with the undertaker's cosmetics painted on,
a turned-up putty nose,
dressed in a pink and white nightie.
Doesn't she look pretty? everyone said.
Consummation at last.
To every woman a happy ending.

[1969]

Joining the Conversation: Critical Thinking and Writing

1. Why is the poem called "Barbie Doll"?
2. What voice do you hear in lines 1–4? Line 6 is, we are told, the voice of "a classmate." How do these voices differ? What voice do you hear in the first three lines of the second stanza?

3. Explain in your own words what Piercy is saying about women in this poem. Does her view seem to you fair, slightly exaggerated, or greatly exaggerated? Support your thesis with reasons.

PLAY

HENRIK IBSEN

Henrik Ibsen (1828–1906) was born in Skien, Norway, of wealthy parents who soon after his birth lost their money. Ibsen worked as a pharmacist's apprentice, but at the age of 22 he had written his first play, a promising melodrama entitled Cataline. *He engaged in theater work first in Norway and then in Denmark and Germany. By 1865 his plays had won him a state pension that enabled him to settle in Rome. After writing romantic, historic, and poetic plays, he turned to realistic drama with* The League of Youth *(1869). Among the major realistic "problem plays" are* A Doll's House *(1879),* Ghosts *(1881), and* An Enemy of the People *(1882). In* The Wild Duck *(1884) he moved toward a more symbolic tragicomedy, and his last plays, written in the nineties, are highly symbolic.* Hedda Gabler *(1890) looks backward to the plays of the eighties rather than forward to the plays of the nineties.*

A Doll's House

Translated by R. Farquharson Sharp

CHARACTERS

TORVALD HELMER, *a lawyer and bank manager*
NORA, *his wife*
DOCTOR RANK
MRS. CHRISTINE LINDE
NILS KROGSTAD, *a lawyer and bank clerk*
IVAR, BOB, AND EMMY, *the Helmers' three young children*
ANNE, *their nurse*
HELEN, *a housemaid*
A PORTER

The action takes place in HELMER'S *apartment.*

Act 1

SCENE. *A room furnished comfortably and tastefully, but not extravagantly. At the back, a door to the right leads to the entrance hall, another to the left leads to* HELMER'S *study. Between the doors stands a piano. In the middle of the left-hand wall is a door, and beyond it a window. Near the window are a round table, armchairs and a small sofa. In the right-hand wall, at the farther end, another door; and on the same side, nearer the footlights, a stove, two easy chairs and a rocking-chair; between the stove and the door, a small table. Engravings on the walls; a cabinet with china and other small objects; a small book case with well-bound books. The floors are carpeted, and a fire burns in the stove. It is winter.*

A Doll's House (Harvard Theatre Collection, Houghton Library)

A bell rings in the hall; shortly afterwards the door is heard to open. Enter NORA, *humming a tune and in high spirits. She is in outdoor dress and carries a number of parcels; these she lays on the table to the right. She leaves the outer door open after her, and through it is seen a* PORTER *who is carrying a Christmas Tree and a basket, which he gives to the* MAID *who has opened the door.*

NORA: Hide the Christmas Tree carefully, Helen. Be sure the children do not see it till this evening, when it is dressed. [*to the* PORTER, *taking out her purse.*] How much?

PORTER: Sixpence.

NORA: There is a shilling. No, keep the change. [*The* PORTER *thanks her, and goes out.* NORA *shuts the door. She is laughing to herself, as she takes off her hat and coat. She takes a packet of macaroons from her pocket and eats one or two; then goes cautiously to her husband's door and listens.*] Yes, he is in.

[*Still humming, she goes to the table on the right.*]

HELMER [*calls out from his room*]: Is that my little lark twittering out there?

NORA [*busy opening some of the parcels*]: Yes, it is!

HELMER: Is my little squirrel bustling about?

NORA: Yes!

HELMER: When did my squirrel come home?

NORA: Just now. [*puts the bag of macaroons into her pocket and wipes her mouth.*] Come in here, Torvald, and see what I have bought.

HELMER: Don't disturb me. [*A little later, he opens the door and looks into the room, pen in hand.*] Bought, did you say? All these things? Has my little spendthrift been wasting money again?

NORA: Yes, but, Torvald, this year we really can let ourselves go a little. This is the first Christmas that we have not needed to economise.

HELMER: Still, you know, we can't spend money recklessly.

NORA: Yes, Torvald, we may be a wee bit more reckless now, mayn't we? Just a tiny wee bit! You are going to have a big salary and earn lots and lots of money.

HELMER: Yes, after the New Year; but then it will be a whole quarter before the salary is due.

NORA: Pooh! we can borrow till then.

HELMER: Nora! [*goes up to her and takes her playfully by the ear.*] The same little featherhead! Suppose, now, that I borrowed fifty pounds to-day, and you spent it all in the Christmas week, and then on New Year's Eve a slate fell on my head and killed me, and—

NORA [*putting her hands over his mouth*]: Oh! don't say such horrid things.

HELMER: Still, suppose that happened—what then?

NORA: If that were to happen, I don't suppose I should care whether I owed money or not.

HELMER: Yes, but what about the people who had lent it?

NORA: They? Who would bother about them? I should not know who they were.

HELMER: That is like a woman! But seriously, Nora, you know what I think about that. No debt, no borrowing. There can be no freedom or beauty about a home life that depends on borrowing and debt. We two have kept bravely on the straight road so far, and we will go on the same way for the short time longer that there need be any struggle.

NORA [*moving towards the stove*]: As you please, Torvald.

HELMER [*following her*]: Come, come, my little skylark must not droop her wings. What is this! Is my little squirrel out of temper? [*taking out his purse.*] Nora, what do you think I have got here?

NORA [*turning around quickly*]: Money!

HELMER: There you are. [*gives her some money*] Do you think I don't know what a lot is wanted for housekeeping at Christmas-time?

NORA [*counting*]: Ten shillings—a pound—two pounds! Thank you, thank you, Torvald; that will keep me going for a long time.

HELMER: Indeed it must.

NORA: Yes, yes, it will. But come here and let me show you what I have bought. And all so cheap! Look, here is a new suit for Ivar, and a sword; and a horse and a trumpet for Bob; and a doll and dolly's bedstead for Emmy—they are very plain, but anyway she will soon break them in pieces. And here are dress-lengths and handkerchiefs for the maids; old Anne ought really to have something better.

HELMER: And what is in this parcel?

NORA [*crying out*]: No, no! you mustn't see that till this evening.

HELMER: Very well. But now tell me, you extravagant little person, what would you like for yourself?

NORA: For myself? Oh, I am sure I don't want anything.

HELMER: Yes, but you must. Tell me something reasonable that you would particularly like to have.

NORA: No, I really can't think of anything—unless, Torvald—

HELMER: Well?

NORA [*playing with his coat buttons, and without raising her eyes to his*]: If you really want to give me something, you might—you might—

HELMER: Well, out with it!

NORA [*speaking quickly*]: You might give me money, Torvald. Only just as much as you can afford; and then one of these days I will buy something with it.

HELMER: But, Nora—

NORA: Oh, do! dear Torvald; please, please do! Then I will wrap it up in beautiful gilt paper and hang it on the Christmas Tree. Wouldn't that be fun?

HELMER: What are little people called that are always wasting money?

NORA: Spendthrifts—I know. Let us do as you suggest, Torvald, and then I shall have time to think what I am most in want of. That is a very sensible plan, isn't it?

HELMER [*smiling*]: Indeed it is—that is to say, if you were really to save out of the money I give you, and then really buy something for yourself. But if you spend it all on the housekeeping and any number of unnecessary things, then I merely have to pay up again.

NORA: Oh but, Torvald—

HELMER: You can't deny it, my dear little Nora. [*puts his arm round her waist*] It's a sweet little spendthrift, but she uses up a deal of money. One would hardly believe how expensive such little persons are!

NORA: It's a shame to say that. I do really save all I can.

HELMER [*laughing*]: That's very true—all you can. But you can't save anything!

NORA [*smiling quietly and happily*]: You haven't any idea how many expenses we skylarks and squirrels have, Torvald.

HELMER: You are an odd little soul. Very like your father. You always find some new way of wheedling money out of me, and, as soon as you have got it, it seems to melt in your hands. You never know where it has gone. Still, one must take you as you are. It is in the blood; for indeed it is true that you can inherit these things, Nora.

NORA: Ah, I wish I had inherited many of papa's qualities.

HELMER: And I would not wish you to be anything but just what you are, my sweet little skylark. But, do you know, it strikes me that you are looking rather—what shall I say—rather uneasy to-day?

NORA: Do I?

HELMER: You do, really. Look straight at me.

NORA [*looks at him*]: Well?

HELMER [*wagging his finger at her*]: Hasn't Miss Sweet-Tooth been breaking rules in town to-day?

NORA: No; what makes you think that?

HELMER: Hasn't she paid a visit to the confectioner's?

NORA: No, I assure you, Torvald—

HELMER: Not been nibbling sweets?

NORA: No, certainly not.

HELMER: Not even taken a bite at a macaroon or two?

NORA: No, Torvald, I assure you really—

HELMER: There, there, of course I was only joking.

NORA [*going to the table on the right*]: I should not think of going against your wishes.

HELMER: No, I am sure of that! besides, you gave me your word—[*going up to her*] Keep your little Christmas secrets to yourself, my darling. They will all be revealed to-night when the Christmas Tree is lit, no doubt.

NORA: Did you remember to invite Doctor Rank?

HELMER: No. But there is no need; as a matter of course he will come to dinner with us. However, I will ask him when he comes in this morning. I have ordered some good wine. Nora, you can't think how I am looking forward to this evening.

NORA: So am I! And how the children will enjoy themselves, Torvald!

HELMER: It is splendid to feel that one has a perfectly safe appointment, and a big enough income. It's delightful to think of, isn't it?

NORA: It's wonderful!

HELMER: Do you remember last Christmas? For a full three weeks beforehand you shut yourself up every evening till long after midnight, making ornaments for the Christmas Tree and all the other fine things that were to be a surprise to us. It was the dullest three weeks I ever spent!

NORA: I didn't find it dull.

HELMER [*smiling*]: But there was precious little result, Nora.

NORA: Oh, you shouldn't tease me about that again. How could I help the cat's going in and tearing everything to pieces?

HELMER: Of course you couldn't, poor little girl. You had the best of intentions to please us all, and that's the main thing. But it is a good thing that our hard times are over.

NORA: Yes, it is really wonderful.

HELMER: This time I needn't sit here and be dull all alone, and you needn't ruin your dear eyes and your pretty little hands—

NORA [*clapping her hands*]: No, Torvald, I needn't any longer, need I! It's wonderfully lovely to hear you say so! [*taking his arm*] Now I will tell you how I have been thinking we ought to arrange things, Torvald. As soon as Christmas is over—[*A bell rings in the hall.*] There's the bell. [*She tidies the room a little.*] There's someone at the door. What a nuisance!

HELMER: If it is a caller, remember I am not at home.

MAID [*in the doorway*]: A lady to see you, ma'am—a stranger.

NORA: Ask her to come in.

MAID: [*to* HELMER] The doctor came at the same time, sir.

HELMER: Did he go straight into my room?

MAID: Yes sir.

[HELMER *goes into his room. The* MAID *ushers in* MRS. LINDE*, who is in travelling dress, and shuts the door.*]

MRS. LINDE [*in a dejected and timid voice*]: How do you do, Nora?

NORA [*doubtfully*]: How do you do—

MRS. LINDE: You don't recognise me, I suppose.

NORA: No, I don't know—yes, to be sure, I seem to—[*suddenly*] Yes! Christine! Is it really you?

MRS. LINDE: Yes, it is I.

NORA: Christine! To think of my not recognising you! And yet how could I—[*in a gentle voice*] How you have altered, Christine!

MRS. LINDE: Yes, I have indeed. In nine, ten long years—

NORA: Is it so long since we met? I suppose it is. The last eight years have been a happy time for me, I can tell you. And so now you have come into the town, and have taken this long journey in winter—that was plucky of you.

MRS. LINDE: I arrived by steamer this morning.

NORA: To have some fun at Christmas-time, of course. How delightful! We will have such fun together! But take off your things. You are not cold, I hope.

[*helps her*] Now we will sit down by the stove, and be cosy. No, take this arm-chair; I will sit here in the rocking-chair. [*takes her hands*] Now you look like your old self again; it was only the first moment—You are a little paler, Christine, and perhaps a little thinner.

MRS. LINDE: And much, much older, Nora.

NORA: Perhaps a little older; very, very little; certainly not much. [*stops suddenly and speaks seriously*] What a thoughtless creature I am, chattering away like this. My poor, dear Christine, do forgive me.

MRS. LINDE: What do you mean, Nora?

NORA [*gently*]: Poor Christine, you are a widow.

MRS. LINDE: Yes; it is three years ago now.

NORA: Yes, I knew; I saw it in the papers. I assure you, Christine, I meant ever so often to write to you at the time, but I always put it off and something always prevented me.

MRS. LINDE: I quite understand, dear.

NORA: It was very bad of me, Christine. Poor thing, how you must have suffered. And he left you nothing?

MRS. LINDE: No.

NORA: And no children?

MRS. LINDE: No.

NORA: Nothing at all, then?

MRS. LINDE: Not even any sorrow or grief to live upon.

NORA [*looking incredulously at her*]: But, Christine, is that possible?

MRS. LINDE [*smiles sadly and strokes her hair*]: It sometimes happens, Nora.

NORA: So you are quite alone. How dreadfully sad that must be. I have three lovely children. You can't see them just now, for they are out with their nurse. But now you must tell me all about it.

MRS. LINDE: No, no; I want to hear you.

NORA: No, you must begin. I mustn't be selfish to-day; to-day I must only think of your affairs. But there is one thing I must tell you. Do you know we have just had a great piece of good luck?

MRS. LINDE: No, what is it?

NORA: Just fancy, my husband has been made manager of the Bank!

MRS. LINDE: Your husband? What good luck!

NORA: Yes, tremendous! A barrister's profession is such an uncertain thing, especially if he won't undertake unsavoury cases; and naturally Torvald has never been willing to do that, and I quite agree with him. You may imagine how pleased we are! He is to take up his work in the Bank at the New Year, and then he will have a big salary and lots of commissions. For the future we can live quite differently—we can do just as we like. I feel so relieved and so happy, Christine! It will be splendid to have heaps of money and not need to have any anxiety, won't it?

MRS. LINDE: Yes, anyhow I think it would be delightful to have what one needs.

NORA: No, not only what one needs, but heaps and heaps of money.

MRS. LINDE [*smiling*]: Nora, Nora haven't you learnt sense yet? In our schooldays you were a great spendthrift.

NORA [*laughing*]: Yes, that is what Torvald says now. [*wags her finger at her*] But "Nora, Nora" is not so silly as you think. We have not been in a position for me to waste money. We have both had to work.

MRS. LINDE: You too?

NORA: Yes; odds and ends, needlework, crochet-work, embroidery, and that kind of thing. [*dropping her voice*] And other things as well. You know Torvald left his office when we were married? There was no prospect of promotion there, and he had to try and earn more than before. But during the first year he overworked himself dreadfully. You see, he had to make money every way he could, and he worked early and late; but he couldn't stand it, and fell dreadfully ill, and the doctors said it was necessary for him to go south.

MRS. LINDE: You spent a whole year in Italy didn't you?

NORA: Yes. It was no easy matter to get away, I can tell you. It was just as Ivar was born; but naturally we had to go. It was a wonderfully beautiful journey, and it saved Torvald's life. But it cost a tremendous lot of money, Christine.

MRS. LINDE: So I should think.

NORA: It cost about two hundred and fifty pounds. That's a lot, isn't it?

MRS. LINDE: Yes, and in emergencies like that it is lucky to have the money.

NORA: I ought to tell you that we had it from papa.

MRS. LINDE: Oh, I see. It was just about that time that he died, wasn't it?

NORA: Yes; and, just think of it, I couldn't go and nurse him. I was expecting little Ivar's birth every day and I had my poor sick Torvald to look after. My dear, kind father—I never saw him again, Christine. That was the saddest time I have known since our marriage.

MRS. LINDE: I know how fond you were of him. And then you went off to Italy?

NORA: Yes; you see we had money then, and the doctors insisted on our going, so we started a month later.

MRS. LINDE: And your husband came back quite well?

NORA: As sound as a bell!

MRS. LINDE: But—the doctor?

NORA: What doctor?

MRS. LINDE: I thought your maid said the gentleman who arrived here just as I did was the doctor?

NORA: Yes, that was Doctor Rank, but he doesn't come here professionally. He is our greatest friend, and comes in at least once every day. No, Torvald has not had an hour's illness since then, and our children are strong and healthy and so am I. [*jumps up and claps her hands*] Christine! Christine! it's good to be alive and happy!—But how horrid of me; I am talking of nothing but my own affairs. [*sits on a stool near her, and rests her arms on her knees*] You mustn't be angry with me. Tell me, is it really true that you did not love your husband? Why did you marry him?

MRS. LINDE: My mother was alive then, and was bedridden and helpless, and I had to provide for my two younger brothers; so I did not think I was justified in refusing his offer.

NORA: No, perhaps you were quite right. He was rich at that time, then?

MRS. LINDE: I believe he was quite well off. But his business was a precarious one; and, when he died, it all went to pieces and there was nothing left.

NORA: And then?—

MRS. LINDE: Well, I had to turn my hand to anything I could find—first a small shop, then a small school, and so on. The last three years have seemed like one long working-day, with no rest. Now it is at an end, Nora. My poor mother needs me no more, for she is gone; and the boys do not need me either; they have got situations and can shift for themselves.

NORA: What a relief you must feel it—

MRS. LINDE: No, indeed; I only feel my life unspeakably empty. No one to live for any more. [*gets up restlessly*] That was why I could not stand the life in my little backwater any longer. I hope it may be easier here to find something which will busy me and occupy my thoughts. If only I could have the good luck to get some regular work—office work of some kind—

NORA: But, Christine, that is so frightfully tiring, and you look tired out now. You had far better go away to some watering-place.

MRS. LINDE [*walking to the window*]: I have no father to give me money for a journey, Nora.

NORA [*rising*]: Oh, don't be angry with me.

MRS. LINDE [*going up to her*]: It is you that must not be angry with me, dear. The worst of a position like mine is that it makes one so bitter. No one to work for, and yet obliged to be always on the look-out for chances. One must live, and so one becomes selfish. When you told me of the happy turn your fortunes have taken—you will hardly believe it—I was delighted not so much on your account as on my own.

NORA: How do you mean?—Oh, I understand. You mean that perhaps Torvald could get you something to do.

MRS. LINDE: Yes, that was what I was thinking of.

NORA: He must, Christine. Just leave it to me; I will broach the subject very cleverly—I will think of something that will please him very much. It will make me so happy to be of some use to you.

MRS. LINDE: How kind you are, Nora, to be so anxious to help me! It is doubly kind in you, for you know so little of the burdens and troubles of life.

NORA: I—? I know so little of them?

MRS. LINDE [*smiling*]: My dear! Small household cares and that sort of thing!—You are a child, Nora.

NORA [*tosses her head and crosses the stage*]: You ought not to be so superior.

MRS. LINDE: No?

NORA: You are just like the others. They all think that I am incapable of anything really serious—

MRS. LINDE: Come, come—

NORA: —that I have gone through nothing in this world of cares.

MRS. LINDE: But, my dear Nora, you have just told me all your troubles.

NORA: Pooh!—those were trifles. [*lowering her voice*] I have not told you the important thing.

MRS. LINDE: The important thing? What do you mean?

NORA: You look down upon me altogether, Christine—but you ought not to. You are proud, aren't you, of having worked so hard and so long for your mother?

MRS. LINDE: Indeed, I don't look down on any one. But it is true that I am both proud and glad to think that I was privileged to make the end of my mother's life almost free from care.

NORA: And you are proud to think of what you have done for your brothers.

MRS. LINDE: I think I have the right to be.

NORA: I think so, too. But now, listen to this; I too have something to be proud of and glad of.

MRS. LINDE: I have no doubt you have. But what do you refer to?

NORA: Speak low. Suppose Torvald were to hear! He mustn't on any account—no one in the world must know, Christine, except you.

MRS. LINDE: But what is it?

NORA: Come here [*pulls her down on the sofa beside her*] Now I will show you that I too have something to be proud and glad of. It was I who saved Torvald's life.

MRS. LINDE: "Saved"? How?

NORA: I told you about our trip to Italy. Torvald would never have recovered if he had not gone there—

MRS. LINDE: Yes, but your father gave you the necessary funds.

NORA [*smiling*]: Yes, that is what Torvald and all the others think, but—

MRS. LINDE: But—

NORA: Papa didn't give us a shilling. It was I who procured the money.

MRS. LINDE: You? All that large sum?

NORA: Two hundred and fifty pounds. What do you think of that?

MRS. LINDE: But, Nora, how could you possibly do it? Did you win a prize in the Lottery?

NORA [*contemptuously*]: In the Lottery? There would have been no credit in that.

MRS. LINDE: But where did you get it from, then?

NORA [*humming and smiling with an air of mystery*]: Hm, hm! Aha!

MRS. LINDE: Because you couldn't have borrowed it.

NORA: Couldn't I? Why not?

MRS. LINDE: No, a wife cannot borrow without her husband's consent.

NORA [*tossing her head*]: Oh, if it is a wife who has any head for business—a wife who has the wit to be a little bit clever—

MRS. LINDE: I don't understand it at all, Nora.

NORA: There is no need you should. I never said I had borrowed the money. I may have got it some other way. [*lies back on the sofa*] Perhaps I got it from some other admirer. When anyone is as attractive as I am—

MRS. LINDE: You are a mad creature.

NORA: Now, you know you're full of curiosity, Christine.

MRS. LINDE: Listen to me, Nora dear. Haven't you been a little bit imprudent?

NORA [*sits up straight*]: Is it imprudent to save your husband's life?

MRS. LINDE: It seems to me imprudent, without his knowledge, to—

NORA: But it was absolutely necessary that he should not know! My goodness, can't you understand that? It was necessary he should have no idea what a dangerous condition he was in. It was to me that the doctors came and said that his life was in danger, and that the only thing to save him was to live in the south. Do you suppose I didn't try, first of all, to get what I wanted as if it were for myself? I told him how much I should love to travel abroad like other young wives; I tried tears and entreaties with him; I told him that he ought to remember the condition I was in, and that he ought to be kind and indulgent to me; I even hinted that he might raise a loan. That nearly made him angry, Christine. He said I was thoughtless, and that it was his duty as my husband not to indulge me in my whims and caprices—as I believe he called them. Very well I thought, you must be saved—and that was how I came to devise a way out of the difficulty—

MRS. LINDE: And did your husband never get to know from your father that the money had not come from him?

NORA: No, never. Papa died just at that time. I had meant to let him into the secret and beg him never to reveal it. But he was so ill then—alas, there never was any need to tell him.

MRS. LINDE: And since then have you never told your secret to your husband?

NORA: Good Heavens, no! How could you think so? A man who has such strong opinions about these things! And besides, how painful and humiliating it would be for Torvald, with his manly independence, to know that he owed me anything! It would upset our mutual relations altogether; our beautiful happy home would no longer be what it is now.

MRS. LINDE: Do you mean never to tell him about it?

NORA [*meditatively, and with a half smile*]: Yes—some day, perhaps, after many years, when I am no longer as nice-looking as I am now. Don't laugh at me! I mean of course, when Torvald is no longer as devoted to me as he is now; when my dancing and dressing-up and reciting have palled on him; then it may be a good thing to have something in reserve—[*breaking off*] What nonsense! That time will never come. Now, what do you think of my great secret, Christine? Do you still think I am of no use? I can tell you, too, that this affair has caused me a lot of worry. It has been by no means easy for me to meet my engagements punctually. I may tell you that there is something that is called, in business, quarterly interest, and another thing called payment in instalments, and it is always so dreadfully difficult to manage them. I have had to save a little here and there, where I could, you understand. I have not been able to put aside much from my housekeeping money, for Torvald must have a good table. I couldn't let my children be shabbily dressed; I have felt obliged to use up all he gave me for them, the sweet little darlings!

MRS. LINDE: So it has all had to come out of your own necessaries of life, poor Nora?

NORA: Of course. Besides, I was the one responsible for it. Whenever Torvald has given me the money for new dresses and such things, I have never spent more than half of it; I have always bought the simplest and cheapest things. Thank Heaven, any clothes look well on me, and so Torvald has never noticed it. But it was often very hard on me, Christine—because it is delightful to be really well dressed, isn't it?

MRS. LINDE: Quite so.

NORA: Well, then I have found other ways of earning money. Last winter I was lucky enough to get a lot of copying to do; so I locked myself up and sat writing every evening until quite late at night. Many a time I was desperately tired; but all the same it was a tremendous pleasure to sit there working and earning money. It was like being a man.

MRS. LINDE: How much have you been able to pay off in that way?

NORA: I can't tell you exactly. You see, it is very difficult to keep an account of a business matter of that kind. I only know that I have paid every penny that I could scrape together. Many a time I was at my wit's end. [*smiles*] Then I used to sit here and imagine that a rich old gentleman had fallen in love with me—

MRS. LINDE: What! Who was it?

NORA: Be quiet!—that he had died; and that when his will was opened it contained, written in big letters, the instruction: "The lovely Mrs. Nora Helmer is to have all I possess paid over to her at once in cash."

MRS. LINDE: But, my dear Nora—who could the man be?

NORA: Good gracious, can't you understand? There was no old gentleman at all; it was only something that I used to sit here and imagine, when I couldn't think of any way of procuring money. But it's all the same now; the tiresome old person can stay where he is, as far as I am concerned; I don't care about him or his will either, for I am free from care now. [*jumps up*] My goodness, it's delightful to think of, Christine! Free from care! To be able to be free from care, quite free from care; to be able to play and romp with the children; to be able to keep the house beautifully and have everything just as Torvald likes it! And, think of it, soon the spring will come and the big blue sky! Perhaps we shall be able to take a little trip—perhaps I shall see the sea again! Oh, it's a wonderful thing to be alive and be happy. [*A bell is heard in the hall.*]

MRS. LINDE [*rising*]: There is the bell; perhaps I had better go.

NORA: No, don't go; no one will come in here; it is sure to be for Torvald.

SERVANT [*at the hall door*]: Excuse me, ma'am—there is a gentleman to see the master, and as the doctor is with him—

NORA: Who is it?

KROGSTAD [*at the door*]: It is I, Mrs. Helmer. [*Mrs. Linde starts, trembles, and turns to the window.*]

NORA [*takes a step towards him, and speaks in a strained, low voice*]: You? What is it? What do you want to see my husband about?

KROGSTAD: Bank business—in a way. I have a small post in the Bank, and I hear your husband is to be our chief now—

NORA: Then it is—

KROGSTAD: Nothing but dry business matters, Mrs. Helmer; absolutely nothing else.

NORA: Be so good as to go into the study, then. [*She bows indifferently to him and shuts the door into the hall; then comes back and makes up the fire in the stove.*]

MRS. LINDE: Nora—who was that man?

NORA: A lawyer, of the name of Krogstad.

MRS. LINDE: Then it really was he.

NORA: Do you know the man?

MRS. LINDE: I used to—many years ago. At one time he was a solicitor's clerk in our town.

NORA: Yes, he was.

MRS. LINDE: He is greatly altered.

NORA: He made a very unhappy marriage.

MRS. LINDE: He is a widower now, isn't he?

NORA: With several children. There now, it is burning up.

[*Shuts the door of the stove and moves the rocking-chair aside.*]

MRS. LINDE: They say he carries on various kinds of business.

NORA: Really! Perhaps he does; I don't know anything about it. But don't let us think of business; it is so tiresome.

DOCTOR RANK [*comes out of* HELMER'*s study. Before he shuts the door he calls to him.*]: No, my dear fellow, I won't disturb you; I would rather go in to your wife for a little while. [*shuts the door and sees* MRS. LINDE:] I beg your pardon; I am afraid I am disturbing you too.

NORA: No, not at all. [*introducing him*] Doctor Rank, Mrs. Linde.

RANK: I have often heard Mrs. Linde's name mentioned here. I think I passed you on the stairs when I arrived, Mrs. Linde?

MRS. LINDE: Yes, I go up very slowly; I can't manage stairs well.

RANK: Ah! some slight internal weakness?

MRS. LINDE: No, the fact is I have been overworking myself.

RANK: Nothing more than that? Then I suppose you have come to town to amuse yourself with our entertainments?

MRS. LINDE: I have come to look for work.

RANK: Is that a good cure for overwork?

MRS. LINDE: One must live, Doctor Rank.

RANK: Yes, the general opinion seems to be that it is necessary.

NORA: Look here, Doctor Rank—you know you want to live.

RANK: Certainly. However wretched I may feel, I want to prolong the agony as long as possible. All my patients are like that. And so are those who are morally diseased; one of them, and a bad case too, is at this very moment with Helmer—

MRS. LINDE [*sadly*]: Ah!

NORA: Whom do you mean?

RANK: A lawyer of the name of Krogstad, a fellow you don't know at all. He suffers from a diseased moral character, Mrs. Helmer; but even he began talking of its being highly important that he should live.

NORA: Did he? What did he want to speak to Torvald about?

RANK: I have no idea; I only heard that it was something about the Bank.

NORA: I didn't know this—what's his name—Krogstad had anything to do with the Bank.

RANK: Yes, he has some sort of appointment there. [*to* MRS. LINDE] I don't know whether you find also in your part of the world that there are certain people who go zealously snuffing about to smell out moral corruption, and, as soon as they have found some, put the person concerned into some lucrative position where they can keep their eye on him. Healthy natures are left out in the cold.

MRS. LINDE: Still I think the sick are those who most need taking care of.

RANK [*shrugging his shoulders*]: Yes, there you are. That is the sentiment that is turning Society into a sickhouse.

[NORA, *who has been absorbed in her thoughts, breaks out into smothered laughter and claps her hands.*]

RANK: Why do you laugh at that? Have you any notion what Society really is?

NORA: What do I care about tiresome Society? I am laughing at something quite different, something extremely amusing. Tell me, Doctor Rank, are all the people who are employed in the Bank dependent on Torvald now?

RANK: Is that what you find so extremely amusing?

NORA [*smiling and humming*]: That's my affair! [*walking about the room*] It's perfectly glorious to think that we have—that Torvald has so much power over so many people. [*takes the packet from her pocket*] Doctor Rank, what do you say to a macaroon?

RANK: What, macaroons? I thought they were forbidden here.

NORA: Yes, but these are some Christine gave me.

MRS. LINDE: What! I?—

NORA: Oh, well, don't be alarmed! You couldn't know that Torvald had forbidden them. I must tell you that he is afraid they will spoil my teeth. But, bah!—once in a way—That's so, isn't it, Doctor Rank? By your leave? [*puts a macaroon into his mouth*] You must have one too, Christine. And I shall have one, just a little one—or at most two. [*walking about*] I am tremendously happy. There is just one thing in the world now that I should dearly love to do.

RANK: Well, what is that?

NORA: It's something I should dearly love to say, if Torvald could hear me.

RANK: Well, why can't you say it?

NORA: No, I daren't; it's so shocking.

MRS. LINDE: Shocking?

RANK: Well, I should not advise you to say it. Still, with us you might. What is it you would so much like to say if Torvald could hear you?

NORA: I should just love to say—Well, I'm damned!

RANK: Are you mad?

MRS. LINDE: Nora, dear—!

RANK: Say it, here he is!

NORA [*hiding the packet*]: Hush! Hush! Hush!

[HELMER *comes out of his room, with his coat over his arm and his hat in his hands.*]

NORA: Well, Torvald dear, have you got rid of him?

HELMER: Yes, he has just gone.

NORA: Let me introduce you—this is Christine, who has come to town.

HELMER: Christine—? Excuse me, but I don't know—

NORA: Mrs. Linde, dear; Christine Linde.

HELMER: Of course. A school friend of my wife's, I presume?

MRS. LINDE: Yes, we have known each other since then.

NORA: And just think, she has taken a long journey in order to see you.

HELMER: What do you mean?

MRS. LINDE: No, really, I—

NORA: Christine is tremendously clever at book-keeping, and she is frightfully anxious to work under some clever man, so as to perfect herself—

HELMER: Very sensible, Mrs. Linde.

NORA: And when she heard you had been appointed manager of the Bank—the news was telegraphed, you know—she travelled here as quick as she could. Torvald, I am sure you will be able to do something for Christine, for my sake, won't you?

HELMER: Well, it is not altogether impossible. I presume you are a widow, Mrs. Linde?

MRS. LINDE: Yes.

HELMER: And have had some experience of book-keeping?

MRS. LINDE: Yes, a fair amount.

HELMER: Ah! well, it's very likely I may be able to find something for you—

NORA [*clapping her hands*]: What did I tell you? What did I tell you?

HELMER: You have just come at a fortunate moment, Mrs. Linde.

MRS. LINDE: How am I to thank you?

HELMER: There is no need. [*puts on his coat*] But to-day you must excuse me—

RANK: Wait a minute; I will come with you.

[*Brings his fur coat from the hall and warms it at the fire.*]

NORA: Don't be long away, Torvald dear.

HELMER: About an hour, not more.

NORA: Are you going too, Christine?

MRS. LINDE [*putting on her cloak*]: Yes, I must go and look for a room.

HELMER: Oh, well then, we can walk down the street together.

NORA [*helping her*]: What a pity it is we are so short of space here: I am afraid it is impossible for us—

MRS. LINDE: Please don't think of it! Good-bye, Nora dear, and many thanks.

NORA: Good-bye for the present. Of course you will come back this evening. And you too, Dr. Rank. What do you say? If you are well enough? Oh, you must be! Wrap yourself up well.

[*They go to the door all talking together. Children's voices are heard on the staircase.*]

NORA: There they are. There they are! [*She runs to open the door. The* NURSE *comes in with the children.*] Come in! Come in! [*stoops and kisses them*] Oh, you sweet blessings! Look at them, Christine! Aren't they darlings?

RANK: Don't let us stand here in the draught.

HELMER: Come along, Mrs. Linde; the place will only be bearable for a mother now!

[RANK, HELMER *and* MRS. LINDE *go downstairs. The* NURSE *comes forward with the children;* NORA *shuts the hall door.*]

NORA: How fresh and well you look! Such red cheeks!—like apples and roses. [*The children all talk at once while she speaks to them.*] Have you had great fun? That's splendid! What, you pulled both Emmy and Bob along on the sledge?—both at once?—that was good. You are a clever boy, Ivar. Let me take her for a little, Anne. My sweet little baby doll! [*takes the baby from the* MAID *and dances it up and down*] Yes, yes, mother will dance with Bob too. What! Have you been snowballing? I wish I had been there too! No, no, I will take their things off, Anne; please let me do it, it is such fun. Go in now, you look half frozen. There is some coffee for you on the stove.

[*The* NURSE *goes into the room on the left.* NORA *takes off the children's things and throws them about, while they all talk to her at once.*]

NORA: Really! Did a big dog run after you? But it didn't bite you? No, dogs don't bite nice little dolly children. You mustn't look at the parcels, Ivar. What are they? Ah, I daresay you would like to know. No, no—it's something nasty! Come, let us have a game! What shall we play at? Hide and Seek? Yes, we'll play Hide and Seek. Bob shall hide first. Must I hide? Very well, I'll hide first.

[*She and the children laugh and shout, and romp in and out of the room; at last* NORA *hides under the table, the children rush in and look for her, but do not see her; they hear her smothered laughter, run to the table, lift up the cloth and find her. Shouts of laughter. She crawls forward and pretends to frighten them. Fresh laughter. Meanwhile there has been a knock at the hall door, but none of them has noticed it. The door is half opened, and* KROGSTAD *appears. He waits a little; the game goes on.*]

KROGSTAD: Excuse me, Mrs. Helmer.

NORA [*with a stifled cry, turns round and gets up on to her knees*]: Ah! what do you want?

KROGSTAD: Excuse me, the outer door was ajar; I suppose someone forgot to shut it.

NORA [*rising*]: My husband is out, Mr. Krogstad.

KROGSTAD: I know that.

NORA: What do you want here, then?

KROGSTAD: A word with you.

NORA: With me?—[*to the children, gently*] Go in to nurse. What? No, the strange man won't do mother any harm. When he has gone we will have another game. [*She takes the children into the room on the left, and shuts the door after them.*] You want to speak to me?

KROGSTAD: Yes, I do.

NORA: To-day? It is not the first of the month yet.

KROGSTAD: No, it is Christmas Eve, and it will depend on yourself what sort of a Christmas you will spend.

NORA: What do you want? To-day it is absolutely impossible for me—

KROGSTAD: We won't talk about that till later on. This is something different. I presume you can give me a moment?

NORA: Yes—yes, I can—although—

KROGSTAD: Good. I was in Olsen's Restaurant and saw your husband going down the street—

NORA: Yes?

KROGSTAD: With a lady.

NORA: What then?

KROGSTAD: May I make so bold as to ask if it was a Mrs. Linde?

NORA: It was.

KROGSTAD: Just arrived in town?

NORA: Yes, to-day.

KROGSTAD: She is a great friend of yours, isn't she?

NORA: She is. But I don't see—

KROGSTAD: I knew her too, once upon a time.

NORA: I am aware of that.

KROGSTAD: Are you? So you know all about it; I thought as much. Then I can ask you, without beating about the bush—is Mrs. Linde to have an appointment in the Bank?

NORA: What right have you to question me, Mr. Krogstad?—You, one of my husband's subordinates! But since you ask, you shall know. Yes, Mrs. Linde *is* to have an appointment. And it was I who pleaded her cause, Mr. Krogstad, let me tell you that.

KROGSTAD: I was right in what I thought, then.

NORA [*walking up and down the stage*]: Sometimes one has a tiny little bit of influence, I should hope. Because one is a woman, it does not necessarily follow that—. When anyone is in a subordinate position, Mr. Krogstad, they should really be careful to avoid offending anyone who—who—

KROGSTAD: Who has influence?

NORA: Exactly.

KROGSTAD [*changing his tone*]: Mrs. Helmer, you will be so good as to use your influence on my behalf.

NORA: What? What do you mean?

KROGSTAD: You will be so kind as to see that I am allowed to keep my subordinate position in the Bank.

NORA: What do you mean by that? Who proposes to take your post away from you?

KROGSTAD: Oh, there is no necessity to keep up the pretence of ignorance. I can quite understand that your friend is not very anxious to expose herself to the chance of rubbing shoulders with me; and I quite understand, too, whom I have to thank for being turned out.

NORA: But I assure you—

KROGSTAD: Very likely; but, to come to the point, the time has come when I should advise you to use your influence to prevent that.

NORA: But, Mr. Krogstad, I *have* no influence.

KROGSTAD: Haven't you? I thought you said yourself just now—

NORA: Naturally I did not mean you to put that construction on it. I! What should make you think I have any influence of that kind with my husband?

KROGSTAD: Oh, I have known your husband from our student days. I don't suppose he is any more unassailable than other husbands.

NORA: If you speak slightingly of my husband, I shall turn you out of the house.

KROGSTAD: You are bold, Mrs. Helmer.

NORA: I am not afraid of you any longer. As soon as the New Year comes, I shall in a very short time be free of the whole thing.

KROGSTAD [*controlling himself*]: Listen to me, Mrs. Helmer. If necessary, I am prepared to fight for my small post in the Bank as if I were fighting for my life.

NORA: So it seems.

KROGSTAD: It is not only for the sake of the money; indeed, that weighs least with me in the matter. There is another reason—well, I may as well tell you. My position is this. I daresay you know, like everybody else, that once, many years ago, I was guilty of an indiscretion.

NORA: I think I have heard something of the kind.

KROGSTAD: The matter never came into court; but every way seemed to be closed to me after that. So I took to the business that you know of. I had to do something; and, honestly, I don't think I've been one of the worst. But now I must cut myself free from all that. My sons are growing up; for their sake I must try and win back as much respect as I can in the town. This post in the Bank was like the first step up for me—and now your husband is going to kick me downstairs again into the mud.

NORA: But you must believe me, Mr. Krogstad; it is not in my power to help you at all.

KROGSTAD: Then it is because you haven't the will; but I have means to compel you.

NORA: You don't mean that you will tell my husband that I owe you money?

KROGSTAD: Hm!—suppose I were to tell him?

NORA: It would be perfectly infamous of you. [*sobbing*] To think of his learning my secret, which has been my joy and pride, in such an ugly, clumsy way—that he should learn it from you! And it would put me in a horribly disagreeable position—

KROGSTAD: Only disagreeable?

NORA [*impetuously*]: Well, do it, then!—and it will be the worse for you. My husband will see for himself what a blackguard you are, and you certainly won't keep your post then.

KROGSTAD: I asked you if it was only a disagreeable scene at home that you were afraid of?

NORA: If my husband does get to know of it, of course he will at once pay you what is still owing, and we shall have nothing more to do with you.

KROGSTAD [*coming a step nearer*]: Listen to me, Mrs. Helmer. Either you have a very bad memory or you know very little of business. I shall be obliged to remind you of a few details.

NORA: What do you mean?

KROGSTAD: When your husband was ill, you came to me to borrow two hundred and fifty pounds.

NORA: I didn't know any one else to go to.

KROGSTAD: I promised to get you that amount—

NORA: Yes, and you did so.

KROGSTAD: I promised to get you that amount, on certain conditions. Your mind was so taken up with your husband's illness, and you were so anxious to get the money for your journey, that you seem to have paid no attention to the conditions of our bargain. Therefore it will not be amiss if I remind you of them. Now, I promised to get the money on the security of a bond which I drew up.

NORA: Yes, and which I signed.

KROGSTAD: Good. But below your signature there were a few lines constituting your father a surety for the money; those lines your father should have signed.

NORA: Should? He did sign them.

KROGSTAD: I had left the date blank; that is to say your father should himself have inserted the date on which he signed the paper. Do you remember that?

NORA: Yes, I think I remember—

KROGSTAD: Then I gave you the bond to send by post to your father. Is that not so?

NORA: Yes.

KROGSTAD: And you naturally did so at once, because five or six days afterwards you brought me the bond with your father's signature. And then I gave you the money.

NORA: Well, haven't I been paying it off regularly?

KROGSTAD: Fairly so, yes. But—to come back to the matter in hand—that must have been a very trying time for you, Mrs. Helmer?

NORA: It was, indeed.

KROGSTAD: Your father was very ill, wasn't he?

NORA: He was very near his end.

KROGSTAD: And died soon afterwards?

NORA: Yes.

KROGSTAD: Tell me, Mrs. Helmer, can you by any chance remember what day your father died?—on what day of the month, I mean.

NORA: Papa died on the 29th of September.

KROGSTAD: That is correct; I have ascertained it for myself. And, as that is so, there is a discrepancy [*taking a paper from his pocket*] which I cannot account for.

NORA: What discrepancy? I don't know—

KROGSTAD: The discrepancy consists, Mrs. Helmer, in the fact that your father signed this bond three days after his death.

NORA: What do you mean? I don't understand—

KROGSTAD: Your father died on the 29th of September. But, look here; your father has dated his signature the 2nd of October. It is a discrepancy, isn't it? [NORA *is silent*.] Can you explain it to me? [NORA *is still silent*.] It is a remarkable thing, too, that the words "2nd of October," as well as the year, are not written in your father's handwriting but in one that I think I know. Well, of course it can be explained; your father may have forgotten to date his signature, and someone else may have dated it haphazard before they knew of his death. There is no harm in that. It all depends on the signature of the name; and *that* is genuine, I suppose, Mrs. Helmer? It was your father himself who signed his name here?

NORA [*after a short pause, throws her head up and looks defiantly at him*]: No, it was not. It was I that wrote papa's name.

KROGSTAD: Are you aware that is a dangerous confession?

NORA: In what way? You shall have your money soon.

KROGSTAD: Let me ask you a question; why did you not send the paper to your father?

NORA: It was impossible; papa was so ill. If I had asked him for his signature, I should have had to tell him what the money was to be used for; and when he was so ill himself I couldn't tell him that my husband's life was in danger—it was impossible.

KROGSTAD: It would have been better for you if you had given up your trip abroad.

NORA: No, that was impossible. That trip was to save my husband's life; I couldn't give that up.

KROGSTAD: But did it never occur to you that you were committing a fraud on me?

NORA: I couldn't take that into account; I didn't trouble myself about you at all. I couldn't bear you, because you put so many heartless difficulties in my way, although you knew what a dangerous condition my husband was in.

KROGSTAD: Mrs. Helmer, you evidently do not realise clearly what it is that you have been guilty of. But I can assure you that my one false step, which lost me all my reputation, was nothing more or nothing worse than what you have done.

NORA: You? Do you ask me to believe that you were brave enough to run a risk to save your wife's life?

KROGSTAD: The law cares nothing about motives.

NORA: Then it must be a very foolish law.

KROGSTAD: Foolish or not, it is the law by which you will be judged, if I produce this paper in court.

NORA: I don't believe it. Is a daughter not to be allowed to spare her dying father anxiety and care? Is a wife not to be allowed to save her husband's life? I don't know much about law; but I am certain that there must be laws permitting such things as that. Have you no knowledge of such laws—you who are a lawyer? You must be a very poor lawyer, Mr. Krogstad.

KROGSTAD: Maybe. But matters of business—such business as you and I have had together—do you think I don't understand that? Very well. Do as you please. But let me tell you this—if I lose my position a second time, you shall lose yours with me.

[*He bows, and goes out through the hall.*]

NORA [*appears buried in thought for a short time, then tosses her head*]: Nonsense! Trying to frighten me like that!—I am not so silly as he thinks. [*begins to busy herself putting the children's things in order*] And yet—? No, it's impossible! I did it for love's sake.

THE CHILDREN [*in the doorway on the left*]: Mother, the stranger man has gone out through the gate.

NORA: Yes, dears, I know. But, don't tell anyone about the stranger man. Do you hear? Not even papa.

CHILDREN: No, mother; but will you come and play again?

NORA: No, no—not now.

CHILDREN: But, mother, you promised us.

NORA: Yes, but I can't now. Run away in; I have such a lot to do. Run away in, my sweet little darlings. [*She gets them into the room by degrees and shuts the door on them; then sits down on the sofa, takes up a piece of needlework and sews a few stitches, but soon stops.*] No! [*throws down the work, gets up, goes to the hall door and calls out*] Helen! bring the Tree in. [*goes to the table on the left, opens a drawer, and stops again*] No, no! it is quite impossible!

MAID [*coming in with the Tree*]: Where shall I put it, ma'am?

NORA: Here, in the middle of the floor.

MAID: Shall I get you anything else?

NORA: No, thank you. I have all I want.

[*Exit* MAID.]

NORA [*begins dressing the tree*]: A candle here—and flowers here—. The horrible man! It's all nonsense—there's nothing wrong. The Tree shall be splendid! I will do everything I can think of to please you, Torvald!—I will sing for you, dance for you— [HELMER *comes in with some papers under his arm*] Oh! are you back already?

HELMER: Yes. Has anyone been here?

NORA: Here? No.

HELMER: That is strange. I saw Krogstad going out of the gate.

NORA: Did you? Oh yes, I forgot, Krogstad was here for a moment.

HELMER: Nora, I can see from your manner that he has been here begging you to say a good word for him.

NORA: Yes.

HELMER: And you were to appear to do it of your own accord; you were to conceal from me the fact of his having been here; didn't he beg that of you too?

NORA: Yes, Torvald, but—

HELMER: Nora, Nora, and you would be a party to that sort of thing? To have any talk with a man like that, and give him any sort of promise? And to tell me a lie into the bargain?

NORA: A lie—?

HELMER: Didn't you tell me no one had been here? [*shakes his finger at her*] My little song-bird must never do that again. A song-bird must have a clean beak to chirp with—no false notes! [*puts his arm round her waist*] That is so, isn't it? Yes, I am sure it is. [*lets her go*] We will say no more about it. [*sits down by the stove*] How warm and snug it is here!

[*Turns over his papers.*]

NORA [*after a short pause, during which she busies herself with the Christmas Tree*]: Torvald!

HELMER: Yes.

NORA: I am looking forward tremendously to the fancy dress ball at the Stenborgs' the day after to-morrow.

HELMER: And I am tremendously curious to see what you are going to surprise me with.

NORA: It was very silly of me to want to do that.

HELMER: What do you mean?

NORA: I can't hit upon anything that will do; everything I think of seems so silly and insignificant.

HELMER: Does my little Nora acknowledge that at last?

NORA [*standing behind his chair with her arms on the back of it*]: Are you very busy, Torvald?

HELMER: Well—

NORA: What are all those papers?

HELMER: Bank business.

NORA: Already?

HELMER: I have got authority from the retiring manager to undertake the necessary changes in the staff and in the rearrangement of the work; and I must make use of the Christmas week for that, so as to have everything in order for the new year.

NORA: Then that was why this poor Krogstad—

HELMER: Hm!

NORA [*leans against the back of his chair and strokes his hair*]: If you hadn't been so busy I should have asked you a tremendously big favour, Torvald.

HELMER: What is that? Tell me.

NORA: There is no one has such good taste as you. And I do so want to look nice at the fancy-dress ball. Torvald, couldn't you take me in hand and decide what I shall go as, and what sort of a dress I shall wear?

HELMER: Aha! so my obstinate little woman is obliged to get someone to come to her rescue?

NORA: Yes, Torvald, I can't get along a bit without your help.

HELMER: Very well, I will think it over, we shall manage to hit upon something.

NORA: That is nice of you. [*Goes to the Christmas Tree. A short pause.*] How pretty the red flowers look—. But, tell me, was it really something very bad that this Krogstad was guilty of?

HELMER: He forged someone's name. Have you any idea what that means?

NORA: Isn't it possible that he was driven to do it by necessity?

HELMER: Yes; or, as in so many cases, by imprudence. I am not so heartless as to condemn a man altogether because of a single false step of that kind.

NORA: No you wouldn't, would you, Torvald?

HELMER: Many a man has been able to retrieve his character, if he has openly confessed his fault and taken his punishment.

NORA: Punishment—?

HELMER: But Krogstad did nothing of that sort; he got himself out of it by a cunning trick, and that is why he has gone under altogether.

NORA: But do you think it would—?

HELMER: Just think how a guilty man like that has to lie and play the hypocrite with everyone, how he has to wear a mask in the presence of those near and dear to him, even before his own wife and children. And about the children—that is the most terrible part of it all, Nora.

NORA: How?

HELMER: Because such an atmosphere of lies infects and poisons the whole life of a home. Each breath the children take in such a house is full of the germs of evil.

NORA [*coming nearer him*]: Are you sure of that?

HELMER: My dear, I have often seen it in the course of my life as a lawyer. Almost everyone who has gone to the bad early in life has had a deceitful mother.

NORA: Why do you only say—mother?

HELMER: It seems most commonly to be the mother's influence, though naturally a bad father's would have the same result. Every lawyer is familiar with the fact. This Krogstad, now, has been persistently poisoning his own children with lies and dissimulation; that is why I say he has lost all moral character. [*holds out his hands to her*] That is why my sweet little Nora must promise me not to plead his cause. Give me your hand on it. Come, come, what is this? Give me your hand. There now, that's settled. I assure you it would be quite impossible for me to work with him; I literally feel physically ill when I am in the company of such people.

NORA [*takes her hand out of his and goes to the opposite side of the Christmas Tree*]: How hot it is in here; and I have such a lot to do.

HELMER [*getting up and putting his papers in order*]: Yes, and I must try and read through some of these before dinner; and I must think about your costume, too. And it is just possible I may have something ready in gold paper to hang up on the Tree. [*Puts his hand on her head.*] My precious little singing-bird!

[*He goes into his room and shuts the door after him.*]

NORA [*after a pause, whispers*]: No, no—it isn't true. It's impossible; it must be impossible.

[*The* NURSE *opens the door on the left.*]

NURSE: The little ones are begging so hard to be allowed to come in to mamma.

NORA: No, no, no! Don't let them come in to me! You stay with them, Anne.

NURSE: Very well, ma'am.

[*Shuts the door.*]

NORA [*pale with terror*]: Deprave my little children? Poison my home? [*a short pause. Then she tosses her head.*] It's not true. It can't possibly be true.

Act 2

THE SAME SCENE. *The Christmas Tree is in the corner by the piano, stripped of its ornaments and with burnt-down candle-ends on its dishevelled branches.* NORA'*s cloak and hat are lying on the sofa. She is alone in the room, walking about uneasily. She stops by the sofa and takes up her cloak.*

NORA [*drops the cloak*]: Someone is coming now! [*goes to the door and listens*] No—it is no one. Of course, no one will come to-day, Christmas Day—nor tomorrow either. But, perhaps—[*opens the door and looks out*] No, nothing in the letter-box; it is quite empty. [*comes forward*] What rubbish! of course he can't be in earnest about it. Such a thing couldn't happen; it is impossible—I have three little children.

[*Enter the* NURSE *from the room on the left, carrying a big cardboard box.*]

NURSE: At last I have found the box with the fancy dress.

NORA: Thanks; put it on the table.

NURSE [*doing so*]: But it is very much in want of mending.

NORA: I should like to tear it into a hundred thousand pieces.

NURSE: What an idea! It can easily be put in order—just a little patience.

NORA: Yes, I will go and get Mrs. Linde to come and help me with it.

NURSE: What, out again? In this horrible weather? You will catch cold, ma'am, and make yourself ill.

NORA: Well, worse than that might happen. How are the children?

NURSE: The poor little souls are playing with their Christmas presents, but—

NORA: Do they ask much for me?

NURSE: You see, they are so accustomed to have their mamma with them.

NORA: Yes, but, nurse, I shall not be able to be so much with them now as I was before.

NURSE: Oh well, young children easily get accustomed to anything.

NORA: Do you think so? Do you think they would forget their mother if she went away altogether?

NURSE: Good heavens!—went away altogether?

NORA: Nurse, I want you to tell me something I have often wondered about—how could you have the heart to put your own child out among strangers?

NURSE: I was obliged to, if I wanted to be little Nora's nurse.

NORA: Yes, but how could you be willing to do it?

NURSE: What, when I was going to get such a good place by it? A poor girl who has got into trouble should be glad to. Besides, that wicked man didn't do a single thing for me.

NORA: But I suppose your daughter has quite forgotten you.

NURSE: No, indeed she hasn't. She wrote to me when she was confirmed, and when she was married.

NORA [*putting her arms round her neck*]: Dear old Anne, you were a good mother to me when I was little.

NURSE: Little Nora, poor dear, had no other mother but me.

NORA: And if my little ones had no other mother, I am sure you would—What nonsense I am talking! [*opens the box*] Go in to them. Now I must—. You will see tomorrow how charming I shall look.

NURSE: I am sure there will be no one at the ball so charming as you, ma'am.

[*Goes into the room on the left.*]

NORA [*begins to unpack the box, but soon pushes it away from her*]: If only I dared go out. If only no one would come. If only I could be sure nothing would happen here in the meantime. Stuff and nonsense! No one will come. Only I mustn't think about it. I will brush my muff. What, lovely gloves! Out of my thoughts, out of my thoughts! One, two, three, four, five, six—[*Screams.*] Ah! there is someone coming—

[*Makes a movement towards the door, but stands irresolute.*]

[*Enter* MRS. LINDE *from the hall, where she has taken off her cloak and hat.*]

NORA: Oh, it's you, Christine. There is no one else out there, is there? How good of you to come!

MRS. LINDE: I heard you were up asking for me.

NORA: Yes, I was passing by. As a matter of fact, it is something you could help me with. Let us sit down here on the sofa. Look here. To-morrow evening there is to be a fancy-dress ball at the Stenborgs', who live about us; and Torvald wants me to go as a Neapolitan fisher-girl, and dance the Tarantella that I learnt at Capri.

MRS. LINDE: I see; you are going to keep up the character.

NORA: Yes, Torvald wants me to. Look, here is the dress; Torvald had it made for me there, but now it is all so torn, and I haven't any idea—

MRS. LINDE: We will easily put that right. It is only some of the trimming come unsewn here and there. Needle and thread? Now then, that's all we want.

NORA: It *is* nice of you.

MRS. LINDE [*sewing*]: So you are going to be dressed up to-morrow, Nora. I will tell you what—I shall come in for a moment and see you in your fine feathers. But I have completely forgotten to thank you for a delightful evening yesterday.

NORA [*gets up, and crosses the stages*]: Well I don't think yesterday was as pleasant as usual. You ought to have come to town a little earlier, Christine. Certainly Torvald does understand how to make a house dainty and attractive.

MRS. LINDE: And so do you, it seems to me; you are not your father's daughter for nothing. But tell me, is Doctor Rank always as depressed as he was yesterday?

NORA: No; yesterday it was very noticeable. I must tell you that he suffers from a very dangerous disease. He has consumption of the spine, poor creature. His father was a horrible man who committed all sorts of excesses; and that is why his son was sickly from childhood, do you understand?

MRS. LINDE [*dropping her sewing*]: But, my dearest Nora, how do you know anything about such things?

NORA [*walking about*]: Pooh! When you have three children, you get visits now and then from—from married women, who know something of medical matters, and they talk about one thing and another.

MRS. LINDE [*goes on sewing. A short silence*]: Does Doctor Rank come here every day?

NORA: Every day regularly. He is Torvald's most intimate friend, and a great friend of mine too. He is just like one of the family.

MRS. LINDE: But tell me this—is he perfectly sincere? I mean, isn't he the kind of man that is very anxious to make himself agreeable?

NORA: Not in the least. What makes you think that?

MRS. LINDE: When you introduced him to me yesterday, he declared he had often heard my name mentioned in this house; but afterwards I noticed that your husband hadn't the slightest idea who I was. So how could Doctor Rank—?

NORA: That is quite right, Christine. Torvald is so absurdly fond of me that he wants me absolutely to himself, as he says. At first he used to seem almost jealous if I mentioned any of the dear folk at home, so naturally I gave up doing so. But I often talk about such things with Doctor Rank, because he likes hearing about them.

MRS. LINDE: Listen to me, Nora. You are still very like a child in many things, and I am older than you in many ways and have a little more experience. Let me tell you this—you ought to make an end of it with Doctor Rank.

NORA: What ought I to make an end of?

MRS. LINDE: Of two things, I think. Yesterday you talked some nonsense about a rich admirer who was to leave you money—

NORA: An admirer who doesn't exist, unfortunately! But what then?

MRS. LINDE: Is Doctor Rank a man of means?

NORA: Yes, he is.

MRS. LINDE: And has no one to provide for?

NORA: No, no one; but—

MRS. LINDE: And comes here every day?

NORA: Yes, I told you so.

MRS. LINDE: But how can this well-bred man be so tactless?

NORA: I don't understand you at all.

MRS. LINDE: Don't prevaricate, Nora. Do you suppose I don't guess who lent you the two hundred and fifty pounds?

NORA: Are you out of your senses? How can you think of such a thing! A friend of ours, who comes here every day! Do you realise what a horribly painful position that would be?

MRS. LINDE: Then it really isn't he?

NORA: No, certainly not. It would never have entered into my head for a moment. Besides, he had no money to lend then; he came into his money afterwards.

MRS. LINDE: Well, I think that was lucky for you, my dear Nora.

NORA: No, it would never have come into my head to ask Doctor Rank. Although I am quite sure that if I had asked him—

MRS. LINDE: But of course you won't.

NORA: Of course not. I have no reason to think it could possibly be necessary. But I am quite sure that if I told Doctor Rank—

MRS. LINDE: Behind your husband's back?

NORA: I *must* make an end of it with the other one, and that will be behind his back too. I *must* make an end of it with him.

MRS. LINDE: Yes, that is what I told you yesterday, but—

NORA [*walking up and down*]: A man can put a thing like that straight much easier than a woman—

MRS. LINDE: One's husband, yes.

NORA: Nonsense! [*standing still*] When you pay off a debt you get your bond back, don't you?

MRS. LINDE: Yes, as a matter of course.

NORA: And can tear it into a hundred thousand pieces, and burn it up—the nasty dirty paper!

MRS. LINDE [*looks hard at her, lays down her sewing and gets up slowly*]: Nora, you are concealing something from me.

NORA: Do I look as if I were?

MRS. LINDE: Something has happened to you since yesterday morning. Nora, what is it?

NORA [*going nearer to her*]: Christine! [*listens*] Hush! there's Torvald come home. Do you mind going in to the children for the present? Torvald can't bear to see dressmaking going on. Let Anne help you.

MRS. LINDE [*gathering some of the things together*]: Certainly—but I am not going away from here till we have had it out with one another.

[*She goes into the room on the left, as* HELMER *comes in from the hall.*]

NORA [*going up to* HELMER]: I have wanted you so much, Torvald dear.

HELMER: Was that the dressmaker?

NORA: No, it was Christine; she is helping me to put my dress in order. You will see I shall look quite smart.

HELMER: Wasn't that a happy thought of mine, now?

NORA: Splendid! But don't you think it is nice of me, too, to do as you wish?

HELMER: Nice?—because you do as your husband wishes? Well, well, you little rogue, I am sure you did not mean it in that way. But I am not going to disturb you; you will want to be trying on your dress, I expect.

NORA: I suppose you are going to work.

HELMER: Yes. [*shows her a bundle of papers*] Look at that. I have just been into the bank. [*Turns to go into his room.*]

NORA: Torvald.

HELMER: Yes.

NORA: If your little squirrel were to ask you for something very, very prettily—?

HELMER: What then?

NORA: Would you do it?

HELMER: I should like to hear what it is, first.

NORA: Your squirrel would run about and do all her tricks if you would be nice, and do what she wants.

HELMER: Speak plainly.

NORA: Your skylark would chirp about in every room, with her song rising and falling—

HELMER: Well, my skylark does that anyhow.

NORA: I would play the fairy and dance for you in the moonlight, Torvald.

HELMER: Nora—you surely don't mean that request you made of me this morning?

NORA [*going near him*]: Yes, Torvald, I beg you so earnestly—

HELMER: Have you really the courage to open up that question again?

NORA: Yes, dear, you *must* do as I ask; you *must* let Krogstad keep his post in the Bank.

HELMER: My dear Nora, it is his post that I have arranged Mrs. Linde shall have.

NORA: Yes, you have been awfully kind about that; but you could just as well dismiss some other clerk instead of Krogstad.

HELMER: This is simply incredible obstinacy! Because you chose to give him a thoughtless promise that you would speak for him, I am expected to—

NORA: That isn't the reason, Torvald. It is for your own sake. This fellow writes in the most scurrilous newspapers; you have told me so yourself. He can do you an unspeakable amount of harm. I am frightened to death of him—

HELMER: Ah, I understand; it is recollections of the past that scare you.

NORA: What do you mean?

HELMER: Naturally you are thinking of your father.

NORA: Yes—yes, of course. Just recall to your mind what these malicious creatures wrote in the papers about papa, and how horribly they slandered him. I believe they would have procured his dismissal if the Department had not sent you over to inquire into it, and if you had not been so kindly disposed and helpful to him.

HELMER: My little Nora, there is an important difference between your father and me. Your father's reputation as a public official was not above suspicion. Mine is, and I hope it will continue to be so, as long as I hold my office.

NORA: You never can tell what mischief these men may contrive. We ought to be so well off, so snug and happy here in our peaceful home, and have no cares—you and I and the children, Torvald! That is why I beg you so earnestly—

HELMER: And it is just by interceding for him that you make it impossible for me to keep him. It is already known at the Bank that I mean to dismiss Krogstad. Is it to get about now that the new manager has changed his mind at his wife's bidding—

NORA: And what if it did?

HELMER: Of course!—if only this obstinate little person can get her way! Do you suppose I am going to make myself ridiculous before my whole staff, to let people think that I am a man to be swayed by all sorts of outside influence? I should very soon feel the consequences of it, I can tell you! And besides, there is one thing that makes it quite impossible for me to have Krogstad in the Bank as long as I am manager.

NORA: Whatever is that?

HELMER: His moral failings I might perhaps have overlooked, if necessary—

NORA: Yes, you could—couldn't you?

HELMER: And I hear he is a good worker, too. But I knew him when we were boys. It was one of those rash friendships that so often prove an incubus in after life. I may as well tell you plainly, we were once on very intimate terms with one another. But this tactless fellow lays no restraint on himself when other people are present. On the contrary, he thinks it gives him the right to adopt a familiar tone with me, and every minute it is "I say, Helmer, old fellow!" and that sort of thing. I assure you it is extremely painful for me. He would make my position in the Bank intolerable.

NORA: Torvald, I don't believe you mean that.

HELMER: Don't you? Why not?

NORA: Because it is such a narrow-minded way of looking at things.

HELMER: What are you saying? Narrow-minded? Do you think I am narrow-minded?

NORA: No, just the opposite, dear—and it is exactly for that reason.

HELMER: It's the same thing. You say my point of view is narrow-minded, so I must be so too. Narrow-minded! Very well—I must put an end to this. [*Goes to the hall-door and calls.*] Helen!

NORA: What are you going to do?

HELMER [*looking among his papers*]: Settle it. [*Enter* MAID.] Look here; take this letter and go downstairs with it at once. Find a messenger and tell him to deliver it, and be quick. The address is on it, and here is the money.

MAID: Very well, sir.

[*Exits with the letter.*]

HELMER [*putting his papers together*]: Now then, little Miss Obstinate.

NORA [*breathlessly*]: Torvald—what was that letter?

HELMER: Krogstad's dismissal.

NORA: Call her back, Torvald! There is still time. Oh Torvald, call her back! Do it for my sake—for your own sake—for the children's sake! Do you hear me, Torvald? Call her back!! You don't know what that letter can bring upon us.

HELMER: It's too late.

NORA: Yes, it's too late.

HELMER: My dear Nora, I can forgive the anxiety you are in, although really it is an insult to me. It is, indeed. Isn't it an insult to think that I should be afraid of a starving quill-driver's vengeance? But I forgive you nevertheless, because it is such eloquent witness to your great love for me. [*takes her in his arms*] And that is as it should be, my own darling Nora. Come what will, you may be sure I shall have both courage and strength if they be needed. You will see I am man enough to take everything upon myself.

NORA [*in a horror-stricken voice*]: What do you mean by that?

HELMER: Everything, I say—

NORA [*recovering herself*]: You will never have to do that.

HELMER: That's right. Well, we will share it, Nora, as man and wife should. That is how it shall be. [*caressing her*] Are you content now? There! there!—not these frightened dove's eyes! The whole thing is only the wildest fancy!—Now, you must go and play through the Tarantella and practise with your tambourine. I shall go into the inner office and shut the door, and I shall hear nothing; you can make as much noise as you please. [*turns back at the door*] And when Rank comes, tell him where he will find me.

[*Nods to her, takes his papers and goes into his room, and shuts the door after him*]

NORA [*bewildered with anxiety, stands as if rooted to the spot, and whispers*]: He is capable of doing it. He will do it. He will do it in spite of everything.—No, not that! Never, never! Anything rather than that! Oh, for some help, some way out of it! [*The door-bell rings.*] Doctor Rank! Anything rather than that—anything, whatever it is!

[*She puts her hands over her face, pulls herself together, goes to the door and opens it.* RANK *is standing without, hanging up his coat. During the following dialogue it begins to grow dark.*]

NORA: Good-day, Doctor Rank. I knew your ring. But you mustn't go in to Torvald now; I think he is busy with something.

RANK: And you?

NORA [*brings him in and shuts the door after him*]: Oh, you know very well I always have time for you.

RANK: Thank you. I shall make use of as much of it as I can.

NORA: What do you mean by that? As much of it as you can?

RANK: Well, does that alarm you?

NORA: It was such a strange way of putting it. Is anything likely to happen?

RANK: Nothing but what I have long been prepared for. But I certainly didn't expect it to happen so soon.

NORA [*gripping him by the arm*]: What have you found out? Doctor Rank, you must tell me.

RANK [*sitting down by the stove*]: It is all up with me. And it can't be helped.

NORA [*with a sigh of relief*]: Is it about yourself?

RANK: Who else? It is no use lying to one's self. I am the most wretched of all my patients, Mrs. Helmer. Lately I have been taking stock of my internal economy. Bankrupt! Probably within a month I shall lie rotting in the churchyard.

NORA: What an ugly thing to say!

RANK: The thing itself is cursedly ugly, and the worst of it is that I shall have to face so much more that is ugly before that. I shall only make one more examination of myself; when I have done that, I shall know pretty certainly when it will be that the horrors of dissolution will begin. There is something I want to tell you. Helmer's refined nature gives him an unconquerable disgust at everything that is ugly; I won't have him in my sick-room.

NORA: Oh, but, Doctor Rank—

RANK: I won't have him there. Not on any account. I bar my door to him. As soon as I am quite certain that the worst has come, I shall send you my card with a black cross on it, and then you will know that the loathsome end has begun.

NORA: You are quite absurd to-day. And I wanted you so much to be in a really good humour.

RANK: With death stalking beside me?—To have to pay this penalty for another man's sin! Is there any justice in that? And in every single family, in one way or another, some such inexorable retribution is being exacted—

NORA [*putting her hands over her ears*]: Rubbish! Do talk of something cheerful.

RANK: Oh, it's a mere laughing matter, the whole thing. My poor innocent spine has to suffer for my father's youthful amusements.

NORA [*sitting at the table on the left*]: I suppose you mean that he was too partial to asparagus and pâté de foie gras, don't you.

RANK: Yes, and to truffles.

NORA: Truffles, yes. And oysters too, I suppose?

RANK: Oysters, of course, that goes without saying.

NORA: And heaps of port and champagne. It is sad that all these nice things should take their revenge on our bones.

RANK: Especially that they should revenge themselves on the unlucky bones of those who have not had the satisfaction of enjoying them.

NORA: Yes, that's the saddest part of it all.

RANK [*with a searching look at her*]: Hm!—

NORA [*after a short pause*]: Why did you smile?

RANK: No, it was you that laughed.

NORA: No, it was you that smiled, Doctor Rank!

RANK [*rising*]: You are a greater rascal than I thought.

NORA: I am in a silly mood to-day.

RANK: So it seems.

NORA [*putting her hands on his shoulders*]: Dear, dear Doctor Rank, death mustn't take you away from Torvald and me.

RANK: It is a loss you would easily recover from. Those who are gone are soon forgotten.

NORA [*looking at him anxiously*]: Do you believe that?

RANK: People form new ties, and then—

NORA: Who will form new ties?

RANK: Both you and Helmer, when I am gone. You yourself are already on the high road to it, I think. What did that Mrs. Linde want here last night?

NORA: Oho!—you don't mean to say you are jealous of poor Christine?

RANK: Yes, I am. She will be my successor in this house. When I am done for, this woman will—

NORA: Hush! don't speak so loud. She is in that room.

RANK: To-day again. There, you see.

NORA: She has only come to sew my dress for me. Bless my soul, how unreasonable you are! [*sits down on the sofa*] Be nice now, Doctor Rank, and tomorrow you will see how beautifully I shall dance, and you can imagine I am doing it all for you—and for Torvald too, of course. [*takes various things out of the box*] Doctor Rank, come and sit down here, and I will show you something.

RANK [*sitting down*]: What is it?

NORA: Just look at those!

RANK: Silk stockings.

NORA: Flesh-coloured. Aren't they lovely? It is so dark here now, but to-morrow—. No, no, no! you must only look at the feet. Oh well, you may have leave to look at the legs too.

RANK: Hm!—

NORA: Why are you looking so critical? Don't you think they will fit me?

RANK: I have no means of forming an opinion about that.

NORA [*looks at him for a moment*]: For shame! [*hits him lightly on the ear with the stockings*] That's to punish you. [*folds them up again*]

RANK: And what other nice things am I to be allowed to see?

NORA: Not a single thing more, for being so naughty. [*She looks among the things, humming to herself*.]

RANK [*after a short silence*]: When I am sitting here, talking to you as intimately as this, I cannot imagine for a moment what would have become of me if I had never come into this house.

NORA [*smiling*]: I believe you do feel thoroughly at home with us.

RANK [*in a lower voice, looking straight in front of him*]: And to be obliged to leave it all—

NORA: Nonsense, you are not going to leave it.

RANK [*as before*]: And not be able to leave behind one the slightest token of one's gratitude, scarcely even a fleeting regret—nothing but an empty place which the first comer can fill as well as any other.

NORA: And if I asked you now for a—? No!

RANK: For what?

NORA: For a big proof of your friendship—

RANK: Yes, yes!

NORA: I mean a tremendously big favour—

RANK: Would you really make me so happy for once?

NORA: Ah, but you don't know what it is yet.

RANK: No—but tell me.

NORA: I really can't, Doctor Rank. It is something out of all reason; it means advice, and help, and a favour—

RANK: The bigger a thing it is the better. I can't conceive what it is you mean. Do tell me. Haven't I your confidence?

NORA: More than anyone else. I know you are my truest and best friend, and so I will tell you what it is. Well, Doctor Rank, it is something you must help me to prevent. You know how devotedly, how inexpressibly deeply Torvald loves me; he would never for a moment hesitate to give his life for me.

RANK [*leaning towards her*]: Nora—do you think he is the only one—?

NORA [*with a slight start*]: The only one—?

RANK: The only one who would gladly give his life for your sake.

NORA [*sadly*]: Is that it?

RANK: I was determined you should know it before I went away, and there will never be a better opportunity than this. Now you know it, Nora. And now you know, too, that you can trust me as you would trust no one else.

NORA [*rises, deliberately and quietly*]: Let me pass.

RANK [*makes room for her to pass him, but sits still*]: Nora!

NORA [*at the hall door*]: Helen, bring in the lamp. [*goes over to the stove*] Dear Doctor Rank, that was really horrid of you.

RANK: To have loved you as much as anyone else does? Was that horrid?

NORA: No, but to go and tell me so. There was really no need—

RANK: What do you mean? Did you know—? [MAID *enters with lamp, puts it down on the table, and goes out.*] Nora—Mrs. Helmer—tell me, had you any idea of this?

NORA: Oh, how do I know whether I had or whether I hadn't? I really can't tell you—To think you could be so clumsy, Doctor Rank! We were getting on so nicely.

RANK: Well, at all events you know now that you can command me, body and soul. So won't you speak out?

NORA [*looking at him*]: After what happened?

RANK: I beg you to let me know what it is.

NORA: I can't tell you anything now.

RANK: Yes, yes. You mustn't punish me in that way. Let me have permission to do for you whatever a man may do.

NORA: You can do nothing for me now. Besides, I really don't need any help at all. You will find that the whole thing is merely fancy on my part. It really is so—of course it is! [*Sits down in the rocking-chair, and looks at him with a smile*] You are a nice sort of man, Doctor Rank!—don't you feel ashamed of yourself, now the lamp has come?

RANK: Not a bit. But perhaps I had better go—for ever?

NORA: No, indeed, you shall not. Of course you must come here just as before. You know very well Torvald can't do without you.

RANK: Yes, but you?

NORA: Oh, I am always tremendously pleased when you come.

RANK: It is just that, that put me on the wrong track. You are a riddle to me. I have often thought that you would almost as soon be in my company as in Helmer's.

NORA: Yes—you see there are some people one loves best, and others whom one would almost always rather have as companions.

RANK: Yes, there is something in that.

NORA: When I was at home, of course I loved papa best. But I always thought it tremendous fun if I could steal down into the maid's room, because they never moralised at all, and talked to each other about such entertaining things.

RANK: I see—it is *their* place I have taken.

NORA [*jumping up and going to him*]: Oh, dear, nice Doctor Rank, I never meant that at all. But surely you can understand that being with Torvald is a little like being with papa—

[*Enter* MAID *from the hall*]

MAID: If you please, ma'am. [*whispers and hands her a card*]

NORA [*glancing at the card*]: Oh! [*puts it in her pocket*]

RANK: Is there anything wrong?

NORA: No, no, not in the least. It is only something—it is my new dress—

RANK: What? Your dress is lying there.

NORA: Oh, yes, that one; but this is another. I ordered it. Torvald mustn't know about it—

RANK: Oho! Then that was the great secret.

NORA: Of course. Just go in to him; he is sitting in the inner room. Keep him as long as—

RANK: Make your mind easy; I won't let him escape. [*goes into* HELMER'*s room*]

NORA [*to the* MAID]: And he is standing waiting in the kitchen?

MAID: Yes; he came up the back stairs.

NORA: But didn't you tell him no one was in?

MAID: Yes, but it was no good.

NORA: He won't go away?

MAID: No; he says he won't until he has seen you, ma'am.

NORA: Well, let him come in—but quietly. Helen, you mustn't say anything about it to anyone. It is a surprise for my husband.

MAID: Yes, ma'am, I quite understand. [*Exit.*]

NORA: This dreadful thing is going to happen! It will happen in spite of me! No, no, no, it can't happen—it shan't happen!

[*She bolts the door of* HELMER'*s room. The* MAID *opens the hall door for* KROGSTAD *and shuts it after him. He is wearing a fur coat, high boots and a fur cap.*]

NORA [*advancing towards him*]: Speak low—my husband is at home.

KROGSTAD: No matter about that.

NORA: What do you want of me?

KROGSTAD: An explanation of something.

NORA: Make haste then. What is it?

KROGSTAD: You know, I suppose, that I have got my dismissal.

NORA: I couldn't prevent it, Mr. Krogstad. I fought as hard as I could on your side, but it was no good.

KROGSTAD: Does your husband love you so little, then? He knows that what I can expose you to, and yet he ventures—

NORA: How can you suppose that he has any knowledge of the sort?

KROGSTAD: I didn't suppose so at all. It would not be the least like our dear Torvald Helmer to show so much courage—

NORA: Mr. Krogstad, a little respect for my husband, please.

KROGSTAD: Certainly—all the respect he deserves. But since you have kept the matter so carefully to yourself, I make bold to suppose that you have a little clearer idea, than you had yesterday, of what it actually is that you have done?

NORA: More than you could ever teach me.

KROGSTAD: Yes, such a bad lawyer as I am.

NORA: What is it you want of me?

KROGSTAD: Only to see how you were, Mrs. Helmer. I have been thinking about you all day long. A mere cashier, a quill-driver, a—well, a man like me—even he has a little of what is called feeling, you know.

NORA: Show it, then; think of my little children.

KROGSTAD: Have you and your husband thought of mine? But never mind about that. I only wanted to tell you that you need not take this matter too seriously. In the first place there will be no accusation made on my part.

NORA: No, of course not; I was sure of that.

KROGSTAD: The whole thing can be arranged amicably; there is no reason why anyone should know anything about it. It will remain a secret between us three.

NORA: My husband must never get to know anything about it.

KROGSTAD: How will you be able to prevent it? Am I to understand that you can pay the balance that is owing?

NORA: No, not just at present.

KROGSTAD: Or perhaps that you have some expedient for raising the money soon?

NORA: No expedient that I mean to make use of.

KROGSTAD: Well, in any case, it would have been of no use to you now. If you stood there with ever so much money in your hand, I would never part with your bond.

NORA: Tell me what purpose you mean to put it to.

KROGSTAD: I shall only preserve it—keep it in my possession. No one who is not concerned in the matter shall have the slightest hint of it. So that if the thought of it has driven you to any desperate resolution—

NORA: It has.

KROGSTAD: If you had it in your mind to run away from your home—

NORA: I had.

KROGSTAD: Or even something worse—

NORA: How could you know that?

KROGSTAD: Give up the idea.

NORA: How did you know I had thought of *that?*

KROGSTAD: Most of us think of that at first. I did, too—but I hadn't the courage.

NORA [*faintly*]: No more had I.

KROGSTAD [*in a tone of relief*]: No, that's it, isn't it—you hadn't the courage either?

NORA: No, I haven't—I haven't.

KROGSTAD: Besides, it would have been a great piece of folly. Once the first storm at home is over—. I have a letter for your husband in my pocket.

NORA: Telling him everything?

KROGSTAD: In as lenient a manner as I possibly could.

NORA [*quickly*]: He mustn't get the letter. Tear it up. I will find some means of getting money.

KROGSTAD: Excuse me, Mrs. Helmer, but I think I told you just now—

NORA: I am not speaking of what I owe you. Tell me what sum you are asking my husband for, and I will get the money.

KROGSTAD: I am not asking your husband for a penny.

NORA: What do you want, then?

KROGSTAD: I will tell you. I want to rehabilitate myself, Mrs. Helmer; I want to get on; and in that your husband must help me. For the last year and a half I have not had a hand in anything dishonourable, and all that time I have been struggling in most restricted circumstances. I was content to work my way up step by step. Now I am turned out, and I am not going to be satisfied with merely being taken into favour again. I want to get on, I tell you. I want to get into the Bank again, in a higher position. Your husband must make a place for me—

NORA: That he will never do!

KROGSTAD: He will; I know him; he dare not protest. And as soon as I am in there again with him, then you will see! Within a year I shall be the manager's right hand. It will be Nils Krogstad and not Torvald Helmer who manages the Bank.

NORA: That's a thing you will never see!

KROGSTAD: Do you mean that you will—?

NORA: I have courage enough for it now.

KROGSTAD: Oh, you can't frighten me. A fine, spoilt lady like you—

NORA: You will see, you will see.

KROGSTAD: Under the ice, perhaps? Down into the cold, coal-black water? And then, in the spring, to float up to the surface, all horrible and unrecognisable, with your hair fallen out—

NORA: You can't frighten me.

KROGSTAD: Nor you me. People don't do such things, Mrs. Helmer. Besides, what use would it be? I should have him completely in my power all the same.

NORA: Afterwards? When I am no longer—

KROGSTAD: Have you forgotten that it is I who have the keeping of your reputation? [NORA *stands speechlessly looking at him.*] Well, now, I have warned you. Do not do anything foolish. When Helmer has had my letter, I shall expect a message from him. And be sure you remember that it is your husband himself who has forced me into such ways as this again. I will never forgive him for that. Good-bye, Mrs. Helmer.

[*Exit through the hall*]

NORA [*goes to the hall door, opens it slightly and listens*]: He is going. He is not putting the letter in the box. Oh no, no! that's impossible! [*opens the door by degrees*] What is that? He is standing outside. He is not going downstairs. Is he hesitating? Can he—

[*A letter drops into the box; then* KROGSTAD'*s footsteps are heard, till they die away as he goes downstairs.* NORA *utters a stifled cry and runs across the room to the table by the sofa. A short pause.*]

NORA: In the letter-box. [*steals across to the hall door*] There it lies—Torvald, Torvald, there is no hope for us now!

[MRS. LINDE *comes in from the room on the left, carrying the dress.*]

MRS. LINDE: There, I can't see anything more to mend now. Would you like to try it on—?

NORA [*in a hoarse whisper*]: Christine, come here.

MRS. LINDE [*throwing the dress down on the sofa*]: What is the matter with you? You look so agitated!

NORA: Come here. Do you see that letter? There, look—you can see it through the glass in the letter-box.

MRS. LINDE: Yes, I see it.

NORA: That letter is from Krogstad.

MRS. LINDE: Nora—it was Krogstad who lent you the money!

NORA: Yes, and now Torvald will know all about it.

MRS. LINDE: Believe me, Nora, that's the best thing for both of you.

NORA: You don't know all. I forged a name.

MRS. LINDE: Good heavens—!

NORA: I only want to say this to you, Christine—you must be my witness.

MRS. LINDE: Your witness? What do you mean? What am I to—?

NORA: If I should go out of my mind—and it might easily happen—

MRS. LINDE: Nora!

NORA: Or if anything else should happen to me—anything, for instance, that might prevent my being here—

MRS. LINDE: Nora! Nora! you are quite out of your mind.

NORA: And if it should happen that there were someone who wanted to take all the responsibility, all the blame, you understand—

MRS. LINDE: Yes, yes—but how can you suppose—?

NORA: Then you must be my witness, that it is not true, Christine. I am not out of my mind at all; I am in my right senses now, and I tell you no one else has known anything about it; I, and I alone, did the whole thing. Remember that.

MRS. LINDE: I will, indeed. But I don't understand all this.

NORA: How should you understand it? A wonderful thing is going to happen.

MRS. LINDE: A wonderful thing?

NORA: Yes, a wonderful thing!—But it is so terrible, Christine; it *mustn't* happen, not for all the world.

MRS. LINDE: I will go at once and see Krogstad.

NORA: Don't go to him; he will do you some harm.

MRS. LINDE: There was a time when he would gladly do anything for my sake.

NORA: He?

MRS. LINDE: Where does he live?

NORA: How should I know—? Yes [*feeling in her pocket*] here is his card. But the letter, the letter—!

HELMER [*calls from his room, knocking at the door*]: Nora!

NORA [*cries out anxiously*]: Oh, what's that? What do you want?

HELMER: Don't be so frightened. We are not coming in; you have locked the door. Are you trying on your dress?

NORA: Yes, that's it. I look so nice, Torvald.

MRS. LINDE [*who has read the card*]: I see he lives at the corner here.

NORA: Yes, but it's no use. It is hopeless. The letter is lying there in the box.

MRS. LINDE: And your husband keeps the key?

NORA: Yes, always.

MRS. LINDE: Krogstad must ask for his letter back unread, he must find some pretence—

NORA: But it is just at this time that Torvald generally—

MRS. LINDE: You must delay him. Go in to him in the meantime. I will come back as soon as I can.

[*She goes out hurriedly through the hall door.*]

NORA [*goes to* HELMER'*s door, opens it and peeps in*]: Torvald!

HELMER [*from the inner room*]: Well? May I venture at last to come into my own room again? Come along, Rank, now you will see—[*halting in the doorway*] But what is this?

NORA: What is what, dear?

HELMER: Rank led me to expect a splendid transformation.

RANK [*in the doorway*]: I understood so, but evidently I was mistaken.

NORA: Yes, nobody is to have the chance of admiring me in my dress until tomorrow.

HELMER: But, my dear Nora, you look so worn out. Have you been practising too much?

NORA: No, I have not practised at all.

HELMER: But you will need to—

NORA: Yes, indeed I shall, Torvald. But I can't get on a bit without you to help me; I have absolutely forgotten the whole thing.

HELMER: Oh, we will soon work it up again.

NORA: Yes, help me, Torvald. Promise that you will! I am so nervous about it—all the people—. You must give yourself up to me entirely this evening. Not the tiniest bit of business—you mustn't even take a pen in your hand. Will you promise, Torvald dear?

HELMER: I promise. This evening I will be wholly and absolutely at your service, you helpless little mortal. Ah, by the way, first of all I will just—

[*Goes towards the hall door*]

NORA: What are you going to do there?

HELMER: Only see if any letters have come.

NORA: No, no! don't do that, Torvald!

HELMER: Why not?

NORA: Torvald, please don't. There is nothing there.

HELMER: Well, let me look. [*Turns to go to the letter-box.* NORA, *at the piano, plays the first bars of the Tarantella.* HELMER *stops in the doorway.*] Aha!

NORA: I can't dance to-morrow if I don't practise with you.

HELMER [*going up to her*]: Are you really so afraid of it, dear.

NORA: Yes, so dreadfully afraid of it. Let me practise at once; there is time now, before we go to dinner. Sit down and play for me, Torvald dear; criticise me, and correct me as you play.

HELMER: With great pleasure, if you wish me to.

[*Sits down at the piano.*]

NORA [*takes out of the box a tambourine and a long variegated shawl. She hastily drapes the shawl round her. Then she springs to the front of the stage and calls out.*]: Now play for me! I am going to dance!

[HELMER *plays and* NORA *dances.* RANK *stands by the piano behind* HELMER *and looks on.*]

HELMER [*as he plays*]: Slower, slower!

NORA: I can't do it any other way.

HELMER: Not so violently, Nora!

NORA: This is the way.

HELMER [*stops playing*]: No, no—that is not a bit right.

NORA [*laughing and swinging the tambourine*]: Didn't I tell you so?

RANK: Let me play for her.

HELMER [*getting up*]: Yes, do. I can correct her better then.

[RANK *sits down at the piano and plays.* NORA *dances more and more wildly.* HELMER *has taken up a position beside the stove, and during her dance gives her frequent instructions. She does not seem to hear him; her hair comes down and falls over her shoulders; she pays no attention to it, but goes on dancing. Enter* MRS. LINDE.]

MRS. LINDE [*standing as if spell-bound in the doorway*]: Oh!—

NORA [*as she dances*]: Such fun, Christine!

HELMER: My dear darling Nora, you are dancing as if your life depended on it.

NORA: So it does.

HELMER: Stop, Rank; this is sheer madness. Stop, I tell you! [RANK *stops playing, and* NORA *suddenly stands still.* HELMER *goes up to her.*] I could never have believed it. You have forgotten everything I taught you.

NORA [*throwing away the tambourine*]: There, you see.

HELMER: You will want a lot of coaching.

NORA: Yes, you see how much I need it. You must coach me up to the last minute. Promise me that, Torvald!

HELMER: You can depend on me.

NORA: You must not think of anything but me, either to-day or to-morrow; you mustn't open a single letter—not even open the letter-box—

HELMER: Ah, you are still afraid of that fellow—

NORA: Yes, indeed I am.

HELMER: Nora, I can tell from your looks that there is a letter from him lying there.

NORA: I don't know; I think there is; but you must not read anything of that kind now. Nothing horrid must come between us till this is all over.

RANK [*whispers to* HELMER]: You mustn't contradict her.

HELMER [*taking her in his arms*]: The child shall have her way. But to-morrow night, after you have danced—

NORA: Then you will be free.

[MAID *appears in the doorway to the right*.]

MAID: Dinner is served, ma'am.

NORA: We will have champagne, Helen.

MAID: Very good, ma'am.

[*Exit*.]

HELMER: Hullo!—are we going to have a banquet?

NORA: Yes, a champagne banquet till the small hours. [*calls out*] And a few macaroons, Helen—lots, just for once!

HELMER: Come, come, don't be so wild and nervous. Be my own little skylark, as you used.

NORA: Yes, dear, I will. But go in now and you too, Doctor Rank. Christine, you must help me to do up my hair.

RANK [*whispers to* HELMER *as they go out*]: I suppose there is nothing—she is not expecting anything?

HELMER: Far from it, my dear fellow; it is simply nothing more than this childish nervousness I was telling you of.

[*They go into the right-hand room*.]

NORA: Well!

MRS. LINDE: Gone out of town.

NORA: I could tell from your face.

MRS. LINDE: He is coming home to-morrow evening. I wrote a note for him.

NORA: You should have let it alone; you must prevent nothing. After all, it is splendid to be waiting for a wonderful thing to happen.

MRS. LINDE: What is it that you are waiting for?

NORA: Oh, you wouldn't understand. Go in to them, I will come in a moment. [MRS. LINDE *goes into the dining-room*. NORA *stands still for a little while, as if to compose herself. Then she looks at her watch*.] Five o'clock. Seven hours till midnight; and then four-and-twenty hours till the next midnight. Then the Tarantella will be over. Twenty-four and seven? Thirty-one hours to live.

HELMER [*from the doorway on the right*]: Where's my little skylark?

NORA [*going to him with her arms outstretched*]: Here she is!

Act 3

THE SAME SCENE. *The table has been placed in the middle of the stage, with chairs round it. A lamp is burning on the table. The door into the hall stands open. Dance music is heard in the room above.* MRS. LINDE *is sitting at the table idly turning over the leaves of a book; she tries to read, but does not seem able to collect her thoughts. Every now and then she listens intently for a sound at the outer door.*

MRS. LINDE [*looking at her watch*]: Not yet—and the time is nearly up. If only he does not—. [*listens again*] Ah, there he is. [*Goes into the hall and opens the outer door carefully. Light footsteps are heard on the stairs. She whispers.*] Come in. There is no one here.

KROGSTAD [*in the doorway*]: I found a note from you at home. What does this mean?

MRS. LINDE: It is absolutely necessary that I should have a talk with you.

KROGSTAD: Really? And is it absolutely necessary that it should be here?

MRS. LINDE: It is impossible where I live; there is no private entrance to my rooms. Come in; we are quite alone. The maid is asleep, and the Helmers are at the dance upstairs.

KROGSTAD [*coming into the room*]: Are the Helmers really at a dance to-night?

MRS. LINDE: Yes, why not?

KROGSTAD: Certainly—why not?

MRS. LINDE: Now, Nils, let us have a talk.

KROGSTAD: Can we two have anything to talk about?

MRS. LINDE: We have a great deal to talk about.

KROGSTAD: I shouldn't have thought so.

MRS. LINDE: No, you have never properly understood me.

KROGSTAD: Was there anything else to understand except what was obvious to all the world—a heartless woman jilts a man when a more lucrative chance turns up?

MRS. LINDE: Do you believe I am as absolutely heartless as all that? And do you believe that I did it with a light heart?

KROGSTAD: Didn't you?

MRS. LINDE: Nils, did you really think that?

KROGSTAD: If it were as you say, why did you write to me as you did at the time?

MRS. LINDE: I could do nothing else. As I had to break with you, it was my duty also to put an end to all that you felt for me.

KROGSTAD [*wringing his hands*]: So that was it, and all this—only for the sake of money!

MRS. LINDE: You must not forget that I had a helpless mother and two little brothers. We couldn't wait for you, Nils; your prospects seemed hopeless then.

KROGSTAD: That may be so, but you had no right to throw me over for any one else's sake.

MRS. LINDE: Indeed I don't know. Many a time did I ask myself if I had the right to do it.

KROGSTAD [*more gently*]: When I lost you, it was as if all the solid ground went from under my feet. Look at me now—I am a shipwrecked man clinging to a bit of wreckage.

MRS. LINDE: But help may be near.

KROGSTAD: It *was* near; but then you came and stood in my way.

MRS. LINDE: Unintentionally, Nils. It was only to-day that I learnt it was your place I was going to take in the Bank.

KROGSTAD: I believe you, if you say so. But now that you know it, are you not going to give it up to me?

MRS. LINDE: No, because that would not benefit you in the least.

KROGSTAD: Oh, benefit, benefit—I would have done it whether or no.

MRS. LINDE: I have learnt to act prudently. Life, and hard, bitter necessity have taught me that.

KROGSTAD: And life has taught me not to believe in fine speeches.

MRS. LINDE: Then life has taught you something very reasonable. But deeds you must believe in?

KROGSTAD: What do you mean by that?

MRS. LINDE: You said you were like a shipwrecked man clinging to some wreckage.

KROGSTAD: I had good reason to say so.

MRS. LINDE: Well, I am like a shipwrecked woman clinging to some wreckage—no one to mourn for, no one to care for.

KROGSTAD: It was your own choice.

MRS. LINDE: There was no other choice—then.

KROGSTAD: Well, what now?

MRS. LINDE: Nils, how would it be if we two shipwrecked people could join forces?

KROGSTAD: What are you saying?

MRS. LINDE: Two on the same piece of wreckage would stand a better chance than each on their own.

KROGSTAD: Christine!

MRS. LINDE: What do you suppose brought me to town?

KROGSTAD: Do you mean that you gave me a thought?

MRS. LINDE: I could not endure life without work. All my life, as long as I can remember, I have worked, and it has been my greatest and only pleasure. But now I am quite alone in the world—my life is so dreadfully empty and I feel so forsaken. There is not the least pleasure in working for one's self. Nils, give me someone and something to work for.

KROGSTAD: I don't trust that. It is nothing but a woman's overstrained sense of generosity that prompts you to make such an offer of yourself.

MRS. LINDE: Have you ever noticed anything of the sort in me?

KROGSTAD: Could you really do it? Tell me—do you know all about my past life?

MRS. LINDE: Yes.

KROGSTAD: And do you know what they think of me here?

MRS. LINDE: You seemed to me to imply that with me you might have been quite another man.

KROGSTAD: I am certain of it.

MRS. LINDE: Is it too late now?

KROGSTAD: Christine, are you saying this deliberately? Yes, I am sure you are. I see it in your face. Have you really the courage, then—?

MRS. LINDE: I want to be a mother to someone, and your children need a mother. We two need each other. Nils, I have faith in your real character—I can dare anything together with you.

KROGSTAD [*grasps her hands*]: Thanks, thanks, Christine! Now I shall find a way to clear myself in the eyes of the world. Ah, but I forgot—

MRS. LINDE [*listening*]: Hush! The Tarantella! Go, go!

KROGSTAD: Why? What is it?

MRS. LINDE: Do you hear them up there? When that is over, we may expect them back.

KROGSTAD: Yes, yes—I will go. But it is all no use. Of course you are not aware what steps I have taken in the matter of the Helmers.

MRS. LINDE: Yes. I know all about that.

KROGSTAD: And in spite of that have you the courage to—?

MRS. LINDE: I understand very well to what lengths a man like you might be driven by despair.

KROGSTAD: If I could only undo what I have done!

MRS. LINDE: You can. Your letter is lying in the letter-box now.

KROGSTAD: Are you sure of that?

MRS. LINDE: Quite sure, but—

KROGSTAD [*with a searching look at her*]: Is that what it all means?—that you want to save your friend at any cost? Tell me frankly. Is that it?

MRS. LINDE: Nils, a woman who has once sold herself for another's sake, doesn't do it a second time.

KROGSTAD: I will ask for my letter back.

MRS. LINDE: No, no.

KROGSTAD: Yes, of course I will. I will wait here till Helmer comes; I will tell him he must give me my letter back—that it only concerns my dismissal—that he is not to read it—

MRS. LINDE: No, Nils, you must not recall your letter.

KROGSTAD: But, tell me, wasn't it for that very purpose that you asked me to meet you here?

MRS. LINDE: In my first moment of fright, it was. But twenty-four hours have elapsed since then, and in that time I have witnessed incredible things in this house. Helmer must know all about it. This unhappy secret must be disclosed; they must have a complete understanding between them, which is impossible with all this concealment and falsehood going on.

KROGSTAD: Very well, if you will take the responsibility. But there is one thing I can do in any case, and I shall do it at once.

MRS. LINDE [*listening*]: You must be quick and go! The dance is over; we are not safe a moment longer.

KROGSTAD: I will wait for you below.

MRS. LINDE: Yes, do. You must see me back to my door.

KROGSTAD: I have never had such an amazing piece of good fortune in my life.

[*Goes out through the outer door. The door between the room and the hall remains open.*]

MRS. LINDE [*tidying up the room and laying her hat and cloak ready*]: What a difference! what a difference! Someone to work for and live for—a home to bring comfort into. That I will do, indeed. I wish they would be quick and come—[*listens*] Ah, there they are now. I must put on my things.

[*Takes up her hat and cloak.* HELMER'*s and* NORA'*s voices are heard outside; a key is turned, and* HELMER *brings* NORA *almost by force into the hall. She is in an Italian costume with a large black shawl round her; he is in evening dress and a black domino which is flying open.*]

NORA [*hanging back in the doorway, and struggling with him*]: No, no, no!—don't take me in. I want to go upstairs again; I don't want to leave so early.

HELMER: But, my dearest Nora—

NORA: Please, Torvald dear—please, *please*—only an hour more.

HELMER: Not a single minute, my sweet Nora. You know that was our agreement. Come along into the room; you are catching cold standing there.

[*He brings her gently into the room, in spite of her resistance.*]

MRS. LINDE: Good evening.

NORA: Christine!

HELMER: You here, so late, Mrs. Linde?

MRS. LINDE: Yes, you must excuse me; I was so anxious to see Nora in her dress.

NORA: Have you been sitting here waiting for me?

MRS. LINDE: Yes, unfortunately I came too late, you had already gone upstairs; and I thought I couldn't go away without having seen you.

HELMER [*taking off* NORA'*s shawl*]: Yes, take a good look at her. I think she is worth looking at. Isn't she charming, Mrs. Linde?

MRS. LINDE: Yes, indeed she is.

HELMER: Doesn't she look remarkably pretty? Everyone thought so at the dance. But she is terribly self-willed, this sweet little person. What are we to do with her? You will hardly believe that I had almost to bring her away by force.

NORA: Torvald, you will repent not having let me stay, even if it were only for half an hour.

HELMER: Listen to her, Mrs. Linde! She had danced her Tarantella, and it had been a tremendous success, as it deserved—although possibly the performance was a trifle too realistic—a little more so, I mean, than was strictly compatible with the limitations of art. But never mind about that! The chief thing is, she had made a success—she had made a tremendous success. Do you think I was going to let her remain there after that, and spoil the effect? No indeed! I took my charming little Capri maiden—my capricious little Capri maiden, I should say—on my arm; took one quick turn round the room; a curtsey on either side, and, as they say in novels, the beautiful apparition disappeared. An exit ought always to be effective, Mrs. Linde; but that is what I cannot make Nora understand. Pooh! this room is hot. [*throws his domino on a chair and opens the door of his room*] Hullo! it's all dark in here. Oh, of course—excuse me—.

[*He goes in and lights some candles.*]

NORA [*in a hurried and breathless whisper*]: Well?

MRS. LINDE [*in a low voice*]: I have had a talk with him.

NORA: Yes, and—

MRS. LINDE: Nora, you must tell your husband all about it.

NORA [*in an expressionless voice*]: I knew it.

MRS. LINDE: You have nothing to be afraid of as far as Krogstad is concerned; but you must tell him.

NORA: I won't tell him.

MRS. LINDE: Then the letter will.

NORA: Thank you, Christine. Now I know what I must do. Hush—!

HELMER [*coming in again*]: Well, Mrs. Linde, have you admired her?

MRS. LINDE: Yes, and now I will say good-night.

HELMER: What already? Is this yours, this knitting?

MRS. LINDE [*taking it*]: Yes, thank you, I had very nearly forgotten it.

HELMER: So you knit?

MRS. LINDE: Of course.

HELMER: Do you know, you ought to embroider.

MRS. LINDE: Really? Why?

HELMER: Yes, it's far more becoming. Let me show you. You hold the embroidery thus in your left hand, and use the needle with the right—like this—with a long, easy sweep. Do you see?

MRS. LINDE: Yes, perhaps—

HELMER: But in the case of knitting—that can never be anything but ungraceful; look here—the arms close together, the knitting-needles going up and down—it has a sort of Chinese effect—. That was really excellent champagne they gave us.

MRS. LINDE: Well,—good-night, Nora, and don't be self-willed any more.

HELMER: That's right, Mrs. Linde.

MRS. LINDE: Good-night, Mr. Helmer.

HELMER [*accompanying her to the door*]: Good-night, good-night. I hope you will get home all right. I should be very happy to—but you haven't any great distance to go. Good-night, good-night. [*She goes out; he shuts the door after her, and comes in again.*] Ah!—at last we have got rid of her. She is a frightful bore, that woman.

NORA: Aren't you very tired, Torvald?

HELMER: No, not in the least.

NORA: Nor sleepy?

HELMER: Not a bit. On the contrary, I feel extraordinarily lively. And you?—you really look both tired and sleepy.

NORA: Yes, I am very tired. I want to go to sleep at once.

HELMER: There, you see it was quite right of me not to let you stay there any longer.

NORA: Everything you do is quite right, Torvald.

HELMER [*kissing her on the forehead*]: Now my little skylark is speaking reasonably. Did you notice what good spirits Rank was in this evening?

NORA: Really? Was he? I didn't speak to him at all.

HELMER: And I very little, but I have not for a long time seen him in such good form. [*looks for a while at her and then goes nearer to her*] It is delightful to be at home by ourselves again, to be all alone with you—you fascinating, charming little darling!

NORA: Don't look at me like that, Torvald.

HELMER: Why shouldn't I look at my dearest treasure?—at all the beauty that is mine, all my very own?

NORA [*going to the other side of the table*]: You mustn't say things like that to me to-night.

HELMER [*following her*]: You have still got the Tarantella in your blood, I see. And it makes you more captivating than ever. Listen—the guests are beginning to go now. [*in a lower voice*] Nora—soon the whole house will be quiet.

NORA: Yes, I hope so.

HELMER: Yes, my own darling Nora. Do you know, when I am out at a party with you like this, why I speak so little to you, keep away from you, and only send a stolen glance in your direction now and then?—do you know why I do that? It is because I make believe to myself that we are secretly in love, and you are my secretly promised bride, and that no one suspects there is anything between us.

NORA: Yes, yes—I know very well your thoughts are with me all the time.

HELMER: And when we are leaving, and I am putting the shawl over your beautiful young shoulders—on your lovely neck—then I imagine that you are my young bride and that we have just come from the wedding, and I am bringing you for the first time into our home—to be alone with you for the first time—quite alone with my shy little darling! All this evening I have longed for nothing but you. When I watched the seductive figures of the Tarantella, my blood was on fire; I could endure it no longer, and that was why I brought you down so early—

NORA: Go away, Torvald! You must let me go. I won't—

HELMER: What's that? You're joking, my little Nora! You won't—you won't? Am I not your husband—?

[*A knock is heard at the outer door.*]

NORA [*starting*]: Did you hear—?

HELMER [*going into the hall*]: Who is it?

RANK [*outside*]: It is I. May I come in for a moment?

HELMER [*in a fretful whisper*]: Oh, what does he want now? [*aloud*] Wait a minute! [*unlocks the door*] Come, that's kind of you not to pass by our door.

RANK: I thought I heard your voice, and felt as if I should like to look in. [*with a swift glance round*] Ah, yes!—these dear familiar rooms. You are very happy and cosy in here, you two.

HELMER: It seems to me that you looked after yourself pretty well upstairs too.

RANK: Excellently. Why shouldn't I? Why shouldn't one enjoy everything in this world?—at any rate as much as one can, and as long as one can. The wine was capital—

HELMER: Especially the champagne.

RANK: So you noticed that too? It is almost incredible how much I managed to put away!

NORA: Torvald drank a great deal of champagne tonight, too.

RANK: Did he?

NORA: Yes, and he is always in such good spirits afterwards.

RANK: Well, why should one not enjoy a merry evening after a well-spent day?

HELMER: Well spent? I am afraid I can't take credit for that.

RANK [*clapping him on the back*]: But I can, you know!

NORA: Doctor Rank, you must have been occupied with some scientific investigation to-day.

RANK: Exactly.

HELMER: Just listen!—little Nora talking about scientific investigations!

NORA: And may I congratulate you on the result?

RANK: Indeed you may.

NORA: Was it favourable, then?

RANK: The best possible, for both doctor and patient—certainty.

NORA [*quickly and searchingly*]: Certainty?

RANK: Absolute certainty. So wasn't I entitled to make a merry evening of it after that?

NORA: Yes, you certainly were, Doctor Rank.

HELMER: I think so too, so long as you don't have to pay for it in the morning.

RANK: Oh well, one can't have anything in this life without paying for it.

NORA: Doctor Rank—are you fond of fancy-dress balls?

RANK: Yes, if there is a fine lot of pretty costumes.

NORA: Tell me—what shall we two wear at the next?

HELMER: Little featherbrain!—are you thinking of the next already?

RANK: We two? Yes, I can tell you. You shall go as a good fairy—

HELMER: Yes, but what do you suggest as an appropriate costume for that?

RANK: Let your wife go dressed just as she is in everyday life.

HELMER: That was really very prettily turned. But can't you tell us what you will be?

RANK: Yes, my dear friend, I have quite made up my mind about that.

HELMER: Well?

RANK: At the next fancy dress ball I shall be invisible.

HELMER: That's a good joke!

RANK: There is a big black hat—have you never heard of hats that make you invisible? If you put one on, no one can see you.

HELMER [*suppressing a smile*]: Yes, you are quite right.

RANK: But I am clean forgetting what I came for. Helmer, give me a cigar—one of the dark Havanas.

HELMER: With the greatest pleasure [*offers him his case*].

RANK [*takes a cigar and cuts off the end*]: Thanks.

NORA [*striking a match*]: Let me give you a light.

RANK: Thank you. [*She holds the match for him to light his cigar.*] And now good-bye!

HELMER: Good-bye, good-bye, dear old man!

NORA: Sleep well, Doctor Rank.

RANK: Thank you for that wish.

NORA: Wish me the same.

RANK: You? Well, if you want me to: sleep well! And thanks for the light.

[*He nods to them both and goes out.*]

HELMER [*in a subdued voice*]: He has drunk more than he ought.

NORA [*absently*]: Maybe. [HELMER *takes a bunch of keys out of his pocket and goes into the hall.*] Torvald! what are you going to do there?

HELMER: Empty the letter-box; it is quite full; there will be no room to put the newspaper in to-morrow morning.

NORA: Are you going to work to-night?

HELMER: You know quite well I'm not. What is this? Some one has been at the lock.

NORA: At the lock—?

HELMER: Yes, someone has. What can it mean? I should never have thought the maid—. Here is a broken hairpin. Nora, it is one of yours.

NORA [*quickly*]: Then it must have been the children—

HELMER: Then you must get them out of those ways. There, at last I have got it open. [*Takes out the contents of the letter-box, and calls to the kitchen.*] Helen!—Helen, put out the light over the front door. [*Goes back into the room and shuts the door into the hall. He holds out his hand full of letters.*] Look at that—look what a heap of them there are. [*turning them over*] What on earth is that?

NORA [*at the window*]: The letter—No! Torvald, no!

HELMER: Two cards—of Rank's.

NORA: Of Doctor Rank's?

HELMER [*looking at them*]: Doctor Rank. They were on the top. He must have put them in when he went out.

NORA: Is there anything written on them?

HELMER: There is a black cross over the name. Look there—what an uncomfortable idea! It looks as if he were announcing his own death.

NORA: It is just what he is doing.

HELMER: What? Do you know anything about it? Has he said anything to you?

NORA: Yes. He told me that when the cards came it would be his leave-taking from us. He means to shut himself up and die.

HELMER: My poor old friend. Certainly I knew we should not have him very long with us. But so soon! And so he hides himself away like a wounded animal.

NORA: If it has to happen, it is best it should be without a word—don't you think so, Torvald?

HELMER [*walking up and down*]: He had so grown into our lives. I can't think of him as having gone out of them. He, with his sufferings and his loneliness, was like a cloudy background to our sunlit happiness. Well, perhaps it is best so. For him, anyway. [*standing still*] And perhaps for us too, Nora. We two are thrown quite upon each other now. [*puts his arms round her*] My darling wife, I don't feel as if I could hold you tight enough. Do you know, Nora, I have often wished that you might be threatened by some great danger, so that I might risk my life's blood, and everything, for your sake.

NORA [*disengages herself, and says firmly and decidedly*]: Now you must read your letters, Torvald.

HELMER: No, no; not to-night. I want to be with you, my darling wife.

NORA: With the thought of your friend's death—

HELMER: You are right, it has affected us both. Something ugly has come between us—the thought of the horrors of death. We must try and rid our minds of that. Until then—we will each go to our own room.

NORA [*hanging on his neck*]: Good-night, Torvald—Good-night!

HELMER [*kissing her on the forehead*]: Good-night, my little singing-bird. Sleep sound, Nora. Now I will read my letters through.

[*He takes his letters and goes into his room, shutting the door after him.*]

NORA [*gropes distractedly about, seizes* HELMER'*s domino, throws it round her, while she says in quick, hoarse, spasmodic whispers*]: Never to see him again. Never! Never! [*puts her shawl over her head*] Never to see my children again either—never again. Never! Never!—Ah! the icy, black water—the unfathomable depths—If only it were over! He has got it now—now he is reading it. Good-by, Torvald and my children!

[*She is about to rush out through the hall, when* HELMER *opens his door hurriedly and stands with an open letter in his hand.*]

HELMER: Nora!

NORA: Ah!—

HELMER: What is this? Do you know what is in this letter?

NORA: Yes, I know. Let me go! Let me get out!

HELMER [*holding her back*]: Where are you going?

NORA [*trying to get free*]: You shan't save me, Torvald!

HELMER [*reeling*]: True? Is this true, that I read here? Horrible! No, no—it is impossible that it can be true.

NORA: It is true. I have loved you above everything else in the world.

HELMER: Oh, don't let us have any silly excuses.

NORA [*taking a step towards him*]: Torvald—!

HELMER: Miserable creature—what have you done?

NORA: Let me go. You shall not suffer for my sake. You shall not take it upon yourself.

HELMER: No tragedy airs, please. [*locks the hall door*] Here you shall stay and give me an explanation. Do you understand what you have done? Answer me? Do you understand what you have done?

NORA [*looks steadily at him and says with a growing look of coldness in her face*]: Yes, now I am beginning to understand thoroughly.

HELMER [*walking about the room*]: What a horrible awakening! All these eight years—she who was my joy and pride—a hypocrite, a liar—worse, worse—a criminal! The unutterable ugliness of it all! For shame! For shame! [NORA *is silent and looks steadily at him. He stops in front of her.*] I ought to have suspected that something of the sort would happen. I ought to have foreseen it. All your father's want of principle—be silent!—all your father's want of principle has come out in you. No religion, no morality, no sense of duty—. How I am punished for having winked at what he did! I did it for your sake, and this is how you repay me.

NORA: Yes, that's just it.

HELMER: Now you have destroyed all my happiness. You have ruined all my future. It is horrible to think of! I am in the power of an unscrupulous man; he can do what he likes with me, ask anything he likes of me, give me any orders he pleases— I dare not refuse. And I must sink to such miserable depths because of a thoughtless woman!

NORA: When I am out of the way, you will be free.

HELMER: No fine speeches, please. Your father had always plenty of those ready, too. What good would it be to me if you were out of the way, as you say? Not the slightest. He can make the affair known everywhere; and if he does, I may be falsely suspected of having been a party to your criminal action. Very likely people will think I was behind it all—that it was I who prompted you! And I have to thank you for all this—you whom I have cherished during the whole of our married life. Do you understand now what it is you have done for me?

NORA [*coldly and quietly*]: Yes.

HELMER: It is so incredible that I can't take it in. But we must come to some understanding. Take off that shawl. Take it off, I tell you. I must try and appease him some way or another. The matter must be hushed up at any cost. And as for you and me, it must appear as if everything between us were just as before—but naturally only in the eyes of the world. You will still remain in my house, that is a matter of course. But I shall not allow you to bring up the children; I dare not trust them to you. To think that I should be obliged to say so to one whom I have loved so dearly, and whom I still—. No, that is all over. From this moment happiness is not the question; all that concerns us is to save the remains, the fragments, the appearance—

[*A ring is heard at the front-door bell.*]

HELMER [*with a start*]: What is that? So late! Can the worst—? Can he—? Hide yourself, Nora. Say you are ill.

[NORA *stands motionless.* HELMER *goes and unlocks the hall door.*]

MAID [*half-dressed, comes to the door*]: A letter for the mistress.

HELMER: Give it to me. [*takes the letter, and shuts the door*] Yes, it is from him. You shall not have it; I will read it myself.

NORA: Yes, read it.

HELMER [*standing by the lamp*]: I scarcely have the courage to do it. It may mean ruin for both of us. No, I must know. [*tears open the letter, runs his eye over a few lines, looks at a paper enclosed and gives a shout of joy*] Nora! [*She looks at him questioningly.*] Nora!—No, I must read it once again—. Yes, it is true! I am saved! Nora, I am saved!

NORA: And I?

HELMER: You too, of course; we are both saved, both you and I. Look, he sends you your bond back. He says he regrets and repents—that a happy change in his life—never mind what he says! We are saved, Nora! No one can do anything to you. Oh, Nora, Nora!—no, first I must destroy these hateful things. Let me see—. [*takes a look at the bond*] No, no, I won't look at it. The whole thing shall be nothing but a bad dream to me. [*tears up the bond and both letters, throws them all into the stove, and watches them burn*] There—now it doesn't exist any longer. He says that since Christmas Eve you—. These must have been three dreadful days for you, Nora.

NORA: I have fought a hard fight these three days.

HELMER: And suffered agonies, and seen no way out but—. No, we won't call any of the horrors to mind. We will only shout with joy, and keep saying "It's all over! It's all over!" Listen to me, Nora. You don't seem to realise that it is all over. What is this?—such a cold, set face! My poor little Nora, I quite understand; you don't feel as if you could believe that I have forgiven you. But it is true, Nora, I swear it; I have forgiven you everything. I know that what you did, you did out of love for me.

NORA: That is true.

HELMER: You have loved me as a wife ought to love her husband. Only you had not sufficient knowledge to judge of the means you used. But do you suppose you are any the less dear to me, because you don't understand how to act on your own responsibility? No, no; only lean on me; I will advise you and direct you. I should not be a man if this womanly helplessness did not just give you a double attractiveness in my eyes. You must not think any more about the hard things I said in my first moment of consternation, when I thought everything was going to overwhelm me. I have forgiven you, Nora; I swear to you I have forgiven you.

NORA: Thank you for your forgiveness.

[*She goes out through the door to the right.*]

HELMER: No, don't go—. [*looks in*] What are you doing in there?

NORA [*from within*]: Taking off my fancy dress.

HELMER [*standing at the open door*]: Yes, do. Try and calm yourself, and make your mind easy again, my frightened little singing-bird. Be at rest, and feel secure; I have broad wings to shelter you under. [*walks up and down by the door*] How warm and cosy our home is, Nora. Here is shelter for you; here I will protect you like a hunted dove that I have saved from a hawk's claws. I will bring peace to your poor beating heart. It will come, little by little, Nora, believe me. Tomorrow morning you will look upon it all quite differently; soon everything will be just as it was before. Very soon you won't need me to assure you that I have forgiven you; you will yourself feel the certainty that I have done so. Can you suppose I should ever think of such a thing as repudiating you, or even reproaching you? You have no idea what a true man's heart is like, Nora. There is something so indescribably sweet and satisfying, to a man, in the knowledge that he has forgiven his wife—forgiven her freely, and with all his heart. It seems as if that had made her, as it were, doubly his own; he has given her a new life, so to speak; and she has in a way become both wife and child to him. So you shall be for me after this, my little scared, helpless darling. Have no anxiety about anything, Nora; only be frank and open with me, and I will serve as will and conscience both to you—. What is this? Not gone to bed? Have you changed your things?

NORA [*in everyday dress*]: Yes, Torvald, I have changed my things now.

HELMER: But what for?—so late as this.

NORA: I shall not sleep to-night.

HELMER: But, my dear Nora—

NORA [*looking at her watch*]: It is not so very late. Sit down here, Torvald. You and I have much to say to one another.

[*She sits down at one side of the table.*]

HELMER: Nora—what is this?—this cold, set face?

NORA: Sit down. It will take some time; I have a lot to talk over with you.

HELMER [*sits down at the opposite side of the table*]: You alarm me, Nora!—and I don't understand you.

NORA: No, that is just it. You don't understand me, and I have never understood you either—before to-night. No, you mustn't interrupt me. You must simply listen to what I say. Torvald, this is a settling of accounts.

HELMER: What do you mean by that?

NORA [*after a short silence*]: Isn't there one thing that strikes you as strange in our sitting here like this?

Torvald Helmer (Sam Waterston) begs Nora (Liv Ullmann) to reconsider her decision to leave home in the Joseph Papp New York Shakespeare Festival production (1995) of *A Doll's House* (director, Tormod Skagestad).

HELMER: What is that?

NORA: We have been married now eight years. Does it not occur to you that this is the first time we two, you and I, husband and wife, have had a serious conversation?

HELMER: What do you mean by serious?

NORA: In all these eight years—longer than that—from the very beginning of our acquaintance, we have never exchanged a word on any serious subject.

HELMER: Was it likely that I would be continually and for ever telling you about worries that you could not help me to bear?

NORA: I am not speaking about business matters. I say that we have never sat down in earnest together to try and get at the bottom of anything.

HELMER: But, dearest Nora, would it have been any good to you?

NORA: That is just it; you have never understood me. I have been greatly wronged, Torvald—first by papa and then by you.

HELMER: What! By us two—by us two, who have loved you better than anyone else in the world?

NORA [*shaking her head*]: You have never loved me. You have only thought it pleasant to be in love with me.

HELMER: Nora, what do I hear you saying?

NORA: It is perfectly true, Torvald. When I was at home with papa, he told me his opinion about everything, and so I had the same opinions; and if I differed from him I concealed the fact, because he would not have liked it. He called me his doll-child, and he played with me just as I used to play with my dolls. And when I came to live with you—

HELMER: What sort of an expression is that to use about our marriage?

NORA [*undisturbed*]: I mean that I was simply transferred from papa's hands into yours. You arranged everything according to your own taste, and so I got the same tastes as you—or else I pretended to, I am really not quite sure which—I think sometimes the one and sometimes the other. When I look back on it, it seems to me as if I had been living here like a poor woman—just from hand to mouth. I have existed merely to perform tricks for you, Torvald. But you would have it so. You and papa have committed a great sin against me. It is your fault that I have made nothing of my life.

HELMER: How unreasonable and how ungrateful you are, Nora! Have you not been happy here?

NORA: No, I have never been happy. I thought I was, but it has never really been so.

HELMER: Not—not happy!

NORA: No, only merry. And you have always been so kind to me. But our home has been nothing but a playroom. I have been your doll-wife, just as at home I was papa's doll-child; and here the children have been my dolls. I thought it great fun when you played with me, just as they thought it great fun when I played with them. That is what our marriage has been, Torvald.

HELMER: There is some truth in what you say—exaggerated and strained as your view of it is. But for the future it shall be different. Playtime shall be over, and lesson-time shall begin.

NORA: Whose lessons? Mine, or the children's?

HELMER: Both yours and the children's, my darling Nora.

NORA: Alas, Torvald, you are not the man to educate me into being a proper wife for you.

HELMER: And you can say that!

NORA: And I—how am I fitted to bring up the children?

HELMER: Nora!

NORA: Didn't you say so yourself a little while ago—that you dare not trust me to bring them up?

HELMER: In a moment of anger! Why do you pay any heed to that?

NORA: Indeed, you were perfectly right. I am not fit for the task. There is another task I must undertake first. I must try and educate myself—you are not the man to help me in that. I must do that for myself. And that is why I am going to leave you now.

HELMER [*springing up*]: What do you say?

NORA: I must stand quite alone, if I am to understand myself and everything about me. It is for that reason that I cannot remain with you any longer.

HELMER: Nora! Nora!

NORA: I am going away from here now, at once. I am sure Christine will take me in for the night—

HELMER: You are out of your mind! I won't allow it! I forbid you!

NORA: It is no use forbidding me anything any longer. I will take with me what belongs to myself. I will take nothing from you, either now or later.

HELMER: What sort of madness is this!

NORA: To-morrow I shall go home—I mean, to my old home. It will be easiest for me to find something to do there.

HELMER: You blind, foolish woman!

NORA: I must try and get some sense, Torvald.

HELMER: To desert your home, your husband and your children! And you don't consider what people will say!

NORA: I cannot consider that at all. I only know that it is necessary for me.

HELMER: It's shocking. This is how you would neglect your most sacred duties.

NORA: What do you consider my most sacred duties?

HELMER: Do I need to tell you that? Are they not your duties to your husband and your children?

NORA: I have other duties just as sacred.

HELMER: That you have not. What duties could those be?

NORA: Duties to myself.

HELMER: Before all else, you are a wife and a mother.

NORA: I don't believe that any longer. I believe that before all else I am a reasonable human being, just as you are—or, at all events, that I must try and become one. I know quite well, Torvald, that most people would think you right, and that views of that kind are to be found in books; but I can no longer content myself with what most people say, or with what is found in books. I must think over things for myself and get to understand them.

HELMER: Can you not understand your place in your own home? Have you not a reliable guide in such matters as that?—have you no religion?

NORA: I am afraid, Torvald, I do not exactly know what religion is.

HELMER: What are you saying?

NORA: I know nothing but what the clergyman said when I went to be confirmed. He told us that religion was this, and that, and the other. When I am away from all this, and am alone, I will look into that matter too. I will see if what the clergyman said is true, or at all events if it is true for me.

HELMER: This is unheard of in a girl of your age! But if religion cannot lead you aright, let me try and awaken your conscience. I suppose you have some moral sense? Or—answer me—am I to think you have none?

NORA: I assure you, Torvald, that is not an easy question to answer. I really don't know. The thing perplexes me altogether. I only know that you and I look at it in quite a different light. I am learning, too, that the law is quite another thing from what I supposed; but I find it impossible to convince myself that the law is right. According to it a woman has no right to spare her old dying father, or to save her husband's life. I can't believe that.

HELMER: You talk like a child. You don't understand the conditions of the world in which you live.

NORA: No, I don't. But now I am going to try. I am going to see if I can make out who is right, the world or I.

HELMER: You are ill, Nora; you are delirious; I almost think you are out of your mind.

NORA: I have never felt my mind so clear and certain as to-night.

HELMER: And is it with a clear and certain mind that you forsake your husband and your children?

NORA: Yes, it is.

HELMER: Then there is only one possible explanation.

NORA: What is that?

HELMER: You do not love me any more.

NORA: No, that is just it.

HELMER: Nora!—and you can say that?

NORA: It gives me great pain, Torvald, for you have always been so kind to me, but I cannot help it. I do not love you any more.

HELMER [*regaining his composure*]: Is that a clear and certain conviction too?

NORA: Yes, absolutely clear and certain. That is the reason why I will not stay here any longer.

HELMER: And can you tell me what I have done to forfeit your love?

NORA: Yes, indeed I can. It was to-night, when the wonderful thing did not happen; then I saw you were not the man I had thought you.

HELMER: Explain yourself better—I don't understand you.

NORA: I have waited so patiently for eight years; for, goodness knows, I knew very well that wonderful things don't happen every day. Then this horrible misfortune came upon me; and then I felt quite certain that the wonderful thing was going to happen at last. When Krogstad's letter was lying out there, never for a moment did I imagine that you would consent to accept this man's conditions. I was so absolutely certain that you would say to him: Publish the thing to the whole world. And when that was done—

HELMER: Yes, what then?—when I had exposed my wife to shame and disgrace?

NORA: When that was done, I was so absolutely certain, you would come forward and take everything upon yourself, and say: I am the guilty one.

HELMER: Nora—!

NORA: You mean that I would never have accepted such a sacrifice on your part? No, of course not. But what would my assurances have been worth against yours? That was the wonderful thing which I hoped for and feared; and it was to prevent that, that I wanted to kill myself.

HELMER: I would gladly work night and day for you, Nora—bear sorrow and want for your sake. But no man would sacrifice his honour for the one he loves.

NORA: It is a thing hundreds of thousands of women have done.

HELMER: Oh, you think and talk like a heedless child.

NORA: Maybe. But you neither think nor talk like the man I could bind myself to. As soon as your fear was over—and it was not fear for what threatened me, but for what might happen to you—when the whole thing was past, as far as you were concerned it was exactly as if nothing at all had happened. Exactly as before, I was your little skylark, your doll, which you would in future treat with doubly gentle care, because it was so brittle and fragile. [*getting up*] Torvald—it was then it dawned upon me that for eight years I had been living here with a strange man, and had borne him three children—. Oh, I can't bear to think of it! I could tear myself into little bits!

HELMER [*sadly*]: I see, I see. An abyss has opened between us—there is no denying it. But, Nora, would it not be possible to fill it up?

NORA: As I am now, I am no wife for you.

HELMER: I have it in me to become a different man.

NORA: Perhaps—if your doll is taken away from you.

HELMER: But to part!—to part from you! No, no, Nora, I can't understand that idea.

NORA [*going out to the right*]: That makes it all the more certain that it must be done.

[*She comes back with her cloak and hat and a small bag which she puts on a chair by the table.*]

HELMER: Nora, Nora, not now! Wait till to-morrow.

NORA [*putting on her cloak*]: I cannot spend the night in a strange man's room.

HELMER: But can't we live here like brother and sister—?

NORA [*putting on her hat*]: You know very well that would not last long. [*puts the shawl round her*] Good-bye, Torvald. I won't see the little ones. I know they are in better hands than mine. As I am now, I can be of no use to them.

HELMER: But some day, Nora—some day?

NORA: How can I tell? I have no idea what is going to become of me.

HELMER: But you are my wife, whatever becomes of you.

NORA: Listen, Torvald. I have heard that when a wife deserts her husband's house, as I am doing now, he is legally freed from all obligations towards her. In any case I set you free from all your obligations. You are not to feel yourself bound in the slightest way, any more than I shall. There must be perfect freedom on both sides. See here is your ring back. Give me mine.

HELMER: That too?

NORA: That too.

HELMER: Here it is.

NORA: That's right. Now it is all over. I have put the keys here. The maids know all about everything in the house—better than I do. To-morrow, after I have left her, Christine will come here and pack up my own things that I brought with me from home. I will have them sent after me.

HELMER: All over! All over!—Nora, shall you never think of me again?

NORA: I know I shall often think of you and the children and this house.

HELMER: May I write to you, Nora?

NORA: No—never. You must not do that.

HELMER: But at least let me send you—

NORA: Nothing—nothing—

HELMER: Let me help you if you are in want.

NORA: No. I can receive nothing from a stranger.

HELMER: Nora—can I never be anything more than a stranger to you?

NORA [*taking her bag*]: Ah, Torvald, the most wonderful thing of all would have to happen.

HELMER: Tell me what that would be!

NORA: Both you and I would have to be so changed that—. Oh, Torvald, I don't believe any longer in wonderful things happening.

HELMER: But I will believe in it. Tell me? So changed that—?

NORA: That our life together would be a real wedlock. Good-bye.

[*She goes out through the hall.*]

HELMER [*sinks down on a chair at the door and buries his face in his hands*]: Nora! Nora! [*looks round, and rises*] Empty. She is gone. [*A hope flashes across his mind.*] The most wonderful thing of all—?

[*The sound of a door slamming is heard from below.*]

[1879]

Joining the Conversation: Critical Thinking and Writing

1. Near the beginning of the play, how does Mrs. Linde's presence help to define Nora's character? How does Nora's response to Krogstad's entrance tell us something about Nora?
2. What does Dr. Rank contribute to the play? If he were eliminated, what would be lost?

3. Can it be argued that although at the end Nora goes out to achieve self-realization, her abandonment of her children—especially to Torvald's loathsome conventional morality—is a crime?
4. Why does Nora leave the children? She seems to imply, in some passages, that because she forged a signature she is unfit to bring them up. But do you agree with her?
5. Michael Meyer, in his splendid biography *Henrik Ibsen,* says that the play is not so much about women's rights as about "the need of every individual to find out the kind of person he or she really is, and to strive to become that person." What evidence can you offer to support or refute this interpretation?
6. In *The Quintessence of Ibsenism* Bernard Shaw says that Ibsen, reacting against a common theatrical preference for strange situations,

> saw that . . . the more familiar the situation, the more interesting the play. Shakespeare had put ourselves on the stage but not our situations. Our uncles seldom murder our fathers and . . . marry our mothers. . . . Ibsen . . . gives us not only ourselves, but ourselves in our own situations. The things that happen to his stage figures are things that happen to us. One consequence is that his plays are much more important to us than Shakespeare's. Another is that they are capable both of hurting us cruelly and of filling us with excited hopes of escape from idealistic tyrannies, and with visions of intenser life in the future.

How much of this do you believe? Support your response with reasons.

Chapter Overview: Looking Backward/Looking Forward

1. Do you think it is beneficial for men and women to be together in the same college classroom? Can you recall a class discussion or debate when you were aware of sharp differences between how women and men were responding to an issue? Are there some subjects that you believe are best taught in a single-sex environment?
2. Plays, films, and TV shows often make use of the plot device of a man transformed into a woman, or of a woman who disguises herself as a man, and so on. Do you think you would gain from such an experience? How long would you like this experience to last?
3. What does it mean to be a feminist? Has feminism gone too far? Can a man be a feminist, or is that impossible?
4. Do you think that men and women should be free to enter into whatever kind of relationship, married or unmarried (that is, living together), gay or straight, they desire? Or is it your view that the government should play a leading role in defining proper and improper relationships?
5. Can you identify a literary work, or a film, that only a man, or a woman, can really understand or appreciate?
6. Who is better at keeping a secret, a man or a woman?
7. Many colleges and universities now offer courses in gay and lesbian literature. Have you taken such a course yourself? What did you learn from it? If you have not taken such a course, do you intend to?
8. If a straight student in a literature course is assigned to write a paper about a book by a gay author, but then tells the teacher that he or she disapproves of homosexuality on religious grounds, should this student be excused from having to do the paper?

CHAPTER 22

Innocence and Experience

SHORT VIEWS

Children, I grant, should be innocent; but when the epithet is applied to men, or women, it is but a civil term for weakness.

Mary Wollstonecraft

People who shut their eyes to reality simply invite their own destruction, and anyone who insists on remaining in a state of innocence long after that innocence is dead turns himself into a monster.

James Baldwin

"Experience iz a good schoolmaster," but reason iz a better one.

Josh Billings

Experience keeps a dear school, but Fools will learn in no other.

Ben Franklin

A moment's insight is sometimes worth a life's experience.

Oliver Wendell Holmes

What is the good of drawing conclusions from experience? I don't deny we sometimes draw the right conclusions, but don't we just as often draw the wrong ones?

G. C. Lichtenberg

The power to guess the unseen from the seen, to trace the implications of things, to judge the whole piece by the pattern, the condition of feeling life in general so completely that you are well on your way to knowing any particular corner of it—this cluster of gifts may almost be said to constitute experience.

Henry James

We should be careful to get out of an experience only the wisdom that is in it—and stop there; lest we be like the cat that sits down on a hot stove-lid. She will never sit down on a hot stove-lid again—and that is well; but also she will never sit down on a cold one anymore.

Mark Twain

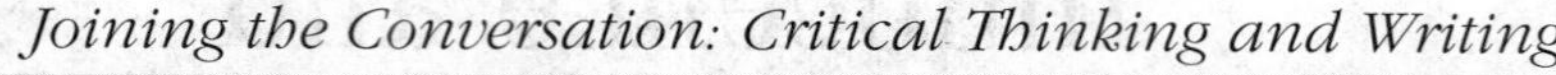

Joining the Conversation: Critical Thinking and Writing

1. Select a quotation that especially appeals to you, and make it the focus of an essay of about 500 words.
2. Take two of the passages—perhaps one that you especially like and one that you think is wrongheaded—and write a dialogue of about 500 words in which the two authors converse or argue. They may each try to convince the other, or they may find that to some degree they share views and they may then work out a statement that both can accept. If you do take the first position—that one writer is on the correct track but the other is utterly mistaken—try to be fair to the view that you think is mistaken. (As an experiment in critical thinking, imagine that you accept it, and make the best case for it that you possibly can.)

ESSAY

GEORGE ORWELL

George Orwell (1903–1950), an Englishman, adopted this name; he was born Eric Blair, in India. He was educated at Eton, in England, but in 1921 he went to Burma (now Myanmar), where he served for five years as a police officer. He then returned to Europe, doing odd jobs while writing novels and stories. In 1936 he fought in the Spanish Civil War on the side of the Republicans, an experience reported in Homage to Catalonia *(1938). Orwell is best known for his novels* Animal Farm *(1945) and* Nineteen Eighty-Four *(1949).*

Shooting an Elephant

In Moulmein, in Lower Burma, I was hated by large numbers of people—the only time in my life that I have been important enough for this to happen to me. I was sub-divisional police officer of the town, and in an aimless, petty kind of way anti-European feeling was very bitter. No one had the guts to raise a riot, but if a European woman went through the bazaars alone somebody would probably spit betel juice over her dress. As a police officer I was an obvious target and was baited whenever it seemed safe to do so. When a nimble Burman tripped me up on the football field and the referee (another Burman) looked the other way, the crowd yelled with hideous laughter. This happened more than once. In the end the sneering yellow faces of young men that met me everywhere, the insults hooted after me when I was at a safe distance, got badly on my nerves. The young Buddhist priests were the worst of all. There were several thousands of them in the town and none of them seemed to have anything to do except stand on street corners and jeer at Europeans.

All this was perplexing and upsetting. For at that time I had already made up my mind that imperialism was an evil thing and the sooner I chucked up my job and got out of it the better. Theoretically—and secretly, of course—I was all for the Burmese and all against their oppressors, the British. As for the job I was doing, I hated it more bitterly than I can perhaps make clear. In a job like that you see the dirty work of the Empire at close quarters. The wretched prisoners huddling in the stinking cages of the lockups, the grey, cowed faces of the long-term convicts, the scarred buttocks of the men who had been flogged with bamboos—all these oppressed me with an intolerable sense of guilt. But I could get nothing into perspective. I was young and ill-educated and I had had to think out my problems in the utter silence that is imposed on every Englishman in the East. I did not even know that the British Empire is dying, still less did I know that it is a great deal better than the younger empires that are going to supplant it. All I knew was that I was stuck between my hatred of the empire I served and my rage against the evil-spirited little beasts who tried to make my job impossible. With one part of my mind I thought of the British Raj as an unbreakable tyranny, as something clamped down, in *saecula saeculorum,*[1] upon the will of prostrate peoples; with another part I thought that the greatest joy in the world would be to drive a bayonet into a Buddhist priest's guts. Feelings like these are the normal by-products of imperialism; ask any Anglo-Indian official, if you can catch him off duty.

One day something happened which in a roundabout way was enlightening. It was a tiny incident in itself, but it gave me a better glimpse than I had had before of the real nature of imperialism—the real motives for which despotic governments act. Early one morning the sub-inspector at a police station at the other end of the town rang me up on the 'phone and said that an elephant was ravaging the bazaar. Would I please come and do something about it? I did not know what I could do, but I wanted to see what was happening and I got onto a pony and started out. I took my rifle, an old .44 Winchester and much too small to kill an elephant, but I thought the noise might be useful *in terrorem.*[2] Various Burmans stopped me on the way and told me about the elephant's doings. It was not, of course, a wild elephant, but a tame one which had gone "must." It had been chained up, as tame elephants always are when their attack of "must" is due, but on the previous night it had broken its chain and escaped. Its mahout, the only person who could manage it when it was in that state, had set out in pursuit, but had taken the wrong direction and was now twelve hours' journey away, and in the morning the elephant had suddenly reappeared in the town. The Burmese population had no weapons and were quite helpless against it. It had already destroyed somebody's bamboo hut, killed a cow and raided some fruit-stalls and devoured the stock; also it had met the municipal rubbish van and, when the driver jumped out and took to his heels, had turned the van over and inflicted violences upon it.

The Burmese sub-inspector and some Indian constables were waiting for me in the quarter where the elephant had been seen. It was a very poor quarter, a labyrinth of squalid bamboo huts, thatched with palmleaf, winding all over a steep hillside. I remember that it was a cloudy, stuffy morning at the beginning of the rains. We began questioning the people as to where the elephant had gone and, as usual, failed to get any definite information. That is invariably the case in the East; a story always sounds clear enough at a distance, but the nearer you get to the scene of events the vaguer it becomes. Some of the people said that the elephant had gone in one direction, some said that he had gone in another, some professed not even to have heard of any elephant. I had almost made up my mind that the whole story was a pack of lies, when we heard yells a little distance away. There was a loud, scandalized cry of "Go away, child! Go away this instant!" and an old woman with a switch in her hand came round the corner of a hut,

[1]*Saecula saeculorum* Latin, "For world without end," In the next paragraph *in terrorem* is Latin for "as a warning" (editors' note). [2]***in terrorem*** as a warning.

violently shooing away a crowd of naked children. Some more women followed, clicking their tongues and exclaiming; evidently there was something that the children ought not to have seen. I rounded the hut and saw a man's dead body sprawling in the mud. He was an Indian, a black Dravidian coolie, almost naked, and he could not have been dead many minutes. The people said that the elephant had come suddenly upon him round the corner of the hut, caught him with its trunk, put its foot on his back and ground him into the earth. This was the rainy season and the ground was soft, and his face had scored a trench a foot deep and a couple of yards long. He was lying on his belly with arms crucified and head sharply twisted to one side. His face was coated with mud, the eyes wide open, the teeth bared and grinning with an expression of unendurable agony. (Never tell me, by the way, that the dead look peaceful. Most of the corpses I have seen look devilish.) The friction of the great beast's foot had stripped the skin from his back as neatly as one skins a rabbit. As soon as I saw the dead man I sent an orderly to a friend's house nearby to borrow an elephant rifle. I had already sent back the pony, not wanting it to go mad with fright and throw me if it smelt the elephant.

5 The orderly came back in a few minutes with a rifle and five cartridges, and meanwhile some Burmans had arrived and told us that the elephant was in the paddy fields below, only a few hundred yards away. As I started forward practically the whole population of the quarter flocked out of the houses and followed me. They had seen the rifle and were all shouting excitedly that I was going to shoot the elephant. They had not shown much interest in the elephant when he was merely ravaging their homes, but it was different now that he was going to be shot. It was a bit of fun to them, as it would be to an English crowd; besides they wanted the meat. It made me vaguely uneasy. I had no intention of shooting the elephant—I had merely sent for the rifle to defend myself if necessary—and it is always unnerving to have a crowd following you. I marched down the hill, looking and feeling a fool, with the rifle over my shoulder and an ever-growing army of people jostling at my heels. At the bottom, when you got away from the huts, there was a metalled road and beyond that a miry waste of paddy fields a thousand yards across, not yet ploughed but soggy from the first rains and dotted with coarse grass. The elephant was standing eight yards from the road, his left side towards us. He took not the slightest notice of the crowd's approach. He was tearing up bunches of grass, beating them against his knees to clean them and stuffing them into his mouth.

I had halted on the road. As soon as I saw the elephant I knew with perfect certainty that I ought not to shoot him. It is a serious matter to shoot a working elephant—it is comparable to destroying a huge and costly piece of machinery—and obviously one ought not to do it if it can possibly be avoided. And at that distance, peacefully eating, the elephant looked no more dangerous than a cow. I thought then and I think now that his attack of "must" was already passing off; in which case he would merely wander harmlessly about until the mahout came back and caught him. Moreover, I did not in the least want to shoot him. I decided that I would watch him for a little while to make sure that he did not turn savage again, and then go home.

But at that moment I glanced round at the crowd that had followed me. It was an immense crowd, two thousand at the least and growing every minute. It blocked the road for a long distance on either side. I looked at the sea of yellow faces above the garish clothes—faces all happy and excited over this bit of fun, all certain that the elephant was going to be shot. They were watching me as they would watch a conjurer about to perform a trick. They did not like me, but with the magical rifle in my hands I was momentarily worth watching. And suddenly I realized that I should have to shoot the elephant after all. The people expected it of me and I had got to do it; I could feel their two thousand wills pressing me forward, irresistibly. And it was at this moment, as I stood there with the rifle in my hands, that I first grasped the hollowness, the futility of the white man's dominion in the East. Here was I, the white man with his gun, standing in front of the unarmed native crowd—seemingly the leading actor of the piece; but in reality I was only an absurd puppet pushed to and fro by the will of those yellow faces behind. I perceived in this moment that when the white man turns tyrant it is his own freedom that he destroys. He becomes a sort of hollow, posing dummy, the conventionalized figure of a sahib. For it is the condition of his rule that he shall spend his life in trying to impress the "natives," and so in every crisis he has got to do what the "natives" expect of him. He wears a mask, and his face grows to fit it. I had got to shoot the elephant. I had committed myself to doing it when I sent for the rifle. A sahib has got to act like a sahib; he has got to appear resolute, to know his own mind and do definite things. To come all that way, rifle in hand, with two thousand people marching at my heels, and then to trail feebly away, having done nothing—no, that was impossible. The crowd would laugh at me. And my whole life, every white man's life in the East, was one long struggle not to be laughed at.

But I did not want to shoot the elephant. I watched him beating his bunch of grass against his knees, with that preoccupied grandmotherly air that elephants have. It seemed to me that it would be murder to shoot him. At that age I was not squeamish about killing animals, but I had never shot an elephant and never wanted to. (Somehow it always seems worse to kill a *large* animal.) Besides, there was the beast's owner to be considered. Alive, the elephant was worth at least a hundred pounds; dead, he would only be worth the value of his tusks, five pounds, possibly. But I had got to act quickly. I turned to some experienced-looking Burmans who had been there when we arrived, and asked them how the elephant had been behaving. They all said the same thing; he took no notice of you if you left him alone, but he might charge if you went too close to him.

It was perfectly clear to me what I ought to do. I ought to walk up to within, say, twenty-five yards of the elephant and test his behavior. If he charged, I could shoot; if he took no notice of me, it would be safe to leave him until the mahout came back. But also I knew that I was going to do no such thing. I was a poor shot with a rifle and the ground was soft mud into which one would sink at every step. If the elephant charged and I missed him, I should have about as much chance as a toad under a steam-roller. But even then I was not thinking particularly of my own skin, only of the watchful yellow faces behind. For at that moment, with the crowd watching me, I was not afraid in the ordinary sense, as I would have been if I had been alone. A white man mustn't be frightened in front of "natives"; and so, in general, he isn't frightened. The sole thought in my mind was that if anything went wrong those two thousand Burmans would see me pursued, caught, trampled on and reduced to a grinning corpse like that Indian up the hill. And if that happened it was quite probable that some of them would laugh. That would never do. There was only one alternative. I shoved the cartridges into the magazine and lay down on the road to get a better aim.

10 The crowd grew very still, and a deep, low, happy sigh, as of people who see the theatre curtain go up at last breathed from innumerable throats. They were going to have their bit of fun after all. The rifle was a beautiful German thing with cross-hair sights. I did not then know that in shooting an elephant one would

shoot to cut an imaginary bar running from ear-hole to ear-hole. I ought, therefore, as the elephant was sideways on, to have aimed straight at his ear-hole; actually I aimed several inches in front of this, thinking the brain would be further forward.

When I pulled the trigger I did not hear the bang or feel the kick—one never does when a shot goes home—but I heard the devilish roar of glee that went up from the crowd. In that instant, in too short a time, one would have thought, even for the bullet to get there, a mysterious, terrible change had come over the elephant. He neither stirred nor fell, but every line of his body had altered. He looked suddenly stricken, shrunken, immensely old, as though the frightful impact of the bullet had paralysed him without knocking him down. At last, after what seemed a long time—it might have been five seconds, I dare say—he sagged flabbily to his knees. His mouth slobbered. An enormous senility seemed to have settled upon him. One could have imagined him thousands of years old. I fired again into the same spot. At the second shot he did not collapse but climbed with desperate slowness to his feet and stood weakly upright, with legs sagging and head dropping. I fired a third time. That was the shot that did for him. You could see the agony of it jolt his whole body and knock the last remnant of strength from his legs. But in falling he seemed for a moment to rise, for as his hind legs collapsed beneath him he seemed to tower upward like a huge rock toppling, his trunk reaching skywards like a tree. He trumpeted, for the first and only time. And then down he came, his belly towards me, with a crash that seemed to shake the ground even where I lay.

I got up. The Burmans were already racing past me across the mud. It was obvious that the elephant would never rise again, but he was not dead. He was breathing very rhythmically with long rattling gasps, his great mound of a side painfully rising and falling. His mouth was wide open. I could see far down into caverns of pale pink throat. I waited a long time for him to die, but his breathing did not weaken. Finally I fired my two remaining shots into the spot where I thought his heart must be. The thick blood welled out of him like red velvet, but still he did not die. His body did not even jerk when the shots hit him, the tortured breathing continued without a pause. He was dying, very slowly and in great agony, but in some world remote from me where not even a bullet could damage him further. I felt I had got to put an end to that dreadful noise. It seemed dreadful to see the great beast lying there, powerless to move and yet powerless to die, and not even to be able to finish him. I sent back for my small rifle and poured shot after shot into his heart and down his throat. They seemed to make no impression. The tortured gasps continued as steadily as the ticking of a clock.

In the end I could not stand it any longer and went away. I heard later that it took him half an hour to die. Burmans were bringing dahs[3] and baskets even before I left, and I was told they had stripped his body almost to the bones by the afternoon.

Afterwards, of course, there were endless discussions about the shooting of the elephant. The owner was furious, but he was only an Indian and could do nothing. Besides, legally I had done the right thing, for a mad elephant has to be killed, like a mad dog, if its owner fails to control it. Among the Europeans opinion was divided. The older men said I was right, the younger men said it was a damn shame to shoot an elephant for killing a coolie, because an elephant was worth more than any damn Coringhee coolie. And afterwards I was very glad that the coolie had been killed; it put me legally in the right and it gave me a sufficient

[3]**dahs** knives.

pretext for shooting the elephant. I often wondered whether any of the others grasped that I had done it solely to avoid looking a fool.

[1936]

Joining the Conversation: Critical Thinking and Writing

1. How does Orwell characterize himself at the time of the events he describes? What evidence in the essay suggests that he wrote it some years later?
2. Orwell says the incident was "enlightening." What does he mean? Picking up this clue, state in a sentence or two the thesis or main point of the essay.
3. Compare Orwell's description of the dead coolie (in the fourth paragraph) with his description of the elephant's death (in the eleventh and twelfth paragraphs). Why does Orwell devote more space to the death of the elephant?
4. How would you describe the tone of the last paragraph, particularly of the last two sentences? Do you find the paragraph an effective conclusion to the essay? Explain.

STORIES

HANS CHRISTIAN ANDERSEN

Hans Christian Andersen (1805–1875) was born in humble circumstances and apprenticed as a weaver and tailor at the age of 11. A patron enabled him to return to elementary school, but he was unhappy there, taunted because of his unattractive appearance. In 1829 he published a short story that gained some attention, and in 1835 he published his first book of fairy tales, but the book did not sell widely. A book of travel sketches (1851) did better, and so did his second book of fairy tales (1837). His third book of fairy tales (1845) brought him widespread fame. Among his best-known tales are "The Ugly Duckling" "The Little Mermaid," "The Princess and the Pea," and the one that we present here, "The Emperor's New Clothes."

The Emperor's New Clothes

Many years ago, there was an Emperor, who was so excessively fond of new clothes that he spent all his money in dress. He did not trouble himself in the least about his soldiers; nor did he care to go either to the theatre or the chase, except for the opportunities then afforded him for displaying his new clothes. He had a different suit for each hour of the day; and as of any other king or emperor one is accustomed to say, "He is sitting in council," it was always said of him, "The Emperor is sitting in his wardrobe."

Time passed away merrily in the large town which was his capital; strangers arrived every day at the court. One day two rogues, calling themselves weavers, made their appearance. They gave out that they knew how to weave stuffs of the most beautiful colors and elaborate patterns, the clothes manufactured from which should have the wonderful property of remaining invisible to every one who was unfit for the office he held, or who was extraordinarily simple in character.

"These must, indeed, be splendid clothes!" thought the Emperor. "Had I such a suit, I might at once find out what men in my realm are unfit for their office, and also be able to distinguish the wise from the foolish! This stuff must be woven for me immediately." And he caused large sums of money to be given to both the weavers, in order that they might begin their work directly.

So the two pretended weavers set up two looms, and affected to work very busily, though in reality they did nothing at all. They asked for the most delicate silk and the purest gold thread; put both into their own knapsacks; and then continued their pretended work at the empty looms until late at night.

5 "I should like to know how the weavers are getting on with my cloth," said the emperor to himself, after some little time had elapsed; he was, however, rather embarrassed when he remembered that a simpleton, or one unfit for his office, would be unable to see the manufacture. To be sure, he thought, he had nothing to risk in his own person; but yet he would prefer sending somebody else to bring him intelligence about the weavers, and their work, before he troubled himself in the affair. All the people throughout the city had heard of the wonderful property the cloth was to possess; and all were anxious to learn how wise, or how ignorant, their neighbors might prove to be.

"I will send my faithful old Minister to the weavers," said the Emperor at last, after some deliberation; "he will be best able to see how the cloth looks; for he is a man of sense, and no one can be more suitable for his office than he is."

So the honest old Minister went into the hall, where the knaves were working with all their might at their empty looms. "What can be the meaning of this?" thought the old man, opening his eyes very wide; "I cannot discover the least bit of thread on the looms!" However, he did not express his thoughts aloud.

The impostors requested him very courteously to be so good as to come nearer their looms; and then asked him whether the design pleased him, and whether the colors were not very beautiful; at the same time pointing to the empty frames. The poor old Minister looked and looked; he could not discover anything on the looms, for a very good reason: there was nothing there. "What!" thought he again, "is it possible that I am a simpleton? I have never thought so myself; and, at any rate, if I am so, no one must know it. Can it be that I am unfit for my office? No, that must not be said either. I will never confess that I could not see the stuff."

"Well, Sir Minister!" said one of the knaves, still pretending to work, "you do not say whether the stuff pleases you."

10 "Oh, it is admirable!" replied the old Minister, looking at the loom through his spectacles. "This pattern, and the colors—yes, I will tell the Emperor without delay how very beautiful I think them."

"We shall be much obliged to you," said the impostors, and then they named the different colors and described the patterns of the pretended stuff. The old Minister listened attentively to their words, in order that he might repeat them to the Emperor; and then the knaves asked for more silk and gold, saying that it was necessary to complete what they had begun. However, they put all that was given them into their knapsacks, and continued to work with as much apparent diligence as before at their empty looms.

The Emperor now sent another officer of his court to see how the men were getting on, and to ascertain whether the cloth would soon be ready. It was just the same with this gentleman as with the Minister; he surveyed the looms on all sides, but could see nothing at all but the empty frames.

"Does not the stuff appear as beautiful to you as it did to my Lord the Minister?" asked the impostors of the Emperor's second ambassador; at the same time making the same gestures as before, and talking of the design and colors which were not there.

"I certainly am not stupid!" thought the messenger. "It must be that I am not fit for my good, profitable office! That is very odd; however, no one shall know anything about it." And accordingly he praised the stuff he could not see, and declared that he was delighted with both colors and patterns. "Indeed, please your Imperial Majesty," said he to his sovereign, when he returned, "the cloth which the weavers are preparing is extraordinarily magnificent."

15 The whole city was talking of the splendid cloth which the Emperor had ordered to be woven at his own expense.

And now the Emperor himself wished to see the costly manufacture, whilst it was still on the loom. Accompanied by a select number of officers of the court, among whom were the two honest men who had already admired the cloth, he went to the crafty impostors, who, as soon as they were aware of the Emperor's approach, went on working more diligently than ever; although they still did not pass a single thread through the looms.

"Is not the work absolutely magnificent?" said the two officers of the crown already mentioned. "If your Majesty will only be pleased to look at it! What a splendid design! What glorious colors!" and at the same time they pointed to the empty frames; for they imagined that every one but themselves could see this exquisite piece of workmanship.

"How is this?" said the Emperor to himself; "I can see nothing! This is, indeed, a terrible affair! Am I a simpleton? Or am I unfit to be an Emperor? That would be the worst thing that could happen." "Oh, the cloth is charming!" said he aloud; "it has my entire approbation." And he smiled most graciously, and looked closely at the empty looms; for on no account would he say that he could not see what two of the officers of his court had praised so much. All his retinue now strained their eyes, hoping to discover something on the looms, but they could see no more than the others; nevertheless, they all exclaimed, "Oh! how beautiful!" and advised his Majesty to have some new clothes made from this splendid material for the approaching procession. "Magnificent! charming! excellent!" resounded on all sides; and every one was uncommonly gay. The Emperor shared in the general satisfaction, and presented the impostors with the riband of an order of knighthood to be worn in their buttonholes, and the title of "Gentlemen Weavers."

The rogues sat up the whole of the night before the day on which the procession was to take place, and had sixteen lights burning, so that every one might see how anxious they were to finish the Emperor's new suit. They pretended to roll the cloth off the looms; cut the air with their scissors; and sewed with needles without any thread in them. "See!" cried they at last, "the Emperor's new clothes are ready!"

20 And now the Emperor, with all the grandees of his court, came to the weavers; and the rogues raised their arms, as if in the act of holding something up, saying, "Here are your Majesty's trousers! Here is the scarf! Here is the mantle! The whole suit is as light as a cobweb; one might fancy one has nothing at all on, when dressed in it; that, however, is the great virtue of this delicate cloth."

"Yes, indeed!" said all the courtiers, although not one of them could see anything of this exquisite manufacture.

"If your Imperial Majesty will be graciously pleased to take off your clothes, we will fit on the new suit, in front of the looking-glass."

The Emperor was accordingly undressed, and the rogues pretended to array him in his new suit; the Emperor turning round, from side to side, before the looking-glass.

"How splendid his Majesty looks in his new clothes! and how well they fit!" every one cried out. "What a design! what colors! These are, indeed, royal robes!"

25 "The canopy which is to be borne over your majesty, in the procession, is waiting," announced the Chief Master of the Ceremonies.

"I am quite ready," answered the Emperor. "Do my new clothes fit well?" asked he, turning himself round again before the looking-glass, in order that he might appear to be examining his handsome suit.

The lords of the bed-chamber, who were to carry his Majesty's train, felt about on the ground, as if they were lifting up the ends of the mantle, and pretended to be carrying something; for they would by no means betray anything like simplicity, or unfitness for their office.

So now the Emperor walked under his high canopy in the midst of the procession, through the streets of his capital; and all the people standing by, and those at the windows, cried out, "Oh! How beautiful are our Emperor's new clothes! What a magnificent train there is to the mantle! And how gracefully the scarf hangs!" In short, no one would allow that he could not see these much-admired clothes, because, in doing so, he would have declared himself either a simpleton or unfit for his office. Certainly, none of the Emperor's various suits had ever excited so much admiration as this.

"But the Emperor has nothing at all on!" said a little child. "Listen to the voice of innocence!" exclaimed his father; and what the child had said was whispered from one to another.

30 "But he has nothing at all on!" at last cried out all the people. The Emperor was vexed, for he knew that the people were right; but he thought, "the procession must go on now!" And the lords of the bed-chamber took greater pains than ever to appear holding up a train, although, in reality, there was no train to hold.

[1837]

Joining the Conversation: Critical Thinking and Writing

1. What reason does the emperor give to himself for not being the first to examine the clothes? What is his real reason?
2. Why is it significant that a child rather than an adult is the first to see the truth that the emperor is naked?
3. In an essay of 500 words, consider whether the story would be better or worse if, after the child's perception, the crowd roared with laughter at the vain and foolish emperor, and the emperor fled in humiliation. Argue for the superiority of the ending you prefer.
4. Drawing on your own experience, set forth and analyze an episode that illustrates the gist of this story; that is, an episode showing the hypocrisy or folly of adults and the insight of a child or adolescent. Your essay should include an analysis of the reasons for the behavior of the adults.

JAMAICA KINCAID

Jamaica Kincaid was born in 1949 in St. Johns, Antigua, in the West Indies. She was educated at the Princess Margaret school in Antigua and, briefly, at Westchester Community College and Franconia College. Since 1974 she has been a contributor to the New Yorker, *where "Girl" first was published in 1978. "Girl" was later included in the first of Kincaid's books,* At the Bottom of the River.

Kincaid informs us that "benna," mentioned early in "Girl," refers to "songs of the sort your parents didn't want you to sing, at first calypso and later rock and roll." "Doukona" is a spicy pudding made of plantains.

Girl

Wash the white clothes on Monday and put them on the stone heap; wash the color clothes on Tuesday and put them on the clothesline to dry; don't walk bare-head in the hot sun; cook pumpkin fritters in very hot sweet oil; soak your little clothes right after you take them off; when buying cotton to make yourself a nice blouse, be sure that is doesn't have gum on it, because that way it won't hold up well after a wash; soak salt fish overnight before you cook it; is it true that you sing benna in Sunday school?; always eat your food in such a way that it won't turn someone else's stomach; on Sundays try to walk like a lady and not like the slut you are so bent on becoming; don't sing benna in Sunday school; you mustn't speak to wharf-rat boys, not even to give directions; don't eat fruits on the street—flies will follow you; *but I don't sing benna on Sundays at all and never in Sunday school;* this is how to sew on a button; this is how to make a buttonhole for the button you have just sewed on; this is how to hem a dress when you see the hem coming down and so to prevent yourself from looking like the slut I know you are so bent on becoming; this is how you iron your father's khaki shirt so that it doesn't have a crease; this is how you iron your father's khaki pants so that they don't have a crease; this is how you grow okra—far from the house, because okra tree harbors red ants; when you are growing dasheen, make sure it gets plenty of water or else it makes your throat itch when you are eating it; this is how you sweep a corner; this is how you sweep a whole house; this is how you sweep a yard; this is how you smile to someone you don't like too much; this is how you smile to someone you don't like at all; this is how you smile to someone you like completely; this is how you set a table for tea; this is how you set a table for dinner; this is how you set a table for dinner with an important guest; this is how you set a table for lunch; this is how you set a table for breakfast; this is how to behave in the presence of men who don't know you very well, and this way they won't recognize immediately the slut I have warned you against becoming; be sure to wash every day, even if it is with your own spit; don't squat down to play marbles—you are not a boy, you know; don't pick people's flowers—you might catch something; don't throw stones at blackbirds, because it might not be a blackbird at all; this is how to make a bread pudding; this is how to make doukona; this is how to make pepper pot; this is how to make a good medicine for a cold; this is how to make a good medicine to throw away a child before it even becomes a child; this is how to catch a fish; this is how to throw back a fish you don't like, and that way something bad won't fall on you; this is how to bully a man; this is how a man bullies you; this is how to love a man, and if this doesn't work there are other ways, and if they don't work don't feel too bad about giving up; this is how to spit up in the air if you feel like it, and this is how to move quick so that it doesn't fall on you; this is how to make ends meet; always squeeze bread to make sure it's fresh; *but what if the baker won't let me feel the bread?*; you mean to say that after all you are really going to be the kind of woman who the baker won't let near the bread?

[1978]

Joining the Conversation: Critical Thinking and Writing

1. In a paragraph, identify the two characters whose voices we hear in this story. Explain what we know about them (their circumstances and their relationship). Cite specific evidence from the text. For example, what is the effect of the frequent repetition of "this is how"? Are there other words or phrases frequently repeated?
2. Try reading a section of "Girl" out loud in a rhythmical pattern, giving the principal and the second voices. Then reread the story, trying to incorporate this rhythm mentally into your reading. How does this rhythm contribute to the overall effect of the story? How does it compare to or contrast with speech rhythms that are familiar to you?

Daniel Orozco

Daniel Orozco, born in 1957, is chiefly known for his short stories. A professor of creative writing at the University of Idaho, Orozco has received several important awards, including a grant from the National Endowment for the Arts.

Orientation

Those are the offices and these are the cubicles. That's my cubicle there, and this is your cubicle. This is your phone. Never answer your phone. Let the Voicemail System answer it. This is your Voicemail System Manual. There are no personal phone calls allowed. We do, however, allow for emergencies. If you must make an emergency phone call, ask your supervisor first. If you can't find your supervisor, ask Phillip Spiers, who sits over there. He'll check with Clarissa Nicks, who sits over there. If you make an emergency phone call without asking, you may be let go.

These are your IN and OUT boxes. All the forms in your IN box must be logged in by the date shown in the upper left-hand corner, initialed by you in the upper right-hand corner, and distributed to the Processing Analyst whose name is numerically coded in the lower left-hand corner. The lower right-hand corner is left blank. Here's your Processing Analyst Numerical Code Index. And here's your Forms Processing Procedures Manual.

You must pace your work. What do I mean? I'm glad you asked that. We pace our work according to the eight-hour workday. If you have twelve hours of work in your IN box, for example, you must compress that work into the eight-hour day. If you have one hour of work in your IN box, you must expand that work to fill the eight-hour day. That was a good question. Feel free to ask questions. Ask too many questions, however, and you may be let go.

That is our receptionist. She is a temp. We go through receptionists here. They quit with alarming frequency. Be polite and civil to the temps. Learn their names, and invite them to lunch occasionally. But don't get close to them, as it only makes it more difficult when they leave. And they always leave. You can be sure of that.

5 The men's room is over there. The women's room is over there. John LaFountaine, who sits over there, uses the women's room occasionally. He says it

is accidental. We know better, but we let it pass. John LaFountaine is harmless, his forays into the forbidden territory of the women's room simply a benign thrill, a faint blip on the dull flat line of his life.

Russell Nash, who sits in the cubicle to your left, is in love with Amanda Pierce, who sits in the cubicle to your right. They ride the same bus together after work. For Amanda Pierce, it is just a tedious bus ride made less tedious by the idle nattering of Russell Nash. But for Russell Nash, it is the highlight of his day. It is the highlight of his life. Russell Nash has put on forty pounds, and grows fatter with each passing month, nibbling on chips and cookies while peeking glumly over the partitions at Amanda Pierce, and gorging himself at home on cold pizza and ice cream while watching adult videos on TV.

Amanda Pierce, in the cubicle to your right, has a six-year-old son named Jamie, who is autistic. Her cubicle is plastered from top to bottom with the boy's crayon artwork—sheet after sheet of precisely drawn concentric circles and ellipses, in black and yellow. She rotates them every other Friday. Be sure to comment on them. Amanda Pierce also has a husband, who is a lawyer. He subjects her to an escalating array of painful and humiliating sex games, to which Amanda Pierce reluctantly submits. She comes to work exhausted and freshly wounded each morning, wincing from the abrasions on her breasts, or the bruises on her abdomen, or the second-degree burns on the backs of her thighs.

But we're not supposed to know any of this. Do not let on. If you let on, you may be let go.

Amanda Pierce, who tolerates Russell Nash, is in love with Albert Bosch, whose office is over there. Albert Bosch, who only dimly registers Amanda Pierce's existence, has eyes only for Ellie Tapper, who sits over there. Ellie Tapper, who hates Albert Bosch, would walk through fire for Curtis Lance. But Curtis Lance hates Ellie Tapper. Isn't the world a funny place? Not in the ha-ha sense, of course.

10 Anika Bloom sits in that cubicle. Last year, while reviewing quarterly reports in a meeting with Barry Hacker, Anika Bloom's left palm began to bleed. She fell into a trance, stared into her hand, and told Barry Hacker when and how his wife would die. We laughed it off. She was, after all, a new employee. But Barry Hacker's wife is dead. So unless you want to know exactly when and how you'll die, never talk to Anika Bloom.

Colin Heavey sits in that cubicle over there. He was new once, just like you. We warned him about Anika Bloom. But at last year's Christmas Potluck, he felt sorry for her when he saw that no one was talking to her. Colin Heavey brought her a drink. He hasn't been himself since. Colin Heavey is doomed. There's nothing he can do about it, and we are powerless to help him. Stay away from Colin Heavey. Never give any of your work to him. If he asks to do something, tell him you have to check with me. If he asks again, tell him I haven't gotten back to you.

This is the Fire Exit. There are several on this floor, and they are marked accordingly. We have a Floor Evacuation Review every three months, and an Escape Route Quiz once a month. We have our Biannual Fire Drill twice a year, and our Annual Earthquake Drill once a year. These are precautions only. These things never happen.

For your information, we have a comprehensive health plan. Any catastrophic illness, any unforeseen tragedy is completely covered. All dependents are completely covered. Larry Bagdikian, who sits over there, has six daughters. If anything were to happen to any of his girls, or to all of them, if all six were to simultaneously fall victim to illness or injury—stricken with a hideous degenerative muscle disease or some rare toxic blood disorder, sprayed with semiautomatic gunfire while on a class field trip, or attacked in their bunk beds by some prowling nocturnal lunatic—if any of this were to pass, Larry's girls would all be taken care of. Larry Bagdikian would not have to pay one dime. He would have nothing to worry about.

We also have a generous vacation and sick leave policy. We have an excellent disability insurance plan. We have a stable and profitable pension fund. We get group discounts for the symphony, and block seating at the ballpark. We get commuter ticket books for the bridge. We have Direct Deposit. We are all members of Costco.

15 This is our kitchenette. And this, this is our Mr. Coffee. We have a coffee pool, into which we each pay two dollars a week for coffee, filters, sugar, and CoffeeMate. If you prefer Cremora or half-and-half to CoffeeMate, there is a special pool for three dollars a week. If you prefer Sweet 'n Low to sugar, there is a special pool for two-fifty a week. We do not do decaf. You are allowed to join the coffee pool of your choice, but you are not allowed to touch the Mr. Coffee.

This is the microwave oven. You are allowed to *heat* food in the microwave oven. You are not, however, allowed to *cook* food in the microwave oven.

We get one hour for lunch. We also get one fifteen-minute break in the morning, and one fifteen-minute break in the afternoon. Always take your breaks. If you skip a break, it is gone forever. For your information, your break is a privilege, not a right. If you abuse the break policy, we are authorized to rescind your breaks. Lunch, however, is a right, not a privilege. If you abuse the lunch policy, our hands will be tied, and we will be forced to look the other way. We will not enjoy that.

This is the refrigerator. You may put your lunch in it. Barry Hacker, who sits over there, steals food from this refrigerator. His petty theft is an outlet for his grief. Last New Year's Eve, while kissing his wife, a blood vessel burst in her brain. Barry Hacker's wife was two months pregnant at the time, and lingered in a coma for half a year before dying. It was a tragic loss for Barry Hacker. He hasn't been himself since. Barry Hacker's wife was a beautiful woman. She was also completely covered. Barry Hacker did not have to pay one dime. But his dead wife haunts him. She haunts all of us. We have seen her, reflected in the monitors of our computers, moving past our cubicles. We have seen the dim shadow of her face in our photocopies. She pencils herself in the receptionist's appointment book, with the notation: To see Barry Hacker. She has left messages in the receptionist's Voicemail box, messages garbled by the electronic chirrups and buzzes in the phone line, her voice echoing from an immense distance within the ambient hum. But the voice is hers. And beneath her voice, beneath the tidal *whoosh* of static and hiss, the gurgling and crying of a baby can be heard.

In any case, if you bring a lunch, put a little something extra in the bag for Barry Hacker. We have four Barrys in this office. Isn't that a coincidence?

20 This is Matthew Payne's office. He is our Unit Manager, and his door is always closed. We have never seen him, and you will never see him. But he is here. You can be sure of that. He is all around us.

This is the Custodian's Closet. You have no business in the Custodian's Closet.

And this, this is our Supplies Cabinet. If you need supplies, see Curtis Lance. He will log you in on the Supplies Cabinet Authorization Log, then give you a Supplies Authorization Slip. Present your pink copy of the Supplies Authorization Slip to Ellie Tapper. She will log you in on the Supplies Cabinet Key Log, then give you the key. Because the Supplies Cabinet is located outside the Unit Manager's office, you must be very quiet. Gather your supplies quietly. The Supplies Cabinet is divided into four sections. Section One contains letterhead stationery, blank paper and envelopes, memo and note pads, and so on. Section Two contains pens and pencils and typewriter and printer ribbons, and the like. In Section Three we have erasers, correction fluids, transparent tapes, glue sticks, et cetera. And in Section Four we have paper clips and push pins and scissors and razor blades. And here are the spare blades for the shredder. Do not touch the shredder, which is located over there. The shredder is of no concern to you.

Gwendolyn Stich sits in that office there. She is crazy about penguins, and collects penguin knickknacks: penguin posters and coffee mugs and stationery, penguin stuffed animals, penguin jewelry, penguin sweaters and T-shirts and socks. She has a pair of penguin fuzzy slippers she wears when working late at the office. She has a tape cassette of penguin sounds which she listens to for relaxation. Her favorite colors are black and white. She has personalized license plates that read PEN GWEN. Every morning, she passes through all the cubicles to wish each of us a good morning. She brings Danish on Wednesdays for Hump Day morning break, and doughnuts on Fridays for TGIF afternoon break. She organizes the Annual Christmas Potluck, and is in charge of the Birthday List. Gwendolyn Stich's door is always open to all of us. She will always lend an ear, and put in a good word for you; she will always give you a hand, or the shirt off her back, or a shoulder to cry on. Because her door is always open, she hides and cries in a stall in the women's room. And John LaFountaine—who, enthralled when a woman enters, sits quietly in his stall with his knees to his chest—John LaFountaine has heard her vomiting in there. We have come upon Gwendolyn Stich huddled in the stairwell, shivering in the updraft, sipping a Diet Mr. Pibb and hugging her knees. She does not let any of this interfere with her work. If it interfered with her work, she might have to be let go.

Kevin Howard sits in that cubicle over there. He is a serial killer, the one they call the Carpet Cutter, responsible for the mutilations across town. We're not supposed to know that, so do not let on. Don't worry. His compulsion inflicts itself on strangers only, and the routine established is elaborate and unwavering. The victim must be a white male, a young adult no older than thirty, heavyset, with dark hair and eyes, and the like. The victim must be chosen at random, before sunset, from a public place; the victim is followed home, and must put up a struggle; et cetera. The carnage inflicted is precise: the angle and direction of the incisions; the layering of skin and muscle tissue; the rearrangement of the visceral organs; and so on. Kevin Howard does not let any of this interfere with his work. He is, in fact, our fastest typist. He types as if he were on fire. He has a secret crush on Gwendolyn Stich, and leaves a red-foil-wrapped Hershey's Kiss on her desk every afternoon. But he hates Anika Bloom, and keeps well away from her. In his presence, she has uncontrollable fits of shaking and trembling. Her left palm does not stop bleeding.

25 In any case, when Kevin Howard gets caught, act surprised. Say that he seemed like a nice person, a bit of a loner, perhaps, but always quiet and polite.

This is the photocopier room. And this, this is our view. It faces southwest. West is down there, toward the water. North is back there. Because we are on the seventeenth floor, we are afforded a magnificent view. Isn't it beautiful? It overlooks the park, where the tops of those trees are. You can see a segment of the bay between those two buildings there. You can see the sun set in the gap between those two buildings over there. You can see this building reflected in the glass panels of that building across the way. There. See? That's you, waving. And look there. There's Anika Bloom in the kitchenette, waving back.

Enjoy this view while photocopying. If you have problems with the photocopier, see Russell Nash. If you have any questions, ask your supervisor. If you can't find your supervisor, ask Phillip Spiers. He sits over there. He'll check with Clarissa Nicks. She sits over there. If you can't find them, feel free to ask me. That's my cubicle. I sit in there.

[1994]

Joining the Conversation: Critical Thinking and Writing

1. How would you characterize the narrator. Thoroughly experienced? Innocent in some ways?
2. Write your own "Orientation" instructions (250–500 words) to someone who is about to take a job that you have had.

JAMES BALDWIN

James Baldwin (1924–1987) was born in New York City. He was the author of short stories and novels, including Go Tell It on the Mountain *(1953), which drew upon his own experiences growing up in Harlem, in poverty and in the midst of a highly religious household. Perhaps his most influential work was done in his many literary and autobiographical essays, especially in the collections* Notes of a Native Son *(1955) and* Nobody Knows My Name *(1961).*

Sonny's Blues

I read about it in the paper, in the subway, on my way to work. I read it, and I couldn't believe it, and I read it again. Then perhaps I just stared at it, at the newsprint spelling out his name, spelling out the story. I stared at it in the swinging lights of the subway car, and in the faces and bodies of the people, and in my own face, trapped in the darkness which roared outside.

It was not to be believed and I kept telling myself that, as I walked from the subway station to the high school. And at the same time I couldn't doubt it. I was scared, scared for Sonny. He became real to me again. A great block of ice got settled in my belly and kept melting there slowly all day long, while I taught my classes algebra. It was a special kind of ice. It kept melting, sending trickles of ice water all up and down my veins, but it never got less. Sometimes it hardened and seemed to expand until I felt my guts were going to come spilling out or that I was going to choke or scream. This would always be at a moment when I was remembering some specific thing Sonny had once said or done.

When he was about as old as the boys in my classes his face had been bright and open, there was a lot of copper in it; and he'd had wonderfully direct brown eyes, and great gentleness and privacy. I wondered what he looked like now. He had been picked up, the evening before, in a raid on an apartment downtown, for peddling and using heroin.

I couldn't believe it: but what I mean by that is that I couldn't find any room for it anywhere inside me. I had kept it outside me for a long time. I hadn't wanted to know. I had had suspicions, but I didn't name them, I kept putting them away. I told myself that Sonny was wild, but he wasn't crazy. And he'd always been a good boy, he hadn't ever turned hard or evil or disrespectful, the way kids can, so quick, so quick, especially in Harlem. I didn't want to believe that I'd ever see my brother going down, coming to nothing, all that light in his face gone out, in the condition I'd already seen so many others. Yet it had happened and here I was, talking about algebra to a lot of boys who might, every one of them for all I knew, be popping off needles every time they went to the head. Maybe it did more for them than algebra could.

5 I was sure that the first time Sonny had ever had horse, he couldn't have been much older than these boys were now. These boys, now, were living as we'd been living then, they were growing up with a rush and their heads bumped abruptly against the low ceiling of their actual possibilities. They were filled with rage. All they really knew were two darknesses, the darkness of their lives, which was now closing in on them, and the darkness of the movies, which had blinded them to that other darkness, and in which they now, vindictively, dreamed, at once more together than they were at any other time, and more alone.

When the last bell rang, the last class ended, I let out my breath. It seemed I'd been holding it for all that time. My clothes were wet—I may have looked as though I'd been sitting in a steam bath, all dressed up, all afternoon. I sat alone in the classroom a long time. I listened to the boys outside, downstairs, shouting and cursing and laughing. Their laughter struck me for perhaps the first time. It was not the joyous laughter which—God knows why—one associates with children. It was mocking and insular, its intent to denigrate. It was disenchanted, and in this, also, lay the authority of their curses. Perhaps I was listening to them because I was thinking about my brother and in them I heard my brother. And myself.

One boy was whistling a tune, at once very complicated and very simple, it seemed to be pouring out of him as though he were a bird, and it sounded very cool and moving through all that harsh, bright air, only just holding its own through all those other sounds.

I stood up and walked over to the window and looked down into the courtyard. It was the beginning of the spring and the sap was rising in the boys. A teacher passed through them every now and again, quickly, as though he or she couldn't wait to get out of that courtyard, to get those boys out of their sight and off their minds. I started collecting my stuff. I thought I'd better get home and talk to Isabel.

The courtyard was almost deserted by the time I got downstairs. I saw this boy standing in the shadow of a doorway, looking just like Sonny. I almost called his name. Then I saw that it wasn't Sonny, but somebody we used to know, a boy from around our block. He'd been Sonny's friend. He'd never been mine, having been too young for me, and, anyway, I'd never liked him. And now, even though he was a grown-up man, he still hung around that block, still spent hours on the street corners, was always high and raggy. I used to run into him from time to time and he'd often work around to asking me for a quarter or fifty cents. He always had some real good excuse, too, and I always gave it to him, I don't know why.

10 But now, abruptly, I hated him. I couldn't stand the way he looked at me, partly like a dog, partly like a cunning child. I wanted to ask him what the hell he was doing in the school courtyard.

He sort of shuffled over to me, and he said, "I see you got the papers. So you already know about it."

"You mean about Sonny? Yes, I already know about it. How come they didn't get you?"

He grinned. It made him repulsive and it also brought to mind what he'd looked like as a kid. "I wasn't there. I stay away from them people."

"Good for you." I offered him a cigarette and I watched him through the smoke. "You come all the way down here just to tell me about Sonny?"

15 "That's right." He was sort of shaking his head and his eyes looked strange, as though they were about to cross. The bright sun deadened his damp dark brown skin and it made his eyes look yellow and showed up the dirt in his kinked hair. He smelled funky. I moved a little away from him and I said, "Well, thanks. But I already know about it and I got to get home."

"I'll walk you a little ways," he said. We started walking. There were a couple of kids still loitering in the courtyard and one of them said goodnight to me and looked strangely at the boy beside me.

"What're you going to do?" he asked me. "I mean, about Sonny?"

"Look. I haven't seen Sonny for over a year. I'm not sure I'm going to do anything. Anyway, what the hell *can* I do?"

"That's right," he said quickly, "ain't nothing you can do. Can't much help old Sonny no more, I guess."

20 It was what I was thinking and so it seemed to me he had no right to say it.

"I'm surprised at Sonny, though," he went on—he had a funny way of talking, he looked straight ahead as though he were talking to himself—"I thought Sonny was a smart boy, I thought he was too smart to get hung."

"I guess he thought so too," I said sharply, "and that's how he got hung. And how about you? You're pretty goddamn smart, I bet."

Then he looked directly at me, just for a minute. "I ain't smart," he said. "If I was smart, I'd have reached for a pistol a long time ago."

"Look. Don't tell *me* your sad story, if it was up to me, I'd give you one." Then I felt guilty—guilty, probably, for never having supposed that the poor bastard *had* a story of his own, much less a sad one, and I asked, quickly, "What's going to happen to him now?"

25 He didn't answer this. He was off by himself some place. "Funny thing," he said, and from his tone we might have been discussing the quickest way to get to Brooklyn, "when I saw the papers this morning, the first thing I asked myself was if I had anything to do with it. I felt sort of responsible."

I began to listen more carefully. The subway station was on the corner, just before us, and I stopped. He stopped, too. We were in front of a bar and he ducked slightly, peering in, but whoever he was looking for didn't seem to be there. The juke box was blasting away with something black and bouncy and I half watched the barmaid as she danced her way from the juke box to her place behind the bar. And I watched her face as she laughingly responded to something someone said to her, still keeping time to the music. When she smiled one saw the little girl, one sensed the doomed, still-struggling woman beneath the battered face of the semi-whore.

"I never *give* Sonny nothing," the boy said finally, "but a long time ago I come to school high and Sonny asked me how it felt." He paused, I couldn't bear to watch him, I watched the barmaid, and I listened to the music which seemed to be causing the pavement to shake. "I told him it felt great." The music stopped, the barmaid paused and watched the juke box until the music began again. "It did."

All this was carrying me some place I didn't want to go. I certainly didn't want to know how it felt. It filled everything, the people, the houses, the music, the dark, quicksilver barmaid, with menace; and this menace was their reality.

"What's going to happen to him now?" I asked again.

30 "They'll send him away some place and they'll try to cure him." He shook his head. "Maybe he'll even think he's kicked the habit. Then they'll let him loose"—he gestured, throwing his cigarette into the gutter. "That's all."

"What do you mean, that's *all?*"

But I knew what he meant.

"I *mean,* that's *all.*" He turned his head and looked at me, pulling down the corners of his mouth. "Don't you know what I mean?" he asked, softly.

"How the hell *would* I know what you mean?" I almost whispered it, I don't know why.

35 "That's right," he said to the air, "how would *he* know what I mean?" He turned toward me again, patient and calm, and yet I somehow felt him shaking, shaking as though he were going to fall apart. I felt that ice in my guts again, the dread I'd felt all afternoon; and again I watched the barmaid, moving about the bar, washing glasses, and singing. "Listen. They'll let him out and then it'll just start all over again. That's what I mean."

"You mean—they'll let him out. And then he'll just start working his way back in again. You mean he'll never kick the habit. Is that what you mean?"

"That's right," he said, cheerfully. "*You* see what I mean."

"Tell me," I said at last, "why does he want to die? He must want to die, he's killing himself, why does he want to die?"

He looked at me in surprise. He licked his lips. "He don't want to die. He wants to live. Don't nobody want to die, ever."

40 Then I wanted to ask him—too many things. He could not have answered, or if he had, I could not have borne the answers. I started walking. "Well, I guess it's none of my business."

"It's going to be rough on old Sonny," he said. We reached the subway station. "This is your station?" he asked. I nodded. I took one step down. "Damn!" he said, suddenly. I looked up at him. He grinned again. "Damn it if I didn't leave all my money home. You ain't got a dollar on you, have you? Just for a couple of days, is all."

All at once something inside gave and threatened to come pouring out of me. I didn't hate him any more. I felt that in another moment I'd start crying like a child.

"Sure," I said. "Don't sweat." I looked in my wallet and didn't have a dollar, I only had a five. "Here," I said. "That hold you?"

He didn't look at it—he didn't want to look at it. A terrible closed look came over his face, as though he were keeping the number on the bill a secret from him and me. "Thanks," he said, and now he was dying to see me go. "Don't worry about Sonny. Maybe I'll write him or something."

45 "Sure," I said. "You do that. So long."

"Be seeing you," he said. I went on down the steps.

And I didn't write Sonny or send him anything for a long time. When I finally did, it was just after my little girl died, he wrote me back a letter which made me feel like a bastard.

Here's what he said:

Dear brother,

You don't know how much I needed to hear from you. I wanted to write you many a time but I dug how much I must have hurt you and so I didn't write.

But now I feel like a man who's been trying to climb up out of some deep, real deep and funky hole and just saw the sun up there, outside. I got to get outside.

I can't tell you much about how I got here. I mean I don't know how to tell you. I guess I was afraid of something or I was trying to escape from something and you know I have never been very strong in the head (smile). I'm glad Mama and Daddy are dead and can't see what's happened to their son and I swear if I'd known what I was doing I would never have hurt you so, you and a lot of other fine people who were nice to me and who believed in me.

I don't want you to think it had anything to do with me being a musician. It's more than that. Or maybe less than that. I can't get anything straight in my head down here and I try not to think about what's going to happen to me when I get outside again. Sometime I think I'm going to flip and *never* get outside and sometime I think I'll come straight back. I tell you one thing, though, I'd rather blow my brains out than go through this again. But that's what they all say, so they tell me. If I tell you when I'm coming to New York and if you could meet me, I sure would appreciate it. Give my love to Isabel and the kids and I was sure sorry to hear about little Gracie. I wish I could be like Mama and say the Lord's will be done, but I don't know it seems to me that trouble is the one thing that never does get stopped and I don't know what good it does to blame it on the Lord. But maybe it does some good if you believe it.

Your brother,
Sonny

Then I kept in constant touch with him and I sent him whatever I could and I went to meet him when he came back to New York. When I saw him many things I thought I had forgotten came flooding back to me. This was because I had begun, finally, to wonder about Sonny, about the life that Sonny lived inside. This life, whatever it was, had made him older and thinner and it had deepened the distant stillness in which he had always moved. He looked very unlike my baby brother. Yet, when he smiled, when we shook hands, the baby brother I'd never known looked out from the depths of his private life, like an animal waiting to be coaxed into the light.

50 "How you been keeping?" he asked me.

"All right. And you?"

"Just fine." He was smiling all over his face. "It's good to see you again."

"It's good to see you."

The seven years' difference in our ages lay between us like a chasm: I wondered if these years would ever operate between us as a bridge. I was remembering, and it made it hard to catch my breath, that I had been there when he was born; and I had heard the first words he had ever spoken. When he started to walk, he walked from our mother straight to me. I caught him just before he fell when he took the first steps he ever took in this world.

55 "How's Isabel?"

"Just fine. She's dying to see you."

"And the boys?"

"They're fine, too. They're anxious to see their uncle."

"Oh, come on. You know they don't remember me."

60 "Are you kidding? Of course they remember you."

He grinned again. We got into a taxi. We had a lot to say to each other, far too much to know how to begin.

As the taxi began to move, I asked, "You still want to go to India?"

He laughed. "You still remember that. Hell, no. This place is Indian enough for me."

"It used to belong to them," I said.

65 And he laughed again. "They damn sure knew what they were doing when they got rid of it."

Years ago, when he was around fourteen, he'd been all hipped on the idea of going to India. He read books about people sitting on rocks, naked, in all kinds of weather, but mostly bad, naturally, and walking barefoot through hot coals and arriving at wisdom. I used to say that it sounded to me as though they were getting away from wisdom as fast as they could. I think he sort of looked down on me for that.

"Do you mind," he asked, "if we have the driver drive alongside the park? On the west side—I haven't seen the city in so long."

"Of course not," I said. I was afraid that I might sound as though I were humoring him, but I hoped he wouldn't take it that way.

So we drove along, between the green of the park and the stony, lifeless elegance of hotels and apartment buildings, toward the vivid, killing streets of our childhood. These streets hadn't changed, though housing projects jutted up out of them now like rocks in the middle of a boiling sea. Most of the houses in which we had grown up had vanished, as had the stores from which we had stolen, the basements in which we had first tried sex, the rooftops from which we had hurled tin cans and bricks. But houses exactly like the houses of our past yet dominated the landscape, boys exactly like the boys we once had been found themselves smothering in these houses, came down into the streets for light and air and found themselves encircled by disaster. Some escaped the trap, most didn't. Those who got out always left something of themselves behind, as some animals amputate a leg and leave it in the trap. It might be said, perhaps, that I had escaped, after all, I was a school teacher; or that Sonny had, he hadn't lived in Harlem for years. Yet, as the cab moved uptown through streets which seemed, with a rush, to darken with dark people, and as I covertly studied Sonny's face, it came to me that what we both were seeking through our separate cab windows was that part of ourselves which had been left behind. It's always at the hour of trouble and confrontation that the missing member aches.

70 We hit 110th Street and started rolling up Lenox Avenue. And I'd known this avenue all my life, but it seemed to me again, as it had seemed on the day I'd first heard about Sonny's trouble, filled with a hidden menace which was its very breath of life.

"We almost there," said Sonny.

"Almost." We were both too nervous to say anything more.

We live in a housing project. It hasn't been up long. A few days after it was up it seemed uninhabitably new, now, of course, it's already rundown. It looks like a parody of the good, clean, faceless life—God knows the people who live in it do their best to make it a parody. The beat-looking grass lying around isn't enough to make their lives green, the hedges will never hold out the streets, and they know it. The big windows fool no one, they aren't big enough to make space out of no space. They don't bother with the windows, they watch the TV screen instead. The playground is most popular with the children who don't play at jacks, or skip rope, or roller skate, or swing, and they can be found in it after dark. We moved in partly because it's not too far from where I teach, and partly for the kids; but it's really just like the houses in which Sonny and I grew up. The same things happen, they'll have the same things to remember. The moment Sonny and I started into the house I had the feeling that I was simply bringing him back into the danger he had almost died trying to escape.

Sonny has never been talkative. So I don't know why I was sure he'd be dying to talk to me when supper was over the first night. Everything went fine, the oldest boy remembered him, and the youngest boy liked him, and Sonny had remembered to bring something for each of them; and Isabel, who is really much nicer than I am, more open and giving, had gone to a lot of trouble about dinner and was genuinely glad to see him. And she's always been able to tease Sonny in a way that I haven't. It was nice to see her face so vivid again and to hear her laugh and watch her make Sonny laugh. She wasn't, or, anyway, she didn't seem to be, at all uneasy or embarrassed. She chatted as though there were no subject which had to be avoided and she got Sonny past his first, faint stiffness. And thank God she was there, for I was filled with that icy dread again. Everything I did seemed awkward to me, and everything I said sounded freighted with hidden meaning. I was trying to remember everything I'd heard about dope addiction and I couldn't help watching Sonny for signs. I wasn't doing it out of malice. I was trying to find out something about my brother. I was dying to hear him tell me he was safe.

"Safe!" my father grunted, whenever Mama suggested trying to move to a neighborhood which might be safer for children. "Safe, hell! Ain't no place safe for kids, nor nobody."

He always went on like this, but he wasn't, ever, really as bad as he sounded, not even on weekends, when he got drunk. As a matter of fact, he was always on the lookout for "something a little better," but he died before he found it. He died suddenly, during a drunken weekend in the middle of the war, when Sonny was fifteen. He and Sonny hadn't ever got on too well. And this was partly because Sonny was the apple of his father's eye. It was because he loved Sonny so much and was frightened for him, that he was always fighting with him. It doesn't do any good to fight with Sonny. Sonny just moves back, inside himself, where he can't be reached. But the principal reason that they never hit it off is that they were so much alike. Daddy was big and rough and loud-talking, just the opposite of Sonny, but they both had—that same privacy.

Mama tried to tell me something about this, just after Daddy died. I was home on leave from the army.

This was the last time I ever saw my mother alive. Just the same, this picture gets all mixed up in my mind with pictures I had of her when she was younger. The way I always see her is the way she used to be on a Sunday afternoon, say, when the old folks were talking after the big Sunday dinner. I always see her wearing pale blue. She'd be sitting on the sofa. And my father would be sitting in the easy chair, not far from her. And the living room would be full of church folks and relatives. There they sit, in chairs all around the living room, and the night is creeping up outside, but nobody knows it yet. You can see the darkness growing against the windowpanes and you hear the street noises every now and again, or maybe the jangling beat of a tambourine from one of the churches close by, but it's real quiet in the room. For a moment nobody's talking, but every face looks darkening, like the sky outside. And my mother rocks a little from the waist, and my father's eyes are closed. Everyone is looking at something a child can't see. For a minute they've forgotten the children. Maybe a kid is lying on the rug, half asleep. Maybe somebody's got a kid in his lap and is absent-mindedly stroking the kid's head. Maybe there's a kid, quiet and big-eyed, curled up in a big chair in the corner. The silence, the darkness coming, and the darkness in the faces frightens the child obscurely. He hopes that the hand which strokes his forehead will never stop—will never die. He hopes that there will never come a time when the old folks won't be sitting around the living room, talking about where they've come from, and what they've seen, and what's happened to them and their kinfolk.

But something deep and watchful in the child knows that this is bound to end, is already ending. In a moment someone will get up and turn on the light. Then the old folks will remember the children and they won't talk any more that day. And when light fills the room, the child is filled with darkness. He knows that every time this happens he's moved just a little closer to that darkness outside. The darkness outside is what the old folks have been talking about. It's what they've come from. It's what they endure. The child knows that they won't talk any more because if he knows too much about what's happened to *them*, he'll know too much too soon, about what's going to happen to *him*.

80 The last time I talked to my mother, I remember I was restless. I wanted to get out and see Isabel. We weren't married then and we had a lot to straighten out between us.

There Mama sat, in black, by the window. She was humming an old church song, *Lord, you brought me from a long ways off*. Sonny was out somewhere. Mama kept watching the streets.

"I don't know," she said, "if I'll ever see you again, after you go off from here. But I hope you'll remember the things I tried to teach you."

"Don't talk like that," I said, and smiled. "You'll be here a long time yet."

She smiled, too, but she said nothing. She was quiet for a long time. And I said, "Mama, don't you worry about nothing. I'll be writing all the time, and you be getting the checks. . . ."

85 "I want to talk to you about your brother," she said, suddenly. "If anything happens to me he ain't going to have nobody to look out for him."

"Mama," I said, "ain't nothing going to happen to you *or* Sonny. Sonny's all right. He's a good boy and he's got good sense."

"It ain't a question of his being a good boy," Mama said, "nor of his having good sense. It ain't only the bad ones, nor yet the dumb ones that gets sucked under." She stopped, looking at me. "Your Daddy once had a brother," she said, and she smiled in a way that made me feel she was in pain. "You didn't never know that, did you?"

"No," I said, "I never knew that," and I watched her face.

"Oh, yes," she said, "your Daddy had a brother." She looked out of the window again. "I know you never saw your Daddy cry. But *I* did—many a time, through all these years."

90 I asked her, "What happened to his brother? How come nobody's ever talked about him?"

This was the first time I ever saw my mother look old.

"His brother got killed," she said, "when he was just a little younger than you are now. I knew him. He was a fine boy. He was maybe a little full of the devil, but he didn't mean nobody no harm."

Then she stopped and the room was silent, exactly as it had sometimes been on those Sunday afternoons. Mama kept looking out into the streets.

"He used to have a job in the mill," she said, "and, like all young folks, he just liked to perform on Saturday nights. Saturday nights, him and your father would drift around to different places, go to dances and things like that, or just sit around with people they knew, and your father's brother would sing, he had a fine voice, and play along with himself on his guitar. Well, this particular Saturday night, him and your father was coming home from some place, and they were both a little drunk and there was a moon that night, it was bright like day. Your father's brother was feeling kind of good, and he was whistling to himself, and he had his guitar slung over his shoulder. They was coming down a hill and beneath them was a road that turned off from the highway. Well, your father's brother, being always kind of frisky, decided to run down this hill, and he did, with that guitar banging and clanging behind him, and he ran across the road, and he was making water behind a tree. And your father was sort of amused at him and he was still coming down the hill, kind of slow. Then he heard a car motor and that same minute his brother stepped from behind the tree, into the road, in the moonlight. And he started to cross the road. And your father started to run down the hill, he says he don't know why. This car was full of white men. They was all drunk, and when they seen your father's brother they let out a great whoop and holler and they aimed the car straight at him. They was having fun, they just wanted to scare him, the way they do sometimes, you know. But they was drunk. And I guess the boy, being drunk, too, and scared, kind of lost his head. By the time he jumped it was too late. Your father says he heard his brother scream when the car rolled over him, and he heard the wood of that guitar when it give, and he heard them strings go flying, and he heard them white men shouting, and the car kept on a-going and it ain't stopped till this day. And, time your father got down the hill, his brother weren't nothing but blood and pulp."

95 Tears were gleaming on my mother's face. There wasn't anything I could say.

"He never mentioned it," she said, "because I never let him mention it before you children. Your Daddy was like a crazy man that night and for many a night thereafter. He says he never in his life seen anything as dark as that road after the lights of that car had gone away. Weren't nothing, weren't nobody on that road, just your Daddy and his brother and that busted guitar. Oh, yes. Your Daddy never did really get right again. Till the day he died he weren't sure but that every white man he saw was the man that killed his brother."

She stopped and took out her handkerchief and dried her eyes and looked at me.

"I ain't telling you all this," she said, "to make you scared or bitter or to make you hate nobody. I'm telling you this because you got a brother. And the world ain't changed."

I guess I didn't want to believe this. I guess she saw this in my face. She turned away from me, toward the window again, searching those streets.

100 "But I praise my Redeemer," she said at last, "that He called your Daddy home before me. I ain't saying it to throw no flowers at myself, but, I declare, it keeps me from feeling too cast down to know I helped your father get safely through this world. Your father always acted like he was the roughest, strongest man on earth. And everybody took him to be like that. But if he hadn't had *me* there—to see his tears!"

She was crying again. Still, I couldn't move. I said, "Lord, Lord, Mama, I didn't know it was like that."

"Oh, honey," she said, "there's a lot that you don't know. But you are going to find it out." She stood up from the window and came over to me. "You got to hold on to your brother," she said, "and don't let him fall, no matter what it looks like is happening to him and no matter how evil you gets with him. You going to be evil with him many a time. But don't you forget what I told you, you hear?"

"I won't forget," I said. "Don't you worry, I won't forget. I won't let nothing happen to Sonny."

My mother smiled as though she were amused at something she saw in my face. Then, "You may not be able to stop nothing from happening. But you got to let him know you's *there*."

105 Two days later I was married, and then I was gone. And I had a lot of things on my mind and I pretty well forgot my promise to Mama until I got shipped home on a special furlough for her funeral.

And, after the funeral, with just Sonny and me alone in the empty kitchen, I tried to find out something about him.

"What do you want to do?" I asked him.

"I'm going to be a musician," he said.

For he had graduated, in the time I had been away, from dancing to the juke box to finding out who was playing what, and what they were doing with it, and he had bought himself a set of drums.

110 "You mean, you want to be a drummer?" I somehow had the feeling that being a drummer might be all right for other people but not for my brother Sonny.

"I don't think," he said, looking at me very gravely, "that I'll ever be a good drummer. But I think I can play a piano."

I frowned. I'd never played the role of the older brother quite so seriously before, had scarcely ever, in fact, *asked* Sonny a damn thing. I sensed myself in the presence of something I didn't really know how to handle, didn't understand. So I made my frown a little deeper as I asked: "What kind of musician do you want to be?"

He grinned. "How many kinds do you think there are?"

"Be *serious*," I said.

115 He laughed, throwing his head back, and then looked at me. "I *am* serious."

"Well, then, for Christ's sake, stop kidding around and answer a serious question. I mean, do you want to be a concert pianist, you want to play classical music and all that, or—or what?" Long before I finished he was laughing again. "For Christ's *sake*, Sonny!"

He sobered, but with difficulty. "I'm sorry. But you sound so—*scared!*" and he was off again.

"Well, you may think it's funny now, baby, but it's not going to be so funny when you have to make your living at it, let me tell you *that*." I was furious because I knew he was laughing at me and I didn't know why.

"No," he said, very sober now, and afraid, perhaps, that he'd hurt me, "I don't want to be a classical pianist. That isn't what interests me. I mean"—he paused, looking hard at me, as though his eyes would help me to understand, and then gestured helplessly, as though perhaps his hand would help—"I mean, I'll have a lot of studying to do, and I'll have to study *everything*, but, I mean, I want to play *with*—jazz musicians." He stopped. "I want to play jazz," he said.

120 Well, the word had never before sounded as heavy, as real, as it sounded that afternoon in Sonny's mouth. I just looked at him and I was probably frowning a real frown by this time. I simply couldn't see why on earth he'd want to spend his time hanging around nightclubs, clowning around on bandstands, while people pushed each other around a dance floor. It seemed—beneath him, somehow. I had never thought about it before, had never been forced to,

but I suppose I had always put jazz musicians in a class with what Daddy called "good-time people."

"Are you *serious?*"

"Hell, *yes,* I'm serious."

He looked more helpless than ever, and annoyed, and deeply hurt.

I suggested, helpfully: "You mean—like Louis Armstrong?"

125 His face closed as though I'd struck him. "No. I'm not talking about none of that old-time, down home crap."

"Well, look, Sonny, I'm sorry, don't get mad. I just don't altogether get it, that's all. Name somebody—you know, a jazz musician you admire."

"Bird."

"Who?"

"Bird! Charlie Parker! Don't they teach you nothing in the goddamn army?"

130 I lit a cigarette. I was surprised and then a little amused to discover that I was trembling. "I've been out of touch," I said. "You'll have to be patient with me. Now. Who's this Parker character?"

"He's just one of the greatest jazz musicians alive," said Sonny, sullenly, his hands in his pockets, his back to me. "Maybe *the* greatest," he added, bitterly, "that's probably why *you* never heard of him."

"All right," I said, "I'm ignorant. I'm sorry. I'll go out and buy all the cat's records right away, all right?"

"It don't," said Sonny, with dignity, "make any difference to me. I don't care what you listen to. Don't do me no favors."

I was beginning to realize that I'd never seen him so upset before. With another part of my mind I was thinking that this would probably turn out to be one of those things kids go through and that I shouldn't make it seem important by pushing it too hard. Still, I didn't think it would do any harm to ask: "Doesn't all this take a lot of time? Can you make a living at it?"

135 He turned back to me and half leaned, half sat, on the kitchen table. "Everything takes time," he said, "and—well, yes, sure, I can make a living at it. But what I don't seem to be able to make you understand is that it's the only thing I want to do."

"Well, Sonny," I said, gently, "you know people can't always do exactly what they *want* to do—"

"*No,* I don't know that," said Sonny, surprising me. "I think people *ought* to do what they want to do, what else are they alive for?"

"You getting to be a big boy," I said desperately, "it's time you started thinking about your future."

"I'm thinking about my future," said Sonny, grimly. "I think about it all the time."

140 I gave up. I decided, if he didn't change his mind, that we could always talk about it later. "In the meantime," I said, "you got to finish school." We had already decided that he'd have to move in with Isabel and her folks. I knew this wasn't the ideal arrangement because Isabel's folks are inclined to be dicty and they hadn't especially wanted Isabel to marry me. But I didn't know what else to do. "And we have to get you fixed up at Isabel's."

There was a long silence. He moved from the kitchen table to the window. "That's a terrible idea. You know it yourself."

"Do you have a *better* idea?"

He just walked up and down the kitchen for a minute. He was as tall as I was. He had started to shave. I suddenly had the feeling that I didn't know him at all.

He stopped at the kitchen table and picked up my cigarettes. Looking at me with a kind of mocking, amused defiance, he put one between his lips. "You mind?"

145 "You smoking already?"

He lit the cigarette and nodded, watching me through the smoke. "I just wanted to see if I'd have the courage to smoke in front of you." He grinned and blew a great cloud of smoke to the ceiling. "It was easy." He looked at my face. "Come on, now. I bet you was smoking at my age, tell the truth."

I didn't say anything but the truth was on my face, and he laughed. But now there was something very strained in his laugh. "Sure. And I bet that ain't all you was doing."

He was frightening me a little. "Cut the crap," I said. "We already decided that you was going to go and live at Isabel's. Now what's got into you all of a sudden?"

"*You* decided it," he pointed out. "*I* didn't decide nothing." He stopped in front of me, leaning against the stove, arms loosely folded. "Look, brother. I don't want to stay in Harlem no more, I really don't." He was very earnest. He looked at me, then over toward the kitchen window. There was something in his eyes I'd never seen before, some thoughtfulness, some worry all his own. He rubbed the muscle of one arm. "It's time I was getting out of here."

150 "Where do you want to *go*, Sonny?"

"I want to join the army. Or the navy, I don't care. If I say I'm old enough, they'll believe me."

Then I got mad. It was because I was so scared. "You must be crazy. You goddamn fool, what the hell do you want to go and join the *army* for?"

"I just told you. To get out of Harlem."

"Sonny, you haven't even finished *school*. And if you really want to be a musician, how do you expect to study if you're in the *army?*"

155 He looked at me, trapped, and in anguish. "There's ways. I might be able to work out some kind of deal. Anyway, I'll have the G.I. Bill when I come out."

"*If* you come out." We stared at each other. "Sonny, please. Be reasonable. I know the setup is far from perfect. But we got to do the best we can."

"I ain't learning nothing in school," he said. "Even when I go." He turned away from me and opened the window and threw his cigarette out into the narrow alley. I watched his back. "At least, I ain't learning nothing you'd want me to learn." He slammed the window so hard I thought the glass would fly out, and turned back to me. "And I'm sick of the stink of these garbage cans!"

"Sonny," I said, "I know how you feel. But if you don't finish school now, you're going to be sorry later that you didn't." I grabbed him by the shoulders. "And you only got another year. It ain't so bad. And I'll come back and I swear I'll help you do *whatever* you want to do. Just try to put up with it till I come back. Will you please do that? For me?"

He didn't answer and he wouldn't look at me.

160 "Sonny. You hear me?"

He pulled away. "I hear you. But you never hear anything *I* say."

I didn't know what to say to that. He looked out of the window and then back at me. "OK," he said, and sighed. "I'll try."

Then I said, trying to cheer him up a little, "They got a piano at Isabel's. You can practice on it."

And as a matter of fact, it did cheer him up for a minute. "That's right," he said to himself. "I forgot that." His face relaxed a little. But the worry, the thoughtfulness, played on it still, the way shadows play on a face which is staring into the fire.

* * *

165 But I thought I'd never hear the end of that piano. At first, Isabel would write me, saying how nice it was that Sonny was so serious about his music and how, as soon as he came in from school, or wherever he had been when he was supposed to be at school, he went straight to that piano and stayed there until suppertime. And, after supper, he went back to that piano and stayed there until everybody went to bed. He was at the piano all day Saturday and all day Sunday. Then he bought a record player and started playing records. He'd play one record over and over again, all day long sometimes, and he'd improvise along with it on the piano. Or he'd play one section of the record, one chord, one change, one progression, then he'd do it on the piano. Then back to the record. Then back to the piano.

Well, I really don't know how they stood it. Isabel finally confessed that it wasn't like living with a person at all, it was like living with sound. And the sound didn't make any sense to her, didn't make any sense to any of them—naturally. They began, in a way, to be afflicted by this presence that was living in their home. It was as though Sonny were some sort of god, or monster. He moved in an atmosphere which wasn't like theirs at all. They fed him and he ate, he washed himself, he walked in and out of their door; he certainly wasn't nasty or unpleasant or rude, Sonny isn't any of those things; but it was as though he were all wrapped up in some cloud, some fire, some vision all his own; and there wasn't any way to reach him.

At the same time, he wasn't really a man yet, he was still a child, and they had to watch out for him in all kinds of ways. They certainly couldn't throw him out. Neither did they dare to make a great scene about that piano because even they dimly sensed, as I sensed, from so many thousands of miles away, that Sonny was at that piano playing for his life.

But he hadn't been going to school. One day a letter came from the school board and Isabel's mother got it—there had, apparently, been other letters but Sonny had torn them up. This day, when Sonny came in, Isabel's mother showed him the letter and asked where he'd been spending his time. And she finally got it out of him that he'd been down in Greenwich Village, with musicians and other characters, in a white girl's apartment. And this scared her and she started to scream at him and what came up, once she began—though she denies it to this day—was what sacrifices they were making to give Sonny a decent home and how little he appreciated it.

Sonny didn't play the piano that day. By evening, Isabel's mother had calmed down but then there was the old man to deal with, and Isabel herself. Isabel says she did her best to be calm but she broke down and started crying. She says she just watched Sonny's face. She could tell, by watching him, what was happening with him. And what was happening was that they penetrated his cloud, they had reached him. Even if their fingers had been a thousand times more gentle than human fingers ever are, he could hardly help feeling that they had stripped him naked and were spitting on that nakedness. For he also had to see that his presence, that music, which was life or death to him, had been torture for them and that they had endured it, not at all for his sake, but only for mine. And Sonny couldn't take that. He can take it a little better today than he could then but he's still not very good at it and, frankly, I don't know anybody who is.

170 The silence of the next few days must have been louder than the sound of all the music ever played since time began. One morning, before she went to work, Isabel was in his room for something and she suddenly realized that all of his records were gone. And she knew for certain that he was gone. And he was. He went as far as the navy would carry him. He finally sent me a postcard from

some place in Greece and that was the first I knew that Sonny was still alive. I didn't see him any more until we were both back in New York and the war had long been over.

He was a man by then, of course, but I wasn't willing to see it. He came by the house from time to time, but we fought almost every time we met. I didn't like the way he carried himself, loose and dreamlike all the time, and I didn't like his friends, and his music seemed to be merely an excuse for the life he led. It sounded just that weird and disordered.

Then we had a fight, a pretty awful fight, and I didn't see him for months. By and by I looked him up, where he was living, in a furnished room in the Village, and I tried to make it up. But there were lots of people in the room and Sonny just lay on his bed, and he wouldn't come downstairs with me, and he treated these other people as though they were his family and I weren't. So I got mad and then he got mad, and then I told him that he might just as well be dead as live the way he was living. Then he stood up and he told me not to worry about him any more in life, that he *was* dead as far as I was concerned. Then he pushed me to the door and the other people looked on as though nothing were happening, and he slammed the door behind me. I stood in the hallway, staring at the door. I heard somebody laugh in the room and then the tears came to my eyes. I started down the steps, whistling to keep from crying, I kept whistling to myself, *You going to need me, baby, one of these cold, rainy days.*

I read about Sonny's trouble in the spring. Little Grace died in the fall. She was a beautiful little girl. But she only lived a little over two years. She died of polio and she suffered. She had a slight fever for a couple of days, but it didn't seem like anything and we just kept her in bed. And we would certainly have called the doctor, but the fever dropped, she seemed to be all right. So we thought it had just been a cold. Then, one day, she was up, playing, Isabel was in the kitchen fixing lunch for the two boys when they'd come in from school, and she heard Grace fall down in the living room. When you have a lot of children you don't always start running when one of them falls, unless they start screaming or something. And, this time, Grace was quiet. Yet, Isabel says that when she heard that *thump* and then that silence, something happened in her to make her afraid. And she ran to the living room and there was little Grace on the floor, all twisted up, and the reason she hadn't screamed was that she couldn't get her breath. And when she did scream, it was the worst sound, Isabel says, that she'd ever heard in all her life, and she still hears it sometimes in her dreams. Isabel will sometimes wake me up with a low, moaning, strangled sound and I have to be quick to awaken her and hold her to me and where Isabel is weeping against me seems a mortal wound.

I think I may have written Sonny the very day that little Grace was buried. I was sitting in the living room in the dark, by myself, and I suddenly thought of Sonny. My trouble made his real.

175 One Saturday afternoon, when Sonny had been living with us, or, anyway, been in our house, for nearly two weeks, I found myself wandering aimlessly about the living room, drinking from a can of beer, and trying to work up the courage to search Sonny's room. He was out, he was usually out whenever I was home, and Isabel had taken the children to see their grandparents. Suddenly I was standing still in front of the living room window, watching Seventh Avenue. The idea of searching Sonny's room made me still. I scarcely dared to admit to myself what I'd be searching for. I didn't know what I'd do if I found it. Or if I didn't.

On the sidewalk across from me, near the entrance to a barbecue joint, some people were holding an old-fashioned revival meeting. The barbecue cook, wearing a dirty white apron, his conked hair reddish and metallic in the pale sun, and a cigarette between his lips, stood in the doorway, watching them. Kids and older people paused in their errands and stood there, along with some older men and a couple of very tough-looking women who watched everything that happened on the avenue, as though they owned it, or were maybe owned by it. Well, they were watching this, too. The revival was being carried on by three sisters in black, and a brother. All they had were their voices and their Bibles and a tambourine. The brother was testifying and while he testified two of the sisters stood together, seeming to say, amen, and the third sister walked around with the tambourine outstretched and a couple of people dropped coins into it. Then the brother's testimony ended and the sister who had been taking up the collection dumped the coins into her palm and transferred them to the pocket of her long black robe. Then she raised both hands, striking the tambourine against the air, and then against one hand, and she started to sing. And the two other sisters and the brother joined in.

It was strange, suddenly, to watch, though I had been seeing these street meetings all my life. So, of course, had everybody else down there. Yet, they paused and watched and listened and I stood still at the window. *"Tis the old ship of Zion,"* they sang, and the sister with the tambourine kept a steady, jangling beat, *"it has rescued many a thousand!"* Not a soul under the sound of their voices was hearing this song for the first time, not one of them had been rescued. Nor had they seen much in the way of rescue work being done around them. Neither did they especially believe in the holiness of the three sisters and the brother, they knew too much about them, knew where they lived, and how. The woman with the tambourine, whose voice dominated the air, whose face was bright with joy, was divided by very little from the woman who stood watching her, a cigarette between her heavy, chapped lips, her hair a cuckoo's nest, her face scarred and swollen from many beatings, and her black eyes glittering like coal. Perhaps they both knew this, which was why, when, as rarely, they addressed each other, they addressed each other as Sister. As the singing filled the air the watching, listening faces underwent a change, the eyes focusing on something within; the music seemed to soothe a poison out of them; and time seemed, nearly, to fall away from the sullen, belligerent, battered faces, as though they were fleeing back to their first condition, while dreaming of their last. The barbecue cook half shook his head and smiled, and dropped his cigarette and disappeared into his joint. A man fumbled in his pockets for change and stood holding it in his hand impatiently, as though he had just remembered a pressing appointment further up the avenue. He looked furious. Then I saw Sonny, standing on the edge of the crowd. He was carrying a wide, flat notebook with a green cover, and it made him look, from where I was standing, almost like a schoolboy. The coppery sun brought out the copper in his skin, he was very faintly smiling, standing very still. Then the singing stopped, the tambourine turned into a collection plate again. The furious man dropped in his coins and vanished, so did a couple of the women, and Sonny dropped some change in the plate, looking directly at the woman with a little smile. He started across the avenue, toward the house. He has a slow, loping walk, something like the way Harlem hipsters walk, only he's imposed on this his own half-beat. I had never really noticed it before.

I stayed at the window, both relieved and apprehensive. As Sonny disappeared from my sight, they began singing again. And they were still singing when his key turned in the lock.

"Hey," he said.

180 "Hey, yourself. You want some beer?"

"No. Well, maybe." But he came up to the window and stood beside me, looking out. "What a warm voice," he said.

They were singing *If I could only hear my mother pray again!*

"Yes," I said, "and she can sure beat that tambourine."

"But what a terrible song," he said, and laughed. He dropped his notebook on the sofa and disappeared into the kitchen. "Where's Isabel and the kids?"

185 "I think they went to see their grandparents. You hungry?"

"No." He came back into the living room with his can of beer. "You want to come some place with me tonight?"

I sensed, I don't know how, that I couldn't possibly say no. "Sure. Where?"

He sat down on the sofa and picked up his notebook and started leafing through it. "I'm going to sit in with some fellows in a joint in the Village."

"You mean, you're going to play, tonight?"

190 "That's right." He took a swallow of his beer and moved back to the window. He gave me a sidelong look. "If you can stand it."

"I'll try," I said.

He smiled to himself and we both watched as the meeting across the way broke up. The three sisters and the brother, heads bowed, were singing *God be with you till we meet again*. The faces around them were very quiet. Then the song ended. The small crowd dispersed. We watched the three women and the lone man walk slowly up the avenue.

"When she was singing before," said Sonny, abruptly, "her voice reminded me for a minute of what heroin feels like sometimes—when it's in your veins. It makes you feel sort of warm and cool at the same time. And distant. And—and sure." He sipped his beer, very deliberately not looking at me. I watched his face. "It makes you feel—in control. Sometimes you've got to have that feeling."

"Do you?" I sat down slowly in the easy chair.

195 "Sometimes." He went to the sofa and picked up his notebook again. "Some people do."

"In order," I asked, "to play?" And my voice was very ugly, full of contempt and anger.

"Well"—he looked at me with great, troubled eyes, as though, in fact, he hoped his eyes would tell me things he could never otherwise say—"they *think* so. And *if* they think so—!"

"And what do *you* think?" I asked.

He sat on the sofa and put his can of beer on the floor. "I don't know," he said, and I couldn't be sure if he were answering my question or pursuing his thoughts. His face didn't tell me. "It's not so much to *play*. It's to *stand* it, to be able to make it at all. On any level." He frowned and smiled: "In order to keep from shaking to pieces."

200 "But these friends of yours," I said, "they seem to shake themselves to pieces pretty goddamn fast."

"Maybe." He played with the notebook. And something told me that I should curb my tongue, that Sonny was doing his best to talk, that I should listen. "But of course you only know the ones that've gone to pieces. Some don't—or at least they haven't *yet* and that's just about all *any* of us can say." He paused. "And then there are some who just live, really, in hell, and they know it and they see what's happening and they go right on. I don't know." He sighed, dropped the notebook, folded his arms. "Some guys, you can tell from the way they play, they on something *all* the time. And you can see that, well, it makes something real for them. But of course," he picked up his beer from the floor and sipped it and put the can down again, "they *want* to, too, you've got to see that. Even some of them that say they don't—*some,* not all."

"And what about you?" I asked—I couldn't help it. "What about you? Do *you* want to?"

He stood up and walked to the window and remained silent for a long time. Then he sighed. "Me," he said. Then: "While I was downstairs before, on my way here, listening to that woman sing, it struck me all of a sudden how much suffering she must have had to go through—to sing like that. It's *repulsive* to think you have to suffer that much."

I said: "But there's no way not to suffer—is there, Sonny?"

205 "I believe not," he said and smiled, "but that's never stopped anyone from trying." He looked at me. "Has it?" I realized, with this mocking look, that there stood between us, forever, beyond the power of time or forgiveness, the fact that I had held silence—so long!—when he had needed human speech to help him. He turned back to the window. "No, there's no way not to suffer. But you try all kinds of ways to keep from drowning in it, to keep on top of it, and to make it seem—well, like *you*. Like you did something, all right, and now you're suffering for it. You know?" I said nothing. "Well you know," he said, impatiently, "why *do* people suffer? Maybe it's better to do something to give it a reason, *any* reason."

"But we just agreed," I said, "that there's no way not to suffer. Isn't it better, then, just to—take it?"

"But nobody just takes it," Sonny cried, "that's what I'm telling you! *Everybody* tries not to. You're just hung up on the *way* some people try—it's not *your* way!"

The hair on my face began to itch, my face felt wet. "That's not true," I said, "that's not true. I don't give a damn what other people do, I don't even care how they suffer. I just care how *you* suffer." And he looked at me. "Please believe me," I said, "I don't want to see you—die—trying not to suffer."

"I won't," he said, flatly, "die trying not to suffer. At least, not any faster than anybody else."

210 "But there's no need," I said, trying to laugh, "is there? in killing yourself."

I wanted to say more, but I couldn't. I wanted to talk about will power and how life could be—well, beautiful. I wanted to say that it was all within; but was it? or, rather, wasn't that exactly the trouble? And I wanted to promise that I would never fail him again. But it would all have sounded—empty words and lies.

So I made the promise to myself and prayed that I would keep it.

"It's terrible sometimes, inside," he said, "that's what's the trouble. You walk these streets, black and funky and cold, and there's not really a living ass to talk to, and there's nothing shaking, and there's no way of getting it out—that storm inside. You can't talk it and you can't make love with it, and when you finally try to get with it and play it, you realize *nobody's* listening. So *you've* got to listen. You got to find a way to listen."

And then he walked away from the window and sat on the sofa again, as though all the wind had suddenly been knocked out of him. "Sometimes you'll do *anything* to play, even cut your mother's throat." He laughed and looked at me. "Or your brother's." Then he sobered. "Or your own." Then: "Don't worry. I'm all right now and I think I'll *be* all right. But I can't forget—where I've been. I don't mean just the physical place I've been, I mean where I've *been*. And *what* I've been."

215 "What have you been, Sonny?" I asked.

He smiled—but sat sideways on the sofa, his elbow resting on the back, his fingers playing with his mouth and chin, not looking at me. "I've been something I didn't recognize, didn't know I could be. Didn't know anybody could be." He stopped, looking inward, looking helplessly young, looking old. "I'm not talking about it now because I feel *guilty* or anything like that—maybe it would be better if I did, I don't know. Anyway, I can't really talk about it. Not to you, not to anybody," and now he turned and faced me. "Sometimes, you know, and it was actually when I was most *out* of the world, I felt that I was in it, that I was *with* it, really, and I could play or I didn't really have to *play*, it just came out of me, it was there. And I don't know how I played, thinking about it now, but I know I did awful things, those times, sometimes, to people. Or it wasn't that I *did* anything to them—it was that they weren't real." He picked up the beer can; it was empty; he rolled it between his palms: "And other times—well, I needed a fix, I needed to find a place to lean, I needed to clear a space to *listen*—and I couldn't find it, and I—went crazy, I did terrible things to *me*, I was terrible *for* me." He began pressing the beer can between his hands, I watched the metal begin to give. It glittered, as he played with it, like a knife, and I was afraid he would cut himself, but I said nothing. "Oh well. I can never tell you. I was all by myself at the bottom of something, stinking and sweating and crying and shaking, and I smelled it, you know? *my* stink, and I thought I'd die if I couldn't get away from it and yet, all the same, I knew that everything I was doing was just locking me in with it. And I didn't know," he paused, still flattening the beer can, "I didn't know, I still *don't* know, something kept telling me that maybe it was good to smell your own stink, but I didn't think that *that* was what I'd been trying to do—and—who can stand it?" and he abruptly dropped the ruined beer can, looking at me with a small, still smile, and then rose, walking to the window as though it were the lodestone rock. I watched his face, he watched the avenue. "I couldn't tell you when Mama died—but the reason I wanted to leave Harlem so bad was to get away from drugs. And then, when I ran away, that's what I was running from—really. When I came back, nothing had changed, *I* hadn't changed, I was just—older." And he stopped, drumming with his fingers on the windowpane. The sun had vanished, soon darkness would fall. I watched his face. "It can come again," he said, almost as though speaking to himself. Then he turned to me. "It can come again," he repeated. "I just want you to know that."

"All right," I said, at last. "So it can come again. All right."

He smiled, but the smile was sorrowful. "I had to try to tell you," he said.

"Yes," I said. "I understand that."

220 "You're my brother," he said, looking straight at me, and not smiling at all.

"Yes," I repeated, "yes. I understand that."

He turned back to the window, looking out. "All that hatred down there," he said, "all that hatred and misery and love. It's a wonder it doesn't blow the avenue apart."

We went to the only nightclub on a short, dark street, downtown. We squeezed through the narrow, chattering, jam-packed bar to the entrance of the big room, where the bandstand was. And we stood there for a moment, for the lights were very dim in this room and we couldn't see. Then, "Hello, boy," said a voice and an enormous black man, much older than Sonny or myself, erupted out of all that atmospheric lighting and put an arm around Sonny's shoulder. "I been sitting right here," he said, "waiting for you."

He had a big voice, too, and heads in the darkness turned toward us.

225 Sonny grinned and pulled a little away, and said, "Creole, this is my brother. I told you about him."

Creole shook my hand. "I'm glad to meet you, son," he said, and it was clear that he was glad to meet me *there,* for Sonny's sake. And he smiled, "You got a real musician in *your* family," and he took his arm from Sonny's shoulder and slapped him, lightly, affectionately, with the back of his hand.

"Well. Now I've heard it all," said a voice behind us. This was another musician, and a friend of Sonny's, a coal-black, cheerful-looking man, built close to the ground. He immediately began confiding to me, at the top of his lungs, the most terrible things about Sonny, his teeth gleaming like a lighthouse and his laugh coming up out of him like the beginning of an earthquake. And it turned out that everyone at the bar knew Sonny, or almost everyone; some were musicians, working there, or nearby, or not working, some were simply hangers-on, and some were there to hear Sonny play. I was introduced to all of them and they were all very polite to me. Yet, it was clear that, for them, I was only Sonny's brother. Here, I was in Sonny's world. Or, rather: his kingdom. Here, it was not even a question that his veins bore royal blood.

They were going to play soon and Creole installed me, by myself, at a table in a dark corner. Then I watched them, Creole, and the little black man, and Sonny, and the others, while they horsed around, standing just below the bandstand. The light from the bandstand spilled just a little short of them and, watching them laughing and gesturing and moving about, I had the feeling that they, nevertheless, were being most careful not to step into that circle of light too suddenly: that if they moved into the light too suddenly, without thinking, they would perish in flame. Then, while I watched, one of them, the small, black man, moved into the light and crossed the bandstand and started fooling around with his drums. Then—being funny and being, also, extremely ceremonious—Creole took Sonny by the arm and led him to the piano. A woman's voice called Sonny's name and a few hands started clapping. And Sonny, also being funny and being ceremonious, and so touched, I think, that he could have cried, but neither hiding it nor showing it, riding it like a man, grinned, and put both hands to his heart and bowed from the waist.

Creole then went to the bass fiddle and a lean, very bright-skinned brown man jumped up on the bandstand and picked up his horn. So there they were, and the atmosphere on the bandstand and in the room began to change and tighten. Someone stepped up to the microphone and announced them. Then there were all kinds of murmurs. Some people at the bar shushed others. The waitress ran around, frantically getting in the last orders, guys and chicks got closer to each other, and the lights on the bandstand, on the quartet, turned to a kind of indigo. Then they all looked different there. Creole looked about him for the last time, as though he were making certain that all his chickens were in the coop, and then he—jumped and struck the fiddle. And there they were.

230 All I know about music is that not many people ever really hear it. And even then, on the rare occasions when something opens within, and the music enters, what we mainly hear, or hear corroborated, are personal, private, vanishing evocations. But the man who creates the music is hearing something else, is dealing with the roar rising from the void and imposing order on it as it hits the air. What is evoked in him, then, is of another order, more terrible because it has no words, and triumphant, too, for that same reason. And his triumph, when he triumphs, is ours. I just watched Sonny's face. His face was troubled, he was working hard, but he wasn't with it. And I had the feeling that, in a way, everyone on the bandstand was waiting for him, both waiting for him and pushing him along. But as

I began to watch Creole, I realized that it was Creole who held them all back. He had them on a short rein. Up there, keeping the beat with his whole body, wailing on the fiddle, with his eyes half closed, he was listening to everything, but he was listening to Sonny. He was having a dialogue with Sonny. He wanted Sonny to leave the shoreline and strike out for the deep water. He was Sonny's witness that deep water and drowning were not the same thing—he had been there, and he knew. And he wanted Sonny to know. He was waiting for Sonny to do the things on the keys which would let Creole know that Sonny was in the water.

And, while Creole listened, Sonny moved, deep within, exactly like someone in torment. I had never before thought of how awful the relationship must be between the musician and his instrument. He has to fill it, this instrument, with the breath of life, his own. He has to make it do what he wants it to do. And a piano is just a piano. It's made out of so much wood and wires and little hammers and big ones, and ivory. While there's only so much you can do with it, the only way to find this out is to try; to try and make it do everything.

And Sonny hadn't been near a piano for over a year. And he wasn't on much better terms with his life, not the life that stretched before him now. He and the piano stammered, started one way, got scared, stopped; started another way, panicked, marked time, started again; then seemed to have found a direction, panicked again, got stuck. And the face I saw on Sonny I'd never seen before. Everything had been burned out of it, and, at the same time, things usually hidden were being burned in, by the fire and fury of the battle which was occurring in him up there.

Yet, watching Creole's face as they neared the end of the first set, I had the feeling that something had happened, something I hadn't heard. Then they finished, there was scattered applause, and then, without an instant's warning, Creole started into something else, it was almost sardonic, it was *Am I Blue*. And, as though he commanded, Sonny began to play. Something began to happen. And Creole let out the reins. The dry, low, black man said something awful on the drums, Creole answered, and the drums talked back. Then the horn insisted, sweet and high, slightly detached perhaps, and Creole listened, commenting now and then, dry, and driving, beautiful and calm and old. Then they all came together again, and Sonny was part of the family again. I could tell this from his face. He seemed to have found, right there beneath his fingers, a damn brand-new piano. It seemed that he couldn't get over it. Then, for awhile, just being happy with Sonny, they seemed to be agreeing with him that brand-new pianos certainly were a gas.

Then Creole stepped forward to remind them that what they were playing was the blues. He hit something in all of them, he hit something in me, myself, and the music tightened and deepened, apprehension began to beat the air. Creole began to tell us what the blues were all about. They were not about anything very new. He and his boys up there were keeping it new, at the risk of ruin, destruction, madness, and death, in order to find new ways to make us listen. For, while the tale of how we suffer, and how we are delighted, and how we may triumph is never new, it always must be heard. There isn't any other tale to tell, it's the only light we've got in all this darkness.

235 And this tale, according to that face, that body, those strong hands on those strings, has another aspect in every country, and a new depth in every generation. Listen, Creole seemed to be saying, listen. Now these are Sonny's blues. He made the little black man on the drums know it, and the bright, brown man on the horn. Creole wasn't trying any longer to get Sonny in the water. He was wishing him Godspeed. Then he stepped back, very slowly, filling the air with the immense suggestion that Sonny speak for himself.

Then they all gathered around Sonny and Sonny played. Every now and again one of them seemed to say, amen. Sonny's fingers filled the air with life, his life. But that life contained so many others. And Sonny went all the way back, he really began with the spare, flat statement of the opening phrase of the song. Then he began to make it his. It was very beautiful because it wasn't hurried and it was no longer a lament. I seemed to hear with what burning he had made it his, with what burning we had yet to make it ours, how we could cease lamenting. Freedom lurked around us and I understood, at last, that he could help us to be free if we would listen, that he would never be free until we did. Yet, there was no battle in his face now. I heard what he had gone through, and would continue to go through until he came to rest in earth. He had made it his: that long line, of which we knew only Mama and Daddy. And he was giving it back, as everything must be given back, so that, passing through death, it can live forever. I saw my mother's face again, and felt, for the first time, how the stones of the road she had walked on must have bruised her feet. I saw the moonlit road where my father's brother died. And it brought something else back to me, and carried me past it. I saw my little girl again and felt Isabel's tears again, and I felt my own tears begin to rise. And I was yet aware that this was only a moment, that the world waited outside, as hungry as a tiger, and that trouble stretched above us, longer than the sky.

Then it was over. Creole and Sonny let out their breath, both soaking wet, and grinning. There was a lot of applause and some of it was real. In the dark, the girl came by and I asked her to take drinks to the bandstand. There was a long pause, while they talked up there in the indigo light and after awhile I saw the girl put a Scotch and milk on top of the piano for Sonny. He didn't seem to notice it, but just before they started playing again, he sipped from it and looked toward me, and nodded. Then he put it back on top of the piano. For me, then, as they began to play again, it glowed and shook above my brother's head like the very cup of trembling.

[1957]

Joining the Conversation: Critical Thinking and Writing

1. Do you think that this story begins effectively? Does it end effectively? Please explain your response as carefully as you can.
2. Why does the narrator become angry with the unnamed friend who says that he "can't much help old Sonny no more"?
3. Why does Baldwin use the technique of the flashback in the scene after Sonny's release from prison, when the narrator recalls his childhood?
4. How is religion presented in this story?
5. Why does Sonny become addicted to heroin? What is the relation between his drug habit and his love of jazz?
6. Do you sympathize more with Sonny or with the narrator? Can you point to a key moment where Baldwin creates this sympathy in you?
7. A scholar of blues and jazz has said, "Only someone who knows and loves this music can really understand Baldwin's story." Do you agree?
8. This is a powerful story about African American experience and history. Does it also deal with issues and challenges that all of us face, whatever our race or ethnicity might happen to be? Please explain, citing evidence from the text.

JAMES JOYCE

For a biographical note on James Joyce, see page 658.

Araby

North Richmond Street, being blind,[1] was a quiet street except at the hour when the Christian Brothers' School set the boys free. An uninhabited house of two stories stood at the blind end, detached from its neighbors in a square ground. The other houses of the street, conscious of decent lives within them, gazed at one another with brown imperturbable faces.

The former tenant of our house, a priest, had died in the back drawing-room. Air, musty from having long been enclosed, hung in all the rooms, and the waste room behind the kitchen was littered with old useless papers. Among these I found a few papercovered books, the pages of which were curled and damp: *The Abbot,* by Walter Scott, *The Devout Communicant* and *The Memoirs of Vidocq*.[2] I liked the last best because its leaves were yellow. The wild garden behind the house contained a central apple-tree and a few straggling bushes under one of which I found the late tenant's rusty bicycle-pump. He had been a very charitable priest; in his will he had left all his money to institutions and the furniture of his house to his sister.

When the short days of winter came dusk fell before we had well eaten our dinners. When we met in the street the houses had grown sombre. The space of sky above us was the colour of everchanging violet and towards it the lamps of the street lifted their feeble lanterns. The cold air stung us and we played till our bodies glowed. Our shouts echoed in the silent street. The career of our play brought us through the dark muddy lanes behind the houses where we ran the gauntlet of the rough tribes from the cottages, to the back doors of the dark dripping gardens where odours arose from the ashpits, to the dark odorous stables where a coachman smoothed and combed the horse or shook music from the buckled harness. When we returned to the street light from the kitchen windows had filled the areas. If my uncle was seen turning the corner we hid in the shadow until we had seen him safely housed. Or if Mangan's sister came out on the doorstep to call her brother in to his tea we watched her from our shadow peer up and down the street. We waited to see whether she would remain or go in and, if she remained, we left our shadow and walked up to Mangan's steps resignedly. She was waiting for us, her figure defined by the light from the half-opened door. Her brother always teased her before he obeyed and I stood by the railings looking at her. Her dress swung as she moved her body and the soft rope of her hair tossed from side to side.

Every morning I lay on the floor in the front parlour watching her door. The blind was pulled down to within an inch of the sash so that I could not be seen. When she came out on the doorstep my heart leaped. I ran to the hall, seized my books and followed her. I kept her brown figure always in my eye and, when we came near the point at which our ways diverged, I quickened my pace and passed her. This happened morning after morning. I had never spoken to her,

[1]**blind** a dead-end street. (All notes are by the editors.) [2]***The Abbot*** one of Scott's popular historical romances (1820); ***The Devout Communicant*** a Catholic religious manual published in the eighteenth century; ***The Memoirs of Vidocq*** the memoirs of the chief of the French detective force (1829).

except for a few casual words, and yet her name was like a summons to all my foolish blood.

Her image accompanied me even in places the most hostile to romance. On Saturday evenings when my aunt went marketing I had to go to carry some of the parcels. We walked through the flaring streets, jostled by drunken men and bargaining women, amid the curses of labourers, the shrill litanies of shop-boys who stood on guard by the barrels of pigs' cheeks, the nasal chanting of street-singers, who sang a *come-all-you* about O'Donovan Rossa,[3] or a ballad about the troubles in our native land. These noises converged in a single sensation of life for me: I imagined that I bore my chalice safely through a throng of foes. Her name sprang to my lips at moments in strange prayers and praises which I myself did not understand. My eyes were often full of tears (I could not tell why) and at times a flood from my heart seemed to pour itself out into my bosom. I thought little of the future. I did not know whether I would ever speak to her or not or, if I spoke to her, how I could tell her of my confused adoration. But my body was like a harp and her words and gestures were like fingers running upon the wires.

One evening I went into the back drawing-room in which the priest had died. It was a dark rainy evening and there was no sound in the house. Through one of the broken panes I heard the rain impinge upon the earth, the fine incessant needles of water playing in the sodden beds. Some distant lamp or lighted window gleamed below me. I was thankful that I could see so little. All my senses seemed to desire to veil themselves and, feeling that I was about to slip from them, I pressed the palms of my hands together until they trembled, murmuring: *O love! O love!* many times.

At last she spoke to me. When she addressed the first words to me I was so confused that I did not know what to answer. She asked me was I going to Araby. I forget whether I answered yes or no. It would be a splendid bazaar, she said; she would love to go.

—And why can't you? I asked.

While she spoke she turned a silver bracelet round and round her wrist. She could not go, she said, because there would be a retreat that week in her convent. Her brother and two other boys were fighting for their caps and I was alone at the railings. She held one of the spikes, bowing her head towards me. The light from the lamp opposite our door caught the white curve of her neck, lit up her hair that rested there and, falling, lit up the hand upon the railing. It fell over one side of her dress and caught the white border of a petticoat, just visible as she stood at ease.

—It's well for you, she said.

—If I go, I said, I will bring you something.

What innumerable follies laid waste my waking and sleeping thoughts after that evening! I wished to annihilate the tedious intervening days. I chafed against the work of school. At night in my bedroom and by day in the classroom her image came between me and the page I strove to read. The syllables of the word *Araby* were called to me through the silence in which my soul luxuriated and cast an Eastern enchantment over me. I asked for leave to go to the bazaar on Saturday night. My aunt was surprised and hoped it was not some Freemason[4] affair.

[3]***come-all-you*** a topical song that began "Come all you gallant Irishmen;" **O'Donovan Rossa** Jeremiah O'Donovan (1831–1915), a popular Irish leader who was jailed by the British for advocating violent rebellion. [4]**Freemason** Irish Catholics viewed the Masons as their Protestant enemies.

I answered few questions in class, I watched my master's face pass from amiability to sternness; he hoped I was not beginning to idle. I could not call my wandering thoughts together. I had hardly any patience with the serious work of life which, now that it stood between me and my desire, seemed to me child's play, ugly monotonous child's play.

On Saturday morning I reminded my uncle that I wished to go to the bazaar in the evening. He was fussing at the hallstand, looking for the hat-brush, and answered me curtly:

15 —Yes, boy, I know.

As he was in the hall I could not go into the front parlour and lie at the window. I left the house in bad humour and walked slowly towards the school. The air was pitilessly raw and already my heart misgave me.

When I came home to dinner my uncle had not yet been home. Still it was early. I sat staring at the clock for some time and, when its ticking began to irritate me, I left the room. I mounted the staircase and gained the upper part of the house. The high cold empty gloomy rooms liberated me and I went from room to room singing. From the front window I saw my companions playing below in the street. Their cries reached me weakened and indistinct and, leaning my forehead against the cool glass, I looked over at the dark house where she lived. I may have stood there for an hour, seeing nothing but the brown-clad figure cast by my imagination, touched discreetly by the lamplight at the curved neck, at the hand upon the railings and at the border below the dress.

When I came downstairs again I found Mrs Mercer sitting at the fire. She was an old garrulous woman, a pawnbroker's widow, who collected used stamps for some pious purpose. I had to endure the gossip of the tea-table. The meal was prolonged beyond an hour and still my uncle did not come. Mrs Mercer stood up to go: she was sorry she couldn't wait any longer, but it was after eight o'clock and she did not like to be out late, as the night air was bad for her. When she had gone I began to walk up and down the room, clenching my fists. My aunt said:

—I'm afraid you may put off your bazaar for this night of Our Lord.

20 At nine o'clock I heard my uncle's latchkey in the halldoor. I heard him talking to himself and heard the hallstand rocking when it had received the weight of his overcoat. I could interpret these signs. When he was midway through his dinner I asked him to give me the money to go to the bazaar. He had forgotten.

—The people are in bed and after their first sleep now, he said.

I did not smile. My aunt said to him energetically:

—Can't you give him the money and let him go? You've kept him late enough as it is.

My uncle said he was very sorry he had forgotten. He said he believed in the old saying: *All work and no play makes Jack a dull boy.* He asked me where I was going and, when I had told him a second time he asked me did I know *The Arab's Farewell to His Steed.*[5] When I left the kitchen he was about to recite the opening lines of the piece to my aunt.

25 I held a florin tightly in my hand as I strode down Buckingham Street towards the station. The sight of the streets thronged with buyers and glaring with gas recalled to me the purpose of my journey. I took my seat in a third-class carriage of a deserted train. After an intolerable delay the train moved out of the station slowly.

[5]***The Arab's Farewell to His Steed*** "The Arab to His Favorite Steed" was a popular sentimental poem by Caroline Norton (1808–1877).

It crept onward among ruinous houses and over the twinkling river. At Westland Row Station a crowd of people pressed to the carriage doors; but the porters moved them back, saying that it was a special train for the bazaar. I remained alone in the bare carriage. In a few minutes the train drew up beside an improvised wooden platform. I passed out on to the road and saw by the lighted dial of a clock that it was ten minutes to ten. In front of me was a large building which displayed the magical name.

I could not find any sixpenny entrance and, fearing that the bazaar would be closed, I passed in quickly through a turnstile, handing a shilling to a weary-looking man. I found myself in a big hall girdled at half its height by a gallery. Nearly all the stalls were closed and the greater part of the hall was in darkness. I recognised a silence like that which pervades a church after a service. I walked into the center of the bazaar timidly. A few people were gathered about the stalls which were still open. Before a curtain, over which the words *Café Chantant* were written in coloured lamps, two men were counting money on a salver. I listened to the fall of the coins.

Remembering with difficulty why I had come I went over to one of the stalls and examined porcelain vases and flowered tea-sets. At the door of the stall a young lady was talking and laughing with two young gentlemen. I remarked their English accents and listened vaguely to their conversation.

—O, I never said such a thing!

—O, but you did!

—O, but I didn't!

—Didn't she say that?

—Yes! I heard her.

—O, there's a . . . fib!

Observing me the young lady came over and asked me did I wish to buy anything. The tone of her voice was not encouraging; she seemed to have spoken to me out of a sense of duty. I looked humbly at the great jars that stood like eastern guards at either side of the dark entrance to the stall and murmured:

—No, thank you.

The young lady changed the position of one of the vases and went back to the two young men. They began to talk of the same subject. Once or twice the young lady glanced at me over her shoulder.

I lingered before her stall, though I knew my stay was useless, to make my interest in her wares seem the more real. Then I turned away slowly and walked down the middle of the bazaar. I allowed the two pennies to fall against the sixpence in my pocket. I heard a voice call from one end of the gallery that the light was out. The upper part of the hall was now completely dark.

Gazing up into the darkness I saw myself as a creature driven and derided by vanity; and my eyes burned with anguish and anger.

[1905]

Joining the Conversation: Critical Thinking and Writing

1. Joyce wrote a novel called *A Portrait of the Artist as a Young Man* (1916). Write an essay of about 500 words on "Araby" as a portrait of the artist as a boy.
2. In an essay of about 500 words, consider the role of images of darkness and blindness and what they reveal to us about "Araby" as a story of the fall from innocence into painful awareness.

3. How old, approximately, is the narrator of "Araby" at the time of the experience he describes? How old is he at the time he tells his story? On what evidence do you base your estimates?
4. The boy, apparently an only child, lives with an uncle and aunt, rather than with parents. Why do you suppose Joyce put him in this family setting rather than some other?
5. The story is rich in images of religion. This in itself is not surprising, for the story is set in Roman Catholic Ireland, but the religious images are not simply references to religious persons or objects. In an essay of 500 to 750 words, discuss how these images reveal the narrator's state of mind.

ISAAC BASHEVIS SINGER

Isaac Bashevis Singer (1904–1991) was born in a Jewish village in Poland. His father and both of his grandfathers were Hasidic rabbis, and Singer received a traditional Jewish education in a rabbinical seminary in Warsaw, although he left the seminary after one year and turned to writing fiction and journalism. In 1935 he immigrated to New York, where he wrote articles and essays for the Yiddish Daily Forward *as well as radio scripts for Yiddish soap operas.*

Singer wrote many stories and novels, as well as books for juveniles and four autobiographies (including Lost in America, *1981). In 1978 his work received world attention when he was awarded the Nobel Prize in Literature.*

The Son from America

The village of Lentshin was tiny—a sandy marketplace where the peasants of the area met once a week. It was surrounded by little huts with thatched roofs or shingles green with moss. The chimneys looked like pots. Between the huts there were fields, where the owners planted vegetables or pastured their goats.

In the smallest of these huts lived old Berl, a man in his eighties, and his wife, who was called Berlcha (wife of Berl). Old Berl was one of the Jews who had been driven from their villages in Russia and had settled in Poland. In Lentshin, they mocked the mistakes he made while praying aloud. He spoke with a sharp "r." He was short, broad-shouldered, and had a small white beard, and summer and winter he wore a sheepskin hat, a padded cotton jacket, and stout boots. He walked slowly, shuffling his feet. He had a half acre of field, a cow, a goat, and chickens.

The couple had a son, Samuel, who had gone to America forty years ago. It was said in Lentshin that he became a millionaire there. Every month, the Lentshin letter carrier brought old Berl a money order and a letter that no one could read because many of the words were English. How much money Samuel sent his parents remained a secret. Three times a year, Berl and his wife went on foot to Zakroczym and cashed the money orders there. But they never seemed to use the money. What for? The garden, the cow, and the goat provided most of their needs. Besides, Berlcha sold chickens and eggs, and from these there was enough to buy flour for bread.

No one cared to know where Berl kept the money that his son sent him. There were no thieves in Lentshin. The hut consisted of one room, which contained all their belongings: the table, the shelf for meat, the shelf for milk foods, the two beds, and the clay oven. Sometimes the chickens roosted in the woodshed and sometimes, when it was cold, in a coop near the oven. The goat, too, found shelter inside when the weather was bad. The more prosperous villages had kerosene lamps, but Berl and his wife did not believe in newfangled gadgets. What was wrong with a wick in a dish of oil? Only for the Sabbath would Berlcha buy three tallow candles at the store. In summer, the couple got up at sunrise and retired with the chickens. In the long winter evenings, Berlcha spun flax at her spinning wheel and Berl sat beside her in the silence of those who enjoy their rest.

5 Once in a while when Berl came home from the synagogue after evening prayers, he brought news to his wife. In Warsaw there were strikers who demanded that the czar abdicate. A heretic by the name of Dr. Herzl[1] had come up with the idea that Jews should settle again in Palestine. Berlcha listened and shook her bonneted head. Her face was yellowish and wrinkled like a cabbage leaf. There were bluish sacks under her eyes. She was half deaf. Berl had to repeat each word he said to her. She would say, "The things that happen in the big cities!"

Here in Lentshin nothing happened except usual events: a cow gave birth to a calf, a young couple had a circumcision party, or a girl was born and there was no party. Occasionally, someone died. Lentshin had no cemetery, and the corpse had to be taken to Zakroczym. Actually, Lentshin had become a village with few young people. The young men left for Zakroczym, for Nowy Dwor, for Warsaw, and sometimes for the United States. Like Samuel's, their letters were illegible, the Yiddish mixed with the languages of the countries where they were now living. They sent photographs in which the men wore top hats and the women fancy dresses like squiresses.

Berl and Berlcha also received such photographs. But their eyes were failing and neither he nor she had glasses. They could barely make out the pictures. Samuel had sons and daughters with gentile names—and grandchildren who had married and had their own offspring. Their names were so strange that Berl and Berlcha could never remember them. But what difference do names make? America was far, far away on the other side of the ocean, at the edge of the world. A Talmud[2] teacher who came to Lentshin had said that Americans walked with their heads down and their feet up. Berl and Berlcha could not grasp this. How was it possible? But since the teacher said so it must be true. Berlcha pondered for some time and then she said, "One can get accustomed to everything."

And so it remained. From too much thinking—God forbid—one may lose one's wits.

One Friday morning, when Berlcha was kneading the dough for the Sabbath loaves, the door opened and a nobleman entered. He was so tall that he had to bend down to get through the door. He wore a beaver hat and a cloak bordered with fur. He was followed by Chazkel, the coachman from Zakroczym, who carried two leather valises with brass locks. In astonishment Berlcha raised her eyes.

10 The nobleman looked around and said to the coachman in Yiddish, "Here it is." He took out a silver ruble and paid him. The coachman tried to hand him change but he said, "You can go now."

When the coachman closed the door, the nobleman said, "Mother, it's me, your son Samuel—Sam."

[1]**Dr. Herzl** Theodore Herzl (1860–1904), the founder of Zionism. [2]**Talmud** the collection of ancient rabbinic writings that constitute the basis of traditional Judaism.

Berlcha heard the words and her legs grew numb. Her hands, to which pieces of dough were sticking, lost their power. The nobleman hugged her, kissed her forehead, both her cheeks. Berlcha began to cackle like a hen, "My son!" At that moment Berl came in from the woodshed, his arms piled with logs. The goat followed him. When he saw a nobleman kissing his wife, Berl dropped the wood and exclaimed, "What is this?"

The nobleman let go of Berlcha and embraced Berl. "Father!"

For a long time Berl was unable to utter a sound. He wanted to recite holy words that he had read in the Yiddish Bible, but he could remember nothing. Then he asked, "Are you Samuel?"

"Yes, Father, I am Samuel."

"Well, peace be with you." Berl grasped his son's hand. He was still not sure that he was not being fooled. Samuel wasn't as tall and heavy as this man, but then Berl reminded himself that Samuel was only fifteen years old when he had left home. He must have grown in that faraway country. Berl asked, "Why didn't you let us know that you were coming?"

"Didn't you receive my cable?" Samuel asked.

Berl did not know what a cable was.

Berlcha had scraped the dough from her hands and enfolded her son. He kissed her again and asked, "Mother, didn't you receive a cable?"

"What? If I lived to see this, I am happy to die," Berlcha said, amazed by her own words. Berl, too, was amazed. These were just the words he would have said earlier if he had been able to remember. After a while Berl came to himself and said, "Pescha, you will have to make a double Sabbath pudding in addition to the stew."

It was years since Berl had called Berlcha by her given name. When he wanted to address her, he would say, "Listen," or "Say." It is the young or those from the big cities who call a wife by her name. Only now did Berlcha begin to cry. Yellow tears ran from her eyes, and everything became dim. Then she called out, "It's Friday—I have to prepare for the Sabbath." Yes, she had to knead the dough and braid the loaves. With such a guest, she had to make a larger Sabbath stew. The winter day is short and she must hurry.

Her son understood what was worrying her, because he said, "Mother, I will help you."

Berlcha wanted to laugh, but a choked sob came out. "What are you saying? God forbid."

The nobleman took off his cloak and jacket and remained in his vest, on which hung a solid-gold watch chain. He rolled up his sleeves and came to the trough. "Mother, I was a baker for many years in New York," he said, and he began to knead the dough.

"What! You are my darling son who will say Kaddish[3] for me." She wept raspingly. Her strength left her, and she slumped onto the bed.

Berl said, "Women will always be women." And he went to the shed to get more wood. The goat sat down near the oven; she gazed with surprise at this strange man—his height and his bizarre clothes.

The neighbors had heard the good news that Berl's son had arrived from America and they came to greet him. The women began to help Berlcha prepare for the Sabbath. Some laughed, some cried. The room was full of people, as at a

[3]**Kaddish** the prayer for the dead.

wedding. They asked Berl's son, "What is new in America?" And Berl's son answered, "America is all right."

"Do Jews make a living?"

"One eats white bread there on weekdays."[4]

"Do they remain Jews?"

"I am not a gentile."

After Berlcha blessed the candles, father and son went to the little synagogue across the street. A new snow had fallen. The son took large steps, but Berl warned him, "Slow down."

In the synagogue the Jews recited "Let Us Exult" and "Come, My Groom." All the time, the snow outside kept falling. After prayers, when Berl and Samuel left the Holy Place, the village was unrecognizable. Everything was covered in snow. One could see only the contours of the roofs and the candles in the windows. Samuel said, "Nothing has changed here."

Berlcha had prepared gefilte fish, chicken soup with rice, meat, carrot stew. Berl recited the benediction over a glass of ritual wine. The family ate and drank, and when it grew quiet for a while one could hear the chirping of the house cricket. The son talked a lot, but Berl and Berlcha understood little. His Yiddish was different and contained foreign words.

After the final blessing Samuel asked, "Father, what did you do with all the money I sent you?"

Berl raised his white brows. "It's here."

"Didn't you put it in a bank?"

"There is no bank in Lentshin."

"Where do you keep it?"

Berl hesitated. "One is not allowed to touch money on the Sabbath but I will show you." He crouched beside the bed and began to shove something heavy. A boot appeared. Its top was stuffed with straw. Berl removed the straw and the son saw that the boot was full of gold coins. He lifted it.

"Father, this is a treasure!" he called out.

"Well."

"Why didn't you spend it?"

"On what? Thank God, we have everything."

"Why didn't you travel somewhere?"

"Where to? This is our home."

The son asked one question after the other, but Berl's answer was always the same: they wanted for nothing. The garden, the cow, the goat, the chickens provided them with all they needed. The son said, "If thieves knew about this, your lives wouldn't be safe."

"There are no thieves here."

"What will happen to the money?"

"You take it."

Slowly, Berl and Berlcha grew accustomed to their son and his American Yiddish. Berlcha could hear him better now. She even recognized his voice. He was saying, "Perhaps we should build a larger synagogue."

"The synagogue is big enough," Berl replied.

"Perhaps a home for old people."

"No one sleeps in the street."

[4]**One eats white bread there on weekdays** In the poor communities of Europe, white bread was a luxury reserved for holidays such as the Sabbath.

55 The next day after the Sabbath meal was eaten, a gentile from Zakroczym brought a paper—it was the cable. Berl and Berlcha lay down for a nap. They soon began to snore. The goat, too, dozed off. The son put on his cloak and his hat and went for a walk. He strode with his long legs across the marketplace. He stretched out a hand and touched a roof. He wanted to smoke a cigar, but he remembered it was forbidden on the Sabbath. He had a desire to talk to someone, but it seemed that the whole of Lentshin was asleep. He entered the synagogue. An old man was sitting there, reciting psalms. Samuel asked, "Are you praying?"

"What else is there to do when one gets old?"

"Do you make a living?"

The old man did not understand the meaning of those words. He smiled, showing his empty gums, and then he said, "If God gives health, one keeps on living."

Samuel returned home. Dusk had fallen. Berl went to the synagogue for the evening prayers and the son remained with his mother. The room was filled with shadows.

60 Berlcha began to recite in a solemn singsong, "God of Abraham, Isaac, and Jacob, defend the poor people of Israel and Thy name. The Holy Sabbath is departing; the welcome week is coming to us. Let it be one of health, wealth, and good deeds."

"Mother, you don't need to pray for wealth," Samuel said. "You are wealthy already."

Berlcha did not hear—or pretended not to. Her face had turned into a cluster of shadows.

In the twilight Samuel put his hand into his jacket pocket and touched his passport, his checkbook, his letters of credit. He had come here with big plans. He had a valise filled with presents for his parents. He wanted to bestow gifts on the village. He brought not only his own money but funds from the Lentshin Society in New York, which had organized a ball for the benefit of the village. But this village in the hinterland needed nothing. From the synagogue one could hear hoarse chanting. The cricket, silent all day, started again its chirping. Berlcha began to sway and utter holy rhymes inherited from mothers and grandmothers:

Thy holy sheep
In mercy keep,
In Torah[5] good deeds;
Provide for all their needs,
Shoes, clothes, and bread
And the Messiah's tread.

[1973]

[5]**Torah** Jewish teachings, especially the first five books of the Hebrew Bible.

Joining the Conversation: Critical Thinking and Writing

1. What is your attitude toward Berl and Berlcha? Admiration? Pity? Or what? (Of course you need not limit your answer to a single word. You may find that your response is complex.) What is your attitude toward Samuel?
2. Compare Samuel's values with those of his parents. What resemblances do you find? What differences?

POEMS

WILLIAM BLAKE

William Blake (1757–1827) was born in London and at 14 was apprenticed for seven years to an engraver. A Christian visionary poet, he made his living by giving drawing lessons and by illustrating books, including his own Songs of Innocence *(1789) and* Songs of Experience *(1794). These two books represent, he said, "two contrary states of the human soul." ("Infant Joy" comes from Innocence, "Infant Sorrow" and "The Echoing Green" come from* Experience.*) In 1809 Blake exhibited his art, but the show was a failure. Not until he was in his sixties, when he stopped writing poetry, did he achieve any public recognition—and then it was as a painter.*

"Infant Joy" by William Blake, from *Songs of Innocence*. (By kind permission of the Provost and Scholars of King's College, Cambridge.)

Infant Joy

"I have no name,
I am but two days old."
What shall I call thee?
"I happy am,
Joy is my name."

Sweet joy befall thee!
Pretty joy!
Sweet joy but two days old,
Sweet joy I call thee;
Thou dost smile,
I sing the while—
Sweet joy befall thee.

[1789]

"Infant Sorrow" by William Blake, from *Songs of Experience.* (By kind permission of the Provost and Scholars of King's College, Cambridge.)

Infant Sorrow

My mother groand! my father wept.
Into the dangerous world I leapt,
Helpless, naked, piping loud;
Like a fiend hid in a cloud.

Struggling in my father's hands,
Striving against my swadling bands;
Bound and weary I thought best
To sulk upon my mother's breast.

[1794]

Joining the Conversation: Critical Thinking and Writing

1. "Infant Joy" begins "I have no name," but by line 5 the infant says "Joy is my name." What does the mother reply? Does she know the infant's name?
2. In line 9 the mother says, "Sweet joy I call thee." Does the line suggest how the mother has learned the name? What is the child's response?
3. In "Infant Sorrow," why is the infant sorrowful? What does the baby struggle against? Does "Like a fiend" suggest that it is inherently wicked and therefore should be repressed? Or does the adult world wickedly repress energy?
4. Why does the mother groan? Why does the father weep? Is the world "dangerous" to the infant in other than an obviously physical sense? To what degree are its parents its enemies? To what degree does the infant yield to them? In the last line, one might expect a newborn baby to nurse. What does this infant do?
5. Compare "Infant Joy" with "Infant Sorrow." What differences in sound do you hear? In "Infant Sorrow," for instance, look at lines 3, 5, 6, and 7. What repeated sounds do you hear?
6. One scholar has said that each of these poems is a "refutation" of the other one. Do you agree? Please explain.

The Echoing Green

The Sun does arise,
And make happy the skies;
The merry bells ring
To welcome the Spring;
The skylark and thrush,
The birds of the bush,
Sing louder around
To the bells' cheerful sound,
While our sports shall be seen
On the Echoing Green.

Old John, with white hair,
Does laugh away care,
Sitting under the oak,
Among the old folk.
They laugh at our play,
And soon they all say:
"Such, such were the joys
When we all, girls and boys,
In our youth time were seen
On the Echoing Green."

Till the little ones, weary,
No more can be merry;
The sun does descend,
And our sports have an end.
Round the laps of their mothers
Many sisters and brothers,
Like birds in their nest,
Are ready for rest,
And sport no more seen
On the darkening Green.

[1789]

Joining the Conversation: Critical Thinking and Writing

1. Who speaks the poem? (Go through the poem, picking up the clues that identify the speaker.)
2. When does the poem begin? And when does it end?
3. What is a "green," and why in this poem does it "echo"?
4. Try writing a piece entitled "Such, such were the joys . . ." You may need to pretend to be a bit older than you are, but try to get down what really were the joys of your childhood.
5. Please argue why childhood is the best time of our lives. After you have done that, argue why it is not.

The Lamb

Little Lamb, who made thee?
Dost thou know who made thee?
Gave thee life, and bid thee feed
By the stream and o'er the mead;
Gave thee clothing of delight,
Softest clothing, wooly, bright;
Gave thee such a tender voice,
Making all the vales rejoice?
  Little Lamb, who made thee?
  Dost thou know who made thee?

Little Lamb, I'll tell thee,
Little Lamb, I'll tell thee:
He is calléd by thy name,
For he calls himself a Lamb.
He is meek, and he is mild;
He became a little child.
I a child, and thou a lamb,
We are calléd by his name.
Little Lamb, God bless thee!
Little Lamb, God bless thee!

[1789]

The Tyger

Tyger! Tyger! burning bright
In the forests of the night,
What immortal hand or eye
Could frame thy fearful symmetry?

In what distant deeps or skies
Burnt the fire of thine eyes?
On what wings dare he aspire?
What the hand dare seize the fire?

And what shoulder, and what art,
Could twist the sinews of thy heart?
And, when thy heart began to beat,
What dread hand? and what dread feet?

What the hammer? what the chain?
In what furnace was thy brain?
What the anvil? what dread grasp
Dare its deadly terrors clasp?

When the stars threw down their spears,
And watered heaven with their tears,
Did he smile his work to see?
Did he who made the lamb make thee?

Tyger! Tyger! burning bright
In the forests of the night,
What immortal hand or eye,
Dare frame thy fearful symmetry?

[1794]

Joining the Conversation: Critical Thinking and Writing

Why does Blake answer his question in "The Lamb" but not in "The Tyger"?

Gerard Manley Hopkins

Gerard Manley Hopkins (1844–1889) was born near London and was educated at Oxford, where he studied the classics. A convert from Anglicanism to Roman Catholicism, he was ordained a Jesuit priest in 1877. After serving as a parish priest and teacher, he was appointed Professor of Greek at the Catholic University in Dublin.

Hopkins published only a few poems during his lifetime, partly because he believed that the pursuit of literary fame was incompatible with his vocation as a priest, and partly because he was aware that his highly individual style might puzzle readers.

Spring and Fall

To a Young Child

Márgarét áre you griéving°
Over Goldengrove unleaving?
Leáves, líke the thíngs of mán, you
With your fresh thoughts care for, can you?
Áh! ás the héart grows older
It will come to such sights colder
By and by, nor spare a sigh
Though worlds of wanwood leafmeal lie;
And yet you will weep and know why.
Now no matter, child, the name:
Sórrow's spríngs áre the same.
Nor mouth had, no nor mind, expressed
What héart heárd of, ghost° guéssed:
It ís the blíght mán was bórn for,
It is Margaret you mourn for.

[1880]

1 The stress marks in this poem were indicated by Hopkins. **13 ghost** spirit.

Joining the Conversation: Critical Thinking and Writing

1. What is the speaker's age? His tone? What is the relevance of the title to Margaret? What meanings are in "Fall"? Is there more than one meaning to "Spring"? (Notice especially the title and line 11.)
2. What is meant by Margaret's "fresh thoughts" (line 4)? Paraphrase lines 3–4 and lines 12–13.
3. "Wanwood" and "leafmeal" are words coined by Hopkins. What are their suggestions?
4. What does "blight" mean in line 14?
5. Why is it not contradictory for the speaker to say that Margaret weeps for herself (line 15) after saying that she weeps for "Goldengrove unleaving" (line 2)?
6. Do you find this poem to be difficult? Using details from the text, please explain why or why not.

E. E. Cummings

Edwin Estlin Cummings (1894–1962), who used the pen name e. e. cummings, grew up in Cambridge, Massachusetts, and graduated from Harvard, where he became interested in modern literature and art, especially in the movements called Cubism and Futurism. His father, a conservative clergyman and a professor at Harvard, seems to have been baffled by the youth's interests, but Cummings's mother encouraged his artistic activities, including unconventional punctuation.

Politically liberal in his youth, Cummings became more conservative after a visit to Russia in 1931, but early and late his work emphasizes individuality and freedom of expression.

in Just-

in Just-
spring   when the world is mud-
luscious the little
lame balloonman

whistles   far   and wee

and eddieandbill come
running from marbles and
piracies and it's
spring

when the world is puddle-wonderful

the queer
old balloonman whistles
far   and   wee
and bettyandisbel come dancing

from hop-scotch and jump-rope and

it's
spring
and

    the

        goat-footed

balloonMan   whistles
far
and
wee

[1920]

Joining the Conversation: Critical Thinking and Writing

1. Why "eddieandbill" and "bettyandisbel" rather than "eddie and bill" and "betty and isabel"? And why not "eddie and betty," and "bill and isabel"?

2. What are some effects that Cummings may be getting at by his unusual arrangement of words on the page? Compare, for instance, the physical appearance of "Whistles far and wee" in line 5 with the appearance of the same words in lines 12–13 and 21–24.
3. Because the balloonman is "lame" (line 4) or "goat-footed" (line 20), many readers find an allusion to the Greek god Pan, the goat-footed god of woods, fields, and flocks, and the inventor of a primitive wind instrument consisting of a series of reeds, "Pan's pipes." (If you are unfamiliar with Pan, consult an encyclopedia or a guide to mythology.) Do you agree that Cummings is alluding to Pan? If so, what is the point of the allusion?
4. A critic has said: "Cummings cares more about words than about their meanings." What is this critic saying? Please argue why you agree or disagree.

Louise Glück

Louise Glück (b. 1943) was born in New York City and attended Sarah Lawrence College and Columbia University. She has taught at Goddard College in Vermont and at Warren Wilson College in North Carolina. Her volume of poems, The Triumph of Achilles *(1985), won the National Book Critics Circle Award for poetry. She now teaches creative writing at Yale and Boston University.*

The School Children

The children go forward with their little satchels.
And all morning the mothers have labored
to gather the late apples, red and gold,
like words of another language.

And on the other shore
are those who wait behind great desks
to receive these offerings.

How orderly they are—the nails
on which the children hang
their overcoats of blue or yellow wool.

And the teachers shall instruct them in silence
and the mothers shall scour the orchards for a way out,
drawing to themselves the gray limbs of the fruit trees
bearing so little ammunition.

[1975]

Joining the Conversation: Critical Thinking and Writing

1. Which words in the poem present a cute picture-postcard view of small children going to school?
2. Which words undercut this happy scene?
3. In the last stanza we read that "the teachers shall instruct" and "the mothers shall scour." What, if anything, is changed if we substitute "will" for "shall"?
4. In this poem about schoolchildren, is the poet herself seeking to teach us something? Explain.

Gretel in Darkness

This is the world we wanted. All who would have seen us dead
Are dead. I hear the witch's cry
Break in the moonlight through a sheet of sugar: God rewards.
Her tongue shrivels into gas. . . .

Now, far from women's arms
And memory of women, in our father's hut
We sleep, are never hungry.
Why do I not forget?
My father bars the door, bars harm
From this house, and it is years.

No one remembers. Even you, my brother,
Summer afternoons you look at me as though you meant
To leave, as though it never happened. But I killed for you.
I see armed firs, the spires of that gleaming kiln come back, come back—
Nights I turn to you to hold me but you are not there.
Am I alone? Spies
Hiss in the stillness, Hansel we are there still, and it is real, real,
That black forest, and the fire in earnest.

[1975]

Joining the Conversation: Critical Thinking and Writing

1. How, as the poem develops, is the first sentence of the poem modified? Is this the world "we" wanted? What does Gretel believe that Hansel wants?
2. In stanza 3 Gretel says

   But I killed for you.
   I see . . . the spires of that gleaming kiln come back, come back—

   Whether or not you know the story from *Grimm's Fairy Tales,* how do you understand Gretel's plight?
3. Why is the poem called "Gretel in Darkness"? What does the poem seem to tell us about how men and women face danger?

PLAY

Thinking Critically: Case Study on Writing Arguments about Hamlet

This case study contains (in addition to illustrations of the original texts of *Hamlet*, the Elizabethan theater, and modern productions) the following material:

1. A note on the Elizabethan theater
2. A note on *Hamlet* on the stage
3. A note on the text of *Hamlet*
4. The text of *Hamlet*
5. A Freudian interpretation by Ernest Jones
6. Anne Barton's general comments on the play
7. Stanley Wells's analysis of the first soliloquy
8. Elaine Showalter's discussion of Ophelia
9. Claire Bloom's comments on her performance as Gertrude, in the BBC TV production
10. Bernice W. Kliman review of the BBC TV production of *Hamlet* (1980)
11. A review by student Will Saretta of Branagh's *Hamlet*

A Note on the Elizabethan Theater

Shakespeare's theater was wooden, round or polygonal (the Chorus in *Henry V* calls it a "wooden O"). About eight hundred spectators could stand in the yard in front of—and perhaps along the two sides of—the stage that jutted from the rear

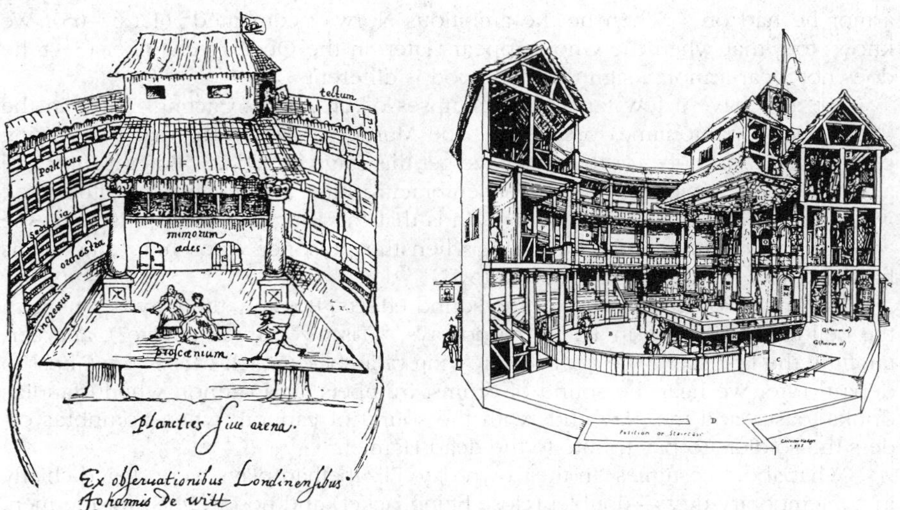

Left, Johannes de Witt, a Continental visitor to London, made a drawing of the Swan Theater in about the year 1596. The original drawing is lost; this is Arend van Buchel's copy of it. (Copyright the British Museum.) *Right*, C. Walter Hodges's drawing (1965) of an Elizabethan playhouse. (Courtesy C. Walter Hodges.)

wall, and another fifteen hundred or so spectators could sit in the three roofed galleries that ringed the stage.

That portion of the galleries that was above the rear of the stage was sometimes used by actors. For instance, in *The Tempest,* 3.3, a stage direction following line 17 mentions "Prospero on the top, invisible"—that is, he is imagined to be invisible to the characters in the play.

Entry to the stage was normally gained by doors at the rear, but apparently on rare occasions use was made of a curtained alcove—or perhaps a booth—between the doors, which allowed characters to be "discovered" (revealed) as in the modern proscenium theater, which normally employs a curtain. Such "discovery" scenes are rare.

Although the theater as a whole was unroofed, the stage was protected by a roof, supported by two pillars. These could serve (by an act of imagination) as trees behind which actors might pretend to conceal themselves.

A performance was probably uninterrupted by intermissions or by long pauses for the changing of scenery; a group of characters leaves the stage, another enters, and if the locale has changed the new characters somehow tell us. (Modern editors customarily add indications of locales to help a reader, but it should be remembered that the action on the Elizabethan stage was continuous.)

A Note on *Hamlet* on the Stage

We know that *Hamlet* was popular during Shakespeare's lifetime, but the earliest illustration (1709) showing a scene from the play was engraved more than a century after the play was written, so we know little about what *Hamlet* looked like on Shakespeare's stage. Still, we do have at least some idea. We know, for instance, that at least in the first scene Hamlet wore black (he speaks of his "inky cloak"), and we know that when the Ghost first appears it is dressed in "the very armor he had on / When he the ambitious Norway combated" (1.1.64–65). We know, too, that when the Ghost appears later, in the Queen's chamber (3.4), he does not wear armor, a sign that his mood is different.

We also have a few tantalizing glimpses of Elizabethan acting. Thus, in the dumb show (pantomime) preceding "The Murder of Gonzago" that the touring players in 3.2 produce for the court, we get this stage direction: "Enter a King and a Queen [very lovingly]; the Queen embracing him, and he her." A little later, when the Queen in this dumb show finds that the King has been poisoned, she "makes passionate action," but then, when the poisoner woos her, "she seems harsh awhile, but in the end accepts love."

We know something, too, of the sound effects. Possibly the play begins with the bell tolling twelve (in 1.1 Bernardo says, "'Tis now struck twelve"), and certainly in the first scene we hear the crowing of a cock, which causes the Ghost to depart. Later we hear the sound of drums, trumpets, and cannon when Claudius drinks toasts, and the play ends with the sound of cannon, when Fortinbras orders the soldiers to pay tribute to the dead Hamlet.

What about costumes? In their own day, Elizabethan plays were staged chiefly in contemporary dress—doublet (close-fitting jacket) and hose (tights) for the men, gowns of various sorts for the women (whose roles were played by boy actors)—though for classical plays such as *Julius Caesar* some attempt was made in the direction of ancient costume, at least for the major characters. The seventeenth and eighteenth centuries, too, staged the plays in the costume of the day, which of course was not Elizabethan. But in much of the nineteenth century, and in the first third of the twentieth, a strong sense that the plays were "Elizabethan" caused producers to use Elizabethan costumes, although these costumes—contemporary when the plays were first performed—now had become historical costume, marking the plays as of an age remote from our own. In 1925 Barry Jackson staged a modern-dress production in London, in an effort to emphasize the play's contemporary relevance. Today, productions tend to be in modern dress in the sense that they avoid Elizabethan costume. Usually, in an effort to add some color to the stage as well as some (but not a great) sense of remoteness, they use costumes of the nineteenth century, which allow for splendid gowns and for military uniforms with sashes.

Figure 1

Figure 1. "The Murder of Gonzago" in 3.2. Because this episode is a play-within-the-play, Shakespeare uses a distinctive form of verse (pairs of rhyming line, eight syllables to a line) that sets it off from the language of the rest of the play (chiefly prose, or unrhymed lines of ten syllables). The language, too, is different, for it is conspicuously old-fashioned (the sun is called "Phoebus' cart," the ocean is called "Neptune's salt wash"). In this modern-dress production done at Stratford, England, in 1975, Claudius wore a blue business suit and Fortinbras wore combat gear, but the characters in the play-within-the-play were masked, to emphasize their theatricality.

Figure 2

Figure 2. The "closet" scene, in 3.4. A line in the preceding scene specifically tells us that Hamlet is "going to his mother's closet." (In Elizabethan language, a "closet" is a private room, rather than a public room—for instance a room in which a monarch might pray, or relax, as opposed to an audience chamber in which he or she would engage in official actions.) In the twentieth century, at least as early as John Gielgud's production in New York in 1935, and probably in response to Freudian interpretations of the play, the Queen's closet has been fitted with a bed on which Hamlet and Gertrude tussle, and indeed the scene is often wrongly called "the bedroom scene." In this 1989 Royal Shakespeare Company production, with Mark Rylance as Hamlet, a ranting Hamlet (at the left) confronts Gertrude. The Ghost, unknown to Gertrude, sits on the bed, presumably seeking to protect her from Hamlet's assault. The setting was not realistic but expressionistic; that is, the curtains stirred and the lighting changed not because a physical wind was blowing or the sources of illumination were changing, but to express the characters' passions.

Figure 3

Figures 3 and 4 (page 902). Hamlet meditates on death in the grave yard, in 5.1. Both of these productions used costumes that suggested the late nineteenth century. Kenneth Branagh portrayed Hamlet in 1993 for the Royal Shakespeare Theatre. In the photograph showing Kevin Kline as Hamlet (New York Shakespeare Festival), Horatio is played by an African American. Other than plays by black authors, and a very few plays by whites about blacks (such as Eugene O'Neill's *The Emperor Jones*), there are few roles in drama expressly written for blacks. Shakespeare offers only three: Othello, Aaron (a Moor in *Titus Andronicus*), and the Prince of Morocco (in *The Merchant of Venice*). The few black actors who played other Shakespearean roles, such as the great Ira Aldridge who in the nineteenth century was known for his King Lear, performed the roles in whiteface. Since the 1980s, however, directors have engaged in open casting, using blacks (and Asians) in any and all roles, and not requiring white makeup.

Figure 4

A Note on the Text of *Hamlet*

Shakespeare's *Hamlet* comes to us in three versions. The first, known as the First Quarto (Q1), was published in 1603. It is an illegitimate garbled version, perhaps derived from the memory of the actor who played Marcellus (this part is conspicuously more accurate than the rest of the play) in a short version of the play.

The second printed version (Q2), which appeared in 1604–1605, is almost twice as long as Q1; all in all, it is the best text we have, doubtless published (as Q1 was not) with the permission of Shakespeare's theatrical company.

The third printed version, in the First Folio (the collected edition of Shakespeare's plays, published in 1623), is also legitimate, but it seems to be an acting version, for it lacks some two hundred lines of Q2.

On the other hand, the Folio text includes some ninety lines not found in Q2.

Because Q2 is the longest version, giving us more of the play as Shakespeare conceived it than either of the other texts, it serves as the basic version for this text. Unfortunately, the printers of it often worked carelessly: Words and phrases are omitted, there are plain misreadings of what must have been in Shakespeare's manuscript, and speeches are sometimes wrongly assigned. It was therefore necessary to turn to the First Folio for many readings. It has been found useful, also, to divide the play into acts and scenes; these divisions, not found in Q2 (and only a few are found in the Folio), are purely editorial additions, and they are therefore enclosed in square brackets.

We use the text edited by David Bevington.

The Tragedy of Hamlet

And so by continuance, and weakenesse of the braine
Into this frensie, which now possesseth him:
And if this be not true, take this from this.
King Thinke you t'is so?
Cor. How? so my Lord, I would very faine know
That thing that I haue saide t'is so, positiuely,
And it hath fallen out otherwise.
Nay, if circumstances leade me on,
Ile finde it out, if it were hid
As deepe as the centre of the earth.
King. how should wee trie this same?
Cor. Mary my good lord thus,
The Princes walke is here in the galery,
There let *Ofelia*, walke vntill hee comes:
Your selfe and I will stand close in the study,
There shall you heare the effect of all his hart,
And if it proue any otherwise then loue,
Then let my censure faile an other time.
King. see where hee comes poring vppon a booke.
Enter Hamlet.
Cor. Madame, will it please your grace
To leaue vs here?
Que. With all my hart. *exit.*
Cor. And here *Ofelia*, reade you on this booke,
And walke aloofe, the King shal be vnseene.
Ham. To be, or not to be, I there's the point,
To Die, to sleepe, is that all? I all:
No, to sleepe, to dreame, I mary there it goes,
For in that dreame of death, when wee awake,
And borne before an euerlasting Iudge,
From whence no passenger euer retur'nd,
The vndiscouered country, at whose sight
The happy smile, and the accursed damn'd.
But for this, the ioyfull hope of this,
Whol'd beare the scornes and flattery of the world,
Scorned by the right rich, the rich cursed of the poore?
The

On this page and on the next, we give the text of "To be or not to be" from the First Quarto (Q1, 1603). On pages 905–906 we give the text from the Second Quarto (Q2, 1604–1605), and on page 907 we give a third version, from the First Folio (F1, 1623), beginning at the bottom of the left-hand column.

Prince of Denmarke

The widow being oppressed, the orphan wrong'd,
The taste of hunger, or a tirants raigne,
And thousand more calamities besides,
To grunt and sweate vnder this weary life,
When that he may his full *Quietus* make,
With a bare bodkin, who would this indure,
But for a hope of something after death?
Which pusles the braine, and doth confound the sence,
Which makes vs rather beare those euilles we haue,
Than flie to others that we know not of.
I that, O this conscience makes cowardes of vs all,
Lady in thy orizons, be all my sinnes remembred.

Ofel. My Lord, I haue sought opportunitie, which now I haue, to redeliuer to your worthy handes, a small remembrance, such tokens which I haue receiued of you.

Ham. Are you faire?

Ofel. My Lord.

Ham. Are you honest?

Ofel. What meanes my Lord?

Ham. That if you be faire and honest,
Your beauty should admit no discourse to your honesty.

Ofel. My Lord, can beauty haue better priuiledge than with honesty?

Ham. Yea mary may it; for Beauty may transforme
Honesty, from what she was into a bawd:
Then Honesty can transforme Beauty:
This was sometimes a Paradox,
But now the time giues it scope.
I neuer gaue you nothing.

Ofel. My Lord, you know right well you did,
And with them such earnest vowes of loue,
As would haue moou'd the stoniest breast aliue,
But now too true I finde,
Rich giftes waxe poore, when giuers grow vnkinde.

Ham. I neuer loued you.

Ofel. You made me beleeue you did.

E *Ham.*

First Quarto continued.

That ſhow of ſuch an exerciſe may cullour
Your lowlines; we are oft too blame in this,
Tis too much proou'd, that with deuotions viſage
And pious action, we doe ſugar ore
The deuill himſelfe.
King. O tis too true,
How ſmart a laſh that ſpeech doth giue my conſcience.
The harlots cheeke beautied with plaſtring art,
Is not more ougly to the thing that helps it,
Then is my deede to my moſt painted word:
O heauy burthen.

Enter Hamlet.

Pol. I heare him comming, with-draw my Lord.
Ham. To be, or not to be, that is the queſtion,
Whether tis nobler in the minde to ſuffer
The ſlings and arrowes of outragious fortune,
Or to take Armes againſt a ſea of troubles,
And by oppoſing, end them; to die to ſleepe
No more, and by a ſleepe, to ſay we end
The hart-ake, and the thouſand naturall ſhocks
That fleſh is heire to; tis a conſumation
Deuoutly to be wiſht to die to ſleepe,
To ſleepe, perchance to dreame, I there's the rub,
For in that ſleepe of death what dreames may come
When we haue ſhuffled off this mortall coyle
Muſt giue vs pauſe, there's the reſpect
That makes calamitie of ſo long life:
For who would beare the whips and ſcornes of time,
Th'oppreſſors wrong, the proude mans contumely,
The pangs of deſpiz'd loue, the lawes delay,
The inſolence of office, and the ſpurnes
That patient merrit of th'vnworthy takes,
When he himſelfe might his quietas make
With a bare bodkin; who would fardels beare,
To grunt and ſweat vnder a wearie life,
But that the dread of ſomething after death,
The vndiſcouer'd country, from whoſe borne

G 2 No

On this page and the next we give "To be or not to be," as it appears in the Second Quarto (Q2, 1604–1605).

The Tragedie of Hamlet

No trauiler returnes, puzzels the will,
And makes vs rather beare those ills we haue,
Then flie to others that we know not of.
Thus conscience dooes make cowards,
And thus the natiue hiew of resolution
Is sickled ore with the pale cast of thought,
And enterprises of great pitch and moment,
With this regard theyr currents turne awry,
And loose the name of action. Soft you now,
The faire *Ophelia*, Nimph in thy orizons
Be all my sinnes remembred.

Oph. Good my Lord,
How dooes your honour for this many a day?

Ham. I humbly thanke you well.

Oph. My Lord, I haue remembrances of yours
That I haue longed long to redeliuer,
I pray you now receiue them.

Ham. No, not I, I neuer gaue you ought.

Oph. My honor'd Lord, you know right well you did,
And with them words of so sweet breath compos'd
As made these things more rich, their perfume lost,
Take these againe, for to the noble mind
Rich gifts wax poore when giuers prooue vnkind,
There my Lord.

Ham. Ha, ha, are you honest.

Oph. My Lord.

Ham. Are you faire?

Oph. What meanes your Lordship?

Ham. That if you be honest & faire, you should admit no discourse to your beautie.

Oph. Could beauty my Lord haue better comerse
Then with honestie?

Ham. I truly, for the power of beautie will sooner transforme honestie from what it is to a bawde, then the force of honestie can translate beautie into his likenes, this was sometime a paradox, but now the time giues it proofe, I did loue you once.

Oph. Indeed my Lord you made me belieue so.

Ham. You should not haue beleeu'd me, for vertue cannot so euocutat our old stock, but we shall relish of it, I loued you not.

Second Quarto continued.

The Tragedie of Hamlet. 265

With turbulent and dangerous Lunacy.
Rosin. He does confesse he feeles himselfe distracted,
But from what cause he will by no meanes speake.
Gul. Nor do we finde him forward to be sounded,
But with a crafty Madnesse keepes aloofe:
When we would bring him on to some Confession
Of his true state.
Qu. Did he receiue you well?
Rosin. Most like a Gentleman.
Guild. But with much forcing of his disposition.
Rosin. Niggard of question, but of our demands
Most free in his reply.
Qu. Did you assay him to any pastime?
Rosin. Madam, it so fell out, that certaine Players
We ore-wrought on the way: of these we told him,
And there did seeme in him a kinde of ioy
To heare of it: They are about the Court,
And (as I thinke) they haue already order
This night to play before him.
Pol. 'Tis most true:
And he beseech'd me to intreate your Maiesties
To heare, and see the matter.
King. With all my heart, and it doth much content me
To heare him so inclin'd. Good Gentlemen,
Giue him a further edge, and driue his purpose on
To these delights.
Rosin. We shall my Lord. *Exeunt.*
King. Sweet *Gertrude* leaue vs too,
For we haue closely sent for *Hamlet* hither,
That he, as 'twere by accident, may there
Affront *Ophelia*. Her Father, and my selfe (lawful espials)
Will so bestow our selues, that seeing vnseene
We may of their encounter frankely iudge,
And gather by him, as he is behaued,
If't be th'affliction of his loue, or no.
That thus he suffers for.
Qu. I shall obey you,
And for your part *Ophelia*, I do wish
That your good Beauties be the happy cause
Of *Hamlets* wildenesse: so shall I hope your Vertues
Will bring him to his wonted way againe,
To both your Honors.
Ophe. Madam, I wish it may.
Pol. *Ophelia*, walke you heere. Gracious so please ye
We will bestow our selues: Reade on this booke,
That shew of such an exercise may colour
Your lonelinesse. We are oft too blame in this,
'Tis too much prou'd, that with Deuotions visage,
And pious Action, we do surge o're
The diuell himselfe.
King. Oh 'tis true:
How smart a lash that speech doth giue my Conscience?
The Harlots Cheeke beautied with plaist'ring Art
Is not more vgly to the thing that helpes it,
Then is my deede, to my most painted word.
Oh heauie burthen!
Pol. I heare him comming, let's withdraw my Lord.
Exeunt.

Enter Hamlet.

Ham. To be, or not to be, that is the Question:
Whether 'tis Nobler in the minde to suffer
The Slings and Arrowes of outragious Fortune,
Or to take Armes against a Sea of troubles,
And by opposing end them: to dye, to sleepe
No more; and by a sleepe, to say we end
The Heart-ake, and the thousand Naturall shockes
That Flesh is heyre too? 'Tis a consummation
Deuoutly to be wish'd. To dye to sleepe,
To sleepe, perchance to Dreame; I, there's the rub,
For in that sleepe of death, what dreames may come,
When we haue shuffel'd off this mortall coile,
Must giue vs pawse. There's the respect
That makes Calamity of so long life:
For who would beare the Whips and Scornes of time,
The Oppressors wrong, the poore mans Contumely,
The pangs of dispriz'd Loue, the Lawes delay,
The insolence of Office, and the Spurnes
That patient merit of the vnworthy takes,
When he himselfe might his *Quietus* make
With a bare Bodkin? Who would these Fardles beare
To grunt and sweat vnder a weary life,
But that the dread of something after death,
The vndiscouered Countrey, from whose Borne
No Traueller returnes, Puzels the will,
And makes vs rather beare those illes we haue,
Then flye to others that we know not of.
Thus Conscience does make Cowards of vs all,
And thus the Natiue hew of Resolution
Is sicklied o're, with the pale cast of Thought,
And enterprizes of great pith and moment,
With this regard their Currants turne away,
And loose the name of Action. Soft you now,
The faire *Ophelia?* Nimph, in thy Orizons
Be all my sinnes remembred.
Ophe. Good my Lord,
How does your Honor for this many a day?
Ham. I humbly thanke you: well, well, well.
Ophe. My Lord, I haue Remembrances of yours,
That I haue longed long to re-deliuer.
I pray you now, receiue them.
Ham. No, no, I neuer gaue you ought.
Ophe. My honor'd Lord, I know right well you did,
And with them words of so sweet breath compos'd,
As made the things more rich, then perfume left:
Take these againe, for to the Noble minde
Rich gifts wax poore, when giuers proue vnkinde.
There my Lord.
Ham. Ha, ha: Are you honest?
Ophe. My Lord.
Ham. Are you faire?
Ophe. What meanes your Lordship?
Ham. That if you be honest and faire, your Honesty should admit no discourse to your Beautie.
Ophe. Could Beautie my Lord, haue better Comerce then your Honestie?
Ham. I trulie: for the power of Beautie, will sooner transforme Honestie from what it is, to a Bawd, then the force of Honestie can translate Beautie into his likenesse. This was sometime a Paradox, but now the time giues it proofe. I did loue you once.
Ophe. Indeed my Lord, you made me beleeue so.
Ham. You should not haue beleeued me. For vertue cannot so innocculate our old stocke, but we shall rellish of it. I loued you not.
Ophe. I was the more deceiued.
Ham. Get thee to a Nunnerie. Why would'st thou be a breeder of Sinners? I am my selfe indifferent honest, but yet I could accuse me of such things, that it were better my Mother had not borne me. I am very prowd, reuengefull, Ambitious, with more offences at my becke, then I haue thoughts to put them in imagination, to giue them shape, or time to acte them in. What should such Fel-

"To be or not to be," as given in the First Folio (F1, 1623).

WILLIAM SHAKESPEARE

William Shakespeare (1564–1616) was born in Stratford-on-Avon, England, of middle-class parents. Nothing of interest is known about his early years, but by 1590 he was acting and writing plays in London. By the end of the following decade he had worked in all three Elizabethan dramatic genres—tragedy, comedy, and history. Romeo and Juliet, *for example, was written about 1595, the year of* Richard II. Hamlet *was probably written in 1600–1601. Among the plays that followed were* Othello *(1603–1604),* King Lear *(1605–1606),* Macbeth *(1605–1606), and several "romances"—plays that have happy endings but that seem more meditative and closer to tragedy than such comedies as* A Midsummer Night's Dream *(c.1595),* As You Like It *(1598–1600), and* Twelfth Night *(1600–1602).*

The Tragedy of Hamlet, Prince of Denmark

DRAMATIS PERSONAE

GHOST *of Hamlet, the former King of Denmark*
CLAUDIUS, *King of Denmark, the former King's brother*
GERTRUDE, *Queen of Denmark, widow of the former King and now wife of Claudius*
HAMLET, *Prince of Denmark, son of the late King and of Gertrude*
POLONIUS, *councillor to the King*
LAERTES, *his son*
OPHELIA, *his daughter*
REYNALDO, *his servant*

HORATIO, *Hamlet's friend and fellow student*

VOLTIMAND, CORNELIUS, ROSENCRANTZ, GUILDENSTERN, OSRIC, A GENTLEMAN, A LORD, — *members of the Danish court*

BERNARDO, FRANCISCO, MARCELLUS, — *officers and soldiers on watch*

FORTINBRAS, *Prince of Norway*
CAPTAIN *in his army*
Three or Four PLAYERS, *taking the roles of* PROLOGUE, PLAYER KING, PLAYER QUEEN, and LUCIANUS
Two MESSENGERS
FIRST SAILOR
Two CLOWNS, *a gravedigger and his companion*
PRIEST
FIRST AMBASSADOR from England
Lords, Soldiers, Attendants, Guards, other Players, Followers of Laertes, other Sailors, another Ambassador or Ambassadors from England
SCENE: *Denmark*

[1.1]

Enter BERNARDO *and* FRANCISCO, *two sentinels* [*meeting*].

BERNARDO: Who's there?
FRANCISCO: Nay, answer me.° Stand and unfold yourself.°
BERNARDO: Long live the King!
FRANCISCO: Bernardo?
BERNARDO: He.
FRANCISCO: You come most carefully upon your hour.
BERNARDO: 'Tis now struck twelve. Get thee to bed, Francisco.
FRANCISCO: For this relief much thanks. 'Tis bitter cold,
And I am sick at heart.
BERNARDO: Have you had quiet guard?
FRANCISCO: Not a mouse stirring.
BERNARDO: Well, good night.
If you do meet Horatio and Marcellus,
The rivals° of my watch, bid them make haste.

Enter HORATIO *and* MARCELLUS.

FRANCISCO: I think I hear them.—Stand, ho! Who is there?
HORATIO: Friends to this ground.°
MARCELLUS: And liegemen to the Dane.°
FRANCISCO: Give° you good night.
MARCELLUS: O, farewell, honest soldier. Who hath relieved you?
FRANCISCO: Bernardo hath my place. Give you good night. *Exit* FRANCISCO.
MARCELLUS: Holla! Bernardo!
BERNARDO: Say, what, is Horatio there?
HORATIO: A piece of him.
BERNARDO: Welcome, Horatio. Welcome, good Marcellus.
HORATIO: What, has this thing appeared again tonight?
BERNARDO: I have seen nothing.
MARCELLUS: Horatio says 'tis but our fantasy,°
And will not let belief take hold of him
Touching this dreaded sight twice seen of us.
Therefore I have entreated him along°
With us to watch° the minutes of this night,
That if again this apparition come
He may approve° our eyes and speak to it.
HORATIO: Tush, tush, 'twill not appear.
BERNARDO: Sit down awhile,
And let us once again assail your ears,
That are so fortified against our story,
What° we have two nights seen.

> **Note:** Stage directions that are enclosed within square brackets are not in the original text. They have been added by the editor.

[1.1] Location: Elsinore castle. A guard platform. **2 me** (Francisco emphasizes that *he* is the sentry currently on watch.); **unfold yourself** reveal your identity. **14 rivals** partners. **16 ground** ground, land. **17 liegemen to the Dane** men sworn to serve the Danish king. **18 Give** i.e., may God give. **27 fantasy** imagination. **30 along** to come along. **31 watch** keep watch during. **33 approve** corroborate. **37 What** with what.

HORATIO: Well, sit we down,
And let us hear Bernardo speak of this.

BERNARDO: Last night of all,°
When yond same star that's westward from the pole°
Had made his° course t' illume° that part of heaven
Where now it burns, Marcellus and myself,
The bell then beating one—

Enter GHOST.

MARCELLUS: Peace, break thee off! Look where it comes again!

BERNARDO: In the same figure like the King that's dead.

MARCELLUS: Thou art a scholar.° Speak to it, Horatio.

BERNARDO: Looks 'a° not like the King? Mark it, Horatio.

HORATIO: Most like. It harrows me with fear and wonder.

BERNARDO: It would be spoke to.°

MARCELLUS: Speak to it, Horatio.

HORATIO: What art thou that usurp'st° this time of night,
Together with that fair and warlike form
In which the majesty of buried Denmark°
Did sometime° march? By heaven, I charge thee, speak!

MARCELLUS: It is offended.

BERNARDO: See, it stalks away.

HORATIO: Stay! Speak, speak! I charge thee, speak! *Exit* GHOST.

MARCELLUS: 'Tis gone and will not answer.

BERNARDO: How now, Horatio? You tremble and look pale.
Is not this something more than fantasy?
What think you on 't?°

HORATIO: Before my God, I might not this believe
Without the sensible° and true avouch°
Of mine own eyes.

MARCELLUS: Is it not like the King?

HORATIO: As thou art to thyself.
Such was the very armor he had on
When he the ambitious Norway° combated.
So frowned he once when, in an angry parle,°
He smote the sledded° Polacks° on the ice.
'Tis strange.

MARCELLUS: Thus twice before, and jump° at this dead hour,
With martial stalk° hath he gone by our watch.

HORATIO: In what particular thought to work° I know not,
But in the gross and scope° of mine opinion
This bodes some strange eruption to our state.

39 Last . . . all i.e., this *very* last night (emphatic). **40 pole** Pole Star, North Star. **41 his** its; **illume** illuminate. **46 scholar** one learned enough to know how to question a ghost properly. **47 'a** he. **49 It . . . to** (It was commonly believed that a ghost could not speak until spoken to.) **50 usurp'st** wrongfully takes over. **52 buried Denmark** the buried King of Denmark. **53 sometime** formerly. **59 on 't** of it. **61 sensible** confirmed by the sense; **avouch** warrant evidence. **65 Norway** King of Norway. **66 parle** parley. **67 sledded** traveling on sleds; **Polacks** Poles. **69 jump** exactly. **70 stalk** stride. **71 to work** i.e., to collect my thoughts and try to understand this. **72 gross and scope** general drift.

MARCELLUS: Good now,° sit down, and tell me, he that knows,
Why this same strict and most observant watch
So nightly toils° the subject° of the land,
And why such daily cast° of brazen cannon
And foreign mart° for implements of war,
Why such impress° of shipwrights, whose sore task
Does not divide the Sunday from the week.
What might be toward,° that this sweaty haste
Doth make the night joint-laborer with the day?
Who is 't that can inform me?

HORATIO: That can I;
At least, the whisper goes so. Our last king,
Whose image even but now appeared to us,
Was, as you know, by Fortinbras of Norway,
Thereto pricked on° by a most emulate° pride,°
Dared to the combat; in which our valiant Hamlet—
For so this side of our known world° esteemed him—
Did slay this Fortinbras; who by a sealed° compact
Well ratified by law and heraldry
Did forfeit, with his life, all those his lands
Which he stood seized° of, to the conqueror;
Against the° which a moiety competent°
Was gagèd° by our king, which had returned°
To the inheritance° of Fortinbras
Had he been vanquisher, as, by the same cov'nant°
And carriage of the article designed,°
His fell to Hamlet. Now, sir, young Fortinbras,
Of unimprovèd mettle° hot and full,
Hath in the skirts° of Norway here and there
Sharked up° a list° of lawless resolutes°
For food and diet° to some enterprise
That hath a stomach° in 't, which is no other—
As it doth well appear unto our state—
But to recover of us, by strong hand
And terms compulsatory, those foresaid lands
So by his father lost. And this, I take it,
Is the main motive of our preparations,

74 Good now (An expression denoting entreaty or expostulation.) **76 toils** causes to toil; **subject** subjects. **77 cast** casting. **78 mart** buying and selling. **79 impress** impressment, conscription. **81 toward** in preparation. **87 pricked on** incited; **emulate** emulous, ambitious; **Thereto . . . pride** (refers to old Fortinbras, not the Danish King.) **89 this . . . world** i.e., all Europe, the Western world. **90 sealed** certified, confirmed. **93 seized** possessed. **94 Against the** in return for; **moiety competent** corresponding portion. **95 gagèd** engaged, pledged; **had returned** would have passed. **96 inheritance** possession. **97 cov'nant** i.e., the *sealed compact* on line 90. **98 carriage . . . designed** carrying out of the article or clause drawn up to cover the point. **100 unimprovèd mettle** untried, undisciplined spirits. **101 skirts** outlying regions, outskirts. **102 Sharked up** gathered up, as a shark takes fish; **list** i.e., troop; **resolutes** Desperadoes. **103 For food and diet** i.e., they are to serve as *food,* or "means," *to some enterprises,* also they serve in return for the rations they get. **104 stomach** (1) a spirit of daring; (2) an appetite that is fed by the ***lawless resolutes.***

The source of this our watch, and the chief head°
Of this posthaste and rummage° in the land.

BERNARDO: I think it be no other but e'en so.
Well may it sort° that this portentous figure
Comes armèd through our watch so like the King
That was and is the question° of these wars.

HORATIO: A mote° it is to trouble the mind's eye.
In the most high and palmy° state of Rome,
A little ere the mightiest Julius fell,
The graves stood tenantless, and the sheeted° dead
Did squeak and gibber in the Roman streets;
As° stars with trains° of fire and dews of blood,
Disasters° in the sun; and the moist star°
Upon whose influence Neptune's° empire stands°
Was sick almost to doomsday° with eclipse.
And even the like precurse° of feared events,
As harbingers° preceding still° the fates
And prologue to the omen° coming on,
Have heaven and earth together demonstrated
Unto our climatures° and countrymen.

Enter GHOST.

But soft,° behold! Lo, where it comes again!
I'll cross° it, though it blast° me. [*It spreads his° arms.*]
Stay, *illusion!*
If thou hast any sound or use of voice,
Speak to me!
If there be any good thing to be done
That may to thee do ease and grace to me,
Speak to me!
If thou art privy to° thy country's fate,
Which, happily,° foreknowing may avoid,
O, speak!
Or if thou hast uphoarded in thy life
Extorted treasure in the womb of earth,
For which, they say, you spirits oft walk in death,
Speak of it! [*The cock crows.*] Stay and speak!—Stop it, Marcellus.

MARCELLUS: Shall I strike at it with my partisan?°

HORATIO: Do, if it will not stand. [*They strike at it.*]

BERNARDO: 'Tis here!

110 head source. **111 rummage** bustle, commotion. **113 sort** suit. **115 question** focus of contention. **116 mote** speck of dust. **117 palmy** flourishing. **119 sheeted** shrouded.
121 As (This abrupt transition suggests that matter is possibly omitted between lines 120 and 121.); **trains** trails. **122 Disasters** unfavorable signs or aspects; **moist star** i.e., moon, governing tides. **123 Neptune** god of the sea; **stands** depends. **124 sick . . . doomsday** (See Matthew 24:29 and Revelation 6:12.) **125 precurse** heralding, foreshadowing.
126 harbingers forerunners; **still** continually. **127 omen** calamitous event. **129 climatures** regions. **130 soft** i.e., enough, break off. **131 cross** stand in its path, confront; **blast** wither, strike with a curse; **s.d. his** its. **137 privy to** in on the secret of. **138 happily** haply, perchance. **144 partisan** long-handled spear.

HORATIO: 'Tis here! [*Exit* GHOST.]
MARCELLUS: 'Tis gone.
We do it wrong, being so majestical,
To offer it the show of violence,
For it is as the air invulnerable,
And our vain blows malicious mockery.
BERNARDO: It was about to speak when the cock crew.
HORATIO: And then it started like a guilty thing
Upon a fearful summons. I have heard
The cock, that is the trumpet° to the morn,
Doth with his lofty and shrill-sounding throat
Awake the god of day, and at his warning,
Whether in sea or fire, in earth or air,
Th' extravagant and erring° spirit hies°
To his confine; and of the truth herein
This present object made probation.°
MARCELLUS: It faded on the crowing of the cock.
Some say that ever 'gainst° that season comes
Wherein our Savior's birth is celebrated,
This bird of dawning singeth all night long,
And then, they say, no spirit dare stir abroad;
The nights are wholesome, then no planets strike,°
No fairy takes,° nor witch hath power to charm,
So hallowed and so gracious° is that time.
HORATIO: So have I heard and do in part believe it.
But, look, the morn in russet mantle clad
Walks o'er the dew of yon high eastward hill.
Break we our watch up, and by my advice
Let us impart what we have seen tonight
Unto young Hamlet; for upon my life,
This spirit, dumb to us, will speak to him.
Do you consent we shall acquaint him with it,
As needful in our loves, fitting our duty?
MARCELLUS: Let's do 't, I pray, and I this morning know
Where we shall find him most conveniently. *Exeunt.*

[1.2]

Flourish. Enter CLAUDIUS, *King of Denmark,* GERTRUDE *the Queen,*
[*the*] *Council, as*° POLONIUS *and his son* LAERTES, HAMLET, *cum aliis*°
[*including* VOLTIMAND *and* CORNELIUS].

KING: Though yet of Hamlet our° dear brother's death
The memory be green, and that it us befitted
To bear our hearts in grief and our whole kingdom
To be contracted in one brow of woe,
Yet so far hath discretion fought with nature
That we with wisest sorrow think on him

156 trumpet trumpeter. **160 extravagant and erring** wandering beyond bounds. (The words have similar meaning.); **hies** hastens. **162 probation** proof. **164 'gainst** just before. **168 strike** destroy by evil influence. **169 takes** bewitches. **170 gracious** full of grace. **[1.2] Location: The castle. s.d. as** i.e., such as, including; **cum aliis** with others. **1 our** my. (The royal "we"; also in the following lines.)

Together with remembrance of ourselves.
Therefore our sometime° sister, now our queen,
Th' imperial jointress° to this warlike state,
Have we, as 'twere with a defeated joy—
With an auspicious and a dropping eye,°
With mirth in funeral and with dirge in marriage,
In equal scale weighing delight and dole°—
Taken to wife: Nor have we herein barred
Your better wisdoms, which have freely gone
With this affair along. For all, our thanks.
Now follows that you know° young Fortinbras,
Holding a weak supposal° of our worth,
Or thinking by our late dear brother's death
Our state to be disjoint and out of frame,
Co-leaguèd with° this dream of his advantage,°
He hath not failed to pester us with message
Importing° the surrender of those lands
Lost by his father, with all bonds° of law,
To our most valiant brother. So much for him.
Now for ourself and for this time of meeting.
Thus much the business is: we have here writ
To Norway, uncle of young Fortinbras—
Who, impotent° and bed-rid, scarcely hears
Of this his nephew's purpose—to suppress
His° further gait° herein, in that the levies,
The lists, and full proportions are all made
Out of his subject;° and we here dispatch
You, good Cornelius, and you, Voltimand,
For bearers of this greeting to old Norway,
Giving to you no further personal power
To business with the King more than the scope
Of these dilated° articles allow. [*He gives a paper.*]
Farewell, and let your haste commend your duty.°

CORNELIUS, VOLTIMAND: In that, and all things, will we show our duty.

KING: We doubt it nothing.° Heartily farewell.

[*Exeunt* VOLTIMAND *and* CORNELIUS.]

And now, Laertes, what's the news with you?
You told us of some suit; what is 't, Laertes?
You cannot speak of reason to the Dane°
And lose your voice.° What wouldst thou beg, Laertes,

8 sometime former. **9 jointress** woman possessing property with her husband. **11 With . . . eye** with one eye smiling and the other weeping. **13 dole** grief. **17 that you know** what you know already, that; or, that you be informed as follows. **18 weak supposal** low estimate. **21 Co-leaguèd with** joined to, allied with; **dream . . . advantage** illusory hope of having the advantage. (His only ally is this hope.) **23 Importing** pertaining to. **24 bonds** contracts. **29 impotent** helpless. **31 His** i.e., Fortinbras'; **gait** proceeding. **31–33 in that . . . subject** since the levying of troops and supplies is drawn entirely from the King of Norway's own subjects. **38 dilated** set out at length. **39 let . . . duty** let your swift obeying of orders, rather than mere words, express your dutifulness. **41 nothing** not at all. **44 the Dane** the Danish king. **45 lose your voice** waste your speech.

That shall not be my offer, not thy asking?
The head is not more native° to the heart,
The hand more instrumental° to the mouth,
Than is the throne of Denmark to thy father.
What wouldst thou have, Laertes?

LAERTES: My dread lord,
Your leave and favor° to return to France,
From whence though willingly I came to Denmark
To show my duty in your coronation,
Yet now I must confess, that duty done,
My thoughts and wishes bend again toward France
And bow them to your gracious leave and pardon.°

KING: Have you your father's leave? What says Polonius?

POLONIUS: H'ath,° my lord, wrung from me my slow leave
By laborsome petition, and at last
Upon his will I sealed° my hard° consent.
I do beseech you, give him leave to go.

KING: Take thy fair hour,° Laertes. Time be thine,
And thy best graces spend it at thy will!°
But now, my cousin° Hamlet, and my son—

HAMLET: A little more than kin, and less than kind.°

KING: How is it that the clouds still hang on you?

HAMLET: Not so, my lord. I am too much in the sun.°

QUEEN: Good Hamlet, cast thy nighted color° off,
And let thine eye look like a friend on Denmark.°
Do not forever with thy vailèd lids°
Seek for thy noble father in the dust.
Thou know'st 'tis common,° all that lives must die,
Passing through nature to eternity.

HAMLET: Ay, madam, it is common.

QUEEN: If it be,
Why seems it so particular° with thee?

HAMLET: Seems, madam? Nay, it is. I know not "seems."
'Tis not alone my inky cloak, good Mother,
Nor customary° suits of solemn black,
Nor windy suspiration° of forced breath,

47 native closely connected, related. **48 instrumental** serviceable. **51 leave and favor** kind permission. **56 bow . . . pardon** entreatingly make a deep bow, asking your permission to depart. **58 H'ath** he has. **60 sealed** (as if sealing a legal document.); **hard** reluctant. **62 Take thy fair hour** enjoy your time of youth. **63 And . . . will** and may your finest qualities guide the way you choose to spend your time. **64 cousin** any kin not of the immediate family. **65 A little . . . kind** i.e., closer than an ordinary nephew (since I am stepson), and yet more separated in natural feeling (with pun on *kind* meaning "affectionate" and "natural," "lawful." This line is often read as an aside, but it need not be. The King chooses perhaps not to respond to Hamlet's cryptic and bitter remark.) **67 the sun** i.e., the sunshine of the King's royal favor (with pun on *son*). **68 nighted color** (1) mourning garments of black, (2) dark melancholy. **69 Denmark** the King of Denmark. **70 vailèd lids** lowered eyes. **72 common** of universal occurrence. (But Hamlet plays on the sense of "vulgar" in line 74.) **75 particular** personal. **78 customary** (1) socially conventional, (2) habitual with me. **79 suspiration** sighing.

No, nor the fruitful° river in the eye,
Nor the dejected havior° of the visage,
Together with all forms, moods,° shapes of grief,
That can denote me truly. These indeed seem,
For they are actions that a man might play.
But I have that within which passes show;
These but the trappings and the suits of woe.

KING: 'Tis sweet and commendable in your nature, Hamlet,
To give these mourning duties to your father.
But you must know your father lost a father,
That father lost, lost his, and the survivor bound
In filial obligation for some term
To do obsequious° sorrow. But to persever°
In obstinate condolement° is a course
Of impious stubbornness. 'Tis unmanly grief.
It shows a will most incorrect to heaven,
A heart unfortified,° a mind impatient,
An understanding simple° and unschooled.
For what we know must be and is as common
As any the most vulgar thing to sense,°
Why should we in our peevish opposition
Take it to heart? Fie, 'tis a fault to heaven,
A fault against the dead, a fault to nature,
To reason most absurd, whose common theme
Is death of fathers, and who still° hath cried,
From the first corpse° till he that died today,
"This must be so." We pray you, throw to earth
This unprevailing° woe and think of us
As of a father; for let the world take note,
You are the most immediate° to our throne,
And with no less nobility of love
Than that which dearest father bears his son
Do I impart toward° you. For° your intent
In going back to school° in Wittenberg,°
It is most retrograde° to our desire,
And we beseech you bend you° to remain
Here in the cheer and comfort of our eye,
Our chiefest courtier, cousin, and our son.

QUEEN: Let not thy mother lose her prayers, Hamlet.
I pray thee, stay with us, go not to Wittenberg.

80 fruitful abundant. **81 havior** expression. **82 moods** outward expression of feeling. **92 obsequious** suited to obsequies or funerals; **persever** persevere. **93 condolement** sorrowing. **96 unfortified** i.e., against adversity. **97 simple** ignorant. **99 As . . . sense** as the most ordinary experience. **104 still** always. **105 the first corpse** (Abel's.) **107 unprevailing** unavailing, useless. **109 most immediate** next in succession. **112 impart toward** i.e., bestow my affection on; **For** as for. **113 to school** i.e., to your studies; **Wittenberg** famous German university founded in 1502. **114 retrograde** contrary. **115 bend you** incline yourself.

HAMLET: I shall in all my best° obey you, madam.
KING: Why, 'tis a loving and a fair reply.
Be as ourself in Denmark. Madam, come.
This gentle and unforced accord of Hamlet
Sits smiling to° my heart, in grace° whereof
No jocund° health that Denmark drinks today
But the great cannon to the clouds shall tell,
And the King's rouse° the heaven shall bruit again,°
Respeaking earthly thunder.° Come away.
Flourish. Exeunt all but HAMLET.

HAMLET: O, that this too too sullied° flesh would melt,
Thaw, and resolve itself into a dew!
Or that the Everlasting had not fixed
His canon° 'gainst self-slaughter! O God, God,
How weary, stale, flat, and unprofitable
Seem to me all the uses° of this world!
Fie on 't, ah fie! 'Tis an unweeded garden
That grows to seed. Things rank and gross in nature
Possess it merely.° That it should come to this!
But two months dead—nay, not so much, not two.
So excellent a king, that was to° this
Hyperion° to a satyr,° so loving to my mother
That he might not beteem° the winds of heaven
Visit her face too roughly. Heaven and earth,
Must I remember? Why, she would hang on him
As if increase of appetite had grown
By what it fed on, and yet within a month—
Let me not think on 't; frailty, thy name is woman!—
A little month, or ere° those shoes were old
With which she followed my poor father's body,
Like Niobe;° all tears, why she, even she—
O God, a beast, that wants discourse of reason,°
Would have mourned longer—married with my uncle,
My father's brother, but no more like my father
Than I to Hercules. Within a month,
Ere yet the salt of most unrighteous tears
Had left the flushing in her gallèd° eyes,
She married. O, most wicked speed, to post°

120 in all my best to the best of my ability. **124 to** i.e., at; **grace** thanksgiving.
125 jocund merry. **127 rouse** drinking of a draft of liquor; **bruit again** loudly echo.
128 thunder i.e., of trumpet and kettledrum, sounded when the King drinks; see 1.4.8–12.
129 sullied defiled. (The early quartos read *sallied;* the Folio, *solid.*) **132 canon** law. **134 all the uses** the whole routine. **137 merely** completely. **139 to** in comparison to.
140 Hyperion Titan sun-god, father of Helios; **satyr** a lecherous creature of classical mythology, half-human but with a goat's legs, tail, ears, and horns. **141 beteem** allow. **147 or ere** even before. **149 Niobe** Tantalus' daughter, Queen of Thebes, who boasted that she had more sons and daughters than Leto; for this, Apollo and Artemis, children of Leto, slew her fourteen children. She was turned by Zeus into a stone that continually dropped tears.
150 wants . . . reason lacks the faculty of reason. **155 gallèd** irritated, inflamed.
156 post hasten.

With such dexterity to incestuous° sheets!
It is not, nor it cannot come to good.
But break, my heart, for I must hold my tongue.

Enter HORATIO, MARCELLUS *and* BERNARDO.

HORATIO: Hail to your lordship!
HAMLET: I am glad to see you well.
Horatio!—or I do forget myself.
HORATIO: The same, my lord, and your poor servant ever.
HAMLET: Sir, my good friend; I'll change that name° with you.
And what make you from° Wittenberg, Horatio?
Marcellus.
MARCELLUS: My good lord.
HAMLET: I am very glad to see you. [*To* BERNARDO.] Good even, sir.—
But what in faith make you from Wittenberg?
HORATIO: A truant disposition, good my lord.
HAMLET: I would not hear your enemy say so,
Nor shall you do my ear that violence
To make it truster of your own report
Against yourself. I know you are no truant.
But what is your affair in Elsinore?
We'll teach you to drink deep ere you depart.
HORATIO: My lord, I came to see your father's funeral.
HAMLET: I prithee, do not mock me, fellow student;
I think it was to see my mother's wedding.
HORATIO: Indeed, my lord, it followed hard° upon.
HAMLET: Thrift, thrift, Horatio! The funeral baked meats°
Did coldly° furnish forth the marriage tables.
Would I had met my dearest° foe in heaven
Or ever° I had seen that day, Horatio!
My father!—Methinks I see my father.
HORATIO: Where, my lord?
HAMLET: In my mind's eye, Horatio.
HORATIO: I saw him once. 'A° was a goodly king.
HAMLET: 'A was a man. Take him for all in all,
I shall not look upon his like again.
HORATIO: My lord, I think I saw him yesternight.
HAMLET: Saw? Who?
HORATIO: My lord, the King your father.
HAMLET: The King my father?
HORATIO: Season your admiration° for a while
With an attent° ear till I may deliver,
Upon the witness of these gentlemen,
This marvel to you.
HAMLET: For God's love, let me hear!

157 incestuous (In Shakespeare's day, the marriage of a man like Claudius to his deceased brother's wife was considered incestuous.) **163 change that name** i.e., give and receive reciprocally the name of "friend" (rather than talk of "servant"). **164 make you from** are you doing away from. **179 hard** close. **180 baked meats** meat pies. **181 coldly** i.e., as cold leftovers. **182 dearest** closest (and therefore deadliest). **183 Or ever** before. **186 'A** he. **193 Season your admiration** restrain your astonishment. **194 attent** attentive.

HORATIO: Two nights together had these gentlemen,
Marcellus and Bernardo, on their watch,
In the dead waste° and middle of the night,
Been thus encountered. A figure like your father,
Armèd at point° exactly, cap-à-pie,°
Appears before them, and with solemn march
Goes slow and stately by them. Thrice he walked
By their oppressed and fear-surprisèd eyes
Within his truncheon's° length, whilst they, distilled°
Almost to jelly with the act° of fear,
Stand dumb and speak not to him. This to me
In dreadful° secrecy impart they did,
And I with them the third night kept the watch,
Where, as they had delivered, both in time,
Form of the thing, each word made true and good,
The apparition comes. I knew your father;
These hands are not more like.
HAMLET: But where was this?
MARCELLUS: My lord, upon the platform where we watch.
HAMLET: Did you not speak to it?
HORATIO: My lord, I did,
But answer made it none. Yet once methought
It lifted up its head and did address
Itself to motion, like as it would speak;°
But even then° the morning cock crew loud,
And at the sound it shrunk in haste away
And vanished from our sight.
HAMLET: 'Tis very strange.
HORATIO: As I do live, my honored lord, 'tis true,
And we did think it writ down in our duty
To let you know of it.
HAMLET: Indeed, indeed, sirs. But this troubles me.
Hold you the watch tonight?
ALL: We do, my lord.
HAMLET: Armed, say you?
ALL: Armed, my lord.
HAMLET: From top to toe?
ALL: My lord, from head to foot.
HAMLET: Then saw you not his face?
HORATIO: O, yes, my lord, he wore his beaver° up.
HAMLET: What° looked he, frowningly?
HORATIO: A countenance more in sorrow than in anger.
HAMLET: Pale or red?
HORATIO: Nay, very pale.
HAMLET: And fixed his eyes upon you?

199 dead waste desolate stillness. **201 at point** correctly in every detail; **cap-à-pie** from head to foot. **205 truncheon** officer's staff; **distilled** dissolved. **206 act** action, operation. **208 dreadful** full of dread. **217–218 did . . . speak** began to move as though it were about to speak. **219 even then** at that very instant. **232 beaver** visor on the helmet. **233 What** how.

HORATIO: Most constantly.
HAMLET: I would I had been there.
HORATIO: It would have much amazed you.
HAMLET: Very like, very like. Stayed it long?
HORATIO: While one with moderate haste might tell° a hundred.
MARCELLUS, BERNARDO: Longer, longer.
HORATIO: Not when I saw 't.
HAMLET: His beard was grizzled°—no?
HORATIO: It was, as I have seen it in his life,
A sable silvered.°
HAMLET: I will watch tonight.
Perchance 'twill walk again.
HORATIO: I warrant° it will.
HAMLET: If it assume my noble father's person,
I'll speak to it though hell itself should gape
And bid me hold my peace. I pray you all,
If you have hitherto concealed this sight,
Let it be tenable° in your silence still,
And whatsoever else shall hap tonight,
Give it an understanding but no tongue.
I will requite your loves. So, fare you well.
Upon the platform twixt eleven and twelve
I'll visit you.
ALL: Our duty to your honor.
HAMLET: Your loves, as mine to you. Farewell. *Exeunt [all but* HAMLET*].*
My father's spirit in arms! All is not well.
I doubt° some foul play. Would the night were come!
Till then sit still, my soul. Foul deeds will rise,
Though all the earth o'erwhelm them, to men's eyes. *Exit.*

[1.3]

Enter LAERTES *and* OPHELIA, *his sister.*

LAERTES: My necessaries are embarked. Farewell.
And, sister, as the winds give benefit
And convoy is assistant,° do not sleep
But let me hear from you.
OPHELIA: Do you doubt that?
LAERTES: For Hamlet, and the trifling of his favor,
Hold it a fashion and a toy in blood,°
A violet in the youth of primy° nature,
Forward,° not permanent, sweet, not lasting,
The perfume and suppliance° of a minute—
No more.
OPHELIA: No more but so?
LAERTES: Think it no more.

242 tell count. **245 grizzled** gray. **247 sable silvered** black mixed with white. **248 warrant** assure you. **253 tenable** held. **261 doubt** suspect. **[1.3] Location: Polonius' chambers.** **3 convoy is assistant** means of conveyance are available. **6 toy in blood** passing amorous fancy. **7 primy** in its prime, springtime. **8 Forward** precocious. **9 suppliance** supply, filler.

For nature crescent° does not grow alone
In thews° and bulk, but as this temple° waxes
The inward service of the mind and soul
Grows wide withal.° Perhaps he loves you now,
And now no soil° nor cautel° doth besmirch
The virtue of his will,° but you must fear,
His greatness weighed,° his will is not his own.
For he himself is subject to his birth.
He may not, as unvalued persons do,
Carve° for himself, for on his choice depends
The safety and health of this whole state,
And therefore must his choice be circumscribed
Unto the voice and yielding° of that body
Whereof he is the head. Then if he says he loves you,
It fits your wisdom so far to believe it
As he in his particular act and place°
May give his saying deed, which is no further
Than the main voice° of Denmark goes withal.°
Then weigh what loss your honor may sustain
If with too credent° ear you list° his songs,
Or lose your heart, or your chaste treasure open
To his unmastered importunity.
Fear it, Ophelia, fear it, my dear sister,
And keep you in the rear of your affection,°
Out of the shot and danger of desire.
The chariest° maid is prodigal enough
If she unmask her beauty° to the moon.°
Virtue itself scapes not calumnious strokes.
The canker galls° the infants of the spring
Too oft before their buttons° be disclosed,°
And in the morn and liquid dew° of youth
Contagious blastments° are most imminent.
Be wary then; best safety lies in fear.
Youth to itself rebels,° though none else near.

OPHELIA: I shall the effect of this good lesson keep
As watchman to my heart. But, good my brother,
Do not, as some ungracious° pastors do,
Show me the steep and thorny way to heaven,
Whiles like a puffed° and reckless libertine

11 crescent growing, waxing. **12 thews** bodily strength; **temple** i.e., body. **14 Grows wide withal** grows along with it. **15 soil** blemish; **cautel** deceit. **16 will** desire. **17 His greatness weighed** if you take into account his high position. **20 Carve** i.e., choose. **23 voice and yielding** assent, approval. **26 in . . . place** in his particular restricted circumstances. **28 main voice** general assent; **withal** along with. **30 credent** credulous; **list** listen to. **34 keep . . . affection** don't advance as far as your affection might lead you (A military metaphor.)
36 chariest most scrupulously modest. **37 If she unmask her beauty** if she does no more than show her beauty; **moon** (symbol of chastity.) **39 canker galls** canker-worm destroys.
40 buttons buds; **disclosed** opened. **41 liquid dew** i.e., time when dew is fresh and bright.
42 blastments blights. **44 Youth . . . rebels** youth is inherently rebellious. **47 ungracious** ungodly. **49 puffed** bloated, or swollen with pride.

Himself the primrose path of dalliance treads,
And recks° not his own rede.°

Enter POLONIUS.

LAERTES: O, fear me not.°
I stay too long. But here my father comes.
A double° blessing is a double grace;
Occasion smiles upon a second leave.°

POLONIUS: Yet here, Laertes? Aboard, aboard, for shame!
The wind sits in the shoulder of your sail,
And you are stayed for. There—my blessing with thee!
And these few precepts in thy memory
Look° thou character.° Give thy thoughts no tongue,
Nor any unproportioned° thought his° act.
Be thou familiar,° but by no means vulgar.°
Those friends thou hast, and their adoption tried,°
Grapple them unto thy soul with hoops of steel,
But do not dull thy palm° with entertainment
Of each new-hatched, unfledged courage.° Beware
Of entrance to a quarrel, but being in,
Bear 't that° th' opposèd may beware of thee.
Give every man thy ear, but few thy voice;
Take each man's censure,° but reserve thy judgment.
Costly thy habit° as thy purse can buy,
But not expressed in fancy;° rich, not gaudy,
For the apparel oft proclaims the man,
And they in France of the best rank and station
Are of a most select and generous chief in that.°
Neither a borrower nor a lender be,
For loan oft loses both itself and friend,
And borrowing dulleth edge of husbandry.°
This above all: to thine own self be true,
And it must follow, as the night the day,
Thou canst not then be false to any man.
Farewell. My blessing season° this in thee!

LAERTES: Most humbly do I take my leave, my lord.

POLONIUS: The time invests° you. Go, your servants tend.°

LAERTES: Farewell, Ophelia, and remember well
What I have said to you.

51 recks heeds; **rede** counsel; **fear me not** don't worry on my account. **53 double** (Laertes has already bid his father good-bye.) **54 Occasion . . . leave** happy is the circumstance that provides a second leave-taking. (The goddess Occasion, or Opportunity, smiles.) **59 Look** be sure that; **character** inscribe. **60 unproportioned** badly calculated, intemperate; **his** its. **61 familiar** sociable; **vulgar** common. **62 and their adoption tried** and also their suitability for adoption as friends having been tested. **64 dull thy palm** i.e., shake hands so often as to make the gesture meaningless. **65 courage** young man of spirit. **67 Bear 't that** manage it so that. **69 censure** opinion, judgment. **70 habit** clothing. **71 fancy** excessive ornament, decadent fashion. **74 Are . . . that** are of a most refined and well-bred preeminence in choosing what to wear. **77 husbandry** thrift. **81 season** mature. **83 invests** besieges, presses upon; **tend** attend, wait.

OPHELIA: 'Tis in my memory locked,
And you yourself shall keep the key of it.
LAERTES: Farewell. *Exit* LAERTES.
POLONIUS: What is 't, Ophelia, he hath said to you?
OPHELIA: So please you, something touching the Lord Hamlet.
POLONIUS: Marry,° well bethought.
'Tis told me he hath very oft of late
Given private time to you, and you yourself
Have of your audience been most free and bounteous.
If it be so—as so 'tis put on° me,
And that in way of caution—I must tell you
You do not understand yourself so clearly
As it behooves° my daughter and your honor.
What is between you? Give me up the truth.
OPHELIA: He hath, my lord, of late made many tenders°
Of his affection to me.
POLONIUS: Affection? Pooh! You speak like a green girl,
Unsifted° in such perilous circumstance.
Do you believe his tenders, as you call them?
OPHELIA: I do not know, my lord, what I should think.
POLONIUS: Marry, I will teach you. Think yourself a baby
That you have ta'en these tenders for true pay
Which are not sterling.° Tender° yourself more dearly,
Or—not to crack the wind° of the poor phrase,
Running it thus—you'll tender me a fool.°
OPHELIA: My lord, he hath importuned me with love
In honorable fashion.
POLONIUS: Ay, fashion° you may call it. Go to,° go to.
OPHELIA: And hath given countenance° to his speech, my lord,
With almost all the holy vows of heaven.
POLONIUS: Ay, springes° to catch woodcocks.° I do know,
When the blood burns, how prodigal° the soul
Lends the tongue vows. These blazes, daughter,
Giving more light than heat, extinct in both
Even in their promise as it° is a-making,
You must not take for fire. From this time
Be something° scanter of your maiden presence.
Set your entreatments° at a higher rate
Than a command to parle.° For Lord Hamlet,

91 Marry i.e., by the Virgin Mary. (A mild oath.) **95 put on** impressed on, told to. **98 behooves** befits. **100 tenders** offers. **103 Unsifted** i.e., untried. **108 sterling** legal currency; **Tender** hold, look after, offer. **109 crack the wind** i.e., run it until it is broken-winded. **110 tender me a fool** (1) show yourself to me as a fool, (2) show me up as a fool, (3) present me with a grandchild. (*Fool* was a term of endearment for a child.) **113 fashion** mere form, pretense; **Go to** (an expression of impatience.) **114 countenance** credit, confirmation. **116 springes** snares; **woodcocks** birds easily caught; here used to connote gullibility. **117 prodigal** prodigally. **120 it** i.e., the promise. **122 something** somewhat. **123 entreatments** negotiations for surrender. (A military term.) **124 parle** discuss terms with the enemy. (Polonius urges his daughter, in the metaphor of military language, not to meet with Hamlet and consider giving in to him merely because he requests an interview.)

Believe so much in him° that he is young,
And with a larger tether may he walk
Than may be given you. In few,° Ophelia,
Do not believe his vows, for they are brokers,°
Not of that dye° which their investments° show,
But mere implorators° of unholy suits,
Breathing° like sanctified and pious bawds,
The better to beguile. This is for all:°
I would not, in plain terms, from this time forth
Have you so slander° any moment° leisure
As to give words or talk with the Lord Hamlet.
Look to 't, I charge you. Come your ways.°

OPHELIA: I shall obey, my lord. *Exeunt.*

[1.4]

Enter HAMLET, HORATIO, *and* MARCELLUS.

HAMLET: The air bites shrewdly,° it is very cold.
HORATIO: It is a nipping and an eager° air.
HAMLET: What hour now?
HORATIO: I think it lacks of° twelve.
MARCELLUS: No, it is struck.
HORATIO: Indeed? I heard it not.
It then draws near the season°
Wherein the spirit held his wont° to walk.
A flourish of trumpets, and two pieces° go off [within].
What does this mean, my lord?
HAMLET: The King doth wake° tonight and takes his rouse,°
Keeps wassail,° and the swaggering upspring° reels,°
And as he drains his drafts of Rhenish° down,
The kettledrum and trumpet thus bray out
The triumph of his pledge.°
HORATIO: It is a custom?
HAMLET: Ay, marry, is't,
But to my mind, though I am native here
And to the manner° born, it is a custom
More honored in the breach than the observance.°
This heavy-headed revel east and west°
Makes us traduced and taxed of° other nations.
They clepe° us drunkards, and with swinish phrase°

125 so . . . him this much concerning him. **127 In few** briefly. **128 brokers** go-betweens, procurers. **129 dye** color or sort; **investments** clothes. (The vows are not what they seem.) **130 mere implorators** out-and-out solicitors. **131 Breathing** speaking. **132 for all** once for all, in sum. **134 slander** abuse, misuse; **moment** moment's. **136 Come your ways** come along. **[1.4] Location: The guard platform.** **1 shrewdly** keenly, sharply. **2 eager** biting. **3 lacks of** is just short of. **5 season** time. **6 held his wont** was accustomed; **s.d. pieces** i.e., of ordnance, cannon. **8 wake** stay awake and hold revel; **takes his rouse** carouses. **9 wassail** carousal; **upspring** wild German dance; **reels** dances. **10 Rhenish** Rhine wine. **12 The triumph . . . pledge** i.e., his feat in draining the wine in a single draft. **15 manner** custom (of drinking). **16 More . . . observance** better neglected than followed. **17 east and west** i.e., everywhere. **18 taxed of** censured by. **19 clepe** call; **with swinish phrase** i.e., by calling us swine.

Soil our addition;° and indeed it takes
From our achievements, though performed at height,°
The pith and marrow of our attribute.°
So, oft it chances in particular men,
That for° some vicious mole of nature° in them,
As in their birth—wherein they are not guilty,
Since nature cannot choose his° origin—
By their o'ergrowth of some complexion,°
Oft breaking down the pales° and forts of reason,
Or by some habit that too much o'erleavens°
The form of plausive° manners, that these men,
Carrying, I say, the stamp of one defect,
Being nature's livery° or fortune's star,°
His virtues else,° be they as pure as grace,
As infinite as man may undergo,°
Shall in the general censure° take corruption
From that particular fault. The dram of evil
Doth all the noble substance often dout
To his own scandal.°

Enter GHOST.

HORATIO: Look, my lord, it comes!
HAMLET: Angels and ministers of grace° defend us!
Be thou° a spirit of health° or goblin damned,
Bring° with thee airs from heaven or blasts from hell,
Be thy intents° wicked or charitable,
Thou com'st in such a questionable° shape
That I will speak to thee. I'll call thee Hamlet,
King, father, royal Dane. O, answer me!
Let me not burst in ignorance, but tell
Why thy canonized° bones, hearsèd° in death,
Have burst their cerements;° why the sepulcher
Wherein we saw thee quietly inurned°
Hath oped his ponderous and marble jaws
To cast thee up again. What may this mean,
That thou, dead corpse, again in complete steel,°

20 addition reputation. **21 at height** outstandingly. **22 The pith . . . attribute** the essence of the reputation that others attribute to us. **24 for** on account of; **mole of nature** natural blemish in one's constitution. **26 his** its. **27 their o'ergrowth . . . complexion** the excessive growth in individuals of some natural trait. **28 pales** palings, fences (as of a fortification). **29 o'erleavens** induces a change throughout (as yeast works in dough). **30 plausive** pleasing. **32 nature's livery** sign of one's servitude to nature; **fortune's star** the destiny that chance brings. **33 His virtues else** i.e., the other qualities of *these men* (line 30). **34 may undergo** can sustain. **35 general censure** general opinion that people have of him. **36–38 The dram . . . scandal** i.e., the small drop of evil blots out or works against the noble substance of the whole and brings it into disrepute. To *dout* is to blot out. (A famous crux.) **39 ministers of grace** messengers of God. **40 Be thou** whether you are; **spirit of health** good angel. **41 Bring** whether you bring. **42 Be thy intents** whether your intentions are. **43 questionable** inviting question. **47 canonized** buried according to the canons of the church; **hearsèd** coffined. **48 cerements** grave clothes. **49 inurned** entombed. **52 complete steel** full armor.

Revisits thus the glimpses of the moon,°
Making night hideous, and we fools of nature°
So horridly to shake our disposition°
With thoughts beyond the reaches of our souls?
Say, why is this? Wherefore? What should we do?

[*The* GHOST] *beckons* [HAMLET].

HORATIO: It beckons you to go away with it,
As if it some impartment° did desire
To you alone.

MARCELLUS: Look with what courteous action
It wafts you to a more removèd ground.
But do not go with it.

HORATIO: No, by no means.

HAMLET: It will not speak. Then I will follow it.

HORATIO: Do not, my lord!

HAMLET: Why, what should be the fear?
I do not set my life at a pin's fee,°
And for my soul, what can it do to that,
Being a thing immortal as itself?
It waves me forth again. I'll follow it.

HORATIO: What if it tempt you toward the flood,° my lord,
Or to the dreadful summit of the cliff
That beetles o'er° his° base into the sea,
And there assume some other horrible form
Which might deprive your sovereignty of reason°
And draw you into madness? Think of it.
The very place puts toys of desperation,°
Without more motive, into every brain
That looks so many fathoms to the sea
And hears it roar beneath.

HAMLET: It wafts me still.—Go on, I'll follow thee.

MARCELLUS: You shall not go, my lord. [*They try to stop him*.]

HAMLET: Hold off your hands!

HORATIO: Be ruled. You shall not go.

HAMLET: My fate cries out,°
And makes each petty° artery° in this body
As hardy as the Nemean lion's° nerve.°
Still am I called. Unhand me, gentlemen.
By heaven, I'll make a ghost of him that lets° me!
I say, away!—Go on, I'll follow thee. *Exeunt* GHOST *and* HAMLET.

HORATIO: He waxes desperate with imagination.

53 glimpses of the moon pale and uncertain moonlight. **54 fools of nature** mere men, limited to natural knowledge and subject to nature. **55 So . . . disposition** to distress our mental composure so violently. **59 impartment** communication. **65 fee** value. **69 flood** sea. **71 beetles o'er** overhangs threateningly (like bushy eyebrows); **his** its. **73 deprive . . . reason** take away the rule of reason over your mind. **75 toys of desperation** fancies of desperate acts, i.e., suicide. **81 My fate cries out** my destiny summons me. **82 petty** weak; **artery** (through which the vital spirits were thought to have been conveyed). **83 Nemean lion** one of the monsters slain by Hercules in his twelve labors; **nerve** sinew. **85 lets** hinders.

MARCELLUS: Let's follow. 'Tis not fit thus to obey him.
HORATIO: Have after.° To what issue° will this come?
MARCELLUS: Something is rotten in the state of Denmark.
HORATIO: Heaven will direct it.°
MARCELLUS: Nay, let's follow him. *Exeunt.*

[1.5]

Enter GHOST *and* HAMLET.

HAMLET: Whither wilt thou lead me? Speak. I'll go no further.
GHOST: Mark me.
HAMLET: I will.
GHOST: My hour is almost come,
When I to sulfurous and tormenting flames
Must render up myself.
HAMLET: Alas, poor ghost!
GHOST: Pity me not, but lend thy serious hearing
To what I shall unfold.
HAMLET: Speak. I am bound° to hear.
GHOST: So art thou to revenge, when thou shalt hear.
HAMLET: What?
GHOST: I am thy father's spirit,
Doomed for a certain term to walk the night,
And for the day confined to fast° in fires,
Till the foul crimes° done in my days of nature°
Are burnt and purged away. But that° I am forbid
To tell the secrets of my prison house,
I could a tale unfold whose lightest word
Would harrow up° thy soul, freeze thy young blood,
Make thy two eyes like stars start from their spheres,°
Thy knotted and combinèd locks° to part,
And each particular hair to stand on end
Like quills upon the fretful porcupine.
But this eternal blazon° must not be
To ears of flesh and blood. List, list, O, list!
If thou didst ever thy dear father love—
HAMLET: O God!
GHOST: Revenge his foul and most unnatural murder.
HAMLET: Murder?
GHOST: Murder most foul, as in the best° it is,
But this most foul, strange, and unnatural.
HAMLET: Haste me to know't, that I, with wings as swift
As meditation or the thoughts of love,
May sweep to my revenge.

89 Have after let's go after him; **issue** outcome. **91 it** i.e., the outcome. **[1.5] Location: The battlements of the castle.** **7 bound** (1) ready, (2) obligated by duty and fate. (the Ghost, in line 8, answers in the second sense.) **12 fast** do penance by fasting. **13 crimes** Sins; **of nature** as a mortal. **14 But that** were it not that. **17 harrow up** lacerate, tear. **18 spheres** i.e., eye-sockets, here compared to the orbits or transparent revolving spheres in which, according to Ptolemaic astronomy, the heavenly bodies were fixed. **19 knotted . . . locks** hair neatly arranged and confined. **22 eternal blazon** revelation of the secrets of eternity. **28 in the best** even at best.

GHOST: I find thee apt;
And duller shouldst thou be° than the fat° weed
That roots itself in ease on Lethe° wharf,
Wouldst thou not stir in this. Now, Hamlet, hear.
'Tis given out that, sleeping in my orchard,°
A serpent stung me. So the whole ear of Denmark
Is by a forgèd process° of my death
Rankly abused.° But know, thou noble youth,
The serpent that did sting thy father's life
Now wears his crown.

HAMLET: O, my prophetic soul! My uncle!

GHOST: Ay, that incestuous, that adulterate° beast,
With witchcraft of his wit, with traitorous gifts°—
O wicked wit and gifts, that have the power
So to seduce!—won to his shameful lust
The will of my most seeming-virtuous queen.
O Hamlet, what a falling off was there!
From me, whose love was of that dignity
That it went hand in hand even with the vow°
I made to her in marriage, and to decline
Upon a wretch whose natural gifts were poor
To° those of mine!
But virtue, as it° never will be moved,
Though lewdness court it in a shape of heaven,°
So lust, though to a radiant angel linked,
Will sate itself in a celestial bed°
And prey on garbage.
But soft, methinks I scent the morning air.
Brief let me be. Sleeping within my orchard,
My custom always of the afternoon,
Upon my secure° hour thy uncle stole,
With juice of cursèd hebona° in a vial,
And in the porches of my ears° did pour
The leprous distillment,° whose effect
Holds such an enmity with blood of man
That swift as quicksilver it courses through
The natural gates and alleys of the body,
And with a sudden vigor it doth posset°
And curd, like eager° droppings into milk,
The thin and wholesome blood. So did it mine,

33 shouldst thou be you would have to be; **fat** torpid, lethargic. **348 Lethe** the river of forgetfulness in Hades. **36 orchard** garden. **38 forgèd process** falsified account. **39 abused** deceived. **43 adulterate** adulterous. **44 gifts** (1) talents, (2) presents. **50 even with the vow** with the very vow. **53 To** compared to. **54 virtue, as it** as virtue. **55 shape of heaven** heavenly form. **57 sate . . . bed** cease to find sexual pleasure in a virtuously lawful marriage. **62 secure** confident, unsuspicious. **63 hebona** a poison. (The word seems to be a form of *ebony,* though it is thought perhaps to be related to *henbane,* a poison, or to *ebenus,* "yew.") **64 porches of my ears** ears as a porch or entrance of the body. **65 leprous distillment** distillation causing leprosylike disfigurement. **69 posset** coagulate, curdle. **70 eager** sour, acid.

And a most instant tetter° barked° about,
Most lazar-like,° with vile and loathsome crust,
All my smooth body.
Thus was I, sleeping, by a brother's hand
Of life, of crown, of queen at once dispatched,°
Cut off even in the blossoms of my sin,
Unhouseled,° disappointed,° unaneled,°
No reckoning° made, but sent to my account
With all my imperfections on my head.
O, horrible! O, horrible, most horrible!
If thou hast nature° in thee, bear it not.
Let not the royal bed of Denmark be
A couch for luxury° and damnèd incest.
But, howsoever thou pursues this act,
Taint not thy mind nor let thy soul contrive
Against thy mother aught. Leave her to heaven
And to those thorns that in her bosom lodge,
To prick and sting her. Fare thee well at once.
The glowworm shows the matin° to be near,
And 'gins to pale his° uneffectual fire.
Adieu, adieu, adieu! Remember me. [*Exit.*]

HAMLET: O all you host of heaven! O earth! What else?
And shall I couple° hell? O, fie! Hold,° hold, my heart,
And you, my sinews, grow not instant° old,
But bear me stiffly up. Remember thee?
Ay, thou poor ghost, whiles memory holds a seat
In this distracted globe.° Remember thee?
Yea, from the table° of my memory
I'll wipe away all trivial fond° records,
All saws° of books, all forms,° all pressures° past
That youth and observation copied there,
And thy commandment all alone shall live
Within the book and volume of my brain,
Unmixed with baser matter. Yes, by heaven!
O most pernicious woman!
O villain, villain, smiling, damnèd villain!
My tables°—meet it is° I set it down
That one may smile, and smile, and be a villain.
At least I am sure it may be so in Denmark. [*Writing.*]
So uncle, there you are.° Now to my word:
It is "Adieu, adieu! Remember me."
I have sworn 't.

72 tetter eruption of scabs; **barked** recovered with a rough covering, like bark on a tree. **73 lazar-like** leperlike. **76 dispatched** suddenly deprived. **78 Unhouseled** without having received the Sacrament; **disappointed** unready (spiritually) for the last journey; **unaneled** without having received extreme unction. **79 reckoning** settling of accounts. **82 nature** i.e., the promptings of a son. **84 luxury** lechery. **90 matin** morning. **91 his** its. **94 couple** add; **Hold** hold together. **95 instant** instantly. **98 globe** (1) head, (2) world. **99 table** tablet, slate. **100 fond** foolish. **101 saws** wise sayings; **forms** shapes or images copied onto the slate; general ideas; **pressures** impressions stamped. **108 tables** writing tablets; **meet it is** it is fitting. **111 there you are** i.e., there, I've written that down against you.

Enter HORATIO *and* MARCELLUS.

HORATIO: My lord, my lord!
MARCELLUS: Lord Hamlet!
HORATIO: Heavens secure him!°
HAMLET: So be it.
MARCELLUS: Hilo, ho, ho, my lord!
HAMLET: Hillo, ho, ho, boy! Come, bird, come.°
MARCELLUS: How is 't, my noble lord?
HORATIO: What news, my lord?
HAMLET: O, wonderful!
HORATIO: Good my lord, tell it.
HAMLET: No, you will reveal it.
HORATIO: Not I, my lord, by heaven.
MARCELLUS: Nor I, my lord.
HAMLET: How say you, then, would heart of man once° think it?
But you'll be secret?
HORATIO, MARCELLUS: Ay, by heaven, my lord.
HAMLET: There's never a villain dwelling in all Denmark
But he's an arrant° knave.
HORATIO: There needs no ghost, my lord, come from the grave
To tell us this.
HAMLET: Why, right, you are in the right.
And so, without more circumstance° at all,
I hold it fit that we shake hands and part,
You as your business and desire shall point you—
For every man hath business and desire,
Such as it is—and for my own poor part,
Look you, I'll go pray.
HORATIO: These are but wild and whirling words, my lord.
HAMLET: I am sorry they offend you, heartily;
Yes, faith, heartily.
HORATIO: There's no offense, my lord.
HAMLET: Yes, by Saint Patrick,° but there is, Horatio,
And much offense° too. Touching this vision here,
It is an honest ghost,° that let me tell you.
For your desire to know what is between us,
O'ermaster 't as you may. And now, good friends,
As you are friends, scholars, and soldiers,
Give me one poor request.
HORATIO: What is 't, my lord? We will.
HAMLET: Never make known what you have seen tonight.
HORATIO, MARCELLUS: My lord, we will not.
HAMLET: Nay, but swear 't.

116 secure him keep him safe. **119 Hillo . . . come** (A falconer's call to a hawk in air. Hamlet mocks the halloing as though it were a part of hawking.) **127 once** ever. **130 arrant** thoroughgoing. **133 circumstance** ceremony, elaboration. **142 Saint Patrick** (the keeper of Purgatory and patron saint of all blunders and confusion.) **143 offense** (Hamlet deliberately changes Horatio's "no offense against all decency.") **144 an honest ghost** i.e., a real ghost and not an evil spirit.

HORATIO: In faith, my lord, not I.°
MARCELLUS: Nor I, my lord, in faith.
HAMLET: Upon my sword.° [*He holds out his sword.*]
MARCELLUS: We have sworn, my lord, already.°
HAMLET: Indeed, upon my sword, indeed.
GHOST [*cries under the stage*]: Swear.
HAMLET: Ha, ha, boy, sayst thou so? Art thou there, truepenny?°
Come on, you hear this fellow in the cellarage.
Consent to swear.
HORATIO: Propose the oath, my lord.
HAMLET: Never to speak of this that you have seen,
Swear by my sword.
GHOST [*beneath*]: Swear. [*They swear.*°]
HAMLET: *Hic et ubique?*° Then we'll shift our ground.
[*He moves to another spot.*]
Come hither, gentlemen,
And lay your hands again upon my sword.
Swear by my sword
Never to speak of this that you have heard.
GHOST [*beneath*]: Swear by his sword. [*They swear.*]
HAMLET: Well said, old mole. Canst work i' th' earth so fast?
A worthy pioneer!°—Once more removed, good friends.
[*He moves again.*]
HORATIO: O day and night, but this is wondrous strange!
HAMLET: And therefore as a stranger° give it welcome.
There are more things in heaven and earth, Horatio,
Than are dreamt of in your philosophy.°
But come;
Here, as before, never, so help you mercy,°
How strange or odd soe'er I bear myself—
As I perchance hereafter shall think meet
To put an antic° disposition on—
That you, at such times seeing me, never shall,
With arms encumbered° thus, or this headshake,
Or by pronouncing of some doubtful phrase
As "Well, we know," or "We could, an if° we would,"
Or "If we list° to speak," or "There be, an if they might,"°
Or such ambiguous giving out,° to note°

153 In faith . . . I i.e., I swear not to tell what I have seen. (Horatio is not refusing to swear.) **155 sword** i.e., the hilt in the form of a cross. **156 We . . . already** i.e., we swore in ***faith***. **159 truepenny** honest old fellow. **164 s.d. They swear** (seemingly they swear here, and at lines 170 and 190, as they lay their hands on Hamlet's sword. Triple oaths would have particular force; these three oaths deal with what they have seen, what they have heard, and what they promise about Hamlet's *antic disposition*.) **165 *Hic et ubique*** here and everywhere (Latin). **172 pioneer** foot soldier assigned to dig tunnels and excavations. **174 as a stranger** i.e., needing your hospitality. **176 your philosophy** this subject called "natural philosophy" or "science" that people talk about. **178 so help you mercy** as you hope for God's mercy when you are judged. **181 antic** fantastic. **183 encumbered** folded. **185 an if** if. **186 list** wished; **There . . . might** i.e., there are people here (we, in fact) who could tell news if we were at liberty to do so. **187 giving out** intimation; **note** draw attention to the fact.

That you know aught° of me—this do swear,
So grace and mercy at your most need help you.
GHOST [*beneath*]: Swear. [*They swear.*]
HAMLET: Rest, rest, perturbèd spirit! So, gentlemen,
With all my love I do commend me to you;°
And what so poor a man as Hamlet is
May do t' express his love and friending° to you,
God willing, shall not lack.° Let us go in together,
And still° your fingers on your lips, I pray.
The time° is out of joint. O cursèd spite°
That ever I was born to set it right! [*They wait for him to leave first.*]
Nay, come, let's go together.° *Exeunt.*

[2.1]

Enter old POLONIUS *with his man* [REYNALDO].

POLONIUS: Give him this money and these notes, Reynaldo.
[*He gives money and papers.*]
REYNALDO: I will, my lord.
POLONIUS: You shall do marvelous° wisely, good Reynaldo,
Before you visit him, to make inquire°
Of his behavior.
REYNALDO: My lord, I did intend it.
POLONIUS: Marry, well said, very well said. Look you, sir,
Inquire me first what Danskers° are in Paris,
And how, and who, what means,° and where they keep,°
What company, at what expense; and finding
By this encompassment° and drift° of question
That they do know my son, come you more nearer
Than your particular demands will touch it.°
Take you,° as 'twere, some distant knowledge of him,
As thus, "I know his father and his friends,
And in part him." Do you mark this, Reynaldo?
REYNALDO: Ay, very well, my lord.
POLONIUS: "And in part him, but," you may say, "not well.
But if 't be he I mean, he's very wild,
Addicted so and so," and there put on° him
What forgeries° you please—marry, none so rank°
As may dishonor him, take heed of that,
But, sir, such wanton,° wild, and usual slips
As are companions noted and most known
To youth and liberty.

188 aught i.e., something secret. **192 do . . . you** entrust myself to you. **194 friending** friendliness. **195 lack** be lacking. **196 still** always. **197 The time** the state of affairs; **spite** i.e., the spite of Fortune. **199 let's go together** (probably they wait for him to leave first, but he refuses this ceremoniousness.) **[2.1] Location: Polonius' chambers. 3 marvelous** marvelously. **4 inquire** inquiry. **7 Danskers** Danes. **8 what means** what wealth (they have); **keep** dwell. **10 encompassment** roundabout talking; **drift** gradual approach or course. **11–12 come . . . it** you will find out more this way than by asking pointed questions (*particular demands*). **13 Take you** assume, pretend. **19 put on** impute to. **20 forgeries** invented tales; **rank** gross. **22 wanton** sportive, unrestrained.

REYNALDO: As gaming, my lord.
POLONIUS: Ay, or drinking, fencing, swearing,
Quarreling, drabbing°—you may go so far.
REYNALDO: My lord, that would dishonor him.
POLONIUS: Faith, no, as you may season° it in the charge.
You must not put another scandal on him
That he is open to incontinency;°
That's not my meaning. But breathe his faults so quaintly°
That they may seem the taints of liberty,°
The flash and outbreak of a fiery mind,
A savageness in unreclaimèd blood,
Of general assault.°
REYNALDO: But, my good lord—
POLONIUS: Wherefore should you do this?
REYNALDO: Ay, my lord, I would know that.
POLONIUS: Marry, sir, here's my drift,
And I believe it is a fetch of warrant.°
You laying these slight sullies on my son,
As 'twere a thing a little soiled wi' the working,°
Mark you,
Your party in converse,° him you would sound,°
Having ever° seen in the prenominate crimes°
The youth you breathe° of guilty, be assured
He closes with you in this consequence:°
"Good sir," or so, or "friend," or "gentleman,"
According to the phrase or the addition°
Of man and country.
REYNALDO: Very good, my lord.
POLONIUS: And then, sir, does 'a this—'a does—what was I about to say? By the Mass, I was about to say something. Where did I leave?
REYNALDO: At "closes in the consequence."
POLONIUS: At "closes in the consequence," ay, marry.
He closes thus: "I know the gentleman,
I saw him yesterday," or "th' other day,"
Or then, or then, with such or such, "and as you say,
There was 'a gaming," "there o'ertook in 's rouse,"°
"There falling out° at tennis," or perchance
"I saw him enter such a house of sale,"
Videlicet° a brothel, or so forth. See you now,
Your bait of falsehood takes this carp° of truth;
And thus do we of wisdom and of reach,°

27 drabbing whoring. **29 season** temper, soften. **31 incontinency** habitual sexual excess. **32 quaintly** artfully, subtly. **33 taints of liberty** faults resulting from free living. **35–36 A savageness . . . assault** a wildness in untamed youth that assails all indiscriminately. **41 fetch of warrant** legitimate trick. **43 soiled wi' the working** soiled by handling while it is being made, i.e., by involvement in the ways of the world. **45 converse** conversation; **sound** i.e., sound out. **46 Having ever** if he has ever; **prenominate crimes** before-mentioned offenses. **47 breathe** speak. **48 closes . . . consequence** takes you into his confidence in some fashion, as follows. **50 addition** title. **59 o'ertook in 's rouse** overcome by drink. **60 falling out** quarreling. **62 Videlicet** namely. **63 carp** a fish. **64 reach** capacity, ability.

With windlasses° and with assays of bias,°
By indirections find directions° out.
So by my former lecture and advice
Shall you my son. You have° me, have you not?

REYNALDO: My lord, I have.

POLONIUS: God b'wi'° ye; fare ye well.

REYNALDO: Good my lord.

POLONIUS: Observe his inclination in yourself.°

REYNALDO: I shall, my lord.

POLONIUS: And let him ply his music.

REYNALDO: Well, my lord.

POLONIUS: Farewell. *Exit* REYNALDO.

Enter OPHELIA.

How now, Ophelia, what's the matter?

OPHELIA: O my lord, my lord, I have been so affrighted!

POLONIUS: With what, i' the name of God?

OPHELIA: My lord, as I was sewing in my closet,°
Lord Hamlet, with his doublet° all unbraced,°
No hat upon his head, his stockings fouled,
Ungartered, and down-gyvèd° to his ankle,
Pale as his shirt, his knees knocking each other,
And with a look so piteous in purport°
As if he had been loosèd out of hell
To speak of horrors—he comes before me.

POLONIUS: Mad for thy love?

OPHELIA: My lord, I do not know,
But truly I do fear it.

POLONIUS: What said he?

OPHELIA: He took me by the wrist and held me hard.
Then goes he to the length of all his arm,
And, with his other hand thus o'er his brow
He falls to such perusal of my face
As° 'a would draw it. Long stayed he so.
At last, a little shaking of mine arm
And thrice his head thus waving up and down,
He raised a sigh so piteous and profound
As it did seem to shatter all his bulk°
And end his being. That done, he lets me go,
And with his head over his shoulder turned
He seemed to find his way without his eyes,
For out o' doors he went without their helps,
And to the last bended their light on me.

65 windlasses i.e., circuitous paths. (Literally, circuits made to head off the game in hunting); **assays of bias** attempts through indirection (like the curving path of the bowling ball, which is biased or weighted to one side). **66 directions** i.e., the way things really are. **68 have** understand. **69 b' wi'** be with. **71 in yourself** in your own person (as well as by asking questions). **78 closet** private chamber. **79 doublet** close-fitting jacket; **unbraced** unfastened. **81 down-gyvèd** fallen to the ankles (like gyves or fetters). **83 in purport** in what it expressed. **92 As** as if (also in line 97). **96 bulk** body.

POLONIUS: Come, go with me. I will go seek the King.
This is the very ecstasy° of love,
Whose violent property° fordoes° itself
And leads the will to desperate undertakings
As oft as any passion under heaven
That does afflict our natures. I am sorry.
What, have you given him any hard words of late?
OPHELIA: No, my good lord, but as you did command
I did repel his letters and denied
His access to me.
POLONIUS: That hath made him mad.
I am sorry that with better heed and judgment
I had not quoted° him. I feared he did but trifle
And meant to wrack° thee. But beshrew my jealousy!°
By heaven, it is as proper to our age°
To cast beyond° ourselves in our opinions
As it is common for the younger sort
To lack discretion. Come, go we to the King.
This must be known,° which, being kept close,° might move
More grief to hide than hate to utter love.°
Come. *Exeunt.*

[2.2]

Flourish. Enter KING *and* QUEEN, ROSENCRANTZ, *and* GUILDENSTERN *[with others].*

KING: Welcome, dear Rosencrantz and Guildenstern.
Moreover that° we much did long to see you,
The need we have to use you did provoke
Our hasty sending. Something have you heard
Of Hamlet's transformation—so call it,
Sith nor° th' exterior nor the inward man
Resembles that° it was. What it should be,
More than his father's death, that thus hath put him
So much from th' understanding of himself,
I cannot dream of. I entreat you both
That, being of so young days° brought up with him,
And sith so neighbored to° his youth and havior,°
That you vouchsafe your rest° here in our court
Some little time, so by your companies
To draw him on to pleasures, and to gather

103 ecstasy madness. **104 property** nature; **fordoes** destroys. **113 quoted** observed. **114 wrack** ruin, seduce; **beshrew my jealousy** a plague upon my suspicious nature. **115 proper . . . age** characteristic of us (old) men. **116 cast beyond** overshoot, miscalculate. (A metaphor from hunting.) **119 known** made known (to the King); **close** secret. **119–120 might . . . love** i.e., might cause more grief (because of what Hamlet might do) by hiding the knowledge of Hamlet's strange behavior toward Ophelia than unpleasantness by telling it. **[2.2] Location: The castle.** **2 Moreover that** besides the fact that. **6 Sith nor** since neither. **7 that** what. **11 of . . . days** From such early youth. **12 And sith so neighbored to** and since you are (or, and since that time you are) intimately acquainted with; **havior** demeanor. **13 vouchsafe your rest** please to stay.

So much as from occasion° you may glean,
Whether aught to us unknown afflicts him thus
That, opened,° lies within our remedy.

QUEEN: Good gentlemen, he hath much talked of you,
And sure I am two men there is not living
To whom he more adheres. If it will please you
To show us so much gentry° and good will
As to expend your time with us awhile
For the supply and profit of our hope,°
Your visitation shall receive such thanks
As fits a king's remembrance.°

ROSENCRANTZ: Both Your Majesties
Might, by the sovereign power you have of° us,
Put your dread° pleasures more into command
Than to entreaty.

GUILDENSTERN: But we both obey,
And here give up ourselves in the full bent°
To lay our service freely at your feet,
To be commanded.

KING: Thanks, Rosencrantz and gentle Guildenstern.

QUEEN: Thanks, Guildenstern and gentle Rosencrantz.
And I beseech you instantly to visit
My too much changèd son. Go, some of you,
And bring these gentlemen where Hamlet is.

GUILDENSTERN: Heavens make our presence and our practices°
Pleasant and helpful to him!

QUEEN: Ay, amen!

Exeunt ROSENCRANTZ *and* GUILDENSTERN [*with some attendants*].

Enter POLONIUS.

POLONIUS: Th' ambassadors from Norway, my good lord,
Are joyfully returned.

KING: Thou still° hast been the father of good news.

POLONIUS: Have I, my lord? I assure my good liege
I hold° my duty, as° I hold my soul,
Both to my God and to my gracious king;
And I do think, or else this brain of mine
Hunts not the trail of policy° so sure
As it hath used to do, that I have found
The very cause of Hamlet's lunacy.

KING: O, speak of that! That do I long to hear.

POLONIUS: Give first admittance to th' ambassadors.
My news shall be the fruit° to that great feast.

KING: Thyself do grace° to them and bring them in. [*Exit* POLONIUS.]

16 occasion opportunity. **18 opened** being revealed. **22 gentry** courtesy. **24 supply . . . hope** aid and furtherance of what we hope for. **26 As fits . . . remembrance** as would be a fitting gift of a king who rewards true service. **27 of** over. **28 dread** inspiring awe. **30 in . . . bent** to the utmost degree of our capacity. (An archery metaphor.) **38 practices** doings. **42 still** always. **44 hold** maintain; **as** firmly as. **47 policy** sagacity. **52 fruit** dessert. **53 grace** honor (punning on *grace* said before a *feast*, line 52.)

He tells me, my dear Gertrude, he hath found
The head and source of all your son's distemper.

QUEEN: I doubt° it is no other but the main,°
His father's death and our o'erhasty marriage.

Enter Ambassadors VOLTIMAND *and* CORNELIUS, *with* POLONIUS.

KING: Well, we shall sift him.°—Welcome, my good friends!
Say, Voltimand, what from our brother° Norway?

VOLTIMAND: Most fair return of greetings and desires.°
Upon our first,° he sent out to suppress
His nephew's levies, which to him appeared
To be a preparation 'gainst the Polack,
But, better looked into, he truly found
It was against Your Highness. Whereat grieved
That so his sickness, age, and impotence°
Was falsely borne in hand,° sends out arrests°
On Fortinbras, which he, in brief, obeys,
Receives rebuke from Norway, and in fine°
Makes vow before his uncle never more
To give th' assay° of arms against Your Majesty.
Whereon old Norway, overcome with joy,
Gives him three thousand crowns in annual fee
And his commission to employ those soldiers,
So levied as before, against the Polack,
With an entreaty, herein further shown, [*giving a paper*]
That it might please you to give quiet pass
Through your dominions for this enterprise
On such regards of safety and allowance°
As therein are set down.

KING: It likes° us well,
And at our more considered° time we'll read,
Answer, and think upon this business.
Meantime we thank you for your well-took labor.
Go to your rest; at night we'll feast together.
Most welcome home! *Exeunt Ambassadors.*

POLONIUS: This business is well ended.
My liege, and madam, to expostulate°
What majesty should be, what duty is,
Why day is day, night night, and time is time,
Were nothing but to waste night, day, and time.
Therefore, since brevity is the soul of wit,°
And tediousness the limbs and outward flourishes,
I will be brief. Your noble son is mad.

56 doubt fear, suspect; **main** chief point, principal concern. **58 sift him** question Polonius closely. **59 brother** fellow king. **60 desires** good wishes. **61 Upon our first** at our first words on the business. **66 impotence** helplessness. **67 borne in hand** deluded, taken advantage of; **arrests** orders to desist. **69 in fine** in conclusion. **71 give th' assay** make trial of strength, challenge. **78 On . . . allowance** i.e., with such considerations for the safety of Denmark and permission for Fortinbras. **80 likes** pleases. **81 considered** suitable for deliberation. **86 expostulate** expound, inquire into. **90 wit** sense or judgment.

Mad call I it, for, to define true madness,
What is't but to be nothing else but mad?
But let that go.

QUEEN: More matter, with less art.

POLONIUS: Madam, I swear I use no art at all.
That he's mad, 'tis true; 'tis true 'tis pity.
And pity 'tis 'tis true—a foolish figure,°
But farewell it, for I will use no art.
Mad let us grant him, then, and now remains
That we find out the cause of this effect,
Or rather say, the cause of this defect,
For this effect defective comes by cause.°
Thus it remains, and the remainder thus.
Perpend.°
I have a daughter—have while she is mine—
Who, in her duty and obedience, mark,
Hath given me this. Now gather and surmise.°
[*He reads the letter.*] "To the celestial and my soul's idol, the most beautified Ophelia"—
That's an ill phrase, a vile phrase; "beautified" is a vile phrase. But you shall hear. Thus: [*He reads.*]
"In her excellent white bosom,° these,° etc."

QUEEN: Came this from Hamlet to her?

POLONIUS: Good madam, stay° awhile, I will be faithful.° [*He reads.*]

"Doubt thou the stars are fire,
Doubt that the sun doth move,
Doubt° truth to be a liar,
But never doubt I love.

O dear Ophelia, I am ill at these numbers.° I have not art to reckon° my groans. But that I love thee best, O most best, believe it. Adieu.

Thine evermore, most dear lady, whilst this machine° is to him,
Hamlet."

This in obedience hath my daughter shown me,
And, more above,° hath his solicitings,
As they fell out° by° time, by means, and place,
All given to mine ear.°

KING: But how hath she
Received his love?

POLONIUS: What do you think of me?

KING: As of a man faithful and honorable.

POLONIUS: I would fain° prove so. But what might you think,

98 figure figure of speech. **103 For . . . cause** i.e., for this defective behavior, his madness, has a cause. **105 Perpend** consider. **108 gather and surmise** draw your own conclusions. **113 In . . . bosom** (The letter is poetically addressed to her heart.); **these** i.e., the letter. **115 stay** wait; **faithful** i.e., in reading the letter accurately. **118 Doubt** suspect. **120 ill . . . numbers** unskilled at writing verses. **121 reckon** (1) count, (2) number metrically, scan. **122 machine** i.e., body. **125 more above** moreover. **126 fell out** occurred; **by** according to. **127 given . . . ear** i.e., told me about. **130 fain** gladly.

When I had seen this hot love on the wing—
As I perceived it, I must tell you that,
Before my daughter told me—what might you,
Or my dear Majesty your queen here, think,
If I had played the desk or table book,°
Or given my heart a winking,° mute and dumb,
Or looked upon this love with idle sight?°
What might you think? No, I went round° to work,
And my young mistress thus I did bespeak:°
"Lord Hamlet is a prince out of thy star;°
This must not be." And then I prescripts° gave her,
That she should lock herself from his resort,°
Admit no messengers, receive no tokens.
Which done, she took the fruits of my advice;
And he, repellèd—a short tale to make—
Fell into a sadness, then into a fast,
Thence to a watch,° thence into a weakness,
Thence to a lightness,° and by this declension°
Into the madness wherein now he raves,
And all we° mourn for.

KING [*to the* QUEEN]: Do you think 'tis this?

QUEEN: It may be, very like.

POLONIUS: Hath there been such a time—I would fain know that—
That I have positively said "'Tis so,"
When it proved otherwise?

KING: Not that I know.

POLONIUS: Take this from this,° if this be otherwise.
If circumstances lead me, I will find
Where truth is hid, though it were hid indeed
Within the center.°

KING: How may we try° it further?

POLONIUS: You know sometimes he walks four hours together
Here in the lobby.

QUEEN: So he does indeed.

POLONIUS: At such a time I'll loose° my daughter to him.
Be you and I behind an arras° then.
Mark the encounter. If he love her not
And be not from his reason fall'n thereon,°

135 played . . . table book i.e., remained shut up, concealing the information. **136 given . . . winking** closed the eyes of my heart to this. **137 with idle sight** complacently or incomprehendingly. **138 round** roundly, plainly. **139 bespeak** address. **140 out of thy star** above your sphere, position. **141 prescripts** orders. **142 his resort** his visits. **147 watch** state of sleeplessness. **148 lightness** lightheadedness; **declension** decline, deterioration (with a pun on the grammatical sense). **150 all we** all of us, or, into everything that we. **155 Take this from this** (The actor probably gestures, indicating that he means his head from his shoulders, or his staff of office or chain from his hands or neck, or something similar.) **158 center** middle point of the earth (which is also the center of the Ptolemaic universe); **try** test, judge. **161 loose** (as one might release an animal that is being mated.) **162 arras** hanging, tapestry. **164 thereon** on that account.

Let me be no assistant for a state,
But keep a farm and carters.°

KING: We will try it.

Enter HAMLET [*reading on a book*].

QUEEN: But look where sadly° the poor wretch comes reading.

POLONIUS: Away, I do beseech you both, away.
I'll board° him presently.° O, give me leave.°

Exeunt KING *and* QUEEN [*with attendants*].

How does my good Lord Hamlet?

HAMLET: Well, God-a-mercy.°

POLONIUS: Do you know me, my lord?

HAMLET: Excellent well. You are a fishmonger.°

POLONIUS: Not I, my lord.

HAMLET: Then I would you were so honest a man.

POLONIUS: Honest, my lord?

HAMLET: Ay, sir. To be honest, as this world goes, is to be one man picked out of ten thousand.

POLONIUS: That's very true, my lord.

HAMLET: For if the sun breed maggots in a dead dog, being a good kissing carrion°—Have you a daughter?

POLONIUS: I have, my lord.

HAMLET: Let her not walk i' the sun.° Conception° is a blessing, but as your daughter may conceive, friend, look to 't.

POLONIUS [*aside*]: How say you by that? Still harping on my daughter. Yet he knew me not at first; 'a° said I was a fishmonger. 'A is far gone. And truly in my youth I suffered much extremity for love, very near this. I'll speak to him again.—What do you read, my lord?

HAMLET: Words, words, words.

POLONIUS: What is the matter,° my lord?

HAMLET: Between who?

POLONIUS: I mean, the matter that you read, my lord.

HAMLET: Slanders, sir; for the satirical rogue says here that old men have gray beards, that their faces are wrinkled, their eyes purging° thick amber° and plum-tree gum, and that they have a plentiful lack of wit,° together with most weak hams. All which, sir, though I most powerfully and potently believe, yet I hold it not honesty° to have it thus set down, for yourself, sir, shall grow old° as I am, if like a crab you could go backward.

POLONIUS [*aside*]: Though this be madness, yet there is method in 't.—Will you walk out of the air,° my lord?

166 carters wagon drivers. **167 sadly** seriously. **169 board** accost; **presently** at once; **give me leave** i.e., excuse me, leave me alone. (Said to those he hurries offstage, including the King and Queen.) **171 God-a-mercy** God have mercy, i.e., thank you. **173 fishmonger** fish merchant. **180–181 a good kissing carrion** i.e., a good piece of flesh for kissing, or for the sun to kiss. **183 i' the sun** in public (with additional implication of the sunshine of princely favors); **Conception** (1) understanding, (2) pregnancy. **186 'a** he. **190 matter** dubstance. (But Hamlet plays on the sense of "basis for a dispute.") **194 purging** discharging; **amber** i.e., resin, like the resinous **plum-tree gum.** **195 wit** understanding. **197 honesty** decency, decorum. **198 old** as old. **200 out of the air** (The open air was considered dangerous for sick people.)

HAMLET: Into my grave.

POLONIUS: Indeed, that's out of the air. [*Aside.*] How pregnant° sometimes his replies are! A happiness° that often madness hits on, which reason and sanity could not so prosperously° be delivered of. I will leave him and suddenly° contrive the means of meeting between him and my daughter.—My honorable lord, I will most humbly take my leave of you.

HAMLET: You cannot, sir, take from me anything that I will more willingly part withal°—except my life, except my life, except my life.

Enter GUILDENSTERN *and* ROSENCRANTZ.

POLONIUS: Fare you well, my lord.

HAMLET: These tedious old fools!°

POLONIUS: You go to seek the Lord Hamlet. There he is.

ROSENCRANTZ [*to* POLONIUS]: God save you, sir! [*Exit* POLONIUS.]

GUILDENSTERN: My honored lord!

ROSENCRANTZ: My most dear lord!

HAMLET: My excellent good friends! How dost thou, Guildenstern? Ah, Rosencrantz! Good lads, how do you both?

ROSENCRANTZ: As the indifferent° children of the earth.

GUILDENSTERN: Happy in that we are not overhappy.
On Fortune's cap we are not the very button.

HAMLET: Nor the soles of her shoe?

ROSENCRANTZ: Neither, my lord.

HAMLET: Then you live about her waist, or in the middle of her favors?°

GUILDENSTERN: Faith, her privates we.°

HAMLET: In the secret parts of Fortune? O, most true, she is a strumpet.° What news?

ROSENCRANTZ: None, my lord, but the world's grown honest.

HAMLET: Then is doomsday near. But your news is not true. Let me question more in particular. What have you, my good friends, deserved at the hands of Fortune that she sends you to prison hither?

GUILDENSTERN: Prison, my lord?

HAMLET: Denmark's a prison.

ROSENCRANTZ: Then is the world one.

HAMLET: A goodly one, in which there are many confines,° wards,° and dungeons, Denmark being one o' the worst.

ROSENCRANTZ: We think not so, my lord.

HAMLET: Why then 'tis none to you, for there is nothing either good or bad but thinking makes it so. To me it is a prison.

ROSENCRANTZ: Why then, your ambition makes it one. 'Tis too narrow for your mind.

HAMLET: O God, I could be bounded in a nutshell and count myself a king of infinite space, were it not that I have bad dreams.

202 pregnant quick-witted, full of meaning. **203 happiness** felicity of expression. **204 prosperously** successfully. **205 suddenly** immediately. **208 withal** with. **210 old fools** i.e., old men like Polonius. **217 indifferent** ordinary, at neither extreme of fortune or misfortune. **222 favors** i.e., sexual favors. **223 her privates we** i.e., (1) we are sexually intimate with Fortune, the fickle goddess who bestows her favors indiscriminately, (2) we are her private citizens. **224 strumpet** prostitute. (A common epithet for indiscriminate Fortune; see line 452.) **233 confines** places of confinement; **wards** cells.

GUILDENSTERN: Which dreams indeed are ambition, for the very substance of the ambitious° is merely the shadow of a dream.

HAMLET: A dream itself is but a shadow.

ROSENCRANTZ: Truly, and I hold ambition of so airy and light a quality that it is but a shadow's shadow.

HAMLET: Then are our beggars bodies,° and our monarchs and outstretched° heroes the beggars' shadows. Shall we to the court? For, by my fay,° I cannot reason.

ROSENCRANTZ, GUILDENSTERN: We'll wait upon° you.

HAMLET: No such matter. I will not sort° you with the rest of my servants, for, to speak to you like an honest man, I am most dreadfully attended.° But, in the beaten way° of friendship, what make° you at Elsinore?

ROSENCRANTZ: To visit you, my lord, no other occasion.

HAMLET: Beggar that I am, I am even poor in thanks; but I thank you, and sure, dear friends, my thanks are too dear a halfpenny.° Were you not sent for? Is it your own inclining? Is it a free° visitation? Come, come, deal justly with me. Come, come. Nay, speak.

GUILDENSTERN: What should we say, my lord?

HAMLET: Anything but to the purpose.° You were sent for, and there is a kind of confession in your looks which your modesties° have not craft enough to color.° I know the good King and Queen have sent for you.

ROSENCRANTZ: To what end, my lord?

HAMLET: That you must teach me. But let me conjure° you, by the rights of our fellowship, by the consonancy of our youth,° by the obligation of our ever-preserved love, and by what more dear a better° proposer could charge° you withal, be even° and direct with me whether you were sent for or no.

ROSENCRANTZ [*aside to* GUILDENSTERN]: What say you?

HAMLET [*aside*]: Nay, then, I have an eye of° you.—If you love me, hold not off.°

GUILDENSTERN: My lord, we were sent for.

HAMLET: I will tell you why; so shall my anticipation prevent your discovery,° and your secrecy to the King and Queen molt no feather,° I have of late—but wherefore I know not—lost all my mirth, for-gone all custom of exercises; and indeed it goes so heavily with my disposition that this goodly frame, the earth, seems to me a sterile promontory; this most excellent canopy, the air, look you, this brave° o'erhanging firmament, this majesti cal roof fretted° with golden fire, why, it appeareth nothing-to me but a

241–242 the very . . . ambitious that seemingly very substantial thing that the ambitious pursue. **246 bodies** i.e., solid substances rather than shadows (since beggars are not ambitious). **outstretched** (1) far-reaching in their ambition, (2) elongated as shadows. **247 fay** faith. **249 wait upon** accompany, attend. (But Hamlet uses the phrase in the sense of providing menial service.) **250 sort** class, categorize. **251 dreadfully attended** waited upon in slovenly fashion. **252 beaten way** familiar path, tried-and-true course; **make** do. **255 too dear a halfpenny** (1) too expensive at even a halfpenny, i.e., of little worth, (2) too expensive *by* a halfpenny in return for worthless kindness. **256 free** voluntary. **259 Anything but to the purpose** anything except a straightforward answer. (Said ironically.) **260 modesties** sense of shame. **261 color** disguise. **263 conjure** adjure, entreat. **264 the consonancy of our youth** our closeness in our younger days. **265 better** more skillful; **charge** urge. **266 even** straight, honest. **268 of** on; **hold not off** don't hold back. **270 so . . . discovery** in that way my saying it first will spare you from revealing the truth. **271 molt no feather** i.e., not diminish in the least. **275 brave** splendid. **276 fretted** adorned (with fretwork, as in a vaulted ceiling).

foul and pestilent congregation° of vapors. What a piece of work° is a man! How noble in reason, how infinite in faculties, in form and moving how express° and admirable, in action how like an angel, in apprehension° how like a god! The beauty of the world, the paragon of animals! And yet, to me, what is this quintessence° of dust? Man delights not me—no, nor woman neither, though by your smiling you seem to say so.

ROSENCRANTZ: My lord, there was no such stuff in my thoughts.

HAMLET: Why did you laugh, then, when I said man delights not me?

ROSENCRANTZ: To think, my lord, if you delight not in man, what Lenten entertainment° the players shall receive from you. We coted° them on the way, and hither are they coming to offer you service.

HAMLET: He that plays the king shall be welcome; His Majesty shall have tribute° of° me. The adventurous knight shall use his foil and target,° the lover shall not sigh gratis,° the humorous man° shall end his part in peace,° the clown shall make those laugh whose lungs are tickle o' the sear,° and the lady shall say her mind freely, or the blank verse shall halt° for 't. What players are they?

ROSENCRANTZ: Even those you were wont to take such delight in, the tragedians° of the city.

HAMLET: How chances it they travel? Their residence,° both in reputation and profit, was better both ways.

ROSENCRANTZ: I think their inhibition° comes by the means of the late° innovation.°

HAMLET: Do they hold the same estimation they did when I was in the city? Are they so followed?

ROSENCRANTZ: No, indeed are they not.

HAMLET: How comes it? Do they grow rusty?

ROSENCRANTZ: Nay, their endeavor keeps° in the wonted° pace. But there is, sir, an aerie° of children, little eyases,° that cry out on the top of question° and are most tyrannically° clapped for 't. These are now the fashion, and so berattle° the common stages°—so they call them—that many wearing rapiers° are afraid of goose quills° and dare scarce come thither.

HAMLET: What, are they children? Who maintains 'em? How are they escoted?° Will they pursue the quality° no longer than they can sing?° Will they not

277 congregation mass; **piece of work** masterpiece. **279 express** well-framed, exact, expressive. **279–280 apprehension** power of comprehending. **281 quintessence** the fifth essence of ancient philosophy, beyond earth, water, air, and fire, supposed to be the substance of the heavenly bodies and to be latent in all things. **285–286 Lenten entertainment** meager reception (appropriate to Lent); **coted** overtook and passed by. **288 tribute** (1) applause, (2) homage paid in money. **289 of** from; **foil and target** sword and shield. **290 gratis** for nothing; **humorous man** eccentric character, dominated by one trait or "humor"; **in peace** i.e., with full license. **291 tickle o' the sear** easy on the trigger, ready to laugh easily. (A *sear* is part of a gunlock.) **292 halt** limp. **294 tragedians** actors. **296 residence** remaining in their usual place, i.e., in the city. **298 inhibition** formal prohibition (from acting plays in the city); **late** Recent; **innovation** i.e., the new fashion in satirical plays performed by boy actors in the "private" theaters; or possibly a political uprising; or the strict limitations set on theaters in London in 1600. **303 keeps** continues; **wonted** usual. **304 aerie** nest; **eyases** young hawks; **cry . . . question** speak shrilly, dominating the controversy (in decrying the public theaters). **305 tyrannically** outrageously. **306 berattle** berate, clamor against; **common stages** public theaters. **306–307 many wearing repiers** i.e., many men of fashion, afraid to patronize the common players for fear of being satirized by the poets writing for the boy actors; **goose quills** i.e., pens of satirists. **308 escoted** maintained. **309 quality** (acting) profession; **no longer . . . sing** i.e., only until their voices change.

say afterwards, if they should grow themselves to common° players—as it is most like,° if their means are no better°—their writers do them wrong to make them exclaim against their own succession?°

ROSENCRANTZ: Faith, there has been much to-do° on both sides, and the nation holds it no sin to tar° them to controversy. There was for a while no money bid for argument unless the poet and the player went to cuffs in the question.°

HAMLET: Is 't possible?

GUILDENSTERN: O, there has been much throwing about of brains.

HAMLET: Do the boys carry it away?°

ROSENCRANTZ: Ay, that they do, my lord—Hercules and his load° too.°

HAMLET: It is not very strange; for my uncle is King of Denmark, and those that would make mouths° at him while my father lived give twenty, forty, fifty, a hundred ducats° apiece for his picture in little.° 'Sblood,° there is something in this more than natural, if philosophy° could find it out.

A flourish [*of trumpets within*].

GUILDENSTERN: There are the players.

HAMLET: Gentlemen, you are welcome to Elsinore. Your hands, come then. Th' appurtenance° of welcome is fashion and ceremony. Let me comply° with you in this garb,° lest my extent° to the players, which, I tell you, must show fairly outwards,° should more appear like entertainment° than yours. You are welcome. But my uncle-father and aunt-mother are deceived.

GUILDENSTERN: In what, my dear lord?

HAMLET: I am but mad north-north-west.° When the wind is southerly I know a hawk from a handsaw.°

Enter POLONIUS.

POLONIUS: Well be with you, gentlemen!

HAMLET: Hark you, Guildenstern, and you too; at each ear a hearer. That great baby you see there is not yet out of his swaddling clouts.°

ROSENCRANTZ: Haply° he is the second time come to them, for they say an old man is twice a child.

HAMLET: I will prophesy he comes to tell me of the players. Mark it.—You say right, sir, o' Monday morning, 'twas then indeed.

310 common regular, adult. **311 like** likely; **if . . . better** if they find no better way to support themselves. **312 succession** i.e., future careers. **313 to-do** ado. **314 tar** set on (as dogs). **314–315 There . . . question** i.e., for a while, no money was offered by the acting companies to playwrights for the plot to a play unless the satirical poets who wrote for the boys and the adult actors came to blows in the play itself. **318 carry it away** i.e., win the day. **319 Hercules . . . load** (thought to be an allusion to the sign of the Globe Theatre, which was Hercules bearing the world on his shoulders.) **302–319 How . . . load too** (The passage, omitted from the early quartos, alludes to the so-called War of the Theaters, 1599–1602, the rivalry between the children's companies and the adult actors.) **321 mouths** faces. **322 ducats** gold coins; **in little** in miniature; **'Sblood** by God's (Christ's) blood. **323 philosophy** i.e., scientific inquiry. **326 appurtenance** proper accompaniment; **comply** observe the formalities of courtesy. **327 garb** i.e., manner; **my extent** that which I extend, i.e., my polite behavior. **328 show fairly outwards** show every evidence of cordiality; **entertainment** a (warm) reception. **332 north-north-west** just off true north, only partly. **333 hawk, handsaw** i.e., two very different things, though also perhaps meaning a mattock (or *hack*) and carpenter's cutting tools, respectively; also birds, with a play on *bernshaw*, or heron. **336 swaddling clouts** cloths in which to wrap a newborn baby. **337 Haply** perhaps.

POLONIUS: My lord, I have news to tell you.

HAMLET: My lord, I have news to tell you. When Roscius° was an actor in Rome—

POLONIUS: The actors are come hither, my lord.

HAMLET: Buzz,° buzz!

POLONIUS: Upon my honor—

HAMLET: Then came each actor on his ass.

POLONIUS: The best actors in the world, either for tragedy, comedy, history, pastoral, pastoral-comical, historical-pastoral, tragical-historical, tragical-comical-historical-pastoral, scene individable,° or poem unlimited.° Seneca° cannot be too heavy, nor Plautus° too light. For the law of writ and the liberty,° these° are the only men.

HAMLET: O Jephthah, judge of Israel,°
what a treasure hadst thou!

POLONIUS: What a treasure had he, my lord?

HAMLET: Why,
"One fair daughter, and no more,
The which he lovèd passing° well."

POLONIUS [*aside*]: Still on my daughter.

HAMLET: Am I not i' the right, old Jephthah?

POLONIUS: If you call me Jephthah, my lord, I have a daughter that I love passing well.

HAMLET: Nay, that follows not.

POLONIUS: What follows then, my lord?

HAMLET: Why,
"As by lot,° God wot,"°
and then, you know,
"It came to pass, as most like° it was"—
the first row° of the pious chanson° will show you more, for look where my abridgement° comes.

Enter the PLAYERS.

You are welcome, masters; welcome, all. I am glad to see thee well. Welcome, good friends. O, old friend! Why, thy face is valanced° since I saw thee last. Com'st thou to beard° me in Denmark? What, my young lady° and mistress! By 'r Lady,° your ladyship is nearer to heaven than when I saw you last, by the altitude of a chopine.° Pray God your voice, like a piece of uncurrent° gold, be not cracked within the ring.° Masters,

342 Roscius a famous Roman actor who died in 62 B.C.E **344 Buzz** (an interjection used to denote stale news.) **349 scene individable** a play observing the unity of place; or perhaps one that is unclassifiable, or performed without intermission; **poem unlimited** a play disregarding the unities of time and place; one that is all-inclusive. **350 Seneca** writer of Latin tragedies; **Plautus** writer of Latin comedies. **350–351 law . . . liberty** dramatic composition both according to the rules and disregarding the rules; **these** i.e., the actors. **352 Jephthah . . . Israel** (Jephthah had to sacrifice his daughter; see Judges 11. Hamlet goes on to quote from a ballad on the theme.) **357 passing** surpassingly. **365 lot** chance; **wot** knows. **367 like** likely, probable. **368 row** stanza; **chanson** ballad, song. **369 my abridgement** something that cuts short my conversation; also, a diversion. **371 valanced** Fringed (with a beard). **372 beard** confront, challenge (with obvious pun). **372–373 young lady** i.e., boy playing women's parts; **By 'r Lady** by Our Lady. **374 chopine** thick-soled shoe of Italian fashion. **375 uncurrent** not passable as lawful coinage; **cracked . . . ring** i.e., changed from adolescent to male voice, no longer suitable for women's roles. (Coins featured rings enclosing the sovereign's head; if the coin was cracked within this ring, it was unfit for currency.)

you are all welcome. We'll e'en to 't° like French falconers, fly at anything we see. We'll have a speech straight.° Come, give us a taste of your quality.° Come, a passionate speech.

FIRST PLAYER: What speech, my good lord?

HAMLET: I heard thee speak me a speech once, but it was never acted, or if it was, not above once, for the play, I remember, pleased not the million; 'twas caviar to the general.° But it was—as I received it, and others, whose judgments in such matters cried in the top of° mine—an excellent play, well digested° in the scenes, set down with as much modesty° as cunning.° I remember one said there were no sallets° in the lines to make the matter savory, nor no matter in the phrase that might indict° the author of affectation, but called it an honest method, as wholesome as sweet, and by very much more handsome° than fine.° One speech in 't I chiefly loved: 'twas Aeneas' tale to Dido, and thereabout of it especially when he speaks of Priam's slaughter.° If it live in your memory, begin at this line: let me see, let me see—

"The rugged Pyrrhus,° like th' Hyrcanian beast°"—

'Tis not so. It begins with Pyrrhus:

"The rugged° Pyrrhus, he whose sable° arms,
Black as his purpose, did the night resemble
When he lay couchèd° in the ominous horse,°
Hath now this dread and black complexion smeared
With heraldry more dismal.° Head to foot
Now is he total gules,° horridly tricked°
With blood of fathers, mothers, daughters, sons,
Baked and impasted° with the parching streets,°
That lend a tyrannous° and a damnèd light
To their lord's° murder. Roasted in wrath and fire,
And thus o'ersizèd° with coagulate gore,
With eyes like carbuncles,° the hellish Pyrrhus
Old grandsire Priam seeks."

So proceed you.

376 e'en to 't go at it. **377 straight** at once. **378 quality** professional skill. **382 caviar to the general** caviar to the multitude, i.e., a choice dish too elegant for coarse tastes. **383 cried in the top of** i.e., spoke with greater authority than. **384 digested** arranged, ordered; **modesty** moderation, restraint. **385 cunning** skill; **sallets** i.e., something savory, spicy improprieties. **386 indict** convict. **388 handsome** well-proportioned; **fine** elaborately ornamented, showy. **390 Priam's slaughter** the slaying of the ruler of Troy, when the Greeks finally took the city. **392 Pyrrhus** a Greek hero in the Trojan War, also known as Neoptolemus, son of Achilles—another avenging son; **Hyrcanian beast** i.e., tiger. (On the death of Priam, see Virgil, *Aeneid*, 2.506 ff.; compare the whole speech with Marlowe's *Dido Queen of Carthage*, 2.1.214. ff. On the *Hyrcanian* tiger, see *Aeneid*, 4.366–67. Hyrcania is on the Caspian Sea.) **394 rugged** shaggy, savage; **sable** black (for reasons of camouflage during the episode of the Trojan horse). **396 couchèd** concealed; **ominous horse** fateful Trojan horse, by which the Greeks gained access to Troy. **398 dismal** ill-omened. **399 total gules** entirely red. (A heraldic term); **tricked** spotted and smeared. (Heraldic.) **401 impasted** crusted, like a thick paste; **with . . . streets** by the parching heat of the streets (because of the fires everywhere). **402 tyrannous** cruel. **403 their lord's** i.e., Priam's. **404 o'ersizèd** covered as with size or glue. **405 carbuncles** large fiery-red precious stones thought to emit their own light.

POLONIUS: 'Fore God, my lord, well spoken, with good accent and good discretion.

FIRST PLAYER: "Anon he finds him
Striking too short at Greeks. His antique° sword,
Rebellious to his arm, lies where it falls,
Repugnant° to command. Unequal matched,
Pyrrhus at Priam drives, in rage strikes wide,
But with the whiff and wind of his fell° sword
Th' unnervèd° father falls. Then senseless Ilium,°
Seeming to feel this blow, with flaming top
Stoops to his° base, and with a hideous crash
Takes prisoner Pyrrhus' ear. For, lo! His sword,
Which was declining° on the milky° head
Of reverend Priam, seemed i' th' air to stick.
So as a painted° tyrant Pyrrhus stood,
And, like a neutral to his will and matter,°
Did nothing.
But as we often see against° some storm
A silence in the heavens, the rack° stand still,
The bold winds speechless, and the orb° below
As hush as death, anon the dreadful thunder
Doth rend the region,° so, after Pyrrhus' pause,
A rousèd vengeance sets him new a-work
And never did the Cyclops'° hammers fall
On Mars's armor forged for proof eterne°
With less remorse° than Pyrrhus' bleeding sword
Now falls on Priam.
Out, out, thou strumpet Fortune! All you gods
In general synod° take away her power!
Break all the spokes and fellies° from her wheel,
And bowl the round nave° down the hill of heaven°
As low as to the fiends!"

POLONIUS: This is too long.

HAMLET: It shall to the barber's with your beard.—Prithee, say on. He's for a jig° or a tale of bawdry, or he sleeps. Say on; come to Hecuba.°

FIRST PLAYER: "But who, ah woe! had° seen the moblèd° queen"—

HAMLET: "The moblèd queen?"

POLONIUS: That's good. "Moblèd queen" is good.

FIRST PLAYER: "Run barefoot up and down, threat'ning the flames°

410 antique ancient, long-used. **412 Repugnant** disobedient, resistant. **414 fell** cruel. **415 unnervèd** strengthless; **senseless Ilium** inanimate citadel of Troy. **417 his** its. **419 declining** descending; **milky** white-haired. **421 painted** i.e., painted in a picture. **422 like . . . matter** i.e., as though suspended between his intention and its fulfullment. **424 against** just before. **425 rack** mass of clouds. **426 orb** globe, earth. **428 region** sky. **430 Cyclops** giant armor makers in the smithy of Vulcan. **431 proof eterne** Eternal resistance to assault. **432 remorse** Pity. **435 synod** assembly. **436 fellies** pieces of wood forming the rim of a wheel. **437 nave** hub; **hill of heaven** Mount Olympus. **440 jig** comic song and dance often given at the end of a play. **441 Hecuba** wife of Priam. **442 who . . . had** anyone who had (also in line 469); **moblèd** muffled. **445 threat'ning the flames** i.e., weeping hard enough to dampen the flames.

With bisson rheum,° a clout° upon that head
Where late° the diadem stood, and, for a robe,
About her lank and all o'erteemd° loins
A blanket, in the alarm of fear caught up—
Who this had seen, with tongue in venom steeped,
'Gainst Fortune's state° would treason have pronounced.°
But if the gods themselves did see her then
When she saw Pyrrhus make malicious sport
In mincing with his sword her husband's limbs,
The instant burst of clamor that she made,
Unless things mortal move them not at all,
Would have made milch° the burning eyes of heaven,°
And passion° in the gods."

POLONIUS: Look whe'er° he has not turned his color and has tears in 's eyes. Prithee, no more.

HAMLET: 'Tis well; I'll have thee speak out the rest of this soon.—Good my lord, will you see the players well bestowed?° Do you hear, let them be well used, for they are the abstract° and brief chronicles of the time. After your death you were better have a bad epitaph than their ill report while you live.

POLONIUS: My lord, I will use them according to their desert.

HAMLET: God's bodikin,° man, much better. Use every man after his desert, and who shall scape whipping? Use them after° your own honor and dignity. The less they deserve, the more merit is in your bounty. Take them in.

POLONIUS: Come, sirs. [*Exit.*]

HAMLET: Follow him, friends. We'll hear a play tomorrow. [*As they start to leave,* HAMLET *detains the* FIRST PLAYER.] Dost thou hear me, old friend? Can you play *The Murder of Gonzago?*

FIRST PLAYER: Ay, my lord.

HAMLET: We'll ha 't° tomorrow night. You could, for a need, study° a speech of some dozen or sixteen lines which I would set down and insert in 't, could you not?

FIRST PLAYER: Ay, my lord.

HAMLET: Very well. Follow that lord, and look you mock him not. [*Exeunt* PLAYERS.] My good friends, I'll leave you till night. You are welcome to Elsinore.

ROSENCRANTZ: Good my lord! *Exeunt* [ROSENCRANTZ *and* GUILDENSTERN].

HAMLET: Ay, so, goodbye to you.—Now I am alone.
O, what a rogue and peasant slave am I!
Is it not monstrous that this player here,
But° in a fiction, in a dream of passion,
Could force his soul so to his own conceit°
That from her working° all his visage wanned,°

446 bisson rheum blinding tears; **clout** cloth. **447 late** lately. **448 all o'erteemèd** utterly worn out with bearing children. **451 state** rule, managing; **pronounced** proclaimed. **457 milch** milky, moist with tears; **burning eyes of heaven** i.e., heavenly bodies. **458 passion** overpowering emotion. **459 whe'er** whether. **462 bestowed** lodged. **463 abstract** summary account. **466 God's bodikin** by God's (Christ's) little body, *bodykin.* (Not to be confused with *bodkin,* "dagger.") **467 after** according to. **474 ha 't** have it; **study** memorize. **484 But** merely. **485 force . . . conceit** bring his innermost being so entirely into accord with his conception (of the role). **486 from her working** as a result of, or in response to, his soul's activity; **wanned** grew pale.

Tears in his eyes, distraction in his aspect,°
A broken voice, and his whole function suiting
With forms to his conceit?° And all for nothing!
For Hecuba!
What's Hecuba to him, or he to Hecuba,
That he should weep for her? What would he do
Had he the motive and the cue for passion
That I have? He would drown the stage with tears
And cleave the general ear° with horrid° speech,
Make mad the guilty and appall° the free,°
Confound the ignorant,° and amaze° indeed
The very faculties of eyes and ears. Yet I,
A dull and muddy-mettled° rascal, peak°
Like John-a-dreams,° unpregnant of° my cause,
And can say nothing—no, not for a king
Upon whose property° and most dear life
A damned defeat° was made. Am I a coward?
Who calls me villain? Breaks my pate° across?
Plucks off my beard and blows it in my face?
Tweaks me by the nose? Gives me the lie i' the throat°
As deep as to the lungs? Who does me this?
Ha, 'swounds,° I should take it; for it cannot be
But I am pigeon-livered° and lack gall
To make oppression bitter,° or ere this
I should ha' fatted all the region kites°
With this slave's offal.° Bloody, bawdy villain!
Remorseless,° treacherous, lecherous, kindless° villain!
O, vengeance!
Why, what an ass am I! This is most brave,°
That I, the son of a dear father murdered,
Prompted to my revenge by heaven and hell,
Must like a whore unpack my heart with words
And fall a-cursing, like a very drab,°
A scullion!° Fie upon 't, foh! About,° my brains!
Hum, I have heard
That guilty creatures sitting at a play
Have by the very cunning° of the scene°

487 aspect look, glance. **488–489 his whole . . . conceit** all his bodily powers responding with actions to suit his thought. **495 the general ear** everyone's ear; **horrid** horrible. **496 appall** (literally, make pale.); **free** innocent. **497 Confound the ignorant**, i.e., dumbfound those who know nothing of the crime that has been committed; **amaze** stun. **499 muddy-mettled** dull-spirited; **peak** mope, pine. **500 John-a-dreams** a sleepy, dreaming idler; **unpregnant of** not quickened by. **502 property** i.e., the crown; also character, quality. **503 damned defeat** damnable act of destruction. **504 pate** head. **506 Gives . . . throat** calls me an out-and-out liar. **508 'swounds** by his (Christ's) wounds. **509 pigeon-livered** (The pigeon or dove was popularly supposed to be mild because it secreted no gall.) **510 bitter** i.e., bitter to me. **511 region kites** kites (birds of prey) of the air. **512 offal** entrails. **513 Remorseless** pitiless; **kindless** unnatural. **515 brave** fine, admirable. (Said ironically.) **519 drab** whore. **520 scullion** menial kitchen servant (apt to be foul-mouthed); **About** about it, to work. **523 cunning** art, skill; **scene** dramatic presentation.

Been struck so to the soul that presently°
They have proclaimed their malefactions;
For murder, though it have no tongue, will speak
With most miraculous organ. I'll have these players
Play something like the murder of my father
Before mine uncle. I'll observe his looks;
I'll tent° him to the quick.° If 'a do blench,°
I know my course. The spirit that I have seen
May be the devil, and the devil hath power
T' assume a pleasing shape; yea, and perhaps,
Out of my weakness and my melancholy,
As he is very potent with such spirits,°
Abuses° me to damn me. I'll have grounds
More relative° than this. The play's the thing
Wherein I'll catch the conscience of the King. *Exit.*

[3.1]

Enter KING, QUEEN, POLONIUS, OPHELIA, ROSENCRANTZ, GUILDENSTERN, *lords.*

KING: And can you by no drift of conference°
Get from him why he puts on this confusion,
Grating so harshly all his days of quiet
With turbulent and dangerous lunacy?

ROSENCRANTZ: He does confess he feels himself distracted,
But from what cause 'a will by no means speak.

GUILDENSTERN: Nor do we find him forward° to be sounded,°
But with a crafty madness keeps aloof
When we would bring him on to some confession
Of his true state.

QUEEN: Did he receive you well?

ROSENCRANTZ: Most like a gentleman.

GUILDENSTERN: But with much forcing of his disposition.°

ROSENCRANTZ: Niggard° of question,° but of our demands
Most free in his reply.

QUEEN: Did you assay° him
To any pastime?

ROSENCRANTZ: Madam, it so fell out that certain players
We o'erraught° on the way. Of these we told him,
And there did seem in him a kind of joy
To hear of it. They are here about the court,
And, as I think, they have already order
This night to play before him.

POLONIUS: 'Tis most true,
And he beseeched me to entreat Your Majesties
To hear and see the matter.

524 presently at once. **530 tent** probe; **the quick** the tender part of a wound, the core; **blench** quail, flinch. **535 spirits** humors (of melancholy). **536 Abuses** deludes. **537 relative** cogent, pertinent. **[3.1] Location: The castle.** **1 drift of conference** directing of conversation. **7 forward** willing; **sounded** questioned. **12 dispositon** inclination. **13 Niggard** stingy; **question** conversation. **14 assay** try to win. **17 o'erraught** overtook.

KING: With all my heart, and it doth much content me
To hear him so inclined.
Good gentlemen, give him a further edge°
And drive his purpose into these delights.

ROSENCRANTZ: We shall, my lord. *Exeunt* ROSENCRANTZ *and* GUILDENSTERN.

KING: Sweet Gertrude, leave us too
For we have closely° sent for Hamlet hither,
That he, as 'twere by accident, may here
Affront° Ophelia.
Her father and myself, lawful espials,°
Will so bestow ourselves that seeing, unseen,
We may of their encounter frankly judge,
And gather by him, as he is behaved,
If't be th' affliction of his love or no
That thus he suffers for.

QUEEN: I shall obey you.
And for your part, Ophelia, I do wish
That your good beauties be the happy cause
Of Hamlet's wildness. So shall I hope your virtues
Will bring him to his wonted° way again,
To both your honors.

OPHELIA: Madam, I wish it may. [*Exit* QUEEN.]

POLONIUS: Ophelia, walk you here.—Gracious,° so please you,
We will bestow° ourselves. [*To* OPHELIA.] Read on this book,
[*giving her a book*]
That show of such an exercise° may color°
Your loneliness.° We are oft to blame in this—
'Tis too much proved°—that with devotion's visage
And pious action we do sugar o'er
The devil himself.

KING [*aside*]: O 'tis too true!
How smart a lash that speech doth give my conscience!
The harlot's cheek, beautied with plastering art,
Is not more ugly to° the thing° that helps it
Than is my deed to my most painted word.
O heavy burden!

POLONIUS: I hear him coming. Let's withdraw, my lord.
[*The* KING *and* POLONIUS *withdraw.*°]

Enter HAMLET. [OPHELIA *pretends to read a book.*]

HAMLET: To be, or not to be, that is the question:
Whether 'tis nobler in the mind to suffer
The slings° and arrows of outrageous fortune,
Or to take arms against a sea of troubles

26 edge incitement. **29 closely** privately. **31 Affront** confront, meet. **32 espials** spies. **41 wonted** accustomed. **43 Gracious** your Grace (i.e., the King). **44 bestow** conceal. **45 exercise** religious exercise. (The book she reads is one of devotion.); **color** give a plausible appearance to. **46 loneliness** being alone. **47 too much proved** too often shown to be true, too often practiced. **53 to** compared to; **the thing** i.e., the cosmetic. **56 s.d. withdraw** (The King and Polonius may retire behind an arras. The stage directions specify that they "enter" again near the end of the scene.) **59 slings** missiles.

And by opposing end them. To die, to sleep—
No more—and by a sleep to say we end
The heartache and the thousand natural shocks
That flesh is heir to. 'Tis a consummation
Devoutly to be wished. To die, to sleep;
To sleep, perchance to dream. Ay, there's the rub,°
For in that sleep of death what dreams may come,
When we have shuffled° off this mortal coil,°
Must give us pause. There's the respect°
That makes calamity of so long life.°
For who would bear the whips and scorns of time,
Th' oppressor's wrong, the proud man's contumely,°
The pangs of disprized° love, the law's delay,
The insolence of office,° and the spurns°
That patient merit of th' unworthy takes,°
When he himself might his quietus° make
With a bare bodkin?° Who would fardels° bear,
To grunt and sweat under a weary life,
But that the dread of something after death,
The undiscovered country from whose bourn°
No traveler returns, puzzles the will,
And makes us rather bear those ills we have
Than fly to others that we know not of?
Thus conscience does make cowards of us all;
And thus the native hue° of resolution
Is sicklied o'er with the pale cast° of thought,
And enterprises of great pitch° and moment°
With this regard° their currents° turn awry
And lose the name of action.—Soft you° now,
The fair Ophelia. Nymph, in thy orisons°
Be all my sins remembered.

OPHELIA: Good my lord,
How does your honor for this many a day?

HAMLET: I humbly thank you; well, well, well.

OPHELIA: My lord, I have remembrances of yours,
That I have longèd long to redeliver.
I pray you, now receive them. [*She offers tokens.*]

HAMLET: No, not I, I never gave you aught.

OPHELIA: My honored lord, you know right well you did,
And with them words of so sweet breath composed
As made the things more rich. Their perfume lost,

66 rub (literally, an obstacle in the game of bowls.) **68 shuffled** sloughed, cast; **coil** turmoil. **69 respect** consideration. **70 of . . . life** so long-lived, something we willingly endure for so long (also suggesting that long life is itself a calamity). **72 contumely** insolent abuse. **73 disprized** unvalued. **74 office** officialdom; **spurns** insults. **75 of . . . takes** receives from unworthy persons. **76 quietus** acquitance; here, death. **77 a bare bodkin** a mere dagger, unsheathed; **fardels** burdens. **80 bourn** frontier, boundary. **85 native hue** natural color, complexion. **86 cast** tinge, shade of color. **87 pitch** height (as of a falcon's flight.); **moment** importance. **88 regard** respect, consideration; **currents** courses. **89 Soft you** i.e., wait a minute, gently. **90 orisons** prayers.

Take these again, for to the noble mind
Rich gifts wax poor when givers prove unkind.
There, my lord. [*She gives tokens.*]

HAMLET: Ha, ha! Are you honest?°

OPHELIA: My lord?

HAMLET: Are you fair?°

OPHELIA: What means your lordship?

HAMLET: That if you be honest and fair, your honesty° should admit no discourse to° your beauty.

OPHELIA: Could beauty, my lord, have better commerce° than with honesty?

HAMLET: Ay, truly, for the power of beauty will sooner transform honesty from what it is to a bawd than the force of honesty can translate beauty into his° likeness. This was sometime° a paradox,° but now the time° gives it proof. I did love you once.

OPHELIA: Indeed, my lord, you made me believe so.

HAMLET: You should not have believed me, for virtue cannot so inoculate° our old stock but we shall relish of it.° I loved you not.

OPHELIA: I was the more deceived.

HAMLET: Get thee to a nunnery.° Why wouldst thou be a breeder of sinners? I am myself indifferent honest,° but yet I could accuse me of such things that it were better my mother had not borne me: I am very proud, revengeful, ambitious, with more offenses at my beck° than I have thoughts to put them in, imagination to give them shape, or time to act them in. What should such fellows as I do crawling between earth and heaven? We are arrant knaves all; believe none of us. Go thy ways to a nunnery. Where's your father?

OPHELIA: At home, my lord.

HAMLET: Let the doors be shut upon him, that he may play the fool nowhere but in's own house. Farewell.

OPHELIA: O, help him, you sweet heavens!

HAMLET: If thou dost marry, I'll give thee this plague for thy dowry: be thou as chaste as ice, as pure as snow, thou shalt not escape calumny. Get thee to a nunnery, farewell. Or, if thou wilt needs marry, marry a fool, for wise men know well enough what monsters° you° make of them. To a nunnery, go, and quickly too. Farewell.

OPHELIA: Heavenly powers, restore him!

HAMLET: I have heard of your paintings too, well enough. God hath given you one face, and you make yourselves another. You jig,° you amble,° and you lisp, you nickname God's creatures,° and make your wantonness your ignorance.° Go to, I'll no more on 't;° it hath made me mad. I say

104 honest (1) truthful, (2) chaste. **106 fair** (1) beautiful, (2) just, honorable. **108 your honesty** your chastity. **108–109 discourse to** familiar dealings with. **110 commerce** dealings, intercourse. **113 his** its; **sometime** formerly; **a paradox** a view opposite to commonly held opinion; **the time** the present age. **116 inoculate** graft, be engrafted to. **117 but . . . it** that we do not still have about us a taste of the old stock, i.e., retain our sinfulness. **119 nunnery** convent (with possibly an awareness that the word was also used derisively to denote a brothel). **120 indifferent honest** reasonably virtuous. **122 beck** command. **133 monsters** (an illusion to the horns of a cuckold.); **you** i.e., you women. **137 jig** dance; **amble** move coyly. **138 you nickname . . . creatures** i.e., you give trendy names to things in place of their god-given names. **139 make . . . ignorance** i.e., excuse your affectation on the grounds of pretended ignorance; **on 't** of it.

we will have no more marriage. Those that are married already—all but one—shall live. The rest shall keep as they are. To a nunnery, go.

Exit.

OPHELIA: O, what a noble mind is here o'erthrown!
The courtier's, soldier's, scholar's, eye, tongue, sword,
Th' expectancy° and rose° of the fair state,
The glass of fashion and the mold of form,°
Th' observed of all observers,° quite, quite down!
And I, of ladies most deject and wretched,
That sucked the honey of his music° vows,
Now see that noble and most sovereign reason
Like sweet bells jangled out of tune and harsh,
That unmatched form and feature of blown° youth
Blasted° with ecstasy.° O, woe is me,
T' have seen what I have seen, see what I see!

Enter KING *and* POLONIUS.

KING: Love? His affections° do not that way tend;
Nor what he spake, though it lacked form a little,
Was not like madness. There's something in his soul
O'er which his melancholy sits on brood,°
And I do doubt° the hatch and the disclose°
Will be some danger; which for to prevent,
I have in quick determination
Thus set it down:° he shall with speed to England
For the demand of° our neglected tribute.
Haply the seas and countries different
With variable objects° shall expel
This something-settled matter in his heart,°
Whereon his brains still° beating puts him thus
From fashion of himself.° What think you on 't?

POLONIUS: It shall do well. But yet do I believe
The origin and commencement of his grief
Sprung from neglected love.—How now, Ophelia?
You need not tell us what Lord Hamlet said;
We heard it all.—My lord, do as you please,
But, if you hold it fit, after the play
Let his queen-mother° all alone entreat him
To show his grief. Let her be round° with him;
And I'll be placed, so please you, in the ear
Of all their conference. If she find him not,°

144 expectancy hope; **rose** ornament. **145 The glass . . . form** the mirror of true fashioning and the pattern of courtly behavior. **146 Th' observed . . . observers** i.e., the center of attention and honor in the court. **148 music** musical, sweetly uttered. **151 blown** blooming. **152 Blasted** withered; **ecstasy** madness. **154 affections** emotions, feelings. **157 sits on brood** sits like a bird on a nest, about to *hatch* mischief (line 169). **158 doubt** fear; **disclose** disclosure, hatching. **161 set it down** resolved. **162 For . . . of** to demand. **164 variable objects** various sights and surroundings to divert him. **165 This something . . . heart** the strange matter settled in his heart. **166 still** continually. **167 From . . . himself** out of his natural manner. **174 queen-mother** queen and mother. **175 round** blunt. **177 find him not** fails to discover what is troubling him.

To England send him, or confine him where
Your wisdom best shall think.

KING: It shall be so.
Madness in great ones must not unwatched go. *Exeunt.*

[3.2]

Enter HAMLET *and three of the* PLAYERS.

HAMLET: Speak the speech, I pray you, as I pronounced it to you, trippingly on the tongue. But if you mouth it, as many of our players° do, I had as lief° the town crier spoke my lines. Nor do not saw the air too much with your hand, thus, but use all gently; for in the very torrent, tempest, and, as I may say, whirlwind of your passion, you must acquire and beget a temperance that may give it smoothness. O, it offends me to the soul to hear a robustious° periwig-pated° fellow tear a passion to tatters, to very rags, to split the ears of the groundlings,° who for the most part are capable of° nothing but inexplicable dumb shows° and noise. I would have such a fellow whipped for o'erdoing Termagant.° It out-Herods Herod.° Pray you, avoid it.

FIRST PLAYER: I warrant your honor.

HAMLET: Be not too tame neither, but let your own discretion be your tutor. Suit the action to the word, the word to the action, with this special observance, that you o'erstep not the modesty° of nature. For anything so o'erdone is from° the purpose of playing, whose end, both at the first and now, was and is to hold as 't were the mirror up to nature, to show virtue her feature, scorn° her own image, and the very age and body of the time° his° form and pressure.° Now this overdone or come tardy off,° though it makes the unskillful° laugh, cannot but make the judicious grieve, the censure of the which one° must in your allowance° o'erweigh a whole theater of others. O, there be players that I have seen play, and heard others praise, and that highly, not to speak it profanely,° that, neither having th' accent of Christians° nor the gait of Christian, pagan, nor man,° have so strutted and bellowed that I have thought some of nature's journeymen° had made men and not made them well, they imitated humanity so abominably.°

[3.2] Location: The castle. 2 our players players nowadays. **2–3 I had as lief** I would just as soon. **7 robustious** violent, boisterous; **periwig-pated** wearing a wig. **8 groundlings** spectators who paid least and stood in the yard of the theater. **9 capable of** able to understand; **dumb shows** mimed performances, often used before Shakespeare's time to precede a play or each act. **10 Termagant** a supposed deity of the Mohammedans, not found in any English medieval play but elsewhere portrayed as violent and blustering. **11 Herod** herod of Jewry. (A character in *The Slaughter of the Innocents* and other cycle plays. The part was played with great noise and fury.) **15 modesty** restraint, moderation. **16 from** contrary to. **18 scorn** i.e., something foolish and deserving of scorn. **18–19 the very . . . time** i.e., the present state of affairs; **his** its; **pressure** stamp, impressed character; **come tardy off** inadequately done. **20 the unskillful** those lacking in judgment. **21 the censure . . . one** the judgment of even one of whom; **your allowance** your scale of values. **23 not . . . profanely** (Hamlet anticipates his idea in lines 25–27 that some men were not made by God at all.) **24 Christians** i.e., ordinary decent folk. **24–25 nor man** i.e., nor any human being at all. **26 journeymen** laborers who are not yet masters in their trade. **27 abominably** (Shakespeare's usual spelling, *abhominably*, suggests a literal though etymologically incorrect meaning, "removed from human nature.")

FIRST PLAYER: I hope we have reformed that indifferently° with us, sir.

HAMLET: O, reform it altogether. And let those that play your clowns speak no more than is set down for them; for there be of them° that will themselves laugh, to set on some quantity of barren° spectators to laugh too, though in the meantime some necessary question of the play be then to be considered. That's villainous, and shows a most pitiful ambition in the fool that uses it. Go make you ready. [*Exeunt* PLAYERS.]

Enter POLONIUS, GUILDENSTERN *and* ROSENCRANTZ.

How now, my lord, will the King hear this piece of work?

POLONIUS: And the Queen too, and that presently.°

HAMLET: Bid the players make haste. [*Exit* POLONIUS.]
Will you two help to hasten them?

ROSENCRANTZ: Ay, my lord. *Exeunt they two.*

HAMLET: What ho, Horatio!

Enter HORATIO.

HORATIO: Here, sweet lord, at your service.

HAMLET: Horatio, thou art e'en as just a man
As e'er my conversation coped withal.°

HORATIO: O, my dear lord—

HAMLET: Nay, do not think I flatter,
For what advancement may I hope from thee
That no revenue hast but thy good spirits
To feed and clothe thee? Why should the poor be flattered?
No, let the candied° tongue lick absurd pomp,
And crook the pregnant° hinges of the knee
Where thrift° may follow fawning. Dost thou hear?
Since my dear soul was mistress of her choice
And could of men distinguish her election,°
Sh' hath sealed thee° for herself, for thou hast been
As one, in suffering all, that suffers nothing,
A man that Fortune's buffets and rewards
Hast ta'en with equal thanks; and blest are those
Whose blood° and judgment are so well commeddled°
That they are not a pipe for Fortune's finger
To sound what stop° she please. Give me that man
That is not passion's slave, and I will wear him
In my heart's core, ay, in my heart of heart,
As I do thee.—Something too much of this.—
There is a play tonight before the King.
One scene of it comes near the circumstance
Which I have told thee of my father's death.
I prithee, when thou seest that act afoot,

28 indifferently tolerably. **30 of them** some among them. **31 barren** i.e., of wit. **36 presently** at once. **42 my . . . withal** my dealings encountered. **47 candied** sugared, flattering. **48 pregnant** compliant. **49 thrift** profit. **51 could . . . election** could make distinguishing choices among persons. **52 sealed thee** (literally, as one would seal a legal document to mark possession.) **56 blood** passion; **commeddled** commingled. **58 stop** hole in a wind instrument for controlling the sound.

Even with the very comment of thy soul°
Observe my uncle. If his occulted° guilt
Do not itself unkennel° in one speech,
It is a damnéd° ghost that we have seen,
And my imaginations are as foul
As Vulcan's stithy.° Give him heedful note,
For I mine eyes will rivet to his face,
And after we will both our judgments join
In censure of his seeming.°

HORATIO: Well, my lord.
If 'a steal aught° the whilst this play is playing
And scape detecting, I will pay the theft.

[*Flourish.*] *Enter trumpets and kettledrums,* KING, QUEEN, POLONIUS, OPHELIA, [ROSENCRANTZ, GUILDENSTERN, *and other lords, with guards carrying torches*].

HAMLET: They are coming to the play. I must be idle.°
Get you a place. [*The* KING, QUEEN, *and courtiers sit.*]

KING: How fares our cousin° Hamlet?

HAMLET: Excellent, i' faith, of the chameleon's dish:° I eat the air, promise-crammed. You cannot feed capons° so.

KING: I have nothing with° this answer, Hamlet. These words are not mine.°

HAMLET: No, nor mine now.° [*To* POLONIUS.] My lord, you played once i' th' university, you say?

POLONIUS: That did I, my lord, and was accounted a good actor.

HAMLET: What did you enact?

POLONIUS: I did enact Julius Caesar. I was killed i' the Capitol; Brutus killed me.

HAMLET: It was a brute° part° of him to kill so capital a calf° there.—Be the players ready?

ROSENCRANTZ: Ay, my lord. They stay upon° your patience.

QUEEN: Come hither, my dear Hamlet, sit by me.

HAMLET: No, good Mother, here's metal° more attractive.

POLONIUS [*to the* KING]: O, ho, do you mark that?

HAMLET: Lady, shall I lie in your lap? [*Lying down at* OPHELIA'*s feet.*]

OPHELIA: No, my lord.

HAMLET: I mean, my head upon your lap?

OPHELIA: Ay, my lord.

HAMLET: Do you think I meant country matters?°

66 very . . . soul your most penetrating observation and consideration. **67 occulted** hidden. **68 unkennel** (as one would say of a fox driven from its lair.) **69 damnéd** in league with Satan. **71 stithy** smithy, place of stiths (anvils). **74 censure of his seeming** judgment of his appearance or behavior. **75 If 'a steal aught** if he gets away with anything. **77 idle** (1) unoccupied, (2) mad. **79 cousin** i.e., close relative. **80 chameleon's dish** (Chameleons were supposed to feed on air. Hamlet deliberately misinterprets the King's *fares* as "feeds." By his phrase *eat the air* he also plays on the idea of feeding himself with the promise of succession, of being the *heir.*) **81 capons** roosters castrated and ***crammed*** with feed to make them succulent. **82 have . . . with** make nothing of, or gain nothing from; **are not mine** do not respond to what I asked. **83 nor mine now** (once spoken, words are proverbially no longer the speaker's own—and hence should be uttered warily.) **88 brute** (the Latin meaning of *brutus,* "stupid," was often used punningly with the name Brutus.); **part** (1) deed, (2) role; **calf** fool. **90 stay upon** await. **92 metal** substance that is *attractive,* i.e., magnetic, but with suggestion also of *mettle,* "disposition."

OPHELIA: I think nothing, my lord.
HAMLET: That's a fair thought to lie between maids' legs.
OPHELIA: What is, my lord?
HAMLET: Nothing.°
OPHELIA: You are merry, my lord.
HAMLET: Who, I?
OPHELIA: Ay, my lord.
HAMLET: O God, your only jig maker.° What should a man do but be merry? For look you how cheerfully my mother looks, and my father died within 's° two hours.
OPHELIA: Nay, 'tis twice two months, my lord.
HAMLET: So long? Nay then, let the devil wear black, for I'll have a suit of sables.° O heavens! Die two months ago, and not forgotten yet? Then there's hope a great man's memory may outlive his life half a year. But, by 'r Lady, 'a must build churches, then, or else shall 'a suffer not thinking on,° with the hobbyhorse, whose epitaph is
"For O, for O, the hobbyhorse is forgot."°

The trumpets sound. Dumb show follows.

Enter a King and a Queen [very lovingly]; the Queen embracing him, and he her. [She kneels, and makes show of protestation unto him.] He takes her up, and declines his head upon her neck. He lies him down upon a bank of flowers. She, seeing him asleep, leaves him. Anon comes in another man, takes off his crown, kisses it, pours poison in the sleeper's ears, and leaves him. The Queen returns, finds the King dead, makes passionate action. The Poisoner with some three or four come in again, seem to condole with her. The dead body is carried away. The Poisoner woos the Queen with gifts; she seems harsh awhile, but in the end accepts love.

[*Exeunt* PLAYERS.]

OPHELIA: What means this, my lord?
HAMLET: Marry, this' miching mallico;° it means mischief.
OPHELIA: Belike° this show imports the argument° of the play.

Enter PROLOGUE.

HAMLET: We shall know by this fellow. The players cannot keep counsel;° they'll tell all.
OPHELIA: Will 'a tell us what this show meant?

98 country matters sexual intercourse (making a bawdy pun on the first syllable of *country*). **102 Nothing** the figure zero or naught, suggesting the female sexual anatomy. (*Thing* not infrequently has a bawdy connotation of male or female anatomy, and the reference here could be male.) **106 only jig maker** very best composer of jigs, i.e., pointless merriment. (Hamlet replies sardonically to Ophelia's observation that he is merry by saying, "If you're looking for someone who is really merry, you've come to the right person.") **107 within 's** within this (i.e., these). **110 suit of sables** garments trimmed with the fur of the sable and hence suited for a wealthy person, not a mourner (but with a pun on *sable*, "black," ironically suggesting mourning once again). **113–114 suffer . . . on** undergo oblivion. **115 For . . . forgot** (verse of a song occurring also in *Love's Labor's Lost*, 3.1.27–28. The hobbyhorse was a character made up to resemble a horse and rider, appearing in the morris dance and such May-game sports. This song laments the disappearance of such customs under pressure from the Puritans.) **117 this' miching mallico** this is sneaking mischief. **118 Belike** probably; **argument** plot. **119 counsel** secret.

HAMLET: Ay, or any show that you will show him. Be not you° ashamed to show, he'll not shame to tell you what it means.

OPHELIA: You are naught,° you are naught. I'll mark the play.

PROLOGUE: For us, and for our tragedy,
Here stooping° to your clemency,
We beg your hearing patiently. [*Exit.*]

HAMLET: Is this a prologue, or the posy of a ring?°

OPHELIA: 'Tis brief, my lord.

HAMLET: As woman's love.

Enter [*two* PLAYERS *as*] *King and Queen.*

PLAYER KING: Full thirty times hath Phoebus' cart° gone round
Neptune's salt wash° and Tellus'° orbèd ground,
And thirty dozen moons with borrowed° sheen
About the world have times twelve thirties been,
Since love our hearts and Hymen° did our hands
Unite commutual° in most sacred bands.°

PLAYER QUEEN: So many journeys may the sun and moon
Make us again count o'er ere love be done!
But, woe is me, you are so sick of late,
So far from cheer and from your former state,
That I distrust° you. Yet, though I distrust,
Discomfort° you, my lord, it nothing° must.
For women's fear and love hold quantity;°
In neither aught, or in extremity.°
Now, what my love is, proof° hath made you know,
And as my love is sized,° my fear is so.
Where love is great, the littlest doubts are fear;
Where little fears grow great, great love grows there.

PLAYER KING: Faith, I must leave thee, love, and shortly too;
My operant powers° their functions leave to do.°
And thou shalt live in this fair world behind,°
Honored, beloved; and haply one as kind
For husband shalt thou—

PLAYER QUEEN: O, confound the rest!
Such love must needs be treason in my breast.
In second husband let me be accurst!
None° wed the second but who° killed the first.

HAMLET: Wormwood,° wormwood.

122 Be not you provided you are not. **124 naught** indecent. (Ophelia is reacting to Hamlet's pointed remarks about not being ashamed to show all.) **126 stooping** bowing. **128 posy . . . ring** brief motto in verse inscribed in a ring. **131 Phoebus' cart** the sun-god's chariot, making its yearly cycle. **132 salt wash** the sea; **Tellus** goddess of the earth, of the **orbèd ground. 133 borrowed** i.e., reflected. **135 Hymen** god of matrimony. **136 commutual** mutually; **bands** bonds. **141 distrust** am anxious about. **142 Discomfort** distress; **nothing** not at all. **143 hold quantity** keep proportion with one another. **144 In . . . extremity** i.e., women fear and love either too little or too much, but the two, fear and love, are equal in either case. **145 proof** experience. **146 sized** in size. **150 operant powers** vital functions; **leave to do** cease to perform. **151 behind** after I have gone. **156 None** i.e., let no woman; **but who** except the one who. **157 Wormwood** i.e., how bitter. (Literally, a bitter-tasting plant.)

PLAYER QUEEN: The instances° that second marriage move°
Are base respects of thrift,° but none of love.
A second time I kill my husband dead
When second husband kisses me in bed.
PLAYER KING: I do believe you think what now you speak,
But what we do determine oft we break.
Purpose is but the slave to memory,°
Of violent birth, but poor validity,°
Which° now, like fruit unripe, sticks on the tree,
But fall unshaken when they mellow be.
Most necessary 'tis that we forget
To pay ourselves what to ourselves is debt.°
What to ourselves in passion we propose,
The passion ending, doth the purpose lose.
The violence of either grief or joy
Their own enactures° with themselves destroy.
Where joy most revels, grief doth most lament;
Grief joys, joy grieves, on slender accident.°
This world is not for aye,° nor 'tis not strange
That even our loves should with our fortunes change;
For 'tis a question left us yet to prove,
Whether love lead fortune, or else fortune love
The great man down,° you mark his favorite flies;
The poor advanced makes friends of enemies.°
And hitherto° doth love on fortune tend;°
For who not needs° shall never lack a friend,
And who in want° a hollow friend doth try°
Directly seasons him° his enemy.
But, orderly to end where I begun,
Our wills and fates do so contrary run°
That our devices still° are overthrown;
Our thoughts are ours, their ends° none of our own.
So think thou wilt no second husband wed,
But die thy thoughts when thy first lord is dead.
PLAYER QUEEN: Nor° earth to me give food, nor heaven light,
Sport and repose lock from me day and night,°
To desperation turn my trust and hope,

158 instances motives; **move** motivate. **159 base . . . thrift** ignoble considerations of material prosperity. **164 Purpose . . . memory** our good intentions are subject to forgetfulness. **165 validity** strength, durability. **166 Which** i.e., purpose. **168–169 Most . . . debt** it's inevitable that in time we forget the obligations we have imposed on ourselves. **173 enactures** fulfillments. **174–175 Where . . . accident** the capacity for extreme joy and grief go together, and often one extreme is instantly changed into its opposite on the slightest provocation. **176 aye** ever. **180 down** fallen in fortune. **181 The poor . . . enemies** when one of humble station is promoted, you see his enemies suddenly becoming his friends. **182 hitherto** up to this point in the argument, or, to this extent; **tend** attend. **183 who not needs** he who is not in need (of wealth). **184 who in want** he who, being in need; **try** test (his generosity). **185 seasons him** ripens him into. **187 Our . . . run** what we want and what we get go so contrarily. **188 devices still** intentions continually. **189 ends** results. **192 Nor** let neither. **193 Sport . . . night** may day deny me its pastimes and night its repose.

An anchor's cheer° in prison be my scope!°
Each opposite that blanks° the face of joy
Meet what I would have well and it destroy!°
Both here and hence° pursue me lasting strife
If, once a widow, ever I be wife!

HAMLET: If she should break it now!

PLAYER KING: 'Tis deeply sworn. Sweet, leave me here awhile;
My spirits° grow dull, and fain I would beguile
The tedious day with sleep.

PLAYER QUEEN: Sleep rock thy brain,
And never come mischance between us twain!

[*He sleeps.*] *Exit* [PLAYER QUEEN].

HAMLET: Madam, how like you this play?

QUEEN: The lady doth protest too much,° methinks.

HAMLET: O, but she'll keep her word.

KING: Have you heard the argument?° Is there no offense in 't?

HAMLET: No, no, they do but jest,° poison in jest. No offense° i' the world.

KING: What do you call the play?

HAMLET: *The Mousetrap.* Marry, how? Tropically.° This play is the image of a murder done in Vienna. Gonzago is the Duke's° name, his wife, Baptista. You shall see anon. 'Tis a knavish piece of work, but what of that? Your Majesty, and we that have free° souls, it touches us not. Let the galled jade° wince, our withers° are unwrung.°

Enter LUCIANUS.

This is one Lucianus, nephew to the King.

OPHELIA: You are as good as a chorus,° my lord.

HAMLET: I could interpret° between you and your love, if I could see the puppets dallying.°

OPHELIA: You are keen,° my lord, you are keen.

HAMLET: It would cost you a groaning to take off mine edge.

OPHELIA: Still better, and worse.°

195 anchor's cheer Anchorite's or hermit's fare; **my scope** the extent of my happiness. **196 blanks** causes to blanch or grow pale. **196–197 Each . . . destroy** may every adverse thing that causes the face of joy to turn pale meet and destroy everything that I desire to see prosper. **198 hence** in the life hereafter. **202 spirits** vital spirits. **206 doth . . . much** makes too many promises and protestations. **208 argument** plot. **209 jest** make believe. **208–209 offense . . . offense** cause for objection . . . actual injury, crime. **211 Tropically** figuratively. (The First Quarto reading, *trapically,* suggests a pun on *trap* in *Mousetrap.*) **212 Duke's** i.e., King's (A slip that may be due to Shakespeare's possible source, the alleged murder of the Duke of Urbino by Luigi Gonzaga in 1538.) **214 free** guiltless. **214–215 galled jade** horse whose hide is rubbed by saddle or harness. **215 withers** the part between the horse's shoulder blades; **unwrung** not rubbed sore. **217 chorus** (In many Elizabethan plays, the forthcoming action was explained by an actor known as the "chorus"; at a puppet show, the actor who spoke the dialogue was known as an "interpreter," as indicated by the lines following.) **218 interpret** (1) ventriloquize the dialogue, as in a puppet show, (2) act as pander. **218–219 puppets dallying** (with suggestion of sexual play, continued in *keen,* "sexually aroused," *groaning,* "moaning in pregnancy," and *edge,* "sexual desire" or "impetuosity.") **220 keen** sharp, bitter. **222 Still . . . worse** more keen, always *bettering* what other people say with witty wordplay, but at the same time more offensive.

HAMLET: So° you mis-take° your husbands. Begin, murder; leave thy damnable faces and begin. Come, the croaking raven doth bellow for revenge.

LUCIANUS: Thoughts black, hands apt, drugs fit, and time agreeing,
Confederate season,° else° no creature seeing,°
Thou mixture rank, of midnight weeds collected,
With Hecate's ban° thrice blasted, thrice infected,
Thy natural magic and dire property°
On wholesome life usurp immediately.

[*He pours the poison into the sleeper's ear.*]

HAMLET: 'A poisons him i' the garden for his estate.° His° name's Gonzago. The story is extant, and written in very choice Italian. You shall see anon how the murderer gets the love of Gonzago's wife.

[CLAUDIUS *rises.*]

OPHELIA: The King rises.
HAMLET: What, frighted with false fire?°
QUEEN: How fares my lord?
POLONIUS: Give o'er the play.
KING: Give me some light. Away!
POLONIUS: Lights, lights, lights!

Exeunt all but HAMLET *and* HORATIO.

HAMLET:

"Why,° let the strucken deer go weep,
The hart ungallèd° play.
For some must watch,° while some must sleep;
Thus runs the world away."°

Would not this,° sir, and a forest of feathers°—if the rest of my fortunes turn Turk with° me—with two Provincial roses° on my razed° shoes, get me a fellowship in a cry° of players?°

HORATIO: Half a share.
HAMLET: A whole one, I.

"For thou dost know, O Damon° dear,
This realm dismantled° was

223 So even thus (in marriage); **mis-take** take falseheartedly and cheat on. (The marriage vows say "for better, for worse.") **226 Confederate season** the time and occasion conspiring (to assist the murderer); **else** otherwise; **seeing** seeing me. **228 Hecate's ban** the curse of Hecate, the goddess of witchcraft. **229 dire property** baleful quality. **231 estate** i.e., the kingship; **His** i.e., the King's. **235 false fire** the blank discharge of a gun loaded with powder but no shot. **240–243 Why . . . away** (probably from an old ballad, with allusion to the popular belief that a wounded deer retires to weep and die; compare with *As You Like It*, 2.1.33–66.) **241 ungallèd** unafflicted. **242 watch** remain awake. **243 Thus . . . away** thus the world goes. **244 this** i.e., the play; **feathers** (allusion to the plumes that Elizabethan actors were fond of wearing.) **245 turn Turk with** turn renegade against, go back on; **Provincial roses** rosettes of ribbon, named for roses grown in a part of France; **razed** with ornamental slashing. **246 cry** pack (of hounds); **fellowship . . . players** partnership in a theatrical company. **249 Damon** the friend of Pythias, as Horatio is friend of Hamlet; or, a traditional pastoral name. **250 dismantled** stripped, divested.

Of Jove himself, and now reigns here
A very, very—pajock."°

HORATIO: You might have rhymed.

HAMLET: O good Horatio, I'll take the ghost's word for a thousand pound. Didst perceive?

HORATIO: Very well, my lord.

HAMLET: Upon the talk of the poisoning?

HORATIO: I did very well note him.

Enter ROSENCRANTZ *and* GUILDENSTERN.

HAMLET: Aha! Come, some music! Come, the recorders.°

"For if the King like not the comedy,
Why then, belike, he likes it not, perdy."°

Come, some music.

GUILDENSTERN: Good my lord, vouchsafe me a word with you.

HAMLET: Sir, a whole history.

GUILDENSTERN: The King, sir—

HAMLET: Ay, sir, what of him?

GUILDENSTERN: Is in his retirement° marvelous distempered.°

HAMLET: With drink, sir?

GUILDENSTERN: No, my lord, with choler.°

HAMLET: Your wisdom should show itself more richer to signify this to the doctor, for for me to put him to his purgation° would perhaps plunge him into more choler.

GUILDENSTERN: Good my lord, put your discourse into some frame° and start° not so wildly from my affair.

HAMLET: I am tame, sir. Pronounce.

GUILDENSTERN: The Queen, your mother, in most great affliction of spirit, hath sent me to you.

HAMLET: You are welcome.

GUILDENSTERN: Nay, good my lord, this courtesy is not of the right breed.° If it shall please you to make me a wholesome answer, I will do your mother's commandment; if not, your pardon° and my return shall be the end of my business.

HAMLET: Sir, I cannot.

ROSENCRANTZ: What, my lord?

250–252 This realm . . . pajock i.e., Jove, representing divine authority and justice, has abandoned this realm to its own devices, leaving in his stead only a peacock or vain pretender to virtue (though the rhyme-word expected in place of *pajock* or "peacock" suggests that the realm is now ruled over by an "ass"). **259 recorders** wind instruments of the flute kind. **261 perdy** (a corruption of the French *par dieu*, "by God.") **267 retirement** withdrawal to his chambers; **distempered** out of humor. (But Hamlet deliberately plays on the wider application to any illness of mind or body, as in line 298, especially to drunkenness.) **269 choler** anger. (But Hamlet takes the word in its more basic humoral sense of "bilious disorder.") **271 purgation** (Hamlet hints at something going beyond medical treatment to bloodletting and the extraction of confession.) **273 frame** order; **start** shy or jump away (like a horse; the opposite of *tame* in line 275). **279 breed** (1) kind, (2) breeding, manners. **281 pardon** permission to depart.

HAMLET: Make you a wholesome answer; my wit's diseased. But, sir, such answer as I can make, you shall command, or rather, as you say, my mother. Therefore no more, but to the matter. My mother, you say—

ROSENCRANTZ: Then thus she says: your behavior hath struck her into amazement and admiration.°

HAMLET: O wonderful son, that can so stonish a mother! But is there no sequel at the heels of this mother's admiration? Impart.

ROSENCRANTZ: She desires to speak with you in her closet° ere you go to bed.

HAMLET: We shall obey, were she ten times our mother. Have you any further trade with us?

ROSENCRANTZ: My lord, you once did love me.

HAMLET: And do still, by these pickers and stealers.°

ROSENCRANTZ: Good my lord, what is your cause of distemper? You do surely bar the door upon your own liberty° if you deny° your griefs to your friend.

HAMLET: Sir, I lack advancement.

ROSENCRANTZ: How can that be, when you have the voice of the King himself for your succession in Denmark?

HAMLET: Ay, sir, but "While the grass grows"°—the proverb is something° musty.

Enter the PLAYERS° *with recorders.*

O, the recorders. Let me see one. [*He takes a recorder.*] To withdraw° with you: why do you go about to recover the wind° of me, as if you would drive me into a toil?°

GUILDENSTERN: O, my lord, if my duty be too bold, my love is too unmannerly.°

HAMLET: I do not well understand that.° Will you play upon this pipe?

GUILDENSTERN: My lord, I cannot.

HAMLET: I pray you.

GUILDENSTERN: Believe me, I cannot.

HAMLET: I do beseech you.

GUILDENSTERN: I know no touch of it, my lord.

HAMLET: It is as easy as lying. Govern these ventages° with your fingers and thumb, give it breath with your mouth, and it will discourse most eloquent music. Look you, these are the stops.

GUILDENSTERN: But these cannot I command to any utterance of harmony. I have not the skill.

HAMLET: Why, look you now, how unworthy a thing you make of me! You would play upon me, you would seem to know my stops, you would pluck out the heart of my mystery, you would sound° me from my lowest note to the top of my compass,° and there is much music, excellent voice, in this little organ,° yet cannot you make it speak. 'Sblood, do you think I am

289 admiration bewilderment. **292 closet** private chamber. **296 pickers and stealers** i.e., hands. (So called from the catechism, "to keep my hands from picking and stealing.") **298 liberty** i.e., being freed from *distemper*, line 297, but perhaps with a veiled threat as well; **deny** refuse to share. **302 While . . . grows** (the rest of the proverb is "the silly horse starves"; Hamlet may not live long enough to succeed to the kingdom.); **something** somewhat; **s.d. Players** actors. **304 withdraw** speak privately; **recover the wind** get to the windward side (thus driving the game into the *toil*, or "net"). **305 toil** snare. **306 if . . . unmannerly** if I am using an unmannerly boldness, it is my love that occasions it. **307 I . . . that** i.e., I don't understand how genuine love can be unmannerly. **313 ventages** finger-holes or *stops* (line 319) of the recorder. **320 sound** (1) fathom, (2) produce sound in. **321 compass** range (of voice). **322 organ** musical instrument.

easier to be played on than a pipe? Call me what instrument you will, though you can fret° me, you cannot play upon me.

Enter POLONIUS.

God bless you, sir!

POLONIUS: My lord, the Queen would speak with you, and presently.°

HAMLET: Do you see yonder cloud that's almost in shape of a camel?

POLONIUS: By the Mass and 'tis, like a camel indeed.

HAMLET: Methinks it is like a weasel.

POLONIUS: It is backed like a weasel.

HAMLET: Or like a whale.

POLONIUS: Very like a whale.

HAMLET: Then I will come to my mother by and by.° [*Aside.*] They fool me° to the top of my bent.°—I will come by and by.

POLONIUS: I will say so. [*Exit.*]

HAMLET: "By and by" is easily said. Leave me, friends.

[*Exeunt all but* HAMLET.]

'Tis now the very witching time° of night,
When churchyards yawn and hell itself breathes out
Contagion to this world. Now could I drink hot blood
And do such bitter business as the day
Would quake to look on. Soft, now to my mother.
O heart, lose not thy nature!° Let not ever
The soul of Nero° enter this firm bosom.
Let me be cruel, not unnatural;
I will speak daggers to her, but use none.
My tongue and soul in this be hypocrites:
How in my words soever° she be shent,°
To give them seals° never my soul consent! *Exit.*

[3.3]

Enter KING, ROSENCRANTZ, *and* GUILDENSTERN.

KING: I like him° not, nor stands it safe with us
To let his madness range. Therefore prepare you.
I your commission will forthwith dispatch,°
And he to England shall along with you.
The terms of our estate° may not endure
Hazard so near 's as doth hourly grow
Out of his brows.°

GUILDENSTERN: We will ourselves provide.
Most holy and religious fear° it is

324 fret irritate (with a quibble on *fret,* meaning the piece of wood, gut, or metal that regulates the fingering on an instrument). **326 presently** at once. **333 by and by** quite soon. **fool me** trifle with me, humor my fooling. **334 top of my bent** limit of my ability or endurance. (Literally, the extent to which a bow may be bent.) **337 witching time** time when spells are cast and evil is abroad. **342 nature** natural feeling. **343 Nero** murderer of his mother, Agrippina. **347 How . . . soever** however much by my words; **shent** rebuked. **348 give them seals** i.e., confirm them with deeds. **[3.3] Location: The castle. 1 him** i.e., his behavior. **3 dispatch** prepare, cause to be drawn up. **5 terms of our estate** circumstances of my royal position. **7 Out of his brows** i.e., from his brain, in the form of plots and threats. **8 religious fear** sacred concern.

To keep those many many bodies safe
That live and feed upon Your Majesty.

ROSENCRANTZ: The single and peculiar° life is bound
With all the strength and armor of the mind
To keep itself from noyance,° but much more
That spirit upon whose weal depends and rests
The lives of many. The cess° of majesty
Dies not alone, but like a gulf° doth draw
What's near it with it; or it is a massy° wheel
Fixed on the summit of the highest mount,
To whose huge spokes ten thousand lesser things
Are mortised° and adjoined, which, when it falls,°
Each small annexment, petty consequence,°
Attends° the boisterous ruin. Never alone
Did the King sigh, but with a general groan.

KING: Arm° you, I pray you, to this speedy voyage,
For we will fetters put about this fear,
Which now goes too free-footed.

ROSENCRANTZ: We will haste us.

Exeunt gentlemen [ROSENCRANTZ *and* GUILDENSTERN].

Enter POLONIUS.

POLONIUS: My lord, he's going to his mother's closet.
Behind the arras° I'll convey myself
To hear the process.° I'll warrant she'll tax him home,°
And, as you said—and wisely was it said—
'Tis meet° that some more audience than a mother,
Since nature makes them partial, should o'erhear
The speech, of vantage.° Fare you well, my liege.
I'll call upon you ere you go to bed
And tell you what I know.

KING: Thanks, dear my lord. *Exit* [POLONIUS].
O, my offense is rank! It smells to heaven.
It hath the primal eldest curse° upon't,
A brother's murder. Pray can I not,
Though inclination be as sharp as will;°
My stronger guilt defeats my strong intent,
And like a man to double business bound°
I stand in pause where I shall first begin,

11 single and peculiar individual and private. **13 noyance** harm. **15 cess** decease, cessation. **16 gulf** whirlpool. **17 massy** massive. **20 mortised** fastened (as with a fitted joint); **when it falls** i.e., when it descends, like the wheel of Fortune, bringing a king down with it. **21 Each . . . consequence** i.e., every hanger-on and unimportant person or thing connected with the King. **22 Attends** participates in. **24 Arm** prepare. **28 arras** screen of tapestry placed around the walls of household apartments. (On the Elizabethan stage, the arras was presumably over a door or discovery space in the tiring-house facade.) **29 process** proceedings; **tax him home** reprove him severely. **31 meet** fitting. **33 of vantage** from an advantageous place, or, in addition. **37 the primal eldest curse** the curse of Cain, the first murderer; he killed his brother Abel. **39 Though . . . will** though my desire is as strong as my determination. **41 bound** (1) destined, (2) obliged. (The King wants to repent and still enjoy what he has gained.)

And both neglect. What if this cursèd hand
Were thicker than itself with brother's blood,
Is there not rain enough in the sweet heavens
To wash it white as snow? Whereto serves mercy
But to confront the visage of offense?°
And what's in prayer but this twofold force,
To be forestallèd° ere we come to fall,
Or pardoned being down? Then I'll look up.
My fault is past. But O, what form of prayer
Can serve my turn? "Forgive me my foul murder"?
That cannot be, since I am still possessed
Of those effects for which I did the murder:
My crown, mine own ambition, and my Queen.
May one be pardoned and retain th' offense?°
In the corrupted currents° of this world
Offense's gilded hand° may shove by° justice,
And oft 'tis seen the wicked prize° itself
Buys out the law. But 'tis not so above.
There° is no shuffling,° there the action lies°
In his° true nature, and we ourselves compelled,
Even to the teeth and forehead° of our faults,
To give in° evidence. What then? What rests?°
Try what repentance can. What can it not?
Yet what can it, when one cannot repent?
O wretched state, O bosom black as death,
limèd° soul that, struggling to be free,
Art more engaged!° Help, angels! Make assay.°
Bow, stubborn knees, and heart with strings of steel,
Be soft as sinews of the newborn babe!
All may be well. [*He kneels.*]

Enter HAMLET.

HAMLET: Now might I do it pat,° now 'a is a-praying;
And now I'll do 't. [*He draws his sword.*] And so 'a goes to heaven,
And so am I revenged. That would be scanned:°
A villain kills my father, and for that,
I, his sole son, do this same villain send
To heaven.
Why, this is hire and salary, not revenge.
'A took my father grossly, full of bread,°

46–47 Whereto . . . offense What function does mercy serve other than to meet sin face to face? **49 forestallèd** prevented (from sinning). **56 th' offense** the thing for which one offended. **57 currents** courses. **58 gilded hand** hand offering gold as a bribe; **shove by** thrust aside. **59 wicked prize** prize won by wickendness. **61 There** i.e., in heaven; **shuffling** escape by trickery; **the action lies** the accusation is made manifest. (A legal metaphor.) **62 his** its. **63 to the teeth and forehead** face to face, concealing nothing. **64 give in** provide; **rests** remains. **68 limèd** caught as with birdlime, a sticky substance used to ensnare birds. **69 engaged** entangled; **assay** trial. (Said to himself.) **73 pat** opportunely. **75 would be scanned** needs to be looked into, or, would be interpreted as follows. **80 grossly, full of bread** i.e., enjoying his worldly pleasures rather than fasting. (See Ezekiel 16:49.)

With all his crimes broad blown,° as flush° as May;
And how his audit° stands who knows save° heaven?
But in our circumstance and course of thought°
'Tis heavy with him. And am I then revenged,
To take him in the purging of his soul
When he is fit and seasoned° for his passage?
No!
Up, sword, and know thou a more horrid hent.°
[*He puts up his sword.*]
When he is drunk asleep, or in his rage,°
Or in th' incestuous pleasure of his bed,
At game,° a-swearing, or about some act
That has no relish° of salvation in 't—
Then trip him, that his heels may kick at heaven,
And that his soul may be as damned and black
As hell, whereto it goes. My mother stays.°
This physic° but prolongs thy sickly days. *Exit.*

KING: My words fly up, my thoughts remain below.
Words without thoughts never to heaven go. *Exit.*

[3.4]

Enter [QUEEN] GERTRUDE *and* POLONIUS.

POLONIUS: 'A will come straight. Look you lay home° to him.
Tell him his pranks have been too broad° to bear with,
And that Your Grace hath screened and stood between
Much heat° and him. I'll shroud° me even here.
Pray you, be round° with him.

HAMLET [*within*]: Mother, Mother, Mother!

QUEEN: I'll warrant you, fear me not.
Withdraw, I hear him coming. [POLONIUS *hides behind the arras.*]

Enter HAMLET.

HAMLET: Now, Mother, what's the matter?

QUEEN: Hamlet, thou hast thy father° much offended.

HAMLET: Mother, you have my father much offended.

QUEEN: Come, come, you answer with an idle° tongue.

HAMLET: Go, go, you question with a wicked tongue.

QUEEN: Why, how now, Hamlet?

HAMLET: What's the matter now?

81 crimes broad blown sins in full bloom; **flush** vigorous. **82 audit** account; **save** except for. **83 in . . . thought** As we see it from our mortal perspective. **86 seasoned** matured, readied. **88 know . . . hent** await to be grasped by me on a more horrid occasion; **hent** act of seizing. **89 drunk . . . rage** dead drunk, or in a fit of sexual passions. **91 game** gambling. **92 relish** trace, savor. **95 stays** awaits (me). **96 physic** purging (by prayer), or, Hamlet's postponement of the killing. **[3.4] Location: The Queen's private chamber. 1 lay home** thrust to the heart, reprove him soundly. **2 broad** unrestrained. **4 Much heat** i.e., the King's anger; **shround** conceal. (With ironic fitness to Polonius' imminent death. The word is only in the First Quarto: the Second Quarto and the Folio read "silence.") **5 round** blunt. **10 thy father** i.e., your stepfather, Claudius. **12 idle** foolish.

QUEEN: Have you forgot me?°
HAMLET: No, by the rood,° not so:
You are the Queen your husband's brother's wife,
And—would it were not so!—you are my mother.
QUEEN: Nay, then, I'll set those to you that can speak.°
HAMLET: Come, come, and sit you down; you shall not budge.
You go not till I set you up a glass
Where you may see the inmost part of you.
QUEEN: What wilt thou do? Thou wilt not murder me?
Help, ho!
POLONIUS [*behind the arras*]: What ho! Help!
HAMLET [*drawing*]: How now? A rat? Dead for a ducat,° dead!
[*He thrusts his rapier through the arras.*]
POLONIUS [*behind the arras*]: O, I am slain! [*He falls and dies.*]
QUEEN: O me, what hast thou done?
HAMLET: Nay, I know not. Is it the King?
QUEEN: O, what a rash and bloody deed is this!
HAMLET: A bloody deed—almost as bad, good Mother,
As kill a King, and marry with his brother.
QUEEN: As kill a King!
HAMLET: Ay, lady, it was my word.
[*He parts the arras and discovers* POLONIUS.]
Thou wretched, rash, intruding fool, farewell!
I took thee for thy better. Take thy fortune.
Thou find'st to be too busy° is some danger.—
Leave wringing of your hands. Peace, sit you down,
And let me wring your heart, for so I shall,
If it be made of penetrable stuff,
If damnèd custom° have not brazed° it so
That it be proof° and bulwark against sense.°
QUEEN: What have I done, that thou dar'st wag thy tongue
In noise so rude against me?
HAMLET: Such an act
That blurs the grace and blush of modesty,
Calls virtue hypocrite, takes off the rose
From the fair forehead of an innocent love
And sets a blister° there, makes marriage vows
As false as dicers' oaths. O, such a deed
As from the body of contraction° plucks
The very soul, and sweet religion makes°
A rhapsody° of words. Heaven's face does glow
O'er this solidity and compound mass

15 forgot me i.e., forgotten that I am your mother; **rood** cross of Christ. **18 speak** i.e., to someone so rude. **25 Dead for a ducat** i.e., I bet a ducat he's dead; or, a ducat is his life's fee. **34 busy** nosey. **38 damnèd custom** habitual wickedness; **brazed** brazened, hardened. **39 proof** armor; **sense** feeling. **45 sets a blister** i.e., brands as a harlot. **47 contraction** the marriage contract. **48 sweet religion makes** i.e., makes marriage vows. **49 rhapsody** senseless string.

With tristful visage, as against the doom,
Is thought-sick at the act.°

QUEEN: Ay me, what act,
That roars so loud and thunders in the index?°

HAMLET [*showing her two likenesses*]: Look here upon this picture, and on this,
The counterfeit presentment° of two brothers.
See what a grace was seated on this brow:
Hyperion's° curls, the front° of Jove himself,
An eye like Mars° to threaten and command,
A station° like the herald Mercury°
New-lighted° on a heaven-kissing hill—
A combination and a form indeed
Where every god did seem to set his seal°
To give the world assurance of a man.
This was your husband. Look you now what follows:
Here is your husband, like a mildewed ear,°
Blasting° his wholesome brother. Have you eyes?
Could you on this fair mountain leave° to feed
And batten° on this moor?° Ha, have you eyes?
You cannot call it love, for at your age
The heyday° in the blood° is tame, it's humble,
And waits upon the judgment, and what judgment
Would step from this to this? Sense,° sure, you have,
Else could you not have motion, but sure that sense
Is apoplexed,° for madness would not err,°
Nor sense to ecstasy was ne'er so thralled,
But° it reserved some quantity of choice
To serve in such a difference.° What devil was 't
That thus hath cozened° you at hoodman-blind?°
Eyes without feeling, feeling without sight,
Ears without hands or eyes, smelling sans° all
Or but a sickly part of one true sense
Could not so mope.° O shame, where is thy blush?
Rebellious hell,

49–52 Heaven's . . . act Heaven's face blushes at this solid world compounded of the various elements, with sorrowful face as though the day of doom were near, and is sick with horror at the deed (i.e., Gertrude's marriage). **54 index** table of contents, prelude or preface. **55 counterfeit presentment** portrayed representation. **57 Hyperion's** the sungod's; **front** brow. **58 Mars** god of war. **59 station** manner of standing; **Mercury** winged messenger of the gods. **60 New-lighted** newly alighted. **62 set his seal** i.e., affix his approval. **65 ear** i.e., of grain. **66 Blasting** blighting. **67 leave** cease. **68 batten** gorge; **moor** barren or marshy ground (suggesting also "dark-skinned"). **70 heyday** state of excitement; **blood** passion. **72 Sense** perception through the five senses (the functions of the middle sensible soul). **74 apoplexed** paralyzed (Hamlet goes on to explain that, without such a paralysis of will, mere madness would not so err, nor would the five senses so enthrall themselves to **ecstasy** or lunacy; even such deranged states of mind would be able to make the obvious choice between Hamlet Senior and Claudius.); **err** so err. **76 But** but that. **77 To . . . difference** to help in making a choice between two such men. **78 cozened** cheated; **hoodman-blind** blindman's buff. (In this game, says Hamlet, the devil must have pushed Claudius toward Gertrude while she was blind-folded.) **80 sans** without. **82 mope** be dazed, act aimlessly.

If thou canst mutine° in a matron's bones,
To flaming youth let virtue be as wax
And melt in her own fire.° Proclaim no shame
When the compulsive ardor gives the charge,
Since frost itself as actively doth burn,
And reason panders will.°

QUEEN: O Hamlet, speak no more!
Thou turn'st mine eyes into my very soul,
And there I see such black and grainèd° spots
As will not leave their tinct.°

HAMLET: Nay, but to live
In the rank sweat of an enseamèd° bed,
Stewed° in corruption, honeying and making love
Over the nasty sty!

QUEEN: O, speak to me no more!
These words like daggers enter in my ears.
No more, sweet Hamlet!

HAMLET: A murderer and a villain,
A slave that is not twentieth part the tithe°
Of your precedent lord,° a vice° of kings,
A cutpurse of the empire and the rule,
That from a shelf the precious diadem stole
And put it in his pocket!

QUEEN: No more!

Enter GHOST [*in his nightgown*].

HAMLET: A king of shreds and patches°—
Save me, and hover o'er me with your wings,
You heavenly guards! What would your gracious figure?

QUEEN: Alas, he's mad!

HAMLET: Do you not come your tardy son to chide,
That, lapsed° in time and passion, lets go by
Th' important° acting of your dread command?
O, say!

GHOST: Do not forget. This visitation
Is but to whet thy almost blunted purpose.
But look, amazement° on thy mother sits.
O, step between her and her fighting soul!
Conceit° in weakest bodies strongest works.
Speak to her, Hamlet.

84 mutine incite mutiny. **85–86 be as wax . . . fire** melt like a candle or stick of sealing wax held over the candle flame. **86–89 Proclaim . . . will** call it no shameful business when the compelling ardor of youth delivers the attack, i.e., commits lechery, since the *frost* of advanced age burns with as active a fire of lust and reason perverts itself by fomenting lust rather than restraining it. **92 grainèd** dyed in grain, indelible. **93 leave their tinct** surrender their color. **94 enseamèd** saturated in the grease and filth of passionate lovemaking. **95 Stewed** soaked, bathed (with a suggestion of "stew," brothel). **100 tithe** tenth part. **101 precedent lord** former husband; **vice** buffoon. (A reference to the Vice of the morality plays.) **106 shreds and patches** i.e., motley, the traditional costume of the clown or fool. **111 lapsed** delaying. **112 important** importunate, urgent. **116 amazement** distraction. **118 Conceit** imagination.

HAMLET: How is it with you, lady?
QUEEN: Alas, how is 't with you,
That you do bend your eye on vacancy,
And with th' incorporal° air do hold discourse?
Forth at your eyes your spirits wildly peep,
And, as the sleeping soldiers in th' alarm,°
Your bedded° hair, like life in excrements,°
Start up and stand on end. O gentle son,
Upon the heat and flame of thy distemper°
Sprinkle cool patience. Whereon do you look?
HAMLET: On him, on him! Look you how pale he glares!
His form and cause conjoined,° preaching to stones,
Would make them capable.°—Do not look upon me,
Lest with this piteous action you convert
My stern effects.° Then what I have to do
Will want true color—tears perchance for blood.°
QUEEN: To whom do you speak this?
HAMLET: Do you see nothing there?
QUEEN: Nothing at all, yet all that is I see.
HAMLET: Nor did you nothing hear?
QUEEN: No, nothing but ourselves.
HAMLET: Why, look you there, look how it steals away!
My father, in his habit° as° he lived!
Look where he goes even now out at the portal! *Exit* GHOST.
QUEEN: This is the very° coinage of your brain.
This bodiless creation ecstasy
Is very cunning in.°
HAMLET: Ecstasy?
My pulse as yours doth temperately keep time,
And makes as healthful music. It is not madness
That I have uttered. Bring me to the test,
And I the matter will reword,° which madness
Would gambol° from. Mother, for love of grace,
Lay not that flattering unction° to your soul
That not your trespass but my madness speaks.
It will but skin° and film the ulcerous place,
Whiles rank corruption, mining° all within,
Infects unseen. Confess yourself to heaven,
Repent what's past, avoid what is to come,

122 incorporal immaterial. **124 as . . . alarm** like soldiers called out of sleep by an alarum. **125 bedded** laid flat; **like life in excrements** i.e., as though hair, an outgrowth of the body, had a life of its own. (Hair was thought to be lifeless because it lacks sensation, and so its standing on end would be unnatural and ominous.) **127 distemper** disorder. **130 His . . . conjoined** his appearance joined to his cause for speaking. **131 capable** receptive. **132–133 convert . . . effects** divert me from my stern duty. **134 want . . . blood** lack plausibility so that (with a play on the normal sense of *color*) I shall shed colorless tears instead of blood. **141 habit** clothes; **as** as when. **143 very** mere. **144–145 This . . . in** madness is skillful in creating this kind of hallucination. **150 reword** repeat word for word. **151 gambol** skip away. **152 unction** ointment. **154 skin** grow a skin for. **155 mining** working under the surface.

And do not spread the compost° on the weeds
To make them ranker. Forgive me this my virtue;°
For in the fatness° of these pursy° times
Virtue itself of vice must pardon beg,
Yea, curb° and woo for leave° to do him good.

QUEEN: O Hamlet, thou hast cleft my heart in twain.

HAMLET: O, throw away the worser part of it,
And live the purer with the other half.
Good night. But go not to my uncle's bed;
Assume a virtue, if you have it not.
That monster, custom, who all sense doth eat,°
Of habits devil,° is angel yet in this,
That to the use of actions fair and good
He likewise gives a frock or livery°
That aptly° is put on. Refrain tonight,
And that shall lend a kind of easiness
To the next abstinence; the next more easy;
For use° almost can change the stamp of nature,°
And either° . . . the devil, or throw him out
With wondrous potency. Once more, good night;
And when you are desirous to be blest,
I'll blessing beg of you.° For this same lord, [*pointing to* POLONIUS.]
I do repent; but heaven hath pleased it so
To punish me with this, and this with me,
That I must be their scourge and minister.°
I will bestow° him, and will answer° well
The death I gave him. So, again, good night.
I must be cruel only to be kind.
This° bad begins, and worse remains behind.°
One word more, good lady.

QUEEN: What shall I do?

HAMLET: Not this by no means that I bid you do:
Let the bloat° King tempt you again to bed,
Pinch wanton° on your cheek, call you his mouse,
And let him, for a pair of reechy° kisses,
Or paddling° in your neck with his damned fingers,

158 compost manure. **159 this my virtue** my virtuous talk in reproving you. **160 fatness** grossness; **pursy** flabby, out of shape. **162 curb** bow, bend the knee; **leave** permission. **168 who . . . eat** which consumes all proper or natural feeling, all sensibility. **169 Of habits devil** devil-like in prompting evil habits. **171 livery** an outer appearance, a customary garb (and hence a predisposition easily assumed in time of stress). **172 aptly** readily. **175 use** habit; **the stamp of nature** our inborn traits. **176 And either** (a defective line, usually emended by inserting the word *master* after *either*, following the Fourth Quarto and early editors.) **178–179 when . . . you** i.e., when you are ready to be penitent and seek God's blessing, I will ask your blessing as a dutiful son should. **182 their scourge and minister** i.e., agent of heavenly retribution. (By *scourge*, Hamlet also suggests that he himself will eventually suffer punishment in the process of fulfilling heaven's will.) **183 bestow** stow, dispose of; **answer** account or pay for. **186 This** i.e., the killing of Polonius; **behind** to come. **189 bloat** bloated. **190 Pinch wanton** i.e., leave his love pinches on your cheeks, branding you as wanton. **191 reechy** dirty, filthy. **192 paddling** fingering amorously.

Make you to ravel all this matter out°
That I essentially am not in madness,
But mad in craft.° 'Twere good° you let him know,
For who that's but a Queen, fair, sober, wise,
Would from a paddock,° from a bat, a gib,°
Such dear concernings° hide? Who would do so?
No, in despite of sense and secrecy,°
Unpeg the basket° on the house's top,
Let the birds fly, and like the famous ape,°
To try conclusions,° in the basket creep
And break your own neck down.°

QUEEN: Be thou assured, if words be made of breath,
And breath of life, I have no life to breathe
What thou hast said to me.

HAMLET: I must to England. You know that?

QUEEN: Alack,
I had forgot. 'Tis so concluded on.

HAMLET: There's letters sealed, and my two schoolfellows,
Whom I will trust as I will adders fanged,
They bear the mandate; they must sweep my way
And marshal me to knavery.° Let it work.°
For 'tis the sport to have the enginer°
Hoist with° his own petard,° and 't shall go hard
But I will° delve one yard below their mines°
And blow them at the moon. O, 'tis most sweet
When in one line° two crafts° directly meet.
This man shall set me packing.°
I'll lug the guts into the neighbor room.
Mother, good night indeed. This counselor
Is now most still, most secret, and most grave,
Who was in life a foolish prating knave.—
Come, sir, to draw toward an end° with you.—
Good night, Mother.

Exeunt [*separately,* HAMLET *dragging in* POLONIUS].

193 ravel . . . out unravel, disclose. **195 in craft** by cunning; **good** (said sarcastically; also the following eight lines.) **197 paddock** toad; **gib** tomcat. **198 dear concernings** important affairs. **199 sense and secrecy** secrecy that common sense requires. **200 Unpeg the basket** open the cage, i.e., let out the secret. **201 famous ape** (in a story now lost.) **202 try conclusions** test the outcome (in which the ape apparently enters a cage from which birds have been released and then tries to fly out of the cage as they have done, falling to its death). **203 down** in the fall; utterly. **211–212 sweep . . . knavery** sweep a path before me and conduct me to some *knavery* or treachery prepared for me; **work** proceed. **213 enginer** maker of military contrivances. **214 Hoist with** blown up by; **petard** an explosive used to blow in a door or make a breach. **214–215 't shall . . . will** unless luck is against me, I will; **mines** tunnels used in warfare to undermine the enemy's emplacements; Hamlet will countermine by going under their mines. **217 in one line** i.e., mines and countermines on a collision course, or the countermines directly below the mines; **crafts** acts of guile, plots. **218 set me packing** set me to making schemes, and set me to lugging (him), and, also, send me off in a hurry. **223 draw . . . end** finish up (with a pun on *draw,* "pull").

[4.1]

Enter KING *and* QUEEN,° *with* ROSENCRANTZ *and* GUILDENSTERN.

KING: There's matter° in these sighs, these profound heaves.°
You must translate; 'tis fit we understand them.
Where is your son?
QUEEN: Bestow this place on us a little while.
[*Exeunt* ROSENCRANTZ *and* GUILDENSTERN.]
Ah, mine own lord, what have I seen tonight!
KING: What, Gertrude? How does Hamlet?
QUEEN: Mad as the sea and wind when both contend
Which is the mightier. In his lawless fit,
Behind the arras hearing something stir,
Whips out his rapier, cries, "A rat, a rat!"
And in this brainish apprehension° kills
The unseen good old man.
KING: O heavy° deed!
It had been so with us,° had we been there.
His liberty is full of threats to all—
To you yourself, to us, to everyone.
Alas, how shall this bloody deed be answered?°
It will be laid to us, whose providence°
Should have kept short,° restrained, and out of haunt°
This mad young man. But so much was our love,
We would not understand what was most fit,
But, like the owner of a foul disease,
To keep it from divulging,° let it feed
Even on the pith of life. Where is he gone?
QUEEN: To draw apart the body he hath killed,
O'er whom his very madness, like some ore°
Among a mineral° of metals base,
Shows itself pure: 'a weeps for what is done.
KING: O Gertrude, come away!
The sun no sooner shall the mountains touch
But we will ship him hence, and this vile deed
We must with all our majesty and skill
Both countenance° and excuse.—Ho, Guildenstern!

Enter ROSENCRANTZ *and* GUILDENSTERN.

Friends both, go join you with some further aid.
Hamlet in madness hath Polonius slain,

[4.1] Location: The castle. s.d. Enter . . . Queen (Some editors argue that Gertrude never exits in 3.4 and that the scene is continuous here, as suggested in the Folio, but the Second Quarto marks an entrance for her and at line 35 Claudius speaks of Gertrude's *closet* as though it were elsewhere. A short time has elapsed, during which the King has become aware of her highly wrought emotional state.) **1 matter** significance; **heaves** heavy sighs. **11 brainish apprehension** headstrong conception. **12 heavy** grievous. **13 us** i.e., me. (The royal "we"; also in line 15.) **16 answered** explained. **17 providence** foresight. **18 short** i.e., on a short tether; **out of haunt** secluded. **22 divulging** becoming evident. **25 ore** vein of gold. **26 mineral** mine. **32 countenance** put the best face on.

And from his mother's closet hath he dragged him.
Go seek him out, speak fair, and bring the body
Into the chapel. I pray you, haste in this.

[*Exeunt* ROSENCRANTZ *and* GUILDENSTERN.]

Come, Gertrude, we'll call up our wisest friends
And let them know both what we mean to do
And what's untimely done°. . . . . . .
Whose whisper o'er the world's diameter,°
As level° as the cannon to his blank,°
Transports his poisoned shot, may miss our name
And hit the woundless° air. O, come away!
My soul is full of discord and dismay. *Exeunt.*

[4.2]

Enter HAMLET.

HAMLET: Safely stowed.

ROSENCRANTZ, GUILDENSTERN [*within*]: Hamlet! Lord Hamlet!

HAMLET: But soft, what noise? Who calls on Hamlet? O, here they come.

Enter ROSENCRANTZ *and* GUILDENSTERN.

ROSENCRANTZ: What have you done, my lord, with the dead body?

HAMLET: Compounded it with dust, whereto 'tis kin.

ROSENCRANTZ: Tell us where 'tis, that we may take it thence
And bear it to the chapel.

HAMLET: Do not believe it.

ROSENCRANTZ: Believe what?

HAMLET: That I can keep your counsel and not mine own.° Besides, to be demanded of° a sponge, what replication° should be made by the son of a king?

ROSENCRANTZ: Take you me for a sponge, my lord?

HAMLET: Ay, sir, that soaks up the King's countenance,° his rewards, his authorities.° But such officers do the King best service in the end. He keeps them, like an ape, an apple, in the corner of his jaw, first mouthed to be last swallowed. When he needs what you have gleaned, it is but squeezing you, and, sponge, you shall be dry again.

ROSENCRANTZ: I understand you not, my lord.

HAMLET: I am glad of it. A knavish speech sleeps in° a foolish ear.

ROSENCRANTZ: My lord, you must tell us where the body is and go with us to the King.

HAMLET: The body is with the King, but the King is not with the body.°
The King is a thing—

40 And . . . done (a defective line; conjectures as to the missing words include *So, haply, slander* [Capell and other early editors]; *For, haply, slander* [Theobald and others]; and *So envious slander* [Jenkins].) **41 diameter** extent from side to side. **42 As level** with as direct aim; **his blank** its target at point-blank range. **44 woundless** invulnerable. **[4.2] Location: The castle. 10 That . . . own** i.e., that I can follow your advice (by telling where the body is) and still keep my own secret. **10–11 demanded of** questioned by; **replication** reply. **13 countenance** favor. **13–14 authorities** delegated power, influence. **19 sleeps in** has no meaning to. **22 The . . . body** (Perhaps alludes to the legal commonplace of "the king's two bodies," which drew a distinction between the sacred office of kingship and the particular mortal who possessed it at any given time. Hence, although Claudius' body is necessarily a part of him, true kingship is not contained in it. Similarly, Claudius will have Polonius' body when it is found, but there is no kingship in this business either.)

GUILDENSTERN: A thing, my lord?
HAMLET: Of nothing.° Bring me to him. Hide fox, and all after!°

Exeunt [*running*].

[4.3]

Enter KING, *and two or three.*

KING: I have sent to seek him, and to find the body.
How dangerous is it that this man goes loose!
Yet must not we put the strong law on him.
He's loved of° the distracted° multitude,
Who like not in their judgment, but their eyes,°
And where 'tis so, th' offender's scourge° is weighed,°
But never the offense. To bear all smooth and even,°
This sudden sending him away must seem
Deliberate pause.° Diseases desperate grown
By desperate appliance° are relieved,
Or not at all.

Enter ROSENCRANTZ, GUILDENSTERN, *and all the rest.*

How now, what hath befall'n?

ROSENCRANTZ: Where the dead body is bestowed, my lord,
We cannot get from him.
KING: But where is he?
ROSENCRANTZ: Without, my lord; guarded, to know your pleasure.
KING: Bring him before us.
ROSENCRANTZ: Ho! Bring in the lord.

They enter [*with* HAMLET].

KING: Now, Hamlet, where's Polonius?
HAMLET: At supper.
KING: At supper? Where?
HAMLET: Not where he eats, but where 'a is eaten. A certain convocation of politic worms° are e'en° at him. Your worm° is your only emperor for diet.° We fat all creatures else to fat us, and we fat ourselves for maggots. Your fat king and your lean beggar is but variable service°—two dishes, but to one table. That's the end.
KING: Alas, alas!
HAMLET: A man may fish with the worm that hath eat° of a king, and eat of the fish that hath fed of that worm.
KING: What dost thou mean by this?

25 Of nothing (1) of no account, (2) lacking the essence of kingship, as in lines 24–25 and note; **Hide . . . after** (an old signal cry in the game of hide-and-seek, suggesting that Hamlet now runs away from them.) **[4.3] Location: The castle.** **4 of** by; **distracted** fickle, unstable. **5 Who . . . eyes** who choose not by judgment but by appearance. **6 scourge** punishment. (Literally, blow with a whip.); **weighed** sympathetically considered. **7 To . . . even** to manage the business in an unprovocative way. **9 Deliberate pause** carefully considered action. **10 appliance** remedies. **19–20 politic worms** crafty worms (suited to a master spy like Polonius); **e'en** even now; **Your worm** your average worm. (Compare *your fat king and your lean beggar* in lines 21–22.); **diet** food, eating (with a punning reference to the Diet of Worms, a famous *convocation* held in 1521). **22 variable service** different courses of a single meal. **25 eat** eaten. (Pronounced *et.*)

HAMLET: Nothing but to show you how a king may go a progress° through the guts of a beggar.

KING: Where is Polonius?

HAMLET: In heaven. Send thither to see. If your messenger find him not there, seek him i' th' other place yourself. But if indeed you find him not within this month, you shall nose him as you go up the stairs into the lobby.

KING [*to some attendants*]: Go seek him there.

HAMLET: 'A will stay till you come. [*Exeunt attendants.*]

KING: Hamlet, this deed, for thine especial safety—
Which we do tender,° as we dearly° grieve
For that which thou hast done—must send thee hence
With fiery quickness. Therefore prepare thyself.
The bark° is ready, and the wind at help,
Th' associates tend,° and everything is bent°
For England.

HAMLET: For England!

KING: Ay, Hamlet.

HAMLET: Good.

KING: So is it, if thou knew'st our purposes.

HAMLET: I see a cherub° that sees them. But come, for England!
Farewell, dear mother.

KING: Thy loving father, Hamlet.

HAMLET: My mother. Father and mother is man and wife, man and wife is one flesh, and so, my mother. Come, for England! *Exit.*

KING: Follow him at foot;° tempt him with speed aboard.
Delay it not. I'll have him hence tonight.
Away! For everything is sealed and done
That else leans on° th' affair. Pray you, make haste.
[*Exeunt all but the* KING.]
And, England,° if my love thou hold'st at aught°—
As my great power thereof may give thee sense,°
Since yet thy cicatrice° looks raw and red
After the Danish sword, and thy free awe°
Pays homage to us—thou mayst not coldly set°
Our sovereign process,° which imports at full,°
By letters congruing° to that effect,
The present° death of Hamlet. Do it, England,
For like the hectic° in my blood he rages,
And thou must cure me. Till I know 'tis done,
Howe'er my haps,° my joys were ne'er begun. *Exit.*

28 progress royal journey of state. **38 tender** regard, hold dear; **dearly** intensely. **41 bark** sailing vessel. **42 tend** wait; **bent** in readiness. **48 cherub** (Cherubim are angels of knowledge. Hamlet hints that both he and heaven are onto Claudius' tricks.) **53 at foot** close behind, at heel. **56 leans on** bears upon, is related to. **57 England** i.e., King of England; **at aught** at any value. **58 As . . . sense** for so my great power may give you a just appreciation of the importance of valuing my love. **59 cicatrice** scar. **60 free awe** voluntary show of respect. **61 coldly set** regard with indifference. **62 process** command; **imports at full** conveys specific directions for. **63 congruing** agreeing. **64 present** immediate. **65 hectic** persistent fever. **67 haps** fortunes.

[4.4]

Enter FORTINBRAS *with his army over the stage.*

FORTINBRAS: Go, Captain, from me greet the Danish king.
Tell him that by his license° Fortinbras
Craves the conveyance of° a promised march
Over his kingdom. You know the rendezvous.
If that His Majesty would aught with us,
We shall express our duty° in his eye;°
And let him know so.

CAPTAIN: I will do 't, my lord.

FORTINBRAS: Go softly° on. [*Exeunt all but the* CAPTAIN.]

Enter HAMLET, ROSENCRANTZ, [GUILDENSTERN,] *etc.*

HAMLET: Good sir, whose powers° are these?

CAPTAIN: They are of Norway, sir.

HAMLET: How purposed, sir, I pray you?

CAPTAIN: Against some part of Poland.

HAMLET: Who commands them, sir?

CAPTAIN: The nephew to old Norway, Fortinbras.

HAMLET: Goes it against the main° of Poland, sir,
Or for some frontier?

CAPTAIN: Truly to speak, and with no addition,°
We go to gain a little patch of ground
That hath in it no profit but the name.
To pay° five ducats, five, I would not farm it;°
Nor will it yield to Norway or the Pole
A ranker° rate, should it be sold in fee.°

HAMLET: Why, then the Polack never will defend it.

CAPTAIN: Yes, it is already garrisoned.

HAMLET: Two thousand souls and twenty thousand ducats
Will not debate° the question of this straw.°
This is th' impostume° of much wealth and peace,
That inward breaks, and shows no cause without
Why the man dies. I humbly thank you, sir.

CAPTAIN: God b' wi' you, sir. [*Exit.*]

ROSENCRANTZ: Will 't please you go, my lord?

HAMLET: I'll be with you straight. Go a little before.

[*Exeunt all except* HAMLET.]

How all occasions do inform against° me
And spur my dull revenge! What is a man,
If his chief good and market of° his time
Be but to sleep and feed? A beast, no more.
Sure he that made us with such large discourse,°
Looking before and after,° gave us not

[4.4] Location: The coast of Denmark. **2 license** permission. **3 the conveyance of** escort during. **6 duty** respect; **eye** presence. **9 softly** slowly, circumspectly. **10 powers** forces. **16 main** main part. **18 addition** exaggeration. **21 To pay** i.e., for a yearly rental of; **farm it** take a lease on it. **23 ranker** higher; **in fee** fee simple, outright. **27 debate . . . straw** settle this trifling matter. **28 impostume** abscess. **34 inform against** denounce, betray; take shape against. **36 market of** profit of, compensation for. **38 discourse** power of reasoning. **39 Looking before and after** able to review past events and anticipate the future.

That capability and godlike reason
To fust° in us unused. Now, whether it be
Bestial oblivion,° or some craven° scruple
Of thinking too precisely° on th' event°—
A thought which, quartered, hath but one part wisdom
And ever three parts coward—I do not know
Why yet I live to say "This thing's to do,"
Sith° I have cause, and will, and strength, and means
To do 't. Examples gross° as earth exhort me:
Witness this army of such mass and charge,°
Led by a delicate and tender° prince,
Whose spirit with divine ambition puffed
Makes mouths° at the invisible event,°
Exposing what is mortal and unsure
To all that fortune, death, and danger dare,°
Even for an eggshell. Rightly to be great
Is not to stir without great argument,
But greatly to find quarrel in a straw
When honor's at the stake.° How stand I, then,
That have a father killed, a mother stained,
Excitements of° my reason and my blood,
And let all sleep, while to my shame I see
The imminent death of twenty thousand men
That for a fantasy° and trick° of fame
Go to their graves like beds, fight for a plot°
Whereon the numbers cannot try the cause,°
Which is not tomb enough and continent°
To hide the slain? O, from this time forth
My thoughts be bloody or be nothing worth! *Exit.*

[4.5]

Enter HORATIO, [QUEEN] GERTRUDE, *and a* GENTLEMAN.

QUEEN: I will not speak with her.
GENTLEMAN: She is importunate,
Indeed distract.° Her mood will needs be pitied.
QUEEN: What would she have?
GENTLEMAN: She speaks much of her father, says she hears
There's tricks° i' the world, and hems,° and beats her heart,°
Spurns enviously at straws,° speaks things in doubt°

41 fust grow moldy. **42 oblivion** forgetfulness; **craven** cowardly. **43 precisely** scrupulously; **event** outcome. **47 Sith** since. **48 gross** obvious. **49 charge** expense. **50 delicate and tender** of fine and youthful qualities. **52 Makes mouths** makes scornful faces; **invisible event** unforeseeable outcome. **54 dare** could do (to him). **55–58 Rightly . . . stake** true greatness does not normally consist of rushing into action over some trivial provocation; however, when one's honor is involved, even a trifling insult requires that one respond greatly (?); **at the stake** (A metaphor from gambling or bear-baiting.) **60 Excitements of** promptings by. **63 fantasy** fanciful caprice, illusion; **trick** trifle, deceit. **64 plot** plot of ground. **65 Whereon . . . cause** on which there is insufficient room for the soldiers needed to engage in a military contest. **66 continent** receptacle; container. **[4.5] Location: The castle.** **2 distract** distracted. **5 tricks** deceptions; **hems** makes "hmm" sounds; **heart** i.e., breast. **6 Spurns . . . straws** kicks spitefully, takes offense at trifles; **in doubt** obscurely.

That carry but half sense. Her speech is nothing,
Yet the unshapèd use° of it doth move
The hearers to collection;° they yawn° at it,
And botch° the words up fit to their own thoughts,
Which,° as her winks and nods and gestures yield° them,
Indeed would make one think there might be thought,°
Though nothing sure, yet much unhappily.°

HORATIO: 'Twere good she were spoken with, for she may strew
Dangerous conjectures in ill-breeding° minds.

QUEEN: Let her come in. [*Exit* GENTLEMAN.]
[*Aside.*] To my sick soul, as sin's true nature is,
Each toy° seems prologue to some great amiss.°
So full of artless jealousy is guilt,
It spills itself in fearing to be spilt.°

Enter OPHELIA° [*distracted*].

OPHELIA: Where is the beauteous majesty of Denmark?

QUEEN: How now, Ophelia?

OPHELIA [*she sings*]:

"How should I your true love know
From another one?
By his cockle hat° and staff,
And his sandal shoon."°

QUEEN: Alas, sweet lady, what imports this song?

OPHELIA: Say you? Nay, pray you, mark.

"He is dead and gone, lady, [*Song.*]
He is dead and gone;
At his head a grass-green turf,
At his heels a stone."

O, ho!

QUEEN: Nay, but Ophelia—

OPHELIA: Pray you, mark. [*Sings.*]
"White his shroud as the mountain snow"—

Enter KING.

QUEEN: Alas, look here, my lord.

OPHELIA:

"Larded° with sweet flowers; [*Song.*]
Which bewept to the ground did not go
With true-love showers."°

9 unshapèd use incoherent manner. **9 collection** inference, a guess at some sort of meaning; **yawn** gape, wonder; grasp. (The Folio reading, *aim*, is possible.) **10 botch** patch. **11 Which** which words; **yield** deliver, represent. **12 thought** intended. **13 unhappily** unpleasantly near the truth, shrewdly. **15 ill-breeding** prone to suspect the worst and to make mischief. **18 toy** trifle; **amiss** calamity. **19–20 So . . . split** guilt is so full of suspicion that it unskilfully betrays itself in fearing betrayal. **s.d. Enter Ophelia** (In the First Quarto, Ophelia enters, "playing on a lute, and her hair down, singing.") **25 cockle hat** hat with cockle-shell stuck in it as a sign that the wearer had been a pilgrim to the shrine of Saint James of Compostela in Spain. **26 shoon** shoes. **38 Larded** decorated. **40 showers** i.e., tears.

KING: How do you, pretty lady?

OPHELIA: Well, God 'ild° you! They say the owl° was a baker's daughter. Lord, we know what we are, but know not what we may be. God be at your table!

KING: Conceit° upon her father.

OPHELIA: Pray let's have no words of this; but when they ask you what it means, say you this:

"Tomorrow is Saint Valentine's day, [*Song.*]
All in the morning betime,°
And I a maid at your window,
To be your Valentine.
Then up he rose, and donned his clothes,
And dupped° the chamber door,
Let in the maid, that out a maid
Never departed more."

KING: Pretty Ophelia—

OPHELIA: Indeed, la, without an oath, I'll make an end on 't: [*Sings.*]

"By Gis° and by Saint Charity,
Alack, and fie for shame!
Young men will do 't, if they come to 't;
By Cock,° they are to blame.
Quoth she, 'Before you tumbled me,
You promised me to wed.'"

He answers:

"'So would I ha' done, by yonder sun,
An° thou hadst not come to my bed.'"

KING: How long hath she been thus?

OPHELIA: I hope all will be well. We must be patient, but I cannot choose but weep to think they would lay him i' the cold ground. My brother shall know of it. And so I thank you for your good counsel. Come, my coach! Good night, ladies, good night, sweet ladies, good night, good night. [*Exit.*]

KING [*to* HORATIO]: Follow her close. Give her good watch, I pray you. [*Exit* HORATIO.]

O, this is the poison of deep grief; it springs
All from her father's death—and now behold!
O Gertrude, Gertrude,
When sorrows come, they come not single spies,°
But in battalions. First, her father slain;
Next, your son gone, and he most violent author

42 God 'ild god yield or reward; **owl** (refers to a legend about a baker's daughter who was turned into an owl for being ungenerous when Jesus begged a loaf of bread.) **45 Conceit** brooding. **49 betime** early. **53 dupped** did up, opened. **58 Gis** Jesus. **61 Cock** (a perversion of "God" in oaths; here also with a quibble on the slang word for penis.) **66 An** if. **77 spies** scouts sent in advance of the main force.

Of his own just remove;° the people muddied,°
Thick and unwholesome in their thoughts and whispers
For good Polonius' death—and we have done but greenly,°
In hugger-mugger° to inter him; poor Ophelia
Divided from herself and her fair judgment,
Without the which we are pictures or mere beasts;
Last, and as much containing° as all these,
Her brother is in secret come from France,
Feeds on this wonder, keeps himself in clouds,°
And wants° not buzzers° to infect his ear
With pestilent speeches of his father's death,
Wherein necessity,° of matter beggared,°
Will nothing stick our person to arraign
In ear and ear.° O my dear Gertrude, this,
Like to a murdering piece,° in many places
Gives me superfluous death.° *A noise within.*

QUEEN: Alack, what noise is this?

KING: Attend!°
Where is my Switzers?° Let them guard the door.

Enter a MESSENGER.

What is the matter?

MESSENGER: Save yourself, my lord!
The ocean, overpeering of his list,°
Eats not the flats° with more impetuous° haste
Than young Laertes, in a riotous head,°
O'erbears your officers. The rabble call him lord,
And, as° the world were now but to begin,
Antiquity forgot, custom not known,
The ratifiers and props of every word,°
They cry, "Choose we! Laertes shall be king!"
Caps,° hands, and tongues applaud it to the clouds,
"Laertes shall be king, Laertes king!"

QUEEN: How cheerfully on the false trail they cry! *A noise within.*
O, this is counter,° you false Danish dogs!

Enter LAERTES *with others.*

80 remove removal; **muddied** stirred up, confused. **82 greenly** in an inexperienced way, foolishly. **83 hugger-mugger** secret haste. **86 as much containing** as full of serious matter. **88 Feeds . . . clouds** feeds his resentment or shocked grievance, holds himself inscrutable and aloof amid all this rumor. **89 wants** lacks; **buzzers** gossipers, informers. **91 necessity** i.e., the need to invent some plausible explanation; **of matter beggared** unprovided with facts. **92–93 Will . . . ear** will not hesitate to accuse my (royal) person in everybody's ears. **94 murdering piece** cannon loaded so as to scatter its shot. **95 Gives . . . death** kills me over and over. **97 Attend** i.e., guard me. **98 Switzers** Swiss guards, mercenaries. **100 overpeering of his list** overflowing its shore, boundary. **101 flats** i.e., flatlands near shore; **impetuous** violent. (Perhaps also with the meaning of *impiteous* [*impitious*, Q2], "pitiless.") **102 head** insurrection. **104 as** as if. **106 The ratifiers . . . word** i.e., *antiquity* (or tradition) and *custom* ought to confirm (*ratify*) and underprop our every word or promise. **108 Caps** (The caps are thrown in the air.) **111 counter** (a hunting term, meaning to follow the trail in a direction opposite to that which the game has taken.)

KING: The doors are broke.
LAERTES: Where is this King?—Sirs, stand you all without.
ALL: No, let's come in.
LAERTES: I pray you, give me leave.
ALL: We will, we will.
LAERTES: I thank you. Keep the door. [*Exeunt followers.*] O thou vile king,
Give me my father!
QUEEN [*restraining him*]: Calmly, good Laertes.
LAERTES: That drop of blood that's calm proclaims me bastard,
Cries cuckold to my father, brands the harlot
Even here, between° the chaste unsmirchèd brow
Of my true mother.
KING: What is the cause, Laertes,
That thy rebellion looks so giantlike?
Let him go, Gertrude. Do not fear our° person.
There's such divinity doth hedge° a king
That treason can but peep to what it would,°
Acts little of his will.° Tell me, Laertes,
Why thou art thus incensed. Let him go, Gertrude.
Speak, man.
LAERTES: Where is my father?
KING: Dead.
QUEEN: But not by him.
KING: Let him demand his fill.
LAERTES: How came he dead? I'll not be juggled with.°
To hell, allegiance! Vows, to the blackest devil!
Conscience and grace, to the profoundest pit!
I dare damnation. To this point I stand,°
That both the worlds I give to negligence,°
Let come what comes, only I'll be revenged
Most throughly° for my father.
KING: Who shall stay you?
LAERTES: My will, not all the world's.°
And for° my means, I'll husband them so well
They shall go far with little.
KING: Good Laertes,
If you desire to know the certainty
Of your dear father, is 't writ in your revenge
That, swoopstake,° you will draw both friend and foe,
Winner and loser?
LAERTES: None but his enemies.
KING: Will you know them, then?

122 between in the middle of. **125 fear our** fear for my. **126 hedge** protect, as with a surrounding barrier. **127 can . . . would** can only peep furtively, as through a barrier, at what it would intend. **128 Acts . . . will** (but) performs little of what it intends. **132 juggled with** cheated, deceived. **135 To . . . stand** I am resolved in this. **136 both . . . negligence** i.e. both this world and the next are of no consequence to me. **138 throughly** thoroughly. **140 My will . . . world's** I'll stop (*stay*) when my will is accomplished, not for anyone else's. **141 for** as for. **145 swoopstake** i.e., indiscriminately. (Literally, taking all stakes on the gambling table at once. *Draw* is also a gambling term, meaning "taken from.")

LAERTES: To his good friends thus wide I'll ope my arms,
And like the kind life-rendering pelican°
Repast° them with my blood.
KING: Why, now you speak
Like a good child and a true gentleman.
That I am guiltless of your father's death,
And am most sensibly° in grief for it,
It shall as level° to your judgment 'pear
As day does to your eye. *A noise within.*
LAERTES: How now, what noise is that?

Enter OPHELIA.

KING: Let her come in.
LAERTES: O heat, dry up my brains! Tears seven times salt
Burn out the sense and virtue° of mine eye!
By heaven, thy madness shall be paid with weight°
Till our scale turn the beam.° O rose of May!
Dear maid, kind sister, sweet Ophelia!
O heavens, is 't possible a young maid's wits
Should be as mortal as an old man's life?
Nature is fine in° love, and where 'tis fine
It sends some precious instance° of itself
After the thing it loves.°
OPHELIA: [*Song.*]

"They bore him barefaced on the bier,
  Hey non nonny, nonny, hey nonny,
And in his grave rained many a tear—"

Fare you well, my dove!
LAERTES: Hadst thou thy wits and didst persuade° revenge,
It could not move thus.
OPHELIA: You must sing "A-down a-down," and you "call him a-down-a."° O, how the wheel° becomes it! It is the false steward° that stole his master's daughter.
LAERTES: This nothing's more than matter.°
OPHELIA: There's rosemary,° that's for remembrance; pray you, love, remember. And there is pansies;° that's for thoughts.
LAERTES: A document° in madness, thoughts and remembrance fitted.

150 pelican (refers to the belief that the female pelican fed its young with its own blood.) **151 Repast** feed. **154 sensibly** feelingly. **155 level** plain. **159 virtue** faculty, power. **160 paid with weight** repaid, avenged equally or more. **161 beam** crossbar of a balance. **165 fine in** refined by. **166 instance** token. **167 After . . . loves** i.e., into the grave, along with Polonius. **172 persuade** argue cogently for. **174 You . . . a-down-a** (Ophelia assigns the singing of refrains, like her own "Hey non nonny," to others present.) **175 wheel** spinning wheel as accompaniment to the song, or refrain; **false steward** (The story is unknown.) **177 This . . . matter** This seeming nonsense is more eloquent than sane utterance. **178 rosemary** (used as a symbol of remembrance both at weddings and at funerals.) **179 pansies** (emblems of love and courtship; perhaps from French *pensées*, "thoughts.") **180 document** instruction, lesson.

OPHELIA: There's fennel° for you, and columbines.° There's rue° for you, and here's some for me; we may call it herb of grace o' Sundays. You must wear your rue with a difference.° There's a daisy.° I would give you some violets,° but they withered all when my father died. They say 'a made a good end—

[*Sings.*] "For bonny sweet Robin is all my joy."

LAERTES: Thought° and affliction, passion,° hell itself,
She turns to favor° and to prettiness.

OPHELIA: [*Song.*]

"And will 'a not come again?
And will 'a not come again?
No, no, he is dead.
Go to thy deathbed,
He never will come again.

"His beard was as white as snow,
All flaxen was his poll.°
He is gone, he is gone,
And we cast away moan.
God ha' mercy on his soul!"

And of all Christian souls, I pray God. God b' wi' you.

[*Exit, followed by* GERTRUDE.]

LAERTES: Do you see this, O God?

KING: Laertes, I must commune with your grief,
Or you deny me right. Go but apart,
Make choice of whom° your wisest friends you will,
And they shall hear and judge twixt you and me.
If by direct or by collateral hand°
They find us touched,° we will our kingdom give,
Our crown, our life, and all that we call ours
To you in satisfaction; but if not,
Be you content to lend your patience to us,
And we shall jointly labor with your soul
To give it due content.

LAERTES: Let this be so.
His means of death, his obscure funeral—
No trophy,° sword, nor hatchment° o'er his bones,
No noble rite, nor formal ostentation°—

181 fennel (emblem of flattery.); **columbines** (emblems of unchastity or ingratitude.); **rue** (emblem of repentance—a signification that is evident in its popular name, *herb of grace.*) **183 with a difference** (a device used in heraldry to distinguish one family from another on the coat of arms, here suggesting that Ophelia and the others have different causes of sorrow and repentance; perhaps with a play on *rue* in the sense of "ruth," "pity."); **daisy** (emblem of dissembling, faithlessness.) **184 violets** (emblems of faithfulness.) **187 Thought** melancholy; **passion** suffering. **188 favor** grace, beauty. **195 poll** head. **203 whom** whichever of. **205 collateral hand** indirect agency. **206 us touched** me implicated. **213 trophy** memorial; **hatchment** tablet displaying the armorial bearings of a deceased person. **214 ostentation** ceremony.

Cry to be heard, as 'twere from heaven to earth,
That° I must call 't in question.°

KING: So you shall,
And where th' offense is, let the great ax fall.
I pray you, go with me. *Exeunt.*

[4.6]

Enter HORATIO *and others.*

HORATIO: What are they that would speak with me?

GENTLEMAN: Seafaring men, sir. They say they have letters for you.

HORATIO: Let them come in. [*Exit* GENTLEMAN.]
I do not know from what part of the world
I should be greeted, if not from Lord Hamlet.

Enter Sailors.

FIRST SAILOR: God bless you, sir.

HORATIO: Let him bless thee too.

FIRST SAILOR: 'A shall, sir, an 't° please him. There's a letter for you, sir—it came from th' ambassador° that was bound for England—if your name be Horatio, as I am let to know it is. [*He gives a letter.*]

HORATIO [*reads*]: "Horatio, when thou shalt have overlooked° this, give these fellows some means° to the King; they have letters for him. Ere we were two days old at sea, a pirate of very warlike appointment° gave us chase. Finding ourselves too slow of sail, we put on a compelled valor, and in the grapple I boarded them. On the instant they got clear of our ship, so I alone became their prisoner. They have dealt with me like thieves of mercy,° but they knew what they did: I am to do a good turn for them. Let the King have the letters I have sent, and repair° thou to me with as much speed as thou wouldest fly death. I have words to speak in thine ear will make thee dumb, yet are they much too light for the bore° of the matter. These good fellows will bring thee where I am. Rosencrantz and Guildenstern hold their course for England. Of them I have much to tell thee. Farewell.

He that thou knowest thine, Hamlet."

Come, I will give you way° for these your letters,
And do 't the speedier that you may direct me
To him from whom you brought them. *Exeunt.*

[4.7]

Enter KING *and* LAERTES.

KING: Now must your conscience my acquittance seal,°
And you must put me in your heart for friend,
Sith° you have heard, and with a knowing ear,
That he which hath your noble father slain
Pursued my life.

216 That so that; **call 't in question** demand an explanation. **[4.6] Location: The castle. 8 an 't** if it. **9 th' ambassador** (evidently Hamlet. The sailor is being circumspect.) **11 overlooked** looked over. **12 means** means of access. **13 appointment** equipage. **16–17 thieves of mercy** merciful thieves. **18 repair** come. **20 bore** caliber, i.e., importance. **25 way** means of access. **[4.7] Location: The castle. 1 my acquittance seal** confirm or acknowledge my innocence. **3 Sith** since.

LAERTES: It well appears. But tell me
Why you proceeded not against these feats°
So crimeful and so capital° in nature,
As by your safety, greatness, wisdom, all things else,
You mainly° were stirred up.
KING: O, for two special reasons,
Which may to you perhaps seem much unsinewed,°
But yet to me they're strong. The Queen his mother
Lives almost by his looks, and for myself—
My virtue or my plague, be it either which—
She is so conjunctive° to my life and soul
That, as the star moves not but in his° sphere,°
I could not but by her. The other motive
Why to a public count° I might not go
Is the great love the general gender° bear him,
Who, dipping all his faults in their affection,
Work° like the spring° that turneth wood to stone,
Convert his gyves° to graces, so that my arrows,
Too slightly timbered° for so loud° a wind,
Would have reverted° to my bow again
But not where I had aimed them.
LAERTES: And so have I a noble father lost,
A sister driven into desperate terms,°
Whose worth, if praises may go back° again,
Stood challenger on mount° of all the age
For her perfections. But my revenge will come.
KING: Break not your sleeps for that. You must not think
That we are made of stuff so flat and dull
That we can let our beard be shook with danger
And think it pastime. You shortly shall hear more.
I loved your father, and we love ourself;
And that, I hope, will teach you to imagine—

Enter a MESSENGER *with letters.*

How now? What news?
MESSENGER: Letters, my lord, from Hamlet:
This to Your Majesty, this to the queen. [*He gives letters.*]
KING: From Hamlet? Who brought them?
MESSENGER: Sailors, my lord, they say. I saw them not.
They were given me by Claudio. He received them
Of him that brought them.

6 feats acts. **7 capital** punishable by death. **9 mainly** greatly. **11 unsinewed** weak. **15 conjunctive** closely united. (An astronomical metaphor.) **16 his** its; **sphere** one of the hollow spheres in which, according to Ptolematic astronomy, the planets were supposed to move. **18 count** account, reckoning, indictment. **19 general gender** common people. **21 Work** operate, act; **spring** i.e., a spring with such a concentration of lime that it coats a piece of wood with limestone, in effect gilding and petrifying it. **22 gyves** fetters (which, gilded by the people's praise, would look like badges of honor). **23 slightly timbered** light; **loud** (suggesting public outcry on Hamlet's behalf). **24 reverted** returned. **27 terms** state, condition. **28 go back** i.e., recall what she was. **29 on mount** set up on high.

KING: Laertes, you shall hear them.—
Leave us. [*Exit* MESSENGER.]
[*He reads.*] "High and mighty, you shall know I am set naked° on your kingdom. Tomorrow shall I beg leave to see your kingly eyes, when I shall, first asking your pardon,° thereunto recount the occasion of my sudden and more strange return. Hamlet."
What should this mean? Are all the rest come back?
Or is it some abuse,° and no such thing?°

LAERTES: Know you the hand?

KING: 'Tis Hamlet's character.° "Naked!"
And in a postscript here he says "alone."
Can you devise° me?

LAERTES: I am lost in it, my lord. But let him come.
It warms the very sickness in my heart
That I shall live and tell him to his teeth,
"Thus didst thou."°

KING: If it be so, Laertes—
As how should it be so? How otherwise?°—
Will you be ruled by me?

LAERTES: Ay, my lord,
So° you will not o'errule me to a peace.

KING: To thine own peace. If he be now returned,
As checking at° his voyage, and that° he means
No more to undertake it, I will work him
To an exploit, now ripe in my device,°
Under the which he shall not choose but fall;
And for his death no wind of blame shall breathe,
But even his mother shall uncharge the practice°
And call it accident.

LAERTES: My lord, I will be ruled,
The rather if you could devise it so
That I might be the organ.°

KING: It falls right.
You have been talked of since your travel much,
And that in Hamlet's hearing, for a quality
Wherein they say you shine. Your sum of parts°
Did not together pluck such envy from him
As did that one, and that, in my regard,
Of the unworthiest siege.°

LAERTES: What part is that, my lord?

KING: A very ribbon in the cap of youth,

45 naked destitute, unarmed, without following. **47 pardon** permission. **50 abuse** deceit; **no such thing** not what it appears. **51 character** handwriting. **53 devise** explain to. **57 Thus didst thou** i.e., here's for what you did to my father. **58 As . . . otherwise** How can this (Hamlet's return) be true? Yet how otherwise than true (since we have the evidence of his letter)? **60 So** provided that. **62 checking at** i.e., turning aside from (like a falcon leaving the quarry to fly at a chance bird); **that** if. **64 device** devising, invention. **67 uncharge the practice** acquit the stratagem of being a plot. **70 organ** agent, instrument. **73 Your . . . parts** i.e., all your other virtues. **76 unworthiest siege** least important rank.

Yet needful too, for youth no less becomes°
The light and careless livery that it wears
Than settled age his sables° and his weeds°
Importing health and graveness.° Two months since
Here was a gentleman of Normandy.
I have seen myself, and served against, the French,
And they can well° on horseback, but this gallant
Had witchcraft in 't; he grew unto his seat,
And to such wondrous doing brought his horse
As had he been incorpsed and demi-natured°
With the brave beast. So far he topped° my thought
That I in forgery° of shapes and tricks
Come short of what he did.

LAERTES: A Norman was 't?

KING: A Norman.

LAERTES: Upon my life, Lamord.

KING: The very same.

LAERTES: I know him well. He is the brooch° indeed
And gem of all the nation.

KING: He made confession° of you,
And gave you such a masterly report
For art and exercise in your defense,°
And for your rapier most especial,
That he cried out 'twould be a sight indeed
If one could match you. Th' escrimers° of their nation,
He swore, had neither motion, guard, nor eye
If you opposed them. Sir, this report of his
Did Hamlet so envenom with his envy
That he could nothing do but wish and beg
Your sudden° coming o'er, to play° with you.
Now, out of this—

LAERTES: What out of this, my lord?

KING: Laertes, was your father dear to you?
Or are you like the painting of a sorrow,
A face without a heart?

LAERTES: Why ask you this?

KING: Not that I think you did not love your father,
But that I know love is begun by time,°
And that I see, in passages of proof,°
Time qualifies° the spark and fire of it.
There lives within the very flame of love

79 no less becomes is no less suited by. **81 his sables** its rich robes furred with sable; **weeds** garments. **82 Importing . . . graveness** signifying a concern for health and dignified prosperity; also, giving an impression of comfortable prosperity. **85 can well** are skilled. **88 As . . . demi-natured** as if he had been of one body and nearly of one nature (like the centaur). **89 topped** surpassed. **90 forgery** imagining. **94 brooch** ornament. **96 confession** testimonial, admission of superiority. **98 For . . . defense** with respect to your skill and practice with your weapon. **101 escrimers** fencers. **106 sudden** immediate; **play** fence. **112 begun by time** i.e., created by the right circumstance and hence subject to change. **113 passages of proof** actual instances that prove it. **114 qualifies** weakens, moderates.

A kind of wick or snuff° that will abate it,
And nothing is at a like goodness still,°
For goodness, growing to a pleurisy,°
Dies in his own too much.° That° we would do,
We should do when we would; for this "would" changes
And hath abatements° and delays as many
As there are tongues, are hands, are accidents,°
And then this "should" is like a spendthrift sigh,°
That hurts by easing.° But, to the quick o' th' ulcer:°
Hamlet comes back. What would you undertake
To show yourself in deed your father's son
More than in words?

LAERTES: To cut his throat i' the church.

KING: No place, indeed, should murder sanctuarize;°
Revenge should have no bounds. But good Laertes,
Will you do this,° keep close within your chamber.
Hamlet returned shall know you are come home.
We'll put on those shall° praise your excellence
And set a double varnish on the fame
The Frenchman gave you, bring you in fine° together,
And wager on your heads. He, being remiss,°
Most generous,° and free from all contriving,
Will not peruse the foils, so that with ease,
Or with a little shuffling, you may choose
A sword unbated,° and in a pass of practice°
Requite him for your father.

LAERTES: I will do 't,
And for that purpose I'll anoint my sword.
I bought an unction° of a mountebank°
So mortal that, but dip a knife in it,
Where it draws blood no cataplasm° so rare,
Collected from all simples° that have virtue°
Under the moon,° can save the thing from death
That is but scratched withal. I'll touch my point
With this contagion, that if I gall° him slightly,
It may be death.

116 snuff the charred part of a candlewick. **117 nothing . . . still** nothing remains at a constant level of perfection. **118 pleurisy** excess, plethora. (Literally, a chest inflammation.) **119 in . . . much** of its own excess; **That** that which. **121 abatements** diminutions. **122 As . . . accidents** as there are tongues to dissuade, hands to prevent, and chance events to intervene. **123 spendthrift sigh** (an allusion to the belief that sighs draw blood from the heart.) **124 hurts by easing** i.e., costs the heart blood and wastes precious opportunity even while it affords emotional relief; **quick o' th' ulcer** i.e., heart of the matter. **128 sanctuarize** protect from punishment. (Alludes to the right of sanctuary with which certain religious places were invested.) **130 Will you do this** if you wish to do this. **132 put on those shall** arrange for some to. **134 in fine** finally. **135 remiss** negligently unsuspicious. **136 generous** noble-minded. **139 unbated** not blunted, having no button; **pass of practice** treacherous thrust. **142 unction** ointment; **mountebank** quack doctor. **144 cataplasm** plaster or poultice. **145 simples** herbs; **virtue** potency. **146 Under the moon** i.e., anywhere (with reference perhaps to the belief that herbs gathered at night had a special power). **148 gall** graze, wound.

KING: Let's further think of this,
Weigh what convenience both of time and means
May fit us to our shape.° If this should fail,
And that our drift look through our bad performance,°
'Twere better not assayed. Therefore this project
Should have a back or second, that might hold
If this did blast in proof.° Soft, let me see.
We'll make a solemn wager on your cunnings°—
I ha 't!
When in your motion you are hot and dry—
As° make your bouts more violent to that end—
And that he calls for drink, I'll have prepared him
A chalice for the nonce,° whereon but sipping,
If he by chance escape your venomed stuck,°
Our purpose may hold there. [*A cry within.*] But stay, what noise?

Enter QUEEN.

QUEEN: One woe doth tread upon another's heel,
So fast they follow. Your sister's drowned, Laertes.

LAERTES: Drowned! O, where?

QUEEN: There is a willow grows askant° the brook,
That shows his hoar leaves° in the glassy stream;
Therewith fantastic garlands did she make
Of crowflowers, nettles, daisies, and long purples,°
That liberal° shepherds give a grosser name,°
But our cold° maids do dead men's fingers call them.
There on the pendent° boughs her crownet° weeds
Clamb'ring to hang, an envious sliver° broke,
When down her weedy° trophies and herself
Fell in the weeping brook. Her clothes spread wide,
And mermaidlike awhile they bore her up,
Which time she chanted snatches of old lauds,°
As one incapable of° her own distress,
Or like a creature native and endued°
Unto that element. But long it could not be
Till that her garments, heavy with their drink,
Pulled the poor wretch from her melodious lay
To muddy death.

LAERTES: Alas, then she is drowned?

QUEEN: Drowned, drowned.

152 shape part we propose to act. **153 drift . . . performance** intention should be made visible by our bungling. **156 blast in proof** burst in the test (like a cannon). **157 cunnings** respective skills. **160 As** i.e., and you should. **162 nonce** occasion. **163 stuck** thrust. (From *stoccado*, a fencing term.) **168 askant** aslant. **169 hoar leaves** white or gray undersides of the leaves. **171 long purples** early purple orchids. **172 liberal** free-spoken; **a grosser name** (the testicle-resembling tubers of the orchid, which also in some cases resemble *dead men's fingers*, have earned various slang names like "dogstones" and "cullions.") **173 cold** chaste. **174 pendent** over-hanging; **crownet** made into a chaplet or coronet. **175 envious sliver** malicious branch. **176 weedy** i.e., of plants. **179 lauds** hymns. **180 incapable of** lacking capacity to apprehend. **181 endued** adapted by nature.

LAERTES: Too much of water hast thou, poor Ophelia,
And therefore I forbid my tears. But yet
It is our trick;° nature her custom holds,
Let shame say what it will. [*He weeps.*] When these are gone,
The woman will be out.° Adieu, my lord.
I have a speech of fire that fain would blaze,
But that this folly douts° it. *Exit.*

KING: Let's follow, Gertrude.
How much I had to do to calm his rage!
Now fear I this will give it start again;
Therefore let's follow. *Exeunt.*

[5.1]

Enter two CLOWNS ° [*with spades and mattocks*].

FIRST CLOWN: Is she to be buried in Christian burial, when she willfully seeks her own salvation?°

SECOND CLOWN: I tell thee she is; therefore make her grave straight.° The crowner° hath sat on her,° and finds it° Christian burial.

FIRST CLOWN: How can that be, unless she drowned herself in her own defense?

SECOND CLOWN: Why, 'tis found so.°

FIRST CLOWN: It must be *se offendendo,*° it cannot be else. For here lies the point: if I drown myself wittingly, it argues an act, and an act hath three branches—it is to act, to do, and to perform. Argal,° she drowned herself wittingly.

SECOND CLOWN: Nay, but hear you, goodman° delver—

FIRST CLOWN: Give me leave. Here lies the water; good. Here stands the man; good. If the man go to this water and drown himself, it is, will he, nill he,° he goes, mark you that. But if the water come to him and drown him, he drowns not himself. Argal, he that is not guilty of his own death shortens not his own life.

SECOND CLOWN: But is this law?

FIRST CLOWN: Ay, marry, is 't—crowner's quest° law.

SECOND CLOWN: Will you ha' the truth on 't? If this had not been a gentlewoman, she should have been buried out o' Christian burial.

FIRST CLOWN: Why, there thou sayst.° And the more pity that great folk should have countenance° in this world to drown or hang themselves, more than their even-Christian.° Come, my spade. There is no ancient° gentlemen but gardeners, ditchers, and grave makers. They hold up° Adam's profession.

189 It is our trick i.e., weeping is our natural way (when sad). **190–191 When . . . out** When my tears are all shed, the woman in me will be expended, satisfied. **193 douts** extinguishes. (The Second Quarto reads "drowns.") **[5.1] Location: A churchyard.** **s.d. Clowns** rustics. **2 salvation** (a blunder for "damnation," or perhaps a suggestion that Ophelia was taking her own shortcut to heaven.) **3 straight** straightway, immediately. (But with a pun on *strait,* "narrow.") **4 crowner** coroner; **sat on her** conducted an inquest on her case; **finds it** gives his official verdict that her means of death was consistent with. **6 found so** determined so in the coroner's verdict. **7 *se offendendo*** (a comic mistake for *se defendendo,* a term used in verdicts of justifiable homicide.) **9 Argal** (corruption of *ergo,* "therefore.") **11 goodman** (an honorific title often used with the name of a profession or craft.) **13 will he, nill he** whether he will or no, willy-nilly. **18 quest** inquest. **21 there thou sayst** i.e., that's right. **22 countenance** privilege. **23 even-Christian** fellow Christians; **ancient** going back to ancient times. **24 hold up** maintain.

SECOND CLOWN: Was he a gentleman?

FIRST CLOWN: 'A was the first that ever bore arms.°

SECOND CLOWN: Why, he had none.

FIRST CLOWN: What, art a heathen? How dost thou understand the Scripture? The Scripture says Adam digged. Could he dig without arms?° I'll put another question to thee. If thou answerest me not to the purpose, confess thyself°—

SECOND CLOWN: Go to.

FIRST CLOWN: What is he that builds stronger than either the mason, the shipwright, or the carpenter?

SECOND CLOWN: The gallows maker, for that frame° outlives a thousand tenants.

FIRST CLOWN: I like thy wit well, in good faith. The gallows does well.° But how does it well? It does well to those that do ill. Now thou dost ill to say the gallows is built stronger than the church. Argal, the gallows may do well to thee. To 't again, come.

SECOND CLOWN: "Who builds stronger than a mason, a shipwright, or a carpenter?"

FIRST CLOWN: Ay, tell me that, and unyoke.°

SECOND CLOWN: Marry, now I can tell.

FIRST CLOWN: To 't.

SECOND CLOWN: Mass,° I cannot tell.

Enter HAMLET *and* HORATIO [*at a distance*].

FIRST CLOWN: Cudgel thy brains no more about it, for your dull ass will not mend his pace with beating; and when you are asked this question next, say "a grave maker." The houses he makes lasts till doomsday. Go get thee in and fetch me a stoup° of liquor.

[*Exit* SECOND CLOWN: FIRST CLOWN *digs.*]

Song.

"In youth, when I did love, did love,°
 Methought it was very sweet,
To contract—O—the time for—a—my behove,°
 O, methought there—a—was nothing—a—meet."°

HAMLET: Has this fellow no feeling of his business, 'a° sings in gravemaking?

HORATIO: Custom hath made it in him a property of easiness.°

HAMLET: 'Tis e'en so. The hand of little employment hath the daintier sense.°

FIRST CLOWN: *Song.*

"But age with his stealing steps
 Hath clawed me in his clutch,

26 bore arms (to be entitled to bear a coat of arms would make Adam a gentleman, but as one who bore a spade, our common ancestor was an ordinary delver in the earth.) **29 arms** i.e., the arms of the body. **30–31 confess thyself** (the saying continues, "and be hanged.") **35 frame** (1) gallows, (2) structure. **36 does well** (1) is an apt answer, (2) does a good turn. **41 unyoke** i.e., after this great effort, you may unharness the team of your wits. **44 Mass** by the Mass. **48 stoup** two-quart measure. **49 In . . . love** (This and the two following stanzas, with nonsensical variations, are from a poem attributed to Lord Vaux and printed in *Tottel's Miscellany,* 1557. The *O* and *a* [for "ah"] seemingly are the grunts of the digger.) **51 To contract . . . behove** i.e., to shorten the time for my own advantage. (Perhaps he means to *prolong* it.) **52 meet** suitable, i.e., more suitable. **53 'a** that he. **54 property of easiness** something he can do easily and indifferently. **55 daintier sense** more delicate sense of feeling.

And hath shipped me into the land,°
As if I had never been such." [*He throws up a skull.*]

HAMLET: That skull had a tongue in it and could sing once. How the knave jowls° it to the ground, as if 'twere Cain's jawbone, that did the first murder! This might be the pate of a politician,° which this ass now o'erreaches,° one that would circumvent God, might it not?

HORATIO: It might, my lord.

HAMLET: Or of a courtier, which could say, "Good morrow, sweet lord! How dost thou, sweet lord?" This might be my Lord Such-a-one, that praised my Lord Such-a-one's horse when 'a meant to beg it, might it not?

HORATIO: Ay, my lord.

HAMLET: Why, e'en so, and now my Lady Worm's, chapless,° and knocked about the mazard° with a sexton's spade. Here's fine revolution,° an° we had the trick to see° 't. Did these bones cost no more the breeding but to° play at loggets° with them? Mine ache to think on 't.

FIRST CLOWN: *Song.*

"A pickax and a spade, a spade,
For and° a shrouding sheet;
O, a pit of clay for to be made
For such a guest is meet." [*He throws up another skull.*]

HAMLET: There's another. Why may not that be the skull of a lawyer? Where be his quiddities° now, his quillities,° his cases, his tenures,° and his tricks? Why does he suffer this mad knave now to knock him about the sconce° with a dirty shovel, and will not tell him of his action of battery?° Hum, this fellow might be in 's time a great buyer of land, with his statutes, his recognizances,° his fines, his double° vouchers,° his recoveries.° Is this the fine of his fines and the recovery of his recoveries, to have his fine pate full of fine dirt?° Will his vouchers vouch him no more of his purchases, and double ones too, than the length and breadth of a pair of indentures?° The very conveyances° of his lands will scarcely lie in this box,° and must th' inheritor° himself have no more, ha?

58 into the land i.e., toward my grave (?) (But note the lack of rhyme in *steps, land.*) **60 jowls** dashes (with a pun on *jowl,* "jawbone"). **62 politician** schemer, plotter; **o'erreaches** circumvents, gets the better of (with a quibble on the literal sense). **69 chapless** having no lower jaw. **70 mazard** i.e., head (Literally, a drinking vessel.); **revolution** turn of Fortune's wheel, change; **an** if. **71 trick to see** knack of seeing; **cost . . . to** involve so little expense and care in upbringing that we may. **72 loggets** a game in which pieces of hard wood shaped like Indian clubs or bowling pins are thrown to lie as near as possible to a stake. **74 For and** and moreover. **78 quiddities** subtleties, quibbles. (From Latin *quid,* "a thing."); **quillities** verbal niceties, subtle distinctions. (Variation of *quiddities.*); **tenures** the holding of a piece of property or office, or the conditions or period of such holding. **79 sconce** head. **80 action of battery** lawsuit about physical assault. **81–82 statutes, recognizances** legal documents guaranteeing a debt by attaching land and property. **82 fines, recoveries** ways of converting entailed estates into "fee simple" or freehold; **double** signed by two signatories; **vouchers** guarantees of the legality of a title to real estate. **83–84 fine of his fines . . . fine pate . . . fine dirt** end of his legal maneuvers . . . elegant head . . . minutely sifted dirt. **85–86 pair of indentures** legal document drawn up in duplicate on a single sheet and then cut apart on a zigzag line so that each pair was uniquely matched. (Hamlet may refer to two rows of teeth or dentures.) **86 conveyances** deeds. **87 box** (1) deed box, (2) coffin. ("Skull" has been suggested.); **inheritor** possessor, owner.

HORATIO: Not a jot more, my lord.

HAMLET: Is not parchment made of sheepskins?

HORATIO: Ay, my lord, and of calves' skins too.

HAMLET: They are sheep and calves which seek out assurance in that.° I will speak to this fellow.—Whose grave's this, sirrah?°

FIRST CLOWN: Mine, sir. [*Sings.*]
"O, pit of clay for to be made
For such a guest is meet."

HAMLET: I think it be thine, indeed, for thou liest in 't.

FIRST CLOWN: You lie out on 't, sir, and therefore 'tis not yours. For my part, I do not lie in 't, yet it is mine.

HAMLET: Thou dost lie in 't, to be in 't and say it is thine. 'Tis for the dead, not for the quick;° therefore thou liest.

FIRST CLOWN: 'Tis a quick lie, sir; 'twill away again from me to you.

HAMLET: What man dost thou dig it for?

FIRST CLOWN: For no man, sir.

HAMLET: What woman, then?

FIRST CLOWN: For none, neither.

HAMLET: Who is to be buried in 't?

FIRST CLOWN: One that was a woman, sir, but, rest her soul, she's dead.

HAMLET: How absolute° the knave is! We must speak by the card,° or equivocation° will undo us. By the Lord, Horatio, this three years I have took° note of it: the age is grown so picked° that the toe of the peasant comes so near the heel of the courtier, he galls his kibe.°—How long hast thou been grave maker?

FIRST CLOWN: Of all the days i' the year, I came to 't that day that our last king Hamlet overcame Fortinbras.

HAMLET: How long is that since?

FIRST CLOWN: Cannot you tell that? Every fool can tell that. It was that very day that young Hamlet was born—he that is mad and sent into England.

HAMLET: Ay, marry, why was he sent into England?

FIRST CLOWN: Why, because 'a was mad. 'A shall recover his wits there, or if 'a do not, 'tis no great matter there.

HAMLET: Why?

FIRST CLOWN: 'Twill not be seen in him there. There the men are as mad as he.

HAMLET: How came he mad?

FIRST CLOWN: Very strangely, they say.

HAMLET: How strangely?

FIRST CLOWN: Faith, e'en with losing his wits.

HAMLET: Upon what ground?°

FIRST CLOWN: Why, here in Denmark. I have been sexton here, man and boy, thirty years.

91 assurance in that safety in legal parchments. **92 sirrah** (a term of address to inferiors.) **100 quick** living. **108 absolute** strict, precise; **by the card** i.e., with precision. (Literally, by the mariner's compass-card, on which the points of the compass were marked.) **109–110 equivocation** ambiguity in the use of terms. **109 took** taken; **110 picked** refined, fastidious. **111 galls his kibe** chafes the courtier's chilblain. **127 ground** cause. (But, in the next line, the gravedigger takes the word in the sense of "land," "country.")

HAMLET: How long will a man lie i' th' earth ere he rot?

FIRST CLOWN: Faith, if 'a be not rotten before 'a die—as we have many pocky° corpses nowadays, that will scarce hold the laying in°—'a will last you° some eight year or nine year. A tanner will last you nine year.

HAMLET: Why he more than another?

FIRST CLOWN: Why, sir, his hide is so tanned with his trade that 'a will keep out water a great while, and your water is a sore° decayer of your whoreson° dead body. [*He picks up a skull.*] Here's a skull now hath lien you° i' th' earth three-and-twenty years.

HAMLET: Whose was it?

FIRST CLOWN: A whoreson mad fellow's it was. Whose do you think it was?

HAMLET: Nay, I know not.

FIRST CLOWN: A pestilence on him for a mad rogue! 'A poured a flagon of Rhenish° on my head once. This same skull, sir, was, sir, Yorick's skull, the King's jester.

HAMLET: This?

FIRST CLOWN: E'en that.

HAMLET: Let me see. [*He takes the skull.*] Alas, poor Yorick! I knew him, Horatio, a fellow of infinite jest, of most excellent fancy. He hath bore° me on his back a thousand times, and now how abhorred in my imagination it is! My gorge rises° at it. Here hung those lips that I have kissed I know not how oft. Where be your gibes now? Your gambols, your songs, your flashes of merriment that were wont° to set the table on a roar? Not one now, to mock your own grinning?° Quite chopfallen?° Now get you to my lady's chamber and tell her, let her paint an inch thick, to this favor° she must come. Make her laugh at that. Prithee, Horatio, tell me one thing.

HORATIO: What's that, my lord?

HAMLET: Dost thou think Alexander looked o' this fashion i' th' earth?

HORATIO: E'en so.

HAMLET: And smelt so? Pah! [*He throws down the skull.*]

HORATIO: E'en so, my lord.

HAMLET: To what base uses we may return, Horatio! Why may not imagination trace the noble dust of Alexander till 'a find it stopping a bunghole?°

HORATIO: 'Twere to consider too curiously° to consider so.

HAMLET: No, faith, not a jot, but to follow him thither with modesty° enough, and likelihood to lead it. As thus: Alexander died, Alexander was buried, Alexander returneth to dust, the dust is earth, of earth we make loam,° and why of that loam whereto he was converted might they not stop a beer barrel?

Imperious° Caesar, dead and turned to clay,

131 pocky rotten, diseased. (Literally, with the pox, or syphilis.) **132 hold the laying in** hold together long enough to be interred; **last you** last. (*You* is used colloquially here and in the following lines.) **136 sore** i.e., terrible, great; **whoreson** i.e., vile, scurvy. **137 lien you** lain. (See the note at line 144.) **143 Rhenish** Rhine wine. **148 bore** borne. **150 My gorge rises** i.e., I feel nauseated. **152 were wont** used. **153 mock your own grinning** mock at the way your skull seems to be grinning (just as you used to mock at yourself and those who grinned at you); **chopfallen** (1) lacking the lower jaw, (2) dejected. **154 favor** aspect, appearance. **162 bunghole** hole for filling or emptying a cask. **163 curiously** minutely. **164 modesty** plausible moderation. **166 loam** mortar consisting chiefly of moistened clay and straw. **169 Imperious** imperial.

Might stop a hole to keep the wind away.
O, that that earth which kept the world in awe
Should patch a wall t' expel the winter's flaw!°

Enter KING, QUEEN, LAERTES, *and the corpse* [*of* OPHELIA, *in procession, with* PRIEST, *lords, etc.*].

But soft,° but soft awhile! Here comes the King,
The Queen, the courtiers. Who is this they follow?
And with such maimèd° rites? This doth betoken
The corpse they follow did with desperate hand
Fordo° its own life. 'Twas of some estate.°
Couch we° awhile and mark.

[*He and* HORATIO *conceal themselves.* OPHELIA*'s body is taken to the grave.*]

LAERTES: What ceremony else?
HAMLET [*to* HORATIO]: That is Laertes, a very noble youth. Mark.
LAERTES: What ceremony else?
PRIEST: Her obsequies have been as far enlarged
As we have warranty.° Her death was doubtful,
And but that great command o'ersways the order°
She should in ground unsanctified been lodged°
Till the last trumpet. For° charitable prayers,
Shards,° flints, and pebbles should be thrown on her.
Yet here she is allowed her virgin crants,°
Her maiden strewments,° and the bringing home
Of bell and burial.°
LAERTES: Must there no more be done?
PRIEST: No more be done.
We should profane the service of the dead
To sing a requiem and such rest° to her
As to peace-parted souls.°
LAERTES: Lay her i' th' earth,
And from her fair and unpolluted flesh
May violets° spring! I tell thee, churlish priest,
A ministering angel shall my sister be
When thou liest howling.°
HAMLET [*to* HORATIO]: What, the fair Ophelia!
QUEEN [*scattering flowers*]: Sweets to the sweet! Farewell.
I hoped thou shouldst have been my Hamlet's wife.
I thought thy bride-bed to have decked, sweet maid,
And not t' have strewed thy grave.

172 flaw gust of wind. **173 soft** i.e., wait, be careful. **175 maimèd** mutilated, incomplete. **177 Fordo** destroy; **estate** rank. **178 Couch we** let's hide, lie low. **183 warranty** i.e., ecclesiastical authority. **184 great . . . order** orders from on high overrule the prescribed procedures. **185 She should . . . lodged** she should have been buried in unsanctified ground. **186 For** in place of. **187 Shards** broken bits of pottery. **188 crants** garlands betokening maidenhood. **189 strewments** flowers strewn on a coffin. **190 bringing . . . burial** laying the body to rest, to the sound of the bell. **193 such rest** i.e., to pray for such rest. **194 peace-parted souls** those who have died at peace with God. **196 violets** (see 4.5.191 and note.) **198 howling** i.e., in hell.

LAERTES: O, treble woe
Fall ten times treble on that cursèd head
Whose wicked deed thy most ingenious sense°
Deprived thee of! Hold off the earth awhile,
Till I have caught her once more in mine arms.

[*He leaps into the grave and embraces* OPHELIA.]

Now pile your dust upon the quick and dead,
Till of this flat a mountain you have made
T' o'ertop old Pelion or the skyish head
Of blue Olympus.°

HAMLET [*coming forward*]: What is he whose grief
Bears such an emphasis,° whose phrase of sorrow
Conjures the wandering stars° and makes them stand
Like wonder-wounded° hearers? This is I,
Hamlet the Dane.°

LAERTES [*grappling with him*°]: The devil take thy soul!

HAMLET: Thou pray'st not well.
I prithee, take thy fingers from my throat,
For though I am not splenitive° and rash,
Yet have I in me something dangerous,
Which let thy wisdom fear. Hold off thy hand.

KING: Pluck them asunder.

QUEEN: Hamlet, Hamlet!

ALL: Gentlemen!

HORATIO: Good my lord, be quiet.

[HAMLET *and* LAERTES *are parted.*]

HAMLET: Why, I will fight with him upon this theme
Until my eyelids will no longer wag.°

QUEEN: O my son, what theme?

HAMLET: I loved Ophelia. Forty thousand brothers
Could not with all their quantity of love
Make up my sum. What wilt thou do for her?

KING: O, he is mad, Laertes.

QUEEN: For love of God, forbear him.°

HAMLET: 'Swounds,° show me what thou'lt do.
Woo't° weep? Woo't fight? Woo't fast? Woo't tear thyself?
Woo't drink up° eisel?° Eat a crocodile?°
I'll do 't. Dost come here to whine?

204 ingenious sense a mind that is quick, alert, of fine qualities. **209–210 Pelion, Olympus** sacred mountains in the north of Thessaly; see also *Ossa*, below, at line 241. **211 emphasis** i.e., rhetorical and florid emphasis. (*Phrase* has a similar rhetorical connotation.) **212 wandering stars** planets. **213 wonder-wounded** struck with amazement. **214 the Dane** (This title normally signifies the King; see 1.1.17 and note.) **s.d. grappling with him** (The testimony of the First Quarto that "*Hamlet leaps in after Laertes*" and the "Elegy on Burbage" ("Oft have I seen him leap into the grave") seem to indicate one way in which this fight was staged; however, the difficulty of fitting two contenders and Ophelia's body into a confined space (probably the trapdoor) suggests to many editors the alternative, that Laertes jumps out of the grave to attack Hamlet.) **217 splenitive** quick-tempered. **225 wag** move. (A fluttering eyelid is a conventional sign that life has not yet gone.) **231 forbear him** leave him alone. **232 'Swounds** by His (Christ's) wounds. **233 Woo't** wilt thou. **234 drink up** drink deeply; **eisel** vinegar; **crocodile** (Crocodiles were tough and dangerous, and were supposed to shed hypocritical tears.)

To outface me with leaping in her grave?
Be buried quick° with her, and so will I.
And if thou prate of mountains, let them throw
Millions of acres on us, till our ground,
Singeing his pate° against the burning zone,°
Make Ossa° like a wart! Nay, an° thou'lt mouth,°
I'll rant as well as thou.

QUEEN: This is mere° madness,
And thus awhile the fit will work on him;
Anon, as patient as the female dove
When that her golden couplets° are disclosed,°
His silence will sit drooping.

HAMLET: Hear you, sir,
What is the reason that you use me thus?
I loved you ever. But it is no matter.
Let Hercules himself do what he may,
The cat will mew, and dog will have his day.° *Exit* HAMLET.

KING: I pray thee, good Horatio, wait upon him. [*Exit*] HORATIO.
[*To* LAERTES.] Strengthen your patience in° our last night's speech;
We'll put the matter to the present push.°—
Good Gertrude, set some watch over your son.—
This grave shall have a living° monument.
An hour of quiet° shortly shall we see;
Till then, in patience our proceeding be. *Exeunt.*

[5.2]

Enter HAMLET *and* HORATIO.

HAMLET: So much for this, sir; now shall you see the other.°
You do remember all the circumstance?

HORATIO: Remember it, my lord!

HAMLET: Sir, in my heart there was a kind of fighting
That would not let me sleep. Methought I lay
Worse than the mutines° in the bilboes.° Rashly,°
And praised be rashness for it—let us know°
Our indiscretion° sometimes serves us well
When our deep plots do pall,° and that should learn° us
There's a divinity that shapes our ends,

237 quick alive. **240 his pate** its head, I.e., top; **burning zone** zone in the celestial sphere containing the sun's orbit, between the tropics of Cancer and Capricorn. **241 Ossa** another mountain in Thessaly. (In their war against the Olympian gods, the giants attempted to heap Ossa on Pelion to scale Olympus.); **an** if; **mouth** i.e., rant. **242 mere** utter. **245 golden couplets** two baby pigeons, covered with yellow down; **disclosed** hatched. **249–250 Let . . . day** i.e., (1) even Hercules couldn't stop Laertes' theatrical rant, (2) I, too, will have my turn; i.e., despite any blustering attempts at interference, every person will sooner or later do what he or she must do. **252 in** i.e., by recalling. **253 present push** immediate test. **255 living** lasting. (For Laertes' private understanding, Claudius also hints that Hamlet's death will serve as such a monument.) **256 hour of quiet** time free of conflict. **[5.2] Location: The castle.**
1 see the other hear the other news. **6 mutines** mutineers; **bilboes** shackles; **Rashly** on impulse. (This adverb goes with lines 12 ff.) **7 know** acknowledge **8 indiscretion** lack of foresight and judgment (not an indiscreet act). **9 pall** fail, falter, go stale; **learn** teach.

Rough-hew° them how we will—

HORATIO: That is most certain.

HAMLET: Up from my cabin,
My sea-gown° scarfed° about me, in the dark
Groped I to find out them,° had my desire,
Fingered° their packet, and in fine° withdrew
To mine own room again, making so bold,
My fears forgetting manners, to unseal
Their grand commission; where I found, Horatio—
Ah, royal knavery!—an exact command,
Larded° with many several° sorts of reasons
Importing° Denmark's health and England's too,
With, ho! such bugs° and goblins in my life,°
That on the supervise,° no leisure bated,°
No, not to stay° the grinding of the ax,
My head should be struck off.

HORATIO: Is't possible?

HAMLET [*giving a document*]:
Here's the commission. Read it at more leisure.
But wilt thou hear now how I did proceed?

HORATIO: I beseech you.

HAMLET: Being thus benetted round with villainies—
Ere I could make a prologue to my brains,
They had begun the play°—I sat me down,
Devised a new commission, wrote it fair.°
I once did hold it, as our statists° do,
A baseness° to write fair, and labored much
How to forget that learning; but, sir, now
It did me yeoman's° service. Wilt thou know
Th' effect° of what I wrote?

HORATIO: Ay, good my lord.

HAMLET: An earnest conjuration° from the King,
As England was his faithful tributary,
As love between them like the palm° might flourish,
As peace should still° her wheaten garland° wear
And stand a comma° 'tween their amities,
And many suchlike "as"es° of great charge,°
That on the view and knowing of these contents,
Without debatement further more or less,
He should those bearers put to sudden death,

11 Rough-hew shape roughly. **13 sea-gown** seaman's coat; **scarfed** loosely wrapped. **14 them** i.e., Rosencrantz and Guildenstern. **15 Fingered** pilfered, pinched; **in fine** finally, in conclusion. **20 Larded** garnished; **several** different. **21 Importing** relating to. **22 bugs** bugbears, hobgoblins; **in my life** i.e., to be feared if I were allowed to live. **23 supervise** reading; **leisure bated** delay allowed. **24 stay** await. **30–31 Ere . . . play** before I could consciously turn my brain to the matter, it had started working on a plan. **32 fair** in a clear hand. **33 statists** statesmen. **34 baseness** i.e., lower-class trait. **36 yeoman's** i.e., substantial, faithful, loyal. **37 effect** purport. **38 conjuration** entreaty. **40 palm** (an image of health; see Psalm 92:12.) **41 still** always; **wheaten garland** (symbolic of fruitful agriculture, of peace and plenty.) **42 comma** (indicating continuity, link.) **43 "as"es** (1) the "whereases" of a formal document, (2) asses; **charge** (1) import, (2) burden (appropriate to asses).

Not shriving time° allowed.
HORATIO: How was this sealed?
HAMLET: Why, even in that was heaven ordinant.°
I had my father's signet° in my purse,
Which was the model° of that Danish seal;
Folded the writ° up in the form of th' other,
Subscribed° it, gave 't th' impression,° placed it safely,
The changeling° never known. Now, the next day
Was our sea fight, and what to this was sequent°
Thou knowest already.
HORATIO: So Guildenstern and Rosencrantz go to 't.
HAMLET: Why, man, they did make love to this employment.
They are not near my conscience. Their defeat°
Does by their own insinuation° grow.
'Tis dangerous when the baser° nature comes
Between the pass° and fell° incensèd points
Of mighty opposites.°
HORATIO: Why, what a king is this!
HAMLET: Does it not, think thee, stand me now upon°—
He that hath killed my king and whored my mother,
Popped in between th' election° and my hopes,
Thrown out his angle° for my proper° life,
And with such cozenage°—is 't not perfect conscience
To quit° him with this arm? And is 't not to be damned
To let this canker° of our nature come
In° further evil?
HORATIO: It must be shortly known to him from England
What is the issue of the business there.
HAMLET: It will be short. The interim is mine,
And a man's life's no more than to say "one."°
But I am very sorry, good Horatio,
That to Laertes I forgot myself,
For by the image of my cause I see
The portraiture of his. I'll court his favors.
But, sure, the bravery° of his grief did put me
Into a tow'ring passion.
HORATIO: Peace, who comes here?

Enter a Courtier [OSRIC].

OSRIC: Your lordship is right welcome back to Denmark.

47 shriving time time for confession and absolution. **48 ordinant** directing. **49 signet** small seal. **50 model** replica. **51 writ** writing. **52 Subscribed** signed (with forged signature); **impression** i.e., with a wax seal. **53 changeling** i.e., substituted letter. (Literally, a fairy child substituted for a human one.) **54 was sequent** followed. **58 defeat** destruction. **59 insinuation** intrusive intervention, sticking their noses in my business. **60 baser** of lower social station. **61 pass** thrust; **fell** fierce. **62 opposites** antagonists. **63 stand me now upon** become incumbent on me now. **65 election** (The Danish monarch was "elected" by a small number of high-ranking electors.) **66 angle** fishhook; **proper** very. **67 cozenage** trickery. **68 quit** requite, pay back. **69 canker** ulcer. **69–70 come In** grow into. **74 a man's . . . "one"** one's whole life occupies such a short time, only as long as it takes to count to 1. **79 bravery** bravado.

HAMLET: I humbly thank you, sir. [*To* HORATIO.] Dost know this water fly?

HORATIO: No, my good lord.

HAMLET: Thy state is the more gracious, for 'tis a vice to know him. He hath much land, and fertile. Let a beast be lord of beasts, and his crib° shall stand at the King's mess.° 'Tis a chuff,° but, as I say, spacious in the possession of dirt.

OSRIC: Sweet lord, if your lordship were at leisure, I should impart a thing to you from His Majesty.

HAMLET: I will receive it, sir, with all diligence of spirit. Put your bonnet° to his° right use; 'tis for the head.

OSRIC: I thank your lordship, it is very hot.

HAMLET: No, believe me, 'tis very cold. The wind is northerly.

OSRIC: It is indifferent° cold, my lord, indeed.

HAMLET: But yet methinks it is very sultry and hot for my complexion.°

OSRIC: Exceedingly, my lord. It is very sultry, as 'twere—I cannot tell how. My lord, His Majesty bade me signify to you that 'a has laid a great wager on your head. Sir, this is the matter—

HAMLET: I beseech you, remember.

[HAMLET *moves him to put on his hat.*]

OSRIC: Nay, good my lord; for my ease,° in good faith. Sir, here is newly come to court Laertes—believe me, an absolute° gentleman, full of most excellent differences,° of very soft society° and great showing.° Indeed, to speak feelingly° of him, he is the card° or calendar° of gentry,° for you shall find in him the continent of what part a gentleman would see.°

HAMLET: Sir, his definement° suffers no perdition° in you,° though I know to divide him inventorially° would dozy° th' arithmetic of memory, and yet but yaw° neither° in respect of° his quick sail. But, in the verity of extolment,° I take him to be a soul of great article,° and his infusion° of such dearth and rareness° as, to make true diction° of him, his semblable° is his mirror and who else would trace° him his umbrage,° nothing more.

OSRIC: Your lordship speaks most infallibly of him.

85 crib manger. **85–86 Let . . . mess** i.e., if a man, no matter how beastlike, is as rich in livestock and possessions as Osric, he may eat at the King's table. **86 chuff** boor, churl. (The Second Quarto spelling, *chough,* is a variant spelling that also suggests the meaning here of "chattering jackdaw.") **91 bonnet** any kind of cap or hat; **his** its. **94 indifferent** somewhat. **95 complexion** temperament. **100 for my ease** (a conventional reply declining the invitation to put his hat back on.) **101 absolute** perfect. **102 differences** special qualities; **soft society** agreeable manners; **great showing** distinguished appearance. **103 feelingly** with just perception; **card** chart, map; **calendar** guide. **104 gentry** good breeding. **104–105 the continent . . . see** one who contains in him all the qualities a gentleman would like to see. (A *continent* is that which contains.) **106 definement** definition (Hamlet proceeds to mock Osric by throwing his lofty diction back at him); **perdition** loss, diminution; **you** your description. **106–107 divide him inventorially** enumerate his graces; **107 dozy** dizzy. **108 yaw** swing unsteadily off course. (Said of a ship.); **neither** for all that; **in respect of** in comparison with. **108–109 in . . . extolment** in true praise (of him). **109 of great article** one with many articles in his inventory; **infusion** essence, character infused into him by nature. **110 dearth and rareness** rarity; **make true diction** speak truly; **semblable** only true likeness. **111 who . . . trace** any other person who would wish to follow; **umbrage** shadow.

HAMLET: The concernancy,° sir? Why do we wrap the gentleman in our more rawer breath?°

OSRIC: Sir?

HORATIO: Is 't not possible to understand in another tongue?° You will do 't,° sir, really.

HAMLET: What imports the nomination° of this gentleman?

OSRIC: Of Laertes?

HORATIO [*to* HAMLET]: His purse is empty already; all 's golden words are spent.

HAMLET: Of him, sir.

OSRIC: I know you are not ignorant—

HAMLET: I would you did, sir. Yet in faith if you did, it would not much approve° me. Well, sir?

OSRIC: You are not ignorant of what excellence Laertes is—

HAMLET: I dare not confess that, lest I should compare with him in excellence. But to know a man well were to know himself.°

OSRIC: I mean, sir, for° his weapon; but in the imputation laid on him by them,° in his meed° he's unfellowed.°

HAMLET: What's his weapon?

OSRIC: Rapier and dagger.

HAMLET: That's two of his weapons—but well.°

OSRIC: The King, sir, hath wagered with him six Barbary horses, against the which he° has impawned,° as I take it, six French rapiers and poniards,° with their assigns,° as girdle, hangers,° and so.° Three of the carriages,° in faith, are very dear to fancy,° very responsive° to the hilts, most delicate° carriages, and of very liberal conceit.°

HAMLET: What call you the carriages?

HORATIO [*to* HAMLET]: I knew you must be edified by the margent° ere you had done.

OSRIC: The carriages, sir, are the hangers.

HAMLET: The phrase would be more germane to the matter if we could carry a cannon by our sides; I would it might be hangers till then. But, on: six Barbary horses against six French swords, their assigns, and three liberal-conceited carriages; that's the French bet against the Danish. Why is this impawned, as you call it?

113 concernancy import, relevance. **114 rawer breath** unrefined speech that can only come short in praising him. **116 to understand . . . tongue** i.e., for you, Osric, to understand when someone else speaks your language. (Horatio twits Osric for not being able to understand the kind of flowery speech he himself uses, when Hamlet speaks in such a vein. Alternatively, all this could be said to Hamlet:); **You will do 't** i.e., you can if you try, or, you may well have to try (to speak plainly). **118 nomination** naming. **123 approve** commend. **126–127 I dare . . . himself** I dare not boast of knowing Laertes' excellence lest I seem to imply a comparable excellence in myself. Certainly, to know another person well, one must know oneself. **128 for** i.e., with; **imputation . . . them** reputation given him by others. **129 meed** merit; **unfellowed** unmatched. **132 but well** but never mind. **134 he** i.e., Laertes; **impawned** staked, wagered; **poniards** daggers. **135 assigns** appurtenances; **hangers** straps on the sword belt (*girdle*), from which the sword hung; **and so** and so on; **carriages** (an affected way of saying *hangers*, literally, gun carriages.) **136 dear to fancy** delightful to the fancy; **responsive** corresponding closely, matching or well adjusted. **136–137 delicate** (i.e., in workmanship); **liberal conceit** elaborate design. **139 margent** margin of a book, place for explanatory notes.

OSRIC: The King, sir, hath laid,° sir, that in a dozen passes° between yourself and him, he shall not exceed you three hits. He hath laid on twelve for nine, and it would come to immediate trial, if your lordship would vouchsafe the answer.°

HAMLET: How if I answer no?

OSRIC: I mean, my lord, the opposition of your person in trial.

HAMLET: Sir, I will walk here in the hall. If it please His Majesty, it is the breathing time° of day with me. Let° the foils be brought, the gentleman willing, and the King hold his purpose. I will win for him an I can; if not, I will gain nothing but my shame and the odd hits.

OSRIC: Shall I deliver you° so?

HAMLET: To this effect, sir—after what flourish your nature will.

OSRIC: I commend° my duty to your lordship.

HAMLET: Yours, yours. [*Exit* OSRIC.] 'A does well to commend it himself; there are no tongues else for 's turn.°

HORATIO: This lapwing° runs away with the shell on his head.

HAMLET: 'A did comply with his dug° before 'a sucked it. Thus has he—and many more of the same breed that I know the drossy° age dotes on—only got the tune° of the time and, out of an habit of encounter,° a kind of yeasty° collection,° which carries them through and through the most fanned and winnowed opinions;° and do° but blow them to their trial, the bubbles are out.°

Enter a LORD.

LORD: My lord, His Majesty commended him to you by young Osric, who brings back to him that you attend him in the hall. He sends to know if your pleasure hold to play with Laertes, or that° you will take longer time.

HAMLET: I am constant to my purposes; they follow the King's pleasure. If his fitness speaks, mine is ready;° now or whensoever, provided I be so able as now.

LORD: The King and Queen and all are coming down.

HAMLET: In happy time.°

147 laid wagered; **passes** bouts. (The odds of the betting are hard to explain. Possibly the King bets that Hamlet will win at least five out of twelve, at which point Laertes raises the odds against himself by betting he will win nine.) **149–150 vouchsafe the answer** be so good as to accept the challenge. (Hamlet deliberately takes the phrase in its literal sense of replying.) **153–154 breathing time** exercise period; **Let** i.e., if. **157 deliver you** report what you say. **159 commend** commit to your favor. (A conventional salutation, but Hamlet wryly uses a more literal meaning, "recommend," "praise," in line 160.) **161 for 's turn** for his purposes, i.e., to do it for him. **162 lapwing** (a proverbial type of youthful forwardness. Also, a bird that draws intruders away from its nest and was thought to run about with its head in the shell when newly hatched; a seeming reference to Osric's hat.) **163 comply . . . dug** observe ceremonious formality toward his nurse's or mother's teat. **164 drossy** laden with scum and impurities, frivolous. **165 tune** temper, mood, manner of speech; **an habit of encounter** a demeanor in conversing (with courtiers of his own kind); **yeasty** frothy. **166 collection** i.e., of current phrases. **166–167 carries . . . opinions** sustains them right through the scrutiny of persons whose opinions are select and refined. (Literally, like grain separated from its chaff. Osric is both the chaff and the bubbly froth on the surface of the liquor that is soon blown away.) **167 and do** yet do. **167–168 blow . . . out** test them by merely blowing on them, and their bubbles burst. **171 that** if. **172–173 If . . . ready** If he declares his readiness, my convenience waits on his. **175 In happy time** (a phrase of courtesy indicating that the time is convenient.)

LORD: The Queen desires you to use some gentle entertainment° to Laertes before you fall to play.

HAMLET: She well instructs me. [*Exit* LORD.]

HORATIO: You will lose, my lord.

HAMLET: I do not think so. Since he went into France, I have been in continual practice; I shall win at the odds. But thou wouldst not think how ill all's here about my heart; but it is no matter.

HORATIO: Nay, good my lord—

HAMLET: It is but foolery, but it is such a kind of gaingiving° as would perhaps trouble a woman.

HORATIO: If your mind dislike anything, obey it. I will forestall their repair° hither and say you are not fit.

HAMLET: Not a whit, we defy augury. There is special providence in the fall of a sparrow. If it be now, 'tis not to come; if it be not to come, it will be now; if it be not now, yet it will come. The readiness is all. Since no man of aught he leaves knows, what is 't to leave betimes? Let be.°

A table prepared. [*Enter*] *trumpets, drums, and officers with cushions;* KING, QUEEN, [OSRIC,] *and all the state; foils, daggers,* [*and wine borne in;*] *and* LAERTES.

KING: Come, Hamlet, come and take this hand from me.

[*The* KING *puts* LAERTES' *hand into* HAMLET'*s.*]

HAMLET [*to* LAERTES]: Give me your pardon, sir. I have done you wrong,
But pardon 't as you are a gentleman.
This presence° knows,
And you must needs have heard, how I am punished°
With a sore distraction. What I have done
That might your nature, honor, and exception°
Roughly awake, I here proclaim was madness.
Was 't Hamlet wronged Laertes? Never Hamlet.
If Hamlet from himself be ta'en away,
And when he's not himself does wrong Laertes,
Then Hamlet does it not, Hamlet denies it.
Who does it, then? His madness. If 't be so,
Hamlet is of the faction° that is wronged;
His madness is poor Hamlet's enemy.
Sir, in this audience
Let my disclaiming from a purposed evil
Free me so far in your most generous thoughts
That I have° shot my arrow o'er the house
And hurt my brother.

LAERTES: I am satisfied in nature,°
Whose motive° in this case should stir me most
To my revenge. But in my terms of honor
I stand aloof, and will no reconcilement

176 entertainment greeting. **184 gaingiving** misgiving. **186 repair** coming. **190–191 Since . . . Let be** Since no one has knowledge of what he is leaving behind, what does an early death matter after all? Enough; don't struggle against it. **195 presence** royal assembly. **196 punished** afflicted. **198 exception** disapproval. **205 faction** party. **210 That I have** as if I had. **211 in nature** i.e., as to my personal feelings. **212 motive** prompting.

Till by some elder masters of known honor
I have a voice° and precedent of peace°
To keep my name ungored.° But till that time
I do receive your offered love like love,
And will not wrong it.

HAMLET: I embrace it freely,
And will this brothers' wager frankly° play.—
Give us the foils. Come on.

LAERTES: Come, one for me.

HAMLET: I'll be your foil,° Laertes. In mine ignorance
Your skill shall, like a star i' the darkest night,
Stick fiery off° indeed.

LAERTES: You mock me, sir.

HAMLET: No, by this hand.

KING: Give them the foils, young Osric. Cousin Hamlet,
You know the wager?

HAMLET: Very well, my lord.
Your Grace has laid the odds o'° the weaker side.

KING: I do not fear it; I have seen you both.
But since he is bettered,° we have therefore odds.

LAERTES: This is too heavy. Let me see another.
[*He exchanges his foil for another.*]

HAMLET: This likes me° well. These foils have all a length?
[*They prepare to play.*]

OSRIC: Ay, my good lord.

KING: Set me the stoups of wine upon that table.
If Hamlet give the first or second hit,
Or quit in answer of the third exchange,°
Let all the battlements their ordnance fire.
The King shall drink to Hamlet's better breath,°
And in the cup an union° shall he throw
Richer than that which four successive kings
In Denmark's crown have worn. Give me the cups,
And let the kettle° to the trumpet speak,
The trumpet to the cannoneer without,
The cannons to the heavens, the heaven to earth,
"Now the King drinks to Hamlet." Come, begin. *Trumpets the while.*
And you, the judges, bear a wary eye.

HAMLET: Come on, sir.

LAERTES: Come, my lord. [*They play.* HAMLET *scores a hit.*]

HAMLET: One.

216 voice authoritative pronouncement; **of peace** for reconciliation. **217 name ungored** reputation unwounded. **220 frankly** without ill feeling or the burden of rancor. **222 foil** thin metal background which sets a jewel off (with pun on the blunted rapier for fencing).
224 Stick fiery off stand out brilliantly. **228 laid the odds o'** bet on, backed. **230 is bettered** has improved; is the odds-on favorite. (Laertes' handicap is the "three hits" specified in line 148.) **232 likes me** pleases me. **236 Or . . . exchange** i.e., or requites Laertes in the third bout for having won the first two. **238 better breath** improved vigor. **239 union** pearl. (So called, according to Pliny's *Natural History*, 9, because pearls are *unique*, never identical.)
242 kettle kettledrum.

LAERTES: No.
HAMLET: Judgment.
OSRIC: A hit, a very palpable hit.
Drum, trumpets, and shot. Flourish. A piece goes off.
LAERTES: Well, again.
KING: Stay, give me drink. Hamlet, this pearl is thine.

[*He drinks, and throws a pearl in* HAMLET*'s cup.*]

Here's to thy health. Give him the cup.
HAMLET: I'll play this bout first. Set it by awhile.
Come. [*They play.*] Another hit; what say you?
LAERTES: A touch, a touch, I do confess 't.
KING: Our son shall win.
QUEEN: He's fat° and scant of breath.
Here, Hamlet, take my napkin,° rub thy brows.
The Queen carouses° to thy fortune, Hamlet.
HAMLET: Good madam!
KING: Gertrude, do not drink.
QUEEN: I will, my lord, I pray you pardon me. [*She drinks.*]
KING [*aside*]: It is the poisoned cup. It is too late.
HAMLET: I dare not drink yet, madam; by and by.
QUEEN: Come, let me wipe thy face.
LAERTES [*to* KING]: My lord, I'll hit him now.
KING: I do not think 't.
LAERTES [*aside*]: And yet it is almost against my conscience.
HAMLET: Come, for the third, Laertes. You do but dally.
I pray you, pass° with your best violence;
I am afeard you make a wanton of me.°
LAERTES: Say you so? Come on. [*They play.*]
OSRIC: Nothing neither way.
LAERTES: Have at you now!

[LAERTES *wounds* HAMLET; *then, in scuffling, they change rapiers,° and* HAMLET *wounds* LAERTES.]

KING: Part them! They are incensed.
HAMLET: Nay, come, again. [*The* QUEEN *falls.*]
OSRIC: Look to the Queen there, ho!
HORATIO: They bleed on both sides. How is it, my lord?
OSRIC: How is 't, Laertes?
LAERTES: Why, as a woodcock° to mine own springe,° Osric;
I am justly killed with mine own treachery.
HAMLET: How does the Queen?
KING: She swoons to see them bleed.
QUEEN: No, no, the drink, the drink—O my dear Hamlet—
The drink, the drink! I am poisoned. [*She dies.*]

258 fat not physically fit, out of training. **259 napkin** handkerchief. **260 carouses** drinks a toast. **270 pass** thrust. **271 make . . . me** i.e., treat me like a spoiled child, trifle with me. **274 s.d. in scuffling, they change rapiers** (This stage direction occurs in the Folio. According to a widespread stage tradition, Hamlet receives a scratch, realizes that Laertes' sword is unbated, and accordingly forces an exchange.) **278 woodcock** a bird, a type of stupidity or as a decoy; **springe** trap, snare.

HAMLET: O villainy! Ho, let the door be locked!
Treachery! Seek it out. [LAERTES *falls. Exit* OSRIC.]
LAERTES: It is here, Hamlet. Hamlet, thou art slain.
No med'cine in the world can do thee good;
In thee there is not half an hour's life.
The treacherous instrument is in thy hand,
Unbated° and envenomed. The foul practice°
Hath turned itself on me. Lo, here I lie,
Never to rise again. Thy mother's poisoned.
I can no more. The King, the King's to blame.
HAMLET: The point envenomed too? Then, venom, to thy work.
[*He stabs the* KING.]
ALL: Treason! Treason!
KING: O, yet defend me, friends! I am but hurt.
HAMLET [*forcing the* KING *to drink.*]
Here, thou incestuous, murderous, damnèd Dane,
Drink off this potion. Is thy union° here?
Follow my mother. [*The* KING *dies.*]
LAERTES: He is justly served.
It is a poison tempered° by himself.
Exchange forgiveness with me, noble Hamlet.
Mine and my father's death come not upon thee,
Nor thine on me! [*He dies.*]
HAMLET: Heaven make thee free of it! I follow thee.
I am dead, Horatio. Wretched Queen, adieu!
You that look pale and tremble at this chance,°
That are but mutes° or audience to this act,
Had I but time—as this fell° sergeant,° Death,
Is strict° in his arrest°—O, I could tell you—
But let it be. Horatio, I am dead;
Thou livest. Report me and my cause aright
To the unsatisfied.
HORATIO: Never believe it.
I am more an antique Roman° than a Dane.
Here's yet some liquor left.
[*He attempts to drink from the poisoned cup.* HAMLET *prevents him.*]
HAMLET: As thou'rt a man,
Give me the cup! Let go! By heaven, I'll ha 't.
O God, Horatio, what a wounded name,
Things standing thus unknown, shall I leave behind me!
If thou didst ever hold me in thy heart,
Absent thee from felicity awhile,
And in this harsh world draw thy breath in pain

289 Unbated not blunted with a button; **practice** plot. **297 union** pearl. (See line 239; with grim puns on the word's other meanings: marriage, shared death.) **299 tempered** mixed. **305 chance** mischance. **306 mutes** silent observers. (Literally, actors with nonspeaking parts.) **307 fell** cruel; **sergeant** sheriff's officer. **308 strict** (1) severely just, (2) unavoidable; **arrest** (1) taking into custody, (2) stopping my speech. **312 Roman** (suicide was an honorable choice for many Romans as an alternative to a dishonorable life.)

To tell my story. *A march afar off* [*and a volley within*].
What warlike noise is this?

Enter OSRIC.

OSRIC: Young Fortinbras, with conquest come from Poland,
To th' ambassadors of England gives
This warlike volley.

HAMLET: O, I die, Horatio!
The potent poison quite o'ercrows° my spirit.
I cannot live to hear the news from England,
But I do prophesy th' election lights
On Fortinbras. He has my dying voice.°
So tell him, with th' occurents° more and less
Which have solicited°—the rest is silence. [*He dies.*]

HORATIO: Now cracks a noble heart. Good night, sweet prince,
And flights of angels sing thee to thy rest! [*March within.*]
Why does the drum come hither?

Enter FORTINBRAS, *with the* [*English*] *Ambassadors* [*with drum, colors, and attendants*].

FORTINBRAS: Where is this sight?

HORATIO: What is it you would see?
If aught of woe or wonder, cease your search.

FORTINBRAS: This quarry° cries on havoc.° O proud Death,
What feast° is toward° in thine eternal cell,
That thou so many princes at a shot
So bloodily hast struck?

FIRST AMBASSADOR: The sight is dismal,
And our affairs from England come too late.
The ears are senseless that should give us hearing,
To tell him his commandment is fulfilled,
That Rosencrantz and Guildenstern are dead.
Where should we have our thanks?

HORATIO: Not from his° mouth,
Had it th' ability of life to thank you.
He never gave commandment for their death.
But since, so jump° upon this bloody question,°
You from the Polack wars, and you from England,
And here arrived, give order that these bodies
High on a stage° be placèd to the view,
And let me speak to th' yet unknowing world
How these things came about. So shall you hear
Of carnal, bloody, and unnatural acts,
Of accidental judgments,° casual° slaughters,

325 o'ercrows triumphs over (like the winner in a cockfight). **328 voice** vote. **329 occurrents** events, incidents. **330 solicited** moved, urged. (Hamlet doesn't finish saying what the events have prompted—presumably, his acts of vengeance, or his reporting of those events to Fortinbras.) **336 quarry** heap of dead; **cries on havoc** proclaims a general slaughter. **337 feast** i.e., Death feasting on those who have fallen; **toward** in preparation. **344 his** i.e., Claudius'. **347 jump** precisely, immediately; **question** dispute, affair. **350 stage** platform. **354 judgments** retributions; **casual** occurring by chance.

Of deaths put on° by cunning and forced cause,°
And, in this upshot, purposes mistook
Fall'n on th' inventors' heads. All this can I
Truly deliver.

FORTINBRAS: Let us haste to hear it,
And call the noblest to the audience.
For me, with sorrow I embrace my fortune.
I have some rights of memory° in this kingdom,
Which now to claim my vantage° doth invite me.

HORATIO: Of that I shall have also cause to speak,
And from his mouth whose voice will draw on more.°
But let this same be presently° performed,
Even while men's minds are wild, lest more mischance
On° plots and errors happen.

FORTINBRAS: Let four captains
Bear Hamlet, like a soldier, to the stage,
For he was likely, had he been put on,°
To have proved most royal; and for his passage,°
The soldiers' music and the rite of war
Speak° loudly for him.
Take up the bodies. Such a sight as this
Becomes the field,° but here shows much amiss.
Go bid the soldiers shoot.

Exeunt [*marching, bearing off the dead bodies; a peal of ordnance is shot off*].

[1603]

355 put on instigated; **forced cause** contrivance. **361 of memory** traditional, remembered, unforgotten. **362 vantage** favorable opportunity. **364 voice . . . more** vote will influence still others. **365 presently** immediately. **367 On** on the basis of; on top of. **369 put on** i.e., invested in royal office and so put to the test. **370 Passage** i.e., from life to death. **372 Speak** let them speak. **374 Becomes the field** suits the field of battle.

Joining the Conversation: Critical Thinking and Writing

Act 1

1. The first scene (like many other scenes in this play) is full of expressions of uncertainty. What are some are these uncertainties? The Ghost first appears at 1.1.43. Does his appearance surprise us, or have we been prepared for it? Or is there both preparation and surprise? Do the last four speeches of 1.1 help to introduce a note of hope? If so, how?
2. Does the King's opening speech in 1.2 reveal him to be an accomplished public speaker—or are lines 10–14 offensive? In his second speech (lines 41–49), what is the effect of naming Laertes four times? Claudius sometimes uses the royal pronouns ("we," "our"), sometimes the more intimate "I" and "my." Study his use of these in lines 1–4 and in 106–117. What do you think he is getting at?
3. Hamlet's first soliloquy (1.2.129–59) reveals that more than just his father's death distresses him. Be as specific as possible about the causes of Hamlet's anguish here.
4. What traits does Hamlet reveal in his conversation with Horatio (1.2.160–258)?

5. What do you make of Polonius's advice to Laertes (1.3.55–81)? Is it sound? Sound advice, but here uttered by a fool? Ignoble advice? How would one follow the advice of line 78: "to thine own self be true"? In his words to Ophelia in 1.3.102–36, what does he reveal about himself?
6. Can 1.4.17–38 reasonably be taken as a speech on the "tragic flaw"? (On this idea, see page 435.) Or is the passage a much more limited discussion, a comment simply on Danish drinking habits?
7. Hamlet is convinced in 1.5.93–105 that the Ghost has told the truth, indeed, the only important truth. But do we detect in 105–12 a hint of a tone suggesting that Hamlet delights in hating villainy? If so, can it be said that later this delight grows, and that in some scenes (e.g., 3.3) we feel that Hamlet has almost become a diabolic revenger? Explain.

Act 2

1. Characterize Polonius on the basis of 2.1.1–75.
2. In light of what we have seen of Hamlet, is Ophelia's report of his strange behavior when he visits her understandable?
3. Why does 2.2.33–34 seem almost comic? How do these lines help us to form a view about Rosencrantz and Guildenstern?
4. Is "the hellish Pyrrhus" (2.2.405) Hamlet's version of Claudius? Or is he Hamlet, who soon will be responsible for the deaths of Polonius, Rosencrantz and Guildenstern, Claudius, Gertrude, Ophelia, and Laertes? Explain.
5. Is the speech that Hamlet and the First Player recite, with some interruptions (2.2.392–453), an absurdly bombastic speech? If so, why? To distinguish it from the poetry of the play itself? To characterize the bloody deeds that Hamlet cannot descend to?
6. In 2.2.482–520 Hamlet rebukes himself for not acting. Why has he not acted? Because he is a coward (line 503)? Because he has a conscience? Because no action can restore his father and his mother's purity? Because he doubts the Ghost? What reason(s) can you offer?

Act 3

1. What do you make out of Hamlet's assertion to Ophelia: "I loved you not" (3.1.117)? Of his characterization of himself as full of "offenses" (3.1.121–25)? Why is Hamlet so harsh to Ophelia?
2. In 3.3.36–72 Claudius's conscience afflicts him. But is he repentant? What makes you say so?
3. Is Hamlet other than abhorrent in 3.3.73–96? Do we want him to kill Claudius at this moment, when Claudius (presumably with his back to Hamlet) is praying? Why?
4. The Ghost speaks of Hamlet's "almost blunted purpose" (3.4.115). Is the accusation fair? Explain.
5. How would you characterize Hamlet in 3.4.209–24?

Act 4

1. Is Gertrude protecting Hamlet when she says he is mad (4.1.7), or does she believe that he is mad? If she believes he is mad, does it follow that she no longer feels ashamed and guilty? Explain.
2. Why should Hamlet hide Polonius's body (in 4.2)? Is he feigning madness? Is he on the edge of madness? Explain.

3. How can we explain Hamlet's willingness to go to England (4.3.52)?
4. Judging from 4.5, what has driven Ophelia mad? Is Laertes heroic, or somewhat foolish? Consider also the way Claudius treats him in 4.7.

Act 5

1. Would anything be lost if the gravediggers in 5.1 were omitted?
2. To what extent do we judge Hamlet severely for sending Rosencrantz and Guildenstern to their deaths, as he reports in 5.2? On the whole, do we think of Hamlet as an intriguer? What other intrigues has he engendered? How successful were they?
3. Does 5.2.188–91 show a paralysis of the will, or a wise recognition that more is needed than mere human scheming? Explain.
4. Does 5.2.274 suggest that Laertes takes advantage of a momentary pause and unfairly stabs Hamlet? Is the exchange of weapons accidental, or does Hamlet (as in Olivier's film version), realizing that he has been betrayed, deliberately get possession of Laertes's deadly weapon?
5. Fortinbras is often cut from the play. How much is lost by the cut? Explain.
6. Fortinbras gives Hamlet a soldier's funeral. Is this ridiculous? Can it fairly be said that, in a sense, Hamlet has been at war? Explain.

General Questions

1. Hamlet in 5.2.10–11 speaks of a "divinity that shapes our ends." To what extent does "divinity" (or Fate or mysterious Chance) play a role in the happenings?
2. How do Laertes, Fortinbras, and Horatio help to define Hamlet for us?
3. T. S. Eliot says (in "Shakespeare and the Stoicism of Seneca") that Hamlet, having made a mess, "dies fairly well pleased with himself." Evaluate.

ERNEST JONES

*Hamlet and the Oedipus Complex**

In short, the whole picture presented by Hamlet, his deep depression, the hopeless note in his attitude towards the world and towards the value of life, his dread of death, his repeated reference to bad dreams, his self-accusations, his desperate efforts to get away from the thoughts of his duty, and his vain attempts to find an excuse for his procrastination: all this unequivocally points to a *tortured conscience,* to some hidden ground for shirking his task, a ground which he dare not or cannot avow to himself.

. . .

Extensive studies of the past half century, inspired by Freud, have taught us that a psychoneurosis means a state of mind where the person is unduly, and often painfully, driven or thwarted by the "unconscious" part of his mind, that buried part that was once the infant's mind and still lives on side by side with the adult mentality that has developed out of it and should have taken its place.

*The title is the editors'. Footnotes are abridged.

It signifies *internal* mental conflict. We have here the reason why it is impossible to discuss intelligently the state of mind of anyone suffering from a psychoneurosis, whether the description is of a living person or an imagined one, without correlating the manifestations with what must have operated in his infancy and is *still operating*. That is what I propose to attempt here.

For some deep-seated reason, which is to him unacceptable, Hamlet is plunged into anguish at the thought of his father being replaced in his mother's affections by someone else. It is as if his devotion to his mother had made him so jealous for her affection that he had found it hard enough to share this even with his father and could not endure to share it with still another man. Against this thought, however, suggestive as it is, may be urged three objections. First, if it were in itself a full statement of the matter, Hamlet would have been aware of the jealousy, whereas we have concluded that the mental process we are seeking is hidden from him. Secondly, we see in it no evidence of the arousing of an old and forgotten memory. And, thirdly, Hamlet is being deprived by Claudius of no greater share in the Queen's affection than he had been by his own father, for the two brothers made exactly similar claims in this respect—namely, those of a loved husband. The last-named objection, however, leads us to the heart of the situation. How if, in fact, Hamlet had in years gone by, as a child, bitterly resented having had to share his mother's affection even with his own father, had regarded him as a rival, and had secretly wished him out of the way so that he might enjoy undisputed and undisturbed the monopoly of that affection? If such thoughts had been present in his mind in childhood days they evidently would have been "repressed," and all traces of them obliterated, by filial piety and other educative influences. The actual realization of his early wish in the death of his father at the hands of a jealous rival would then have stimulated into activity these "repressed" memories, which would have produced, in the form of depression and other suffering, an obscure aftermath of his childhood's conflict. This is at all events the mechanism that is actually found in the real Hamlets who are investigated psychologically.

The explanation, therefore, of the delay and self-frustration exhibited in the endeavour to fulfil his father's demand for vengeance is that to Hamlet the thought of incest and parricide combined is too intolerable to be borne. One part of him tries to carry out the task, the other flinches inexorably from the thought of it. How fain would he blot it out in that "bestial oblivion" which unfortunately for him his conscience contemns. He is torn and tortured in an insoluble inner conflict.

• • •

5 Now comes the father's death and the mother's second marriage. The association of the idea of sexuality with his mother, buried since infancy, can no longer be concealed from his consciousness. As Bradley well says: "Her son was forced to see in her action not only an astounding shallowness of feeling, but an eruption of coarse sensuality, 'rank and gross,' speeding post-haste to its horrible delight." Feelings which once, in the infancy of long ago, were pleasurable desires can now, because of his repressions, only fill him with repulsion. The long "repressed" desire to take his father's place in his mother's affection is stimulated to unconscious activity by the sight of someone usurping this place exactly as he himself had once longed to do. More, this someone was a member of the same family, so that the actual usurpation further resembled the imaginary one in being incestuous. Without his being in the least aware of it these ancient desires are ringing in his mind, are once more struggling to find conscious expression, and

need such an expenditure of energy again to "repress" them that he is reduced to the deplorable mental state he himself so vividly depicts.

There follows the Ghost's announcement that the father's death was a willed one, was due to murder. Hamlet, having at the moment his mind filled with natural indignation at the news, answers normally enough with the cry (Act I, Sc. 5):

> Haste me to know't, that I, with wings as swift
> As meditation or the thoughts of love,
> May sweep to my revenge.

The momentous words follow revealing who was the guilty person, namely a relative who had committed the deed at the bidding of lust.[1] Hamlet's second guilty wish had thus also been realized by his uncle, namely to procure the fulfilment of the first—the possession of the mother—by a personal deed, in fact by murder of the father. The two recent events, the father's death and the mother's second marriage, seemed to the world to have no inner causal relation to each other, but they represented ideas which in Hamlet's unconscious phantasy had always been closely associated. These ideas now in a moment forced their way to conscious recognition in spite of all "repressing forces," and found immediate expression in his almost reflex cry: "O my prophetic soul! My uncle?" The frightful truth his unconscious had already intuitively divined, his consciousness had now to assimiliate as best it could. For the rest of the interview Hamlet is stunned by the effect of the internal conflict thus re-awakened, which from now on never ceases, and into the essential nature of which he never penetrates.

[1949]

[1]It is not maintained that this was by any means Claudius's whole motive, but it was evidently a powerful one and the one that most impressed Hamlet.

ANNE BARTON

*The Promulgation of Confusion**

The length of the play suggests that it was never, not even in Shakespeare's time, performed uncut. Other plays by Shakespeare are long; no other violates so strikingly the limits of audience attention, or asks for so much from its leading actor. Like *Titus*, like *The Spanish Tragedy* and that lost source play, the so-called *Ur-Hamlet*, which was probably the work of Kyd, Shakespeare's *Hamlet* is a tragedy of revenge. It concentrates, like them, upon a single, essentially sympathetic hero and it confronts precisely the same structural problem: how to linger out his vengeance for the necessary five acts. Kyd's Hieronymo (and probably his Hamlet), Shakespeare's Titus and Hamlet all require proof of the villain's identity before they can act. They are temporarily deflected from their purpose, not only by difficulties of strategy, but by a madness partly assumed and partly real. All make use of some kind of dramatic show to further their intention and all accomplish, in the end, a vengeance which, whatever the original provocation, has by this time become more than a little suspect.

As a tragic predicament, revenge has several inherent advantages. Intrigue and spectacle, madness and violence, are not the only elements native to the genre. The isolation naturally imposed upon the revenger not only encourages introspection, it destroys normal human relationships in a fundamentally tragic way. A detached, satirist's view of the society against which they war almost forces itself upon these

*The title is the editors'.

characters. Their situation generates a corrosive doubt, reaching out to attack religious, moral and legal institutions. Kyd, Marlowe in *The Jew of Malta,* and the young Shakespeare of *Titus,* had all recognized and explored these inbuilt opportunities, at least to some extent. It was only with *Hamlet,* however, that a dramatist seized upon the form to trigger off an enquiry into the whole basis of human existence. Debate over man's right to encroach upon the prerogative of Heaven by undertaking himself what was properly God's act of retributive justice had been and, in the Jacobean period, would continue to be a feature of revenge tragedy.

• • •

Only *Hamlet* side-steps the ethic of revenge entirely. It is one of several great silences at the heart of this play. Deliberately, Shakespeare has shifted attention away from an expected centre, from the problem of whether the prince *ought* to kill Claudius—or even whether in practical terms he *can*—to the far more complicated and subjective issue of whether or not he ultimately *will*. It is not the peculiar status of acts of private vengeance that is under review here, but the validity of all and any human action.

Although other dramatists (Marston, Webster and Tourneur especially) later used *Hamlet* as a spring-board for their own exploration of the revenge form, none of them dared to attempt a focus so wide. The range of the play and, above all, of the role of Hamlet himself, is so great that any performance must necessarily be a matter of selection, of emphases more or less arbitrarily imposed. The impossibility of presenting *Hamlet* whole and uncut is not entirely a feature of its great length. It is also bound up with its inclusiveness, with the fact that Shakespeare seems to have been determined to subject a bewildering number of people, ideas, values, kinds of relationship, emotions and social forms to the distorted but strangely clear scrutiny of a revenger so complicated himself that no attempt to describe, or act, him can be more than partial. Even more than most plays of Shakespeare, *Hamlet* is a warning against the fallacy that any critical interpretation or stage production can be definitive, or even complete.

5 When Hamlet cautioned Rosencrantz and Guildenstern, after the play scene, against the attempt to "pluck out the heart of my mystery . . . sound me from my lowest note to the top of my compass" (3.2.319–21), he also provided a useful counsel for literary critics. The play as a whole is built upon contradiction, upon the promulgation of confusion. Shakespeare gives every indication of having constructed an imaginary Denmark intended to baffle, to resist explanation as stubbornly as those mysterious facts of human existence which it illuminates without rationalizing. A distrust of what might be described as a "play-shaped" view of the world of the falseness of clearly defined moral, theological or formal patterns imposed upon reality in the interests of art is, I think, characteristic of him throughout his dramatic career. It was to become particularly strong in his Jacobean plays. This antipathy may account, in part, for Shakespeare's apparent suspicion of *tragedy* as a term, and also for the variety and restlessness of his own formal development.

Certainly, the eschatology of *Hamlet* defies explication. The ghost of a murdered king appears from an almost embarrassingly specific Catholic Purgatory, a place of "sulph'rous and tormenting flames" (1.5.3) to which it has been confined "till the foul crimes done in my days of nature / Are burnt and purged away" (1.5.13–14). This spirit urges upon its beloved only son a revenge for which, by immutable Christian law, that son must be damned perpetually—sent not to Purgatory, but to the far greater torments of Hell. Neither Hamlet, the sensible Horatio nor the ghost itself ever remark upon this illogicality. Hamlet's worry is only about the truth of the ghost's accusation. If Claudius is guilty, and the Mouse-trap proves that he is, he must be killed. Not for an instant does Hamlet doubt the justice of such a course, let alone the propriety of a repentant soul spending its time in Purgatory meditating a murder. A similar inconsistency adds complications to what is already, on psychological grounds, a most ambiguous scene in Act 3. Hamlet declines to kill the king at prayers because he fears that Claudius' soul will ascend to Heaven. This, at least, is the reason he gives. He will wait to find his enemy

> drunk asleep, or in his rage,
> Or in th'incestuous pleasure of his bed,
> At game, a-swearing, or about some act
> That has no relish of salvation in't,
> Then trip him that his heels may kick at heaven,
> And that his soul may be as damned and black
> As hell whereto it goes.
>
> (3.3.89–95)

Here, the odd fact that Hamlet never considers that his own soul would be damned irrecoverably by the requirements of such a theology, is cunningly mingled with doubts as to whether he really means what he is saying in this speech, or whether it is a feeble excuse for postponing an explicably distasteful task.

In *Hamlet,* Shakespeare affirms a Christian supernatural in one moment to deny it in the next. The hereafter involves Purgatory, hell fire, and flights of angels. It is also silence, an eternal sleep that has nothing to do with punishment or reward. The prince talks about death as "the undiscovered country, from whose bourn / No traveller returns" (3.1.80–81) out of an anguish of mind created by the return of just such a traveller. A special Providence guides the fall of the sparrow, or at least Hamlet asserts that it does just before the fatal game with the foils in Act 5. He seems to die, however, in the agnostic spirit which, a moment later, prompts Horatio's account of the catastrophe as "accidental judgements, casual slaughters" (5.2.354). These conflicting views follow one another so closely in the action, and they are treated by the dramatist with such a non-committal equality, that it becomes impossible to characterize the supernatural in the play. Although we stumble from time to time over the partially submerged rocks of old beliefs, their presence only makes the obscurity of the total picture more poignant. In effect, Shakespeare has created his own, infinitely more complex version of the divided worlds of [Pickering's] *Horestes* and [Kyd's] *The Spanish Tragedy*. Hamlet's questions, instead of being halted artificially as Hieronymo's were by a tidy, Senecan supernatural visible to us in the audience although not to the hero, grope their way into a darkness without form or limit. Like Pickering, Shakespeare placed his spirit of Revenge inside the play itself, as a character who addresses the protagonist directly. Having done so, he proceeded disconcertingly to associate the ghost with a Christian hereafter, and refused to judge its ethic of blood vengeance. *Hamlet* never explains the nature of that silence towards which the hero moves gradually, away from us, and into which he finally vanishes. This is one reason why the tragedy has a terror, and also a relevance to the world as we know it, lacking in Pickering and Kyd.

More perhaps than any other Shakespearean tragedy, *Hamlet* is a play obsessed with words themselves. It displaces the accustomed centre of earlier revenge drama by subordinating plot for its own sake to a new concern with the mysterious gap between thought and action, between the verbal formulation of intent and its concrete realization. The prince himself is the most articulate of Shakespeare's tragic heroes, but he combines verbal fluency with a curious paralysis of the will. When Claudius asks Laertes in Act 4 what he would do "to show yourself your father's son in deed / More than in words" (4.7.130–131), Laertes replies instantly that, to be avenged, he would be happy to cut Hamlet's throat "i' the church." A demonstration that "in deed more than words" he is his father's son is conspicuously what the Hamlet of "O, what a rogue and peasant slave am I" and "How all occasions do inform against me" has not managed. We may respect him for this failing. Certainly, the sharply contrasted readiness of Laertes to act without thinking is unlovely. The fact remains that Hamlet is a man suffering from a peculiar malaise. In his mind, speech and event, language and its realization have become separate and disjunct. He can initiate action only when he has no time to subject it, first, to words: when he stabs impulsively through the arras and kills Polonius, when he sends Rosencrantz and Guildenstern to death *before* "I could make a prologue to my brains" (5.2.31), boards the pirate ship in the heat of the moment or finally, without premeditation, kills the king. The Norwegian captain tells Hamlet in the fourth scene of Act 4 that Fortinbras is hazarding twenty thousand ducats and an army of two thousand men to gain "a little patch of ground / That hath in it no profit but the name" (4.4.19–20). Fortinbras here, as in other respects, is Hamlet's diametric opposite. He has converted a mere word, a name, into a pretext for action. Hamlet, on the other hand, allows a tangible situation, the fact of a father's murder, to dissolve into words alone.

[1971]

Stanley Wells

On the First Soliloquy

More than most plays, *Hamlet* is a series of opportunities for virtuosity. This is true above all of the role of Hamlet himself. "Hamlet," wrote Max Beerbohm, is "a hoop through which every very eminent actor must, sooner or later, jump." There is no wonder that it has been such a favourite part with actors, and even with actresses. The performer has the opportunity to demonstrate a wide range of ability, to be melancholy and gay, charming and cynical, thoughtful and flippant, tender and cruel, calm and impassioned, noble and vindictive, downcast and witty, all within a few hours. He can wear a variety of costumes, he need not disguise good looks, he can demonstrate athletic ability, he has perhaps the longest role in drama—he could scarcely ask for more, except perhaps the opportunity to sing and dance.

And if the role of Hamlet is the greatest reason for the play's popularity with actors, the character of Hamlet is surely the greatest reason for its popularity with audiences. Hamlet is the most sympathetic of tragic heroes. We are drawn to him by his youth, his intelligence, and his vulnerability. As soon as he appears we are conscious of one of the sources of his appeal: his immense capacity for taking life seriously. It may sound like a slightly repellent quality, but I don't mean to imply that he is excessively gloomy or over-earnest. Often he is deeply dejected: but he has good cause. There is nothing exceptional about his emotional reactions except perhaps their intensity. He has a larger-than-life capacity for experience, a fullness of response, a depth of feeling, a vibrancy of living, which mark him out from the ordinary. He is a raw nerve in the court of Denmark, disconcertingly liable to make the instinctive rather than the conditioned response. This cuts him off from those around him, but it puts him into peculiar contact with the audience. And as Hamlet is to the other figures of the play, so his soliloquies are to the role, for in them Shakespeare shows us the raw nerves of Hamlet himself.

The use of soliloquy is one of the most brilliant features of the play, for in these speeches Shakespeare solves a major technical problem in the presentation of his central character. The young man who takes himself seriously, who persists in explaining himself and his problems, is someone we are apt—perhaps too apt—to regard as a bore. We have all had experience of him, and so probably have most of our friends. On the other hand, the desire to know someone to the depths is fundamental to human nature. Here was both a problem and a challenge: how to let Hamlet reveal himself without becoming an almighty bore? Shakespeare found a double solution. First, he caused Hamlet to conduct his deepest self-communings in solitude, so that there is none of the awkwardness associated with the presence of a confidant. And secondly, the soliloquies are written in a style which presents us not with conclusions but with the very processes of Hamlet's mind.

There had been nothing like this in drama before: nothing which, while retaining a verse form, at the same time so vividly revealed what Shakespeare elsewhere calls "the quick forge and working-house of thought" (*Henry the Fifth* [5.Pro.23]). Vocabulary, syntax, and rhythm all contribute to the effect. Consider the second half of Hamlet's first soliloquy, beginning with his contrast between his uncle and his dead father:

That it should come to this—
But two months dead—nay, not so much, not two—
So excellent a king, that was to this
Hyperion to a satyr, so loving to my mother
That he might not beteem the winds of heaven
Visit her face too roughly! Heaven and earth,
Must I remember? Why, she would hang on him
As if increase of appetite had grown
By what it fed on, and yet within a month—
Let me not think on't; frailty, thy name is woman—
A little month, or ere those shoes were old
With which she followed my poor father's body,
Like Niobe, all tears, why she, even she—
O God, a beast that wants discourse of reason
Would have mourned longer!—married with mine uncle,
My father's brother, but no more like my father
Than I to Hercules; within a month,
Ere yet the salt of most unrighteous tears
Had left the flushing of her gallèd eyes,
She married. O most wicked speed, to post
With such dexterity to incestuous sheets!
It is not, nor it cannot come to good.
But break, my heart, for I must hold my tongue.

(1.2.137–159)

5 The anguish that it causes Hamlet to think of his mother's over-hasty marriage is conveyed as much by the tortured syntax as by direct statement; we share his difficulty as he tries—and fails—to assimilate these unwelcome facts into his consciousness, seeking to bring under emotional control the discordant elements of his disrupted universe: his love of his dead father, his love of his mother combined with disgust at her marriage to the uncle whom he loathes, and the disillusion with womankind that this has provoked in him. The short exclamations interrupting the sentence structure point his horror: the rhythms of ordinary speech within the verse give immediacy to the contrasts in phrases such as "Hyperion to a satyr" and "Than I to Hercules"; and the concreteness of the imagery betrays the effort it costs him to master the unwelcome nature of the facts which it expresses: his mother's haste to marry "or ere those shoes were old / With which she followed my poor father's body"—it is as if only by concentrating on the matter-of-fact, physical aspects of the scene can he bear to contemplate it, or bring it within his belief. He ends on a note of utter helplessness: he alone sees the truth; he knows that his mother's actions, which both he and she see as evil, must bring forth evil; but he, the only emotionally honest person there, cannot express his emotion—except to us.

[1995]

Elaine Showalter

Representing Ophelia

"Of all the characters in *Hamlet,*" Bridget Lyons has pointed out, "Ophelia is most persistently presented in terms of symbolic meanings." Her behavior, her appearance, her gestures, her costume, her props, are freighted with emblematic significance, and for many generations of Shakespearean critics her part in the play has seemed to be primarily iconographic. Ophelia's symbolic meanings, moreover, are specifically feminine. Whereas for Hamlet madness is metaphysical, linked with culture, for Ophelia it is a product of the female body and female nature, perhaps that nature's purest form. On the Elizabethan stage, the conventions of female insanity were sharply defined. Ophelia dresses in white, decks herself with "fantastical garlands" of wild flowers, and enters, according to the stage directions of the "Bad" Quarto, "distracted" playing on a lute with her "hair down singing." Her speeches are marked by extravagant metaphors, lyrical free associations, and "explosive sexual imagery." She sings wistful and bawdy ballads, and ends her life by drowning.

All of these conventions carry specific messages about femininity and sexuality. Ophelia's virginal and vacant white is contrasted with Hamlet's scholar's garb, his "suits of solemn black." Her flowers suggest the discordant double images of female sexuality as both innocent blossoming and whorish contamination; she is the "green girl" of pastoral, the virginal "Rose of May" and the sexually explicit madwoman who, in giving away her wild flowers and herbs, is symbolically deflowering herself. The "weedy trophies" and phallic "long purples" which she wears to her death intimate an improper and discordant sexuality that Gertrude's lovely elegy cannot quite obscure. In Elizabethan and Jacobean drama, the stage direction that a woman enters with dishevelled hair indicates that she might either be mad or the victim of a rape; the disordered hair, her offense against decorum, suggests sensuality in each case. The mad Ophelia's bawdy songs and verbal license, while they give her access to "an entirely different range of experience" from what she is allowed as the dutiful daughter, seem to be her one sanctioned form of self-assertion as a woman, quickly followed, as if in retribution, by her death.

Drowning too was associated with the feminine, with female fluidity as opposed to masculine aridity. In his discussion of the "Ophelia complex," the phenomenologist Gaston Bachelard traces the symbolic connections between women, water, and death. Drowning, he suggests, becomes the truly feminine death in the dramas of literature and life, one which is a beautiful immersion and submersion in the female element. Water is the profound and organic symbol of the liquid woman whose eyes are so easily drowned in tears, as her body is the repository of blood, amniotic fluid, and milk. A man contemplating this feminine suicide understands it by reaching for what is feminine in himself, like Laertes, by a temporary surrender to his own fluidity—that is, his tears; and he becomes a man again in becoming once more dry—when his tears are stopped.

Clinically speaking, Ophelia's behavior and appearance are characteristic of the malady the Elizabethans would have diagnosed as female love-melancholy, or erotomania. From about 1580, melancholy had become a fashionable disease among young men, especially in London, and Hamlet himself is a prototype of the melancholy hero. Yet the epidemic of melancholy associated with intellectual and imaginative genius "curiously bypassed women." Women's melancholy was seen instead as biological, and emotional in origins.

[1985]

Claire Bloom

Playing Gertrude on Television

Editors' note: Claire Bloom played Gertrude in the BBC TV production (1980), directed by Rodney Bennett, with Patrick Stewart as Claudius. In the following passage she discusses the role.

It's very hard to play because strangely enough Gertrude has very few lines; I've always known it was a wonderful part and it *is,* but when you come to play it you realise you have to find many ways around the fact that she in actual fact says little!

You come to rehearse a part like this with certain preconceived notions, which you usually leave! I can only describe them as a battering ram—you knock down the first wall then what is inside is something quite different from what you'd imagined. I was convinced that she was guilty, not of the murder, but certainly that she had found out from Claudius that he had killed her husband. But there's nothing in the text that bears that out and many things that contradict it. I had thought it would make her less of a victim, more of a performer in the world, but [she laughs at herself] it isn't so. Like anyone if you live with a man, she must know there was something more, but I now believe that when Hamlet confronts her with "as kill a king . . . ay, madam, it was my word," it's the first time she's realised. I think from then on she knows and she must accept the fact that Claudius did it, and there is a change in their relationship. But there isn't a break—you don't break with someone suddenly like that. It changes; perhaps if they'd lived another twenty years they would have drifted apart. But there isn't a complete withdrawal. The hold they have on each other is too strong for that to happen. That caused me great difficulty; the scene after the closet scene is with Claudius, when he repeats twice "Gertrude, come away," and she doesn't reply. It's very mysterious. It's a kind of underwritten scene until you realise, or I realised, that there is no real choice for her. For the moment she doesn't go with him, but the next day she does. Hamlet knows it when he says, "Go not to my uncle's bed." She never replies and says "I won't"; she just says, "Thou hast cleft my heart in twain." She's a woman who goes with whatever is happening at the time. She's a weak-willed woman, but most of us are weak-willed if we're in the power of somebody who is very strong—and Claudius and Hamlet are both pretty strong fellows.

The "mysterious" scene with Claudius was one of the hardest to deal with in rehearsal. . . . We tried backwards, forwards, upside down and inside out and didn't really find it until a couple of days before we shot it. The minute we found it we knew it was the right one, but at other times we'd go away saying, "We've got it," then both Patrick and I would come in the next day depressed and say to Rodney, "Could we please do that scene again because it doesn't make sense when you think about it." There are questions that I'm sure have been asked by every cast of every *Hamlet* since Burbage[1] and for Gertrude they are: Was there a decision to go with Claudius or not to go with Claudius? How far was she lying about Hamlet's madness? I do think part of her believes he's mad, but when she says to the king "He's mad," I think that's protection, or overstating a fact she believes is possibly true. And of course she withholds information from Claudius; she says, "Behind the arras hearing something stir . . . . [he] kills the unseen good old man," but she *doesn't* say he said "Is it the king?" That is a very important bit of information which she certainly doesn't pass on!

[1980]

[1]**Burbage** Richard Burbage (c. 1567–1619), the first actor to play Shakepeare's Hamlet.

Bernice W. Kliman

The BBC Hamlet: *A Television Production*

With *Hamlet,* the producers of the BBC Shakespeare Plays have finally met the demands of Shakespeare-on-television by choosing a relatively bare set, conceding only a few richly detailed movable panels and props to shape key locales. By avoiding both location and realistic settings, they point up the natural affinity between Shakespeare's stage and the undisguised sound set. This starkness of setting admits poetry, heightened intensity—and "what not that's sweet and happy."

The producers have thus made a valid choice from among television's three faces: one, broadcast films, whether made for television or not, which exploit location settings, long shots, and all the clichés we associate with movies, including sudden shifts of space and time and full use of distance, from the most extreme long shots to "eyes only" closeups; two, studio-shot television drama with naturalistic settings, such as the hospital corridors and middle-class living rooms of sitcoms and soap operas, mostly in mid- to close-shots, often interspersed, to be sure, with a bit of stock footage of highways and skylines to establish a realistic environment. This second style varies from a close representation of real action to frankly staged action, where canned laughter or even shadowy glimpses of the studio audience can heighten the staged effect. Three, there is bare space with little or no effort made to disguise that this is a televised activity with a television crew out of sight but nearby. News broadcasts, talk shows and some television drama fit into this third category. Because of its patently unrepresentational quality, this last type offers the most freedom in shooting style. To all three kinds of settings we bring particular expectations in response to their conventions.

Shakespeare's plays work best in the last kind of television space, I believe, because it avoids the clash between realism and poetry, between the unity often expected in realistic media and the disunity and ambiguity of many of the plays, especially *Hamlet*. Yet, while closest to the kind of stage Shakespeare wrote for, the bare television set can be stretched through creative camera work. For example, when Hamlet follows the ghost in the BBC play, the two repeatedly walk across the frame and out of it, first from one direction, then from another; framing fosters the illusion of extended space. Freeing this *Hamlet* from location (as in the BBC *As You Like It*) and from realistic sets (as in the BBC *Measure for Measure*—however well those sets worked for that play) allows the play to be as inconsistent as it is, with, as Bernard Beckerman has so brilliantly explained in *Shakespeare at the Globe, 1599–1609,* a rising and falling action in each individual scene rather than through the course of the drama as a whole. It also allows for acting, the bravura kind that Derek Jacobi is so capable of.

Although gradually coalescing like the pointillism of impressionistic paintings into a subtly textured portrait, at first his mannerisms suggesting madness seem excessive. It is to be expected, perhaps, that Hamlet is a bit unhinged after the ghost scene, but Jacobi's rapid, hard blows to his forehead with the flat of his hand as he says "My tables" recall the desperation of Lear's cry: "O, let me not be mad, not mad, sweet heaven." And soon after, following the last couplet of the scene, Hamlet, maniacally playful, widens his eyes and points, pretending to see the ghost again, then guffaws at Marcellus's fears. Even more unsettling is his laughter when he is alone, as while he is saying "The play's the thing / Wherein I'll catch the conscience of the King." More significantly, he breaks up his own "Mousetrap" by getting right into the play, destroying the distance between audience and stage (a very real raked proscenium-arch stage), spoiling it as a test, because Claudius has a right to be incensed at Hamlet's behavior. Of course, Hamlet does so because Claudius never gives himself away, an unusual and provocative but not impossible interpretation. Thus, Claudius can only have the court's sympathy as he calmly calls for light and uses it to examine Hamlet closely. Hamlet, in response, covers his face, then laughs.

5 Hamlet himself thinks he is mad. To Ophelia he says, as if the realization had suddenly struck him, "It *hath* made me mad [emphasis his]" (III.i.147). To his mother he stresses the word "essentially" in "I *essentially* am not in madness" (III.iv.187). That is, in all essential matters he can be considered sane, though mad around the edges. This indeed turns out to be the explanation.

However doubtful about Hamlet's sanity Jacobi's acting leaves us, in this production this question does not seem to make a difference because it does not have a bearing on the tragedy, and this is true at least partly because in each scene on this nonrealistic set we seem to start anew, ready to let Hamlet's behavior tell us if he is mad or not. Moreover, if Hamlet is mad, it is not so totally as to obscure reason or sensibility. Far from it. It is more as if exacerbated reason and sensibility sometimes tip him into madness. This madness is no excuse for action or delay; it is simply part of the suffering that Hamlet is heir to.

Hamlet, then, is left to struggle against himself—surely where Shakespeare intended the struggle to abide. One of the conflicts in this Hamlet results from his affinity, perhaps, more to the bureaucratic Claudius who handles war-scares with diplomacy and who sits at a desk while brooding over his sins than to the warlike King Hamlet who comes in full armor. Hamlet may admire Fortinbras but is himself more like the bookish Horatio. Through nuance of gesture, through body movement, through a face that is indeed a map of all emotions,

Jacobi shapes a Hamlet who loves his father too much to disregard his command, yet who cannot hate his step-father enough to attend to it. Because Jacobi conveys so fully Hamlet's aloneness and vulnerability, one could be struck, for the first time, by the ghost's silence about his son. There is no declaration of love, no concern about Hamlet's ascension to the throne. Hamlet is doomed, it seems, to care about those who consistently care more for others than for him.

All of this production's richness and suggestiveness was realized not only because Jacobi is a marvelous actor—as indeed he is—but also because within the set's spareness that acting could unfold, an acting style that subsumes and transcends the "real." This production's space tells us what is possible for television presentations of Shakespeare. The more bare the set, it seems, the more glowing the words, the more immediate our apprehension of the enacted emotion.

[1988]

Will Saretta

What follows is an undergraduate's review, published in a college newspaper, of Kenneth Branagh's film version of Hamlet *(1996).*

Branagh's Film of Hamlet

Kenneth Branagh's *Hamlet* opened last night at the Harmon Auditorium, and will be shown again on Wednesday and Thursday at 7:30 p.m. According to the clock the evening will be long—the film runs for four hours, and in addition there is one ten-minute intermission—but you will enjoy every minute of it.

Well, almost every minute. Curiously, the film begins and ends relatively weakly, but most of what occurs in between is good and much of it is wonderful. The beginning is weak because it is too strong; Bernardo, the sentinel, offstage says "Who's there?" but before he gets a reply he crashes onto the screen and knocks Francisco down. The two soldiers grapple, swords flash in the darkness, and Francisco finally says, "Nay, answer me. Stand and unfold yourself." Presumably Branagh wanted to begin with a bang, but here, as often, more is less. A quieter, less physical opening in which Bernardo, coming on duty, hears a noise and demands that the maker of the noise identify himself and Francisco, the sentinel on duty, rightly demands that the newcomer identify *himself,* would catch the uneasiness and the mystery that pervades the play much better than does Branagh's showy beginning.

Similarly, at the end of the film, we get too much. For one thing, shots of Fortinbras's army invading Elsinore alternate with shots of the duel between Hamlet and King Claudius's pawn, Laertes, and they merely distract us from what really counts in this scene, the duel itself, which will result in Hamlet's death but also in Hamlet's successful completion of his mission to avenge his father. Second, at the very end we get shots of Fortinbras's men pulling down a massive statue of Hamlet Senior, probably influenced by television and newspaper shots of statues of Lenin being pulled down when the Soviet Union was dissolved a few years earlier. This is ridiculous; *Hamlet* is not a play about the fall of Communism, or about one form of tyranny replacing another. Shakespeare's *Hamlet* is not about the triumph of Fortinbras. It is about Hamlet's brave and ultimately successful efforts to do what is right, against overwhelming odds, and to offer us the consolation that in a world where death always triumphs there nevertheless is something that can be called nobility.

What, then, is good about the film? First of all, the film gives us the whole play, whereas almost all productions, whether on the stage or in the movie house, give us drastically abbreviated versions. Although less is often more, when it comes to the text of *Hamlet*, more is better, and we should be grateful to Branagh for letting us hear all of the lines. Second, it is very well performed, with only a few exceptions. Jack Lemmon as Marcellus is pretty bad, but fortunately the part is small. Other big-name actors in small parts—Charlton Heston as the Player King, Robin Williams as Osric, and Billy Crystal as the First Grave-digger—are admirable. But of course the success or failure of any production of *Hamlet* will depend chiefly on the actor who plays Hamlet, and to a considerable degree on the actors who play Claudius, Gertrude, Polonius, Ophelia, Laertes, and Horatio. There isn't space here to comment on all of these roles, but let it be said that Branagh's Prince Hamlet is indeed princely, a man who strikes us as having the ability to become a king, not a wimpy whining figure. When at the end Fortinbras says that if Hamlet had lived to become the king, he would "have proved most royal," we believe him. And his adversary, King Claudius, though morally despicable, is a man of great charm and great ability. The two men are indeed "mighty opposites," to use Hamlet's own words.

5 Branagh's decision to set the play in the late nineteenth century rather than in the Elizabethan period of Shakespeare's day and rather than in our own day contributes to this sense of powerful forces at work. If the play were set in Shakespeare's day, the men would wear tights, and if it were set in our day they would wear suits or trousers and sports jackets and sweaters, but in the film all of the men wear military costumes (black for Hamlet, scarlet for Claudius, white for Laertes) and the women wear ball gowns of the Victorian period. Branagh gives us a world that is closer to our own than would Elizabethan costumes, but yet it is, visually at least, also distant enough to convey a sense of grandeur, which modern dress cannot suggest. Of course *Hamlet* can be done in modern dress, just as *Romeo and Juliet* was done, successfully, in the recent film starring Claire Danes and Leonardo DiCaprio, set in a world that seemed to be Miami Beach, but *Romeo and Juliet* is less concerned with heroism and grandeur than *Hamlet* is, so Branagh probably did well to avoid contemporary costumes.

Although Branagh is faithful to the text, in that he gives us the entire text, he knows that a good film cannot be made merely by recording on film a stage production, and so he gives us handsome shots of landscape, and of rich interiors—for instance, a great mirrored hall—that would be beyond the resources of any theatrical production. I have already said that at the end, when Fortinbras's army swarms over the countryside and then invades the castle we get material that is distracting, indeed irrelevant, but there are also a few other distractions. It is all very well to let us *see* the content of long narrative speeches (for instance, when the Player King talks of the fall of Troy and the death of King Priam and the lament of Queen Hecuba, Branagh shows us these things, with John Gielgud as Priam and Judi Dench as Hecuba, performing in pantomime), but there surely is no need for us to see a naked Hamlet and a naked Ophelia in bed, when Polonius is warning Ophelia that Hamlet's talk of love cannot be trusted. Polonius's warning is not so long or so undramatic that we need to be entertained visually with an invention that finds not a word of support in the text. On the contrary, all of Ophelia's lines suggest that she would not be other than a dutiful young woman, obedient to the morals of the times and to her father's authority. Yet another of Branagh's unfortunate inventions is the prostitute who appears in Polonius's bedroom, during Polonius's interview with Reynaldo. A final example of unnecessary spectacle is Hamlet's killing of Claudius: He hurls his rapier the length of the hall, impaling

Claudius, and then like some 1930's movie star he swings on the chandelier and drops down on Claudius to finish him off.

But it is wrong to end this review by pointing out faults in Branagh's film of *Hamlet*. There is so much in this film that is exciting, so much that is moving, so much that is . . . , well, so much that is *Hamlet* (which is to say that is a great experience), that the film must be recommended without reservation. Go to see it. The four hours will fly.

A postscript. It is good to see that Branagh uses color-blind casting. Voltemand, Fortinbras's Captain, and the messenger who announces Laertes's return are all blacks—the messenger is a black woman—although of course medieval Denmark and Elizabethan England, and, for that matter, Victorian England, would not have routinely included blacks. These performers are effective, and it is appropriate that actors of color take their place in the world's greatest play.

[2000]

Chapter Overview: Looking Backward/Looking Forward

1. Sometimes we say a person is "so innocent." Is this a compliment, or a criticism?
2. Was there a moment in your own life when you moved in a significant way from "innocence" to "experience"? How did you feel when this event occurred? How do you feel about it now?
3. Do you think it is possible to know something well even without having direct experience of it? Can someone know what being a parent means, for example, if he or she does not have a child? Can someone comment expertly on baseball without having played on a major-league team?
4. Name and describe some things that you have experienced once, but never want to experience again.
5. Name and describe some things that you have not experienced, but that you hope to experience some day. If you do not experience them, will your life be affected a lot or a little?
6. Name and describe some things that you feel you must experience at some point in your life. Why are these so important to you?
7. If you could have been present at any historical event, however long ago, what would it be? Why would you want to be there? What would this experience give you that you do not now possess?

CHAPTER 23

The Sporting Life

SHORT VIEWS

Sports remain a great metaphor for life's more difficult lessons. It was through athletics that many of us first came to understand that fear can be tamed; that on a team the whole is more than the sum of its parts; and that the ability to be heroic lies, to a surprising degree, within.
Susan Casey

Champions aren't made in the gyms. Champions are made from something they have deep inside them—a desire, a dream, a vision.
Muhammad Ali

Champions keep playing until they get it right.
Billie Jean King

Training gives us an outlet for suppressed energies created by stress and thus tones the spirit just as exercise conditions the body.
Arnold Schwarzenegger

Talent wins games, but teamwork and intelligence wins championships.
Michael Jordan

The most important thing in the Olympic Games is not winning but taking part; the essential thing in life is not conquering but fighting well.
Pierre de Coubertin

Whoever said, "It's not whether you win or lose that counts," probably lost.
Martina Navratilova

Most games are lost, not won.
Casey Stengel

Sport strips away personality, letting the white bone of character shine through. Sport gives players an opportunity to know and test themselves.
Rita Mae Brown

The one nice thing about sports is that they prove men do have emotions and are not afraid to show them.
Jane O'Reilly

The difference between men and women is that, if given the choice between saving the life of an infant or catching a fly ball, a woman will automatically choose to save the infant, without even considering if there's a man on base.

Dave Barry

I used to joke that if you could bottle all the emotion let loose in a basketball game you'd have enough hate to fight a war and enough joy to prevent one.

Bill Russell

Serious sport has nothing to do with fair play. It is bound up with hatred, jealousy, boastfulness, disregard of all rules, and sadistic pleasure in witnessing violence. In other words, it is war minus the shooting.

George Orwell

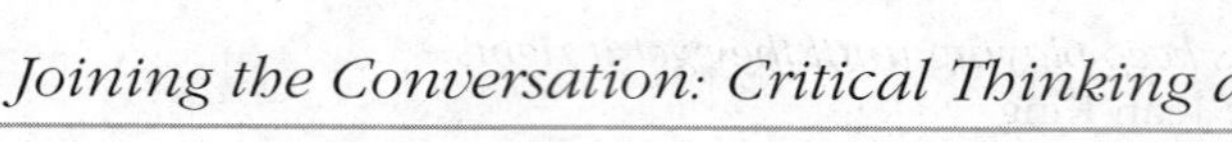

Joining the Conversation: Critical Thinking and Writing

1. Select a quotation that especially appeals to you, and make it the focus of an essay of about 500 words.
2. Take two of the passages—perhaps one that you especially like and one that you think is wrongheaded—and write a dialogue of about 500 words in which the two authors converse or argue. They may each try to convince the other, or they may find that to some degree they share views and they may then work out a statement that both can accept. If you do take the first position—that one writer is on the correct track but the other is utterly mistaken—try to be fair to the view that you think is mistaken. (As an experiment in critical thinking, imagine that you accept it, and make the best case for it that you possibly can.)

ESSAY

JAMES MICHENER

James Michener (1907–1997), born in Doylestown, Pennsylvania, wrote some forty titles, chiefly fiction (including Tales of the South Pacific, *which won the Pulitzer Prize for Fiction in 1948), but he also wrote travel books, a memoir, and* Sports in America *(1976). We reprint the introductory material from this last title.*

Sports in America

Every statement I make henceforth will be subject to three criteria, and I hope the reader will keep these in mind, because they will explain some of the arguments I advance.

I. *Sports should be fun for the participant.* They should provide release from tensions, a joyful exuberance as the game progresses, and a discharge of those aggressions which, if kept bottled up, damage the human being. If sports become a drudgery, or a perverted competition, or a mere commercial enterprise, something is wrong. I believe that sports should be fun whether one is actively participating, like the ancient Greeks, or watching, like the ancient Romans. In either case they ought to provide a spiritual catharsis, which cannot occur if participants are overly dedicated to winning, or if spectators allow their partisanship to get out of hand. This criterion of fun will become especially important when we inspect Little Leagues in baseball and Pop Warner teams in football, but it will also apply at every other level of sports in America. If the game isn't fun, it has lost at least half its justification, and there are many signs that in America some sports are no longer fun, to either the participant or the spectator.

II. *Sports should enhance the health of both the individual participant and the general society.* I place this criterion at the apex of my value system. For me it takes precedence over everything else, and most of my conclusions will be incomprehensible if this goal is forgotten. I believe without question that the general health of the nation ought to be a concern of those who govern the nation, and the way in which we have allowed national health standards to decline in recent decades is a scandal for which schools, colleges and universities will one day be called to account. Specifically, a sport, to be effective, should place a demand upon big muscles, lung capacity, sweat glands, and particularly the heart. If it does not, much of the potential value of that sport is lost. Of course, prudent limits should be observed. Not many should engage in a marathon run of 26 miles 385 yards, because that requires too much exertion. But I cannot consider croquet a serious sport, because it requires none. A rigorous application of this criterion to all the sports we engage in will produce surprising results, and in a later chapter tables will be given showing that some of our most popular sports contribute little, whereas others of small reputation contribute much. For myself, I no longer have much interest in any sport that does not generate a vigorous sweat.

III. *Sports have an obligation to provide public entertainment.* I am by nature a participant rather than a spectator, and my whole sympathy lies with the sandlot where boys are playing rather than the stadium where professionals are offering an exhibition. One might therefore expect me to be prejudiced against spectator sports, and I might have been had I not spent much of my adult life abroad, studying various cultures and countries. The more I learned, the more apparent it became that all societies in all periods of history have needed some kind of public entertainment, and it has usually been provided by sports.

5 Ancient Greece had its Olympiad and Rome its Colosseum. In the most distant corners of Asia Minor, I saw amphitheaters constructed by these civilizations because the rulers knew that the general citizenry required some kind of public entertainment. In Mérida, in western Spain, I visited the enormous flat plain that had once been walled to a height of four feet and waterproofed so that when a river was led into the area a small lake resulted on which actual ships could engage in simulated naval battles. In Crete young men and women skillfully leaped on and off the backs of charging bulls, and I have always been impressed by the frequency with which games are mentioned in the Bible. Some of the most effective analogies of St. Paul were borrowed from the arena. Shakespeare, too, found

examples in sports, and I have found only one society in which sports were not a functional part. The Hebrews of Biblical time held a low opinion of games and said so, but when they entered Greek and Roman society they became advocates, like their neighbors. The most dramatic example of a spectator sport I have ever witnessed occurred in the most primitive society I have known, one of the savage islands in the New Hebrides group. There the entire community gathered at the bottom of a cliff to watch admiringly as young men of the village climbed to the top of the cliff, and then to the top of a tall tree at the edge of the cliff. Posing there, the athlete would utter a defiant scream, then throw himself headfirst toward the rocks below, trusting that the vine rope attached to his heels would bring him up short just before he crashed onto the rocks. In all ages societies have looked to sports for entertainment, so that when the State of Alabama demands that its university provide first-class, big-time football, it is acting within a historical tradition, and when the State of Louisiana spends $163,000,000 to build a Superdome, it is aping only what Greece and Rome did ages ago. I am completely in favor of public sporting spectacles, for they fill a timeless need, but I am confused as to who should provide them and under what type of public sponsorship.

While doing research for this book I sometimes outlined these three criteria to public groups. Frequently I was asked, "Why don't you have one about sports building character?" Originally I had that as my fourth criterion, but the more I considered it, and the more I weighed the evidence that has been forthcoming in recent years, the more doubtful I became as to its validity, and here we come to the nitty-gritty of this book.

In favor of including character-building as one of the great contributions of sports is this kind of evidence: The Duke of Wellington has been quoted as having said, "The battle of Waterloo was won on the playing fields of Eton." General MacArthur was lavish in his praise of West Point and its playing fields. The men who played for Vince Lombardi testified to the fact that he made them better men than they were when they joined his team. A thousand masters of ceremonies have introduced their local coaches as molders of character first and athletes second. Aging alumni, returning to their colleges, pay tribute first to long-dead coaches and much later to certain memorable professors. Hundreds of professional athletes have testified to the impact their high school coaches had on them. And I myself, a few pages back, stated that my character was formed in part by athletics.

On the other hand, emerging evidence begins to erode the legend that participation in sports automatically builds character. The present Duke of Wellington has disclosed that within his family it has long been known that the famous duke never made his statement about the playing fields of Eton. That attractive quotation did not surface until forty-one years after the Battle of Waterloo, and then in the book of a Frenchman known for his ability to turn a neat phrase.

I often thought about this during my navy service in World War II. I noticed that whenever an admiral had played on the football team at Annapolis, a great deal was made of the fact, and there were numerous stories to the effect that he had acquired his capacity for leadership and military strategy from playing football. The same was true, to an even greater degree, of generals who had played at West Point, and this impressed the public, as it did me.

10 But then I began to look at the record, and many of the finest admirals and generals had never stepped on a football field, or a baseball field either. Some of the greatest had been primarily scholars, who had paid commendable attention to

their bodies and who now even during the heat of war took care to get their daily exercise. Leadership and military brilliance, I discovered, had very little to do with football training. Some of the great leaders had played on teams; more had not. Capacity for leadership came principally from the fact that they were well-disciplined, intelligent men to begin with, and those who had happened to play football played it well, as now they fought well.

I had also begun to suspect the legend that playing on a university football team, or basketball or baseball, created civic leaders. In company after company that I knew, the guiding man had played no organized games in college, although he was apt to play golf in his later years. I found little correlation between being a quarterback in college and a quarterback in life. Some college athletes graduated into good jobs and became absolutely topnotch human beings; but a larger number of topnotch leaders had never participated in organized college sports. And as every college graduate knows, a distressing number of college athletes failed to find themselves in adult life. For them the adulation of college athletics was a positive deterrent; it was an albatross which they could never shake off. For them football was not character-building; it was character-destroying.

For some twenty years I kept these tentative suspicions to myself, insecure in my evidence and suspicious that I might be reasoning from inadequate data. Certainly, the whole popular legend was that athletics did build character, and it had done so for me. So I kept silent.

And then, a few years ago, a slow but constant trickle of books and stories began to surface, calling into question the assumptions we had accepted automatically before. The intellectuals' agitation of the 1960s, with their attack on all fronts against the establishment, made it inevitable that sports should be subjected to a more severe scrutiny, and the result was spectacular.

I do not believe that anyone has the right to be doctrinaire on this question of character-building unless he has read at least some of the following books, most of which have appeared in paperback. He can reject them as sensational. He can deny their argument as prejudiced. He can inveigh against them as anti-American. And he can dismiss the individual authors as sensation mongers. But he cannot ignore the basic questions they raise.

15 Paul Hoch. *Rip Off the Big Game: The Exploitation of Sports by the Power Elite.* A Canadian Marxist launches a frontal attack on almost every hallowed preconception of American sports. I know of no book which so totally rejects all the beliefs I sustained from my early experience. Always infuriating, sometimes unfair, grotesquely anti-capitalist, it is nevertheless a good book to read if you want the cobwebs blasted from your eyes.

Harry Edwards. *The Revolt of the Black Athlete.* One of the first hard-nosed analyses of what the black athlete gains and loses when he becomes a part of big-time sports. Edwards, himself a black athlete, was bitterly criticized for having led the strike of black athletes at the Mexico City Olympics, but here he raises fundamental questions which destroy many illusions previously held by well-intentioned whites.

Martin Ralbovsky. *Destiny's Darlings. A World Championship Little League Team Twenty Years Later.* A carefully researched, compassionate portrait of the Schenectady Little League team which won the world championship at Williamsport in 1954. Vivid portraits of the players and coaches, then and now. In no sense scandalmongering, this book nevertheless raises important questions and indicates solutions.

Dave Meggyesy. *Out of Their League.* A cynical attack on college football (Syracuse) and professional (St. Louis). Shows a superjock as he slowly wakens to the realities of big-time sports. An eye-opener whose theses have been disputed by critics who castigate Meggyesy as a no-talent ingrate.

Robert Vare. *Buckeye, a Study of Coach Woody Hayes and the Ohio State Football Machine.* A good book to read regarding character-building and the problems attached to the vigorous recruiting of high school athletes.

20 Gary Shaw. *Meat on the Hoof.* A shocking personal account of how high school stars are recruited into the University of Texas and then abused when they don't make the first team and shamed into voluntarily surrendering their scholarships. Some critics have accused Shaw of being a crybaby who couldn't make it, but the basic accusations have not yet been refuted. If you can read only one book of adverse criticism, read this one for an inside look at what "big-time football" means.

David Wolf. *Foul! The Connie Hawkins Story.* A sad, angry guided tour through the irresponsibility of big-time basketball. The conductor, Connie Hawkins, is a talented black college star who becomes a case history in exploitation, gambling, disenchantment and legal gymnastics. Anyone misty-eyed about the influence of a benign coach must read Chapter 15. Of course, if you do, you'll read the rest of the book.

Peter Gent. *North Dallas Forty.* A shocking fictional account of what life is supposed to be like when playing for the Dallas Cowboys. Gent, a football star at Michigan State and with the Cowboys, writes with an insider's know-how, but his unrelieved emphasis on brutality, venality, drugs and sex sometimes seems unreal. My comment on finishing the book: "If they had that much sex that constantly, how did they have the energy to suit up for the Sunday game?" A book for those who retain a schoolboy's dedication to sports.

Dan Jenkins, *Semi-Tough.* A rollicking, hilariously written novel about big-time football, less brutal in its approach than *North Dallas Forty,* but based on the same assumptions. Difficult reading for those who still believe that sports build character.

I assure the reader that later on I shall be citing an equal number of books highly favorable to sports, but I believe that familiarity with some of the above books, or at least the tenor of their criticisms, is essential.

25 If the militaristic type of leadership evidenced in the Little League book, in the biography of Woody Hayes and the study of football at the University of Texas is what sports idealize and sponsor, then our democracy is doomed. If the professional football players presented in the two novels epitomize the kinds of all-Americans graduated by Oklahoma, Notre Dame and Michigan, our civilization has progressed to a point that leaves us some thousand leagues behind the Roman Empire.

As I was typing these doubts, and wondering if I was being fair, *The New York Times* carried this brief notice about New York City basketball, with no headline, as if the story were too ordinary to deserve comment:

> New York, February 7, 1975. Another Public Schools Athletic League basketball team has forfeited its spot in the playoffs. Brandeis High School, which gained a playoff spot when Franklin gave up all its victories, admitted yesterday that one of its players was in his fifth year in high school and was thus ineligible. Franklin's forfeits had been for the same reason. This week, in addition to Franklin and Brandeis, Bayside forfeited two games and George Washington forfeited all its games.

Thus in one week, four major high schools in one city admitted that they had been playing ineligible players, and the nature of that offense is such that at least some officials in each school must have known about it. But the lure of fielding a winning team is so great, and the rewards to any coaching staff so attractive, that outright cheating is condoned. A coach whose team goes 23–2 but who gets reprimanded for playing an ineligible player, or two or three, suffers a momentary rebuke, but he also gains long-lasting accolades for having produced a winner. And if such coaches are building character, I must not understand the meaning of that word.

I am very doubtful that big-time sports, whether high school, college, university or professional, do much to alter or enhance the character of the young men who participate. Those who enter the system with strong characters formed at home and who fall under the guidance of a good coach emerge strengthened in their convictions. Later on I shall refer to several who have had this experience.

But if the boy already has a weak character, and if he falls into the hands of an irresponsible coach, the effect of sports can be disastrous, and he may well wind up a weaker person than when he began. I know of many such and will be referring to a few.

Three conclusions have been offered to this problem. Heywood Hale Broun, who has written much in this field, has said: "Sports do not build character. They reveal it." Darrell Royal, of Texas, phrased it this way: "Football doesn't build character. It eliminates the weak ones." And a comedian has said, "Sport develops not character, but characters." A sentimentalist, remembering only the best, can be forgiven if he argues that sports do build character. The most I will concede is that a balance is reached, the Fellowship of Christian Athletes offsetting the savagery, the drugs, the broken contracts, the chicanery and the awful abuses in recruiting high school athletes. The literature on this subject is ably summarized in Charles R. Kniker's "The Values of Athletics in Schools: A Continuing Debate," in *Phi Delta Kappan,* October 1974.

30 The days of bland acceptance of sports are past. The entire program in this country will have to be subjected to most careful scrutiny and the most biting criticism. Those who defend sports and their enormous budgets will have to justify them as never before and many hallowed preconceptions will be challenged. From the nine critical books cited, and from other sources, including especially the daily press and to less extent television and radio, the following major accusations against sports as now conducted are being made:

- Children are being introduced into highly organized sports too young.
- Adults conducting children's programs place too much stress on winning.
- Girls and women are unjustly deprived of an adequate share of the sports budget.
- The popular contention that sports are an escape hatch for ghetto youth is overstated.
- Small colleges ought to quit trying to field two-platoon football teams.
- Most medium-sized universities are spending too much money trying to maintain big-time football programs and many should de-escalate to something more manageable.
- Large universities with successful big-time programs should finance them more realistically.
- The recruiting of high school athletes is a national scandal.
- Television threatens to engulf many of the inherent values of sports.

- The media, up until recent years, have been delinquent in reporting the facts about sports.
- It is improper for political units like cities, counties and states to use public money to pay for large stadiums which are then turned over to professional teams for a fraction of a realistic rental.
- The federal government may have to intervene to provide guidance for national sporting programs, including supervision of professional contracts with players, the awarding of franchises to cities, and sponsorship of our Olympic teams.
- Throughout our sports programs there is an undue emphasis on violence.
- Even if, as some charge, the excesses of sports merely reflect the excesses of our society, that is no justification. Sports, as an idealistic exercise, should transcend any meannesses in our society and offer a more responsible ideal.

These are the conditions with which our society must grapple in the next decades, and naturally they form the basis for this book. I should like to add two other criticisms that may be the most important.

- Our present program for sports has deplorably evaded its responsibility for improving the health of individuals and of the general society.
- Especially grievous has been the lack of any program to encourage young people to continue sports activity into adult life. Such a vigorous program could prolong many lives and make each day lived more meaningful and enjoyable. We place an undue emphasis on gifted athletes aged fifteen to twenty-two, a preposterous emphasis on a few professionals aged twenty-three to thirty-five, and never enough on the mass of our population aged twenty-three to seventy-five.

[1975]

Joining the Conversation: Critical Thinking and Writing

1. In paragraph 11 Michener suggests that sports may *not* be important in building character, especially in developing leadership qualities. Do you have anything to add, perhaps based on personal experience?
2. Probably no one condones cheating—for instance, using illegal drugs, or throwing a prize fight—but how about (in an effort to rattle the opposing team) booing? Is such behavior unfair? Fair, but unsportsmanly? Or what?
3. Michener published these comments in 1975. Do you think they still apply? Please explain.

Stories

Sherwood Anderson

Sherwood Anderson (1876–1941) was born in Camden, Ohio. At 14 he dropped out of school—his attendance had already been irregular, partly because, like the narrator in "The Egg," his family drifted from small town to small town. Anderson worked at odd jobs such as newsboy, house painter, and stable groom, and in 1898 served briefly in the Spanish-American War. He then turned to advertising and business and by 1904 was a fairly prosperous manager of paint factories in Ohio. In 1912, however, in the midst of dictating a business letter, he walked out of the office and disappeared for several days. He went to Chicago, where he fell in with such writers as Carl Sandburg and Theodore Dreiser and soon began writing poems, stories, and novels. After publishing two unsuccessful novels, at the age of 43 he achieved fame with Winesburg, Ohio *(1919), a collection of related stories about life in a small town. "I Want To Know Why" and "The Egg" come from a later collection of stories,* The Triumph of the Egg *(1921).*

I Want to Know Why

We got up at four in the morning, that first day in the east. On the evening before we had climbed off a freight train at the edge of town, and with the true instinct of Kentucky boys had found our way across town and to the race track and the stables at once. Then we knew we were all right. Hanley Turner right away found a nigger we knew. It was Bildad Johnson who in the winter works at Ed Becker's livery barn in our home town, Beckersville. Bildad is a good cook as almost all our niggers are and of course he, like everyone in our part of Kentucky who is anyone at all, likes the horses. In the spring Bildad begins to scratch around. A nigger from our country can flatter and wheedle anyone into letting him do most anything he wants. Bildad wheedles the stable men and the trainers from the horse farms in our country around Lexington. The trainers come into town in the evening to stand around and talk and maybe get into a poker game. Bildad gets in with them. He is always doing little favors and telling about things to eat, chicken browned in a pan, and how is the best way to cook sweet potatoes and corn bread. It makes your mouth water to hear him.

When the racing season comes on and the horses go to the races and there is all the talk on the streets in the evenings about the new colts, and everyone says when they are going over to Lexington or to the spring meeting at Churchill Downs or to Latonia, and the horsemen that have been down to New Orleans or maybe at the winter meeting at Havana in Cuba come home to spend a week before they start out again, at such a time when everything talked about in Beckersville is just horses and nothing else and the outfits start out and horse racing is in every breath of air you breathe, Bildad shows up with a job as cook for some outfit. Often when I think about it, his always going all season to the races and working in the livery barn in the winter where horses are and where men like to come and talk about horses, I wish I was a nigger. It's a foolish thing to say, but that's the way I am about being around horses, just crazy. I can't help it.

Well, I must tell you about what we did and let you in on what I'm talking about. Four of us boys from Beckersville, all whites and sons of men who live in Beckersville regular, made up our minds we were going to the races, not just to Lexington or Louisville, I don't mean, but to the big eastern track we were always hearing our Beckersville men talk about, to Saratoga. We were all pretty young then. I was just turned fifteen and I was the oldest of the four. It was my scheme. I admit that and I talked the others into trying it. There was Hanley Turner and Henry Rieback and Tom Tumberton and myself. I had thirty-seven dollars I had earned during the winter working nights and Saturdays in Enoch Myer's grocery. Henry Rieback had eleven dollars and the others, Hanley and Tom, had only a dollar or two each. We fixed it all up and laid low until the Kentucky spring meetings were over and some of our men, the sportiest ones, the ones we envied the most, had cut out—then we cut out too.

I won't tell you the trouble we had beating our way on freights and all. We went through Cleveland and Buffalo and other cities and saw Niagara Falls. We bought things there, souvenirs and spoons and cards and shells with pictures of the falls on them for our sisters and mothers, but thought we had better not send any of the things home. We didn't want to put the folks on our trail and maybe be nabbed.

5 We got into Saratoga as I said at night and went to the track. Bildad fed us up. He showed us a place to sleep in hay over a shed and promised to keep still. Niggers are all right about things like that. They won't squeal on you. Often a white man you might meet, when you had run away from home like that, might appear to be all right and give you a quarter or a half-dollar or something, and then go right and give you away. White men will do that, but not a nigger. You can trust them. They are squarer with kids. I don't know why.

At the Saratoga meeting that year there were a lot of men from home. Dave Williams and Arthur Mulford and Jerry Myers and others. Then there was a lot from Louisville and Lexington Henry Rieback knew but I didn't. They were professional gamblers and Henry Rieback's father is one too. He is what is called a sheet writer[1] and goes away most of the year to the tracks. In the winter when he is home in Beckersville he don't stay there much but goes away to cities and deals faro.[2] He is a nice man and generous, is always sending Henry presents, a bicycle and a gold watch and a boy scout suit of clothes and things like that.

My own father is a lawyer. He's all right, but don't make much money and can't buy me things and anyway I'm getting so old now I don't expect it. He never said nothing to me against Henry, but Hanley Turner and Tom Tumberton's fathers did. They said to their boys that money so come by is no good and they didn't want their boys brought up to hear gamblers' talk and be thinking about such things and maybe embrace them.

That's all right and I guess the men know what they are talking about, but I don't see what it's got to do with Henry or with horses either. That's what I'm writing this story about. I'm puzzled. I'm getting to be a man and want to think straight and be O.K., and there's something I saw at the race meeting at the eastern track I can't figure out.

I can't help it, I'm crazy about thoroughbred horses. I've always been that way. When I was ten years old and saw I was growing to be big and couldn't be a rider I was so sorry I nearly died. Harry Hellinfinger in Beckersville, whose father is Postmaster, is grown up and too lazy to work, but likes to stand around in the street and get up jokes on boys like sending them to a hardware store for a gimlet to bore square holes and other jokes like that. He played one on me. He told me that if I would eat a half a cigar I would be stunted and not grow any more and maybe could be a rider. I did it. When father wasn't looking I took a cigar out of his pocket and gagged it down some way. It made me awful sick and the doctor had to be sent

[1]**a sheet writer** a bookie. [2]**faro** a card game.

for, and then it did no good. I kept right on growing. It was a joke. When I told what I had done and why most fathers would have whipped me but mine didn't.

10 Well, I didn't get stunted and didn't die. It serves Harry Hellinfinger right. Then I made up my mind I would like to be a stable boy, but had to give that up too. Mostly niggers do that work and I knew father wouldn't let me go into it. No use to ask him.

If you've never been crazy about thoroughbreds it's because you've never been around where they are much and don't know any better. They're beautiful. There isn't anything so lovely and clean and full of spunk and honest and everything as some race horses. On the big horse farms that are all around our town Beckersville there are tracks and the horses run in the early morning. More than a thousand times I've got out of bed before daylight and walked two or three miles to the tracks. Mother wouldn't of let me go but father always says, "Let him alone." So I got some bread out of the bread box and some butter and jam, gobbled it and lit out.

At the tracks you sit on the fence with men, whites and niggers, and they chew tobacco and talk, and then the colts are brought out. It's early and the grass is covered with shiny dew and in another field a man is plowing and they are frying things in a shed where the track niggers sleep, and you know how a nigger can giggle and laugh and say things that make you laugh. A white man can't do it and some niggers can't but a track nigger can every time.

And so the colts are brought out and some are just galloped by stable boys, but almost every morning on a big track owned by a rich man who lives maybe in New York, there are always, nearly every morning, a few colts and some of the old race horses and geldings and mares that are cut loose.

It brings a lump up into my throat when a horse runs. I don't mean all horses but some. I can pick them nearly every time. It's in my blood like in the blood of race track niggers and trainers. Even when they just go slob-jogging along with a little nigger on their backs I can tell a winner. If my throat hurts and it's hard for me to swallow, that's him. He'll run like Sam Hill when you let him out. If he don't win every time it'll be a wonder and because they've got him in a pocket behind another or he was pulled or got off bad at the post or something. If I wanted to be a gambler like Henry Rieback's father I could get rich. I know I could and Henry says so, too. All I would have to do is to wait 'til that hurt comes when I see a horse and then bet every cent. That's what I would do if I wanted to be a gambler, but I don't.

15 When you're at the tracks in the morning—not the race tracks but the training tracks around Beckersville—you don't see a horse, the kind I've been talking about, very often, but it's nice anyway. Any thoroughbred, that is sired right and out of a good mare and trained by a man that knows how, can run. If he couldn't what would he be there for and not pulling a plow?

Well, out of the stables they come and the boys are on their backs and it's lovely to be there. You hunch down on top of the fence and itch inside you. Over in the sheds the niggers giggle and sing. Bacon is being fried and coffee made. Everything smells lovely. Nothing smells better than coffee and manure and horses and niggers and bacon frying and pipes being smoked out of doors on a morning like that. It just gets you, that's what it does.

But about Saratoga. We was there six days and not a soul from home seen us, and everything came off just as we wanted it to, fine weather and horses and races and all. We beat our way home and Bildad gave us a basket with fried chicken and bread and other eatables in, and I had eighteen dollars when we got back to Beckersville. Mother jawed and cried but Pop didn't say much. I told everything we done except one thing. I did and saw that alone. That's what I'm writing about. It got me upset, I think about it at night. Here it is.

At Saratoga we laid up nights in the hay in the shed Bildad had showed us and ate with the niggers early and at night when the race people had all gone away. The men from home stayed mostly in the grandstand and betting field, and didn't come out around the places where the horses are kept except to the paddocks just before a race when the horses are saddled. At Saratoga they don't have paddocks under an open shed as at Lexington and Churchill Downs and other tracks down in our country, but saddle the horses right out in an open place under trees on a lawn as smooth and nice as Banker Bohon's front yard here in Beckersville. It's lovely. The horses are sweaty and nervous and shine and the men come out and smoke cigars and look at them and the trainers are there and the owners, and your heart thumps so you can hardly breathe.

Then the bugle blows for post and the boys that ride come running out with their silk clothes on and you run to get a place by the fence with the niggers.

20 I always am wanting to be a trainer or owner, and at the risk of being seen and caught and sent home I went to the paddocks before every race. The other boys didn't but I did.

We got to Saratoga on a Friday and on Wednesday the next week the big Mullford Handicap was to be run. Middlestride was in it and Sunstreak. The weather was fine and the track fast. I couldn't sleep the night before.

What had happened was that both these horses are the kind it makes my throat hurt to see. Middlestride is long and looks awkward and is a gelding. He belongs to Joe Thompson, a little owner from home who only has a half-dozen horses. The Mullford Handicap is for a mile and Middlestride can't untrack fast. He goes away slow and is always back at the half, then he begins to run and if the race is a mile and a quarter he'll just eat up everything and get there.

Sunstreak is different. He is a stallion and nervous and belongs on the biggest farm we've got in our country, the Van Riddle place that belongs to Mr. Van Riddle of New York. Sunstreak is like a girl you think about sometimes but never see. He is hard all over and lovely too. When you look at his head you want to kiss him. He is trained by Jerry Tillford who knows me and has been good to me lots of times, lets me walk into a horse's stall to look at him close and other things. There isn't anything as sweet as that horse. He stands at the post quiet and not letting on, but he is just burning up inside. Then when the barrier goes up he is off like his name, Sunstreak. It makes you ache to see him. It hurts you. He just lays down and runs like a bird dog. There can't anything I ever see run like him except Middlestride when he gets untracked and stretches himself.

Gee! I ached to see that race and those two horses run, ached and dreaded it too. I didn't want to see either of our horses beaten. We had never sent a pair like that to the races before. Old men in Beckersville said so and the niggers said so. It was a fact.

25 Before the race I went over to the paddocks to see. I looked a last look at Middlestride, who isn't such a much standing in a paddock that way, then I went to Sunstreak.

It was his day. I knew when I see him. I forgot all about being seen myself and walked right up. All the men from Beckersville were there and no one noticed me except Jerry Tillford. He saw me and something happened. I'll tell you about that.

I was standing looking at that horse and aching. In some way, I can't tell how, I knew just how Sunstreak felt inside. He was quiet and letting the niggers rub his legs and Mr. Van Riddle himself put the saddle on, but he was just a raging torrent inside. He was like the water in the river at Niagara Falls just before it goes plunk down. That horse wasn't thinking about running. He don't have to think about that. He was just thinking about holding himself back 'til the time for the running came. I knew that. I could just in a way see right inside him. He was going to do some awful running and I knew it. He wasn't bragging or letting on much or prancing or making a fuss, but just waiting. I knew it and Jerry Tillford his trainer knew. I looked up and then that man and I looked into each other's eyes. Something happened to me. I guess I loved the man as much as I did the horse because he knew what I knew. Seemed to me there wasn't anything in the world but that man and the horse and me. I cried and Jerry Tillford had a shine in his eyes. Then I came away to the fence to wait for the race. The horse was better than me, more steadier, and now I know better than Jerry. He was the quietest and he had to do the running.

Sunstreak ran first of course and he busted the world's record for a mile. I've seen that if I never see anything more. Everything came out just as I expected. Middlestride got left at the post and was way back and closed up to be second, just as I knew he would. He'll get a world's record too some day. They can't skin the Beckersville country on horses.

I watched the race calm because I knew what would happen. I was sure. Hanley Turner and Henry Rieback and Tom Tumberton were all more excited than me.

30 A funny thing had happened to me. I was thinking about Jerry Tillford the trainer and how happy he was all through the race. I liked him that afternoon even more than I ever liked my own father. I almost forgot the horses thinking that way about him. It was because of what I had seen in his eyes as he stood in the paddocks beside Sunstreak before the race started. I knew he had been watching and working with Sunstreak since the horse was a baby colt, had taught him to run and be patient and when to let himself out and not to quit, never. I knew that for him it was like a mother seeing her child do something brave or wonderful. It was the first time I ever felt for a man like that.

After the race that night I cut out from Tom and Hanley and Henry. I wanted to be by myself and I wanted to be near Jerry Tillford if I could work it. Here is what happened.

The track in Saratoga is near the edge of town. It is all polished up and trees around, the evergreen kind, and grass and everything painted and nice. If you go past the track you get to a hard road made of asphalt for automobiles, and if you go along this for a few miles there is a road turns off to a little rummy-looking farm house set in a yard.

That night after the race I went along that road because I had seen Jerry and some other men go that way in an automobile. I didn't expect to find them. I walked for a ways and then sat down by a fence to think. It was the direction they went in. I wanted to be as near Jerry as I could. I felt close to him. Pretty soon I went up the side road—I don't know why—and came to the rummy farm house. I was just lonesome to see Jerry, like wanting to see your father at night when you are a young kid. Just then an automobile came along and turned in. Jerry was in it and Henry Rieback's father, and Arthur Bedford from home, and Dave Williams and two other men I didn't know. They got out of the car and went into the house, all but Henry Rieback's father who quarreled with them and said he wouldn't go. It was only about nine o'clock, but they were all drunk and the rummy-looking farm house was a place for bad women to stay in. That's what it was. I crept up along a fence and looked through a window and saw.

It's what give me the fantods.[3] I can't make it out. The women in the house were all ugly mean-looking women, not nice to look at or be near. They were homely too, except one who was tall and looked a little like the gelding Middlestride, but not clean like him, but with a hard ugly mouth. She had red hair. I saw everything plain. I got up by an old rose bush by an open window and looked. The women had on loose dresses and sat around in chairs. The men came in and some sat on the women's laps. The place smelled rotten and there was rotten talk, the kind a kid hears around a livery stable in a town like Beckersville in the winter but don't ever expect to hear talked when there are women around. It was rotten. A nigger wouldn't go into such a place.

I looked at Jerry Tillford. I've told you how I had been feeling about him on account of his knowing what was going on inside of Sunstreak in the minute before he went to the post for the race in which he made a world's record.

Jerry bragged in that bad woman house as I know Sunstreak wouldn't never have bragged. He said that he made that horse, that it was him that won the race and made the record. He lied and bragged like a fool. I never heard such silly talk.

And then, what do you suppose he did! He looked at the woman in there, the one that was lean and hard-mouthed and looked a little like the gelding Middlestride, but not clean like him, and his eyes began to shine just as they did when he looked at me and at Sunstreak in the paddocks at the track in the afternoon. I stood there by the window—gee!—but I wished I hadn't gone away from the tracks, but had stayed with the boys and the niggers and the horses. The tall rotten-looking woman was between us just as Sunstreak was in the paddocks in the afternoon.

Then, all of a sudden, I began to hate that man. I wanted to scream and rush in the room and kill him. I never had such a feeling before. I was so mad clean through that I cried and my fists were doubled up so my finger nails cut my hands.

And Jerry's eyes kept shining and he waved back and forth, and then he went and kissed that woman and I crept away and went back to the tracks and to bed and didn't sleep hardly any, and then next day I got the other kids to start home with me and never told them anything I seen.

I been thinking about it ever since. I can't make it out. Spring has come again and I'm nearly sixteen and go to the tracks mornings same as always, and I see Sunstreak and Middlestride and a new colt named Strident I'll bet will lay them all out, but no one thinks so but me and two or three niggers.

But things are different. At the tracks the air don't taste as good or smell as good It's because a man like Jerry Tillford, who knows what he does, could see a horse like Sunstreak run, and kiss a woman like that the same day. I can't make it out. Darn him, what did he want to do like that for? I keep thinking about it and it spoils looking at horses and smelling things and hearing niggers laugh and everything. Sometimes I'm so mad about it I want to fight someone. It gives me the fantods. What did he do it for? I want to know why.

[1920]

[3]**the fantods** the jitters.

Joining the Conversation: Critical Thinking and Writing

1. How does the scene of Tillford in the farmhouse connect with the earlier scene at the paddock? What parallels or contrasts do you see?
2. Why does the boy tell his story?
3. About one-third of the way through the story, the boy says, "I'm getting to be a man and want to think straight and be O.K." Drawing only on what he has said up to this point, set forth what you think the "straight" thoughts (the accepted values) of the white society he is born into are. In what ways do the boy's values differ from these?
4. The boy sees African Americans as different from whites. Putting aside your own views—and drawing only on the story—discuss the differences. How, again using only the story as evidence, can the distinction be explained?
5. The narrator "wants to know why." If you were able to talk to him, what explanation would you offer? If you believe that his question is unanswerable, explain your belief.

RALPH ELLISON

Ralph Ellison (1914–1994) was born in Oklahoma City. His father died when Ellison was 3, and his mother supported herself and her child by working as a domestic. A trumpeter since boyhood, after graduating from high school Ellison went to study music at Tuskegee Institute, a black college in Alabama founded by Booker T. Washington. In 1936 he dropped out of Tuskegee and went to Harlem to study music composition and the visual arts; there he met Langston Hughes and Richard Wright, who encouraged him to turn to fiction. Ellison published stories and essays, and in 1942 became the managing editor of Negro Quarterly. *During World War II he served in the Merchant Marine. After the war he returned to writing and later taught in universities.*

"Battle Royal" was first published in 1947 and slightly revised (a transitional paragraph was added at the end of the story) for the opening chapter of Ellison's novel, Invisible Man *(1952), a book cited by* Book-Week *as "the most significant work of fiction written by an American" in the years between 1945 and 1965. In addition to publishing stories and one novel, Ellison published critical essays, which are brought together in* The Collected Essays of Ralph Ellison *(1995).*

Battle Royal

It goes a long way back, some twenty years. All my life I had been looking for something, and everywhere I turned someone tried to tell me what it was. I accepted their answers too, though they were often in contradiction and even self-contradictory. I was naïve. I was looking for myself and asking everyone except myself questions which I, and only I, could answer. It took me a long time and much painful boomeranging of my expectations to achieve a realization everyone else appears to have been born with: That I am nobody but myself. But first I had to discover that I am an invisible man!

Gordon Parks, *Ralph Ellison.* Parks, an African American photographer with an international reputation, published many books of photographs, including *Camera Portraits,* where this picture appears.

And yet I am no freak of nature, nor of history. I was in the cards, other things having been equal (or unequal) eighty-five years ago. I am not ashamed of my grandparents for having been slaves. I am only ashamed of myself for having at one time been ashamed. About eighty-five years ago they were told that they were free, united with others of our country in everything pertaining to the common good, and, in everything social, separate like the fingers of the hand. And they believed it. They exulted in it. They stayed in their place, worked hard, and brought up my father to do the same. But my grandfather is the one. He was an odd old guy, my grandfather, and I am told I take after him. It was he who caused the trouble. On his deathbed he called my father to him and said, "Son, after I'm gone I want you to keep up the good fight. I never told you, but our life is a war and I have been a traitor all my born days, a spy in the enemy's country ever since I give up my gun back in the Reconstruction. Live with your head in the lion's mouth. I want you to overcome 'em with yeses, undermine 'em with grins, agree 'em to death and destruction, let 'em swoller you till they vomit or bust wide open." They thought the old man had gone out of his mind. He had been the meekest of men. The younger children were rushed from the room, the shades drawn and the flame of the lamp turned so low that it sputtered on the wick like the old man's breathing. "Learn it to the younguns," he whispered fiercely; then he died.

But my folks were more alarmed over his last words than over his dying. It was as though he had not died at all, his words caused so much anxiety. I was warned emphatically to forget what he had said and, indeed, this is the first time it has been mentioned outside the family circle. It has a tremendous effect upon me, however. I could never be sure of what he meant. Grandfather had been a quiet old man who never made any trouble, yet on his deathbed he had called himself a traitor and a spy, and he had spoken of his meekness as a dangerous activity. It became a constant puzzle which lay unanswered in the back of my mind. And whenever things went well for me I remembered my grandfather and felt guilty and uncomfortable. It was as though I was carrying out his advice in spite of myself. And to make it worse, everyone loved me for it. I was praised by the most lily-white men of the town. I was considered an example of desirable conduct—just as my grandfather had been. And what puzzled me was that the old man had defined it as *treachery*. When I was praised for my conduct I felt a guilt that in some way I was doing something that was really against the wishes of the white folks, that if they had understood they would have desired me to act just the opposite, that I should have been sulky and mean, and that that really would have been what they wanted, even though they were fooled and thought they wanted me to act as I did. It made me afraid that some day they would look upon me as a traitor and I would be lost. Still I was more afraid to act any other way because they didn't like that at all. The old man's words were like a curse. On my graduation day I delivered an oration in which I showed that humility was the secret, indeed, the very essence of progress. (Not that I believed this—how could I, remembering my grandfather?—I only believed that it worked.) It was a great success. Everyone praised me and I was invited to give the speech at a gathering of the town's leading white citizens. It was a triumph for our whole community.

It was in the main ballroom of the leading hotel. When I got there I discovered that it was on the occasion of a smoker, and I was told that since I was to be there anyway I might as well take part in the battle royal to be fought by some of my schoolmates as part of the entertainment. The battle royal came first.

5 All of the town's big shots were there in their tuxedoes, wolfing down the buffet foods, drinking beer and whiskey and smoking black cigars. It was a large room with a high ceiling. Chairs were arranged in neat rows around three sides of a portable boxing ring. The fourth side was clear, revealing a gleaming space of polished floor. I had some misgivings over the battle royal, by the way. Not from a distaste for fighting, but because I didn't care too much for the other fellows who were to take part. They were tough guys who seemed to have no grandfather's curse worrying their minds. No one could mistake their toughness. And besides, I suspected that fighting a battle royal might detract from the dignity of my speech. In those pre-invisible days I visualized myself as a potential Booker T. Washington. But the other fellows didn't care too much for me either, and there were nine of them. I felt superior to them in my way, and I didn't like the manner in which we were all crowded together into the servants' elevator. Nor did they like my being there. In fact, as the warmly lighted floors flashed past the elevator we had words over the fact that I, by taking part in the fight, had knocked one of their friends out of a night's work.

We were led out of the elevator through a rococo hall into an anteroom and told to get into our fighting togs. Each of us was issued a pair of boxing gloves and ushered out into the big mirrored hall, which we entered looking cautiously about us and whispering, lest we might accidentally be heard above the noise of the room. It was foggy with cigar smoke. And already the whiskey was taking effect. I was shocked to see some of the most important men of the town quite tipsy. They were all there—bankers, lawyers, judges, doctors, fire chiefs, teachers, merchants. Even one of the more fashionable pastors. Something we could not see was going on up front. A clarinet was vibrating sensuously and the men were standing up and moving eagerly forward. We were a small tight group, clustered together, our bare upper bodies touching and shining with anticipatory sweat; while up front the big shots were becoming increasingly excited over something we still could not see. Suddenly I heard the school superintendent, who had told me to come, yell. "Bring up the shines, gentlemen! Bring up the little shines!"

We were rushed up to the front of the ballroom, where it smelled even more strongly of tobacco and whiskey. Then we were pushed into place. I almost wet my pants. A sea of faces, some hostile, some amused, ringed around us, and in the center, facing us, stood a magnificent blonde—stark naked. There was dead silence. I felt a blast of cold air chill me. I tried to back away, but they were behind me and around me. Some of the boys stood with lowered heads, trembling. I felt a wave of irrational guilt and fear. My teeth chattered, my skin turned to goose flesh, my knees knocked. Yet I was strongly attracted and looked in spite of myself. Had the price of looking been blindness, I would have looked. The hair was yellow like that of a circus kewpie doll, the face heavily powdered and rouged, as though to form an abstract mask, the eyes hollow and smeared a cool blue, the color of a baboon's butt. I felt a desire to spit upon her as my eyes brushed slowly over her body. Her breasts were firm and round as the domes of East Indian temples, and I stood so close as to see the fine skin texture and beads of pearly perspiration glistening like dew around the pink and erected buds of her nipples. I wanted at one and the same time to run from the room, to sink through the floor, or go to her and cover her from my eyes and the eyes of the others with my body; to feel the soft thighs, to caress her and destroy her, to love her and murder her, to hide from her, and yet to stroke where below the small American flag tattooed upon her belly her thighs formed a capital V. I had a notion that of all in the room she saw only me with her impersonal eyes.

And then she began to dance, a slow sensuous movement; the smoke of a hundred cigars clinging to her like the thinnest of veils. She seemed like a fair bird-girl girdled in veils calling to me from the angry surface of some gray and threatening sea. I was transported. Then I became aware of the clarinet playing and the big shots yelling at us. Some threatened us if we looked and others if we did not. On my right I saw one boy faint. And now a man grabbed a silver pitcher from a table and stepped close as he dashed ice water upon him and stood him up and forced two of us to support him as his head hung and moans issued from his thick bluish lips. Another boy began to plead to go home. He was the largest of the group, wearing dark red fighting trunks much too small to conceal the erection which projected from him as though in answer to the insinuating low-registered moans of the clarinet. He tried to hide himself with his boxing gloves.

And all the while the blonde continued dancing, smiling faintly at the big shots who watched her with fascination, and faintly smiling at our fear. I noticed a certain merchant who followed her hungrily, his lips loose and drooling. He was a large man who wore diamond studs in a shirtfront which swelled with the ample paunch underneath, and each time the blonde swayed her undulating hips he ran his hand through the thin hair of his bald head and, with his arms upheld, his posture clumsy like that of an intoxicated panda, wound his belly in a slow and obscene grind. This creature was completely hypnotized. The music had quickened. As the dancer flung herself about with a detached expression on her face, the men began reaching out to touch her. I could see their beefy fingers sink into her soft flesh. Some of the others tried to stop them and she began to move around the floor in graceful circles, as they gave chase, slipping and sliding over the polished floor. It was mad. Chairs went crashing, drinks were spilt, as they ran laughing and howling after her. They caught her just as she reached a door, raised her from the floor, and tossed her as college boys are tossed at a hazing, and above her red, fixed-smiling lips I saw the terror and disgust in her eyes, almost like my own terror and that which I saw in some of the other boys. As I watched, they tossed her twice and her soft breasts seemed to flatten against the air and her legs flung wildly as she spun. Some of the more sober ones helped her to escape. And I started off the floor, heading for the anteroom with the rest of the boys.

10 Some were still crying and in hysteria. But as we tried to leave we were stopped and ordered to get into the ring. There was nothing to do but what we were told. All ten of us climbed under the ropes and allowed ourselves to be blindfolded with broad bands of white cloth. One of the men seemed to feel a bit sympathetic and tried to cheer us up as we stood with our backs against the ropes. Some of us tried to grin. "See that boy over there?" one of the men said. "I want you to run across at the bell and give it to him right in the belly. If you don't get him, I'm going to get you. I don't like his looks." Each of us was told the same. The blindfolds were put on. Yet even then I had been going over my speech. In my mind each word was as bright as flame. I felt the cloth pressed into place, and frowned so that it would be loosened when I relaxed.

But now I felt a sudden fit of blind terror. I was unused to darkness. It was as though I had suddenly found myself in a dark room filled with poisonous cotton-mouths. I could hear the bleary voices yelling insistently for the battle royal to begin.

"Get going in there!"

"Let me at that big nigger!"

I strained to pick up the school superintendent's voice, as though to squeeze some security out of that slightly more familiar sound.

15 "Let me at those black sonsabitches!" someone yelled.

"No, Jackson, no!" another voice yelled. "Here, somebody, help me hold Jack."

"I want to get at that ginger-colored nigger. Tear him limb from limb," the first voice yelled.

I stood against the ropes trembling. For in those days I was what they called ginger-colored, and he sounded as though he might crunch me between his teeth like a crisp ginger cookie.

Quite a struggle was going on. Chairs were being kicked about and I could hear voices grunting as with a terrific effort. I wanted to see, to see more desperately than ever before. But the blindfold was as tight as a thick skin-puckering scab and when I raised my gloved hands to push the layers of white aside a voice yelled, "Oh, no you don't, black bastard! Leave that alone!"

20 "Ring the bell before Jackson kills him a coon!" someone boomed in the sudden silence. And I heard the bell clang and the sound of the feet scuffling forward.

A glove smacked against my head. I pivoted, striking out stiffly as someone went past, and felt the jar ripple along the length of my arm to my shoulder. Then it seemed as though all nine of the boys had turned upon me at once. Blows pounded me from all sides while I struck out as best I could. So many blows landed upon me that I wondered if I were not the only blindfolded fighter in the ring, or if the man called Jackson hadn't succeeded in getting me after all.

Blindfolded, I could no longer control my motions. I had no dignity. I stumbled about like a baby or a drunken man. The smoke had become thicker and with each new blow it seemed to sear and further restrict my lungs. My saliva became like hot bitter glue. A glove connected with my head, filling my mouth with warm blood. It was everywhere. I could not tell if the moisture I felt upon my body was sweat or blood. A blow landed hard against the nape of my neck. I felt myself going over, my head hitting the floor. Streaks of blue light filled the black world behind the blindfold. I lay prone, pretending that I was knocked out, but felt myself seized by hands and yanked to my feet. "Get going, black boy! Mix it up!" My arms were like lead, my head smarting from blows. I managed to feel my way to the ropes and held on, trying to catch my breath. A glove landed in my mid-section and I went over again, feeling as though the smoke had become a knife jabbed into my guts. Pushed this way and that by the legs milling around me, I finally pulled erect and discovered that I could see the black, sweat-washed forms weaving in the smoky-blue atmosphere like drunken dancers weaving to the rapid drum-like thuds of blows.

Everyone fought hysterically. It was complete anarchy. Everybody fought everybody else. No group fought together for long. Two, three, four, fought one, then turned to fight each other, were themselves attacked. Blows landed below the belt and in the kidney, with the gloves open as well as closed, and with my eye partly opened now there was not so much terror. I moved carefully, avoiding blows, although not too many to attract attention, fighting from group to group. The boys groped about like blind, cautious crabs crouching to protect their mid-sections, their heads pulled in short against their shoulders, their arms stretched nervously before them, with their fists testing the smoke-filled air like the knobbed feelers of hypersensitive snails. In one corner I glimpsed a boy violently punching the air and heard him scream in pain as he smashed his hand against a ring post. For a second I saw him bent over holding his hand, then going down as a blow caught his unprotected head. I played one group against the other, slipping and throwing a punch then stepping out of range while pushing the others into the melee to take the blows blindly aimed at me. The smoke was agonizing and there were no rounds, no bells at three minute intervals to relieve our exhaustion. The room spun round me, a swirl of lights, smoke, sweating bodies surrounded by tense white faces. I bled from both nose and mouth, the blood spattering upon my chest.

The men kept yelling, "Slug him, black boy! Knock his guts out!"

"Uppercut him! Kill him! Kill that big boy!"

Taking a fake fall, I saw a boy going down heavily beside me as though we were felled by a single blow, saw a sneaker-clad foot shoot into his groin as the two who had knocked him down stumbled upon him. I rolled out of range, feeling a twinge of nausea.

The harder we fought the more threatening the men became. And yet, I had begun to worry about my speech again. How would it go? Would they recognize my ability? What would they give me?

I was fighting automatically and suddenly I noticed that one after another of the boys was leaving the ring. I was surprised, filled with panic, as though I had been left alone with an unknown danger. Then I understood. The boys had arranged it among themselves. It was the custom for the two men left in the ring to slug it out for the winner's prize. I discovered this too late. When the bell sounded two men in tuxedoes leaped into the ring and removed the blindfold. I found myself facing Tatlock, the biggest of the gang. I felt sick at my stomach. Hardly had the bell stopped ringing in my ears than it clanged again and I saw him moving swiftly toward me. Thinking of nothing else to do I hit him smash on the nose. He kept coming, bringing the rank sharp violence of stale sweat. His face was a black blank of a face, only his eyes alive—with hate of me and aglow with a feverish terror from what had happened to us all. I became anxious. I wanted to deliver my speech and he came at me as though he meant to beat it out of me. I smashed him again and again, taking his blows as they came. Then on a sudden impulse I struck him lightly as we clinched, I whispered, "Fake like I knocked you out, you can have the prize."

"I'll break your behind," he whispered hoarsely.

30 "For *them?*"

"For *me*, sonofabitch!"

They were yelling for us to break it up and Tatlock spun me half around with a blow, and as a joggled camera sweeps in a reeling scene, I saw the howling red faces crouching tense beneath the cloud of blue-gray smoke. For a moment the world wavered, unraveled, flowed, then my head cleared and Tatlock bounced before me. That fluttering shadow before my eyes was his jabbing left hand. Then falling forward, my head against his damp shoulder, I whispered,

"I'll make it five dollars more."

"Go to hell!"

35 But his muscles relaxed a trifle beneath my pressure and I breathed, "Seven!"

"Give it to your ma," he said, ripping me beneath the heart.

And while I still held him I butted him and moved away. I felt myself bombarded with punches. I fought back with hopeless desperation. I wanted to deliver my speech more than anything else in the world, because I felt that only these men could judge truly my ability, and now this stupid clown was ruining my chances. I began fighting carefully now, moving in to punch him and out again with my greater speed. A lucky blow to his chin and I had him going too—until I heard a loud voice yell, "I got my money on the big boy."

Hearing this, I almost dropped my guard. I was confused: Should I try to win against the voice out there? Would not this go against my speech, and was not this a moment for humility, for nonresistance? A blow to my head as I danced about sent my right eye popping like a jack-in-the-box and settled my dilemma. The room went red as I fell. It was a dream fall, my body languid and fastidious as to where to land, until the floor became impatient and smashed up to meet me. A moment later I came to. An hypnotic voice said FIVE emphatically. And I lay there, hazily watching a dark red spot of my own blood shaping itself into a butterfly, glistening and soaking into the soiled gray world of the canvas.

When the voice drawled TEN I was lifted up and dragged to a chair. I sat dazed. My eye pained and swelled with each throb of my pounding heart and I wondered if now I would be allowed to speak. I was wringing wet, my mouth still bleeding. We were grouped along the wall now. The other boys ignored me as they congratulated Tatlock and speculated as to how much they would be paid. One boy whimpered over his smashed hand. Looking up front, I saw attendants in white jackets rolling the portable ring away and placing a small square rug in the vacant space surrounded by chairs. Perhaps, I thought, I will stand on the rug to deliver my speech.

40 Then the M.C. called to us, "Come on up here boys and get your money."

We ran forward to where the men laughed and talked in their chairs, waiting. Everyone seemed friendly now.

"There it is on the rug," the man said. I saw the rug covered with coins of all dimensions and a few crumpled bills. But what excited me, scattered here and there, were the gold pieces.

"Boys, it's all yours," the man said. "You get all you grab."

"That's right, Sambo," a blond man said, winking at me confidentially.

45 I trembled with excitement, forgetting my pain. I would get the gold and the bills, I thought. I would use both hands. I would throw my body against the boys nearest me to block them from the gold.

"Get down around the rug now," the man commanded, "and don't anyone touch it until I give the signal."

"This ought to be good," I heard.

As told, we got around the square rug on our knees. Slowly the man raised his freckled hand as we followed it upward with our eyes.

I heard, "These niggers look like they're about to pray!"

50 Then, "Ready," the man said. "Go!"

I lunged for a yellow coin lying on the blue design of the carpet, touching it and sending a surprised shriek to join those rising around me. I tried frantically to remove my hand but could not let go. A hot, violent force tore through my body, shaking me like a wet rat. The rug was electrified. The hair bristled up on my head as I shook myself free. My muscles jumped, my nerves jangled, writhed. But I saw that this was not stopping the other boys. Laughing in fear and embarrassment, some were holding back and scooping up the coins knocked off by the painful contortions of the others. The men roared above us as we struggled.

"Pick it up, goddamnit, pick it up!" someone called like a bass-voiced parrot. "Go on, get it!"

I crawled rapidly around the floor, picking up the coins, trying to avoid the coppers and to get greenbacks and the gold. Ignoring the shock by laughing, as I brushed the coins off quickly, I discovered that I could contain the electricity—a contradiction, but it works. Then the men began to push us onto the rug. Laughing embarrassedly, we struggled out of their hands and kept after the coins. We were all wet and slippery and hard to hold. Suddenly I saw a boy lifted into the air, glistening with sweat like a circus seal, and dropped, his wet back landing flush upon the charged rug, heard him yell and saw him literally dance upon his back, his elbows beating a frenzied tattoo upon the floor, his muscles twitching like the flesh of a horse stung by many flies. When he finally rolled off, his face was gray and no one stopped him when he ran from the floor amid booming laughter.

"Get the money," the M.C. called. "That's good hard American cash!"

55 And we snatched and grabbed, snatched and grabbed. I was careful not to come too close to the rug now, and when I felt the hot whiskey breath descend upon me like a cloud of foul air I reached out and grabbed the leg of a chair. It was occupied and I held on desperately.

"Leggo, nigger! Leggo!"

The huge face wavered down to mine as he tried to push me free. But my body was slippery and he was too drunk. It was Mr. Colcord, who owned a chain of movie houses and "entertainment palaces." Each time he grabbed me I slipped out of his hands. It became a real struggle. I feared the rug more than I did the drunk, so I held on, surprising myself for a moment by trying to topple *him* upon the rug. It was such an enormous idea that I found myself actually carrying it out. I tried not to be obvious, yet when I grabbed his leg, trying to tumble him out of the chair, he raised up roaring with laughter, and, looking at me with soberness dead in the eye, kicked me viciously in the chest. The chair leg flew out of my hand. I felt myself going and rolled. It was as though I had rolled through a bed of hot coals. It seemed a whole century would pass before I would roll free, a century in which I was seared through the deepest levels of my body to the fearful breath within me and the breath seared and heated to the point of explosion. It'll all be over in a flash, I thought as I rolled clear. It'll all be over in a flash.

But not yet, the men on the other side were waiting, red faces swollen as though from apoplexy as they bent forward in their chairs. Seeing their fingers coming toward me I rolled away as a fumbled football rolls off the receiver's fingertips, back into the coals. That time I luckily sent the rug sliding out of place and heard the coins ringing against the floor and the boys scuffling to pick them up and the M.C. calling, "All right, boys, that's all. Go get dressed and get your money."

I was limp as a dish rag. My back felt as though it had been beaten with wires.

60 When we had dressed the M.C. came in and gave us each five dollars, except Tatlock, who got ten for being the last in the ring. Then he told us to leave. I was not to get a chance to deliver my speech, I thought. I was going out into the dim alley in despair when I was stopped and told to go back. I returned to the ballroom, where the men were pushing back their chairs and gathering in groups to talk.

The M.C. knocked on a table for quiet. "Gentlemen," he said, "we almost forgot an important part of the program. A most serious part, gentlemen. This boy was brought here to deliver a speech which he made at his graduation yesterday. . . ."

"Bravo!"

"I'm told that he is the smartest boy we've got out there in Greenwood. I'm told that he knows more big words than a pocket-sized dictionary."

Much applause and laughter.

65 "So now, gentlemen, I want you to give him your attention."

There was still laughter as I faced them, my mouth dry, my eye throbbing. I began slowly, but evidently my throat was tense, because they began shouting, "Louder! Louder!"

"We of the younger generation extol the wisdom of that great leader and educator," I shouted, "who first spoke these flaming words of wisdom: 'A ship lost at sea for many days suddenly sighted a friendly vessel. From the mast of the unfortunate vessel was seen a signal: "Water, water; we die of thirst!" The answer from the friendly vessel came back: "Cast down your bucket where you are." The captain of the distressed vessel, at last heeding the injunction, cast down his bucket, and it came up full of fresh sparkling water from the mouth of the Amazon River.' And like him I say, and in his words. 'To those of my race who depend upon bettering their condition in a foreign land, or who underestimate the importance of cultivating friendly relations with the Southern white man, who is his next-door neighbor. I would say: "Cast down your bucket where you are"—cast it down in making friends in every manly way of the people of all races by whom we are surrounded. . . .'"

I spoke automatically and with such fervor that I did not realize that the men were still talking and laughing until my dry mouth, filling up with blood from the cut, almost strangled me. I coughed, wanting to stop and go to one of the tall brass, sand-filled spittoons to relieve myself, but a few of the men, especially the superintendent, were listening and I was afraid. So I gulped it down, blood, saliva and all, and continued. (What powers of endurance I had during those days! What enthusiasm! What a belief in the rightness of things!) I spoke even louder in spite of the pain. But still they talked and still they laughed, as though deaf with cotton in dirty ears. So I spoke with greater emotional emphasis. I closed my ears and swallowed blood until I was nauseated. The speech seemed a hundred times as long as before, but I could not leave out a single word. All had to be said, each memorized nuance considered, rendered. Nor was that all. Whenever I uttered a word of three or more syllables a group of voices would yell for me to repeat it. I used the phrase "social responsibility" and they yelled:

"What's the word you say, boy?"

"Social responsibility," I said.

"What?"

"Social . . ."

"Louder."

". . . responsibility."

"More!"

"Respon—"

"Repeat!"

"—sibility."

The room filled with the uproar of laughter until, no doubt, distracted by having to gulp down my blood, I made a mistake and yelled a phrase I had often seen denounced in newspaper editorials, heard debated in private.

"Social . . ."

"What?" they yelled.

". . . equality—"

The laughter hung smokelike in the sudden stillness. I opened my eyes, puzzled. Sounds of displeasure filled the room. The M.C. rushed forward. They shouted hostile phrases at me. But I did not understand.

A small dry mustached man in the front row blared out, "Say that slowly, son!"

"What sir?"

"What you just said!"

"Social responsibility, sir," I said.

"You weren't being smart, were you, boy?" he said, not unkindly.

"No, sir!"

"You sure that about 'equality' was a mistake?"

"Oh, yes, sir," I said. "I was swallowing blood."

"Well, you had better speak more slowly so we can understand. We mean to do right by you, but you've got to know your place at all times. All right, now, go on with your speech."

I was afraid. I wanted to leave but I wanted also to speak and I was afraid they'd snatch me down.

"Thank you, sir," I said, beginning where I had left off, and having them ignore me as before.

Yet when I finished there was a thunderous applause. I was surprised to see the superintendent come forth with a package wrapped in white tissue paper, and gesturing for quiet, address the men.

"Gentlemen, you see that I did not overpraise this boy. He makes a good speech and some day he'll lead his people in the proper paths. And I don't have to tell you that that is important in these days and times. This is a good, smart boy, and so to encourage him in the right direction, in the name of the Board of Education I wish to present him a prize in the form of this . . ."

He paused, removing the tissue paper and revealing a gleaming calfskin brief case.

". . . in the form of this first-class article from Shad Whitmore's shop."

"Boy," he said, addressing me, "take this prize and keep it well. Consider it a badge of office. Prize it. Keep developing as you are and some day it will be filled with important papers that will help shape the destiny of your people."

I was so moved that I could hardly express my thanks. A rope of bloody saliva forming a shape like an undiscovered continent drooled upon the leather and I wiped it quickly away. I felt an importance that I had never dreamed.

"Open it and see what's inside," I was told.

My fingers a-tremble, I complied, smelling the fresh leather and finding an official-looking document inside. It was a scholarship to the state college for Negroes. My eyes filled with tears and I ran awkwardly off the floor.

I was overjoyed; I did not even mind when I discovered that the gold pieces I had scrambled for were brass pocket tokens advertising a certain make of automobile.

When I reached home everyone was excited. Next day the neighbors came to congratulate me. I even felt safe from grandfather, whose deathbed curse usually spoiled my triumphs. I stood beneath his photograph with my brief case in hand and smiled triumphantly into his stolid black peasant's face. It was a face that fascinated me. The eyes seemed to follow everywhere I went.

That night I dreamed I was at a circus with him and that he refused to laugh at the clowns no matter what they did. Then later he told me to open my brief case and read what was inside and I did, finding an official envelope stamped with the state seal; and inside the envelope I found another and another, endlessly, and I thought I would fall of weariness. "Them's years," he said. "Now open that one." And I did and in it I found an engraved document containing a short message in letters of gold. "Read it," my grandfather said. "Out loud."

"To Whom It May Concern," I intoned, "Keep This Nigger-Boy Running."

I awoke with the old man's laughter ringing in my ears.

(It was a dream I was to remember and dream again for many years after. But at the time I had no insight into its meaning. First I had to attend college.)

[1947]

Joining the Conversation: Critical Thinking and Writing

1. Now that you have read the entire story, the opening paragraph may be clearer than it was when you first read it. What does the narrator mean when he declares at the end of this paragraph, "I am an invisible man?" Explain how the events described in the story taught him this painful truth.

2. The narrator says of his grandfather's dying speech, "I could never be sure of what he meant." What do you think the grandfather meant by calling himself a traitor and a spy in the enemy's territory?

3. What is the significance of the scene involving the naked blonde woman? How is this scene related to the narrator's discovery that he is invisible?

4. This story is a powerful, indeed shocking study of racism, but in essays and interviews Ellison often noted that he intended his stories and his novel *Invisible Man* to illuminate "universal truths" about human experience as well. In your view, does "Battle Royal" achieve this goal? What insights does it offer about the nature of self-knowledge and human identity?

Mary Robison

Mary Robison (b. 1949) was born in Washington, D.C., and educated at Ohio State University (a bachelor's degree, with a major in art history) and Johns Hopkins University (a master's degree in creative writing). In 1977 she published two stories in the New Yorker. *Robison has continued to write stories and novels while teaching creative writing at various colleges. She now teaches at the University of Florida.*

Coach

1

The August two-a-day practice sessions were sixty-seven days away, Coach calculated. He was drying breakfast dishes. He swabbed a coffee cup and made himself listen to his wife, who was across the kitchen, sponging the stove's burner coils.

"I know I'm no Rembrandt," Sherry said, "but I have so damn much fun trying, and this little studio—this room—we can afford. I could get out of your way by going there and get you and Daphne out of my way. No offense."

"I'm thinking," Coach said.

His wife coasted from appliance to appliance. She swiped the face of the oven clock with her sponge. "You're thinking too slow. Your reporter's coming at nine and it's way after eight now. Should I give them a deposit on the studio or not? Yes or no?"

5 Coach was staring at the sink, at a thread of water that came from one of the taps. He thought of the lake place where they used to go in North Carolina. He saw green water being thickly sliced by a power boat; the boat towing Sherry, who was blond and laughing on her skis, her rounded back strong, her suit shining red.

"Of course, of course, give them the money," he said.

Their daughter, Daphne, wandered into the kitchen. She was dark-haired, lazy-looking, fifteen. Her eyes were lost behind bangs. She drew open the enormous door of the refrigerator.

"Don't hang, Daphne, you'll unhinge things," her mother said. "What are you after?"

"Food mainly," Daphne said.

10 Sherry went away, to the little sun patio off the kitchen. Coach pushed the glass door sideways after her and it smacked shut.

"Eat and run," he said to Daphne. "I've got a reporter coming in short order. Get dressed." He spoke firmly but in the smaller voice he always used for his child.

"Yes, sir," Daphne said. She broke into the freezer compartment and ducked to let its gate pass over her head. "Looks bad. Nothing in here but Eggos."

"I ate Eggos. Just hustle up," Coach said.

"Can I be here for this guy?" Daphne asked.

15 "Who guy? The reporter? Nuh-uh. He's just from the college, Daph. Coming to see if the new freshman coach has three heads or just two."

Daphne was nodding at the food jars racked on the wide refrigerator door. "Hey, lookit," she said. She blew a breath in front of the freezer compartment and made a short jet of mist.

Coach remembered a fall night, a Friday-game night, long ago, when he had put Daphne on the playing field. It was during the ceremonies before his unbeaten squad had taken on Ignatius South High School Parents' Night. He had laced shoulder pads on Daphne and draped the trainer's gag jersey—number 1/2—over her, and balanced Tim-somebody's helmet on her eight-year-old head. She was lost in the getup, a small pile of equipment out on the fifty-yard line. She had applauded when the loudspeaker announced her name, when the p.a. voice, garbled by amplification and echo, had rung out, "Daughter of our coach, Harry Noonan, and his wife—number one-half, Daphne Noonan!" She had stood in the bath of floodlights, shaking as the players and their folks strolled by—the players grim in their war gear, the parents tiny and apologetic-seeming in civilian clothes. The co-captain of the team, awesome in his pads and cleats and steaming from warm-up running, had palmed Daphne's big helmet and twisted it sideways. From behind, from the home stands, Coach had heard, "Haaa!" as Daphne turned circles of happy confusion, trying to right the helmet. Through the ear hole her left eye had twinkled, Coach remembered. He had heard, "God, that's funny," and "Coach's kid."

On the sun porch now, his wife was doing a set of tennis exercises. She was between Coach and the morning sun, framed by the glass doors. He could see through the careless weave of her caftan, enough to make out the white flesh left by her swimsuit.

"I knew you wouldn't let me," Daphne said. She had poured a glass of chocolate milk. She pulled open a chilled banana. "I bet Mom gets to be here."

20 "Daph, this isn't a big deal. We've been through it all before," Coach said.

"Not for a college paper," Daphne said. "Wait a minute, I'll be right back." She left the kitchen.

"I'll hold my breath and count the heartbeats," Coach said to the space she had left behind.

They were new to the little town, new to Pennsylvania. Coach was assuming charge of the freshman squad, in a league where freshmen weren't eligible for the varsity. He had taken the job, not sure if it was a step up for him or a serious misstep. The money was so-so. But he wanted the college setting for his family—especially for Daphne. She had been seeming to lose interest in the small celebrity they achieved in high-school towns. She had acted bored at the Noonans' Sunday spaghetti dinner for standout players. She had stopped fetching plates of food for the boys, who were too game-sore to get their own. She had even stopped wearing the charm bracelet her parents had put together for her—a silver bracelet with a tiny megaphone, the numerals 68—a league championship year—and, of course, a miniature football.

Coach took a seat at the kitchen table. He ate grapes from a bowl. He spilled bottled wheat germ into his palm. On the table were four chunky ring binders, their black leatherette covers printed with the college seal—which still looked strange to him. These were his playbooks, and he was having trouble getting the play tactics into his head.

25 "Will you turn off the radio?" he yelled.

The bleat from Daphne's upstairs bedroom ceased. A minute later she came down and into the kitchen. She had a cardboard folder and some textbooks with her. "Later on, would you look at this stuff and help me? Can you do these?" she asked Coach.

He glanced over one of her papers. It was penciled with algebra equations, smutty with erasures and scribbled-out parts. "I'd have to see the book, but no. Not now, not later. I don't want to and I don't have time."

"That's just great," Daphne said.

"Your mother and I got our algebra homework done already, Daph. We turned ours in," Coach said. "This was in nineteen fifty-six."

30 "Mom!" Daphne said, pushing aside the glass door.

"Forget it," Sherry said.

2

Toby, the boy sent from *The Rooter* to interview Coach, was unshaven and bleary-eyed. He wore a rumpled cerise polo shirt and faded Levi's. He asked few questions, dragging his words. Now and then he grumbled of a hangover and no sleep. He yawned during Coach's answers. He took no notes.

"You're getting this now?" Coach said.

"Oh, yeah, it's writing itself, I'm such a pro," Toby said, and Coach wasn't certain if the boy was kidding.

"So you've been here just a little while. Lucky you," Toby said. "Less than a month?"

"Is that like a question? It seems less than a month—less than a week—a day and a half," Coach said. For the interview, he had put on white sports slacks and a maroon pullover with a gold collar—the college's colors. The pullover he had bought at Campus World. The clothes had a snug fit that flattered Coach and showed off his flat stomach and heavy biceps.

He and Toby were on either end of the sofa in the living room of the house, a wooden two-story Coach had found and would be paying off for decades, he was sure.

Toby said, "Well, believe it or not, I've got enough for a couple sticks, which is shoptalk among we press men for two columns. If you're going to be home tomorrow, there's a girl who'll come and take your picture—Marcia. She's a drag, I warn you."

"One thing about this town, there aren't any damn sidewalks, and the cars don't give you much room if you're jogging," Coach said, standing up.

"Hey, tell me about it. When I'm hitching, I wear an orange safety poncho and carry a red flag and paint a big X on my back. Of course, I'm probably just making a better target," the reporter said.

"I jog down at the track now. It's a great facility, comparable to a Big Ten's. I like the layout," Coach said.

"Okay, but the interview's over," Toby said.

"Well, I came from high schools, remember. In Indiana and Ohio—good schools with good budgets, mind you, but high schools, nonetheless."

"Yeah, I got where you're coming from," Toby said.

"Did you need to know what courses I'll be handling? Fall quarter, they've got me lined up for two things: The Atlantic World is the first one, and Colloquium or European Industrial Development, I think it is. Before, I always taught World History. P.O.D.,[1] once or twice."

"That three-eighty-one you're going to teach is a tit course, in case nobody's informed you. It's what we call lunch," Toby said.

"It's, in nature, a refresher course," Coach said.

"Yeah, or out of nature," Toby said.

Daphne came from the long hall steps into the living room. Her dark hair was brushed and lifting with static. He eyes seemed to Coach larger than usual, and a little sooty around the lashes.

"You're just leaving, aren't you, buster?" Coach said to her.

"Retrieving a pencil," Daphne said.

"Is your name really Buster?" Toby asked.

[1]**P.O.D.** Principles of Democracy.

"Get your pencil and scoot. This is Toby here. Toby, this is my daughter, Daphne," Coach said.

"Nice to meet you," Daphne said. She slipped into a deep chair at the far corner of the long living room.

"Can she hear us over in that county?" Toby said. "Do you read me?" he shouted.

Daphne smiled. Coach saw bangs, and her very white teeth.

"Come on, Daph, hit the trail," he said.

"I've got a joke for her first," Toby said. "What's green and moves very fast?"

"Frog in a blender," Daphne said. "Dad? Some friends invited me to go swimming with them at the Natatorium. May I?"

"You've got to see the Nat. It's the best thing," Toby said.

"What about your class, though? She's in makeup school here, Toby, catching up on some algebra that didn't take the first time around."

Toby wrinkled his nose at Daphne. "At first, I thought you meant *makeup* school, like lipstick and rouge."

"I wish," Daphne said.

She slipped her left foot from her leather sandal and casually stroked the toes.

"She's a nut for swimming," Coach said.

"You'll be so bored here. Most nights, your options are either ordering a pizza or slashing your wrists," Toby told Daphne.

"Oh," she said, rolling her chin on her shoulder in a rather seductive way.

"Take it from Toby," he said.

Coach let Toby through the front door, and watched until he was down the street.

"He was nice," Daphne said.

"Aw, Daph. That's what you say about everybody. There's a lot better things you could say—more on-the-beam things."

"I guess you're mad," she said.

Coach went to the kitchen, to sit down with his play-books again. Daphne came after him.

"Aren't you?" she said.

"I guess you thought he was cute," Coach said. He flapped through some mimeographed pages, turning them on the notebook's silver rings. "I don't mean to shock you about it, but you'd be wasting your time there, Daph. You'd be trying to start a fire with a wet match."

Daphne stared at her father. "That's sick!" she said.

"I'm not criticizing him for it. I'm just telling you," Coach said.

3

"This is completely wrong," Coach said sadly. He read further "Oh, no," he said. He drowned the newspaper in his bath water and slogged the pages over into a corner by the commode.

His wife handed him a dry edition, one of the ten or twelve *Rooters* Daphne had brought home.

Sherry was parallel to Coach on the edge of the tub, sitting with her back braced against the wall. "Oh, cheer up," she said. "Nobody reads a free newspaper."

"Coach quartered the dry *Rooter* into a package around Toby's article, "Well, I wasn't head coach at Elmgrove, and I sure wasn't Phi Beta Kappa. And look at this picture," Coach said.

"What's so wrong with it?" Sherry said.

"Where did he get that you were at Mt. Holyoke? And I didn't bitch about the sidewalks this much."

"You didn't?" Sherry said. "That's almost too bad. I thought that was the best part of the article."

Coach slunk further into the warm water until it crowded his chin. He kept the newspaper aloft, "Oh, come on, give me some credit here! Don't they have any supervision over in journalism? I don't see how he could get away with this shit. It's an unbelievably sloppy job."

"It's just a dinky article in a handout paper, Coach. What do you care? It wouldn't matter if he said we were a bright-green family with scales," Sherry said.

"He didn't think of that or he would have. This breaks my heart," Coach said.

"Daph liked it," Sherry said.

Coach wearily chopped bath water with the side of his hand and threw a splash at the soap recess in the tiled wall. "I tell you, I'm going to be spending my whole first year here explaining how none of it's true."

"What difference does true make?" Sherry said.

4

Coach was seated awkwardly on an iron stool at a white table on the patio of the Dairy Frost. Daphne was across from him, fighting the early evening heat for her mocha-fudge cone. She tilted her head at the cone, lapping at it.

"You aren't saying anything," Coach said.

"Wait," Daphne said.

She worked on the cone.

"I've been waiting."

"If you two want to separate, it's none of my business," she said.

They were facing the busy parking lot when a new Pontiac turned in off the highway, glided easily onto the gravel, took a parking slot close by. In the driver's seat was a boy with built-up shoulders—a boy who looked very familiar to Coach. In back was a couple in their fifties—the boy's parents, Coach thought—both talking at once.

"Have I been spilling all this breath for nothing! *Not* a separation," Coach said. "Not anything like it."

"All right, not," Daphne said. She stopped in her attack on the cone long enough to watch the Pontiac boy step out. Dark brown ice cream streamed between her knuckles and down the inside of her wrist.

"You're losing it, honey," Coach said.

Daphne dabbed around the cone and her hand, making repairs.

"Hell, *real* trouble your father wouldn't tell you about at a *Dairy* Frost. This apartment your mom found is like an office or something. A studio for her to go to and get away every now and then. That kid's in my backfield. What the *hell's* his name?"

They watched as the young man took orders from his parents, then went inside the Dairy Frost. He looked both wider and taller than the other patrons, out of their scale. His rump and haunches were thick with muscle. His neck was fat but tight.

"Bobby Stark!" Coach said, and smiled very quickly at the parents in the Pontiac. He turned back to his daughter.

"She wants to get away from us," Daphne said.

"Definitely not. She gave me a list, is how this whole thing started. She's got stuff she wants to do, and you with your school problems and me with the team—we're too much for her, see? She could spend her entire day on us, if you think about it, and never have one second for herself. If you think about it fairly, Daphne, you'll agree."

Daphne seemed to consider. She was focused on the inside of the Dairy Frost building, and for a while she kept still.

"That guy looks dumb. One of the truly dumb," she said.

"My halfback? He's not. He was his class salutatorian," Coach said.

"He doesn't know *you.*"

"Just embarrassed," Coach said. "Can we stick to the point, Daph? And quit rocking the boat. Look what you're doing." Daphne's arm was on the table and she was violently swinging her legs under her chair.

She made a sigh and marched over to a trash can to deposit her slumping cone. Then she washed up at the children's drinking fountain and rejoined Coach, who had finished his Brown Cow but had kept the plastic spoon in his mouth.

"What was on this list of Mom's?" Daphne asked.

"Adult stuff," Coach said.

"Just give me an example."

"Coach removed the plastic spoon and cracked it in half.

"Your mother's list is for five years. In that time, she wants to be speaking French regularly. She wants to follow up on her printmaking."

"This is adult stuff?" Daphne said.

Coach raised a hand to Bobby Stark. Stark had three malt cups in a cardboard carrier and he was moving toward the parking lot.

"Hey, those all for you?" Coach called out.

"I got a month to get fat, Coach. You'll have five months to beat it off me," the boy called back.

The people at some of the tables around Coach's lit up with grins. Bobby Stark's parents were grinning.

"Every hit of that junk takes a second off your time in the forty—remember that!" Coach shouted.

Stark wagged his head ruefully, his cheeks blushing. He pretended to hide the malts behind his arm.

"Duh," Daphne said in a hoarse voice. "What way to the door, Coach?"

"He can hear you," Coach said.

"Duh, kin I have a candy bar, Coach," she rasped.

They faced Stark, who smiled a little crookedly at Daphne, and threw her a wink so dazzling, she went silent.

5

Coach was in the basement laundry room, both arms busy hugging a bundle of jogging clothes. He was waiting on the washer, waiting for Sherry to unload her clothes.

"The Cowboys are soaking their players in a sense-deprivation tub of warm saltwater," she said.

"We know," Coach said.

"If Dallas is doing it, I just thought you might want to consider it."

"We have. Hustle up a little with your stuff, will you?" Coach said.

"It's like my apartment," Sherry said. "A place apart."

135 Coach cut her off. "Don't go on about how much you love your apartment."

"I wasn't going to," Sherry said. She slung her wet slacks and blouses into the dryer.

Coach had just two weeks before the start of the heavy practices. His team would have him then, he knew, almost straight through to the Christmas holidays.

"I like that," Coach said. "A place apart."

A half hour later, Coach and his wife were on the side patio. They could hear the tick of the clothes dryer downstairs. Sherry had changed into a halter top. She was taking sun on her back, adding to her tan.

140 "You know what's odd?" she said. "Daphne's popularity here. I don't mean it's odd."

"She's always done terrific with people, always gone over well," Coach said.

"*Your* people, though. These are hers," Sherry said. "Like that reporter."

"Yeah, they're like sisters," Coach said.

6

It was a week before the two-a-day practice sessions would begin. The sky was colorless and glazed, like milk glass. When Coach looked at the sun, his eyes ached, his head screamed.

145 He had run some wind sprints on the stadium field, and now he was doing an easy lap. A stopwatch on a noose of ribbon swung against his chest. He cut through the goalposts and trotted for the sidelines, for the twenty, where he had dumped his clipboard and a towel.

Someone called to him.

Blond Bobby Stark came out from under the stands. His football shoes were laced together and draped around his neck. He wore a midriff-cut T-shirt and shorts. He walked gingerly in white wool socks.

"Did everybody go? Or am I the first one here?" he called to Coach.

"Bout a half hour," Coach said, heaving.

150 Stark sat down to untangle his shoes, and Coach, sweating, stood over him.

Coach spat. He folded his arms in a way that pushed out his muscles. He sniffed, twisting his whole nose and mouth to the left. He said, "You know, Stark, you were salutatorian for your class."

"High school," the boy said. He grinned up at Coach, an eye pinched against the glare.

"That counts, believe me. Maybe we can use you to help some of our slower players along—some of the linemen, maybe I'm thinking."

"What do you mean—tutor?" Stark said.

155 "Naw. Teach them to eat without biting off their fingers. How to tie a necktie. Some of your style," Coach said, and Stark bobbed his head.

Stark settled the fit of his right shoe. He said, "But there aren't any really dumb ones on our squad, because they'd just get flunked out. Recruiters won't touch them in this league. There wouldn't be any percentage in it.

"Then I'm greatly relieved," Coach said.

He planted his feet along a furrow of lime-eaten grass. He faced the open end of the stadium, where the enormous library building stood shimmering and uncertain behind sheets of heat that rose from the parking area.

Stark stood up and studied his shoes as he began jogging in place. He danced twenty yards down the field; loped back.

Other players were arriving for the informal session. Coach meant to time them in the mile, and in some dashes.

Stark looked jittery. He walked in semicircles, crowding Coach.

"What're you worried about?" Coach asked him. "Girl problems you got? You pull a muscle already?"

Stark glanced quickly around them. He said, "I live all my life two doors down from Coach Burton's house. My mom and Burton's wife are best friends, so I always know what's going on."

Burton had been the head coach of the varsity team for over a decade.

"You probably know about it already, anyway," Stark said. "Do you?"

"What the hell are you talking about, Stark?"

"You don't know? Typical. Burton's leaving, see? Like at the end of this year. His wife wants him out real bad, and the alumni want him out because they're tired of losing seasons. So what I heard was you were brought in because of it. And if we do okay this season, like you'll be varsity coach next year."

"That's conjecture," Coach said. But he was excited.

It was three o'clock, still hot. Coach was moving along a sidewalk with Bobby Stark, who was balanced on a racing bicycle, moving just enough to keep the machine upright.

"Three things," Coach said. "I've seen all the game films from last year, and I came here personally and witnessed the Tech game. No one lost because of the coaching. A coach can work miracles with a good team, but he is *helpless* if his personnel don't want it bad enough. That's the worst part about running a team—you can't climb down into your people's hearts and change them."

Some college girls in a large expensive car went past. They shrieked and whistled at Bobby Stark.

"Lifeguards at the pool," he explained.

"I don't know if Burton's leaving or not," Coach continued. "But if his wife wants him to go, he probably will. If you're ever thinking about a career in coaching someday, Bob, think about that. Your family's either with you or you've had it. And remember, whether you stay someplace or not depends completely on a bunch of *kids*. I swear, I'd give up a leg for a chance to get in a game myself—just one play, with what I know now."

Stark nodded. They went on a block, and he said, "I turn off here. You going to tell your daughter about the job?"

"My daughter?" Coach said, and smiled.

7

No one was home. A magnet under a plastic ladybug held a note to the face of the refrigerator. The note read:

> Harry, I'm at my place. Daph's with Toby.
> K. Somewhere, fooling around. Be good now,
> Sherry Baby.

"Dope," Coach said.

He felt very good.

He took a beer upstairs and drank it while he showered. He cinched on a pair of sweat pants and, wearing only these, went back down and fetched another beer.

180 He watched some of a baseball game on cable. He thought over his conversation with Bobby Stark. "Boy, is that true!" Coach said, and then was not at all sure why he had said it.

He frowned, remembering that in his second year of college, the only year he had been on the varsity team, he had proved an indifferent player.

"Not now," he whispered. "Not anymore."

He squashed the shape out of his beer can and stood it on top of the television.

There was a thump over his head. The ceiling creaked.

185 "Someone came home while I was in the shower," he said to himself, and ran his hand over his belly, feeling for signs of bloat from the beer.

He took the stairs in three leaps, strode into the master bedroom, calling, "Sherry?"

The dark figure in the room surprised Coach.

He yelled, "Hey!"

Daphne was dancing in front of the full-length mirror. She had improvised a look—sweeping her hair over her right ear, and stretching the neck of her shirt until her right shoulder was bared. A thing by the Commodores shrieked from her transistor.

190 "Nothing," she said.

"You're not home. Aren't you with whoosis? You're supposed to be out. You are *beet* red," Coach said.

Daphne lowered her head and squared her shirt, which bagged around her small torso. "Okay, Dad," she said.

"No, but how did your audience like the show? I bet they loved it," Coach said. He smiled at himself in the mirror. "I'm just kidding you, Daph. You looked great."

"Come *on,* Dad," she said, and tried to pass.

195 Coach chimed in with the radio. He shuffled his feet. "Hey, Daph, you know what time it is?" he said.

"Let me out, please," Daphne said.

"It's monkey time!" Coach did a jerky turn, keeping in the way of the exit door. "Do the shing-a-ling. Do the Daphne." He rolled his shoulder vampishly. He kissed his own hand. He sang along.

"Thanks a lot," Daphne said. She gave up trying to get around him. She leaned over and snapped off her radio. "You've got to use a mirror so you don't look stupid," she said. "Everybody does."

"I was only kidding. Seriously. I know dancing is important," Coach said.

200 "May I go now? I've got algebra." Daphne brought her hair from behind her ear.

"Before that, you have to hear the news. Here's news bulletin, flash extra."

"You're drunk. You and Mom are going to live in different cities," Daphne said. "Somebody shot somebody."

"No, this is good news. I'm going to be coach here of the varsity. Me." Coach pointed to his chest.

"Now let me out, please," Daphne said.

205 Coach let her pass. He followed her down the narrow hallway to her bedroom.

"More money," he said. "I'll even be on TV. I'll have my own show on Sundays. And I'll get written up in the press all the time. By *real* reporters. Hey! Why am I yelling at wood, here?"

8

Coach was drunk at the kitchen table. He was enjoying the largeness of the room, and he was making out a roster for his dream team. He had put the best kids from his fifteen years of coaching in the positions they had played for him. He was puzzling over the tight-end spot. "Jim Wyckoff or Jerry Kinney?" he said aloud. He penciled "Kinney" into his diagram.

He heard Daphne on the stairs. It occurred to him to clear the beer cans from the table. Instead, he snapped open a fresh can. "Daphne?" he called.

"Wait a second. What?" she said from the living room.

"Just wondered who else was alive besides me," Coach said. "Your mom's still not home."

Daphne entered the kitchen.

"You're sorry you were rude before? That's perfectly okay, honey, just forget it. All right, Father, but I really an ashamed of myself anyway," Coach said.

"You guzzled all those?" Daphne said.

"Hold still. What've you got on?" Coach asked her. He hauled his chair around so that he could see his daughter.

"Two, four, five," Daphne said, counting the cans.

She was wearing one of the fan shirts that Coach had seen on a few summer coeds. On the front, against a maroon field, in gold, was GO. Across the back was GRIFFINS.

"Now you're talking," Coach said.

"It was free. This guy I met—well, these two guys, really—who work at Campus World, they gave it to me. It's dumb, but I want you to see I care. I do care. Not just for you, but because I want to stay here. Do you think we can maybe? Do your people look any good this year?"

"Winners," Coach said.

"Yeah," Daphne said.

Coach skidded his chair forward. "Have a beer," he said. "Sit down here and let me show you on paper the material they've given me to work with. Then maybe you'll be a believer. Now these guys are fast and big for once. I'm not overestimating them, either. I've seen what I've seen," Coach said.

A car crept into the drive, and then its engine noise filled the garage. Coach and Daphne were quiet until Sherry bustled down the short hall that connected the garage to the kitchen.

"Really late. Sorry, sorry," she said.

"It's a party in here, I warn you," Coach said.

"So I noticed." Sherry had a grocery sack, but it was almost empty. There were bright streaks of paint on her brown arms.

Daphne plucked a bag of Oreo cookies from the groceries.

"Shoot me one of those," Coach said.

"Is there any beer left for me?" Sherry said. "I want to drown my disappointment. I can't paint!"

"You *can* paint," Coach said.

"Let's face it," Sherry said. "An artist? The wife of a coach?"

[1981]

Joining the Conversation: Critical Thinking and Writing

1. In the fifth paragraph the narrator shifts from an objective point of view to one of selective (or limited) omniscience, telling us what Coach is thinking. In your opinion, why is Coach thinking these thoughts rather than thinking about what his wife is telling him?
2. How would you characterize the relationship between Coach and Sherry? Do you think the marriage is going on the rocks? Why, or why not?
3. What do you make of the last line of the story? Is Sherry blaming Coach?
4. If you were asked to relate (in a few sentences) the history of Coach's relationship with his daughter—*not* just their present relationship—what would you write?
5. Why, in your opinion, does Robison divide the story into short, numbered scenes? After all, she could easily have provided a few transitional sentences and eliminated the numbers.

TOBIAS WOLFF

Tobias Wolff was born in Alabama in 1945, but he was raised in the state of Washington. He served for four years in the army (1964-68), including a tour of duty in Vietnam. He graduated from Oxford University in 1972 and then studied creative writing at Stanford. Wolff's first two books were collections of short stories, In the Garden of North American Martyrs *(1981) and* Back in the World *(1985), and both received good reviews, but he achieved greater success and acclaim with the publication of* The Boy's Life *(1989), his memoir of his teenage years. He also has written a memoir of his military service,* In Pharaoh's Army *(1994). The author of many short stories and two novels, his recent publications include* Our Story Begins: New and Selected Stories *(2008). From 1980 to 1997, Wolff taught courses in English and creative writing at Syracuse University, and, since then, he has taught at Stanford, where he is the Ward W. and Priscilla B. Woods Professor in the School of Humanities and Sciences.*

Powder

Just before Christmas my father took me skiing at Mount Baker. He'd had to fight for the privilege of my company, because my mother was still angry with him for sneaking me into a nightclub during his last visit, to see Thelonius Monk.

He wouldn't give up. He promised, hand on heart, to take good care of me and have me home for dinner on Christmas Eve, and she relented. But as we were checking out of the lodge that morning it began to snow, and in this snow he observed some quality that made it necessary for us to get in one last run. We got in several last runs. He was indifferent to my fretting. Snow whirled around us in bitter, blinding squalls, hissing like sand, and still we skied. As the lift bore us to the peak yet again, my father looked at his watch and said: "Criminey. This'll have to be a fast one."

By now I couldn't see the trail. There was no point in trying. I stuck to him like white on rice and did what he did and somehow made it to the bottom without sailing off a cliff. We returned our skis and my father put chains on the Austin-Healy while I swayed from foot to foot, clapping my mittens and wishing I were home. I could see everything. The green tablecloth, the plates with the holly pattern, the red candles waiting to be lit.

We passed a diner on our way out. "You want some soup?" my father asked. I shook my head. "Buck up," he said. "I'll get you there. Right, doctor?"

I was supposed to say, "Right, doctor," but I didn't say anything.

A state trooper waved us down outside the resort. A pair of sawhorses were blocking the road. The trooper came up to our car and bent down to my father's window. His face was bleached by the cold. Snowflakes clung to his eyebrows and to the fur trim of his jacket and cap.

"Don't tell me," my father said.

The trooper told him. The road was closed. It might get cleared, it might not. Storm took everyone by surprise. So much, so fast. Hard to get people moving. Christmas Eve. What can you do?

My father said: "Look. We're talking about four, five inches. I've taken this car through worse than that."

The trooper straightened up, boots creaking. His face was out of sight but I could hear him. "The road is closed."

My father sat with both hands on the wheel, rubbing the wood with his thumbs. He looked at the barricade for a long time. He seemed to be trying to master the idea of it. Then he thanked the trooper, and with a weird, old-maidy show of caution turned the car around. "Your mother will never forgive me for this," he said.

"We should have left before," I said. "Doctor."

He didn't speak to me again until we were both in a booth at the diner, waiting for our burgers. "She won't forgive me," he said. "Do you understand? Never."

"I guess," I said, but no guesswork was required; she wouldn't forgive him.

"I can't let that happen." He bent toward me. "I'll tell you what I want. I want us to be all together again. Is that what you want?"

"Yes, sir."

He bumped my chin with his knuckles. "That's all I needed to hear."

When we finished eating he went to the pay phone in the back of the dinner, then joined me in the booth again. I figured he'd called my mother, but he didn't give a report. He sipped at his coffee and stared out the window at the empty road. "Come on, come on," he said. A little while later he said, "Come on!" When the trooper's car went past, lights flashing, he got up and dropped some money on the check. "O.K. Vámanos."

The wind had died. The snow was falling straight down, less of it now; lighter. We drove away from the resort, right up to the barricade. "Move it," my father told me. When I looked at him he said, "What are you waiting for?" I got out and dragged one of the sawhorses aside, then put it back after he drove through. He pushed the door open for me. "Now you're an accomplice," he said. "We go down together." He put the car into gear and gave me a look. "Joke, doctor."

"Funny, doctor."

Down the first long stretch I watched the road behind us, to see if the trooper was on our tail. The barricade vanished. Then there was nothing but snow: snow on the road, snow kicking up from the chains, snow on the trees, snow in the sky; and our trail in the snow. I faced around and had a shock. The lie of the road behind us had been marked by our own tracks, but there were no tracks ahead of us. My father was breaking virgin snow between a line of tall trees. He was humming "Stars Fell on Alabama." I felt snow brush along the floorboards under my feet. To keep my hands from shaking, I clamped them between my knees.

My father grunted in a thoughtful way and said, "Don't ever try this yourself."

"I won't."

"That's what you say now, but someday you'll get your license and then you'll think you can do anything. Only you won't be able to do this. You need, I don't know—a certain instinct."

25 "Maybe I have it."

"You don't. You have your strong points, but not . . . this. I only mention it, because I don't want you to get the idea this is something just anybody can do. I'm a great driver. That's not a virtue, O.K.? It's just a fact, and one you should be aware of. Of course you have to give the old heap some credit, too—there aren't many cars I'd try this with. Listen!"

I listened. I heard the slap of the chains, the stiff, jerky rasps of the wipers, the purr of the engine. It really did purr. The car was almost new. My father couldn't afford it, and kept promising to sell it, but here it was.

I said, "Where do you think that policeman went to?"

"Are you warm enough?" He reached over and cranked up the blower. Then he turned off the wipers. We didn't need them. The clouds had brightened. A few sparse, feathery flakes drifted into our slipstream and were swept away. We left the trees and entered a broad field of snow that ran level for a while and then tilted sharply downward. Orange stakes had been planted at intervals in two parallel lines and my father steered a course between them, though they were far enough apart to leave considerable doubt in my mind as to where exactly the road lay. He was humming again, doing little scat riffs around the melody.

30 "O.K. then. What are my strong points?"

"Don't get me started," he said. "It'd take all day."

"Oh, right. Name one."

"Easy. You always think ahead."

True. I always thought ahead. I was a boy who kept his clothes on numbered hangers to insure proper rotation. I bothered my teachers for homework assignments far ahead of their due dates so I could make up schedules. I thought ahead, and that was why I knew that there would be other troopers waiting for us at the end of our ride, if we got there. What I did not know was that my father would wheedle and plead his way past them—he didn't sing "O Tannenbaum" but just about—and get me home for dinner, buying a little more time before my mother decided to make the split final. I knew we'd get caught; I was resigned to it. And maybe for this reason I stopped moping and began to enjoy myself.

35 Why not? This was one for the books. Like being in a speedboat, but better. You can't go downhill in a boat. And it was all ours. And it kept coming, the laden trees, the unbroken surface of snow, the sudden white vistas. Here and there I saw hints of the road, ditches, fences, stakes, but not so many that I could have found my way. But then I didn't have to. My father was driving. My father in his 48th year, rumpled, kind, bankrupt of honor, flushed with certainty. He was a great driver. All persuasion, no coercion. Such subtlety at the wheel, such tactful pedalwork. I actually trusted him. And the best was yet to come—the switchbacks and hairpins. Impossible to describe. Except maybe to say this: If you haven't driven fresh powder, you haven't driven.

[1992]

Joining the Conversation: Critical Thinking and Writing

1. How would you characterize the father?
2. How does the boy feel about his father?

3. What argument might you offer to someone who said that this story glorified an irresponsible father?
4. What is the main point of the story? What is your evidence? Or does this story have more than one "main point"? Again, please support your view with evidence.

POEMS

LINDA PASTAN

For a biographical note on Linda Pastan see page 99.

Baseball

When you tried to tell me
baseball was a metaphor

for life: the long, dusty travail
around the bases, for instance,

to try to go home again;
the Sacrifice for which you win

approval but not applause;
the way the light closes down

in the last days of the season—
I didn't believe you.

It's just a way of passing
the time, I said.

And you said: that's it.
Yes.

[1995]

Joining the Conversation: Critical Thinking and Writing

1. What does it mean to say that baseball is "a metaphor for life"? Does the speaker agree? She seems not to at first, but perhaps by the end she changes her mind. Or is that a misreading of the poem?
2. Take a step back. What is the story that this poem is telling? How does it begin? What takes place in the middle? How does it conclude?
3. Do you understand this poem? How would you explain its meaning to someone who found it perplexing?
4. Why is the word "Sacrifice" capitalized?
5. "Baseball" consists of seven short two-line stanzas. Why did Pastan structure it this way? Would her poem have been more effective if she had presented it as a single stanza?

Lillian Morrison

Lillian Morrison, born in Jersey City, New Jersey, in 1908, was an anthologist and folklorist and a writer of children's books as well as a poet in her own right. The first books she published were collections of folk rhymes which she assembled and edited while working as a librarian at the New York Public Library. In 1987 Morrison received the Grolier Award for "outstanding contributions to the stimulation of reading by young people." She died in 2006.

The Sidewalk Racer

or *On the Skateboard*

Skimming
an asphalt sea
I swerve, I curve, I
sway; I speed to whirring
sound an inch above the
ground; I'm the sailor
and the sail, I'm the
driver and the wheel
I'm the one and only
single engine
human auto
mobile.

[1978]

Joining the Conversation: Critical Thinking and Writing

1. This poem has a title, and a second, alternative title. What is your response to this device?
2. When you glance at the poem as a whole, what do you see?
3. What does the word "skimming" mean? Do you think that this word gets the poem off to an effective start?
4. Morrison's poem is written in the first person. Would it have been better in the third person? Yes or no? Please argue both sides of the question.
5. Does this poem have a point? Please explain what it is.

Diane Ackerman

The poet, essayist, and naturalist Diane Ackerman was born in Waukegan, Illinois, in 1948. She graduated from Pennsylvania State University and later received an MFA and a PhD from Cornell University. She is the author of six volumes of verse, including Jaguar of Sweet Laughter: New and Selected Poems *(1991) and, most recently,* I Praise My Destroyer *(1998). She has also written nonfiction and is especially admired for* A Natural History of the Senses *(1990). She lives in Ithaca, New York.*

Pumping Iron

She doesn't want
the bunchy look
of male lifters:
torso an unyielding love-knot,
arms hard at mid-boil.
Doesn't want
the dancing bicepses
of pros.
Just to run her flesh
up the flagpole
of her body,
to pull her roaming flab
into tighter cascades,
machete a waist
through the jungle
of her hips,
a trim waist
two hands might grip
as a bouquet.

[1985]

Joining the Conversation: Critical Thinking and Writing

1. Explain why the "she" of the poem does not want to look like "male lifters"?
2. Which phrase or image in the poem do you like the most?
3. Did the ending surprise you? Why or why not?
4. Please write a short poem about weightlifting, similar in form and length to Ackerman's, but from a male point of view.

A. E. Housman

A. E. Housman (1859–1936) was one of the most distinguished classical scholars of his time. Though he left Oxford without a degree (having failed his examinations), through hard work, discipline, and rigorous study he earned an appointment in 1892 as professor of Latin at University College, London, and in 1911 as professor of Latin at Cambridge and fellow of Trinity College. Only two volumes of Housman's poems appeared during his lifetime: A Shropshire Lad *(1896) and* Last Poems *(1922).*

To an Athlete Dying Young

The time you won your town the race
We chaired you through the market-place;
Man and boy stood cheering by,
And home we brought you shoulder-high.

Today, the road all runners come,
Shoulder-high we bring you home,
And set you at your threshold down,
Townsman of a stiller town.

Smart lad, to slip betimes away
From fields where glory does not stay
And early though the laurel grows
It withers quicker than the rose.

Eyes the shady night has shut
Cannot see the record cut,
And silence sounds no worse than cheers
After earth has stopped the ears:

Now you will not swell the rout
Of lads that wore their honours out,
Runners whom renown outran
And the name died before the man.

So set, before its echoes fade,
The fleet foot on the sill of shade,
And hold to the low lintel up
The still-defended challenge-cup.

And round that early laurelled head
Will flock to gaze the strengthless dead
And find unwithered on its curls
The garland briefer than a girl's.

[1896]

Joining the Conversation: Critical Thinking and Writing

1. When you read this poem out loud, what sorts of things do you hear?
2. Does it seem odd to you that this poem addresses a "you"? Please explain why or why not.
3. A scholar of modern poetry says that while Housman's poem focuses on death, its message ultimately is "upbeat and celebratory." Do you agree?
4. This poem is sometimes termed an elegy, and sometimes termed a dramatic monologue. Which seems the more accurate one to you?
5. Do you find this poem to be sentimental? Is that a bad thing or a good thing, or neither?

PLAY

JANE MARTIN

Jane Martin has never given an interview and has never been photographed. The name presumably is the pseudonym of a writer who works with the Actors Theatre of Louisville, Kentucky. Rodeo is one of a collection of monologues, Talking With . . . , *first presented at the Actors Theatre during the 1981 Humana Festival of New American Plays. Jane Martin has also written full-length plays.*

Rodeo

A young woman in her late twenties sits working an a piece of tack.[1] *Beside her is a Lone Star beer in the can. As the lights come up we hear the last verse of a Tanya Tucker song or some other female country-western vocalist. She is wearing old worn jeans and boots plus a long-sleeved workshirt with the sleeves rolled up. She works until the song is over and then speaks.*

BIG EIGHT: Shoot—Rodeo's just goin' to hell in a handbasket. Rodeo used to be somethin'. I loved it. I did. Once Daddy an' a bunch of 'em was foolin' around with some old bronc over to our place and this ol' red nose named Cinch got bucked off and my Daddy hooted and said he had him a nine-year-old girl, namely me, wouldn't have no damn trouble cowboyin' that horse. Well, he put me on up there, stuck that ridin' rein in my hand, gimme a kiss, and said, "Now there's only one thing t' remember Honey Love, if ya fall off you jest don't come home." Well I stayed up. You gotta stay on a bronc eight seconds. Otherwise the ride don't count. So from that day on my daddy called me Big Eight. Heck! That's all the name I got anymore . . . Big Eight.

Used to be fer cowboys, the rodeo did. Do it in some open field, folks would pull their cars and pick-ups round it, sit on the hoods, some ranch hand'd bulldog him some rank steer and everybody'd wave their hats and call him by name. Ride us some buckin' stock, rope a few calves, git throwed off a bull, and then we'd jest git us to a bar and tell each other lies about how good we were.

Used to be a family thing. Wooly Billy Tilson and Tammy Lee had them five kids on the circuit. Three boys, two girls and Wooly and Tammy. Wasn't no two-beer rodeo in Oklahoma didn't have a Tilson entered. Used to call the oldest girl Tits. Tits Tilson. Never seen a girl that top-heavy could ride so well. Said she only fell off when the gravity got her. Cowboys used to say if she landed face down you could plant two young trees in the holes she'd leave. Ha! Tits Tilson.

Used to be people came to a rodeo had a horse of their own back home. Farm people, ranch people—lord, they knew what they were lookin' at. Knew a good ride from a bad ride, *knew* hard from easy. You broke some bones er spent the day eatin' dirt, at least ya got appreciated.

Now they bought the rodeo. Them. Coca-Cola, Pepsi Cola, Marlboro damn cigarettes. You know the ones I mean. Them. Hire some New York faggot t' sit on some ol' stuffed horse in front of a sagebrush photo n' smoke that junk. Hell, tobacco wasn't made to smoke, honey, it was made to chew. Lord wanted ya filled up with smoke he would've set ya on fire. Damn it gets me!

[1]**tack** harness for a horse, including the bridle and saddle.

Margo Martinale, in Jane Martin's *Rodeo,* at the 6th Humana Festival of New American Plays (1982). Photographer: Sam Garst.

There's some guy in a banker's suit runs the rodeo now. Got him a pinky ring and a digital watch, honey. Told us we oughta have a watchamacallit, choriographus or somethin', ol' ballbuster used to be with the Ice damn Capades. Wants us to ride around dressed up like Mickey Mouse, Pluto, crap like that. Told me I had to haul my butt through the barrel race done up like Minnie damn Mouse in a tu-tu. Huh uh, honey! Them people is so screwed-up they probably eat what they run over in the road.

Listen, they got the clowns wearin' Astronaut suits! I ain't lyin'. You know what a rodeo clown does! You go down, fall off whatever—the clown runs in front of the bull so's ya don't git stomped. Pinstripes, he got 'em in space suits tellin' jokes on a microphone. First horse see 'em, done up like the Star Wars went crazy. Best buckin' horse on the circuit, name of Piss 'N' Vinegar, took one look at them clowns, had him a heart attack and died. Cowboy was ridin' him got hisself squashed. Twelve hundred pounds of coronary arrest jes fell right through 'em. Blam! Vio con dios. Crowd thought that was funnier than the astronauts. I swear it won't be long before they're strappin' ice-skates on the ponies. Big crowds now. Ain't hardly no ranch people, no farm people, nobody I know. Buncha disco babies and deevorce lawyers—designer jeans and day-glo Stetsons. Hell, the whole bunch of 'em wears French perfume. Oh it smells like money now! Got it on the cable T and V—hey, you know what, when ya rodeo yer just bound to kick yerself up some dust—well now, seems like that fogs up the ol' TV camera, so they told us a while back that from now on we was gonna ride on some new stuff called Astro-dirt. Dust free. Artificial damn dirt, honey. Lord have mercy.

Banker Suit called me in the other day said "Lurlene . . ." "Hold it," I said. "Who's this Lurlene? Round here they call me Big Eight." "Well, Big

Eight," he said, "my name's Wallace." "Well that's a real surprise t' me," I said, "cause aroun' here everybody jes calls you Dumbass." My, he laughed real big, slapped his big ol' desk, an' then he said I wasn't suitable for the rodeo no more. Said they was lookin' fer another type, somethin' a little more in the showgirl line, like the Dallas Cowgirls maybe. Said the ridin' and ropin' wasn't the thing no more. Talked on about floats, costumes, dancin' choreogaphy. If I was a man I woulda pissed on his shoe. Said he'd give me a lifetime pass though. Said I could come to his rodeo any time I wanted.

Rodeo used to be people ridin' horses for the pleasure of people who rode horses—made you feel good about what you could do. Rodeo wasn't worth no money to nobody. Money didn't have nothing to do with it! Used to be seven Tilsons riding in the rodeo. Wouldn't none of 'em dress up like Donald damn Duck so they quit. That there's the law of gravity!

There's a bunch of assholes in this country sneak around until they see ya havin' fun and then they buy the fun and start in sellin' it. See, they figure if ya love it, they can sell it. Well you look out, honey! They want to make them a dollar out of what you love. Dress *you* up like Minnie Mouse. Sell your rodeo. Turn *yer* pleasure into Ice damn Capades. You hear what I'm sayin'? You're jus' merchandise to them, sweetie. You're jus' merchandise to them.

Blackout.

[1981]

Joining the Conversation: Critical Thinking and Writing

1. Try to recall your response to the title and the first paragraph or two of the play. Did Big Eight fit your view (perhaps a stereotypical view) of what a cowgirl might sound like?
2. Reread *Rodeo,* this time paying attention not only to what Big Eight says but also to your responses to her. By the end of the play has she become a somewhat more complicated figure than she seems to be after the first paragraph, or does she pretty much seem the same? Do you find that you become increasingly sympathetic? Increasingly unsympathetic? Or does your opinion not change?
3. If you have ever seen a rodeo, do you think Big Eight's characterization is on the mark? Or is she simply bitter because she has been fired?
4. If a local theater group were staging *Rodeo,* presumably with some other short plays, would you go to see it? Why, or why not?
5. If you were directing a production of *Rodeo,* would you keep the actor seated, or would you have her get up, move around the stage, perhaps hang up one piece of tack and take down another? Why?
6. If you were directing *Rodeo,* would you tell Big Eight that her speech is essentially an interior monologue—a soliloquy—or would you tell her that she is speaking directly to the audience—i.e., that the audience is, collectively, a character in the play?
7. The play ends with a stage direction, "Blackout"; that is, the stage suddenly darkens. One director of a recent production, however, chose to end with a "fade out"; the illumination decreased slowly by means of dimmers (mechanical devices that regulate the intensity of a lighting unit). If you were directing a production, what sort of lighting would you use at the end? Why?

Chapter Overview: Looking Backward/Looking Forward

1. In a single paragraph set forth the chief value that you see in sports.
2. In an essay of 500 words, explain which spectator sport offers you the most pleasure.
3. If you actively participate in a sport, explain why you find this sport especially stimulating.
4. Should women be allowed to play on teams that now are all-male? Should men be allowed to play on teams that now are all-female? Why?
5. Do you think that Americans place too much emphasis on sports? Are there other activities and pursuits that, in your view, are more important than sports?
6. Often it is said that playing on a sports team "builds character." (James Michener, in the essay that we include here, goes into this issue.) Do you agree, or is this just a cliché?
7. Do you believe that the top athletes in their sports make good "role models"? Please explain why or why not.

CHAPTER 24

Identity in America

SHORT VIEWS

America is God's crucible, the great melting pot where all the races of Europe are melting and re-forming.
Israel Zangwill

We have room for but one language here and that is the English language, for we intend to see that the crucible turns out our people as Americans, of American nationality and not as dwellers in a polyglot boarding house, and we have room for but one loyalty and that is a loyalty to the American people.
Theodore Roosevelt

No metaphor can capture completely the complexity of ethnic dynamics in the U.S. "Melting pot" ignores the persistence and reconfiguration of ethnicity over the generations. "Mosaic," much more apt for pluralistic societies such as Kenya or India, is too static a metaphor; it fails to take into account the easy penetration of many ethnic boundaries. Nor is "salad bowl" appropriate; the ingredients of a salad bowl are mixed but do not change. "Rainbow" is a tantalizing metaphor, but rainbows disappear. "Symphony," like "rainbow," implies near perfect harmony; both fail to take into account the variety and range of ethnic conflict in the Untied States.

The most accurately descriptive metaphor, the one that best explains the dynamics of ethnicity, is " kaleidoscope." American ethnicity is kaleidoscopic, i.e. "complex and varied, changing form, pattern, color . . . continually shifting from one set of relations to another; rapidly changing" When a kaleidoscope is in motion, the parts give the appearance of rapid change and extensive variety in color and shape and in their interrelationhips. The viewer sees an endless variety of variegated patterns, just as takes place on the American ethnic landscape.
Lawrence Fuchs

Through our own efforts and concerted good faith in learning to know, thus to respect, the wonderfully rich and diverse subcommunities of America, we can establish a new vision of America: a place where "community" may mean many things, yet retains its deeper spiritual significance. We may even learn to coincide with the 500th anniversary of the "discovery" of America by Columbus, that America, in its magnificent variety, has yet to be discovered.
Joyce Carol Oates

It is impossible for a stranger traveling through the United States to tell from the appearance of the people or the country whether he is in Toledo, Ohio, or Portland, Oregon. Ninety million Americans cut their hair in the same way, eat each morning exactly the same breakfast, tie up the small girls' curls with precisely the same kind of ribbon fashioned into bows exactly alike; and in every way all try to look and act as much like all the others as they can.

Alfred Harmsworth, Lord Northcliffe

Racism is so universal in this country, so wide-spread and deep-seated, that it is invisible because it is so normal.

Shirley Chisholm

Light came to me when I realized that I did not have to consider any racial group as a whole. God made them duck by duck and that was the only way I could see them.

Zora Neale Hurston

I have a dream that my four little children will one day live in a nation where they will not be judged by the color of their skin but by the content of their character.

Martin Luther King Jr.

Joining the Conversation: Critical Thinking and Writing

1. Select a quotation that especially appeals to you, and make it the focus of an essay of about 500 words.
2. Take two of the passages—perhaps one that you especially like and one that you thing is wrongheaded—and write a dialogue of about 500 words in which the two authors converse or argue. They may each try to convince the other, or they may find that to some degree they share views and they may then work out a statement that both can accept. If you do take the first position—that one writer is on the correct track but the other is utterly mistaken—try to be fair to the view that you think is mistaken. (As an experiment in critical thinking, imagine that you accept it, and make the best case for it that you possibly can.)

Essays

Anna Lisa Raya

Anna Lisa Raya, daughter of a second-generation Mexican American father and a Puerto Rican mother, grew up in Los Angeles but went to Columbia University in New York. While an undergraduate at Columbia she wrote and published this essay on identity.

It's Hard Enough Being Me

When I entered college, I *discovered* I was Latina. Until then, I had never questioned who I was or where I was from: My father is a second-generation Mexican-American, born and raised in Los Angeles, and my mother was born in Puerto Rico and raised in Compton, Calif. My home is El Sereno, a predominantly Mexican neighborhood in L.A. Every close friend I have back home is Mexican. So I was always just Mexican. Though sometimes I was just Puerto Rican—like when we would visit Mamo (my grandma) or hang out with my Aunt Titi.

Upon arriving in New York as a first-year student, 3000 miles from home, I not only experienced extreme culture shock, but for the first time I had to define myself according to the broad term "Latina." Although culture shock and identity crisis are common for the newly minted collegian who goes away to school, my experience as a newly minted Latina was, and still is, even more complicating. In El Sereno, I felt like I was part of a majority, whereas at the College I am a minority.

I've discovered that many Latinos like myself have undergone similar experiences. We face discrimination for being a minority in this country while also facing criticism for being "whitewashed" or "sellouts" in the countries of our heritage. But as an ethnic group in college, we are forced to define ourselves according to some vague, generalized Latino experience. This requires us to know our history, our language, our music, and our religion. I can't even be a content "Puerto Mexican" because I have to be a politically-and-socially-aware-Latina-with-a-chip-on-my-shoulder-because-of-how-repressed-I-am-in-this-country.

I am none of the above. I am the quintessential imperfect Latina. I can't dance salsa to save my life, I learned about Montezuma and the Aztecs in sixth grade, and I haven't prayed to the *Virgen de Guadalupe* in years.

5 Apparently I don't even look Latina. I can't count how many times people have just assumed that I'm white or asked me if I'm Asian. True, my friends back home call me *güera* ("whitey") because I have green eyes and pale skin, but that was as bad as it got. I never thought I would wish my skin were a darker shade or my hair a curlier texture, but since I've been in college, I have—many times.

Another thing: my Spanish is terrible. Every time I call home, I berate my mama for not teaching me Spanish when I was a child. In fact, not knowing how to speak the language of my home countries is the biggest problem that I have encountered, as have many Latinos. In Mexico there is a term, *pocha,* which is used by native Mexicans to ridicule Mexican-Americans. It expresses a deep-rooted antagonism and dislike for those of us who were raised on the other side of the border. Our failed attempts to speak pure, Mexican Spanish are largely responsible for the dislike. Other Latin American natives have this same attitude. No matter how well a Latino speaks Spanish, it can never be good enough.

Yet Latinos can't even speak Spanish in the U.S. without running the risk of being called "spic" or "wetback." That is precisely why my mother refused to teach me Spanish when I was a child. The fact that she spoke Spanish was constantly used against her: It prevented her from getting good jobs, and it would have placed me in bilingual education—a construct of the Los Angeles public school system that has proved to be more of a hindrance to intellectual development than a help.

To be fully Latina in college, however, I *must* know Spanish. I must satisfy the equation: Latina [equals] Spanish-speaking.

So I'm stuck in this black hole of an identity crisis, and college isn't making my life any easier, as I thought it would. In high school, I was being prepared for an adulthood in which I would be an individual, in which I wouldn't have to wear a Catholic school uniform anymore. But though I led an anonymous adolescence, I knew who I was. I knew I was different from white, black, or Asian people. I knew there was a language other than English that I could call my own if I only knew how to speak it better. I knew there were historical reasons why I was in this country, distinct reasons that make my existence here easier or more difficult than other people's existence. Ultimately, I was content.

10 Now I feel pushed into a corner, always defining, defending, and proving myself to classmates, professors, or employers. Trying to understand who and why I am, while understanding Plato or Homer, is a lot to ask of myself.

A month ago, I heard three Nuyorican (Puerto Ricans born and raised in New York) writers discuss how New York City has influenced their writing. One problem I have faced as a young writer is finding a voice that is true to my community. I was surprised and reassured to discover that as Latinos, these writers had faced similar pressures and conflicts as myself; some weren't even taught Spanish in childhood. I will never forget the advice that one of them gave me that evening: She said that I need to be true to myself. "Because people will always complain about what you are doing—you're a 'gringa' or a 'spic' no matter what," she explained. "So you might as well do things for yourself and not for them."

I don't know why it has taken 20 years to hear this advice, but I'm going to give it a try. *Soy yo* and no one else. *Punto*.[1]

[1994]

Joining the Conversation: Critical Thinking and Writing

1. In her first paragraph Raya says that although her parents are American citizens, until she went to New York she "was always just Mexican" or "just Puerto Rican." Why do you suppose she thought this way?
2. In her second paragraph Raya says that in New York she "had to" define herself as "Latina," and in her third paragraph she says that many members of "minority" communities "are forced" to define themselves. In paragraph 10 she says, "Now I feel pushed into a corner, always defining, defending, and proving myself to classmates, professors, or employers. Trying to understand who and why I am, while understanding Plato or Homer, is a lot to ask. . . ." Is Raya saying that both the majority culture and the minority culture force her to define herself? Drawing on your own experience, give your views on whether it is a good thing or a bad thing (or some of each) to be forced to define oneself in terms of ethnicity.
3. Today the words *Latino* and *Latina* are common, but until perhaps ten years ago Spanish-speaking people from Mexico, Central America, and South America were called *Hispanics* or *Latin Americans*. Do you think these terms are useful, or do you think that the differences between, say, a poor black woman from Cuba and a rich white man from Argentina are so great that it makes very little sense to put them into the same category, whether the category

[1]***Soy yo . . . Punto*** I'm me . . . Period. (Editors' note.)

is called *Latino, Hispanic,* or *Latin American?* Why, incidentally, do you think that *Latino/Latina* is now preferred to *Hispanic?*

4. In paragraph 7 Raya speaks of the Los Angeles bilingual educational program as "a construct of the Los Angeles public school system that has proved to be more of a hindrance to intellectual development than a help." If you have been in a bilingual educational program, evaluate the program. Did it chiefly help you, or chiefly hinder you? Explain.
5. In her last two paragraphs Raya explains that after an acquaintance told her to be true to herself, she concluded, *Soy yo* ("I'm me," or "I'm myself"). You may recall that in *Hamlet* Polonius says to his son Laertes, "This above all: to thine own self be true" (1.3.78). But what does it mean to be true to oneself? Presumably one doesn't behave immorally, but beyond that, what does one do? For instance, if a friend suggested to Raya that she might enjoy (and intellectually profit from) taking a course in Latin American literature, in making a decision, what *self* would she be true to?
6. In your own life, you make many decisions each day. Are many of them based on being true to yourself? Again, putting aside questions concerning immorality, do you think you have a "self" that you are true to? If so, is this self at least in part based on ethnicity?

Andrew Lam

Born in South Vietnam in 1964, Andrew Lam, essayist and short story writer, edits the Pacific News Service. We reprint a PNS essay that originally appeared on 7 May 2003.

Who Will Light Incense When Mother's Gone?

My mother turned 70 recently, and though she remains a vivacious woman—her hair is still mostly black and there is a girlish twang in her laughter—mortality nevertheless weighs heavily on her soul. After the gifts were opened and the cake eaten, mother whispered this confidence to her younger sister: "Who will light incense to the dead when we're gone?"

"Honestly, I don't know," my aunt replied. "None of my children will do it, and we can forget the grandchildren. They don't even understand what we are doing. I guess when we're gone, the ritual ends."

Such is the price of living in America. I can't remember the last time I lit incense sticks and talked to my dead ancestors. Having fled so far from Vietnam, I no longer know to whom I should address my prayers or what promises I could possibly make to the long departed.

My mother, on the other hand, lives in America the way she would in Vietnam. Every morning in my parents' suburban home north of San Jose, she climbs a chair and piously lights a few joss sticks for the ancestral altar that sits on top of the living room bookcase. Every morning she talks to ghosts. She mumbles solemn prayers to the spirits of our dead ancestors, asks them for protection.

5 By contrast, on the shelves below stand my older siblings' engineering and business degrees, my own degree in biochemistry, our combined sports trophies and, last but not least, the latest installments of my own unending quest for self-reinvention—plaques and obelisk-shaped crystals—my journalism awards.

What mother's altar and the shelves beneath it seek to tell is the narrative of many an Asian immigrant family's journey to America. The collective, agrarian-based ethos in which ancestor worship is central slowly gives way to the glories of individual ambitions.

At that far end of the Asian immigrant trajectory, however, I cannot help but feel a certain twinge of guilt and regret upon hearing my mother's remark. Once when I was still a rebellious teenager and living at home, Mother asked me to speak more Vietnamese inside the house. "No," I answered in English, "what good is it to speak it? It's not as if I'm going to use it after I move out."

Mother, I remember, had a pained look in her eyes and called me the worst thing she could muster. "You've become a little American now, haven't you? A cowboy."

Vietnamese appropriated the word "cowboy" from the movies to imply selfishness. A cowboy in Vietnamese estimation is a rebel who, as in the spaghetti westerns, leaves town—the communal life—to ride alone into the sunset.

10 America, it had seemed, had stolen my mother's children, especially her youngest and once obedient son. America seduced him with its optimism, twisted his thinking, bent his tongue and dulled his tropic memories. America gave him freeways and fast food and silly cartoons and sitcoms, imbuing him with sappy, happy-ending incitements.

If we have reconciled since then, it does not mean I have become a traditional, incense-lighting Vietnamese son. I visit. I take her to lunch. I come home for important dates—New Year, Thanksgiving, Tet.

But these days in front of the family altar, with all those faded photos of the dead staring down at me, I often feel oddly removed, as if staring at a relic of my distant past. And when, upon my mother's insistence, I light incense, I do not feel as if I am participating in a living tradition so much as pleasing a traditional mother.

We live in two different worlds, Mother and I. Mine is a world of travel and writing and public speaking, of immersing myself in contemporary history. Hers is a world of consulting the Vietnamese horoscope, of attending Buddhist temple on the day of her parents' death anniversaries and of telling and retelling stories of the past.

But on her 70th birthday, having listened to her worries, I have to wonder: What will survive my mother?

15 I wish I could assure my mother that, after she is gone, each morning I would light incense for her and all the ancestor spirits before her, but I can't.

In that odd, contradictory space in which immigrants' children find themselves, I feel strangely comforted when watching my mother's pious gesture each morning in front of the ancestors' altar. She is what connects me and my generation to a traditional past. And essentially, I share her fear that her generation and its memories of the Old World, what preserves us as a community, will fade away like incense smoke. I fear she'll leave me stranded in America, becoming more American than I expected, a lonely cowboy cursed with amnesia.

[2003]

Joining the Conversation: Critical Thinking and Writing

1. What does Andrew Lam mean when he refers to his mother as "a vivacious woman"? What does he mean when he refers to his own "unending quest for self-reinvention"? And "collective, agrarian-based ethos": what does this phrase mean?

2. How does Lam's mother feel about America? What about Lam himself: What are his feelings about America?
3. Does this essay give you a new perspective on the immigrant experience, or a familiar one? Do you think Lam intends to show the reader something new? Or does he have a different purpose in mind?
4. Imagine that you know the author, and that, before publishing this essay, he sent it to you and asked for your "response and any suggestions" you might have. Compose a letter of 1–2 pages, beginning "Dear Andrew . . . ," in which you reply to him.

STORIES

AMY TAN

Amy Tan was born in Oakland, California, in 1952, of Chinese immigrant parents. When she was 8, she won first prize among elementary students with an essay entitled "What the Library Means to Me." She attended Linfield College in Oregon, then transferred to San Jose State University where, while working two part-time jobs, she became an honors student and a President's Scholar. In 1973 she earned a master's degree in linguistics, also at San Jose, and she later enrolled as a doctoral student at the University of California, Berkeley, though she left this program after the murder of a close friend. For the next five years she worked as a language development consultant and a project director, and then she became a freelance business writer. In 1986 she published her first short story, and it was reprinted in Seventeen *where it was noticed by an agent, who encouraged her to continue writing fiction. In 1989* The Joy Luck Club *(a collection of linked short stories, including "Two Kinds") was published. Other books include* The Kitchen God's Wife *(1991),* The Hundred Secret Senses *(1995), and* The Bonesetter's Daughter *(2001). She has also written two books for children,* The Moon Lady *(1992) and* SAGWA The Chinese Siamese Cat *(1994).*

Two Kinds

My mother believed you could be anything you wanted to be in America. You could open a restaurant. You could work for the government and get good retirement. You could buy a house with almost no money down. You could become rich. You could become instantly famous.

"Of course, you can be prodigy, too," my mother told me when I was nine. "You can be best anything. What does Auntie Lindo know? Her daughter, she is only best tricky."

America was where all my mother's hopes lay. She had come here in 1949 after losing everything in China: her mother and father, her family home, her first husband, and two daughters, twin baby girls. But she never looked back with regret. There were so many ways for things to get better.

We didn't immediately pick the right kind of prodigy. At first my mother thought I could be a Chinese Shirley Temple. We'd watch Shirley's old movies on TV as though they were training films. My mother would poke my arm and say, "*Ni kan.*" —You watch. And I would see Shirley tapping her feet, or singing a sailor song, or pursing her lips into a very round O while saying "Oh, my goodness."

5 "*Ni kan,*" said my mother as Shirley's eyes flooded with tears. "You already know how. Don't need talent for crying!"

Soon after my mother got this idea about Shirley Temple, she took me to a beauty training school in the Mission district and put me in the hands of a student who could barely hold the scissors without shaking. Instead of getting big fat curls, I emerged with an uneven mass of crinkly black fuzz. My mother dragged me off to the bathroom and tried to wet down my hair.

"You look like Negro Chinese," she lamented, as if I had done this on purpose.

The instructor of the beauty training school had to lop off these soggy clumps to make my hair even again. "Peter Pan is very popular these days," the instructor assured my mother. I now had hair the length of a boy's, with straight-across bangs that hung at a slant two inches above my eyebrows. I liked the haircut and it made me actually look forward to my future fame.

In fact, in the beginning, I was just as excited as my mother, maybe even more so. I pictured this prodigy part of me as many different images, trying each one on for size. I was a dainty ballerina girl standing by the curtains, waiting to hear the music that would send me floating on my tiptoes. I was like the Christ child lifted out of the straw manger, crying with holy indignity. I was Cinderella stepping from her pumpkin carriage with sparkly cartoon music filling the air.

10 In all of my imaginings, I was filled with a sense that I would soon become *perfect.* My mother and father would adore me. I would be beyond reproach. I would never feel the need to sulk for anything.

But sometimes the prodigy in me became impatient. "If you don't hurry up and get me out of here, I'm disappearing for good," it warned. "And then you'll always be nothing."

Every night after dinner, my mother and I would sit at the Formica kitchen table. She would present new tests, taking her examples from stories of amazing children she had read in *Ripley's Believe It or Not,* or *Good Housekeeping, Reader's Digest,* and a dozen other magazines she kept in a pile in our bathroom. My mother got these magazines from people whose houses she cleaned. And since she cleaned many houses each week, we had a great assortment. She would look through them all, searching for stories about remarkable children.

The first night she brought out a story about a three-year-old boy who knew the capitals of all the states and even most of the European countries. A teacher was quoted as saying the little boy could also pronounce the names of the foreign cities correctly.

"What's the capital of Finland?" my mother asked me, looking at the magazine story.

15 All I knew was the capital of California, because Sacramento was the name of the street we lived on in Chinatown. "Nairobi!" I guessed, saying the most foreign word I could think of. She checked to see if that was possibly one way to pronounce "Helsinki" before showing me the answer.

The tests got harder—multiplying numbers in my head, finding the queen of hearts in a deck of cards, trying to stand on my head without using my hands, predicting the daily temperatures in Los Angeles, New York, and London.

One night I had to look at a page from the Bible for three minutes and then report everything I could remember. "Now Jehoshaphat had riches and honor in abundance and . . . that's all I remember, Ma," I said.

And after seeing my mother's disappointed face once again, something inside of me began to die. I hated the tests, the raised hopes and failed expectations. Before going to bed that night, I looked in the mirror above the bathroom sink and when I saw only my face staring back—and that it would always be this ordinary face—I began to cry. Such a sad, ugly girl! I made high-pitched noises like a crazed animal, trying to scratch out the face in the mirror.

And then I saw what seemed to be the prodigy side of me—because I had never seen that face before. I looked at my reflection, blinking so I could see more clearly. The girl staring back at me was angry, powerful. This girl and I were the same. I had new thoughts, willful thoughts, or rather thoughts filled with lots of won'ts. I won't let her change me, I promised myself. I won't be what I'm not.

20 So now on nights when my mother presented her tests, I performed listlessly, my head propped on one arm. I pretended to be bored. And I was. I got so bored I started counting the bellows of the foghorns out on the bay while my mother drilled me in other areas. The sound was comforting and reminded me of the cow jumping over the moon. And the next day, I played a game with myself, seeing if my mother would give up on me before eight bellows. After a while I usually counted only one, maybe two bellows at most. At last she was beginning to give up hope.

Two or three months had gone by without any mention of my being a prodigy again. And then one day my mother was watching *The Ed Sullivan Show*[1] on TV. The TV was old and the sound kept shorting out. Every time my mother got halfway up from the sofa to adjust the set, the sound would go back on and Ed would be talking. As soon as she sat down, Ed would go silent again. She got up, the TV broke into loud piano music. She sat down. Silence. Up and down, back and forth, quiet and loud. It was like a stiff embraceless dance between her and the TV set. Finally she stood by the set with her hand on the sound dial.

She seemed entranced by the music, a little frenzied piano piece with this mesmerizing quality, sort of quick passages and then teasing lilting ones before it returned to the quick playful parts.

"*Ni kan,*" my mother said, calling me over with hurried hand gestures, "Look here."

I could see why my mother was fascinated by the music. It was being pounded out by a little Chinese girl, about nine years old, with a Peter Pan haircut. The girl had the sauciness of a Shirley Temple. She was proudly modest like a proper Chinese child. And she also did this fancy sweep of a curtsy, so that the fluffy skirt of her white dress cascaded slowly to the floor like the petals of a large carnation.

25 In spite of these warning signs, I wasn't worried. Our family had no piano and we couldn't afford to buy one, let alone reams of sheet music and piano lessons. So I could be generous in my comments when my mother bad-mouthed the little girl on TV.

"Play note right, but doesn't sound good! No singing sound," my mother complained.

"What are you picking on her for?" I said carelessly. "She's pretty good. Maybe she's not the best, but she's trying hard." I knew almost immediately I would be sorry I said that.

[1]***The Ed Sullivan Show*** popular television variety show (1948–1971).

"Just like you," she said. "Not the best. Because you not trying." She gave a little huff as she let go of the sound dial and sat down on the sofa.

The little Chinese girl sat down also to play an encore of "Anitra's Dance,"[2] by Grieg. I remember the song, because later on I had to learn how to play it.

30 Three days after watching *The Ed Sullivan Show,* my mother told me what my schedule would be for piano lessons and piano practice. She had talked to Mr. Chong, who lived on the first floor of our apartment building. Mr. Chong was a retired piano teacher and my mother had traded housecleaning services for weekly lessons and a piano for me to practice on every day, two hours a day, from four until six.

When my mother told me this, I felt as though I had been sent to hell. I whined and then kicked my foot a little when I couldn't stand it anymore.

"Why don't you like me the way I am? I'm *not* a genius! I can't play the piano. And even if I could, I wouldn't go on TV if you paid me a million dollars!" I cried.

My mother slapped me. "Who ask you be genius?" she shouted. "Only ask you be your best. For you sake. You think I want you be genius? Hnnh! What for! Who ask you!"

"So ungrateful," I heard her mutter in Chinese. "If she had as much talent as she has temper, she would be famous now."

35 Mr. Chong, whom I secretly nicknamed Old Chong, was very strange, always tapping his fingers to the silent music of an invisible orchestra. He looked ancient in my eyes. He had lost most of the hair on top of his head and he wore thick glasses and had eyes that always looked tired and sleepy. But he must have been younger than I thought, since he lived with his mother and was not yet married.

I met Old Lady Chong once and that was enough. She had this peculiar smell like a baby that had done something in its pants. And her fingers felt like a dead person's, like an old peach I once found in the back of the refrigerator; the skin just slid off the meat when I picked it up.

I soon found out why Old Chong had retired from teaching piano. He was deaf. "Like Beethoven!" he shouted to me. "We're both listening only in our head!" And he would start to conduct his frantic silent sonatas.

Our lessons went like this. He would open the book and point to different things, explaining their purpose: "Key! Treble! Bass! No sharps or flats! So this is C major! Listen now and play after me!"

And then he would play the C scale a few times, a simple chord, and then, as if inspired by an old, unreachable itch, he gradually added more notes and running trills and a pounding bass until the music was really something quite grand.

40 I would play after him, the simple scale, the simple chord, and then I just played some nonsense that sounded like a cat running up and down on top of garbage cans. Old Chong smiled and applauded and then said, "Very good! But now you must learn to keep time!"

So that's how I discovered that Old Chong's eyes were too slow to keep up with the wrong notes I was playing. He went through the motions in half-time. To help me keep rhythm, he stood behind me, pushing down on my right shoulder for every beat. He balanced pennies on top of my wrists so I would keep them still as I slowly played scales and arpeggios. He had me curve my hand around an apple and keep that shape when playing chords. He marched stiffly to show me how to make each finger dance up and down, staccato like an obedient little soldier.

[2]**"Anitra's Dance"** a section from the incidental music that Edvard Grieg (1843–1907) wrote for *Peer Gynt*, a play by Henrik Ibsen.

He taught me all these things, and that was how I also learned I could be lazy and get away with mistakes, lots of mistakes. If I hit the wrong notes because I hadn't practiced enough, I never corrected myself. I just kept playing in rhythm. And Old Chong kept conducting his own private reverie.

So maybe I never really gave myself a fair chance. I did pick up the basics pretty quickly, and I might have become a good pianist at that young age. But I was so determined not to try, not to be anybody different that I learned to play only the most ear-splitting preludes, the most discordant hymns.

Over the next year I practiced like this, dutifully in my own way. And then one day I heard my mother and her friend Lindo Jong both talking in a loud bragging tone of voice so others could hear. It was after church, and I was leaning against the brick wall wearing a dress with stiff white petticoats. Auntie Lindo's daughter, Waverly, who was about my age, was standing farther down the wall about five feet away. We had grown up together and shared all the closeness of two sisters squabbling over crayons and dolls. In other words, for the most part, we hated each other. I thought she was snotty. Waverly Jong had gained a certain amount of fame as "Chinatown's Littlest Chinese Chess Champion."

45 "She bring home too many trophy," lamented Auntie Lindo that Sunday. "All day she play chess. All day I have no time do nothing but dust off her winnings." She threw a scolding look at Waverly, who pretended not to see her.

"You lucky you don't have this problem," said Auntie Lindo with a sigh to my mother.

And my mother squared her shoulders and bragged: "Our problem worser than yours. If we ask Jing-mei wash dish, she hear nothing but music. It's like you can't stop this natural talent."

And right then, I was determined to put a stop to her foolish pride.

A few weeks later, Old Chong and my mother conspired to have me play in a talent show which would be held in the church hall. By then, my parents had saved up enough to buy me a secondhand piano, a black Wurlitzer spinet with a scarred bench. It was the showpiece of our living room.

50 For the talent show, I was to play a piece called "Pleading Child" from Schumann's *Scenes from Childhood*.[3] It was a simple, moody piece that sounded more difficult than it was. I was supposed to memorize the whole thing, playing the repeat parts twice to make the piece sound longer. But I dawdled over it, playing a few bars and then cheating, looking up to see what notes followed. I never really listened to what I was playing. I daydreamed about being somewhere else, about being someone else.

The part I liked to practice best was the fancy curtsy: right foot out, touch the rose on the carpet with a pointed foot, sweep to the side, left leg bends, look up and smile.

My parents invited all the couples from the Joy Luck Club to witness my debut. Auntie Lindo and Uncle Tin were there. Waverly and her two older brothers had also come. The first two rows were filled with children both younger and older than I was. The littlest ones got to go first. They recited simple nursery rhymes, squawked out tunes on miniature violins, twirled Hula Hoops, pranced in pink ballet tutus, and when they bowed or curtsied, the audience would sigh in unison, "Awww," and then clap enthusiastically.

[3]***Scenes from Childhood*** a piano work by Robert Shumann (1810–1856) with twelve titled sections and an epilogue.

When my turn came, I was very confident. I remember my childish excitement. It was as if I knew, without a doubt, that the prodigy side of me really did exist. I had no fear whatsoever, no nervousness. I remember thinking to myself, This is it! This is it! I looked out over the audience, at my mother's blank face, my father's yawn, Auntie Lindo's stiff-lipped smile, Waverly's sulky expression. I had on a white dress layered with sheets of lace, and a pink bow in my Peter Pan haircut. As I sat down I envisioned people jumping to their feet and Ed Sullivan rushing up to introduce me to everyone on TV.

And I started to play. It was so beautiful. I was so caught up in how lovely I looked that at first I didn't worry how I would sound. So it was a surprise to me when I hit the first wrong note and I realized something didn't sound quite right. And then I hit another and another followed that. A chill started at the top of my head and began to trickle down. Yet I couldn't stop playing, as though my hands were bewitched. I kept thinking my fingers would adjust themselves back, like a train switching to the right track. I played this strange jumble through two repeats, the sour notes staying with me all the way to the end.

55 When I stood up, I discovered my legs were shaking. Maybe I had just been nervous and the audience, like Old Chong, had seen me go through the right motions and had not heard anything wrong at all. I swept my right foot out, went down on my knee, looked up and smiled. The room was quiet, except for Old Chong, who was beaming and shouting, "Bravo! Bravo! Well done!" But then I saw my mother's face, her stricken face. The audience clapped weakly, and as I walked back to my chair, with my whole face quivering as I tried not to cry, I heard a little boy whisper loudly to his mother, "That was awful," and the mother whispered back, "Well, she certainly tried."

And now I realized how many people were in the audience, the whole world it seemed. I was aware of eyes burning into my back. I felt the shame of my mother and father as they sat stiffly throughout the rest of the show.

We could have escaped during intermission. Pride and some strange sense of honor must have anchored my parents to their chairs. And so we watched it all: the eighteen-year-old boy with a fake moustache who did a magic show and juggled flaming hoops while riding a unicycle. The breasted girl with white makeup who sang from *Madame Butterfly* and got honorable mention. And the eleven-year-old boy who won first prize playing a tricky violin song that sounded like a busy bee.

After the show, the Hsus, the Jongs, and the St. Clairs from the Joy Luck Club, came up to my mother and father.

"Lots of talented kids," Auntie Lindo said vaguely, smiling broadly.

60 "That was somethin' else," said my father, and I wondered if he was referring to me in a humorous way, or whether he even remembered what I had done.

Waverly looked at me and shrugged her shoulders. "You aren't a genius like me," she said matter-of-factly. And if I hadn't felt so bad, I would have pulled her braids and punched her stomach.

But my mother's expression was what devastated me: a quiet, blank look that said she had lost everything. I felt the same way, and it seemed as if everybody were now coming up, like gawkers at the scene of an accident, to see what parts were actually missing. When we got on the bus to go home, my father was humming the busy-bee tune and my mother was silent. I kept thinking she wanted to wait until we got home before shouting at me. But when my father unlocked the door to our apartment, my mother walked in and then went to the back, into the bedroom. No accusations. No blame. And in a way, I felt disappointed. I had been waiting for her to start shouting, so I could shout back and cry and blame her for all my misery.

I assumed my talent-show fiasco meant I never had to play the piano again. But two days later, after school, my mother came out of the kitchen and saw me watching TV.

"Four clock," she reminded me as if it were any other day. I was stunned, as though she were asking me to go through the talent-show torture again. I wedged myself more tightly in front of the TV.

"Turn off TV," she called from the kitchen five minutes later.

I didn't budge. And then I decided. I didn't have to do what my mother said anymore. I wasn't her slave. This wasn't China. I had listened to her before and look what happened. She was the stupid one.

She came out from the kitchen and stood in the arched entryway of the living room. "Four clock," she said once again, louder.

"I'm not going to play anymore," I said nonchalantly. "Why should I? I'm not a genius."

She walked over and stood in front of the TV. I saw her chest was heaving up and down in an angry way.

"No!" I said, and I now felt stronger, as if my true self had finally emerged. So this was what had been inside me all along.

"No! I won't!" I screamed.

She yanked me by the arm, pulled me off the floor, snapped off the TV. She was frighteningly strong, half pulling, half carrying me toward the piano as I kicked the throw rugs under my feet. She lifted me up and onto the hard bench. I was sobbing by now, looking at her bitterly. Her chest was heaving even more and her mouth was open, smiling crazily as if she were pleased I was crying.

"You want me to be someone that I'm not!" I sobbed. "I'll never be the kind of daughter you want me to be!"

"Only two kinds of daughters," she shouted in Chinese. "Those who are obedient and those who follow their own mind! Only one kind of daughter can live in this house. Obedient daughter!"

"Then I wish I wasn't your daughter. I wish you weren't my mother," I shouted. As I said these things I got scared. It felt like worms and toads and slimy things crawling out of my chest, but it also felt good, as if this awful side of me had surfaced, at last.

"Too late change this," said my mother shrilly.

And I could sense her anger rising to its breaking point. I wanted to see it spill over. And that's when I remembered the babies she had lost in China, the ones we never talked about. "Then I wish I'd never been born!" I shouted. "I wish I were dead! Like them."

It was as if I had said the magic words. Alakazam!—and her face went blank, her mouth closed, her arms went slack, and she backed out of the room, stunned, as if she were blowing away like a small brown leaf, thin, brittle, lifeless.

It was not the only disappointment my mother felt in me. In the years that followed, I failed her so many times, each time asserting my own will, my right to fall short of expectations. I didn't get straight As. I didn't become class president. I didn't get into Stanford. I dropped out of college.

For unlike my mother, I did not believe I could be anything I wanted to be. I could only be me.

And for all those years, we never talked about the disaster at the recital or my terrible accusations afterward at the piano bench. All of that remained unchecked, like a betrayal that was now unspeakable. So I never found a way to ask her why she had hoped for something so large that failure was inevitable.

And even worse, I never asked her what frightened me the most: Why had she given up hope?

For after our struggle at the piano, she never mentioned my playing again. The lessons stopped. The lid to the piano was closed, shutting out the dust, my misery, and her dreams.

So she surprised me. A few years ago, she offered to give me the piano, for my thirtieth birthday. I had not played in all those years. I saw the offer as a sign of forgiveness, a tremendous burden removed.

85 "Are you sure?" I asked shyly. "I mean, won't you and Dad miss it?"

"No, this your piano," she said firmly. "Always your piano. You only one can play."

"Well, I probably can't play anymore," I said. "It's been years."

"You pick up fast," said my mother, as if she knew this was certain. "You have natural talent. You could been genius if you want to."

"No I couldn't."

90 "You just not trying," said my mother. And she was neither angry nor sad. She said it as if to announce a fact that could never be disproved. "Take it," she said.

But I didn't at first. It was enough that she had offered it to me. And after that, every time I saw it in my parents' living room, standing in front of the bay windows, it made me feel proud, as if it were a shiny trophy I had won back.

Last week I sent a tuner over to my parents' apartment and had the piano reconditioned, for purely sentimental reasons. My mother had died a few months before and I had been getting things in order for my father, a little bit at a time. I put the jewelry in special silk pouches. The sweaters she had knitted in yellow, pink, bright orange—all the colors I hated—I put those in moth-proof boxes. I found some old Chinese silk dresses, the kind with little slits up the sides. I rubbed the old silk against my skin, then wrapped them in tissue and decided to take them home with me.

After I had the piano tuned, I opened the lid and touched the keys. It sounded even richer than I remembered. Really, it was a very good piano. Inside the bench were the same exercise notes with handwritten scales, the same secondhand music books with their covers held together with yellow tape.

I opened up the Schumann book to the dark little piece I had played at the recital. It was on the left-hand side of the page, "Pleading Child." It looked more difficult than I remembered. I played a few bars, surprised at how easily the notes came back to me.

95 And for the first time, or so it seemed, I noticed the piece on the right-hand side. It was called "Perfectly Contented." I tried to play this one as well. It had a lighter melody but the same flowing rhythm and turned out to be quite easy. "Pleading Child" was shorter but slower; "Perfectly Contented" was longer, but faster. And after I played them both a few times, I realized they were two halves of the same song.

[1989]

Joining the Conversation: Critical Thinking and Writing

1. Try to recall your responses when you had finished reading the first three paragraphs. At that point, how did the mother strike you? Now that you have read the entire story, is your view of her different? If so, in what way(s)?
2. When the narrator looks in the mirror, she discovers "the prodigy side," a face she had never seen before. What do you think she is discovering?
3. If you enjoyed the story, point out two or three passages that you found particularly engaging, and briefly explain why they appeal to you. Argue someone into sharing your view.
4. Do you think this story is interesting only because it may give a glimpse of life in a Chinese American family? Or do you find it interesting for additional reasons? Explain.
5. Conceivably the story could have ended with the fifth paragraph from the end. What do the last four paragraphs contribute? Argue your case.

Alice Walker

Alice Walker was born in 1944 in Eatonton, Georgia, where her parents eked out a living as sharecroppers and dairy farmers; her mother also worked as a domestic. Walker attended Spelman College in Atlanta, and in 1965 she finished her undergraduate work at Sarah Lawrence College near New York City. She then became active in the welfare rights movement in New York and in the voter registration movement in Georgia. Later she taught writing and literature in Mississippi, at Jackson State College and Tougaloo College, and at Wellesley College, the University of Massachusetts, and Yale University.

Walker has written essays, poetry, and fiction. Her best-known novel, The Color Purple *(1982), won a Pulitzer Prize and the National Book Award. She has said that her chief concern is "exploring the oppressions, the insanities, the loyalties, and the triumphs of black women."*

Everyday Use

For your grandmama

I will wait for her in the yard that Maggie and I made so clean and wavy yesterday afternoon. A yard like this is more comfortable than most people know. It is not just a yard. It is like an extended living room. When the hard clay is swept clean as a floor and the fine sand around the edges lined with tiny, irregular grooves, anyone can come and sit and look up into the elm tree and wait for the breezes that never come inside the house.

Maggie will be nervous until after her sister goes: she will stand hopelessly in corners homely and ashamed of the burn scars down her arms and legs, eyeing her sister with a mixture of envy and awe. She thinks her sister had held life always in the palm of one hand, that "no" is a word the world never learned to say to her.

You've no doubt seen those TV shows where the child who has "made it" is confronted, as a surprise, by her own mother and father, tottering in weakly from backstage. (A pleasant surprise, of course: What would they do if parent and child came on the show only to curse out and insult each other?) On TV mother and child embrace and smile into each other's faces. Sometimes the mother and father weep, the child wraps them in her arms and leans across the table to tell how she would not have made it without their help. I have seen these programs.

Sometimes I dream a dream in which Dee and I are suddenly brought together on a TV program of this sort. Out of a dark and soft-seated limousine I am ushered into a bright room filled with many people. There I meet a smiling, gray, sporty man like Johnny Carson who shakes my hand and tells me what a fine girl I have. Then we are on the stage and Dee is embracing me with tears in her eyes. She pins on my dress a large orchid, even though she has told me once that she thinks orchids are tacky flowers.

5 In real life I am a large, big-boned woman with rough, man-working hands. In the winter I wear flannel nightgowns to bed and overalls during the day. I can kill and clean a hog as mercilessly as a man. My fat keeps me hot in zero weather. I can work outside all day, breaking ice to get water for washing. I can eat pork liver cooked over the open fire minutes after it comes steaming from the hog. One winter I knocked a bull calf straight in the brain between the eyes with a sledge hammer and had the meat hung up to chill before nightfall. But of course all this does not show on television. I am the way my daughter would want me to be: a hundred pounds lighter, my skin like an uncooked barley pancake. My hair glistens in the hot bright lights. Johnny Carson has much to do to keep up with my quick and witty tongue.

But that is a mistake. I know even before I wake up. Who ever knew a Johnson with a quick tongue? Who can even imagine me looking a strange white man in the eye? It seems to me I have talked to them always with one foot raised in flight, with my head turned in whichever way is farthest from them. Dee, though. She would always look anyone in the eye. Hesitation was no part of her nature.

"How do I look, Mama?" Maggie says, showing just enough of her thin body enveloped in pink skirt and red blouse for me to know she's there, almost hidden by the door.

"Come out into the yard," I say.

Have you ever seen a lame animal, perhaps a dog run over by some careless person rich enough to own a car, sidle up to someone who is ignorant enough to be kind to him? That is the way my Maggie walks. She has been like this, chin on chest, eyes on ground, feet in shuffle, ever since the fire that burned the other house to the ground.

10 Dee is lighter than Maggie, with nicer hair and a fuller figure. She's a woman now, though sometimes I forget. How long ago was it that the other house burned? Ten, twelve years? Sometimes I can still hear the flames and feel Maggie's arms sticking to me, her hair smoking and her dress falling off her in little black papery flakes. Her eyes seemed stretched open, blazed open by the flames reflected in them. And Dee. I see her standing off under the sweet gum tree she used to dig gum out of; a look of concentration on her face as she watched the last dingy gray board of the house fall in toward the red-hot brick chimney. Why don't you do a dance around the ashes? I'd wanted to ask her. She had hated the house that much.

I used to think she hated Maggie, too. But that was before we raised the money, the church and me, to send her to Augusta to school. She used to read to us without pity; forcing words, lies, other folks' habits, whole lives upon us two, sitting trapped and ignorant underneath her voice. She washed us in a river of make-believe, burned us with a lot of knowledge we didn't necessarily need to know. Pressed us to her with the serious way she read, to shove us away at just the moment, like dimwits, we seemed about to understand.

Dee wanted nice things. A yellow organdy dress to wear to her graduation from high school; black pumps to match a green suit she'd made from an old suit somebody gave me. She was determined to stare down any disaster in her efforts. Her eyelids would not flicker for minutes at a time. Often I fought off the temptation to shake her. At sixteen she had a style of her own: and knew what style was.

I never had an education myself. After second grade the school was closed down. Don't ask me why: in 1927 colored asked fewer questions than they do now. Sometimes Maggie reads to me. She stumbles along goodnaturedly but can't see well. She knows she is not bright. Like good looks and money, quickness passed her by. She will marry John Thomas (who has mossy teeth in an earnest face) and then I'll be free to sit here and I guess just sing church songs to myself. Although I never was a good singer. Never could carry a tune. I was always better at a man's job. I used to love to milk till I was hoofed in the side in '49. Cows are soothing and slow and don't bother you, unless you try to milk them the wrong way.

I have deliberately turned my back on the house. It is three rooms, just like the one that burned, except the roof is tin; they don't make shingle roofs any more. There are no real windows, just some holes cut in the sides, like the portholes in a ship, but not round and not square, with rawhide holding the shutters up on the outside. This house is in a pasture, too, like the other one. No doubt when Dee sees it she will want to tear it down. She wrote me once that no matter where we "choose" to live, she will manage to come see us. But she will never bring her friends. Maggie and I thought about this and Maggie asked me, "Mama, when did Dee ever *have* any friends?"

15 She had a few. Furtive boys in pink shirts hanging about on washday after school. Nervous girls who never laughed. Impressed with her they worshiped the well-turned phrase, the cute shape, the scalding humor that erupted like bubbles in lye. She read to them.

When she was courting Jimmy T she didn't have much time to pay to us, but turned all her faultfinding power on him. He *flew* to marry a cheap gal from a family of ignorant flashy people. She hardly had time to recompose herself.

When she comes I will meet—but there they are!

Maggie attempts to make a dash for the house, in her shuffling way, but I stay her with my hand. "Come back here," I say. And she stops and tries to dig a well in the sand with her toe.

It is hard to see them clearly through the strong sun. But even the first glimpse of leg out of the car tells me it is Dee. Her feet were always neat-looking, as if God himself had shaped them with a certain style. From the other side of the car comes a short, stocky man. Hair is all over his head a foot long and hanging from his chin like a kinky mule tail. I hear Maggie suck in her breath. "Uhnnnh," is what it sounds like. Like when you see the wriggling end of a snake just in front of your foot on the road. "Uhnnnh."

20 Dee next. A dress down to the ground, in this hot weather. A dress so loud it hurts my eyes. There are yellows and oranges enough to throw back the light of the sun. I feel my whole face warming from the heat waves it throws out. Earrings, too, gold and hanging down to her shoulders. Bracelets dangling and making noises when she moves her arm up to shake the folds of the dress out of her armpits. The dress is loose and flows, and as she walks closer, I like it. I hear Maggie go "Uhnnnh" again. It is her sister's hair. It stands straight up like the wool on a sheep. It is black as night and around the edges are two long pigtails that rope about like small lizards disappearing behind her ears.

"Wa-su-zo-Tean-o!" she says, coming on in that gliding way the dress makes her move. The short stocky fellow with the hair to his navel is all grinning and he follows up with "Asalamalakim, my mother and sister!" He moves to hug Maggie but she falls back, right up against the back of my chair. I feel her trembling there and when I look up I see the perspiration falling off her chin.

"Don't get up," says Dee. Since I am stout it takes something of a push. You can see me trying to move a second or two before I make it. She turns, showing white heels through her sandals, and goes back to the car. Out she peeks next with a Polaroid. She stoops down quickly and lines up picture after picture of me sitting there in front of the house with Maggie cowering behind me. She never takes a shot without making sure the house is included. When a cow comes nibbling around the edge of the yard she snaps it and me and Maggie *and* the house. Then she puts the Polaroid in the back seat of the car, and comes up and kisses me on the forehead.

Meanwhile Asalamalakim is going through the motions with Maggie's hand. Maggie's hand is as limp as a fish, and probably as cold, despite the sweat, and she keeps trying to pull it back. It looks like Asalamalakim wants to shake hands but wants to do it fancy. Or maybe he don't know how people shake hands. Anyhow, he soon gives up on Maggie.

"Well," I say. "Dee."

25 "No, Mama," she says. "Not 'Dee,' Wangero Leewanika Kemanjo!"

"What happened to 'Dee'?" I wanted to know.

"She's dead," Wangero said. "I couldn't bear it any longer being named after the people who oppress me."

"You know as well as me you was named after your aunt Dicie," I said. Dicie is my sister. She named Dee. We called her "Big Dee" after Dee was born.

"But who was *she* named after?" asked Wangero.

30 "I guess after Grandma Dee," I said.

"And who was she named after?" asked Wangero.

"Her mother," I said, and saw Wangero was getting tired. "That's about as far back as I can trace it," I said. Though, in fact, I probably could have carried it back beyond the Civil War through the branches.

"Well," said Asalamalakim, "there you are."

"Uhnnnh," I heard Maggie say.

35 "There I was not," I said, "before 'Dicie' cropped up in our family, so why should I try to trace it that far back?"

He just stood there grinning, looking down on me like somebody inspecting a Model A car. Every once in a while he and Wangero sent eye signals over my head.

"How do you pronounce this name?" I asked.

"You don't have to call me by it if you don't want to," said Wangero.

"Why shouldn't I?" I asked. "If that's what you want us to call you, we'll call you."

40 "I know it might sound awkward at first," said Wangero.

"I'll get used to it," I said. "Ream it out again."

Well, soon we got the name out of the way. Asalamalakim had a name twice as long and three times as hard. After I tripped over it two or three times he told me to just call him Hakim-a-barber. I wanted to ask him was he a barber, but I didn't really think he was, so I didn't ask.

"You must belong to those beef-cattle peoples down the road," I said. They said "Asalamalakim" when they met you, too, but they didn't shake hands. Always too busy: feeding the cattle, fixing the fences, putting up saltlick shelters, throwing down hay. When the white folks poisoned some of the herd the men stayed up all night with rifles in their hands. I walked a mile and a half just to see the sight.

Hakim-a-barber said, "I accept some of their doctrines, but farming and raising cattle is not my style." (They didn't tell me, and I didn't ask, whether Wangero [Dee] had really gone and married him.)

45 We sat down to eat and right away he said he didn't eat collards and pork was unclean. Wangero, though, went on through the chitlins and corn bread, the greens and everything else. She talked a blue streak over the sweet potatoes. Everything delighted her. Even the fact that we still used the benches her daddy made for the table when we couldn't afford to buy chairs.

"Oh, Mama!" she cried. Then turned to Hakim-a-barber. "I never knew how lovely these benches are. You can feel the rump prints," she said, running her hands underneath her and along the bench. Then she gave a sigh and her hand closed over Grandma Dee's butter dish. "That's it!" she said. "I knew there was something I wanted to ask you if I could have." She jumped up from the table and went over in the corner where the churn stood, the milk in it clabber by now. She looked at the churn and looked at it.

"This churn top is what I need," she said. "Didn't Uncle Buddy whittle it out of a tree you all used to have?"

"Yes," I said.

"Uh huh," she said happily. "And I want the dasher, too."

50 "Uncle Buddy whittle that, too?" asked the barber.

Dee (Wangero) looked up at me.

"Aunt Dee's first husband whittled the dash," said Maggie so low you almost couldn't hear her. "His name was Henry, but they called him Stash."

"Maggie's brain is like an elephant's," Wangero said, laughing. "I can use the churn top as a centerpiece for the alcove table," she said, sliding a plate over the churn, "and I'll think of something artistic to do with the dasher."

When she finished wrapping the dasher the handle stuck out. I took it for a moment in my hands. You didn't even have to look close to see where hands pushing the dasher up and down to make butter had left a kind of sink in the wood. In fact, there were a lot of small sinks; you could see where thumbs and fingers had sunk into the wood. It was beautiful light yellow wood, from a tree that grew in the yard where Big Dee and Stash had lived.

55 After dinner Dee (Wangero) went to the trunk at the foot of my bed and started rifling through it. Maggie hung back in the kitchen over the dishpan. Out came Wangero with two quilts. They had been pieced by Grandma Dee and then Big Dee and me had hung them on the quilt frames on the front porch and quilted them. One was in the Lone Star pattern. The other was Walk Around the Mountain. In both of them were scraps of dresses Grandma Dee had worn fifty and more years ago. Bits and pieces of Grandpa Jarrell's paisley shirts. And one

teeny faded blue piece, about the size of a penny matchbox, that was from Great Grandpa Ezra's uniform that he wore in the Civil War.

"Mama," Wangero said sweet as a bird. "Can I have these old quilts?"

I heard something fall in the kitchen, and a minute later the kitchen door slammed.

"Why don't you take one or two of the others?" I asked. "These old things was just done by me and Big Dee from some tops your grandma pieced before she died."

"No," said Wangero. "I don't want those. They are stitched around the borders by machine."

60 "That'll make them last better," I said.

"That's not the point," said Wangero. "These are all pieces of dresses Grandma used to wear. She did all this stitching by hand. Imagine!" She held the quilts securely in her arms, stroking them.

"Some of the pieces, like those lavender ones, come from old clothes her mother handed down to her," I said, moving up to touch the quilts. Dee (Wangero) moved back just enough so that I couldn't reach the quilts. They already belonged to her.

"Imagine!" she breathed again, clutching them closely to her bosom.

"The truth is," I said, "I promised to give them quilts to Maggie, for when she marries John Thomas."

65 She gasped like a bee had stung her.

"Maggie can't appreciate these quilts!" she said. "She'd probably be backward enough to put them to everyday use."

"I reckon she would," I said. "God knows I been saving 'em for long enough with nobody using 'em. I hope she will!" I didn't want to bring up how I had offered Dee (Wangero) a quilt when she went away to college. Then she had told me they were old-fashioned, out of style.

"But they're *priceless!*" she was saying now, furiously; for she has a temper. "Maggie would put them on the bed and in five years they'd be in rags. Less than that!"

"She can always make some more," I said. "Maggie knows how to quilt."

70 Dee (Wangero) looked at me with hatred. "You just will not understand. The point is these quilts, *these* quilts!"

"Well," I said, stumped. "What would *you* do with them?"

"Hang them," she said. As if that was the only thing you *could* do with quilts.

Maggie by now was standing in the door. I could almost hear the sound her feet made as they scraped over each other.

"She can have them, Mama," she said, like somebody used to never winning anything, or having anything reserved for her. "I can 'member Grandma Dee without the quilts."

75 I looked at her hard. She had filled her bottom lip with checkerberry snuff and it gave her face a kind of dopey, hangdog look. It was Grandma Dee and Big Dee who taught her how to quilt herself. She stood there with her scarred hands hidden in the folds of her skirt. She looked at her sister with something like fear but she wasn't mad at her. This was Maggie's portion. This was the way she knew God to work.

When I looked at her like that something hit me in the top of my head and ran down to the soles of my feet. Just like when I'm in church and the spirit of God touches me and I get happy and shout. I did something I never had done before: hugged Maggie to me, then dragged her on into the room, snatched the quilts out of Miss Wangero's hands and dumped them into Maggie's lap. Maggie just sat there on my bed with her mouth open.

"Take one or two of the others," I said to Dee.

But she turned without a word and went out to Hakim-a-barber.

"You just don't understand," she said, as Maggie and I came out to the car.

80 "What don't I understand?" I wanted to know.

"Your heritage," she said. And then she turned to Maggie, kissed her, and said, "You ought to try to make something of yourself, too, Maggie. It's really a new day for us. But from the way you and Mama still live you'd never know it."

She put on some sunglasses that hid everything above the tip of her nose and her chin.

Maggie smiled; maybe at the sunglasses. But a real smile, not scared. After we watched the car dust settle I asked Maggie to bring me a dip of snuff. And then the two of us sat there just enjoying, until it was time to go in the house and go to bed.

[1973]

Joining the Conversation: Critical Thinking and Writing

1. Alice Walker wrote the story, but the story is narrated by one of the characters, Mama. How would you characterize Mama?
2. At the end of the story, Dee tells Maggie, "It's really a new day for us. But from the way you and Mama still live you'd never know it." What does Dee mean? And how do Maggie and Mama respond?
3. In paragraph 76 the narrator says, speaking of Maggie, "When I looked at her like that something hit me in the top of my head and ran down to the soles of my feet." What "hit" Mama? That is, what does she understand at this moment that she had not understood before?
4. In "Everyday Use" why does the family conflict focus on who will possess the quilts? Why are the quilts important? What do they symbolize?

KATHERINE MIN

A graduate of Amherst College and the Columbia School of Journalism, Katherine Min has published stories in several magazines notable for their excellent fiction, including Tri-Quarterly *and* Ploughshares. *She has received grants from the National Endowment for the Arts and from the New Hampshire State Arts Council, and she has twice been a fellow at the MacDowell Colony.*

Courting a Monk

When I first saw my husband he was sitting cross-legged under a tree on the quad, his hair as short as peach fuzz, large blue eyes staring upward, the smile on his face so wide and undirected as to seem moronic. I went flying by him every minute or two, guarding man-to-man, or chasing down a pass, and out of the corner of my eye I would see him watching and smiling. What I noticed about him most was his tremendous capacity for stillness. His hands were like still-life objects resting on his knees; his posture was impeccable. He looked so rooted there, like some cheerful, exotic mushroom, that I began to feel awkward in my exertion. Sweat funneled into the valley of my back, cooling and sticking when I stopped, hands on knees, to regain my breath. I tried to stop my gape-mouthed panting, refashioned my pony-tail, and wiped my hands on the soft front of my sweatpants.

He was still there two plays later when my team was down by one. Sully stole a pass and flipped to Graham. Graham threw me a long bomb that sailed wide and I leapt for it, sailing with the Frisbee for a moment in a parallel line—floating, flying, reaching—before coming down whap! against the ground. I groaned. I'd taken a tree root in the solar plexus. The wind was knocked out of me. I lay there, the taste of dry leaves in my mouth.

"Sorry, Gina. Lousy pass," Graham said, coming over. "You O.K.?"

"Fine," I gasped, fingering my ribs. "Just let me sit out for a while."

5 I sat down in the leaves, breathing carefully as I watched them play. The day was growing dark and the Frisbee was hard to see. Everyone was tired and played in a sloppy rhythm of errant throws and dropped passes.

Beside me on the grass crept the guy from under the tree. I had forgotten about him. He crouched shyly next to me, leaves cracking under his feet, and, when I looked up, he whispered, "You were magnificent," and walked away smiling.

I spotted him the next day in the vegetarian dining hall. I was passing through with my plate of veal cordon bleu when I saw him sitting by himself next to the window. He took a pair of wooden chopsticks out of the breast pocket of his shirt and poked halfheartedly at his tofu and wilted mung beans. I sat down across from him and demanded his life story.

It turned out he wanted to be a monk. Not the Chaucerian kind, bald-pated and stout, with a hooded robe, ribald humor and penchant for wine. Something even more baffling—a Buddhist. He had just returned from a semester in Nepal, studying in a monastery in the Himalayas. His hair was coming back in soft spikes across his head and he had a watchful manner—not cautious but receptive, waiting.

He was from King of Prussia, off the Philadelphia Main Line, and this made me mistrust the depth of his beliefs. I have discovered that a fascination for the East is often a prelude to a pass, a romantic overture set in motion by an "I think Oriental girls are so beautiful," and a vise-like grip on the upper thigh. But Micah was different. He understood I was not impressed by his belief, and he did not aim to impress.

10 "My father was raised Buddhist," I told him. "But he's a scientist now."

"Oh," said Micah. "So, he's not spiritual."

"Spirit's insubstantial," I said. "He doesn't hold with intangibility."

"Well, you can't hold atoms in your hand," Micah pointed out.

"Ah," I said, smiling, "but you can count them."

. . .

15 I told Micah my father was a man of science, and this was true. He was a man, also, of silence. Unlike Micah, whose reticence seemed calming, so undisturbed, like a pool of light on still water, my father's silence was like the lid on a pot, sealing off some steaming, inner pressure.

Words were not my father's medium. "Language," my father liked to say, "is an imprecise instrument." (For though he said little, when he hit upon a phrase he liked, he said it many times.) He was fond of Greek letters and numerals set together in intricate equations, symbolizing a certain physical law or experimental hypothesis. He filled yellow legal pads in a strong vertical hand, writing these beauties down in black, indelible felt-tip pen. I think it was a source of tremendous irritation to him that he could not communicate with other people in so ordered a fashion, that he could not simply draw an equals sign after something he'd said, have them solve for x or y.

That my father's English was not fluent was only part of it. He was not a garrulous man, even in Korean, among visiting relatives, or alone with my mother. And with me, his only child—who could speak neither of his preferred languages, Korean or science—my father had conspicuously little to say. "Pick up this mess," he would tell me, returning from work in the evening. "Homework finished?" he would inquire, raising an eyebrow over his rice bowl as I excused myself to go watch television.

He limited himself to the imperative mood, the realm of injunction and command; the kinds of statement that required no answer, that left no opening for discussion or rejoinder. These communications were my father's verbal equivalent to his neat numerical equations. They were hermetically sealed.

When I went away to college, my father's parting words constituted one of the longest speeches I'd heard him make. Surrounded by station wagons packed with suitcases, crates of books and study lamps, amid the excited chattering and calling out of students, among the adults with their nervous parental surveillance of the scene, my father leaned awkwardly forward with his hands in his pockets, looking at me intently. He said, "Study hard. Go to bed early. Do not goof off. And do not let the American boys take advantages."

20 This was the same campus my father had set foot on twenty years before, when he was a young veteran of the Korean War, with fifty dollars in his pocket and about that many words of English. Stories of his college years constituted family legend and, growing up, I had heard them so often they were as vivid and dream-like as my own memories. My father in the dorm bathroom over Christmas, vainly trying to hard-boil an egg in a sock by running it under hot water; his triumph in the physics lab where his ability with the new language did not impede him, and where his maturity and keen scientific mind garnered him highest marks and the top physics prize in his senior year—these were events I felt I'd witnessed, like some obscure, envious ghost.

In the shadow of my father's achievements then, on the same campus where he had first bowed his head to a microscope, lost in a chalk-dust mathematical dream, I pursued words. English words. I committed myself to expertise. I studied Shakespeare and Eliot, Hardy and Conrad, Joyce and Lawrence and Hemingway and Fitzgerald. It was important to get it right, every word, every nuance, to fill in my father's immigrant silences, the gaps he had left for me.

Other gaps he'd left. Staying up late and studying little, I did things my father would have been too shocked to merely disapprove. As for American boys, I heeded my father's advice and did not let them take advantage. Instead I took advantage of them, of their proximity, their good looks, and the amiable way they would fall into bed with you if you gave them the slightest encouragement. I liked the way they moved in proud possession of their bodies, the rough feel of their unshaven cheeks, their shoulders and smooth, hairless chests, the curve of their backs like burnished wood. I liked the way I could look up at them, or down, feeling their shuddering climax like a distant earthquake; I could make it happen, moving in undulant circles from above or below, watching them, holding them, making them happy. I collected boys like baubles, like objects not particularly valued, which you stash away in the back of some drawer. It was the pleasant interchangeability of their bodies I liked. They were all white boys.

Micah refused to have sex with me. It became a matter of intellectual disagreement with us. "Sex saps the will," he said.

"Not necessarily," I argued. "Just reroutes it."

25 "There are higher forms of union," he said.

"Not with your clothes off," I replied.

"Gina," he said, looking at me with kindness, a concern that made me flush with anger. "What need do you have that sex must fill?"

"Fuck you, Micah," I said. "Be a monk, not a psychologist."

He laughed. His laughter was always a surprise to me, like a small disturbance to the universe. I wanted to seduce him, this was true. I considered Micah the only real challenge among an easy field. But more than seduction, I wanted to rattle him, to get under that sense of peace, that inward contentment. No one my age, I reasoned, had the right to such self-possession.

30 We went for walks in the bird sanctuary, rustling along the paths slowly discussing Emily Dickinson or maple syrup-making, but always I brought the subject around.

"What a waste of life," I said once. "Such indulgence. All that monkly devotion and quest for inner peace. Big deal. It's selfish. Not only is it selfish, it's a cop-out. An escape from this world and its messes."

Micah listened, a narrow smile on his lips, shaking his head regretfully. "You're so wonderfully passionate, Gina, so alive and in the world. I can't make you see. Maybe it is a cop-out as you say, but Buddhism makes no distinction between the world outside or the world within the monastery. And historically, monks have been in the middle of political protest and persecution. Look at Tibet."

"I was thinking about, ahem, something more basic," I said.

Micah laughed. "Of course," he said. "You don't seem to understand, Gina, Buddhism is all about the renunciation of desire."

35 I sniffed. "What's wrong with desire? Without desire, you might as well not be alive."

The truth was that I was fascinated by this idea, the renunciation of desire. My life was fueled by longing, by vast and clamorous desires; a striving toward things I did not have and, perhaps, had no hope of having. I could vaguely imagine an end, some point past desiring, of satiety, but I could not fathom the laying down of desire, walking away in full appetite.

"The desire to renounce desire," I said now, "is still desire, isn't it?"

Micah sunk his hands into his pockets and smiled. "It's not," he said, walking ahead of me. "It's a conscious choice."

We came to a pond, sun-dappled in a clearing, bordered by white birch and maples with the bright leaves of mid-autumn. A fluttering of leaves blew from the trees, landing on the water as gently as if they'd been placed. The color of the pond was a deep canvas green; glints of light snapped like sparks above the surface. There was the lyric coo of a mourning dove, the chitter-chitter of late-second insects. Micah's capacity for appreciation was vast. Whether this had anything to do with Buddhism, I didn't know, but watching him stand on the edge of the pond, his head thrown back, his eyes eagerly taking in the light, I felt his peace and also his sense of wonder. He stood motionless for a long time.

40 I pulled at ferns, weaved their narrow leaves in irregular samplers, braided tendrils together, while Micah sat on a large rock and, taking his chopsticks from

his breast pocket, began to tap them lightly against one another in a solemn rhythm.

"Every morning in the monastery," he said, "we woke to the prayer drum. Four o'clock and the sky would be dark and you'd hear the hollow wooden sound—plock, plock, plock—summoning you to meditation." He smiled dreamily. The chopsticks made a somewhat less effectual sound, a sort of ta ta ta. I imagined sunrise across a Himalayan valley—the wisps of pink-tinged cloud on a cold spring morning, the austerity of a monk's chamber.

Micah had his eyes closed, face to the sun. He continued to tap the chopsticks together slowly. He looked singular and new, sitting on that rock, like an advance scout for some new tribe, with his crest of hair and calm, and the attentiveness of his body to his surroundings.

I think it was then I fell in love with him, or, it was in that moment that my longing for him became so great that it was no longer a matter of simple gratification. I needed his response. I understood what desire was then, the disturbance of a perfect moment in anticipation of another.

"Wake-up call," I said. I peeled off my turtleneck and sweater in one clever motion and tossed them at Micah's feet. Micah opened his eyes. I pulled my pants off and my underwear and stood naked. "Plock, plock, who's there?"

Micah did not turn away. He looked at me, his chopsticks poised in the air. He raised one toward me and held it, as though he were an artist with a paintbrush raised for a proportion, or a conductor ready to lead an orchestra. He held the chopstick suspended in the space between us, and it was as though I couldn't move for as long as he held it. His eyes were fathomless blue. My nipples constricted with the cold. Around us leaves fell in shimmering lights to the water, making a soft rustling sound like the rub of stiff fabric. He brought his hand down and I was released. I turned and leapt into the water.

A few nights later I bought a bottle of cheap wine and goaded Micah into drinking it with me. We started out on the steps of the library after it had closed for the night, taking sloppy swigs from a brown paper bag. The lights of the Holyoke range blinked in the distance, across the velvet black of the freshman quad. From there we wandered the campus, sprawling on the tennis courts, bracing a stiff wind from the terrace of the science center, sedately rolling down Memorial Hill like a pair of tumbleweeds.

"J'a know what a koan is?" he asked me, when we were perched at the top of the bleachers behind home plate. We unsteadily contemplated the steep drop off the back side.

"You mean like ice cream?" I said.

"No, a ko-an. In Buddhism."

"Nope."

"It's a question that has no answer, sort of like a riddle. You know, like 'What is the sound of one hand clapping?' Or 'What was your face before you were born?'"

"'What was my face before it was born?' That makes no sense."

"Exactly. You're supposed to contemplate the koan until you achieve a greater awareness."

"Of what?"

"Of life, of meaning."

"Oh, O.K.," I said, "I've got it." I was facing backwards, the bag with the bottle in both my hands. "How 'bout, 'What's the sound of one cheek farting?'"

He laughed for a long time, then retched off the side of the bleachers. I got him home and put him to bed; his forehead was feverish, his eyes glassy with sickness.

"Sorry," I said. "I'm a bad influence." I kissed him. His lips were hot and slack.

"Don't mind," he murmured, half-asleep.

60 The next night we slept in the same bed together for the first time. He kept his underwear on and his hands pressed firmly to his sides, like Gandhi among his young virgins. I was determined to make it difficult for him. I kept brushing my naked body against him, draping a leg across his waist, stroking his narrow chest with my fingertips. He wiggled and pushed away, feigning sleep. When I woke in the morning, he was gone and the *Ode to Joy* was blasting from my stereo.

Graham said he missed me. We'd slept together a few times before I met Micah, enjoying the warm, healthful feeling we got from running or playing Ultimate, taking a quick sauna and falling into bed. He was good-looking, dark and broad, with sinewy arms and a tight chest. He made love to a woman like he was lifting Nautilus, all grim purpose and timing. It was hard to believe that had ever been appealing. I told him I was seeing someone else.

"Not the guy with the crew cut?" he said. "The one who looks like a baby seal?"

I shrugged.

Graham looked at me skeptically "He doesn't seem like your type," he said.

65 "No," I agreed. "But at least he's not yours."

Meanwhile I stepped up my attack. I asked endless questions about Buddhist teaching. Micah talked about *dukkha;*[1] the four noble truths; the five aggregates of attachment; the noble eightfold path to enlightenment. I listened dutifully, willing to acknowledge that it all sounded nice, that the goal of perfect awareness and peace seemed worth attaining. While he talked, I stretched my feet out until my toes touched his thigh; I slid my hand along his back; or leaned way over so he could see down my loose, barely-buttoned blouse.

"Too bad you aren't Tantric," I said. I'd been doing research.

Micah scoffed. "Hollywood Buddhism," he said. "Heavy breathing and theatrics."

"They believe in physical desire," I said. "They have sex."

70 "Buddha believes in physical desire," Micah said. "It's impermanent, that's all. Something to get beyond."

"To get beyond it," I said petulantly, "you have to do it."

Micah signed. "Gina," he said, "you are beautiful, but I can't. There are a lot of guys who will."

"A lot of them do."

He smiled a bit sadly. "Well, then . . ."

75 I leaned down to undo his shoelaces. I tied them together in double knots. "But I want you," I said.

My parents lived thirty miles from campus and my mother frequently asked me to come home for dinner. I went only once that year, and that was with Micah. My parents were not the kind of people who enjoyed the company of strangers. They were insular people who did not like to socialize much or go out—or anyway, my father was that way, and my mother accommodated herself to his preferences.

[1]***dukkha*** a Pali word meaning "suffering," particularly the suffering that is caused by desire.

My mother had set the table in the dining room with blue linen. There were crystal wine glasses and silver utensils in floral patterns. She had made some dry baked chicken with overcooked peas and carrots—the meal she reserved for when Americans came to dinner. When it came to Korean cooking, my mother was a master. She made fabulous marinated short ribs and sautéed transparent bean noodles with vegetables and beef, pork dumplings and batter-fried shrimp, and cucumber and turnip kimchis[2] which she made herself and fermented in brown earthenware jars. But American cuisine eluded her; it bored her. I think she thought it was meant to be tasteless.

"Just make Korean," I had urged her on the phone. "He'll like that."

My mother was skeptical. "Too spicy," she said. "I know what Americans like."

"Not the chicken dish," I pleaded. "He's a vegetarian."

"We'll see," said my mother, conceding nothing.

Micah stared down at his plate. My mother smiled serenely. Micah nodded. He ate a forkful of vegetables, took a bite of bread. His Adam's apple seemed to be doing a lot of work. My father, too, was busy chewing, his Adam's apple moving up and down his throat like the ratchets of a tire jack. No one had said a thing since my father had uncorked the Chardonnay and read to us the description from his well-creased paperback edition of *The New York Times Guide to Wine*.

The sound of silverware scraping on ceramic plates seemed amplified. I was aware of my own prolonged chewing. My father cleared his throat. My mother looked at him expectantly. He coughed.

"Micah studied Buddhism in Nepal," I offered into the silence.

"Oh!" my mother exclaimed. She giggled.

My father kept eating. He swallowed exaggeratedly and looked up. "That so?" he said, sounding almost interested.

Micah nodded. "I was only there four months," he said. "Gina tells me you were brought up Buddhist."

My father grunted. "Well, of course," he said. "In Korea in those days, our families were all Buddhist. I do not consider myself a Buddhist now."

Micah and I exchanged a look.

"It's become quite fashionable, I understand," my father went on. "With you American college kids. Buddhism has become fad."

I saw Micah wince.

"I think it is wonderful, Hi Joon," my mother interceded, "for Americans to learn about Asian religion and philosophy. I was a philosophy major in college, Micah. I studied Whitehead,[3] American pragmatism."

My father leaned back in his chair and watched, frowning, while my mother and Micah talked. It was like he was trying to analyze Micah, not as a psychiatrist analyzes—my father held a dim view of psychology—but as a chemist would, breaking him down to his basic elements, the simple chemical formula that would define his makeup.

Micah was talking about the aggregates of matter, sensation, perception, mental formations, and consciousness that comprise being in Buddhist teaching. "It's a different sense of self than in Christian religions," he explained, looking at my mother.

"Nonsense," my father interrupted. "There is no self in Buddhist doctrine. . . ."

[2]**kimchis** pickles. [3]**Whitehead** Alfred North Whitehead (1861–1947), British mathematician and philosopher.

My mother and I watched helplessly as they launched into discussion. I was surprised that my father seemed to know so much about it, and by how much he was carrying forth. I was surprised also by Micah's deference. He seemed to have lost all his sureness, the walls of his conviction. He kept nodding and conceding to my father certain points that he had rigorously defended to me before. "I guess I don't know as much about it," he said more than once, and "Yes, I see what you mean" several times, with a sickening air of humility.

I turned from my father's glinting, pitiless intelligence, to Micah's respectfulness, his timid manner, and felt a rising irritation I could not place, anger at my father's belligerence, at Micah's backing down, at my own strange motives for having brought them together. Had I really expected them to get along? And yet, my father was concentrating on Micah with such an intensity—almost as though he were a rival—in a way in which he never focused on me.

When the dialogue lapsed, and after we had consumed as much of the food as we deemed polite, my mother took the dishes away and brought in a bowl of rice with kimchi for my father. Micah's eyes lit up. "May I have some of that, too, Mrs. Kim?"

My mother looked doubtful. "Too spicy," she said.

"Oh, I love spicy food," Micah assured her. My mother went to get him a bowl.

"You can use chopsticks?" my mother said, as Micah began eating with them.

"Mom, it's no big deal," I said.

My father looked up from his bowl. Together, my parents watched while Micah ate a large piece of cabbage kimchi.

"Hah!" my father said, suddenly smiling. "Gina doesn't like kimchi," he said. He looked at me. "Gina," he said. "This boy more Korean than you."

"Doesn't take much," I said.

My father ignored me. "Gina always want to be American," he told Micah. "Since she was little girl, she want blue eyes, yellow hair." He stabbed a chopstick toward Micah's face. "Like yours."

"If I had hair" said Micah, grinning, rubbing a hand across his head.

My father stared into his bowl. "She doesn't want to be Korean girl. She thinks she can be 100 percent American, but she cannot. She has Korean blood—100 percent. Doesn't matter where you grow up—blood is most important. What is in the blood." He gave Micah a severe look. "You think you can become Buddhist. Same way. But it is not in your blood. You cannot know real Buddha's teaching. You should study Bible."

"God, Dad!" I said. "You sound like a Nazi!"

"Gina!" my mother warned.

"You're embarrassing me," I said. "Being rude to my guest. Discussing me as if I wasn't here. You can say what you want, Dad, I'm American whether you like it or not. Blood's got nothing to do with it. It's what's up here." I tapped my finger to my temple.

"It's not Nazi," my father said. "Is fact! What you have here," he pointed to his forehead, "is all from blood, from genetics. You got from me!"

"Heaven help me," I said.

"Gina!" my mother implored.

"Mr. Kim—" Micah began.

"You just like American girl in one thing," my father shouted. "You have no respect for father. In Korea, daughters do not talk back to their parents, is big shame!"

"In Korea, girls are supposed to be submissive doormats for fathers to wipe their feet on!" I shouted back.

"What do you know about Korea? You went there only once when you were six years old."

"It's in my blood," I said. I stood up. "I'm not going to stay here for this. Come on, Micah."

Micah looked at me uncertainly, then turned to my father.

My father was eating again, slowly levering rice to his mouth with his chopsticks. He paused. "She was always this way," he said, seeming to address the table. "So angry. Even as a little girl."

"Mr. Kim," Micah said, "Um, thank you very much. We're . . . I think we're heading out now."

My father chewed ruminatively. "I should never have left Korea," he said quietly, with utter conviction.

"Gina," my mother said. "Sit down. Hi Joon, please!"

"Micah," I said. "You coming?"

We left my father alone at the dining-room table.

"I should have sent you to live with Auntie Soo!" he called after me.

My mother followed us out to the driveway with a Tupperware container of chicken Micah hadn't eaten.

On the way home we stopped for ice cream. Koans, I told Micah. "What is the sound of Swiss chocolate almond melting?" I asked him. "What was the vanilla before it was born?"

Inside the ice-cream parlor the light was too strong, a ticking fluorescence bleaching everything bone-white. Micah leaned down to survey the cardboard barrels of ice cream in their plastic cases. He looked shrunken, subdued. He ordered a scoop of mint chocolate chip and one of black cherry on a sugar cone and ate it with the long, regretful licks of a child who'd spent the last nickel of his allowance. There was a ruefulness to his movements, a sense of apology. He had lost his monk-like stillness and seemed suddenly adrift.

The cold of the ice cream gave me a headache, all the blood vessels in my temples seemed strung out and tight. I shivered and the cold was like fury, spreading through me with the chill.

Micah rubbed my back.

"You're hard on your father," he said. "He's not a bad guy."

"Forget it," I said. "Let's go."

We walked from the dorm parking lot in silence. There were lights going on across the quad and music spilling from the windows out into the cool air. What few stars there were seemed too distant to wage a constant light.

Back in my room, I put on the Rolling Stones at full blast. Mick Jagger's voice was taunting and cruel. I turned out the lights and lit a red candle.

"O.K., this is going to stop," I said. I felt myself trembling. I pushed Micah back on the bed. I was furious. He had ruined it for me, the lightness, the skimming quality of my life. It had seemed easy, with the boys, the glib words and feelings, the simple heat and surface pleasures. It was like the sensation of flying, leaping for the Frisbee and sailing through the air. For a moment you lose a feeling for gravity, for the consciousness of your own skin or species. For a moment you are free.

I started to dance, fast, swinging and swaying in front of the bed. I closed my eyes and twirled wildly, bouncing off the walls like a pinball, stumbling on my own stockings. I danced so hard the stereo skipped, Jagger forced to stutter in throaty monosyllables, gulping repetitions. I whirled and circled, threw my head from side to side until I could feel the baffled blood, brought my hair up off my neck and held it with both hands.

Micah watched me dance. His body made an inverted-S upon my bed, his head propped by the pillar of his own arm. The expression on his face was the same as he'd had talking with my father, that look of deference, of fawn-eyed yielding. But I could see there was something hidden.

140 With white-knuckled fingers, I undid the buttons of my sweater and ripped my shirt lifting it off my head. I danced out of my skirt and underthings, kicking them into the corner, danced until the song was over, until I was soaked with sweat and burning—and then I jumped him.

It was like the taste of food after a day's starvation—unexpectedly strong and substantial. Micah responded to my fury, met it with his own mysterious passion; it was like a brawl, a fight, with something at stake that neither of us wanted to lose. Afterward we sat up in bed and listened to *Ode to Joy* while Micah, who had a surplus supply of chopsticks lying around the room, did his Leonard Bernstein[4] impersonation. Later, we went out for a late-night snack to All-Star Dairy and Micah admitted to me that he was in love.

. . .

My father refused to attend the wedding. He liked Micah, but he did not want me to marry a Caucasian. It became a joke I would tell people. Korean custom, I said, to give the bride away four months before the ceremony.

Micah became a high-school biology teacher. I am an associate dean of students at the local college. We have two children. When Micah tells the story of our courtship, he tells it with great self-deprecation and humor. He makes it sound as though he were crazy to ever consider becoming a monk. "Think of it," he tells our kids. "Your dad."

Lately I've taken to reading books about Buddhism. Siddhartha Gotama was thirty-five years old when he sat under the Bodhi-tree on the bank of the river Neranjara and gained Enlightenment. Sometimes, when I see my husband looking at me across the breakfast table, or walking toward me from the other side of the room, I catch a look of distress on his face, a blinking confusion, as though he cannot remember who I am. I have happened on him a few times, on a Sunday when he has disappeared from the house, sitting on a bench with the newspaper in his lap staring across the town common, so immersed in his thoughts that he is not roused by my calling of his name.

145 I remember the first time I saw him, the tremendous stillness he carried, the contentment in his face. I remember how he looked on the rocks by that pond, like a pioneer in a new land, and I wonder if he regrets, as I do, the loss of his implausible faith. Does he miss the sound of the prayer drum, the call to an inner life without the configuration of desire? I think of my father, running a sock under heated water thousands of miles from home, as yet unaware of the daughter he will raise with the same hopeful, determined, and ultimately futile, effort. I remember the way I used to play around with koans, and I wonder, "What is the sound of a life not lived?"

[1996]

[4]**Leonard Bernstein** American composer and conductor (1918–1990), known for his highly dramatic style of leading an orchestra.

Joining the Conversation: Critical Thinking and Writing

1. Halfway through the story, in paragraph 43, the narrator says, "I think it was then I fell in love with him. . . ." Why does she fall in love with Micah at this moment? And how does she describe the feeling of love?
2. When we return to the beginning of the story—first, the Frisbee game, and, second, the scene at the dining hall—what signs do we see of the kind of relationship that will develop between the narrator and Micah? What do we learn about each of these persons and about what might draw them to one another?
3. What is your response to the narrator's father? Why do you think that Min chose to make him a scientist? Is our response to the father meant to be critical? Highly critical? Or, a lot or a little sympathetic? Please present your responses in the form of a good argument.
4. Do you agree with Min's decision to include the brief scene with the narrator's former boyfriend, Graham, paragraphs 61–65? Would you agree that this scene is important for the meaning of the story as a whole, or would you recommend that it be omitted?
5. Describe what happens during the love-making scene, beginning with paragraph 135. What is the narrator trying to do through her dance, and why? What leads Micah at last to respond to her?
6. Do sexual scenes in literature make you uncomfortable? Is there a right and a wrong way, in your view, to present such scenes? What arguments can you offer to support your position?

POEMS

EMMA LAZARUS

Emma Lazarus (1849–1887) was of German-Jewish descent on her mother's side, and of Sephardic descent on her father's side. (Sephardic Jews trace their ancestry back to Spain under Moslem rule, before the Jews were expelled by the Christians in 1492.)

In 1883 a committee was formed to raise funds for a pedestal for the largest statue in the world, Liberty Enlightening the People, *to be installed on a small island in New York Harbor. Authors were asked to donate manuscripts that were then auctioned to raise money. Emma Lazarus, keenly aware of ancient persecutions and of contemporary Jewish refugees fleeing Russian persecutions, contributed the following poem. It was read when the statue was unveiled in 1886, and the words of Liberty, spoken in the last five lines, were embossed on a plaque inside the pedestal.*

For the ancients, a colossus was a statue larger than life. "The brazen giant of Greek fame," mentioned in Lazarus's first line, was a statue of the sun god, erected in the harbor of the Greek island of Rhodes, celebrating the island's success in resisting the Macedonians in 305–304 B.C.E. More than 100 feet tall, it stood in the harbor until it toppled during an earthquake in 225 B.C.E. In later years its size became mythical; it was said to have straddled the harbor (Lazarus speaks of "limbs astride from land to land"), so that ships supposedly entered the harbor by sailing between its legs.

In Lazarus's poem, the "imprisoned lightning" (line 5) in the torch is electricity. The harbor is said to be "air-bridged" because in 1883, the year of the poem, the Brooklyn Bridge was completed, connecting Brooklyn with New York. (These are the "twin cities" of the poem.)

The New Colossus

Not like the brazen giant of Greek fame,
With conquering limbs astride from land to land;
Here at our sea-washed, sunset gates shall stand
A mighty woman with a torch, whose flame
Is the imprisoned lightning, and her name
Mother of Exiles. From her beacon-hand
Glows world-wide welcome; her mild eyes command
The air-bridged harbor that twin cities frame.
"Keep, ancient lands, your storied pomp!" cries she
With silent lips. "Give me your tired, your poor,
Your huddled masses yearning to breathe free,
The wretched refuse of your teeming shore.
Send these, the homeless, tempest-tost to me,
I lift my lamp beside the golden door!"

[1883]

Joining the Conversation: Critical Thinking and Writing

1. Does this poem have a message? In a paragraph, please state what this message is.
2. Do you find this poem to be clear, or confusing, or both? Please point to details that either are clear in their meaning or that are confusing to you.
3. Emma Lazarus uses the word "new" in her title. What is the relationship between the old Colossus and this new one?
4. Have you ever visited the Statue of Liberty? If you have, describe this experience. If you have not, please explain why you have not, and explain too why you do or do not intend to visit this site sometime soon.
5. A prominent historian has said that the Statue of Liberty is the nation's "greatest monument to the true meaning of America." Do you agree with this statement? Please argue for or against it.

THOMAS BAILEY ALDRICH

Thomas Bailey Aldrich (1836–1907) was born in Portsmouth, New Hampshire. He wrote poetry from his youth to his old age, and he also wrote short stories and essays, but his literary career was chiefly that of a journalist and an editor. (One magazine that he edited from 1881 to 1890, Atlantic Monthly, *continues to be important.) As the following poem indicates, Aldrich was deeply conservative. The view that he here expresses is known as Nativism, or the Nativist view, favoring the interests of established inhabitants rather than those of immigrants and newcomers.*

The Unguarded Gates

Wide open and unguarded stand our gates,
And through them press a wild, a motley throng—
Men from the Volga and the Tartar steppes,
Featureless figures of the Hoang-Ho,
Malayan, Scythian, Teuton, Kelt, and Slav,
Flying the Old World's poverty and scorn;
These bringing with them unknown gods and rites,
Those tiger passions, here to stretch their claws.
In street and alley what strange tongues are these,
Accents of menace alien to our air,
Voices that once the tower of Babel knew!

O, Liberty, white goddess, is it well
To leave the gate unguarded? On thy breast
Fold sorrow's children, soothe the hurts of fate,
Lift the downtrodden, but with the hand of steel
Stay those who to thy sacred portals come
To waste the fight of freedom. Have a care
Lest from thy brow the clustered stars be torn
And trampled in the dust. For so of old
The thronging Goth and Vandal trampled Rome,
And where the temples of the Caesars stood
The lean wolf unmolested made her lair.

[1885]

Joining the Conversation: Critical Thinking and Writing

1. Using a good dictionary and other Internet resources or reference books, identify the terms in lines 3, 4, 5, 11, 20, and 21.
2. Do you think that this poet is a racist? Please explain.
3. Could someone say, "Aldrich is a racist, but he is making a defensible point"? What is Aldrich's point? In the poem does he argue effectively for it?
4. How would Aldrich respond to Lazarus's poem? How would she respond to him?

JOSEPH BRUCHAC III

Joseph Bruchac III (the name is pronounced "Brewshack") was born in Saratoga Springs, New York, in 1942, and educated at Cornell University, Syracuse University, and Union Graduate School. Like many other Americans, he has a multicultural ethnic heritage, and he includes Native Americans as well as Slovaks among his ancestors. Bruchac, who has taught in Ghana and also in the United States, has chiefly worked as an editor and educator. He lives in Saratoga County, New York.

"Much of my writing and my life," Bruchac says, "relates to the problem of being an American. . . . While in college I was active in Civil Rights work and in the antiwar movement. . . .

I went to Africa to teach—but more than that to be taught. It showed me many things. How much we have as Americans and take for granted. How much our eyes refuse to see because they are blinded to everything in a man's face except his color."

Slavic women arrive at Ellis Island in the winter of 1910. (Brown Brothers)

Ellis Island

Beyond the red brick of Ellis Island
where the two Slovak children
who became my grandparents
waited the long days of quarantine,
after leaving the sickness,
the old Empires of Europe,
a Circle Line ship slips easily
on its way to the island
of the tall woman, green
as dreams of forests and meadows
waiting for those who'd worked
a thousand years
yet never owned their own.

Like millions of others,
I too come to this island,
nine decades the answerer
of dreams.

Yet only one part of my blood loves that memory.
Another voice speaks
of native lands
within this nation.
Lands invaded
when the earth became owned.
Lands of those who followed
the changing Moon,
knowledge of the seasons
in their veins.

[1978]

Joining the Conversation: Critical Thinking and Writing

1. The poet tells of a visit he made to Ellis Island. What did he learn there?
2. Do you think that the poem would be effective if it ended at line 17? If so, effective in what way?
3. How is the effect of the poem changed by lines 18–27?
4. Should every American be required to visit Ellis Island? What would be the benefit of such a requirement?
5. Consider this question, in relation to the poem: Should America be celebrated or criticized? Is Bruchac doing one or the other, or both?

AURORA LEVINS MORALES

Aurora Levins Morales, born in Puerto Rico in 1954, came to the United States with her family in 1967. She has lived in Chicago and New Hampshire and now lives in the San Francisco Bay Area. A member of the Latina Feminist Group, Levins Morales has published stories, essays, prose poems, and poems.

Child of the Americas

I am a child of the Americas,
a light-skinned mestiza of the Caribbean,
a child of many diaspora,° born into this continent at a crossroads.

I am a U.S. Puerto Rican Jew,
a product of the ghettos of New York I have never known.

3 diaspora literally, "scattering"; the term is used especially to refer to the dispersion of the Jews outside of Israel from the sixth century B.C.E., when they were exiled to Babylonia, to the present time.

An immigrant and the daughter and granddaughter of immigrants.
I speak English with passion: it's the tongue of my consciousness,
a flashing knife blade of crystal, my tool, my craft.

I am Caribeña,° island grown. Spanish is in my flesh,
ripples from my tongue, lodges in my hips:
the language of garlic and mangoes,
the singing in my poetry, the flying gestures of my hands.

I am of Latinoamerica, rooted in the history of my continent:
I speak from that body.

I am not african. African is in me, but I cannot return.
I am not taína.° Taíno is in me, but there is no way back.
I am not european. Europe lives in me, but I have no home there.

I am new. History made me. My first language was spanglish.°
I was born at the crossroads
and I am whole.

[1986]

9 Caribeña Caribbean woman. **16 taína** The Taínos were the Indian tribe native to Puerto Rico. **18 spanglish** a mixture of Spanish and English.

Joining the Conversation: Critical Thinking and Writing

1. In the first stanza, Levins Morales speaks of herself as "a child of many diaspora." *Diaspora* often means "a scattering," or "a dispersion of a homogeneous people." What does it refer to here?
2. In the second stanza, Levins Morales says that she is "a product of the ghettos of New York I have never known." What does she apparently refer to?
3. What attitude does "Child of the Americas" have toward the writer's ethnicity? What words or lines particularly communicate it?

GLORIA ANZALDÚA

Gloria Anzaldúa, a seventh-generation American, was born in 1942 on a ranch settlement in Texas. When she was 11 her family moved to Hargill, Texas, and in the next few years the family traveled as migrant workers between Texas and Arkansas. In 1969 she earned a BA from Pan American University, and later she earned an MA from the University of Texas at Austin and did further graduate work at the University of California, Santa Cruz. Anzaldúa taught at the University of Texas at Austin; San Francisco State University; Oakes College at the University of California, Santa Cruz; and Vermont College. She died in 2004.

We give a poem from Anzaldúa's Borderlands: La Frontera—The New Mestiza *(1987), a work that combines seven prose essays with poems. For Anzaldúa—a woman, a Latina, and a lesbian—the "borderlands" of course are spiritual as well as geographic.*

To Live in the Borderlands Means You

To live in the Borderlands means you
are neither *hispana india negra española*
ni gabacha,° *eres mestiza, mulata,*° half-breed
caught in the crossfire between camps
while carrying all five races on your back
not knowing which side to turn to, run from;

To live in the Borderlands means knowing
that the *india* in you, betrayed for 500 years,
is no longer speaking to you,
that *mexicanas* call you *rajetas,*°
that denying the Anglo inside you
is as bad as having denied the Indian or Black;

Cuando vives en la frontera°
people walk through you, the wind steals your voice,
you're a *burra, buey,*° scapegoat,
forerunner of a new race,
half and half—both woman and man, neither—
a new gender;

To live in the Borderlands means to
put *chile* in the borscht,
eat whole wheat *tortillas,*
speak Tex-Mex with a Brooklyn accent;
be stopped by *la migra*° at the border checkpoints;

Living in the Borderlands means you fight hard to
resist the gold elixer beckoning from the bottle,
the pull of the gun barrel,
the rope crushing the hollow of your throat;

In the Borderlands
you are the battleground
where enemies are kin to each other;
you are at home, a stranger,
the border disputes have been settled
the volley of shots have shattered the truce
you are wounded, lost in action
dead, fighting back;

To live in the Borderlands means
the mill with the razor white teeth wants to shred off
your olive-red skin, crush out the kernel, your heart
pound you pinch you roll you out
smelling like white bread but dead;

2–3 neither . . . ***mulata*** neither Spanish indian black Spanish woman, nor white, you are mixed, a mixed breed. **3 *gabacha*** a Chicano term for a white woman. **10 *rajetas*** literally, "split," that is having betrayed your word (author's note). **13 *Cuando . . . frontera*** when you live in the borderlands. **15 *burra, buey*** donkey, oxen (author's note). **23 *la migra*** immigration officials.

To survive the Borderlands
  you must live *sin fronteras*°
  be a crossroads.

[1987]

42 ***sin fronteras*** without borders.

Joining the Conversation: Critical Thinking and Writing

1. When you first read the title, what was your response to it? After studying the poem, has your understanding of the title changed?
2. What is your response to Anzaldúa's use of Spanish terms? Why might she have wanted this mix of English and Spanish languages?
3. In no more than a paragraph, summarize what it means "to live in the Borderlands."
4. Is the tone of the poem celebratory, despairing, or something else? Does the tone change as the poem unfolds?
5. From your own personal background and experience, do you feel a special connection to Anzaldúa's poem? If you do not have such a background and experience, how does this fact affect your response to the poem?
6. Do some people live more in the Borderlands than do others? Why is that?

JIMMY SANTIAGO BACA

Jimmy Santiago Baca, of Chicano and Apache descent, was born in 1952. When he was 2 his parents divorced, and a grandparent brought him up until he was 5, when he was placed in an orphanage in New Mexico. He ran away when he was 11, lived on the streets, took drugs, and at the age of 20 was convicted of drug possession. In prison he taught himself to read and write, and he began to compose poetry. A fellow inmate urged him to send some poems to Mother Jones *magazine, and the work was accepted. In 1979 Louisiana State University Press published a book of his poems,* Immigrants in Our Own Land. *He has since published several other books.*

So Mexicans Are Taking Jobs from Americans

O Yes? Do they come on horses
with rifles, and say,
      Ese gringo,° gimmee your job?
And do you, gringo, take off your ring,
drop your wallet into a blanket
spread over the ground, and walk away?

3 Ese gringo Hey, whitey.

I hear Mexicans are taking your jobs away.
Do they sneak into town at night,
and as you're walking home with a whore,
do they mug you, a knife at your throat,
saying, I want your job?

Even on TV, an asthmatic leader
crawls turtle heavy, leaning on an assistant,
and from a nest of wrinkles on his face,
a tongue paddles through flashing waves
of lightbulbs, of cameramen, rasping
"They're taking our jobs away."

Well, I've gone about trying to find them,
asking just where the hell are these fighters.

The rifles I hear sound in the night
are white farmers shooting blacks and browns
whose ribs I see jutting out
and starving children,
I see the poor marching for a little work,
I see small white farmers selling out
to clean-suited farmers living in New York,
who've never been on a farm,
don't know the look of a hoof or the smell
of a woman's body bending all day long in fields.

I see this, and I hear only a few people
got all the money in this world, the rest
count their pennies to buy bread and butter.

Below that cool green sea of money,
millions and millions of people fight to live,
search for pearls in the darkest depths
of their dreams, hold their breath for years
trying to cross poverty to just having something.

The children are dead already. We are killing them,
that is what America should be saying;
on TV, in the streets, in offices, should be saying,
"We aren't giving the children a chance to live."

Mexicans are taking our jobs, they say instead.
What they really say is, let them die,
and the children too.

[1979]

Joining the Conversation: Critical Thinking and Writing

1. When you read the title, what was your response to it? What happened to this first response as you read and then reread the poem?
2. To whom is the poem addressed?
3. Is the speaker angry? If so, is the speaker too angry?

4. Please identify and comment on the section of the poem that you think is the most effective. Is the poem effective throughout, or is there a section or are there sections where, in your view, it is not?
5. One critic, in praise of the poem, has said that in it Baca "uses words as a weapon." Please explain what you think this phrase means. Does it strike you as a good insight about the poem? Please point to evidence in the text to support your argument.
6. Prepare an essay of 1–2 pages in which you argue that Baca's poem should be included on the required reading list for first-year high school students. Then, prepare an essay of the same length in which you argue that it should not.

Langston Hughes

Langston Hughes (1902–1967) was born in Joplin, Missouri. He lived part of his youth in Mexico, spent a year at Columbia University, served as a merchant seaman, and worked in a Paris nightclub. Soon he received support from Alain Locke, a strong advocate of African American literature to whom Hughes had shown some of his poems. Hughes went on to publish poetry, fiction, plays, essays, and biographies.

Theme for English B

The instructor said,

Go home and write
a page tonight.
And let that page come out of you—
Then, it will be true.

I wonder if it's that simple?
I am twenty-two, colored, born in Winston-Salem.
I went to school there, then Durham, then here
to this college on the hill above Harlem.
I am the only colored student in my class.
The steps from the hill lead down into Harlem,
through a park, then I cross St. Nicholas,
Eighth Avenue, Seventh, and I come to the Y,
the Harlem Branch Y, where I take the elevator
up to my room, sit down, and write this page:

It's not easy to know what is true for you or me
at twenty-two, my age. But I guess I'm what
I feel and see and hear, Harlem, I hear you:
hear you, hear me—we two—you, me, talk on this page.
(I hear New York, too.) Me—who?
Well, I like to eat, sleep, drink, and be in love.
I like to work, read, learn, and understand life.
I like a pipe for a Christmas present,
or records—Bessie,° bop, or Bach.
I guess being colored doesn't make me *not* like
the same things other folks like who are other races.

24 Bessie Bessie Smith (1898?–1937), African American blues singer.

So will my page be colored that I write?
Being me, it will not be white.
But it will be
a part of you, instructor.
You are white—
yet a part of me, as I am a part of you.
That's American.
Sometimes perhaps you don't want to be a part of me.
Nor do I often want to be a part of you.
But we are, that's true!
As I learn from you,
I guess you learn from me—
although you're older—and white—
and somewhat more free.

This is my page for English B.

[1949]

Joining the Conversation: Critical Thinking and Writing

1. The teacher instructs the students (line 4) to "let that page come out of you," and adds, "Then, it will be true" (6). Does it follow that what we let "come" out of us is "true"? If you were a student, what would be your response to the teacher's instruction?
2. In lines 21–24 Hughes specifies some of the things he likes—things that many people who are not black doubtless also like. Why, then, does he say (line 28) that his page "will not be white"?
3. Pretend that you are the English B instructor who received Hughes's theme. What comment (about 250 words) do you put at the end of the theme?
4. Aside from the statement that he is a "colored" student (10, 27) from Harlem (9, 11, 14, 18), is there anything particularly African American about this poem? Putting aside these references, might the poem have been written by an Asian American, or (say) an American of Middle Eastern descent?
5. In line 10 the speaker says he is "the only colored student in [his] class." If you have ever been the only student of your race or religion or ethnic background or sex in a group, in an essay of 250–500 words set forth the feelings you had, and the feelings you now have about the experience.

Pat Parker

Pat Parker (1944–1989), author of several books of poems and essays, was a founder of the Black Women's Revolutionary Council in 1980, and a medical co-ordinator at the Oakland Feminist Women's Health Center.

For the White Person Who Wants to Know How to Be My Friend

The first thing you do is to forget that i'm Black.
Second, you must never forget that i'm Black.

You should be able to dig Aretha,°
but don't play her every time i come over.
And if you decide to play Beethoven—don't tell me
his life story. They made us take music appreciation too.

Eat soul food if you like it, but don't expect me
to locate your restaurants
or cook it for you.

And if some Black person insults you,
mugs you, rapes your sister, rapes you,
rips your house or is just being an ass—
please, do not apologize to me
for wanting to do them bodily harm.
It makes me wonder if you're foolish.

And even if you really believe Blacks are better lovers than
whites—don't tell me. I start thinking of charging stud fees.

In other words—if you really want to be my friend—*don't*
make a labor of it. I'm lazy. Remember.

[1978]

3 Aretha Aretha Franklin, born in 1942, African American singer of blues and rock.

Joining the Conversation: Critical Thinking and Writing

1. The first two lines are contradictory. What sense do you make out of them?
2. Explain lines 4–5.
3. What stereotypes of African Americans does Parker evoke in the last two stanzas? What is her point?
4. If you have ever been involved in an episode of the sort that Parker mentions in her second stanza, in an essay of 500 words narrate the experience and offer a reflection on it.

Mitsuye Yamada

Mitsuye Yamada, the daughter of Japanese immigrants to the United States, was born in Japan in 1923, during her mother's return visit to her native land. Yamada was raised in Seattle, but in 1942 she and her family were incarcerated and then relocated in a camp in Idaho, when Executive Order 9066 gave military authorities the right to remove any and all persons from "military areas." In 1955 she became an American citizen. Later, she became a member of the Asian American Studies Program at the University of California at Irvine. She is the author of poems and stories.

Dorothea Lange. "Grandfather and Grandchildren Awaiting Evacuation Bus." (War Relocation Authority/The National Archives)

To the Lady

The one in San Francisco who asked:
Why did the Japanese Americans let
the government put them in
those camps without protest?

Come to think of it I
should've run off to Canada
should've hijacked a plane to Algeria
should've pulled myself up from my
bra straps
and kicked'm in the groin
should've bombed a bank
should've tried self-immolation
should've holed myself up in a
woodframe house
and let you watch me
burn up on the six o'clock news
should've run howling down the street
naked and assaulted you at breakfast
by AP wirephoto

should've screamed bloody murder
like Kitty Genovese°

Then
YOU would've
come to my aid in shining armor
laid yourself across the railroad track
marched on Washington
tatooed a Star of David on your arm
written six million enraged
letters to Congress

But we didn't draw the line
anywhere
law and order Executive Order 9066°
social order moral order internal order

You let'm
I let'm
All are punished.

[1976]

21 Kitty Genovese In 1964 Kitty Genovese of Kew Gardens, New York, was stabbed to death when she left her car and walked toward her home. Thirty-eight persons heard her screams, but no one came to her assistance. **32 Executive Order 9066** an authorization, signed in 1941 by President Franklin D. Roosevelt, allowing military authorities to relocate Japanese and Japanese Americans who resided on the Pacific Coast of the United States.

Joining the Conversation: Critical Thinking and Writing

1. Has the lady's question (lines 2–4) ever crossed your mind? If so, what answers did you think of?
2. What, in effect, is the speaker really saying in lines 5–21? And in lines 24–29?
3. Explain the last line.

NILA NORTHSUN

nila northSun was born in 1951 in Schurz, Nevada, of Shoshone-Chippewa stock. She studied at the California State University campuses at Hayward and Humboldt and the University of Montana at Missoula, beginning as a psychology major but switching to art history, specializing in Native American art. She is a photographer, a teacher, and the author of three books of poetry.

Moving Camp Too Far

i can't speak of
many moons
moving camp on travois°

1 travois a frame slung between trailing poles that are pulled by a horse. Plains Indians used the device to transport their goods.

i can't tell of
  the last great battle
  counting coup° or
  taking scalp
i don't know what it
  was to hunt buffalo
  or do the ghost dance
but
i can see an eagle
  almost extinct
  on slurpee plastic cups
i can travel to powwows
  in campers & winnebagos
i can eat buffalo meat
  at the tourist burger stand
i can dance to indian music
  rock-n-roll hey-a-hey-o
i can
  & unfortunately
  i do

[1977]

6 counting coup recounting one's exploits in battle.

Joining the Conversation: Critical Thinking and Writing

1. What is the speaker's attitude toward the world she has lost? What is her attitude toward herself?
2. The first ten lines are presented in a negative form, and the final ten in a positive form. How would you respond to someone who argued, "This poem is too formulaic"?

PLAYS

LUIS VALDEZ

Luis Valdez was born into a family of migrant farm workers in Delano, California, in 1940. After completing high school he entered San José State College on a scholarship. He wrote his first plays while still an undergraduate, and after receiving his degree (in English and drama) from San José in 1964 he joined the San Francisco Mime Troupe, a left-wing group that performed in parks and streets. Revolutionary in technique as well as in political content, the Mime Troupe rejected the traditional forms of drama and instead drew on the traditions of the circus and the carnival.

In 1965 Valdez returned to Delano, where Cesar Chavez had organized a strike of farm workers and a boycott against grape growers. It was here, under the wing of the United Farm Workers, that he established El Teatro Campesino (the Farm

Workers' Theater), which at first specialized in doing short, improvised, satirical skits called actos. When the teatro moved to Del Rey, California, it expanded its repertoire beyond farm issues, and it became part of a cultural center that gave workshops (in English and Spanish) in such subjects as history, drama, and politics.

The actos, performed by amateurs on college campuses and on flatbed trucks and at the edges of vineyards, were highly political. Making use of stereotypes (the boss, the scab), the actos sought not to present the individual thoughts of a gifted playwright but to present the social vision of ordinary people—the pueblo*—though it was acknowledged that in an oppressive society the playwright might have to help guide the people to see their own best interests.*

Valdez moved from actos *to* mitos *(myths)—plays that drew on Aztec mythology, Mexican folklore, and Christianity—and then to* Zoot Suit, *a play that ran for many months in California and that became the first Mexican American play to be produced on Broadway. More recently he wrote and directed a hit movie,* La Bamba, *and in 1991 received an award from the AT&T Foundation for his musical,* Bandido, *presented by El Teatro Campesino. Valdez teaches at California State University, Monterey Bay.*

Los Vendidos *was written in 1967, when Ronald Reagan, a conservative Republican, was governor of California.*

Los Vendidos[1]

LIST OF CHARACTERS

HONEST SANCHO
SECRETARY
FARM WORKER
JOHNNY
REVOLUCIONARIO
MEXICAN-AMERICAN

SCENE: *Honest Sancho's Used Mexican Lot and Mexican Curio Shop. Three models are on display in Honest* SANCHO*'s shop: to the right, there is a* REVOLUCIONARIO, *complete with sombrero, carrilleras,*[2] *and carabina 30-30. At center, on the floor, there is the* FARM WORKER *under a broad straw sombrero. At stage left is the* PACHUCO,[3] *filero*[4] *in hand.*

[*Honest* SANCHO *is moving among his models, dusting them off and preparing for another day of business.*]

SANCHO: Bueno, bueno, mis monos, vamos a ver a quien vendemos ahora, ¿no?[5] [*To audience.*] ¡Quihubo! I'm Honest Sancho and this is my shop. Antes fui contratista pero ahora logré tener mi negocito.[6] All I need now is a customer. [*A bell rings offstage.*] Ay, a customer!

SECRETARY: [*Entering*] Good morning, I'm Miss Jiménez from—

SANCHO: ¡Ah, una chicana! Welcome, welcome Señorita Jiménez.

SECRETARY: [*Anglo pronunciation*] JIM-enez.

[1]**Los Vendidos** the sellouts. [2]**carrilleras** cartridge belts. [3]**Pachuco** an urban tough guy. [4]**filero** blade. [5]**Bueno . . . ¿no?** Well, well darlings, let's see who we can sell now, O.K.? [6]**Antes . . . negocito** I used to be a contractor, but now I've succeeded in having my little business.

SANCHO: ¿Qué?

SECRETARY: My name is Miss JIM-enez. Don't you speak English? What's wrong with you?

SANCHO: Oh, nothing, Señorita JIM-enez. I'm here to help you.

SECRETARY: That's better. As I was starting to say, I'm a secretary from Governor Reagan's office, and we're looking for a Mexican type for the administration.

SANCHO: Well, you come to the right place, lady. This is Honest Sancho's Used Mexican lot, and we got all types here. Any particular type you want?

SECRETARY: Yes, we were looking for somebody suave—

SANCHO: Suave.

SECRETARY: Debonair.

SANCHO: De buen aire.

SECRETARY: Dark.

SANCHO: Prieto.

SECRETARY: But of course not too dark.

SANCHO: No muy prieto.

SECRETARY: Perhaps, beige.

SANCHO: Beige, just the tone. Así como cafecito con leche,[7] ¿no?

SECRETARY: One more thing. He must be hard-working.

SANCHO: That could only be one model. Step right over here to the center of the shop, lady. [*They cross to the* FARM WORKER.] This is our standard farm worker model. As you can see, in the words of our beloved Senator George Murphy, he is "built close to the ground." Also take special notice of his four-ply Goodyear huaraches, made from the rain tire. This wide-brimmed sombrero is an extra added feature—keeps off the sun, rain, and dust.

SECRETARY: Yes, it does look durable.

SANCHO: And our farm worker model is friendly. Muy amable.[8] Watch. [*Snaps his fingers.*]

FARM WORKER [*Lifts up head*]: Buenos días, señorita. [*His head drops.*]

SECRETARY: My, he's friendly.

SANCHO: Didn't I tell you? Loves his patrones! But his most attractive feature is that he's hard working. Let me show you. [*Snaps fingers,* FARM WORKER *stands.*]

FARM WORKER: ¡El jale![9] [*He begins to work.*]

SANCHO: As you can see, he is cutting grapes.

SECRETARY: Oh, I wouldn't know.

SANCHO: He also picks cotton. [*Snap.* FARM WORKER *begins to pick cotton.*]

SECRETARY: Versatile isn't he?

SANCHO: He also picks melons. [*Snap.* FARM WORKER *picks melons.*] That's his slow speed for late in the season. Here's his fast speed. [*Snap.* FARM WORKER *picks faster.*]

SECRETARY: ¡Chihuahua! . . . I mean, goodness, he sure is a hard worker.

SANCHO [*Pulls the* FARM WORKER *to his feet*]: And that isn't the half of it. Do you see these little holes on his arms that appear to be pores? During those hot sluggish days in the field, when the vines or the branches get so entangled, it's almost impossible to move; these holes emit a certain grease that allow our model to slip and slide right through the crop with no trouble at all.

SECRETARY: Wonderful. But is he economical?

[7]**Así . . . leche** like coffee with milk. [8]**Muy amable** very friendly. [9]**¡El jale!** the job!

SANCHO: Economical? Señorita, you are looking at the Volkswagen of Mexicans. Pennies a day is all it takes. One plate of beans and tortillas will keep him going all day. That, and chile. Plenty of chile. Chile jalapeños, chile verde, chile colorado. But, of course, if you do give him chile [*Snap.* FARM WORKER *turns left face. Snap.* FARM WORKER *bends over.*] then you have to change his oil filter once a week.

SECRETARY: What about storage?

SANCHO: No problem. You know these new farm labor camps our Honorable Governor Reagan has built out by Parlier or Raisin City? They were designed with our model in mind. Five, six, seven, even ten in one of those shacks will give you no trouble at all. You can also put him in old barns, old cars, river banks. You can even leave him out in the field overnight with no worry!

SECRETARY: Remarkable.

SANCHO: And here's an added feature: Every year at the end of the season, this model goes back to Mexico and doesn't return, automatically, until next Spring.

SECRETARY: How about that. But tell me: does he speak English?

SANCHO: Another outstanding feature is that last year this model was programmed to go out on STRIKE! [*Snap.*]

FARM WORKER: ¡HUELGA! ¡HUELGA! Hermanos, sálganse de esos files.[10] [*Snap. He stops.*]

SECRETARY: No! Oh no, we can't strike in the State Capitol.

SANCHO: Well, he also scabs. [*Snap.*]

FARM WORKER: Me vendo barato, ¿y qué?[11] [*Snap.*]

SECRETARY: That's much better, but you didn't answer my question. Does he speak English?

SANCHO: Bueno . . . no, pero[12] he has other—

SECRETARY: No.

SANCHO: Other features.

SECRETARY: NO! He just won't do!

SANCHO: Okay, okay pues. We have other models.

SECRETARY: I hope so. What we need is something a little more sophisticated.

SANCHO: Sophisti—¿qué?

SECRETARY: An urban model.

SANCHO: Ah, from the city! Step right back. Over here in this corner of the shop is exactly what you're looking for. Introducing our new 1969 JOHNNY PACHUCO model! This is our fast-back model. Streamlined. Built for speed, low-riding, city life. Take a look at some of these features. Mag shoes, dual exhausts, green chartreuse paint-job, dark-tint windshield, a little poof on top. Let me just turn him on. [*Snap.* JOHNNY *walks to stage center with a pachuco bounce.*]

SECRETARY: What was that?

SANCHO: That, señorita, was the Chicano shuffle.

SECRETARY: Okay, what does he do?

SANCHO: Anything and everything necessary for city life. For instance, survival: He knife fights. [*Snap.* JOHNNY *pulls out switchblade and swings at* SECRETARY.]

[SECRETARY *screams.*]

SANCHO: He dances. [*Snap.*]

[10]**¡HUELGA! . . . files** Strike! Strike! Brothers, leave those rows. [11]**Me . . . qué?** I come cheap. So what? [12]**Bueno . . . no, pero** well, no, but.

JOHNNY [*Singing*]: "Angel Baby, my Angel Baby . . ." [*Snap.*]

SANCHO: And here's a feature no city model can be without. He gets arrested, but not without resisting, of course. [*Snap.*]

JOHNNY: ¡En la madre, la placa![13] I didn't do it! I didn't do it! [JOHNNY *turns and stands up against an imaginary wall, legs spread out, arms behind his back.*]

SECRETARY: Oh no, we can't have arrests! We must maintain law and order.

SANCHO: But he's bilingual!

SECRETARY: Bilingual?

SANCHO: Simón que yes.[14] He speaks English! Johnny, give us some English. [*Snap.*]

JOHNNY [*Comes downstage*]: Fuck-you!

SECRETARY [*Gasps*]: Oh! I've never been so insulted in my whole life!

SANCHO: Well, he learned it in your school.

SECRETARY: I don't care where he learned it.

SANCHO: But he's economical!

SECRETARY: Economical?

SANCHO: Nickels and dimes. You can keep Johnny running on hamburgers, Taco Bell tacos, Lucky Lager beer, Thunderbird wine, yesca—

SECRETARY: Yesca?

SANCHO: Mota.

SECRETARY: Mota?

SANCHO: Leños[15] . . . Marijuana. [*Snap;* JOHNNY *inhales on an imaginary joint.*]

SECRETARY: That's against the law!

JOHNNY [*Big smile, holding his breath*]: Yeah.

SANCHO: He also sniffs glue. [*Snap.* JOHNNY *inhales glue, big smile.*]

JOHNNY: That's too much man, ése.[16]

SECRETARY: No, Mr. Sancho, I don't think this—

SANCHO: Wait a minute, he has other qualities I know you'll love. For example, an inferiority complex. [*Snap.*]

JOHNNY [*To* SANCHO]: You think you're better than me, huh ése? [*Swings switchblade.*]

SANCHO: He can also be beaten and he bruises, cut him and he bleeds; kick him and he—[*He beats, bruises and kicks* PACHUCO.] would you like to try it?

SECRETARY: Oh, I couldn't.

SANCHO: Be my guest. He's a great scapegoat.

SECRETARY: No, really.

SANCHO: Please.

SECRETARY: Well, all right. Just once. [*She kicks* PACHUCO.] Oh, he's so soft.

SANCHO: Wasn't that good? Try again.

SECRETARY [*Kicks* PACHUCO]: Oh, he's so wonderful! [*She kicks him again.*]

SANCHO: Okay, that's enough, lady. You ruin the merchandise. Yes, our Johnny Pachuco model can give you many hours of pleasure. Why, the L.A.P.D. just bought twenty of these to train their rookie cops on. And talk about maintenance. Señorita, you are looking at an entirely self-supporting machine. You're never going to find our Johnny Pachuco model on the relief rolls. No, sir, this model knows how to liberate.

SECRETARY: Liberate?

[13]**¡En . . . la placa!** Wow, the cops! [14]**Simón que yes** Yea, sure. [15]**Leños** joints (marijuana).
[16]**ése** fellow.

SANCHO: He steals. [*Snap.* JOHNNY *rushes the* SECRETARY *and steals her purse.*]

JOHNNY: ¡Dame esa bolsa, vieja![17] [*He grabs the purse and runs. Snap by* SANCHO. *He stops.*]

[SECRETARY *runs after* JOHNNY *and grabs purse away from him, kicking him as she goes.*]

SECRETARY: No, no, no! We can't have any *more* thieves in the State Administration. Put him back.

SANCHO: Okay, we still got other models. Come on, Johnny, we'll sell you to some old lady. [SANCHO *takes* JOHNNY *back to his place.*]

SECRETARY: Mr. Sancho, I don't think you quite understand what we need. What we need is something that will attract the women voters. Something more traditional, more romantic.

SANCHO: Ah, a lover. [*He smiles meaningfully.*] Step right over here, señorita. Introducing our standard Revolucionario and/or Early California Bandit type. As you can see he is well-built, sturdy, durable. This is the International Harvester of Mexicans.

SECRETARY: What does he do?

SANCHO: You name it, he does it. He rides horses, stays in the mountains, crosses deserts, plains, rivers, leads revolutions, follows revolutions, kills, can be killed, serves as a martyr, hero, movie star—did I say movie star? Did you ever see *Viva Zapata? Viva Villa? Villa Rides? Pancho Villa Returns? Pancho Villa Goes Back? Pancho Villa Meets Abbott and Costello*—

SECRETARY: I've never seen any of those.

SANCHO: Well, he was in all of them. Listen to this. [*Snap.*]

REVOLUCIONARIO [*Scream*]: ¡VIVA VILLAAAAA!

SECRETARY: That's awfully loud.

SANCHO: He has a volume control. [*He adjusts volume. Snap.*]

REVOLUCIONARIO [*Mousey voice*]: ¡Viva Villa!

SECRETARY: That's better.

SANCHO: And even if you didn't see him in the movies, perhaps you saw him on TV. He makes commercials. [*Snap.*]

REVOLUCIONARIO: Is there a Frito Bandito in your house?

SECRETARY: Oh yes, I've seen that one!

SANCHO: Another feature about this one is that he is economical. He runs on raw horsemeat and tequila.

SECRETARY: Isn't that rather savage?

SANCHO: Al contrario,[18] it makes him a lover. [*Snap.*]

REVOLUCIONARIO [*To* SECRETARY]: ¡Ay, mamasota, cochota, ven pa'ca![19] [*He grabs* SECRETARY *and folds her back—Latin-Lover style.*]

SANCHO [*Snap.* REVOLUCIONARIO *goes back upright.*]: Now wasn't that nice?

SECRETARY: Well, it was rather nice.

SANCHO: And finally, there is one outstanding feature about this model I KNOW the ladies are going to love: He's a GENUINE antique! He was made in Mexico in 1910!

SECRETARY: Made in Mexico?

SANCHO: That's right. Once in Tijuana, twice in Guadalajara, three times in Cuernavaca.

[17]**¡Dame . . . vieja!** Give me that bag, old lady! [18]**Al contrario** On the contrary.
[19]**¡Ay . . . pa'ca!** Get over here!

SECRETARY: Mr. Sancho, I thought he was an American product.

SANCHO: No, but—

SECRETARY: No, I'm sorry. We can't buy anything but American-made products. He just won't do.

SANCHO: But he's an antique!

SECRETARY: I don't care. You still don't understand what we need. It's true we need Mexican models such as these, but it's more important that he be *American.*

SANCHO: American?

SECRETARY: That's right, and judging from what you've shown me, I don't think you have what we want. Well, my lunch hour's almost over: I better—

SANCHO: Wait a minute! Mexican but American?

SECRETARY: That's correct.

SANCHO: Mexican but . . . [*A sudden flash.*] AMERICAN! Yeah, I think we've got exactly what you want. He just came in today! Give me a minute. [*He exits. Talks from backstage.*] Here he is in the shop. Let me just get some papers off. There. Introducing our new 1970 Mexican-American! Ta-ra-ra-ra-ra-ra-RA-RAAA!

[SANCHO *brings out the* MEXICAN-AMERICAN *model, a clean-shaven middle-class type in a business suit, with glasses.*]

SECRETARY [*Impressed*]: Where have you been hiding this one?

SANCHO: He just came in this morning. Ain't he a beauty? Feast your eyes on him! Sturdy US STEEL frame, streamlined, modern. As a matter of fact, he is built exactly like our Anglo models except that he comes in a variety of darker shades: naugahyde, leather, or leatherette.

SECRETARY: Naugahyde.

SANCHO: Well, we'll just write that down. Yes, señorita, this model represents the apex of American engineering! He is bilingual, college educated, ambitious! Say the word "acculturate" and he accelerates. He is intelligent, well-mannered, clean—did I say clean? [*Snap.* MEXICAN-AMERICAN *raises his arm.*] Smell.

SECRETARY [*Smells*]: Old Sobaco, my favorite.

SANCHO [*Snap.* MEXICAN-AMERICAN *turns toward* SANCHO]: Eric! [*To* SECRETARY.] We call him Eric García. [*To* ERIC.] I want you to meet Miss JIM-enez, Eric.

MEXICAN-AMERICAN: Miss JIM-enez, I am delighted to make your acquaintance. [*He kisses her hand.*]

SECRETARY: Oh, my, how charming!

SANCHO: Did you feel the suction? He has seven especially engineered suction cups right behind his lips. He's a charmer all right!

SECRETARY: How about boards? Does he function on boards?

SANCHO: You name them, he is on them. Parole boards, draft boards, school boards, taco quality control boards, surf boards, two-by-fours.

SECRETARY: Does he function in politics?

SANCHO: Señorita, you are looking at a political MACHINE. Have you ever heard of the OEO, EOC, COD, WAR ON POVERTY? That's our model! Not only that, he makes political speeches.

SECRETARY: May I hear one?

SANCHO: With pleasure. [*Snap.*] Eric, give us a speech.

MEXICAN-AMERICAN: Mr. Congressman, Mr. Chairman, members of the board, honored guests, ladies and gentlemen. [SANCHO *and* SECRETARY *applaud.*] Please, please. I come before you as a Mexican-American to tell you about the problems of the Mexican. The problems of the Mexican stem from one thing and one thing alone: He's stupid. He's uneducated. He needs to stay in school.

He needs to be ambitious, forward-looking, harder-working. He needs to think American, American, American, AMERICAN, AMERICAN, AMERICAN. GOD BLESS AMERICA! GOD BLESS AMERICA! GOD BLESS AMERICA!! [*He goes out of control.*]

[SANCHO *snaps frantically and the* MEXICAN-AMERICAN *finally slumps forward, bending at the waist.*]

SECRETARY: Oh my, he's patriotic too!

SANCHO: Sí, señorita, he loves his country. Let me just make a little adjustment here. [*Stands* MEXICAN-AMERICAN *up.*]

SECRETARY: What about upkeep? Is he economical?

SANCHO: Well, no, I won't lie to you. The Mexican-American costs a little bit more, but you get what you pay for. He's worth every extra cent. You can keep him running on dry Martinis, Langendorf bread.

SECRETARY: Apple pie?

SANCHO: Only Mom's. Of course, he's also programmed to eat Mexican food on ceremonial functions, but I must warn you: an overdose of beans will plug up his exhaust.

SECRETARY: Fine! There's just one more question: HOW MUCH DO YOU WANT FOR HIM?

SANCHO: Well, I tell you what I'm gonna do. Today and today only, because you've been so sweet, I'm gonna let you steal this model from me! I'm gonna let you drive him off the lot for the simple price of—let's see taxes and license included—$15,000.

SECRETARY: Fifteen thousand DOLLARS? For a MEXICAN!

SANCHO: Mexican? What are you talking, lady? This is a Mexican-AMERICAN! We had to melt down two pachucos, a farm worker and three gabachos[20] to make this model! You want quality, but you gotta pay for it! This is no cheap runabout. He's got class!

SECRETARY: Okay, I'll take him.

SANCHO: You will?

SECRETARY: Here's your money.

SANCHO: You mind if I count it?

SECRETARY: Go right ahead.

SANCHO: Well, you'll get your pink slip in the mail. Oh, do you want me to wrap him up for you? We have a box in the back.

SECRETARY: No, thank you. The Governor is having a luncheon this afternoon, and we need a brown face in the crowd. How do I drive him?

SANCHO: Just snap your fingers. He'll do anything you want.

[SECRETARY *snaps.* MEXICAN-AMERICAN *steps forward.*]

MEXICAN-AMERICAN: RAZA QUERIDA, ¡VAMOS LEVANTANDO ARMAS PARA LIBERARNOS DE ESTOS DESGRACIADOS GABACHOS QUE NOS EXPLOTAN! VAMOS.[21]

SECRETARY: What did he say?

SANCHO: Something about lifting arms, killing white people, etc.

SECRETARY: But he's not supposed to say that!

[20]**gabachos** whites. [21]**RAZA . . . VAMOS** Beloved Raza [persons of Mexican descent], let's take up arms to liberate ourselves from those damned whites who exploit us. Let's get going.

SANCHO: Look, lady, don't blame me for bugs from the factory. He's your Mexican-American; you bought him, now drive him off the lot!

SECRETARY: But he's broken!

SANCHO: Try snapping another finger.

[SECRETARY *snaps.* MEXICAN-AMERICAN *comes to life again.*]

MEXICAN-AMERICAN: ¡ESTA GRAN HUMANIDAD HA DICHO BASTA! Y SE HA PUESTO EN MARCHA! ¡BASTA! ¡BASTA! ¡VIVA LA RAZA! ¡VIVA LA CAUSA! ¡VIVA LA HUELGA! ¡VIVAN LOS BROWN BERETS! ¡VIVAN LOS ESTUDIANTES![22] ¡CHICANO POWER!

[*The* MEXICAN-AMERICAN *turns toward the* SECRETARY, *who gasps and backs up. He keeps turning toward the* PACHUCO, FARM WORKER, *and* REVOLUCIONARIO *snapping his fingers and turning each of them on, one by one.*]

PACHUCO [*Snap. To* SECRETARY]: I'm going to get you, baby! ¡Viva La Raza!

FARM WORKER [*Snap. To* SECRETARY]. ¡Viva la huelga! ¡Viva la Huelga! ¡VIVA LA HUELGA!

REVOLUCIONARIO [*Snap. To* SECRETARY]: ¡Viva la revolución! ¡VIVA LA REVOLUCIÓN!

[*The three models join together and advance toward the* SECRETARY *who backs up and runs out of the shop screaming.* SANCHO *is at the other end of the shop holding his money in his hand. All freeze. After a few seconds of silence, the* PACHUCO *moves and stretches, shaking his arms and loosening up. The* FARM WORKER *and* REVOLUCIONARIO *do the same.* SANCHO *stays where he is, frozen to his spot.*]

JOHNNY: Man, that was a long one, ése.[23] [*Others agree with him.*]

FARM WORKER: How did we do?

JOHNNY: Perty good, look at all that lana,[24] man! [*He goes over to* SANCHO *and removes the money from his hand.* SANCHO *stays where he is.*]

REVOLUCIONARIO: En la madre, look at all the money.

JOHNNY: We keep this up, we're going to be rich.

FARM WORKER: They think we're machines.

REVOLUCIONARIO: Burros.

JOHNNY: Puppets.

MEXICAN-AMERICAN: The only thing I don't like is—how come I always got to play the godamn Mexican-American?

JOHNNY: That's what you get for finishing high school.

FARM WORKER: How about our wages, ése?

JOHNNY: Here it comes right now. $3,000 for you, $3,000 for you, $3,000 for you, and $3,000 for me. The rest we put back into the business.

MEXICAN-AMERICAN: Too much, man. Heh, where you vatos[25] going tonight?

FARM WORKER: I'm going over to Concha's. There's a party.

JOHNNY: Wait a minute, vatos. What about our salesman? I think he needs an oil job.

REVOLUCIONARIO: Leave him to me.

[22]**¡ESTA . . . ESTUDIANTES!** This great mass of humanity has said enough! And it has begun to march. Enough! Enough! Long live La Raza! Long live the Cause! Long live the strike! Long live the Brown Berets! Long live the students! [23]**ése** man. [24]**lana** money. [25]**vatos** guys.

[*The* PACHUCO, FARM WORKER, *and* MEXICAN-AMERICAN *exit, talking loudly about their plans for the night. The* REVOLUCIONARIO *goes over to* SANCHO, *removes his derby hat and cigar, lifts him up and throws him over his shoulder.* SANCHO *hangs loose, lifeless.*]

REVOLUCIONARIO [*To audience*]: He's the best model we got! ¡Ajua![26]

[*Exit.*]

THE END

[1967]

[26]**¡Ajua!** Wow!

Joining the Conversation: Critical Thinking and Writing

1. If you are an Anglo (shorthand for a Caucasian with traditional northern European values), do you find the play deeply offensive? Why, or why not? If you are a Mexican American, do you find the play entertaining—or do you find parts of it offensive? What might Anglos enjoy in the play, and what might Mexican Americans find offensive? Set forth your views in a detailed argument.
2. What stereotypes of Mexican Americans are presented here? At the end of the play, what image of the Mexican American is presented? How does it compare with the stereotypes?
3. If you are a member of some other minority group, in a few sentences indicate how *Los Vendidos* might be adapted into a play about that group.
4. Putting aside the politics of the play (and your own politics), what do you think are the strengths of *Los Vendidos?* What do you think are the weaknesses?
5. The play was written in 1967. Do you find it dated? If not, why not? Please point to specific passages to support your analysis and argument.
6. In 1971 when *Los Vendidos* was produced by El Teatro de la Esperanza, the group altered the ending by having the men decide to use the money to build a community center. Evaluate this ending.
7. When the play was videotaped by KNBC in Los Angeles for broadcast in 1973, Valdez changed the ending. In the revised version we discover that a scientist (played by Valdez) masterminds the operation, placing Mexican American models wherever there are persons of Mexican descent. These models soon will become Chicanos (as opposed to persons with Anglo values) and will aid rather than work against their fellows. Evaluate this ending.
8. In his short essay "The Actos," Valdez says, "Actos: Inspire the audience to social action. Illuminate specific points about social problems. Satirize the opposition. Show or hint at a solution. Express what people are feeling." How many of these do you think *Los Vendidos* does?
9. Many people assume that politics gets in the way of serious art. That is, they assume that artists ought to be concerned with issues that transcend politics. Does this point make any sense to you? Why, or why not?

LORRAINE HANSBERRY

Lorraine Hansberry (1930–1965) was born in Chicago, Illinois, to middle-class black parents who lived on the city's South Side. When she was still a child, her father was barred from purchasing a house in a white neighborhood. He sued and pursued the case all the way to the Supreme Court, which ruled in his favor. Hansberry attended the University of Wisconsin as an undergraduate. Following college, she pursued a career as a painter studying at the Art Institute of Chicago and in Mexico before she decided to move to New York to pursue her interest in writing. There she wrote for Freedom, *a magazine founded by the great singer-actor turned political activist, Paul Robeson. When her first play,* A Raisin in the Sun, *premiered at the Ethel Barrymore Theater in 1959, it was the first play written by an African-American woman to be performed on Broadway. She wrote only one other play,* The Sign in Sidney Brustein's Window *(1965), before she died of cancer at the age of thirty-four. The title of* A Raisin in the Sun *is taken from the poem "A Dream Deferred," by Langston Hughes.*

The 1959 opening night cast for the Broadway production of *A Raisin in the Sun* included Sidney Poitier, Claudia MacNeil, Ruby Dee, Diana Sands, Louis Gossett Jr., Ivan Dixon, Glynn Turman, John Fielder, Lonne Elder III, Ed Hall and Douglas Turner Ward.

A Raisin in the Sun

CHARACTERS IN ORDER OF APPEARANCE

RUTH YOUNGER, *Walter's wife, about thirty*
TRAVIS YOUNGER, *her son and Walter's*
WALTER LEE YOUNGER, *(brother) Ruth's husband, mid-thirties*
BENEATHA YOUNGER, *Walter's sister, about twenty*
LENA YOUNGER, *(Mama) mother of Walter and Beneatha*
JOSEPH ASAGAI, *Nigerian, Beneatha's suitor*
GEORGE MURCHISON, *Beneatha's date, wealthy*
KARL LINDNER, *white, chairman of the Clybourne Park New Neighbors Orientation Committee*
BOBO, *one of Walter's business partners*
MOVING MEN

The action of the play is set in Chicago's South Side, sometime between World War II and the present.

ACT I
SCENE 1. *Friday morning*
SCENE 2. *The following morning*

ACT II
SCENE 1. *Later, the same day*
SCENE 2. *Friday night, a few weeks later*
SCENE 3. *Moving day, one week later*

ACT III
An hour later

ACT I

SCENE 1

The Younger living room would be a comfortable and well-ordered room if it were not for a number of indestructible contradictions to this state of being. Its furnishings are typical and undistinguished and their primary feature now is that they have clearly had to accommodate the living of too many people for too many years—and they are tired. Still, we can see that at some time, a time probably no longer remembered by the family (except perhaps for MAMA*) the furnishings of this room were actually selected with care and love and even hope—and brought to this apartment and arranged with taste and pride.*

That was a long time ago. Now the once loved pattern of the couch upholstery has to fight to show itself from under acres of crocheted doilies and couch covers which have themselves finally come to be more important than the upholstery. And here a table or a chair has been moved to disguise the worn places in the carpet; but the carpet has fought back by showing its weariness, with depressing uniformity, elsewhere on its surface.

Weariness has, in fact, won in this room. Everything has been polished, washed, sat on, used, scrubbed too often. All pretenses but living itself have long since vanished from the very atmosphere of this room.

Moreover, a section of this room, for it is not really a room unto itself, though the landlord's lease would make it seem so, slopes backward to provide a small kitchen area, where the family prepares the meals that are eaten in the living room proper, which must also serve as dining room. The single window that has been provided for these "two" rooms is located in this kitchen area. The sole natural light the family may enjoy in the course of a day is only that which fights its way through this little window.

At left, a door leads to a bedroom which is shared by MAMA *and her daughter,* BENEATHA. *At right, opposite, is a second room (which in the beginning of the life of this apartment was probably a breakfast room) which serves as a bedroom for* WALTER *and his wife,* RUTH.

TIME: *Sometime between World War II and the present.*
PLACE: *Chicago's South Side.*

AT RISE: *It is morning dark in the living room.* TRAVIS *is asleep on the makedown bed at center. An alarm clock sounds from within the bedroom at right, and presently* RUTH *enters from that room and closes the door behind her. She crosses sleepily toward the window. As she passes her sleeping son she reaches down and shakes him a little. At the window she raises the shade and a dusky South Side morning light comes in feebly. She fills a pot with water and puts it on to boil. She calls to the boy, between yawns, in a slightly muffled voice.*

RUTH *is about thirty. We can see that she was a pretty girl, even exceptionally so, but now it is apparent that life has been little that she expected, and disappointment has already begun to hang in her face. In a few years, before thirty-five even, she will be known among her people as a "settled woman."*

She crosses to her son and gives him a good, final, rousing shake.

RUTH: Come on now, boy, it's seven thirty! [*Her son sits up at last, in a stupor of sleepiness.*] I say hurry up, Travis! You ain't the only person in the world got to use a bathroom! [*The child, a sturdy, handsome little boy of ten or eleven, drags himself out of the bed and almost blindly takes his towels and "today's clothes" from drawers and a closet and goes out to the bathroom, which is in an outside hall and which is shared by another family or families on the same floor.* RUTH *crosses to the bedroom door at right and opens it and calls in to her husband.*] Walter Lee! . . . It's after seven thirty! Lemme see you do some waking up in there now! [*She waits.*] You better get up from there, man! It's after seven thirty I tell you. [*She waits again.*] All right, you just go ahead and lay there and next thing you know Travis be finished and Mr. Johnson'll be in there and you'll be fussing and cussing round here like a mad man! And be late too! [*She waits, at the end of patience.*] Walter Lee—it's time for you to get up! [*She waits another second and then starts to go into the bedroom, but is apparently satisfied that her husband has begun to get up. She stops, pulls the door to, and returns to the kitchen area. She wipes her face with a moist cloth and runs her fingers through her sleep-disheveled hair in a vain effort and ties an apron around her housecoat. The bedroom door at right opens and her husband stands in the doorway in his pajamas, which are rumpled and mismated. He is a lean, intense young man in his middle thirties, inclined to quick nervous movements and erratic speech habits—and always in his voice there is a quality of indictment.*]

WALTER: Is he out yet?

RUTH: What you mean *out?* He ain't hardly got in there good yet.

WALTER [*wandering in, still more oriented to sleep than to a new day*]: Well, what was you doing all that yelling for if I can't even get in there yet? [*stopping and thinking*] Check coming today?

RUTH: They *said* Saturday and this is just Friday and I hopes to God you ain't going to get up here first thing this morning and start talking to me 'bout no money—'cause I 'bout don't want to hear it.

WALTER: Something the matter with you this morning?

RUTH: No—I'm just sleepy as the devil. What kind of eggs you want?

WALTER: Not scrambled. [RUTH *starts to scramble eggs.*] Paper come? [RUTH *points impatiently to the rolled up* Tribune *on the table, and he gets it and spreads it out and vaguely reads the front page.*] Set off another bomb yesterday.

RUTH [*maximum indifference*]: Did they?

WALTER [*looking up*]: What's the matter with you?

RUTH: Ain't nothing the matter with me. And don't keep asking me that this morning.

WALTER: Ain't nobody bothering you. [*reading the news of the day absently again*] Say Colonel McCormick is sick.

RUTH [*affecting tea-party interest*]: Is he now? Poor thing.

WALTER [*sighing and looking at his watch*]: Oh, me. [*He waits.*] Now what is that boy doing in that bathroom all this time? He just going to have to start getting up earlier. I can't be being late to work on account of him fooling around in there.

RUTH [*turning on him*]: Oh, no he ain't going to be getting up earlier no such thing! It ain't his fault that he can't get to bed no earlier nights 'cause he got a bunch of crazy good-for-nothing clowns sitting up running their mouths in what is supposed to be his bedroom after ten o'clock at night . . .

WALTER: That's what you mad about, ain't it? The things I want to talk about with my friends just couldn't be important in your mind, could they? [*He rises and finds a cigarette in her handbag on the table and crosses to the little window and looks out, smoking and deeply enjoying this first one.*]

RUTH [*almost matter of factly, a complaint too automatic to deserve emphasis*]: Why you always got to smoke before you eat in the morning?

WALTER [*at the window*]: Just look at 'em down there. . . . Running and racing to work . . . [*He turns and faces his wife and watches her a moment at the stove, and then, suddenly.*] You look young this morning, baby.

RUTH [*indifferently*]: Yeah?

WALTER: Just for a second—stirring them eggs. It's gone now—just for a second it was—you looked real young again. [*then, drily*] It's gone now—you look like yourself again.

RUTH: Man, if you don't shut up and leave me alone.

WALTER [*looking out to the street again*]: First thing a man ought to learn in life is not to make love to no colored woman first thing in the morning. You all some evil people at eight o'clock in the morning. [TRAVIS *appears in the hall doorway, almost fully dressed and quite wide awake now, his towels and pajamas across his shoulders. He opens the door and signals for his father to make the bathroom in a hurry.*]

TRAVIS [*watching the bathroom*]: Daddy, come on! [WALTER *gets his bathroom utensils and flies out to the bathroom.*]

RUTH: Sit down and have your breakfast, Travis.

TRAVIS: Mama, this is Friday. [*gleefully*] Check coming tomorrow, huh?

RUTH: You get your mind off money and eat your breakfast.

TRAVIS [*eating*]: This is the morning we supposed to bring the fifty cents to school.

RUTH: Well, I ain't got no fifty cents this morning.

TRAVIS: Teacher say we have to.

RUTH: I don't care what teacher say. I ain't got it. Eat your breakfast, Travis.

TRAVIS: I *am* eating.

RUTH: Hush up now and just eat! [*The boy gives her an exasperated look for her lack of understanding, and eats grudgingly.*]

TRAVIS: You think Grandmama would have it?

RUTH: No! And I want you to stop asking your grandmother for money, you hear me?

TRAVIS [*outraged*]: Gaaaleee! I don't ask her, she just gimme it sometimes!

RUTH: Travis Willard Younger—I got too much on me this morning to be—

TRAVIS: Maybe Daddy—

RUTH: *Travis.* [*The boy hushes abruptly. They are both quiet and tense for several seconds.*]

TRAVIS [*presently*]: Could I maybe go carry some groceries in front of the supermarket for a little while after school then?

RUTH: Just hush, I said. [TRAVIS *jabs his spoon into his cereal bowl viciously, and rests his head in anger upon his fists.*] If you through eating, you can get over there and make up your bed. [*The boy obeys stiffly and crosses the room, almost mechanically, to the bed and more or less carefully folds the covering. He carries the bedding into his mother's room and returns with his books and cap.*]

TRAVIS [*sulking and standing apart from her unnaturally*]: I'm gone.

RUTH [*looking up from the stove to inspect him automatically*]: Come here. [*He crosses to her and she studies his head.*] If you don't take this comb and fix this here head, you better! [TRAVIS *puts down his books with a great sigh of oppression, and crosses to the mirror. His mother mutters under her breath about his "stubbornness."*] 'Bout to march out of here with that head looking just like chickens slept in it! I just don't know where you get your stubborn ways . . . And get your jacket, too. Looks chilly out this morning.

TRAVIS [*with conspicuously brushed hair and jacket*]: I'm gone.

RUTH: Get carfare and milk money—[*waving one finger*]—and not a single penny for no caps, you hear me?

TRAVIS [*with sullen politeness*]: Yes'm. [*He turns in outrage to leave. His mother watches after him as in his frustration he approaches the door almost comically. When she speaks to him, her voice has become a very gentle tease.*]

RUTH [*mocking, as she thinks he would say it*]: Oh, Mama makes me so mad sometimes, I don't know what to do! [*She waits and continues to his back as he stands stock-still in front of the door.*] I wouldn't kiss that woman good-bye for nothing in this world this morning! [*The boy finally turns around and rolls his eyes at her, knowing the mood has changed and he is vindicated; he does not, however, move toward her yet.*] Not for nothing in this world! [*She finally laughs aloud at him and holds out her arms to him and we see that it is a way between them, very old and practiced. He crosses to her and allows her to embrace him warmly but keeps his face fixed with masculine rigidity. She holds him back from her presently and looks at him and runs her fingers over the features of his face. With utter gentleness—*] Now—whose little old angry man are you?

TRAVIS [*The masculinity and gruffness start to fade at last.*]: Aw gaalee—Mama . . .

RUTH [*mimicking*]: Aw—gaaaaalleeeee, Mama! [*She pushes him, with rough playfulness and finality, toward the door.*] Get on out of here or you going to be late.

TRAVIS [*in the face of love, new aggressiveness*]: Mama, could I *please* go carry groceries?

RUTH: Honey, it's starting to get so cold evenings.

WALTER [*coming in from the bedroom and drawing a make-believe gun from a make-believe holster and shooting at his son*]: What is it he wants to do?

RUTH: Go carry groceries after school at the supermarket.

WALTER: Well, let him go . . .

TRAVIS [*quickly, to the ally*]: I *have* to—she won't gimme the fifty cents . . .

WALTER [*to his wife only*]: Why not?

RUTH [*simply, and with flavor*]: 'Cause we don't have it.

WALTER [*to* RUTH *only*]: What you tell the boy things like that for? [*reaching down into his pants with a rather important gesture*] Here, son—[*He hands the boy the coin, but his eyes are directed to his wife's.* TRAVIS *takes the money happily.*]

TRAVIS: Thanks, Daddy. [*He starts out.* RUTH *watches both of them with murder in her eyes.* WALTER *stands and stares back at her with defiance, and suddenly reaches into his pocket again on an afterthought.*]

WALTER [*without even looking at his son, still staring hard at his wife*]: In fact, here's another fifty cents . . . Buy yourself some fruit today—or take a taxicab to school or something!

TRAVIS: Whoopee—[*He leaps up and clasps his father around the middle with his legs, and they face each other in mutual appreciation; slowly* WALTER LEE *peeks around the boy to catch the violent rays from his wife's eyes and draws his head back as if shot.*]

WALTER: You better get down now—and get to school, man.

TRAVIS [*at the door*]: O.K. Good-bye. [*He exits.*]

WALTER [*after him, pointing with pride*]: That's *my* boy. [*She looks at him in disgust and turns back to her work.*] You know what I was thinking 'bout in the bathroom this morning?

RUTH: No.

WALTER: How come you always try to be so pleasant!

RUTH: What is there to be pleasant 'bout!

WALTER: You want to know what I was thinking 'bout in the bathroom or not!

RUTH: I know what you thinking 'bout.

WALTER [*ignoring her*]: 'Bout what me and Willy Harris was talking about last night.

RUTH [*immediately—a refrain*]: Willy Harris is a good-for-nothing loudmouth.

WALTER: Anybody who talks to me has got to be a good-for-nothing loudmouth, ain't he? And what you know about who is just a good-for-nothing loudmouth? Charlie Atkins was just a "good-for-nothing loudmouth" too, wasn't he! When he wanted me to go in the dry-cleaning business with him. And now—he's grossing a hundred thousand a year. A hundred thousand dollars a year! You still call *him* a loudmouth!

RUTH [*bitterly*]: Oh, Walter Lee . . . [*She folds her head on her arms over the table.*]

WALTER [*rising and coming to her and standing over her*]: You tired, ain't you? Tired of everything. Me, the boy, the way we live—this beat-up hole—everything. Ain't you? [*She doesn't look up, doesn't answer.*] So tired—moaning and groaning all the time, but you wouldn't do nothing to help, would you? You couldn't be on my side that long for nothing, could you?

RUTH: Walter, please leave me alone.

WALTER: A man needs for a woman to back him up . . .

RUTH: Walter—

WALTER: Mama would listen to you. You know she listen to you more than she do me and Bennie. She think more of you. All you have to do is just sit down with her when you drinking your coffee one morning and talking 'bout things like you do and—[*He sits down beside her and demonstrates graphically what he thinks her methods and tone should be.*]—you just sip your coffee, see, and say easy like that you been thinking 'bout that deal Walter Lee is so interested in, 'bout the store and all, and sip some more coffee, like what you saying ain't really that important to you—And the next thing you know, she be listening good and asking you questions and when I come home—I can tell her the details. This ain't no fly-by-night proposition, baby. I mean we figured it out, me and Willy and Bobo.

RUTH [*with a frown*]: Bobo?

WALTER: Yeah. You see, this little liquor store we got in mind cost seventy-five thousand and we figured the initial investment on the place be 'bout thirty thousand, see. That be ten thousand each. Course, there's a couple of hundred you got to pay so's you don't spend your life just waiting for them clowns to let your license get approved—

RUTH: You mean graft?

WALTER [*frowning impatiently*]: Don't call it that. See there, that just goes to show you what women understand about the world. Baby, don't *nothing* happen for you in this world 'less you pay *somebody* off!

RUTH: Walter, leave me alone! [*She raises her head and stares at him vigorously—then says, more quietly.*] Eat your eggs, they gonna be cold.

WALTER [*straightening up from her and looking off*]: That's it. There you are. Man say to his woman: I got me a dream. His woman say: Eat your eggs. [*sadly, but gaining in power*] Man say: I got to take hold of this here world, baby! And a woman will say: Eat your eggs and go to work. [*passionately now*] Man say: I got to change my life, I'm choking to death, baby! And his woman say—[*in utter anguish as he brings his fists down on his thighs*]—Your eggs is getting cold!

RUTH [*softly*]: Walter, that ain't none of our money.

WALTER [*not listening at all or even looking at her*]: This morning, I was lookin' in the mirror and thinking about it . . . I'm thirty-five years old; I been married eleven years and I got a boy who sleeps in the living room—[*very, very quietly*]—and all I got to give him is stories about how rich white people live . . .

RUTH: Eat your eggs, Walter.

WALTER: *Damn my eggs . . . damn all the eggs that ever was!*

RUTH: Then go to work.

WALTER [*looking up at her*]: See—I'm trying to talk to you 'bout myself—[*shaking his head with the repetition*]—and all you can say is eat them eggs and go to work.

RUTH [*wearily*]: Honey, you never say nothing new. I listen to you every day, every night and every morning, and you never say nothing new. [*shrugging*] So you would rather *be* Mr. Arnold than be his chauffeur. So—I would *rather* be living in Buckingham Palace.

WALTER: That is just what is wrong with the colored woman in this world . . . Don't understand about building their men up and making 'em feel like they somebody. Like they can do something.

RUTH [*drily, but to hurt*]: There *are* colored men who do things.

WALTER: No thanks to the colored woman.

RUTH: Well, being a colored woman, I guess I can't help myself none. [*She rises and gets the ironing board and sets it up and attacks a huge pile of roughdried clothes, sprinkling them in preparation for the ironing and then rolling them into tight fat balls.*]

WALTER [*mumbling*]: We one group of men tied to a race of women with small minds.

[*His sister* BENEATHA *enters. She is about twenty, as slim and intense as her brother. She is not as pretty as her sister-in-law, but her lean, almost intellectual face has a handsomeness of its own. She wears a bright-red flannel nightie, and her thick hair stands wildly about her head. Her speech is a mixture of many things; it is different from the rest of the family's insofar as education has permeated her sense of English—and perhaps the Midwest rather than the South has finally—at last—won out in her inflection; but not altogether, because over all of it is a soft slurring and transformed use of vowels which is the decided influence of the South Side. She passes through the room without looking at either* RUTH *or* WALTER *and goes to the outside door and looks, a little blindly, out to the bathroom. She sees that it has been lost to the Johnsons. She closes the door with a sleepy vengeance and crosses to the table and sits down a little defeated.*]

BENEATHA: I am going to start timing those people.

WALTER: You should get up earlier.

BENEATHA [*her face in her hands; she is still fighting the urge to go back to bed*]: Really—would you suggest dawn? Where's the paper?

WALTER [*pushing the paper across the table to her as he studies her almost clinically, as though he has never seen her before*]: You a horrible-looking chick at this hour.

BENEATHA [*drily*]: Good morning, everybody.

WALTER [*senselessly*]: How is school coming?

BENEATHA [*in the same spirit*]: Lovely, Lovely. And you know, biology is the greatest. [*looking up at him*] I dissected something that looked just like you yesterday.

WALTER: I just wondered if you've made up your mind and everything.

BENEATHA [*gaining in sharpness and impatience*]: And what did I answer yesterday morning—and the day before that?

RUTH [*from the ironing board, like someone disinterested and old*]: Don't be so nasty, Bennie.

BENEATHA [*still to her brother*]: And the day before that and the day before that!

WALTER [*defensively*]: I'm interested in you. Something wrong with that? Ain't many girls who decide—

WALTER AND BENEATHA [*in unison*]: —"to be a doctor." [*silence*]

WALTER: Have we figured out yet just exactly how much medical school is going to cost?

RUTH: Walter Lee, why don't you leave that girl alone and get out of here to work?

BENEATHA [*exits to the bathroom and bangs on the door*]: Come on out of there, please! [*She comes back into the room.*]

WALTER [*looking at his sister intently*]: You know the check is coming tomorrow.

BENEATHA [*turning on him with a sharpness all her own*]: That money belongs to Mama, Walter and it's for her to decide how she wants to use it. I don't care if she wants to buy a house or a rocket ship or just nail it up somewhere and look at it. It's hers. Not ours—hers.

WALTER [*bitterly*]: Now ain't that fine! You just got your mother's interest at heart, ain't you, girl? You such a nice girl—but if Mama got that money she can always take a few thousand and help you through school too—can't she?

BENEATHA: I have never asked anyone around here to do anything for me!

WALTER: No! And the line between asking and just accepting when the time comes is big and wide—ain't it!

BENEATHA [*with fury*]: What do you want from me, Brother—that I quit school or just drop dead, which!

WALTER: I don't want nothing but for you to stop acting holy 'round here. Me and Ruth done made some sacrifices for you—why can't you do something for the family?

RUTH: Walter, don't be dragging me in it.

WALTER: You are in it—Don't you get up and go work in somebody's kitchen for the last three years to help put clothes on her back?

RUTH: Oh, Walter—that's not fair . . .

WALTER: It ain't that nobody expects you to get on your knees and say thank you, Brother; thank you, Ruth; thank you, Mama—and thank you, Travis, for wearing the same pair of shoes for two semesters—

BENEATHA [*dropping to her knees*]: Well—I do—all right?—thank everybody . . . and forgive me for ever wanting to be anything at all . . . forgive me, forgive me!

RUTH: Please stop it! Your mama'll hear you.

WALTER: Who the hell told you you had to be a doctor? If you so crazy 'bout messing 'round with sick people—then go be a nurse like other women—or just get married and be quiet . . .

BENEATHA: Well—you finally got it said . . . It took you three years but you finally got it said. Walter, give up; leave me alone—it's Mama's money.

WALTER: *He was my father, too!*

BENEATHA: So what? He was mine, too—and Travis' grandfather—but the insurance money belongs to Mama. Picking on me is not going to make her give it to you to invest in any liquor stores—[*under breath, dropping into a chair*]—and I for one say, God bless Mama for that!

WALTER [*to* RUTH]: See—did you hear? Did you hear!

RUTH: Honey, please go to work.

WALTER: Nobody in this house is ever going to understand me.

BENEATHA: Because you're a nut.

WALTER: Who's a nut?

BENEATHA: You—you are a nut. Thee is mad, boy.

WALTER [*looking at his wife and his sister from the door, very sadly*]: The world's most backward race of people, and that's a fact.

BENEATHA [*turning slowly in her chair*]: And then there are all those prophets who would lead us out of the wilderness—[WALTER *slams out of the house.*]—into the swamps!

RUTH: Bennie, why you always gotta be pickin' on your brother? Can't you be a little sweeter sometimes? [*Door opens.* WALTER *walks in.*]

WALTER [*to* RUTH]: I need some money for carfare.

RUTH [*looks at him, then warms; teasing, but tenderly*]: Fifty cents? [*She goes to her bag and gets money.*] Here, take a taxi. [WALTER *exits.* MAMA *enters. She is a woman in her early sixties, full-bodied and strong. She is one of those women of a certain grace and beauty who wear it so unobtrusively that it takes a while to notice. Her dark-brown face is surrounded by the total whiteness of her hair, and, being a woman who has adjusted to many things in life and overcome many more, her face is full of strength. She has, we can see, wit and faith of a kind that keep her eyes lit and full of interest and expectancy. She is, in a word, a beautiful woman. Her bearing is perhaps most like the noble bearing of the women of the Hereros of Southwest Africa—rather as if she imagines that as she walks she still bears a basket or a vessel upon her head. Her speech, on the other hand, is as careless as her carriage is precise—she is inclined to slur everything—but her voice is perhaps not so much quiet as simply soft.*]

MAMA: Who that 'round here slamming doors at this hour? [*She crosses through the room, goes to the window, opens it, and brings in a feeble little plant growing doggedly in a small pot on the window sill. She feels the dirt and puts it back out.*]

RUTH: That was Walter Lee. He and Bennie was at it again.

MAMA: My children and they tempers. Lord, if this little old plant don't get more sun that it's been getting it ain't never going to see spring again. [*She turns from the window.*] What's the matter with you this morning, Ruth? You looks right peaked. You aiming to iron all them things? Leave some for me. I'll get to 'em this afternoon. Bennie honey, it's too drafty for you to be sitting 'round half dressed. Where's your robe?

BENEATHA: In the cleaners.

MAMA: Well, go get mine and put it on.

BENEATHA: I'm not cold, Mama, honest.

MAMA: I know—but you so thin . . .

BENEATHA [*irritably*]: Mama, I'm not cold.

MAMA [*seeing the make-down bed as* TRAVIS *has left it*]: Lord have mercy, look at that poor bed. Bless his heart—he tries, don't he? [*She moves to the bed* TRAVIS *has sloppily made up.*]

RUTH: No—he don't half try at all 'cause he knows you going to come along behind him and fix everything. That's just how come he don't know how to do nothing right now—you done spoiled that boy so.

MAMA: Well—he's a little boy. Ain't supposed to know 'bout housekeeping. My baby, that's what he is. What you fix for his breakfast this morning?

RUTH [*angrily*]: I feed my son, Lena!

MAMA: I ain't meddling—[*under breath, busy-bodyish*]: I just noticed all last week he had cold cereal, and when it starts getting this chilly in the fall a child ought to have some hot grits or something when he goes out in the cold—

RUTH [*furious*]: I gave him hot oats—is that all right!

MAMA: I ain't meddling. [*pause*] Put a lot of nice butter on it? [RUTH *shoots her an angry look and does not reply.*] He likes lots of butter.

RUTH [*exasperated*]: Lena—

MAMA [*to* BENEATHA; MAMA *is inclined to wander conversationally sometimes*]: What was you and your brother fussing 'bout this morning?

BENEATHA: It's not important, Mama. [*She gets up and goes to look out at the bathroom, which is apparently free, and she picks up her towels and rushes out.*]

MAMA: What was they fighting about?

RUTH: Now you know as well as I do.

MAMA [*shaking her head*]: Brother still worrying hisself sick about that money?

RUTH: You know he is.

MAMA: You had breakfast?

RUTH: Some coffee.

MAMA: Girl, you better start eating and looking after yourself better. You almost thin as Travis.

RUTH: Lena—

MAMA: Uh-hunh?

RUTH: What are you going to do with it?

MAMA: Now don't you start, child. It's too early in the morning to be talking about money. It ain't Christian.

RUTH: It's just that he got his heart set on that store—

MAMA: You mean that liquor store that Willy Harris want him to invest in?

RUTH: Yes—

MAMA: We ain't no business people, Ruth. We just plain working folks.

RUTH: Ain't nobody business people till they go into business. Walter Lee say colored people ain't never going to start getting ahead till they start gambling on some different kinds of things in the world—investments and things.

MAMA: What done got into you, girl? Walter Lee done finally sold you on investing.

RUTH: No. Mama, something is happening between Walter and me. I don't know what it is—but he needs something—something I can't give him any more. He needs this chance, Lena.

MAMA [*frowning deeply*]: But liquor, honey—

RUTH: Well—like Walter say—I spec people going to always be drinking themselves some liquor.

MAMA: Well—whether they drinks it or not ain't none of my business. But whether I go into business selling it to 'em is, and I don't want that on my ledger this late in life. [*stopping suddenly and studying her daughter-in-law*] Ruth Younger, what's the matter with you today? You look like you could fall over right there.

RUTH: I'm tired.

MAMA: Then you better stay home from work today.

RUTH: I can't stay home. She'd be calling up the agency and screaming at them, "My girl didn't come in today—send me somebody! My girl didn't come in!" Oh, she just have a fit . . .

MAMA: Well, let her have it. I'll just call her up and say you got the flu—

RUTH [*laughing*]: Why the flu?

MAMA: 'Cause it sounds respectable to 'em. Something white people get, too. They know 'bout the flu. Otherwise they think you been cut up or something when you tell 'em you sick.

RUTH: I got to go in. We need the money.

MAMA: Somebody would of thought my children done all but starved to death the way they talk about money here late. Child, we got a great big old check coming tomorrow.

RUTH [*sincerely, but also self-righteously*]: Now that's your money. It ain't got nothing to do with me. We all feel like that—Walter and Bennie and me—even Travis.

MAMA [*thoughtfully, and suddenly very far away*]: Ten thousand dollars—

RUTH: Sure is wonderful.

MAMA: Ten thousand dollars.

RUTH: You know what you should do, Miss Lena? You should take yourself a trip somewhere. To Europe or South America or someplace—

MAMA [*throwing up her hands at the thought*]: Oh, child!

RUTH: I'm serious. Just pack up and leave! Go on away and enjoy yourself some. Forget about the family and have yourself a ball for once in your life—

MAMA [*drily*]: You sound like I'm just about ready to die. Who'd go with me? What I look like wandering 'round Europe by myself?

RUTH: Shoot—these here rich white women do it all the time. They don't think nothing of packing up they suitcases and piling on one of them big steamships and—swoosh!—they gone, child.

MAMA: Something always told me I wasn't no rich white woman.

RUTH: Well—what are you going to do with it then?

MAMA: I ain't rightly decided. [*Thinking. She speaks now with emphasis.*] Some of it got to be put away for Beneatha and her schoolin'—and ain't nothing going to touch that part of it. Nothing. [*She waits several seconds, trying to make up her mind about something, and looks at* RUTH *little tentatively before going on.*] Been thinking that we maybe could meet the notes on a little old two-story somewhere, with a yard where Travis could play in the summertime, if we use part of the insurance for a down payment and everybody kind of pitch in. I could maybe take on a little day work again, few days a week—

RUTH [*studying her mother-in-law furtively and concentrating on her ironing, anxious to encourage without seeming to*]: Well, Lord knows, we've put enough rent into this here rat trap to pay for four houses by now . . .

MAMA [*looking up at the words "rat trap" and then looking around and leaning back and sighing—in a suddenly reflective mood*]: "Rat trap"—yes, that's all it is. [*smiling*] I remember just as well the day me and Big Walter moved in here. Hadn't been married but two weeks and wasn't planning on living here no more than a year. [*She shakes her head at the dissolved dream.*] We was going to set away, little by little, don't you know, and buy a little place out in Morgan Park. We had even picked out the house. [*chuckling a little*] Looks right dumpy today. But Lord, child, you should know all the dreams I had 'bout buying that house and fixing it up and making me a little garden in the back—[*She waits and stops smiling.*] And didn't none of it happen [*dropping her hands in a futile gesture*].

RUTH [*keeps her head down, ironing*]: Yes, life can be a barrel of disappointments, sometimes.

MAMA: Honey, Big Walter would come in here some nights back then and slump down on that couch there and just look at the rug, and look at me and look at the rug and then back at me—and I'd know he was down then . . . really down. [*After a second very long and thoughtful pause; she is seeing back to times that only she can see.*] And then, Lord, when I lost that baby—little Claude—I almost thought I was going to lose Big Walter too. Oh, that man grieved hisself! He was one man to love his children.

RUTH: Ain't nothin' can tear at you like losin' your baby.

MAMA: I guess that's how come that man finally worked hisself to death like he done. Likely he was fighting his own war with this here world that took his baby from him.

RUTH: He sure was a fine man, all right. I always liked Mr. Younger.

MAMA: Crazy 'bout his children! God knows there was plenty wrong with Walter Younger—hard-headed, mean, kind of wild with women—plenty wrong with him. But he sure loved his children. Always wanted them to have something—be something. That's where Brother gets all these notions, I reckon. Big Walter used to say, he'd get right wet in the eyes sometimes, lean his head back with the water standing in his eyes and say, "Seem like God didn't see fit to give the black man nothing but dreams—but He did give us children to make them dreams seem worth while." [*She smiles.*] He could talk like that, don't you know.

RUTH: Yes, he sure could. He was a good man, Mr. Younger.

MAMA: Yes, a fine man—just couldn't never catch up with his dreams, that's all. [BENEATHA *comes in, brushing her hair and looking up to the ceiling, where the sound of a vacuum cleaner has started up.*]

BENEATHA: What could be so dirty on that woman's rugs that she has to vacuum them every single day?

RUTH: I wish certain young women 'round here who I could name would take inspiration about certain rugs in a certain apartment I could also mention.

BENEATHA [*shrugging*]: How much cleaning can a house need, for Christ's sakes?

MAMA [*not liking the Lord's name used thus*]: Bennie!

RUTH: Just listen to her—just listen!

BENEATHA: Oh, God!

MAMA: If you use the Lord's name just one more time—

BENEATHA [*a bit of a whine*]: Oh, Mama—

RUTH: Fresh—just fresh as salt, this girl!

BENEATHA [*drily*]: Well—if the salt loses its savor—

MAMA: Now that will do. I just ain't going to have you 'round here reciting the scriptures in vain—you hear me?

BENEATHA: How did I manage to get on everybody's wrong side by just walking into a room?

RUTH: If you weren't so fresh—

BENEATHA: Ruth, I'm twenty years old.

MAMA: What time you be home from school today?

BENEATHA: Kind of late. [*with enthusiasm*] Madeline is going to start my guitar lessons today. [MAMA *and* RUTH *look up with the same expression.*]

MAMA: Your *what* kind of lessons?

BENEATHA: Guitar.

RUTH: Oh, Father!

MAMA: How come you done taken it in your mind to learn to play the guitar?

BENEATHA: I just want to, that's all.

MAMA [*smiling*]: Lord, child, don't you know what to do with yourself? How long it going to be before you get tired of this now—like you got tired of that little play-acting group you joined last year? [*looking at* RUTH] And what was it the year before that?

RUTH: The horseback-riding club for which she bought that fifty-five-dollar riding habit that's been hanging in the closet ever since!

MAMA [*to* BENEATHA]: Why you got to flit so from one thing to another, baby?

BENEATHA [*sharply*]: I just want to learn to play the guitar. Is there anything wrong with that?

MAMA: Ain't nobody trying to stop you. I just wonders sometimes why you has to flit so from one thing to another all the time. You ain't never done nothing with all that camera equipment you brought home—

BENEATHA: I don't flit! I—I experiment with different forms of expression—

RUTH: Like riding a horse?

BENEATHA: —People have to express themselves one way or another.

MAMA: What is it you want to express?

BENEATHA [*angrily*]: Me! [MAMA *and* RUTH *look at each other and burst into raucous laughter*] Don't worry—I don't expect you to understand.

MAMA [*to change the subject*]: Who you going out with tomorrow night?

BENEATHA [*with displeasure*]: George Murchison again.

MAMA [*pleased*]: Oh—you getting a little sweet on him?

RUTH: You ask me, this child ain't sweet on nobody but herself—[*under breath*] Express herself! [*They laugh.*]

BENEATHA: Oh—I like George all right, Mama. I mean I like him enough to go out with him and stuff, but—

RUTH [*for devilment*]: What does and stuff mean?

BENEATHA: Mind your own business.

MAMA: Stop picking at her now, Ruth. [*a thoughtful pause, and then a suspicious sudden look at her daughter as she turns in her chair for emphasis*] What does it mean?

BENEATHA [*wearily*]: Oh, I just mean I couldn't ever really be serious about George. He's—he's so shallow.

RUTH: Shallow—what do you mean he's shallow? He's *Rich!*

MAMA: Hush, Ruth.

BENEATHA: I know he's rich. He knows he's rich, too.

RUTH: Well—what other qualities a man got to have to satisfy you, little girl?

BENEATHA: You wouldn't even begin to understand. Anybody who married Walter could not possibly understand.

MAMA [*outraged*]: What kind of way is that to talk about your brother?

BENEATHA: Brother is a flip—let's face it.

MAMA [*to* RUTH, *helplessly*]: What's a flip?

RUTH [*glad to add kindling*]: She's saying he's crazy.

BENEATHA: Not crazy. Brother isn't really crazy yet—he—he's an elaborate neurotic.

MAMA: Hush your mouth!

BENEATHA: As for George. Well. George looks good—he's got a beautiful car and he takes me to nice places and, as my sister-in-law says, he is probably the richest boy I will ever get to know and I even like him sometimes—but if the Youngers are sitting around waiting to see if their little Bennie is going to tie up the family with the Murchisons, they are wasting their time.

RUTH: You mean you wouldn't marry George Murchison if he asked you someday? That pretty, rich thing? Honey, I knew you was odd—

BENEATHA: No I would not marry him if all I felt for him was what I feel now. Besides, George's family wouldn't really like it.

MAMA: Why not?

BENEATHA: Oh, Mama—The Murchisons are honest-to-God-real-*live*-rich colored people, and the only people in the world who are more snobbish than rich white people are rich colored people. I thought everybody knew that. I've met Mrs. Murchison. She's a scene!

MAMA: You must not dislike people 'cause they well off, honey.

BENEATHA: Why not? It makes just as much sense as disliking people 'cause they are poor, and lots of people do that.

RUTH [*a wisdom-of-the-ages manner; to* MAMA]: Well, she'll get over some of this—

BENEATHA: Get over it? What are you talking about, Ruth? Listen, I'm going to be a doctor. I'm not worried about who I'm going to marry yet—if I ever get married.

MAMA AND RUTH: *If!*

MAMA: Now, Bennie—

BENEATHA: Oh, I probably will . . . but first I'm going to be a doctor, and George, for one, still thinks that's pretty funny. I couldn't be bothered with that. I am going to be a doctor and everybody around here better understand that!

MAMA [*kindly*]: 'Course you going to be a doctor, honey, God willing.

BENEATHA [*drily*]: God hasn't got a thing to do with it.

MAMA: Beneatha—that just wasn't necessary.

BENEATHA: Well—neither is God. I get sick of hearing about God.

MAMA: Beneatha!

BENEATHA: I mean it! I'm just tired of hearing about God all the time. What has He got to do with anything? Does he pay tuition?

MAMA: You 'bout to get your fresh little jaw slapped!

RUTH: That's just what she needs, all right!

BENEATHA: Why? Why can't I say what I want to around here, like everybody else?

MAMA: It don't sound nice for a young girl to say things like that—you wasn't brought up that way. Me and your father went to trouble to get you and Brother to church every Sunday.

BENEATHA: Mama, you don't understand. It's all a matter of ideas, and God is just one idea I don't accept. It's not important. I am not going out and be immoral or commit crimes because I don't believe in God. I don't even think about it. It's just that I get tired of Him getting credit for all the things the human race achieves through its own stubborn effort. There simply is no blasted God—there is only man and it is he who makes miracles! [MAMA *absorbs this speech, studies her daughter and rises slowly and crosses to* BENEATHA *and slaps her powerfully across the face. After, there is only silence and the daughter drops her eyes from her mother's face, and* MAMA *is very tall before her.*]

MAMA: Now—you say after me, in my mother's house there is still God. [*There is a long pause and* BENEATHA *stares at the floor wordlessly.* MAMA *repeats the phrase with precision and cool emotion.*] In my mother's house there is still God.

BENEATHA: In my mother's house there is still God [*a long pause*].

MAMA [*walking away from* BENEATHA, *too disturbed for triumphant posture; stopping and turning back to her daughter*]: There are some ideas we ain't going to have in this house. Not long as I am at the head of this family.

BENEATHA: Yes, ma'am. [MAMA *walks out of the room.*]

RUTH [*almost gently, with profound understanding*]: You think you a woman, Bennie—but you still a little girl. What you did was childish—so you got treated like a child.

BENEATHA: I see. [*quietly*] I also see that everybody thinks it's all right for Mama to be a tyrant. But all the tyranny in the world will never put a God in the heavens! [*She picks up her books and goes out.*]

RUTH [*goes to* MAMA*'s door*]: She said she was sorry.

MAMA [*coming out, going to her plant*]: They frightens me, Ruth. My children.

RUTH: You got good children, Lena. They just a little off sometimes—but they're good.

MAMA: No—There's something come down between me and them that don't let us understand each other and I don't know what it is. One done almost lost his mind thinking 'bout money all the time and the other done commence to talk about things I can't seem to understand in no form or fashion. What is it that's changing, Ruth?

RUTH [*soothingly, older than her years*]: Now . . . you taking it all too seriously. You just got strong-willed children and it takes a strong woman like you to keep 'em in hand.

MAMA [*looking at her plant and sprinkling a little water on it*]: They spirited all right, my children. Got to admit they got spirit—Bennie and Walter. Like this little old plant that ain't never had enough sunshine or nothing—and look at it . . . [*She has her back to* RUTH, *who has had to stop ironing and lean against something and put the back of her hand to her forehead.*]

RUTH [*trying to keep* MAMA *from noticing*]: You . . . sure . . . loves that little old thing, don't you? . . .

MAMA: Well, I always wanted me a garden like I used to see sometimes at the back of the houses-down home. This plant is close as I ever got to having one. [*She looks out of the window as she replaces the plant.*] Lord, ain't nothing as dreary as the view from this window on a dreary day, is there? Why ain't you singing this morning, Ruth? Sing that "No Ways Tired." That song always lifts me up so—[*She turns at last to see that* RUTH *has slipped quietly into a chair, in a state of semiconsciousness.*] Ruth! Ruth honey—what's the matter with you . . . Ruth!

CURTAIN

SCENE 2

It is the following morning; a Saturday morning, and house cleaning is in progress at the Youngers. Furniture has been shoved hither and yon and MAMA *is giving the kitchen-area walls a washing down.* BENEATHA, *in dungarees, with a handkerchief tied around her face, is spraying insecticide into the cracks in the walls. As they work, the radio is on and a South Side disk jockey program is inappropriately filling the house with a rather exotic saxophone blues.* TRAVIS, *the sole idle one, is leaning on his arms, looking out of the window.*

TRAVIS: Grandmama, that stuff Bennie is using smells awful. Can I go downstairs, please?

MAMA: Did you get all them chores done already? I ain't seen you doing much.

TRAVIS: Yes'm—finished early. Where did Mama go this morning?

MAMA [*looking at* BENEATHA]: She had to go on a little errand.

TRAVIS: Where?

MAMA: To tend to her business.

TRAVIS: Can I go outside then?

MAMA: Oh, I guess so. You better stay right in front of the house, though . . . and keep a good lookout for the postman.

TRAVIS: Yes'm. [*He starts out and decides to give his* AUNT BENEATHA *a good swat on the legs as he passes her.*] Leave them poor little old cockroaches alone, they ain't bothering you none. [*He runs as she swings the spray gun at him both viciously and playfully.* WALTER *enters from the bedroom and goes to the phone.*]

MAMA: Look out there, girl, before you be spilling some of that stuff on that child!

TRAVIS [*teasing*]: That's right—look out now! [*He exits.*]

BENEATHA [*drily*]: I can't imagine that it would hurt him—it has never hurt the roaches.

MAMA: Well, little boys' hides ain't as tough as South Side roaches.

WALTER [*into phone*]: Hello—Let me talk to Willy Harris.

MAMA: You better get over there behind the bureau. I seen one marching out of there like Napoleon yesterday.

WALTER: Hello, Willy? It ain't come yet. It'll be here in a few minutes. Did the lawyer give you the papers?

BENEATHA: There's really only one way to get rid of them, Mama—

MAMA: How?

BENEATHA: Set fire to this building.

WALTER: Good. Good. I'll be right over.

BENEATHA: Where did Ruth go, Walter?

WALTER: I don't know. [*He exits abruptly.*]

BENEATHA: Mama, where did Ruth go?

MAMA [*looking at her with meaning*]: To the doctor, I think.

BENEATHA: The doctor? What's the matter? [*They exchange glances.*] You don't think—

MAMA [*with her sense of drama*]: Now I ain't saying what I think. But I ain't never been wrong 'bout a woman neither. [*The phone rings.*]

BENEATHA [*at the phone*]: Hay-lo . . . [*pause, and a moment of recognition*] Well—when did you get back! . . . And how was it? . . . Of course I've missed you—in my way . . . This morning? No . . . house cleaning and all that and Mama hates it if I let people come over when the house is like this . . . You *have?* Well, that's different . . . What is it—Oh, what the hell, come on over . . . Right, see you then. [*She hangs up.*]

MAMA [*who has listened vigorously, as is her habit*]: Who is that you inviting over here with this house looking like this? You ain't got the pride you was born with!

BENEATHA: Asagai doesn't care how houses look, Mama—he's an intellectual.

MAMA: *Who?*

BENEATHA: Asagai—Joseph Asagai. He's an African boy I met on campus. He's been studying in Canada all summer.

MAMA: What's his name?

BENEATHA: Asagai, Joseph. Ah-sah-guy . . . He's from Nigeria.

MAMA: Oh, that's the little country that was founded by slaves way back . . .

BENEATHA: No, Mama—that's Liberia.

MAMA: I don't think I never met no African before.

BENEATHA: Well, do me a favor and don't ask him a whole lot of ignorant questions about Africans. I mean, do they wear clothes and all that—

MAMA: Well, now, I guess if you think we so ignorant 'round here maybe you shouldn't bring your friends here—

BENEATHA: It's just that people ask such crazy things. All anyone seems to know about when it comes to Africa is Tarzan—

MAMA [*indignantly*]: Why should I know anything about Africa?

BENEATHA: Why do you give money at church for the missionary work?

MAMA: Well, that's to help save people.

BENEATHA: You mean save them from *heathenism*—

MAMA [*innocently*]: Yes.

BENEATHA: I'm afraid they need more salvation from the British and the French. [RUTH *comes in forlornly and pulls off her coat with dejection. They both turn to look at her.*]

RUTH [*dispiritedly*]: Well, I guess from all the happy faces—everybody knows.

BENEATHA: You pregnant?

MAMA: Lord have mercy, I sure hope it's a little old girl. Travis ought to have a sister [BENEATHA *and* RUTH *give her a hopeless look for this grandmotherly enthusiasm*].

BENEATHA: How far along are you?

RUTH: Two months.

BENEATHA: Did you mean to? I mean did you plan it or was it an accident?

MAMA: What do you know about planning or not planning?

BENEATHA: Oh, Mama.

RUTH [*wearily*]: She's twenty years old, Lena.

BENEATHA: Did you plan it, Ruth?

RUTH: Mind your own business.

BENEATHA: It is my business—where is he going to live, on the roof? [*There is silence following the remark as the three women react to the sense of it.*] Gee—I didn't mean that, Ruth, honest. Gee, I don't feel like that at all. I—I think it is wonderful.

RUTH [*dully*]: Wonderful.

BENEATHA: Yes—really.

MAMA [*looking at* RUTH, *worried*]: Doctor say everything going to be all right?

RUTH [*far away*]: Yes—she says everything is going to be fine . . .

MAMA [*immediately suspicious*]: "She"—What doctor you went to? [RUTH *folds over, near hysteria.*]

MAMA [*worriedly hovering over* RUTH]: Ruth, honey—what's the matter with you—you sick? [RUTH *has her fists clenched on her thighs and is fighting hard to suppress a scream that seems to be rising in her.*]

BENEATHA: What's the matter with her, Mama?

MAMA [*working her fingers in* RUTH*'s shoulder to relax her*]: She be all right. Women gets right depressed sometimes when they get her way. [*speaking softly, expertly, rapidly*] Now you just relax. That's right . . . just lean back, don't think 'bout nothing at all . . . nothing at all—

RUTH: I'm all right . . . [*The glassy-eyed look melts and then she collapses into a fit of heavy sobbing. The bell rings.*]

BENEATHA: Oh, my God—that must be Asagai.

MAMA [*to* RUTH]: Come on now, honey. You need to lie down and rest awhile . . . then have some nice hot food. [*They exit,* RUTH*'s weight on her mother-in-law.* BENEATHA, *herself profoundly disturbed, opens the door to admit a rather dramatic-looking young man with a large package.*]

ASAGAI: Hello, Alaiyo—

BENEATHA [*holding the door open and regarding him with pleasure*]: Hello . . . [*long pause*] Well—come in. And please excuse everything. My mother was very upset about my letting anyone come here with the place like this.

ASAGAI [*coming into the room*]: You look disturbed too . . . Is something wrong?

BENEATHA [*still at the door, absently*]: Yes . . . we've all got acute ghetto-itus. [*She smiles and comes toward him, finding a cigarette and sitting.*] So—sit down! How was Canada?

ASAGAI [*a sophisticate*]: Canadian.

BENEATHA [*looking at him*]: I'm very glad you are back.

ASAGAI [*looking back at her in turn*]: Are you really?

BENEATHA: Yes—very.

ASAGAI: Why—you were quite glad when I went away. What happened?

BENEATHA: You went away.

ASAGAI: Ahhhhhhhh.

BENEATHA: Before—you wanted to be so serious before there was time.

ASAGAI: How much time must there be before one knows what one feels?

BENEATHA [*stalling this particular conversation; her hands pressed together, in a deliberately childish gesture*]: What did you bring me?

ASAGAI [*handing her the package*]: Open it and see.

BENEATHA [*eagerly opening the package and drawing out some records and the colorful robes of a Nigerian woman*]: Oh, Asagai! . . . You got them for me! . . . How beautiful . . . and the records too! [*She lifts out the robes and runs to the mirror with them and holds the drapery up in front of herself.*]

ASAGAI [*coming to her at the mirror*]: I shall have to teach you how to drape it properly. [*He flings the material about her for the moment and stands back to look at her.*] Ah—*Oh-pay-gay-day, oh-gbah-mu-shay.* [*a Yoruba exclamation for admiration*] You wear it well . . . very well . . . mutilated hair and all.

BENEATHA [*turning suddenly*]: My hair—what's wrong with my hair?

ASAGAI [*shrugging*]: Were you born with it like that?

BENEATHA [*reaching up to touch it*]: No . . . of course not. [*She looks back to the mirror, disturbed.*]

ASAGAI [*smiling*]: How then?

BENEATHA: You know perfectly well how . . . as crinkly as yours . . . that's how.

ASAGAI: And it is ugly to you that way?

BENEATHA [*quickly*]: Oh, no—not ugly . . . [*more slowly, apologetically*] But it's so hard to manage when it's, well—raw.

ASAGAI: And so to accommodate that—you mutilate it every week?

BENEATHA: It's not mutilation!

ASAGAI [*laughing aloud at her seriousness*]: Oh . . . please! I am only teasing you because you are so very serious about these things. [*He stands back from her and folds his arms across his chest as he watches her pulling at her hair and frowning in the mirror.*] Do you remember the first time you met me at school? . . . [*He laughs.*] You came up to me and said—and I thought you were the most serious little thing I had ever seen—you said: [*He imitates her.*] "Mr. Asagai—I want very much to talk with you. About Africa. You see, Mr. Asagai, I am looking for my *identity!*" [*He laughs.*]

BENEATHA [*turning to him, not laughing*]: Yes—[*Her face is quizzical, profoundly disturbed.*]

ASAGAI [*still teasing and reaching out and taking her face in his hands and turning her profile to him*]: Well . . . it is true that this is not so much a profile of a Hollywood queen as perhaps a queen of the Nile—[*a mock dismissal of the importance of the question*] But what does it matter? Assimilationism is so popular in your country.

BENEATHA [*wheeling, passionately, sharply*]: I am not an assimilationist!

ASAGAI [*the protest hangs in the room for a moment and* ASAGAI *studies her, his laughter fading*]: Such a serious one. [*There is a pause.*] So—you like the robes? You must take excellent care of them—they are from my sister's personal wardrobe.

BENEATHA [*with incredulity*]: You—you sent all the way home—for me?

ASAGAI [*with charm*]: For you—I would do much more . . . Well, that is what I came for. I must go.

BENEATHA: Will you call me Monday?

ASAGAI: Yes . . . We have a great deal to talk about. I mean about identity and time and all that.

BENEATHA: Time?

ASAGAI: Yes. About how much time one needs to know what one feels.

BENEATHA: You never understood that there is more than one kind of feeling which can exist between a man and a woman—or, at least, there should be.

ASAGAI [*shaking his head negatively but gently*]: No. Between a man and a woman there need be only one kind of feeling. I have that for you . . . Now even . . . right this moment . . .

BENEATHA: I know—and by itself—it won't do. I can find that anywhere.

ASAGAI: For a woman it should be enough.

BENEATHA: I know—because that's what it says in all the novels that men write. But it isn't. Go ahead and laugh—but I'm not interested in being someone's little episode in America or—[*with feminine vengeance*]—one of them! [ASAGAI *has burst into laughter again.*] That's funny as hell, huh!

ASAGAI: It's just that every American girl I have known has said that to me. White—black—in this you are all the same. And the same speech, too!

BENEATHA [*angrily*]: Yuk, yuk, yuk!

ASAGAI: It's how you can be sure that the world's most liberated women are not liberated at all. You all talk about it too much! [MAMA *enters and is immediately all social charm because of the presence of a guest.*]

BENEATHA: Oh—Mama—this is Mr. Asagai.

MAMA: How do you do?

ASAGAI [*total politeness to an elder*]: How do you do, Mrs. Younger. Please forgive me for coming at such an outrageous hour on a Saturday.

MAMA: Well, you are quite welcome. I just hope you understand that our house don't always look like this. [*chatterish*] You must come again. I would love to hear all about—[*not sure of the name*]—your country. I think it's so sad the way our American Negroes don't know nothing about Africa 'cept Tarzan and all that. And all that money they pour into these churches when they ought to be helping you people over there drive out them French and Englishmen done taken away your land. [*The mother flashes a slightly superior look at her daughter upon completion of the recitation.*]

ASAGAI [*taken aback by this sudden and acutely unrelated expression of sympathy*]: Yes . . . yes . . .

MAMA [*smiling at him suddenly and relaxing and looking him over*]: How many miles is it from here to where you come from?

ASAGAI: Many thousands.

MAMA [*looking at him as she would* WALTER]: I bet you don't half look after yourself, being away from your mama either. I spec you better come 'round here from time to time and get yourself some decent home-cooked meals . . .

ASAGAI [*moved*]: Thank you. Thank you very much. [*They are all quiet, then—*] Well . . . I must go. I will call you Monday, Alaiyo.

MAMA: What's that he call you?

ASAGAI: Oh—"Alaiyo." I hope you don't mind. It is what you would call a nickname, I think. It is a Yoruba word. I am a Yoruba.

MAMA [*looking at* BENEATHA]: I—I thought he was from—

ASAGAI [*understanding*]: Nigeria is my country. Yoruba is my tribal origin—

BENEATHA: You didn't tell us what Alaiyo means . . . for all I know, you might be calling me Little Idiot or something . . .

ASAGAI: Well . . . let me see . . . I do not know how just to explain it . . . The sense of a thing can be so different when it changes languages.

BENEATHA: You're evading.

ASAGAI: No—really it is difficult . . . [*thinking*] It means . . . it means One for Whom Bread—Food—Is Not Enough. [*He looks at her.*] Is that all right?

BENEATHA [*understanding, softly*]: Thank you.

MAMA [*looking from one to the other and not understanding any of it*]: Well . . . that's nice . . . You must come see us again—Mr.—

ASAGAI: Ah-sah-guy . . .

MAMA: Yes . . . Do come again.

ASAGAI: Good-bye. [*He exits.*]

MAMA [*after him*]: Lord, that's a pretty thing just went out here! [*insinuatingly, to her daughter*] Yes, I guess I see why we done commence to get so interested in Africa 'round here. Missionaries my aunt Jenny! [*She exits.*]

BENEATHA: Oh, Mama! . . . [*She picks up the Nigerian dress and holds it up to her in front of the mirror again. She sets the headdress on haphazardly and then notices her hair again and clutches at it and then replaces the headdress and frowns at herself. Then she starts to wriggle in front of the mirror as she thinks a Nigerian woman might.* TRAVIS *enters and regards her.*]

TRAVIS: You cracking up?

BENEATHA: Shut up. [*She pulls the headdress off and looks at herself in the mirror and clutches at her hair again and squinches her eyes as if trying to imagine something. Then, suddenly, she gets her raincoat and kerchief and hurriedly prepares for going out.*]

MAMA [*coming back into the room*]: She's resting now. Travis, baby, run next door and ask Miss Johnson to please let me have a little kitchen cleanser. This here can is empty as Jacob's kettle.

TRAVIS: I just came in.

MAMA: Do as you told. [*He exits and she looks at her daughter.*] Where you going?

BENEATHA [*halting at the door*]: To become a queen of the Nile! [*She exits in a breathless blaze of glory.* RUTH *appears in the bedroom doorway.*]

MAMA: Who told you to get up?

RUTH: Ain't nothing wrong with me to be lying in no bed for. Where did Bennie go?

MAMA [*drumming her fingers*]: Far as I could make out—to Egypt. [RUTH *just looks at her.*] What time is it getting to?

RUTH: Ten twenty. And the mailman going to ring that bell this morning just like he done every morning for the last umpteen years. [TRAVIS *comes in with the cleanser can.*]

TRAVIS: She say to tell you that she don't have much.

MAMA [*angrily*]: Lord, some people I could name sure is tight-fisted! [*directing her grandson*] Mark two cans of cleanser down on the list there. If she that hard up for kitchen cleanser, I sure don't want to forget to get her none!

RUTH: Lena—maybe the woman is just short on cleanser—

MAMA [*not listening*]: —Much baking powder as she done borrowed from me all these years, she could of done gone into the baking business! [*The bell sounds suddenly and sharply and all three are stunned—serious and silent—mid-speech. In spite of all the other conversation and distractions of the morning, this is what they have been waiting for, even* TRAVIS, *who looks helplessly from his mother to his grandmother.* RUTH *is the first to come to life again.*]

RUTH [*to* TRAVIS]: Get down them steps, boy! [TRAVIS *snaps to life and flies out to get the mail.*]

MAMA [*her eyes wide, her hand to her breast*]: You mean it done really come?

RUTH [*excited*]: Oh, Miss Lena!

MAMA [*collecting herself*]: Well . . . I don't know what we all so excited about 'round here for. We known it was coming for months.

RUTH: That's a whole lot different from having it come and being able to hold it in your hands . . . a piece of paper worth ten thousand dollars . . . [TRAVIS *bursts back into the room. He holds the envelope high above his head, like a little dancer, his face is radiant and he is breathless. He moves to his grandmother with sudden slow ceremony and puts the envelope into her hands. She accepts it, and then merely holds it and looks at it.*] Come on! Open it . . . Lord have mercy, I wish Walter Lee was here!

TRAVIS: Open it, Grandmama!

MAMA [*staring at it*]: Now you all be quiet. It's just a check.

RUTH: Open it . . .

MAMA [*still staring at it*]: Now don't act silly . . . We ain't never been no people to act silly 'bout no money—

RUTH [*swiftly*]: We ain't never had none before—*open it!* [MAMA *finally makes a good strong tear and pulls out the thin blue slice of paper and inspects it closely. The boy and his mother study it raptly over* MAMA*'s shoulders.*]

MAMA: Travis! [*She is counting off with doubt.*] Is that the right number of zeros?

TRAVIS: Yes'm . . . ten thousand dollars. Gaalee, Grandmama, you rich.

MAMA [*She holds the check away from her, still looking at it. Slowly her face sobers into a mask of unhappiness.*]: Ten thousand dollars. [*She hands it to* RUTH.] Put it away somewhere, Ruth. [*She does not look at* RUTH*; her eyes seem to be seeing something somewhere very far off.*] Ten thousand dollars they give you. Ten thousand dollars.

TRAVIS [*to his mother, sincerely*]: What's the matter with Grandmama—don't she want to be rich?

RUTH [*distractedly*]: You go on out and play now, baby. [TRAVIS *exits.* MAMA *starts wiping dishes absently, humming intently to herself.* RUTH *turns to her, with kind exasperation.*] You've gone and got yourself upset.

MAMA [*not looking at her*]: I spec if it wasn't for you all . . . I would just put that money away or give it to the church or something.

RUTH: Now what kind of talk is that. Mr. Younger would just be plain mad if he could hear you talking foolish like that.

MAMA [*stopping and staring off*]: Yes . . . he sure would. [*sighing*] We got enough to do with that money, all right. [*She halts then, and turns and looks at her daughter-in-law hard;* RUTH *avoids her eyes and* MAMA *wipes her hands with finality and starts to speak firmly to* RUTH.] Where did you go today, girl?

RUTH: To the doctor.

MAMA [*impatiently*]: Now, Ruth . . . you know better than that. Old Doctor Jones is strange enough in his way but there ain't nothing 'bout him make somebody slip and call him "she"—like you done this morning.

RUTH: Well, that's what happened—my tongue slipped.

MAMA: You went to see that woman, didn't you?

RUTH [*defensively, giving herself away*]: What woman you talking about?

MAMA [*angrily*]: That woman who—[WALTER *enters in great excitement.*]

WALTER: Did it come?

MAMA [*quietly*]: Can't you give people a Christian greeting before you start asking about money?

WALTER [*to* RUTH]: Did it come? [RUTH *unfolds the check and lays it quietly before him, watching him intently with thoughts of her own.* WALTER *sits down and grasps it close and counts off the zeros.*] Ten thousand dollars—[*He turns suddenly, frantically to his mother and draws some papers out of his breast pocket.*] Mama—look. Old Willy Harris put everything on paper—

MAMA: Son—I think you ought to talk to your wife . . . I'll go on out and leave you alone if you want—

WALTER: I can talk to her later—Mama, look—

MAMA: Son—

WALTER: WILL SOMEBODY PLEASE LISTEN TO ME TODAY!

MAMA [*quietly*]: I don't 'low no yellin' in this house, Walter Lee, and you know it—[WALTER *stares at them in frustration and starts to speak several times.*] And there ain't going to be no investing in no liquor stores. I don't aim to have to speak on that again [*a long pause*].

WALTER: Oh—so you don't aim to have to speak on that again? So you have decided . . . [*crumpling his papers*] Well, *you* tell that to my boy tonight when you put him to sleep on the living-room couch . . . [*turning to* MAMA *and speaking directly to her*]: Yeah—and tell it to my wife, Mama, tomorrow when she has to go out of here to look after somebody else's kids. And tell it to *me,* Mama, every time we need a new pair of curtains and I have to watch *you* go out and work in somebody's kitchen. Yeah, you tell me then! [WALTER *starts out.*]

RUTH: Where you going?

WALTER: I'm going out!

RUTH: Where?

WALTER: Just out of this house somewhere—

RUTH [*getting her coat*]: I'll come too.

WALTER: I don't want you to come!

RUTH: I got something to talk to you about, Walter.

WALTER: That's too bad.

MAMA [*still quietly*]: Walter Lee—[*She waits and he finally turns and looks at her.*] Sit down.

WALTER: I'm a grown man, Mama.

MAMA: Ain't nobody said you wasn't grown. But you still in my house and my presence. And as long as you are—you'll talk to your wife civil. Now sit down.

RUTH [*suddenly*]: Oh, let him go on out and drink himself to death! He makes me sick to my stomach! [*She flings her coat against him.*]

WALTER [*violently*]: And you turn mine, too, baby! [RUTH *goes into their bedroom and slams the door behind her.*] That was my greatest mistake—

MAMA [*still quietly*]: Walter, what is the matter with you?

WALTER: Matter with me? Ain't nothing the matter with *me!*

MAMA: Yes there is. Something eating you up like a crazy man. Something more than me not giving you this money. The past few years I been watching it happen to you. You get all nervous acting and kind of wild in the eyes—[WALTER *jumps up impatiently at her words.*] I said sit there now, I'm talking to you!

WALTER: Mama—I don't need no nagging at me today.

MAMA: Seem like you getting to a place where you always tied up in some kind of knot about something. But if anybody ask you 'bout it you just yell at 'em and bust out the house and go out and drink somewheres. Walter Lee, people can't live with that. Ruth's a good, patient girl in her way—but you getting to be too much. Boy, don't make the mistake of driving that girl away from you.

WALTER: Why—what she do for me?

MAMA: She loves you.

WALTER: Mama—I'm going out. I want to go off somewhere and be by myself for a while.

MAMA: I'm sorry 'bout your liquor store, son. It just wasn't the thing for us to do. That's what I want to tell you about—

WALTER: I got to go out, Mama—[*He rises.*]

MAMA: It's dangerous, son.

WALTER: What's dangerous?

MAMA: When a man goes outside his home to look for peace.

WALTER [*beseechingly*]: Then why can't there never be no peace in this house then?

MAMA: You done found it in some other house?

WALTER: No—there ain't no woman! Why do women always think there's a woman somewhere when a man gets restless. [*coming to her*] Mama—Mama—I want so many things . . .

MAMA: Yes, son—

WALTER: I want so many things that they are driving me kind of crazy . . . Mama—look at me.

MAMA: I'm looking at you. You a good-looking boy. You got a job, a nice wife, a fine boy and—

WALTER: A job. [*looks at her*] Mama, a job? I open and close car doors all day long. I drive a man around in his limousine and I say, "Yes, sir; no, sir; very good, sir; shall I take the Drive, sir?" Mama, that ain't no kind of job . . . that ain't nothing at all. [*very quietly*] Mama, I don't know if I can make you understand.

MAMA: Understand what, baby?

WALTER [*quietly*]: Sometimes it's like I can see the future stretched out in front of me—just plain as day. The future, Mama. Hanging over there at the edge of my days. Just waiting for me—a big, looming blank space—full of *nothing*. Just waiting for *me*. [*pause*] Mama—sometimes when I'm down-town and I pass them cool, quiet-looking restaurants where them white boys are sitting back and talking 'bout things . . . sitting there turning deals worth millions of dollars . . . sometimes I see guys don't look much older than me—

MAMA: Son—how come you talk so much 'bout money?

WALTER [*with immense passion*]: Because it is life, Mama!

MAMA [*quietly*]: Oh—[*very quietly*] So now it's life. Money is life. Once upon a time freedom used to be life—now it's money. I guess the world really do change . . .

WALTER: No—it was always money, Mama. We just didn't know about it.

MAMA: No . . . something has changed. [*She looks at him.*] You something new, boy. In my time we was worried about not being lynched and getting to the North if we could and how to stay alive and still have a pinch of dignity too . . . Now here come you and Beneatha—talking 'bout things we ain't never even thought about hardly, me and your daddy. You ain't satisfied or proud of nothing we done. I mean that you had a home; that we kept you out of trouble till you was grown; that you don't have to ride to work on the back of nobody's streetcar—You my children—but how different we done become.

WALTER: You just don't understand, Mama, you just don't understand.

MAMA: Son—do you know your wife is expecting another baby? [WALTER *stands, stunned, and absorbs what his mother has said.*] That's what she wanted to talk to you about. [WALTER *sinks down into a chair.*] This ain't for me to be telling—but you ought to know. [*She waits*] I think Ruth is thinking 'bout getting rid of that child.

WALTER [*slowly understanding*]: No—no—Ruth wouldn't do that.

MAMA: When the world gets ugly enough—a woman will do anything for her family. *The part that's already living.*

WALTER: You don't know Ruth, Mama, if you think she would do that. [RUTH *opens the bedroom door and stands there a little limp.*]

RUTH [*beaten*]: Yes I would too, Walter, [*pause*] I gave her a five-dollar down payment. [*There is total silence as the man stares at his wife and the mother stares at her son.*]

MAMA [*presently*]: Well—[*tightly*] Well—son, I'm waiting to hear you say something . . . I'm waiting to hear how you be your father's son. Be the man he was . . . [*pause*] Your wife say she going to destroy your child. And I'm waiting to hear you talk like him and say we a people who give children life, not who destroys them—[*She rises.*] I'm waiting to see you stand up and look like your daddy and say we done give up one baby to poverty and that we ain't going to give up nary another one . . . I'm waiting.

WALTER: Ruth—

MAMA: If you a son of mine, tell her! [WALTER *turns, looks at her and can say nothing. She continues, bitterly.*] You . . . you are a disgrace to your father's memory. Somebody get me my hat.

CURTAIN

ACT II

SCENE 1

TIME: *Later the same day.*

AT RISE: RUTH *is ironing again. She has the radio going. Presently* BENEATHA'S *bedroom door opens and* RUTH*'s mouth falls and she puts down the iron in fascination.*

RUTH: What have we got on tonight!

BENEATHA [*emerging grandly from the doorway so that we can see her thoroughly robed in the costume* ASAGAI *brought*]: You are looking at what a well-dressed Nigerian woman wears—[*She parades for* RUTH, *her hair completely hidden by the headdress; she is coquettishly fanning herself with an ornate oriental fan, mistakenly more like Butterfly than any Nigerian that ever was.*] Isn't it beautiful? [*She promenades to the radio and, with an arrogant flourish, turns off the good loud blues that is playing.*] Enough of this assimilationist junk! [RUTH *follows her with her eyes as she goes to the phonograph and puts on a record and turns and waits ceremoniously for the music to come up. Then with a shout*—] OCOMOGOSIAY! [RUTH *jumps. The music comes up, a lovely Nigerian melody.* BENEATHA *listens, enraptured, her eyes far away—"back to the past." She begins to dance.* RUTH *is dumbfounded.*]

RUTH: What kind of dance is that?

BENEATHA: A folk dance.

RUTH [*Pearl Bailey*]: What kind of folks do that, honey?

BENEATHA: It's from Nigeria. It's a dance of welcome.

RUTH: Who you welcoming?

BENEATHA: The men back to the village.

RUTH: Where they been?

BENEATHA: How should I know—out hunting or something. Anyway, they are coming back now. . .

RUTH: Well, that's good.

BENEATHA [*with the record*]: *Alundi, alundi*
Alundi alunya
Jop pu a jeepua
Ang gu soooooooooo
Ai yai yae . . .
Ayehaye—alundi . . .

[WALTER *comes in during this performance; he has obviously been drinking. He leans against the door heavily and watches his sister, at first with distaste. Then his eyes look off—"back to the past"—as he lifts both his fists to the roof, screaming.*]

WALTER: YEAH . . . AND ETHIOPIA STRETCH FORTH HER HANDS AGAIN! . . .

RUTH [*drily, looking at him*]: Yes—and Africa sure is claiming her own tonight. [*She gives them both up and starts ironing again.*]

WALTER [*all in a drunken, dramatic shout*]: Shut up! . . . I'm digging them drums . . . them drums move me! . . . [*He makes his weaving way to his wife's face and leans in close to her.*] In my heart of hearts—[*He thumps his chest.*]—I am much warrior!

RUTH [*without even looking up*]: In your heart of hearts you are much drunkard.

WALTER [*coming away from her and starting to wander around the room, shouting*]: Me and Jomo . . . [*Intently, in his sister's face. She has stopped dancing to watch him in this unknown mood.*] That's my man, Kenyatta. [*Shouting and thumping his chest.*] FLAMING SPEAR! HOT DAMN! [*He is suddenly in possession of an imaginary spear and actively spearing enemies all over the room.*] OCOMOGOSIAY . . . THE LION IS WAKING . . . OWIMOWEH! [*He pulls his shirt open and leaps up on a table and gestures with his spear. The bell rings.* RUTH *goes to answer.*]

BENEATHA [*to encourage* WALTER, *thoroughly caught up with this side of him*]: OCOMOGOSIAY, FLAMING SPEAR!

WALTER [*On the table, very far gone, his eyes pure glass sheets. He sees what we cannot, that he is a leader of his people, a great chief, a descendant of Chaka, and that the hour to march has come.*]: Listen, my black brothers—

BENEATHA: OCOMOGOSIAY!

WALTER: —Do you hear the waters rushing against the shores of the coast-lands—

BENEATHA: OCOMOGOSIAY!

WALTER: —Do you hear the screeching of the cocks in yonder hills beyond where the chiefs meet in council for the coming of the mighty war—

BENEATHA: OCOMOGOSIAY!

WALTER: —Do you hear the beating of the wings of the birds flying low over the mountains and the low places of our land—[RUTH *opens the door,* GEORGE MURCHISON *enters.*]

BENEATHA: OCOMOGOSIAY!

WALTER: —Do you hear the singing of the women, singing the war songs of our fathers to the babies in the great houses . . . singing the sweet war songs? OH, DO YOU HEAR, MY BLACK BROTHERS?

BENEATHA [*completely gone*]: We hear you, Flaming Spear—

WALTER: Telling us to prepare for the greatness of the time—[*to* GEORGE] Black Brother! [*He extends his hand for the fraternal clasp.*]

GEORGE: Black Brother, hell!

RUTH [*having had enough, and embarrassed for the family*]: Beneatha, you got company—what's the matter with you? Walter Lee Younger, get down off that table and stop acting like a fool . . . [WALTER *comes down off the table suddenly and makes a quick exit to the bathroom.*]

RUTH: He's had a little to drink . . . I don't know what her excuse is.

GEORGE [*to* BENEATHA]: Look honey, we're going *to* the theatre—we're not going to be *in* it . . . so go change, huh?

RUTH: You expect this boy to go out with you looking like that?

BENEATHA [*looking at* GEORGE]: That's up to George. If he's ashamed of his heritage—

GEORGE: Oh, don't be so proud of yourself, Bennie—just because you look eccentric.

BENEATHA: How can something that's natural be eccentric?

GEORGE: That's what being eccentric means—being natural. Get dressed.

BENEATHA: I don't like that, George.

RUTH: Why must you and your brother make an argument out of everything people say?

BENEATHA: Because I hate assimilationist Negroes!

RUTH: Will somebody please tell me what assimila-who-ever means!

GEORGE: Oh, it's just a college girl's way of calling people Uncle Toms—but that isn't what it means at all.

RUTH: Well, what does it mean?

BENEATHA [*cutting* GEORGE *off and staring at him as she replies to* RUTH]: It means someone who is willing to give up his own culture and submerge himself completely in the dominant, and in this case, *oppressive* culture!

GEORGE: Oh, dear, dear, dear! Here we go! A lecture on the African past! On our Great West African Heritage! In one second we will hear all about the great Ashanti empires; the great Songhay civilizations; and the great sculpture of Benin—and then some poetry in the Bantu—and the whole monologue will end with the word *heritage!* [*nastily*] Let's face it, baby, your heritage is nothing but a bunch of raggedy-assed spirituals and some grass huts!

BENEATHA: *Grass huts!* [RUTH *crosses to her and forcibly pushes her toward the bedroom.*] See there . . . you are standing there in your splendid ignorance talking about people who were the first to smelt iron on the face of the earth! [RUTH *is pushing her through the door.*] The Ashanti were performing surgical operations when the English—[RUTH *pulls the door to, with* BENEATHA *on the other side, and smiles graciously at* GEORGE. BENEATHA *opens the door and shouts the end of the sentence defiantly at* GEORGE.]—were still tattooing themselves with blue dragons . . . [*She goes back inside.*]

RUTH: Have a seat, George. [*They both sit.* RUTH *folds her hands rather primly on her lap, determined to demonstrate the civilization of the family.*] Warm, ain't it? I mean for September. [*pause*] Just like they always say about Chicago weather: If it's too hot or cold for you, just wait a minute and it'll change. [*She smiles happily at this cliché of clichés.*] Everybody say it's got to do with them bombs and things they keep setting off. [*pause*] Would you like a nice cold beer?

GEORGE: No, thank you. I don't care for beer. [*He looks at his watch.*] I hope she hurries up.

RUTH: What time is the show?

GEORGE: It's an eight-thirty curtain. That's just Chicago, though. In New York standard curtain time is eight forty. [*He is rather proud of this knowledge.*]

RUTH [*properly appreciating it*]: You get to New York a lot?

GEORGE [*offhand*]: Few times a year.

RUTH: Oh—that's nice. I've never been to New York. [WALTER *enters. We feel he has relieved himself, but the edge of unreality is still with him.*]

WALTER: New York ain't got nothing Chicago ain't. Just a bunch of hustling people all squeezed up together—being "Eastern." [*He turns his face into a screw of displeasure.*]

GEORGE: Oh—you've been?

WALTER: Plenty of times.

RUTH [*shocked at the lie*]: Walter Lee Younger!

WALTER [*staring her down*]: Plenty! [*pause*] What we got to drink in this house? Why don't you offer this man some refreshment. [*to* GEORGE] They don't know how to entertain people in this house, man.

GEORGE: Thank you—I don't really care for anything.

WALTER [*feeling his head; sobriety coming*]: Where's Mama?

RUTH: She ain't come back yet.

WALTER [*looking* MURCHISON *over from head to toe, scrutinizing his carefully casual tweed sports jacket over cashmere V-neck sweater over soft eyelet shirt and tie, and soft slacks, finished off with white buckskin shoes*]: Why all you college boys wear them fairyish-looking white shoes?

RUTH: Walter Lee! [GEORGE MURCHISON *ignores the remark.*]

WALTER [*to* RUTH]: Well, they look crazy as hell—white shoes, cold as it is.

RUTH [*crushed*]: You have to excuse him—

WALTER: No he don't! Excuse me for what? What you always excusing me for! I'll excuse myself when I needs to be excused! [*a pause*] They look as funny as them black knee socks Beneatha wears out of here all the time.

RUTH: It's the college *style,* Walter.

WALTER: Style, hell. She looks like she got burnt legs or something!

RUTH: Oh, Walter—

WALTER [*an irritable mimic*]: Oh, Walter! Oh, Walter! [*to* MURCHISON] How's your old man making out? I understand you all going to buy that big hotel on the Drive?[1] [*He finds a beer in the refrigerator, wanders over to* MURCHISON, *sipping and wiping his lips with the back of his hand, and straddling a chair backwards to talk to the other man.*] Shrewd move. Your old man is all right, man. [*tapping his head and half winking for emphasis*] I mean he knows how to operate. I mean he thinks big, you know what I mean, I mean for a home,[2] you know? But I think he's kind of running out of ideas now. I'd like to talk to him. Listen, man, I got some plans that could turn this city upside down. I mean I think like he does. *Big.* Invest big, gamble big, hell, lose *big* if you have to, you know what I mean. It's hard to find a man on this whole Southside who understands my kind of thinking—you dig? [*He scrutinizes* MURCHISON *again, drinks his beer, squints his eyes and leans in close, confidential, man to man.*] Me and you ought to sit down and talk sometimes, man. Man, I got me some ideas . . .

MURCHISON [*with boredom*]: Yeah—sometimes we'll have to do that, Walter.

WALTER [*understanding the indifference, and offended*]: Yeah—well, when you get the time, man. I know you a busy little boy.

RUTH: Walter, please—

WALTER [*bitterly, hurt*]: I know ain't nothing in this world as busy as you colored college boys with your fraternity pins and white shoes . . .

RUTH [*covering her face with humiliation*]: Oh, Walter Lee—

WALTER: I see you all all the time—with the books tucked under your arms—going to your [*British A—a mimic*] "clahsses." And for what! What the hell you learning over there? Filling up your heads—[*counting off on his fingers*]—with the sociology and the psychology—but they teaching you how to be a man? How to take over and run the world? They teaching you how to run a rubber plantation or a steel mill? Naw—just to talk proper and read books and wear white shoes . . .

GEORGE [*looking at him with distaste, a little above it all*]: You're all wacked up with bitterness, man.

WALTER [*intently, almost quietly, between the teeth, glaring at the boy*]: And you—ain't you bitter, man? Ain't you just about had it yet? Don't you see no stars gleaming that you can't reach out and grab? You happy?—You contented son-of-a-bitch—you happy? You got it made? Bitter? Man, I'm a volcano. Bitter?

[1]**Drive** Chicago's Outer Drive running along Lake Michigan. [2]**Home** home-boy; one of us.

Here I am a giant—surrounded by ants! Ants who can't even understand what it is the giant is talking about.

RUTH [*passionately and suddenly*]: Oh, Walter—ain't you with nobody!

WALTER [*violently*]: No! 'Cause ain't nobody with me! Not even my own mother!

RUTH: Walter, that's a terrible thing to say! [BENEATHA *enters, dressed for the evening in a cocktail dress and earrings.*]

GEORGE: Well—hey, you look great.

BENEATHA: Let's go, George. See you all later.

RUTH: Have a nice time.

GEORGE: Thanks. Good night. [*to* WALTER, *sarcastically*] Good night, *Prometheus*. [BENEATHA *and* GEORGE *exit.*]

WALTER [*to* RUTH]: Who is Prometheus?

RUTH: I don't know. Don't worry about it.

WALTER [*in fury, pointing after* GEORGE]: See there—they get to a point where they can't insult you man to man—they got to go talk about something ain't nobody never heard of!

RUTH: How do you know it was an insult? [*to humor him*] Maybe Prometheus is a nice fellow.

WALTER: Prometheus! I bet there ain't even no such thing! I bet that simple-minded clown—

RUTH: Walter—[*She stops what she is doing and looks at him.*]

WALTER [*yelling*]: Don't start!

RUTH: Start what?

WALTER: Your nagging! Where was I? Who was I with? How much money did I spend?

RUTH [*plaintively*]: Walter Lee—why don't we just try to talk about it . . .

WALTER [*not listening*]: I been out talking with people who understand me. People who care about the things I got on my mind.

RUTH [*wearily*]: I guess that means people like Willy Harris.

WALTER: Yes, people like Willy Harris.

RUTH [*with a sudden flash of impatience*]: Why don't you all just hurry up and go into the banking business and stop talking about it!

WALTER: Why? You want to know why? 'Cause we all tied up in a race of people that don't know how to do nothing but moan, pray and have babies! [*The line is too bitter even for him and he looks at her and sits down.*]

RUTH: Oh, Walter . . . [*softy*] Honey, why can't you stop fighting me?

WALTER [*without thinking*]: Who's fighting you? Who even cares about you? [*This line begins the retardation of his mood.*]

RUTH: Well—[*She waits a long time, and then with resignation starts to put away her things.*] I guess I might as well go on to bed . . . [*more or less to herself*] I don't know where we lost it . . . but we have . . . [*Then, to him.*] I—I'm sorry about this new baby, Walter. I guess maybe I better go on and do what I started . . . I guess I just didn't realize how bad things was with us . . . I guess I just didn't really realize—[*She starts out to the bedroom and stops.*] You want some hot milk?

WALTER: Hot milk?

RUTH: Yes—hot milk.

WALTER: Why hot milk?

RUTH: 'Cause after all that liquor you come home with you ought to have something hot in your stomach.

WALTER: I don't want no milk.

RUTH: You want some coffee then?

WALTER: No, I don't want no coffee. I don't want nothing hot to drink. [*almost plaintively*] Why you always trying to give me something to eat?

RUTH [*standing and looking at him helplessly*]: What else can I give you, Walter Lee Younger? [*She stands and looks at him and presently turns to go out again. He lifts his head and watches her going away from him in a new mood which began to emerge when he asked her, "Who cares about you?"*]

WALTER: It's been rough, ain't it, baby? [*She hears and stops but does not turn around and he continues to her back.*] I guess between two people there ain't never as much understood as folks generally thinks there is. I mean like between me and you—[*She turns to face him.*] How we gets to the place where we scared to talk softness to each other. [*He waits, thinking hard himself.*] Why you think it got to be like that? [*He is thoughtful, almost as a child would be.*] Ruth, what is it gets into people ought to be close?

RUTH: I don't know, honey. I think about it a lot.

WALTER: On account of you and me, you mean? The way things are with us. The way something done come down between us.

RUTH: There ain't so much between us, Walter . . . Not when you come to me and try to talk to me. Try to be with me . . . a little even.

WALTER [*total honesty*]: Sometimes . . . sometimes . . . I don't even know how to try.

RUTH: Walter—

WALTER: Yes?

RUTH [*coming to him, gently and with misgiving, but coming to him*]: Honey . . . life don't have to be like this. I mean sometimes people can do things so that things are better . . . You remember how we used to talk when Travis was born . . . about the way we were going to live . . . the kind of house . . . [*She is stroking his head.*] Well, it's all starting to slip away from us . . . [MAMA *enters, and* WALTER *jumps up and shouts at her.*]

WALTER: Mama, where have you been?

MAMA: My—them steps is longer than they used to be. Whew! [*She sits down and ignores him.*] How you feeling this evening, Ruth! [RUTH *shrugs, disturbed some at having been prematurely interrupted and watching her husband knowingly.*]

WALTER: Mama, where have you been all day?

MAMA [*still ignoring him and leaning on the table and changing to more comfortable shoes*]: Where's Travis?

RUTH: I let him go out earlier and he ain't come back yet. Boy, is he going to get it!

WALTER: Mama!

MAMA [*as if she has heard him for the first time*]: Yes, son?

WALTER: Where did you go this afternoon?

MAMA: I went downtown to tend to some business that I had to tend to.

WALTER: What kind of business?

MAMA: You know better than to question me like a child, Brother.

WALTER [*rising and bending over the table*]: Where were you, Mama? [*bringing his fists down and shouting*] Mama, you didn't go do something with that insurance money, something crazy? [*The front door opens slowly, interrupting him, and* TRAVIS *peeks his head in, less than hopefully.*]

TRAVIS [*to his mother*]: Mama, I—

RUTH: "Mama I" nothing! You're going to get it, boy! Get on in that bedroom and get yourself ready!

TRAVIS: But I—

MAMA: Why don't you all never let the child explain hisself.

RUTH: Keep out of it now, Lena. [MAMA *clamps her lips together, and* RUTH *advances toward her son menacingly.*]

RUTH: A thousand times I have told you not to go off like that—

MAMA [*holding out her arms to her grandson*]: Well—at least let me tell him something. I want him to be the first one to hear . . . Come here, Travis. [*the boy obeys, gladly*] Travis—[*She takes him by the shoulder and looks into his face.*]—you know that money we got in the mail this morning?

TRAVIS: Yes'm—

MAMA: Well—what you think your grandmama gone and done with that money?

TRAVIS: I don't know, Grandmama.

MAMA [*putting her finger on his nose for emphasis*]: She went out and she bought you a house! [*The explosion comes from* WALTER *at the end of the revelation and he jumps up and turns away from all of them in a fury.* MAMA *continues, to* TRAVIS.] You glad about the house? It's going to be yours when you get to be a man.

TRAVIS: Yeah—I always wanted to live in a house.

MAMA: All right, gimme some sugar then—[TRAVIS *puts his arms around her neck as she watches her son over the boy's shoulder. Then, to* TRAVIS, *after the embrace.*] Now when you say your prayers tonight, you thank God and your grandfather—'cause it was him who give you the house—in his way.

RUTH [*taking the boy from* MAMA *and pushing him toward the bedroom*]: Now you get out of here and get ready for your beating.

TRAVIS: Aw, Mama—

RUTH: Get on in there—[*closing the door behind him and turning radiantly to her mother-in-law*] So you went and did it!

MAMA [*quietly, looking at her son with pain*]: Yes, I did.

RUTH [*raising both arms classically*]: *Praise God!* [*Looks at* WALTER *a moment, who says nothing. She crosses rapidly to her husband.*] Please, honey—let me be glad . . . you be glad too. [*She has laid her hands on his shoulders, but he shakes himself free of her roughly, without turning to face her.*] Oh, Walter . . . a home . . . *a home.* [*She comes back to* MAMA.] Well—where is it? How big is it? How much it going to cost?

MAMA: Well—

RUTH: When we moving?

MAMA [*smiling at her*]: First of the month.

RUTH [*throwing back her head with jubilance*]: *Praise God!*

MAMA [*tentatively, still looking at her son's back turned against her and* RUTH]: It's—it's a nice house too . . . . [*She cannot help speaking directly to him. An imploring quality in her voice, her manner, makes her almost like a girl now.*] Three bedrooms—nice big one for you and Ruth . . . . Me and Beneatha still have to share our room, but Travis have one of his own—and [*with difficulty*] I figure if the—new baby—is a boy, we could get one of them double-decker outfits . . . And there's a yard with a little patch of dirt where I could maybe get to grow me a few flowers . . . And a nice big basement . . .

RUTH: Walter honey, be glad—

MAMA [*still to his back, fingering things on the table*]: 'Course I don't want to make it sound fancier than it is . . . It's just a plain little old house—but it's made good and solid—and it will be *ours*. Walter Lee—it makes a difference in a man when he can walk on floors that belong to *him* . . .

RUTH: Where is it?

MAMA [*frightened at this telling*]: Well—well—it's out there in Clybourne Park— [RUTH*'s radiance fades abruptly, and* WALTER *finally turns slowly to face his mother with incredulity and hostility*.]

RUTH: Where?

MAMA [*matter-of-factly*]: Four o six Clybourne Street, Clybourne Park.

RUTH: Clybourne Park? Mama, there ain't no colored people living in Clybourne Park.

MAMA [*almost idiotically*]: Well, I guess there's going to be some now.

WALTER [*bitterly*]: So that's the peace and comfort you went out and bought for us today!

MAMA [*raising her eyes to meet his finally*]: Son—I just tried to find the nicest place for the least amount of money for my family.

RUTH [*trying to recover from the shock*]: Well—well—'course I ain't one never been 'fraid of no crackers, mind you—but—well, wasn't there no other houses nowhere?

MAMA: Them houses they put up for colored in them areas way out all seem to cost twice as much as other houses. I did the best I could.

RUTH [*struck senseless with the news, in its various degrees of goodness and trouble, she sits a moment, her fists propping her chin in thought, and then she starts to rise, bringing her fists down with vigor, the radiance spreading from cheek to cheek again*]: Well—well!—All I can say is—if this is my time in life—my time—to say good-bye—[*And she builds with momentum as she starts to circle the room with an exuberant, almost tearfully happy release.*]—to these God-damned cracking walls!—[*she pounds the walls*]—and these marching roaches—[*she wipes at an imaginary army of marching roaches*]—and this cramped little closet which ain't now or never was no kitchen! . . . then I say it loud and good, *Hallelujah! and good-bye misery . . . I don't never want to see your ugly face again!* [*She laughs joyously, having practically destroyed the apartment, and flings her arms up and lets them come down happily, slowly, reflectively, over her abdomen, aware for the first time perhaps that the life therein pulses with happiness and not despair.*] Lena?

MAMA [*moved, watching her happiness*]: Yes, honey?

RUTH [*looking off*]: Is there—is there a whole lot of sunlight?

MAMA [*understanding*]: Yes, child, there's a whole lot of sunlight [*long pause*].

RUTH [*collecting herself and going to the door of the room* TRAVIS *is in*]: Well—I guess I better see 'bout Travis. [*to* MAMA] Lord, I sure don't feel like whipping nobody today! [*She exits.*]

MAMA [*the mother and son are left alone now and the mother waits a long time, considering deeply, before she speaks*]: Son—you—you understand what I done, don't you? [WALTER *is silent and sullen.*] I—I just seen my family falling apart today . . . just falling to pieces in front of my eyes . . . We couldn't of gone on like we was today. We was going backwards 'stead of forwards—talking 'bout killing babies and wishing each other was dead . . . When it gets like that in life—you just got to do something different, push on out and do something bigger . . . [*She waits.*] I wish you say something, son . . . I wish you'd say how deep inside you you think I done the right thing—

WALTER [*crossing slowly to his bedroom door and finally turning there and speaking measuredly*]: What you need me to say you done right for? You the head of this family. You run our lives like you want to. It was your money and you did what you wanted with it. So what you need for me to say it was all right for? [*bitterly, to hurt her as deeply as he knows is possible*] So you butchered up a dream of mine—you—who always talking 'bout your children's dreams . . .

MAMA: Walter Lee—[*He just closes the door behind him.* MAMA *sits alone, thinking heavily.*]

CURTAIN

SCENE 2

TIME: *Friday night. A few weeks later.*

AT RISE: *Packing crates mark the intention of the family to move.* BENEATHA *and* GEORGE *come in, presumably from an evening out again.*

GEORGE: O.K. . . . O.K., whatever you say . . . [*They both sit on the couch. He tries to kiss her. She moves away.*] Look, we've had a nice evening; let's not spoil it, huh? . . . [*He again turns her head and tries to nuzzle in and she turns away from him, not with distaste but with momentary lack of interest; in a mood to pursue what they were talking about.*]

BENEATHA: I'm trying to talk to you.

GEORGE: We always talk.

BENEATHA: Yes—and I love to talk.

GEORGE [*exasperated; rising*]: I know it and I don't mind it sometimes . . . I want you to cut it out, see—The moody stuff, I mean. I don't like it. You're a nice-looking girl . . . all over. That's all you need, honey, forget the atmosphere. Guys aren't going to go for the atmosphere—they're going to go for what they see. Be glad for that. Drop the Garbo routine. It doesn't go with you. As for myself, I want a nice—[*groping*]—simple [*thoughtfully*]—sophisticated girl . . . not a poet—O.K.? [*She rebuffs him again and he starts to leave.*]

BENEATHA: Why are you angry?

GEORGE: Because this is stupid! I don't go out with you to discuss the nature of "quiet desperation" or to hear all about your thoughts—because the world will go on thinking what it thinks regardless—

BENEATHA: Then why read books? Why go to school?

GEORGE [*with artificial patience, counting on his fingers*]: It's simple. You read books—to learn facts—to get grades—to pass the course—to get a degree. That's all—it has nothing to do with thoughts [*a long pause*].

BENEATHA: I see. [*a longer pause as she looks at him*] Good night, George. [GEORGE *looks at her a little oddly, and starts to exit. He meets* MAMA *coming in.*]

GEORGE: Oh—hello, Mrs. Younger.

MAMA: Hello, George, how you feeling?

GEORGE: Fine—fine, how are you?

MAMA: Oh, a little tired. You know them steps can get you after a day's work. You all have a nice time tonight?

GEORGE: Yes—a fine time. Well, good night.

MAMA: Good night. [*He exits.* MAMA *closes the door behind her.*] Hello, honey. What you sitting like that for?

BENEATHA: I'm just sitting.

MAMA: Didn't you have a nice time?

BENEATHA: No.

MAMA: No? What's the matter?

BENEATHA: Mama, George is a fool—honest. [*She rises.*]

MAMA [*bustling around unloading the packages she has entered with; she stops*]: Is he, baby?

BENEATHA: Yes. [BENEATHA *makes up* TRAVIS' *bed as she talks.*]

MAMA: You sure?

BENEATHA: Yes.

MAMA: Well—I guess you better not waste your time with no fools. [BENEATHA *looks up at her mother, watching her put groceries in the refrigerator. Finally she gathers up her things and starts into the bedroom. At the door she stops and looks back at her mother.*]

BENEATHA: Mama—

MAMA: Yes, baby—

BENEATHA: Thank you.

MAMA: For what?

BENEATHA: For understanding me this time. [*She exits quickly and the mother stands, smiling a little, looking at the place where* BENEATHA *had stood.* RUTH *enters.*]

RUTH: Now don't you fool with any of this stuff, Lena—

MAMA: Oh, I just thought I'd sort a few things out. [*The phone rings.* RUTH *answers.*]

RUTH [*at the phone*]: Hello—Just a minute. [*goes to door*] Walter, it's Mrs. Arnold. [*Waits. Goes back to the phone. Tense.*] Hello. Yes, this is his wife speaking . . . He's lying down now. Yes . . . well, he'll be in tomorrow. He's been very sick. Yes—I know we should have called, but we were so sure he'd be able to come in today. Yes—yes, I'm very sorry. Yes . . . Thank you very much. [*She hangs up.* WALTER *is standing in the doorway of the bedroom behind her.*] That was Mrs. Arnold.

WALTER [*indifferently*]: Was it?

RUTH: She said if you don't come in tomorrow that they are getting a new man . . .

WALTER: Ain't that sad—ain't that crying sad.

RUTH: She said Mr. Arnold has had to take a cab for three days . . . Walter, you ain't been to work for three days! [*This is a revelation to her.*] Where you been, Walter Lee Younger? [WALTER *looks at her and starts to laugh.*] You're going to lose your job.

WALTER: That's right . . .

RUTH: Oh, Walter, and with your mother working like a dog every day—

WALTER: That's sad too—Everything is sad.

MAMA: What you been doing for these three days, son?

WALTER: Mama—you don't know all the things a man what got leisure can find to do in this city . . . What's this—Friday night? Well—Wednesday I borrowed Willy Harris' car and I went for a drive . . . just me and myself and I drove and drove . . . Way out . . . way past South Chicago, and I parked the car and I sat and looked at the steel mills all day long. I just sat in the car and looked at them big black chimneys for hours. Then I drove back and I went to the Green Hat. [*pause*] And Thursday—Thursday I borrowed the car again and I got in it and I pointed it the other way and I drove the other way—for hours—way, way up to Wisconsin, and I looked at the farms. I just drove and looked at the farms. Then I drove back and I went to the Green Hat. [*pause*] And today—today I didn't get the car. Today I just walked. All over the Southside. And I looked at the Negroes and they looked at me and finally I just sat down on the curb at Thirty-ninth and South Parkway and I just sat there and watched the Negroes go by. And then I went to the Green Hat. You all sad? You all depressed? And you know where I am going right now—[RUTH *goes out quietly*].

MAMA: Oh, Big Walter, is this the harvest of our days?

WALTER: You know what I like about the Green Hat? [*He turns the radio on and a steamy, deep blues pours into the room.*] I like this little cat they got there who blows a sax . . . He blows. He talks to me. He ain't but 'bout five feet tall and he's got a conked head and his eyes is always closed and he's all music—

MAMA [*rising and getting some papers out of her handbag*]: Walter—

WALTER: And there's this other guy who plays the piano . . . and they got a sound. I mean they can work on some music . . . They got the best little combo in the world in the Green Hat . . . You can just sit there and drink and listen to them three men play and you realize that don't nothing matter worth a damn, but just being there—

MAMA: I've helped do it to you, haven't I, son? Walter, I been wrong.

WALTER: Naw—you ain't never been wrong about nothing, Mama.

MAMA: Listen to me, now. I say I been wrong, son. That I been doing to you what the rest of the world been doing to you. [*She stops and he looks up slowly at her and she meets his eyes pleadingly.*] Walter—what you ain't understood is that I ain't got nothing, don't own nothing, ain't never really wanted nothing that wasn't for you. There ain't nothing as precious to me . . . There ain't nothing worth holding on to, money, dreams, nothing else—if it means—if it means it's going to destroy my boy. [*She puts her papers in front of him and he watches her without speaking or moving.*] I paid the man thirty-five hundred dollars down on the house. That leaves sixty-five hundred dollars. Monday morning I want you to take this money and take three thousand dollars and put it in a savings account for Beneatha's medical schooling. The rest you put in a checking account—with your name on it. And from now on any penny that come out of it or that go in it is for you to look after. For you to decide. [*She drops her hands a little helplessly.*] It ain't much, but it's all I got in the world and I'm putting it in your hands. I'm telling you to be the head of this family from now on like you supposed to be.

WALTER [*stares at the money*]: You trust me like that, Mama?

MAMA: I ain't never stop trusting you. Like I ain't never stop loving you. [*She goes out, and* WALTER *sits looking at the money on the table as the music continues in its idiom, pulsing in the room. Finally, in a decisive gesture, he gets up, and, in mingled joy and desperation, picks up the money. At the same moment,* TRAVIS *enters for bed.*]

TRAVIS: What's the matter, Daddy? You drunk?

WALTER [*sweetly, more sweetly than we have ever known him*]: No, Daddy ain't drunk. Daddy ain't going to never be drunk again. . . .

TRAVIS: Well, good night, Daddy. [*The father has come from behind the couch and leans over, embracing his son.*]

WALTER: Son, I feel like talking to you tonight.

TRAVIS: About what?

WALTER: Oh, about a lot of things. About you and what kind of man you going to be when you grow up. . . . Son—son, what do you want to be when you grow up?

TRAVIS: A bus driver.

WALTER [*laughing a little*]: A what? Man, that ain't nothing to want to be!

TRAVIS: Why not?

WALTER: 'Cause, man—it ain't big enough—you know what I mean.

TRAVIS: I don't know then. I can't make up my mind. Sometimes Mama asks me that too. And sometimes when I tell her I just want to be like you—she says she don't want me to be like that and sometimes she says she does . . . .

WALTER [*gathering him up in his arms*]: You know what, Travis? In seven years you going to be seventeen years old. And things is going to be very different with us in seven years, Travis. . . . One day when you are seventeen I'll come home—home from my office downtown somewhere—

TRAVIS: You don't work in no office, Daddy.

WALTER: No—but after tonight. After what your daddy gonna do tonight, there's going to be offices—a whole lot of offices. . . .

TRAVIS: What you gonna do tonight, Daddy?

WALTER: You wouldn't understand yet, son, but your daddy's gonna make a transaction . . . a business transaction that's going to change our lives . . . That's how come one day when you 'bout seventeen years old I'll come home and I'll be pretty tired, you know what I mean, after a day of conferences and secretaries getting things wrong the way they do . . . 'cause an executive's life is hell, man—[*The more he talks the farther away he gets.*] And I'll pull the car up on the driveway . . . just a plain black Chrysler, I think, with white walls—no—black tires. More elegant. Rich people don't have to be flashy . . . though I'll have to get something a little sportier for Ruth—maybe a Cadillac convertible to do her shopping in. . . . And I'll come up the steps to the house and the gardener will be clipping away at the hedges and he'll say, "Good evening, Mr. Younger." And I'll say, "Hello, Jefferson, how are you this evening?" And I'll go inside and Ruth will come downstairs and meet me at the door and we'll kiss each other and she'll take my arm and we'll go up to your room to see you sitting on the floor with the catalogues of all the great schools in America around you. . . . All the great schools in the world! And—and I'll say, all right son—it's your seventeenth birthday, what is it you've decided? . . . Just tell me where you want to go to school and you'll *go*. Just tell me, what it is you want to be—and you'll be it. . . . Whatever you want to be—Yessir! [*He holds his arms open for* TRAVIS.] You just name it, son . . . [TRAVIS *leaps into them*] and I hand you the world! [WALTER*'s voice has risen in pitch and hysterical promise and on the last line he lifts* TRAVIS *high*.]

BLACKOUT

SCENE 3

TIME: *Saturday, moving day, one week later.*

Before the curtain rises, RUTH*'s voice, a strident, dramatic church alto, cuts through the silence.*

It is, in the darkness, a triumphant surge, a penetrating statement of expectation: "Oh, Lord, I don't feel no ways tired! Children, oh, glory hallelujah!"

As the curtain rises we see that RUTH *is alone in the living room, finishing up the family's packing. It is moving day. She is nailing crates and tying cartons.* BENEATHA *enters, carrying a guitar case, and watches her exuberant sister-in-law.*

RUTH: Hey!

BENEATHA [*putting away the case*]: Hi.

RUTH [*pointing at a package*]: Honey—look in that package there and see what I found on sale this morning at the South Center. [RUTH *gets up and moves to the package and draws out some curtains.*] Lookahere—hand-turned hems!

BENEATHA: How do you know the window size out there?

RUTH [*who hadn't thought of that*]: Oh—Well, they bound to fit something in the whole house. Anyhow, they was too good a bargain to pass up. [RUTH *slaps her head, suddenly remembering something.*] Oh, Bennie—I meant to put a special note on that carton over there. That's your mama's good china and she wants 'em to be very careful with it.

BENEATHA: I'll do it. [BENEATHA *finds a piece of paper and starts to draw large letters on it.*]

RUTH: You know what I'm going to do soon as I get in that new house?

BENEATHA: What?

RUTH: Honey—I'm going to run me a tub of water up to here . . . [*with her fingers practically up to her nostrils*] And I'm going to get in it—and I am going to sit . . . and sit . . . and sit in that hot water and the first person who knocks to tell *me* to hurry up and come out—

BENEATHA: Gets shot at sunrise.

RUTH [*laughing happily*]: You said it, sister! [*noticing how large* BENEATHA *is absent-mindedly making the note*] Honey, they ain't going to read that from no airplane.

BENEATHA [*laughing herself*]: I guess I always think things have more emphasis if they are big, somehow.

RUTH [*looking up at her and smiling*]: You and your brother seem to have that as a philosophy of life. Lord, that man—done changed so 'round here. You know—you know what we did last night? Me and Walter Lee?

BENEATHA: What?

RUTH [*smiling to herself*]: We went to the movies. [*looking at* BENEATHA *to see if she understands*] We went to the movies. You know the last time me and Walter went to the movies together?

BENEATHA: No.

RUTH: Me neither. That's how long it been. [*smiling again*] But we went last night. The picture wasn't much good, but that didn't seem to matter. We went—and we held hands.

BENEATHA: Oh, Lord!

RUTH: We held hands—and you know what?

BENEATHA: What?

RUTH: When we come out of the show it was late and dark and all the stores and things was closed up . . . and it was kind of chilly and there wasn't many people on the streets . . . and we was still holding hands, me and Walter.

BENEATHA: You're killing me. [WALTER *enters with a large package. His happiness is deep in him; he cannot keep still with his new-found exuberance. He is singing and wiggling and snapping his fingers. He puts his package in a corner and puts a phonograph record, which he has brought in with him, on the record player. As the music comes up he dances over to* RUTH *and tries to get her to dance with him. She gives in at last to his raunchiness and in a fit of giggling allows herself to be drawn into his mood and together they deliberately burlesque an old social dance of their youth.*]

BENEATHA [*regarding them a long time as they dance, then drawing in her breath for a deeply exaggerated comment which she does not particularly mean*]: Talk about—olddddddddd—fashionedddddd—Negroes!

WALTER [*stopping momentarily*]: What kind of Negroes? [*He says this in fun. He is not angry with her today, nor with anyone. He starts to dance with his wife again.*]

BENEATHA: Old-fashioned.

WALTER [*as he dances with* RUTH]: You know, when these *New Negroes* have their convention—[*pointing at his sister*]—that is going to be the chairman of the Committee on Unending Agitation. [*He goes on dancing, then stops.*] Race, race, race! . . . Girl, I do believe you are the first person in the history of the entire human race to successfully brainwash yourself. [BENEATHA *breaks up and he goes on dancing. He stops again, enjoying his tease.*] Damn, even the N double A C P takes a holiday sometimes! [BENEATHA *and* RUTH *laugh. He dances with* RUTH *some more and starts to laugh and stops and pantomimes someone over an operating table.*] I can just see that chick someday looking down at some poor cat on an operating table before she starts to slice him, saying . . . [*pulling his sleeves back maliciously*] "By the way, what are your views on civil rights down there? . . ." [*He laughs at her again and starts to dance happily. The bell sounds.*]

BENEATHA: Sticks and stones may break my bones but . . . words will never hurt me! [BENEATHA *goes to the door and opens it as* WALTER *and* RUTH *go on with the clowning.* BENEATHA *is somewhat surprised to see a quiet-looking middle-aged white man in a business suit holding his hat and a briefcase in his hand and consulting a small piece of paper.*]

MAN: Uh—how do you do, miss. I am looking for a Mrs.—[*He looks at the slip of paper.*] Mrs. Lena Younger?

BENEATHA [*smoothing her hair with slight embarrassment*]: Oh—yes, that's my mother. Excuse me. [*She closes the door and turns to quiet the other two.*] Ruth! Brother! Somebody's here. [*Then she opens the door. The man casts a curious quick glance at all of them.*] Uh—come in please.

MAN [*coming in*]: Thank you.

BENEATHA: My mother isn't here just now. Is it business?

MAN: Yes . . . well, of a sort.

WALTER [*freely, the Man of the House*]: Have a seat. I'm Mrs. Younger's son. I look after most of her business matters. [RUTH *and* BENEATHA *exchange amused glances.*]

MAN [*regarding* WALTER, *and sitting*]: Well—My name is Karl Lindner . . .

WALTER [*stretching out his hand*]: Walter Younger. This is my wife—[RUTH *nods politely.*]—and my sister.

LINDNER: How do you do.

WALTER [*amiably, as he sits himself easily on a chair, leaning with interest forward on his knees and looking expectantly into the newcomer's face*]: What can we do for you, Mr. Lindner!

LINDNER [*some minor shuffling of the hat and briefcase on his knees*]: Well—I am a representative of the Clybourne Park Improvement Association—

WALTER [*pointing*]: Why don't you sit your things on the floor?

LINDNER: Oh—yes. Thank you. [*He slides the briefcase and hat under the chair.*] And as I was saying—I am from the Clybourne Park Improvement Association and we have had it brought to our attention at the last meeting that you people—or at least your mother—has bought a piece of residential property at—[*He digs for the slip of paper again.*]—four o six at Clybourne Street . . .

WALTER: That's right. Care for something to drink? Ruth, get Mr. Lindner a beer.

LINDNER [*upset for some reason*]: Oh—no, really, I mean thank you very much, but no thank you.

RUTH [*innocently*]: Some coffee?

LINDNER: Thank you, nothing at all. [BENEATHA *is watching the man carefully.*]

LINDNER: Well, I don't know how much you folks know about our organization. [*He is a gentle man; thoughtful and somewhat labored in his manner.*] It is one of these community organizations set up to look after—oh, you know, things like block upkeep and special projects and we also have what we call our New Neighbors Orientation Committee . . .

BENEATHA [*drily*]: Yes—and what do they do?

LINDNER [*turning a little to her and then returning the main force to* WALTER]: Well—it's what you might call a sort of welcoming committee, I guess. I mean they, we, I'm the chairman of the committee—go around and see the new people who move into the neighborhood and sort of give them the lowdown on the way we do things out in Clybourne Park.

BENEATHA [*with appreciation of the two meanings, which escape* RUTH *and* WALTER]: Uh-huh.

LINDNER: And we also have the category of what the association calls—[*He looks elsewhere.*]—uh—special community problems . . .

BENEATHA: Yes—and what are some of those?

WALTER: Girl, let the man talk.

LINDNER [*with understated relief*]: Thank you. I would sort of like to explain this thing in my own way. I mean I want to explain to you in a certain way.

WALTER: Go ahead.

LINDNER: Yes. Well. I'm going to try to get right to the point. I'm sure we'll all appreciate that in the long run.

BENEATHA: Yes.

WALTER: Be still now!

LINDNER: Well—

RUTH [*still innocently*]: Would you like another chair—you don't look comfortable.

LINDNER [*more frustrated than annoyed*]: No, thank you very much. Please. Well—to get right to the point I—[*a great breath, and he is off at last*] I am sure you people must be aware of some of the incidents which have happened in various parts of the city when colored people have moved into certain areas—[BENEATHA *exhales heavily and starts tossing a piece of fruit up and down in the air.*] Well—because we have what I think is going to be a unique type of organization in American community life—not only do we deplore that kind of thing—but we are trying to do something about it. [BENEATHA *stops tossing and turns with a new and quizzical interest to the man.*] We feel—[*gaining confidence in his mission because of the interest in the faces of the people he is talking to*]—we feel that most of the trouble in this world, when you come right down to it—[*He hits his knee for emphasis.*]—most of the trouble exists because people just don't sit down and talk to each other.

RUTH [*nodding as she might in church, pleased with the remark*]: You can say that again, mister.

LINDNER [*more encouraged by such affirmation*]: That we don't try hard enough in this world to understand the other fellow's problem. The other guy's point of view.

RUTH: Now that's right. [BENEATHA *and* WALTER *merely watch and listen with genuine interest.*]

LINDNER: Yes—that's the way we feel out in Clybourne Park. And that's why I was elected to come here this afternoon and talk to you people. Friendly like, you know, the way people should talk to each other and see if we couldn't find some way to work this thing out. As I say, the whole business is a matter of caring about the other fellow. Anybody can see that you are a nice family of folks, hard working and honest I'm sure. [BENEATHA *frowns slightly, quizzically, her head tilted regarding him.*] Today everybody knows what it means to be on the outside of *something*. And of course, there is always somebody who is out to take the advantage of people who don't always understand.

WALTER: What do you mean?

LINDNER: Well—you see our community is made of people who've worked hard as the dickens for years to build up that little community. They're not rich and fancy people; just hardworking, honest people who don't really have much but those little homes and a dream of the kind of community they want to raise their children in. Now, I don't say we are perfect and there is a lot wrong in some of the things they want. But you've got to admit that a man, right or wrong, has the right to want to have the neighborhood he lives in a certain kind of way. And at the moment the overwhelming majority of our people out there feel that people get along better, take more of a common interest in the life of the community, when they share a common background. I want you to believe me when I tell you that race prejudice simply doesn't enter into it. It is a matter of the people of Clybourne Park believing, rightly or wrongly, as I say, that for the happiness of all concerned that our Negro families are happier when they live in their *own* communities.

BENEATHA [*with a grand and bitter gesture*]: This, friends, is the Welcoming Committee!

WALTER [*dumbfounded, looking at* LINDNER]: Is this what you came marching all the way over here to tell us?

LINDNER: Well, now we've been having a fine conversation. I hope you'll hear me all the way through.

WALTER [*tightly*]: Go ahead, man.

LINDNER: You see—in the face of all things I have said, we are prepared to make your family a very generous offer . . .

BENEATHA: Thirty pieces and not a coin less!

WALTER: Yeah?

LINDNER [*putting on his glasses and drawing a form out of the briefcase*]: Our association is prepared, through the collective effort of our people, to buy the house from you at a financial gain to your family.

RUTH: Lord have mercy, ain't this the living gall!

WALTER: All right, you through?

LINDNER: Well, I want to give you the exact terms of the financial arrangement—

WALTER: We don't want to hear no exact terms of no arrangements. I want to know if you got any more to tell us 'bout getting together?

LINDNER [*taking off his glasses*]: Well—I don't suppose that you feel . . .

WALTER: Never mind how I feel—you got any more to say 'bout how people ought to sit down and talk to each other? . . . Get out of my house, man. [*He turns his back and walks to the door.*]

LINDNER [*looking around at the hostile faces and reaching and assembling his hat and briefcase*]: Well—I don't understand why you people are reacting this way. What do you think you are going to gain by moving into a neighborhood where you just aren't wanted and where some elements—well—people can get awful worked up when they feel that their whole way of life and everything they've ever worked for is threatened.

WALTER: Get out.

LINDNER [*at the door, holding a small card*]: Well—I'm sorry it went like this.

WALTER: Get out.

LINDNER [*almost sadly regarding* WALTER]: You just can't force people to change their hearts, son. [*He turns and put his card on a table and exits.* WALTER *pushes the door to with stinging hatred, and stands looking at it.* RUTH *just sits and* BENEATHA *just stands. They say nothing.* MAMA *and* TRAVIS *enter.*]

MAMA: Well—this all the packing got done since I left out of here this morning. I testify before God that my children got all the energy of the dead. What time the moving men due?

BENEATHA: Four o'clock. You had a caller, Mama. [*She is smiling, teasingly.*]

MAMA: Sure enough—who?

BENEATHA [*her arms folded saucily*]: The Welcoming Committee. [WALTER *and* RUTH *giggle.*]

MAMA [*innocently*]: Who?

BENEATHA: The Welcoming Committee. They said they're sure going to be glad to see you when you get there.

WALTER [*devilishly*]: Yeah, they said they can't hardly wait to see your face. [*laughter*]

MAMA [*sensing their facetiousness*]: What's the matter with you all?

WALTER: Ain't nothing the matter with us. We just telling you 'bout the gentleman who came to see you this afternoon. From the Clybourne Park Improvement Association.

MAMA: What he want?

RUTH [*in the same mood as* BENEATHA *and* WALTER]: To welcome you, honey.

WALTER: He said they can't hardly wait. He said the one thing they don't have, that they just dying to have out there is a fine family of colored people! [*to* RUTH *and* BENEATHA] Ain't that right!

RUTH AND BENEATHA [*mockingly*]: Yeah! He left his card in case—[*They indicate the card, and* MAMA *picks it up and throws it on the floor—understanding and looking off as she draws her chair up to the table on which she has put her plant and some sticks and some cord.*]

MAMA: Father, give us strength. [*knowingly—and without fun*] Did he threaten us?

BENEATHA: Oh—Mama—they don't do it like that any more. He talked Brotherhood. He said everybody ought to learn how to sit down and hate each other with good Christian fellowship. [*She and* WALTER *shake hands to ridicule the remark.*]

MAMA [*sadly*]: Lord, protect us . . .

RUTH: You should hear the money those folks raised to buy the house from us. All we paid and then some.

BENEATHA: What they think we going to do—eat 'em?

RUTH: No, honey, marry 'em.

MAMA [*shaking her head*]: Lord, Lord, Lord . . .

RUTH: Well—that's the way the crackers crumble. Joke.

BENEATHA [*laughingly noticing what her mother is doing*]: Mama, what are you doing?

MAMA: Fixing my plant so it won't get hurt none on the way . . .

BENEATHA: Mama, you going to take that to the new house?

MAMA: Uh-huh—

BENEATHA: That raggedy-looking old thing?

MAMA [*stopping and looking at her*]: It expresses *me.*

RUTH [*with delight, to* BENEATHA]: So there, Miss Thing! [WALTER *comes to* MAMA *suddenly and bends down behind her and squeezes her in his arms with all his strength. She is overwhelmed by the suddenness of it and, though delighted, her manner is like that of* RUTH *with* TRAVIS.]

MAMA: Look out now, boy! You make me mess up my thing here!

WALTER [*his face lit, he slips down on his knees beside her, his arms still about her*]: Mama . . . you know what it means to climb up in the chariot?

MAMA [*gruffly, very happy*]: Get on away from me now . . .

RUTH [*near the gift-wrapped package, trying to catch* WALTER*'s eye*]: Psst—

WALTER: What the old song say, Mama . . .

RUTH: Walter—Now? [*She is pointing at the package.*]

WALTER [*speaking the lines, sweetly, playfully, in his mother's face*]:
I got wings . . . you got wings . . .
All God's children got wings . . .

MAMA: Boy—get out of my face and do some work . . .

WALTER: *When I get to heaven gonna put on my wings,*
Gonna fly all over God's heaven . . .

BENEATHA [*teasingly, from across the room*]: Everybody talking 'bout heaven ain't going there!

WALTER [*to* RUTH, *who is carrying the box across to them*]: I don't know, you think we ought to give her that . . . Seems to me she ain't been very appreciative around here.

MAMA [*eying the box, which is obviously a gift*]: What is that?

WALTER [*taking it from* RUTH *and putting it on the table in front of* MAMA]: Well—what you all think? Should we give it to her?

RUTH: Oh—she was pretty good today.

MAMA: I'll good you—[*She turns her eyes to the box again.*]

BENEATHA: Open it, Mama. [*She stands up, looks at it, turns and looks at all of them, and then presses her hands together and does not open the package.*]

WALTER [*sweetly*]: Open it, Mama. It's for you. [MAMA *looks in his eyes. It is the first present in her life without its being Christmas. Slowly she opens her package and lifts out, one by one, a brand-new sparkling set of gardening tools.* WALTER *continues, prodding.*] Ruth made up the note—read it . . .

MAMA [*picking up the card and adjusting her glasses*]: "To our own Mrs. Miniver—Love from Brother, Ruth and Beneatha." Ain't that lovely . . .

TRAVIS [*tugging at his father's sleeve*]: Daddy, can I give her mine now?

WALTER: All right, son. [TRAVIS *flies to get his gift.*] Travis didn't want to go in with the rest of us, Mama. He got his own. [*somewhat amused*] We don't know what it is . . .

TRAVIS [*racing back in the room with a large hatbox and putting it in front of his grandmother*]: Here!

MAMA: Lord have mercy, baby. You done gone and bought your grandmother a hat?

TRAVIS [*very proud*]: Open it! [*She does and lifts out an elaborate, but very elaborate, wide gardening hat, and all the adults break up at the sight of it.*]

RUTH: Travis, honey, what is that?

TRAVIS [*who thinks it is beautiful and appropriate*]: It's a gardening hat! Like the ladies always have on in the magazines when they work in their gardens.

BENEATHA [*giggling fiercely*]: Travis—we were trying to make Mama Mrs. Miniver—not Scarlett O'Hara!

MAMA [*indignantly*]: What's the matter with you all! This here is a beautiful hat! [*absurdly*] I always wanted me one just like it! [*She pops it on her head to prove it to her grandson, and the hat is ludicrous and considerably oversized.*]

RUTH: Hot dog! Go, Mama!

WALTER [*doubled over with laughter*]: I'm sorry, Mama—but you look like you ready to go out and chop you some cotton sure enough! [*They all laugh except* MAMA, *out of deference to* TRAVIS*'s feelings.*]

MAMA [*gathering the boy up to her*]: Bless your heart—this is the prettiest hat I ever owned—[WALTER, RUTH *and* BENEATHA *chime in—noisily, festively and insincerely congratulating* TRAVIS *on his gift.*] What are we all standing around here for? We ain't finished packin' yet. Bennie, you ain't packed one book. [*The bell rings.*]

BENEATHA: That couldn't be the movers . . . it's not hardly two o'clock yet—[BENEATHA *goes into her room.* MAMA *starts for door.*]

WALTER [*turning, stiffening*]: Wait—wait—I'll get it. [*He stands and looks at the door.*]

MAMA: You expecting company, son?

WALTER [*just looking at the door*]: Yeah—yeah . . . [MAMA *looks at* RUTH, *and they exchange innocent and unfrightened glances.*]

MAMA [*not understanding*]: Well, let them in, son.

BENEATHA [*from her room*]: We need some more string.

MAMA: Travis—you run to the hardware and get me some string cord. [MAMA *goes out and* WALTER *turns and looks at* RUTH. TRAVIS *goes to a dish for money.*]

RUTH: Why don't you answer the door, man?

WALTER [*suddenly bounding across the floor to her*]: 'Cause sometimes it hard to let the future begin! [*stooping down in her face*].

I got wings! You got wings!
All God's children got wings!

[*He crosses to the door and throws it open. Standing there is a very slight little man in a not too prosperous business suit and with haunted frightened eyes and a hat pulled down tightly, brim up, around his forehead.* TRAVIS *passes between the men and exits.* WALTER *leans deep in the man's face, still in his jubilance.*]

When I get to heaven gonna put on my wings,
Gonna fly all over God's heaven . . .

[*The little man just stares at him*]

Heaven—

[*Suddenly he stops and looks past the little man into the empty hallway.*]

Where's Willy, man?

BOBO: He ain't with me.

WALTER [*not disturbed*]: Oh—come on in. You know my wife.

BOBO [*dumbly, taking off his hat*]: Yes—h'you, Miss Ruth.

RUTH [*quietly, a mood apart from her husband already, seeing* BOBO]: Hello, Bobo.

WALTER: You right on time today . . . Right on time. That's the way! [*He slaps* BOBO *on his back.*] Sit down . . . lemme hear. [RUTH *stands stiffly and quietly in back of them, as though somehow she senses death, her eyes fixed on her husband.*]

BOBO [*his frightened eyes on the floor, his hat in his hands*]: Could I please get a drink of water, before I tell you about it, Walter Lee? [WALTER *does not take his eyes off the man.* RUTH *goes blindly to the tap and gets a glass of water and brings it to* BOBO.]

WALTER: There ain't nothing wrong, is there?

BOBO: Lemme tell you—

WALTER: Man—didn't nothing go wrong?

BOBO: Lemme tell you—Walter Lee. [*Looking at* RUTH *and talking to her more than to* WALTER.] You know how it was. I got to tell you how it was. I mean first I got to tell you how it was all the way . . . I mean about the money I put in, Walter Lee . . .

WALTER [*with taut agitation now*]: What about the money you put in?

BOBO: Well—it wasn't much as we told you—me and Willy—[*He stops.*] I'm sorry, Walter. I got a bad feeling about it. I got a real bad feeling about it . . .

WALTER: Man, what you telling me about all this for? . . . Tell me what happened in Springfield . . .

BOBO: Springfield.

RUTH [*like a dead woman*]: What was supposed to happen in Springfield?

BOBO [*to her*]: This deal that me and Walter went into with Willy—Me and Willy was going to go down to Springfield and spread some money 'round so's we wouldn't have to wait so long for the liquor license . . . That's what we were going to do. Everybody said that was the way you had to do, you understand, Miss Ruth?

WALTER: Man—what happened down there?

BOBO [*a pitiful man, near tears*]: I'm trying to tell you, Walter.

WALTER [*screaming at him suddenly*]: THEN TELL ME, GODDAMMIT . . . WHAT'S THE MATTER WITH YOU?

BOBO: Man . . . I didn't go to no Springfield, yesterday.

WALTER [*halted, life hanging in the moment*]: Why not?

BOBO [*the long way, the hard way to tell*]: 'Cause I didn't have no reasons to . . .

WALTER: Man, what are you talking about!

BOBO: I'm talking about the fact that when I got to the train station yesterday morning—eight o'clock like we planned . . . Man—*Willy didn't never show up.*

WALTER: Why . . . where was he . . . where is he?

BOBO: That's what I'm trying to tell you . . . I don't know . . . I waited six hours . . . I called his house . . . and I waited . . . six hours . . . I waited in that train station six hours . . . [*breaking into tears*] That was all the extra money I had in the world . . . [*looking up at* WALTER *with the tears running down his face*] Man, *Willy is gone.*

WALTER: Gone, what you mean Willy is gone? Gone where? You mean he went by himself. You mean he went off to Springfield by himself—to take care of getting the license—[*turns and looks anxiously at* RUTH] You mean maybe he didn't want too many people in on the business down there? [*looks to* RUTH *again, as before*] You know Willy got his own ways. [*looks back to* BOBO] Maybe you was late yesterday and he just went on down there without you. Maybe—maybe—he's been callin' you at home tryin' to tell you what happened or something. Maybe—maybe—he just got sick. He's somewhere—he's got to be somewhere. We just got to find him—me and you got to find him. [*grabs* BOBO *senselessly by the collar and starts to shake him*] We got to!

BOBO [*in sudden angry, frightened agony*]: What's the matter with you, Walter! *When a cat take off with your money he don't leave you no maps!*

WALTER [*turning madly, as though he is looking for* WILLY *in the very room*]: Willy! . . . Willy . . . don't do it . . . Please don't do it . . . Man, not with that money . . . Man, please, not with that money . . . Oh, God . . . Don't let it be true . . . [*He is wandering around, crying out for* WILLY *and looking for him or perhaps for help from God.*] Man . . . I trusted you . . . Man, I put my life in your hands . . . [*He starts to crumple down on the floor as* RUTH *just covers her face in horror,* MAMA *opens the door and comes into the room, with* BENEATHA *behind her.*] Man . . . [*He starts to pound the floor with his fists, sobbing wildly.*] *That money is made out of my father's flesh* . . .

BOBO [*standing over him helplessly*]: I'm sorry, Walter . . . [*Only* WALTER*'s sobs reply.* BOBO *puts on his hat.*] I had my life staked on this deal, too . . . [*He exits.*]

MAMA [*to* WALTER]: Son—[*She goes to him, bends down to him, talks to his bent head.*] Son . . . Is it gone? Son, I gave, you sixty-five hundred dollars. Is it gone? All of it? Beneatha's money too?

WALTER [*lifting his head slowly*]: Mama . . . I never . . . went to the bank at all

MAMA [*not wanting to believe him*]: You mean . . . your sister's school money . . . you used that too . . . Walter? . . .

WALTER: Yessss! . . . All of it . . . It's all gone . . . [*There is total silence.* RUTH *stands with her face covered with her hands;* BENEATHA *leans forlornly against a wall, fingering a piece of red ribbon from the mother's gift.* MAMA *stops and looks at her son without recognition and then, quite without thinking about it, starts to beat him senselessly in the face.* BENEATHA *goes to them and stops it.*]

BENEATHA: Mama! [MAMA *stops and looks at both of her children and rises slowly and wanders vaguely, aimlessly away from them.*]

MAMA: I seen . . . him . . . night after night . . . come in . . . and look at that rug . . . and then look at me . . . the red showing in his eyes . . . the veins moving in his head . . . I seen him grow thin and old before he was forty . . . working and working and working like somebody's old horse . . . killing himself . . . and you—you give it all away in a day . . .

BENEATHA: Mama—

MAMA: Oh, God . . . [*She looks up to Him.*] Look down here—and show me the strength.

BENEATHA: Mama—

MAMA [*folding over*]: Strength . . .

BENEATHA [*plaintively*]: Mama . . .

MAMA: Strength!

CURTAIN

ACT III

An hour later.

At curtain, there is a sullen light of gloom in the living room, gray light not unlike that which began the first scene of Act I. At left we can see WALTER *within his room, alone with himself. He is stretched out on the bed, his shirt out and open, his arms under his head. He does not smoke, he does not cry out, he merely lies there, looking up at the ceiling, much as if he were alone in the world.*

In the living room BENEATHA *sits at the table, still surrounded by the now almost ominous packing crates. She sits looking off. We feel that this is a mood struck perhaps an hour before, and it lingers now, full of the empty sound of profound disappointment. We see on a line from her brother's bedroom the sameness of their attitudes. Presently the bell rings and* BENEATHA *rises without ambition or interest in answering. It is* ASAGAI, *smiling broadly, striding into the room with energy and happy expectation and conversation.*

ASAGAI: I came over . . . I had some free time. I thought I might help with the packing. Ah, I like the look of packing crates! A household in preparation for a journey! It depresses some people . . . but for me . . . it is another feeling.

Something full of the flow of life, do you understand? Movement, progress . . . It makes me think of Africa.

BENEATHA: Africa!

ASAGAI: What kind of a mood is this? Have I told you how deeply you move me?

BENEATHA: He gave away the money, Asagai . . .

ASAGAI: Who gave away what money?

BENEATHA: The insurance money. My brother gave it away.

ASAGAI: Gave it away?

BENEATHA: He made an investment! With a man even Travis wouldn't have trusted.

ASAGAI: And it's gone?

BENEATHA: Gone!

ASAGAI: I'm very sorry . . . And you, now?

BENEATHA: Me? . . . Me? . . . Me, I'm nothing . . . Me. When I was very small . . . we used to take our sleds out in the wintertime and the only hills we had were the ice-covered stone steps of some houses down the street. And we used to fill them in with snow and make them smooth and slide down them all day . . . and it was very dangerous you know . . . far too steep . . . and sure enough one day a kid named Rufus came down too fast and hit the sidewalk . . . and we saw his face just split open right there in front of us . . . And I remember standing there looking at his bloody open face thinking that was the end of Rufus. But the ambulance came and they took him to the hospital and they fixed the broken bones and they sewed it all up . . . and the next time I saw Rufus he just had a little line down the middle of his face . . . I never got over that . . . [WALTER *sits up, listening on the bed. Throughout this scene it is important that we feel his reaction at all times, that he visibly respond to the words of his sister and* ASAGAI.]

ASAGAI: What?

BENEATHA: That that was what one person could do for another, fix him up—sew up the problem, make him all right again. That was the most marvelous thing in the world . . . I wanted to do that. I always thought it was the one concrete thing in the world that a human being could do. Fix up the sick, you know—and make them whole again. This was truly being God . . .

ASAGAI: You wanted to be God?

BENEATHA: No—I wanted to cure. It used to be so important to me. I wanted to cure. It used to matter. I used to care. I mean about people and how their bodies hurt . . .

ASAGAI: And you've stopped caring?

BENEATHA: Yes—I think so.

ASAGAI: Why? [WALTER *rises, goes to the door of his room and is about to open it, then stops and stands listening, leaning on the door jamb.*]

BENEATHA: Because it doesn't seem deep enough, close enough to what ails mankind—I mean this thing of sewing up bodies or administering drugs. Don't you understand? It was a child's reaction to the world. I thought that doctors had the secret to all the hurts . . . That's the way a child sees things—or an idealist.

ASAGAI: Children see things very well sometimes—and idealists even better.

BENEATHA: I know that's what you think. Because you are still where I left off—you still care. This is what you see for the world, for Africa. You with the dreams of the future will patch up all Africa—you are going to cure the Great Sore of colonialism with Independence—

ASAGAI: Yes!

BENEATHA: Yes—and you think that one word is the penicillin of the human spirit: "Independence!" But then what?

ASAGAI: That will be the problem for another time. First we must get there.

BENEATHA: And where does it end?

ASAGAI: End? Who even spoke of an end? To life? To living?

BENEATHA: An end to misery!

ASAGAI [*smiling*]: You sound like a French intellectual.

BENEATHA: No! I sound like a human being who just had her future taken right out of her hands! While I was sleeping in my bed in there, things were happening in this world that directly concerned me—and nobody asked me, consulted me—they just went out and did things—and changed my life. Don't you see there isn't any real progress, Asagai, there is only one large circle that we march in, around and around, each of us with our own little picture—in front of us—our own little mirage that we think is the future.

ASAGAI: That is the mistake.

BENEATHA: What?

ASAGAI: What you just said—about the circle. It isn't circle—it is simply a long line—as in geometry, you know, one that reaches into infinity. And because we cannot see the end—we also cannot see how it changes. And it is very odd but those who see the changes are called "idealists"—and those who cannot, or refuse to think, they are the "realists." It is very strange, and amusing too, I think.

BENEATHA: You—you are almost religious.

ASAGAI: Yes . . . I think I have the religion of doing what is necessary in the world—and of worshipping man—because he is so marvelous, you see.

BENEATHA: Man is foul! And the human race deserves its misery!

ASAGAI: You see: *you* have become the religious one in the old sense. Already, and after such a small defeat, you are worshipping despair.

BENEATHA: From now on, I worship the truth—and the truth is that people are puny, small and selfish . . .

ASAGAI: Truth? Why is it that you despairing ones always think that only you have the truth? I never thought to see *you* like that. You! Your brother made a stupid, childish mistake—and you are grateful to him. So that now you can give up the ailing human race on account of it. You talk about what good is struggle; what good is anything? Where are we all going? And why are we bothering?

BENEATHA: *And you cannot answer it!* All your talk and dreams about Africa and Independence. Independence and then what? What about all the crooks and petty thieves and just plain idiots who will come into power to steal and plunder the same as before—only now they will be black and do it in the name of the new Independence—You cannot answer that.

ASAGAI [*shouting over her*]: *I live the answer!* [*pause*] In my village at home it is the exceptional man who can even read a newspaper . . . or who ever *sees* a book at all. I will go home and much of what I will have to say will seem strange to the people of my village. . . . But I will teach and work and things will happen, slowly and swiftly. At times it will seem that nothing changes at all . . . and then again . . . the sudden dramatic events which make history leap into the future. And then quiet again. Retrogression even. Guns, murder, revolution. And I even will have moments when I wonder if the quiet was not better than all that death and hatred. But I will look about my village at the illiteracy and disease and ignorance and I will not wonder long. And perhaps . . . perhaps I will be a great man . . . I mean perhaps I will hold on to the substance of truth and find my way always with the right course . . . and perhaps for it I will be butchered in my bed some night by the servants of empire . . .

BENEATHA: *The martyr!*

ASAGAI: . . . or perhaps I shall live to be a very old man, respected and esteemed in my new nation . . . And perhaps I shall hold office and this is what I'm trying to tell you, Alaiyo; perhaps the things I believe now for my country will be wrong and outmoded, and I will not understand and do terrible things to have things my way or merely to keep my power. Don't you see that there will be young men and women, not British soldiers then, but my own black countrymen . . . to step out of the shadows some evening and slit my then useless throat? Don't you see they have always been there . . . that they always will be. And that such a thing as my own death will be an advance? They who might kill me even . . . actually replenish me!

BENEATHA: Oh, Asagai, I know all that.

ASAGAI: Good! Then stop moaning and groaning and tell me what you plan to do.

BENEATHA: Do?

ASAGAI: I have a bit of a suggestion.

BENEATHA: What?

ASAGAI [*rather quietly for him*]: That when it is all over—that you come home with me—

BENEATHA [*slapping herself on the forehead with exasperation born of misunderstanding*]: Oh—Asagai—at this moment you decide to be romantic!

ASAGAI [*quickly understanding the misunderstanding*]: My dear, young creature of the New World—I do not mean across the city—I mean across the ocean; home—to Africa.

BENEATHA [*slowly understanding and turning to him with murmured amazement*]: To—to Nigeria?

ASAGAI: Yes! . . . [*smiling and lifting his arms playfully*]. Three hundred years later the African Prince rose up out of the seas and swept the maiden back across the middle passage over which her ancestors had come—

BENEATHA [*unable to play*]: Nigeria?

ASAGAI: Nigeria. Home. [*coming to her with genuine romantic flippancy*] I will show you our mountains and our stars; and give you cool drinks from gourds and teach you the old songs and the ways of our people—and, in time, we will pretend that—[*very softly*]—you have only been away for a day—[*She turns her back to him, thinking. He swings her around and takes her full in his arms in a long embrace which proceeds to passion.*]

BENEATHA [*pulling away*]: You're getting me all mixed up—

ASAGAI: Why?

BENEATHA: Too many things—too many things have happened today. I must sit down and think. I don't know what I feel about anything right this minute. [*She promptly sits down and props her chin on her fist.*]

ASAGAI [*charmed*]: All right, I shall leave you. No—don't get up. [*touching her, gently, sweetly*] Just sit awhile and think . . . Never be afraid to sit awhile and think. [*He goes to door and looks at her.*] How often I have looked at you and said, "Ah—so this is what the New World hath finally wrought . . ." [*He exits.* BENEATHA *sits on alone. Presently* WALTER *enters from his room and starts to rummage through things, feverishly looking for something. She looks up and turns in her seat.*]

BENEATHA [*hissingly*]: Yes—just look at what the New World hath wrought! . . . Just look! [*She gestures with bitter disgust.*] There he is! *Monsieur le petit bougeois noir*—himself! There he is—Symbol of a Rising Class! Entrepreneur! Titan of the system! [WALTER *ignores her completely and continues frantically and destructively looking for something and hurling things to the floor and tearing things out of their place in his search.* BENEATHA *ignores the eccentricity of his actions and goes on with the monologue of insult.*] Did you dream of yachts on Lake Michigan, Brother? Did you see yourself on that Great Day sitting down at the Conference Table, surrounded by all the mighty bald-headed men in America? All halted, waiting, breathless, waiting for your pronouncements on industry? Waiting for you—Chairman of the Board? [WALTER *finds what he is looking for—a small piece of white paper—and pushes it in his pocket and puts on his coat and rushes out without ever having looked at her. She shouts after him.*] I look at you and I see the final triumph of stupidity in the world! [*The door slams and she returns to just sitting again.* RUTH *comes quickly out of* MAMA*'s room.*]

RUTH: Who was that?

BENEATHA: Your husband.

RUTH: Where did he go?

BENEATHA: Who knows—maybe he has an appointment at U.S. Steel.

RUTH [*anxiously, with frightened eyes*]: You didn't say nothing bad to him, did you?

BENEATHA: Bad? Say anything bad to him? No—I told him he was a sweet boy and full of dreams and everything is strictly peachy keen, as the ofay[3] kids say!

[MAMA *enters from her bedroom. She is lost, vague, trying to catch hold, to make some sense of her former command of the world, but it still eludes her. A sense of waste overwhelms her gait; a measure of apology rides on her shoulders. She goes to her plant, which has remained on the table, looks at it, picks it up and takes it to the window sill and sets it outside, and she stands and looks at it a long moment. Then she closes the window, straightens her body with effort and turns around to her children.*]

MAMA: Well—ain't it a mess in here, though? [*a false cheerfulness, a beginning of something*] I guess we all better stop moping around and get some work done. All this unpacking and everything we got to do. [RUTH *raises her head slowly in response to the sense of the line; and* BENEATHA *in similar manner turns very slowly to look at her mother.*] One of you all better call the moving people and tell 'em not to come.

RUTH: Tell 'em not to come?

MAMA: Of course, baby. Ain't no need in 'em coming all the way here and having to go back. They charges for that too. [*She sits down, fingers to her brow, thinking.*] Lord, ever since I was a little girl, I always remembers people saying, "Lena—Lena Eggleston, you aims too high all the time. You needs to slow down and see life a little more like it is. Just slow down some." That's what they always used to say down home—"Lord, that Lena Eggleston is a high-minded thing. She'll get her due one day!"

RUTH: No, Lena . . .

[3]**ofay** White (pig Latin meaning "foe").

MAMA: Me and Big Walter just didn't never learn right.

RUTH: Lena, no! We gotta go. Bennie—tell her . . . [*She rises and crosses to* BENEATHA *with her arms outstretched.* BENEATHA *doesn't respond.*] Tell her we can still move . . . the notes ain't but a hundred and twenty-five a month. We got four grown people in this house—we can work . . .

MAMA [*to herself*]: Just aimed too high all the time—

RUTH [*turning and going to* MAMA *fast—the words pouring out with urgency and desperation*]: Lena—I'll work . . . I'll work twenty hours a day in all the kitchens in Chicago . . . I'll strap my baby on my back if I have to and scrub all the floors in America and wash all the sheets in America if I have to—but we got to move . . . We got to get out of here . . . [MAMA *reaches out absently and pats* RUTH*'s hand.*]

MAMA: No—I sees things differently now. Been thinking 'bout some of the things we could do to fix this place up some. I seen a second-hand bureau over on Maxwell Street just the other day that could fit right there. [*She points to where the new furniture might go.* RUTH *wanders away from her.*] Would need some new handles on it and then a little varnish and then it look like something brand-new. And—we can put up them new curtains in the kitchen . . . Why this place be looking fine. Cheer us all up so that we forget trouble ever came . . . [*to* RUTH] And you could get some nice screens to put up in your room round the baby's bassinet . . . [*She looks at both of them, pleadingly.*] Sometimes you just got to know when to give up some things . . . and hold on to what you got. [WALTER *enters from the outside, looking spent and leaning against the door, his coat hanging from him.*]

MAMA: Where you been, son?

WALTER [*breathing hard*]: Made a call.

MAMA: To who, son?

WALTER: To the Man.

MAMA: What man, baby?

WALTER: The Man, Mama. Don't you know who The Man is?

RUTH: Walter Lee?

WALTER: *The Man.* Like the guys in the street say—*the Man.* Captain Boss—Mistuh Charley . . . Old Captain Please Mr. Bossman . . .

BENEATHA [*suddenly*]: Lindner!

WALTER: That's right! That's good. I told him to come right over.

BENEATHA [*fiercely, understanding*]: For what? What do you want to see him for?

WALTER [*looking at his sister*]: We are going to do business with him.

MAMA: What you talking 'bout, son?

WALTER: Talking 'bout life, Mama. You all always telling me to see life like it is. Well—I laid in there on my back today . . . and I figured it out. Life just like it is. Who gets and who don't get. [*He sits down with his coat on and laughs.*] Mama, you know it's all divided up. Life is. Sure enough. Between the takers and the "tooken." [*He laughs.*] I've figured it out finally. [*He looks around at them.*] Yeah. Some of us always getting "tooken." [*He laughs.*] People like Willy Harris, they don't never get "tooken." And you know why the rest of us do? 'Cause we all mixed up. Mixed up bad. We get to looking 'round for the right and the wrong; and we worry about it and cry about it and stay up nights trying to figure out 'bout the wrong and the right of things all the time . . . And all the time, man, them takers is out there operating, just taking and taking. Willy Harris? Shoot—Willy Harris don't even count. He don't even count in the big scheme of things. But I'll say one thing for old Willy Harris . . . he's taught me something. He's taught me to keep my eye on what counts in this world. Yeah—[*shouting out a little*] Thanks, Willy!

RUTH: What did you call that man for, Walter Lee!

WALTER: Called him to tell him to come on over to the show. Gonna put on a show for the man. Just what he wants to see. You see, Mama, the man came here today and he told us that them people out there where you want us to move—well they so upset they willing to pay us not to move out there. [*He laughs again.*] And—and oh, Mama—you would of been proud of the way me and Ruth and Bennie acted. We told him to get out . . . Lord have mercy! We told the man to get out. Oh, we was some proud folks this afternoon, yeah. [*He lights a cigarette.*] We were still full of that old-time stuff . . .

RUTH [*coming toward him slowly*]: You talking 'bout taking them people's money to keep us from moving in that house?

WALTER: I ain't just talking 'bout it, baby—I'm telling you that's what's going to happen.

BENEATHA: Oh, God! Where is the bottom! Where is the real honest-to-God bottom so he can't go any farther!

WALTER: See—that's the old stuff. You and that boy that was here today. You all want everybody to carry a flag and a spear and sing some marching songs, huh? You wanna spend your life looking into things and trying to find the right and the wrong part, huh? Yeah. You know what's going to happen to that boy someday—he'll find himself sitting in a dungeon, locked in forever—and the takers will have the key! Forget it, baby! There ain't no causes—there ain't nothing but taking in this world, and he who takes most is smartest—and it don't make a damn bit of difference *how*.

MAMA: You making something inside me cry, son. Some awful pain inside me.

WALTER: Don't cry, Mama. Understand. That white man is going to walk in that door able to write checks for more money than we ever had. It's important to him and I'm going to help him . . . I'm going to put on the show, Mama.

MAMA: Son—I come from five generations of people who was slaves and sharecroppers—but ain't nobody in my family never let nobody pay 'em no money that was a way of telling us we wasn't fit to walk the earth. We ain't never been that poor. [*raising her eyes and looking at him*] We ain't never been that dead inside.

BENEATHA: Well—we are dead now. All the talk about dreams and sunlight that goes on in this house. All dead.

WALTER: What's the matter with you all! I didn't make this world! It was give to me this way! Hell, yes, I want me some yachts someday! Yes, I want to hang some real pearls 'round my wife's neck. Ain't she supposed to wear no pearls? Somebody tell me—tell me, who decides which women is suppose to wear pearls in this world. I tell you I am a *man*—and I think my wife should wear some pearls in this world! [*This last line hangs a good while and* WALTER *begins to move about the room. The word "Man" has penetrated his consciousness; he mumbles it to himself repeatedly between strange agitated pauses as he moves about.*]

MAMA: Baby, how you going to feel on the inside?

WALTER: Fine! . . . Going to feel fine . . . a man . . .

MAMA: You won't have nothing left then, Walter Lee.

WALTER [*coming to her*]: I'm going to feel fine, Mama. I'm going to look that son-of-a-bitch in the eyes and say—[*He falters.*]—and say, "All right, Mr. Lindner—

[*He falters even more.*]—that's your neighborhood out there. You got the right to keep it like you want. You got the right to have it like you want. Just write the check and—the house is yours." And, and I am going to say—[*His voice almost breaks.*] And you—you people just put the money in my hand and you won't have to live next to this bunch of stinking niggers! . . . [*He straightens up and moves away from his mother, walking around the room.*] Maybe—maybe I'll just get down on my black knees . . . [*He does so;* RUTH *and* BENNIE *and* MAMA *watch him in frozen horror.*] Captain, Mistuh, Bossman. [*He starts crying.*] A-hee-hee-hee! [*wringing his hands in profoundly anguished imitation*] Yassss-suh! Great White Father, just gi' ussen de money, fo' God's sake, and we's ain't gwine come out deh and dirty up yo' white folks neighborhood . . . [*He breaks down completely, then gets up and goes into the bedroom.*]

BENEATHA: That is not a man. That is nothing but a toothless rat.

MAMA: Yes—death done come in this here house. [*She is nodding, slowly, reflectively.*] Done come walking in my house. On the lips of my children. You what supposed to be my beginning again. You—what supposed to be my harvest. [*to* BENEATHA] You—you mourning your brother?

BENEATHA: He's no brother of mine.

MAMA: What you say?

BENEATHA: I said that that individual in that room is no brother of mine.

MAMA: That's what I thought you said. You feeling like you better than he is today? [BENEATHA *does not answer.*] Yes? What you tell him a minute ago? That he wasn't a man? Yes? You give him up for me? You done wrote his epitaph too—like the rest of the world? Well, who give you the privilege?

BENEATHA: Be on my side for once! You saw what he just did, Mama! You saw him—down on his knees. Wasn't it you who taught me—to despise any man who would do that? Do what he's going to do.

MAMA: Yes—I taught you that. Me and your daddy. But I thought I taught you something else too . . . I thought I taught you to love him.

BENEATHA: Love him? There is nothing left to love.

MAMA: There is always something left to love. And if you ain't learned that, you ain't learned nothing. [*looking at her*] Have you cried for that boy today? I don't mean for yourself and for the family 'cause we lost the money. I mean for him; what he been through and what it done to him. Child, when do you think is the time to love somebody the most; when they done good and made things easy for everybody? Well then, you ain't through learning—because that ain't the time at all. It's when he's at his lowest and can't believe in hisself 'cause the world done whipped him so. When you starts measuring somebody, measure him right, child, measure him right. Make sure you done taken into account what hills and valleys he come through before he got to wherever he is. [TRAVIS *bursts into the room at the end of the speech, leaving the door open.*]

TRAVIS: Grandmama—the moving men are downstairs! The truck just pulled up.

MAMA [*turning and looking at him*]: Are they, baby? They downstairs? [*She sighs and sits.* LINDNER *appears in the doorway. He peers in and knocks lightly, to gain attention, and comes in. All turn to look at him.*]

LINDNER [*hat and briefcase in hand*]: Uh—hello . . . [RUTH *crosses mechanically to the bedroom door and opens it and lets it swing open freely and slowly as the lights come up on* WALTER *within, still in his coat, sitting at the far corner of the room. He looks up and out through the room to* LINDNER.]

RUTH: He's here. [*A long minute passes and* WALTER *slowly gets up.*]

LINDNER [*coming to the table with efficiency, putting his briefcase on the table and starting to unfold papers and unscrew fountain pens*]: Well, I certainly was glad to hear from you people. [WALTER *has begun the trek out of the room, slowly and awkwardly, rather like a small boy, passing the back of his sleeve across his mouth from time to time.*] Life can really be so much simpler than people let it be most of the time. Well—with whom do I negotiate? You, Mrs. Younger, or your son here? [MAMA *sits with her hands folded on her lap and her eyes closed as* WALTER *advances.* TRAVIS *goes close to* LINDNER *and looks at the papers curiously.*] Just some official papers, sonny.

RUTH: Travis, you go downstairs.

MAMA [*opening her eyes and looking into* WALTER*'s*]: No. Travis, you stay right here. And you make him understand what you doing. Walter Lee. You teach him good. Like Willy Harris taught you. You show where our five generations done come to. Go ahead, son—

WALTER [*Looks down into his boy's eyes.* TRAVIS *grins at him merrily and* WALTER *draws him beside him with his arm lightly around his shoulders.*]: Well, Mr. Lindner. [BENEATHA *turns away.*] We called you—[*There is a profound, simple groping quality in his speech.*]—because, well, me and my family [*He looks around and shifts from one foot to the other.*] Well—we are very plain people . . .

LINDNER: Yes—

WALTER: I mean—I have worked as a chauffeur most of my life—and my wife here, she does domestic work in people's kitchens. So does my mother. I mean—we are plain people . . .

LINDNER: Yes, Mr. Younger—

WALTER [*really like a small boy, looking down at his shoes and then up at the man*]: And—uh—well, my father, well, he was a laborer most of his life.

LINDNER [*absolutely confused*]: Uh, yes—

WALTER [*looking down at his toes once again*]: My father almost beat a man to death once because this man called him a bad name or something, you know what I mean?

LINDNER: No, I'm afraid I don't.

WALTER [*finally straightening up*]: Well, what I mean is that we come from people who had a lot of pride. I mean—we are very proud people. And that's my sister over there and she's going to be a doctor—and we are very proud—

LINDNER: Well—I am sure that is very nice, but—

WALTER [*starting to cry and facing the man eye to eye*]: What I am telling you is that we called you over here to tell you that we are very proud and that this is—this is my son, who makes the sixth generation of our family in this country, and that we have all thought about your offer and we have decided to move into our house because my father—my father—he earned it. [MAMA *has her eyes closed and is rocking back and forth as though she were in church, with her head nodding the amen yes.*] We don't want to make no trouble for nobody or fight no causes—but we will try to be good neighbors. That's all we got to say. [*He looks the man absolutely in the eyes.*] We don't want your money. [*He turns and walks away from the man.*]

LINDNER [*looking around at all of them*]: I take it then that you have decided to occupy.

BENEATHA: That's what the man said.

LINDNER [*to* MAMA *in her reverie*]: Then I would like to appeal to you, Mrs. Younger. You are older and wiser and understand things better I am sure . . .

MAMA [*rising*]: I am afraid you don't understand. My son said we was going to move and there ain't nothing left for me to say. [*Shaking her head with double meaning.*] You know how these young folks is nowadays, mister. Can't do a thing with 'em. Good-bye.

LINDNER [*folding up his materials*]: Well—if you are that final about it . . . There is nothing left for me to say. [*He finishes. He is almost ignored by the family, who are concentrating on* WALTER LEE. *At the door* LINDNER *halts and looks around.*] I sure hope you people know what you're doing. [*He shakes his head and exits.*]

RUTH [*looking around and coming to life*]: Well, for God's sake—if the moving men are here—LET'S GET THE HELL OUT OF HERE!

MAMA [*into action*]: Ain't it the truth! Look at all this here mess. Ruth, put Travis' good jacket on him . . . Walter Lee, fix your tie and tuck your shirt in, you look just like somebody's hoodlum. Lord have mercy, where is my plant? [*She flies to get it amid the general bustling of the family, who are deliberately trying to ignore the nobility of the past moment.*] You all start on down . . . Travis child, don't go empty-handed . . . Ruth, where did I put that box with my skillets in it? I want to be in charge of it myself . . . I'm going to make us the biggest dinner we ever ate tonight . . . Beneatha, what's the matter with them stockings? Pull them things up, girl . . . [*The family starts to file out as two moving men appear and begin to carry out the heavier pieces of furniture, bumping into the family as they move about.*]

BENEATHA: Mama, Asagai—asked me to marry him today and go to Africa—

MAMA [*in the middle of her getting-ready activity*]: He did? You ain't old enough to marry nobody—[*Seeing the moving men lifting one of her chairs precariously.*] Darling, that ain't no bale of cotton, please handle it so we can sit in it again. I had that chair twenty-five years . . . [*The movers sigh with exasperation and go on with their work.*]

BENEATHA [*girlishly and unreasonably trying to pursue the conversation*]: To got to Africa, Mama—be a doctor in Africa . . .

MAMA [*distracted*]: Yes, baby—

WALTER: Africa! What he want to go to Africa for?

BENEATHA: To practice there . . .

WALTER: Girl, if you don't get all them silly ideas out your head! You better marry yourself a man with some loot . . .

BENEATHA [*angrily, precisely as in the first scene of the play*]: What have you got to do with who I marry!

WALTER: Plenty. Now I think George Murchison—[*He and* BENEATHA *go out yelling at each other vigorously;* BENEATHA *is heard saying that she would not marry* GEORGE MURCHISON *if he were Adam and she were Eve, etc. The anger is loud and real till their voices diminish.* RUTH *stands at the door and turns to* MAMA *and smiles knowingly.*]

MAMA [*fixing her hat at last*]: Yeah—they something all right, my children . . .

RUTH: Yeah—they're something. Let's go, Lena.

MAMA [*stalling, starting to look around at the house*]: Yes—I'm coming. Ruth—

RUTH: Yes?

MAMA [*quietly, woman to woman*]: He finally come into his manhood today, didn't he? Kind of like a rainbow after the rain . . .

RUTH [*biting her lip lest her own pride explode in front of* MAMA]: Yes, Lena. [BENEATHA*'s voice calls for them raucously.*]

MAMA [*waving* RUTH *out vaguely*]: All right, honey—go on down. I be down directly. [RUTH *hesitates, then exits.* MAMA *stands, at last alone in the living room, her plant on the table before her as the lights start to come down. She looks around at all the walls and ceilings and suddenly, despite herself, while the children call below, a great heaving thing rises in her and she puts her fist to her mouth, takes a final desperate look, pulls her coat about her, pats her hat and goes out. The lights dim down. The door opens and she comes back in, grabs her plant, and goes out for the last time.*]

CURTAIN

[1958]

Joining the Conversation: Critical Thinking and Writing

1. On pages 106–114 we discuss Langston Hughes's "Harlem," the poem from which Hansberry chose her title. Please describe why this choice of title is a good one.
2. Imagine that Hansberry has asked your help in selecting a title for her play—and that the title she actually selected, *A Raisin in the Sun,* is not an option. Write a letter to her, of about 1–2 pages, in which you recommend a title of your own choosing based on your reading of the text.
3. A scholar has observed, "the main point of the play is that the characters find they must defer their dreams." Present an argument in which you discuss and provide evidence for this claim.
4. Please list, in two or three sentences each, three key insights that Hansberry offers about race. Describe how you would organize and connect these insights into an effective argument.
5. If you were assigned to give an analysis in class of a crucial passage or scene in the play, which one would you choose? What would be the key questions about it that you would ask the students? What would you be trying to help them discover and understand about Hansberry's work?
6. Mama says, "money is life." What does she mean? Is her view supported by the play as a whole?
7. Consider the phrase "money is life" in a more general sense. In an essay of 1–2 pages, please argue that it is indeed the case that "money is life," and then in a second essay of the same length, argue that it is not.
8. Mama also says: "There is always something left to love." What does she mean by this statement? Does the play as a whole support her view?
9. Commenting on the historical context of *A Raisin the Sun,* a scholar has stated: "The play is best understood in relation to the American civil rights movement of the 1950s and 1960s." Making use of at least three sources, write a 2–3 page essay that summarizes this context for the play. Remember to include a bibliography of the Internet and print sources that you consulted.
10. Another scholar has noted that Hansberry's play "has been translated into over thirty languages on every continent, and has been produced in such diverse countries as the former Czechoslovakia, England, the former Soviet Union, and France." In your view, what explains this worldwide appeal? Please point to specific passages to support your argument.

11. Do you agree that *A Raisin in the Sun* is not only about race, but also about gender and class? Locate passages in the text that support your response.
12. Are you familiar with the phrase "the American dream"? What does it mean? How does it apply to the characters in this play?
13. Is "the American dream" for these characters the same as or different from what it is for you? Do you expect that you will be able to achieve your dream when you want to, or that you will be obliged to defer it? Please explain as clearly as you can.
14. Why is having a home of one's own so important in this play? Is it important for you as well?
15. Often it is said that each of us—whatever our race, religion, ethnicity, or gender—"wants the same thing in life." Do you agree or disagree? How would you go about developing an argument to explain and support your view? What kinds of evidence would you present?
16. Imagine that you are preparing a new edition of Hansberry's play. Making use of library or Internet sources, locate a photograph or an image of some other kind for the cover of this edition. Please explain your choice. (Be sure to include the image with your essay.)

Chapter Overview: Looking Backward/Looking Forward

1. How would you define patriotism? Stephen Decatur (1779–1820), a heroic officer in the U.S. Navy, once offered a toast, "Our country! In her intercourse with foreign nations may she always be in the right; but our country, right or wrong." Would you say that this toast exemplifies patriotism? In any case, to what degree do you share this sentiment? Do you think it is important for Americans to be patriotic? Please explain.
2. If you are an American, are you proud to be an American? Explain why.
3. If you are not an American, are you thinking about becoming one? Why or why not?
4. Do you feel you are more or less of an "American" than other Americans whom you know, or know about? How does one become a "real" American? Is it just a matter of place of birth, or (for someone coming here from abroad) of place of residence? Have you attended an event, or been part of an experience, when you said to yourself, "This is what it feels like to be an American"?
5. If you are an American who has traveled abroad, where, and in what ways, were you conscious of being an American? More so in some places than in others? If you have traveled abroad at different times, have you found yourself more conscious now of your American identity than you were in the past? What sorts of interactions and experiences led you to feel this?
6. Sometimes we hear references to the "heartland of America," or the "true America." Are there some parts of the country that are more "American" than others? If this is the case, is it a bad or a good thing?
7. We see, hear, and read a great deal about racial, ethnic, and religious differences, both within the United States and overseas. But isn't it the case that everyone, finally, is the same?

8. A recent survey concluded that "identity" is now the topic studied the most in college and university courses. Do you agree that it should be? Why is this topic receiving so much attention? Are there other topics that you believe are equally important, and maybe even more important? What are they, and what kinds of courses would you design and develop for studying them?

CHAPTER 25

American Dreams and Nightmares

SHORT VIEWS

The land of the free, and the home of the brave.
Francis Scott Key

The Star-Spangled Banner and all its successors have come to embody our country, what we think of as America. It may not be quite the same for every one of us who looks at it, but in the end we all pretty much come out where the framers did. We know we have a country founded on the then revolutionary idea that all of us are created equal, and equally entitled to life, liberty, and the pursuit of happiness. . . . You can neither honor the past, nor imagine the future, without the kind of citizenship embodied by all our memories of this flag. So as you see this flag and leave this place, promise yourself that when your great-grandchildren are here, they will not only be able to see the Star-Spangled Banner, it will mean just as much to them as it does to you today.
William Jefferson Clinton, at the National Museum of American History, 13 July 1998, standing in front of the Star-Spangled Banner

I always consider the settlement of America with reverence and wonder, as the opening of a grand scene and design in providence, for the illumination of the ignorant and the emancipation of the slavish part of mankind all over the earth.
John Adams

America is neither free nor brave, but a land of tight, iron-clanking little wills, everybody trying to put it over everybody else, and a land of men absolutely devoid of the real courage of trust, trust in life's sacred spontaneity. They can't trust *life until they can* control *it.*
D. H. Lawrence

America is still mostly xenophobic and racist. That's the nature of America, I think.
Jerry Garcia

A man is not expected to love his country, lest he make an ass of himself. Yet our country, seen through the mists of smog, is curiously lovable, in somewhat the way an individual who has got himself into an unconscionable scrape seems lovable—or at least deserving of support.
E. B. White

Americans are all too soft.
Pearl Buck

If American men are obsessed with money, American women are obsessed with weight. The men talk of gain, the women talk of loss.
Marya Mannes

I don't feel we did wrong in taking this great country away from them. These were great numbers of people who needed new land, and the Indians were selfishly trying to keep it for themselves.
John Wayne

America is the only nation in history which, miraculously, has gone directly from barbarism to degeneration without the usual interval of civilization.
attributed to Georges Clemenceau

The greatest honor history can bestow is the title of peacemaker. This honor now beckons America—the chance to help lead the world at last out of the valley of the turmoil and on to that high ground of peace that man has dreamed of since the dawn of civilization.
Richard M. Nixon

Joining the Conversation: Critical Thinking and Writing

1. Select a quotation that especially appeals to you, and make it the focus of an essay of about 500 words.
2. Take two of the passages—perhaps one that you especially like and one that you think is wrongheaded—and write a dialogue of about 500 words in which the two authors converse or argue. They may each try to convince the other, or they may find that to some degree they share views and they may then work out a statement that both can accept. If you do take the first position—that one writer is on the correct track but the other is utterly mistaken—try to be fair to the view that you think is mistaken. (As an experiment in critical thinking, imagine that you accept it, and make the best case for it that you possibly can.)
3. Imagine you are teaching a class, with this group of quotations as your subject for the day. Which quotation would you choose as your starting point? What would you say about it? What would you do next?

4. In a phrase that is familiar to all of us, Francis Scott Key says that America is "the land of the free, and the home of the brave." What does this phrase mean? What kinds of arguments could you present to support it? Could you imagine counterarguments?
5. Former president Clinton says that American flags "embody our country, what we think of as America." Sometimes American citizens, for instance during the Vietnam War, protest the government's actions by burning the flag. The Supreme Court has protected such action, saying that it is symbolic and is equivalent to speech. Occasionally a bill criminalizing flag-burning is introduced into Congress. Do you think flag-burning should be criminalized? Please explain.
6. Jerry Garcia (1942–1995), the rock guitarist and vocalist who was the leader of "The Grateful Dead," says that America is "mostly xenophobic and racist." If you had to argue in support of Garcia's claim, what would be your evidence? If you had to argue against this claim, what would be your evidence?
7. E. B. White says that America is "curiously lovable." Why does he use the word "curiously"? Do you think that White explains his point of view clearly? Could someone find what he says to be confusing? Do you? Why is that?
8. Marya Mannes offers a generalization about American men and women. What is your response to what she says? Do you believe that such generalizations illuminate the truth or distort it?
9. Imagine that you are in a debate with John Wayne. He has just begun by making his statement about the Indians, and now it is your turn. What would you say? First, present your reply in a paragraph of five or so sentences. Then, present your reply at greater length, in about a page and a half. Now compare the two versions: Which is more effective and why?
10. The remark attributed to Clemenceau is supposed to be witty, but of course it may also be true—or false. Do you find any truth in it? Please explain.
11. Do you see in the statements by former presidents Adams and Nixon suggestions that can easily lead to the view that it is America's destiny to bring democracy to the rest of the world? Is there, implicit in their remarks, a hint of what Rudyard Kipling called "the white man's burden"?

ESSAYS

CHIEF SEATTLE

Seattle (1786–1866), for whom the city in Washington is named, was a chief of the Suquamish and Duwamish tribes on the coast of the Pacific Northwest region of what is now the United States. There is some uncertainty about exactly when he delivered this speech—perhaps late in 1853, when the white governor of the Washington Territory first visited the territory, or perhaps early in 1855, when Seattle signed the Port Elliott Treaty, which confined the tribes to a reservation.

Seattle spoke little or no English. The speech was given through an interpreter and was transcribed by Henry Smith, who published it in 1887, with a concluding note saying, "The above is but a fragment of his speech." Because Smith's notes are not extant, it is now impossible to know exactly what Seattle said, but one point can be made: The text we print here is based entirely on Smith's version, the only text with any claim to authenticity. Since 1931 Smith's version has occasionally been reprinted with embellishments, the most popular of which is the addition of three sentences at the end: "Dead—did I say? There is no death. Only a change of worlds." Fine words, but they belong to an editor of 1931, not to Seattle.

My People

Yonder sky has wept tears of compassion on our fathers for centuries untold, and which, to us, looks eternal, may change. To-day it is fair, to-morrow it may be overcast with clouds. My words are like the stars that never set. What Seattle says the great chief, Washington, (the Indians in early times thought that Washington was still alive. They knew the name to be that of a president, and when they heard of the president at Washington they mistook the name of the city for the name of the reigning chief. They thought, also, that King George was still England's monarch, because the Hudson Bay traders called themselves "King George men." This innocent deception the company was shrewd enough not to explain away for the Indians had more respect for them than they would have had, had they known England was ruled by a woman. Some of us have learned better.) can rely upon, with as much certainty as our pale-face brothers can rely upon the return of the seasons. The son of the white chief says his father sends us greetings of friendship and good-will. This is kind, for we know he has little need of our friendship in return, because his people are many. They are like the grass that covers the vast prairies, while my people are few, and resemble the scattering trees of a wind-swept plain.

The great, and I presume also good, white chief sends us word that he wants to buy our lands but is willing to allow us to reserve enough to live on comfortably. This indeed appears generous, for the red man no longer has rights that he need respect, and the offer may be wise, also, for we are no longer in need of a great country. There was a time when our people covered the whole land as the waves of a wind-ruffled sea cover its shell-paved floor. But that time has long since passed away with the greatness of tribes almost forgotten. I will not mourn over our untimely decay, nor reproach my pale-face brothers with hastening it, for we, too, may have been somewhat to blame.

When our young men grow angry at some real or imaginary wrong and disfigure their faces with black paint, their hearts, also, are disfigured and turn black, and then their cruelty is relentless and knows no bounds, and our old men are not able to restrain them.

But let us hope that hostilities between the red man and his pale face brothers may never return. We would have everything to lose and nothing to gain.

True it is that revenge, with our young braves, is considered gain, even at the cost of their own lives, but old men who stay at home in times of war, and old women who have sons to lose, know better.

Our great father Washington, for I presume he is now our father as well as yours, since George has moved his boundaries to the north; our great and good father, I say, sends us word by his son, who, no doubt, is a great chief among his people, that if we do as he desires, he will protect us. His brave armies will be to us a bristling wall of strength, and his great ships of war will fill our harbors so that our ancient enemies far to the northward, the Simsiams and Hydas, will no longer frighten our women and old men. Then he will be our father and we will be his children. But can this ever be? Your God loves your people and hates mine; he folds his strong arms lovingly around the white man and leads him as a father leads his infant son, but he has forsaken his red children; he makes your people wax strong every day, and soon they will fill the land; while our people are ebbing away like a fast-receding tide, that will never flow again. The white man's God cannot love his red children or he would protect them. They seem to be orphans and can look nowhere for help. How then can we become brothers? How can your father become our father and bring us prosperity and awaken in us dreams of returning greatness?

Your God seems to be partial. He came to the white man. We never saw Him; never even heard His voice; He gave the white man laws but He had no word for His red children whose teeming millions filled this vast continent as the stars fill the firmament. No, we are two distinct races and must ever remain so. There is little in common between us. The ashes of our ancestors are sacred and their final resting place is hallowed ground, while you wander away from the tombs of your fathers seemingly without regret.

Your religion was written on tables of stone by the iron finger of an angry God, lest you might forget it. The red man could never remember nor comprehend it.

Our religion is the traditions of our ancestors, the dreams of our old men, given them by the great Spirit, and the visions of our sachems, and is written in the hearts of our people.

10 Your dead cease to love you and the homes of their nativity as soon as they pass the portals of the tomb. They wander off beyond the stars, are soon forgotten and never return. Our dead never forget the beautiful world that gave them being. They still love its winding rivers, its great mountains and its sequestered vales, and they ever yearn in tenderest affection over the lonely hearted living and often return to visit and comfort them.

Day and night cannot dwell together. The red man has ever fled the approach of the white man, as the changing mists on the mountain side flee before the blazing morning sun.

However, your proposition seems a just one, and I think my folks will accept it and will retire to the reservation you offer them, and we will dwell apart and in peace, for the words of the great white chief seem to be the voice of nature speaking to my people out of the thick darkness that is fast gathering around them like a dense fog floating inward from a midnight sea.

It matters but little where we pass the remainder of our days. They are not many. The Indian's night promises to be dark. No bright star hovers about the horizon. Sad-voiced winds moan in the distance. Some grim Nemesis of our race is on the red man's trail, and wherever he goes he will still hear the sure approaching footsteps of the fell destroyer and prepare to meet his doom, as does the wounded doe that hears the approaching footsteps of the hunter. A few more moons, a few more winters and not one of all the mighty hosts that once filled this broad land or that now roam in fragmentary bands through these vast solitudes will remain to weep over the tombs of a people once as powerful and as hopeful as your own.

But why should we repine? Why should I murmur at the fate of my people? Tribes are made up of individuals and are no better than they. Men come and go like the waves of the sea. A tear, a tamanamus, a dirge, and they are gone from our longing eyes forever. Even the white man, whose God walked and talked with him, as friend to friend, is not exempt from the common destiny. We *may* be brothers after all. We shall see.

15 We will ponder your proposition, and when we have decided we will tell you. But should we accept it, I here and now make this the first condition: That we will not be denied the privilege, without molestation, of visiting at will the graves of our ancestors and friends. Every part of this country is sacred to my people. Every hillside, every valley, every plain and grove has been hallowed by some fond memory or some sad experience of my tribe. Even the rocks that seem to lie dumb as they swelter in the sun along the silent seashore in solemn grandeur thrill with memories of past events connected with the fate of my people, and the very dust under your feet responds more lovingly to our footsteps than to yours, because it is the ashes of our ancestors, and our bare feet are conscious of the sympathetic touch, for the soil is rich with the life of our kindred.

The sable braves, and fond mothers, and glad-hearted maidens, and the little children who lived and rejoiced here, and whose very names are now forgotten, still love these solitudes, and their deep fastnesses at eventide grow shadowy with the presence of dusky spirits. And when the last red man shall have perished from the earth and his memory among white men shall have become a myth, these shores shall swarm with the invisible dead of my tribe, and when your children's children shall think themselves alone in the field, the shop, upon the highway or in the silence of the woods they will not be alone. In all the earth there is no place dedicated to solitude. At night when the streets of your cities and villages shall be silent, and you think them deserted, they will throng with the returning hosts that once filled and still love this beautiful land. The white man will never be alone. Let him be just and deal kindly with my people, for the dead are not altogether powerless.

[c. 1835]

Joining the Conversation: Critical Thinking and Writing

1. In a paragraph explain why Chief Seattle believes white people have a different God from that of Native Americans.
2. Chief Seattle says that he thinks the offer of the whites is "fair" and that he thinks his people will accept the offer and retire to the reservation. Judging from his speech, do you think his main reason for approving the proposal is that it is fair?
3. In 250 words explain why Chief Seattle believes that whites and Native Americans can never be reconciled, and evaluate his view.
4. Chief Seattle's speech is rich in metaphors and other figures of speech. List three examples. From what areas are most of his figures of speech drawn?

ELIZABETH CADY STANTON

Elizabeth Cady Stanton (1815–1902), a lawyer's daughter and journalist's wife, proposed in 1848 a convention to address the "social, civil, and religious condition and rights of women." Responding to Stanton's call, women from all over the Northeast convened in the village of Seneca Falls, New York. Her Declaration of Sentiments and Resolutions *adopted by the Seneca Falls Convention—but only after vigorous debate and some amendments by others—became the platform for the women's movement in this country.*

Declaration of Sentiments and Resolutions

When, in the course of human events, it becomes necessary for one portion of the family of man to assume among the people of the earth a position different from that which they have hitherto occupied, but one to which the laws of nature and of nature's God entitle them, a decent respect to the opinions of mankind requires that they should declare the causes that impel them to such a course.

We hold these truths to be self-evident: that all men and women are created equal; that they are endowed by their Creator with certain inalienable rights; that among these are life, liberty and the pursuit of happiness; that to secure these rights governments are instituted, deriving their just powers from the consent of the governed. Whenever any form of government becomes destructive of these ends, it is the right of those who suffer from it to refuse allegiance to it, and to insist upon the institution of a new government, laying its foundation on such principles, and organizing its powers in such form, as to them shall seem most likely to effect their safety and happiness. Prudence, indeed, will dictate that governments long established should not be changed for light and transient causes; and accordingly all experience hath shown that mankind are more disposed to suffer, while evils are sufferable, than to right themselves by abolishing the forms to which they were accustomed. But when a long train of abuses and usurpations, pursuing invariably the same object, evinces a design to reduce them under absolute despotism, it is their duty to throw off such government, and to provide new guards for their future security. Such has been the patient sufferance of the women under this government, and such is now the necessity which constrains them to demand the equal station to which they are entitled.

The history of mankind is a history of repeated injuries and usurpations on the part of man toward woman, having in direct object the establishment of an absolute tyranny over her. To prove this, let facts be submitted to a candid world.

He has never permitted her to exercise her inalienable right to the elective franchise.

5 He has compelled her to submit to laws, in the formation of which she had no voice.

He has withheld from her rights which are given to the most ignorant and degraded men—both natives and foreigners.

Having deprived her of this first right of a citizen, the elective franchise, thereby leaving her without representation in the halls of legislation, he has oppressed her on all sides.

He has made her, if married, in the eye of the law, civilly dead.

He has taken from her all right in property, even to the wages she earns.

10 He has made her, morally, an irresponsible being, as she can commit many crimes with impunity, provided they be done in the presence of her husband. In the covenant of marriage, she is compelled to promise obedience to her husband, he becoming to all intents and purposes, her master—the law giving him power to deprive her of her liberty, and to administer chastisement.

He has so framed the laws of divorce, as to what shall be the proper causes, and in case of separation, to whom the guardianship of the children shall be given, as to be wholly regardless of the happiness of women—the law, in all cases, going upon a false supposition of the supremacy of man, and giving all power into his hands.

After depriving her of all rights as a married woman, if single, and the owner of property, he has taxed her to support a government which recognizes her only when her property can be made profitable to it.

He has monopolized nearly all the profitable employments, and from those she is permitted to follow, she receives but a scanty remuneration. He closes against her all the avenues to wealth and distinction which he considers most honorable to himself. As a teacher of theology, medicine, or law, she is not known.

He has denied her the facilities for obtaining a thorough education, all colleges being closed against her.

15 He allows her in Church, as well as State, but a subordinate position, claiming Apostolic authority for her exclusion from the ministry, and, with some exceptions, from any public participation in the affairs of the Church.

He has created a false public sentiment by giving to the world a different code of morals for men and women, by which moral delinquencies which exclude women from society, are not only tolerated, but deemed of little account in man.

He has usurped the prerogative of Jehovah himself, claiming it as his right to assign for her a sphere of action, when that belongs to her conscience and to her God.

He has endeavored, in every way that he could, to destroy her confidence in her own powers, to lessen her self-respect, and to make her willing to lead a dependent and abject life.

Now, in view of this entire disfranchisement of one-half the people of this country, their social and religious degradation—in view of the unjust laws above mentioned, and because women do feel themselves aggrieved, oppressed, and fraudulently deprived of their most sacred rights, we insist that they have immediate admission to all the rights and privileges which belong to them as citizens of the United States.

20 In entering upon the great work before us, we anticipate no small amount of misconception, misrepresentation, and ridicule; but we shall use every instrumentality within our power to effect our object. We shall employ agents, circulate tracts, petition the State and National legislatures, and endeavor to enlist the pulpit and the press in our behalf. We hope this Convention will be followed by a series of Conventions embracing every part of the country.

[The following resolutions were discussed by Lucretia Mott, Thomas and Mary Ann McClintock, Amy Post, Catharine A. F. Stebbins, and others, and were adopted:]

Whereas, The great precept of nature is conceded to be, that "man shall pursue his own true and substantial happiness." Blackstone in his Commentaries remarks, that this law of Nature being coeval with mankind, and dictated by God himself, is of course superior in obligation to any other. It is binding over all the globe, in all countries, and at all times; no human laws are of any validity if contrary to this, and such of them as are valid, derive all their force, and all their validity, and all their authority, mediately and immediately, from this original; therefore.

Resolved, That such laws as conflict, in any way, with the true and substantial happiness of woman, are contrary to the great precept of nature and of no validity, for this is "superior in obligation to any other."

Resolved, That all laws which prevent woman from occupying such a station in society as her conscience shall dictate, or which place her in a position inferior to that of man, are contrary to the great precept of nature, and therefore of no force or authority.

Resolved, That woman is man's equal—was intended to be so by the Creator, and the highest good of the race demands that she should be recognized as such.

25 *Resolved,* That the women of this country ought to be enlightened in regard to the laws under which they live, that they may no longer publish their degradation

by declaring themselves satisfied with their present position, nor their ignorance, by asserting that they have all the rights they want.

Resolved, That inasmuch as man, while claiming for himself intellectual superiority, does accord to woman moral superiority, it is preeminently his duty to encourage her to speak and teach, as she has an opportunity, in all religious assemblies.

Resolved, That the same amount of virtue, delicacy, and refinement of behavior that is required of woman in the social state, should also be required of man, and the same transgressions should be visited with equal severity on both man and woman.

Resolved, That the objection of indelicacy and impropriety, which is so often brought against woman when she addresses a public audience, comes with a very ill-grace from those who encourage, by their attendance, her appearance on the stage, in the concert, or in feats of the circus.

Resolved, That woman has too long rested satisfied in the circumscribed limits which corrupt customs and a perverted application of the Scriptures have marked out for her, and that it is time she should move in the enlarged sphere which her great Creator has assigned her.

Resolved, That it is the duty of the women of this country to secure to themselves their sacred right to the elective franchise.

Resolved, That the equality of human rights results necessarily from the fact of the identity of the race in capabilities and responsibilities.

Resolved, therefore, That, being invested by the Creator with the same capabilities, and the same consciousness of responsibility for their exercise, it is demonstrably the right and duty of woman, equally with man, to promote every righteous cause by every righteous means; and especially in regard to the great subjects of morals and religion, it is self-evidently her right to participate with her brother in teaching them, both in private and in public, by writing and by speaking, by any instrumentalities proper to be used, and in any assemblies proper to be held; and this being a self-evident truth growing out of the divinely implanted principles of human nature, any custom or authority adverse to it, whether modern or wearing the hoary sanction of antiquity, is to be regarded as a self-evident falsehood, and at war with mankind.

[At the last session Lucretia Mott offered and spoke to the following resolution:]

Resolved, That the speedy success of our cause depends upon the zealous and untiring efforts of both men and women, for the overthrow of the monopoly of the pulpit, and for the securing to woman an equal participation with men in the various trades, professions, and commerce.

[1848]

Joining the Conversation: Critical Thinking and Writing

1. Stanton echoes the Declaration of Independence because she wishes to associate her ideas and the movement she supports with a document and a movement that her readers esteem. And of course she must have believed that if readers esteem the Declaration of Independence, they must grant the justice of her goals. Does her strategy work, or does it backfire by making her essay seem strained?

2. When Stanton insists that women have an "inalienable right to the elective franchise" (paragraph 4), what does she mean by "inalienable"?
3. Stanton complains that men have made women, "in the eye of the law, civilly dead" (paragraph 8). What does she mean by "civilly dead"? How is it possible for a person to be biologically alive yet civilly dead?
4. Stanton objects that women are "not known" as teachers of "theology, medicine, or law" (paragraph 13). Is this still true today? Do some research in the library or online, and then write three 100-word biographical sketches, one each on a well-known woman professor of theology, medicine, and law.
5. How might you go about proving (rather than merely asserting) that, as paragraph 24 says, "woman is man's equal—was intended to be so by the Creator"?
6. Stanton's *Declaration* claims that women have "the same capabilities" as men (paragraph 32). Yet in 1848 Stanton and the others at Seneca Falls knew, or should have known, that history recorded no example of an outstanding woman philosopher to compare with Plato or Kant, a great composer to compare with Beethoven or Chopin, a scientist to compare with Galileo or Newton, or a creative mathematician to compare with Euclid or Descartes. Do these facts contradict the Declaration's claim? If not, why not? How else but by different intellectual capabilities do you think such facts are to be explained?
7. Stanton's *Declaration* is about 160 years old. Have all of the issues she raised been satisfactorily resolved? If not, which ones remain?
8. In our society, children have very few rights. For instance, a child cannot decide to drop out of elementary school or high school, and a child cannot decide to leave his or her parents to reside with some other family that he or she finds more compatible. Whatever your view of children's rights, compose the best declaration of the rights of children that you can.

MARTIN LUTHER KING JR.

Martin Luther King Jr. (1929–1968), was born in Atlanta and educated at Morehouse College, Crozer Theological Seminary, and Boston University. In 1954 he was called to serve as a Baptist minister in Montgomery, Alabama. During the next two years he achieved national fame when, using a policy of nonviolent resistance, he successfully led the boycott against segregated bus lines in Montgomery. He then organized the Southern Christian Leadership Conference, which furthered civil rights, first in the South and then nationwide. In 1964 he was awarded the Nobel Peace Prize. Four years later he was assassinated in Memphis, Tennessee.

"I Have a Dream" was delivered from the steps of the Lincoln Memorial, in Washington, D.C., in 1963, the hundredth anniversary of the Emancipation Proclamation. King's immediate audience consisted of more than two hundred thousand people who had come to demonstrate for civil rights.

I Have a Dream

I am happy to join with you today in what will go down in history as the greatest demonstration for freedom in the history of our nation.

Five score years ago, a great American, in whose symbolic shadow we stand today, signed the Emancipation Proclamation. This momentous decree came as a great beacon light of hope to millions of Negro slaves who had been seared in the flames of withering injustice. It came as a joyous daybreak to end the long night of their captivity. But one hundred years later, the Negro still is not free. One hundred years later, the life of the Negro is still sadly crippled by the manacles of segregation and the chains of discrimination. One hundred years later, the Negro lives on a lonely island of poverty in the midst of a vast ocean of material prosperity. One hundred years later, the Negro is still anguished in the corners of American society and finds himself in exile in his own land. And so we have come here today to dramatize a shameful condition.

In a sense we have come to our nation's capital to cash a check. When the architects of our republic wrote the magnificent words of the Constitution and the Declaration of Independence, they were signing a promissory note to which every American was to fall heir. This note was the promise that all men—yes, black men as well as white men—would be guaranteed the inalienable rights of life, liberty, and the pursuit of happiness.

It is obvious today that America has defaulted on this promissory note insofar as her citizens of color are concerned. Instead of honoring this sacred obligation, America has given the Negro people a bad check, a check which has come back marked "insufficient funds." But we refuse to believe that the bank of justice is bankrupt. We refuse to believe that there are insufficient funds in the great vaults of opportunity of this nation; and so we have come to cash this check, a check that will give us upon demand the riches of freedom and the security of justice.

5 We have also come to this hallowed spot to remind America of the fierce urgency of *now.* This is no time to engage in the luxury of cooling off or to take the tranquilizing drug of gradualism. *Now* is the time to make real promises of democracy. *Now* is the time to rise from the dark and desolate valley of segregation to the sunlit path of racial justice. *Now* is the time to lift our nation from the quicksands of racial injustice to the solid rock of brotherhood. *Now* is the time to make justice a reality for all of God's children.

It would be fatal for the nation to overlook the urgency of the moment. This sweltering summer of the Negro's legitimate discontent will not pass until there is an invigorating autumn of freedom and equality. Nineteen sixty-three is not an end, but a beginning. And those who hope that the Negro needed to blow off steam and will now be content will have a rude awakening if the nation returns to business as usual. There will be neither rest nor tranquility in America until the Negro is granted his citizenship rights. The whirlwinds of revolt will continue to shake the foundations of our nation until the bright day of justice emerges.

But there is something that I must say to my people who stand on the warm threshold which leads into the palace of justice. In the process of gaining our rightful place, we must not be guilty of wrongful deeds. Let us not seek to satisfy our thirst for freedom by drinking from the cup of bitterness and hatred. We must forever conduct our struggle on the high plane of dignity and discipline. We must not allow our creative protest to degenerate into physical violence. Again and again we must rise to the majestic heights of meeting physical force with soul force. And the marvelous new militancy which has engulfed the Negro community must not lead us to a distrust of all white people; for many of our white brothers, as evidenced by their presence here today, have come to realize that their destiny is tied up with our destiny, and they have come to realize that their freedom is inextricably bound to our freedom.

We cannot walk alone. And as we walk we must make the pledge that we shall always march ahead. We cannot turn back. There are those who are asking the devotees of civil rights, "When will you be satisfied?" We can never be satisfied as long as the Negro is the victim of the unspeakable horrors of police brutality. We can never be satisfied as long as our bodies, heavy with the fatigue of travel, cannot gain lodging in the motels of the highways and the hotels of the cities. We cannot be satisfied as long as the Negro's basic mobility is from a smaller ghetto to a larger one. We can never be satisfied as long as our children are stripped of their selfhood and robbed of their dignity by signs stating "For Whites Only." We cannot be satisfied as long as the Negro in Mississippi cannot vote and a Negro in New York believes he has nothing for which to vote. No, no, we are not satisfied, and we will not be satisfied until justice rolls down like waters and righteousness like a mighty stream.[1]

I am not unmindful that some of you have come here out of great trials and tribulations. Some of you have come fresh from narrow jail cells. Some of you have come from areas where your quest for freedom left you battered by the storms of persecution and staggered by the winds of police brutality. You have been the veterans of creative suffering. Continue to work with the faith that unearned suffering is redemptive.

10 Go back to Mississippi, and go back to Alabama. Go back to South Carolina. Go back to Georgia. Go back to Louisiana. Go back to the slums and ghettos of our Northern cities, knowing that somehow this situation can and will be changed. Let us not wallow in the valley of despair.

I say to you today, my friends, even though we face the difficulties of today and tomorrow, I still have a dream. It is a dream deeply rooted in the American dream. I have a dream that one day this nation will rise up and live out the true meaning of its creed: "We hold these truths to be self-evident, that all men are created equal." I have a dream that one day, on the red hills of Georgia, sons of former slaves and the sons of former slave owners will be able to sit down together at the table of brotherhood. I have a dream that one day even the state of Mississippi, a state sweltering with the heat of injustice, sweltering with the heat of oppression, will be transformed into an oasis of freedom and justice. I have a dream that my four little children will one day live in a nation where they will not be judged by the color of their skin, but by the content of their character.

I have a dream today. I have a dream that one day down in Alabama—with its vicious racists, with its governor's lips dripping with the words of interposition and nullification—one day right there in Alabama, little black boys and black girls will be able to join hands with little white boys and white girls as sisters and brothers.

I have a dream today. I have a dream that one day every valley shall be exalted and every hill and mountain shall be made low, the rough places will be made plain and the crooked places will be made straight, and the glory of the Lord shall be revealed, and all flesh shall see it together.[2]

This is our hope. This is the faith that I go back to the South with. And with this faith we will be able to hew out of the mountain of despair a stone of hope. With this faith we will be able to transform the jangling discords of our nation into a beautiful symphony of brotherhood. With this faith we will be able to work together, to play together, to struggle together, to go to jail together, to stand up for freedom together, knowing that we will be free one day.

[1]**justice . . . stream** a quotation from the Hebrew Bible: Amos 5:24. (All notes to this reading are by the editors.) [2]**every valley . . . see it together** another quotation from the Hebrew Bible: Isaiah 40.4–5.

15 And this will be the day—this will be the day when all of God's children will be able to sing with new meaning:

> My country, 'tis of thee,
> Sweet land of liberty,
> Of thee I sing;
> Land where my fathers died,
> Land of the Pilgrim's pride,
> From every mountainside
> Let freedom ring.

And if America is to be a great nation, this must become true.

And so let freedom ring from the prodigious hilltops of New Hampshire. Let freedom ring from the mighty mountains of New York. Let freedom ring from the heightening Alleghenies of Pennsylvania. Let freedom ring from the snow-capped Rockies of Colorado. Let freedom ring from the curvaceous slopes of California.

But not only that. Let freedom ring from Stone Mountain of Georgia. Let freedom ring from Lookout Mountain of Tennessee. Let freedom ring from every hill and molehill of Mississippi. "From every mountainside let freedom ring."

And when this happens—when we allow freedom to ring, when we let it ring from every village and every hamlet, from every state and every city—we will be able to speed up that day when all of God's children, Black men and white men, Jews and Gentiles, Protestants and Catholics, will be able to join hands and sing in the words of the old Negro spiritual: "Free at last! Free at last! Thank God Almighty. We are free at last!"

[1963]

Joining the Conversation: Critical Thinking and Writing

1. Analyze the rhetoric—the oratorical art—of the second paragraph. What, for instance, is gained by saying "five score years ago" instead of "a hundred years ago"? By metaphorically calling the Emancipation Proclamation "a great beacon light?" By saying that "Negro slaves . . . had been seared in the flames of withering injustice"? And what of the metaphors "daybreak" and "the long night of . . . captivity"?
2. Do the first two paragraphs make an effective opening? Why?
3. In the third and fourth paragraphs King uses the metaphor of a bad check. Rewrite the third paragraph *without* using any of King's metaphors, and then in a paragraph evaluate the difference between King's version and yours.
4. King's highly metaphoric speech of course appeals to emotions. But it also offers *reasons*. What reason(s), for instance, does King give to support his belief that blacks should not resort to physical violence?
5. When King delivered the speech, his audience at the Lincoln Memorial was primarily black. Do you think that the speech is also addressed to whites? Explain.
6. The speech can be divided into three parts: paragraphs 1 through 6; paragraphs 7 ("But there is") through 10; and paragraph 11 ("I say to you today, my friends") to the end. Summarize each of these three parts in a sentence or two, so that the basic organization is evident.

7. King says (paragraph 11) that his dream is "deeply rooted in the American dream." First, what is the American dream, as King seems to understand it? Second, how does King establish his point—that is, what evidence does he use to convince us—that his dream is the American dream? (On this second issue, for a start one might point out that in the second paragraph King refers to the Emancipation Proclamation. What other relevant documents does he refer to?)
8. King delivered his speech in 1963, more than forty years ago. In an essay of 500 words argue that the speech still is—or is not—relevant. Or write an essay of 500 words in which you state what you take to be the "American dream," and argue that it now is or is not readily available to blacks.
9. Do you believe that members of the clergy should be politically active? Why, or why not?

Studs Terkel

Studs Terkel (1912–2008) was born Louis Terkel in New York City in 1912. After earning a PhD and a law degree from the University of Chicago he worked as a civil servant and an actor before becoming a radio and television broadcaster. Much of his broadcasting work consisted of interviewing people for "Studs' Place," and he later published numerous books of interviews.

*Arnold Schwarzenegger's Dream**

Call me Arnold.

I was born in a little Austrian town, outside Graz. It was a 300-year-old house.

When I was ten years old, I had the dream of being the best in the world in something. When I was fifteen, I had a dream that I wanted to be the best body builder in the world and the most muscular man. It was not only a dream I dreamed at night. It was also a daydream. It was so much in my mind that I felt it had to become a reality. It took me five years of hard work. Five years later, I turned this dream into reality and became Mr. Universe, the best-built man in the world.

"Winning" is a very important word. There is one that achieves what he wanted to achieve and there are hundreds of thousands that failed. It singles you out: the winner.

5 I came out second three times, but that is not what I call losing. The bottom line for me was: Arnold has to be the winner. I have to win more often the Mr. Universe title than anybody else. I won it five times consecutively. I hold the record as Mr. Olympia, the top professional body-building championship. I won it six times. That's why I retired. There was nobody even close to me. Everybody gave up competing against me. That's what I call a winner.

When I was a small boy, my dream was not to be big physically, but big in a way that everybody listens to me when I talk, that I'm a very important person, that people recognize me and see me as something special. I had a big need for being singled out.

Also my dream was to end up in America. When I was ten years old, I dreamed of being an American. At the time I didn't know much about America, just that it was a wonderful country. I felt it was where I belonged. I didn't like

*Terkel's *American Dreams* presents transcriptions that Terkel recorded. This interview took place in the 1970s, decades before Schwarzenegger was elected governor of California.

being in a little country like Austria. I did everything possible to get out. I did so in 1968, when I was twenty-one years old.

If I would believe in life after death, I would say my before-life I was living in America. That's why I feel so good here. It is the country where you can turn your dream into reality. Other countries don't have those things. When I came over here to America, I felt I was in heaven. In America, we don't have an obstacle. Nobody's holding you back.

Number One in America pretty much takes care of the rest of the world. You kind of run through the rest of the world like nothing. I'm trying to make people in America aware that they should appreciate what they have here. You have the best tax advantages here and the best prices here and the best products here.

10 One of the things I always had was a business mind. When I was in high school, a majority of my classes were business classes. Economics and accounting and mathematics. When I came over here to this country, I really didn't speak English almost at all. I learned English and then started taking business courses, because that's what America is best known for: business. Turning one dollar into a million dollars in a short period of time. Also when you make money, how do you keep it?

That's one of the most important things when you have money in your hand, how can you keep it? Or make more out of it? Real estate is one of the best ways of doing that. I own apartment buildings, office buildings, and raw land. That's my love, real estate.

I have emotions. But what you do, you keep them cold or you store them away for a time. You must control your emotions, you must have command over yourself. Three, four months before a competition, I could not be interfered by other people's problems. This is sometimes called selfish. It's the only way you can be if you want to achieve something. Any emotional things inside me, I try to keep cold so it doesn't interfere with my training.

Many times things really touched me. I felt them and I felt sensitive about them. But I had to talk myself out of it. I had to suppress those feelings in order to go on. Sport is one of those activities where you really have to concentrate. You must pay attention a hundred percent to the particular thing you're doing. There must be nothing else on your mind. Emotions must not interfere. Otherwise, you're thinking about your girlfriend. You're in love, your positive energies get channeled into another direction rather than going into your weight room or making money.

You have to choose at a very early date what you want: a normal life or to achieve things you want to achieve. I never wanted to win a popularity contest in doing things the way people want me to do it. I went the road I thought was best for me. A few people thought I was cold, selfish. Later they found out that's not the case. After I achieve my goal, I can be Mr. Nice Guy. You know what I mean?

15 California is to me a dreamland. It is the absolute combination of everything I was always looking for. It has all the money in the world there, show business there, wonderful weather there, beautiful country, ocean is there. Snow skiing in the winter, you can go in the desert the same day. You have beautiful-looking people there. They all have a tan.

I believe very strongly in the philosophy of staying hungry. If you have a dream and it becomes a reality, don't stay satisfied with it too long. Make up a new dream and hunt after that one and turn it into reality. When you have that dream achieved, make up a new dream.

I am a strong believer in Western philosophy, the philosophy of success, of progress, of getting rich. The Eastern philosophy is passive, which I believe in maybe three percent of the times, and the ninety-seven percent is Western, conquering and going on. It's a beautiful philosophy, and America should keep it up.

[1980]

Joining the Conversation: Critical Thinking and Writing

1. After saying that America "is the country where you can turn your dream into reality. Other countries don't have those things," Schwarzenegger goes on to say, "In America . . . nobody's holding you back." What do you suppose he means by "those things," and by saying that here "nobody's holding you back"?
2. If you have some firsthand knowledge of another country, in an essay of 250–500 words indicate in what ways that country might differ from America in the matter of allowing individuals to fulfill their dreams. By the way, is it your guess that Schwarzenegger's particular dream ("to be the best body builder in the world") is more easily fulfilled in the United States than elsewhere—say in Canada, or Cuba, or Russia, or Austria? Why?
3. In a paragraph, set forth what you think Schwarzenegger's view of America is.
4. In one paragraph, sketch Schwarzenegger as objectively as possible, as you perceive him in this interview. In a second paragraph, again drawing only on this interview, evaluate him, calling attention to what you think are his strengths and weaknesses.

STORIES

KURT VONNEGUT JR.

Kurt Vonnegut Jr. (1922–2007) was born in Indianapolis and studied biochemistry at Cornell University. He was drafted into the army and was captured by the Germans in the Battle of the Bulge in late 1944. A survivor of the Allied fire-bombing of Dresden in February 1945, along with other prisoners he was required to search for corpses hidden in the rubble. Two months later he was freed. After the war, he studied anthropology at the University of Chicago, then worked as a publicist for General Electric from 1947 until 1950, when he became a full-time writer.

Vonnegut wrote stories, novels, and plays. His two most famous works probably are Cat's Cradle *(1963), which ends with the freezing of the world, and* Slaughterhouse Five *(1969), which draws on his experience in Dresden.*

Harrison Bergeron

The year was 2081, and everybody was finally equal. They weren't only equal before God and the law. They were equal every which way. Nobody was smarter than anybody else. Nobody was better looking than anybody else. Nobody was stronger or quicker than anybody else. All this equality was due to the 211th, 212th, and 213th Amendments to the Constitution, and to the unceasing vigilance of agents of the United States Handicapper General.

Some things about living still weren't quite right, though. April, for instance, still drove people crazy by not being springtime. And it was in that clammy month that the H-G men took George and Hazel Bergeron's fourteen-year-old son, Harrison, away.

It was tragic, all right, but George and Hazel couldn't think about it very hard. Hazel had a perfectly average intelligence, which meant she couldn't think about anything except in short bursts. And George, while his intelligence was way above normal, had a little mental handicap radio in his ear. He was required by law to wear it at all times. It was tuned to a government transmitter. Every twenty seconds or so, the transmitter would send out some sharp noise to keep people like George from taking unfair advantage of their brains.

George and Hazel were watching television. There were tears on Hazel's cheeks, but she'd forgotten for the moment what they were about.

On the television screen, were ballerinas.

A buzzer sounded in George's head. His thoughts fled in panic, like bandits from a burglar alarm.

"That was a real pretty dance, that dance they just did," said Hazel.

"Huh?" said George.

"That dance—it was nice," said Hazel.

"Yup," said George. He tried to think a little about the ballerinas. They weren't really very good—no better than anybody else would have been, anyway. They were burdened with sashweights and bags of birdshot, and their faces were masked, so that no one, seeing a free and graceful gesture or a pretty face, would feel like something and cat drug in. George was toying with the vague notion that maybe dancers shouldn't be handicapped. But he didn't get very far with it before another noise in his ear radio scattered his thoughts.

George winced. So did two out of the eight ballerinas.

Hazel saw him wince. Having no mental handicap herself, she had to ask George what the latest sound had been.

"Sounded like somebody hitting a milk bottle with a ball peen hammer," said George.

"I'd think it would be real interesting, hearing all the different sounds," said Hazel, a little envious. "All the things they think up."

"Um," said George.

"Only, if I was Handicapper General, you know what I would do?" said Hazel. Hazel, as a matter of fact, bore a strong resemblance to the Handicapper General, a woman named Diana Moon Glampers. "If I was Diana Moon Glampers," said Hazel, "I'd have chimes on Sunday—just chimes. Kind of in honor or religion."

"I could think, if it was just chimes," said George.

"Well—maybe make 'em real loud," said Hazel. "I think I'd make a good Handicapper General."

"Good as anybody else," said George.

"Who knows better'n I do what normal is?" said Hazel.

"Right," said George. He began to think glimmeringly about his abnormal son who was now in jail, about Harrison, but a twenty-one-gun salute in his head stopped that.

"Boy!" said Hazel, "that was a doozy, wasn't it?"

It was such a doozy that George was white and trembling, and tears stood on the rims of his red eyes. Two of the eight ballerinas had collapased to the studio floor, [and] were holding their temples.

"All of a sudden you look so tired," said Hazel. "Why don't you stretch out on the sofa, so's you can rest your handicap bag on the pillows, honeybunch." She was referring to the forty-seven pounds of birdshot in a canvas bag, which was padlocked around George's neck. "Go on and rest the bag for a little while," she said. "I don't care if you're not equal to me for a while."

25 George weighed the bag with his hands. "I don't mind it," he said. "I don't notice it any more. It's just a part of me."

"You been so tired lately—kind of wore out," said Hazel. "If there was just some way we could make a little hole in the bottom of the bag, and just take out a few of them lead balls. Just a few."

"Two years in prison and two thousand dollars fine for every ball I took out," said George. "I don't call that a bargain."

"If you could just take a few out when you came home from work," said Hazel. "I mean—you don't compete with anybody around here. You just set around."

"If I tried to get away with it," said George, "then other people'd get away with it—and pretty soon we'd be right back to the dark ages again, with everybody competing against everybody else. You wouldn't like that, would you?"

30 "I'd hate it," said Hazel.

"There you are," said George. "The minute people start cheating on laws, what do you think happens to society?"

If Hazel hadn't been able to come up with an answer to this question George couldn't have supplied one. A siren was going off in his head.

"Reckon it'd fall apart," said Hazel.

"What would?" said George blankly.

35 "Society," said Hazel uncertainly. "Wasn't that what you just said?"

"Who knows?" said George.

The television program was suddenly interrupted for a news bulletin. It wasn't clear at first as to what the bulletin was about, since the announcer, like all announcers, had a serious speech impediment. For about half a minute, and in a state of high excitement, the announcer tried to say, "Ladies and gentlemen—"

He finally gave up, handed the bulletin to a ballerina to read.

"That's all right—" Hazel said of the announcer, "he tried. That's the big thing. He tried to do the best he could with what God gave him. He should get a nice raise for trying so hard."

40 "Ladies and gentlemen—" said the ballerina, reading the bulletin. She must have been extraordinarily beautiful, because the mask she wore was hideous. And it was easy to see that she was the strongest and most graceful of all the dancers, for her handicap bags were as big as those worn by two-hundred-pound men.

And she had to apologize at once for her voice, which was a very unfair voice for a woman to use. Her voice was a warm, luminous, timeless melody. "Excuse me—" she said, and she began again, making her voice absolutely uncompetitive.

"Harrison Bergeron, age fourteen," she said in a grackle squawk, "has just escaped from jail, where he was held on suspicion of plotting to overthrow the government. He is a genius and an athlete, is under-handicapped, and should be regarded as extremely dangerous."

A police photograph of Harrison Bergeron was flashed on the screen upside down, then sideways, upside down again, then right side up. The picture showed the full length of Harrison against a background calibrated in feet and inches. He was exactly seven feet tall.

The rest of Harrison's appearance was Halloween and hardware. Nobody had ever borne heavier handicaps. He had outgrown hindrances faster than the H-G men could think them up. Instead of a little ear radio for a mental handicap, he wore a tremendous pair of earphones, and spectacles with thick wavy lenses. The spectacles were intended to make him not only half blind, but to give him whanging headaches besides.

45 Scrap mental was hung all over him. Ordinarily, there was a certain symmetry, a military neatness to the handicaps issued to strong people, but Harrison looked like a walking junkyard. In the race of life, Harrison carried three hundred pounds.

And to offset his good looks, the H-G men required that he wear at all times a red rubber ball for a nose, keep his eyebrows shaved off, and cover his even white teeth with black caps at snaggle-tooth random.

"If you see this boy," said the ballerina, "do not—I repeat, do not—try to reason with him."

There was the shriek of a door being torn from its hinges.

Screams and barking cries of consternation came from the television set. The photograph of Harrison Bergeron on the screen jumped again and again, as though dancing to the tune of an earthquake.

50 George Bergeron correctly identified the earthquake, and well he might have—for many was the time his own home had danced to the same crashing tune. "My God—" said George, "that must be Harrison!"

The realization was blasted from his mind instantly by the sound of an automobile collision in his head.

When George could open his eyes again, the photograph of Harrison was gone. A living, breathing Harrison filled the screen.

Clanking, clownish, and huge, Harrison stood in the center of the studio. The knob of the uprooted studio door was still in his hand. Ballerinas, technicians, musicians, and announcers cowered on their knees before him, expecting to die.

"I am the Emperor!" cried Harrison. "Do you hear? I am the Emperor! Everybody must do what I say at once!" He stamped his foot and the studio shook.

55 "Even as I stand here—" he bellowed, "crippled, hobbled, sickened—I am a greater ruler than any man who ever lived! Now watch me become what I *can* become!"

Harrison tore the straps of his handicap harness like wet tissue paper, tore straps guaranteed to support five thousand pounds.

Harrison's scrap-iron handicaps crashed to the floor.

Harrison thrust his thumbs under the bar of the padlock that secured his head harness. The bar snapped like celery. Harrison smashed his headphones and spectacles against the wall.

He flung away his rubber-ball nose, revealed a man that would have awed Thor, the god of thunder.

60 "I shall now select my Empress!" he said, looking down on the cowering people. "Let the first woman who dares rise to her feet claim her mate and her throne!"

A moment passed, and then a ballerina arose, swaying like a willow.

Harrison plucked the mental handicap from her ear, snapped off her physical handicaps with marvelous delicacy. Last of all, he removed her mask.

She was blindingly beautiful.

"Now—" said Harrison, taking her hand, "shall we show the people the meaning of the word dance? Music!" he commanded.

65 The musicians scrambled back into their chairs, and Harrison stripped them of their handicaps, too. "Play your best," he told them, "and I'll make you barons and dukes and earls."

The music began. It was normal at first—cheap, silly, false. But Harrison snatched two musicians from their chairs, waved them like batons as he sang the music as he wanted it played. He slammed them back into their chairs.

The music began again and was much improved.

Harrison and his Empress merely listened to the music for a while—listened gravely, as though synchronizing their heartbeats with it.

They shifted their weights to their toes.

70 Harrison placed his big hands on the girl's tiny waist, letting her sense the weightlessness that would soon be hers.

And then, in an explosion of joy and grace, into the air they sprang!

Not only were the laws of the land abandoned, but the law of gravity and the laws of motion as well.

They reeled, whirled, swiveled, flounced, capered, gamboled, and spun.

They leaped like deer on the moon.

75 The studio ceiling was thirty feet high, but each leap brought the dancers nearer to it.

It became their obvious intention to kiss the ceiling.

They kissed it.

And then, neutralizing gravity with love and pure will, they remained suspended in air inches below the ceiling, and they kissed each other for a long, long time.

It was then that Diana Moon Glampers, the Handicapper General, came into the studio with a double-barreled ten-gauge shotgun. She fired twice, and the Emperor and the Empress were dead before they hit the floor.

80 Diana Moon Glampers loaded the gun again. She aimed it at the musicians and told them they had ten seconds to get their handicaps back on.

It was then that the Bergerons' television tube burned out.

Hazel turned to comment about the blackout to George. But George had gone out into the kitchen for a can of beer.

George came back in with the beer, paused while a handicap signal shook him up. And then he sat down again. "You been crying?" he said to Hazel.

"Yup," she said.

85 "What about?" he said.

"I forget," she said. "Something real sad on television."

"What was it?" he said.

"It's all kind of mixed up in my mind," said Hazel.

"Forget sad things," said Geroge.

90 "I always do," said Hazel.

"That's my girl," said George. He winced. There was the sound of a riveting gun in his head.

"Gee—I could tell that one was a doozy," said Hazel.

"You can say that again," said George.

"Gee—" said Hazel, "I could tell that one was a doozy."

[1961]

Joining the Conversation: Critical Thinking and Writing

1. The Declaration of Independence, drafted by Thomas Jefferson, tells us that "all men are created equal." What does this statement mean? Does the society of Harrison Bergeron—a society in which, according to the first sentence of the story, "everybody was finally equal"—show us a society in which Jefferson's words are at last fulfilled? Exactly what are the values of the world in 2081?
2. One sometimes hears that it is the duty of government to equalize society. Hence, for instance, inheritance taxes are sometimes said to be a device employed in an effort to equalize wealth. What forces, if any, can you point to, for example in educational or political systems, that seek to equalize people? If there are such forces at work, do you think they represent unwise and perhaps unlawful government meddling, and are essentially at odds with a basic American idea of rugged individualism and of wholesome competition?
3. Speaking of competition, George says (paragraph 31) to Hazel, "The minute people start cheating on laws, what do you think happens to society?" Hazel replies, "Reckon it'd fall all apart" (33). What do you think that we, as readers, are supposed to make out of this statement? In your response—an essay of 500 words—consider the actions of Harrison Bergeron, who declares himself Emperor and who says (54), "Everybody must do what I say at once!" Is Vonnegut suggesting, in George's behavior, that only laws can keep talented individuals from tyrannizing over others?

LANGSTON HUGHES

For a biographical note on Langston Hughes, see page 106.

One Friday Morning

The thrilling news did not come directly to Nancy Lee, but it came in little indirections that finally added themselves up to one tremendous fact: she had won the prize! But being a calm and quiet young lady, she did not say anything, although the whole high school buzzed with rumors, guesses, reportedly authentic announcements on the part of students who had no right to be making announcements at all—since no student really knew yet who had won this year's art scholarship.

But Nancy Lee's drawing was so good, her lines so sure, her colors so bright and harmonious, that certainly no other student in the senior art class at George Washington High was thought to have very much of a chance. Yet you never could tell. Last year nobody had expected Joe Williams to win the Artist Club scholarship with that funny modernistic water color he had done of the high-level bridge. In fact, it was hard to make out there was a bridge until you had looked at the picture a long time. Still, Joe Williams got the prize, was feted by the community's leading painters, club women, and society folks at a big banquet at the Park-Rose Hotel, and was now an award student at the Art School—the city's only art school.

Nancy Lee Johnson was a colored girl, a few years out of the South. But seldom did her high-school classmates think of her as colored. She was smart, pretty, and brown, and fitted in well with the life of the school. She stood high in scholarship, played a swell game of basketball, had taken part in the senior musical in a soft, velvety voice, and had never seemed to intrude or stand out, except in pleasant ways, so it was seldom even mentioned—her color.

Nancy Lee sometimes forgot she was colored herself. She liked her classmates and her school. Particularly she liked her art teacher, Miss Dietrich, the tall red-haired woman who taught her law and order in doing things; and the beauty of working step by step until a job is done; a picture finished; a design created; or a block print carved out of nothing but an idea and a smooth square of linoleum, inked, proofs made, and finally put down on paper—clean, sharp, beautiful, individual, unlike any other in the world, thus making the paper have a meaning nobody else could give it except Nancy Lee. That was the wonderful thing about true creation. You made something nobody else on earth could make—but you.

5 Miss Dietrich was the kind of teacher who brought out the best in her students—but their own best, not anybody else's copied best. For anybody else's best, great though it might be, even Michelangelo's, wasn't enough to please Miss Dietrich, dealing with the creative impulses of young men and women living in an American city in the Middle West, and being American.

Nancy Lee was proud of being American, a Negro American with blood out of Africa a long time ago, too many generations back to count. But her parents had taught her the beauties of Africa, its strength, its song, its mighty rivers, its early smelting of iron, its building of the pyramids, and its ancient and important civilizations. And Miss Dietrich had discovered for her the sharp and humorous lines of African sculpture, Benin, Congo, Makonde. Nancy Lee's father was a mail carrier, her mother a social worker in a city settlement house. Both parents had been to Negro colleges in the South. And her mother had gotten a further degree in social work from a Northern university. Her parents were, like most Americans, simple, ordinary people who had worked hard and steadily for their education. Now they were trying to make it easier for Nancy Lee to achieve learning than it had been for them. They would be very happy when they heard of the award to their daughter—yet Nancy did not tell them. To surprise them would be better. Besides, there had been a promise.

Casually, one day, Miss Dietrich asked Nancy Lee what color frame she thought would be best on her picture. That had been the first inkling.

"Blue," Nancy Lee said. Although the picture had been entered in the Artist Club contest a month ago, Nancy Lee did not hesitate in her choice of a color for the possible frame, since she could still see her picture clearly in her mind's eye—for that picture waiting for the blue frame had come out of her soul, her own life, and had bloomed into miraculous being with Miss Dietrich's help. It was, she knew, the best water color she had painted in her four years as a high-school art student, and she was glad she had made something Miss Dietrich liked well enough to permit her to enter in the contest before she graduated.

It was not a modernistic picture in the sense that you had to look at it a long time to understand what it meant. It was just a simple scene in the city park on a spring day, with the trees still leaflessly lacy against the sky, the new grass fresh and green, a flag on a tall pole in the center, children playing, and an old Negro woman sitting on a bench with her head turned. A lot for one picture, to be sure, but it was not there in heavy and final detail like a calendar. Its charm was that everything was light and airy, happy like spring, with a lot of blue sky; paper-white clouds, and air showing through. You could tell that the old Negro woman was looking at the flag, and that the flag was proud in the spring breeze, and that the breeze helped to make the children's dresses billow as they played.

10 Miss Dietrich had taught Nancy Lee how to paint spring, people, and a breeze on what was only a plain white piece of paper from the supply closet. But Miss Dietrich had not said make it like any other spring-people-breeze ever seen before. She let it remain Nancy Lee's own. That is how the old Negro woman happened to be there looking at the flag—for in her mind the flag, the spring, and the woman formed a kind of triangle holding a dream Nancy Lee wanted to express. White stars on a blue field, spring, children, ever-growing life, and an old woman. Would the judges at the Artist Club like it?

One wet, rainy April afternoon Miss O'Shay, the girls' vice-principal, sent for Nancy Lee to stop by her office as school closed. Pupils without umbrellas or raincoats were clustered in doorways, hoping to make it home between showers. Outside the skies were gray. Nancy Lee's thoughts were suddenly gray, too.

She did not think she had done anything wrong, yet that tight little knot came in her throat just the same as she approached Miss O'Shay's door. Perhaps she had banged her locker too often and too hard. Perhaps the note in French she had written to Sallie halfway across the study hall just for fun had never gotten to Sallie but into Miss O'Shay's hands instead. Or maybe she was failing in some subject and wouldn't be allowed to graduate. Chemistry! A pang went through the pit of her stomach.

She knocked on Miss O'Shay's door. That familiarly solid and competent voice said, "Come in."

Miss O'Shay had a way of making you feel welcome, even if you came to be expelled.

15 "Sit down, Nancy Lee Johnson," said Miss O'Shay. "I have something to tell you." Nancy Lee sat down. "But I must ask you to promise not to tell anyone yet."

"I won't, Miss O'Shay," Nancy Lee said, wondering what on earth the principal had to say to her.

"You are about to graduate," Miss O'Shay said. "And we shall miss you. You have been an excellent student, Nancy, and you will not be without honors on the senior list, as I am sure you know."

At that point there was a light knock on the door. Miss O'Shay called out, "Come in," and Miss Dietrich entered. "May I be a part of this, too?" she asked, tall and smiling.

"Of course," Miss O'Shay said. "I was just telling Nancy Lee what we thought of her. But I hadn't gotten around to giving her the news. Perhaps, Miss Dietrich, you'd like to tell her yourself."

20 Miss Dietrich was always direct. "Nancy Lee," she said, "your picture has won the Artist Club scholarship."

The slender brown girl's eyes widened, her heart jumped, then her throat tightened again. She tried to smile, but instead tears came to her eyes.

"Dear Nancy Lee," Miss O'Shay said, "we are so happy for you." The elderly white woman took her hand and shook it warmly while Miss Dietrich beamed with pride.

Nancy Lee must have danced all the way home. She never remembered quite how she got there through the rain. She hoped she had been dignified. But certainly she hadn't stopped to tell anybody her secret on the way. Raindrops, smiles, and tears mingled on her brown cheeks. She hoped her mother hadn't yet gotten home and that the house was empty. She wanted to have time to calm down and look natural before she had to see anyone. She didn't want to be bursting with excitement—having a secret to contain.

Miss O'Shay's calling her to the office had been in the nature of a preparation and a warning. The kind, elderly vice-principal said she did not believe in catching young ladies unawares, even with honors, so she wished her to know about the coming award. In making acceptance speeches she wanted her to be calm, prepared, not nervous, overcome, and frightened. So Nancy Lee was asked to think what she would say when the scholarship was conferred upon her a few days hence, both at the Friday morning high-school assembly hour, when the announcement would be made, and at the evening banquet of the Artist Club. Nancy Lee promised the vice-principal to think calmly about what she would say.

25 Miss Dietrich had then asked for some facts about her parents, her background, and her life, since such material would probably be desired for the papers. Nancy Lee had told her how, six years before, they had come up from the Deep South, her father having been successful in achieving a transfer from the one post office to another, a thing he had long sought in order to give Nancy Lee a chance to go to school in the North. Now they lived in a modest Negro neighborhood, went to see the best plays when they came to town, and had been saving to send Nancy Lee to art school, in case she were permitted to enter. But the scholarship would help a great deal, for they were not rich people.

"Now Mother can have a new coat next winter," Nancy Lee thought, "because my tuition will all be covered for the first year. And once in art school, there are other scholarships I can win."

Dreams began to dance through her head, plans and ambitions, beauties she would create for herself, her parents, and the Negro people—for Nancy Lee possessed a deep and reverent race pride. She could see the old woman in her picture (really her grandmother in the South) lifting her head to the bright stars on the flag in the distance. A Negro in America! Often hurt, discriminated against, sometimes lynched—but always there were the stars on the blue body of the flag. Was there any other flag in the world that had so many stars? Nancy Lee thought deeply, but she could remember none in all the encyclopedias or geographies she had ever looked into.

"Hitch your wagon to a star," Nancy Lee thought, dancing home in the rain. "Who were our flag-makers?"

Friday morning came, the morning when the world would know—her high-school world, the newspaper world, her mother and dad. Dad could not be there at the assembly to hear the announcement, nor see her prize picture displayed on the stage, nor to listen to Nancy Lee's little speech of acceptance, but Mother would be able to come, although Mother was much puzzled as to why Nancy Lee was so insistent she be at school on that particular Friday morning.

30 When something is happening, something new and fine, something that will change your very life, it is hard to go to sleep at night for thinking about it, and hard to keep your heart from pounding, or a strange little knot of joy from gathering in your throat. Nancy Lee had taken her bath, brushed her hair until it glowed, and had gone to bed thinking about the next day, the big day, when before three thousand students, she would be the one student honored, her painting the one painting to be acclaimed as the best of the year from all the art classes of the city. Her short speech of gratitude was ready. She went over it in her mind, not word for word (because she didn't want it to sound as if she had learned it by heart), but she let the thoughts flow simply and sincerely through her consciousness many times.

When the president of the Artist Club presented her with the medal and scroll of the scholarship award, she would say:

"Judges and members of the Artist Club. I want to thank you for this award that means so much to me personally and through me to my people, the colored people of this city, who, sometimes, are discouraged and bewildered, thinking that color and poverty are against them. I accept this award with gratitude and pride, not for myself alone, but for my race that believes in American opportunity and American fairness—and the bright stars in our flag. I thank Miss Dietrich and the teachers who made it possible for me to have the knowledge and training that lie behind this honor you have conferred upon my painting. When I came here from the South a few years ago, I was not sure how you would receive me. You received me well. You have given me a chance and helped me along the road I wanted to follow. I suppose the judges know that every week here at assembly the students of this school pledge allegiance to the flag. I shall try to be worthy of that pledge, and of the help and friendship and understanding of my fellow citizens of whatever race or creed, and of our American dream of 'Liberty and justice for all'!"

That would be her response before the students in the morning. How proud and happy the Negro pupils would be, perhaps almost as proud as they were of the one colored star on the football team. Her mother would probably cry with happiness. Thus Nancy Lee went to sleep dreaming of a wonderful tomorrow.

The bright sunlight of an April morning woke her. There was breakfast with her parents—their half-amused and puzzled faces across the table, wondering what could be this secret that made her eyes so bright. The swift walk to school; the clock in the tower almost nine; hundreds of pupils streaming into the long, rambling old building that was the city's largest high school; the sudden quiet of the homeroom after the bell rang; then the teacher opening her record book to call the roll. But just before she began, she looked across the room until her eyes located Nancy Lee.

"Nancy," she said, "Miss O'Shay would like to see you in her office, please."

Nancy Lee rose and went out while the names were being called and the word *present* added its period to each name. Perhaps, Nancy Lee thought, the reporters from the papers had already come. Maybe they wanted to take her picture before assembly, which wasn't until ten o'clock. (Last year they had had the photograph of the winner of the award in the morning papers as soon as the announcement had been made.)

Nancy Lee knocked at Miss O'Shay's door.

"Come in."

The vice-principal stood at her desk. There was no one else in the room. It was very quiet.

"Sit down, Nancy Lee," she said. Miss O'Shay did not smile. There was a long pause. The seconds went by slowly. "I do not know how to tell you what I have to say," the elderly woman began, her eyes on the papers on her desk. "I am indignant and ashamed for myself and for this city." Then she lifted her eyes and looked at Nancy Lee in the neat blue dress, sitting there before her. "You are not to receive the scholarship this morning."

Outside in the hall the electric bells announcing the first period rang, loud and interminably long. Miss O'Shay remained silent. To the brown girl there in the chair, the room grew suddenly smaller, smaller, smaller, and there was no air. She could not speak.

Miss O'Shay said, "When the committee learned that you were colored, they changed their plans."

Still Nancy Lee said nothing, for there was no air to give breath to her lungs.

"Here is the letter from the committee, Nancy Lee." Miss O'Shay picked it up and read the final paragraph to her.

45 "'It seems to us wiser to arbitrarily rotate the award among the various high schools of the city from now on. And especially in this case since the student chosen happens to be colored, a circumstance which unfortunately, had we known, might have prevented this embarrassment. But there have never been any Negro students in the local art school, and the presence of one there might create difficulties for all concerned. We have high regard for the quality of Nancy Lee Johnson's talent, but we do not feel it would be fair to honor it with the Artist Club award.'" Miss O'Shay paused. She put the letter down.

"Nancy Lee, I am very sorry to have to give you this message."

"But my speech," Nancy Lee said, "was about. . . ." The words stuck in her throat. ". . . about America. . . ."

Miss O'Shay had risen; she turned her back and stood looking out the window at the spring tulips in the school yard.

"I thought, since the award would be made at assembly right after our oath of allegiance," the words tumbled almost hysterically from Nancy Lee's throat now, "I would put part of the flag salute in my speech. You know, Miss O'Shay, that part about 'liberty and justice for all.'"

50 "I know," said Miss O'Shay, slowly facing the room again. "But America is only what we who believe in it make it. I am Irish. You may not know, Nancy Lee, but years ago we were called the dirty Irish, and mobs rioted against us in the big cities, and we were invited to go back where we came from. But we didn't go. And we didn't give up, because we believed in the American dream, and in our power to make that dream come true. Difficulties, yes. Mountains to climb, yes. Discouragements to face, yes. Democracy to make, yes. That is it, Nancy Lee! We still have in this world of ours democracy to *make*. You and I, Nancy Lee. But the premise and the base are here, the lines of the Declaration of Independence and the words of Lincoln are here, and the stars in our flag. Those who deny you this scholarship do not know the meaning of those stars, but it's up to us to make them know. As a teacher in the public schools of this city, I myself will go before the school board and ask them to remove from our system the offer of any prizes or awards denied to any student because of race or color."

Suddenly Miss O'Shay stopped speaking. Her clear, clear blue eyes looked into those of the girl before her. The woman's eyes were full of strength and courage. "Lift up your head, Nancy Lee, and smile at me."

Miss O'Shay stood against the open window with the green lawn and the tulips beyond, the sunlight tangled in her gray hair, her voice an electric flow of strength to the hurt spirit of Nancy Lee. The Abolitionists who believed in freedom when there was slavery must have been like that. The first white teachers who went into the Deep South to teach the freed slaves must have been like that. All those who stand against ignorance, narrowness, hate, and mud on stars must be like that.

Nancy Lee lifted her head and smiled. The bell for assembly rang. She went through the long hall filled with students, toward the auditorium.

"There will be other awards," Nancy Lee thought. "There're schools in other cities. This won't keep me down. But when I'm a woman, I'll fight to see that these things don't happen to other girls as this has happened to me. And men and women like Miss O'Shay will help me."

She took her seat among the seniors. The doors of the auditorium closed. As the principal came onto the platform, the students rose and turned their eyes to the flag on the stage.

One hand went to the heart, the other outstretched toward the flag. Three thousand voices spoke. Among them was the voice of a dark girl whose cheeks were suddenly wet with tears, ". . . one nation indivisible, with liberty and justice for all."

"That is the land we must make," she thought.

[1941]

Joining the Conversation: Critical Thinking and Writing

1. The third paragraph begins: "Nancy Lee Johnson was a colored girl. . . ." How would your response to the opening of the story change if this paragraph were placed at the very beginning?
2. Nancy Lee takes pride in her identity as both a "Negro" and an "American." How does she define and understand each of these terms? Does she perceive them to be at all at odds with one another? Is she admirable in her convictions, or is she simply naive?
3. This is a story about racism, but it is also a study (and an affirmation) of American ideals and principles. What is your response to Miss O'Shay's inspiring words to Nancy Lee at the end of the story? What is Nancy Lee's response to them, and your response to her? Does Hughes succeed in making us believe in, and accept, Nancy Lee's feelings at the conclusion?

WILLIAM CARLOS WILLIAMS

William Carlos Williams (1883–1963) was the son of an English traveling salesman and a Basque-Jewish woman. The couple met in Puerto Rico and settled in Rutherford, New Jersey, where Williams was born. He spent his life there, practicing as a pediatrician and writing poems in the moments between seeing patients.

The Use of Force

They were new patients to me, all I had was the name, Olson. Please come down as soon as you can, my daughter is very sick. When I arrived I was met by the mother, a big startled looking woman, very clean and apologetic who merely said, Is this the doctor? and let me in. In the back, she added. You must excuse us, doctor, we have her in the kitchen where it is warm. It is very damp here sometimes.

The child was fully dressed and sitting on her father's lap near the kitchen table. He tried to get up, but I motioned for him not to bother, took off my overcoat and started to look things over. I could see that they were all very nervous, eyeing me up and down distrustfully. As often, in such cases, they weren't telling me more than they had to, it was up to me to tell them; that's why they were spending three dollars on me.

The child was fairly eating me up with her cold, steady eyes, and no expression to her face whatever. She did not move and seemed, inwardly, quiet; an unusually attractive little thing, and as strong as a heifer in appearance. But her face was flushed, she was breathing rapidly, and I realized that she had a high fever. She had magnificent blond hair, in profusion. One of those picture children often reproduced in advertising leaflets and the photogravure sections of the Sunday papers.

She's had a fever for three days, began the father and we don't know what it comes from. My wife has given her things, you know, like people do, but it don't do no good. And there's been a lot of sickness around. So we tho't you'd better look her over and tell us what is the matter.

As doctors often do I took a trial shot at it as a point of departure. Has she had a sore throat?

Both parents answered me together, No . . . No, she says her throat don't hurt her.

Does your throat hurt you? added the mother to the child. But the little girl's expression didn't change nor did she move her eyes from my face.

Have you looked?

I tried to, said the mother, but I couldn't see.

As it happens we had been having a number of cases of diphtheria in the school to which the child went during that month and we were all, quite apparently, thinking of that, though no one had as yet spoken of the thing.

Well, I said, suppose we take a look at the throat first. I smiled in my best professional manner and asking for the child's first name I said, come on, Mathilda, open your mouth and let's take a look at your throat.

Nothing doing.

Aw, come on, I coaxed, just open your mouth wide and let me take a look. Look, I said opening both hands wide, I haven't anything in my hands. Just open up and let me see.

Such a nice man, put in the mother. Look how kind he is to you. Come on, do what he tells you to, he won't hurt you.

At that I ground my teeth in disgust. If only they wouldn't use the word "hurt" I might be able to get somewhere. But I did not allow myself to be hurried or disturbed but speaking quietly and slowly I approached the child again.

As I moved my chair a little nearer suddenly with one catlike movement both her hands clawed instinctively for my eyes and she almost reached them too. In fact she knocked my glasses flying and they fell, though unbroken, several feet away from me on the kitchen floor.

Both the mother and father almost turned themselves inside out in embarrassment and apology. You bad girl, said the mother, taking her and shaking her by one arm. Look what you've done. The nice man . . .

For heaven's sake, I broke in. Don't call me a nice man to her. I'm here to look at her throat on the chance that she might have diphtheria and possibly die of it. But that's nothing to her. Look here, I said to the child, we're going to look at your throat. You're old enough to understand what I'm saying. Will you open it now by yourself or shall we have to open it for you?

Not a move. Even her expression hadn't changed. Her breaths however were coming faster and faster. Then the battle began. I had to do it. I had to have a throat culture for her own protection. But first I told the parents that it was entirely up to them. I explained the danger but said that I would not insist on a throat examination so long as they would take the responsibility.

20 If you don't do what the doctor says you'll have to go to the hospital, the mother admonished her severely.

Oh yeah? I had to smile to myself. After all, I had already fallen in love with the savage brat, the parents were contemptible to me. In the ensuing struggle they grew more and more abject, crushed, exhausted while she surely rose to magnificent heights of insane fury of effort bred of her terror of me.

The father tried his best, and he was a big man but the fact that she was his daughter, his shame at her behavior and his dread of hurting her made him release her just at the critical times when I had almost achieved success, till I wanted to kill him. But his dread also that she might have diphtheria made him tell me to go on, go on though he himself was almost fainting, while the mother moved back and forth behind us raising and lowering her hands in an agony of apprehension.

Put her in front of you on your lap, I ordered, and hold both her wrists.

But as soon as he did the child let out a scream. Don't, you're hurting me. Let go of my hands. Let them go I tell you. Then she shrieked terrifyingly, hysterically. Stop it! Stop it! You're killing me!

25 Do you think she can stand it, doctor! said the mother.

You get out, said the husband to his wife. Do you want her to die of diphtheria?

Come on now, hold her, I said.

Then I grasped the child's head with my left hand and tried to get the wooden tongue depressor between her teeth. She fought, with clenched teeth, desperately! But now I also had grown furious—at a child. I tried to hold myself down but I couldn't. I know how to expose a throat for inspection. And I did my best. When finally I got the wooden spatula behind the last teeth and just the point of it into the mouth cavity, she opened up for an instant but before I could see anything she came down again and gripped the wooden blade between her molars. She reduced it to splinters before I could get it out again.

Aren't you ashamed, the mother yelled at her. Aren't you ashamed to act like that in front of the doctor?

30 Get me a smooth-handled spoon of some sort, I told the mother. We're going through with this. The child's mouth was already bleeding. Her tongue was cut and she was screaming in wild hysterical shrieks. Perhaps I should have desisted and come back in an hour or more. No doubt it would have been better. But I have seen at least two children lying dead in bed of neglect in such cases, and feeling that I must get a diagnosis now or never I went at it again. But the worst of it was that I too had got beyond reason. I could have torn the child apart in my own fury and enjoyed it. It was a pleasure to attack her. My face was burning with it.

The damned little brat must be protected against her own idiocy, one says to one's self at such times. Others must be protected against her. It is a social necessity. And all these things are true. But a blind fury, a feeling of adult shame, bred of a longing for muscular release are the operatives. One goes on to the end.

In the final unreasoning assault I overpowered the child's neck and jaws. I forced the heavy silver spoon back of her teeth and down her throat till she gagged. And there it was—both tonsils covered with membrane. She had fought valiantly to keep me from knowing her secret. She had been hiding that sore throat for three days at least and lying to her parents in order to escape just such an outcome as this.

Now truly she was furious. She had been on the defensive before but now she attacked. Tried to get off her father's lap and fly at me while tears of defeat blinded her eyes.

[1938]

Joining the Conversation: Critical Thinking and Writing

1. The characters are the doctor, the girl, and her parents. What can you say about each of them—their characters, their classes—on the basis of the first paragraph? What can you say about the doctor as we perceive him by the end of the fifteenth paragraph?
2. According to popular stereotypes, children are supposed to be nice, sweet, innocent things, and doctors are supposed to be kind, wise, relatively unemotional persons. Do Williams's figures seem to you to be utterly improbable? Explain.
3. The narrator is the doctor, but he occasionally lets us hear other voices. For instance we hear the voice of one of the parents in the second sentence ("Please come down as soon as you can, my daughter is very sick"), the voice of the father in the fourth paragraph ("She's had a fever for three days, began the father and we don't know what it comes from. My wife has given her things, you know, like people do, but it don't do no good"), and the voice of the mother in the fourteenth paragraph ("Such a nice man, put in the mother"). Still, the doctor is the narrator, and we chiefly hear his voice. Now consider the fact that he says such things as "I wanted to kill [the father]" (paragraph 22), "But now I also had grown furious—at a child" (paragraph 28), and "the worst of it was that I too had got beyond reason" (paragraph 30). Can we reasonably say that there are *two* conflicts in the story—the doctor versus the child, and the doctor versus himself, i.e., the doctor as a dispassionate professional, and the doctor as a human being? The first conflict is resolved—the child is defeated—but would you add that the second conflict is never resolved? If you believe it is not resolved, do you think this is a weakness in the story?
4. One of our students, in an analysis of the story, argued that it is really a story about rape, perhaps in the form of a rapist's memoir, written for himself. Her evidence included such passages as "I had already fallen in love with the savage brat" (paragraph 21) and "Will you open it now by yourself or shall we have to open it for you?" (paragraph 18). Do you think the episode describes a rape? Your evidence?

SHIRLEY JACKSON

Shirley Jackson (1919–1965) was born in San Francisco and went to college in New York, first at the University of Rochester and then at Syracuse University. Although one of her stories was published in The Best American Short Stories 1944, *she did not receive national attention until 1948 when the* New Yorker *published "The Lottery." The magazine later reported that none of its earlier publications had produced so strong a response.*

In 1962 she experienced a breakdown and was unable to write, but she recovered and worked on a new novel. Before completing the book, however, she died of cardiac arrest at the age of 46. The book was published posthumously under the title Come Along with Me.

Two of her books, Life Among the Savages *(1953) and* Raising Demons *(1957), are engaging self-portraits of a harried mother in a house full of children. But what seems amusing also has its dark underside. After her breakdown Jackson said, "I think all my books laid end to end would be one long documentary of anxiety."*

Her husband, Stanley Edgar Hyman (her college classmate and later a professor of English), said of Jackson, "If she used the resources of supernatural terror, it was to provide metaphors for the all-too-real terrors of the natural."

The Lottery

The morning of June 27th was clear and sunny, with the fresh warmth of a full-summer day; the flowers were blossoming profusely and the grass was richly green. The people of the village began to gather in the square, between the post office and the bank, around ten o'clock; in some towns there were so many people that the lottery took two days and had to be started on June 26th, but in this village, where there were only about three hundred people, the whole lottery took less than two hours, so it could begin at ten o'clock in the morning and still be through in time to allow the villagers to get home for noon dinner.

The children assembled first, of course. School was recently over for the summer, and the feeling of liberty sat uneasily on most of them; they tended to gather together quietly for a while before they broke into boisterous play, and their talk was still of the classroom and the teacher, of books and reprimands. Bobby Martin had already stuffed his pockets full of stones, and the other boys soon followed his example, selecting the smoothest and roundest stones; Bobby and Harry Jones and Dickie Delacroix—the villagers pronounced this name "Dellacroy"—eventually made a great pile of stones in one corner of the square and guarded it against the raids of the other boys. The girls stood aside, talking among themselves, looking over their shoulders at the boys, and the very small children rolled in the dust or clung to the hands of their older brothers or sisters.

Soon the men began to gather, surveying their own children, speaking of planting and rain, tractors and taxes. They stood together, away from the pile of stones in the corner, and their jokes were quiet and they smiled rather than laughed. The women, wearing faded house dresses and sweaters, came shortly after their menfolk. They greeted one another and exchanged bits of gossip as they went to join their husbands. Soon the women, standing by their husbands, began to call to their children, and the children came reluctantly, having to be called four or five times. Bobby Martin ducked under his mother's grasping hand and ran, laughing, back to the pile of stones. His father spoke up sharply, and Bobby came quickly, and took his place between his father and his oldest brother.

The lottery was conducted—as were the square dances, the teenage club, the Halloween program—by Mr. Summers, who had time and energy to devote to civic activities. He was a roundfaced, jovial man and he ran the coal business, and people were sorry for him, because he had no children and his wife was a scold. When he arrived in the square, carrying the black wooden box, there was a murmur of conversation among the villagers and he waved and called, "Little late today, folks." The postmaster, Mr. Graves, followed him, carrying a three-legged stool, and the stool was put in the center of the square and Mr. Summers set the black box down on it. The villagers kept their distance, leaving a space between themselves and the stool, and when Mr. Summers said, "Some of you fellows want to give me a hand?" there was a hesitation before two men, Mr. Martin and his oldest son, Baxter, came forward to hold the box steady on the stool while Mr. Summers stirred up the papers inside it.

5 The original paraphernalia for the lottery had been lost long ago, and the black box now resting on the stool had been put into use even before Old Man Warner, the oldest man in town, was born. Mr. Summers spoke frequently to the

villagers about making a new box, but no one liked to upset even as much tradition as was represented by the black box. There was a story that the present box had been made with some pieces of the box that had preceded it, the one that had been constructed when the first people settled down to make a village here. Every year, after the lottery, Mr. Summers began talking again about a new box, but every year the subject was allowed to fade off without anything's being done. The black box grew shabbier each year; by now it was no longer completely black but splintered badly along one side to show the original wood color, and in some places faded or stained.

Mr. Martin and his oldest son, Baxter, held the black box securely on the stool until Mr. Summers had stirred the papers thoroughly with his hand. Because so much of the ritual had been forgotten or discarded, Mr. Summers had been successful in having slips of paper substituted for the chips of wood that had been used for generations. Chips of wood, Mr. Summers had argued, had been all very well when the village was tiny, but now that the population was more than three hundred and likely to keep on growing, it was necessary to use something that would fit more easily into the black box. The night before the lottery, Mr. Summers and Mr. Graves made up the slips of paper and put them in the box, and it was then taken to the safe of Mr. Summers's coal company and locked up until Mr. Summers was ready to take it to the square next morning. The rest of the year, the box was put away, sometimes one place, sometimes another; it had spent one year in Mr. Graves's barn and another year underfoot in the post office, and sometimes it was set on a shelf in the Martin grocery and left there.

There was a great deal of fussing to be done before Mr. Summers declared the lottery open. There were lists to make up—of heads of families, heads of households in each family, members of each household in each family. There was the proper swearing in of Mr. Summers by the postmaster, as the official of the lottery; at one time, some people remembered, there had been a recital of some sort, performed by the official of the lottery, a perfunctory, tuneless chant that had been rattled off duly each year; some people believed that the official of the lottery used to stand just so when he said or sang it, others believed that he was supposed to walk among the people, but years and years ago this part of the ritual had been allowed to lapse. There had been, also, a ritual salute, which the official of the lottery had had to use in addressing each person who came up to draw from the box, but this also had changed with time, until now it was felt necessary only for the official to speak to each person approaching. Mr. Summers was very good at all this; in his clean white shirt and blue jeans, with one hand resting carelessly on the black box, he seemed very proper and important as he talked interminably to Mr. Graves and the Martins.

Just as Mr. Summers left off talking and turned to the assembled villagers, Mrs. Hutchinson came hurriedly along the path to the square, her sweater thrown over her shoulders, and slid into place in the back of the crowd. "Clean forgot what day it was," she said to Mrs. Delacroix, who stood next to her, and they both laughed softly. "Thought my old man was out back stacking wood," Mrs. Hutchinson went on, "and then I looked out the window and the kids were gone, and then I remembered it was the twenty-seventh and came a-running." She dried her hands on her apron, and Mrs. Delacroix said, "You're in time, though. They're still talking away up there."

Mrs. Hutchinson craned her neck to see through the crowd and found her husband and children standing near the front. She tapped Mrs. Delacroix on the arm as a farewell and began to make her way through the crowd. The people separated good humoredly to let her through, two or three people said, in voices just loud enough to be heard across the crowd, "Here comes your Missus, Hutchinson," and "Bill, she made it after all." Mrs. Hutchinson reached her husband, and Mr. Summers, who had been waiting, said cheerfully, "Thought we were going to have to get on without you, Tessie." Mrs. Hutchinson said, grinning, "Wouldn't have me leave m'dishes in the sink, now would you, Joe?," and soft laughter ran through the crowd as the people stirred back into position after Mrs. Hutchinson's arrival.

10 "Well, now," Mr. Summers said soberly, "guess we better get started, get this over with, so's we can go back to work. Anybody ain't here?"

"Dunbar," several people said. "Dunbar, Dunbar."

Mr. Summers consulted his list. "Clyde Dunbar," he said. "That's right. He's broke his leg, hasn't he? Who's drawing for him?"

"Me, I guess," a woman said, and Mr. Summers turned to look at her. "Wife draws for her husband," Mr. Summers said. "Don't you have a grown boy to do it for you, Janey?" Although Mr. Summers and everyone else in the village knew the answer perfectly well, it was the business of the official of the lottery to ask such questions formally. Mr. Summers waited with an expression of polite interest while Mrs. Dunbar answered.

"Horace's not but sixteen yet," Mrs. Dunbar said regretfully. "Guess I gotta fill in for the old man this year."

15 "Right," Mr. Summers said. He made a note on the list he was holding. Then he asked, "Watson boy drawing this year?"

A tall boy in the crowd raised his hand. "Here," he said. "I'm drawing for m'-mother and me." He blinked his eyes nervously and ducked his head as several voices in the crowd said things like "Good fellow, Jack," and "Glad to see your mother's got a man to do it."

"Well," Mr. Summers said, "guess that's everyone. Old Man Warner make it?"

"Here," a voice said, and Mr. Summers nodded.

A sudden hush fell on the crowd as Mr. Summers cleared his throat and looked at the list. "All ready?" he called. "Now, I'll read the names—heads of families first—and the men come up and take a paper out of the box. Keep the paper folded in your hand without looking at it until everyone has had a turn. Everything clear?"

20 The people had done it so many times that they only half listened to the directions; most of them were quiet, wetting their lips, not looking around. Then Mr. Summers raised one hand high and said, "Adams." A man disengaged himself from the crowd and came forward. "Hi, Steve," Mr. Summers said, and Mr. Adams said, "Hi, Joe." They grinned at one another humorlessly and nervously. Then Mr. Adams reached into the black box and took out a folded paper. He held it firmly by one corner as he turned and went hastily back to his place in the crowd, where he stood a little apart from his family, not looking down at his hand.

"Allen," Mr. Summers said. "Anderson. . . . Bentham."

"Seems like there's no time at all between lotteries any more," Mrs. Delacroix said to Mrs. Graves in the back row. "Seems like we got through with the last one only last week."

"Time sure goes fast," Mrs. Graves said.

"Clark. . . . Delacroix."

25 "There goes my old man," Mrs. Delacroix said. She held her breath while her husband went forward.

"Dunbar," Mr. Summers said, and Mrs. Dunbar went steadily to the box while one of the women said, "Go on, Janey," and another said. "There she goes."

"We're next," Mrs. Graves said. She watched while Mr. Graves came around from the side of the box, greeted Mr. Summers gravely, and selected a slip of paper from the box. By now, all through the crowd there were men holding the small folded papers in their large hands, turning them over and over nervously. Mrs. Dunbar and her two sons stood together. Mrs. Dunbar holding the slip of paper.

"Harburt. . . . Hutchinson."

"Get up there, Bill," Mrs. Hutchinson said, and the people near her laughed.

30 "Jones."

"They do say," Mr. Adams said to Old Man Warner, who stood next to him, "that over in the north village they're talking of giving up the lottery."

Old Man Warner snorted. "Pack of crazy fools," he said. "Listening to the young folks, nothing's good enough for *them*. Next thing you know, they'll be wanting to go back to living in caves, nobody work any more, live *that* way for a while. Used to be a saying about 'Lottery in June, corn be heavy soon.' First thing you know, we'd all be eating stewed chickweed and acorns. There's *always* been a lottery," he added petulantly. "Bad enough to see young Joe Summers up there joking with everybody."

"Some places have already quit lotteries," Mrs. Adams said.

"Nothing but trouble in *that,*" Old Man Warner said stoutly. "Pack of young fools."

35 "Martin." And Bobby Martin watched his father go forward. "Overdyke. . . . Percy."

"I wish they'd hurry," Mrs. Dunbar said to her older son. "I wish they'd hurry."

"They're almost through," her son said.

"You get ready to run tell Dad," Mrs. Dunbar said.

Mr. Summers called his own name and then stepped forward precisely and selected a slip from the box. Then he called, "Warner."

40 "Seventy-seventh year I been in the lottery," Old Man Warner said as he went through the crowd. "Seventy-seventh time."

"Watson." The tall boy came awkwardly through the crowd. Someone said, "Don't be nervous, Jack," and Mr. Summers said, "Take your time, son."

"Zanani."

After that, there was a long pause, a breathless pause, until Mr. Summers, holding his slip of paper in the air, said, "All right, fellows." For a minute, no one moved, and then all of the slips of paper were opened. Suddenly, all women began to speak at once, saying, "Who is it?" "Who's got it?" "Is it the Dunbars?" "Is it the Watsons?" Then the voices began to say, "It's Hutchinson. It's Bill." "Bill Hutchinson's got it."

"Go tell your father," Mrs. Dunbar said to her older son.

45 People began to look around to see the Hutchinsons. Bill Hutchinson was standing quiet, staring down at the paper in his hand. Suddenly, Tessie Hutchinson shouted to Mr. Summers, "You didn't give him time enough to take any paper he wanted. I saw you. It wasn't fair!"

"Be a good sport, Tessie," Mrs. Delacroix called, and Mrs. Graves said, "All of us took the same chance."

"Shut up, Tessie," Bill Hutchinson said.

"Well, everyone," Mr. Summers said, "That was done pretty fast, and now we've got to be hurrying a little more to get done in time." He consulted his next list. "Bill," he said, "you draw for the Hutchinson family. You got any other households in the Hutchinsons?"

"There's Don and Eva," Mrs. Hutchinson yelled. "Make *them* take their chance!"

50 "Daughters draw with their husbands' families, Tessie," Mr. Summers said gently. "You know that as well as anyone else."

"It wasn't fair," Tessie said.

"I guess no, Joe," Bill Hutchinson said regretfully. "My daughter draws with her husband's family, that's only fair. And I've got no other family except the kids."

"Then, as far as drawing for families is concerned, it's you," Mr. Summers said in explanation, "and as far as drawing for households is concerned, that's you, too. Right?"

"Right," Bill Hutchinson said.

55 "How many kids, Bill?" Mr. Summers asked formally.

"Three," Bill Hutchinson said. "There's Bill, Jr., and Nancy, and little Dave. And Tessie and me."

"All right, then," Mr. Summers said. "Harry, you got their tickets back?"

Mr. Graves nodded and held up the slips of paper. "Put them in the box, then," Mr. Summers directed. "Take Bill's and put it in."

"I think we ought to start over," Mrs. Hutchinson said, as quietly as she could. "I tell you it wasn't *fair*. You didn't give him time enough to choose. *Everybody* saw that."

60 Mr. Graves had selected the five slips and put them in the box, and he dropped all the papers but those onto the ground, where the breeze caught them and lifted them off.

"Listen, everybody," Mrs. Hutchinson was saying to the people around her.

"Ready, Bill?" Mr. Summers asked, and Bill Hutchinson, with one quick glance around at his wife and children, nodded.

"Remember," Mr. Summers said, "Take the slips and keep them folded until each person has taken one. Harry, you help little Dave." Mr. Graves took the hand of the little boy, who came willingly with him up to the box. "Take a paper out of the box, Davy," Mr. Summers said. Davy put his hand into the box and laughed. "Take just *one* paper," Mr. Summers said. "Harry, you hold it for him." Mr. Graves took the child's hand and removed the folded paper from the tight fist and held it while little Dave stood next to him and looked up at him wonderingly.

"Nancy next," Mr. Summers said. Nancy was twelve, and her school friends breathed heavily as she went forward, switching her skirt, and took a slip daintily from the box. "Bill, Jr.," Mr. Summers said, and Billy, his face red and his feet overlarge, nearly knocked the box over as he got a paper out. "Tessie," Mr. Summers said. She hesitated for a minute, looking around defiantly, and then set her lips and went up to the box. She snatched a paper out and held it behind her.

65 "Bill," Mr. Summers said, and Bill Hutchinson reached into the box and felt around, bringing his hand out at last with the slip of paper in it.

The crowd was quiet. A girl whispered, "I hope it's not Nancy," and the sound of the whisper reached the edges of the crowd.

"It's not the way it used to be," Old Man Warner said clearly. "People ain't the way they used to be."

"All right," Mr. Summers said. "Open the papers. Harry, you open little Dave's."

Mr. Graves opened the slip of paper and there was a general sigh through the crowd as he held it up and everyone could see that it was blank. Nancy and Bill, Jr., opened theirs at the same time, and both beamed and laughed, turning around to the crowd and holding their slips of paper above their heads.

70 "Tessie," Mr. Summers said. There was a pause, and then Mr. Summers looked at Bill Hutchinson, and Bill unfolded his paper and showed it. It was blank.

"It's Tessie," Mr. Summers said, and his voice was hushed. "Show us her paper, Bill."

Bill Hutchinson went over to his wife and forced the slip of paper out of her hand. It had a black spot on it, the black spot Mr. Summers had made the night before with the heavy pencil in the coal-company office. Bill Hutchinson held it up, and there was a stir in the crowd.

"All right, folks," Mr. Summers said, "let's finish quickly."

Although the villagers had forgotten the ritual and lost the original black box. They still remembered to use stones. The pile of stones the boys had made earlier was ready; there were stones on the ground with the blowing scraps of paper that had come out of the box. Mrs. Delacroix selected a stone so large she had to pick it up with both hands and turned to Mrs. Dunbar. "Come on," she said. "Hurry up."

Mrs. Dunbar had small stones in both hands, and she said, gasping for breath, "I can't run at all. You'll have to go ahead and I'll catch up with you."

The children had stones already, and someone gave little Davy Hutchinson a few pebbles.

Tessie Hutchinson was in the center of a cleared space by now, and she held her hands out desperately as the villagers moved in on her. "It isn't fair," she said. A stone hit her on the side of the head.

Old Man Warner was saying, "Come on, come on, everyone." Steve Adams was in the front of the crowd of villagers, with Mrs. Graves beside him.

"It isn't fair, it isn't right," Mrs. Hutchinson screamed, and then they were upon her.

[1948]

Joining the Conversation: Critical Thinking and Writing

1. Is "The Lottery" more than a shocker?
2. What is the community's attitude toward tradition?
3. Doubtless a good writer could tell this story effectively from the point of view of a participant, but Jackson chose a nonparticipant point of view. What does she gain?
4. Let's say you were writing this story, and you had decided to write it from Tessie's point of view. What would your first paragraph, or your first 250 words, be?
5. Suppose someone claimed that the story is an attack on religious orthodoxy. What might be your response? (Whether you agree or disagree, set forth your reasons in a thoughtful argument.)

Grace Paley

Grace Paley (1922–2007), was born in New York City, where she attended Hunter College and New York University but left without a degree. While raising two children she wrote poetry and then, in the 1950s, turned to writing fiction. In 1959 she published her first collection of stories, The Little Disturbances of Man. *The title indicates her chief concern—"little disturbances"; the title of her second collection,* Enormous Changes at the Last Minute *(1974), is similarly revealing.*

Paley's chief subject is the life of little people struggling to live in the big city. Of life she has said, "How daily life is lived is a mystery to me. You write about what's mysterious to you. What is it like? Why do people do this?" Of the short story she has said, "It can be just telling a little tale, or writing a complicated philosophical story. It can be a song, almost."

A Man Told Me the Story of His Life

Vicente said: I wanted to be a doctor. I wanted to be a doctor with my whole heart.

I learned every bone, every organ in the body. What is it for? Why does it work?

The school said to me: Vicente, be an engineer. That would be good. You understand mathematics.

I said to the school: I want to be a doctor. I already know how the organs connect. When something goes wrong, I'll understand how to make repairs.

5 The school said: Vicente, you will really be an excellent engineer. You show on all the tests what a good engineer you will be. It doesn't show whether you'll be a good doctor.

I said: Oh, I long to be a doctor. I nearly cried. I was seventeen. I said: But perhaps you're right. You're the teacher. You're the principal. I know I'm young.

The school said: And besides, you're going into the Army.

And then I was made a cook. I prepared food for two thousand men.

Now you see me. I have a good job. I have three children. This is my wife, Consuela. Did you know I saved her life?

10 Look, she suffered pain. The doctor said: What is this? Are you tired? Have you had too much company? How many children? Rest overnight, then tomorrow we'll make tests.

The next morning I called the doctor. I said: She must be operated immediately. I have looked in the book. I see where her pain is. I understand what the pressure is, where it comes from. I see clearly the organ that is making trouble.

The doctor made a test. He said: She must be operated at once. He said to me: Vicente, how did you know?

[1985]

Joining the Conversation: Critical Thinking and Writing

1. If the first two words ("Vicente said") of the first sentence were omitted, the story could be called "The Story of My Life," or even "My Life." What does Paley gain (or lose) by introducing a narrator other than Vicente?
2. Is Vicente characterized, or is he simply (as the title puts it) "a man"?
3. Is Paley saying something about America? If so, *what* is she saying?

TIM O'BRIEN

Tim O'Brien, born in 1947 in Austin, Minnesota, was drafted into the army in 1968 and served as an infantryman in Vietnam. Drawing on this experience he wrote a memoir, If I Die in a Combat Zone *(1973), in which he explains that he did not believe in the Vietnam War, considered dodging the draft, but, lacking the courage to do so, he served, largely out of fear and embarrassment. A later book, a novel called* Going after Cacciato, *won the National Book Award in 1979.*

"The Things They Carried," first published in 1986, was republished in 1990 as one of a series of interlocking stories in a book entitled The Things They Carried. *In one of the stories, entitled "How To Tell a True War Story," he writes,*

> *A true war story is never moral. It does not instruct, nor encourage virtue, nor suggest models of proper human behavior. . . . If a story seems moral, do not believe it. If at the end of a war story you feel uplifted, or if you feel that some small bit of rectitude has been salvaged from the larger waste, then you have been made the victim of a very old and terrible lie. There is no rectitude whatsoever. There is no virtue. As a first rule of thumb, therefore, you can tell a true war story by its absolute and uncompromising allegiance to obscenity and evil.*

The Things They Carried

First Lieutenant Jimmy Cross carried letters from a girl named Martha, a junior at Mount Sebastian College in New Jersey. They were not love letters, but Lieutenant Cross was hoping, so he kept them folded in plastic at the bottom of his rucksack. In the late afternoon, after a day's march, he would dig his foxhole, wash his hands under a canteen, unwrap the letters, hold them with the tips of his fingers, and spend the last hour of light pretending. He would imagine romantic camping trips into the White Mountains in New Hampshire. He would sometimes taste the envelope flaps, knowing her tongue had been there. More than anything, he wanted Martha to love him as he loved her, but the letters were mostly chatty, elusive on the matter of love. She was a virgin, he was almost sure. She was an English major at Mount Sebastian, and she wrote beautifully about her professors and roommates and midterm exams, about her respect for Chaucer and her great affection for Virginia Woolf. She often quoted lines of poetry; she never mentioned the war, except to say, Jimmy, take care of yourself. The letters weighed ten ounces. They were signed "Love, Martha," but Lieutenant Cross understood that Love was only a way of signing and did not mean what he sometimes pretended it meant. At dusk, he would carefully return the letters to his rucksack. Slowly, a bit distracted, he would get up and move among his men, checking the perimeter, then at full dark he would return to his hole and watch the night and wonder if Martha was a virgin.

The things they carried were largely determined by necessity. Among the necessities or near-necessities were P-38 can openers, pocket knives, heat tabs, wrist watches, dog tags, mosquito repellent, chewing gum, candy, cigarettes, salt tablets, packets of Kool-Aid, lighters, matches, sewing kits, Military Payment Certificates, C rations, and two or three canteens of water. Together, these items weighed between fifteen and twenty pounds, depending upon a man's habits or rate of metabolism. Henry Dobbins, who was a big man, carried extra rations; he was especially fond of canned peaches in heavy syrup over pound cake. Dave Jensen, who practiced field hygiene, carried a toothbrush, dental floss, and several hotel-size bars of soap he'd stolen on R&R[1] in Sydney, Australia. Ted Lavender, who was scared, carried tranquilizers until he was shot in the head outside the village of Than Khe in mid-April. By necessity, and because it was SOP,[2] they all carried steel helmets that weighed five pounds including the liner and camouflage cover. They carried the standard fatigue jackets and trousers.

[1]**R&R** rest and rehabilitation leave. [2]**SOP** standard operating procedure.

Very few carried underwear. On their feet they carried jungle boots—2.1 pounds—and Dave Jensen carried three pairs of socks and a can of Dr. Scholl's foot powder as a precaution against trench foot. Until he was shot, Ted Lavender carried six or seven ounces of premium dope, which for him was a necessity. Mitchell Sanders, the RTO,[3] carried condoms. Norman Bowker carried a diary. Rat Kiley carried comic books. Kiowa, a devout Baptist, carried an illustrated New Testament that had been presented to him by his father, who taught Sunday school in Oklahoma City, Oklahoma. As a hedge against bad times, however, Kiowa also carried his grandmother's distrust of the white man, his grandfather's old hunting hatchet. Necessity dictated. Because the land was mined and booby-trapped, it was SOP for each man to carry a steel-centered, nylon-covered flak jacket, which weighed 6.7 pounds, but which on hot days seemed much heavier. Because you could die so quickly, each man carried at least one large compress bandage, usually in the helmet band for easy access. Because the nights were cold, and because the monsoons were wet, each carried a green plastic poncho that could be used as a raincoat or groundsheet or makeshift tent. With its quilted liner, the poncho weighed almost two pounds, but it was worth every ounce. In April, for instance, when Ted Lavender was shot, they used his poncho to wrap him up, then to carry him across the paddy, then to lift him into the chopper that took him away.

They were called legs or grunts.

To carry something was to "hump" it, as when Lieutenant Jimmy Cross humped his love for Martha up the hills and through the swamps. In its intransitive form, "to hump" meant "to walk," or "to march," but it implied burdens far beyond the intransitive.

5 Almost everyone humped photographs. In his wallet, Lieutenant Cross carried two photographs of Martha. The first was a Kodachrome snapshot signed "Love," though he knew better. She stood against a brick wall. Her eyes were gray and neutral, her lips slightly open as she stared straight-on at the camera. At night, sometimes, Lieutenant Cross wondered who had taken the picture, because he knew she had boyfriends, because he loved her so much, and because he could see the shadow of the picture taker spreading out against the brick wall. The second photograph had been clipped from the 1968 Mount Sebastian yearbook. It was an action shot—women's volleyball—and Martha was bent horizontal to the floor, reaching, the palms of her hands in sharp focus, the tongue taut, the expression frank and competitive. There was no visible sweat. She wore white gym shorts. Her legs, he thought, were almost certainly the legs of a virgin, dry and without hair, the left knee cocked and carrying her entire weight, which was just over one hundred pounds. Lieutenant Cross remembered touching that left knee. A dark theater, he remembered, and the movie was *Bonnie and Clyde,* and Martha wore a tweed skirt, and during the final scene, when he touched her knee, she turned and looked at him in a sad, sober way that made him pull his hand back, but he would always remember the feel of the tweed skirt and the knee beneath it and the sound of the gunfire that killed Bonnie and Clyde, how embarrassing it was, how slow and oppressive. He remembered kissing her goodnight at the dorm door. Right then, he thought, he should've done something brave. He should've carried her up the stairs to her room and tied her to the bed and touched that left knee all night long. He should've risked it. Whenever he looked at the photographs, he thought of new things he should've done.

[3]**RTO** radio and telephone operator.

What they carried was partly a function of rank, partly of field specialty.

As a first lieutenant and platoon leader, Jimmy Cross carried a compass, maps, code books, binoculars, and a .45-caliber pistol that weighed 2.9 pounds fully loaded. He carried a strobe light and the responsibility for the lives of his men.

As an RTO, Mitchell Sanders carried the PRC-25 radio, a killer, twenty-six pounds with its battery.

As a medic, Rat Kiley carried a canvas satchel filled with morphine and plasma and malaria tablets and surgical tape and comic books and all the things a medic must carry, including M&Ms[4] for especially bad wounds, for a total weight of nearly twenty pounds.

10 As a big man, therefore a machine gunner, Henry Dobbins carried the M-60, which weighed twenty-three pounds unloaded, but which was almost always loaded. In addition, Dobbins carried between ten and fifteen pounds of ammunition draped in belts across his chest and shoulders.

As PFCs or Spec 4s, most of them were common grunts and carried the standard M-16 gas operated assault rifle. The weapon weighed 7.5 pounds unloaded, 8.2 pounds with its full twenty-round magazine. Depending on numerous factors, such as topography and psychology, the riflemen carried anywhere from twelve to twenty magazines, usually in cloth bandoliers, adding on another 8.4 pounds at minimum, fourteen pounds at maximum. When it was available, they also carried M-16 maintenance gear—rods and steel brushes and swabs and tubes of LSA oil—all of which weighed about a pound. Among the grunts, some carried the M-79 grenade launcher, 5.9 pounds unloaded, a reasonably light weapon except for the ammunition, which was heavy. A single round weighed ten ounces. The typical load was twenty-five rounds. But Ted Lavender, who was scared, carried thirty-four rounds when he was shot and killed outside Than Khe, and he went down under an exceptional burden, more than twenty pounds of ammunition, plus the flak jacket and helmet and rations and water and toilet paper and tranquilizers and all the rest, plus the unweighed fear. He was dead weight. There was no twitching or flopping. Kiowa, who saw it happen, said it was like watching a rock fall, or a big sandbag or something—just boom, then down—not like the movies where the dead guy rolls around and does fancy spins and goes ass over teakettle—not like that, Kiowa said, the poor bastard just flat-fuck fell. Boom. Down. Nothing else. It was a bright morning in mid-April. Lieutenant Cross felt the pain. He blamed himself. They stripped off Lavender's canteens and ammo, all the heavy things, and Rat Kiley said the obvious, the guy's dead, and Mitchell Sanders used his radio to report one U.S. KIA[5] and to request a chopper. Then they wrapped Lavender in his poncho. They carried him out to a dry paddy, established security, and sat smoking the dead man's dope until the chopper came. Lieutenant Cross kept to himself. He pictured Martha's smooth young face, thinking he loved her more than anything, more than his men, and now Ted Lavender was dead because he loved her so much and could not stop thinking about her. When the dust-off arrived, they carried Lavender aboard. Afterward they burned Than Khe. They marched until dusk, then dug their holes, and that night Kiowa kept explaining how you had to be there, how fast it was, how the poor guy just dropped like so much concrete. Boom-down, he said. Like cement.

In addition to the three standard weapons—the M-60, M-16, and M-79—they carried whatever presented itself, or whatever seemed appropriate as a means of

[4]**M&M** joking term for medical supplies. [5]**KIA** killed in action.

killing or staying alive. They carried catch-as-catch-can. At various times, in various situations, they carried M-14s and CAR-15s and Swedish Ks and grease guns and captured AK-47s and Chi-Coms and RPGs and Simonov carbines and black-market Uzis and .38-caliber Smith & Wesson handguns and 66 mm LAWs and shotguns and silencers and blackjacks and bayonets and C-4 plastic explosives. Lee Strunk carried a slingshot; a weapon of last resort, he called it. Mitchell Sanders carried brass knuckles. Kiowa carried his grandfather's feathered hatchet. Every third or fourth man carried a Claymore antipersonnel mine—3.5 pounds with its firing device. They all carried fragmentation grenades—fourteen ounces each. They all carried at least one M-18 colored smoke grenade—twenty-four ounces. Some carried CS or tear-gas grenades. Some carried white-phosphorus grenades. They carried all they could bear, and then some, including a silent awe for the terrible power of the things they carried.

In the first week of April, before Lavender died, Lieutenant Jimmy Cross received a good-luck charm from Martha. It was a simple pebble, an ounce at most. Smooth to the touch, it was a milky-white color with flecks of orange and violet, oval-shaped, like a miniature egg. In the accompanying letter, Martha wrote that she had found the pebble on the Jersey shoreline, precisely where the land touched the water at high tide, where things came together but also separated. It was this separate-but-together quality, she wrote, that had inspired her to pick up the pebble and to carry it in her breast pocket for several days, where it seemed weightless, and then to send it through the mail, by air, as a token of her truest feelings for him. Lieutenant Cross found this romantic. But he wondered what her truest feelings were, exactly, and what she meant by separate-but-together. He wondered how the tides and waves had come into play on that afternoon along the Jersey shoreline when Martha saw the pebble and bent down to rescue it from geology. He imagined bare feet. Martha was a poet, with the poet's sensibilities, and her feet would be brown and bare, the toenails unpainted, the eyes chilly and somber like the ocean in March, and though it was painful, he wondered who had been with her that afternoon. He imagined a pair of shadows moving along the strip of sand where things came together but also separated. It was phantom jealousy, he knew, but he couldn't help himself. He loved her so much. On the march, through the hot days of early April, he carried the pebble in his mouth, turning it with his tongue, tasting sea salts and moisture. His mind wandered. He had difficulty keeping his attention on the war. On occasion he would yell at his men to spread out the column, to keep their eyes open, but then he would slip away into daydreams, just pretending, walking barefoot along the Jersey shore, with Martha, carrying nothing. He would feel himself rising. Sun and waves and gentle winds, all love and lightness.

What they carried varied by mission.

15 When a mission took them to the mountains, they carried mosquito netting, machetes, canvas tarps, and extra bugjuice.

If a mission seemed especially hazardous, or if it involved a place they knew to be bad, they carried everything they could. In certain heavily mined AOs,[6] where the land was dense with Toe Poppers and Bouncing Betties, they took turns humping a twenty-eight-pound mine detector. With its headphones and big sensing plate, the equipment was a stress on the lower back and shoulders, awkward to handle, often useless because of the shrapnel in the earth, but they carried it anyway, partly for safety, partly for the illusion of safety.

[6]**AOs** areas of operation.

On ambush, or other night missions, they carried peculiar little odds and ends. Kiowa always took along his New Testament and a pair of moccasins for silence. Dave Jensen carried night-sight vitamins high in carotin. Lee Strunk carried his slingshot; ammo, he claimed, would never be a problem. Rat Kiley carried brandy and M&Ms. Until he was shot, Ted Lavender carried the starlight scope, which weighed 6.3 pounds with its aluminum carrying case. Henry Dobbins carried his girlfriend's panty hose wrapped around his neck as a comforter. They all carried ghosts. When dark came, they would move out single file across the meadows and paddies to their ambush coordinates, where they would quietly set up the Claymores and lie down and spend the night waiting.

Other missions were more complicated and required special equipment. In mid-April, it was their mission to search out and destroy the elaborate tunnel complexes in the Than Khe area south of Chu Lai. To blow the tunnels, they carried one-pound blocks of pentrite high explosives, four blocks to a man, sixty-eight pounds in all. They carried wiring, detonators, and battery-powered clackers. Dave Jensen carried earplugs. Most often, before blowing the tunnels, they were ordered by higher command to search them, which was considered bad news, but by and large they just shrugged and carried out orders. Because he was a big man, Henry Dobbins was excused from tunnel duty. The others would draw numbers. Before Lavender died there were seventeen men in the platoon, and whoever drew the number seventeen would strip off his gear and crawl in headfirst with a flashlight and Lieutenant Cross's .45-caliber pistol. The rest of them would fan out as security. They would sit down or kneel, not facing the hole, listening to the ground beneath them, imagining cobwebs and ghosts, whatever was down there—the tunnel walls squeezing in—how the flashlight seemed impossibly heavy in the hand and how it was tunnel vision in the very strictest sense, compression in all ways, even time, and how you had to wiggle in—ass and elbows—a swallowed-up feeling—and how you found yourself worrying about odd things—will your flashlight go dead? Do rats carry rabies? If you screamed, how far would the sound carry? Would your buddies hear it? Would they have the courage to drag you out? In some respects, though not many, the waiting was worse than the tunnel itself. Imagination was a killer.

On April 16, when Lee Strunk drew the number seventeen, he laughed and muttered something and went down quickly. The morning was hot and very still. Not good, Kiowa said. He looked at the tunnel opening, then out across a dry paddy toward the village of Than Khe. Nothing moved. No clouds or birds or people. As they waited, the men smoked and drank Kool-Aid, not talking much, feeling sympathy for Lee Strunk but also feeling the luck of the draw. You win some, you lose some, said Mitchell Sanders, and sometimes you settle for a rain check. It was a tired line and no one laughed.

20 Henry Dobbins ate a tropical chocolate bar. Ted Lavender popped a tranquilizer and went off to pee.

After five minutes, Lieutenant Jimmy Cross moved to the tunnel, leaned down, and examined the darkness. Trouble, he thought—a cave-in maybe. And then suddenly, without willing it, he was thinking about Martha. The stresses and fractures, the quick collapse, the two of them buried alive under all that weight. Dense, crushing love. Kneeling, watching the hole, he tried to concentrate on Lee Strunk and the war, all the dangers, but his love was too much for him, he felt paralyzed, he wanted to sleep inside her lungs and breathe her blood and be smothered. He wanted her to be a virgin and not a virgin, all at once. He wanted to know her. Intimate secrets—why poetry? Why so sad? Why that grayness in her eyes?

Why so alone? Not lonely, just alone—riding her bike across campus or sitting off by herself in the cafeteria. Even dancing, she danced alone—and it was the aloneness that filled him with love. He remembered telling her that one evening. How she nodded and looked away. And how, later, when he kissed her, she received the kiss without returning it, her eyes wide open, not afraid, not a virgin's eyes, just flat and uninvolved.

Lieutenant Cross gazed at the tunnel. But he was not there. He was buried with Martha under the white sand at the Jersey shore. They were pressed together, and the pebble in his mouth was her tongue. He was smiling. Vaguely, he was aware of how quiet the day was, the sullen paddies, yet he could not bring himself to worry about matters of security. He was beyond that. He was just a kid at war, in love. He was twenty-two years old. He couldn't help it.

A few minutes later Lee Strunk crawled out of the tunnel. He came up grinning, filthy but alive. Lieutenant Cross nodded and closed his eyes while the others clapped Strunk on the back and made jokes about rising from the dead.

Worms, Rat Kiley said. Right out of the grave. Fuckin' zombie.

The men laughed. They all felt great relief.

Spook City, said Mitchell Sanders.

Lee Strunk made a funny ghost sound, a kind of moaning, yet very happy, and right then, when Strunk made that high happy moaning sound, when he went *Ah-hooooo,* right then Ted Lavender was shot in the head on his way back from peeing. He lay with his mouth open. The teeth were broken. There was a swollen black bruise under his left eye. The cheekbone was gone. Oh shit, Rat Kiley said, the guy's dead. The guy's dead, he kept saying, which seemed profound—the guy's dead. I mean really.

The things they carried were determined to some extent by superstition. Lieutenant Cross carried his good-luck pebble. Dave Jensen carried a rabbit's foot. Norman Bowker, otherwise a very gentle person, carried a thumb that had been presented to him as a gift by Mitchell Sanders. The thumb was dark brown, rubbery to the touch, and weighed four ounces at most. It had been cut from a VC corpse, a boy of fifteen or sixteen. They'd found him at the bottom of an irrigation ditch, badly burned, flies in his mouth and eyes. They boy wore black shorts and sandals. At the time of his death he had been carrying a pouch of rice, a rifle, and three magazines of ammunition.

You want my opinion, Mitchell Sanders said, there's a definite moral here.

He put his hand on the dead boy's wrist. He was quiet for a time, as if counting a pulse, then he patted the stomach, almost affectionately, and used Kiowa's hunting hatchet to remove the thumb.

Henry Dobbins asked what the moral was.

Moral?

You know. *Moral.*

Sanders wrapped the thumb in toilet paper and handed it across to Norman Bowker. There was no blood. Smiling, he kicked the boy's head, watched the flies scatter, and said, It's like with that old TV show—Paladin. Have gun, will travel.

Henry Dobbins thought about it.

Yeah, well, he finally said. I don't see no moral.

There it *is,* man.

Fuck off.

They carried USO stationery and pencils and pens. They carried Sterno, safety pins, trip flares, signal flares, spools of wire, razor blades, chewing tobacco, liberated joss sticks and statuettes of the smiling Buddha, candles, grease pencils, *The Stars and Stripes,* fingernail clippers, Psy Ops leaflets, bush hats, bolos, and much more. Twice a week, when the resupply choppers came in, they carried hot chow in green Mermite cans and large canvas bags filled with iced beer and soda pop. They carried plastic water containers, each with a two gallon capacity. Mitchell Sanders carried a set of starched tiger fatigues for special occasions. Henry Dobbins carried Black Flag insecticide. Dave Jensen carried empty sandbags that could be filled at night for added protection. Lee Strunk carried tanning lotion. Some things they carried in common. Taking turns, they carried the big PRC-77 scrambler radio, which weighed thirty pounds with its battery. They shared the weight of memory. They took up what others could no longer bear. Often, they carried each other, the wounded or weak. They carried infections. They carried chess sets, basketballs, Vietnamese-English dictionaries, insignia of rank, Bronze Stars and Purple Hearts, plastic cards imprinted with the Code of Conduct. They carried diseases, among them malaria and dysentery. They carried lice and ringworm and leeches and paddy algae and various rots and molds. They carried the land itself—Vietnam, the place, the soil—a powdery orange-red dust that covered their boots and fatigues and faces. They carried the sky. The whole atmosphere, they carried it, the humidity, the monsoons, the stink of fungus and decay, all of it, they carried gravity. They moved like mules. By daylight they took sniper fire, at night they were mortared, but it was not battle, it was just the endless march, village to village, without purpose, nothing won or lost. They marched for the sake of the march. They plodded along slowly, dumbly, leaning forward against the heat, unthinking, all blood and bone, simple grunts, soldiering with their legs, toiling up the hills and down into the paddies and across the rivers and up again and down, just humping, one step and then the next and then another, but no volition, no will, because it was automatic, it was anatomy, and the war was entirely a matter of posture and carriage, the hump was everything, a kind of inertia, a kind of emptiness, a dullness of desire and intellect and conscience and hope and human sensibility. Their principles were in their feet. Their calculations were biological. They had no sense of strategy or mission. They searched the villages without knowing what to look for, nor caring, kicking over jars of rice, frisking children and old men, blowing tunnels, sometimes setting fires and sometimes not, then forming up and moving on to the next village, then other villages, where it would always be the same. They carried their own lives. The pressures were enormous. In the heat of early afternoon, they would remove their helmets and flak jackets, walking bare, which was dangerous but which helped ease the strain. They would often discard things along the route of march. Purely for comfort, they would throw away rations, blow their Claymores and grenades, no matter, because by nightfall the resupply choppers would arrive with more of the same, then a day or two later still more, fresh watermelons and crates of ammunition and sunglasses and woolen sweaters—the resources were stunning—sparklers for the Fourth of July, colored eggs for Easter. It was the great American war chest—the fruits of sciences, the smokestacks, the canneries, the arsenals at Hartford, the Minnesota forests, the machine shops, the vast fields of corn and wheat—they carried like freight trains; they carried it on their backs and shoulders—and for all the ambiguities of Vietnam, all the mysteries and unknowns, there was at least the single abiding certainty that they would never be at a loss for things to carry.

40 After the chopper took Lavender away, Lieutenant Jimmy Cross led his men into the village of Than Khe. They burned everything. They shot chickens and dogs, they trashed the village well, they called in artillery and watched the wreckage, then they marched for several hours through the hot afternoon, and then at dusk, while Kiowa explained how Lavender died, Lieutenant Cross found himself trembling.

He tried not to cry. With his entrenching tool, which weighed five pounds, he began digging a hole in the earth.

He felt shame. He hated himself. He had loved Martha more than his men, and as a consequence Lavender was now dead, and this was something he would have to carry like a stone in his stomach for the rest of the war.

All he could do was dig. He used his entrenching tool like an ax, slashing, feeling both love and hate, and then later, when it was full dark, he sat at the bottom of his foxhole and wept. It went on for a long while. In part, he was grieving for Ted Lavender, but mostly it was for Martha, and for himself, because she belonged to another world, which was not quite real, and because she was a junior at Mount Sebastian College in New Jersey, a poet and a virgin and uninvolved, and because he realized she did not love him and never would.

Like cement, Kiowa whispered in the dark. I swear to God—boom-down. Not a word.

45 I've heard this, said Norman Bowker.

A pisser, you know? Still zipping himself up. Zapped while zipping.

All right, fine. That's enough.

Yeah, but you had to see it, the guy just—

I *heard,* man. Cement. So why not shut the fuck *up?*

50 Kiowa shook his head sadly and glanced over at the hole where Lieutenant Jimmy Cross sat watching the night. The air was thick and wet. A warm, dense fog had settled over the paddies and there was the stillness that precedes rain.

After a time Kiowa sighed.

One thing for sure, he said. The lieutenant's in some deep hurt. I mean that crying jag—the way he was carrying on—it wasn't fake or anything, it was real heavy-duty hurt. The man cares.

Sure, Norman Bowker said.

Say what you want, the man does care.

55 We all got problems.

Not Lavender.

No, I guess not, Bowker said. Do me a favor, though.

Shut up?

That's a smart Indian. Shut up.

60 Shrugging, Kiowa pulled off his boots. He wanted to say more, just to lighten up his sleep, but instead he opened his New Testament and arranged it beneath his head as a pillow. The fog made things seem hollow and unattached. He tried not to think about Ted Lavender, but then he was thinking how fast it was, no drama, down and dead, and how it was hard to feel anything except surprise. It seemed unchristian. He wished he could find some great sadness, or even anger, but the emotion wasn't there and he couldn't make it happen. Mostly he felt pleased to be alive. He liked the smell of the New Testament under his cheek, the leather and ink and paper and glue, whatever the chemicals were. He liked hearing the sounds of night. Even his fatigue, it felt fine, the stiff muscles and the prickly awareness of his own body, a floating feeling. He enjoyed not being dead. Lying there, Kiowa admired Lieutenant Jimmy Cross's capacity for grief. He wanted

to share the man's pain, he wanted to care as Jimmy Cross cared. And yet when he closed his eyes, all he could think was Boom-down, and all he could feel was the pleasure of having his boots off and the fog curling in around him and damp soil and the Bible smells and the plush comfort of night.

After a moment Norman Bowker sat up in the dark.

What the hell, he said. You want to talk, *talk*. Tell it to me.

Forget it.

No, man, go on. One thing I hate, it's a silent Indian.

65 For the most part they carried themselves with poise, a kind of dignity. Now and then, however, there were times of panic, when they squealed or wanted to squeal but couldn't, when they twitched and made moaning sounds and covered their heads and said Dear Jesus and flopped around on the earth and fired their weapons blindly and cringed and sobbed and begged for the noise to stop and went wild and made stupid promises to themselves and to God and to their mothers and fathers, hoping not to die. In different ways, it happened to all of them. Afterward, when the firing ended, they would blink and peek up. They would touch their bodies, feeling shame, then quickly hiding it. They would force themselves to stand. As if in slow motion, frame by frame, the world would take on the old logic—absolute silence, then the wind, then sunlight, then voices. It was the burden of being alive. Awkwardly, the men would reassemble themselves, first in private, then in groups, becoming soldiers again. They would repair the leaks in their eyes. They would check for casualties, call in dust-offs, light cigarettes, try to smile, clear their throats and spit and begin cleaning their weapons. After a time someone would shake his head and say, No lie, I almost shit my pants, and someone else would laugh, which meant it was bad, yes, but the guy had obviously not shit his pants, it wasn't that bad, and in any case nobody would ever do such a thing and then go ahead and talk about it. They would squint into the dense, oppressive sunlight. For a few moments, perhaps, they would fall silent, lighting a joint and tracking its passage from man to man, inhaling, holding in the humiliation. Scary stuff, one of them might say. But then someone else would grin or flick his eyebrows and say, Roger-dodger, almost cut me a new asshole, *almost*.

There were numerous such poses. Some carried themselves with a sort of wistful resignation, others with pride or still soldierly discipline or good humor or macho zeal. They were afraid of dying but they were even more afraid to show it.

They found jokes to tell.

They used a hard vocabulary to contain the terrible softness. *Greased,* they'd say. *Offed, lit up, zapped while zipping*. It wasn't cruelty, just stage presence. They were actors and the war came at them in 3-D. When someone died, it wasn't quite dying, because in a curious way it seemed scripted, and because they had their lines mostly memorized, irony mixed with tragedy, and because they called it by other names, as if to encyst and destroy the reality of death itself. They kicked corpses. They cut off thumbs. They talked grunt lingo. They told stories about Ted Lavender's supply of tranquilizers, how the poor guy didn't feel a thing, how incredibly tranquil he was.

There's a moral here, said Mitchell Sanders.

70 They were waiting for Lavender's chopper, smoking the dead man's dope.

The moral's pretty obvious, Sanders said, and winked. Stay away from drugs. No joke, they'll ruin your day every time.

Cute, said Henry Dobbins.

Mind-blower, get it? Talk about wiggy—nothing left, just blood and brains.

They made themselves laugh.

75 There it is, they'd say, over and over, as if the repetition itself were an act of poise, a balance between crazy and almost crazy, knowing without going. There it is, which meant be cool, let it ride, because oh yeah, man, you can't change what can't be changed, there it is, there it absolutely and positively and fucking well *is*.

They were tough.

They carried all the emotional baggage of men who might die. Grief, terror, love, longing—these were intangibles, but the intangibles had their own mass and specific gravity, they had tangible weight. They carried shameful memories. They carried the common secret of cowardice barely restrained, the instinct to run or freeze or hide, and in many respects this was the heaviest burden of all, for it could never be put down, it required perfect balance and perfect posture. They carried their reputations. They carried the soldier's greatest fear, which was the fear of blushing. Men killed, and died, because they were embarrassed not to. It was what had brought them to the war in the first place, nothing positive, no dreams of glory or honor, just to avoid the blush of dishonor. They died so as not to die of embarrassment. They crawled into tunnels and walked point and advanced under fire. Each morning, despite the unknowns, they made their legs move. They endured. They kept humping. They did not submit to the obvious alternative, which was simply to close the eyes and fall. So easy, really. Go limp and tumble to the ground and let the muscles unwind and not speak and not budge until your buddies picked you up and lifted you into the chopper that would roar and dip its nose and carry you off to the world. A mere matter of falling, yet no one ever fell. It was not courage, exactly; the object was not valor. Rather, they were too frightened to be cowards.

By and large they carried these things inside, maintaining the masks of composure. They sneered at sick call. They spoke bitterly about guys who had found release by shooting off their own toes or fingers. Pussies, they'd say. Candyasses. It was fierce, mocking talk, with only a trace of envy or awe, but even so, the image played itself out behind their eyes.

They imagined the muzzle against flesh. They imagined the quick, sweet pain, then the evacuation to Japan, then a hospital with warm beds and cute geisha nurses.

80 They dreamed of freedom birds.

At night, on guard, staring into the dark, they were carried away by jumbo jets. They felt the rush of takeoff. *Gone!* they yelled. And then velocity, wings and engines, a smiling stewardess—but it was more than a plane, it was a real bird, a big sleek silver bird with feathers and talons and high screeching. They were flying. The weights fell off, there was nothing to bear. They laughed and held on tight, feeling the cold slap of wind and altitude, soaring, thinking *It's over, I'm gone!*—they were naked, they were light and free—it was all lightness, bright and fast and buoyant, light as light, a helium buzz in the brain, a giddy bubbling in the lungs as they were taken up over the clouds and the war, beyond duty, beyond gravity and mortification and global entanglements—*Sin loi!*[7] They yelled, *I'm sorry, motherfuckers, but I'm out of it, I'm goofed, I'm on a space cruise, I'm gone!*—and it was a restful, disencumbered sensation, just riding the light waves, sailing that big silver freedom bird over the mountains and oceans, over America,

[7] ***Sin loi*** sorry.

over the farms and great sleeping cities and cemeteries and highways and the Golden Arches of McDonald's. It was flight, a kind of fleeing, a kind of falling, falling higher and higher, spinning off the edge of the earth and beyond the sun and through the vast, silent vacuum where there were no burdens and where everything weighed exactly nothing. *Gone!* they screamed, *I'm sorry but I'm gone!* And so at night, not quite dreaming, they gave themselves over to lightness, they were carried, they were purely borne.

On the morning after Ted Lavender died, First Lieutenant Jimmy Cross crouched at the bottom of his foxhole and burned Martha's letters. Then he burned the two photographs. There was a steady rain falling, which made it difficult, but he used heat tabs and Sterno to build a small fire, screening it with his body, holding the photographs over the tight blue flame with the tips of his fingers.

He realized it was only a gesture. Stupid, he thought. Sentimental, too, but mostly just stupid.

Lavender was dead. You couldn't burn the blame.

85 Besides, the letters were in his head. And even now, without photographs, Lieutenant Cross could see Martha playing volleyball in her white gym shorts and yellow T-shirt. He could see her moving in the rain.

When the fire died out, Lieutenant Cross pulled his poncho over his shoulders and ate breakfast from a can.

There was no great mystery, he decided.

In those burned letters Martha had never mentioned the war, except to say, Jimmy, take care of yourself. She wasn't involved. She signed the letters "Love," but it wasn't love, and all the fine lines and technicalities did not matter.

The morning came up wet and blurry. Everything seemed part of everything else, the fog and Martha and the deepening rain.

90 It was a war, after all.

Half smiling, Lieutenant Jimmy Cross took out his maps. He shook his head hard, as if to clear it, then bent forward and began planning the day's march. In ten minutes, or maybe twenty, he would rouse the men and they would pack up and head west, where the maps showed the country to be green and inviting. They would do what they had always done. The rain might add some weight, but otherwise it would be one more day layered upon all the other days.

He was realistic about it. There was the new hardness in his stomach.

No more fantasies, he told himself.

Henceforth, when he thought about Martha, it would be only to think that she belonged elsewhere. He would shut down the daydreams. This was not Mount Sebastian, it was another world, where there were no pretty poems or midterm exams, a place where men died because of carelessness and gross stupidity. Kiowa was right. Boom-down, and you were dead, never partly dead.

95 Briefly, in the rain, Lieutenant Cross saw Martha's gray eyes gazing back at him.

He understood.

It was very sad, he thought. The things men carried inside. The things men did or felt they had to do.

He almost nodded at her, but didn't.

Instead he went back to his maps. He was now determined to perform his duties firmly and without negligence. It wouldn't help Lavender, he knew that, but from this point on he would comport himself as a soldier. He would dispose of his good-luck pebble. Swallow it, maybe, or use Lee Strunk's slingshot, or just drop it along the trail. On the march he would impose strict field discipline. He would be careful to send out flank security, to prevent straggling or bunching up, to keep his troops moving at the proper pace and at the proper interval. He would insist on clean weapons. He would confiscate the remainder of Lavender's dope. Later in the day, perhaps, he would call the men together and speak to them plainly. He would accept the blame for what had happened to Ted Lavender. He would be a man about it. He would look them in the eyes, keeping his chin level, and he would issue the new SOPs in a calm, impersonal tone of voice, an officer's voice, leaving no room for argument or discussion. Commencing immediately, he'd tell them, they would no longer abandon equipment along the route of march. They would police up their acts. They would get their shit together, and keep it together, and maintain it neatly and in good working order.

100 He would not tolerate laxity. He would show strength, distancing himself.

Among the men there would be grumbling, of course, and maybe worse, because their days would seem longer and their loads heavier, but Lieutenant Cross reminded himself that his obligation was not to be loved but to lead. He would dispense with love; it was not now a factor. And if anyone quarreled or complained, he would simply tighten his lips and arrange his shoulders in the correct command posture. He might give a curt little nod. Or he might not. He might just shrug and say Carry on, then they would saddle up and form into a column and move out toward the villages west of Than Khe.

[1986]

Joining the Conversation: Critical Thinking and Writing

1. What is the point of the insistent repetition of the words "the things they carried"? What sorts of things does Lieutenant Cross carry?
2. We are told that "Kiowa admired Lieutenant Jimmy Cross's capacity for grief" (paragraph 60). But we are also told that although Kiowa "wanted to share the man's pain," he could think only of "Boom-down" and of "the pleasure of having his boots off and the fog curling in around him and damp soil and the Bible smells and the plush comfort of night." What might account for the different responses of the two men?
3. Near the end of the story (paragraph 82), Lieutenant Cross "burned the two photographs." Why does he do this?

POEMS

ANONYMOUS

Among the most memorable hymns produced in the United States are the spirituals, or Sorrow Songs, created by black slaves in the United States, chiefly in the first half of the nineteenth century. The origins of the spirituals are still a matter of some dispute, but most specialists agree that the songs represent a distinctive fusion of African rhythms with European hymns, and many of the texts derive ultimately from biblical sources. A central theme is the desire for release, sometimes presented with imagery drawn from ancient Israel. Examples include references to crossing the River Jordan (a river that runs from north of the Sea of Galilee to the Dead Sea), the release of the Israelites from slavery in Egypt (Exodus), Jonah's release from the whale (Book of Jonah), Daniel's deliverance from the lions' den (Book of Daniel, Chapter 6), and the deliverance of Shadrach, Meshach, and Abednego from a fiery furnace (Book of Daniel, Chapter 3).

The first collections of texts were published in the 1860s, in, for instance, Slave Songs of the United States *(1867). These books usually sought to reproduce the singers' pronunciation, and we have followed the early texts in the example that we give here—for instance, where we give "de" for "the."*

Didn't My Lord Deliver Daniel

Didn't my Lord deliver Daniel, deliver Daniel, deliver Daniel,
Didn't my Lord deliver Daniel,
An' why not every man.
He delivered Daniel from de lion's den,
Jonah from de belly of de whale,
An' de Hebrew chillun from de fiery furnace,
An' why not every man.
Didn't my Lord deliver Daniel, deliver Daniel, deliver Daniel,
Didn't my Lord deliver Daniel,
An' why not every man.
De moon run down in a purple stream,
De sun forbear to shine,
An' every star disappear,
King Jesus shall-a be mine.
(Refrain)
De win' blows eas' an' de win' blows wes',
It blows like de judgament day,
An' every po' soul dat never did pray
'll be glad to pray dat day.
(Refrain)

I set my foot on de Gospel ship,
And de ship begin to sail,
It landed me over on Canaan's shore,°
An' I'll never come back no mo'.
(Refrain)

23 Canaan's shore Canaan is the ancient name of a territory that included part of what is now Israel.

Joining the Conversation: Critical Thinking and Writing

As we mentioned a moment ago, we give the text of the song as it was printed in the second half of the nineteenth century, when an effort to indicate pronunciation was made (e.g., "de" for "the"). If you were printing the songs, would you retain these attempts to indicate pronunciation? What, if anything, is gained by keeping them? What, if any, unintentional side effects do you think may be produced? Set forth your responses in an argument of about 500 words.

Robert Hayden

Robert Hayden (1913–1980) was born in Detroit, Michigan. His parents divorced when he was a child, and he was brought up by a neighboring family, whose name he adopted. In 1942, at the age of 29, he graduated from Detroit City College (now Wayne State University), and he received a master's degree from the University of Michigan. He taught at Fisk University from 1946 to 1969 and after that, for the remainder of his life, at the University of Michigan. In 1979 he was appointed Consultant in Poetry to the Library of Congress, the first African American to hold the post.

Frederick Douglass°

When it is finally ours, this freedom, this liberty, this beautiful
and terrible thing, needful to man as air,
usable as earth; when it belongs at last to all,
when it is truly instinct, brain matter, diastole, systole,
reflex action; when it is finally won; when it is more
than the gaudy mumbo jumbo of politicians:
this man, this Douglass, this former slave, this Negro
beaten to his knees, exiled, visioning a world
where none is lonely, none hunted, alien,
this man, superb in love and logic, this man
shall be remembered. Oh, not with statues' rhetoric,
not with legends and poems and wreaths of bronze alone,
but with the lives grown out of his life, the lives
fleshing his dream of the beautiful, needful thing.

[1947]

°Frederick Douglass (1818–1895) Born a slave, Douglass escaped and became an important spokesman for the abolitionist movement and later for civil rights for African Americans.

Joining the Conversation: Critical Thinking and Writing

1. When, according to Hayden, will Douglass "be remembered"? And *how* will he be remembered?
2. "Frederick Douglass" consists of two sentences (or one sentence and a fragment). In what line do you find the subject of the first sentence? What is the main verb (the predicate) and where do you find it? How would you describe the effect of the long delaying of the subject? And of the predicate?
3. Does Hayden assume or seem to predict that there *will* come a time when freedom "is finally ours" (line 1), and "belongs at last to all" (line 3)?
4. Hayden wrote "Frederick Douglass" in 1947. In your opinion are we closer now to Hayden's vision or farther away? (You may find that we are closer in some ways and farther in others.) In your answer—perhaps an essay of 500 words—try to be as specific as possible.
5. "Frederick Douglass" consists of fourteen lines. Is it a sonnet?

LORNA DEE CERVANTES

Lorna Dee Cervantes, born in San Francisco in 1954, founded a press and a poetry magazine, Mango, *chiefly devoted to Chicano literature. In 1978 she received a fellowship from the National Endowment for the Arts, and in 1981 she published her first book of poems. She lives in Boulder, Colorado. "Refugee Ship," originally written in 1974, was revised for the book. We print the revised version.*

Refugee Ship

Like wet cornstarch, I slide
past my grandmother's eyes. Bible
at her side, she removes her glasses.
The pudding thickens.

Mama raised me without language.
I'm orphaned from my Spanish name.
The words are foreign, stumbling
on my tongue. I see in the mirror
my reflection: bronzed skin, black hair.

I feel I am a captive
aboard the refugee ship.
The ship that will never dock.
El barco que nunca atraca.°

[1981]

13 ***El barco que nunca atraca*** The ship that never docks.

Joining the Conversation: Critical Thinking and Writing

1. What do you think the speaker means by the comparison with "wet cornstarch" in line 1? And what do you take her to mean in line 7 when she says, "I'm orphaned from my Spanish name"?
2. Judging from the poem as a whole, why does the speaker feel she is "a captive / aboard the refugee ship"? How would you characterize such feelings?
3. In an earlier version of the poem, instead of "my grandmother's eyes" Cervantes wrote "*mi abuelita's* eyes"; that is, she used the Spanish words for "my grandmother." In line 5 instead of "Mama" she wrote "*mamá*" (again, the Spanish equivalent), and in line 9 she wrote "brown skin" instead of "bronzed skin." The final line of the original version was not in Spanish but in English, a repetition of the preceding line, which ran thus: "A ship that will never dock." How does each of these changes strike you?

EDWIN ARLINGTON ROBINSON

Edwin Arlington Robinson (1869–1935) grew up in Gardiner, Maine, spent two years at Harvard, and then returned to Maine, where he published his first book of poetry in 1896. Though he received encouragement from neighbors, his finances were precarious, even after President Theodore Roosevelt, having been made aware of the book, secured for him an appointment as customs inspector in New York from 1905 to 1909. Additional books won fame for Robinson, and in 1922 he was awarded the first of three Pulitzer Prizes for poetry that he would win.

Richard Cory

Whenever Richard Cory went down town,
We people on the pavement looked at him:
He was a gentleman from sole to crown,
Clean favored, and imperially slim.

And he was always quietly arrayed,
And he was always human when he talked;
But still he fluttered pulses when he said,
"Good-morning," and he glittered when he walked.

And he was rich—yes, richer than a king—
And admirably schooled in every grace:
In fine,° we thought that he was everything
To make us wish that we were in his place.

So on we worked, and waited for the light,
And went without the meat, and cursed the bread;
And Richard Cory, one calm summer night,
Went home and put a bullet through his head.

[1896]

11 In fine in short.

Joining the Conversation: Critical Thinking and Writing

1. What do you think were Richard Cory's thoughts shortly before he "put a bullet through his head"? In 500 words, set forth his thoughts and actions (what he sees and does). If you wish, you can write in the first person, from Cory's point of view. Further, if you wish, your essay can be in the form of a suicide note.
2. Write a sketch (250–350 words) setting forth your early impression or understanding of someone whose later actions revealed that you had not understood the person.

W. H. AUDEN

Wystan Hugh Auden (1907–1973) was born in York, England, and educated at Oxford. In the 1930s his left-wing poetry earned him wide acclaim as the leading poet of his generation. He went to Spain during the Spanish Civil War, intending to serve as an ambulance driver for the Republicans in their struggle against fascism, but he was so distressed by the violence of the Republicans that he almost immediately returned to England. In 1939 he came to America, and in 1946 he became a citizen of the United States, though he returned to England for his last years. Much of his poetry is characterized by a combination of colloquial diction and technical dexterity.

The Unknown Citizen

(To JS/07/M378
This Marble Monument Is Erected by the State)

He was found by the Bureau of Statistics to be
One against whom there was no official complaint,
And all the reports on his conduct agree
That, in the modern sense of an old-fashioned word, he was a saint,
For in everything he did he served the Greater Community.
Except for the War till the day he retired
He worked in a factory and never got fired,
But satisfied his employers, Fudge Motors Inc.
Yet he wasn't a scab or odd in his views,
For his Union reports that he paid his dues,
(Our report on his Union shows it was sound)
And our Social Psychology workers found
That he was popular with his mates and liked a drink.
The Press are convinced that he bought a paper every day
And that his reactions to advertisements were normal in every way.
Policies taken out in His name prove that he was fully insured,
And his Health-card shows he was once in hospital but left it cured.
Both Producers Research and High-Grade Living declare
He was fully sensible to the advantages of the Installment Plan
And had everything necessary to the Modern Man,

A phonograph, radio, a car and a frigidaire.
Our researchers into Public Opinion are content
That he held the proper opinions for the time of year;
When there was peace, he was for peace; when there was war,
  he went.
He was married and added five children to the population,
Which our Eugenist says was the right number for a parent of his
  generation,
And our teachers report that he never interfered with their education.
Was he free? Was he happy? The question is absurd:
Had anything been wrong, we should certainly have heard.

[1940]

Joining the Conversation: Critical Thinking and Writing

1. What is Auden satirizing in "The Unknown Citizen"? (Students might be cautioned to spend some time thinking about whether Auden is satirizing the speaker, the citizen, conformism, totalitarianism, technology, or what.)
2. Write a prose eulogy of 250 words satirizing contemporary conformity, or, if you prefer, contemporary individualism.
3. Was he free? Was he happy? Explain.
4. In a paragraph or two, sketch the values of the speaker of the poem and then sum them up in a sentence or two. Finally, in as much space as you feel you need, judge these values.

ALLEN GINSBERG

Allen Ginsberg (1926–1997) was born in Newark, New Jersey, and graduated from Columbia University in 1948. After eight months in Columbia Psychiatric Institute—Ginsberg had pleaded insanity to avoid prosecution when the police discovered that a friend had stored stolen goods in Ginsberg's apartment—he worked at odd jobs and finally left the nine-to-five world for a freer life in San Francisco. In the 1950s he established a reputation as an uninhibited declamatory poet whose chief theme was a celebration of those who were alienated from a repressive America.

A Supermarket in California

What thoughts I have of you tonight, Walt Whitman, for I walked down
the sidestreets under the trees with a headache self-conscious looking
at the full moon.
  In my hungry fatigue, and shopping for images, I went into the neon
fruit supermarket, dreaming of your enumerations!
  What peaches and what penumbras! Whole families shopping at night!
Aisles full of husbands! Wives in the avocados, babies in the
tomatoes!—and you, García Lorca,° what were you doing
down by the watermelons?

  I saw you, Walt Whitman, childless, lonely old grubber, poking among
the meats in the refrigerator and eyeing the grocery boys.

3 García Lorca Federico García Lorca (1899–1936), Spanish poet (and, like Whitman and Ginsberg, a homosexual).

I heard you asking questions of each: Who killed the pork chops? What price bananas? Are you my Angel?
I wandered in and out of the brilliant stacks of cans following you, and followed in my imagination by the store detective.
We strode down the open corridors together in our solitary fancy tasting artichokes, possessing every frozen delicacy, and never passing the cashier.

Where are we going, Walt Whitman? The doors close in an hour. Which way does your beard point tonight?
(I touch your book and dream of our odyssey in the supermarket and feel absurd.)
Will we walk all night through solitary streets? The trees add shade to shade, lights out in the houses, we'll both be lonely.
Will we stroll dreaming of the lost America of love past blue automobiles in driveways, home to our silent cottage?
Ah, dear father, graybeard, lonely old courage-teacher, what America did you have when Charon quit poling his ferry and you got out on a smoking bank and stood watching the boat disappear on the black water of Lethe?°

[1956]

12 Lethe In classical mythology, Charon ferried the souls of the dead across the river Styx, to Hades, where, after drinking from the river Lethe, they forgot the life they had lived.

Joining the Conversation: Critical Thinking and Writing

1. Ginsberg calls his poem "A Supermarket in California." Need the market be in California, or can it be anywhere?
2. In the second line, Ginsberg explains why he went into the supermarket. Is the explanation clear, or puzzling, or some of each? Explain.
3. In the third section ("What peaches and what penumbras!"), what *is* a penumbra? Are the aisles full of them?
4. In line 8 ("Where are we going, Walt Whitman? The doors close in an hour. Which way does your beard point tonight?"), is Ginsberg hopeful or not about where he and Walt Whitman will stroll?
5. Read two or three Whitman poems (reprinted elsewhere in this book). In what ways does Ginsberg's poem resemble Whitman's poems? In what ways is "A Supermarket" pure Ginsberg?

Marge Piercy

Marge Piercy, born in Detroit in 1936, was the first member of her family to attend college. After earning a bachelor's degree from the University of Michigan in 1957 and a master's degree from Northwestern University in 1958, she moved to Chicago. There she worked at odd jobs while writing novels (unpublished) and engaging in action on behalf of women and blacks and against the Vietnam War. In 1970—the year she moved to Wellfleet, Massachusetts, where she still lives—she published her first book, a novel. Since then she has published many novels, as well as short stories, poems, and essays.

To be of use

The people I love the best
jump into work head first
without dallying in the shallows
and swim off with sure strokes almost out of sight.
They seem to become natives of that element,
the black sleek heads of seals
bouncing like half-submerged balls.

I love people who harness themselves, an ox to a heavy cart,
who pull like water buffalo, with massive patience,
who strain in the mud and the muck to move things forward,
who do what has to be done, again and again.

I want to be with people who submerge
in the task, who go into the fields to harvest
and work in a row and pass the bags along,
who are not parlor generals and field deserters
but move in a common rhythm
when the food must come in or the fire be put out.

The work of the world is common as mud.
Botched, it smears the hands, crumbles to dust.
But the thing worth doing well done
has a shape that satisfies, clean and evident.
Greek amphoras for wine or oil,
Hopi vases that held corn, are put in museums
but you know they were made to be used.
The pitcher cries for water to carry
and a person for work that is real.

[1974]

Joining the Conversation: Critical Thinking and Writing

1. Write a short poem—perhaps seven lines, the length of Piercy's first stanza—beginning with Piercy's first line, "The people I love the best."
2. Suppose someone argued that Piercy's first stanza is the best, and, moreover, that this stanza can stand by itself. How might you argue that the next three stanzas contribute to the poem, making a better poem than the first stanza by itself?

What's That Smell in the Kitchen?

All over America women are burning dinners.
It's lambchops in Peoria; it's haddock
in Providence; it's steak in Chicago;
tofu delight in Big Sur; red
rice and beans in Dallas.

All over America women are burning
food they're supposed to bring with calico
smile on platters glittering like wax.
Anger sputters in her brainpan, confined
but spewing out missiles of hot fat.
Carbonized despair presses like a clinker
from a barbecue against the back of her eyes.
If she wants to grill anything, it's
her husband spitted over a slow fire.
If she wants to serve him anything
it's a dead rat with a bomb in its belly
ticking like the heart of an insomniac.
Her life is cooked and digested,
nothing but leftovers in Tupperware.
Look, she says, once I was roast duck
on your platter with parsley but now I am Spam.
Burning dinner is not incompetence but war.

[1982]

Joining the Conversation: Critical Thinking and Writing

1. Suppose a friend told you that she didn't understand lines 20–21. How would you paraphrase the lines?
2. Who speaks the title?
3. If a poem begins, "All over America women are . . . ," what words might a reader reasonably expect next?
4. Do you take the poem to be chiefly comic? Superficially comic but a work with a serious purpose? Or what?

YUSEF KOMUNYAKAA

Yusef Komunyakaa was born in 1947 in Bogalusa, Louisiana. After graduating from high school he entered the army and served in Vietnam, where he was awarded the Bronze Star. On his return to the United States he earned a bachelor's degree at the University of Colorado, and then earned an MA at Colorado State University and an MFA in creative writing at the University of California, Irvine. The author of several books of poetry, Komunyakaa teaches at New York University. "Facing It" is the last poem in a book of poems about Vietnam, Dien Cai Dau *(1988). The title of the book is a slang word for* crazy.

Facing It

My black face fades,
hiding inside the black granite.
I said I wouldn't,
dammit: No tears.
I'm stone. I'm flesh.

Vietnam Veterans Memorial, Washington, D.C.

My clouded reflection eyes me
like a bird of prey, the profile of night
slanted against morning. I turn
this way—the stone lets me go.
I turn that way—I'm inside
the Vietnam Veterans Memorial
again, depending on the light
to make a difference.
I go down the 58,022 names,
half-expecting to find
my own in letters like smoke.
I touch the name Andrew Johnson;
I see the booby trap's white flash.
Names shimmer on a woman's blouse
but when she walks away
the names stay on the wall.
Brushstrokes flash, a red bird's
wings cutting across my stare.
The sky. A plane in the sky.
A white vet's image floats
closer to me, then his pale eyes
look through mine. I'm a window.
He's lost his right arm
inside the stone. In the black mirror
a woman's trying to erase names:
No, she's brushing a boy's hair.

[1988]

Joining the Conversation: Critical Thinking and Writing

1. The poem's title is "Facing It." What is the speaker facing? How would you describe his attitude?
2. Three people, whose names we don't know, briefly appear on the wall. How might we describe their actions? Try to paraphrase: "I'm a window. / He's lost his right arm / inside the stone."
3. At the poem's end, has the speaker "faced it"? What is your evidence?
4. If you have seen the Vietnam Veterans Memorial, describe it and your reaction to it in a paragraph or two. If you haven't seen it, try to describe it from "Facing It" and any written or photographic accounts you have seen.

BILLY COLLINS

"Billy Collins writes lovely poems," the novelist, critic, and poet John Updike has said: "Limpid, gently and consistently startling, more serious than they seem, they describe all the worlds that are and were and some others besides." The recipient of many honors and awards, and a former poet laureate of the United States, Collins was born in New York City in 1941. He has taught at both the City University of New York and Sarah Lawrence College. His Sailing Alone Around the Room: New and Selected Poems *was published in 2002.*

Collins wrote the following poem on the first anniversary of the terrorist attack on the World Trade Center, September 11, 2001, which killed about 3,000 people and destroyed the Twin Towers.

The Names

Yesterday, I lay awake in the palm of the night.
A soft rain stole in, unhelped by any breeze,
And when I saw the silver glaze on the windows,
I started with A, with Ackerman, as it happened,
Then Baxter and Calabro,
Davis and Eberling, names falling into place
As droplets fell through the dark.

Names printed on the ceiling of the night.
Names slipping around a watery bend.
Twenty-six willows on the banks of a stream.

In the morning, I walked out barefoot
Among thousands of flowers
Heavy with dew like the eyes of tears,
And each had a name—
Fiori inscribed on a yellow petal
Then Gonzalez and Han, Ishikawa and Jenkins.

Names written in the air
And stitched into the cloth of the day.
A name under a photograph taped to a mailbox.
Monogram on a torn shirt,
I see you spelled out on storefront windows

And on the bright unfurled awnings of this city.
I say the syllables as I turn a corner—
Kelly and Lee,
Medina, Nardella, and O'Connor.

When I peer in to the woods,
I see a thick tangle where letters are hidden
As in a puzzle concocted for children.
Parker and Quigley in the twigs of an ash,
Rizzo, Schubert, Torres, and Upton,
Secrets in the boughs of an ancient maple.

Names written in the pale sky.
Names rising in the updraft amid buildings.
Names silent in stone
Or cried out behind a door.
Names blown over the earth and out to sea.

In the evening—weakening light, the last swallows.
A boy on a lake lifts his oars.
A woman by a window puts a match to a candle,
And the names are outlined on the rose clouds—
Vanacore and Wallace,
(let X stand, if it can, for the ones unfound)
Then Young and Ziminsky, the final jolt of Z.

Names etched on the head of a pin.
One name spanning a bridge, another undergoing a tunnel.
A blue name needled into the skin.
Names of citizens, workers, mothers and fathers,
The bright-eyed daughter, the quick son.
Alphabet of names in a green field.
Names in the small tracks of birds.
Names lifted from a hat
Or balanced on the tip of the tongue.
Names wheeled into the dim warehouse of memory.
So many names, there is barely room on the walls of the heart.

[2002]

Joining the Conversation: Critical Thinking and Writing

1. In an interview that appeared several years before "The Names" was published, Collins says of his intention as a poet: "By the end of the poem, the reader should be in a different place from where he started." When you finished reading "The Names," did you find yourself in a "different place"? How would you describe this place?
2. Collins has also observed, again in an interview before he wrote "The Names": "Poetry is clearly very serious for me, but without heaviness or a glib sense of spirituality." Do you perceive a "spiritual" dimension to this poem—one that is not "glib"? What does it mean to say that a poem is "spiritual," that is creates a spiritual effect? Is this the same thing as saying that a poem is "religious," or is it something different?

3. Many readers have expressed their high regard for "The Names," referring to it as a "great poem." Do you agree? What defines a great poem? Do you think a poet does or does not face a special challenge in trying to write a poem, great or simply good, about the tragedy of September 11, 2001? Please explain.
4. One critic, who otherwise admires Collins's work, has objected to "The Names" for being "too sentimental." How would you define "sentimentality"? (Clarify your definition with an example.) Can you locate evidence in the text that might support the judgment that Collins's poem is sentimental? Are there other passages you could cite and analyze in order to argue against it? And what's the matter with sentimentality? Is sentimentality something that poets should always avoid?
5. How do you feel about your own name? Is it something you give much thought to? Any thought? Why is that? Now that you have read Collins's poem, has your relationship to your own name changed in any way?

Gwendolyn Brooks

Gwendolyn Brooks (1917–2000) was born in Topeka, Kansas, but was raised in Chicago's South Side, where she spent most of her life. In 1950, when she won the Pulitzer Prize for Poetry, she became the first African American writer to win a Pulitzer Prize.

The Bean Eaters

They eat beans mostly, this old yellow pair.
Dinner is a casual affair.
Plain chipware on a plain and creaking wood,
Tin flatware.

Two who are Mostly Good.
Two who have lived their day,
But keep on putting on their clothes
And putting things away.

And remembering . . .
Remembering, with twinklings and twinges,
As they lean over the beans in their rented back room that is full of
beads and receipts and dolls and clothes, tobacco crumbs, vases and
fringes.

[1960]

Joining the Conversation: Thinking and Writing

It is often assumed that sentimentality is a fault in literature. First, check the meanings of the word in a dictionary, and then think about the assumption. Second, does the word apply to Brooks's poem, and, if so, is the poem diminished by this quality? Write a paragraph arguing that the poem is or is not sentimental. If you do think it is sentimental, your essay should also face the question of whether sentimentality here is a weakness.

DOROTHY PARKER

For a biographical note on Dorothy Parker, see page 782.

Résumé

Razors pain you;
Rivers are damp;
Acids stain you;
And drugs cause cramp.
Guns aren't lawful;
Nooses give;
Gas smells awful;
You might as well live.

[1926]

Joining the Conversation: Critical Thinking and Writing

1. Exactly what is a *résumé?* How does Parker's *résumé* differ from the usual one?
2. Is the poem amusing? Is it more than amusing, that is, does it offer insight into an interesting state of feeling, or perhaps does it offer a view worth thinking about?

PLAY

TENNESSEE WILLIAMS

Tennessee Williams (1914–1983) was born Thomas Lanier Williams in Columbus, Mississippi. During his childhood his family moved to St. Louis, where his father had accepted a job as manager of a shoe company. Williams has written that neither he nor his sister Rose could adjust to the change from the South to the Midwest, but the children had already been deeply troubled. Nevertheless, at the age of 16 he achieved some distinction as a writer when his prize-winning essay in a nationwide contest was published. After high school he attended the University of Missouri but flunked ROTC and was therefore withdrawn from school by his father. He worked in a shoe factory for a while, then attended Washington University, where he wrote several plays. He finally graduated from the University of Iowa with a major in playwrighting. After graduation he continued to write, supporting himself with odd jobs such as waiting on tables and running elevators. His first commercial success was The Glass Menagerie *(produced in Chicago in 1944, and in New York in 1945); among his other plays are* A Streetcar Named Desire *(1947),* Cat on a Hot Tin Roof *(1955), and* Suddenly, Last Summer *(1958).*

The Glass Menagerie

nobody, not even the rain, has such small hands.
—E. E. Cummings

LIST OF CHARACTERS

AMANDA WINGFIELD, the mother. A little woman of great but confused vitality clinging frantically to another time and place. Her characterization must be carefully created, not copied from type. She is not paranoiac, but her life is paranoia. There is much to admire in Amanda, and as much to love and pity as there is to laugh at. Certainly she has endurance and a kind of heroism, and though her foolishness makes her unwittingly cruel at times, there is tenderness in her slight person.

LAURA WINGFIELD, her daughter. Amanda, having failed to establish contact with reality, continues to live vitally in her illusions, but Laura's situation is even graver. A childhood illness has left her crippled, one leg slightly shorter than the other, and held in a brace. This defect need not be more than suggested on the stage. Stemming from this, Laura's separation increases till she is like a piece of her own glass collection, too exquisitely fragile to move from the shelf.

TOM WINGFIELD, her son. And the narrator of the play. A poet with a job in a warehouse. His nature is not remorseless, but to escape from a trap he has to act without pity.

JIM O'CONNOR, the gentleman caller. A nice, ordinary, young man.

SCENE: *An alley in St. Louis.*
PART I: *Preparation for a Gentleman Caller.*
PART II: *The Gentleman Calls.*
TIME: *Now and the Past.*

Scene I

The Wingfield apartment is in the rear of the building, one of those vast hive-like conglomerations of cellular living-units that flower as warty growths in overcrowded urban centers of lower middle-class population and are symptomatic of the impulse of this largest and fundamentally enslaved section of American society to avoid fluidity and differentiation and to exist and function as one interfused mass of automatism.

The apartment faces an alley and is entered by a fire-escape, a structure whose name is a touch of accidental poetic truth, for all of these huge buildings are always burning with the slow and implacable fires of human desperation. The fire-escape is included in the set—that is, the landing of it and steps descending from it.

The scene is memory and is therefore nonrealistic. Memory takes a lot of poetic license. It omits some details; others are exaggerated, according to the emotional value of the articles it touches, for memory is seated predominantly in the heart. The interior is therefore rather dim and poetic.

At the rise of the curtain, the audience is faced with the dark, grim rear wall of the Wingfield tenement. This building, which runs parallel to the footlights, is flanked on both sides by dark, narrow alleys which run into murky canyons of tangled clotheslines, garbage cans and the sinister latticework of neighboring fire-escapes. It is up and down these side alleys that exterior entrances and exits are made, during the play. At the end of TOM*'s opening commentary, the dark* *tenement wall slowly reveals (by means of a transparency) the interior of the ground floor Wingfield apartment.*

Downstage is the living room, which also serves as a sleeping room for LAURA, *the sofa unfolding to make her bed. Upstage, center, and divided by a wide arch or second proscenium with transparent faded portieres (or second curtain), is the dining room. In an old-fashioned what-not in the living room are seen scores of transparent glass animals. A blown-up photograph of the father hangs on the wall of the living room, facing the audience, to the left of the archway. It is the face of a very handsome young man in a doughboy's First World War cap. He is gallantly smiling, ineluctably smiling, as if to say, "I will be smiling forever."*

The audience hears and sees the opening scene in the dining room through both the transparent fourth wall of the building and the transparent gauze portieres of the dining-room arch. It is during this revealing scene that the fourth wall slowly ascends, out of sight.

This transparent exterior wall is not brought down again until the very end of the play, during TOM*'s final speech.*

The narrator is an undisguised convention of the play. He takes whatever license with dramatic convention as is convenient to his purposes.

TOM *enters dressed as a merchant sailor from alley, stage left, and strolls across the front of the stage to the fire-escape. There he stops and lights a cigarette. He addresses the audience.*

TOM: Yes, I have tricks in my pocket, I have things up my sleeve. But I am the opposite of a stage magician. He gives you illusion that has the appearance of truth. I give you truth in the pleasant disguise of illusion. To begin with, I turn back time. I reverse it to that quaint period, the thirties, when the huge middle class of America was matriculating in a school for the blind. Their eyes had failed them, or they had failed their eyes, and so they were having their fingers pressed forcibly down on the fiery Braille alphabet of a dissolving economy. In Spain there was revolution. Here there was only shouting and confusion. In Spain there was Guernica. Here there were disturbances of labor, sometimes pretty violent, in otherwise peaceful cities such as Chicago, Cleveland, Saint Louis. . . . This is the social background of the play.

[*Music.*]

The play is memory. Being a memory play, it is dimly lighted, it is sentimental, it is not realistic. In memory everything seems to happen to music. That explains the fiddle in the wings. I am the narrator of the play, and also a character in it. The other characters are my mother, Amanda, my sister, Laura, and a gentleman caller who appears in the final scenes. He is the most realistic character in the play, being an emissary from a world of reality that we were somehow set apart from. But since I have a poet's weakness for symbols, I am using this character also as a symbol; he is the long delayed but always expected something that we live for. There is a fifth character in the play who doesn't appear except in this larger-than-life photograph over the mantel. This is our father who left us a long time ago. He was a telephone man who fell in love with long distances; he gave up his job with the telephone company and skipped the light fantastic out of town. . . . The last we heard of him was a picture post-card from Mazatlan, on the Pacific coast of Mexico, containing a message of two words—"Hello—Goodbye!" and no address. I think the rest of the play will explain itself. . . .

AMANDA*'s voice becomes audible through the portieres.*

[*Legend on Screen: "Où Sont les Neiges?"*]

He divides the portieres and enters the upstage area.

AMANDA *and* LAURA *are seated at a drop-leaf table. Eating is indicated by gestures without food or utensils.* AMANDA *faces the audience.* TOM *and* LAURA *are seated in profile.*

The interior has lit up softly and through the scrim we see AMANDA *and* LAURA *seated at the table in the upstage area.*

AMANDA [*calling*]: Tom?

TOM: Yes, Mother.

AMANDA: We can't say grace until you come to the table!

TOM: Coming, Mother. [*He bows slightly and withdraws reappearing a few moments later in his place at the table.*]

AMANDA [*to her son*]: Honey, don't *push* with your *fingers.* If you have to push with something, the thing to push with is a crust of bread. And chew—chew! Animals have sections in their stomachs which enable them to digest food without mastication, but human beings are supposed to chew their food before they swallow it down. Eat food leisurely, son, and really enjoy it. A well-cooked meal has lots of delicate flavors that have to be held in the mouth for appreciation. So chew your food and give your salivary glands a chance to function!

TOM *deliberately lays his imaginary fork down and pushes his chair back from the table.*

TOM: I haven't enjoyed one bite of this dinner because of your constant directions on how to eat it. It's you that makes me rush through meals with your hawk-like attention to every bite I take. Sickening—spoils my appetite—all this discussion of animals' secretion—salivary glands—mastication!

AMANDA [*lightly*]: Temperament like a Metropolitan star! [*He rises and crosses downstage.*] You're not excused from the table.

TOM: I am getting a cigarette.

AMANDA: You smoke too much.

LAURA *rises.*

LAURA: I'll bring in the blanc mange.

He remains standing with his cigarette by the portieres during the following.

AMANDA [*rising*]: No, sister, no, sister—you be the lady this time and I'll be the darky.

LAURA: I'm already up.

AMANDA: Resume your seat, little sister—I want you to stay fresh and pretty—for gentlemen callers!

LAURA: I'm not expecting any gentlemen callers.

AMANDA [*crossing out to kitchenette. Airily*]: Sometimes they come when they are least expected! Why, I remember one Sunday afternoon in Blue Mountain—[*Enters kitchenette.*]

TOM: I know what's coming!

LAURA: Yes. But let her tell it.

TOM: Again?

LAURA: She loves to tell it.

AMANDA *returns with bowl of dessert.*

AMANDA: One Sunday afternoon in Blue Mountain—your mother received—*seventeen!*—gentlemen callers! Why, sometimes there weren't chairs enough to accommodate them all. We had to send the nigger over to bring in folding chairs from the parish house.

TOM [*remaining at portieres*]: How did you entertain those gentlemen callers?

AMANDA: I understood the art of conversation!

TOM: I bet you could talk.

AMANDA: Girls in those days *knew* how to talk, I can tell you.

TOM: Yes?

[*Image:* AMANDA *as a Girl on a Porch Greeting Callers.*]

AMANDA: They knew how to entertain their gentlemen callers. It wasn't enough for a girl to be possessed of a pretty face and a graceful figure—although I wasn't slighted in either respect. She also needed to have a nimble wit and a tongue to meet all occasions.

TOM: What did you talk about?

AMANDA: Things of importance going on in the world! Never anything coarse or common or vulgar. [*She addresses* TOM *as though he were seated in the vacant chair at the table though he remains by portieres. He plays this scene as though he held the book.*] My callers were gentlemen—all! Among my callers were some of the most prominent young planters of the Mississippi Delta—planters and sons of planters!

TOM *motions for music and a spot of light on* AMANDA.

Her eyes lift, her face glows, her voice becomes rich and elegiac. [*Screen Legend: "Où Sont les Neiges?"*]

There was young Champ Laughlin who later became vice-president of the Delta Planters Bank. Hadley Stevenson who was drowned in Moon Lake and left his widow one hundred and fifty thousand in Government bonds. There were the Cutrere brothers, Wesley and Bates. Bates was one of my bright particular beaux! He got in a quarrel with that wild Wainright boy. They shot it out on the floor of Moon Lake Casino. Bates was shot through the stomach. Died in the ambulance on his way to Memphis. His widow was also well-provided for, came into eight or ten thousand acres, that's all. She married him on the rebound—never loved her—carried my picture on him the night he died! And there was that boy that every girl in Delta had set her cap for! That beautiful, brilliant young Fitzhugh boy from Green County!

TOM: What did he leave his widow?

AMANDA: He never married! Gracious, you talk as though all of my old admirers had turned up their toes to the daisies!

TOM: Isn't this the first you mentioned that still survives?

AMANDA: That Fitzhugh boy went North and made a fortune—came to be known as the Wolf of Wall Street! He had the Midas touch, whatever he touched turned to gold! And I could have been Mrs. Duncan J. Fitzhugh, mind you! But—I picked your *father!*

LAURA [*rising*]: Mother, let me clear the table.

AMANDA: No dear, you go in front and study your typewriter chart. Or practice your shorthand a little. Stay fresh and pretty!—It's almost time for our gentlemen callers to start arriving. [*She flounces girlishly toward the kitchenette.*] How many do you suppose we're going to entertain this afternoon?

TOM *throws down the paper and jumps up with a groan.*

LAURA [*alone in the dining room*]: I don't believe we're going to receive any, Mother.

AMANDA [*reappearing, airily*]: What? No one—not one? You must be joking! [LAURA *nervously echoes her laugh. She slips in a fugitive manner through the half-open portieres and draws them gently behind her. A shaft of very clear light is thrown on her face against the faded tapestry of the curtains.*] [*Music: "The Glass Menagerie" Under Faintly.*] [*Lightly.*] Not one gentleman caller? It can't be true! There must be a flood, there must have been a tornado!

LAURA: It isn't a flood, it's not a tornado, Mother. I'm just not popular like you were in Blue Mountain. . . . [TOM *utters another groan.* LAURA *glances at him with a faint, apologetic smile. Her voice catching a little.*] Mother's afraid I'm going to be an old maid.

[*The Scene Dims Out with "Glass Menagerie" Music.*]

Scene II
"Laura, Haven't You Ever Liked Some Boy?"

On the dark stage the screen is lighted with the image of blue roses. Gradually LAURA*'s figure becomes apparent and the screen goes out. The music subsides.*

LAURA *is seated in the delicate ivory chair at the small clawfoot table.*

She wears a dress of soft violet material for a kimono—her hair tied back from her forehead with a ribbon.

She is washing and polishing her collection of glass.

AMANDA *appears on the fire-escape steps. At the sound of her ascent,* LAURA *catches her breath, thrusts the bowl of ornaments away and seats herself stiffly before the diagram of the typewriter keyboard as though it held her spellbound. Something has happened to* AMANDA. *It is written in her face as she climbs to the landing: a look that is grim and hopeless and a little absurd.*

She has on one of those cheap or imitation velvety-looking cloth coats with imitation fur collar. Her hat is five or six years old, one of those dreadful cloche hats that were worn in the late twenties, and she is clasping an enormous black patent-leather pocketbook with nickel clasp and initials. This is her full-dress outfit, the one she usually wears to the D.A.R.

Before entering she looks through the door.

She purses her lips, opens her eyes wide, rolls them upward and shakes her head.

Then she slowly lets herself in the door. Seeing her mother's expression LAURA *touches her lips with a nervous gesture.*

LAURA: Hello, Mother, I was—[*She makes a nervous gesture toward the chart on the wall.* AMANDA *leans against the shut door and stares at* LAURA *with a martyred look.*]

AMANDA: Deception? Deception? [*She slowly removes her hat and gloves, continuing the swift suffering stare. She lets the hat and gloves fall on the floor—a bit of acting.*]

LAURA [*shakily*]: How was the D.A.R. meeting? [AMANDA *slowly opens her purse and removes a dainty white handkerchief which she shakes out delicately and delicately touches to her lips and nostrils.*] Didn't you go to the D.A.R. meeting, Mother?

AMANDA [*faintly, almost inaudibly*]: —No.—No. [*Then more forcibly.*] I did not have the strength—to go to the D.A.R. In fact, I did not have the courage!

I wanted to find a hole in the ground and hide myself in it forever! [*She crosses slowly to the wall and removes the diagram of the typewriter keyboard. She holds it in front of her for a second, staring at it sweetly and sorrowfully—then bites her lips and tears it in two pieces.*]

LAURA [*faintly*]: Why did you do that, Mother? [AMANDA *repeats the same procedure with the chart of the Gregg Alphabet.*] Why are you—

AMANDA: Why? Why? How old are you, Laura?

LAURA: Mother, you know my age.

AMANDA: I thought that you were an adult; it seems that I was mistaken. [*She crosses slowly to the sofa and sinks down and stares at* LAURA.]

LAURA: Please don't stare at me, Mother.

AMANDA *closes her eyes and lowers her head. Count ten.*

AMANDA: What are we going to do, what is going to become of us, what is the future?

Count ten.

LAURA: Has something happened, Mother? [AMANDA *draws a long breath and takes out the handkerchief again. Dabbing process.*] Mother, has—something happened?

AMANDA: I'll be all right in a minute. I'm just bewildered—[*count five*]—by life. . . .

LAURA: Mother, I wish that you would tell me what's happened.

AMANDA: As you know, I was supposed to be inducted into my office at the D.A.R. this afternoon. [*Image: A Swarm of Typewriters.*] But I stopped off at Rubicam's Business College to speak to your teachers about your having a cold and ask them what progress they thought you were making down there.

LAURA: Oh. . . .

AMANDA: I went to the typing instructor and introduced myself as your mother. She didn't know who you were. Wingfield, she said. We don't have any such student enrolled at the school! I assured her she did, that you had been going to classes since early in January. "I wonder," she said, "if you could be talking about that terribly shy little girl who dropped out of school after only a few days' attendance?" "No," I said, "Laura, my daughter, has been going to school every day for the past six weeks!" "Excuse me," she said. She took the attendance book out and there was your name, unmistakably printed, and all the dates you were absent until they decided that you had dropped out of school. I still said, "No, there must have been some mistake! There must have been some mix-up in the records!" And she said, "No—I remember her perfectly now. Her hand shook so that she couldn't hit the right keys! The first time we gave a speed-test, she broke down completely—was sick at the stomach and almost had to be carried into the wash-room! After that morning she never showed up any more. We phoned the house but never got any answer"—while I was working at Famous and Barr, I suppose, demonstrating those—Oh! I felt so weak I could barely keep on my feet. I had to sit down while they got me a glass of water! Fifty dollars' tuition, all of our plans—my hopes and ambitions for you—just gone up the spout, just gone up the spout like that. [LAURA *draws a long breath and gets awkwardly to her feet. She crosses to the victrola and winds it up.*] What are you doing?

LAURA: Oh! [*She releases the handle and returns to her seat.*]

AMANDA: Laura, where have you been going when you've gone out pretending that you were going to business college?

LAURA: I've just been going out walking.

AMANDA: That's not true.

LAURA: It is. I just went walking.

AMANDA: Walking? Walking? In winter? Deliberately courting pneumonia in that light coat? Where did you walk to, Laura?

LAURA: It was the lesser of two evils, Mother. [*Image: Winter Scene in Park.*] I couldn't go back up. I—threw up—on the floor!

AMANDA: From half past seven till after five every day you mean to tell me you walked around in the park, because you wanted to make me think that you were still going to Rubicam's Business College?

LAURA: It wasn't as bad as it sounds. I went inside places to get warmed up.

AMANDA: Inside where?

LAURA: I went in the art museum and the bird-houses at the Zoo. I visited the penguins every day! Sometimes I did without lunch and went to the movies. Lately I've been spending most of my afternoons in the Jewel-box, that big glass house where they raise the tropical flowers.

AMANDA: You did all this to deceive me, just for the deception? [LAURA *looks down.*] Why?

LAURA: Mother, when you're disappointed, you get that awful suffering look on your face, like the picture of Jesus' mother in the museum!

AMANDA: Hush!

LAURA: I couldn't face it.

Pause. A whisper of strings.

[*Legend: "The Crust of Humility."*]

AMANDA [*hopelessly fingering the huge pocketbook*]: So what are we going to do the rest of our lives? Stay home and watch the parades go by? Amuse ourselves with the glass menagerie, darling? Eternally play those worn-out phonograph records your father left as a painful reminder of him? We won't have a business career—we've given that up because it gave us nervous indigestion! [*Laughs wearily.*] What is there left but dependency all our lives? I know so well what becomes of unmarried women who aren't prepared to occupy a position. I've seen such pitiful cases in the South—barely tolerated spinsters living upon the grudging patronage of sister's husband or brother's wife!—stuck away in some little mousetrap of a room—encouraged by one in-law to visit another—little birdlike women without any nest—eating the crust of humility all their life! Is that the future that we've mapped out for ourselves? I swear it's the only alternative I can think of! It isn't a very pleasant alternative, is it? Of course—some girls *do marry.* [LAURA *twists her hands nervously.*] Haven't you ever liked some boy?

LAURA: Yes. I liked one once. [*Rises.*] I came across his picture a while ago.

AMANDA [*with some interest*]: He gave you his picture?

LAURA: No, it's in the year-book.

AMANDA [*disappointed*]: Oh—a high-school boy.

[*Screen Image:* JIM *as a High-School Hero Bearing a Silver Cup.*]

LAURA: Yes. His name was Jim. [LAURA *lifts the heavy annual from the clawfoot table.*] Here he is in *The Pirates of Penzance.*

AMANDA [*absently*]: The what?

LAURA: The operetta the senior class put on. He had a wonderful voice and we sat across the aisle from each other Mondays, Wednesdays and Fridays in the Aud. Here he is with the silver cup for debating! See his grin?

AMANDA [*absently*]: He must have had a jolly disposition.

LAURA: He used to call me—Blue Roses.

[*Image: Blue Roses.*]

AMANDA: Why did he call you such a name as that?

LAURA: When I had that attack of pleurosis—he asked me what was the matter when I came back. I said pleurosis—he thought that I said Blue Roses! So that's what he always called me after that. Whenever he saw me, he'd holler, "Hello, Blue Roses!" I didn't care for the girl that he went out with. Emily Meisenbach. Emily was the best-dressed girl at Soldan. She never struck me, though, as being sincere. . . . It says in the Personal Section—they're engaged. That's—six years ago! They must be married by now.

AMANDA: Girls that aren't cut out for business careers usually wind up married to some nice man. [*Gets up with a spark of revival.*] Sister, that's what you'll do!

LAURA *utters a startled, doubtful laugh. She reaches quickly for a piece of glass.*

LAURA: But, Mother—

AMANDA: Yes? [*Crossing to photograph.*]

LAURA [*in a tone of frightened apology*]: I'm—crippled!

[*Image: Screen.*]

AMANDA: Nonsense! Laura, I've told you never, never to use that word. Why, you're not crippled, you just have a little defect—hardly noticeable, even! When people have some slight disadvantage like that, they cultivate other things to make up for it—develop charm—and vivacity—and—*charm!* That's all you have to do! [*She turns again to the photograph.*] One thing your father had *plenty of*—was *charm!*

TOM *motions to the fiddle in the wings.*

[*The Scene Fades out with Music.*]

Scene III

[*Legend on the Screen: "After the Fiasco—"*]

TOM *speaks from the fire-escape landing.*

TOM: After the fiasco at Rubicam's Business College, the idea of getting a gentleman caller for Laura began to play a more important part in Mother's calculations. It became an obsession. Like some archetype of the universal unconscious, the image of the gentleman caller haunted our small apartment. . . . [*Image: Young Man at Door with Flowers.*] An evening at home rarely passed without some allusion to this image, this specter, this hope. . . . Even when he wasn't mentioned, his presence hung in Mother's preoccupied look and in my sister's frightened, apologetic manner—hung like a sentence passed upon the Wingfields! Mother was a woman of action as well as words. She began to take logical steps in the planned direction. Late that winter and in the early spring—realizing that extra money would be needed to properly feather the nest and plume the bird—she conducted a vigorous campaign on the telephone, roping in subscribers to one of those magazines for matrons called *The Home-maker's Companion,* the type of journal that features the serialized sublimations of ladies of letters who think in terms of delicate cuplike breasts, slim, tapering waists, rich, creamy thighs, eyes like wood-smoke in autumn, fingers that soothe and caress like strains of music, bodies as powerful as Etruscan sculpture.

[*Screen Image: Glamor Magazine Cover.*]

AMANDA *enters with phone on long extension cord. She is spotted in the dim stage.*

AMANDA: Ida Scott? This is Amanda Wingfield! We *missed* you at the D.A.R. last Monday! I said to myself: She's probably suffering with that sinus condition! How is that sinus condition? Horrors! Heaven have mercy!—You're a Christian martyr, yes, that's what you are, a Christian martyr! Well, I just now happened to notice that your subscription to the *Companion*'s about to expire! Yes, it expires with the next issue, honey!—just when that wonderful new serial by Bessie Mae Hopper is getting off to such an exciting start. Oh, honey, it's something that you can't miss! You remember how *Gone With the Wind* took everybody by storm? You simply couldn't go out if you hadn't read it. All everybody *talked* was Scarlett O'Hara. Well, this is a book that critics already compare to *Gone With the Wind*. It's the *Gone With the Wind* of the post-World War generation—What?—Burning?—Oh, honey, don't let them burn, go take a look in the oven and I'll hold the wire! Heavens—I think she's hung up!

[*Dim Out.*]

[*Legend on Screen: "You Think I'm in Love with Continental Shoemakers?"*]

Before the stage is lighted, the violent voices of TOM *and* AMANDA *are heard. They are quarreling behind the portieres. In front of them stands* LAURA *with clenched hands and panicky expression.*

A clear pool of light on her figure throughout this scene.

TOM: What in Christ's name am I—

AMANDA [*shrilly*]: Don't you use that—

TOM: Supposed to do!

AMANDA: Expression! Not in my—

TOM: Ohhh!

AMANDA: Presence! Have you gone out of your senses?

TOM: I have, that's true, *driven* out!

AMANDA: What is the matter with you, you—big—big—IDIOT!

TOM: Look—I've got *no thing,* no single thing—

AMANDA: Lower your voice!

TOM: In my life here that I can call my OWN! Everything is—

AMANDA: Stop that shouting!

TOM: Yesterday you confiscated my books! You had the nerve to—

AMANDA: I took that horrible novel back to the library—yes! That hideous book by that insane Mr. Lawrence. [TOM *laughs wildly.*] I cannot control the output of diseased minds or people who cater to them—[TOM *laughs still more wildly.*] BUT I WON'T ALLOW SUCH FILTH BROUGHT INTO MY HOUSE! No, no, no, no, no!

TOM: House, house! Who pays rent on it, who makes a slave of himself to—

AMANDA [*fairly screeching*]: Don't you DARE to—

TOM: No, no, *I* musn't say things! *I've* got to just—

AMANDA: Let me tell you—

TOM: I don't want to hear any more! [*He tears the portieres open. The upstage area is lit with a turgid smoky red glow.*]

AMANDA*'s hair is in metal curlers and she wears a very old bathrobe, much too large for her slight figure, a relic of the faithless Mr. Wingfield.*

An upright typewriter and a wild disarray of manuscripts are on the dropleaf table. The quarrel was probably precipitated by AMANDA*'s interruption of his creative labor. A chair lying overthrown on the floor.*

Their gesticulating shadows are cast on the ceiling by the fiery glow.

AMANDA: You *will* hear more, you—

TOM: No, I won't hear more, I'm going out!

AMANDA: You come right back in—

TOM: Out, out, out! Because I'm—

AMANDA: Come back here, Tom Wingfield! I'm not through talking to you!

TOM: Oh, go—

LAURA [*desperately*]: Tom!

AMANDA: You're going to listen, and no more insolence from you! I'm at the end of my patience! [*He comes back toward her.*]

TOM: What do you think I'm at? Aren't I supposed to have any patience to reach the end of, Mother? I know, I know. It seems unimportant to you, what I'm *doing*—what I *want* to do—having a little *difference* between them! You don't think that—

AMANDA: I think you've been doing things that you're ashamed of. That's why you act like this. I don't believe that you go every night to the movies. Nobody goes to the movies night after night. Nobody in their right minds goes to the movies as often as you pretend to. People don't go to the movies at nearly midnight, and movies don't let out at two A.M. Come in stumbling. Muttering to yourself like a maniac! You get three hours' sleep and then go to work. Oh, I can picture the way you're doing down there. Moping, doping, because you're in no condition.

TOM [*wildly*]: No, I'm in no condition!

AMANDA: What right have you got to jeopardize your job? Jeopardize the security of us all? How do you think we'd manage if you were—

TOM: Listen! You think I'm crazy *about* the *warehouse?* [*He bends fiercely toward her slight figure.*] You think I'm in love with the Continental Shoemakers? You think I want to spend fifty-five *years* down there in that—*celotex interior!* with—*fluorescent*—*tubes!* Look! I'd rather somebody picked up a crowbar and battered out my brains—than go back mornings! *I go!* Every time you come in yelling that God damn "*Rise and Shine!*" "*Rise and Shine!*" I say to myself "How *lucky dead* people are!" But I get up. I *go!* For sixty-five dollars a month I give up all that I dream of doing and being *ever!* And you say self—*self*'s all I ever think of. Why, listen, if self is what I thought of, Mother, I'd be where he is—GONE! [*Pointing to father's picture.*] As far as the system of transportation reaches! [*He starts past her. She grabs his arm.*] Don't grab at me, Mother!

AMANDA: Where are you going?

TOM: I'm going to the *movies!*

AMANDA: I don't believe that lie!

TOM [*crouching toward her, overtowering her tiny figure. She backs away, gasping*]: I'm going to opium dens! Yes, opium dens, dens of vice and criminals' hang-outs, Mother. I've joined the Hogan gang, I'm a hired assassin, I carry a tommy-gun in a violin case! I run a string of cat-houses in the Valley! They call me Killer, Killer Wingfield, I'm leading a double-life, a simple, honest warehouse worker by day, by night a dynamic *czar* of the *underworld, Mother*. I go to gambling casinos, I spin away fortunes on the roulette table! I wear a patch over one eye and a false mustache, sometimes I put on green whiskers. On those occasions they call me—*El Diablo!* Oh, I could tell you things to make you sleepless! My enemies plan to dynamite this place. They're going to blow us all sky-high some night! I'll be glad, very happy, and so will you! You'll go up, up on a broomstick, over Blue Mountain with seventeen gentlemen callers! You ugly—babbling old—*witch*. . . . [*He goes through a series of violent, clumsy movements, seizing his overcoat, lunging to the door, pulling it fiercely open. The women watch him, aghast. His arm catches in the sleeve of the coat as he struggles to pull it on. For a moment he is pinioned by the bulky garment. With an outraged groan he tears the coat off again, splitting the shoulders of it and hurls it across the room. It strikes against the shelf of* LAURA*'s glass collection, there is a tinkle of shattering glass.* LAURA *cries out as if wounded.*]

[*Music Legend: "The Glass Menagerie."*]

LAURA [*shrilly*]: *My glass!*—menagerie. . . . [*She covers her face and turns away.*]

But AMANDA *is still stunned and stupefied by the "ugly witch" so that she barely notices this occurrence. Now she recovers her speech.*

AMANDA [*in an awful voice*]: I won't speak to you—until you apologize!

[*She crosses through portieres and draws them together behind her.* TOM *is left with* LAURA. LAURA *clings weakly to the mantel with her face averted.* TOM *stares at her stupidly for a moment. Then he crosses to shelf. Drops, awkwardly to his knees to collect the fallen glass, glancing at* LAURA *as if he would speak but couldn't.*]

"The Glass Menagerie" steals in as

[*The Scene Dims Out.*]

Scene IV

The interior is dark. Faint light in the alley.

A deep-voiced bell in a church is tolling the hour of five as the scene commences.

TOM *appears at the top of the alley. After each solemn boom of the bell in the tower, he shakes a little noise-maker or rattle as if to express the tiny spasm of man in contrast to the sustained power and dignity of the Almighty. This and the unsteadiness of his advance make it evident that he has been drinking.*

As he climbs the few steps to the fire-escape landing light steals up inside. LAURA *appears in night-dress, observing* TOM*'s empty bed in the front room.*

TOM *fishes in his pockets for the door-key, removing a motley assortment of articles in the search, including a perfect shower of movie-ticket stubs and an empty bottle. At last he finds the key, but just as he is about to insert it, it slips from his fingers. He strikes a match and crouches below the door.*

TOM [*bitterly*]: One crack—and it falls through!

LAURA *opens the door.*

LAURA: Tom! Tom, what are you doing?

TOM: Looking for a door-key.

LAURA: Where have you been all this time?

TOM: I have been to the movies.

LAURA: All this time at the movies?

TOM: There was a very long program. There was a Garbo picture and a Mickey Mouse and a travelogue and a newsreel and a preview of coming attractions. And there was an organ solo and a collection for the milk-fund—simultaneously—which ended up in a terrible fight between a fat lady and an usher!

LAURA [*innocently*]: Did you have to stay through everything?

TOM: Of course! And, oh, I forgot! There was a big stage show! The headliner on this stage show was Malvolio the Magician. He performed wonderful tricks, many of them, such as pouring water back and forth between pitchers. First it turned to wine and then it turned to beer and then it turned to whiskey. I know it was whiskey it finally turned into because he needed somebody to come up out of the audience to help him, and I came up—both shows! It was Kentucky Straight Bourbon. A very generous fellow, he gave souvenirs. [*He pulls from his back pocket a shimmering rainbow-colored scarf.*] He gave me this. This is his magic scarf. You can have it, Laura. You wave it over a canary cage and you get a bowl of gold-fish. You wave it over the gold-fish bowl and they fly away canaries. . . . But the wonderfullest trick of all was the coffin trick. We nailed him into a coffin and he got out of the coffin without removing one nail. [*He has come inside.*] There is a trick that would come in handy for me—get me out of this 2 by 4 situation! [*Flops onto bed and starts removing shoes.*]

LAURA: Tom—Shhh!

TOM: What you shushing me for?

LAURA: You'll wake up Mother.

TOM: Goody, goody! Pay 'er back for all those "Rise an' Shines." [*Lies down, groaning.*] You know it don't take much intelligence to get yourself into a nailed-up coffin, Laura. But who in hell ever got himself out of one without removing one nail?

As if in answer, the father's grinning photograph lights up.

[*Scene Dims Out*]

Immediately following: The church bell is heard striking six. At the sixth stroke the alarm clock goes off in AMANDA*'s room, and after a few moments we hear her calling: "Rise and Shine! Rise and Shine!* LAURA, *go tell your brother to rise and shine!"*

TOM [*sitting up slowly*]: I'll rise—but I won't shine.

The light increases.

AMANDA: Laura, tell your brother his coffee is ready.

LAURA *slips into front room.*

LAURA: Tom! it's nearly seven. Don't make Mother nervous. [*He stares at her stupidly. Beseechingly.*] Tom, speak to Mother this morning. Make up with her, apologize, speak to her!

TOM: She won't to me. It's her that started not speaking.

LAURA: If you just say you're sorry she'll start speaking.

TOM: Her not speaking—is that such a tragedy?

LAURA: Please—please!

AMANDA [*calling from kitchenette*]: Laura, are you going to do what I asked you to do, or do I have to get dressed and go out myself?

LAURA: Going, going—soon as I get on my coat! [*She pulls on a shapeless felt hat with nervous, jerky movement, pleadingly glancing at* TOM. *Rushes awkwardly for coat. The coat is one of* AMANDA*'s, inaccurately made-over the sleeves too short for* LAURA.] Butter and what else?

AMANDA [*entering upstage*]: Just butter. Tell them to charge it.

LAURA: Mother, they make such faces when I do that.

AMANDA: Sticks and stones may break my bones, but the expression on Mr. Garfinkel's face won't harm us! Tell your brother his coffee is getting cold.

LAURA [*at door*]: Do what I asked you, will you, will you, Tom?

He looks sullenly away.

AMANDA: Laura, go now or just don't go at all!

LAURA [*rushing out*]: Going—going! [*A second later she cries out.* TOM *springs up and crosses to the door.* AMANDA *rushes anxiously in.* TOM *opens the door.*]

TOM: Laura?

LAURA: I'm all right. I slipped, but I'm all right.

AMANDA [*peering anxiously after her*]: If anyone breaks a leg on those fire-escape steps, the landlord ought to be sued for every cent he possesses!

[*She shuts door. Remembers she isn't speaking and returns to other room.*]

As TOM *enters listlessly for his coffee, she turns her back to him and stands rigidly facing the window on the gloomy gray vault of the areaway. Its light on her face with its aged but childish features is cruelly sharp, satirical as a Daumier print.*

[*Music Under: "Ave Maria."*]

TOM *glances sheepishly but sullenly at her averted figure and slumps at the table. The coffee is scalding hot; he sips it and gasps and spits it back in the cup. At his gasp,* AMANDA *catches her breath and half turns. Then catches herself and turns back to window.*

TOM *blows on his coffee, glancing sidewise at his mother. She clears her throat.* TOM *clears his. He starts to rise. Sinks back down again, scratches his head, clears his throat again.* AMANDA *coughs.* TOM *raises his cup in both hands to blow on it, his eyes staring over the rim of it at his mother for several moments. Then he slowly sets the cup down and awkwardly and hesitantly rises from the chair.*

TOM [*hoarsely*]: Mother. I—I apologize. Mother. [AMANDA *draws a quick, shuddering breath. Her face works grotesquely. She breaks into childlike tears.*] I'm sorry for what I said, for everything that I said, I didn't mean it.

AMANDA [*sobbingly*]: My devotion has made me a witch and so I make myself hateful to my children!

TOM: No you *don't.*

AMANDA: I worry so much, don't sleep, it makes me nervous!

TOM [*gently*]: I understand that.

AMANDA: I've had to put up a solitary battle all these years. But you're my right-hand bower! Don't fall down, don't fail!

TOM [*gently*]: I try, Mother.

AMANDA [*with great enthusiasm*]: Try and you will SUCCEED! [*The notion makes her breathless.*] Why, you—you're just *full* of natural endowments! Both of my children—they're *unusual* children! Don't you think I know it? I'm so—*proud!* Happy and—feel I've—so much to be thankful for but—Promise me one thing, son!

TOM: What, Mother?

AMANDA: Promise, son, you'll—never be a drunkard!

TOM [*turns to her grinning*]: I will never be a drunkard, Mother.

AMANDA: That's what frightened me so, that you'd be drinking! Eat a bowl of Purina!

TOM: Just coffee, Mother.

AMANDA: Shredded wheat biscuit?

TOM: No. No, Mother, just coffee.

AMANDA: You can't put in a day's work on an empty stomach. You've got ten minutes—don't gulp! Drinking too-hot liquids makes cancer of the stomach. . . . Put cream in.

TOM: No, thank you.

AMANDA: To cool it.

TOM: No! No, thank you, I want it black.

AMANDA: I know, but it's not good for you. We have to do all that we can to build ourselves up. In these trying times we live in, all that we have to cling to is—each other. . . . That's why it's so important to—Tom, I—I sent out your sister so I could discuss something with you. If you hadn't spoken I would have spoken to you. [*Sits down.*]

TOM [*gently*]: What is it, Mother, that you want to discuss?

AMANDA: Laura!

TOM *puts his cup down slowly.*

[*Legend on Screen: "Laura."*]

[*Music: "The Glass Menagerie."*]

TOM: —Oh.—Laura . . .

AMANDA [*touching his sleeve*]: You know how Laura is. So quiet but—still water runs deep! She notices things and I think she—broods about them. [TOM *looks up.*] A few days ago I came in and she was crying.

TOM: What about?

AMANDA: You.

TOM: Me?

AMANDA: She has an idea that you're not happy here.

TOM: What gave her that idea?

AMANDA: What gives her any idea? However, you do act strangely. I—I'm not criticizing, understand *that!* I know your ambitions do not lie in the warehouse, that like everybody in the whole wide world—you've had to—make sacrifices, but—Tom—Tom—life's not easy, it calls for—Spartan endurance! There's so many things in my heart that I cannot describe to you! I've never told you but I—*loved* your father. . . .

TOM [*gently*]: I know that, Mother.

AMANDA: And you—when I see you taking after his ways! Staying out late—and—well, you *had* been drinking the night you were in that—terrifying condition! Laura says that you hate the apartment and that you go out nights to get away from it! Is that true, Tom?

TOM: No. You say there's so much in your heart that you can't describe to me. That's true of me, too. There's so much in my heart that I can't describe to *you!* So let's respect each other's—

AMANDA: But, why—*why,* Tom—are you always so *restless?* Where do you go to, nights?

TOM: I—go to the movies.

AMANDA: Why do you go to the movies so much, Tom?

TOM: I go to the movies because—I like adventure. Adventure is something I don't have much of at work, so I go to the movies.

AMANDA: But, Tom, you go to the movies *entirely too much!*

TOM: I like a lot of adventure.

AMANDA *looks baffled, then hurt. As the familiar inquisition resumes he becomes hard and impatient again.* AMANDA *slips back into her querulous attitude toward him.*

[*Image on Screen: Sailing Vessel with Jolly Roger.*]

AMANDA: Most young men find adventure in their careers.

TOM: Then most young men are not employed in a warehouse.

AMANDA: The world is full of young men employed in warehouses and offices and factories.

TOM: Do all of them find adventure in their careers?

AMANDA: They do or they do without it! Not everybody has a craze for adventure.

TOM: Man is by instinct a lover, a hunter, a fighter, and none of those instincts are given much play at the warehouse!

AMANDA: Man is by instinct! Don't quote instinct to me! Instinct is something that people have got away from! It belongs to animals! Christian adults don't want it!

TOM: What do Christian adults want, then, Mother?

AMANDA: Superior things! Things of the mind and the spirit! Only animals have to satisfy instincts! Surely your aims are somewhat higher than theirs! Than monkeys—pigs—

TOM: I reckon they're not.

AMANDA: You're joking. However, that isn't what I wanted to discuss.

TOM [*rising*]: I haven't much time.

AMANDA [*pushing his shoulders*]: Sit down.

TOM: You want me to punch in red at the warehouse, Mother?

AMANDA: You have five minutes. I want to talk about Laura.

[*Legend: "Plans and Provisions."*]

TOM: All right! What about Laura?

AMANDA: We have to be making plans and provisions for her. She's older than you, two years, and nothing has happened. She just drifts along doing nothing. It frightens me terribly how she just drifts along.

TOM: I guess she's the type that people call home girls.

AMANDA: There's no such type, and if there is, it's a pity! That is unless the home is hers, with a husband!

TOM: What?

AMANDA: Oh, I can see the handwriting on the wall as plain as I see the nose in the front of my face! It's terrifying! More and more you remind me of your father! He was out all hours without explanation—Then *left! Goodbye!* And me with the bag to hold. I saw that letter you got from the Merchant Marine. I know what you're dreaming of. I'm not standing here blindfolded. Very well, then. Then *do* it! But not till there's somebody to take your place.

TOM: What do you mean?

AMANDA: I mean that as soon as Laura has got somebody to take care of her, married, a home of her own, independent—why, then you'll be free to go wherever you please, on land, on sea, whichever way the wind blows! But until that time you've got to look out for your sister. I don't say me because I'm old and don't matter! I say for your sister because she's young and dependent. I put her in business college—a dismal failure! Frightened her so it made her sick to her stomach. I took her over to the Young People's League at the church. Another fiasco. She spoke to nobody, nobody spoke to her. Now all she does is fool with those pieces of glass and play those worn-out records. What kind of a life is that for a girl to lead!

TOM: What can I do about it?

AMANDA: Overcome selfishness! Self, self, self is all that you ever think of! [TOM *springs up and crosses to get his coat. It is ugly and bulky. He pulls on a cap with earmuffs.*] Where is your muffler? Put your wool muffler on! [*He snatches it angrily from the closet and tosses it around his neck and pulls both ends tight.*] Tom! I haven't said what I had in mind to ask you.

TOM: I'm too late to—

AMANDA [*catching his arms—very importunately. Then shyly*]: Down at the warehouse, aren't there some—nice young men?

TOM: No!

AMANDA: There *must* be—*some*.

TOM: Mother—

Gesture.

AMANDA: Find out one that's clean-living—doesn't drink and—ask him out for sister!

TOM: What?

AMANDA: For *sister!* To *meet!* Get *acquainted!*

TOM [*stamping to door*]: Oh, my *go-osh!*

AMANDA: Will you? [*He opens door. Imploringly.*] Will you? [*He starts down.*] Will you? *Will* you dear?

TOM [*calling back*]: YES!

AMANDA *closes the door hesitantly and with a troubled but faintly hopeful expression.*

[*Screen Image: Glamor Magazine Cover.*]

Spot AMANDA *at phone.*

AMANDA: Ella Cartwright? This is Amanda Wingfield! How are you honey? How is that kidney condition? [*Count five.*] *Horrors!* [*Count five.*] You're a Christian martyr, yes, honey, that's what you are, a Christian martyr! Well, I just happened to notice in my little red book that your subscription to the *Companion* has just run out! I knew that you wouldn't want to miss out on the wonderful serial starting in this new issue. It's by Bessie Mae Hopper, the first thing she's written since *Honeymoon for Three*. Wasn't that a strange and interesting story? Well, this one is even lovelier, I believe. It has a sophisticated society background. It's all about the horsey set on Long Island!

[*Fade Out.*]

Scene V

[*Legend on Screen: "Annunciation."*] *Fade with music.*

It is early dusk of a spring evening. Supper has just been finished at the Wingfield apartment. AMANDA *and* LAURA *in light colored dresses are removing dishes from the table, in the upstage area, which is shadowy, their movements formalized almost as a dance or ritual, their moving forms as pale and silent as moths.*

TOM, *in white shirt and trousers, rises from the table and crosses toward the fire-escape.*

AMANDA [*as he passes her*]: Son, will you do me a favor?

TOM: What?

AMANDA: Comb your hair! You look so pretty when your hair is combed! [TOM *slouches on sofa with evening paper. Enormous caption "Franco Triumphs."*] There is only one respect in which I would like you to emulate your father.

TOM: What respect is that?

AMANDA: The care he always took of his appearance. He never allowed himself to look untidy. [*He throws down the paper and crosses to fire-escape.*] Where are you going?

TOM: I'm going out to smoke.

AMANDA: You smoke too much. A pack a day at fifteen cents a pack. How much would that amount to in a month? Thirty times fifteen is how much, Tom? Figure it out and you will be astounded at what you could save. Enough to give you a night-school course in accounting at Washington U! Just think what a wonderful thing that would be for you, son!

TOM *is unmoved by the thought.*

TOM: I'd rather smoke. [*He steps out on landing, letting the screen door slam.*]

AMANDA [*sharply*]: I know! That's the tragedy of it. . . . [*Alone, she turns to look at her husband's picture.*]

[*Dance Music: "All the World Is Waiting for the Sunrise!"*]

TOM [*to the audience*]: Across the alley from us was the Paradise Dance Hall. On evenings in spring the windows and doors were open and the music came outdoors. Sometimes the lights were turned out except for a large glass sphere that hung from the ceiling. It would turn slowly about and filter the dusk with delicate rainbow colors. Then the orchestra played a waltz or a tango, something that had a slow and sensuous rhythm. Couples would come outside, to the relative privacy of the alley. You could see them kissing behind ashpits and telephone poles. This was the compensation for lives that passed like mine, without any change or adventure. Adventure and change were imminent in this year. They were waiting around the corner for all these kids. Suspended in the mist over Berchtesgaden, caught in the folds of Chamberlain's umbrella—In Spain there was Guernica! But here there was only hot swing music and liquor, dance halls, bars, and movies, and sex that hung in the gloom like a chandelier and flooded the world with brief, deceptive rainbows. . . . All the world was waiting for bombardments!

AMANDA *turns from the picture and comes outside.*

AMANDA [*sighing*]: A fire-escape landing's a poor excuse for a porch. [*She spreads a newspaper on a step and sits down, gracefully and demurely as if she were settling into a swing on a Mississippi veranda.*] What are you looking at?

TOM: The moon.

AMANDA: Is there a moon this evening?

TOM: It's rising over Garfinkel's Delicatessen.

AMANDA: So it is! A little silver slipper of a moon. Have you made a wish on it yet?

TOM: Um-hum.

AMANDA: What did you wish for?

TOM: That's a secret.

AMANDA: A secret, huh? Well, I won't tell mine either. I will be just as mysterious as you.

TOM: I bet I can guess what yours is.

AMANDA: Is my head so transparent?

TOM: You're not a sphinx.

AMANDA: No, I don't have secrets. I'll tell you what I wished for on the moon. Success and happiness for my precious children! I wish for that whenever there's a moon, and when there isn't a moon, I wish for it, too.

TOM: I thought perhaps you wished for a gentleman caller.

AMANDA: Why do you say that?

TOM: Don't you remember asking me to fetch one?

AMANDA: I remember suggesting that it would be nice for your sister if you brought some nice young man from the warehouse. I think I've made that suggestion more than once.

TOM: Yes, you have made it repeatedly.

AMANDA: Well?

TOM: We are going to have one.

AMANDA: *What?*

TOM: A gentleman caller!

[*The Annunciation Is Celebrated with Music.*]

AMANDA *rises.*

[*Image on Screen: Caller with Bouquet.*]

AMANDA: You mean you have asked some nice young man to come over?

TOM: Yep. I've asked him to dinner.

AMANDA: You really did?

TOM: I did!

AMANDA: You did, and did he—*accept?*

TOM: He did!

AMANDA: Well, well—well, well! That's—lovely!

TOM: I thought that you would be pleased.

AMANDA: It's definite, then?

TOM: Very definite.

AMANDA: Soon?

TOM: Very soon.

AMANDA: For heaven's sake, stop putting on and tell me some things, will you?

TOM: What things do you want me to tell you?

AMANDA: Naturally I would like to know when he's *coming!*

TOM: He's coming tomorrow.

AMANDA: *Tomorrow?*

TOM: Yep. Tomorrow.

AMANDA: But, Tom!

TOM: Yes, Mother?

AMANDA: Tomorrow gives me no time!

TOM: Time for what?

AMANDA: Preparations! Why didn't you phone me at once, as soon as you asked him, the minute that he accepted? Then, don't you see, I could have been getting ready!

TOM: You don't have to make any fuss.

AMANDA: Oh, Tom, Tom, Tom, of course I have to make a fuss! I want things nice, not sloppy! Not thrown together. I'll certainly have to do some fast thinking, won't I?

TOM: I don't see why you have to think at all.

AMANDA: You just don't know. We can't have a gentleman caller in a pigsty! All my wedding silver has to be polished, the monogrammed table linen ought to be laundered! The windows have to be washed and fresh curtains put up. And how about clothes? We have to *wear* something, don't we?

TOM: Mother, this boy is no one to make a fuss over!

AMANDA: Do you realize he's the first young man we've introduced to your sister? It's terrible, dreadful, disgraceful that poor little sister has never received a single gentleman caller! Tom, come inside! [*She opens the screen door.*]

TOM: What for?

AMANDA: I want to ask you some things.

TOM: If you're going to make such a fuss, I'll call it off, I'll tell him not to come.

AMANDA: You certainly won't do anything of the kind. Nothing offends people worse than broken engagements. It simply means I'll have to work like a Turk! We won't be brilliant, but we'll pass inspection. Come on inside. [TOM *follows, groaning*.] Sit down.

TOM: Any particular place you would like me to sit?

AMANDA: Thank heavens I've got that new sofa! I'm also making payments on a floor lamp I'll have sent out! And put the chintz covers on, they'll brighten things up! Of course I'd hoped to have these walls repapered. . . . What is the young man's name?

TOM: His name is O'Connor.

AMANDA: That, of course, means fish—tomorrow is Friday! I'll have that salmon loaf—with Durkee's dressing! What does he do? He works at the warehouse?

TOM: Of course! How else would I—

AMANDA: Tom, he—doesn't drink?

TOM: Why do you ask me that?

AMANDA: Your father *did!*

TOM: Don't get started on that!

AMANDA: He *does* drink, then?

TOM: Not that I know of!

AMANDA: Make sure, be certain! The last thing I want for my daughter's a boy who drinks!

TOM: Aren't you being a little premature? Mr. O'Connor has not yet appeared on the scene!

AMANDA: But will tomorrow. To meet your sister, and what do I know about his character? Nothing! Old maids are better off than wives of drunkards!

TOM: Oh, my God!

AMANDA: Be still!

TOM [*leaning forward to whisper*]: Lots of fellows meet girls whom they don't marry!

AMANDA: Oh, talk sensibly, Tom—and don't be sarcastic! [*She has gotten a hair-brush*.]

TOM: What are you doing?

AMANDA: I'm brushing that cow-lick down! What is this young man's position at the warehouse?

TOM [*submitting grimly to the brush and the interrogation*]: This young man's position is that of a shipping clerk, Mother.

AMANDA: Sounds to me like a fairly responsible job, the sort of a job *you* would be in if you just had more *get-up*. What is his salary? Have you got any idea?

TOM: I would judge it to be approximately eighty-five dollars a month.

AMANDA: Well—not princely, but—

TOM: Twenty more than I make.

AMANDA: Yes, how well I know! But for a family man, eighty-five dollars a month is not much more than you can just get by on. . . .

TOM: Yes, but Mr. O'Connor is not a family man.

AMANDA: He might be, mightn't he? Some time in the future?

TOM: I see. Plans and provisions.

AMANDA: You are the only man that I know of who ignores the fact that the future becomes the present, the present the past, and the past turns into everlasting regret if you don't plan for it!

TOM: I will think that over and see what I can make of it.

AMANDA: Don't be supercilious with your mother! Tell me some more about this—what do you call him?

TOM: James D. O'Connor. The D. is for Delaney.

AMANDA: Irish on *both* sides! *Gracious!* And doesn't drink?

TOM: Shall I call him up and ask him right this minute?

AMANDA: The only way to find out about those things is to make discreet inquiries at the proper moment. When I was a girl in Blue Mountain and it was suspected that a young man drank, the girl whose attentions he had been receiving, if any girl *was,* would sometimes speak to the minister of his church, or rather her father would if her father was living, and sort of feel him out on the young man's character. That is the way such things are discreetly handled to keep a young woman from making a tragic mistake!

TOM: Then how did you happen to make a tragic mistake?

AMANDA: That innocent look of your father's had everyone fooled! He *smiled*—the world was *enchanted!* No girl can do worse than put herself at the mercy of a handsome appearance! I hope that Mr. O'Connor is not too good-looking.

TOM: No, he's not too good-looking. He's covered with freckles and hasn't too much of a nose.

AMANDA: He's not right-down homely, though?

TOM: Not right-down homely. Just medium homely, I'd say.

AMANDA: Character's what to look for in a man.

TOM: That's what I've always said, Mother.

AMANDA: You've never said anything of the kind and I suspect you would never give it a thought.

TOM: Don't be suspicious of me.

AMANDA: At least I hope he's the type that's up and coming.

TOM: I think he really goes in for self-improvement.

AMANDA: What reason have you to think so?

TOM: He goes to night school.

AMANDA [*beaming*]: Splendid! What does he do, I mean study?

TOM: Radio engineering and public speaking!

AMANDA: Then he has visions of being advanced in the world! Any young man who studies public speaking is aiming to have an executive job some day! And radio engineering? A thing for the future! Both of these facts are very illuminating. Those are the sort of things that a mother should know concerning any young man who comes to call on her daughter. Seriously or—not.

TOM: One little warning. He doesn't know about Laura. I didn't let on that we had dark ulterior motives. I just said, why don't you come have dinner with us? He said okay and that was the whole conversation.

AMANDA: I bet it was! You're eloquent as an oyster. However, he'll know about Laura when he gets here. When he sees how lovely and sweet and pretty she is, he'll thank his lucky stars he was asked to dinner.

TOM: Mother, you mustn't expect too much of Laura.

AMANDA: What do you mean?

TOM: Laura seems all those things to you and me because she's ours and we love her. We don't even notice she's crippled any more.

AMANDA: Don't say crippled! You know that I never allow that word to be used!

TOM: But face facts, Mother. She is and—that's not all—

AMANDA: What do you mean "not all"?

TOM: Laura is very different from other girls.

AMANDA: I think the difference is all to her advantage.

TOM: Not quite all—in the eyes of others—strangers—she's terribly shy and lives in a world of her own and those things make her seem a little peculiar to people outside the house.

AMANDA: Don't say peculiar.

TOM: Face the facts. She is.

[*The Dance-Hall Music Changes to a Tango that Has a Minor and Somewhat Ominous Tone.*]

AMANDA: In what way is she peculiar—may I ask?

TOM [*gently*]: She lives in a world of her own—a world of—little glass ornaments, Mother. . . . [*Gets up.* AMANDA *remains holding brush, looking at him, troubled.*] She plays old phonograph records and—that's about all—[*He glances at himself in the mirror and crosses to door.*]

AMANDA [*sharply*]: Where are you going?

TOM: I'm going to the movies. [*Out screen door.*]

AMANDA: Not to the movies, every night to the movies! [*Follows quickly to screen door.*] I don't believe you always go to the movies! [*He is gone.* AMANDA *looks worriedly after him for a moment. Then vitality and optimism return and she turns from the door. Crossing to portieres.*] Laura! Laura! [LAURA *answers from kitchenette.*]

LAURA: Yes, Mother.

AMANDA: Let those dishes go and come in front! [*Laura appears with dish towel. Gaily.*] Laura, come here and make a wish on the moon!

LAURA [*entering*]: Moon—moon?

AMANDA: A little silver slipper of a moon. Look over your left shoulder, Laura, and make a wish! [LAURA *looks faintly puzzled as if called out of sleep.* AMANDA *seizes her shoulders and turns her at angle by the door.*] Now! Now, darling, *wish!*

LAURA: What shall I wish for, Mother?

AMANDA: [*her voice trembling and her eyes suddenly filling with tears*]. Happiness! Good Fortune!

The violin rises and the stage dims out.

Scene VI

[*Image: High School Hero.*]

TOM: And so the following evening I brought Jim home to dinner. I had known Jim slightly in high school. In high school Jim was a hero. He had tremendous Irish good nature and vitality with the scrubbed and polished look of white chinaware. He seemed to move in a continual spotlight. He was a star in basketball, captain of the debating club, president of the senior class and the glee club and he sang the male lead in the annual light operas. He was always running or bounding, never just walking. He seemed always at the point of defeating the law of gravity. He was shooting with such velocity through his adolescence that you would logically expect him to arrive at nothing short of the White House by the time he was thirty. But Jim apparently ran into more interference after his graduation from Soldan. His speed had definitely slowed. Six years after he left high school he was holding a job that wasn't much better than mine.

[*Image: Clerk.*]

He was the only one at the warehouse with whom I was on friendly terms. I was valuable to him as someone who could remember his former glory, who had seen him win basketball games and the silver cup in debating. He knew of my secret practice of retiring to a cabinet of the washroom to work on poems when business was slack in the warehouse. He called me Shakespeare. And while the other boys in the warehouse regarded me with suspicious hostility, Jim took a humorous attitude toward me. Gradually his attitude affected the others, their hostility wore off and they also began to smile at me as people smile at an oddly fashioned dog who trots across their path at some distance.

I knew that Jim and Laura had known each other at Soldan, and I had heard Laura speak admiringly of his voice. I didn't know if Jim remembered her or not. In high school Laura had been as unobtrusive as Jim had been astonishing. If he did remember Laura, it was not as my sister, for when I asked him to dinner, he grinned and said, "You know, Shakespeare, I never thought of you as having folks!"

He was about to discover that I did. . . .

[*Light up Stage*]

[*Legend on Screen: "The Accent of a Coming Foot."*]

Friday evening. It is about five o'clock of a late spring evening which comes "scattering poems in the sky."

A delicate lemony light is in the Wingfield apartment.

AMANDA *has worked like a Turk in preparation for the gentleman caller. The results are astonishing. The new floor lamp with its rose-silk shade is in place, a colored paper lantern conceals the broken light fixture in the ceiling, new billowing white curtains are at the windows, chintz covers are on chairs and sofa, a pair of new sofa pillows make their initial appearance.*

Open boxes and tissue paper are scattered on the floor.

LAURA *stands in the middle with lifted arms while* AMANDA *crouches before her, adjusting the hem of the new dress, devout and ritualistic. The dress is colored and designed by memory. The arrangement of* LAURA*'s hair is changed; it is softer and more becoming. A fragile, unearthly prettiness has come out in* LAURA: *she is like a piece of translucent glass touched by light, given a momentary radiance, not actual, not lasting.*

AMANDA [*impatiently*]: Why are you trembling?

LAURA: Mother, you've made me so nervous!

AMANDA: How have I made you nervous?

LAURA: By all this fuss! You make it seem so important!

AMANDA: I don't understand you, Laura. You couldn't be satisfied with just sitting home, and yet whenever I try to arrange something for you, you seem to resist it. [*She gets up.*] Now take a look at yourself. No, wait! Wait just a moment—I have an idea!

LAURA: What is it now?

AMANDA *produces two powder puffs which she wraps in handkerchiefs and stuffs in* LAURA*'s bosom.*

LAURA: Mother, what are you doing?

AMANDA: They call them "Gay Deceivers"!

LAURA: I won't wear them!

AMANDA: You will!

LAURA: Why should I?

AMANDA: Because, to be painfully honest, your chest is flat.

LAURA: You make it seem like we were setting a trap.

AMANDA: All pretty girls are a trap, a pretty trap, and men expect them to be. [*Legend: "A Pretty Trap."*] Now look at yourself, young lady. This is the prettiest you will ever be! I've got to fix myself now! You're going to be surprised by your mother's appearance! [*She crosses through portieres, humming gaily.*]

LAURA *moves slowly to the long mirror and stares solemnly at herself.*

A wind blows the white curtains inward in a slow, graceful motion and with a faint sorrowful sighing.

AMANDA [*off stage*]: It isn't dark enough yet. [*She turns slowly before the mirror with a troubled look.*]

[*Legend on Screen: "This Is My Sister: Celebrate Her with Strings!" Music.*]

AMANDA [*laughing, off*]: I'm going to show you something. I'm going to make a spectacular appearance!

LAURA: What is it, Mother?

AMANDA: Possess your soul in patience—you will see! Something I've resurrected from that old trunk! Styles haven't changed so terribly much after all. . . . [*She parts the portieres.*] Now just look at your mother! [*She wears a girlish frock of yellowed voile with a blue silk sash. She carries a bunch of jonquils—the legend of her youth is nearly revived. Feverishly.*] This is the dress in which I led the cotillion. Won the cakewalk twice at Sunset Hill, wore one spring to the Governor's ball in Jackson! See how I sashayed around the ballroom, Laura? [*She raises her skirt and does a mincing step around the room.*] I wore it on Sundays for my gentlemen callers! I had it on the day I met your father—I had malaria fever all that spring. The change of climate from East Tennessee to the Delta—weakened resistance—I had a little temperature all the time—not enough to be serious—just enough to make me restless and giddy! Invitations poured in—parties all over the Delta!—"Stay in bed," said Mother, "you have fever!"—but I just wouldn't.—I took quinine but kept on going, going!—Evenings, dances!—Afternoons, long, long rides! Picnics—lovely!—So lovely, that country in May.—All lacy with dogwood, literally flooded with jonquils!—That was the spring I had the craze for jonquils. Jonquils became an absolute obsession. Mother said, "Honey, there's no more room for jonquils." And still I kept bringing in more jonquils. Whenever, wherever I saw them, I'd say, "Stop! Stop! I see jonquils!" I made the young men help me gather the jonquils! It was a joke, Amanda and her jonquils! Finally there were no more vases to hold them, every available space was filled with jonquils. No vases to hold them? All right, I'll hold them myself! And then I—[*She stops in front of the picture.*] [*Music.*] met your father! Malaria fever and jonquils and then—this—boy. . . . [*She switches on the rose-colored lamp.*] I hope they get here before it starts to rain. [*She crosses upstage and places the jonquils in bowl on table.*] I gave your brother a little extra change so he and Mr. O'Connor could take the service car home.

LAURA [*with altered look*]: What did you say his name was?

AMANDA: O'Connor.

LAURA: What is his first name?

AMANDA: I don't remember. Oh, yes, I do. It was—Jim!

LAURA *sways slightly and catches hold of a chair.*

[*Legend on Screen: "Not Jim!"*]

LAURA [*faintly*]: Not—Jim!

AMANDA: Yes, that was it, it was Jim! I've never known a Jim that wasn't nice!

[*Music: Ominous.*]

LAURA: Are you sure his name is Jim O'Connor?

AMANDA: Yes. Why?

LAURA: Is he the one that Tom used to know in high school?

AMANDA: He didn't say so. I think he just got to know him at the warehouse.

LAURA: There was a Jim O'Connor we both knew in high school—[*Then, with effort.*] If that is the one that Tom is bringing to dinner—you'll have to excuse me, I won't come to the table.

AMANDA: What sort of nonsense is this?

LAURA: You asked me once if I'd ever liked a boy. Don't you remember I showed you this boy's picture?

AMANDA: You mean the boy you showed me in the year-book?

LAURA: Yes, that boy.

AMANDA: Laura, Laura, were you in love with that boy?

LAURA: I don't know, Mother. All I know is I couldn't sit at the table if it was him!

AMANDA: It won't be him! It isn't the least bit likely. But whether it is or not, you will come to the table. You will not be excused.

LAURA: I'll have to be, Mother.

AMANDA: I don't intend to humor your silliness, Laura. I've had too much from you and your brother, both! So just sit down and compose yourself till they come. Tom has forgotten his key so you'll have to let them in, when they arrive.

LAURA [*panicky*]: Oh, Mother—*you* answer the door!

AMANDA [*lightly*]: I'll be in the kitchen—busy!

LAURA: Oh, Mother, please answer the door, don't make me do it!

AMANDA [*crossing into kitchenette*]: I've got to fix the dressing for the salmon. Fuss, fuss—silliness!—over a gentleman caller!

Door swings shut. LAURA *is left alone.*

[*Legend: "Terror!"*]

She utters a low moan and turns off the lamp—sits stiffly on the edge of the sofa, knotting her fingers together.

[*Legend on Screen: "The Opening of a Door!"*]

TOM *and* JIM *appear on the fire-escape steps and climb to landing. Hearing their approach,* LAURA *rises with a panicky gesture. She retreats to the portieres.*

The doorbell. LAURA *catches her breath and touches her throat. Low drums.*

AMANDA [*calling*]: Laura, sweetheart! The door!

LAURA *stares at it without moving.*

JIM: I think we just beat the rain.

TOM: Uh-huh. [*He rings again, nervously.* JIM *whistles and fishes for a cigarette.*]

AMANDA [*very, very gaily*]: Laura, that is your brother and Mr. O'Connor! Will you let them in, darling?

LAURA *crosses toward kitchenette door.*

LAURA [*breathlessly*]: Mother—you go to the door!

AMANDA *steps out of kitchenette and stares furiously at* LAURA. *She points imperiously at the door.*

LAURA: Please, please!

AMANDA [*in a fierce whisper*]: What is the matter with you, you silly thing?

LAURA [*desperately*]: Please, you answer it, *please!*

AMANDA: I told you I wasn't going to humor you, Laura. Why have you chosen this moment to lose your mind?

LAURA: Please, please, please, you go!

AMANDA: You'll have to go to the door because I can't!

LAURA [*despairingly*]: I can't either!

AMANDA: Why?

LAURA: I'm *sick!*

AMANDA: I'm sick, too—of your nonsense! Why can't you and your brother be normal people? Fantastic whims and behavior! [TOM *gives a long ring.*] Preposterous goings on! Can you give me one reason—[*Calls out lyrically.*] COMING! JUST ONE SECOND!—why should you be afraid to open a door? Now you answer it, Laura!

LAURA: Oh, oh, oh . . . [*She returns through the portieres. Darts to the victrola and winds it frantically and turns it on.*]

AMANDA: Laura Wingfield, you march right to that door!

LAURA: Yes—yes, Mother!

A faraway, scratchy rendition of "Dardanella" softens the air and gives her strength to move through it. She slips to the door and draws it cautiously open. TOM *enters with caller,* JIM O'CONNOR.

TOM: Laura, this is Jim. Jim, this is my sister, Laura.

JIM [*stepping inside*]: I didn't know that Shakespeare had a sister!

LAURA [*retreating stiff and trembling from the door*]. How—how do you do?

JIM [*heartily extending his hand*]. Okay!

LAURA *touches it hesitantly with hers.*

JIM: Your hand's *cold,* Laura!

LAURA: Yes, well—I've been playing the victrola. . . .

JIM: Must have been playing classical music on it! You ought to play a little hot swing music to warm you up!

LAURA: Excuse me—I haven't finished playing the victrola. . . .

She turns awkwardly and hurries into the front room. She pauses a second by the victrola. Then catches her breath and darts through the portieres like a frightened deer.

JIM [*grinning*]: What was the matter?

TOM: Oh—with Laura? Laura is—terribly shy.

JIM: Shy, huh? It's unusual to meet a shy girl nowadays. I don't believe you ever mentioned you had a sister.

TOM: Well, now you know. I have one. Here is the *Post Dispatch*. You want a piece of it?

JIM: Uh-huh.

TOM: What piece? The comics?

JIM: Sports! [*Glances at it*]. Ole Dizzy Dean is on his bad behavior.

TOM [*disinterest*]: Yeah? [*Lights cigarette and crosses back to fire-escape door.*]

JIM: Where are *you* going?

TOM: I'm going out on the terrace.

JIM [*goes after him*]: You know, Shakespeare—I'm going to sell you a bill of goods!

TOM: What goods?

JIM: A course I'm taking.

TOM: Huh?

JIM: In public speaking! You and me, we're not the warehouse type.

TOM: Thanks—that's good news. But what has public speaking got to do with it?

JIM: It fits you for—executive positions!

TOM: Awww.

JIM: I tell you it's done a helluva lot for me.

[*Image: Executive at Desk.*]

TOM: In what respect?

JIM: In every! Ask yourself what is the difference between you an' me and men in the office down front? Brains?—No!—Ability?—No! Then what? Just one little thing—

TOM: What is that one little thing?

JIM: Primarily it amounts to—social poise! Being able to square up to people and hold your own on any social level!

AMANDA [*off stage*]: Tom?

TOM: Yes, Mother?

AMANDA: Is that you and Mr. O'Connor?

TOM: Yes, Mother.

AMANDA: Well, you just make yourselves comfortable in there.

TOM: Yes, Mother.

AMANDA: Ask Mr. O'Connor if he would like to wash his hands.

JIM: Aw—no—no—thank you—I took care of that at the warehouse. Tom—

TOM: Yes?

JIM: Mr. Mendoza was speaking to me about you.

TOM: Favorably?

JIM: What do you think?

TOM: Well—

JIM: You're going to be out of a job if you don't wake up.

TOM: I am waking up—

JIM: You show no signs.

TOM: The signs are interior.

[*Image on Screen: The Sailing Vessel with Jolly Roger Again.*]

TOM: I'm planning to change. [*He leans over the rail speaking with quiet exhilaration. The incandescent marquees and signs of the first-run movie houses light his face from across the alley. He looks like a voyager.*] I'm right at the point of committing myself to a future that doesn't include the warehouse and Mr. Mendoza or even a night-school course in public speaking.

JIM: What are you gassing about?

TOM: I'm tired of the movies.

JIM: Movies!

TOM: Yes, movies! Look at them—[*a wave toward the marvels of Grand Avenue.*] All of those glamorous people—having adventures—hogging it all, gobbling the whole thing up! You know what happens? People go to the *movies* instead of *moving!* Hollywood characters are supposed to have all the adventures for everybody in America, while everybody in America sits in a dark room and watches them have them! Yes, until there's a war. That's when adventure becomes available to the masses! *Everyone's* dish, not only Gable's! Then the people in the dark room come out of the dark room to have some adventures themselves—Goody, goody—It's our turn now, to go to the South Sea Island—to make a safari—to be exotic, far-off—But I'm not patient. I don't want to wait till then. I'm tired of the *movies* and I am *about* to *move!*

JIM [*incredulously*]: Move?

TOM: Yes.

JIM: When?

TOM: Soon!

JIM: Where? Where?

[*Theme three music seems to answer the question, while* TOM *thinks it over. He searches among his pockets.*]

TOM: I'm starting to boil inside. I know I seem dreamy, but inside—well, I'm boiling! Whenever I pick up a shoe, I shudder a little thinking how short life is and what I am doing!—Whatever that means. I know it doesn't mean shoes—except as something to wear on a traveler's feet [*Finds paper.*] Look—

JIM: What?

TOM: I'm a member.

JIM [*reading*]: The Union of Merchant Seamen.

TOM: I paid my dues this month, instead of the light bill.

JIM: You will regret it when they turn the lights off.

TOM: I won't be here.

JIM: How about your mother?

TOM: I'm like my father. The bastard son of a bastard! See how he grins? And he's been absent going on sixteen years!

JIM: You're just talking, you drip. How does your mother feel about it?

TOM: Shhh—Here comes Mother! Mother is not acquainted with my plans!

AMANDA [*enters portieres*]: Where are you all?

TOM: On the terrace, Mother.

They start inside. She advances to them. TOM *is distinctly shocked at her appearance. Even* JIM *blinks a little. He is making his first contact with girlish Southern vivacity and in spite of the night-school course in public speaking is somewhat thrown off the beam by the unexpected outlay of social charm.*

Certain responses are attempted by JIM *but are swept aside by* AMANDA*'s gay laughter and chatter.* TOM *is embarrassed but after the first shock* JIM *reacts very warmly. Grins and chuckles, is altogether won over.*

[*Image:* AMANDA *as a Girl.*]

AMANDA [*coyly smiling, shaking her girlish ringlets*]: Well, well, well, so this is Mr. O'Connor. Introductions entirely unnecessary. I've heard so much about you from my boy. I finally said to him, Tom—good gracious!—why don't you bring this paragon to supper? I'd like to meet this nice young man at the warehouse!—Instead of just hearing him sing your praises so much! I don't know why my son is so standoffish—that's not Southern behavior! Let's sit down and—I think we could stand a little more air in here! Tom, leave the door open. I felt a nice fresh breeze a moment ago. Where has it gone? Mmm, so warm already! And not quite summer, even. We're going to burn up when summer really gets started. However, we're having—we're having a very light supper. I think light things are better fo' this time of year. The same as light clothes are. Light clothes an' light food are what warm weather calls fo'. You know our blood gets so thick during th' winter—it takes a while fo' us to *adjust* ou'selves!—when the season changes. . . . It's come so quick this year, I wasn't prepared. All of a sudden—heavens! Already summer!—I ran to the trunk an' pulled out this light dress—Terribly old! Historical almost! But feels so good—so good an' co-ol, y'know. . . .

TOM: Mother—

AMANDA: Yes, honey?

TOM: How about—supper?

AMANDA: Honey, you go ask Sister if supper is ready! You know that Sister is in full charge of supper! Tell her you hungry boys are waiting for it. [*To* JIM.] Have you met Laura?

JIM: She—

AMANDA: Let you in? Oh, good, you've met already! It's rare for a girl as sweet an' pretty as Laura to be domestic! But Laura is, thank heavens, not only pretty but also very domestic. I'm not at all. I never was a bit. I never could make a thing but angel-food cake. Well, in the South we had so many servants. Gone, gone, gone. All vestiges of gracious living! Gone completely! I wasn't prepared for what the future brought me. All of my gentlemen callers were sons of planters and so of course I assumed that I would be married to one and raise my family on a large piece of land with plenty of servants. But man proposes—and woman accepts the proposal!—To vary that old, old saying a little bit—I married no planter! I married a man who worked for the telephone company!—that gallantly smiling gentleman over there! [*Points to the picture.*] A telephone man who—fell in love with long distance!—Now he travels and I don't even know where!—But what am I going on for about my—tribulations! Tell me yours—I hope you don't have any! Tom?

TOM [*returning*]: Yes, Mother?

AMANDA: Is supper nearly ready?

TOM: It looks to me like supper is on the table.

AMANDA: Let me look—[*She rises prettily and looks through portieres.*] Oh, lovely—But where is Sister?

TOM: Laura is not feeling well and she says that she thinks she'd better not come to the table.

AMANDA: What?—Nonsense!—Laura? Oh, Laura!

LAURA [*off stage, faintly*]: Yes, Mother.

AMANDA: You really must come to the table. We won't be seated until you come to the table! Come in, Mr. O'Connor. You sit over there and I'll—Laura? Laura Wingfield! You're keeping us waiting, honey! We can't say grace until you come to the table!

The back door is pushed weakly open and LAURA *comes in. She is obviously quite faint, her lips trembling, her eyes wide and staring. She moves unsteadily toward the table.*

[*Legend: "Terror!"*]

Outside a summer storm is coming abruptly. The white curtains billow inward at the windows and there is a sorrowful murmur and deep blue dusk.

LAURA *suddenly stumbles—She catches a chair with a faint moan.*

TOM: Laura!

AMANDA: Laura! [*There is a clap of thunder.*] [*Legend: "Ah!"*] [*Despairingly.*] Why, Laura, you *are* sick, darling! Tom, help your sister into the living room, dear! Sit in the living room, Laura—rest on the sofa. Well! [*To the gentleman caller.*] Standing over the hot stove made her ill!—I told her that it was just too warm this evening, but—[TOM *comes back in.* LAURA *is on the sofa.*] Is Laura all right now?

TOM: Yes.

AMANDA: What is that? Rain? A nice cool rain has come up! [*She gives the gentleman caller a frightened look.*] I think we may—have grace—now . . . [TOM *looks at her stupidly.*] Tom, honey—you say grace!

TOM: Oh . . . "For these and all thy mercies—" [*They bow their heads.* AMANDA *stealing a nervous glance at* JIM. *In the living room* LAURA, *stretched on the sofa, clenches her hand to her lips, to hold back a shuddering sob.*] God's Holy Name be praised—

[*The Scene Dims Out.*]

Scene VII
A Souvenir

Half an hour later. Dinner is just being finished in the upstage area which is concealed by the drawn portieres.

As the curtain rises LAURA *is still huddled upon the sofa, her feet drawn under her, her head resting on a pale blue pillow, her eyes wide and mysteriously watchful. The new floor lamp with its shade of rose-colored silk gives a soft, becoming light to her face, bringing out the fragile, unearthly prettiness which usually escapes attention. There is a steady murmur of rain, but it is slackening and stops soon after the scene begins; the air outside becomes pale and luminous as the moon breaks out.*

A moment after the curtain rises, the lights in both rooms flicker and go out.

JIM: Hey, there, Mr. Light Bulb!

AMANDA *laughs nervously.*

[*Legend: "Suspension of a Public Service."*]

AMANDA: Where was Moses when the lights went out? Ha-ha. Do you know the answer to that one, Mr. O'Connor?

JIM: No, ma'am, what's the answer?

AMANDA: In the dark! [JIM *laughs appreciatively.*] Everybody sit still. I'll light the candles. Isn't it lucky we have them on the table? Where's a match? Which of you gentlemen can provide a match?

JIM: Here.

AMANDA: Thank you, sir.

JIM: Not at all, Ma'am!

AMANDA: I guess the fuse has burnt out. Mr. O'Connor, can you tell a burnt-out fuse? I know I can't and Tom is a total loss when it comes to mechanics. [*Sound: Getting Up: Voices Recede a Little to Kitchenette.*] Oh, be careful you don't bump into something. We don't want our gentleman caller to break his neck. Now wouldn't that be a fine howdy-do?

JIM: Ha-ha! Where is the fuse-box?

AMANDA: Right here next to the stove. Can you see anything?

JIM: Just a minute.

AMANDA: Isn't electricity a mysterious thing? Wasn't it Benjamin Franklin who tied a key to a kite? We live in such a mysterious universe, don't we? Some people say that science clears up all the mysteries for us. In my opinion it only creates more! Have you found it yet?

JIM: No, Ma'am. All these fuses look okay to me.

AMANDA: Tom!

TOM: Yes, Mother?

AMANDA: That light bill I gave you several days ago. The one I told you we got the notices about?

TOM: Oh.—Yeah.

[*Legend: "Ha!"*]

AMANDA: You didn't neglect to pay it by any chance?

TOM: Why, I—

AMANDA: Didn't! I might have known it!

JIM: Shakespeare probably wrote a poem on that light bill, Mrs. Wingfield.

AMANDA: I might have known better than to trust him with it! There's such a high price for negligence in this world!

JIM: Maybe the poem will win a ten-dollar prize.

AMANDA: We'll just have to spend the remainder of the evening in the nineteenth century, before Mr. Edison made the Mazda lamp!

JIM: Candlelight is my favorite kind of light.

AMANDA: That shows you're romantic! But that's no excuse for Tom. Well, we got through dinner. Very considerate of them to let us get through dinner before they plunged us into everlasting darkness, wasn't it, Mr. O'Connor?

JIM: Ha-ha!

AMANDA: Tom, as a penalty for your carelessness you can help me with the dishes.

JIM: Let me give you a hand.

AMANDA: Indeed you will not!

JIM: I ought to be good for something.

AMANDA: Good for something? [*Her tone is rhapsodic.*] *You?* Why, Mr. O'Connor, nobody, *nobody's* given me this much entertainment in years—as you have!

JIM: Aw, now, Mrs. Wingfield!

AMANDA: I'm not exaggerating, not one bit! But Sister is all by her lonesome. You go keep her company in the parlor! I'll give you this lovely old candelabrum that used to be on the altar at the Church of the Heavenly Rest. It was melted a little out of shape when the church burnt down. Lightning struck it one spring. Gypsy Jones was holding a revival at the time and he intimated that the church was destroyed because the Episcopalians gave card parties.

JIM: Ha-ha.

AMANDA: And how about coaxing Sister to drink a little wine? I think it would be good for her! Can you carry both at once?

JIM: Sure. I'm Superman!

AMANDA: Now, Thomas, get into this apron!

The door of kitchenette swings closed on AMANDA*'s gay laughter; the flickering light approaches the portieres.*

LAURA *sits up nervously as he enters. Her speech at first is low and breathless from the almost intolerable strain of being alone with a stranger.*

[*Legend: "I Don't Suppose You Remember Me at All!"*]

In her first speeches in this scene, before JIM*'s warmth overcomes her paralyzing shyness,* LAURA*'s voice is thin and breathless as though she has run up a steep flight of stairs.*

JIM*'s attitude is gently humorous. In playing this scene it should be stressed that while the incident is apparently unimportant, it is to* LAURA *the climax of her secret life.*

JIM: Hello, there, Laura.

LAURA [*faintly*]: Hello. [*She clears her throat.*]

JIM: How are you feeling now? Better?

LAURA: Yes. Yes, thank you.

JIM: This is for you. A little dandelion wine. [*He extends it toward her with extravagant gallantry.*]

LAURA: Thank you.

JIM: Drink it—but don't get drunk! [*He laughs heartily.* LAURA *takes the glass uncertainly; laughs shyly.*] Where shall I set the candles?

LAURA: Oh—oh, anywhere . . .

JIM: How about here on the floor? Any objections?

LAURA: No.

JIM: I'll spread a newspaper under to catch the drippings. I like to sit on the floor. Mind if I do?

LAURA: Oh, no.

JIM: Give me a pillow?

LAURA: What?

JIM: A pillow!

LAURA: Oh . . . [*Hands him one quickly.*]

JIM: How about you? Don't you like to sit on the floor?

LAURA: Oh—yes.

JIM: Why don't you, then?

LAURA: I—will.

JIM: Take a pillow! [LAURA *does. Sits on the other side of the candelabrum.* JIM *crosses his legs and smiles engagingly at her.*] I can't hardly see you sitting way over there.

LAURA: I can—see you.

JIM: I know, but that's not fair, I'm in the limelight. [LAURA *moves her pillow closer.*] Good! Now I can see you! Comfortable?

LAURA: Yes.

JIM: So am I. Comfortable as a cow. Will you have some gum?

LAURA: No, thank you.

JIM: I think that I will indulge, with your permission [*Musingly unwraps it and holds it up.*] Think of the fortune made by the guy that invented the first piece of chewing gum. Amazing, huh? The Wrigley Building is one of the sights of Chicago.—I saw it summer before last when I went up to the Century of Progress. Did you take in the Century of Progress?

LAURA: No, I didn't.

JIM: Well, it was quite a wonderful exposition. What impressed me most was the Hall of Science. Gives you an idea of what the future will be in America, even more wonderful than the present time is! [*Pause. Smiling at her.*] Your brother tells me you're shy. Is that right, Laura?

LAURA: I—don't know.

JIM: I judge you to be an old-fashioned type of girl. Well, I think that's a pretty good type to be. Hope you don't think I'm being too personal—do you?

LAURA [*hastily, out of embarrassment*]: I believe I *will* take a piece of gum, if you—don't mind. [*Clearing her throat.*] Mr. O'Connor, have you—kept up with your singing?

JIM: Singing? Me?

LAURA: Yes. I remember what a beautiful voice you had.

JIM: When did you hear me sing?

[*Voice Offstage in the Pause*]

Voice [*offstage*].

O blow, ye winds, heigh-ho.
A-roving I will go!
I'm off to my love
With a boxing glove—
Ten thousand miles away!

JIM: You say you've heard me sing?

LAURA: Oh, yes! Yes, very often . . . I—don't suppose you remember me—at all?

JIM [*smiling doubtfully*]: You know I have an idea I've seen you before. I had that idea soon as you opened the door. It seemed almost like I was about to remember your name. But the name that I started to call you—wasn't a name! And so I stopped myself before I said it.

LAURA: Wasn't it—Blue Roses?

JIM [*springs up, grinning*]: Blue Roses! My gosh, yes—Blue Roses! That's what I had on my tongue when you opened the door! Isn't it funny what tricks your memory plays? I didn't connect you with the high school somehow or other. But that's where it was; it was high school. I didn't even know you were Shakespeare's sister! Gosh, I'm sorry.

LAURA: I didn't expect you to. You—barely knew me!

JIM: But we did have a speaking acquaintance, huh?

LAURA: Yes, we—spoke to each other.

JIM: When did you recognize me?

LAURA: Oh, right away!

JIM: Soon as I came in the door?

LAURA: When I heard your name I thought it was probably you. I knew that Tom used to know you a little in high school. So when you came in the door—Well, then I was—sure.

JIM: Why didn't you *say* something, then?

LAURA [*breathlessly*]: I didn't know what to say, I was—too surprised!

JIM: For goodness' sakes! You know, this sure is funny!

LAURA: Yes! Yes, isn't it, though. . . .

JIM: Didn't we have a class in something together?

LAURA: Yes, we did.

JIM: What class was that?

LAURA: It was—singing—Chorus!

JIM: Aw!

LAURA: I sat across the aisle from you in the Aud.

JIM: Aw.

LAURA: Mondays, Wednesdays and Fridays.

JIM: Now I remember—you always came in late.

LAURA: Yes, it was so hard for me, getting upstairs. I had a brace on my leg—it clumped so loud!

JIM: I never heard any clumping.

LAURA [*wincing at the recollection*]: To me it sounded like—thunder!

JIM: Well, well, well. I never even noticed.

LAURA: And everybody was seated before I came in. I had to walk in front of all those people. My seat was in the back row. I had to go clumping all the way up the aisle with everyone watching!

JIM: You shouldn't have been self-conscious.

LAURA: I know, but I was. It was always such a relief when the singing started.

JIM: Aw, yes, I've placed you now! I used to call you Blue Roses. How was it that I got started calling you that?

LAURA: I was out of school a little while with pleurosis. When I came back you asked me what was the matter. I said I had pleurosis—you thought I said Blue Roses. That's what you always called me after that!

JIM: I hope you didn't mind.

LAURA: Oh, no—I liked it. You see, I wasn't acquainted with many—people. . . .

JIM: As I remember you sort of stuck by yourself.

LAURA: I—I—never had much luck at—making friends.

JIM: I don't see why you wouldn't.

LAURA: Well, I—started out badly.

JIM: You mean being—

LAURA: Yes, it sort of—stood between me—

JIM: You shouldn't have let it!

LAURA: I know, but it did, and—

JIM: You were shy with people!

LAURA: I tried not to be but never could—

JIM: Overcome it?

LAURA: No, I—I never could!

JIM: I guess being shy is something you have to work out of kind of gradually.

LAURA [*sorrowfully*]: Yes—I guess it—

JIM: Takes time!

LAURA: Yes—

JIM: People are not so dreadful when you know them. That's what you have to remember! And everybody has problems, not just you, but practically everybody has got some problems. You think of yourself as having the only problems, as being the only one who is disappointed. But just look around you and you will see lots of people as disappointed as you are. For instance, I hoped when I was going to high school that I would be further along at this time, six years after, than I am now—You remember that wonderful write-up I had in *The Torch?*

LAURA: Yes! [*She rises and crosses to table.*]

JIM: It said I was bound to succeed in anything I went into! [LAURA *returns with the annual.*] Holy Jeez! *The Torch!* [*He accepts it reverently. They smile across it with mutual wonder.* LAURA *crouches beside him and they begin to turn through it.* LAURA*'s shyness is dissolving in his warmth.*]

LAURA: Here you are in *Pirates of Penzance!*

JIM [*wistfully*]: I sang the baritone lead in that operetta.

LAURA [*rapidly*]: So—*beautifully!*

JIM [*protesting*]: Aw—

LAURA: Yes, yes—beautifully—beautifully!

JIM: You heard me?

LAURA: All three times!

JIM: No!

LAURA: Yes!

JIM: All three performances?

LAURA [*looking down*]: Yes.

JIM: Why?

LAURA: I—wanted to ask you to—autograph my program.

JIM: Why didn't you ask me to?

LAURA: You were always surrounded by your own friends so much that I never had a chance to.

JIM: You should have just—

LAURA: Well, I—thought you might think I was—

JIM: Thought I might think you was—what?

LAURA: Oh—

JIM [*with reflective relish*]: I was beleaguered by females in those days.

LAURA: You were terribly popular!

JIM: Yeah—

LAURA: You had such a—friendly way—

JIM: I was spoiled in high school.

LAURA: Everybody—liked you!

JIM: Including you?

LAURA: I—yes, I—I did, too—[*She gently closes the book in her lap.*]

JIM: Well, well, well!—Give me that program, Laura. [*She hands it to him. He signs it with a flourish.*] There you are—better late than never!

LAURA: Oh, I—what a—surprise!

JIM: My signature isn't worth very much right now. But some day—maybe—it will increase in value! Being disappointed is one thing and being discouraged is something else. I am disappointed but I'm not discouraged. I'm twenty-three years old. How old are you?

LAURA: I'll be twenty-four in June.

JIM: That's not old age!

LAURA: No, but—

JIM: You finished high school?

LAURA [*with difficulty*]: I didn't go back.

JIM: You mean you dropped out?

LAURA: I made bad grades in my final examinations. [*She rises and replaces the book and the program. Her voice strained.*] How is—Emily Meisenbach getting along?

JIM: Oh, that kraut-head!

LAURA: Why do you call her that?

JIM: That's what she was.

LAURA: You're not still—going with her?

JIM: I never see her.

LAURA: It said in the Personal Section that you were—engaged!

JIM: I know, but I wasn't impressed by that—propaganda!

LAURA: It wasn't—the truth?

JIM: Only in Emily's optimistic opinion!

LAURA: Oh—

[*Legend: "What Have You Done since High School?"*]

JIM *lights a cigarette and leans indolently back on his elbows smiling at* LAURA *with a warmth and charm which light her inwardly with altar candles. She remains by the table and turns in her hands a piece of glass to cover her tumult.*

JIM [*after several reflective puffs on a cigarette*]: What have you done since high school? [*She seems not to hear him.*] Huh? [LAURA *looks up.*] I said what have you done since high school, Laura?

LAURA: Nothing much.

JIM: You must have been doing something these six long years.

LAURA: Yes.

JIM: Well, then, such as what?

LAURA: I took a business course at business college—

JIM: How did that work out?

LAURA: Well, not very—well—I had to drop out, it gave me—indigestion—

JIM *laughs gently.*

JIM: What are you doing now?

LAURA: I don't do anything—much. Oh, please don't think I sit around doing nothing! My glass collection takes up a good deal of my time. Glass is something you have to take good care of.

JIM: What did you say—about glass?

LAURA: Collection I said—I have one—[*She clears her throat and turns away again, acutely shy.*]

JIM [*abruptly*]: You know what I judge to be the trouble with you? Inferiority complex! Know what that is? That's what they call it when someone low-rates himself! I understand it because I had it, too. Although my case was not so aggravated as yours seems to be. I had it until I took up public speaking, developed my voice, and learned that I had an aptitude for science. Before that time I never thought of myself as being outstanding in any way whatsoever! Now I've never made a regular study of it, but I have a friend who says I can analyze people better than doctors that make a profession of it. I don't claim that to be necessarily true, but I can sure guess a person's psychology, Laura! [*Takes out his gum.*] Excuse me, Laura. I always take it out when the flavor is gone. I'll use this scrap of paper to wrap it in. I know how it is to get it stuck on a shoe. Yep—that's what I judge to be your principal trouble. A lack of confidence in yourself as a person. You don't have the proper amount of faith in yourself. I'm basing that fact on a number of your remarks and also on certain observations I've made. For instance that clumping you thought was so awful in high school. You say that you even dreaded to walk into class. You see what you did? You dropped out of school, you gave up an education because of a clump, which as far as I know was practically nonexistent! A little physical defect is what you have. Hardly noticeable even! Magnified thousands of times by imagination! You know what my strong advice to you is? Think of yourself as *superior* in some way!

LAURA: In what way would I think?

JIM: Why, man alive, Laura! Just look about you a little. What do you see? A world full of common people! All of 'em born and all of 'em going to die! Which of them has one-tenth of your good points! Or mine! Or anyone else's, as far as that goes—Gosh! Everybody excels in some one thing. Some in many! [*Unconsciously glances at himself in the mirror.*] All you've got to do is discover in *what!* Take me, for instance. [*He adjusts his tie at the mirror.*] My interest happens to be in electrodynamics. I'm taking a course in radio engineering at night school, Laura, on top of a fairly responsible job at the warehouse. I'm taking that course and studying public speaking.

LAURA: Ohhhh.

JIM: Because I believe in the future of television! [*Turning back to her.*] I wish to be ready to go up right along with it. Therefore I'm planning to get in on the ground floor. In fact, I've already made the right connections and all that remains is for the industry itself to get under way! Full steam—[*His eyes are starry.*] *Knowledge*—Zzzzzp! *Money*—Zzzzzzp!—*Power!* That's the cycle democracy is built on! [*His attitude is convincingly dynamic.* LAURA *stares at him, even her shyness eclipsed in her absolute wonder. He suddenly grins.*] I guess you think I think a lot of myself!

LAURA: No—o-o-o, I—

JIM: Now how about you? Isn't there something you take more interest in than anything else?

LAURA: Well, I do—as I said—have my—glass collection—

A peal of girlish laughter from the kitchen.

JIM: I'm not right sure I know what you're talking about. What kind of glass is it?

LAURA: Little articles of it, they're ornaments mostly! Most of them are little animals made out of glass, the tiniest little animals in the world. Mother calls them a glass menagerie! Here's an example of one, if you'd like to see it! This one is one of the oldest. It's nearly thirteen. [*He stretches out his hand.*] [*Music: "The Glass Menagerie."*] Oh, be careful—if you breathe, it breaks!

JIM: I'd better not take it. I'm pretty clumsy with things.

LAURA: Go on, I trust you with him! [*Places it in his palm.*] There now—you're holding him gently! Hold him over the light, he loves the light! You see how the light shines through him?

JIM: It sure does shine!

LAURA: I shouldn't be partial, but he is my favorite one.

JIM: What kind of a thing is this one supposed to be?

LAURA: Haven't you noticed the single horn on his forehead?

JIM: A unicorn, huh?

LAURA: Mmm-hmmm!

JIM: Unicorns, aren't they extinct in the modern world?

LAURA: I know!

JIM: Poor little fellow, he must feel sort of lonesome.

LAURA [*smiling*]: Well, if he does he doesn't complain about it. He stays on a shelf with some horses that don't have horns and all of them seem to get along nicely together.

JIM: How do you know?

LAURA [*lightly*]: I haven't heard any arguments among them!

JIM [*grinning*]: No arguments, huh? Well, that's a pretty good sign! Where shall I set him?

LAURA: Put him on the table. They all like a change of scenery once in a while!

JIM [*stretching*]: Well, well, well, well—Look how big my shadow is when I stretch!

LAURA: Oh, oh, yes—it stretches across the ceiling!

JIM [*crossing to door*]: I think it's stopped raining. [*Opens fire-escape door.*] Where does the music come from?

LAURA: From the Paradise Dance Hall across the alley.

JIM: How about cutting the rug a little, Miss Wingfield?

LAURA: Oh, I—

JIM: Or is your program filled up? Let me have a look at it. [*Grasps imaginary card.*] Why, every dance is taken! I'll just have to scratch some out. [*Waltz Music: "La Golondrina."*] Ahhh, a waltz! [*He executes some sweeping turns by himself then holds his arms toward* LAURA.]

LAURA [*breathlessly*]: I—can't dance!

JIM: There you go, that inferiority stuff!

LAURA: I've never danced in my life!

JIM: Come on, try!

LAURA: Oh, but I'd step on you!

JIM: I'm not made out of glass.

LAURA: How—how—how do we start?

JIM: Just leave it to me. You hold your arms out a little.

LAURA: Like this?

JIM: A little bit higher. Right. Now don't tighten up, that's the main thing about it—relax.

LAURA [*laughing breathlessly*]: It's hard not to.

JIM: Okay.

LAURA: I'm afraid you can't budge me.

JIM: What do you bet I can't? [*He swings her into motion.*]

LAURA: Goodness, yes, you can!

JIM: Let yourself go, now, Laura, just let yourself go.

LAURA: I'm—

JIM: Come on!

LAURA: Trying!

JIM: Not so stiff—Easy does it!

LAURA: I know but I'm—

JIM: Loosen th' backbone! There now, that's a lot better.

LAURA: Am I?

JIM: Lots, lots better! [*He moves her about the room in a clumsy waltz.*]

LAURA: Oh, my!

JIM: Ha-ha!

LAURA: Goodness, yes you can!

JIM: Ha-ha-ha! [*They suddenly bump into the table.* JIM *stops.*] What did we hit on?

LAURA: Table.

JIM: Did something fall off it? I think—

LAURA: Yes.

JIM: I hope that it wasn't the little glass horse with the horn!

LAURA: Yes.

JIM: Aw, aw, aw. Is it broken?

LAURA: Now it is just like all the other horses.

JIM: It's lost its—

LAURA: Horn! It doesn't matter. Maybe it's a blessing in disguise.

JIM: You'll never forgive me. I bet that that was your favorite piece of glass.

LAURA: I don't have favorites much. It's no tragedy, Freckles. Glass breaks so easily. No matter how careful you are. The traffic jars the shelves and things fall off them.

JIM: Still I'm awfully sorry that I was the cause.

LAURA [*smiling*]: I'll just imagine he had an operation. The horn was removed to make him feel less—freakish! [*They both laugh.*] Now he will feel more at home with the other horses, the ones that don't have horns . . .

JIM: Ha-ha, that's very funny! [*Suddenly serious.*] I'm glad to see that you have a sense of humor. You know—you're—well—very different! Surprisingly different from anyone else I know! [*His voice becomes soft and hesitant with a genuine feeling.*] Do you mind me telling you that? [LAURA *is abashed beyond speech.*] You make me feel sort of—I don't know how to put it! I'm usually pretty good at expressing things, but—This is something that I don't know how to say! LAURA *touches her throat and clears it—turns the broken unicorn in her hands.*] [*Even softer*] Has anyone ever told you that you were pretty? [*Pause: Music.*] [LAURA *looks up slowly, with wonder, and shakes her head.*] Well, you are! In a very different way from anyone else. And all the nicer because of the difference, too. [*His voice becomes low and husky.* LAURA *turns away, nearly faint with the novelty of her emotions.*] I wish that you were my sister. I'd teach you to have some confidence in yourself. The different people are not like other people, but being different is nothing to be ashamed of. Because other people are not such wonderful people. They're one hundred times one thousand. You're one times one! They walk all over the earth. You just stay here. They're common as—weeds, but—you—well, you're *Blue Roses!*

[*Image on Screen: Blue Roses.*]
[*Music Changes.*]

LAURA: But blue is wrong for—roses . . .

JIM: It's right for you—You're—pretty!

LAURA: In what respect am I pretty?

JIM: In all respects—believe me! Your eyes—your hair—are pretty! Your hands are pretty! [*He catches hold of her hand.*] You think I'm making this up because I'm invited to dinner and have to be nice. Oh, I could do that! I could put on an act for you, Laura, and say lots of things without being very sincere. But this time I am. I'm talking to you sincerely. I happened to notice you had this inferiority complex that keeps you from feeling comfortable with people. Somebody needs to build your confidence up and make you proud instead of shy and turning away and—blushing—Somebody ought to—ought to—*kiss* you. Laura! [*His hand slips slowly up her arm to her shoulder.*] [*Music Swells Tumultuously.*] [*He suddenly turns her about and kisses her on the lips. When he releases her* LAURA *sinks on the sofa with a bright, dazed look.* JIM *backs away and fishes in his pocket for a cigarette.*] [*Legend on Screen: "Souvenir."*] Stumble-john! [*He lights the cigarette, avoiding her look. There is a peal of girlish laughter from* AMANDA *in the kitchen.* LAURA *slowly raises and opens her hand. It still contains the little broken glass animal. She looks at it with a tender, bewildered expression.*] Stumble-john! I shouldn't have done that—That was way off the beam. You don't smoke, do you? [*She looks up, smiling, not hearing the question. He sits beside her a little gingerly. She looks at him speechlessly—waiting. He coughs decorously and moves a little farther aside as he considers the situation and senses her feelings, dimly, with perturbation. Gently.*] Would you—care for a—mint? [*She doesn't seem to hear him but her look grows brighter even.*] Peppermint—Life Saver? My pocket's a regular drug store—wherever I go . . . [*He pops a mint in his mouth. Then gulps and decides to make a clean breast of it. He speaks slowly and gingerly.*] Laura, you know, if I had a sister like you, I'd do the same thing as Tom. I'd bring out fellows—introduce her to them. The right type of boys of a type to—appreciate her. Only—well—he made a mistake about me. Maybe I've got no call to be saying this. That may not have been the idea in having me over. But what if it was? There's nothing wrong about that. The only trouble is that in my case—I'm not in a situation to—do the right thing. I can't take down your number and say I'll phone. I can't call up next week and—ask for a date. I thought I had better explain the situation in case you misunderstood it and—hurt your feelings. . . . [*Pause. Slowly, very slowly,* LAURA*'s look changes, her eyes returning slowly from his to the ornament in her palm.*]

AMANDA *utters another gay laugh in the kitchen.*

LAURA [*faintly*]: You—won't—call again?

JIM: No, Laura, I can't [*He rises from the sofa.*] As I was just explaining, I've—got strings on me, Laura, I've—been going steady! I go out all the time with a girl named Betty. She's a home-girl like you, and Catholic, and Irish, and in a great many ways we—get along fine. I met her last summer on a moonlight boat trip up the river to Alton, on the *Majestic*. Well—right away from the start it was—love! [*Legend: Love!*] [LAURA *sways slightly forward and grips the arm of the sofa. He fails to notice, now enrapt in his own comfortable being.*] Being in love has made a new man of me! [*Leaning stiffly forward, clutching the arm of the sofa,* LAURA *struggles visibly with her storm. But* JIM *is oblivious, she is a long way off.*] The power of love is really pretty tremendous! Love is something that—changes the whole world, Laura! [*The storm abates a little and* LAURA *leans back. He notices her again.*] It happened that Betty's aunt took sick, she got a wire and had to go to Centralia. So Tom—when he asked me to dinner—I naturally just accepted the invitation, not knowing that you—that he—that I—[*He stops awkwardly.*] Huh—I'm a stumble-john! [*He flops back on the sofa. The holy candles in the altar of* LAURA*'s face have been snuffed out! There is a look of almost infinite desolation.* JIM *glances at her uneasily.*] I wish that you would—say something. [*She bites her lip which was trembling and then bravely smiles. She opens her hand again on the broken glass ornament. Then she gently takes his hand and raises it level with her own. She carefully places the unicorn in the palm of his hand, then pushes his fingers closed upon it.*] What are you—doing that for? You want me to have him?—Laura? [*She nods.*] What for?

LAURA: A—souvenir . . .

She rises unsteadily and crouches beside the victrola to wind it up.
[*Legend on Screen: "Things Have a Way of Turning Out So Badly."*]
[*Or Image: "Gentleman Caller Waving Good-Bye!—Gaily."*]

At this moment AMANDA *rushes brightly back in the front room. She bears a pitcher of fruit punch in an old-fashioned cut-glass pitcher and a plate of macaroons. The plate has a gold border and poppies painted on it.*

AMANDA: Well, well, well! Isn't the air delightful after the shower? I've made you children a little liquid refreshment. [*Turns gaily to the gentleman caller.*] Jim, do you know that song about lemonade?

"Lemonade, lemonade
Made in the shade and stirred with a spade—
Good enough for any old maid!"

JIM [*uneasily*]: Ha-ha! No—I never heard it.

AMANDA: Why, Laura! You look so serious!

JIM: We were having a serious conversation.

AMANDA: Good! Now you're better acquainted!

JIM [*uncertainly*]: Ha-ha! Yes.

AMANDA: You modern young people are much more serious-minded than my generation. I was so gay as a girl!

JIM: You haven't changed, Mrs. Wingfield.

AMANDA: Tonight I'm rejuvenated! The gaiety of the occasion, Mr. O'Connor! [*She tosses her head with a peal of laughter. Spills lemonade.*] Oooo! I'm baptizing myself!

JIM: Here—let me—

AMANDA [*setting the pitcher down*]: There now. I discovered we had some maraschino cherries. I dumped them in, juice and all!

JIM: You shouldn't have gone to that trouble, Mrs. Wingfield.

AMANDA: Trouble, trouble? Why it was loads of fun! Didn't you hear me cutting up in the kitchen? I bet your ears were burning! I told Tom how outdone with him I was for keeping you to himself so long a time! He should have brought you over much, much sooner! Well, now that you've found your way, I want you to be a very frequent caller! Not just occasional but all the time. Oh, we're going to have a lot of gay times together! I see them coming! Mmm, just breathe that air! So fresh, and the moon's so pretty! I'll skip back out—I know where my place is when young folks are having a—serious conversation!

JIM: Oh, don't go out, Mrs. Wingfield. The fact of the matter is I've got to be going.

AMANDA: Going, now? You're joking! Why, it's only the shank of the evening, Mr. O'Connor!

JIM: Well, you know how it is.

AMANDA: You mean you're a young workingman and have to keep workingmen's hours. We'll let you off early tonight. But only on the condition that next time you stay later. What's the best night for you? Isn't Saturday night the best night for you workingmen?

JIM: I have a couple of time-clocks to punch, Mrs. Wingfield. One at morning, another one at night!

AMANDA: My, but you *are* ambitious! You work at night, too?

JIM: No, Ma'am, not work but—Betty! [*He crosses deliberately to pick up his hat. The band at the Paradise Dance Hall goes into a tender waltz.*]

AMANDA: Betty? Betty? Who's—Betty! [*There is an ominous cracking sound in the sky.*]

JIM: Oh, just a girl. The girl I go steady with! [*He smiles charmingly. The sky falls.*]

[*Legend: "The Sky Falls."*]

AMANDA [*a long-drawn exhalation*]: Ohhh . . . Is it a serious romance, Mr. O'Connor?

JIM: We're going to be married the second Sunday in June.

AMANDA: Ohhhh—how nice! Tom didn't mention that you were engaged to be married.

JIM: The cat's not out of the bag at the warehouse yet. You know how they are. They call you Romeo and stuff like that. [*He stops at the oval mirror to put on his hat. He carefully shapes the brim and the crown to give a discreetly dashing effect.*] It's been a wonderful evening, Mrs. Wingfield. I guess this is what they mean by Southern hospitality.

AMANDA: It really wasn't anything at all.

JIM: I hope it don't seem like I'm rushing off. But I promised Betty I'd pick her up at the Wabash depot, an' by the time I get my jalopy down there her train'll be in. Some women are pretty upset if you keep 'em waiting.

AMANDA: Yes, I know—The tyranny of women! [*Extends her hand.*] Good-bye, Mr. O'Connor. I wish you luck—and happiness—and success! All three of them, and so does Laura!—Don't you, Laura?

LAURA: Yes!

JIM [*taking her hand*]: Goodbye, Laura. I'm certainly going to treasure that souvenir. And don't you forget the good advice I gave you. [*Raises his voice to a cheery shout.*] So long, Shakespeare! Thanks again, ladies—good night!

He grins and ducks jauntily out.

Still bravely grimacing, AMANDA *closes the door on the gentleman caller. Then she turns back to the room with a puzzled expression. She and* LAURA *don't dare to face each other.* LAURA *crouches beside the victrola to wind it.*

AMANDA [*faintly*]: Things have a way of turning out so badly. I don't believe that I would play the victrola. Well, well—well—Our gentleman caller was engaged to be married! Tom!

TOM [*from back*]: Yes, Mother?

AMANDA: Come in here a minute. I want to tell you something awfully funny.

TOM [*enters with macaroon and a glass of the lemonade*]: Has the gentleman caller gotten away already?

AMANDA: The gentleman caller has made an early departure. What a wonderful joke you played on us!

TOM: How do you mean?

AMANDA: You didn't mention that he was engaged to be married.

TOM: Jim? Engaged?

AMANDA: That's what he just informed us.

TOM: I'll be jiggered! I didn't know about that.

AMANDA: That seems very peculiar.

TOM: What's peculiar about it?

AMANDA: Didn't you call him your best friend down at the warehouse?

TOM: He is, but how did I know?

AMANDA: It seems extremely peculiar that you wouldn't know your best friend was going to be married!

TOM: The warehouse is where I work, not where I know things about people!

AMANDA: You don't know things anywhere! You live in a dream; you manufacture illusions! [*He crosses to door.*] Where are you going?

TOM: I'm going to the movies.

AMANDA: That's right, now that you've had us make such fools of ourselves. The effort, the preparations, all the expense! The new floor lamp, the rug, the clothes for Laura! All for what? To entertain some other girl's fiancé! Go to the movies, go! Don't think about us, a mother deserted, an unmarried sister who's crippled and has no job! Don't let anything interfere with your selfish pleasure! Just go, go, go—to the movies!

TOM: All right, I will! The more you shout about my selfishness to me the quicker I'll go, and I won't go to the movies!

AMANDA: Go, then! Then go to the moon—you selfish dreamer!

TOM *smashes his glass on the floor. He plunges out on the fire-escape, slamming the door.* LAURA *screams—cut by door.*

Dance-hall music up. TOM *goes to the rail and grips it desperately, lifting his face in the chill white moonlight penetrating the narrow abyss of the alley.*

[*Legend on Screen: "And So Good-Bye . . ."*]

TOM*'s closing speech is timed with the interior pantomime. The interior scene is played as though viewed through sound-proof glass.* AMANDA *appears to be making a comforting speech to* LAURA *who is huddled upon the sofa. Now that we cannot hear the mother's speech, her silliness is gone and she has dignity and tragic beauty.* LAURA*'s dark hair hides her face until at the end of the speech she lifts it to smile at her mother.* AMANDA*'s gestures are slow and graceful, almost dancelike, as she comforts the daughter. At the end of her speech she glances a moment at the father's picture—then withdraws through the portieres. At close of* TOM*'s speech,* LAURA *blows out the candles, ending the play.*

TOM: I didn't go to the moon, I went much further—for time is the longest distance between two places—Not long after that I was fired for writing a poem on the lid of a shoe-box. I left Saint Louis. I descended the steps of this fire-escape for a last time and followed, from then on, in my father's footsteps, attempting to find in motion what was lost in space—I traveled around a great deal. The cities swept about me like dead leaves, leaves that were brightly colored but torn away from the branches. I would have stopped, but I was pursued by something. It always came upon me unawares, taking me altogether by surprise. Perhaps it was a familiar bit of music. Perhaps it was only a piece of transparent glass—Perhaps I am walking along a street at night, in some strange city, before I have found companions. I pass the lighted window of a shop where perfume is sold. The window is filled with pieces of colored glass, tiny transparent bottles in delicate colors, like bits of a shattered rainbow. Then all at once my sister touches my shoulder. I turn around and look into her eyes . . . Oh, Laura, Laura, I tried to leave you behind me, but I am more faithful than I intended to be! I reach for a cigarette, I cross the street, I run into the movies or a bar, I buy a drink, I speak to the nearest stranger—anything that can blow your candles out! [LAURA *bends over the candles*.]—for nowadays the world is lit by lightning! Blow out your candles, Laura—and so good-bye . . .

She blows the candles out.
[*The Scene Dissolves.*]

[1944]

Tennessee Williams's Production Notes

Being a "memory play," *The Glass Menagerie* can be presented with unusual freedom of convention. Because of its considerably delicate or tenuous material, atmospheric touches and subtleties of direction play a particularly important part. Expressionism and all other unconventional techniques in drama have only one valid aim, and that is a closer approach to truth. When a play employs unconventional techniques, it is not, or certainly shouldn't be, trying to escape its responsibility of dealing with reality, or interpreting experience, but is actually or should be attempting to find a closer approach, a more penetrating and vivid expression of things as they are. The straight realistic play with its genuine frigidaire and authentic ice cubes, its characters that speak exactly as its audience speaks, corresponds to the academic landscape and has the same virtue of a photographic likeness. Everyone should know nowadays the unimportance of the photographic in art: that truth, life, or reality is an organic thing which the poetic imagination can represent or suggest, in essence, only through transformation, through changing into other forms than those which were merely present in appearance.

These remarks are not meant as comments only on this particular play. They have to do with a conception of a new, plastic theater which must take the place of the exhausted theater of realistic conventions if the theater is to resume vitality as a part of our culture.

The Screen Device

There is *only one important difference between the original and acting version of the play* and that is the *omission* in the latter of the device which I tentatively included in my *original* script. This device was the use of a screen on which were projected magic-lantern slides bearing images or titles. I do not regret the omission of this device from the . . . Broadway production. The extraordinary power of Miss Taylor's performance made it suitable to have the utmost simplicity in the physical production. But I think it may be interesting to some readers to see how this device was conceived. So I am putting it into the published manuscript. These images and legends, projected from behind, were cast on a section of wall between the front-room and dining-room areas, which should be indistinguishable from the rest when not in use.

The purpose of this will probably be apparent. It is to give accent to certain values in each scene. Each scene contains a particular point (or several) which is structurally the most important. In an episodic play, such as this, the basic structure or narrative line may be obscured from the audience; the effect may seem fragmentary rather than architectural. This may not be the fault of the play so much as a lack of attention in the audience. The legend or image upon the screen will strengthen the effect of what is merely allusion in the writing and allow the primary point to be made more simply and lightly than if the entire responsibility were on the spoken lines. Aside from this structural value, I think the screen will have a definite emotional appeal, less definable but just as important. An imaginative producer or director may invent many other uses for this device than those indicated in the present script. In fact the possibilities of the device seem much larger to me than the instance of this play can possibly utilize.

The Music

Another extra-literary accent in this play is provided by the use of music. A single recurring tune, "The Glass Menagerie," is used to give emotional emphasis to suitable passages. This tune is like circus music, not when you are on the grounds or in the immediate vicinity of the parade, but when you are at some distance and very likely thinking of something else. It seems under those circumstances to continue almost interminably and it weaves in and out of your preoccupied consciousness; then it is the lightest, most delicate music in the world and perhaps the saddest. It expresses the surface vivacity of life with the underlying strain of immutable and inexpressible sorrow. When you look at a piece of delicately spun glass you think of two things: how beautiful it is and how easily it can be broken. Both of those ideas should be woven into the recurring tune, which dips in and out of the play as if it were carried on a wind that changes. It serves as a thread of connection and allusion between the narrator with his separate point in time and space and the subject of his story. Between each episode it returns as reference to the emotion, nostalgia, which is the first condition of the play. It is primarily Laura's music and therefore comes out most clearly when the play focuses upon her and the lovely fragility of glass which is her image.

The Lighting

The lighting in the play is not realistic. In keeping with the atmosphere of memory, the stage is dim. Shafts of light are focused on selected areas or actors, sometimes in contradistinction to what is the apparent center. For instance, in the quarrel scene between Tom and Amanda, in which Laura has no active part, the clearest pool of light is on her figure. This is also true of the supper scene. The light upon Laura should be distinct from the others, having a peculiar pristine clarity such as light used in early religious portraits of female saints or madonnas. A certain correspondence to light in religious paintings, such as El Greco's, where the figures are radiant in atmosphere that is relatively dusky, could be effectively used throughout the play. (It will also permit a more effective use of the screen.) A free, imaginative use of light can be of enormous value in giving a mobile, plastic quality to plays of a more or less static nature.

Joining the Conversation: Critical Thinking and Writing

1. When the play was produced in New York, the magic-lantern slides were omitted. Is the device an extraneous gimmick? Might it even interfere with the play, by oversimplifying and thus in a way belittling the actions? Please argue first for why this device is needed, and then for why it is not.
2. What does the Victrola offer to Laura? Why is the typewriter a better symbol (for the purposes of the play) than, say, a piano? After all, Laura could have been taking piano lessons. Explain the symbolism of the unicorn, and the loss of its horn. What is Laura saying to Jim in the gesture of giving him the unicorn?
3. Laura escapes to her glass menagerie. To what do Amanda and Tom escape? How complete is Tom's escape at the end of the play? Evaluate the argument that Tom is as much of an escapist as Laura and Amanda.
4. What is meant at the end when Laura blows out the candles? Is she blowing out illusions? Or life? Or both?
5. Did Williams make a slip in having Amanda say Laura is "crippled" on page 1287?
6. There is an implication that had Jim not been going steady he might have rescued Laura, but Jim also seems to represent (for example, in his lines about money and power) the corrupt outside world that no longer values humanity. Is this a slip on Williams's part, or is it an interesting complexity?
7. On page 1287 Williams says, in a stage direction, "Now that we cannot hear the mother's speech, her silliness is gone and she has dignity and tragic beauty." Is Williams simply dragging in the word "tragic" because of its prestige, or is it legitimate?
8. "Tragedy" is often distinguished from "pathos": In the tragic, the suffering is experienced by persons who act and are in some measure responsible for their suffering; in the pathetic, the suffering is experienced by the passive and the innocent. H. D. F. Kitto in *Greek Tragedy* (1939), says in a discussion of Aeschylus's *The Suppliants*: "The Suppliants are not only pathetic, as the victims of outrage, but also tragic, as the victims of their own misconceptions." Given this distinction, to what extent are Amanda and Laura tragic? pathetic?

Chapter Overview: Looking Backward/Looking Forward

1. Do you think it is important for Americans to love their country? In what ways would this love be shown?
2. Is it possible to love one's country and, at the same time, to be critical of it? Should love of country be complete and unconditional?

3. If you are not an American, but are, for example, attending school here, what is the relationship between your feelings about the United States and your feelings about your homeland?
4. Do you think Americans are the same as, or different from, people everywhere else? How would you argue that they are the same? How would you argue that they are different? Which argument, in your view, is more convincing?
5. Take any one of the Short Views (pages 1184–85) and write an essay of 500–750 words amplifying the point.
6. In 500 words set forth your idea of the American Dream.

CHAPTER 26

Law and Disorder

SHORT VIEWS

The trouble for the thief is not how to steal the bugle, but where to blow it.
African proverb

Whoever desires to found a state and give it laws, must start with assuming that all men are bad and ever ready to display their vicious nature, whenever they may find occasion for it.
Niccolò Machiavelli

It is questionable whether, when we break a murderer on the wheel, we aren't lapsing into precisely the mistake of the child who hits the chair he bumps into.
G. C. Lichtenberg

If a man were permitted to make all the ballads, he need not care who should make the laws of a nation.
Andrew Fletcher

Nature has given women so much power that the law has very wisely given them very little.
Samuel Johnson

One law for the ox and the ass is oppression.
William Blake

The law, in its majestic equality, forbids the rich as well as the poor to sleep under bridges, to beg in the streets, and to steal bread.
Anatole France

The trouble about fighting for human freedom is that you have to spend much of your life defending sons of bitches; for oppressive laws are always aimed at them originally, and oppression must be stopped in the beginning if it is to be stopped at all.
H. L. Mencken

Censorship upholds the dignity of the profession, know what I mean?
Mae West

Joining the Conversation: Critical Thinking and Writing

1. Select a quotation that especially appeals to you, and make it the focus of an essay of about 500 words.
2. Take two of the passages—perhaps one that you especially like and one that you think is wrongheaded—and write a dialogue of about 500 words in which the two authors converse or argue. They may each try to convince the other, or they may find that to some degree they share views and they may then work out a statement that both can accept. If you do take the first position—that one writer is on the correct track but the other is utterly mistaken—try to be fair to the view that you think is mistaken. (As an experiment in critical thinking, imagine that you accept it, and make the best case for it that you possibly can.
3. Do you agree with the Italian statesman and political philosopher Niccolò Machiavelli (1469–1527) when he says that the lawgiver should assume that people are "bad" and inclined toward "vicious" behavior? Isn't this an extreme overstatement? Machiavelli lived long ago: Do you think his claim held true then, but does not hold true today? Or is it as true today as ever?
4. Identify a law, of some significance, that you believe is unjust. Have you ever been tempted to break this law? If you did, what would your act accomplish?

ESSAYS

ZORA NEALE HURSTON

For a biographical note on Zora Neale Hurston, *see page 697.*

A Conflict of Interest

An incident happened that made me realize how theories go by the board when a person's livelihood is threatened. A man, a Negro, came into the shop one afternoon and sank down in Banks's chair. Banks was the manager and had the first chair by the door. It was so surprising that for a minute Banks just looked at him and never said a word. Finally, he found his tongue and asked, "What do you want?"

"Hair-cut and shave," the man said belligerently.

"But you can't get no hair-cut and shave here. Mr. Robinson[1] has a fine shop for Negroes on U Street near Fifteenth," Banks told him.

"I know it, but I want one here. The Constitution of the United States—"

5 But by that time, Banks had him by the arm. Not roughly, but he was helping him out of his chair, nevertheless.

"I don't know how to cut your hair," Banks objected. "I was trained on straight hair. Nobody in here knows how."

"Oh, don't hand me that stuff!" the crusader snarled. "Don't be such an Uncle Tom."

"Run on, fellow. You can't get waited on in here."

[1]**Robinson** George Robinson, an African American, owned a chain of barber shops. Most of his shops catered to whites in Washington, D.C. (Editors' note.)

"I'll stay right here until I do. I know my rights. Things like this have got to be broken up. I'll get waited on all right, or sue the place."

"Go ahead and sue," Banks retorted. "Go on uptown, and get your hair cut, man. Don't be so hard-headed for nothing."

"I'm getting waited on right here!"

"You're next, Mr. Powell," Banks said to a waiting customer. "Sorry, mister, but you better go on uptown."

"But I have a right to be waited on wherever I please," the Negro said, and started towards Updyke's chair which was being emptied. Updyke whirled his chair around so that he could not sit down and stepped in front of it. "Don't you touch *my* chair!" Updyke glared. "Go on about your business."

But instead of going, he made to get into the chair by force.

"Don't argue with him! Throw him out of here!" somebody in the back cried. And in a minute, barbers, customers all lathered and hair half cut, and porters, were all helping to throw the Negro out.

The rush carried him way out into the middle of G street and flung him down. He tried to lie there and be a martyr, but the roar of oncoming cars made him jump up and scurry off. We never heard any more about it. I did not participate in the mêlée, but I wanted him thrown out, too. My business was threatened.

It was only that night in bed that I analyzed the whole thing and realized that I was giving sanction to Jim Crow,[2] which theoretically, I was supposed to resist. But here were ten Negro barbers, three porters and two manicurists all stirred up at the threat of our living through loss of patronage. Nobody thought it out at the moment. It was an instinctive thing. That was the first time it was called to my attention that self-interest rides over all sorts of lines. I have seen the same thing happen hundreds of times since, and now I understand it. One sees it breaking over racial, national, religious and class lines. Anglo-Saxon against Anglo-Saxon, Jew against Jew, Negro against Negro, and all sorts of combinations of the three against other combinations of the three. Offhand, you might say that we fifteen Negroes should have felt the racial thing and served him. He was one of us. Perhaps it would have been a beautiful thing if Banks had turned to the shop crowded with customers and announced that this man was going to be served like everybody else even at the risk of losing their patronage, with all of the other employees lined up in the center of the floor shouting, "So say we all!" It would have been a stirring gesture, and made the headlines for a day. Then we could all have gone home to our unpaid rents and bills and things like that. I could leave school and begin my wanderings again. The "militant" Negro who would have been the cause of it all, would have perched on the smuddled-up wreck of things and crowed. Nobody ever found out who or what he was. Perhaps he did what he did on the spur of the moment, not realizing that serving him would have ruined Mr. Robinson, another Negro who had got what he had the hard way. For not only would the G Street shop have been forced to close, but the F Street shop and all of his other six downtown shops. Wrecking George Robinson like that on a "race" angle would have been ironic tragedy. He always helped out any Negro who was trying to do anything progressive as far as he was able. He had no education himself, but he was for it. He would give any Howard University student a job in his shops if they could qualify, even if it was only a few hours a week.

[2]**Jim Crow** The title of a song in a nineteenth-century minstrel show, "Jim Crow" refers to a practice or policy of segregating or discriminating against blacks, as in public places, public vehicles, or employment.

So I do not know what was the ultimate right in this case. I do know how I felt at the time. There is always something fiendish and loathsome about a person who threatens to deprive you of your way of making a living. That is just human-like, I reckon.

[1942]

Joining the Conversation: Critical Thinking and Writing

1. Hurston published this account in 1942, and she was writing about an event that had taken place a couple of decades earlier. Given the period and given Hurston's analysis of her action, do you find her behavior understandable and excusable, or do you think that she is rationalizing cowardice? Explain.
2. Words like *outrageous, ironic, pathetic,* and even *tragic* probably can be appropriately applied to this episode. Would you agree, however, that, as Hurston narrates it, it also has comic elements? If so, explain.
3. Hurston argues that self-interest overrides "racial, national, religious, and class lines." Do you agree? Does she persuade you that at least in this incident it was true, or might there have been other reasons for the employees' actions?

MARTIN LUTHER KING JR.

Martin Luther King Jr. (1929–1968) was born in Atlanta and educated at Morehouse College, Crozer Theological Seminary, and Boston University. In 1954 he was called to serve as a Baptist minister in Montgomery, Alabama. During the next two years he achieved national fame when, using a policy of nonviolent resistance, he successfully led the boycott against segregated bus lines in Montgomery. He then organized the Southern Christian Leadership Conference, which furthered civil rights, first in the South and then nationwide. In 1964 he was awarded the Nobel Peace Prize. Four years later he was assassinated in Memphis, Tennessee.

In 1963 Dr. King was arrested in Birmingham, Alabama, for participating in a march for which no parade permit had been issued by the city officials. In jail he wrote a response to a letter that eight local clergymen had published in a newspaper.

Their letter, titled "A Call for Unity," is printed here, followed by King's response.

April 12, 1963

We the undersigned clergymen are among those who, in January, issued "An Appeal for Law and Order and Common Sense," in dealing with racial problems in Alabama. We expressed understanding that honest convictions in racial matters could properly be pursued in the courts, but urged that decisions of those courts should in the meantime be peacefully obeyed.

Since that time there had been some evidence of increased forebearance and a willingness to face facts. Responsible citizens have undertaken to work on various problems which cause racial friction and unrest. In Birmingham, recent public events have given indication that we all have opportunity for a new constructive and realistic approach to racial problems.

However, we are now confronted by a series of demonstrations by some of our Negro citizens, directed and led in part by outsiders. We recognize the natural impatience of people who feel that their hopes are slow in being realized. But we are convinced that these demonstrations are unwise and untimely.

We agree rather with certain local Negro leadership which has called for honest and open negotiation of racial issues in our area. And we believe this kind of facing of issues can best be accomplished by citizens of our own metropolitan area, white and Negro, meeting with their knowledge and experience of the local situation. All of us need to face that responsibility and find proper channels for its accomplishment.

Just as we formerly pointed out that "hatred and violence have no sanction in our religious and political traditions," we also point out that such actions as incite to hatred and violence, however technically peaceful those actions may be, have not contributed to the resolution of our local problems. We do not believe that these days of new hope are days when extreme measures are justified in Birmingham.

We commend the community as a whole, and the local news media and law enforcement officials in particular, on the calm manner in which these demonstrations have been handled. We urge the public to continue to show restraint should the demonstrations continue, and the law enforcement officials to remain calm and continue to protect our city from violence.

We further strongly urge our own Negro community to withdraw support from these demonstrations, and to unite locally in working peacefully for a better Birmingham. When rights are consistently denied, a cause should be pressed in the courts and in negotiations among local leaders, and not in the streets. We appeal to both our white and Negro citizenry to observe the principles of law and order and common sense.

C.C.J. Carpenter, D.D., L.L.D., Bishop of Alabama; Joseph A. Durick, D.D., Auxiliary Bishop, Diocese of Mobile-Birmingham; Rabbi Milton L. Grafman, Temple Emanu-El, Birmingham, Alabama; Bishop Paul Hardin, Bishop of the Alabama-West Florida Conference of the Methodist Church; Bishop Nolan B. Harmon, Bishop of the North Alabama Conference of the Methodist Church; George M. Murray, D.D., L.L.D., Bishop Coadjutor, Episcopal Diocese of Alabama; Edward V. Ramage, Moderator, Synod of the Alabama Presbyterian Church in the United States; Earl Stallings, Pastor, First Baptist Church, Birmingham, Alabama.

Letter from Birmingham Jail

April 16, 1963

My Dear Fellow Clergymen:

While confined here in the Birmingham city jail, I came across your recent statement calling my present activities "unwise and untimely."[1] Seldom do I pause to answer criticism of my work and ideas. If I sought to answer all the criticisms

[1]This response to a published statement by eight fellow clergymen from Alabama (Bishop C.C.J. Carpenter, Bishop Joseph A. Durick, Rabbi Milton L. Grafman, Bishop Paul Hardin, Bishop Nolan B. Harmon, the Reverend George M. Murray, the Reverend Edward V. Ramage, and the Reverend Earl Stallings) was composed under somewhat constricting circumstances. Begun on the margins of the newspaper in which the statement appeared while I was in jail, the letter was continued on scraps of writing paper supplied by a friendly Negro trusty, and concluded on a pad my attorneys were eventually permitted to leave me. Although the text remains in substance unaltered, I have indulged in the author's prerogative of polishing it for publication. [King's note.]

that cross my desk, my secretaries would have little time for anything other than such correspondence in the course of the day, and I would have no time for constructive work. But since I feel that you are men of genuine good will and that your criticisms are sincerely set forth, I want to try to answer your statement in what I hope will be patient and reasonable terms.

I think I should indicate why I am here in Birmingham, since you have been influenced by the view which argues against "outsiders coming in." I have the honor of serving as president of the Southern Christian Leadership Conference, an organization operating in every southern state, with headquarters in Atlanta, Georgia. We have some eighty-five affiliated organizations across the South, and one of them is the Alabama Christian Movement for Human Rights. Frequently we share staff, educational, and financial resources with our affiliates. Several months ago the affiliate here in Birmingham asked us to be on call to engage in a nonviolent direct-action program if such were deemed necessary. We readily consented, and when the hour came we lived up to our promise. So I, along with several members of my staff, am here because I was invited here. I am here because I have organizational ties here.

But more basically, I am in Birmingham because injustice is here. Just as the prophets of the eighth century B.C. left their villages and carried their "thus saith the Lord" far beyond the boundaries of their home towns, and just as the Apostle Paul left his village of Tarsus and carried the gospel of Jesus Christ to the far corners of the Greco-Roman world, so am I compelled to carry the gospel of freedom beyond my own home town. Like Paul, I must constantly respond to the Macedonian call for aid.

Moreover, I am cognizant of the interrelatedness of all communities and states. I cannot sit idly by in Atlanta and not be concerned about what happens in Birmingham. Injustice anywhere is a threat to justice everywhere. We are caught in an inescapable network of mutuality; tied in a single garment of destiny. Whatever affects one directly, affects all indirectly. Never again can we afford to live with the narrow, provincial "outside agitator" idea. Anyone who lives inside the United States can never be considered an outsider anywhere within its bounds.

5 You deplore the demonstrations taking place in Birmingham. But your statement, I am sorry to say, fails to express a similar concern for the conditions that brought about the demonstrations. I am sure that none of you would want to rest content with the superficial kind of social analysis that deals merely with effects and does not grapple with underlying causes. It is unfortunate that demonstrations are taking place in Birmingham, but it is even more unfortunate that the city's white power structure left the Negro community with no alternative.

In any nonviolent campaign there are four basic steps: collection of the facts to determine whether injustices exist; negotiation; self-purification; and direct action. We have gone through all these steps in Birmingham. There can be no gainsaying the fact that racial injustice engulfs this community. Birmingham is probably the most thoroughly segregated city in the United States. Its ugly record of brutality is widely known. Negroes have experienced grossly unjust treatment in the courts. There have been more unsolved bombings of Negro homes and churches in Birmingham than in any other city in the nation. These are the hard, brutal facts of the case. On the basis of these conditions, Negro leaders sought to negotiate with the city fathers. But the latter consistently refused to engage in good-faith negotiation.

Then, last September, came the opportunity to talk with leaders of Birmingham's economic community. In the course of the negotiations, certain promises were made by the merchants—for example, to remove the stores' humiliating racial signs. On the basis of these promises, the Reverend Fred Shuttleworth and the leaders of the

Martin Luther King Jr., in Birmingham Jail

Alabama Christian Movement for Human Rights agreed to a moratorium on all demonstrations. As the weeks and months went by, we realized that we were the victims of a broken promise. A few signs, briefly removed, returned; the others remained.

As in so many past experiences, our hopes had been blasted, and the shadow of deep disappointment settled upon us. We had no alternative except to prepare for direct action, whereby we would present our very bodies as a means of laying our case before the conscience of the local and the national community. Mindful of the difficulties involved, we decided to undertake a process of self-purification. We began a series of workshops on nonviolence, and we repeatedly asked ourselves: "Are you able to accept blows without retaliating?" "Are you able to endure the ordeal of jail?" We decided to schedule our direct-action program for the Easter season, realizing that except for Christmas, this is the main shopping period of the year. Knowing that a strong economic-withdrawal program would be the by-product of direct action, we felt that this would be the best time to bring pressure to bear on the merchants for the needed change.

Then it occurred to us that Birmingham's mayoralty election was coming up in March, and we speedily decided to postpone action until after election day. When we discovered that the Commissioner of Public Safety, Eugene "Bull" Connor, had piled up enough votes to be in the run-off, we decided again to postpone action until the day after the run-off so that the demonstrations could not be used to cloud the issues. Like many others, we waited to see Mr. Connor defeated, and to this end we endured postponement after postponement. Having aided in this community need, we felt that our direct-action program could be delayed no longer.

10 You may well ask: "Why direct action? Why sit-ins, marches, and so forth? Isn't negotiation a better path?" You are quite right in calling for negotiation. Indeed, this is the very purpose of direct action. Nonviolent direct action seeks to create such a crisis and foster such a tension that a community which has constantly refused to negotiate is forced to confront the issue. It seeks so to dramatize the issue that it can no longer be ignored. My citing the creation of tension as part of the work of the nonviolent-resister may sound rather shocking. But I must confess that I am not afraid of the word "tension." I have earnestly opposed violent tension, but there is a type of constructive, nonviolent tension which is necessary for growth. Just as Socrates felt that it was necessary to create a tension in the mind so that individuals could rise from the bondage of myths and half-truths to the unfettered realm of creative analysis and objective appraisal, so must we see the need for nonviolent gadflies to create the kind of tension in society that will help men rise from the dark depths of prejudice and racism to the majestic heights of understanding and brotherhood.

The purpose of our direct-action program is to create a situation so crisis-packed that it will inevitably open the door to negotiation. I therefore concur with you in your call for negotiation. Too long has our beloved Southland been bogged down in a tragic effort to live in monologue rather than dialogue.

One of the basic points in your statement is that the action that I and my associates have taken in Birmingham is untimely. Some have asked: "Why didn't you give the new city administration time to act?" The only answer that I can give to this query is that the new Birmingham administration must be prodded about as much as the outgoing one, before it will act. We are sadly mistaken if we feel that the election of Albert Boutwell as mayor will bring the millennium to Birmingham. While Mr. Boutwell is a much more gentle person than Mr. Connor, they are both segregationists, dedicated to maintenance of the status quo. I have hope that Mr. Boutwell will be reasonable enough to see the futility of massive resistance to desegregation. But he will not see this without pressure from devotees of civil rights. My friends, I must say to you that we have not made a single gain in civil rights without determined legal and nonviolent pressure. Lamentably, it is an historical fact that privileged groups seldom give up their privileges voluntarily. Individuals may see the moral light and voluntarily give up their unjust posture; but as Reinhold Niebuhr[2] has reminded us, groups tend to be more immoral than individuals.

We know through painful experience that freedom is never voluntarily given by the oppressor; it must be demanded by the oppressed. Frankly, I have yet to engage in a direct-action campaign that was "well timed" in the view of those who have not suffered unduly from the disease of segregation. For years now I have heard the word "Wait!" It rings in the ear of every Negro with piercing familiarity. This "Wait" has almost always meant "Never." We must come to see, with one of our distinguished jurists, that "justice too long delayed is justice denied."[3]

We have waited for more than 340 years for our constitutional and God-given rights. The nations of Asia and Africa are moving with jetlike speed toward gaining political independence, but we still creep at horse-and-buggy pace toward gaining

[2]**Reinhold Niebuhr** Niebuhr (1892–1971) was a minister, political activist, author, and professor at Union Theological Seminary in New York City. [All notes are the editors' unless otherwise specified.] [3]**Justice . . . denied** a quotation attributed to William E. Gladstone (1809–1898), British statesman and prime minister.

a cup of coffee at a lunch counter. Perhaps it is easy for those who have never felt the stinging darts of segregation to say, "Wait." But when you have seen vicious mobs lynch your mothers and fathers at will and drown your sisters and brothers at whim; when you have seen hate-filled policemen curse, kick, and even kill your black brothers and sisters; when you see the vast majority of your twenty million Negro brothers smothering in an airtight cage of poverty in the midst of an affluent society; when you suddenly find your tongue twisted and your speech stammering as you seek to explain to your six-year-old daughter why she can't go to the public amusement park that has just been advertised on television, and see tears welling up in her eyes when she is told that Funtown is closed to colored children, and see ominous clouds of inferiority beginning to form in her little mental sky, and see her beginning to distort her personality by developing an unconscious bitterness toward white people; when you have to concoct an answer for a five-year-old son who is asking: "Daddy, why do white people treat colored people so mean?"; when you take a cross-country drive and find it necessary to sleep night after night in the uncomfortable corners of your automobile because no motel will accept you; when you are humiliated day in and day out by nagging signs reading "white" and "colored"; when your first name becomes "nigger," your middle name becomes "boy" (however old you are) and your last name becomes "John," and your wife and mother are never given the respected title "Mrs."; when you are harried by day and haunted by night by the fact that you are a Negro, living constantly at tiptoe stance, never quite knowing what to expect next, and are plagued with inner fears and outer resentments; when you are forever fighting a degenerating sense of "nobodiness"—then you will understand why we find it difficult to wait. There comes a time when the cup of endurance runs over, and men are no longer willing to be plunged into the abyss of despair. I hope, sirs, you can understand our legitimate and unavoidable impatience.

15 You express a great deal of anxiety over our willingness to break laws. This is certainly a legitimate concern. Since we so diligently urge people to obey the Supreme Court's decision of 1954 outlawing segregation in the public schools, at first glance it may seem rather paradoxical for us consciously to break laws. One may well ask: "How can you advocate breaking some laws and obeying others?" The answer lies in the fact that there are two types of laws: just and unjust. I would be the first to advocate obeying just laws. One has not only a legal but a moral responsibility to obey just laws. Conversely, one has a moral responsibility to disobey unjust laws. I would agree with St. Augustine that "an unjust law is no law at all."

Now, what is the difference between the two? How does one determine whether a law is just or unjust? A just law is a man-made code that squares with the moral law or the law of God. An unjust law is a code that is out of harmony with the moral law. To put it in the terms of St. Thomas Aquinas: An unjust law is a human law that is not rooted in eternal law and natural law. Any law that uplifts human personality is just. Any law that degrades human personality is unjust. All segregation statutes are unjust because segregation distorts the soul and damages the personality. It gives the segregator a false sense of superiority and the segregated a false sense of inferiority. Segregation, to use the terminology of the Jewish philosopher Martin Buber, substitutes an "I-it" relationship for an "I-thou" relationship and ends up relegating persons to the status of things. Hence segregation is not only politically, economically, and sociologically unsound, it is morally wrong and sinful. Paul Tillich[4] has said that sin is separation. Is not segregation an existential expression of man's tragic separation, his awful estrangement, his terrible sinfulness? Thus it is that I can urge men to obey the 1954 decision of the Supreme Court, for it is morally right; and I can urge them to disobey segregation ordinances, for they are morally wrong.

Let us consider a more concrete example of just and unjust laws. An unjust law is a code that a numerical or power majority group compels a minority group to obey but does not make binding on itself. This is *difference* made legal. By the same token, a just law is a code that a majority compels a minority to follow and that it is willing to follow itself. This is *sameness* made legal.

Let me give another explanation. A law is unjust if it is inflicted on a minority that, as a result of being denied the right to vote, had no part in enacting or devising the law. Who can say that the legislature of Alabama which set up that state's segregation laws was democratically elected? Throughout Alabama all sorts of devious methods are used to prevent Negroes from becoming registered voters, and there are some counties in which, even though Negroes constitute a majority of the population, not a single Negro is registered. Can any law enacted under such circumstances be considered democratically structured?

Sometimes a law is just on its face and unjust in its application. For instance, I have been arrested on a charge of parading without a permit. Now, there is nothing wrong in having an ordinance which requires a permit for a parade. But such an ordinance becomes unjust when it is used to maintain segregation and to deny citizens the First Amendment privilege of peaceful assembly and protest.

20 I hope you are able to see the distinction I am trying to point out. In no sense do I advocate evading or defying the law, as would the rabid segregationist. That would lead to anarchy. One who breaks an unjust law must do so openly, lovingly, and with a willingness to accept the penalty. I submit that an individual who breaks a law that conscience tells him is unjust, and who willingly accepts the penalty of imprisonment in order to arouse the conscience of the community over its injustice, is in reality expressing the highest respect for law.

Of course, there is nothing new about this kind of civil disobedience. It was evidenced sublimely in the refusal of Shadrach, Meshach, and Abednego to obey the laws of Nebuchadnezzar, on the ground that a higher moral law was at stake. It was practiced superbly by the early Christians, who were willing to face hungry lions and the excruciating pain of chopping blocks rather than submit to certain unjust laws of the Roman Empire. To a degree, academic freedom is a reality today because Socrates practiced civil disobedience. In our own nation, the Boston Tea Party represented a massive act of civil disobedience.

We should never forget that everything Adolf Hitler did in Germany was "legal" and everything the Hungarian freedom fighters did in Hungary was "illegal." It was "illegal" to aid and comfort a Jew in Hitler's Germany. Even so, I am sure that, had I lived in Germany at the time, I would have aided and comforted my Jewish brothers. If today I lived in a Communist country where certain principles dear to the Christian faith are suppressed, I would openly advocate disobeying that country's anti-religious laws.

I must make two honest confessions to you, my Christian and Jewish brothers. First, I must confess that over the past few years I have been gravely disappointed with the white moderate. I have almost reached the regrettable conclusion that the

[4]**Paul Tillich** Tillich (1886–1965), born in Germany, taught theology at several German universities, but in 1933 he was dismissed from his post at the University of Frankfurt because of his opposition to the Nazi regime. At the invitation of Reinhold Niebuhr, he came to the United States and taught at Union Theological Seminary.

Negro's great stumbling block in his stride toward freedom is not the White Citizen's Counciler or the Ku Klux Klanner, but the white moderate, who is more devoted to "order" than to justice; who prefers a negative peace which is the absence of tension to a positive peace which is the presence of justice; who constantly says: "I agree with you in the goal you seek, but I cannot agree with your methods or direct action"; who paternalistically believes he can set the timetable for another man's freedom; who lives by a mythical concept of time and who constantly advises the Negro to wait for a "more convenient season." Shallow understanding from people of good will is more frustrating than absolute misunderstanding from people of ill will. Lukewarm acceptance is much more bewildering than outright rejection.

I had hoped that the white moderate would understand that law and order exist for the purpose of establishing justice and that when they fail in this purpose they become the dangerously structured dams that block the flow of social progress. I had hoped that the white moderate would understand that the present tension in the South is a necessary phase of the transition from an obnoxious negative peace, in which the Negro passively accepted his unjust plight, to a substantive and positive peace, in which all men will respect the dignity and worth of human personality. Actually, we who engage in nonviolent direct action are not the creators of tension. We merely bring to the surface the hidden tension that is already alive. We bring it out in the open, where it can be seen and dealt with. Like a boil that can never be cured so long as it is covered up but must be opened with all its ugliness to the natural medicines of air and light, injustice must be exposed, with all the tension its exposure creates, to the light of human conscience and the air of national opinion before it can be cured.

25 In your statement you assert that our actions, even though peaceful, must be condemned because they precipitate violence. But is this a logical assertion? Isn't this like condemning a robbed man because his possession of money precipitated the evil act of robbery? Isn't this like condemning Socrates because his unswerving commitment to truth and his philosophical inquiries precipitated the act by the misguided populace in which they made him drink hemlock? Isn't this like condemning Jesus because his unique God-consciousness and never-ceasing devotion to God's will precipitated the evil act of crucifixion? We must come to see that, as the federal courts have consistently affirmed, it is wrong to urge an individual to cease his efforts to gain his basic constitutional rights because the quest may precipitate violence. Society must protect the robbed and punish the robber.

I had also hoped that the white moderate would reject the myth concerning time in relation to the struggle for freedom. I have just received a letter from a white brother in Texas. He writes: "All Christians know that the colored people will receive equal rights eventually, but it is possible that you are in too great a religious hurry. It has taken Christianity almost two thousand years to accomplish what it has. The teachings of Christ take time to come to earth." Such an attitude stems from a tragic misconception of time, from the strangely irrational notion that there is something in the very flow of time that will inevitably cure all ills. Actually, time itself is neutral; it can be used either destructively or constructively. More and more I feel that the people of ill will have used time much more effectively than have the people of good will. We will have to repent in this generation not merely for the hateful words and actions of the bad people but for the appalling silence of the good people. Human progress never rolls in on wheels of inevitability; it comes through the tireless efforts of men willing to be co-workers with God, and without this hard work, time itself becomes an ally of the forces of social stagnation. We must use time creatively, in the knowledge that the time is always ripe to do right. Now is the time to make real the promise of democracy and transform our pending national elegy into a creative psalm of brotherhood. Now is the time to lift our national policy from the quicksand of racial injustice to the solid rock of human dignity.

You speak of our activity in Birmingham as extreme. At first I was rather disappointed that fellow clergymen would see my nonviolent efforts as those of an extremist. I began thinking about the fact that I stand in the middle of two opposing forces in the Negro community. One is a force of complacency, made up in part of Negroes who, as a result of long years of oppression, are so drained of self-respect and a sense of "somebodiness" that they have adjusted to segregation; and in part of a few middle-class Negroes who, because of a degree of academic and economic security and because in some ways they profit by segregation, have become insensitive to the problems of the masses. The other force is one of bitterness and hatred, and it comes perilously close to advocating violence. It is expressed in the various black nationalist groups that are springing up across the nation, the largest and best-known being Elijah Muhammad's Muslim movement. Nourished by the Negro's frustration over the continued existence of racial discrimination, this movement is made up of people who have lost faith in America, who have absolutely repudiated Christianity, and who have concluded that the white man is an incorrigible "devil."

I have tried to stand between these two forces, saying that we need emulate neither the "do-nothingism" of the complacent nor the hatred and despair of the black nationalist. For there is the more excellent way of love and nonviolent protest. I am grateful to God that, through the influence of the Negro church, the way of nonviolence became an integral part of our struggle.

If this philosophy had not emerged, by now many streets of the South should, I am convinced, be flowing with blood. And I am further convinced that if our white brothers dismiss as "rabble-rousers" and "outside agitators" those of us who employ nonviolent direct action, and if they refuse to support our nonviolent efforts, millions of Negroes will, out of frustration and despair, seek solace and security in black-nationalist ideologies—a development that would inevitably lead to a frightening racial nightmare.

30 Oppressed people cannot remain oppressed forever. The yearning for freedom eventually manifests itself, and that is what has happened to the American Negro. Something within has reminded him of his birthright of freedom, and something without has reminded him that it can be gained. Consciously or unconsciously, he has been caught up by the *Zeitgeist,*[5] and with his black brothers of Africa and his brown and yellow brothers of Asia, South America, and the Caribbean, the United States Negro is moving with a sense of great urgency toward the promised land of racial justice. If one recognizes this vital urge that has engulfed the Negro community, one should readily understand why public demonstrations are taking place. The Negro has many pent-up resentments and latent frustrations, and he must release them. So let him march; let him make prayer pilgrimages to the city hall; let him go on freedom rides—and try to understand why he must do so. If his repressed emotions are not released in nonviolent ways, they will seek expression through violence; this is not a threat but a fact of history. So I have not said to my people: "Get rid of your discontent." Rather, I have tried to say that this normal

[5]***Zeitgeist*** German for "spirit of the age."

and healthy discontent can be channeled into the creative outlet of nonviolent direct action. And now this approach is being termed extremist.

But though I was initially disappointed at being categorized as an extremist, as I continued to think about the matter I gradually gained a measure of satisfaction from the label. Was not Jesus an extremist for love: "Love your enemies, bless them that curse you, do good to them that hate you, and pray for them which despitefully use you, and persecute you." Was not Amos an extremist for justice: "Let justice roll down like waters and righteousness like an ever-flowing stream." Was not Paul an extremist for the Christian gospel: "I bear in my body the marks of the Lord Jesus." Was not Martin Luther an extremist: "Here I stand; I cannot do otherwise, so help me God." And John Bunyan:[6] "I will stay in jail to the end of my days before I make a butchery of my conscience." And Abraham Lincoln: "This nation cannot survive half slave and half free." And Thomas Jefferson: "We hold these truths to be self-evident, that all men are created equal. . . ." So the question is not whether we will be extremists, but what kind of extremists we will be. Will we be extremists for hate or for love? Will we be extremists for the preservation of injustice or for the extension of justice? In that dramatic scene on Calvary's hill three men were crucified. We must never forget that all three were crucified for the same crime—the crime of extremism. Two were extremists for immorality, and thus fell below their environment. The other, Jesus Christ, was an extremist for love, truth, and goodness, and thereby rose above his environment. Perhaps the South, the nation, and the world are in dire need of creative extremists.

I had hoped that the white moderate would see this need. Perhaps I was too optimistic; perhaps I expected too much. I suppose I should have realized that few members of the oppressor race can understand the deep groans and passionate yearnings of the oppressed race, and still fewer have the vision to see that injustice must be rooted out by strong, persistent, and determined action. I am thankful, however, that some of our white brothers in the South have grasped the meaning of this social revolution and committed themselves to it. They are still all too few in quantity, but they are big in quality. Some—such as Ralph McGill, Lillian Smith, Harry Golden, James McBride Dabbs, Ann Braden, and Sarah Patton Boyle—have written about our struggle in eloquent and prophetic terms. Others have marched with us down nameless streets of the South. They have languished in filthy, roach-infested jails, suffering the abuse and brutality of policemen who view them as "dirty nigger-lovers." Unlike so many of their moderate brothers and sisters, they have recognized the urgency of the moment and sensed the need for powerful "action" antidotes to combat the disease of segregation.

Let me take note of my other major disappointment. I have been so greatly disappointed with the white church and its leadership. Of course, there are some notable exceptions. I am not unmindful of the fact that each of you has taken some significant stands on this issue. I commend you, Reverend Stallings, for your Christian stand on this past Sunday, in welcoming Negroes to your worship service on a nonsegregated basis. I commend the Catholic leaders of this state for integrating Spring Hill College several years ago.

But despite these notable exceptions, I must honestly reiterate that I have been disappointed with the church. I do not say this as one of those negative critics who can always find something wrong with the church. I say this as a minister

[6]**John Bunyan** English writer (1628–1688) best known for his *Pilgrim's Progress* (two parts, 1678 and 1684); from 1660 to 1672, he was imprisoned for his political and religious views.

of the gospel, who loves the church; who was nurtured in its bosom; who has been sustained by its spiritual blessings and who will remain true to it as long as the cord of life shall lengthen.

35 When I was suddenly catapulted into the leadership of the bus protest in Montgomery, Alabama, a few years ago, I felt we would be supported by the white church. I felt that the white ministers, priests, and rabbis of the South would be among our strongest allies. Instead, some have been outright opponents, refusing to understand the freedom movement and misrepresenting its leaders; all too many others have been more cautious than courageous and have remained silent behind the anesthetizing security of stained-glass windows.

In spite of my shattered dreams, I came to Birmingham with the hope that the white religious leadership of this community would see the justice of our cause and, with deep moral concern, would serve as the channel through which our just grievances could reach the power structure. I had hoped that each of you would understand. But again I have been disappointed.

I have heard numerous southern religious leaders admonish their worshipers to comply with a desegregation decision because it is the law, but I have longed to hear white ministers declare: "Follow this decree because integration is morally right and because the Negro is your brother." In the midst of blatant injustices inflicted upon the Negro, I have watched white churchmen stand on the sideline and mouth pious irrelevancies and sanctimonious trivialities. In the midst of a mighty struggle to rid our nation of racial and economic injustice, I have heard many ministers say: "Those are social issues, with which the gospel has no real concern." And I have watched many churches commit themselves to a completely otherworldly religion which makes a strange, unbiblical distinction between body and soul, between the sacred and the secular.

I have traveled the length and breadth of Alabama, Mississippi, and all the other southern states. On sweltering summer days and crisp autumn mornings I have looked at the South's beautiful churches with their lofty spires pointing heavenward. I have beheld the impressive outlines of her massive religious-education buildings. Over and over I have found myself saying: "What kind of people worship here? Who is their God? Where were their voices when the lips of Governor Barnett dripped with words of interposition and nullification? Where were they when Governor Wallace gave a clarion call for defiance and hatred? Where were their voices of support when bruised and weary Negro men and women decided to rise from the dark dungeons of complacency to the bright hills of creative protest?"

Yes, these questions are still in my mind. In deep disappointment I have wept over the laxity of the church. But be assured that my tears have been tears of love. There can be no deep disappointment where there is not deep love. Yes, I love the church. How could I do otherwise? I am in the rather unique position of being the son, the grandson, and the great-grandson of preachers. Yes, I see the church as the body of Christ. But, Oh! How we have blemished and scarred that body through social neglect and through fear of being nonconformists.

40 There was a time when the church was very powerful—in the time when the early Christians rejoiced at being deemed worthy to suffer for what they believed. In those days the church was not merely a thermometer that recorded the ideas and principles of popular opinion; it was a thermostat that transformed the mores of society. Whenever the early Christians entered a town, the people in power became disturbed and immediately sought to convict the Christians for being "disturbers of the peace" and "outside agitators." But the Christians

pressed on, in the conviction that they were "a colony of heaven," called to obey God rather than man. Small in number, they were big in commitment. They were too God-intoxicated to be "astronomically intimidated." By their effort and example they brought an end to such ancient evils as infanticide and gladiatorial contests.

Things are different now. So often the contemporary church is a weak, ineffectual voice with an uncertain sound. So often it is an archdefender of the status quo. Far from being disturbed by the presence of the church, the power structure of the average community is consoled by the church's silent—and often even vocal—sanction of things as they are.

But the judgment of God is upon the church as never before. If today's church does not recapture the sacrificial spirit of the early church, it will lose its authenticity, forfeit the loyalty of millions, and be dismissed as an irrelevant social club with no meaning for the twentieth century. Every day I meet young people whose disappointment with the church has turned into outright disgust.

Perhaps I have once again been too optimistic. Is organized religion too inextricably bound to the status quo to save our nation and the world? Perhaps I must turn my faith to the inner spiritual church, the church within the church, as the true *ekklesia* and the hope of the world. But again I am thankful to God that some noble souls from the ranks of organized religion have broken loose from the paralyzing chains of conformity and joined us as active partners in the struggle for freedom. They have left their secure congregations and walked the streets of Albany, Georgia, with us. They have gone down the highways of the South on tortuous rides for freedom. Yes, they have gone to jail with us. Some have been dismissed from their churches, have lost the support of their bishops and fellow ministers. But they have acted in the faith that right defeated is stronger than evil triumphant. Their witness has been the spiritual salt that has preserved the true meaning of the gospel in these troubled times. They have carved a tunnel of hope through the dark mountain of disappointment.

I hope the church as a whole will meet the challenge of this decisive hour. But even if the church does not come to the aid of justice, I have no despair about the future. I have no fear about the outcome of our struggle in Birmingham, even if our motives are at present misunderstood. We will reach the goal of freedom in Birmingham and all over the nation, because the goal of America is freedom. Abused and scorned though we may be, our destiny is tied up with America's destiny. Before the pilgrims landed at Plymouth, we were here. Before the pen of Jefferson etched the majestic words of the Declaration of Independence across the pages of history, we were here. For more than two centuries our forebears labored in this country without wages; they made cotton king; they built the homes of their masters while suffering gross injustice and shameful humiliation—and yet out of a bottomless vitality they continue to thrive and develop. If the inexpressible cruelties of slavery could not stop us, the opposition we now face will surely fail. We will win our freedom because the sacred heritage of our nation and the eternal will of God are embodied in our echoing demands.

45 Before closing I feel impelled to mention one other point in your statement that has troubled me profoundly. You warmly commended the Birmingham police force for keeping "order" and "preventing violence." I doubt that you would have so warmly commended the police force if you had seen its dogs sinking their teeth into unarmed, nonviolent Negroes. I doubt that you would so quickly commend the policemen if you were to observe their ugly and inhumane treatment of

Negroes here in the city jail; if you were to watch them push and curse old Negro women and young Negro girls; if you were to see them slap and kick old Negro men and young boys; if you were to observe them, as they did on two occasions, refuse to give us food because we wanted to sing our grace together. I cannot join you in your praise of the Birmingham police department.

It is true that the police have exercised a degree of discipline in handling the demonstrators. In this sense they have conducted themselves rather "nonviolently" in public. But for what purpose? To preserve the evil system of segregation. Over the past few years I have consistently preached that nonviolence demands that the means we use must be as pure as the ends we seek. I have tried to make clear that it is wrong to use immoral means to attain moral ends. But now I must affirm that it is just as wrong, or perhaps even more so, to use moral means to preserve immoral ends. Perhaps Mr. Connor and his policemen have been rather nonviolent in public, as was Chief Pritchett in Albany, Georgia, but they used the moral means of nonviolence to maintain the immoral end of racial injustice. As T. S. Eliot has said: "The last temptation is the greatest treason: To do the right deed for the wrong reason."

I wish you had commended the Negro sit-inners and demonstrators of Birmingham for their sublime courage, their willingness to suffer, and their amazing discipline in the midst of great provocation. One day the South will recognize its real heroes. They will be the James Merediths, with the noble sense of purpose that enables them to face jeering and hostile mobs, and with the agonizing loneliness that characterizes the life of the pioneer. They will be old, oppressed, battered Negro women, symbolized in a seventy-two-year-old woman in Montgomery, Alabama, who rose up with a sense of dignity and with her people decided not to ride segregated buses, and who responded with ungrammatical profundity to one who inquired about her weariness: "My feets is tired, but my soul is at rest." They will be the young high school and college students, the young ministers of the gospel and a host of their elders, courageously and nonviolently sitting in at lunch counters and willingly going to jail for conscience' sake. One day the South will know that when these disinherited children of God sat down at lunch counters, they were in reality standing up for what is best in the American dream and for the most sacred values in our Judaeo-Christian heritage, thereby bringing our nation back to those great wells of democracy which were dug deep by the founding fathers in their formulation of the Constitution and the Declaration of Independence.

Never before have I written so long a letter. I'm afraid it is much too long to take your precious time. I can assure you that it would have been much shorter if I had been writing from a comfortable desk, but what else can one do when he is alone in a narrow jail cell, other than write long letters, think long thoughts, and pray long prayers?

If I have said anything in this letter that overstates the truth and indicates an unreasonable impatience, I beg you to forgive me. If I have said anything that understates the truth and indicates my having a patience that allows me to settle for anything less than brotherhood, I beg God to forgive me.

50 I hope this letter finds you strong in the faith. I also hope that circumstances will soon make it possible for me to meet each of you, not as an integrationist or a civil-rights leader but as a fellow clergyman and a Christian brother. Let us all

[6]**James Meredith** On October 1, 1962, in the face of widespread opposition, James Meredith became the first African American to attend the University of Mississippi.

hope that the dark clouds of racial prejudice will soon pass away and the deep fog of misunderstanding will be lifted from our fear-drenched communities, and in some not too distant tomorrow the radiant stars of love and brotherhood will shine over our great nation with all their scintillating beauty.

Yours for the cause of Peace and Brotherhood,
Martin Luther King Jr.

[1963]

Joining the Conversation: Critical Thinking and Writing

1. In his first five paragraphs, how does King assure his audience that he is not a meddlesome intruder but a man of good will?
2. In paragraph 3 King refers to Hebrew prophets and to the Apostle Paul, and later (paragraph 10) to Socrates. What is the point of these references?
3. In paragraph 11 what does King mean when he says that "our beloved Southland" has long tried to "live in monologue rather than dialogue"?
4. King begins paragraph 23 with "I must make two honest confessions to you, my Christian and Jewish brothers." What would have been gained or lost if he had used this paragraph as his opening?
5. King's last three paragraphs do not advance his argument. What do they do?
6. Why does King advocate breaking unjust laws "openly, lovingly" (paragraph 20)? What does he mean by these words? What other motives or attitudes do these words rule out?
7. Construct two definitions of "civil disobedience," and explain whether and to what extent it is easier (or harder) to justify civil disobedience, depending on how you have defined the expression.
8. If you feel that you wish to respond to King's letter on some point, write a letter nominally addressed to King. You may, if you wish, adopt the persona of one of the eight clergymen whom King initially addressed.
9. King writes (paragraph 46) that "nonviolence demands that the means we use must be as pure as the ends we seek." How do you think King would evaluate the following acts of civil disobedience: (a) occupying a college administration building in order to protest the administration's unsatisfactory response to a racial incident on campus, or in order to protest the failure of the administration to hire minority persons as staff and faculty; (b) sailing on a collision course with a whaling ship to protest against whaling; (c) trespassing on an abortion clinic to protest abortion? Set down your answer in an essay of 500 words.

STORIES

ELIZABETH BISHOP

Elizabeth Bishop (1911–1979) is chiefly known as a poet. Here, however, we give a prose piece. In a letter (3 February 1937) Bishop mentions the act that served as the immediate trigger for the piece, but of course far more experience of life is in the work than the trivial act she specifies: "I once hung [my cat's] artificial mouse on a string to a chairback, without thinking what I had done—it looked very sad."

The Hanging of the Mouse

Early, early in the morning, even before five o'clock, the mouse was brought out, but already there were large crowds. Some of the animals had not gone to bed the night before, but had stayed up later and later; at first because of a vague feeling of celebration, and then, after deciding several times that they might as well wander about the town for an hour more, to conclude the night by arriving at the square in time for the hanging became only sensible. These animals hiccupped a little and had an air of cynical lassitude. Those who had got up out of bed to come also appeared weary and silent, but not so bored.

The mouse was led in by two enormous brown beetles in the traditional picturesque armor of an earlier day. They came on to the square through the small black door and marched between the lines of soldiers standing at attention: straight ahead, to the right, around two sides of the hollow square, to the left, and out into the middle where the gallows stood. Before each turn the beetle on the right glanced quickly at the beetle on the left; their traditional long, long antennae swerved sharply in the direction they were to turn and they did it to perfection. The mouse, of course, who had had no military training and who, at the moment, was crying so hard he could scarcely see where he was going, rather spoiled the precision and snap of the beetles. At each corner he fell slightly forward, and when he was jerked in the right direction his feet became tangled together. The beetles, however, without even looking at him, each time lifted him quickly into the air for a second until his feet were untangled.

At that hour in the morning the mouse's gray clothes were almost indistinguishable from the light. But his whimpering could be heard, and the end of his nose was rose-red from crying so much. The crowd of small animals tipped back their heads and sniffed with pleasure.

A raccoon, wearing the traditional black mask, was the executioner. He was very fastidious and did everything just so. One of his young sons, also wearing a black mask, waited on him with a small basin and a pitcher of water. First he washed his hands and rinsed them carefully; then he washed the rope and rinsed it. At the last minute he again washed his hands and drew on a pair of elegant black kid gloves.

5 A large praying mantis was in charge of the religious end of the ceremonies. He hurried up on the stage after the mouse and his escorts, but once there a fit of nerves seemed to seize him. He glided to the left a few steps, to the right a few steps, lifted his arms gracefully, but could not seem to begin; and it was quite apparent that he would have liked nothing better than to have jumped quickly down and left the whole affair. When his arms were stretched to Heaven his large eyes flashed toward the crowd, and when he looked up, his body was twitching and he moved about in a really pathetic way. He seemed to feel ill at ease with the low characters around him: the beetles, the hangmen, and the criminal mouse. At last he made a great effort to pull himself together and, approaching the mouse, said a few words in a high, incomprehensible voice. The mouse jumped from nervousness, and cried harder than ever.

At this point the spectators would all undoubtedly have burst out laughing, but just then the King's messenger appeared on the balcony above the small black door the mouse and his guards had lately come through. He was a very large, overweight bullfrog, also dressed in the traditional costume and carrying the traditional long scroll that dragged for several feet on the ground and had the real speech, on a little slip of paper, pasted inside it. The scroll and the white plume on his hat made him look comically like something in a nursery tale, but his voice was impressive enough to awe the crowd into polite attention. It was a deep bass: "Glug! Glug! Berrr-up!" No one could understand a word of the mouse's death sentence.

With the help of some pushes and pinches from the beetles, the executioner got the mouse into position. The rope was tied exquisitely behind one of his little round ears. The mouse raised a hand and wiped his nose with it, and most of the crowd interpreted this gesture as a farewell wave and spoke of it for weeks afterwards. The hangman's young son, at a signal from his father, sprang the trap.

"Squee-eek! Squee-eek!" went the mouse.

His whiskers rowed hopelessly round and round in the air a few times and his feet flew up and curled into little balls like young fern-plants.

10 The praying mantis, with an hysterical fling of his long limbs, had disappeared in the crowd. It was all so touching that a cat, who had brought her child in her mouth, shed several large tears. They rolled down on to the child's back and he began to squirm and shriek, so that the mother thought that the sight of the hanging had perhaps been too much for him, but an excellent moral lesson, nevertheless.

[1937]

Joining the Conversation: Critical Thinking and Writing

1. We have several times quoted Robert Frost's observation that a poem (he could have said any work of literature) is "a performance in words." Reread Bishop's first paragraph, and discuss it in terms of "performance." Why, for instance do you think she repeats the word "early" in the first sentence? In this paragraph notice that Bishop says the animals decided "several times that they might as well wander about the town for an hour more." What do you make of deciding "several times"? And then Bishop says that the idea of concluding the night by "arriving at the square in time for the hanging became only sensible." What do you make of "sensible," especially in the context that immediately follows it: "These animals hiccupped a little and had an air of cynical lassitude." What does "cynical lassitude" mean? How has Bishop juggled her words so as to convey what you assume is her attitude toward the animals?
2. Would you agree that there are humorous touches in the piece? If so, point them out. If you don't think there is anything humorous in it, point to something that someone might conceivably find amusing, and explain why you do not find it so.
3. Describe your response to the sentence, "The rope was tied exquisitely behind one of his little round ears."
4. In the final paragraph Bishop tells us that the cat believed "the sight of the hanging [provided] . . . an excellent moral lesson. . . ." Do you assume that Bishop agrees? By the way, executions used to be public, partly because it was felt that they served to educate the general public. As the proverb puts it, "Who hangs one corrects a thousand." Do you think Bishop would agree or disagree? Why?

URSULA K. LE GUIN

Ursula K. Le Guin was born in 1929 in Berkeley, California, the daughter of a distinguished mother (Theodora Kroeber, a folklorist) and father (Alfred L. Kroeber, an anthropologist). After graduating from Radcliffe College, she earned a master's degree at Columbia University; in 1952 she held a Fulbright Fellowship for study in Paris, where she met and married Charles Le Guin, a historian. She began writing in earnest while bringing up three children. Although her work is most widely known to fans of science fiction, because it usually has larger moral or political dimensions it interests many other readers who normally do not care for sci-fi.

Le Guin has said that she was prompted to write the following story by a remark she encountered in William James's "The Moral Philosopher and the Moral Life." James suggests there that if millions of people could be "kept permanently happy on the one simple condition that a certain lost soul on the far-off edge of things should lead a life of lonely torment," our moral sense "would make us immediately feel" it would be "hideous" to accept such a bargain. This story first appeared in New Dimensions 3 *(1973).*

The Ones Who Walk Away from Omelas

With a clamor of bells that set the swallows soaring, the Festival of Summer came to the city Omelas, bright-towered by the sea. The rigging of the boats in harbor sparkled with flags. In the streets between houses with red roofs and painted walls, between old moss-grown gardens and under avenues of trees, past great parks and public buildings, processions moved. Some were decorous: old people in long stiff robes of mauve and gray, grave master workmen, quiet, merry women carrying their babies and chatting as they walked. In other streets the music beat faster, a shimmering of gong and tambourine, and the people went dancing, the procession was a dance. Children dodged in and out, their high calls rising like the swallows' crossing flights over the music and the singing. All the processions wound towards the north side of the city, where on the great water-meadow called the Green Fields boys and girls, naked in the bright air, with mudstained feet and ankles and long, lithe arms, exercised their restive horses before the race. The horses wore no gear at all but a halter without bit. Their manes were braided with streamers of silver, gold, and green. They flared their nostrils and pranced and boasted to one another; they were vastly excited, the horse being the only animal who has adopted our ceremonies as his own. Far off to the north and west the mountains stood up half encircling Omelas on her bay. The air of morning was so clear that the snow still crowning the Eighteen Peaks burned with white-gold fire across the miles of sunlit air, under the dark blue of the sky. There was just enough wind to make the banners that marked the race-course snap and flutter now and then. In the silence of the broad green meadows one could hear the music winding through the city streets, farther and nearer and ever approaching, a cheerful faint sweetness of the air that from time to time trembled and gathered together and broke out into the great joyous clanging of the bells.

Joyous! How is one to tell about joy? How describe the citizens of Omelas?

They were not simple folk, you see, though they were happy. But we do not say the words of cheer much any more. All smiles have become archaic. Given a description such as this one tends to make certain assumptions. Given a description such as this one tends to look next for the King, mounted on a splendid stallion and surrounded by his noble knights, or perhaps in a golden litter borne by great-muscled slaves. But there was no king. They did not use swords, or keep slaves. They were not barbarians. I do not know the rules and laws of their society, but I suspect that they were singularly few. As they did without monarchy and slavery, so they also got on without the stock exchange, the advertisement, the secret police, and the bomb. Yet I repeat that these were not simple folk, not dulcet shepherds, noble savages, bland utopians. They were not less complex than us. The trouble is that we have a bad habit, encouraged by pedants and sophisticates, of considering happiness as something rather stupid. Only pain is intellectual, only evil interesting. This is the treason of the artist: a refusal to admit the banality of evil and the terrible boredom of pain. If you can't lick 'em, join 'em. If it hurts, repeat it. But to praise despair is to condemn delight, to embrace violence is to lose hold of everything else. We have almost lost hold, we can no longer describe a happy man, nor make any celebration of joy. How can I tell you about the people of Omelas? They were not naïve and happy children—though their children were, in fact, happy. They were mature, intelligent, passionate adults whose lives were not wretched. O miracle! But I wish I could describe it better. I wish I could convince you. Omelas sounds in my words like a city in a fairy tale, long ago and far away, once upon a time. Perhaps it would be best if you imagined it as your own fancy bids, assuming it will rise to the occasion, for certainly I cannot suit you all. For instance, how about technology? I think that there would be no cars or helicopters in and above the streets; this follows from the fact that the people of Omelas are happy people. Happiness is based on a just discrimination of what is necessary, what is neither necessary nor destructive, and what is destructive. In the middle category, however—that of the unnecessary but undestructive, that of comfort, luxury, exuberance, etc.—they could perfectly well have central heating, subway trains, washing machines, and all kinds of marvelous devices not yet invented here, floating light-sources, fuelless power, a cure for the common cold. Or they could have none of that: it doesn't matter. As you like it. I incline to think that people from towns up and down the coast have been coming in to Omelas during the last days before the Festival on very fast little trains and double-decked trams, and that the train station of Omelas is actually the handsomest building in town, though plainer than the magnificent Farmers' Market. But even granted trains, I fear that Omelas so far strikes some of you as goody-goody. Smiles, bells, parades, horses, bleh. If so, please add an orgy. If an orgy would help, don't hesitate. Let us not, however, have temples from which issue beautiful nude priests and priestesses already half in ecstasy and ready to copulate with any man or woman, lover or stranger, who desires union with the deep godhead of the blood, although that was my first idea. But really it would be better not to have any temples in Omelas—at least, not manned temples. Religion yes, clergy no. Surely the beautiful nudes can just wander about, offering themselves like divine soufflés to the hunger of the needy and the rapture of the flesh. Let them join the processions. Let tambourines be struck above the copulations, and the glory of desire be proclaimed upon the gongs, and (a not unimportant point) let the offspring of these delightful rituals be beloved and looked after by all. One thing I know there is none of in Omelas is guilt. But what else should there be? I thought that first there were no drugs, but that is puritanical. For those who like it, the faint insistent sweetness of *drooz* may perfume the ways of the city, *drooz* which first brings a great lightness and brilliance to the mind and limbs, and then after some hours a dreamy languor, and wonderful visions at last of the very arcana and inmost secrets of the Universe, as well as exciting the pleasure of sex beyond all belief; and it is not habit-forming. For more modest tastes I think there ought to be beer. What else, what else belongs in the joyous city? The sense of victory, surely, the celebration of courage. But as we did without clergy, let us do without soldiers. The joy built upon successful slaughter is not the right kind of joy; it will not do; it is fearful and it is trivial. A boundless and generous contentment, a magnanimous triumph felt not against some outer enemy but in communion with the finest and fairest in the souls of all men everywhere and the splendor of the world's summer: this is what swells the hearts of the people of Omelas, and the victory they celebrate is that of life. I really don't think many of them need to take *drooz*.

Most of the processions have reached the Green Fields by now. A marvelous smell of cooking goes forth from the red and blue tents of the provisioners. The faces of small children are amiably sticky; in the benign grey beard of a man a couple of crumbs of rich pastry are entangled. The youths and girls have mounted their horses and are beginning to group around the starting line of the course. An old woman, small, fat, and laughing, is passing out flowers from a basket, and tall young men wear her flowers in their shining hair. A child of nine or ten sits at the edge of the crowd, alone, playing on a wooden flute. People pause to listen, and they smile, but they do not speak to him, for he never ceases playing and never sees them, his dark eyes wholly rapt in the sweet, thin magic of the tune.

5 He finishes, and slowly lowers his hands holding the wooden flute.

As if that little private silence were the signal, all at once a trumpet sounds from the pavilion near the starting line: imperious, melancholy, piercing. The horses rear on their slender legs, and some of them neigh in answer. Sober-faced, the young riders stroke the horses' necks and soothe them, whispering, "Quiet, quiet, there my beauty, my hope. . . ." They begin to form in rank along the starting line. The crowds along the racecourse are like a field of grass and flowers in the wind. The Festival of Summer has begun.

Do you believe? Do you accept the festival, the city, the joy? No? Then let me describe one more thing.

In a basement under one of the beautiful public buildings of Omelas, or perhaps in the cellar of one of its spacious private homes, there is a room. It has one locked door, and no window. A little light seeps in dustily between cracks in the boards, secondhand from a cobwebbed window somewhere across the cellar. In one corner of the little room a couple of mops, with stiff, clotted, foul-smelling heads, stand near a rusty bucket. The floor is dirt, a little damp to the touch, as cellar dirt usually is. The room is about three paces long and two wide: a mere broom closet or disused tool room. In the room a child is sitting. It could be a boy or a girl. It looks about six, but actually is nearly ten. It is feebleminded. Perhaps it was born defective, or perhaps it has become imbecile through fear, malnutrition, and neglect. It picks its nose and occasionally fumbles vaguely with its toes or genitals, as it sits hunched in the corner farthest from the bucket and the two mops. It is afraid of the mops. It finds them horrible. It shuts its eyes, but it knows the mops are still standing there; and the door is locked; and nobody will come. The door is always locked; and nobody ever comes, except that sometimes—the child has no understanding of time or interval—sometimes the door rattles terribly and opens, and a person, or several people, are there. One of them may come in and kick the child to make it stand up. The others never come close, but peer in at it with frightened, disgusted eyes. The food bowl and the water jug are hastily filled, the door is locked, the eyes disappear. The people at the door never say anything, but the child, who has not always lived in the tool room, and can remember sunlight and its mother's voice, sometimes speaks. "I will be good," it says. "Please let me out. I will be good!" They never answer. The child used to scream for help at night, and cry a good deal, but now it only makes a kind of whining "eh-haa, eh-haa," and it speaks less and less often. It is so thin there are no calves to its legs; its belly protrudes; it lives on a half-bowl of corn meal and grease a day. It is naked. Its buttocks and thighs are a mass of festered sores, as it sits in its own excrement continually.

They all know it is there, all the people of Omelas. Some of them have come to see it, others are content merely to know it is there. They all know that it has to be there. Some of them understand why, and some do not, but they all understand that their happiness, the beauty of their city, the tenderness of their friendships, the health of their children, the wisdom of their scholars, the skill of their makers, even the abundance of their harvest and the kindly weathers of their skies, depend wholly on this child's abominable misery.

10 This is usually explained to children when they are between eight and twelve, whenever they seem capable of understanding; and most of those who come to see the child are young people, though often enough an adult comes, or comes back, to see the child. No matter how well the matter has been explained to them, these young spectators are always shocked and sickened at the sight. They feel disgust, which they had thought themselves superior to. They feel anger, outrage, impotence, despite all the explanations. They would like to do something for the child. But there is nothing they can do. If the child were brought up into the sunlight out of that vile place, if it were cleaned and fed and comforted, that would be a good thing, indeed; but if it were done, in that day and hour all the prosperity and beauty and delight of Omelas would wither and be destroyed. Those are the terms. To exchange all the goodness and grace of every life in Omelas for that single, small improvement: to throw away the happiness of thousands for the chance of the happiness of one: that would be to let guilt within the walls indeed.

The terms are strict and absolute; there may not even be a kind word spoken to the child.

Often the young people go home in tears, or in a tearless rage, when they have seen the child and faced this terrible paradox. They may brood over it for weeks or years. But as time goes on they begin to realize that even if the child could be released, it would not get much good of its freedom: a little vague pleasure of warmth and food, no doubt, but little more. It is too degraded and imbecile to know any real joy. It has been afraid too long ever to be free of fear. Its habits are too uncouth for it to respond to humane treatment. Indeed, after so long it would probably be wretched without walls about it to protect it, and darkness for its eyes, and its own excrement to sit in. Their tears at the bitter injustice dry when they begin to perceive the terrible justice of reality, and to accept it. Yet it is their tears and anger, the trying of their generosity and the acceptance of their helplessness, which are perhaps the true source of the splendor of their lives. Theirs is no vapid, irresponsible happiness. They know that they, like the child, are not free. They know compassion. It is the existence of the child, and their knowledge of its existence, that makes possible the nobility of their architecture, the poignancy of their music, the profundity of their science. It is because of the child that they are so gentle with children. They know that if the wretched one were not there snivelling in the dark, the other one, the flute-player, could make no joyful music as the young riders line up in their beauty for the race in the sunlight of the first morning of summer.

Now do you believe in them? Are they not more credible? But there is one more thing to tell, and this is quite incredible.

At times one of the adolescent girls or boys who go to see the child does not go home to weep or rage, does not, in fact, go home at all. Sometimes also a man or woman much older falls silent for a day or two, and then leaves home. These people go out into the street, and walk down the street alone. They keep walking, and walk straight out of the city of Omelas, through the beautiful gates. They keep walking across the farmlands of Omelas. Each one goes alone, youth or girl, man or woman. Night falls; the traveler must pass down village streets, between the houses with yellow-lit windows, and on out into the darkness of the fields. Each alone, they go west or north, towards the mountains. They go on. They leave Omelas, they walk ahead into the darkness, and they do not come back. The place they go towards is a place even less imaginable to most of us than the city of happiness. I cannot describe it at all. It is possible that it does not exist. But they seem to know where they are going, the ones who walk away from Omelas.

[1973]

Joining the Conversation: Critical Thinking and Writing

1. Summarize the point of the story—not the plot, but what the story adds up to, what the author is getting at. Next, set forth what you would probably do (and why) if you were born in Omelas.
2. Consider the narrator's assertion (paragraph 3) that happiness "is based on a just discrimination of what is necessary." Please argue for or against this statement.
3. Do you think the story implies a criticism of contemporary American society? Explain.

WILLIAM FAULKNER

For a biographical note on William Faulkner, see page 237.

Barn Burning

The store in which the Justice of the Peace's court was sitting smelled of cheese. The boy, crouched on his nail keg at the back of the crowded room, knew he smelled cheese, and more: from where he sat he could see the ranked shelves close-packed with the solid, squat, dynamic shapes of tin cans whose labels his stomach read, not from the lettering which mean nothing to his mind but from the scarlet devils and the silver curve of fish—this, the cheese which he knew he smelled and the hermetic meat which his intestines believed he smelled coming in intermittent gusts momentary and brief between the other constant one, the smell and sense just a little of fear because mostly of despair and grief, the old fierce pull of blood. He could not see the table where the Justice sat and before which his father and his father's enemy (*our enemy* he thought in that despair; *ourn! mine and hisn both! He's my father!*) stood, but he could hear them, the two of them that is, because his father had said no word yet:

"But what proof have you, Mr. Harris?"

"I told you. The hog got into my corn. I caught it up and sent it back to him. He had no fence that would hold it. I told him so, warned him. The next time I put the hog in my pen. When he came to get it I gave him enough wire to patch up his pen. The next time I put the hog up and kept it. I rode down to his house and saw the wire I gave him still rolled on to the spool in his yard. I told him he could have the hog when he paid me a dollar pound fee. That evening a nigger came with the dollar and got the hog. He was a strange nigger. He said, 'He say to tell you wood and hay kin burn.' I said, 'What?' 'That whut he say to tell you,' the nigger said. 'Wood and hay kin burn.' That night my barn burned. I got the stock out but I lost the barn."

"Where is the nigger? Have you got him?"

5 "He was a strange nigger, I tell you. I don't know what became of him."

"But that's not proof. Don't you see that's not proof?"

"Get that boy up here. He knows." For a moment the boy thought too that the man meant his older brother until Harris said, "Not him. The little one. The boy," and, crouching, small for his age, small and wiry like his father, in patched and faded jeans even too small for him, with straight, uncombed, brown hair and eyes gray and wild as storm scud, he saw the men between himself and the table part and become a lane of grim faces, at the end of which he saw the Justice, a shabby, collarless, graying man in spectacles, beckoning him. He felt no floor under his bare feet; he seemed to walk beneath the palpable weight of the grim turning faces. His father, stiff in his black Sunday coat donned not for the trial but for the moving, did not even look at him. *He aims for me to lie,* he thought, again with that frantic grief and despair. *And I will have to do hit.*

"What's your name, boy?" the Justice said.

"Colonel Sartoris Snopes," the boy whispered.

10 "Hey?" the Justice said. "Talk louder. Colonel Sartoris? I reckon anybody named for Colonel Sartoris in this country can't help but tell the truth, can they?" The boy said nothing. *Enemy! Enemy!* he thought; for a moment he could not even see, could not see that the Justice's face was kindly nor discern that his voice was troubled when he spoke to the man named Harris: "Do you want me to question this boy?" But he could hear, and during those subsequent long seconds while there was absolutely no sound in the crowded little room save that of quiet and intent breathing it was as if he had swung outward at the end of a grape vine, over a ravine, and at the top of the swing had been caught in a prolonged instant of mesmerized gravity, weightless in time.

"No!" Harris said violently, explosively. "Damnation! Send him out of here!" Now time, the fluid world, rushed beneath him again, the voices coming to him again through the smell of cheese and sealed meat, the fear and despair and the old grief of blood:

"This case is closed. I can't find against you, Snopes, but I can give you advice. Leave this country and don't come back to it."

His father spoke for the first time, his voice cold and harsh, level, without emphasis: "I aim to. I don't figure to stay in a country among people who . . ." he said something unprintable and vile, addressed to no one.

"That'll do," the Justice said. "Take your wagon and get out of this country before dark. Case dismissed."

15 His father turned, and he followed the stiff black coat, the wiry figure walking a little stiffly from where a Confederate provost's man's musket ball had taken him in the heel on a stolen horse thirty years ago, followed the two backs now, since his older brother had appeared from somewhere in the crowd, no taller than the father but thicker, chewing tobacco steadily, between the two lines of grim-faced men and out of the store and across the worn gallery and down the sagging steps and among the dogs and half-grown boys in the mild May dust, where as he passed a voice hissed:

"Barn burner!"

Again he could not see, whirling; there was a face in a red haze, moonlike, bigger than the full moon, the owner of it half again his size, he leaping in the red haze toward the face, feeling no blow, feeling no shock when his head struck the earth, scrabbling up and leaping again, feeling no blow this time either and tasting no blood, scrabbling up to see the other boy in full flight and himself already leaping into pursuit as his father's hand jerked him back, the harsh, cold voice speaking above him: "Go get in the wagon."

It stood in a grove of locusts and mulberries across the road. His two hulking sisters in their Sunday dresses and his mother and her sister in calico and sunbonnets were already in it, sitting on and among the sorry residue of the dozen and more movings which even the boy could remember—the battered stove, the broken beds and chairs, the clock inlaid with mother-of-pearl, which would not run, stopped at some fourteen minutes past two o'clock of a dead and forgotten day and time, which had been his mother's dowry. She was crying, though when she saw him she drew her sleeve across her face and began to descend from the wagon. "Get back," the father said.

"He's hurt. I got to get some water and wash his . . ."

20 "Get back in the wagon," his father said. He got in too, over the tail-gate. His father mounted to the seat where the older brother already sat and struck the gaunt mules two savage blows with the peeled willow, but without heat. It was not even sadistic; it was exactly that same quality which in later years would cause his descendants to over-run the engine before putting a motor car into motion, striking and reining back in the same movement. The wagon went on, the store with its quiet crowd of grimly watching men dropped behind; a curve in the road hid it. *Forever* he thought. *Maybe he's done satisfied now, now that he has* . . . stopping himself, not to say it aloud even to himself. His mother's hand touched his shoulder.

"Does hit hurt?" she said.

"Naw," he said. "Hit don't hurt. Lemme be."

"Can't you wipe some of the blood off before hit dries?"

"I'll wash to-night," he said. "Lemme be, I tell you."

25 The wagon went on. He did not know where they were going. None of them ever did or ever asked, because it was always somewhere, always a house of sorts waiting for them a day or two days or even three days away. Likely his father had already arranged to make a crop on another farm before he . . . Again he had to stop himself. He (the father) always did. There was something about his wolflike independence and even courage when the advantage was at least neutral which impressed strangers, as if they got from his latent ravening ferocity not so much a sense of dependability as a feeling that his ferocious conviction in the rightness of his own actions would be of advantage to all whose interest lay with his.

That night they camped, in a grove of oaks and beeches where a spring ran. The nights were still cool and they had a fire against it, of a rail lifted from a nearby fence and cut into lengths—a small fire, neat, niggard almost, a shrewd fire; such fires were his father's habit and custom always, even in freezing weather. Older, the boy might have remarked this and wondered why not a big one; why should not a man who had not only seen the waste and extravagance of war, but who had in his blood an inherent voracious prodigality with material not his own, have burned everything in sight? Then he might have gone a step farther and thought that that was the reason: that niggard blaze was the living fruit of nights passed during those four years in the woods hiding from all men, blue or gray, with his strings of horses (captured horses, he called them). And older still, he might have divined the true reason: that the element of fire spoke to some deep mainspring of his father's being, as the element of steel or of powder spoke to other men, as the one weapon for the preservation of integrity, else breath were not worth the breathing, and hence to be regarded with respect and used with discretion.

But he did not think this now and he had seen those same niggard blazes all his life. He merely ate his supper beside it and was already half asleep over his iron plate when his father called him, and once more he followed the stiff back, the stiff and ruthless limp, up the slope and on to the starlit road where, turning, he could see his father against the stars but without face or depth—a shape black, flat, and bloodless as though cut from tin in the iron folds of the frockcoat which had not been made for him, the voice harsh like tin and without heat like tin:

"You were fixing to tell them. You would have told him." He didn't answer. his father struck him with the flat of his hand on the side of the head, hard but without heat, exactly as he had struck the two mules at the store, exactly as he would strike either of them with any stick in order to kill a horse fly, his voice still without heat or anger: "You're getting to be a man. You got to learn. You got to learn to stick to your own blood or you ain't going to have any blood to stick to you. Do you think either of them, any man there this morning, would? Don't you know all they wanted was a chance to get at me because they knew I had them beat? Eh?" Later, twenty years later, he was to tell himself, "If I had said they wanted only truth, justice, he would have hit me again." But now he said nothing. He was not crying. He just stood there. "Answer me," his father said.

"Yes," he whispered. His father turned.

"Get on to bed. We'll be there to-morrow."

To-morrow they were there. In the early afternoon the wagon stopped before a paintless two-room house identical almost with the dozen others it had stopped before even in the boy's ten years, and again, as on the other dozen occasions, his mother and aunt got down and began to unload the wagon, although his two sisters and his father and brother had not moved.

"Likely hit ain't fitten for hawgs," one of the sisters said.

"Nevertheless, fit it will and you'll hog it and like it," his father said. "Get out of them chairs and help your Ma unload."

The two sisters got down, big, bovine, in a flutter of cheap ribbons; one of them drew from the jumbled wagon bed a battered lantern, the other a worn broom. His father handed the reins to the older son and began to climb stiffly over the wheel. "When they get unloaded, take the team to the barn and feed them." Then he said, and at first the boy thought he was still speaking to his brother: "Come with me."

"Me?" he said.

"Yes," his father said. "You."

"Abner," his mother said. His father paused and looked back—the harsh level stare beneath the shaggy, graying, irascible brows.

"I reckon I'll have a word with the man that aims to begin to-morrow owning me body and soul for the next eight months."

They went back up the road. A week ago—or before last night, that is—he would have asked where they were going, but not now. His father had struck him before last night but never before had he paused afterward to explain why; it was as if the blow and the following calm, outrageous voice still rang, repercussed, divulging nothing to him save the terrible handicap of being young, the light weight of his few years, just heavy enough to prevent his soaring free of the world as it seemed to be ordered but not heavy enough to keep him footed solid in it, to resist it and try to change the course of its events.

40 Presently he could see the grove of oaks and cedars and the other flowering trees and shrubs where the house would be, though not the house yet. They walked beside a fence massed with honeysuckle and Cherokee roses and came to a gate swinging open between two brick pillars, and now, beyond a sweep of drive, he saw the house for the first time and at that instant he forgot his father and the terror and despair both, and even when he remembered his father again (who had not stopped) the terror and despair did not return. Because, for all the twelve movings, they had sojourned until now in a poor country, a land of small farms and fields and houses, and he had never seen a house like this before. *Hit's big as a courthouse* he thought quietly, with a surge of peace and joy whose reason he could not have thought into words, being too young for that: *They are safe from him. People whose lives are a part of this peace and dignity are beyond his touch, he no more to them than a buzzing wasp: capable of stinging for a little moment but that's all; the spell of this peace and dignity rendering even the barns and stable and cribs which belong to it impervious to the puny flames he might contrive* . . . this, the peace and joy, ebbing for an instant as he looked again at the stiff black back, the stiff and implacable limp of the figure which was not dwarfed by the house, for the reason that it had never looked big anywhere and which now, against the serene columned backdrop, had more than ever that impervious quality of something cut ruthlessly from tin, depthless, as though, sidewise to the sun, it would cast no shadow. Watching him, the boy remarked the absolutely undeviating course which his father held and saw the stiff foot come squarely down in a pile of fresh droppings where a horse had stood in the drive and which his father could have avoided by a simple change of stride. But it ebbed only for a moment, though he could not have thought this into words either, walking on in the spell of the house, which he could even want but without envy, without sorrow, certainly never with that ravening and jealous rage which unknown to him walked in the ironlike black coat before him: *Maybe he will feel it too. Maybe it will even change him now from what maybe he couldn't help but be.*

They crossed the portico. Now he could hear his father's stiff foot as it came down on the boards with clocklike finality, a sound out of all proportion to the displacement of the body it bore and which was not dwarfed either by the white door before it, as though it had attained to a sort of vicious and ravening minimum not to be dwarfed by anything—the flat, wide, black hat, the formal coat of broadcloth which had once been black but which had now that friction-glazed greenish cast of the bodies of old house flies, the lifted sleeve which was too large, the lifted hand like a curled claw. The door opened so promptly that the boy knew the Negro must have been watching them all the time, an old man with neat grizzled hair, in a linen jacket, who stood barring the door with his body, saying, "Wipe yo foots, white man, fo you come in here. Major ain't home nohow."

"Get out of my way, nigger," his father said, without heat too, flinging the door back and the Negro also and entering, his hat still on his head. And now the boy saw the prints of the stiff foot on the doorjamb and saw them appear on the pale rug behind the machinelike deliberation of the foot which seemed to bear (or transmit) twice the weight which the body compassed. The Negro was shouting "Miss Lula! Miss Lula!" somewhere behind them, then the boy, deluged as though by a warm wave by a suave turn of carpeted stair and a pendant glitter of chandeliers and a mute gleam of gold frames, heard the swift feet and saw her too, a lady—perhaps he had never seen her like before either—in a gray, smooth gown with lace at the throat and an apron tied at the waist and the sleeves turned back, wiping cake or biscuit dough from her hands with a towel as she came up the hall, looking not at his father at all but at the tracks on the blond rug with an expression of incredulous amazement.

"I tried," the Negro cried. "I tole him to . . ."

"Will you please go away?" she said in a shaking voice. "Major de Spain is not at home. Will you please go away?"

His father had not spoken again. He did not speak again. He did not even look at her. He just stood stiff in the center of the rug, in his hat, the shaggy iron-gray brows twitching slightly above the pebble-colored eyes as he appeared to examine the house with brief deliberation. Then with the same deliberation he turned; the boy watched him pivot on the good leg and saw the stiff foot drag round the arc of the turning, leaving a final long and fading smear. His father never looked at it, he never once looked down at the rug. The Negro held the door. It closed behind them, upon the hysteric and indistinguishable woman-wail. His father stopped at the top of the steps and scraped his boot clean on the edge of it. At the gate he stopped again. He stood for a moment, planted stiffly on the stiff foot, looking back at the house. "Pretty and white, ain't it?" he said. "That's sweat. Nigger sweat. Maybe it ain't white enough yet to suit him. Maybe he wants to mix some white sweat with it."

Two hours later the boy was chopping wood behind the house within which his mother and aunt and the two sisters (the mother and aunt, not the two girls, he knew that; even at this distance and muffled by walls the flat loud voices of the two girls emanated an incorrigible idle inertia) were setting up the stove to prepare a meal, when he heard the hooves and saw the linen-clad man on a fine sorrel mare, whom he recognized even before he saw the rolled rug in front of the Negro youth following on a fat bay carriage horse—a suffused, angry face vanishing, still at full gallop, behind the corner of the house where his father and brother were sitting in the two tilted chairs; and a moment later, almost before he could have put the axe down, he heard the hooves again and watched the sorrel mare go back out of the yard, already galloping again. Then his father began to shout one of the sisters' names, who presently emerged backward from the kitchen door dragging the rolled rug along the ground by one end while the other sister walked behind it.

"If you ain't going to tote, go on and set up the wash pot," the first said.

"You, Sarty!" the second shouted. "Set up the wash pot!" His father appeared at the door, framed against that shabbiness, as he had been against that other bland perfection, impervious to either, the mother's anxious face at his shoulder.

"Go on," the father said. "Pick it up." The two sisters stooped, broad, lethargic; stooping, they presented an incredible expanse of pale cloth and a flutter of tawdry ribbons.

"If I thought enough of a rug to have to git hit all the way from France I wouldn't keep hit where folks coming in would have to tromp on hit," the first said. They raised the rug.

"Abner," the mother said. "Let me do it."

"You go back and git dinner," his father said. "I'll tend to this."

From the woodpile through the rest of the afternoon the boy watched them, the rug spread flat in the dust beside the bubbling wash-pot, the two sisters stooping over it with that profound and lethargic reluctance, while the father stood over them in turn, implacable and grim, driving them though never raising his voice again. He could smell the harsh homemade lye they were using; he saw his mother come to the door once and look toward them with an expression not anxious now but very like despair; he saw his father turn, and he fell to with the axe and saw from the corner of his eye his father raise from the ground a flattish fragment of field stone and examine it and return to the pot, and this time his mother actually spoke: "Abner. Abner. Please don't. Please, Abner."

Then he was done too. It was dusk; the whippoorwills had already begun. He could smell coffee from the room where they would presently eat the cold food remaining from the midafternoon meal, though when he entered the house he realized they were having coffee again probably because there was a fire on the hearth, before which the rug now lay spread over the backs of the two chairs. The tracks of his father's foot were gone. Where they had been were now long, water-cloudy scoriations resembling the sporadic course of a liliputian mowing machine.

55 It still hung there while they ate the cold food and then went to bed, scattered without order or claim up and down the two rooms, his mother in one bed, where his father would later lie, the older brother in the other, himself, the aunt, and the two sisters on pallets on the floor. But his father was not in bed yet. The last thing the boy remembered was the depthless, harsh silhouette of the hat and coat bending over the rug and it seemed to him that he had not even closed his eyes when the silhouette was standing over him, the fire almost dead behind it, the stiff foot prodding him awake. "Catch up the mule," his father said.

When he returned with the mule his father was standing in the back door, the rolled rug over his shoulder. "Ain't you going to ride?" he said.

"No. Give me your foot."

He bent his knee into his father's hand, the wiry, surprising power flowed smoothly, rising, he rising with it, on to the mule's bare back (they had owned a saddle once; the boy could remember it though not when or where) and with the same effortlessness his father swung the rug up in front of him. Now in the starlight they retraced the afternoon's path, up the dusty road rife with honeysuckle, through the gate and up the black tunnel of the drive to the lightless house, where he sat on the mule and felt the rough warp of the rug drag across his thighs and vanish.

"Don't you want me to help?" he whispered. His father did not answer and now he heard again that stiff foot striking the hollow portico with that wooden and clocklike deliberation, that outrageous overstatement of the weight it carried. The rug, hunched, not flung (the boy could tell that even in the darkness) from his father's shoulder struck the angle of wall and floor with a sound unbelievably loud, thunderous, then the foot again, unhurried and enormous; a light came on in the house and the boy sat, tense, breathing steadily and quietly and just a little fast, though the foot itself did not increase its beat at all, descending the steps now; now the boy could see him.

60 "Don't you want to ride now?" he whispered. "We kin both ride now," the light within the house altering now, flaring up and sinking. *He's coming down the stairs now,* he thought. He had already ridden the mule up beside the horse

block; presently his father was up behind him and he doubled the reins over and slashed the mule across the neck, but before the animal could begin to trot the hard, thin arm came round him, the hard, knotted hand jerking the mule back to a walk.

In the first red rays of the sun they were in the lot, putting plow gear on the mules. This time the sorrel mare was in the lot before he heard it at all, the rider collarless and even bareheaded, trembling, speaking in a shaking voice as the woman in the house had done. His father merely looking up once before stooping again to the hame he was buckling, so that the man on the mare spoke to his stooping back:

"You must realize you have ruined that rug. Wasn't there anybody here, any of your women . . ." he ceased, shaking, the boy watching him, the older brother leaning now in the stable door, chewing, blinking slowly and steadily at nothing apparently. "It cost a hundred dollars. But you never had a hundred dollars. You never will. So I'm going to charge you twenty bushels of corn against your crop. I'll add it in your contract and when you come to the commissary you can sign it. That won't keep Mrs. de Spain quiet but maybe it will teach you to wipe your feet off before you enter her house again."

Then he was gone. The boy looked at his father, who still had not spoken or even looked up again, who was now adjusting the loggerhead in the hame.

"Pap," he said. His father looked at him—the inscrutable face, the shaggy brows beneath which the gray eyes glinted coldly. Suddenly the boy went toward him, fast, stopping as suddenly. "You done the best you could!" he cried. "If he wanted hit done different why didn't he wait and tell you how? He won't git no twenty bushels! He won't git none! We'll gether hit and hide hit! I kin watch . . ."

"Did you put the cutter back in that straight stock like I told you?"

"No, sir," he said.

"Then go do it."

That was Wednesday. During the rest of that week he worked steadily, at what was within his scope and some which was beyond it, with an industry that did not need to be driven nor even commanded twice; he had this from his mother, with the difference that some at least of what he did he liked to do, such as splitting wood with the half-size axe which his mother and aunt had earned, or saved money somehow, to present him with at Christmas. In company with the two older women (and on one afternoon, even one of the sisters), he built pens for the shoat and the cow which were a part of his father's contract with the landlord, and one afternoon, his father being absent, gone somewhere on one of the mules, he went to the field.

They were running a middle buster now, his brother holding the plow straight while he handled the reins, and walking beside the straining mule, the rich black soil shearing cool and damp against his bare ankles, he thought *Maybe this is the end of it. Maybe even that twenty bushels that seems hard to have to pay for just a rug will be a cheap price for him to stop forever and always from being what he used to be;* thinking, dreaming now, so that his brother had to speak sharply to him to mind the mule: *Maybe he even won't collect the twenty bushels. Maybe it will all add up and balance and vanish—corn, rug, fire; the terror and grief, the being pulled two ways like between two teams of horses—gone, done with for ever and ever.*

Then it was Saturday; he looked up from beneath the mule he was harnessing and saw his father in the black coat and hat. "Not that," his father said. "The wagon gear." And then, two hours later, sitting in the wagon bed behind his father and brother on the seat, the wagon accomplished a final curve, and he saw the weathered paintless store with its tattered tobacco- and patent-medicine posters and the tethered wagons and saddle animals below the gallery. He mounted the gnawed steps behind his father and brother, and there again was the lane of quiet, watching faces for the three of them to walk through. He saw the man in spectacles sitting at the plank table and he did not need to be told this was a Justice of the Peace; he sent one glare of fierce, exultant, partisan defiance at the man in collar and cravat now, whom he had seen but twice before in his life, and that on a galloping horse, who now wore on his face an expression not of rage but of amazed unbelief which the boy could not have known was at the incredible circumstance of being sued by one of his own tenants, and came and stood against his father and cried at the Justice: "He ain't done it! He ain't burnt . . ."

"Go back to the wagon," his father said.

"Burnt?" the Justice said. "Do I understand this rug was burned too?"

"Does anybody here claim it was?" his father said. "Go back to the wagon." But he did not, he merely retreated to the rear of the room, crowded as that other had been, but not to sit down this time, instead, to stand pressing among the motionless bodies, listening to the voices:

"And you claim twenty bushels of corn is too high for the damage you did to the rug?"

75 "He brought the rug to me and said he wanted the tracks washed out of it. I washed the tracks out and took the rug back to him."

"But you didn't carry the rug back to him in the same condition it was in before you made the tracks on it."

His father did not answer, and now for perhaps half a minute there was no sound at all save that of breathing, the faint, steady suspiration of complete and intent listening.

"You decline to answer that, Mr. Snopes?" Again his father did not answer. "I'm going to find against you, Mr. Snopes. I'm going to find that you were responsible for the injury to Major de Spain's rug and hold you liable for it. But twenty bushels of corn seems a little high for a man in your circumstances to have to pay. Major de Spain claims it costs a hundred dollars. October corn will be worth about fifty cents. I figure that if Major de Spain can stand a ninety-five-dollar loss on something he paid cash for, you can stand a five-dollar loss you haven't earned yet. I hold you in damages to Major de Spain to the amount of ten bushels of corn over and above your contract with him, to be paid to him out of your crop at gathering time. Court adjourned."

It had taken no time hardly, the morning was but half begun. He thought they would return home and perhaps back to the field, since they were late, far behind all other farmers. But instead his father passed on behind the wagon, merely indicating with his hand for the older brother to follow with it, and crossed the road toward the blacksmith shop opposite, pressing on after his father, overtaking him, speaking, whispering up at the harsh, calm face beneath the weathered hat: "He won't git no ten bushels neither. He won't git one. We'll . . ." until his father glanced for an instant down at him, the face absolutely calm, the grizzled eyebrows tangled above the cold eyes, the voice almost pleasant, almost gentle:

80 "You think so? Well, we'll wait till October anyway."

The matter of the wagon—the setting of a spoke or two and the tightening of the tires—did not take long either, the business of the tires accomplished by driving the wagon into the spring branch behind the shop and letting it stand there, the mules nuzzling into the water from time to time, and the boy on the seat with the idle reins, looking up the slope and through the sooty tunnel of the shed where the slow hammer rang and where his father sat on an upended cypress bolt, easily, either talking or listening, still sitting there when the boy brought the dripping wagon up out of the branch and halted it before the door.

"Take them on to the shade and hitch," his father said. He did so and returned. His father and the smith and a third man squatting on his heels inside the door were talking, about crops and animals; the boy, squatting too in the ammoniac dust and hoof-parings and scales of rust, heard his father tell a long and unhurried story out of the time before the birth of the older brother even when he had been a professional horsetrader. And then his father came up beside him where he stood before a tattered last year's circus poster on the other side of the store, gazing rapt and quiet at the scarlet horses, the incredible poisings and convolutions of tulle and tights and the painted leers of comedians, and said, "It's time to eat."

But not at home. Squatting beside his brother against the front wall, he watched his father emerge from the store and produce from a paper sack a segment of cheese and divide it carefully and deliberately into three with his pocket knife and produce crackers from the same sack. They all three squatted on the gallery and ate, slowly, without talking; then in the store again, they drank from a tin dipper tepid water smelling of the cedar bucket and of living beech trees. And still they did not go home. It was a horse lot this time, a tall rail fence upon and along which men stood and sat and out of which one by one horses were led, to be talked and trotted and then cantered back and forth along the road while the slow swapping and buying went on and the sun began to slant westward, they—the three of them—watching and listening, the older brother with his muddy eyes and his steady, inevitable tobacco, the father commenting now and then on certain of the animals, to no one in particular.

It was after sundown when they reached home. They ate supper by lamplight, then, sitting on the doorstep, the boy watched the night fully accomplish, listening to the whippoorwills and the frogs, when he heard his mother's voice: "Abner! No! No! Oh, God. Oh, God. Abner!" and he rose, whirled, and saw the altered light through the door where a candle stub now burned in a bottle neck on the table and his father, still in the hat and coat, at once formal and burlesque as though dressed carefully for some shabby and ceremonial violence, emptying the reservoir of the lamp back into the five-gallon kerosene can from which it had been filled, while the mother tugged at his arm until he shifted the lamp to the other hand and flung her back, not savagely or viciously, just hard, into the wall, her hands flung out against the wall for balance, her mouth open and in her face the same quality of hopeless despair as had been in her voice. Then his father saw him standing in the door.

"Go to the barn and get that can of oil we were oiling the wagon with," he said. The boy did not move. Then he could speak.

"What . . ." he cried. "What are you . . ."

"Go get that oil," his father said. "Go."

Then he was moving, running, outside the house, toward the stable: this the old habit, the old blood which he had not been permitted to choose for himself, which had been bequeathed him willy nilly and which had run for so long (and who knew where, battening on what of outrage and savagery and lust) before it came to him. *I could keep on,* he thought. *I could run on and on and never look back, never need to see his face again. Only I can't. I can't,* the rusted can in his hand now, the liquid sploshing in it as he ran back to the house and into it, into the sound of his mother's weeping in the next room, and handed the can to his father.

"Ain't you going to even send a nigger?" he cried. "At least you sent a nigger before!"

90 This time his father didn't strike him. The hand came even faster than the blow had, the same hand which had set the can on the table with almost excruciating care flashing from the can toward him too quick for him to follow it, gripping him by the back of his shirt and on to tiptoe before he had seen it quit the can, the face stooping at him in breathless and frozen ferocity, the cold, dead voice speaking over him to the older brother who leaned against the table, chewing with that steady, curious, sidewise motion of cows:

"Empty the can into the big one and go on. I'll catch up with you."

"Better tie him up to the bedpost," the brother said.

"Do like I told you," the father said. Then the boy was moving, his bunched shirt and the hard, bony hand between his shoulderblades, his toes just touching the floor, across the room and into the other one, past the sisters sitting with spread heavy thighs in the two chairs over the cold hearth, and to where his mother and aunt sat side by side on the bed, the aunt's arms about his mother's shoulders.

"Hold him," the father said. The aunt made a startled movement. "Not you," the father said. "Lennie. Take hold of him. I want to see you do it." His mother took him by the wrist. "You'll hold him better than that. If he gets loose don't you know what he is going to do? He will go up yonder." He jerked his head toward the road. "Maybe I'd better tie him."

95 "I'll hold him," his mother whispered.

"See you do then." Then his father was gone, the stiff foot heavy and measured upon the boards, ceasing at last.

Then he began to struggle. His mother caught him in both arms, he jerking and wrenching at them. He would be stronger in the end, he knew that. But he had no time to wait for it. "Lemme go!" he cried. "I don't want to have to hit you!"

"Let him go!" the aunt said. "If he don't go, before God, I am going up there myself!"

"Don't you see I can't?" his mother cried. "Sarty! Sarty! No! No! Help me, Lizzie!"

100 Then he was free. His aunt grasped at him but it was too late. He whirled, running, his mother stumbled forward on to her knees behind him, crying to the nearer sister: "Catch him, Net! Catch him!" But that was too late too, the sister (the sisters were twins, born at the same time, yet either of them now gave the impression of being, encompassing as much living meat and volume and weight as any other two of the family) not yet having begun to rise from the chair, her head, face, alone merely turned, presenting to him in the flying instant an astonishing expanse of young female features untroubled by any surprise even, wearing only an expression of bovine interest. Then he was out of the room, out of the house, in the mild dust of the starlit road and the heavy rifeness of honeysuckle, the pale ribbon unspooling with terrific slowness under his running feet, reaching the gate at last and turning in, running, his heart and lungs drumming, on up the drive toward the lighted house, the lighted door. He did not knock, he burst in, sobbing for breath, incapable for the moment of speech; he saw the astonished face of the Negro in the linen jacket without knowing when the Negro had appeared.

"De Spain!" he cried, panted. "Where's . . ." then he saw the white man too emerging from a white door down the hall. "Barn!" he cried. "Barn!"

"What?" the white man said. "Barn?"

"Yes!" the boy cried. "Barn!"

105 "Catch him!" the white man shouted.

But it was too late this time too. The Negro grasped his shirt, but the entire sleeve, rotten with washing, carried away, and he was out that door too and in the drive again, and had actually never ceased to run even while he was screaming into the white man's face.

Behind him the white man was shouting, "My horse! Fetch my horse!" and he thought for an instant of cutting across the park and climbing the fence into the road, but he did not know the park nor how high the vine-massed fence might be and he dared not risk it. So he ran on down the drive, blood and breath roaring; presently he was in the road again though he could not see it. He could not hear either: the galloping mare was almost upon him before he heard her, and even then he held his course, as if the very urgency of his wild grief and need must in a moment more find him wings, waiting until the ultimate instant to hurl himself aside and into the weed-choked roadside ditch as the horse thundered past and on, for an instant in furious silhouette against the stars, the tranquil early summer night sky which, even before the shape of the horse and rider vanished, stained abruptly and violently upward: a long, swirling roar incredible and soundless, blotting the stars, and he springing up and into the road again, running again, knowing it was too late yet still running even after he heard the shot and, an instant later, two shots, pausing now without knowing he had ceased to run, crying "Pap! Pap!", running again before he knew he had begun to run, stumbling, tripping over something and scrabbling up again without ceasing to run, looking backward over his shoulder at the glares as he got up, running on among the invisible trees, panting, sobbing, "Father! Father!"

At midnight he was sitting on the crest of a hill. He did not know it was midnight and he did not know how far he had come. But there was no glare behind him now and he sat now, his back toward what he had called home for four days anyhow, his face toward the dark woods which he would enter when breath was strong again, small, shaking steadily in the chill darkness, hugging himself into the remainder of his thin, rotten shirt, the grief and despair now no longer terror and fear but just grief and despair. *Father. My father,* he thought. "He was brave!" He cried suddenly, aloud but not loud, no more than a whisper: "He was! He was in the war! He was in Colonel Sartoris' cav'ry!" not knowing that his father had gone to that war a private in the fine old European sense, wearing no uniform, admitting the authority of and giving fidelity to no man or army or flag, going to war as Malbrouck himself did: for booty—it meant nothing and less than nothing to him if it were enemy booty or his own.

The slow constellations wheeled on. It would be dawn and then sun-up after a while and he would be hungry. But that would be to-morrow and now he was only cold, and walking would cure that. His breathing was easier now and he decided to get up and go on, and then he found that he had been asleep because he knew it was almost dawn, the night almost over. He could tell that from the whippoorwills. They were everywhere now among the dark trees below him, constant and inflectioned and ceaseless, so that, as the instant for giving over to the day birds drew nearer and nearer, there was no interval at all between them. He got up. He was a little stiff, but walking would cure that too as it would the cold, and soon there would be the sun. He went on down the hill, toward the dark woods within which the liquid silver voices of the birds called unceasing—the rapid and urgent beating of the urgent and quiring heart of the late spring night. He did not look back.

[1939]

Joining the Conversation: Critical Thinking and Writing

1. Discuss "point of view" in this story. Identify some passages in the text where we are made aware of the narrator's or a character's point of view.
2. Is Faulkner on Major de Spain's side, or Abner Snopes's, or both, or neither?
3. By the end of the story, how has Sarty changed? Does Faulkner show us this process of change in a convincing way? Do we believe it? In your argument, make sure to cite evidence from the text.
4. While you were reading "Barn Burning," did you feel at any point that you needed "background information" in order to understand and appreciate it? Or do you think that the story itself contains everything you need to know?
5. Many people claim that Faulkner is one of the greatest American writers. Do you think that this story supports such a view? Is this a great story, or a good story?

POEMS

ANONYMOUS

Birmingham Jail was famous, not only in the South but throughout the United States, for many decades before Martin Luther King Jr. was arrested and imprisoned there in 1963. A song called "Birmingham Jail" is at least as old as the early twentieth century (a version was published in 1909), and like many popular ballads it draws on older songs, notably "Down in the Valley," which has been sung at least since the late nineteenth century. Like all folk songs, "Birmingham Jail" exists in many versions. Singers make small changes within a line, or sometimes drop or add whole verses. For instance, in what may be the most common version, some lines run thus:

Send me a letter, send it by mail,
Send it in care of the Birmingham jail.

But we have also heard

Send me a letter, send it by mail,
Back it in care of Birmingham jail.

and another version sung by Huddie Ledbetter, known as Leadbelly (1888–1949):

Send me a letter, send it by mail,
'Dress it all over, that Birmingham jail.

We print one version as it was actually sung, and then we print some additional stanzas from other versions, that is, from performances by other singers. You can pick and choose and thus create the version that strikes you as most effective.

(Inventing new lines and stanzas, or adding lines or stanzas from other ballads, is entirely acceptable.)

Birmingham Jail

Down in the valley, the valley so low,
Put your head out the window, and hear the wind blow.
Hear the wind blow, hear the wind blow,
Put your head out the window, and hear the wind blow.

Write me a letter, send it by mail
'Dress it all over, that Birmingham jail.
Birmingham jail, boys, Birmingham jail,
'Dress it all over, that Birmingham jail.

Ty Shek [?] will 'rrest you, bound you over in jail,
Can't get nobody, to go your bail.
To go your bail, boys, to go your bail,
Can't get nobody, to go your bail.

Send for your lawyer, come down to your cell,
He swear he can clear you, in spite of all hell.
Spite of all hell, boys, spite of all hell,
He swear he can clear you, in spite of all hell.

Get the biggest your money, come back for the rest,
Tell you to plead guilty, for he know that is best.
He know that is best, boys, he know that is best,
Tell you plead guilty, he know that is best.

Down in the valley, the valley so low,
Put your head out the window, and hear the wind blow.
Hear the wind blow, hear the wind blow,
Put your head out the window, and hear the wind blow.

Joining the Conversation: Critical Thinking and Writing

1. Here are some additional verses, taken from other singers. If you were singing "Birmingham Jail," which verses might you include, and which exclude? Why?

Writing this letter, containing three lines,
Answer my question, will you be mine?
Will you be mine, dear, will you be mine,
Answer my question, will you be mine?

The roses are red, and the vi'lets are blue,
Angels in Heaven sing "I love you."
Angels in Heaven, Angels in Heaven,
Angels in Heaven, sing "I love you."

Roses love sunshine, violets love dew,
Angels in Heaven know I love you,
Know I love you, dear, know I love you,
Angels in Heaven know I love you.

Go build me a castle, forty feet high,
So I can see her, as she goes by.
As she goes by, love, as she goes by,
So I can see her, as she goes by.

Bird in a cage, love, bird in a cage,
Dying for freedom, ever a slave.
Ever a slave love, ever a slave,
Dying for freedom, ever a slave.

2. We have never heard a version of "Birmingham Jail" in which the singer tells the hearer *why* he is in jail. Other songs talk about gambling debts or drunkenness or disorderly or criminal behavior, but in "Birmingham Jail" no explanation is offered, not even that the singer is unjustly imprisoned. Would the song be better if we were given such information? Why, or why not?
3. How is it that we as readers can feel pleasure in response to a poem that is sorrowful in tone and situation? What kind of pleasure is it? Do we share the speaker's sorrow, or do we remain somewhat at a distance from it?

A. E. Housman

Alfred Edward Housman (1859–1936) was born near rural Shropshire, England, and educated in classics and philosophy at Oxford University. Although he was a brilliant student, his final examination was unexpectedly weak—in fact, he failed his final examination and he did not receive the academic appointment that he had anticipated. He began working as a civil servant at the British Patent Office, but in his spare time he wrote scholarly articles on Latin literature. These writings in 1892 won him an appointment as Professor of Latin at the University of London. In 1911 he was appointed to Cambridge University. During his lifetime he published (in addition to his scholarly writings) only two thin books of poetry, A Shropshire Lad *(1896) and* Last Poems *(1922), and a highly readable lecture called* The Name and Nature of Poetry *(1933). After his death a third book of poems,* More Poems *(1936), was published. The best edition of Housman's poems (containing not only the three books of poems already mentioned but also additional poems, fragments, translations, light verse, and Latin verse) is* The Poems of A. E. Housman *(1997), edited by Archie Burnett.*

The usual explanation for Housman's failure at his examination is that he was in a state of shock resulting from his repressed homosexual love for a fellow student. In any case, Housman, like almost all homosexuals of the period, kept his homosexuality a secret from the outside world. This is not surprising; in England, "unnatural acts" between men were punishable by death until 1885, when the penalty was modified to a maximum of two years at hard labor. (Not until 1967 was homosexual behavior between consenting adults legalized in England.) In the poetry published in Housman's lifetime there is nothing explicitly homosexual, but today readers who are aware of his sexual orientation can easily and reasonably perceive the sexual implications in the voice of the man who believes he is doomed to be an outsider.

The first of the two poems that we print here, "The Carpenter's Son," was written in 1895 and published the next year in A Shropshire Lad. *In this poem Housman sets forth, in nineteenth-century rural imagery, the story of a carpenter's son—Jesus was the son of a carpenter—who is carried in a cart to a gallows, where he will be hanged between two thieves. The youth who speaks the poem differs from his two fellow victims, he says, in that he "dies for love."*

The second poem, "Oh who is that young sinner," was written in August 1895, shortly after Oscar Wilde (1854–1900), the most popular British playwright of the period, was convicted of sodomy and given the maximum prison sentence. Although the poem does not mention homosexuality, Wilde's conviction unquestionably inspired it. Housman never published it, but a year after Housman died his brother, Laurence Housman, published it in A.E.H.: Some Poems, Some Letters and a Personal Memoir By His Brother *(1936).*

The Carpenter's Son°

"Here the hangman stops his cart:
Now the best of friends must part.
Fare you well, for ill fare I:
Live, lads, and I will die.

"Oh, at home had I but stayed
'Prenticed to my father's trade,
Had I stuck to plane and adze,
I had not been lost, my lads.

"Then I might have built perhaps
Gallows-trees for other chaps,
Never dangled on my own,
Had I but left ill alone.

"Now, you see, they hang me high,
And the people passing by
Stop to shake their fists and curse;
So 'is come from ill to worse.

"Here hang I, and right and left
Two poor fellows hang for theft:
All the same's the luck we prove,
Though the midmost hangs for love.

"Comrades all, that stand and gaze,
Walk henceforth in other ways;
See my neck and save your own:
Comrades all, leave ill alone.

°**The Carpenter's Son** The Gospels according to Matthew (13:55) and Mark (6:3) identify Jesus as a carpenter's son. Lines 18–19 in the poem allude to the two thieves between whom Jesus was crucified (Matthew 27:38; Mark 15:27; Luke 23:39–40).

"Make some day a decent end,
Shrewder fellows than your friend.
Fare you well, for ill fare I:
Live, lads, and I will die."

[1895]

Joining the Conversation: Critical Thinking and Writing

1. We think you will agree that even separated from the context of the other poems in *A Shropshire Lad*—a world in which Housman speaks of lads, barns, ploughing, country fairs, and so forth—"The Carpenter's Son" evokes a folksy, rural nineteenth-century world. What words make it seem to be set in relatively modern times, rather than the time of the crucifixion of Jesus? Or put it this way: Why does the speaker sound like a youth of the modern world (nineteenth century) rather than Jesus?
2. The speaker says that he "hangs for love" but he never amplifies what he means. Should he have?
3. Is the poem blasphemous? (If you are not a Christian, try to put yourself into the shoes of a Christian while thinking about this question.)

Oh who is that young sinner

Oh who is that young sinner with the handcuffs on his wrists?
And what has he been after that they groan and shake their fists?
And wherefore is he wearing such a conscience-stricken air?
Oh they're taking him to prison for the colour of his hair.

'Tis a shame to human nature, such a head of hair as his;
In the good old time 'twas hanging for the colour that it is;
Though hanging isn't bad enough and flaying would be fair
For the nameless and abominable colour of his hair.

Oh a deal of pains he's taken and a pretty price he's paid
To hide his poll° or dye it of a mentionable shade;
But they've pulled the beggar's hat off for the world to see and stare,
And they're haling him to justice for the colour of his hair.

Now 'tis oakum for his fingers° and the treadmill for his feet
And the quarry-gang on Portland in the cold and in the heat,
And between his spells of labour in the time he has to spare
He can curse the God that made him for the colour of his hair.

[1895]

10 poll the hair-covered back and top of the human head. **13 oakum for his fingers** Prisoners sentenced to hard labor had to shred jute, a coarse fiber mixed with tar to make oakum, used for caulking wooden ships. The task bloodied their fingers.

Joining the Conversation: Critical Thinking and Writing

1. Characterize the tone of the speaker in the first two stanzas. He begins by asking a simple question, but what causes him to change to the tone we hear in the second stanza? What is the tone of the last line of the poem?
2. In a draft of the first line, Housman wrote "fellow" but he then replaced it with "sinner." Why do you suppose he made the change?
3. No one in England, or probably anywhere else, is or was put into prison "for the colour of his hair." What is Housman getting at?

CLAUDE MCKAY

Born in Jamaica, Claude McKay (1890–1948) wrote his first poems there, in dialect that drew upon the island's folk culture. In 1912 he left Jamaica to pursue a literary career in the United States. McKay attended school and worked at a number of jobs in the 1910s, but above all he continued to write poems, which were well received. During the 1920s, he became part of the Harlem literary and cultural renaissance. A political radical, McKay also was active in left-wing groups and causes; in 1922–1923, he traveled to the Soviet Union, where he lectured on politics and literature. McKay's books of poems include Songs of Jamaica *(1912) and* Harlem Shadows *(1922). His most notable novel is* Home to Harlem *(1928); it tells the story of an African American soldier who deserts from the army in France and then returns to the United States, and it was the first novel by an African American to become a best-seller. McKay's autobiography is* A Long Way from Home *(1937). "If We Must Die," printed here, is McKay's best-known poem. A response to a horrific outbreak of racial violence in the summer of 1919 in Chicago and other major cities, the poem was first published in July of that year in the radical journal* Liberator.

If We Must Die

If we must die, let it not be like hogs
Hunted and penned in an inglorious spot,
While round us bark the mad and hungry dogs,
Making their mock at our accursed lot.
If we must die, O let us nobly die,
So that our precious blood may not be shed
In vain: then even the monsters we defy
Shall be constrained to honor us though dead!
O kinsmen! we must meet the common foe!
Though far outnumbered let us show us brave,
And for their thousand blows deal one deathblow!
What though before us lies the open grave?
Like men we'll face the murderous, cowardly pack,
Pressed to the wall, dying, but fighting back!

[1919]

Joining the Conversation: Critical Thinking and Writing

1. In line 9, the speaker refers to "the common foe." In what other ways in the poem is this "foe" characterized?
2. We know that "If We Must Die" is a poem about racial violence. How would you interpret the poem if you did not know this?
3. Some would argue that violence should never be the response to injustice, no matter how cruel the injustice might be. Do you believe this yourself? Or can you think of instances where violence might be justified?

JIMMY SANTIAGO BACA

For a biographical note on Jimmy Santiago Baca, see page 1110. Immigrants in Our Own Land, *published in 1979, was Baca's first book, and it includes the poem printed here. His other books include* Black Mesa Poems *(1989) and* Healing Earthquakes: Poems *(2001).*

Cloudy Day

It is windy today. A wall of wind crashes against,
windows clunk against, iron frames
as wind swings past broken glass
and seethes, like a frightened cat
in empty spaces of the cellblock.

In the exercise yard
we sat huddled in our prison jackets,
on our haunches against the fence,
and the wind carried our words
over the fence,
while the vigilant guard on the tower
held his cap at the sudden gust.

I could see the main tower from where I sat,
and the wind in my face
gave me the feeling I could grasp
the tower like a cornstalk,
and snap it from its roots of rock.
The wind plays it like a flute,
this hollow shoot of rock.
The brim girded with barbwire
with a guard sitting there also,
listening intently to the sounds
as clouds cover the sun.

I thought of the day I was coming to prison,
in the back seat of a police car,
hands and ankles chained, the policeman pointed,

"See that big water tank? The big
silver one out there, sticking up?
That's the prison."

And here I am, I cannot believe it.
Sometimes it is such a dream, a dream,
where I stand up in the face of the wind,
like now, it blows at my jacket,
and my eyelids flick a little bit.
while I stare disbelieving. . . .

The third day of spring,
and four years later, I can tell you,
how a man can endure, how a man
can become so cruel, how he can die
or become so cold. I can tell you this,
I have seen it every day, every day,
and still I am strong enough to love you,
love myself and feel good;
even as the earth shakes and trembles,
and I have not a thing to my name,
I feel as if I have everything, everything.

[1979]

Joining the Conversation: Critical Thinking and Writing

1. In an interview in 1997, Baca noted that he wrote "Cloudy Day" in prison. How do the details of the poem's language bear witness to Baca's own experience of imprisonment? Do you think that a person who had never been imprisoned could write such a poem?
2. In the same interview, Baca was asked about this poem: "Was that written for a person?" He replied: "It was written for me." Baca did not say any more than that. What do you think he means? And how, specifically, is this meaning reflected in the poem?
3. In the final stanza, Baca recalls that he has now been in prison for four years. What has he learned about himself, and about the realities of prison, during this period of time?
4. Who is the "you" referred to in the final stanza? How do you interpret the last line? And why does Baca repeat the word "everything"?

CAROLYN FORCHÉ

Carolyn Forché was born in Detroit in 1950. After earning a bachelor's degree from Michigan State University and a master's degree from Bowling Green State University, she traveled widely in the Southwest, living among Pueblo Indians. Between 1978 and 1986 she made several visits to El Salvador, documenting human rights violations for Amnesty International. Her first book of poems, Gathering the Tribes, *won the Yale Younger Poets award in 1975. Forché is Director of the Lannan Center for Poetry and Poetics and holds the Lannan Chair in Poetry at Georgetown University in Washington, D.C. Her second book of poems,* The Country Between Us *(1981), includes "The Colonel," which has been called a prose poem i.e., a short work that looks like prose but that is highly rhythmical or rich in images, or both.*

The Colonel

What you have heard is true. I was in his house. His wife carried a tray of coffee and sugar. His daughter filed her nails, his son went out for the night. There were daily papers, pet dogs, a pistol on the cushion beside him. The moon swung bare on its black cord over the house. On the television was a cop show. It was in English. Broken bottles were embedded in the walls around the house to scoop the kneecaps from a man's legs or cut his hands to lace. On the windows there were gratings like those in liquor stores. We had dinner, rack of lamb, good wine, a gold bell was on the table for calling the maid. The maid brought green mangoes, salt, a type of bread. I was asked how I enjoyed the country. There was a brief commercial in Spanish. His wife took everything away. There was some talk then of how difficult it had become to govern. The parrot said hello on the terrace. The colonel told it to shutup, and pushed himself from the table. My friend said to me with his eyes: say nothing. The colonel returned with a sack used to bring groceries home. He spilled many human ears on the table. They were like dried peach halves. There is no other way to say this. He took one of them in his hands, shook it in our faces, dropped it into a water glass. It came alive there. I am tired of fooling around he said. As for the rights of anyone, tell your people they can go fuck themselves. He swept the ears to the floor with his arm and held the last of his wine in the air. Something for your poetry, no? he said. Some of the ears on the floor caught this scrap of his voice. Some of the ears on the floor were pressed to the ground.

May 1978

[*publ. 1981*]

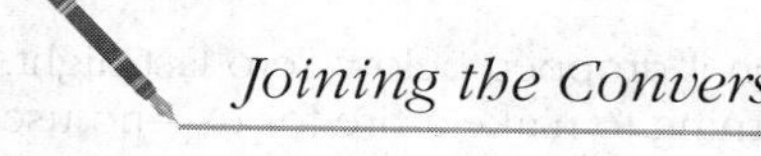

Joining the Conversation: Critical Thinking and Writing

1. How would you characterize the colonel in a few sentences?
2. We are told that the colonel spoke of "how difficult it had become to govern." What do you suppose the colonel assumes is the purpose of government? What do you assume its purpose is?
3. How much do we know about the narrator? Can we guess the narrator's purpose in visiting the colonel? How would you characterize the narrator's tone? Do you believe the narrator?
4. What is your response to the last sentence?

PLAY

SUSAN GLASPELL

Susan Glaspell (1876–1948) was born in Davenport, Iowa, and educated at Drake University in Des Moines. In 1903 she married the novelist, poet, and playwright George Cram Cook and, with Cook and other writers, actors, and artists, in 1915 founded the Provincetown Players, a group that remained vital until 1929. Glaspell wrote Trifles *(1916) for the Provincetown Players, but she also wrote stories, novels, and a biography of her husband. In 1931 she won a Pulitzer Prize for* Alison's House, *a play about the family of a deceased poet who in some ways resembles Emily Dickinson.*

Trifles

SCENE: *The kitchen in the now abandoned farmhouse of* JOHN WRIGHT, *a gloomy kitchen, and left without having been put in order—unwashed pans under the sink, a loaf of bread outside the breadbox, a dish towel on the table—other signs of incompleted work. At the rear the outer door opens, and the* SHERIFF *comes in, followed by the* COUNTY ATTORNEY *and* HALE. *The* SHERIFF *and* HALE *are men in middle life, the* COUNTY ATTORNEY *is a young man; all are much bundled up and go at once to the stove. They are followed by the two women—the* SHERIFF'S WIFE *first; she is a slight wiry woman, a thin nervous face.* MRS. HALE *is larger and would ordinarily be called more comfortable looking, but she is disturbed now and looks fearfully about as she enters. The women have come in slowly and stand close together near the door.*

COUNTY ATTORNEY [*rubbing his hands*]: This feels good. Come up to the fire, ladies.

MRS. PETERS [*after taking a step forward*]: I'm not—cold.

SHERIFF [*unbuttoning his overcoat and stepping away from the stove as if to the beginning of official business*]: Now, Mr. Hale, before we move things about, you explain to Mr. Henderson just what you saw when you came here yesterday morning.

COUNTY ATTORNEY: By the way, has anything been moved? Are things just as you left them yesterday?

SHERIFF [*looking about*]: It's just the same. When it dropped below zero last night, I thought I'd better send Frank out this morning to make a fire for us—no use getting pneumonia with a big case on; but I told him not to touch anything except the stove—and you know Frank.

COUNTY ATTORNEY: Somebody should have been left here yesterday.

SHERIFF: Oh—yesterday. When I had to send Frank to Morris Center for that man who went crazy—I want you to know I had my hands full yesterday. I knew you could get back from Omaha by today, and as long as I went over everything here myself—

COUNTY ATTORNEY: Well, Mr. Hale, tell just what happened when you came here yesterday morning.

The original Provincetown players production (1916) of *Trifles*. (New York Public Library/Art Resource)

HALE: Harry and I had started to town with a load of potatoes. We came along the road from my place; and as I got here, I said, "I'm going to see if I can't get John Wright to go in with me on a party telephone." I spoke to Wright about it once before, and he put me off, saying folks talked too much anyway, and all he asked was peace and quiet—I guess you know about how much he talked himself; but I thought maybe if I went to the house and talked about it before his wife, though I said to Harry that I didn't know as what his wife wanted made much difference to John—

COUNTY ATTORNEY: Let's talk about that later, Mr. Hale. I do want to talk about that, but tell now just what happened when you got to the house.

HALE: I didn't hear or see anything; I knocked at the door, and still it was all quiet inside. I knew they must be up, it was past eight o'clock. So I knocked again, and I thought I heard somebody say, "Come in." I wasn't sure, I'm not sure yet, but I opened the door—this door [*indicating the door by which the two women are still standing*], and there in that rocker—[*pointing to it*] sat Mrs. Wright. [*They all look at the rocker.*]

COUNTY ATTORNEY: What—was she doing?

HALE: She was rockin' back and forth. She had her apron in her hand and was kind of—pleating it.

COUNTY ATTORNEY: And how did she—look?

HALE: Well, she looked queer.

COUNTY ATTORNEY: How do you mean—queer?

HALE: Well, as if she didn't know what she was going to do next. And kind of done up.

COUNTY ATTORNEY: How did she seem to feel about your coming?

HALE: Why, I don't think she minded—one way or other. She didn't pay much attention. I said, "How do, Mrs. Wright, it's cold, ain't it?" And she said, "Is it?"—and went on kind of pleating at her apron. Well, I was surprised; she didn't ask me to come up to the stove, or to set down, but just sat there, not even looking at me, so I said, "I want to see John." And then she—laughed. I guess you would call it a laugh. I thought of Harry and the team outside, so I said a little sharp: "Can't I see John?" "No," she says, kind o' dull like. "Ain't he home?" says I. "Yes," says she, "he's home." "Then why can't I see him?" I asked her, out of patience. "'Cause he's dead," says she. "*Dead?*" says I. She just nodded her head, not getting a bit excited, but rockin' back and forth. "Why—where is he?" says I, not knowing what to say. She just pointed upstairs—like that [*himself pointing to the room above*]. I got up, with the idea of going up there. I walked from there to here—then I says, "Why, what did he die of?" "He died of a rope around his neck," says she, and just went on pleatin' at her apron. Well, I went out and called Harry. I thought I might—need help. We went upstairs, and there he was lyin'—

COUNTY ATTORNEY: I think I'd rather have you go into that upstairs, where you can point it all out. Just go on now with the rest of the story.

HALE: Well, my first thought was to get that rope off. I looked . . . [*Stops, his face twitches.*] . . . but Harry, he went up to him, and he said, "No, he's dead all right, and we'd better not touch anything." So we went back downstairs. She was still sitting that same way. "Has anybody been notified?" I asked. "No," says she, unconcerned. "Who did this, Mrs. Wright?" said Harry. He said it businesslike—and she stopped pleatin' of her apron. "I don't know," she says. "You don't *know?*" says Harry. "No," says she. "Weren't you sleepin' in the bed with him?" says Harry. "Yes," says she, "but I was on the inside." "Somebody slipped a rope round his neck and strangled him, and you didn't wake up?" says Harry. "I didn't wake up," she said after him. We must 'a looked as if we didn't see how that could be, for after a minute she said, "I sleep sound." Harry was going to ask her more questions, but I said maybe we ought to let her tell her story first to the coroner, or the sheriff, so Harry went fast as he could to Rivers' place, where there's a telephone.

COUNTY ATTORNEY: And what did Mrs. Wright do when she knew that you had gone for the coroner?

HALE: She moved from that chair to this over here . . . [*Pointing to a small chair in the corner.*] . . . and just sat there with her hands held together and looking down. I got a feeling that I ought to make some conversation, so I said I had come in to see if John wanted to put in a telephone, and at that she started to laugh, and then she stopped and looked at me—scared. [*The* COUNTY ATTORNEY, *who has had his notebook out, makes a note.*] I dunno, maybe it wasn't scared. I wouldn't like to say it was. Soon Harry got back, and then Dr. Lloyd came, and you, Mr. Peters, and so I guess that's all I know that you don't.

COUNTY ATTORNEY [*looking around*]: I guess we'll go upstairs first—and then out to the barn and around there. [*To the* SHERIFF.] You're convinced that there was nothing important here—nothing that would point to any motive?

SHERIFF: Nothing here but kitchen things. [*The* COUNTY ATTORNEY, *after again looking around the kitchen, opens the door of a cupboard closet. He gets up on a chair and looks on a shelf. Pulls his hand away, sticky.*]

COUNTY ATTORNEY: Here's a nice mess. [*The women draw nearer.*]

MRS. PETERS [*to the other woman*]: Oh, her fruit; it did freeze. [*To the* LAWYER.] She worried about that when it turned so cold. She said the fir'd go out and her jars would break.

SHERIFF: Well, can you beat the women! Held for murder and worryin' about her preserves.

COUNTY ATTORNEY: I guess before we're through she may have something more serious than preserves to worry about.

HALE: Well, women are used to worrying over trifles.

[*The two women move a little closer together.*]

COUNTY ATTORNEY [*with the gallantry of a young politician*]: And yet, for all their worries, what would we do without the ladies? [*The women do not unbend. He goes to the sink, takes a dipperful of water from the pail and, pouring it into a basin, washes his hands. Starts to wipe them on the roller towel, turns it for a cleaner place.*] Dirty towels! [*Kicks his foot against the pans under the sink.*] Not much of a housekeeper, would you say, ladies?

MRS. HALE [*stiffly*]: There's a great deal of work to be done on a farm.

COUNTY ATTORNEY: To be sure. And yet . . . [*With a little bow to her.*] . . . I know there are some Dickson county farmhouses which do not have such roller towels. [*He gives it a pull to expose its full length again.*]

MRS. HALE: Those towels get dirty awful quick. Men's hands aren't always as clean as they might be.

COUNTY ATTORNEY: Ah, loyal to your sex, I see. But you and Mrs. Wright were neighbors. I suppose you were friends, too.

MRS. HALE [*shaking her head*]: I've not seen much of her of late years. I've not been in this house—it's more than a year.

COUNTY ATTORNEY: And why was that? You didn't like her?

MRS. HALE: I liked her all well enough. Farmers' wives have their hands full, Mr. Henderson. And then—

COUNTY ATTORNEY: Yes—?

MRS. HALE [*looking about*]: It never seemed a very cheerful place.

COUNTY ATTORNEY: No—it's not cheerful. I shouldn't say she had the homemaking instinct.

MRS. HALE: Well, I don't know as Wright had, either.

COUNTY ATTORNEY: You mean that they didn't get on very well?

MRS. HALE: No, I don't mean anything. But I don't think a place'd be any cheerfuler for John Wright's being in it.

COUNTY ATTORNEY: I'd like to talk more of that a little later. I want to get the lay of things upstairs now. [*He goes to the left, where three steps lead to a stair door.*]

SHERIFF: I suppose anything Mrs. Peters does'll be all right. She was to take in some clothes for her, you know, and a few little things. We left in such a hurry yesterday.

COUNTY ATTORNEY: Yes, but I would like to see what you take, Mrs. Peters, and keep an eye out for anything that might be of use to us.

MRS. PETERS: Yes, Mr. Henderson.

[*The women listen to the men's steps on the stairs, then look about the kitchen.*]

MRS. HALE: I'd hate to have men coming into my kitchen, snooping around and criticizing. [*She arranges the pans under sink which the* LAWYER *had shoved out of place.*]

MRS. PETERS: Of course it's no more than their duty.

MRS. HALE: Duty's all right, but I guess that deputy sheriff that came out to make the fire might have got a little of this on. [*Gives the roller towel a pull.*] Wish I'd thought of that sooner. Seems mean to talk about her for not having things slicked up when she had to come away in such a hurry.

MRS. PETERS [*who has gone to a small table in the left rear corner of the room, and lifted one end of a towel that covers a pan*]: She had bread set. [*Stands still.*]

MRS. HALE [*eyes fixed on a loaf of bread beside the breadbox, which is on a low shelf at the other side of the room; moves slowly toward it*]: She was going to put this in there. [*Picks up loaf, then abruptly drops it. In a manner of returning to familiar things.*] It's a shame about her fruit. I wonder if it's all gone. [*Gets up on the chair and looks.*] I think there's some here that's all right, Mrs. Peters. Yes—here; [*Holding it toward the window.*] this is cherries, too. [*Looking again.*] I declare I believe that's the only one. [*Gets down, bottle in her hand. Goes to the sink and wipes it off on the outside.*] She'll feel awful bad after all her hard work in the hot weather. I remember the afternoon I put up my cherries last summer. [*She puts the bottle on the big kitchen table, center of the room, front table. With a sigh, is about to sit down in the rocking chair. Before she is seated realizes what chair it is; with a slow look at it, steps back. The chair, which she has touched, rocks back and forth.*]

MRS. PETERS: Well, I must get those things from the front room closet. [*She goes to the door at the right, but after looking into the other room steps back.*] You coming with me, Mrs. Hale? You could help me carry them. [*They go into the other room; reappear,* MRS. PETERS *carrying a dress and skirt,* MRS. HALE *following with a pair of shoes.*]

MRS. PETERS: My, it's cold in there. [*She puts the cloth on the big table, and hurries to the stove.*]

MRS. HALE [*examining the skirt*]: Wright was close. I think maybe that's why she kept so much to herself. She didn't even belong to the Ladies' Aid. I suppose she felt she couldn't do her part, and then you don't enjoy things when you feel shabby. She used to wear pretty clothes and be lively, when she was Minnie Foster, one of the town girls singing in the choir. But that—oh, that was thirty years ago. This all you was to take in?

MRS. PETERS: She said she wanted an apron. Funny thing to want, for there isn't much to get you dirty in jail, goodness knows. But I suppose just to make her feel more natural. She said they was in the top drawer in this cupboard. Yes, here. And then her little shawl that always hung behind the door. [*Opens stair door and looks.*] Yes, here it is. [*Quickly shuts door leading upstairs.*]

MRS. HALE [*abruptly moving toward her*]: Mrs. Peters?

MRS. PETERS: Yes, Mrs. Hale?

MRS. HALE: Do you think she did it?

MRS. PETERS [*in a frightened voice*]: Oh, I don't know.

MRS. HALE: Well, I don't think she did. Asking for an apron and her little shawl. Worrying about her fruit.

MRS. PETERS [*starts to speak, glances up, where footsteps are heard in the room above. In a low voice.*]: Mr. Peters says it looks bad for her. Mr. Henderson is awful sarcastic in speech, and he'll make fun of her sayin' she didn't wake up.

MRS. HALE: Well, I guess John Wright didn't wake when they was slipping that rope under his neck.

MRS. PETERS: No, it's strange. It must have been done awful crafty and still. They say it was such a—funny way to kill a man, rigging it all up like that.

MRS. HALE: That's just what Mr. Hale said. There was a gun in the house. He says that's what he can't understand.

MRS. PETERS: Mr. Henderson said coming out that what was needed for the case was a motive; something to show anger, or—sudden feeling.

MRS. HALE [*who is standing by the table*]: Well, I don't see any signs of anger around here. [*She puts her hand on the dish towel which lies on the table, stands looking down at the table, one half of which is clean, the other half messy.*] It's wiped here. [*Makes a move as if to finish work, then turns and looks at loaf of bread outside the breadbox. Drops towel. In that voice of coming back to familiar things.*] Wonder how they are finding things upstairs? I hope she had it a little more red-up up there. You know, it seems kind of *sneaking.* Locking her up in town and then coming out here and trying to get her own house to turn against her!

MRS. PETERS: But, Mrs. Hale, the law is the law.

MRS. HALE: I s'pose 'is. [*Unbuttoning her coat.*] Better loosen up your things, Mrs. Peters. You won't feel them when you go out.

[MRS. PETERS *takes off her fur tippet, goes to hang it on hook at the back of room, stands looking at the under part of the small corner table.*]

MRS. PETERS: She was piecing a quilt. [*She brings the large sewing basket, and they look at the bright pieces.*]

MRS. HALE: It's log cabin pattern. Pretty, isn't it? I wonder if she was goin' to quilt or just knot it?

[*Footsteps have been heard coming down the stairs. The* SHERIFF *enters, followed by* HALE *and the* COUNTY ATTORNEY.]

SHERIFF: They wonder if she was going to quilt it or just knot it. [*The men laugh, the women look abashed.*]

COUNTY ATTORNEY [*rubbing his hands over the stove*]: Frank's fire didn't do much up there, did it? Well, let's go out to the barn and get that cleared up.

[*The men go outside.*]

MRS. HALE [*resentfully*]: I don't know as there's anything so strange, our takin' up our time with little things while we're waiting for them to get the evidence. [*She sits down at the big table, smoothing out a block with decision.*] I don't see as it's anything to laugh about.

MRS. PETERS [*apologetically*]: Of course they've got awful important things on their minds. [*Pulls up a chair and joins* MRS. HALE *at the table.*]

MRS. HALE [*examining another block*]: Mrs. Peters, look at this one. Here, this is the one she was working on, and look at the sewing! All the rest of it has been so nice and even. And look at this! It's all over the place! Why, it looks as if she didn't know what she was about! [*After she has said this, they look at each other, then started to glance back at the door. After an instant* MRS. HALE *has pulled at a knot and ripped the sewing.*]

MRS. PETERS: Oh, what are you doing, Mrs. Hale?

MRS. HALE [*mildly*]: Just pulling out a stitch or two that's not sewed very good. [*Threading a needle.*] Bad sewing always made me fidgety.

MRS. PETERS [*nervously*]: I don't think we ought to touch things.

MRS. HALE: I'll just finish up this end. [*Suddenly stopping and leaning forward.*] Mrs. Peters?

MRS. PETERS: Yes, Mrs. Hale?

MRS. HALE: What do you suppose she was so nervous about?

MRS. PETERS: Oh—I don't know. I don't know as she was nervous. I sometimes sew awful queer when I'm just tired. [MRS. HALE *starts to say something, looks at* MRS. PETERS, *then goes on sewing.*] Well, I must get these things wrapped up. They may be through sooner than we think. [*Putting apron and other things together.*] I wonder where I can find a piece of paper, and string.

MRS. HALE: In that cupboard, maybe.

MRS. PETERS [*looking in cupboard*]: Why, here's a birdcage. [*Holds it up.*] Did she have a bird, Mrs. Hale?

MRS. HALE: Why, I don't know whether she did or not—I've not been here for so long. There was a man around last year selling canaries cheap, but I don't know as she took one; maybe she did. She used to sing real pretty herself.

MRS. PETERS [*glancing around*]: Seems funny to think of a bird here. But she must have had one, or why should she have a cage? I wonder what happened to it?

MRS. HALE: I s'pose maybe the cat got it.

MRS. PETERS: No, she didn't have a cat. She's got that feeling some people have about cats—being afraid of them. My cat got in her room, and she was real upset and asked me to take it out.

MRS. HALE: My sister Bessie was like that. Queer, ain't it?

MRS. PETERS [*examining the cage*]: Why, look at this door. It's broke. One hinge is pulled apart.

MRS. HALE [*looking, too*]: Looks as if someone must have been rough with it.

MRS. PETERS: Why, yes. [*She brings the cage forward and puts it on the table.*]

MRS. HALE: I wish if they're going to find any evidence they'd be about it. I don't like this place.

MRS. PETERS: But I'm awful glad you came with me, Mrs. Hale. It would be lonesome for me sitting here alone.

MRS. HALE: It would, wouldn't it? [*Dropping her sewing.*] But I tell you what I do wish, Mrs. Peters. I wish I had come over sometimes when *she* was here. I—[*Looking around the room.*]—wish I had.

MRS. PETERS: But of course you were awful busy, Mrs. Hale—your house and your children.

MRS. HALE: I could've come. I stayed away because it weren't cheerful—and that's why I ought to have come. I—I've never liked this place. Maybe because it's down in a hollow, and you don't see the road. I dunno what it is, but it's a lonesome place and always was. I wish I had come over to see Minnie Foster sometimes. I can see now—[*Shakes her head.*]

MRS. PETERS: Well, you mustn't reproach yourself, Mrs. Hale. Somehow we just don't see how it is with other folks until—something comes up.

MRS. HALE: Not having children makes less work—but it makes a quiet house, and Wright out to work all day, and no company when he did come in. Did you know John Wright, Mrs. Peters?

MRS. PETERS: Not to know him; I've seen him in town. They say he was a good man.

MRS. HALE: Yes—good; he didn't drink, and kept his word as well as most, I guess, and paid his debts. But he was a hard man, Mrs. Peters. Just to pass the time of day with him. [*Shivers.*] Like a raw wind that gets to the bone. [*Pauses, her eye falling on the cage.*] I should think she would 'a wanted a bird. But what do you suppose went with it?

MRS. PETERS: I don't know, unless it got sick and died. [*She reaches over and swings the broken door, swings it again; both women watch it.*]

MRS. HALE: You weren't raised round here, were you? [MRS. PETERS *shakes her head.*] You didn't know—her?

MRS. PETERS: Not till they brought her yesterday.

MRS. HALE: She—come to think of it, she was kind of like a bird herself—real sweet and pretty, but kind of timid and—fluttery. How—she—did—change. [*Silence; then as if struck by a happy thought and relieved to get back to every-*

day things.] Tell you what, Mrs. Peters; why don't you take the quilt in with you? It might take up her mind.

MRS. PETERS: Why, I think that's a real nice idea, Mrs. Hale. There couldn't possibly be any objection to it, could there? Now, just what would I take? I wonder if her patches are in here—and her things. [*They look in the sewing basket.*]

MRS. HALE: Here's some red. I expect this has got sewing things in it. [*Brings out a fancy box.*] What a pretty box. Looks like something somebody would give you. Maybe her scissors are in here. [*Opens box. Suddenly puts her hand to her nose.*] Why—[MRS. PETERS *bends nearer, then turns her face away.*] There's something wrapped up in this piece of silk.

MRS. PETERS: Why, this isn't her scissors.

MRS. HALE [*lifting the silk*]: Oh, Mrs. Peters—it's—[MRS. PETERS *bends closer.*]

MRS. PETERS: It's the bird.

MRS. HALE [*jumping up*]: But, Mrs. Peters—look at it. Its neck! Look at its neck! It's all—other side *to*.

MRS. PETERS: Somebody—wrung—its neck.

[*Their eyes meet. A look of growing comprehension of horror. Steps are heard outside.* MRS. HALE *slips box under quilt pieces, and sinks into her chair. Enter* SHERIFF *and* COUNTY ATTORNEY. MRS. PETERS *rises.*]

COUNTY ATTORNEY [*as one turning from serious things to little pleasantries*]: Well, ladies, have you decided whether she was going to quilt it or knot it?

MRS. PETERS: We think she was going to—knot it.

COUNTY ATTORNEY: Well, that's interesting, I'm sure. [*Seeing the birdcage.*] Has the bird flown?

MRS. HALE [*putting more quilt pieces over the box*]: We think the—cat got it.

COUNTY ATTORNEY [*preoccupied*]: Is there a cat?

[MRS. HALE *glances in a quick covert way at* MRS. PETERS.]

MRS. PETERS: Well, not now. They're superstitious, you know. They leave.

COUNTY ATTORNEY [*to* SHERIFF, *continuing an interrupted conversation*]: No sign at all of anyone having come from the outside. Their own rope. Now let's go up again and go over it piece by piece. [*They start upstairs.*] It would have to have been someone who knew just the—[MRS. PETERS *sits down. The two women sit there not looking at one another, but as if peering into something and at the same time holding back. When they talk now, it is the manner of feeling their way over strange ground, as if afraid of what they are saying, but as if they cannot help saying it.*]

MRS. HALE: She liked the bird. She was going to bury it in that pretty box.

MRS. PETERS [*in a whisper*]: When I was a girl—my kitten—there was a boy took a hatchet, and before my eyes—and before I could get there—[*Covers her face an instant.*] If they hadn't held me back, I would have—[*Catches herself, looks upstairs where steps are heard, falters weakly.*]—hurt him.

MRS. HALE [*with a slow look around her*]: I wonder how it would seem never to have had any children around. [*Pause.*] No, Wright wouldn't like the bird—a thing that sang. She used to sing. He killed that, too.

MRS. PETERS [*moving uneasily*]: We don't know who killed the bird.

MRS. HALE: I knew John Wright.

MRS. PETERS: It was an awful thing was done in this house that night, Mrs. Hale. Killing a man while he slept, slipping a rope around his neck that choked the life out of him.

MRS. HALE: His neck. Choked the life out of him.

[*Her hand goes out and rests on the birdcage.*]

MRS. PETERS [*with a rising voice*]: We don't know who killed him. We don't *know.*

MRS. HALE [*her own feeling not interrupted*]: If there'd been years and years of nothing, then a bird to sing to you, it would be awful—still, after the bird was still.

MRS. PETERS [*something within her speaking*]: I know what stillness is. When we homesteaded in Dakota, and my first baby died—after he was two years old, and me with no other then—

MRS. HALE [*moving*]: How soon do you suppose they'll be through, looking for evidence?

MRS. PETERS: I know what stillness is. [*Pulling herself back.*] The law has got to punish crime, Mrs. Hale.

MRS. HALE [*not as if answering that*]: I wish you'd seen Minnie Foster when she wore a white dress with blue ribbons and stood up there in the choir and sang. [*A look around the room.*] Oh, I *wish* I'd come over here once in a while! That was a crime! That was a crime! Who's going to punish that?

MRS. PETERS [*looking upstairs*]: We mustn't—take on.

MRS. HALE: I might have known she needed help! I know how things can be—for women. I tell you, it's queer, Mrs. Peters. We live close together and we live far apart. We all go through the same things—it's all just a different kind of the same thing. [*Brushes her eyes, noticing the bottle of fruit, reaches out for it.*] If I was you, I wouldn't tell her her fruit was gone. Tell her it *ain't.* Tell her it's all right. Take this in to prove it to her. She—she may never know whether it was broke or not.

MRS. PETERS [*takes the bottle, looks about for something to wrap it in; takes petticoat from the clothes brought from the other room, very nervously begins winding this around the bottle. In a false voice*]: My, it's a good thing the men couldn't hear us. Wouldn't they just laugh! Getting all stirred up over a little thing like a—dead canary. As if that could have anything to do with—with—wouldn't they *laugh!*

[*The men are heard coming downstairs.*]

MRS. HALE [*under her breath*]: Maybe they would—maybe they wouldn't.

COUNTY ATTORNEY: No, Peters, it's all perfectly clear except a reason for doing it. But you know juries when it comes to women. If there was some definite thing. Something to show—something to make a story about—a thing that would connect up with this strange way of doing it.

[*The women's eyes meet for an instant. Enter* HALE *from outer door.*]

HALE: Well, I've got the team around. Pretty cold out there.

COUNTY ATTORNEY: I'm going to stay here awhile by myself. [*To the* SHERIFF.] You can send Frank out for me, can't you? I want to go over everything. I'm not satisfied that we can't do better.

SHERIFF: Do you want to see what Mrs. Peters is going to take in?

[*The* LAWYER *goes to the table, picks up the apron, laughs.*]

COUNTY ATTORNEY: Oh I guess they're not very dangerous things the ladies have picked up. [*Moves a few things about, disturbing the quilt pieces which cover the box. Steps back.*] No, Mrs. Peters doesn't need supervising. For that matter, a sheriff's wife is married to the law. Ever think of it that way, Mrs. Peters?

MRS. PETERS: Not—just that way.

SHERIFF [*chuckling*]: Married to the law. [*Moves toward the other room.*] I just want you to come in here a minute, George. We ought to take a look at these windows.

COUNTY ATTORNEY [*scoffingly*]: Oh, windows!

SHERIFF: We'll be right out, Mr. Hale.

[HALE *goes outside. The* SHERIFF *follows the* COUNTY ATTORNEY *into the other room. Then* MRS. HALE *rises, hands tight together, looking intensely at* MRS. PETERS, *whose eyes take a slow turn, finally meeting* MRS. HALE'*s. A moment* MRS. HALE *holds her, then her own eyes point the way to where the box is concealed. Suddenly* MRS. PETERS *throws back quilt pieces and tries to put the box in the bag she is wearing. It is too big. She opens box, starts to take the bird out, cannot touch it, goes to pieces, stands there helpless. Sound of a knob turning in the other room.* MRS. HALE *snatches the box and puts it in the pocket of her big coat. Enter* COUNTY ATTORNEY *and* SHERIFF.]

COUNTY ATTORNEY [*facetiously*]: Well, Henry, at least we found out that she was not going to quilt it. She was going to—what is it you call it, ladies?

MRS. HALE [*her hand against her pocket*]: We call it—knot it, Mr. Henderson.

CURTAIN

[1916]

Joining the Conversation: Critical Thinking and Writing

1. Briefly describe the setting, indicating what it "says" and what atmosphere it evokes.
2. Even before the first word of dialogue is spoken, what do you think the play tells us (in the entrance of the characters) about the distinction between the men and the women?
3. How would you characterize Mr. Henderson, the county attorney?
4. In what way or ways are Mrs. Peters and Mrs. Hale different from each other?
5. Several times the men "laugh" or "chuckle." In their contexts, what do these expressions of amusement convey?
6. In the long stage direction before the next to last speech, "*the women's eyes meet for an instant.*" What do you think this bit of action "says"? What do you understand by the exchange of glances?
7. On page 1343, when Mrs. Peters tells of the boy who killed her cat, she says, "If they hadn't held me back, I would have—(*Catches herself, looks upstairs where steps are heard, falters weakly.*)—hurt him." What do you think she was about to say before she faltered? Why do you suppose Glaspell included this speech about Mrs. Peters's girlhood?
8. On page 1341, Mrs. Hale, looking at a quilt, wonders whether Mrs. Wright "was goin' to quilt or just knot it." The men are amused by the women's concern with this topic, and the last line of the play returns to the issue. What do you make of this emphasis on the matter?
9. We never see Mrs. Wright on stage. Nevertheless, by the end of *Trifles* we know a great deal about her. In an essay of 500–750 words explain both what we know about her—physical characteristics, habits, interests, personality, life before her marriage and after—and *how* we know these things.

10. The title of the play is ironic—the "trifles" are important. What other ironies do you find in the play?
11. Do you think the play is immoral? Explain, supporting your argument with evidence from the text.
12. Assume that the canary has been found, thereby revealing a possible motive, and that Minnie Wright is indicted for murder. You are the defense attorney. In 500 words set forth your defense. (Take any position you wish. For instance, you may want to argue that she committed justifiable homicide or that—on the basis of her behavior as reported by Mr. Hale—she is innocent by reason of insanity.)
13. Assume that the canary had been found and Minnie Wright convicted. Compose the speech you think she might have delivered before the sentence was given.

Chapter Overview: Looking Backward/Looking Forward

1. Should a defense attorney defend a client whose guilt is obvious to everybody? If you were defending a client you believed to be innocent, but then discovered evidence of the client's guilt, would you tell the judge or keep this information to yourself?
2. During the civil rights campaigns of the 1950s and 1960s, Martin Luther King Jr. and many other activists frequently broke the law. What was their aim in doing so? Isn't it always wrong to break the law?
3. Often we say to ourselves or to someone else, "There should be a law against that." Is there an activity or specific form of behavior that you believe should be outlawed? Do you think that most people agree with you about this, or are you clearly in the minority? If your position on this issue became "the law," what would be the consequences?
4. Should a judge strictly abide by the letter of the law all the time? Can you imagine a situation when a judge knew a defendant to be guilty but nonetheless found him or her innocent? Would such a decision make you respect the law more, or less?
5. Does the study of literature affect a person's attitude toward the law? Do you think that it makes a person more respectful of the law, or less? Which literary works have affected your own views about law and order?
6. Has the study of literature made you a better person? How would you prove this to someone?

Writing about Literature: An Overview of Critical Strategies

The Nature of Critical Writing

We have mentioned already that in everyday talk the commonest meaning of **criticism** is something like "finding fault." But a critic can see excellences as well as faults. Because we turn to criticism with the hope that the critic has seen something we have missed, the most valuable criticism is not that which shakes its finger at faults but that which calls our attention to interesting things going on in the work of art. Here is a statement made by W. H. Auden in *The Dyer's Hand* (1963), suggesting that criticism is most useful when it calls our attention to things worth attending to:

> What is the function of a critic? So far as I am concerned, he can do me one or more of the following services:
>
> 1. Introduce me to authors or works of which I was hitherto unaware.
> 2. Convince me that I have undervalued an author or a work because I had not read them carefully enough.
> 3. Show me relations between works of different ages and cultures which I could never have seen for myself because I do not know enough and never shall.
> 4. Give a "reading" of a work which increases my understanding of it.
> 5. Throw light upon the process of artistic "Making."
> 6. Throw light upon the relation of art to life, science, economics, ethics, religion, etc. (8–9)

Auden does not neglect the delight we get from literature, but he extends (especially in his sixth point) the range of criticism to include topics beyond the literary work itself. Notice too the emphasis on observing, showing, and illuminating, which suggests that the function of critical writing is not very different from the commonest view of the function of imaginative writing.

Auden begins by saying that a critic can "introduce" him to an author. How would a critic introduce a reader to an author? It's not enough just to name the author; almost surely the advocate would give *reasons* why we should read the book. "It will really grip you"; "It's the funniest thing I've read in months"; "I was moved to tears." Auden lets the cat out of the bag in his next two assertions: the critic may "convince" him of something, or may "show" him something. Criticism is largely a matter of convincing and showing—really, showing and thereby convincing. We cannot just announce that we like or dislike something and expect people to agree; we have to point to evidence (that's the showing part) if we are going to convince.

In a moment we will return to the matter of evidence, but first let's hear another writer talk about criticism. In *Phoenix: The Posthumous Papers of D. H. Lawrence* (1936), the novelist D. H. Lawrence says this:

> Literary criticism can be no more than a reasoned account of the feeling produced upon the critic by the book he is criticizing. Criticism can never be a science: it is, in the first place, much too personal, and in the second, it is concerned with values that science ignores. (539)

We like Lawrence's assertion that criticism is *a reasoned account*—writing about literature is a rational activity, not a mere pouring out of emotion—but we equally like his assertion that it is rooted in *feeling*. As earlier chapters have suggested, when we read we respond (perhaps with an intense interest, perhaps with a yawn). Our responses are worth examining. *Why* do we find this character memorable, or that character unbelievable?

As we examine our responses, and check the text to make sure that we have properly remembered it, we may find our responses changing, but finally we think we know what we think of the literary work, and we know *why* we think it. We are, in Lawrence's words, able to give "a reasoned account of the feeling produced . . . by the book."

Criticism as Argument: Assumptions and Evidence

In this process of showing and convincing (Auden's words) and of offering a reasoned account (Lawrence's words), even if we are talking about a so-so movie or television show, what we say depends in large measure on certain conscious or unconscious assumptions that we make:

- "I liked it because the characters were very believable" (here the assumption is that characters ought to be believable);
- "I didn't like it; there was too much violence" (here the assumption is that violence ought not to be shown, or if it is shown it should be condemned);
- "I didn't like it; it was awfully slow" (here the assumption probably is that there ought to be a fair amount of physical action, perhaps even changes of scene, rather than characters just talking in the kitchen);
- "I didn't like it; I don't think topics of this sort should be discussed publicly" (here the assumption is a moral one, that it is indecent to present certain topics);
- "I liked it partly because it was refreshing to hear such frankness" (here again the assumption is moral, and more or less the reverse of the previous one).

In short, whether we realize it or not, our responses are rooted in assumptions. These assumptions, we may believe, are so self-evident that they do not need to be stated. Our readers, however, may disagree.

If we are to hold our readers' interest, and perhaps convince them to see things the way we do, we must recognize our assumptions and must offer evidence—point to things in the work—that will convince the reader that our assumptions are reasonable. If we want to say that a short story ought to be realistic, we will call our reader's attention to unrealistic aspects in a particular story and will, with this evidence in front of the reader, argue that the story is not worth much. Or, conversely, we might say that in a satiric story realism of course is not a valid criterion; what readers want is (as in a political caricature in a newspaper) exaggeration and humor, and in our critical study we will call attention to the delight that this or that bit of exaggeration offers.

In brief, as we suggested in Chapters 7 and 8 ("Arguing an Interpretation" and "Arguing an Evaluation"), argument consists of offering statements that are *reasons* for other statements ("The work means X *because* . . ."), and the words that follow "because" normally point to the evidence that we believe supports the earlier assertion.

Some Critical Strategies

Professional critics, like the ordinary moviegoer who recommends a movie to a friend, work from assumptions, but their assumptions are usually highly conscious, and the critics may define their assumptions at length. They regard themselves as, for instance, Freudians or Marxists or gay critics. They read all texts through the lens of a particular theory, and their focus enables them to see things that otherwise might go unnoticed. Most critics realize, however, that if a lens or critical perspective or interpretive strategy helps us to see certain things, it also limits our vision. They therefore regard their method not as an exclusive way of thinking but only as a useful tool.

What follows is a brief survey of the chief current approaches to literature. You may find, as you read these pages, that one or another approach sounds congenial, and you may want to make use of it in your reading and writing. On the other hand, it's important to remember that works of literature are highly varied, and we read them for various purposes—to kill time, to enjoy fanciful visions, to be amused, to learn about alien ways of feeling, and to learn about ourselves.

It may be best, therefore, to try to respond to each text in the way that the text seems to require rather than to read all texts according to a single formula. You'll find, of course, that some works will lead you to want to think about them from several angles. A play by Shakespeare may stimulate you to read a book about the Elizabethan playhouse, and another that offers a Marxist interpretation of the English Renaissance, and still another that offers a feminist analysis of Shakespeare's plays. All of these approaches, and others, may help to deepen your understanding of the literary works that you read.

Formalist Criticism (New Criticism)

Formalist criticism emphasizes the work as an independent creation, a self-contained unity, something to be studied in itself, not as part of some larger context, such as the author's life or a historical period. This kind of study is called formalist criticism because the emphasis is on the *form* of the work, the relationships between the parts—the construction of the plot, the contrasts between characters, the functions of rhymes, the point of view, and so on. Formalist critics explain how and why literary works—*these* words, in *this* order—constitute unique, complex structures that embody or set forth meanings.

Cleanth Brooks, perhaps America's most distinguished formalist critic, in an essay in the *Kenyon Review* (Winter 1951), set forth what he called his "articles of faith":

> That literary criticism is a description and an evaluation of its object.
>
> That the primary concern of criticism is with the problem of unity—the kind of whole which the literary work forms or fails to form, and the relation of the various parts to each other in building up this whole.
>
> That the formal relations in a work of literature may include, but certainly exceed, those of logic.
>
> That in a successful work, form and content cannot be separated.
>
> That form is meaning.

Formalist criticism is, in essence, *intrinsic* criticism, rather than extrinsic, for it concentrates on the work itself, independent of its writer and the writer's background—that is, independent of biography, psychology, sociology, and history. The discussions of a proverb ("A rolling stone") and of a short poem by Frost ("The Span of Life") on page 103 are brief examples.

In practice, of course, we usually bring outside knowledge to the work. For instance, a reader who is familiar with, say, *Hamlet* can hardly study some other tragedy by Shakespeare, such as *Romeo and Juliet,* without bringing to the second play some conception of what Shakespearean tragedy is or can be. A reader of Alice Walker's *The Color Purple* inevitably brings unforgettable outside material (perhaps the experience of being an African American, or some knowledge of the history of African Americans) to the literary work. It is hard to talk only about *Hamlet* or *The Color Purple* and not at the same time talk about, or at least have in mind, aspects of human experience.

Formalist criticism begins with a personal response to the literary work, but it goes on to try to account for the response by closely examining the work. It assumes that the author shaped the poem, play, or story so fully that the work guides the reader's responses.

The assumption that "meaning" is fully and completely presented within the text is not much in favor today, when many literary critics argue that the active or subjective reader (or even what Judith Fetterley, a feminist critic, has called "the resisting reader"), and not the author of the text, makes the "meaning." Still, even if we grant that the reader is active, not passive or coolly objective, we can hold with the formalists that the author is active too, constructing a text that in some measure controls the reader's responses.

Formalist criticism usually takes one of two forms, **explication** (the unfolding of meaning, line by line or even word by word) and **analysis** (the examination of the relations of parts). The essay on Yeats's "The Balloon of the Mind" (page 508) is an explication, a setting forth of the implicit meanings of the words. The essay on Kate Chopin's "The Story of an Hour" (page 45) and on Tennessee Williams's *The Glass Menagerie* (page 1247) are analyses. The two essays on Frost's "Stopping by Woods on a Snowy Evening" (pages 188 and 193) are chiefly analyses but with some passages of explication.

Formalist criticism, also called the **New Criticism** (to distinguish it from the historical and biographical writing that in earlier decades had dominated literary study), began to achieve prominence in the late 1920s and was dominant from the late 1930s until about 1970, and even today it is widely considered the best way for a student to begin to study a work of literature. Formalist criticism empowers the student; that is, the student confronts the work immediately and is not told first to spend days or weeks or months in preparation—for instance, reading Freud and his followers in order to write a psychoanalytic essay or reading Marx and Marxists in order to write a Marxist essay, or doing research on "necessary historical background" in order to write a historical essay.

Deconstruction

Deconstruction or deconstructive or poststructuralist criticism, can almost be characterized as the opposite of everything that formalist criticism stands for. Deconstruction begins with the assumptions that language is unstable, elusive, unfaithful. (Language is all of these things because meaning is largely generated by opposition: *hot* means something in opposition to *cold,* but a hot day may be 90 degrees whereas a hot oven is at least 400 degrees, and a "hot item" may be of any temperature.) Deconstructionists seek to show that a literary work (usually called "a text" or "a discourse") inevitably is self-contradictory. Unlike formalist critics—who hold that an author constructs a coherent work with a stable meaning, and that competent readers can perceive this meaning—deconstructionists hold that a work has no coherent meaning at the center.

Despite the emphasis on indeterminacy, it is sometimes possible to detect in deconstructionist interpretations a view associated with Marxism. This is the idea that authors are "socially constructed" from the "discourses of power" or "signifying practices" that surround them. Thus, although authors may think they are individuals with independent minds, their works usually reveal—unknown to the authors—powerful social, cultural, or philosophic assumptions. Deconstructionists "interrogate" a text, and they reveal what the authors were unaware of or had thought they had kept safely out of sight. That is, deconstructionists often find a rather specific meaning—though this meaning is one that might surprise the author.

Deconstruction is valuable insofar as—like the New Criticism—it encourages close, rigorous attention to the text. The problem with deconstruction, however, is that too often it is reductive, telling the same story about every text—that here, yet again, and again, we see how a text is incoherent and heterogeneous.

Reader-Response Criticism

Probably all reading includes some sort of response—"This is terrific," "This is a bore," "I don't know what's going on here"—and almost all writing about literature begins with some such response, but specialists in literature disagree greatly about the role that response plays, or should play, in experiencing literature and in writing about it.

At one extreme are those who say that our response to a work of literature should be a purely aesthetic response—a response to a work of art—and not the response we would have to something comparable in real life. To take an obvious point: If in real life we heard someone plotting a murder, we would intervene, perhaps by calling the police or by attempting to warn the victim. But when we hear Macbeth and Lady Macbeth plot to kill King Duncan, we watch with deep *interest;* we hear their words with *pleasure,* and maybe with horror and fascination we even look forward to seeing the murder and to what the characters then will say and what will happen to the murderers.

When you think about it, the vast majority of works of literature do not have a close, obvious resemblance to the reader's life. Most readers of *Macbeth* are not Scots, and no readers are Scottish kings or queens. (It's not just a matter of older literature; no readers of Toni Morrison's *Beloved* are nineteenth-century African Americans.) The connections that readers make between themselves and the lives in most of the books they read are not, on the whole, connections based on ethnic or professional identities. Rather, they are connections with states of consciousness—for instance, a young person's sense of isolation from the family, or a young person's sense of guilt for initial sexual experiences.

Before we reject a work either because it seems too close to us ("I'm a man and I don't like the depiction of this man"), or on the other hand too far from our experience ("I'm not a woman, so how can I enjoy reading about these women?"), we probably should try to follow the advice of Virginia Woolf, who said, "Do not dictate to your author; try to become him." Nevertheless, some literary works of the past may today seem intolerable, at least in part. There are passages in Mark Twain's *Huckleberry Finn,* where African Americans are stereotyped or called derogatory names, that deeply upset us today. We should, however, try to reconstruct the cultural assumptions of the age in which the work was written. If we do so, we may find that if in some ways it reflected its historical era, in other ways it challenged it.

Reader-response criticism, then, says that the "meaning" of a work is not merely something put into the work by the writer; rather, the "meaning" is an interpretation created or constructed or produced by the reader as well as the writer. Stanley Fish, an exponent of reader-response theory, in *Is There a Text in This Class?* (1980), puts it this way: "Interpretation is not the art of construing but of constructing. Interpreters do not decode poems; they make them" (327).

But does every reader see his or her individual image in each literary work? Even *Hamlet,* a play that has generated an enormous range of interpretation, is universally seen as a tragedy, a play that deals with painful realities. If someone were to tell us that *Hamlet* is a comedy, and that the end, with a pile of corpses, is especially funny, we would not say, "Oh, well, we all see things in our own way." We would conclude that we have just heard a misinterpretation.

Many people who subscribe to one version or another of a reader-response theory would agree that they are concerned not with all readers but with what they call *informed readers* or *competent readers*. Informed or competent readers are familiar with the conventions of literature. They understand misinterpretation, that in a play such as *Hamlet* the characters usually speak in verse. Such readers, then, do not express amazement that Hamlet often speaks metrically, and that he sometimes uses rhyme. These readers understand that verse is the normal language for most of the characters in the play, and therefore such readers do not characterize Hamlet as a poet. Informed, competent readers, in short, know the rules of the game.

There will still be plenty of room for differences of interpretation. Some people will find Hamlet not at all blameworthy, others will find him somewhat blameworthy, and still others may find him highly blameworthy. In short, we can say that a writer works against a background that is *shared* by readers. As readers, we are familiar with various kinds of literature, and we read or see *Hamlet* as a particular kind of literary work, a tragedy, a play that evokes (in Shakespeare's words) "woe or wonder," sadness and astonishment. Knowing (in a large degree) how we ought to respond, our responses are not merely private.

Archetypal Criticism (Myth Criticism)

Carl G. Jung, the Swiss psychiatrist, in *Contributions to Analytical Psychology* (1928) postulates the existence of a "collective unconscious," an inheritance in our brains consisting of "countless typical experiences [such as birth, escape from danger, selection of a mate] of our ancestors." Few people today believe in an inherited "collective unconscious," but many people agree that certain repeated experiences, such as going to sleep and hours later awakening, or the perception of the setting and of the rising sun, or of the annual death and rebirth of vegetation, manifest themselves in dreams, myths, and literature—in these instances, as stories of apparent death and rebirth. This archetypal plot of death and rebirth is said to be evident in Coleridge's *The Rime of the Ancient Mariner* (1798), for example. The ship suffers a deathlike calm and then is miraculously restored to motion, and, in a sort of parallel rebirth, the mariner moves from spiritual death to renewed perception of the holiness of life. Another archetypal plot is the quest, which usually involves the testing and initiation of a hero, and thus essentially represents the movement from innocence to experience.

In addition to archetypal plots there are archetypal characters, since an **archetype** is any recurring unit. Among archetypal characters are the scapegoat (as in Shirley Jackson's "The Lottery"), the hero (savior, deliverer), the terrible mother (witch, stepmother—even the wolf "grandmother" in the tale of Little Red Riding Hood), and the wise old man (father figure magician).

Because, the theory holds, both writer and reader share unconscious memories, the tale an author tells (derived from the collective unconscious) may strangely move the reader, speaking to his or her collective unconscious. As Maud Bodkin puts it, in *Archetypal Patterns in Poetry* (1934), something within us "leaps in response to the effective presentation in poetry of an ancient theme" (4). But this emphasis on ancient (or repeated) themes has made archetypal criticism vulnerable to the charge that it is reductive. The critic looks for certain characters or patterns of action and values the work if the motifs are there, meanwhile overlooking what is unique, subtle, distinctive, and truly interesting about the work. That is, a work is regarded as good if it closely resembles other works, with the usual motifs and characters. A second weakness in some archetypal criticism is that in its search for the deepest meaning of a work the critic may crudely impose a pattern, seeing the quest in every walk down the street.

If archetypal criticism sometimes seems farfetched, it is nevertheless true that one of its strengths is that it invites us to use comparisons, and comparing is often an excellent way to see not only what a work shares with other works but what is distinctive in the work. The most successful practitioner of archetypal criticism was Northrop Frye (1912–1991), whose numerous books help readers to see fascinating connections between works. For Frye's explicit comments about archetypal criticism, as well as for examples of such criticism in action, see especially his *Anatomy of Criticism* (1957) and *The Educated Imagination* (1964). On archetypes see also Chapter 16, "Archetypal Patterns," in Norman Friedman, *Form and Meaning in Fiction* (1975).

Historical Criticism

Historical criticism studies a work within its historical context. Thus, a student of *Julius Caesar, Hamlet,* or *Macbeth*—plays in which ghosts appear—may try to find out about Elizabethan attitudes toward ghosts. We may find that the Elizabethans took ghosts more seriously than we do, or, on the other hand, we may find that ghosts were explained in various ways—for instance, sometimes as figments of the imagination and sometimes as shapes taken by the devil in order to mislead the virtuous. Similarly, a historical essay concerned with *Othello* may be devoted to Elizabethan attitudes toward Moors, or to Elizabethan ideas of love, or, for that matter, to Elizabethan ideas of a daughter's obligations toward her father's wishes concerning her suitor.

The historical critic assumes (and the assumption can hardly be disputed) that writers, however individualistic, are shaped by the particular social contexts in which they live. Put another way, the goal of historical criticism is to understand how people in the past thought and felt. It assumes that such understanding can enrich our understanding of a particular work. The assumption is, however, disputable, since it may be argued that the artist may *not* have shared the age's view on this or that. All of the half-dozen or so Moors in Elizabethan plays other than *Othello* are villainous or foolish, but this evidence does not prove that *therefore* Othello is villainous or foolish.

Biographical Criticism

One kind of historical research is the study of *biography,* which for our purposes includes not only biographies but also auto biographies, diaries, journals, letters, and so on. What experiences did Mark Twain undergo? Are some of the apparently sensational aspects of *Huckleberry Finn* in fact close to events that Twain experienced? If so, is he a "realist"? If not, is he writing in the tradition of the "tall tale"?

The really good biographies not only tell us about the life of the author—they enable us to return to the literary texts with a deeper understanding of how they came to be what they are. If, for example, you read Richard B. Sewall's biography of Emily Dickinson, you will find a wealth of material concerning her family and the world she moved in—for instance, the religious ideas that were part of her upbringing.

Biographical study may illuminate even the work of a living author. If you are writing about the poetry of Adrienne Rich, for example, you may want to consider what she has told us in many essays about her life, in *On Lies, Secrets, and Silence* (1979) and *Blood, Bread, and Poetry* (1986), especially about her relations with her father and her husband.

Marxist Criticism

One form of historical criticism is **Marxist criticism**, named for Karl Marx (1818–1883). Actually, to say "one form" is misleading, since Marxist criticism today is varied, but essentially it sees history primarily as a struggle between socioeconomic classes, and it sees literature (and everything else, too) as the product of the economic forces of the period.

For Marxists, economics is the "base" or "infrastructure"; on this base rests a "superstructure" of ideology (law, politics, philosophy, religion, and the arts, including literature), reflecting the interests of the dominant class. Thus, literature is a material product, produced—like bread or battleships—in order to be consumed in a given society. Marxist critics are concerned with Shakespeare's plays as part of a market economy—show *business,* the economics of the theater, including payments to authors and actors and revenue from audiences.

Few critics would disagree that works of art in some measure reflect the age that produced them, but most contemporary Marxist critics go further. First, they assert—in a repudiation of what has been called "vulgar Marxist theory"—that the deepest historical meaning of a literary work is to be found in what it does *not* say, what its ideology does not permit it to express. Second, Marxists take seriously Marx's famous comment that "the philosophers have only *interpreted* the world in various ways: the point is to *change* it." The critic's job is to change the world, by revealing the economic basis of the arts. Not surprisingly, most Marxists are skeptical of such concepts as "genius" and "masterpiece." These concepts, they say, are part of the bourgeois myth that idealizes the individual and detaches art from its economic context. For an introduction to Marxist criticism, see Terry Eagleton, *Marxism and Literary Criticism* (1976).

New Historicist Criticism

A recent school of scholarship, called **New Historicism**, insists that there is no "history" in the sense of a narrative of indisputable past events. Rather, New Historicism holds that there is only our version—our narrative, our representation—of the past. In this view, each age projects its own preconceptions on the past: Historians may think they are revealing the past, but they are revealing only their own historical situation and their personal preferences.

For example, in the nineteenth century and in the twentieth almost up to 1992, Columbus was represented as the heroic benefactor of humankind who discovered the New World. But even while plans were being made to celebrate the five-hundredth anniversary of his first voyage across the Atlantic, voices were raised in protest: Columbus did not "discover" a New World; after all, the indigenous people knew where they were, and it was Columbus who was lost, since he thought he was in India. In short, people who wrote history in, say, 1900 projected onto the past their current views (colonialism was a good thing), and people who wrote history in 1992 projected onto that same period a very different set of views (colonialism was a bad thing).

Similarly, ancient Greece, once celebrated by historians as the source of democracy and rational thinking, is now more often regarded as a society that was built on slavery and on the oppression of women. And the Renaissance, once glorified as an age of enlightened thought, is now often seen as an age that tyrannized women, enslaved colonial people, and enslaved itself with its belief in witchcraft and astrology. Thinking about these changing views, we feel the truth of the witticism that the only thing more uncertain than the future is the past.

On the New Historicism, see H. Aram Veeser, ed., *The New Historicism* (1989), and Veeser, *The New Historicism Reader* (1994).

Psychological or Psychoanalytic Criticism

One form that biographical study may take is **psychological criticism** or *psychoanalytic criticism,* which usually examines the author and the author's writings in the framework of Freudian psychology. A central doctrine of Sigmund Freud (1856–1939) is the Oedipus complex, the view that all males (Freud seems not to have made his mind up about females) unconsciously wish to displace their fathers and to sleep with their mothers. According to Freud, hatred for the father and love of the mother, normally repressed, may appear disguised in dreams. Works of art, like dreams, are disguised versions of repressed wishes.

In *Hamlet and Oedipus* (1949) Ernest Jones, amplifying some comments by Freud, argued that Hamlet delays killing Claudius because Claudius (who has killed Hamlet's father and married Hamlet's mother) has done exactly what Hamlet himself wanted to do. For Hamlet to kill Claudius, then, would be to kill himself.

If this approach interests you, take a look at Norman N. Holland's *Psychoanalysis and Shakespeare* (1966) or Frederick Crews's study of Hawthorne, *The Sins of the Fathers* (1966). Crews finds in Hawthorne's work evidence of unresolved Oedipal conflicts, and he accounts for the appeal of the fictions thus: The stories "rest on fantasy, but on the shared fantasy of mankind, and this makes for a more penetrating fiction than would any illusionistic slice of life" (263). For applications to other authors, consider Simon O. Lesser's *Fiction and the Unconscious* (1957), or an anthology of criticism, *Literature and Psychoanalysis,* edited by Edith Kurzweil and William Phillips (1983).

Psychological criticism can also turn from the author and the work to the reader, seeking to explain why we, as readers, respond in certain ways. Why is *Hamlet* so widely popular? A Freudian answer is that it is universal because it deals with a universal (Oedipal) impulse. We can, however, ask whether it appeals as strongly to women as to men (again, Freud was unsure about the Oedipus complex in women) and, if so, why it appeals to them. Or, more generally, we can ask if males and females read in the same way.

Gender Criticism (Feminist, and Lesbian and Gay Criticism)

This last question brings us to **gender criticism**. As we have seen, writing about literature usually seeks to answer questions. Historical scholarship, for instance, tries to answer such questions as "What did Shakespeare and his contemporaries believe about ghosts?" or "How did Victorian novelists and poets respond to Darwin's theory of evolution?" Gender criticism, too, asks questions. It is especially concerned with two issues, one about reading and one about writing: "Do men and women read in different ways?" and "Do they write in different ways?"

Feminist criticism can be traced back to the work of Virginia Woolf (1882–1941), but chiefly it grew out of the women's movement of the 1960s. The women's movement at first tended to hold that women are pretty much the same as men and therefore should be treated equally, but much recent feminist criticism has emphasized and explored the differences between women and men. Because the experiences of the sexes are different, the argument goes, their values and sensibilities are different, and their responses to literature are different. Further, literature written by women is different from literature written by men. Works written by women are seen by some feminist critics as embodying the experiences of a minority culture—a group marginalized by the dominant male culture. If you have read Susan Glaspell's *Trifles* (page 1336) you'll recall that this literary work itself is largely concerned about the differing ways that males and females perceive the world. Not all women are feminist critics, and not all feminist critics are women. Further, there are varieties of feminist criticism, but for a good introduction see *The New Feminist Criticism: Essays on Women, Literature, and Theory* (1985), edited by Elaine Showalter, and *Feminism: An Anthology of Literary Theory and Criticism,* ed. Robyn R. Warhol and Diane Price Herndl, 2nd ed. (1997). For the role of men in feminist criticism, see *Engendering Men,* edited by Joseph A. Boone and Michael Cadden (1990).

Feminist critics rightly point out that men have established the conventions of literature and that men have established the canon—that is, the body of literature that is said to be worth reading. Speaking a bit broadly, in this patriarchal or male-dominated body of literature, men are valued for being strong and active, whereas women are expected to be weak and passive. Thus, in the world of fairy tales, the admirable male is the energetic hero (Jack, the Giant-Killer) but the admirable fe male is the passive Sleeping Beauty. Active women such as the wicked step-mother or—a disguised form of the same thing—the witch are generally villain-ous. (There are exceptions, such as Gretel in "Hansel and Gretel.") A woman hearing or reading the story of Sleeping Beauty or of Little Red Riding Hood (rescued by the powerful woodcutter), or any other work in which women seem to be trivialized, will respond differently than a man. For instance, a woman may be socially conditioned into admiring Sleeping Beauty, but only at great cost to her mental well-being. A more resistant female reader may recognize in herself no kinship with the beautiful, passive Sleeping Beauty and may respond to the story indignantly. Another way to put it is this: The male reader perceives a romantic story, but the resistant female reader perceives a story of oppression.

For discussions of the ways in which, it is argued, women *ought* to read, you may want to look at *Gender and Reading,* edited by Elizabeth A. Flynn and Patrocino Schweikart, and especially at Judith Fetterley's book *The Resisting Reader* (1978). In her discussion of Faulkner's "A Rose for Emily," Fetterley contends that the society made Emily a "lady"—society dehumanized her by elevating her. Emily's father, seeking to shape her life, stood in the doorway of their house and drove away her suitors. So far as he was concerned, Emily was a nonperson, a creature whose own wishes were not to be regarded; he alone would shape her future. Because society (beginning with her father) made her a "lady"—a creature so elevated that she is not taken seriously as a passionate human being—she is able to kill Homer Barron and not be suspected.

Here is Fetterley speaking of the passage in which the townspeople crowd into her house when her death becomes known:

> When the would-be "suitors" finally get into her father's house, they discover the consequences of his oppression of her, for the violence contained in the rotted corpse of Homer Barron is the mirror image of the violence represented in the tableau, the back-flung front door flung back with a vengeance. (42)

"A Rose for Emily" is reprinted on pages 237–44.

Feminist criticism has been concerned not only with the depiction of women and men in a male-determined literary canon and with women's responses to these images but also with yet another topic: women's writing. Women have had fewer opportunities than men to become writers of fiction, poetry, and drama—for one thing, they have been less well educated in the things that the male patriarchy valued—but even when they *have* managed to write, men sometimes have neglected their work simply because it was written by a woman. Feminists have further argued that certain forms of writing have been especially the province of women—for instance journals, diaries, and letters; and predictably, these forms have not been given adequate space in the traditional, male-oriented canon.

In 1972, in an essay entitled "When We Dead Awaken: Writing as Re-Vision," the poet and essayist Adrienne Rich effectively summed up the matter:

> A radical critique of literature, feminist in its impulse, would take the work first of all as a clue to how we live, how we have been living, how we have been led to imagine ourselves, how our language has trapped as well as lib-

> erated us: and how we can begin to see—and therefore live—afresh. . . . We need to know the writing of the past and know it differently than we have ever known it; not to pass on a tradition but to break its hold over us.

Much feminist criticism concerned with women writers has emphasized connections between the writer's biography and her work. Suzanne Juhasz, in her introduction to *Feminist Critics Read Emily Dickinson* (1983), puts it this way:

> The central assumption of feminist criticism is that gender informs the nature of art, the nature of biography, and the relation between them. Dickinson is a woman poet, and this fact is integral to her identity. Feminist criticism's sensitivity to the components of female experience in general and to Dickinson's identity as a woman generates essential insights about her. . . . Attention to the relationship between biography and art is a requisite of feminist criticism. To disregard it further strengthens those divisions continually created by traditional criticism, so that nothing about the woman writer can be seen whole. (1–5)

Feminist criticism has made many readers—men as well as women—increasingly aware of gender relationships within literary works.

Lesbian criticism and **gay criticism** have their roots in feminist criticism; that is, feminist criticism introduced many of the questions that these other, newer developments are now exploring.

Before turning to some of the questions that lesbian and gay critics address, it is necessary to say that lesbian criticism and gay criticism are not symmetrical, because lesbian and gay relationships themselves are not symmetrical. Straight society has traditionally been more tolerant of—or blinder to—lesbianism than male homosexuality. Further, lesbian literary theory has tended to see its affinities more with feminist theory than with gay theory: that is, the emphasis has been on gender (male/female) rather than on sexuality (homosexuality/bisexuality/heterosexuality). On the other hand, some gays and lesbians have been writing what is now being called queer theory.

These are some of the questions that this criticism addresses: (1) Do lesbians and gays read in ways that differ from the ways straight people read? (2) Do they write in ways that differ from those of straight people? (3) How have straight writers portrayed lesbians and gays, and how have lesbian and gay writers portrayed straight women and men? (4) What strategies did lesbian and gay writers use to make their work acceptable to a general public in an age when lesbian and gay behavior was unmentionable?

Examination of gender by gay and lesbian critics can help to illuminate literary works, but it should be added, too, that some—perhaps most—gay and lesbian critics write also as activists, reporting their findings not only to enable us to understand and to enjoy the works of (say) Whitman, but also to change society's view of sexuality. Thus, in *Disseminating Whitman* (1991), Michael Moon is impatient with earlier critical rhapsodies about Whitman's universalism. It used to be said that Whitman's celebration of the male body was a sexless celebration of brotherly love in a democracy, but Moon's view is that we must neither whitewash Whitman's poems with such high-minded talk nor reject them as indecent; rather, we must see exactly what Whitman is saying about a kind of experience to which society had shut its eyes, and we must take Whitman's view seriously.

One assumption in much lesbian and gay critical writing is that although gender greatly influences the ways in which we read, reading is a skill that can be learned, and therefore straight people—aided by lesbian and gay critics—can learn to read, with pleasure and profit, lesbian and gay writers. This assumption also underlies much feminist criticism, which often assumes that men must stop ignoring books by women and must learn (with the help of feminist critics) how to read them, and, in fact, how to read—with newly opened eyes—the sexist writings of men of the past and present.

In addition to the titles mentioned earlier concerning gay and lesbian criticism, consult Eve Kosofsky Sedgwick, *Between Men: English Literature and Male Homosocial Desire* (1985), and an essay by Sedgwick, "Gender Criticism," in *Redrawing the Boundaries,* ed. Stephen Greenblatt and Giles Gunn (1992).

Works that concern gay or lesbian experience include those by A. E. Housman, Gloria Naylor, Adrienne Rich, and Walt Whitman.

This chapter began by making the point that all readers, whether or not they consciously adopt a particular approach to literature, necessarily read through particular lenses. More precisely, a reader begins with a frame of interpretation and from within the frame selects one of the several competing methodologies. Critics often make great—even grandiose—claims for their approaches. For example, Frederic Jameson, a Marxist, begins *The Political Unconscious: Narrative as a Socially Symbolic Act* (1981) thus:

> This book will argue the priority of the political interpretation of literary texts. It conceives of the political perspective not as some supplemental method, not as an optional auxiliary to other interpretive methods current today—the psychoanalytic or the myth-critical, the stylistic, the ethical, the structural—but rather as the absolute horizon of all reading and all interpretation. (7)

Readers who are interested in politics may be willing to assume "the priority of the political interpretation . . . as the absolute horizon of all reading and all interpretation," but other readers may respectfully decline to accept this assumption.

In talking about a critical approach, sometimes the point is made by saying that readers decode a text by applying a grid to it: the grid enables them to see certain things clearly. But what is sometimes forgotten is that a lens or a grid—an angle of vision or interpretive frame and a methodology—also prevents a reader from seeing certain other things. This is to be expected. What is important, then, is to remember this fact, and thus not to deceive ourselves by thinking that our keen tools enable us to see the whole. A psychoanalytic reading of, say, *Hamlet* may be helpful, but it does not reveal all that is in *Hamlet,* and it does not refute the perceptions of another approach, let's say a historical study. Each approach may illuminate aspects neglected by others.

It is too much to expect a reader to apply all useful methods (or even several) at once—that would be rather like looking through a telescope with one eye and through a microscope with the other—but it is not too much to expect readers to be aware of the limitations of their methods. If you read much criticism, you will find two kinds of critics. There are, on the one hand, critics who methodically and mechanically peer through a lens or grid, and they find what can be easily predicted they will find. On the other hand, there are critics who (despite what may be inevitable class and gender biases) are relatively open-minded in their approach—critics who, one might say, do not at the outset of their reading believe that their method assures them that they have got the text's number and that by means of this method they will expose the text for what it is.

The philosopher Richard Rorty engagingly makes a distinction somewhat along these lines, in an essay he contributed to Umberto Eco's *Interpretation and Overinterpretation* (1992). There is a great difference, Rorty suggests,

> between knowing what you want to get out of a person or thing or text in advance and hoping that the person or thing or text will help you want something different—that he or she or it will help you to change your purposes, and thus to change your life. This distinction, I think, helps us highlight the difference between methodical and inspired readings of texts. (106)

Rorty goes on to say he has seen an anthology of readings on Conrad's *Heart of Darkness,* containing a psychoanalytic reading, a reader-response reading, and so on. "None of the readers had, as far as I could see," Rorty says,

> been enraptured or destabilized by *Heart of Darkness*. I got no sense that the book had made a big difference to them, that they cared much about Kurtz or Marlow or the woman "with helmeted head and tawny cheeks" whom Marlow sees on the bank of the river. These people, and that book, had no more changed these readers' purposes than the specimen under the microscope changes the purpose of the histologist. (107)

The kind of criticism that Rorty prefers he calls "unmethodical" criticism and "inspired" criticism. It is, for Rorty, the result of an "encounter" with some aspect of a work of art "which has made a difference to the critic's conception of who she is, what she is good for, what she wants to do with herself . . ." (107). This is not a matter of "respect" for the text, Rorty insists. Rather, he says "love" and "hate" are better words, "for a great love or a great loathing is the sort of thing that changes us by changing our purposes, changing the uses to which we shall put people and things and texts we encounter later" (107).

Your Turn: Putting Critical Strategies to Work

1. Which of the critical strategies described in this chapter do you find the most interesting? Which interests you the least?
2. In Chapter 3, we present two stories by Kate Chopin: "The Story of an Hour" and "The Storm." Which critical strategy do you think is the most rewarding for the study of this author? Explain why, using your favorite story of the two as a "case study" for your arguments.
3. Select a poem in this book that you especially enjoy, and explain why you value it so highly. Next, reread and think about this poem in relation to each of the critical strategies outlined in this chapter. In what ways do these strategies, one by one, enable you to respond to and understand the poem more deeply? Does one of them seem to you especially helpful? Are any of them unhelpful?
4. Imagine that you have been assigned to prepare a mini-anthology of three or four poems and two or three stories that are particularly suited to one of these critical strategies. List your selections, and then explain how your critical strategy gives a special insight into each one, and into the group of works as a whole.
5. Do you think that any of these critical strategies could be usefully combined with one or more of the others? Could, for example, reader-response criticism go hand-in-hand with gender criticism? Select a poem or a story

to show how your combination of two or more strategies can be brought effectively together.

6. Do you find that some of these critical strategies are in conflict with one another? Can you, for instance, be a formalist critic and, say, a reader-response critic or a gender critic at the same time? Is it a problem if our interpretation of a literary work changes, depending on the critical strategy that we use?
7. As you review and think further about the critical strategies we have described, do you find anything missing? How would you respond to someone who says, "What really matters is our own interpretation of a literary work, not the interpretation that this or that critical strategy produces"?

APPENDIX B

Remarks about Manuscript Form

Basic Manuscript Form

Much of what follows is nothing more than common sense.

- Use good quality **8½″ × 11″** paper. Print out a second copy, in case the instructor's copy goes astray. Make sure also to back up the file on an external hard drive or CD, or in your e-mail account.
- If you write on a computer, **double-space,** and print on one side of the page only; set the printer for professional or best quality.
- Use **one-inch margins** on all sides.
- Put your last name and then the **page number** (in arabic numerals), so that the number is flush with the right-hand margin and one-half inch from the top margin.
- On the first page, below the top margin and flush with the left-hand margin, put your **full name,** your **instructor's name,** the **course number** (including the section), and the **date,** one item per line, double-spaced.
- **Center the title** of your essay. Remember that the title is important—it gives the readers their first glimpse of your essay. **Create your own title**—one that reflects your topic or thesis. For example, a paper on Charlotte Perkins Gilman's "The Yellow Wallpaper" should not be called "The Yellow Wallpaper" but might be called

  Disguised Tyranny in Gilman's "The Yellow Wallpaper"

  or

  How to Drive a Woman Mad

  These titles do at least a little in the way of rousing a reader's interest.
- **Capitalize the title thus:** Begin the first word of the title with a capital letter, and capitalize each subsequent word except articles (*a, an, the*), conjunctions (*and, but, if, when,* etc.), and prepositions (*in, on, with,* etc.):

  A Word on Behalf of Love

  Notice that you do *not* enclose your title within quotation marks, and you do *not* underline it—though if it includes the title of a poem or a story, *that* is enclosed within quotation marks, or if it includes the title of a novel or play, *that* is set in italics, thus:

  Gilman's "The Yellow Wallpaper" and Medical Practice

  and

  Gender Stereotypes in *Hamlet*

- **After writing your title, double-space,** indent one-half inch and begin your first sentence.
- Unless your instructor tells you otherwise, **use a staple** to hold the pages together. (Do not use a stiff binder; it will only add to the bulk of the instructor's stack of papers.)
- Extensive revisions should have been made in your drafts, but minor **last-minute revisions** may be made—neatly—on the finished copy if your instructor permits. Proofreading may catch some typographical errors, and you may notice some small weaknesses.

Quotations and Quotation Marks

First, a word about the *point* of using quotations. Don't use quotations to pad the length of a paper. Rather, give quotations from the work you are discussing so that your readers will see the material being considered and (especially in a research paper) so that your readers will know what some of the chief interpretations are and what your responses to them are.

Note: The next few paragraphs do *not* discuss how to include citations of sources, a topic taken up a little later in this appendix, under the heading "Documentation."

The Golden Rule: If you quote, *comment on* the quotation. Let the reader know what you make of it and why you quote it.

Additional principles:

1. Identify the speaker or writer of the quotation so that the reader is not left with a sense of uncertainty. Usually, in accordance with the principle of letting readers know where they are going, this identification precedes the quoted material, but occasionally it may follow the quotation, especially if it will provide something of a pleasant surprise. For instance, in a discussion of Flannery O'Connor's stories, you might quote a disparaging comment on one of the stories and then reveal that O'Connor herself was the speaker.

2. If the quotation is part of your own sentence, **be sure to fit the quotation grammatically and logically into your sentence.**

> *Incorrect:* Holden Caulfield tells us very little about "what my lousy childhood was like."
>
> *Correct:* Holden Caulfield tells us very little about what his "lousy childhood was like."

3. Indicate any omissions or additions. The quotation must be exact. Any material that you add—even one or two words—must be enclosed within square brackets, thus:

> Hawthorne tells us that "owing doubtless to the depth of the gloom at that particular spot [in the forest], neither the travellers nor their steeds were visible."

If you wish to omit material from within a quotation, indicate the ellipsis by three spaced periods. That is, at the point where you are omitting material, type a space, a period, a space, a period, a space, and a third period. If you are omitting material from the end of a sentence, type a space after the last word that you quote, then a period, a space, a period, a space, a third period, and a period to indicate the end of the sentence. The following example is based on a quotation from the sentences immediately above this one:

> The instructions say, "If you . . . omit material from within a quotation, [you must] indicate the ellipsis. . . . If you are omitting material from the end of a sentence, type . . . then a period to indicate the end. . . .

Notice that although material preceded "If you," periods are not needed to indicate the omission because "If you" began a sentence in the original. Customarily, initial and terminal omissions are indicated only when they are part of the sentence you are quoting. Even such omissions need not be indicated when the quoted material is obviously incomplete—when, for instance, it is a word or phrase.

4. Distinguish between short and long quotations, and treat each appropriately. **Short quotations** (usually defined as four or fewer lines of typed prose or three lines of poetry) are enclosed within quotation marks and run into the text (rather than being set off, without quotation marks), as in the following example:

> Hawthorne begins the story by telling us that "Young Goodman Brown came forth at sunset into the street at Salem village" (624), thus at the outset connecting the village with daylight. A few paragraphs later, when Hawthorne tells us that the road Brown takes was "darkened by all of the gloomiest trees of the forest" (624), he begins to associate the forest with darkness—and a very little later with evil.

If your short quotation is from a poem, be sure to follow the capitalization of the original, and use a slash mark (with a space before and after it) to indicate separate lines. Give the line numbers, if your source gives them, in parentheses, immediately after the closing quotation marks and before the closing punctuation, thus:

> In "Diving into the Wreck," Adrienne Rich's speaker says that she puts on "body-armor" (5). Obviously the journey is dangerous.

To set off a **long quotation** (more than four typed lines of prose or more than two lines of poetry), indent the entire quotation ten spaces or one inch from the left margin. Usually, a long quotation is introduced by a clause ending with a colon—for instance,

> The following passage will make this point clear:

or

> The closest we come to hearing an editorial voice is a long passage in the middle of the story:

Or some such lead-in. After typing your lead-in, double-space, and then type the quotation, indented and double-spaced.

5. Commas and periods go inside the quotation marks. If you are quoting some material within a sentence of your own, and you need to use a comma or a period, these marks of punctuation go *before* the closing quotation mark, as in the following example, in which the author uses a comma after "trouble" and a period after "disease."

> Chopin tells us in the first sentence that "Mrs. Mallard was afflicted with heart trouble," and in the last sentence the doctors say that Mrs. Mallard "died of heart disease."

Exception: If the quotation is immediately followed by material in parentheses or in square brackets, close the quotation, then give the parenthetic or bracketed material, and then—after closing the parenthesis or bracket—insert the comma or period.

> Chopin tells us in the first sentence that "Mrs. Mallard was afflicted with heart trouble" (22), and in the last sentence the doctors say that Mrs. Mallard "died of heart disease" (24).

Semicolons, colons, and dashes go outside the closing quotation marks.

Question marks and exclamation points go inside if they are part of the quotation, outside if they are your own.

In the following passage from a student's essay, notice the difference in the position of the question marks. The first question mark is part of the quotation, so it is enclosed within the quotation marks. The second question mark, however, is the student's, so it comes after the closing quotation marks.

> The older man says to Goodman Brown, "Sayest thou so?" Doesn't a reader become uneasy when the man immediately adds, "We are but a little way in the forest yet"?

Quotation Marks or Italics?

Use quotation marks around titles of short stories and other short works—that is, titles of chapters in books, essays, and poems that might not be published by themselves. Use italics for titles of books, periodicals, collections of essays, plays, and long poems such as *The Rime of the Ancient Mariner*.

A Note on the Possessive

It is awkward to use the possessive case for titles of literary works and secondary sources. Rather than "*The Great Gatsby*'s final chapter," write instead "the final chapter of *The Great Gatsby*." Not "*The Oxford Companion to American Literature*'s entry on Emerson," but, instead, "the entry on Emerson in *The Oxford Companion to American Literature*."

Documentation: Internal Parenthetical Citations and a List of Works Cited (MLA Format)

Documentation tells your reader exactly what your sources are. Below we describe how to make internal parenthetical citations and the Works Cited list.

Internal Parenthetical Citations

On page 1364 we distinguish between embedded quotations (which are short, are run right into your own sentence, and are enclosed in quotation marks) and quotations that are set off on the page and are not enclosed in quotation marks (for example, three or more lines of poetry, five or more lines of typed prose).

For an embedded quotation, put the page reference in parentheses immediately after the closing quotation marks *without* any intervening punctuation. Then, after the parenthesis that follows the number, insert the necessary punctuation (for instance, a comma or a period):

> Brent Staples says that he "learned to smother the rage" he felt at "often being taken for a criminal" (303).

The period comes *after* the parenthetical citation. In the next example *no* punctuation comes after the first citation—because none is needed—and a comma comes *after* (not before or within) the second citation, because a comma is needed in the sentence:

> This is ironic because almost at the start of the story, in the second paragraph, Richards with the best of motives "hastened" (23) to bring his sad message; if he had at the start been "too late" (24), Mallard would have arrived at home first.

For a quotation that is not embedded within the text but is set off (by being indented ten spaces), put the parenthetical citation on the last line of the quotation, one space *after* the period that ends the quoted sentence.

Four additional points:

- The abbreviations *p., pg.,* and *pp.* are *not* used in citing pages.
- If a story is very short, perhaps running for only a page or two, your instructor may tell you there is no need to keep citing the page reference for each quotation. Simply mention in the footnote that the story appears on, say, pages 205–206.
- If you are referring to a poem, your instructor may tell you to use parenthetical citations of line numbers rather than of page numbers. But, again, your footnote will tell the reader that the poem can be found in this book, and on what page.

- If you are referring to a play with numbered lines, your instructor may prefer that in your parenthetical citations you give act, scene, and line, rather than page numbers. Use arabic (not roman) numerals, separating the act from the scene, and the scene from the line, by periods. Here, then, is how a reference to Act 3, Scene 2, line 105 would be given: When Hamlet says to Ophelia, "That's a fair thought to lie between maids' legs (3.2.105), she does not understand that he is making a lewd comment.

Parenthetical Citations and List of Works Cited

Parenthetical citations are clarified by means of a list, headed "Works Cited," given at the end of the essay. In this list you give alphabetically (last name first) the authors and titles that you have quoted or referred to in the essay.

Briefly, the idea is that the reader of your paper encounters an author's name and a parenthetical citation of pages. By checking the author's name in Works Cited, the reader can find the passage in the book. Suppose you are writing about Kate Chopin's "The Story of an Hour." Let's assume that you have already mentioned the author and the title of the story—that is, you have let the reader know the subject of the essay—and now you introduce a quotation from the story in a sentence such as this. (Notice the parenthetical citation of page numbers immediately after the quotation.)

> True, Mrs. Mallard at first expresses grief when she hears the news, but soon (unknown to her friends) she finds joy in it. So, Richards's "sad message" (46), though sad in Richards's eyes, is in fact a happy message.

Turning to Works Cited, the reader, knowing the quoted words are by Chopin, looks for Chopin and finds the following:

> Chopin, Kate. "The Story of an Hour." *Literature for Composition*, Ed. Sylvan Barnet, William Burto, and William E. Cain. 9th ed. New York: Longman, 2010. 45–47. Print.

Thus the essayist is informing the reader that the quoted words ("sad message") are to be found on page 46 of this anthology.

If you have not mentioned Chopin's name in some sort of lead-in, you will have to give her name within the parentheses so that the reader will know the author of the quoted words:

> What are we to make out of a story that ends by telling us that the leading character has died "of joy that kills" (Chopin 47)?

The closing quotation marks come immediately after the last word of the quotation; the citation and the final punctuation—in this case, the essayist's question mark—come *after* the closing quotation marks.

If you are comparing Chopin's story with Gilman's "The Yellow Wallpaper," in Works Cited you will give a similar entry for Gilman—her name, the title of the story, the book in which it is reprinted, and the page numbers that the story occupies.

If you are referring to several works reprinted within one volume, instead of listing each item fully, it is acceptable in Works Cited to list each item simply by giving the author's name, the title of the work, then a period, a space, and the name of the anthologist, followed by the page numbers that the selection spans. Thus a reference to Chopin's "The Story of an Hour" would be followed only by: Barnet 45–47. This form requires that the anthology itself be cited under the name of the first-listed editor, thus:

> Barnet, Sylvan, William Burto, and William E. Cain., eds. *Literature for Composition*, 9th ed. New York: Longman, 2010. Print.

If you are writing a research paper, you will use many sources. In the essay itself you will mention an author's name, quote or summarize from this author, and follow the quotation or summary with a parenthetical citation of the pages. In Works Cited you will give the full title, place of publication, and other bibliographic material.

Here are a few examples, all referring to an article by Joan Templeton, "The *Doll House* Backlash: Criticism, Feminism, and Ibsen." The article appeared in *PMLA* 104 (1989): 28–40, but this information is given only in Works Cited, not within the text of the student's essay.

If in the text of your essay you mention the author's name, the citation following a quotation (or a summary of a passage) is merely a page number in parentheses, followed by a period, thus:

> In 1989 Joan Templeton argued that many critics, unhappy with recognizing Ibsen as a feminist, sought "to render Nora inconsequential" (29).

Or:

> In 1989 Joan Templeton noted that many critics, unhappy with recognizing Ibsen as a feminist, have sought to make Nora trivial (29).

If you don't mention the name of the author in a lead-in, you will have to give the name within the parenthetical citation:

> Many critics, attempting to argue that Ibsen was not a feminist, have tried to make Nora trivial (Templeton 29).

Notice in all of these examples that the final period comes after the parenthetical citation. *Exception:* If the quotation is longer than four lines and is therefore set off by being indented ten spaces from the left margin, end the quotation with the appropriate punctuation (period, question mark, or exclamation mark), hit the space bar twice, and type (in parentheses) the page number. In this case, do not put a period after the citation.

Another point: If your list of Works Cited includes more than one work by an author, in your essay when you quote or refer to one or the other you'll have to identify *which* work you are drawing on. You can provide the title in a lead-in, thus:

> In "The *Doll House* Backlash: Criticism, Feminism, and Ibsen," Templeton says, "Nora's detractors have often been, from the first, her husband's defenders" (30).

Or you can provide the information in the parenthetic citation, giving a shortened version of the title. This usually consists of the first word, unless it is *A, An,* or *The,* in which case including the second word is usually enough. Certain titles may require still another word or two, as in this example:

> According to Templeton, "Nora's detractors have often been, from the first, her husband's defenders" ("*Doll House* Backlash" 30).

Forms of Citation in Works Cited

In looking over the following samples of entries in Works Cited, remember:

- The list of Works Cited appears at the end of the paper. It begins on a new page, and the page continues the numbering of the text.
- The list of Works Cited is arranged alphabetically by author (last name first).
- If a work is anonymous, list it under the first word of the title unless the first word is *A, An,* or *The,* in which case list it under the second word.
- If a work is by two authors, although the book is listed alphabetically under the first author's last name, the second author's name is given in the normal order, first name first.
- If you list two or more works by the same author, the author's name is not repeated but is represented by three hyphens followed by a period and a space.
- Each item begins flush left, but if an entry is longer than one line, subsequent lines in the entry are indented five spaces.

For details about almost every imaginable kind of citation, consult Joseph Gibaldi, *MLA Handbook for Writers of Research Papers,* 7th ed. (New York: Modern Language Association, 2009). We give here, however, information concerning the most common kinds of citations.

For citations of electronic sources, see pages 1375–1378.

Here are samples of the kinds of citations you are most likely to include in your list of Works Cited.

A book by one author:

> Douglas, Ann. *The Feminization of American Culture*. New York: Knopf, 1977. Print.

Notice that the author's last name is given first, but otherwise the name is given as on the title page. Do not substitute initials for names written out on the title page, but you may shorten the publisher's name—for example, from Little, Brown and Company to Little.

Take the title from the title page, not from the cover or the spine, but disregard unusual typography—for instance, the use of only capital letters or the use of & for *and*. Italicize the title and subtitle. The place of publication is indicated by the name of the city. If the city is not well known or if several cities have the same name (for instance, Cambridge, Massachusetts, and Cambridge, England) the name of the state or country is added. If the title page lists several cities, give only the first. For print sources, use the word "Print" at the end of each entry.

A book by two or three authors:

Gilbert, Sandra, and Susan Gubar. *The Madwoman in the Attic: The Woman Writer and the Nineteenth-Century Literary Imagination*. New Haven: Yale UP, 1979. Print.

Notice that the book is listed under the last name of the first author (Gilbert) and that the second author's name is then given with first name (Susan) first. *If the book has more than three authors,* give the name of the first author only (last name first) and follow it with *et al.* (Latin for "and others").

A book by more than three authors:

Beidler, Peter G., et al., *A Reader's Companion to J. D. Salinger's* The Catcher in the Rye. Seattle: Coffeetown Press, 2009. Print.

A book in several volumes:

McQuade, Donald, et al., eds. *The Harper American Literature*. 2nd ed. 2 vols. New York: HarperCollins, 1994. Print.

Pope, Alexander. *The Correspondence of Alexander Pope*. 5 vols. Ed. George Sherburn. Oxford: Clarendon, 1955. Print.

The total number of volumes is given after the title, regardless of the number that you have used.

If you have used more than one volume, within your essay you will parenthetically indicate a reference to, for instance, page 30 of volume 3 thus: (3: 30). If you have used only one volume of a multivolume work—let's say you used only volume 2 of McQuade's anthology—in your entry in Works Cited write, after the period following the date, Vol. 2. In your parenthetical citation within the essay you will therefore cite only the page reference (without the volume number), since the reader will (on consulting Works Cited) understand that in this example the reference is in volume 2.

If, instead of using the volumes as a whole, you used only an independent work within one volume—say, an essay in volume 2—in Works Cited omit the abbreviation *Vol.* Instead, give an arabic 2 (indicating volume 2) followed by a colon, a space, and the page numbers that encompass the selection you used:

McPherson, James Alan. "Why I Like Country Music." *The Harper American Literature*. Ed. Donald McQuade et al. 2nd ed. 2 vols. New York: Longman, 1994. 2: 2304-15. Print.

Notice that this entry for McPherson specifies not only that the book consists of two volumes, but also that only one selection ("Why I Like Country Music," occupying pages 2304–2315 in volume 2) was used. If you use this sort of citation in Works Cited, in the body of your essay a documentary reference to this work will be only to the page; the volume number will *not* be added.

A book with a separate title in a set of volumes:

Churchill, Winston. *The Age of Revolution*. Vol. 3 of *A History of the English-Speaking Peoples*. New York: Dodd, 1957. Print.

Jonson, Ben. *The Complete Masques*. Ed. Stephen Orgel. Vol. 4 of *The Yale Ben Jonson*. New Haven: Yale UP, 1969. Print.

A revised edition of a book:

Chaucer, Geoffrey. *The Riverside Chaucer*. Ed. Larry Benson. 3rd ed. Boston: Houghton, 1987. Print.

Ellmann, Richard. *James Joyce*. Rev. ed. New York: Oxford UP, 1982. Print.

A reprint, such as a paperback version of an older hardcover book:

Rourke, Constance. *American Humor*. 1931. Garden City, New York: Doubleday, 1953. Print.

Notice that the entry cites the original date (1931) but indicates that the writer is using the Doubleday reprint of 1953.

An edited book other than an anthology:

Keats, John. *The Letters of John Keats*. Ed. Hyder Edward Rollins. 2 vols. Cambridge, Mass.: Harvard UP, 1958. Print.

An anthology: You can list an anthology either under the editor's name or under the title.

A work in a volume of works by one author:

Sontag, Susan. "The Aesthetics of Silence." In *Styles of Radical Will*. New York: Farrar, 1969. 3-34. Print.

This entry indicates that Sontag's essay, called "The Aesthetics of Silence," appears in a book of hers entitled *Styles of Radical Will*. Notice that the page numbers of the short work are cited (not page numbers that you may happen to refer to, but the page numbers of the entire piece).

A work in an anthology, that is, in a collection of works by several authors: Begin with the author and the title of the work you are citing, not with the name of the anthologist or the title of the anthology. The entry ends with the pages occupied by the selection you are citing:

Ng, Fae Myenne. "A Red Sweater." *Charlie Chan Is Dead: An Anthology of Contemporary Asian American Fiction*. Ed. Jessica Hagedorn. New York: Penguin, 1993. 358-68. Print.

Normally, you will give the title of the work you are citing (probably an essay, short story, or poem) in quotation marks. If you are referring to a book-length work (for instance, a novel or a full-length play), italicize it. If the work is translated, after the period that follows the title, write *Trans.* and give the name of the translator, followed by a period and the name of the anthology.

If the collection is a multivolume work and you are using only one volume, in Works Cited you will specify the volume, as in the example (page 1371) of McPherson's essay. Because the list of Works Cited specifies the volume, your parenthetical documentary reference within your essay will specify (as mentioned earlier) only the page numbers, not the volume. Thus, although McPherson's essay appears on pages 2304–2315 in the second volume of a two-volume work, a parenthetical citation will refer only to the page numbers because the citation in Works Cited specifies the volume.

Remember that the pages specified in the entry in your list of Works Cited are to the *entire selection,* not simply to pages you may happen to refer to within your paper.

If you are referring to a *reprint of a scholarly article,* give details of the original publication, as in the following example:

Mack, Maynard. "The World of Hamlet." *Yale Review* 41 (1952): 502-23. Rpt. in *Hamlet*. By William Shakespeare. Ed. Sylvan Barnet. New York: Penguin Putnam, 1998. 265-87. Print.

Two or more works in an anthology: If you are referring to more than one work in an anthology in order to avoid repeating all the information about the anthology in each entry in Works Cited, under each author's name (in the appropriate alphabetical place) give the author and title of the work, then a period, a space, and the name of the anthologist, followed by the page numbers that the selection spans. Thus, a reference to Shakespeare's *Hamlet* would be followed only by

Barnet 913–1016

rather than by a full citation of Barnet's anthology. This form requires that the anthology itself also be listed, under Barnet.

Two or more works by the same author: Notice that the works are given in alphabetical order (*Fables* precedes *Fools*) and that the author's name is not repeated but is represented by three hyphens followed by a period and a space. If the author is the translator or editor of a volume, the three hyphens are followed not by a period but by a comma, then a space, then the appropriate abbreviation (*Trans.* or *Ed.*), then the title:

Frye, Northrop. *Fables of Identity: Studies in Poetic Mythology*. New York: Harcourt, 1963. Print.

—. *Fools of Time: Studies in Shakespearean Tragedy*. Toronto: U of Toronto P, 1967. Print.

A translated book:

Gogol, Nikolai. *Dead Souls*. Trans. Andrew McAndrew. New York: New American Library, 1961. Print.

If you are discussing the translation itself, as opposed to the book, list the work under the translator's name. Then put a comma, a space, and "trans." After the period following "trans," skip a space, then give the title of the book, a period, a space, and then "By" and the author's name, first name first. Continue with information about the place of publication, publisher, and date, as in any entry for a book.

An introduction, foreword, or afterword, or other editorial apparatus:

Fromm, Erich. Afterword. *1984*. By George Orwell. New York: New American Library, 1961. Print.

Usually a book with an introduction or some such comparable material is listed under the name of the author of the book rather than the name of the author of the editorial material (see the citation to Pope on page 1370). But if you are referring to the editor's apparatus rather than to the work itself, use the form just given.

Words such as *preface, introduction, afterword,* and *conclusion* are capitalized in the entry but are neither enclosed within quotation marks nor underlined.

A book review: First, here is an example of a review that does not have a title.

Vendler, Helen. Rev. of *Essays on Style*. Ed. Roger Fowler. *Essays in Criticism* 16 (1966): 457-63. Print.

If the review has a title, give the title after the period following the reviewer's name, before "Rev." If the review is unsigned, list it under the first word of the title, or the second word if the first word is *A, An,* or *The.* If an unsigned review has no title, begin the entry with "Rev. of" and alphabetize it under the title of the work being reviewed.

An encyclopedia: The first example is for a signed article, the second for an unsigned article.

Lang, Andrew. "Ballads." *Encyclopaedia Britannica.* 1910 ed. Print.

"Metaphor." *The New Encyclopaedia Britannica: Micropaedia.* 1974 ed. Print.

An article in a scholarly journal: Some journals are paginated consecutively; that is, the pagination of the second issue picks up where the first issue left off. Other journals begin each issue with a new page 1. The forms of the citations in Works Cited differ slightly.

First, the citation of a *journal that uses continuous pagination:*

Burbick, Joan. "Emily Dickinson and the Economics of Desire." *American Literature* 58 (1986): 361–78. Print.

This article appeared in volume 58, which was published in 1986. (Notice that the volume number is followed by a space, then by the year in parentheses, and then by a colon, a space, and the page numbers of the entire article.) Although each volume consists of four issues, you do *not* specify the issue number when the journal is paginated continuously.

For a *journal that paginates each issue separately* (a quarterly journal will have four page 1's each year), give the issue number directly after the volume number and a period, with no spaces before or after the period:

Spillers, Hortense J. "Martin Luther King and the Style of the Black Sermon." *The Black Scholar* 3.1 (1971): 14–27. Print.

An article in a weekly, biweekly, or monthly publication:

McCabe, Bernard. "Taking Dickens Seriously." *Commonweal* 14 May 1965: 24. Print.

Notice that the volume number and the issue number are omitted for popular weeklies or monthlies such as *Time* and *Atlantic.*

An article in a newspaper: Because newspapers usually consist of several sections, a section number may precede the page number. The example indicates that an article begins on page 3 of section 2 and is continued on a later page:

Wu, Jim. "Authors Praise New Forms." *New York Times* 8 Mar. 1996, sec. 2: 3+. Print.

You may also have occasion to cite something other than a printed source, for instance, a lecture. Here are the forms for the chief nonprint sources.

An interview:

Saretta, Howard. Personal interview. 3 Nov. 2008.

A lecture:

Heaney, Seamus. Tufts University, Medford, MA. 15 Oct. 1998. Lecture.

A television or radio program:

60 Minutes. CBS. WCBS, New York. 30 Jan. 1994. Television.

A film or video recording:

Modern Times. Dir. Charles Chaplin. United Artists, 1936. Film.

A sound recording:

Frost, Robert. "The Road Not Taken." *Robert Frost Reads His Poetry*. Caedmon, TC 1060, 1956. LP.

A performance:

The Cherry Orchard. By Anton Chekhov. Dir. Ron Daniels. American Repertory Theatre, Cambridge, Mass. 3 Feb. 1994. Performance.

Reminder: For the form of citations of electronic material, see pages 1376–1378.

Citing Sources on the World Wide Web

Many Web sites and pages are not prepared according to the style and form in which you want to cite them. Sometimes the name of the author is unknown, and other information may be missing or hard to find as well. Perhaps the main point to remember is that a source on the WWW is as much a source as is a book or article that you can track down and read in the library. If you have made use of it, you must acknowledge that you have done so and include the bibliographical information, as fully as you can, in your list of Works Cited for the paper.

The Wellesley College Library offers a valuable site for searching the Web and evaluating what you find there:

http://www.wellesley.edu/Library/Research/citation.html

CHECKLIST: *Citing Sources on the Web*

Provide the following information:

- Author's name.
- Title of work in quotation marks or in italics if a longer work or book title.
- Title of Web site set in italics followed by a period.
- Publisher or sponsor of Web site followed by a comma. (Use *N.p.* if that information is not available.)
- Date of publication, followed by a period. (Use *n.d.* if that information is not available.)
- Publication medium—*Web*—followed by a period.
- Date of access—when you accessed the site.
- Include the URL only when your reader cannot locate the source without it.

A short work within a scholarly project:

Whitman, Walt, "Crossing Brooklyn Ferry." *The Walt Whitman Archive*. Ed. Kenneth M. Price and Ed Folson. The Walt Whitman Archive. 16 Mar 1998. Web. 3 April 2008.

1. Author's name
2. Title of work in italics
3. Title of overall Web site in italics
4. Editors of Web site if available
5. Version or edition used
6. Publisher or sponsor of the site. If not available use *N.p.*
7. Date of publication
8. Medium of publication (*Web*)
9. Date of access

A personal or professional site:

Winter, Mick *How to Talk New Age*. The Well. 6 Jan. 2004. Web. 6 April 2009.

An online book published independently:

Smith, Adam. *The Wealth of Nations*. New York: Methuen. 1904. *Bibliomania*. Web. 3 Mar. 2008.

1. Author's name
2. Title of work in italics
3. Edition used
4. City of publication, publisher, and year of publication
5. Title of the database or Web site in italics
6. Medium of publication (*Web*)
7. Date of access (day, month, and year)

An online book within a scholarly project:

Whitman, Walt. *Leaves of Grass.* Philadelphia: McKay, 1891–92. *The Walt Whitman Archive.* Ed. Kenneth M. Price and Ed Folson. The Walt Whitman Archive. 16 Mar 1998. Web. 3 April 2008.

An article in an online scholarly journal:

Jackson, Francis L. "Mexican Freedom: The Ideal of the Indigenous State." Animus 2.3 (1997). n. pag. Web. 4 Apr. 2009.

1. Author's name
2. Title of article in quotation marks
3. Name of the publication in italics
4. Series number or name
5. Volume number
6. Issue number if available
7. Date of publication
8. Inclusive page number if available (use *n.pag.* if no pages are cited)
9. Medium of publication (*Web*)
10. Date of access (day, month, and year)

An unsigned article in a newspaper or on a newswire:

"Drug Czar Wants to Sharpen Drug War." *TopNews* 6 Apr. 1998. Web. 6 Apr. 2008.

An unsigned article in a newspaper or on a Web site:

"Hiking: Richard W. DeKorte Park, Lyndhurst." *NorthJersey.com.* NorthJersey.com, 2 July 2009. Web. 10 July 2009.

An article in a magazine:

Pitta, Julie. "Un-Wired?" *Forbes.com.* Forbes. 20 April 1998. Web. 6 April 2009.

A review:

Beer, Francis A. Rev. of *Evolutionary Paradigms in the Social Sciences, Special Issue, International Studies Quarterly* 40, 3 (Sept. 1996). *Journal of Memetics* 1 (1997). Web. 4 Jan. 2008.

An editorial or letter to the editor:

"The Net Escape Censorship? Ha!" Editorial. *Wired.* Wired. 3.09. Web. 1 Apr. 2009.

A periodical source on CD-ROM or DVD-ROM

Ellis, Richard. "Whale Killing Begins Anew." *Audubon* [GAUD] 94.6 (1992): 20-22. *General Periodicals Ondisc-Magazine Express.* CD-ROM. UMI-Proquest. 1992.

1. Author's name
2. Publication information for analogous printed source (title and date)
3. Publication medium
4. Title of database
5. Name of vendor
6. Publication date of the database

A nonperiodical source on CD-ROM or DVD-ROM

Clements, John. "War of 1812." *Chronology of the United States.* Dallas: Political Research, Inc. 1997. CD-ROM.

1. Author's, editor's, compiler's, or translator's name (if given)
2. Title of the publication
3. Name of the editor, compiler, or translator (if relevant) of entire volume, if work appears in a collection
4. Edition, release, or version
5. Place of publication
6. Name of publisher
7. Date of publication
8. Medium of publication consulted
9. Supplementary information

E-mail:

Mendez, Michael R. "Re: Solar power." Message to Edgar V. Atamian. 11 Sept. 2009. E-mail.

Armstrong, David J. Message to the author. 30 Aug. 2009. E-mail.

An Online Posting For online postings or synchronous communications, try to cite a version stored as a Web file, if one exists, as a courtesy to the reader. Label sources as needed (e.g., *Online posting, Online defense of dissertation,* and so forth, with neither underlining nor quotation marks). Follow these models as appropriate:

Listserv (electronic mailing lists):

Kosten, A. "Major update of the WWWVL Migration and Ethnic Relations." 7 Apr. 1998. Online posting. ERCOMER News. 7 May 1998.

How Much Do You Know about Citing Sources? A Quiz with Answers*

Taking the quiz below will let you test yourself and will assist you in any discussion you have with your classmates about how to cite sources accurately and honestly.

QUIZ YOURSELF: HOW MUCH DO YOU KNOW ABOUT CITING SOURCES?

Section 1: Plagiarism and Academic Dishonesty

Which of the following examples describe violations of academic integrity? Check all the examples that are punishable under university rules.

_____ **1.** You buy a term paper from a Web site and turn it in as your own work.
_____ **2.** You ask a friend to write a paper for you.
_____ **3.** You can't find the information you need, so you invent statistics, quotes, and sources that do not exist and cite these in your paper as if they were real.
_____ **4.** Your professor requires you to use five sources, but you find one book written by one person that has all the information you need, so you cite that book as if it were information coming from other books and authors in order to make it look like you used five different sources.
_____ **5.** Your history professor and your political science professor both assign a term paper. To save time, you write one paper that meets both requirements and hand it in to both professors.
_____ **6.** You don't want to have too many quotes in your paper, so you do not put quotation marks around some sentences you copied from a source. You cite the source correctly at the end of the paragraph and in your bibliography.
_____ **7.** You have copied a long passage from a book into your paper, and you changed some of the wording. You cite the source at the end of the passage and again in the bibliography.

*This quiz and the answers were written by Carmen Lowe, Director of the Tufts University Academic Resource Center. We are grateful to Ms. Lowe for permission to use her material.

_____ **8.** While writing a long research paper, you come across an interesting hypothesis mentioned in a book, and you incorporate this hypothesis into your main argument. After you finish writing the paper, you can't remember where you initially found the hypothesis, so you don't bother to cite the source of your idea.

Section 2: Common Knowledge

Common knowledge is information that is widely known within a society or an intellectual community; therefore, if you include common knowledge in your paper, you do not need to cite where you found that information.

Answer *Yes* or *No* to the following questions:

_____ **1.** In a high school class on American government, you learned about the checks-and-balances system of government which separates power into the judicial, executive, and legislative branches. Now, you are writing a paper for an introductory political science class and you mention the concept of checks-and-balances you learned in high school. Should you cite your old high school textbook?

_____ **2.** In writing a paper about pop culture in the 1980s, you want to include the year that Reagan was shot but you cannot remember if it was 1980 or 1981, so you look up the correct date in an encyclopedia. Do you have to include that encyclopedia as a source for the date on which Reagan was shot?

_____ **3.** You do most of your research online and find lots of interesting Web sites from which you quote several passages. After you write the first draft, you ask your older and more experienced roommate if he knows how to cite Web sites. He says that Web sites are in the public domain and constitute common knowledge, and therefore they do not need to be cited. Is this true?

_____ **4.** In writing a research paper on astrophysics, you come across something called the Eridanus Effect several times. You have never heard of this effect nor discussed it in your class, but after reading about it in six different astrophysics journal articles, you have a pretty clear idea of what it is and its most common characteristics. Is the Eridanus Effect common knowledge within astrophysics?

_____ **5.** Your older sister works for a nonprofit organization that runs adult literacy programs in factories and unemployment centers in several major cities. During winter break, she tells you about the success of one of the programs in St. Louis and the innovative curricula it has designed. Several weeks into spring semester, you remember your conversation as you are writing an economics term paper on empowerment zones and unemployment in the inner city. If you include a description of the program, do you need to cite a source, even if it is just your sister?

_____ **6.** You are writing a paper on Shakespeare's *Hamlet.* Your textbook's introduction to the play mentions that Shakespeare was born in 1564 in Stratford-upon-Avon. You mention these facts in your paper's introduction. Do you need to cite the introduction to your textbook?

_____ 7. You are writing a paper on Shakespeare's *Hamlet.* A footnote in your textbook mentions that some literary historians now believe that Shakespeare himself played the ghost when the play was first performed. If you mention Shakespeare playing the ghost, do you need to cite this footnote in your textbook?

_____ 8. You are writing a paper on the assassination of Robert Kennedy. The three major biographies on him mention when he was killed and by whom. Do you have to cite all these biographies when you mention the date and murderer of RFK?

_____ 9. You are writing a paper on the assassination of Robert Kennedy. The most influential biography on him mentions a controversial conspiracy theory first put forward in the early 1970s by a journalist for the *Washington Post.* When you mention this conspiracy theory, should you cite the biography?

Section 3: Quoting, Paraphrasing, and Summarizing Texts

Read the following passage excerpted from an on-line edition of a foreign policy magazine. Determine whether any of the sample sentences that follow are improperly cited within the sentence or plagiarized.

> The illegal trade in drugs, arms, intellectual property, people, and money is booming. Like the war on terrorism, the fight to control these illicit markets pits governments against agile, stateless, and resourceful networks empowered by globalization. Governments will continue to lose these wars until they adopt new strategies to deal with a larger, unprecedented struggle that now shapes the world as much as confrontations between nation-states once did.
>
> —*from*: Naím, Moisés. "The Five Wars of Globalization." *Foreign Policy* Jan.-Feb. 2003: Online Edition. <http://www.foreignpolicy.com>. January 13, 2003.

Read the following passages and mark ***OK*** if the passage is fine. If the passage is plagiarized, improperly paraphrased, or otherwise cited inadequately, mark it with ***X***.

_____ 1. In his essay on "The Five Wars of Globalization," Moisés Naím argues that governments need to find new ways to handle the kinds of borderless illegal activity increasing under globalization.

_____ 2. In describing the "illegal trade in drugs, arms, intellectual property, people, and money" as "booming," Moisés Naím asserts that governments need to adopt new strategies to deal with this unprecedented struggle that now shapes the world (http://www.foreignpolicy.com).

_____ 3. Like the war on terror, the struggle to control illegal trade in drugs, arms, money, etc., pits governments against cunning, stateless, and enterprising networks empowered by globalization (Moises 2003).

_____ 4. Many experts believe that globalization is changing the face of foreign policy.

Read the following passage from a book on romance novels and soap operas, then read the citations of it that follow to determine whether any are plagiarized or improperly cited within the sentence.

> The complexity of women's responses to romances has not been sufficiently acknowledged. Instead of exploring the possibility that romances, while serving to keep women in their place, may at the same time be concerned with real female problems, analysts of women's romances have generally seen the fantasy embodied in romantic fiction either as evidence of female "masochism" or as a simple reflection of the dominant masculine ideology. For instance, Germaine Greer, referring to the idealized males of women's popular novels, says, "This is the hero that women have chosen for themselves. The traits invented for him have been invented by women cherishing the chains of their bondage."[9] But this places too much blame on women, and assumes a freedom of choice which is not often in evidence—not in their lives and therefore certainly not in their popular arts.
>
> Modleski, Tania. *Loving with a Vengeance: Mass-Produced Fantasies for Women*. New York and London: Methuen, 1982. 37–38. Print.

Read the following passages and mark ***OK*** if the passage is fine as is. If the passage is plagiarized in part or whole or is otherwise cited improperly, mark it with ***X***.

_____ **1.** Tania Modleski claims that Germaine Greer oversimplifies why women read romance novels (38).

_____ **2.** Modleski states that although romance novels may keep women in their place, they also address real female problems (37).

_____ **3.** Feminist critics see the fantasy embodied in romance novels either as evidence of female "masochism" or as a simple reflection of male chauvinism (Modleski 37–38).

_____ **4.** One feminist writer, Germaine Greer, says that the idealized male featured in women's popular romance novels "is the hero that women have chosen for themselves. The traits invented for him have been invented by women cherishing the chains of their bondage."(38).

_____ **5.** Tania Modleski rejects the idea that the fantasies expressed in romance novels are merely a reflection of some innate masochism in women who, in the words of Germaine Greer, "cherish[...] the chains of their bondage" (37; Greer qtd. in Modleski, 38).

Section 4: Miscellaneous

_____ **1. You read *Time* magazine every week and notice that the writers in the magazine never use footnotes or parenthetical citations. Why don't newswriters cite their sources?**

- **a.** Citing sources is only required of students, not professional writers.
- **b.** Professional publications are free to decide if they will require footnotes or citation of any kind.
- **c.** By law, journalists are exempt from revealing their sources of information.
- **d.** Newspapers and magazines have limited space on the page, so they cut off the citations or footnotes to make room for more copy.

_____ **2. What is *not* the proper way to document a Web site in a bibliography?**

a. Naím, Moisés. (2003, Jan.-Feb.) The Five Wars of Globalization [Electronic version]. *Foreign Policy*. Retrieved Jan. 15, 2003 from www.foreignpolicy.com/wwwboard/fivewars.html

b. Naím, Moisés. "The Five Wars of Globalization," *Foreign Policy* Jan.-Feb. 2003: Online Edition. <http://www.foreignpolicy.com>. Jan. 15, 2003.

c. [12]Naím, Moisés. (2003, Jan.-Feb.) The Five Wars of Globalization [Electronic version]. *Foreign Policy*. Retrieved Jan. 15, 2003 From www.foreignpolicy.com/wwwboard/fivewars.html

d. http://www.foreignpolicy.com/wwwboard/fivewars.html

e. Trick question: Web sites are in the public domain and do not need to be cited.

_____ **3. Plagiarism is a violation of which of the following laws:**

a. Copyright.

b. Intellectual property.

c. Both A and B above.

d. None of the above; it is not a legal issue and is not punishable by law because it only pertains to students.

_____ **4. If you use a quote found in a book of quotes or from an online compilation of quotes, such as Bartlett's, how do you cite the quote?**

a. You don't—quotes found in a collection of quotations (whether online or in a book) are considered well-known and in the public domain. Just include the name of the person to whom the quote is attributed. You can also add the date if it seems relevant.

b. You should cite the original source of the quote followed by the bibliographic information from the quotation compilation, such as: Shakespeare, William. *A Midsummer Night's Dream*. Quoted in *Familiar Quotations: Being an Attempt to Trace to Their Sources Passages and Phrases in Common Use,* by John Bartlett (Boston: Little, Brown, 1886), 44.

c. You should find the original source and cite that.

d. All of the above: A is correct, and B and C are possible options if you want to be extra careful or if the quote is extremely important to your paper. Use your common sense in this situation.

Answer Key to Plagiarism Quiz

The Plagiarism Quiz works best when the answers are discussed in class or one-on-one with a student and professor.

Section 1: Plagiarism and Academic Dishonesty

All eight incidents are forms of plagiarism or academic dishonesty. Many students are confused about the last four incidents, so please discuss them with your instructor if you need clarification.

Section 2: Common Knowledge

1. No; the basic facts about the checks-and-balances system are common knowledge and do not need to be cited.

2. No; even if you cannot remember the exact date of the assassination attempt on Reagan, it is common knowledge because the date is undisputed and can be found in a variety of sources.
3. No; writing on the Web is protected by copyright and must be cited, even if no author is listed.
4. Yes; it's common knowledge if it appears *undocumented* in five or more sources.
5. Yes; such a small program would not be widely known, so you should cite your sister as a source if you mention it. If you describe the program in more detail, it would make sense to research documents or newspaper descriptions and cite these rather than Big Sis.
6. No; the date and location of Shakespeare's birth is not in dispute and can be found in many sources, so it is common knowledge even if you did not know it.
7. Hmmm. This is a tricky situation. Since *some,* but not all, literary historians believe Shakespeare himself played the ghost, this is probably common knowledge among Shakespeare experts. You, however, are not a Shakespeare expert, so it would be wise to cite the footnote just to be safe. So, the answer is, Yes—cite it!
8. No; undisputed dates are common knowledge.
9. Yes; conspiracy theories are controversial, and the details of such controversies need to be cited.

Section 3: Quoting, Paraphrasing, and Summarizing Texts

Illegal Trade Passage:

1. OK; an example of summary. The sentence gives the author and the title. (Remember, the bibliography would provide more publication information.)
2. X; two things are wrong: some of the language is too similar to the original, and the citation method is incorrect. Do not list the URL in your paper. The phrase "adopt new strategies to deal with this unprecedented struggle that now shapes the world" is too close to the source, in some places identical to it.
3. X; this paraphrase is too close to the original. The writer used a thesaurus to change key words, but the sentence structure is identical to the original. Plus, the author's last name (not first name) should appear in the parenthetical citation. (Also, using "etc" in the text is annoying!)
4. OK; This is common knowledge. The sentence is so general, it really has nothing to do with the passage from Moises Naim, so there is no reason to cite him.

Romance Novel Passage:

1. OK; this summary is correct; the author's name appears in the sentence so it does not need to appear in the parenthetical citation.
2. X; although the source is documented properly, some of the language is too close to the source, especially the phrases "keep women in their place" and "real female problems." These phrases need to be put into quotation marks or rewritten.
3. X; most of this sentence is copied directly from the source; it needs to be rewritten or partially enclosed in quotes.

4. X; the quote is properly attributed to Greer, but the page number refers to Modleski's book. Also, there's no need to copy the footnote from the original.
5. OK; this example shows how to properly cite one writer quoted within the work of another. Also note how the ellipses and brackets indicate how the "-ing" part of "cherish" was deleted to make the quote flow better. The ellipses indicate that something was deleted; the brackets indicate that the ellipses were not in the original source.

Section 4: Miscellaneous

1. c
2. d; a is an example of APA method of documenting Web sites; b is MLA; c is an APA footnote.
3. c
4. d

Literary Credits

Diane Ackerman: "Pumping Iron" from *Jaguar of Sweet Laughter* by Diane Ackerman, copyright © 1991 by Diane Ackerman. Used by permission of Random House, Inc. **Sherman Alexie:** "On the Amtrack from Boston to New York City" from *First Indian on the Moon* by Sherman Alexie. Copyright © 1993 by Sherman Alexie, by permission of Hanging Loose Press. **Isabel Allende:** "If You Touched My Heart" reprinted with the permission of Scribner, a Division of Simon & Schuster, Inc. from *The Stories of Eva Luna* by Isabel Allende. Translated from the Spanish by Margaret Sayers Peden. Copyright © 1989 by Isabel Allende. English translation Copyright © 1991 by Macmillan Publishing Company. **Julia Alvarez:** "Woman's Work" from *Homecoming.* Copyright © 1984, 1996 by Julia Alvarez. Published by Plume, an imprint of Penguin Group (USA); originally published by Grove Press. Reprinted by permission of Susan Bergholz Literary Services, New York, NY and Lamy, MN. All rights reserved. **Gloria Anzaldua:** "To live in the Borderlands means you" from *Borderlands/La Frontera.* Copyright © 1987, 1999 by Gloria Anzaldua. Reprinted by permission of Aunt Lute Books. **Jose Armas:** "El Tonto del Barrio" originally published in *Pajarito* publications, 1979. From *Cuento Chicanos,* Revised Edition, 1984, edited by Rudolfo A. Anaya and Antonio Marques, University of New Mexico Press. Reprinted by permission of Jose Armas. **W. H. Auden:** "Musee des Beaux Arts," copyright 1940 & renewed 1968 by W. H. Auden. "The Unknown Citizen," copyright 1940 and copyright renewed 1968 by W. H. Auden, from *Collected Poems* by W. H. Auden. Used by permission of Random House, Inc. **Jimmy Santiago Baca:** "Cloudy Day" and "So Mexicans Are Taking Jobs from American" from *Immigrants In Our Own Land,* copyright © 1977, 1979, 1981, 1982, 1990 by Jimmy Santiago Baca. Reprinted by permission of New Directions Publishing Corp. **James Baldwin:** "Sonny's Blues" © 1957 by James Baldwin was originally published in *Partisan Review.* Copyright renewed. Collected in *Going to Meet the Man,* published by Vintage Books. Reprinted by arrangement with the James Baldwin Estate. **Toni Cade Bambara:** "The Lesson" copyright © 1972 by Toni Cade Bambara from *Gorilla, My Love.* Used by permission of Random House, Inc. **Anne Barton:** "The Promulgation of Confusion" by Anne Barton from *English Drama to 1710,* edited by Christopher Ricks. Reprinted by permission of the author. **Elizabeth Bishop:** "The Hanging of the Mouse" and "One Art" from *The Complete Poems 1927–1979* by Elizabeth Bishop. Copyright © 1979, 1983 by Alice Helen Methfessel. Reprinted by permission of Farrar, Straus and Giroux, LLC. **Claire Bloom:** "Playing Gertrude on Television" from *Playing Gertrude for the BBC TV,* 1980 from *BBC TV Shakespeare: Hamlet.* **Louise Bogan:** "Women" from *The Blue Estuaries* by Louise Bogan. Copyright © 1968 by Louise Bogan. Reprinted by permission of Farrar, Straus and Giroux, LLC. **Ray Bradbury:** "There Will Come Soft Rains" published in *Colliers.* Reprinted by permission of Don Congdon Associates, Inc. Copyright © 1950 by the Crowell Collier Publishing Company, renewed 1977 by Ray Bradbury. **Joseph Brodsky:** "Love Song" from *So Forth* by Joseph Brodsky. Copyright ©1996 by Estate of Joseph Brodsky. Reprinted by permission of Farrar, Straus and Giroux, LLC. **Gwendolyn Brooks:** "We Real Cool," "The Mother" and "The Bean Eaters" from *Blacks* by Gwendolyn Brooks. Reprinted by consent of Brooks Permissions. **Joseph Bruchac III:** "Ellis Island" from *The Remembered Earth.* Reprinted by permission of Barbara S. Kouts. **Raymond Carver:** "Cathedral" from *Cathedral* by Raymond Carver, copyright © 1981, 1982, 1983 by Raymond Carver. "Popular Mechanics" from *What We Talk About When We Talk About Love* by Raymond Carver. Copyright © 1974, 1976, 1978, 1980, 1981 by Raymond Carver. Used by permission of Alfred A. Knopf, a division of Random House, Inc. "Mine" from *What We Talk About When We Talk About Love* by Raymond Carver. Copyright © 1981 by Raymond Carver. Reprinted by permission of International Creative Management, Inc. **Oscar Casares:** "Yolanda" from *Brownsville,* by Oscar Casares. Copyright © 2003 by Oscar Casares. Reprinted by permission of Little,

Brown and Company. **Lorna Dee Cervantes:** "Refugee Ship" by Lorna Dee Cervantes is reprinted with permission from the publisher of *The Americas Review* (Houston: Arte Publico Press—University of Houston, 1990). **Diana Chang:** "The Oriental Contingent" from *The Forbidden Stitch* by Diana Chang. Reprinted by permission of The Estate of Diana Chang. **Kate Chopin:** "The Storm" from *The Complete Works of Kate Chopin*, edited by Per Seyersted. Reprinted by permission of Louisiana State University Press. **Arthur C. Clarke:** "The Nine Billion Names of God" from *The Nine Billion Names of God* (Harcourt, 1967) reprinted by permission of the author and the author's agents, Scovil Galen Ghosh Literary Agency, Inc. **Judith Ortiz Cofer:** "I Fell in Love, or My Hormones Awakened" is reprinted with permission from the publisher of *Silent Dancing: A Partial Remembrance of a Puerto Rican Childhood* (Houston: Arte Publico Press–University of Houston, 1991). **Billy Collins:** "Introduction to Poetry" from *The Apple That Astonished Paris* by Billy Collins. "The Names" was read at a special joint session of Congress held in New York City, September 9, 2002. "Sonnet" from *Poetry* Magazine. All Reprinted by permission of the author. **Countee Cullen:** "Incident" from Color by Countee Cullen. Copyrights held by Amistad Research Center, Tulane University. Administered by Thompson and Thompson, New York, NY. **E. E. Cummings:** "Buffalo Bill 's" copyright 1923, 1951, © 1991 by the Trustees for the E. E. Cummings Trust. Copyright © 1976 by George James Firmage, "in Just-" copyright 1923, 1951, © 1991 by the Trustees for the E. E. Cummings Trust. Copyright © 1976 by George James Firmage. "anyone lived in a pretty how town" copyright 1940 © 1968, 1991 by the Trustees for the E. E. Cummings Trust, from *Complete Poems: 1904–1962* by E. E. Cummings, edited by George J. Firmage. Used by permission of Liveright Publishing Corporation. **Lydia Davis:** "Childcare" from *Varieties of Disturbance* by Lydia Davis. Copyright © 2007 by Lydia Davis. "City People" from *Samuel Johnson is Indignant* by Lydia Davis. Copyright © 2001 by Lydia Davis. Both reprinted by permission of Farrar, Straus and Giroux, LLC. **Emily Dickinson:** "I heard a fly buzz—when I died—" (465), "The Soul selects her own Society" (303), "These are the days when Birds come back—" (130), "Papa above!" (61), "There's a certain Slant of light" (258), "This World is not Conclusion" (501), ", "I got so I could hear his name—" (293), "Because I could not stop for death" (712), "Those—dying, then" (1551), "Apparently with no surprise" (1624), "Tell all the Truth, but tell it slant—" (1129), "Wild Nights! Wild Nights!" (249), "I'm Nobody! Who are you?" (288), "'Nature' is what we see" (668) "A narrow Fellow in the Grass (986) reprinted by permission of the publishers and the Trustees of Amherst College from *The Poems of Emily Dickinson*, Thomas H. Johnson, ed., Cambridge, Mass.: The Belknap Press of Harvard University Press, Copyright © 1951, 1955, 1979 by the President and Fellows of Harvard College. **Joan Didion:** "On Going Home" from *Slouching Towards Bethlehem* by Joan Didion. Copyright © 1966, 1968, renewed 1996 by Joan Didion. Reprinted by permission of Farrar, Straus and Giroux, LLC. **Steven Doloff:** "The Opposite Sex" reprinted by permission of the author. **Rita Dove:** "Daystar" from *Thomas and Beulah*, Carnegie Mellon University Press, © 1986 by Rita Dove. Reprinted by permission of the author. **Gretel Ehrlich:** "About Men" from *The Solace of Open Spaces* by Gretel Ehrlich, copyright © 1985 by Gretel Ehrlich. Used by permission of Viking Penguin, a division of Penguin Group (USA) Inc. **Ralph Ellison:** "Battle Royal" copyright 1948 by Ralph Ellison from *Invisible Man* by Ralph Ellison. Used by permission of Random House, Inc. **Louise Erdrich:** "The Red Convertible" from *The Red Convertible: Selected and New Stories, 1978–2008* by Louise Erdrich. Copyright © 2009 by Louise Erdrich. Reprinted by permission of HarperCollins Publishers. **Martin Espada:** "Bully" from *Rebellion is the Circle of a Lover's Hand/Rebellion es le giro de manos del amante* by Martin Espada. Curbstone Press, 1990. Reprinted by permission of Curbstone Press. Distributed by Consortium. **William Faulkner:** "A Rose for Emily" copyright 1930 and renewed 1958 by Wiliam Faulkner. "Barn Burning" copyright 1950 by Random House, Inc. Copyright renewed 1977 by Jill Faulkner Summers. Both from *Collected Stories of William Faulkner* by William Faulkner. Used by permission of Random House, Inc. **Jane Flanders:** "Van Gogh's Bed" from *Timepiece*, by Jane Flanders, © 1988. Reprinted by permission of the University of Pittsburgh Press. **Carolyn Forché:** "The Colonel" from *The Country Between Us* by Carolyn Forché. Copyright © 1981 by Carolyn Forché. Originally appeared in

Women's International Resource Exchange. Reprinted by permission of HarperCollins Publishers. **Robert Frost:** "The Hardship of Accounting," "The Need of Being Versed in Country Things," "The Telephone," "Stopping by Woods on a Snowy Evening," "The Silken Tent," "Design," "The Span of Life," "The Most of It" copyright 1923, 1969, by Henry Holt and Company, copyright 1936, 1944, 1951 by Robert Frost, copright © 1964, 1970 by Lesley Frost Ballantine. "The Figure a Poem Makes" from *Selected Prose of Robert Frost* edited by Hyde Cox and Edward Connery Lathem. Copyright © 1939, 1967 by Henry Holt and Company. Reprinted by arrangement with Henry Holt and Company, LLC. **Gabriel Garcia Marquez:** "A Very Old Man With Enormous Wings" from *Leaf Storm and Other Stories* by Gabriel Garcia Marquez. Translated by Gregory Rabassa. Copyright © 1971 by Gabriel Garcia Marquez. Reprinted by permission of HarperCollins Publishers. **Allen Ginsberg:** "A Supermarket in California" from *Collected Poems 1947–1980* by Allen Ginsberg. Copyright © 1955 by Allen Ginsberg. Reprinted by permission of HarperCollins Publishers. **Dana Gioia:** "Money" copyright 1991 by Dana Gioia. Reprinted from *The Gods of Winter* with the permission of Graywolf Press, Saint Paul, MN. **Nikki Giovanni:** "Love in Place" copyright © 1998 by Nikki Giovanni from *Love Poems*. This poem originally appeared in *The New Yorker*, September 1, 1997. Reprinted by permission. **Louise Glück:** "Gretel in Darkness" and "The School Children" from *The First Four Books of Poems* by Louise Glück . Copyright 1968, 1971, 1972, 1973, 1974, 1975, 1976, 1977, 1978, 1979, 1980, 1985, 1995 by Louise Glück. Reprinted by permission of HarperCollins Publishers Inc. **Frederick L. Gwynn and Joseph L. Blotner:** Excerpts from *Faulkner in the University* © 1965 by the Rector and Visitors of the University of Virginia. Reprinted by permission of the University of Virginia Press. **Lorraine Hansberry:** "A Raisin in the Sun" from *A Raisin in the Sun* by Lorraine Hansberry, copyright © 1958 by Robert Nemiroff, as an unpublished work. Copyright © 1959, 1966, 1984 by Robert Nemiroff. Copyright renewed 1986, 1987 by Robert Nemiroff. Used by permission of Random House, Inc. **Robert Hayden:** "Those Winter Sundays" copyright © 1966 by Robert Hayden, "Frederick Douglass" copyright © 1966 by Robert Hayden. Both from *Collected Poems of Robert Hayden* by Robert Hayden, edited by Frederick Glaser. Used by permission of Liveright Publishing Corporation. **Ernest Hemingway:** "Cat in the Rain" reprinted with permission of Scribner, an imprint of Simon & Schuster Adult Publishing Group, from *In Our Time* by Ernest Hemingway. Copyright 1925 by Charles Scribner's Sons. Copyright renewed 1953 by Ernest Hemingway. **Amy Hempel:** "Today Will be a Quiet Day" reprinted with permission of Scribner, a Division of Simon & Schuster, Incl, from *The Collected Stories of Amy Hempel*, by Amy Hempel, originally published in *Reasons to Live*. Copyright © 1985 by Amy Hempel. All rights reserved. **Andrew Hudgins:** "The Wild Swans Skip School" originally published in *The Paris Review*, 58 (Spring 2001). Reprinted by permission of the author. "At Chancellorsville" from *After the Lost War* by Andrew Hudgins. Copyright © 1988 by Andrew Hudgins. Reprinted by permission of Houghton Mifflin Company. **Langston Hughes:** "Harlem (2) ["What happens to a dream deferred . . ."]" "Theme for English B" from *The Collected Poems of Langston Hughes* by Langston Hughes, edited by Arnold Rampersad with David Roessel, Associate Editor, copyright © 1994 by The Estate of Langston Hughes. Used by permission of Alfred A. Knopf, a division of Random House, Inc. The editors wish to thank The Crisis Publishing Co., Inc., the publisher of the magazine of the National Association for the Advancement of Colored People, for the use of "One Friday Morning" first published in the July 1941 issue of *The Crisis*. **Zora Neale Hurston:** "Pages 162–165 from "School Again" from *Dust Tracks on a Road* by Zora Neale Hurston. Copyright © 1942 by Zora Neale Hurston; renewed © 1970 by John C. Hurston. Reprinted by permission of HarperCollins Publishers, Inc. "Sweat" reprinted by permission of Lucy Hurston. **David Ives:** "Sure Thing" from *All In the Timing: Fourteen Plays* by David Ives, copyright © 1989, 1990, 1992 by David Ives. Used by permission of Vintage Books, a division of Random House, Inc. **Shirley Jackson:** "The Lottery" from *The Lottery* by Shirley Jackson. Copyright © 1948, 1949 by Shirley Jackson. Copyright renewed 1976, 1977 by Laurence Hyman, Barry Hyman, Mrs. Sarah Webster and Mrs. Joanne Schnurer. Reprinted by permission of Farrar, Straus and Giroux, LLC. **Randall Jarrell:** "The Death of the Ball Turret Gunner" from *The Complete Poems* by Randall Jarrell. Copyright © 1969, renewed

1997 by Mary von S. Jarrell. Reprinted by permission of Farrar, Straus and Giroux LLC. **GISH JEN:** "Who's Irish?" copyright © 1998 by Gish Jen. First published in *The New Yorker.* Reprinted with permission by Melanie Jackson Agency, LLC. **ERNEST JONES:** From *Hamlet and Oedipus* by Ernest Jones. Copyright 1949 by Ernest Jones renewed © 1982 by Merwyn Jones. Used by permission of W. W. Norton & Company, Inc. **BEL KAUFMAN:** "Sunday in the Park" reprinted by permission of the author. **X. J. KENNEDY:** "Nude Descending a Staircase" from In a Prominent Bar in Secaucus: New and Selected Poems, 1955–2007. Copyright © 2007 X. J. Kennedy. Reprinted with permission of The Johns Hopkins University Press. **JESSE LEE KERCHEVAL:** "Carpathia" by Jesse Lee Kercheval from *Micro Fiction,* edited by Jerome Stern (Norton, 1996). Reprinted by permission of Jesse Lee Kercheval. **JAMAICA KINCAID:** "Girl" from *At the Bottom of the River* by Jamaica Kincaid. Copyright © 1978, 1983 by Jamaica Kincaid. Reprinted by permission of Farrar, Straus and Giroux, LLC. **MARTIN LUTHER KING, JR.:** "Letter from Birmingham Jail" and "I Have a Dream" copyright © 1963 Dr. Martin Luther King, Jr.; copyright renewed 1991 Coretta Scott King. Reprinted by arrangement with the Heirs to the Estate of Martin Luther King, Jr., c/o Writers House as agent for the proprietor, New York, NY. **BERNICE W. KLIMAN:** Excerpt from Bernice W. Kliman, *Hamlet: Film, Television, and Audio Performance* (Farleigh Dickinson University Press, 1988), pp. 195–201. Reprinted by permission of the author. **ETHERIDGE KNIGHT:** "For Malcolm, a Year After" from *The Essential Etheridge Knight* by Etheridge Knight, © 1986. Reprinted by permission of the University of Pittsburgh Press. **YUSEF KOMUNYAKAA:** "Facing It" from *Dien Cai Dau* in *Pleasure Dome: New and Collected Poems* © 2001 by Yusef Komunyakaa. Reprinted by permission of Wesleyan University Press. **ANDREW LAM:** "Who Will Light Incense When Mother's Gone" from Pacific News Service, May 7 2003. Copyright © 2003. Reprinted by permission of the author. **URSULA K. LE GUIN:** "The Ones Who Walk Away from Omelas" copyright © 1973, 2001 by Ursula K. Le Guin; first appeared in *New Dimensions* 3; from *The Wind's Twelve Quarters*; reprinted by permission of the author and the author's agents, the Virginia Kidd Agency, Inc. **LI-YOUNG LEE:** "I Ask My Mother to Sing" from *Rose.* Copyright © 1986 by Li-Young Lee. Reprinted with the permission of BOA Editions, Ltd., www.BOAEditions.org. **CARMEN LOWE:** Plagiarism Quiz adapted from a quiz created by Carmen Lowe at Tufts University. Reprinted by permission. **JANE MARTIN:** *Rodeo* is reprinted by permission of Alexander Speer, Trustee. CAUTION: Professionals and amateurs are hereby warned that *Rodeo* © 1981 by Alexander Speer, Trustee, is subject to royalty. It is fully protected under the copyright laws of the United States of America, the British Commonwealth, including Canada, and all other countries of the Copyright Union. All rights, including professional, amateur, motion pictures, recitation, lecturing, public reading, radio broadcasting, television, and the rights of translation into foreign languages are strictly reserved. No part of this work may be reproduced, stored in a retrieval system or transmitted in any form, by any means now known or yet to be invented, including mechanical, electronic, photocopying, recording, videotaping or otherwise, without the prior written permission of the publisher. Particular emphasis is laid on the question of amateur or professional readings, permission and terms for which must be secured in writing from Samuel French, Inc., 45 West 25th Street, New York, NY 10010. **BOBBIE ANN MASON:** "Shiloh" from *Shiloh and Other Stories* by Bobbie Ann Mason. Reprinted by permission of International Creative Management, Inc. Copyright © 1982 by Bobbie Ann Mason. **W. SOMERSET MAUGHAM:** "The Appointment in Samarra" from *Sheppey* by W. Somerset Maugham, copyright 1933 by W. Somerset Maugham. Used by permission of Doubleday, a division of Random House, Inc. **BILL MCKIBBEN:** "Now or Never" from *In These Times,* April 10, 2001. Reprinted by permission of *In These Times.* **TERRENCE MCNALLY:** *Andre's Mother* copyright © 1995 by Terrence McNally. Reprinted by permission of William Morris Agency, LLC on behalf of the author. All rights reserved. CAUTION: Professionals and amateurs are hereby warned that *Andre's Mother* is subject to a royalty. It is fully protected under the copyright laws of the United States of America and of all countries covered by the International Copyright Union (including the Dominion of Canada and the rest of the British Commonwealth), the Berne Convention, the Pan-American Copyright Convention and the Universal Copyright Convention as well as all countries with which the United States has reciprocal copyright relations. All rights, including professional/amateur stage rights, motion picture, recitation, lecturing, public reading, radio broadcasting, television, video or sound recording, all other forms of mechanical or electronic reproduction, such as CD-ROM, CD-I, information storage and retrieval systems and photocopying, and the rights of translation into foreign languages, are strictly reserved. Particular emphasis is laid upon the matter of readings, permission for which must be secured from the Author's agent in writing. Inquiries should be addressed to William Morris Agency, LLC. 1325 Avenue of the Americas, New York, NY 10019, Attn: Peter Franklin. Originally produced by The Manhattan Theatre Club. **James Michener:** Excerpt from *Sports in America* by James Michener, copyright © 1976 by Random House, Inc. Used by permission of Random House, Inc. **Edna St. Vincent Millay:** "Love Is Not All: It Is Not Meat nor Drink" (Sonnet XXX of *Fatal Interview*) and "Mindful of you the sodden earth in spring" by Edna St. Vincent Millay. Copyright © 1917, 1928, 1931, 1945, 1952, 1955 by Edna St. Vincent Millay and Norma Millay Ellis. All rights reserved. Reprinted by permission of Elizabeth Barnett, Literary Executor, The Millay Society. **Katherine Min:** "Courting a Monk" from *TriQuarterly, 95* (1996) Reprinted by permission of the author. **Charles De Secondat, Baron de la Brède et de Montesquieu:** Letter 24: Rica to Ibben in Smyrna from *Persian Letters* by Montesquieu, translated by J. Robert Loy. **Pat Mora:** "Immigrants" from *Borders* by Pat Mora is reprinted with permission from the publisher of Borders (Houston: Arte Publico Press—University of Houston, 1986). **Aurora Levins Morales:** "Child of the Americas" from *Getting Home Alive* by Aurora Levins Morales and Rosario Morales, copyright © 1986 by Aurora Levins Morales and Rosario Morales. Reprinted by permission of Firebrand Books, Ann Arbor, Michigan. **Lillian Morrison:** "The Sidewalk Racer, or On the Skateboard" from *The Sidewalk Racer and Other Poems of Sports and Motion* by Lillian Morrison. Copyright © 1965, 1967, 1968, 1977 Lillian Morrison. Used by permission of Marian Reiner for the author. **Alice Munro:** "Boys and Girls" from *Dance of the Happy Shades* copyright © 1968 by Alice Munro. Reprinted by permission of William Morris Agency, LLC. **Gloria Naylor:** "The Two" from *The Women of Brewster Place* by Gloria Naylor. Copyright © 1980, 1982 by Gloria Naylor. Used by permission of Viking Penguin, a division of Penguin Putnam, Inc. **Nila North Sun:** "Moving Camp Too Far" from *Diet Pepsi.* Reprinted by permission of the author. **Joyce Carol Oates:** "Where Are You Going, Where Have You Been?" from *The Wheel of Love and Other Stories.* Copyright © 1970 by Ontario Review. "Smooth Talk: Short Story into film from *The New York Times,* May 23, 1986. Copyright © 1986 by The New York Times. Reprinted by permission of John Hawkins & Associates, Inc. **Tim O'Brien:** "The Things They Carried" from *The Things They Carried* by Tim O'Brien. Copyright © 1990 by Tim O'Brien. Reprinted by permission of Houghton Mifflin Harcourt Company. All rights reserved. **Flannery O'Connor:** "Revelation" from *Everything that Rises Must Converge* by Flannery O'Connor. Copyright © 1965 by the Estate of Mary Flannery O'Connor. Copyright renewed 1993 by Regina O'Connor. Excerpts from *Mystery and Manners* by Flannery O'Connor, edited by Sally and Robert Fitzgerald. Copyright © 1969 by the Estate of Mary Flannery O'Connor. Excerpts from *The Habit of Being: Letters of Flannery O'Connor* edited by Sally Fitzgerald. Copyright © 1979 by Regina O'Connor. All reprinted by permission of Farrar, Straus and Giroux, LLC. "A Good Man Is Hard to Find" from *A Good Man is Hard to Find and Other Stories,* copyright 1953 by Flannery O'Connor and renewed 1981 by Regina O'Connor, reprinted by permission of Houghton Mifflin Harcourt Publishing Company. **John O'Hara:** "Homosexuality" edited by Donald Allen from *The Collected Poems of Frank O'Hara* edited by Donald Allen, copyright © 1971 by Maureen Granville-Smith, Administratrix of the Estate of Frank O'Hara. Used by permission of Alfred A. Knopf, a division of Random House, Inc. **Sharon Olds:** "Rite of Passage" from *The Dead and the Living* by Sharon Olds, copyright © 1987 by Sharon Olds. Used by permission of Alfred A. Knopf, a division of Random House, Inc. **Daniel Orozco:** "Orientation" is reprinted by permission of the author. **George Orwell:** "Shooting an Elephant" from *Shooting an Elephant and Other Essays* by George Orwell, copyright 1950 by Sonia Brownell Orwell and renewed 1978 by Sonia Pitt-Rivers, reprinted by permission of Houghton Mifflin Harcourt Publishing Company. **Wilfred Owen:** "Dulce et Decorum Est" from *The Collected Poems of Wilfred Owen,* copyright © 1963 by Chatto &

Windus, Ltd. Reprinted by permission of New Directions Publishing Corp. **ROBERT PACK:** "The Frog Prince" from *Waking to My Name*, pp%. 246. Copyright © 1980 Rutgers University Press and The Johns Hopkins University Press. Reprinted with permission of the Johns Hopkins University Press. **GRACE PALEY:** "Samuel" from *Enormous Changes at the Last Minute* by Grace Paley. Copyright © 1971, 1974 by Grace Paley. "A Man Told Me the Story of His Life" from *The Collected Stories* by Grace Paley. Copyright © 1994 by Grace Paley. Reprinted by permission of Farrar, Straus and Giroux, LLC. **GREG PAPE:** "American Flamingo" originally published in *The Atlantic Monthly*, July 1988 is reprinted by permission of the author. **DOROTHY PARKER:** "Résumé," copyright 1926, 1928, renewed 1954, © 1956 by Dorothy Parker, from *The Portable Dorothy Parker* by Dorothy Parker, edited by Marion Meade. Used by permission of Viking Penguin, a division of Penguin Group (USA) Inc. "General Review of the Sex Situation" copyright 1926, renewed © 1954 by Dorothy Parker; © 1973, 2006 by The National Association for the Advancement of Colored People, from *The Portable Dorothy Parker* by Dorothy Parker, edited by Marion Meade. Used by permission of Viking Penguin, a division of Penguin Group (USA) Inc. **PAT PARKER:** "For the White Person Who Wants to Be My Friend" by Pat Parker from *Movement In Black*. Copyright © 1989 by Pat Parker. Reprinted by permission of Firebrand Books, Ann Arbor, Michigan. **LINDA PASTAN:** "Jump Cabling" is reprinted from *Light Year '85* copyright © 1985 by Linda Pastan, published by W. W. Norton, by permission of The Jean V. Naggar Literary Agency, Inc. on behalf of Linda Pastan. "Ethics" from *Waiting for My Life* by Linda Pastan. Copyright © 1981 by Linda Pastan. "Baseball" from *An Early Afterlife* by Linda Pastan. Copyright © 1995 by Linda Pastan. Used by permission of W. W. Norton & Company, Inc. **CARL PHILLIPS:** "Luncheon on the Grass" is reprinted by permission of the author. **MARGE PIERCY:** "Barbie doll" "What's that smell in the kitchen," "To be of use" from *Circles on the Water* by Marge Piercy, copyright © 1982 by Marge Piercy. Used by permission of Alfred A. Knopf, a division of Random House, Inc. **SYLVIA PLATH:** "Daddy" from *Ariel* by Sylvia Plath. Copyright © 1963 by Ted Hughes. Reprinted by permission of HarperCollins Publishers. **KATHERINE ANNE PORTER:** "The Jilting of Granny Weatherall" from *Flowering Judas and Other Stories*, copyright 1930 and renewed 1958 by Katherine Anne Porter, reprinted by permission of Houghton Mifflin Harcourt Pubishing Company. **ANNA LISA RAYA:** "It's Hard Enough Being Me" from *Columbia College Today*, Winter/Spring 1994. Reprinted by permission of the author. **HENRY REED:** "Naming of Parts" reproduced by permission of Curtis Brown Group Ltd, London on behalf of the Estate of Henry Reed. Copyright © Henry Reed 1942. **ADRIENNE RICH:** "Poem XI of "Twenty-One Love Poems". Copyright © 2002 by Adrienne Rich. Copyright © 1978 by W. W. Norton & Company, Inc., "Diving into the Wreck". Copyright © 2002 by Adrienne Rich. Copyright © 1973 by W. W. Norton & Company, Inc. from *The Fact of a Doorframe: Selected Poems 1950–2001* by Adrienne Rich. "Mourning Picture" copyright © 1993 by Adrienne Rich. Copyright © 1966 by W. W. Norton & Company, Inc. "Novella" copyright © 1993 by Adrienne Rich. Copyright © 1967, 1963 by Adrienne Rich. "For the Felling of an Elm in the Harvard Yard" copyright © 1993, 1951 by Adrienne Rich, from *Collected Early Poems: 1950–1970* by Adrienne Rich. Used by permission of the author and W. W. Norton & Company, Inc. **MARY ROBISON:** "Coach" from *Tell Me: 30 Stories*. Copyright © 2002 by Mary Robison. Reprinted by permission of Counterpoint. **THEODORE ROETHKE:** "My Papa's Waltz" copyright 1942 by Hearst Magazines, Inc., from *The Complete Collected Poems of Theodore Roethke* by Theodore Roethke. Used by permission of Doubleday, a division of Random House, Inc. **MARY JO SALTER:** "The Rebirth of Venus" from *Unfinished Painting* by Mary Jo Salter, copyright © 1989 by Mary Jo Salter. Used by permission of Alfred A. Knopf, a division of Random House, Inc. **MICHELE SERROS:** "Senior Picture Day" from *How to be a Chicana Role Model*. Copyright © 2000 by Michele Serros. Reprinted by permission of the author. **ANNE SEXTON:** "The Starry Night" from *All My Pretty Ones* by Anne Sexton. Copyright © 1962 by Anne Sexton, renewed 1990 by Linda G. Sexton. "Her Kind" from *To Bedlam and Part Way Back* by Anne Sexton. Copyright © 1960 by Anne Sexton, renewed 1988 by Linda G. Sexton. Reprinted by permission of Houghton Mifflin Harcourt Company. **WILLIAM SHAKESPEARE:** "The Tragedy of Hamlet, Prince of Denmark" from The Complete Works of William Shakespeare, edited by David Bevington. Reprinted by permission of

Pearson Education, Inc. **ELAINE SHOWALTER:** "Representing Ophelia" from *Shakespeare and the Question of Theory*, edited by Parker and Hartman. Reprinted by permission of Taylor & Francis Books UK. **LESLIE MARMON SILKO:** The Man to Send Rain Clouds" by Leslie Marmon Silko reprinted from *Storyteller* by Leslie Marmon Silko. Copyright © 1981 by Leslie Marmon Silko. Published by Seaver Books, New York, NY. **ISAAC BASHEVIS SINGER:** "The Son from America" from *A Crown of Feathers and Other Stories* by Isaac Bashevis Singer. Copyright © 1973 by Isaac Bashevis Singer. Reprinted by permission of Farrar, Straus and Giroux, LLC. **CATHY SONG:** "Beauty and Sadness" from *Picture Bride* by Cathy Song. Copyright © 1983 by Cathy Song. Reprinted by permission of Yale University Press. **SOPHOCLES:** *The Antigone of Sophocles, An English Version* by Dudley Fitts and Robert Fitzgerald, copyright 1939 by Houghton Mifflicn Harcourt, Publishing Company and renewed 1967 by Dudley Fitts and Robert Fitzgerald. Reprinted by permission of the publisher. CAUTION: All rights, including professional, amateur, motion picture, recitation, lecturing, performance, public reading, radio broadcasting, and television are strictly reserved. Inquiries on all rights should be addressed to Harcourt, Inc., Permissions Department, Orlando, FL 32887-6777. **WILLIAM STAFFORD:** "Traveling Through the Dark" from *The Way It Is: New and Selected Poems.* Copyright 1962, 1977, 1991, 1998 by the Estate of William Stafford. Reprinted with the permission of Graywolf Press, Saint Paul, MN. **BRENT STAPLES:** "Black Men and Public Spaces" from *Harper's* December, 1986, reprinted by permission of the author John Steinbeck: "The Chrysanthemums" copyright 1937, renewed © 1965 by John Steinbeck, from *The Long Valley* by John Steinbeck. Used by permission of Viking Penguin, a division of Penguin Group (USA) Inc. **WISLAWA SZYMBORSKA:** "Brueghel's Two Monkeys" from *View with a Grain of Sand*, copyright © 1993 by Wislawa Szymborska, English language translation by Stanislaw Baranczak and Clare Cavanagh copyright © 1995 by Harcourt, Inc. Reprinted by permission of the publisher. **AMY TAN:** "Two Kinds" from *The Joy Luck Club* by Amy Tan, copyright © 1989 by Amy Tan. Used by permission of G.P. Putnam's Sons, a division of Penguin Group (USA) Inc. **STUDS TERKEL:** "Arnold Schwarzenegger's Dream" reprinted by permission of Donadio & Olson, Inc. from *American Dreams Lost and Found.* Copyright © 1980 by Studs Terkel. **JAMES THURBER:** "The Secret Life of Walter Mitty" from My World—And Welcome To It © 1942 by James Thurber. Copyright © renewed 1970 Rosemary A. Thurber. Reprinted by arrangement with Rosemary A. Thurber and The Barbara Hogenson Agency. All rights reserved. **KITTY TSUI:** "A Chinese Banquet" from *The Words of a Woman Who Breathes Free* (Spinsters, Ink, 1983). Reprinted by permission of the author. **JOHN UPDIKE:** "A & P" from *Pigeon Feathers and Other Stories* by John Updike, copyright © 1962 and renewed 1990 by John Updike. "Before the Mirror" from Americana and Other Poems by John Updike, copyright © 2001 by John Updike. Used by permission of Alfred A. Knopf, a division of Random House, Inc. **LUIS VALDEZ:** "Los Vendidos" from *Luis Valdez-Early Works: Actos, Bernabe and Pensamiento Serpintino,* (Houston: Arte Publico Press—University of Houston, 1990). Reprinted with permission from the publisher. **LAURA VANDERKAM:** "Hookups Starve the Soul" from *USA Today*, July 25, 2001. Reprinted by permission of the author. **HELENA MARIA VIRAMONTES:** "The Moths" is used with permission from the publisher (© 1988 Arte Publico Press—University of Houston) of *The Moths and Other Stories* by Helena Maria Viramontes. **KURT VONNEGUT, JR.:** "Harrison Bergeron" from *Welcome to the Monkey House* by Kurt Vonnegut, Jr. Copyright © 1961 by Kurt Vonnegut, Jr. Used by permission of Dell Publishing, a division of Random House, Inc. **DEREK WALCOTT:** "A Far Cry from Africa" from *Collected Poems 1948–1984* by Derek Walcott. Copyright © 1986 by Derek Walcott. Reprinted by permission of Farrar, Straus and Giroux, LLC. **ALICE WALKER:** "Everyday Use" from *In Love & Trouble: Stories of Black Women* copyright © 1973 by Alice Walker, reprinted by permission of Houghton Mifflin Harcourt Publishing Company. **STANLEY WELLS:** "On the First Soliloquy" from *Shakespeare: A Life in Drama.* Copyright © 1995 by Stanley Wells. Reprinted by permission of the author and W. W. Norton & Company, Inc. **EUDORA WELTY:** "A Worn Path" from *A Curtain of Green and Other Stories*, copyright 1941 and renewed 1969 by Eudora Welty, reprinted by permission of Houghton Mifflin Harcourt Publishing Company. **TENNESSEE WILLIAMS:** *The Glass Menagerie* by Tennessee Williams. Copyright © 1945, renewed 1973 The

University of the South. Reprinted by permission of Georges Borchardt, Inc. for the Estate of Tennessee Williams. **WILLIAM CARLOS WILLIAMS:** "The Great Figure" by William Carlos Williams from *Collected Poems: 1909–1939, Volume I,* copyright © 1938 by New Directions Publishing Corp. Reprinted by permission of New Directions Publishing Corp. "The Use of Force" from *The Collected Stories of William Carlos Williams,* copyright © 1938 by William Carlos Williams. Reprinted by permission of New Directions Publishing Corp. **TOBIAS WOLFF:** "Powder" from *Back in the World.* Copyright © 1996 by Tobias Wolff. Reprinted by permission of International Creative Management, Inc. **JAMES WRIGHT:** "Lying in a Hammock at William Duffy's Farm in Pine Island, Minnesota" from *Above the River: The Complete Poems* © 1990 by James Wright. Reprinted by permission of Wesleyan University Press. **RICHARD WRIGHT:** "The Man Who Was Almost a Man" from *Eight Men* by Richard Wright. Copyright 1940 © 1961 by Richard Wright; renewed © 1989 by Ellen Wright. Introduction © 1996 by Paul Gilroy. Reprinted by permission of HarperCollins Publishers. **EMILY WU:** "The Lesson of the Master" is reprinted by permission of the author. **MITSUYE YAMADA:** "To the Lady" from *Camp Notes and Other Poems.* Copyright © 1976, 1980, 1986, 1988, 1992 by Mitsuye Yamada. Reprinted by permission of Rutgers University Press. **W. B. YEATS:** "Sailing to Byzantium" reprinted with the permission of Scribner, a Division of Simon & Schuster, Inc., from *Collected Works of W. B. Yeats, Volume One: The Poems Revised,* edited by Richard J. Finneran. Copyright © 1925 by The Macmillan Company. Copyright © 1956 by Georgie Yeats. All rights reserved.

Photo Credits

Page 23: © The New Yorker Collection 1991 Henry Martin from cartoonbank.com. All Rights Reserved; 37: SCALA Art Resource, N.Y.; 117: Dorothy Alexander; 162: Jill Krementz, Inc.; 169: Jose Armas; 174: Nancy Crampton; 179: Hulton Archive/Getty Images Inc.; 199: By permission of the Houghton Library, Harvard University; 206: The Granger Collection; 225: © Bettmann/CORBIS All Rights Reserved; 237t: Stock Photo/Black Star; 237b, 239, 240, 244: University of Virginia Library; 325: Library of Congress; 351: Hulton Archive/Getty Images; 355: Hulton Archive/Getty Images; 385: © Bettmann/CORBIS All Rights Reserved; 403: AP Wide World Photos; 405: Sylvan Barnet; 459: Photo Researchers, Inc.; 460: Photostage, Ltd.; 523: AP Wide World Photos; 524: CORBIS—NY; 530: AP Wide World Photos; 532: Amherst College Archives and Special Collections, by permission of the Trustees of Amherst College; 606: AP Wide World Photos; 632: AP Wide World Photos; 638: Annie Valva; 648: Jerry Bauer Photography; 658: Library of Congress; 667: Nancy Crampton; 671: Marion Ettinger; 680: Judith Ortiz Cofer; 684: © Bettmann/CORBIS All Rights Reserved; 697: © (Photographer)/CORBIS All Rights Reserved; 709: Jerry Bauer Photography; 729: By kind permission of the Provost and Scholars of King's College, Cambridge.; 733: Robert Pack; 734: Nancy Crampton; 735: Nancy Crampton; 745: © Bettmann/CORBIS All Rights Reserved; 757: © Bettmann/CORBIS All Rights Reserved; 766: AP Wide World Photos; 772: Marion Ettinger; 783: © Bettmann/CORBIS All Rights Reserved; 785: Robert Hayden; 786: The Imogen Cunningham Trust; 787: Nancy Crampton; 788: Hulton Archive/Getty Images; 790: Dorothy Alexander; 791: AP Wide World Photos; 793: Everett Collection; 837: Photofest; 883: Jerry Bauer Photography; 888: By kind permission of the Provost and Scholars of King's College, Cambridge; 889: By kind permission of the Provost and Scholars of King's College, Cambridge; 895: Dorothy Alexander; 897L: © The Trustees of the British Museum/Art Resource, NY; 899: Shakespeare Centre Library; 900: Shakespeare Centre Library; 901: Library of Congress; 902: Library of Congress; 1042: Magnum Photos, Inc.; 1070: Sam Garst; 1079: Frank Capri/Hulton Archive/Getty Images; 1087: AP Wide World Photos; 1105: Prentice Hall School Division; 1106: Brown Brothers; 1107: Linda Haas Photography; 1108: Jean Weisinger; 1110: AP Wide World Photos; 1114: Mitsuye Yamada; 1115: National Archives and Records; Administration/Presidential Library; 1127: AP Wide World Photos; 1242: AP Wide World Photos; 1246: © Bettmann/CORBIS All Rights Reserved; 1300: Library of Congress; 1320: Library of Congress; 1336: Library of Congress; 1355: AP Wide World Photos; 1356: Billy Rose Theatre Collection, The New York Public Library for the Performing Arts, Astor, Lenox and Tilden Foundations.

Color Inserts

Page 544: Vincent van Gogh (1853–1890), "The bedroom of van Gogh at Arles", 1889. Oil on canvas. 57.5 × 74 cm. Musee d'Orsay, Paris, France. Erich Lessing/Art Resource, NY

Page 546: Charles Demuth, American, 1883–1935. "The Figure Five in Gold". 1928. Oil on composition board, 35 1/2″ × 30″ (90.2 × 76.2 cm). The Metropolitan Museum of Modern Art, The Alfred Stieglitz Collection, 1949 49.59.1. The Metropolitan Museum of Art, New York, NY, U.S.A. Image copyright © The Metropolitan Museum of Art. Art Resource, NY

Page 548: Edwin Romanzo Elmer (1850–1923), "Mourning Picture". 1890. Oil on Canvas, 27 8/16″ × 36″ (70.9 × 91.4 cm). Smith College Museum of Art, Northhampton, Massachusetts. Purchase in 1953

Page 550: Kitagawa Utamaro (1753–1806), "Two Women Fixing their Hair", from the series, 'Daily Life of Women', 1794–95, Nishiki-e print, oban format. Photo: Harry Brejat. Musee des Arts Asiatiques-Guimet, Paris. Photo Credit: Reunion des Musees Nationaux/Art Resource, NY

Page 552: Sandro Botticelli, "The Birth of Venus". C. 1484–86. Tempera on Canvas. 5′9 7/8″ × 9′1 7/8″ (1.8 × 2.8 m). Galleria degli Uffizi, Florence. SCALA/Art Resource, NY

Page 554: Vincent Van Gogh (1853–1890), "The Starry Night", 1889, oil on canvas, 29 × 36 1/4. Acquired through the Lillie P. Bliss Bequest (472.1941). The Museum of Modern Art, New York, NY, USA. Digital Image (c) The Museum of Modern Art / Licensed by SCALA/Art Resource, NY

Page 556: Pieter Brueghel the Elder (c. 1525–1569), "Landscape with the Fall of Icarus." Oil on Canvas. Musees Royaux des Beaux-Arts, Brussels, Belgium (c)Scala/Art Resource, NY

Page 558: Marcel Duchamp, "Nude Decending a Staircase No. 2". 1912. 58″ × 35″. Oil on Canvas. Philadelphia Museum of Art: The Louise and Walter Arensberg Collection. Photo: Graydon Wood, 1994. © 2008 ARS Artists Rights Society, NY

Page 560: John James Audubon, "Greater Flamingo, American Flamingo". © 2005 National Audubon Society, Inc. All Rights Reserved. Courtesy of William Reese Company

Page 562: Edouard Manet, "Le Dejeuner sur l'Herbe (The Luncheon on the Grass)". 1863. Oil on Canvas. 7′ × 8′8″ (2.13 × 2.64 m). Musee d'Orsay, Paris. SCALA/Art Resource, NY

Page 564: Pablo Picasso "Girl Before A Mirror". Boisgeloup, March 1932. Oil on canvas, 64 × 51 1/4 in. (162.3 × 130.2 cm). The Museum of Modern Art/Licensed by Scala-Art Resource, NY. Gift of Mrs. Simon Guggenheim. (2.1938). Photograph © 2001 The Museum of Modern Art, New York. © 2010 Estate of Pablo Picasso/Artists Rights Society (ARS), New York.

Page 566: Brueghel, Pieter the Elder (c.1525–1569), "Two Chained Monkeys". 1562. Oil on oak panel, 20 × 23 cm. Inv. 2077. Photo: Joerg P. Anders. Location: Gemaeldegalerie, Staatliche Museen zu Berlin, Berlin, Germany. Bildarchiv Preussischer Kulturbesitz/Art Resource, NY

Index of Authors, Titles, and First Lines

T

Index of Terms